Strategic Management
Competitiveness and Globalization

Third Edition

Michael A. Hitt
Texas A&M University

R. Duane Ireland
Baylor University

Robert E. Hoskisson
The University of Oklahoma

Annotations Prepared by
Kendall W. Artz
Baylor University

South-Western College Publishing
an International Thomson Publishing company I(T)P®

Cincinnati • Albany • Boston • Detroit • Johannesburg • London • Madrid • Melbourne • Mexico City
New York • Pacific Grove • San Francisco • Scottsdale • Singapore • Tokyo • Toronto

Publishing Team Director: Dave Shaut
Acquisitions Editor: John Szilagyi
Developmental Editor: Katherine Pruitt-Schenck
Production Editor: Shelley Brewer
Media Technology Editor: Kevin Von Gillern
Media Production Editor: Robin Browning
Production House: WordCrafters Editorial Services, Inc.
Internal Design: Ellen Pettengell Design
Cover Design: Tin Box Studio
Cover Image: © 1998 Tamsin Jarzebowska/Photonica
Photography Manager: Cary Benbow
Marketing Manager: Rob Bloom
Manufacturing Coodinator: Sue Kirven

Library of Congress Cataloging-in-Publication Data

Hitt, Michael A.
    Strategic management : competitiveness and globalization :
concepts and cases / Michael A. Hitt, R. Duane Ireland, Robert E.
Hoskisson.—3rd ed.
      p.   cm.
    Includes bibliographical references and index.
    ISBN 0-538-88182-8 (Student Edition)
    ISBN 0-324-00011-1 (Annotated Instructor's Edition)
    ISBN 0-538-88188-7 (Concepts Edition)
    ISBN 0-538-88189-5 (Cases Edition)
    1. Strategic planning.   2. Industrial management.   I. Ireland, R.
Duane.   II. Hoskisson, Robert E.   III. Title.
HD30.28.H586   1999
658.4′012—dc21   98-20413
                                                                  CIP

1 2 3 4 5 6 7 8 9 WE 7 6 5 4 3 2 1 0 9 8

Printed in the United States of America

International Thomson Publishing
South-Western College Publishing is an ITP Company. The ITP trademark is used under license.

To Frankie, Shawn, Angie, and Tamara. Thanks for everything: I love you.

To my wife, Mary Ann, and our children, Rebecca and Scott. The three of you are the centerpiece of my life. I love all of you and treasure the blessing of being your husband and father.

To Kathy, Robyn, Luke, Dale, Allison, Becky, Angela, Joseph, and Matthew. Our family is the most important concern of my life.

Brief Contents

Contents

ix

PART II

Strategic Actions: Strategy Formulation

PART III

Strategic
Actions:
Strategy
Implementation

Cases

Case Title	Manufacturing	Service	Consumer Goods	Industrial Goods	International Perspective	High Technology	Entertainment	Food/Retail	Social/Ethical Issues	Entrepreneurial/ Small-Medium Size	Industry Perspective	Chapters
Amazon.com		X								X		2,3,5,13
Americast		X				X	X			X	X	1,2,5,9
Anheuser-Busch	X		X					X			X	2,3,5,9
Australian Pineapple Industry	X		X		X			X			X	2,3,8
Bank of America		X							X			1,12
Birra Moretti	X		X		X			X			X	2,3,7
Cap Gemini Sogeti	X	X		X	X	X						1,8,11, 12,
Carnival Corporation: 1997		X			X		X				X	3,4,5
China Eastern Airlines		X			X						X	2,3,4
Ciba-Geigy and Chiron	X		X		X	X			X		X	3,6,7,9
Circus Circus Enterprises, Inc., 1997		X					X				X	2,3,11, 13,
Columbia/HCA		X							X		X	1,7,12
Compaq	X		X	X		X						1,2,9
Cummins Engine Company, Inc.	X			X	X							4,8,9
Dayton Hudson Corporation		X						X	X		X	3,4
Enron Development Corporation	X			X	X				X			1,8,12
Granada Group		X		X	X		X					6,8,10, 11,
Harold's Stores, Inc.		X			X			X		X	X	4,11, 12,13
Internationalization of Telefónica España, S.A.		X			X	X					X	5,8,9
Jefferson-Pilot Corporation		X									X	3,4,12

Case Title	Manufacturing	Service	Consumer Goods	Industrial Goods	International Perspective	High Technology	Entertainment	Food/Retail	Social/Ethical Issues	Entrepreneurial/ Small-Medium Size	Industry Perspective	Chapters
Královopolská	X			X	X							4,8,11, 12,
Lincoln Electric Company, 1996	X			X	X						X	3,7,8,12
Lockheed and Martin Marietta	X			X	X	X					X	2,6,7
Motorola in China	X			X	X	X						8,9,11
Pasta Perfect, Inc.	X	X	X					X		X	X	3,10,13
PBS	X			X	X							4,8,9
Rover Group	X		X		X							3,8,9,13
Sanyo Manufacturing Corporation 1977–1990	X				X	X					X	2,3,6,8
Sonic		X						X		X	X	4,5
Southwest Airlines, 1996		X									X	3,4,5
Starbucks Corporation		X			X			X		X	X	5,6,8,10
Steinway & Sons	X		X		X					X		4,5,8
Textron, Inc.	X			X		X					X	4,6,7
Tootsie Roll, Inc.	X		X		X					X	X	4,7,12
Tyson Foods, Inc.	X		X		X			X	X		X	6,7
United Colors of Benetton	X	X	X		X				X			4,8,12
VOS Industries					X				X	X		2,8,10, 13,
Walt Disney Co.		X					X				X	6,7,10
Warner-Lambert Company	X		X		X	X					X	1,8,11
Whirlpool's Quest for Global Leadership	X		X		X						X	6,8,11

Preface

The third edition of *Strategic Management: Competitiveness and Globalization* continues the tradition from previous editions of integrating "cutting edge" concepts with an engaging writing style. In addition, we have selected 40 all new full length cases from a wide variety of sources that help explain the strategic management process in today's global environment. As such, the many new features and careful revisions enhance the value of our market-leading textbook.

NEW FEATURES

- All new **chapter opening cases** and **strategic focus segments**
- Many new **company-specific examples** in each chapter
- All new full-length **cases** (40) representing highly current examples of strategy in action
- Expanded **global coverage** throughout the book with more emphasis on the international context and issues in both the text materials and cases
- A complete view of **strategy formulation** and **implementation** at all levels
- New and current research integrated throughout the chapters' conceptual presentations

*These new features provide a unique **competitive advantage** to this book over other alternatives.* With all new opening cases and three new strategic focus segments for each chapter, there are 52 major case examples in the concepts portion of the book. In addition, over 50 percent of the shorter examples used throughout each chapter are completely new. The 40 new full-length cases cover an interesting mix of industries and company sizes (including large corporations and smaller entrepreneurial firms such as Sonic, Pasta Perfect, and Harold's). In addition, many strategic issues such as mergers and acquisitions, competitive dynamics, and expansion into global markets are covered in the cases.

This new edition also emphasizes a **global advantage** with comprehensive coverage of international concepts and issues. In addition to comprehensive coverage in **Chapter 8: International Strategy,** references to and discussions of the international context and issues are included throughout the other chapters. The chapter opening cases, strategic focus segments and individual examples in each chapter cover numerous global issues and markets. In addition, well over 50 percent of the 40 full-length cases focus on international contexts and markets (e.g., Telefónica España, China Eastern Airlines, Královopolská and Sanyo Manufacturing).

Importantly, this new edition solidifies a **research advantage** for the book. For example, each chapter has over 100 references. An average of over 50 new references has been added in each chapter for this edition. Additionally, we maintain our position as the only text on the market that offers a full four-color format that enhances the presentation of our materials and the overall text design plus an Instructor's Edition with valuable annotations for ease of teaching.

Our primary goal in preparing this revised edition was to **define our advantage** by presenting the most complete learning mechanism and instructional tool. Our strategic intent continues to be to present readers with a complete, accurate, and up-to-date explanation of the strategic management process.

INTRODUCTION

The strategic management process is the focus of this book. Described in Chapter 1, organizations (both for-profit companies and not-for-profit agencies) use the strategic management process to understand competitive forces and to develop competitive advantages systematically and consistently. The magnitude of this challenge is greater today than it has been historically. A new competitive landscape is developing as a result of the technological revolution and increasing globalization. The technological revolution has placed increased importance on firm innovation and the ability to rapidly introduce new goods and services to the marketplace. The global economy, one in which goods and services flow freely among nations, continuously pressures firms to become more competitive. By offering either valued goods or services to customers, competitive firms increase the probability of earning above-average returns. Thus, the strategic management process helps organizations identify what they intend to achieve and how they will accomplish valued outcomes.

This book is intended for use primarily in strategic management and business policy courses. The materials presented in the 13 chapters have been researched thoroughly. Both the academic, scholarly literature and the business, practitioner literature were studied and then integrated to design, write, and revise this book. The academic literature provided the foundation to develop an accurate, yet meaningful description of the strategic management process. The business practitioner literature yielded a rich base of current domestic and global examples to show how the concepts, tools, and techniques of the strategic management process are applied in different types of organizations.

THE STRATEGIC MANAGEMENT PROCESS

Our treatment of the strategic management process is both *traditional* and *contemporary*. In maintaining tradition, we examine important materials that have historically been a part of understanding strategic management. For example, we thoroughly examine how to analyze a firm's external environment and internal environment as a part of the strategic management process.

Contemporary Treatment In explaining the aforementioned important activities, we strive to keep our treatments contemporary. In Chapter 3, for example, we emphasize the importance of identifying and determining the value-creating potential of a firm's resources, capabilities, and core competencies. The strategic actions taken as a result of understanding a firm's resources, capabilities, and core competencies have a direct link with the company's ability to establish a sustainable competitive advantage, achieve strategic competitiveness, and earn above-average returns.

Our contemporary treatment of the strategic management process is also exemplified in the chapters on the dynamics of strategic change in the complex global economy. In Chapter 5, for example, we discuss how the dynamics of competition between firms affect the outcomes achieved by individual companies. This chapter's discussion suggests that in most industries, the strategic actions taken by a firm are influenced by a series of competitive actions and responses initiated by competitors. Thus, competition in the global economy is fluid, dynamic, and significantly influences a firm's performance. Similarly, in Chapter 7, we explain the dynamics of strategic change at the corporate level, specifically addressing the motivation and consequences of mergers, acquisitions, and restructuring (e.g., divestitures) in the global economy.

We also emphasize that the total set of strategic actions known as *strategy formulation* and *strategy implementation* (see Figure 1.1 in Chapter 1) must be integrated carefully if a firm is to achieve strategic competitiveness and earn above-average returns. Thus, this book shows that strategic competitiveness is achieved and above-average returns are earned only when firms use implementation tools and actions that are consistent with the firm's chosen business-level (Chapter 4), corporate-level (Chapter 6), acquisition (Chapter 7), international (Chapter 8), and cooperative (Chapter 9) strategies.

Contemporary Concepts Contemporary topics and concepts are the foundation for our in-depth analysis of strategic actions firms take to implement their chosen strategies. In Chapter 10, for example, we describe how different corporate governance mechanisms (e.g., boards of directors, institutional owners, executive compensation, etc.) affect strategy implementation. Chapter 11 explains how firms can gain a competitive advantage by effectively using organizational structures to implement business-level and corporate-level strategies. The vital contributions of strategic leaders are discussed in Chapter 12. Chapter 13 addresses the important topic of corporate entrepreneurship and innovation through internal corporate venturing, strategic alliances, and external acquisition or venture capital investments. Through integration of the traditional and contemporary topics, readers of this book should be able to fully understand the strategic management process and how to use it successfully in an organizational setting.

A number of contemporary topics and issues are examined in the book as well. These include stakeholder analyses, core competencies, total quality management (TQM), strategic flexibility, transnational strategy, strategic refocusing (downsizing, downscoping), strategic change and reengineering, teamwork and horizontal organization, and the importance of business ethics.

KEY FEATURES OF THIS TEXT

To increase the value of this book for readers, several features are included, each of which is described below.

Learning Objectives Each chapter begins with clearly stated learning objectives. These objectives inform readers of key points they should master from each chapter. To both facilitate and verify learning, students can revisit each chapter's learning objectives by preparing answers to the review questions appearing at the end of each chapter.

Opening Cases Following the learning objectives is an opening case. These cases describe current strategic actions taken by modern companies including Bang & Olufsen, Nippon Steel, British Telecommunications, WorldCom, and Hoechst AG, among others. The purpose of these cases is to demonstrate how a specific firm applies the strategic management concepts that are examined in individual chapters. Thus, the opening cases provide a distinct link between the theory and application of the strategic management process in different organizations.

Key Terms Key terms critical to understanding the strategic management process are boldfaced throughout the book. Definitions of these key terms appear in chapter margins as well as in the text. Other terms and concepts throughout the text are italicized, signifying their importance.

Strategic Focus Segments Three all new Strategic Focus segments are presented in each chapter. As with the opening case, the Strategic Focus segments highlight a variety of high-profile organizations. Each segment demonstrates the application of an important part of the strategic management process in the pursuit of strategic competitiveness.

End-of-Chapter Summaries Each chapter ends with a summary that revisits the concepts outlined in the learning objectives. These summaries are presented in a bulleted format to highlight concepts, tools, and techniques examined in each chapter.

Review Questions Review questions are pointedly tied to the learning objectives, prompting students to re-examine the most important concepts in each chapter.

Application Discussion Questions These questions challenge readers to directly apply the part of the strategic management process highlighted in that chapter. They are intended to stimulate thoughtful classroom discussions and to help students develop critical thinking skills.

Ethics Questions At the end of each chapter, readers are challenged by a set of questions about ethical issues that require careful thought and analysis. Preparing answers to these questions helps students recognize and confront ongoing ethical issues facing management teams. Discussing these difficult issues in class heightens awareness of the ethical challenges encountered in global organizations and markets today.

Internet Exercises The Internet is an invaluable source for the exchange of information worldwide. No other mechanism has had the ability to disseminate business information on such a large scale so quickly and effectively as the Internet. As such, a set of Internet exercises, developed by Bruce Barringer of the University of Central Florida, is included at the end of each chapter. Each set of exercises is designed so that students develop the ability to effectively recognize valid information sources and use this to further their business knowledge and management skills.

Examples In addition to the opening cases and Strategic Focus segments, each chapter contains many other real-world examples. Grounded in descriptions of actual organizations' actions, these examples are used to illustrate key strategic management concepts and to provide realistic applications of the strategic management process.

Indices Besides the traditional end of book subject and name indices, a company index is provided. This index includes the names of all organizations discussed in the text for easier accessibility.

Full Four-Color Format Our presentation and discussion of the strategic management process is facilitated by the use of a full four-color format. This format provides the foundation for an interesting and visually appealing treatment of all parts of the strategic management process. Exhibits and photos further enhance the presentation by giving visual insight into the workings of the global business environment.

The Strategic Advantage

The title of this book highlights the importance of strategic competitiveness and globalization to our examination of the strategic management process. The strategic management process is critical to organizational success. As described in Chapter 1, strategic competitiveness is achieved when a firm develops and exploits a sustained competitive advantage. Attaining such an advantage results in the earning of above-average returns; that is, returns that exceed those an investor could expect from other investments with similar amounts of risk. For example, Gillette developed and sustained a competitive advantage over time because of its significant emphasis on innovation even though it operates largely in low-technology industry(ies). Its innovation has helped it to remain one of the top firms in each of the industries in which it competes.

The Competitive Advantage

Success in the new competitive landscape requires specific capabilities, including the abilities to (1) use scarce resources wisely to maintain the lowest possible costs, (2) constantly anticipate frequent changes in customers' preferences, (3) adapt to rapid technological changes, (4) identify, emphasize, and effectively manage what a firm does better than its competitors, (5) continuously structure a firm's operations so objectives can be achieved more efficiently, and (6) successfully manage and gain commitments from a culturally diverse workforce.

The Global Advantage

Also critical to the approach used in this text is the fact that all firms face increasing global competition. Firms no longer operate in relatively safe domestic markets as

U.S. auto firms have discovered. In the past, many companies, including most in the United States, produced large quantities of standardized products. Today, firms typically compete in a global economy that is complex, highly uncertain, and unpredictable. To a greater degree than in a primarily domestic economy, the global economy rewards effective performers, whereas poor performers are forced to restructure significantly to enhance their strategic competitiveness. As noted earlier, increasing globalization and the technological revolution have produced a new competitive landscape. The new competitive landscape presents a challenging and complex environment for firms, but one that also has opportunities. The importance of developing and using these capabilities in the new competitive landscape of the twenty-first century should not be underestimated.

CASES

The text includes 40 case studies that are new to this edition. These cases represent a variety of business and organizational situations and strategic issues. For example, there are cases representing manufacturing, service, consumer goods, and industrial goods industries. Furthermore, many of the cases include an international perspective. Also, cases with high technology, entertainment, and food or retail firms are represented. Some cases focus specifically on social or ethical issues, whereas others emphasize strategic issues of entrepreneurial or small- and medium-sized firms. Finally, a significant number of the cases also provide an effective perspective on the industry examined.

The cases were reviewed carefully and selected personally by the authors. Our goal was to choose cases that were well written and that are focused on clear and important strategic management issues. In addition, the variety of cases provides a rich learning experience for those performing case analyses. The cases are multidimensional. For the readers' convenience, a matrix listing all 40 cases and the dimensions/characteristics of each one is provided following the table of contents. Although most of these cases are concerned with well-known national and multinational companies, several depict the strategic challenges involved in smaller entrepreneurial firms (e.g., Pasta Perfect, Amazon.com, Harold's).

Given the global economy emphasized in this book, approximately 65 percent of the cases include an international perspective (e.g., Enron Development Corporation, Motorola in China, Birra Moretti). There are also cases of special interest or topics (e.g., Bank of America, Southwest Airlines, Starbucks, Benetton, China Eastern Airlines and Columbia/HCA). Several of these cases have won special awards for their excellence (e.g., Telefónica España and Cap Gemini Sogeti). In summary, the cases represent a wide variety of important and challenging strategic issues and provide an exciting setting for case analyses and presentations.

SUPPORT MATERIAL*

The third edition's support materials are authored by most of the same top instructors as the previous editions. We present to you one of the most compre-

---

*Adopters: Please contact your ITP sales representative to learn more about the supplements you are qualified to receive.

hensive and quality learning packages available for teaching strategic management. These materials have been authored by a top support team and were carefully guided by ourselves, to ensure quality and consistency.

For the Instructor

Annotated Instructor's Edition (ISBN: 0-324-00011-1) Comprehensive annotations for the Annotated Instructor's Edition of this edition of our text were prepared by Kendall W. Artz of Baylor University. The annotations provide background information and suggestions to facilitate class discussion of important concepts from the book. The annotations also provide the instructor with additional company examples that give further insight into a particular topic. In addition, most chapter opening cases are accompanied by at least one URL so that further information related to the featured company can be researched using the World Wide Web.

Instructor's Manual with Video Guide & Transparencies (ISBN: 0-538-88183-6) A complete Instructor's Manual has been prepared by Richard A. Menger of St. Mary's University. The instructor's manual provides teaching notes, suggestions, and summaries. The teaching notes include discussion summaries or highlights of each opening case, Strategic Focus segment, table, and figure appearing in the text. Teaching suggestions provide the instructor with a choice of strategies for integrating various text features into a lecture format.

Video Guide (ISBN: 0-538-88183-6) An exclusive video guide has been developed by Bruce Barringer of the University of Central Florida to accompany the video package and provide information on length, alternative points of usage within the text, subjects to address, and discussion questions to stimulate classroom discussion. Suggested answers to these questions are also provided.

Transparency Acetates (ISBN: 0-324-00888-0) The full-color transparency acetates include important figures from the text and additional transparencies from the PowerPoint Presentation Files. To provide comprehensive coverage, 150 transparency acetates are included in the set.

Transparency Masters (ISBN: 0-538-88183-6) More than 200 transparency masters are printed from the PowerPoint Presentation Files and include figures from the text and innovative adaptations to enhance classroom presentation.

Instructor's Case Notes (ISBN: 0-538-88185-2) Samuel M. DeMarie of the University of Nevada at Las Vegas prepared the Case Notes that accompany the text. Each note provides details about the case within the framework of case analysis that is presented in the text. The authors selected the 40 new cases, based on the variety of strategy topics and industry types they represent. The structure of these case notes allows instructors to organize case discussions along common themes and concepts. For example, each case note details the firm's capabilities and resources, its industry and competitive environment (if applicable), and key factors for success in the industry. The case notes also feature aspects of the cases that make them unique.

Test Bank (ISBN: 0-538-88184-4) The Test Bank, prepared by Debora J. Gilliard of Metropolitan State College of Denver, has been thoroughly revised for this new edition. The test bank contains more than 1,200 multiple choice, true/false, and essay questions. Each question has been coded according to Bloom's taxonomy, a widely known testing and measurement device used to classify questions according to level (easy, medium, or hard) and type (application, recall, or comprehension).

World Class Test Computerized Testing Software (ISBN: 0-324-0059-6) New this year, World Class Test allows instructors to create, edit, store, and print exams easily and efficiently.

PowerPoint Presentation Files (ISBN: 0-0-538-88190-9) Jay Dial of Case Western Reserve University has developed more than 800 PowerPoint slides for this text. These unique slides feature figures from the text, lecture outlines, and innovative adaptations to enhance classroom presentation. These files are available on disk in PowerPoint 4.0. The PowerPoint Presentation File slides are integrated with *PowerNotes* (see below).

South-Western College Publishing's Strategy Internet Site and Resource Center The new strategy site includes a wealth of information for both students and instructors. Link directly to the Hitt/Ireland/Hoskisson section and see updates to the cases, strategy terms defined, a full Internet index with important strategy URL listings, and a section on how to write a case analysis. For the instructor, there are sample syllabi that demonstrate both traditional and nontraditional teaching of the course. This online service is available to everyone. We encourage you to access our site and to explore your strategic advantage at: http://strategy.swcollege.com

Videos (ISBN: 0-324-00377-3) A new, very unique video package is available that features video segments exclusive to the South-Western College Publishing management team. Written and directed by Learnet, these video segments run 10-15 minutes each and focus on both small and large companies as they utilize the strategic management process. During the video segment, questions are posed and students are asked to analyze different evolving management situations. Each chapter has its own video segment, focusing on the topics presented therein.

For the Student

Insights: Readings in Strategic Management, Third Edition (ISBN: 0-538-88186-0) Prepared by Timothy B. Palmer of Louisiana State University, *Insights* has been revised and expanded for this edition and includes multiple selected readings from academic and popular business periodicals such as the *Academy of Management Executive*, the *Wall Street Journal*, *Forbes*, and *Fortune*. Each chapter features 3-4 business articles.

PowerNotes (ISBN: 0-538-88187-9) PowerNotes (a student note-taking guide), prepared by Jay Dial of Case Western Reserve University, provides a simple solution for the majority of students who spend their time during lectures copying material from the overheads. PowerNotes contains reduced images of the PowerPoint Presentation Files with space for lecture notes on each page.

ACKNOWLEDGMENTS

We gratefully acknowledge the help of many people in the development of this edition of our book. The professionalism, guidance, and support provided by the editorial team of John Szilagyi (Executive Editor), Katherine Pruitt-Schenck (Project Manager), Shelley Brewer (Production Editor), and Rob Bloom (Marketing Manager) are gratefully acknowledged. We appreciate the excellent work of Sam DeMarie, Jay Dial, Debora Gilliard, Richard Menger, Kendall Artz, Bruce Barringer, and Timothy Palmer in preparing the supplemental materials accompanying this book. Also, we appreciate the excellent secretarial assistance provided by Adrian Elton. In addition, we owe a debt of gratitude to our colleagues at Texas A&M University, Baylor University, and the University of Oklahoma. Finally, we gratefully acknowledge the help of many who read and provided feedback on drafts of our chapters for the three editions of our book. Their insights enhanced our work. Those who contributed through reviews and evaluations are:

Kendall W. Artz
Baylor University

Kimberly B. Boal
Texas Tech University

Garry D. Bruton
Texas Christian University

Victoria L. Buenger
Texas A&M University

Lowell Busenitz
University of Oklahoma

Gary R. Carini
Baylor University

Roy A. Cook
Fort Lewis College

James H. Davis
University of Notre Dame

Samuel M. DeMarie
University of Nevada at Las Vegas

Derrick E. Dsouza
University of North Texas

W. Jack Duncan
University of Alabama at Birmingham

Karin Fladmoe-Lindquist
University of Utah

Karen A. Froehlich
North Dakota State University

Debora J. Gilliard
Metropolitan State College of Denver

Ching-Der Horng
National Sun Yat-Sen University

Veronica Horton
Middle Tennessee State University

Sharon G. Johnson
Cedarville College

Anne T. Lawrence
San Jose State University

Franz T. Lohrke
University of Southern Mississippi

Richard A. Menger
St. Mary's University

Joseph E. Michlitsch
Southern Illinois University at Edwardsville

Paul Miesing
University at Albany, SUNY

Douglas D. Moesel
University of Missouri, Columbia

Benjamin M. Oviatt
Georgia State University

George M. Puia
Indiana State University

Woody Richardson
University of Alabama at Birmingham

Michael V. Russo
University of Oregon

Ronald J. Salazar
Idaho State University

Hugh Sherman
Ohio University

Clayton G. Smith
Oklahoma City University

David C. Snook-Luther
University of Wyoming

Kathleen M. Sutcliffe
University of Michigan

Thomas A. Turk
Chapman University

Margaret A. White
Oklahoma State University

Robert Wiseman
Michigan State University

FINAL COMMENT

Organizations face exciting and dynamic competitive challenges as the 1990s come to a close and the twenty-first century begins. These challenges, and effective responses to them, are explored in this third edition of *Strategic Management: Competitiveness and Globalization*. The strategic management process offers valuable insights for those committed to successfully leading and managing organizations in the 1990s and beyond. We hope that you will enjoy the exposure to the strategic management process provided by this book. In addition, we wish you success in your careers and future endeavors.

Strategic Management Inputs

Chapters

1 Strategic Management and Strategic Competitiveness
2 The External Environment: Opportunities, Threats, Industry Competition, and Competitor Analysis
3 The Internal Environment: Resources, Capabilities, and Core Competencies

PART I

Strategic Management and Strategic Competitiveness

CHAPTER 1

Learning Objectives

After reading this chapter, you should be able to:

1. Define strategic competitiveness, competitive advantage, and above-average returns.

2. Discuss the challenge of strategic management.

3. Describe the new competitive landscape and how it is being shaped by global and technological changes.

4. Use the industrial organization (I/O) model to explain how firms can earn above-average returns.

5. Use the resource-based model to explain how firms can earn above-average returns.

6. Describe strategic intent and strategic mission and discuss their value to the strategic management process.

7. Define stakeholders and describe the three primary stakeholder groups' ability to influence organizations.

8. Describe the work of strategists.

9. Explain the strategic management process.

A New World Order in the Telecommunications Industry

The telecommunications industry will never be the same. Perhaps the changes are best exemplified by the $37 billion acquisition of MCI by WorldCom Inc. This acquisition came on the heels of offers from British Telecommunications and GTE. British Telecommunications and MCI first agreed on a merger reportedly worth between $18 and $19 billion. British Telecommunications then had second thoughts, and GTE offered $28 billion. WorldCom, about 40 percent the size of MCI, made the offer to make it the largest merger in history at that point in time. The combined firms will have total annual revenue of $27.8 billion. The series of offers seemed to spur AT&T into action when it began talks with SBC regarding an acquisition. The talks made progress in the beginning, but they broke down with much external criticism and government scrutiny. Such a merger would have been worth approximately $50 billion.

http://www.mci.com
http://www.worldcom.com

All of this frenetic activity in the telecommunication industry is due to the major changes occurring in and predicted for this industry. In other words, firms are trying to prepare themselves to be competitive as changes occur. Some predict changes in the telecommunications industry as profound as occurred in the computer industry with the advent of the microcomputer. One major change that has occurred in many domestic industries is deregulation and thus increasing competition. Deregulation is also spreading globally. For example, the Federal Communications Commission voted in 1997 to allow foreign companies increased access to the U.S. telecommunications markets. This step is the first among the countries who were a party to a World Trade Organization agreement in which 69 countries pledged to open their telecommunications markets. To compete in a global market, many telecommunications' executives feel that their firms must be large to have the necessary market power. Annual spending in the global telecommunications industry is expected to grow to $1 trillion by 2001. Furthermore there are new markets opening up such as in China that will require massive investments to compete. China alone represents a $1 trillion opportunity. Of course, it is not only the size of the market affecting major investments but also the need to be at the forefront of rapidly advancing technology. In 1996 the required investment in the telecommunications infrastructure globally was $160 billion.

Changes in the industry are clearly not limited to U.S. firms. For example, a consortium of European phone companies agreed to merge their international phone networks to create the largest service provider in Europe. The Unisource consortium was formed by PTT Nederland NV of the Netherlands, Telia AB of Sweden and Swiss Telecom. Unisource will compete mainly with two joint ventures, one between British Telecommunications and MCI and one formed by Sprint, Deutsche Telecom AG, and France Telecom SA. Unisource also has a joint venture with AT&T that will be aided by this new development. Tato, a large Italian firm, formed a strategic alliance with Deutsche Telecom to bid for Italy's third cellular telephone license and to make a $5 billion move into the fixed line market. STET, another Italian company, already controls the largest cellular phone network in Europe. It has bought into systems in Austria, Serbia, and Spain. A final example comes from Asia. Four competitors are cooperating to develop a common format of the code division multiple access (CDMA), a digital transmission technology. The firms, Lucent Technologies, Motorola, Northern Telecom, and Qualcomm, are also cooperating to help Nippon Telephone & Telegraph (NTT) to develop a world CDMA. Improving the CDMA will help Asian carriers such as NTT because of the tremendous growth in Asian markets.

These changes are some of the examples of the transformation occurring in the global telecommunications industry. The changes are required to remain competitive in a rapidly developing and dynamic industry.

SOURCE: C. Arnst, G. McWilliams and A. Barrett, 1997, The return of Ma Bell? *Business Week*, June 3, www.businessweek.com; P. Elstrom, C. Yang and J. Flynn, 1997, The New World Order, *Business Week*, October 13, 26–33; Europe's Unisource confirms its merger of global networks, 1997, *The Wall Street Journal Interactive Edition*, June 5, http://www.interactive5.wsj.com; Four wireless rivals link up to work for CDMA standards, 1997, *The Wall Street Journal Interactive Edition*, June 4, http://www.interactive5.wsj.com; GTE presses its bid for MCI, calling merger a home run, 1997, *The Wall Street Journal Interactive Edition*, http://www.interactive5.wsj.com; D.E. Kalish, 1997, WorldCom-MCI deal makes merger history, *Houston Chronicle*, November 11, C1; J.J. Keller and S. Lipin, 1997, Jumping off sidelines, GTE makes a cash bid for MCI, *The Wall Street Journal Interactive Edition*, October 16, http://www.interactive5.wsj.com; A. Kupfer, 1997, Transforming Telecom: the big switch, *Fortune*, October 13, 105–116; J. Rossant, 1997, Lean, mean— and state-owned Italian companies, *Business Week*, June 16, http://www.businessweek.com; U.S. to open up telecommunications to foreign firms, *Houston Chronicle*, November 26, C3.

Strategic competitiveness is achieved when a firm successfully formulates and implements a value-creating strategy.

The actions undertaken by firms such as WorldCom, PTT Nederland NV, Deutsche Telecom AG, STET, and Nippon Telephone and Telegraph among others are designed to help the firms achieve strategic competitiveness and earn above-average returns. **Strategic competitiveness** is achieved when a firm successfully formulates and implements a value-creating strategy. When a firm implements a value-creating strategy of which other companies are unable to duplicate the benefits or find it too costly to imitate,[1] this firm has a **sustained** or **sustainable competitive advantage** (hereafter called simply competitive advantage). A firm is assured of a competitive advantage only after others' efforts to duplicate its strategy have ceased or failed.[2] Even if a firm achieves a competitive advantage, it normally can sustain it only for a certain period of time.[3] The speed with which competitors are able to acquire the skills needed to duplicate the benefits of a firm's value-creating strategy determines how long a competitive advantage will last.[4] Understanding how to exploit its competitive advantage is necessary for a firm to earn above-average returns.[5]

By achieving strategic competitiveness and successfully exploiting its competitive advantage, a firm is able to accomplish its primary objective—the earning of above-average returns. **Above-average returns** are returns in excess of what an investor expects to earn from other investments with a similar amount of risk. **Risk** is an investor's uncertainty about the economic gains or losses that will result from a particular investment.[6] Firms that are without a competitive advantage or that are not competing in an attractive industry earn, at best, only average returns. **Average returns** are returns equal to those an investor expects to earn from other investments with a similar amount of risk. In the long run, an inability to earn at least average returns results in failure. Failure occurs because investors will choose to invest in firms that earn at least average returns and will withdraw their investments from those earning less.

Dynamic in nature, the **strategic management process** (see Figure 1.1) is the full set of commitments, decisions, and actions required for a firm to achieve strategic competitiveness and earn above-average returns.[7] Relevant *strategic inputs*, from analyses of the internal and external environments, are necessary for effective strategy formulation and strategy implementation actions. In turn, effective *strategic actions* are a prerequisite to achieving the desired outcomes of strategic competitiveness and above-average returns. Thus, the strategic management process is used to match the conditions of an ever-changing market and competitive structure with a firm's continuously evolving resources, capabilities, and competencies (the sources of strategic inputs). Effective *strategic actions* that take place in the context of carefully integrated strategy formulation and strategy implementation processes result in desired *strategic outcomes*.[8]

In the remaining chapters of this book, we use the strategic management process to explain what firms should do to achieve strategic competitiveness and earn above-average returns. Through these explanations, it becomes clear why some firms consistently achieve competitive success and others fail to do so.[9] As you will see, the reality of global competition is a critical part of the strategic management process.[10]

Several topics are discussed in this chapter. First, we examine the challenge of strategic management. This brief discussion highlights the fact that the strategic actions taken to achieve and then to maintain strategic competitiveness demand the best of managers, employees, and their organizations on a continuous basis. Second, we describe the new competitive landscape, created primarily by the emergence of a global economy and rapid technological changes. The new competitive landscape establishes the contextual opportunities and threats within which the strategic management process is used by firms striving to meet the competitive challenge raised by demanding global standards.

We next examine two models that suggest conditions organizations should study to gain the strategic inputs needed to select strategic actions in the pursuit of strategic competitiveness and above-average returns. However, the emphases of these

A **sustained** or **sustainable competitive advantage** occurs when a firm implements a value-creating strategy of which other companies are unable to duplicate the benefits or find it too costly to imitate.

Above-average returns are returns in excess of what an investor expects to earn from other investments with a similar amount of risk.

Risk is an investor's uncertainty about the economic gains or losses that will result from a particular investment.

Average returns are returns equal to those an investor expects to earn from other investments with a similar amount of risk.

The **strategic management process** is the full set of commitments, decisions, and actions required for a firm to achieve strategic competitiveness and earn above-average returns.

5

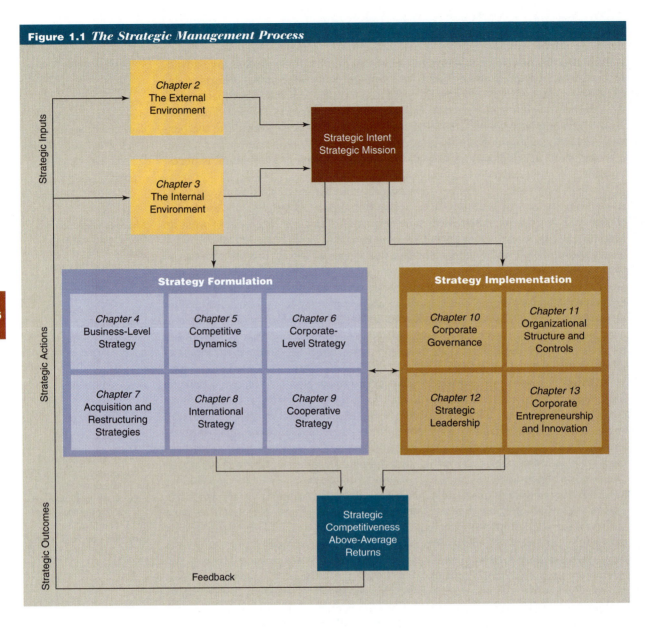

Figure 1.1 *The Strategic Management Process*

two models differ. The first model (industrial organization) suggests that the *external environment* should be the primary determinant of a firm's strategic actions. The key to this model is locating and competing successfully in an attractive (that is, profitable) industry. The second model (resource based) suggests that a firm's unique resources and capabilities are the critical link to strategic competitiveness. Comprehensive explanations of these two models in this first chapter and the next two show that through combined use of these two models, firms obtain the full set of strategic inputs needed to formulate and implement strategies successfully.

Analyses of its external and internal environments provide a firm with the information it needs to develop its strategic intent and strategic mission (intent and mission are defined later in this chapter). As shown in Figure 1.1, strategic intent and strategic mission influence strategy formulation and implementation actions.

The chapter's discussion then turns to the stakeholders served by organizations. The degree to which stakeholders' needs can be met increases directly with enhancements in a firm's strategic competitiveness and its ability to earn above-average returns. Closing the chapter are introductions to organizational strategists and the elements of the strategic management process.

THE CHALLENGE OF STRATEGIC MANAGEMENT

The goals of achieving strategic competitiveness and earning above-average returns are challenging—not only for firms as large as WorldCom, but also for those as small as your local dry cleaners. The performance of some companies, of course, more than meets strategic management's challenge. At the end of a recent year, for example, Coca-Cola and General Electric had created more wealth (as measured by market value added) than other U.S. firms (approximately $125 billion in the case of Coca-Cola; roughly $122 billion for GE). The top 10 wealth creators for 1997, including Coca-Cola and GE, are shown in Table 1.1. Microsoft moved from 14 in 1992 to 3 in 1997. More dramatically, Intel exploded from 74 in 1992 to 4 in 1997.[11] The fact that only 2 of the 25 largest U.S. industrial corporations in 1900 are still competitive today attests to the rigors of business competition and the challenge of strategic management. The remaining 23 companies have failed, been merged with other firms, or are no longer of significant size relative to competitors.[12] Moreover, in a recent year, almost 150,000 U.S. businesses either failed or filed for bankruptcy.[13] Results such as these support the view that competitive success is transient.[14] Thomas J. Watson, Jr., formerly IBM's chairman, once cautioned people to remember that "corporations are expendable and that success—at best—is an impermanent achievement which can always slip out of hand."[15]

TABLE 1.1 *Top Ten Wealth Creators*

1997	1996	1992	Company	Market Value Added (Millions)[a]
1	1	4	Coca-Cola	$124,894
2	2	6	General Electric	121,874
3	5	14	Microsoft	89,957
4	12	74	Intel	86,481
5	3	2	Merck	78,246
6	4	3	Philip Morris	66,608
7	9	12	Exxon	55,532
8	8	10	Procter & Gamble	55,102
9	6	7	Johnson & Johnson	51,119
10	11	5	Bristol-Myers Squibb	42,910

Source: R. Teitelbaum, 1997, America's Greatest Wealth Creators, *Fortune,* November 10, 265–276.
[a]Market Value Added is defined as a company's market value minus the capital tied up in the company.

Successful performance may be transient and impermanent, at least as reflected by *Fortune*'s Most Admired Corporation list. In 1986 IBM held the number one position on *Fortune's* list for the fourth consecutive year. By 1995, IBM's position had slipped to number 281. Of course, IBM has come back as have The Limited and Honda. However, not all companies are fortunate enough for their problems to be temporary. Woolworth and Color Tile are no longer in business as explained in the Strategic Focus on the impermanence of success.

While The Limited and Honda are making changes to return to their days of success, questions remain about whether their efforts will result in the success they once enjoyed. Both have significant competition. The U.S. market drives Honda and so it is vital for the firm to reestablish its relationship with the U.S. consumer. The Limited must do the same by offering consumers smart and unique fashions in the clothing it markets. In both cases, Honda's world car and The Limited's new fashions, the success of these efforts will make the difference in the firm's ability to again achieve strategic competitiveness and to earn above-average returns.[16]

Some firms create their own problems by formulating the wrong strategy or poorly implementing a strategy. Such was the case in Union Pacific Corporation's acquisition of Southern Pacific Rail Corporation. While Union Pacific promised higher efficiency, the opposite occurred after the two firms were merged. There have been many service problems causing widespread shipping delays for many of Union Pacific's largest customers. These delays are costly to Union Pacific's customers, several of whom resorted to trucking their products to their markets. In fact, some of its customers had to halt production for a time because of the firm's inability to transport products to their customers. Union Pacific also experienced a series of fatal accidents, which complicated the problem of untangling the web of delays in freight service. The string of accidents was investigated by 80 inspectors from the Federal Railroad Administration (FRA). The head of the FRA, Jolene Molitoris, suggested that many of the problems being experienced were due to the merger. Thus, Union Pacific acquired Southern Pacific promising improved service but has only angered its best customers and courted problems with the federal regulatory agency. In the final analysis, the cost of the acquisition to Union Pacific may be much greater than the $3.9 billion paid for Southern Pacific.[17]

STRATEGIC FOCUS

The Impermanence of Success

The Limited, the largest specialty retailer in the United States, was started by Les Wexner in 1963 with $5,000 of borrowed capital. The Limited experienced incredible growth and success in its first 29 years of existence. In 1997, it had $8.6 billion in annual revenue from its 13 separate store chains and catalogs (which include Bath & Body Works and Victoria's Secret). However, The Limited has experienced problems in recent years. Competition began to eat into the company's market, with the most damage in the Women's Division. As a result the firm had significantly lower earnings in 1996. Analysts and Wexler agree that some of the problems stemmed from bad fashions; in fact, the clothes being sold by The Limited's stores became boring to the customers. To revive its operations, Wexler is changing the management team and closing unprofitable stores, 200 in 1997 alone. While it has a long way to go, analysts are cautiously optimistic about the firm's future.

Some other retailers have not been as fortunate. For example, in 1997, Woolworth closed all of its existing 400 five and dime stores. A one-time market leader, Color Tile closed its doors in 1997 as well. Woolworth's market niche became less valuable and was usurped by competitors such as Wal-Mart. Furthermore its downtown locations lost customers as shoppers fled to the suburbs. At its pinnacle, Woolworth had 2,100 stores globally. In an attempt to change with the times, Woolworth created Woolco. However, it was never able to compete effectively in the discount variety store market. At its demise, Color Tile had 103 stores. It started to lose market share when superstores such as Lowe's and Home Depot began to offer floor and wall coverings. The industry became hypercompetitive and Color Tile lacked the resources to compete with the superstores and could not make the necessary changes to successfully find a new market niche.

While not as severe as those explained above, Honda also experienced problems and is now making major changes to reassert itself in the global automobile market. A few years ago, it redesigned its popular Accord to make it more sporty. However, it had too little internal space to satisfy U.S. customers and was not adequately sporty for the Japanese consumers. As a result, Honda began to lose market share in several major markets around the world. This was quite an awakening for the Honda executives who had become perhaps too complacent with the strong demand for the firm's autos. Honda took drastic action and is now trying to build a "world car." This car has the same basic design but is adapted for consumer tastes in different markets. For example, in 1997 Honda launched two versions of the Accord, one in the U.S. and one in Japan. The U.S. version is 189 inches long and 70 inches wide to be a mid-size competitor of the Ford Taurus. The Accord in Japan is six inches shorter and four inches thinner. The Japanese version is a sporty compact with many high technology features. In 1998 a European Accord was introduced that had a short narrow body designed for maneuvering on narrow streets. There are other versions as well. Analysts are optimistic; but Honda also must fight to maintain its efficiency as cost is becoming a major factor in global auto sales.

SOURCE: K. Abdullah, 1997, Color Tile to cease operations by Aug. 30, *Dallas Morning News*, August 1, D1, D2; T. Box, 1997, Consumers put increasing emphasis on price when considering new cars, *Dallas Morning News*, September 2, D1, D8; W. Kates, 1997, Woolworth legacy fading with store chain, *Dallas Morning News*, October 20, D1, D4; K. Naughton, E. Thorton, K. Kerwin and H. Dawley, 1997, Can Honda build a world car? *Business Week*, September 8, 100–108; M. Williams, 1997, The Limited tries to rebuild after losing some of its appeal, *Dallas Morning News*, November 2, H5.

In recognition of strategic management's challenge, Andrew Grove, Intel's CEO, observed that only paranoid companies survive and succeed. Intel is the number one computer chip manufacturer in the world with market capitalization greater than the top three U.S. automakers combined. Such firms know that current success does not guarantee future strategic competitiveness and above-average returns. Accordingly, these companies strive continuously to improve so they can remain competitive. To be strategically competitive and earn above-average returns through implementation of a world car, Honda must compete differently than in the past. IBM, The Limited, Motorola, Nippon Telephone and Telegraph, and WorldCom, too, must compete differently in a world being shaped increasingly by globalization, technological changes, and the information revolution. For all these companies and others that are competing in the new competitive landscape, Andrew Grove believes that a key challenge is to try to do the impossible—namely, to anticipate the unexpected.[18]

THE NEW COMPETITIVE LANDSCAPE[19]

The fundamental nature of competition in many of the world's industries is changing.[20] The pace of this change is relentless and is increasing. Even determining the boundaries of an industry has become challenging. Consider, for example, how advances in interactive computer networks and telecommunications have blurred the definition of the "television" industry. Because of these advances, the near future will find firms such as ABC, CBS, NBC, and HBO competing not only among themselves but also with AT&T, Microsoft, and Sony. An example of this new form of competition occurred in late 1995 when News Corporation, which owns Fox Broadcasting Company, formed a strategic alliance with Tele-Communications Inc., the largest U.S. cable system. Viewed as a venture that would control a global web of sports TV networks, this alliance was considered quickly to be a major competitor for ESPN and other sources interested in delivering sports events to customers around the world.[21]

Still other characteristics of the new competitive landscape are noteworthy. Conventional sources of competitive advantage such as economies of scale and huge advertising budgets are not as effective in the new competitive landscape. Moreover, the traditional managerial mind-set cannot lead a firm to strategic competitiveness in the new competitive landscape. In its place, managers must adopt a new mind-set—one that values flexibility, speed, innovation, integration, and the challenges that evolve from constantly changing conditions.[22] The conditions of the new competitive landscape result in a perilous business world, one where the investments required to compete on a global scale are enormous and the consequences of failure are severe.[23]

Hypercompetition is a term that is used often to capture the realities of the new competitive landscape (mentioned briefly here, hypercompetitive environments are discussed further in Chapter 5). According to Richard A. D'Aveni, hypercompetition:

> results from the dynamics of strategic maneuvering among global and innovative combatants. It is a condition of rapidly escalating competition based on price-quality positioning, competition to create new know-how and establish first-mover advantage, competition to protect or invade established product or geographic markets, and competition based on deep pockets and the creation of even deeper pocketed alliances.[24]

Several factors have created hypercompetitive environments and the new competitive landscape. As shown in Figure 1.2, the emergence of a global economy and technology, coupled with rapid technological changes, are the two primary drivers.

The Global Economy

A **global economy** is one in which goods, services, people, skills, and ideas move freely across geographic borders. Relatively unfettered by artificial constraints, such as tariffs, the global economy significantly expands and complicates a firm's competitive environment.[25]

Interesting opportunities and challenges are associated with the global economy's emergence. For example, Europe, instead of the United States, is now the

A **global economy** is one in which goods, services, people, skills, and ideas move freely across geographic borders.

10

Figure 1.2 *The New Competitive Landscape*

Technology and Technological Changes
- Rapid technological changes
- Rapid technology diffusions
- Dramatic changes in information technologies
- Increasing importance of knowledge

The Competitive Landscape

The Global Economy
- People, goods, services, and ideas move freely across geographic borders
- Significant opportunities emerge in multiple global markets
- Markets and industries become more internationalized

world's largest single market. If countries from the former Soviet Union and other Eastern block nations are included, the European market has a gross domestic product (GDP) of $5 trillion with 700 million potential customers.[26] In addition, by 2015 or perhaps sooner, China's total GDP will be greater than Japan's, although its per capita output will be much lower.[27] Some believe that the United States, Japan, and Europe are relatively equal contenders in the battle to be the most competitive nation, or group of nations, in the twenty-first century. Achieving this status will allow the "winner's citizens to have the highest standard of living."[28]

To achieve strategic competitiveness in the global economy, a firm must view the world as its marketplace. For example, Procter & Gamble believes that it still has tremendous potential to grow internationally where the demand for household products is not as mature (such as in China) as it is in the United States.

A commitment to viewing the world as a company's marketplace creates a sense of direction that can serve the firm well. For example, Whirlpool Corporation, the world's largest manufacturer of major home appliances, intends to maintain its global leadership position. With production facilities in 12 countries and through its marketing efforts in 120 nations, the company's sales volume outside the United States is now over 40 percent. Recently Whirlpool had investments in three appliance companies in Brazil, one in Canada, a subsidiary in Argentina, and joint ventures in Mexico, India, Taiwan, and China. Lawrence Bossidy, CEO of AlliedSignal (a manufacturer of aerospace components, automotive parts for original equipment markets, and engineered materials, such as chemicals and plastics), is convinced that globalization is a key to his firm's growth. To achieve his goal of AlliedSignal generating 45 percent of its sales volume outside the United States by 1997, Bossidy aggressively led his company into China and India, two markets he believes have great potential.[29]

Large firms such as Whirlpool and AlliedSignal often commit to competition in the global economy quicker than do midsize and small firms. In the recent past, however, the number of U.S. midsize and small firms competing in the global economy has increased. For example, the percentage of U.S. midsize companies competing in markets outside of their home nation increased to 56 percent of the total in 1995.[30]

Overall, as measured by exports, U.S. companies' strategic actions in globalized markets are increasing. In fact, in a recent time period, 42 percent of the growth in the U.S. economy was based on increasing exported goods. In 1997, exports and imports accounted for 28.4 percent of the U.S. gross domestic product. This percentage was up from 25.5 percent in 1996 and less than 21 percent in 1992. The growth in exports of U.S. firms has been particularly acute in capital goods. Experts suggest that U.S. firms have a strong competitive advantage over foreign rivals in the capital goods industries. These same experts predict that U.S. firms' competitive advantage in global technology will power them into the twenty-first century.[31]

The March of Globalization

Globalization is the spread of economic innovations around the world and the political and cultural adjustments that accompany this diffusion. Globalization encourages international integration, which has increased substantially during the last generation. In globalized markets and industries, financial capital might be obtained in one national market and used to buy raw materials in another one. Manufacturing equipment bought from a third national market can be used to produce products that are sold in yet a fourth market.[32] Thus, globalization increases the range of opportunities for firms competing in the new competitive landscape. As noted in the Strategic Focus, this is the case for Wal-Mart.

STRATEGIC FOCUS

The March of Globalization: Wal-Mart, China, and Beyond

Wal-Mart is the world's largest retailer. The world should be beware, however, because it is now moving aggressively into international markets. For example, the firm recently invested $1.2 billion to buy a controlling interest in Cifra SA a large Mexican retailer with which it had a six-year joint venture. This move is the first direct investment in one of its foreign partners. While the international division of Wal-Mart is currently small compared to the rest of Wal-Mart's organization, analysts estimate that international sales could reach $27 billion (17 percent of Wal-Mart's annual revenues) by 2000. Currently, other retailers have much more foreign sales such as Tengelmann and Aldi from Germany, Ahold from the Netherlands, and Carrefour from France.

Wal-Mart is trying to achieve boundaryless retailing with global pricing, sourcing, and logistics. Most of Wal-Mart's international investments have been in Canada and Mexico, with close proximity to the United States. However, it has moved recently into Argentina, Brazil, Indonesia, and China. Supercenter stores in Buenos Aires sell as many as 15,000 items in a day, twice as many as in comparable U.S. superstores. Wal-Mart plans to export its North American dominance to other regions of the world as well. Additional descriptions of Wal-Mart's international expansion plans are presented in Chapter 8.

One of the regions Wal-Mart intends to enter is China. China is trying to boldly reform its economy, moving toward a more open and entrepreneurial system. Currently, the Chinese government plans to sell a majority of the 13,000 large and mid-sized state-owned enterprises, along with many of the small firms as well. President Jiang Zemen has stated, "We should encourage mergers of enterprises, standardize bankruptcy procedures, divert laid-off workers, increase efficiency by downsizing staff and encourage re-employment projects." Wal-Mart plans to expand operations in China because its managers estimate that purchasing power in China will equal current levels in the U.S. within seven years. Others are venturing into China as well ranging from Motorola's $2 billion fabrication plant to the joint venture between Enron and Singapore Power. This joint venture is designed to develop small scale power projects that are expected to explode in number over the next several years in China.

Another example of the increasing globalization is the fact that the largest gasoline retailer in the U.S. is owned by a foreign firm. Petroleos de Venezuela owns Citgo which has 14,054 gasoline outlets in the U.S. The number two retailer is Texaco with 13,023 outlets. Citgo, Mobil, and Shell (headquartered in the Netherlands) account for 30 percent of the U.S. gasoline market.

SOURCE: S. Faison, 1997, Bold economic reforms proposed at opening of China Congress, *New York Times*, September 13, nytimes.com; M. M. Hamilton, 1997, At gasoline pumps, an urge to merge, *Washington Post*, July 15, washingtonpost.com; L. Lee and J. Millman, 1997, Wal-Mart to invest $1.2 billion for control of Mexican retailer, *Wall Street Journal Interactive Edition*, June 4, http://www.interactive3.wsj.com; *Wall Street Journal*, Singapore Power, Enron units form joint venture in China, June 21, http://www.wsj.com; W. Zellner, L. Shepard, I. Katz and D. Lindorff, 1997, Wal-Mart spoken here, *Business Week*, June 16, http://www.businessweek.com.

13

The internationalization of markets and industries makes it increasingly difficult to think of some firms as domestic companies. For example, in a recent year, Honda Motor Company (1) employed 14,000 people in the United States; (2) sold 660,000 units in the United States, 480,000 (73 percent) of which it produced there; (3) manufactured its automobiles with 75 percent local U.S. content (parts/assemblies manufactured in the United States); (4) purchased $2.9 billion worth of parts from U.S. suppliers; (5) paid $2.5 billion in federal income tax; (6) invested $3 billion in a research and development center in the United States; and (7) exported 40,000 cars from its U.S. facilities to other nations' markets. At the same time, Chrysler Corporation was producing minivans in Canada and LeBarons in Mexico. Similarly, Toyota Motor Corporation continues to reduce its total employment in Japan while expanding its global workforce. Toyota's Kentucky facility is the only place where the company builds its Avalon sedan and Camry Coupe and station wagon. In 1997, this plant became the sole producer of Toyota's new minivan and in 1998, the firm began to build its T100 pickup in the United States.[33] Likewise, a few years ago, Bridgestone Corporation, headquartered in Japan, acquired Firestone Corporation, then an American firm. Now, Bridgestone is planning to build a $400 million manufacturing facility in the U.S. The intent is to enhance its competitive position in the U.S. market with its ninth plant in the U.S. in addition to its $430 million upgrade of existing facilities.[34]

Given their operations, these firms should not be thought of as Japanese or American. Instead, they can be classified more accurately as global companies striv-

Toyota Motor Corporation has reduced its work force in Japan while expanding globally. Its Georgetown, Kentucky, facility is the sole producer of Toyota minivans, Avalon sedans, and Camry coupes and station wagons.

14

ing to achieve strategic competitiveness in the new competitive landscape. Some believe that because of its enormous economic benefits, globalization will not be stopped. It has been predicted, for example, that genuine free trade in manufactured goods among the United States, Europe, and Japan would add 5 to 10 percent to the triad's annual economic outputs; free trade in the triad's service sector would boost aggregate output by another 15 to 20 percent. Realizing these potential gains in economic output requires a commitment from the industrialized nations to cooperatively stimulate the higher levels of trade necessary for global growth. Eliminating national laws that impede free trade is an important stimulus to increased trading among nations.[35]

Global competition has increased performance standards in many dimensions, including those of quality, cost, productivity, product introduction time, and smooth, flowing operations. Moreover, these standards are not static; they are exacting, requiring continuous improvement from a firm and its employees. As they accept the challenges posed by these increasing standards, companies improve their capabilities and individual workers sharpen their skills. Thus, in the new competitive landscape, competitive success will accrue only to those capable of meeting, if not exceeding global standards. This challenge exists for large firms and for small and midsize companies that develop cooperative relationships (e.g., joint ventures) with larger corporations in order to capitalize on international growth opportunities.[36]

The development of newly industrialized countries is changing the global competitive landscape and significantly increasing competition in global markets. The economic development of Asian countries outside of Japan is increasing the significance of Asian markets. Firms in the newly industrialized Asian countries such as South Korea, however, are becoming major competitors in global industries. For instance, Samsung has become a market leader in the semiconductor industry taking market share away from Japanese and American firms. Samsung is also moving into the aerospace industry. With increasing globalization and the spread of information technology, other countries are likely to develop their industrial bases as well. As this occurs, global markets will expand but competition in those markets will also become more intense.

Firms such as Wal-Mart, Motorola, and Enron are making major moves into international markets. In particular, each of these firms is making important investments in Asia. Of course there are also firms such as Petroleos de Venezuela that have made major investments in North America. Thus, international investments come from many directions and are targeted for many different regions of the world. There are risks with these investments, however. We discuss a number of these risks in Chapter 8. Some have referred to these risks as the liability of foreignness.[37] Critical to success in international markets is a firm's ability to manage international operations such that it takes advantage of the opportunities presented by operating in these markets and overcomes or avoids most of the challenges that exist in these markets. Recent research suggests that firm's are challenged in their early ventures into international markets and can have difficulties if they enter too many different or challenging international markets. In other words, performance may suffer in early efforts to globalize until the skills to manage it are developed. Moverover, performance may suffer with substantial amounts of globalization. In this instance, firms may overdiversify internationally beyond their ability to manage the diversified operations that have been created.[38] The outcome can sometimes be quite painful to firms.[39] Thus, movement into international markets, even for firms with substantial experience in such markets, requires careful planning and selection of the appropriate markets to enter and the most effective strategies to operate successfully in those markets.[40]

Global markets are attractive strategic options for some companies, but they are not the only source of strategic competitiveness. In fact, for most companies, even for those capable of competing successfully in global markets, it is critical to remain committed to the domestic market. In the words of the director of economic studies at the Brookings Institution, "Imported goods are components of a larger share of goods produced and sold in the United States, and international trade is likely to grow in significance. Still, the great bulk of the goods and services Americans consume and invest in is entirely domestic."[41] In the new competitive landscape, firms are challenged to develop the optimal level of globalization, a level that results in appropriate concentrations on a company's domestic and global operations.

In many instances then, strategically competitive companies are those that have learned how to apply competitive insights gained locally (or domestically) on a global scale. These companies do not impose homogeneous solutions in a pluralistic world. Instead, they nourish local insights so they can, as appropriate, modify and apply them in different regions around the world.

Technology and Technological Changes

There are three categories of technological trends and conditions through which technology is significantly altering the nature of competition.

Increasing Rate of Technological Change and Diffusion Both the rate of technology changes and the speed at which new technologies become available and are used have increased substantially over the last 15 to 20 years. *Perpetual innovation* is a term used to describe how rapidly and consistently new, information-intensive technologies replace older ones. The shorter product life cycles resulting from these rapid diffusions of new technologies place a competitive premium on being able to quickly introduce new goods and services into the marketplace. In fact, when products become somewhat indistinguishable because of the widespread and rapid diffusion of technologies, speed to market may be the only source of competitive advantage (see Chapter 5).[42]

There are other indicators of rapid technology diffusion. Some evidence suggests that after only 12 to 18 months, companies likely will have gathered information about their competitors' research and development and product decisions. Often, merely a few weeks pass before a new American-made product introduced in U.S. markets is copied, manufactured, and shipped to the United States by one or more companies in Asia.

Once a source of competitive advantage, today's rate of technological diffusion stifles the protection firms possessed previously through their patents. Patents are now thought by many to be an effective way of protecting proprietary technology primarily in the pharmaceutical and chemical industries. Many firms competing in the electronics industry often do not apply for patents to prevent competitors from gaining access to the technological knowledge included in the patent application.

The Information Age Dramatic changes in information technology have occurred in recent years. Personal computers, cellular phones, artificial intelligence, virtual reality, and massive databases (e.g., Lexis/Nexis) are a few examples of how information is used differently as a result of technological developments. Intel's Andrew Grove believes that electronic mail (e-mail) systems are the first manifestation of a revolution in the flow and management of information in companies throughout the world. In Grove's view, "The informed use of e-mail has two simple but startling implications: It turns days into minutes, and allows each person to reach hundreds of co-workers with the same effort it takes to reach just one."[43] An important outcome of these changes is that the ability to access and effectively use information has become an important source of competitive advantage in virtually all industries.

Companies are now being wired to build electronic networks linking them to customers, employees, vendors, and suppliers. IBM has made this a major thrust in its drive to reorient and revive its business. These networks are often referred to as E-business by IBM and others. E-business is big business. For example, Internet trade is predicted to reach $105 billion by 2000 from only $7.8 billion in 1997. It is even predicted that E-business will eventually represent 75-80 percent of the U.S. gross domestic product. This means that most transactions will be accomplished electronically.[44]

Both the pace of change in information technology and its diffusion will continue to increase. It is predicted, for example, that the number of personal computers in use will grow from over 150 million today to 278 million in 2010.

America Online (AOL) is trying to position itself to take advantage of this brave new world. Steve Case started the firm in 1985 and has experienced many problems since then, the most recent of which occurred in 1996. Case was a dreamer, a visionary who wanted to connect common people, not only the techies. There were many naysayers, particularly at the beginning. Regardless of the naysayers and the significant challenges that America Online has had to overcome, the firm's announcement that it was acquiring Compuserve, the oldest and largest online service, has been hailed as a major feat for AOL. It resulted from a three-way deal

Jeff Bezos, founder of Amazon.com, the largest bookstore in the world, began the company when he realized the enormous potential of selling via the Internet. The company, which sells only via the Internet, has an electronic network that connects it to its customers, employees, and suppliers.

17

with WorldCom. WorldCom bought Compuserve and then sold the online company's 2.6 million subscribers to AOL's networking and Internet access division. AOL is now the number one provider of online services. It adds 6,000 subscribers per day and has increased revenues from $53 million in 1993 to $2 billion in 1997. AOL expects to have 25 million subscribers by 2000. Case suggests that AOL "wants to be the Coca-Cola of the online world."[45]

The declining costs of information technologies and the increased accessibility to them are also evident in the new competitive landscape. The global proliferation of relatively inexpensive computing power and its linkage on a global scale via computer networks combine to increase the speed and diffusion of information technologies. Thus, the competitive potential of information technologies is now available to companies throughout the world rather than only to large firms in Europe, Japan, and North America.[46]

An important electronic pathway through which relatively inexpensive data and information are being distributed is the Internet. Combined, the Internet and World Wide Web create an infrastructure that allows the delivery of information to computers in any location. Access to significant quantities of relatively inexpensive information yields strategic opportunities for a range of industries and companies. Retailers, for example, use the Internet to provide abundant shopping privileges to customers in multiple locations. The power of this means of information access and application results in an almost astonishing array of strategic implications and possibilities.[47]

Anticipating and even creating users' future needs for access to and competitive use of information is challenging. The nature of this complex situation in an emerging industry seems to argue against a firm's long-term competitive success. Bill Gates, Microsoft's CEO, observed recently that while his firm may be the most dominant force in the personal computer industry today, "the landscape is changing fast enough that the company's continued role is far from guaranteed." This opinion was offered at a time when Microsoft controlled more than 80 percent of the world market for PC operating systems.[48] Thus, even for companies holding dominant positions such as Microsoft, the information age's rapid changes yield an uncertain and ambiguous future.

Increasing Knowledge Intensity *Knowledge* (information, intelligence, and expertise) is the basis of technology and its application. In the new competitive landscape, knowledge is a critical organizational resource and is increasingly a valuable source of competitive advantage. Because of this, many companies now strive to transmute the accumulated knowledge of individual employees into a corporate asset. Some argue that the value of intangible assets, including knowledge, is growing as a proportion of total shareholder value.[49] The probability of achieving strategic competitiveness in the new competitive landscape is enhanced for the firm that realizes that its survival depends on the ability to capture intelligence, transform it into usable knowledge, and diffuse it rapidly throughout the company.[50] Companies that accept this challenge shift their focus from obtaining the information to exploiting the information to gain a competitive advantage over rival firms.[51]

Our discussion of conditions in the new competitive landscape shows that firms must be able to adapt quickly to achieve strategic competitiveness and earn above-average returns. The term strategic flexibility describes a firm's ability to do this. **Strategic flexibility** is a set of capabilities firms use to respond to various demands and opportunities that are a part of dynamic and uncertain competitive environments.[52] Firms should develop strategic flexibility in all areas of their operations. Such capabilities in terms of manufacturing, for example, allow firms to "switch gears—from, for example, rapid product development to low cost—relatively quickly and with minimum resources."[53]

To achieve strategic flexibility, many firms have to develop organizational slack. Slack resources allow the firm some flexibility to respond to environmental changes.[54] When the changes required are large, firms may have to undergo strategic reorientations. Such reorientations can change drastically a firm's competitive strategy.[55] Strategic reorientations are often the result of a firm's poor performance. For example, when a firm earns negative returns, its stakeholders (see discussion later in this chapter) are likely to place pressure on the top executives to make major changes.[56] To achieve continuous strategic flexibility, a firm has to develop the capacity to learn. As such, the learning is continuous, thereby providing the firm with new and current sets of skills. This allows it to adapt to its environment as the environment changes.[57]

Through careful strategic decisions, Coca-Cola has created strategic flexibility. It has done so by developing effective distribution of its products. For example, several years ago it developed a subsidiary bottling operation. It wanted to build an experienced and large bottling network to benefit from economies of scale and have significant capital to invest in distribution systems to enhance sales of Coca-Cola. Today this small set of anchor bottlers serves as the base for Coca-Cola's global distribution system. While the economies of scale and slack resources for investment provide flexibility of action for Coca-Cola, the real source of flexibility is in the way these anchor bottlers are managed. For example, CCE, the anchor domestic bottler in the United States, is substantially decentralized. In this way, the bottling operation in one region of the country can use different advertising campaigns from bottlers in other regions. Because of its success, CCE is becoming Coca-Cola's primary bottler in Great Britain, France, Belgium, the Netherlands and Luxembourg. Thus, CCE has the resources and expertise to move into different regions of the world, which only increases its economies of scale.[58]

Strategic flexibility is a set of capabilities firms use to respond to various demands and opportunities that are a part of dynamic and uncertain competitive environments.

Next, we describe two models used by firms to generate the strategic inputs needed to successfully formulate and implement strategies and to maintain strategic flexibility in the process of doing so.

THE I/O MODEL OF ABOVE-AVERAGE RETURNS

From the 1960s through the 1980s, the external environment was thought to be the *primary* determinant of strategies firms selected to be successful.[59] The I/O (industrial organization) model explains the dominant influence of the external environment on firms' strategic actions. This model specifies that the chosen industry in which to compete has a stronger influence on a firm's performance than do the choices managers make inside their organizations.[60] Firm performance is believed to be predicted primarily by a range of an industry's properties, including economies of scale, barriers to entry, diversification, product differentiation, and the degree of concentration[61] (these industry characteristics are examined in Chapter 2).

Grounded in the economics discipline, the I/O model has four underlying assumptions. First, the external environment is assumed to impose pressures and constraints that determine the strategies that would result in above-average returns. Second, most firms competing within a particular industry, or within a certain segment of an industry, are assumed to control similar strategically relevant resources and pursue similar strategies in light of those resources. The I/O model's third assumption is that resources used to implement strategies are highly mobile across firms. Because of resource mobility, any resource differences that might develop between firms will be short lived. Fourth, organizational decision makers are assumed to be rational and committed to acting in the firm's best interests as shown by their profit maximizing behaviors.[62]

The I/O model challenges firms to locate the most attractive industry in which to compete. Because most firms are assumed to have similar strategically relevant resources that are mobile across companies, competitiveness generally can be increased only when they find the industry with the highest profit potential and learn how to use their resources to implement the strategy required by the structural characteristics in that industry. The *five forces model of competition* is an analytical tool used to help firms with this task. This model (explained in detail in Chapter 2) encompasses many variables and tries to capture the complexity of competition.[63]

The five forces model suggests that an industry's potential profitability (i.e., its rate of return on invested capital relative to its cost of capital) is a function of interactions among five forces (suppliers, buyers, competitive rivalry among firms currently in the industry, product substitutes, and potential entrants to the industry).[64] Using this tool, a firm is challenged to understand an industry's profit potential and the strategy that should be implemented to establish a defensible competitive position, given the industry's structural characteristics. Typically, this model suggests that firms can earn above-average returns by manufacturing standardized products at costs below those of competitors (a cost leadership strategy) or differentiated products for which customers are willing to pay a price premium (a differentiation strategy). Cost leadership and differentiation strategies are described fully in Chapter 4.

As shown in Figure 1.3, the I/O model suggests that above-average returns are earned when firms implement the strategy dictated by the characteristics of the general, industry, and competitive environments. Companies that develop or acquire the internal skills needed to implement strategies required by the external environment are likely to succeed, while those that do not are likely to fail. As such, above-average returns are determined by external characteristics rather than the firm's unique internal resources and capabilities.

Let us consider the bagel industry as an example. It is a high growth industry with substantial potential to earn above-average returns. U.S. industry sales in-

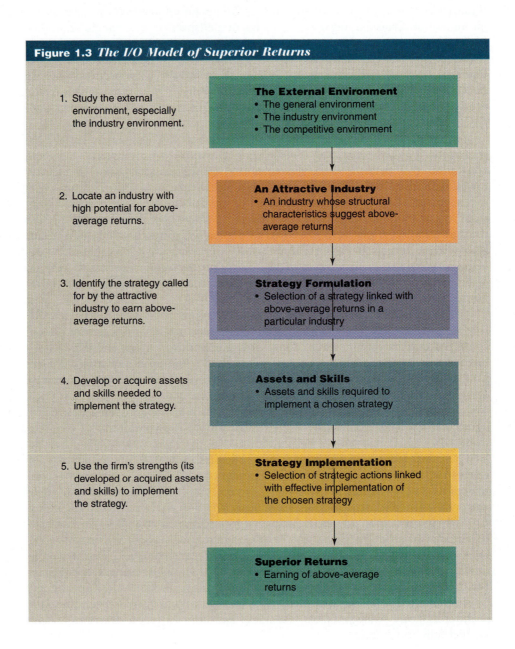

Figure 1.3 *The I/O Model of Superior Returns*

1. Study the external environment, especially the industry environment.

The External Environment
- The general environment
- The industry environment
- The competitive environment

2. Locate an industry with high potential for above-average returns.

An Attractive Industry
- An industry whose structural characteristics suggest above-average returns

3. Identify the strategy called for by the attractive industry to earn above-average returns.

Strategy Formulation
- Selection of a strategy linked with above-average returns in a particular industry

4. Develop or acquire assets and skills needed to implement the strategy.

Assets and Skills
- Assets and skills required to implement a chosen strategy

5. Use the firm's strengths (its developed or acquired assets and skills) to implement the strategy.

Strategy Implementation
- Selection of strategic actions linked with effective implementation of the chosen strategy

Superior Returns
- Earning of above-average returns

creased from $1.6 billion in 1995 to $2.3 billion in 1996, over a 40 percent rise in one year. Industry experts predict this growth trend for global sales as well. Interestingly, the bagel industry is in its infancy and thus has much potential. Evidence of this fact is shown by the growth of The Great Canadian Bagel Ltd. It was started in 1993 and by the end of 1996, it had 112 bakeries in operation. Other bagel firms are opening operations in Europe and Asia. Clearly it is an attractive industry to enter.[65]

Recent research provides support for the I/O model. It showed that approximately 20 percent of firm profitability was explained by industry. In other words, 20 percent of a firm's profitability is determined by the industry(ies) in which it chooses to operate. This research also showed, however, that 36 percent of the variance in profitability could be attributed to firm characteristics and actions.[66] The results of this research suggest that both the environment and firm characteristics play a role in determining a firm's specific level of profitability. Thus, there is likely a reciprocal relationship between the environment and firm strategy, and this interrelationship affects firm performance.[67]

As the research results suggest, successful competition in the new competitive landscape mandates that a firm build a unique set of resources and capabilities. This should be done, however, within the framework of the dynamics of the industry (or industries) in which a firm competes. In this context, a firm is viewed as a bundle of market activities and a bundle of resources. Market activities are understood through application of the I/O model. The development and effective use of a firm's resources, capabilities, and competencies is understood through application of the resource-based model. Through an effective combination of results gained by using both the I/O and resource-based models, firms dramatically increase the probability of achieving strategic competitiveness and earning above-average returns.

THE RESOURCE-BASED MODEL OF ABOVE-AVERAGE RETURNS

The resource-based model assumes that each organization is a collection of unique resources and capabilities that provides the basis for its strategy and is the *primary* source of its returns. In the new competitive landscape, this model argues that a firm is a collection of evolving capabilities that is managed dynamically in pursuit of above-average returns.[68] Thus, according to this model, differences in firms' performances across time are driven *primarily* by their unique resources and capabilities rather than by an industry's structural characteristics.[69] This model also assumes that over time, a firm acquires different resources and develops unique capabilities. As such, all firms competing within a particular industry may not possess the same strategically relevant resources and capabilities. Another assumption of this model is that resources may not be highly mobile across firms. The differences in resources form the basis of competitive advantage.[70]

Resources are inputs into a firm's production process, such as capital equipment, the skills of individual employees, patents, finance, and talented managers. In general, a firm's resources can be classified into three categories: physical, human, and organizational capital.[71] Described fully in Chapter 3, resources are both tangible and intangible in nature.

Resources are inputs into a firm's production process, such as capital equipment, the skills of individual employees, patents, finance, and talented managers.

Individual resources alone may not yield a competitive advantage. For example, a sophisticated piece of manufacturing equipment may become a strategically relevant resource only when its use is integrated effectively with other aspects of a firm's operations (such as marketing and the work of employees). In general, it is through the combination and integration of sets of resources that competitive advantages are formed. A **capability** is the capacity for a set of resources to integratively perform a task or an activity.[72] Through continued use, capabilities become stronger and more difficult for competitors to understand and imitate.[73] As a source of competitive advantage, a capability "... should be neither so simple that it is highly imitable, nor so complex that it defies internal steering and control."[74]

A **capability** is the capacity for a set of resources to integratively perform a task or an activity.

Amazon has taken the retail book market by storm. It was the first firm to sell books on the Internet. As such Amazon has developed important capabilities for marketing and distributing books online. This firm has shown that a large inventory and beautiful facilities are not necessary to sell books. However, Amazon's capabilities can be imitated. In fact, they are being imitated by the large and powerful Barnes & Noble. Barnes & Noble is the leading book marketer in the United States. It recently opened its own online bookshop. Developing Web pages and online order taking is copied easily. Barnes & Noble's action could be bad news for Amazon. It remains to be seen whether Amazon will enjoy many first mover advantages. (See Chapter 5 for a full discussion of first mover advantages.) Analysts are betting that Barnes & Noble will win this competitive battle if for no other reason than it has the resources to wage cutthroat competition.[75]

The resource-based model of competitive advantage is shown in Figure 1.4. In contrast to the I/O model, the resource-based view is grounded in the perspective that a firm's internal environment, in terms of its resources and capabilities, is more critical to the determination of strategic actions than is the external environment. Instead of focusing on the accumulation of resources necessary to implement the strategy dictated by conditions and constraints in the external environment (I/O model), the resource-based view suggests that a firm's unique resources and capabilities provide the basis for a strategy. The strategy chosen should allow the firm to best exploit its core competencies relative to opportunities in the external environment.

Not all of a firm's resources and capabilities have the potential to be the basis for competitive advantage. This potential is realized when resources and capabilities are valuable, rare, costly to imitate, and nonsubstitutable.[76] Resources are *valuable* when they allow a firm to exploit opportunities and/or neutralize threats in its external environment; they are *rare* when possessed by few, if any, current and potential competitors; they are *costly to imitate* when other firms either cannot obtain them or are at a cost disadvantage to obtain them compared to the firm that already possesses them; and they are nonsubstitutable when they have no structural equivalents.[77]

Core competencies are resources and capabilities that serve as a source of competitive advantage for a firm over its rivals.

When these four criteria are met, resources and capabilities become core competencies. **Core competencies** are resources and capabilities that serve as a source of competitive advantage for a firm over its rivals.[78] Often related to a firm's functional skills (e.g., the marketing function is a core competence at Philip Morris), the development, nurturing, and application of core competencies throughout a firm may be highly related to strategic competitiveness. Managerial competencies are important in most firms. For example such competencies have been shown to be critically important to successful entry into foreign markets.[79] Such competen-

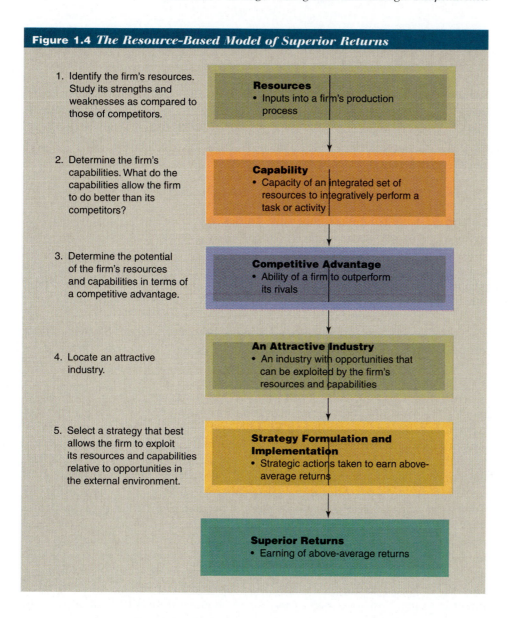

Figure 1.4 *The Resource-Based Model of Superior Returns*

1. Identify the firm's resources. Study its strengths and weaknesses as compared to those of competitors.

Resources
- Inputs into a firm's production process

2. Determine the firm's capabilities. What do the capabilities allow the firm to do better than its competitors?

Capability
- Capacity of an integrated set of resources to integratively perform a task or activity

3. Determine the potential of the firm's resources and capabilities in terms of a competitive advantage.

Competitive Advantage
- Ability of a firm to outperform its rivals

4. Locate an attractive industry.

An Attractive Industry
- An industry with opportunities that can be exploited by the firm's resources and capabilities

5. Select a strategy that best allows the firm to exploit its resources and capabilities relative to opportunities in the external environment.

Strategy Formulation and Implementation
- Strategic actions taken to earn above-average returns

Superior Returns
- Earning of above-average returns

23

cies may include the capability to effectively organize and govern complex and diverse operations and the capability to create and communicate a strategic vision.[80] Another set of important competencies is product related. Included among these competencies are the capability to develop innovative new products and to reengineer existing products to satisfy changing consumer tastes.[81] Competencies must also be under continuous development to keep them up-to-date. This requires a systematic program for updating old skills and learning new ones.[82] Dynamic core competencies are especially important in rapidly changing environments such as those that exist in high technology industries.[83] Thus, the resource-based model argues that core competencies are the basis for a firm's competitive advantage, its strategic competitiveness, and its ability to earn above-average returns.

STRATEGIC INTENT AND STRATEGIC MISSION

Resulting from analyses of a firm's internal and external environments is the information required to form a strategic intent and develop a strategic mission (see Figure 1.1). Both intent and mission are linked with strategic competitiveness.

Strategic Intent

Strategic intent is the leveraging of a firm's internal resources, capabilities, and core competencies to accomplish the firm's goals in the competitive environment.[84] Concerned with winning competitive battles and obtaining global leadership, strategic intent implies a significant stretch of an organization's resources, capabilities, and core competencies. When established effectively, a strategic intent can cause people to perform in ways they never imagined would be possible.[85] Strategic intent exists when all employees and levels of a firm are committed to the pursuit of a specific (and significant) performance criterion. Some argue that strategic intent provides employees with the only goal worthy of personal effort and commitment—to unseat the best or remain the best, worldwide.[86] Strategic intent has been formed effectively when people believe fervently in their product and industry and when they are focused totally on their firm's ability to outdo its competitors.[87]

The following examples are expressions of strategic intent. Unocal Corporation intends "to become a high-performance multinational energy company—not the biggest, but the *best*." According to Eli Lilly and Company, "It's our strategic intent that customers worldwide view us as their most valued pharmaceutical partner." Phillips Petroleum Company seeks "to be the top performer in everything" the company does. Intel intends to become the premier building-block supplier to the computer industry. Microsoft believes that its "holy grail" is to provide the Yellow Pages for an electronic marketplace of on-line information systems. Canon desires to "beat Xerox" and Honda strives to become a second Ford (a company it identified as a pioneer in the automobile industry). The CEO of Pep Boys does not believe in friendly competition; instead, he wants to dominate the competition and, by doing so, put them out of business. At Procter & Gamble (P&G), employees participate in a program the CEO calls "combat training." The program's intent is to focus on ways P&G can beat the competition. AlliedSignal wants to rank with General Electric and Merck as one of America's premier profitmakers. One way AlliedSignal seeks to achieve this strategic intent is to record 6 percent annual productivity improvements "forever." Chrysler Corporation's strategic intent is to be the world's premier car and light truck manufacturer by 2000.[88]

Because of its emotional edge, strategic intent may even be described metaphorically. In a recent annual report, Reebok International showed a series of pictures depicting an athlete crossing a high-jump bar. In her own handwriting, the athlete described her commitment to being the best and to winning:

> It's about raising the bar. I can jump higher. I know it. I can see it. I'm stronger, faster, I've learned more. The key is to focus, to concentrate on each basic element that goes into a jump. Jumping is my gift and it's a privilege to improve the gift. When everything works right, when you're focused and relaxed, it's kind of like flying. One thing that keeps you involved in jumping is that you

Strategic intent is the leveraging of a firm's internal resources, capabilities, and core competencies to accomplish the firm's goals in the competitive environment.

24

are always trying to clear the next height. Even if you miss, you come away from every jump knowing you can go higher.[89]

The words of this athlete appear to reflect Reebok's intent to focus and concentrate on every part of its business in order to constantly improve its performance and, by doing so, achieve strategic competitiveness and earn above-average returns.

But it is not enough for a firm to only know its own strategic intent. To perform well demands that we also identify our competitors' strategic intent. Only when intentions of others are understood can a firm become aware of the resolve, stamina, and inventiveness (traits linked with effective strategic intents) of those competitors.[90] A company's success may be grounded in a keen and deep understanding of the strategic intent of customers, suppliers, partners, and competitors.[91]

Strategic Mission

As our discussion shows, strategic intent is *internally focused*. It is concerned with identifying the resources, capabilities, and core competencies on which a firm can base its strategic actions. Strategic intent reflects what a firm is capable of doing as a result of its core competencies and the unique ways they can be used to exploit a competitive advantage.

Strategic mission flows from strategic intent. Externally focused, the **strategic mission** is a statement of a firm's unique purpose and the scope of its operations in product and market terms.[92] A strategic mission provides general descriptions of the products a firm intends to produce and the markets it will serve using its internally based core competencies. The interdependent relationship between strategic intent and strategic mission is shown in Figure 1.5.

An effective strategic mission establishes a firm's individuality and is exciting, inspiring, and relevant to all stakeholders.[93] Together, strategic intent and strategic mission yield the insights required to formulate and implement the firm's strategies.

Based partially on a firm's strategic intent and mission, top executives develop a *strategic orientation*, a predisposition to adopt a certain strategy(ies) over others.[94] Strategic orientation is also affected by the national culture in an executive's home

The **strategic mission** is a statement of a firm's unique purpose and the scope of its operations in product and market terms.

25

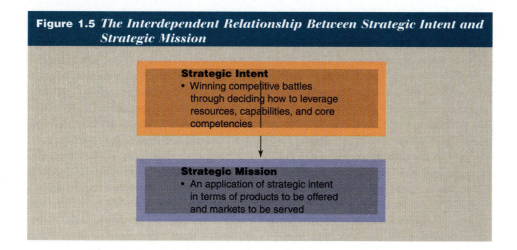

Figure 1.5 *The Interdependent Relationship Between Strategic Intent and Strategic Mission*

Strategic Intent
- Winning competitive battles through deciding how to leverage resources, capabilities, and core competencies

Strategic Mission
- An application of strategic intent in terms of products to be offered and markets to be served

country and the institutional environment where the firm's operations are located.[95] A competitor's strategic orientations can be predicted based on knowledge of its strategic intent and mission, the institutional environment where its home office is located, and the cultural values of the top executives' home country.

When a firm is strategically competitive and earning above-average returns, it has the capacity to satisfy its stakeholders' interests. The stakeholder groups a firm serves are examined next.

STAKEHOLDERS

Stakeholders are the individuals and groups who can affect and are affected by the strategic outcomes achieved and who have enforceable claims on a firm's performance.

An organization is a system of primary stakeholder groups with whom it establishes and manages relationships.[96] **Stakeholders** are the individuals and groups who can affect and are affected by the strategic outcomes achieved and who have enforceable claims on a firm's performance.[97] Claims against an organization's performance are enforced through a stakeholder's ability to withhold participation essential to a firm's survival, competitiveness, and profitability.[98] Stakeholders continue to support an organization when its performance meets or exceeds their expectations.

Thus, organizations have dependency relationships with their stakeholders. Firms, however, are not equally dependent on all stakeholders at all times; as a consequence, every stakeholder does not have the same level of influence. The more critical and valued a stakeholder's participation is, the greater a firm's dependency on it. Greater dependence, in turn, results in more potential influence for the stakeholder over a firm's commitments, decisions, and actions. In one sense, the challenge strategists face is to either accommodate or find ways to insulate the organization from the demands of stakeholders controlling critical resources.[99]

STRATEGIC FOCUS

Stakeholders Are on Both Sides

There are several types of stakeholders and firms must be sensitive to the needs of all of them if they are to earn above-average returns. General Motors, for example, must deal with the United Auto Workers (UAW) union (product market stakeholder) that represents many of its employees while at the same time satisfying its shareholders and potential shareholders (capital market stakeholders). This can be challenging. In 1997, GM had the lowest productivity in the auto industry. GM requires 47 worker-hours to produce an automobile while Nissan can do it in 28 worker-hours. Chrysler and Ford require 38 and 41 worker-hours respectively. This productivity gap costs GM $700 more per car than Nissan. Shareholders and analysts on Wall Street placed significant pressure on GM to improve its productivity. To do so, GM planned to eliminate 50,000 plant jobs over a several year span. However, the UAW fought GM on this decision and threatened to strike.

Unions have employees, too. For example, the Teamsters Union experienced a threatened strike from its office and professional employees. The employees were dissatisfied with the union's proposal that would require employees to have 33 years service to reach the top pay scale, the introduction of time clocks, and restrictions on the use of flextime. The office and professional employees union forced the dispute to be submitted to a mediator. Not all unions are as tough in their negotiations. The German Chemical Union agreed to a reduction in wages. Because of financial problems in German companies, the union agreed to a 10 percent decrease in wages. The union has been pressured by the federal government in Germany to make concessions because of 11 percent unemployment. The German union negotiator called the agreement a reaction to the changing economy.

Another important product market stakeholder is the customer. When a firm has one primary customer, that customer often has significant power as Lockheed Martin Corporation has discovered. The Defense Department, Lockheed's primary customer, expressed substantial concern and scrutinized the potential merger between Lockheed and Northrop Grumman Corporation. Defense leaders are particularly concerned about the potential for less innovation and higher costs. There are discussions about requiring Lockheed to spin off businesses for the deal to be approved. If approved, the new company of Lockheed and Northrop would own 80 percent of the electronic machinery that jams radar equipment and protect aircraft. These firms must be careful not to anger their biggest customer, the powerful federal government.

SOURCE: S. Crock, S. Browder and W. Echikson, 1997, Lockheed: A deal too far? *Business Week*, July 31, businessweek.com; F. Swoboda, 1997, Teamsters on unusual side in labor tiff, *Washington Post*, July 16, washingtonpost.com; *Wall Street Journal Interactive Edition*, 1997, German chemical union agrees to let companies cut wages, http://www.interactive5.wsj.com; B. Vlasic, 1997, GM can't afford to budge: To compete on productivity, it risks strikes, *Business Week*, June 16, http://www.businessweek.com.

The discussion in the Strategic Focus regarding GM's stakeholders suggests the potential differences in power among stakeholders. GM's shareholders and Wall Street are more powerful than the union representing GM workers. GM is willing to accept a strike if necessary in order to achieve the increase in productivity desired by the shareholders. Lockheed's case shows the firm's dependency on its stakeholder, the U.S. government. The Strategic Focus also provides examples of several different types of stakeholders, the topic of our next discussion.

Classification of Stakeholders

The parties involved with a firm's operations can be separated into three groups.[100] As shown in Figure 1.6, these groups are the *capital market stakeholders* (shareholders and the major suppliers of a firm's capital), the *product market stakeholders* (the firm's primary customers, suppliers, host communities, and unions representing the workforce), and the *organizational stakeholders* (all of a firm's employees, including both nonmanagerial and managerial personnel).

Each of these stakeholder groups expects those making strategic decisions in a firm to provide the leadership through which their valued objectives will be accomplished.[101] But these groups' objectives often differ from one another, sometimes placing managers in situations where tradeoffs have to be made.

Grounded in laws governing private property and private enterprise, the most obvious stakeholders, at least in U.S. firms, are *shareholders*—those who have invested capital in a firm in the expectation of earning at least an average return on their investments. Shareholders want the return on their investment (and, hence, their wealth) to be maximized. This could be accomplished at the expense of investing in a firm's future. Gains achieved by reducing investment in research and development, for example, could be returned to shareholders (thereby increasing the short-term return on their investments). However, a short-term enhancement

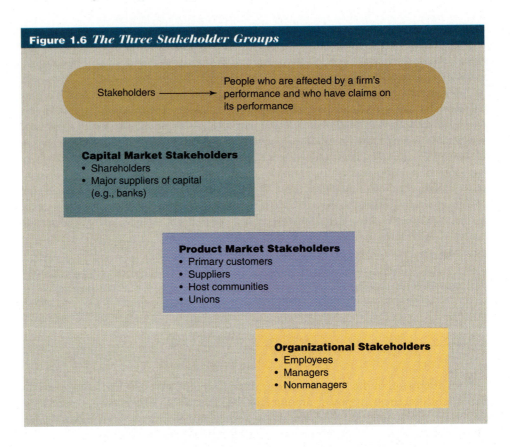

Figure 1.6 The Three Stakeholder Groups

Stakeholders → People who are affected by a firm's performance and who have claims on its performance

Capital Market Stakeholders
- Shareholders
- Major suppliers of capital (e.g., banks)

Product Market Stakeholders
- Primary customers
- Suppliers
- Host communities
- Unions

Organizational Stakeholders
- Employees
- Managers
- Nonmanagers

of shareholders' wealth can negatively affect the firm's future competitive ability. Sophisticated shareholders, with diversified portfolios, may sell their interests if a firm fails to invest in its future. This is exemplified in the Strategic Focus as GM's shareholders are exerting pressure to increase the firm's productivity. Those making strategic decisions are responsible for a firm's survival in both the short and the long terms. Accordingly, it is in the interests of neither the organizational stakeholders nor the product market stakeholders for investments in the company to be unduly minimized.

In contrast to shareholders, customers prefer that investors receive a minimum return on their investments (also see the Strategic Focus discussion of the Defense Department's concerns about Lockheed's strategy). As such, customers could have their interests maximized when the quality and reliability of a firm's products are improved, but without a price increase. High returns to customers might come at the expense of lower returns negotiated with capital market shareholders.

Because of potential conflicts, each firm is challenged to manage its stakeholders. First, a firm must carefully identify all important stakeholders. Second, it must prioritize them in case it cannot satisfy all of them. In doing this, power is the most critical criterion. Other criteria might include the urgency of satisfying each particular stakeholder and the degree of importance to the firm.[102] When earning above-average returns, this challenge is lessened substantially. With the capability and flexibility provided by above-average returns, a firm can more easily satisfy all stakeholders simultaneously.

When earning only average returns, however, a firm may find the management of stakeholders to be more difficult. In these situations, tradeoffs must be made. With average returns, a firm is unlikely to maximize the interests of all stakeholders. The objective becomes one of at least minimally satisfying each stakeholder. Tradeoff decisions are made in light of how dependent the firm is on the support of the stakeholder groups. An example of how stakeholders can demand satisfaction of their claims on a firm's performance is provided in the next subsection. A firm earning below-average returns does not have the capacity to minimally satisfy all stakeholders. The managerial challenge in this case is to make tradeoffs that minimize the amount of support lost from stakeholders.

Societal values influence the general weightings allocated among the three stakeholder groups. Although all three groups are served by firms in at least the major industrialized nations, the priorities in their service vary somewhat because of cultural differences. These differences are shown in the following commentary:

> In America . . . shareholders have a comparatively big say in the running of the enterprises they own; workers . . . have much less influence. In many European countries, shareholders have less say and workers more . . . In Japan . . . managers have been left alone to run their companies as they see fit—namely for the benefit of employees and of allied companies, as much as for shareholders.[103]

29

Thus, it is important that those responsible for managing stakeholder relationships in a country outside their native land use a global mind-set. A **global mind-set** is the "capacity to appreciate the beliefs, values, behaviors, and business practices of individuals and organizations from a variety of regions and cultures."[104] Use of a global mind-set allows managers to better understand the realities and preferences that are a part of the world region and culture in which they are working.

In the next three subsections, additional information is presented about the stakeholder groups that firms manage.

Capital Market Stakeholders Both shareholders and lenders expect a firm to preserve and enhance the wealth they have entrusted to it. The returns expected are commensurate with the degree of risk accepted with those investments (i.e., lower returns are expected with low-risk investments; higher returns are expected with high-risk investments).

If lenders become dissatisfied, they can impose stricter covenants on subsequent capital borrowing. Shareholders can reflect their dissatisfaction through several means, including the sale of their stock. When aware of potential or actual dissatisfactions among capital market stakeholders, a firm may respond to their concerns. The firm's response to dissatisfied stakeholders is affected by the nature of its dependency relationship with them (which, as noted earlier, is also influenced by a society's values). The greater and more significant the dependency relationship, the more direct and significant a firm's response will be.

The power and influence of capital market stakeholders are exemplified in their effects on Rubbermaid in 1997. Rubbermaid announced that its earnings were going to be over 30 percent below the expected amount. At the first announcement of this downward revision of estimated earnings, investors signaled their dissatisfaction by driving down the share price by 11 percent. With the second announcement of bad news, shareholders increased pressure on management to make changes to improve shareholder value. This pressure has led to changes with many

A **global mind-set** is the capacity to appreciate the beliefs, values, behaviors, and business practices of individuals and organizations from a variety of regions and cultures.

managers being forced to resign while others have left voluntarily. Top-level managers are making other changes as well. For example, they are seeking new ways to distribute the firm's products in addition to the traditional outlets such as Wal-Mart. The firm recently formed an alliance with Amway Corp. and is trying to tap specialty stores and the Internet. Thus, shareholders have prompted significant actions on the part of Rubbermaid's top management.[105] At least in the short run, this additional support for the capital market stakeholders may come at the expense of returns to other stakeholders.

Product Market Stakeholders Initial observation of customers, suppliers, host communities, and unions representing workers might suggest little commonality among their interests. However, close inspection indicates that all four parties can benefit as firms engage in competitive battles. For example, depending on product and industry characteristics, marketplace competition may result in lower product prices being charged to a firm's customers and higher prices paid to its suppliers (the firm might be willing to pay higher supplier prices to ensure delivery of the types of goods and services linked with competitive success).

As noted in Chapter 4, customers, as stakeholders, demand reliable products at the lowest possible prices. Suppliers seek assured customers willing to pay the highest sustainable prices for the goods and services they receive. Host communities want companies willing to be long-term employers and providers of tax revenues, without placing excessive demands on public support services. Union officials are interested in secure jobs, under ideal working conditions, for employees they represent. Thus, product market stakeholders are generally satisfied when a firm's profit margin yields the lowest acceptable return to capital market stakeholders (i.e., the lowest return lenders and shareholders will accept and still retain their interests in the firm).

All product market stakeholders are important in a competitive business environment. However, in many firms, customers are being emphasized. Jack Welch, CEO of General Electric, is known for his position that satisfied customers are the only source of job security for the firm's organizational stakeholders. At AT&T, one of the company's top-level executives cautions employees to ask why customers (and/or competitors) are not being discussed after the first 15 minutes of any meeting. If they are not being talked about after a second 15-minute period, the executive believes people should leave the meeting.[106]

In 1946, PepsiCola Co. made a pioneering move that established a new market niche for its product. It hired Edward F. Boyd to develop a sales team to market PepsiCola to African-Americans. Mr. Boyd was one of very few African-Americans in a professional position with a major U.S. corporation. Because of other actions taken by PepsiCola before this time (e.g., scholarships and job programs), the firm had a generally positive image in the African-American community. Mr. Boyd changed the image of African-Americans used in advertisements (e.g., he developed an ad in 1948 for a store display showing a smiling African-American woman serving her family PepsiCola) as opposed to the Aunt Jemima ads, for example. One of his models was Ron Brown, the future Secretary of Commerce. As a result of these efforts, PepsiCola captured a large share of this market niche and outsold Coca-Cola in Chicago for the first time in the late 1940s. Thus, PepsiCola targeted, satisfied, and captured this set of customers.[107] The relationship between satisfaction of customers' needs and strategic competitiveness is examined in detail in Chapter 4.

Organizational Stakeholders Employees, nonmanagerial and managerial, expect a firm to provide a dynamic, stimulating, and rewarding working environment. These stakeholders are usually satisfied working for a company that is growing and developing their skills, especially the skills required to be effective team members and to meet or exceed global work standards. Workers who learn how to productively use rapidly developing knowledge are thought to be critical to organizational success. In a collective sense, the education and skills of a nation's workforce may be its dominant competitive weapon in a global economy.[108]

In the next section, we describe the people responsible for the design and execution of strategic management processes. Various names are given to these people—top-level managers, executives, strategists, the top management team, and general managers are examples. Throughout this book, these names are used interchangeably. But, in all cases, they describe the work of persons responsible for designing and implementing a successful strategic management process.

As is discussed in Chapter 12, top-level managers can be a source of competitive advantage. The decisions and actions these people make to *combine* resources to create capabilities can also result in a competitive advantage.

ORGANIZATIONAL STRATEGISTS

Small organizations may have a single strategist. In many cases, this person owns the firm and is deeply involved with its daily operations. At the other extreme, large, diversified firms have many top-level managers. In addition to the CEO and other top-level officials (e.g., chief operating officer and chief financial officer), they have managers who are responsible for the performance of individual business units.

Typically, stakeholders have high expectations of top-level managers, particularly the CEO. These expectations place significant pressure on top executives. Because of these pressures and the complexity and challenges of the job, many people do not want to be managers, particularly top-level managers. In the current global economy and new competitive landscape, top managers hold insecure positions. Many middle management positions have been eliminated through restructurings, placing more stress on the remaining top- and lower-level managers. These problems are exemplified in Solid State Measurements Inc.'s search for new members for its top management team. The CEO had significant problems locating adequate applicants for the positions. Charles Thomas, Solid State's CEO, said he found the talent pool to be very thin. As a result the search was long, arduous, and frustrating.[109]

Top-level managers play critical roles in firms' efforts to achieve desired strategic outcomes. In fact, some believe that every organizational failure is actually a failure of those who hold the final responsibility for the quality and effectiveness of a firm's decisions and actions.[110]

Decisions for which strategists are responsible include how resources will be developed or acquired, at what price they will be obtained, and how they will be used. Managerial decisions also influence how information flows in a company, the strategies a firm chooses to implement, and the scope of its operations. In making these decisions, managers must assess the risk involved in taking the actions being considered. This risk is then factored into the decision.[111] The firm's strategic intent (discussed earlier) will affect the decisions managers make. Also, managers'

31

strategic orientations, which include their personal values and beliefs, will affect the decisions.[112] Additionally, how strategists complete their work and their patterns of interactions with others significantly influence the way a firm does business and affect its ability to develop a competitive advantage.

How a firm does business is captured by the concept of organizational culture. Critical to strategic leadership practices and the implementation of strategies, **organizational culture** refers to the complex set of ideologies, symbols, and core values shared throughout the firm and that influences the way it conducts business. Thus, culture is the "social energy that drives—or fails to drive—the organization."[113] Andersen Consulting's core values include the requirement that employees attend company-sponsored training classes in professional attire, an expectation of hard work (up to 80 hours per week), and a willingness to work effectively with others in order to accomplish all tasks that are parts of the company-wide demanding workload.[114] These core values at Andersen Consulting provide a particular type of social energy that drives the firm's efforts. As we discuss in Chapters 2, 12, and 13, organizational culture is a potential source of competitive advantage.[115]

After evaluating available information and alternatives, top-level managers must frequently choose from among similarly attractive alternatives. The most effective strategists have the self-confidence necessary to select the best alternatives, allocate the required level of resources to them, and effectively explain to interested parties why certain alternatives were selected.[116]

When choosing among alternatives, strategists are accountable for treating employees, suppliers, customers, and others with fairness and respect. Evidence suggests that trust can be a source of competitive advantage, thereby supporting an organizational commitment to treat stakeholders fairly and with respect.[117] Nonetheless, firms cannot succeed without people who, following careful and

Organizational culture refers to the complex set of ideologies, symbols, and core values shared throughout the firm and that influences the way it conducts business. It is the social energy that drives—or fails to drive—the organization.

32

Organizational culture is the social energy that drives a firm and influences the way it does business. In many high-level corporate environments, core values include attending training classes, wearing professional attire, and working hard and effectively with other employees.

sometimes difficult analyses, are willing to make tough decisions—the types of decisions that result in strategic competitiveness and above-average returns.[118]

The Work of Effective Strategists

Perhaps not surprisingly, hard work, thorough analyses, a willingness to be brutally honest, a penchant for always wanting the firm and its people to accomplish more, and common sense are prerequisites to an individual's success as a strategist.[119] John Sculley, former CEO of Apple Computer, describes the reality of work in the 1990s, suggesting that sleeping through the night is an outmoded remnant of the agrarian and industrial ages. "People don't live that way anymore," Sculley believes. "It's a 24-hour day, not an 8-to-5 day."[120]

In addition to the characteristics mentioned, effective strategists must be able to think clearly and ask many questions. Their strategic effectiveness increases as they find ways for others also to think and inquire about what a firm is doing and why. But, in particular, top-level managers are challenged to "think seriously and deeply ... about the purposes of the organizations they head or functions they perform, about the strategies, tactics, technologies, systems and people necessary to attain these purposes and about the important questions that always need to be asked."[121] Through this type of thinking, strategists, in concert with others, increase the probability of identifying bold, innovative ideas. When these ideas lead to the development of core competencies—that is, when the ideas result in exploiting resources and capabilities that are valuable, rare, costly to imitate, and nonsubstitutable—they become the foundation for taking advantage of environmental opportunities.

Our discussion highlights the nature of a strategist's work. Instead of simplicity, the work is filled with ambiguous decision situations—situations for which the most effective solutions are not always easily determined. However, the opportunities suggested by this type of work are appealing. These jobs offer exciting chances to dream and to act. The following words, given as advice by his father to Steven J. Ross, the former chairman and co-CEO of Time-Warner, describe the opportunities in a strategist's work: "There are three categories of people— the person who goes into the office, puts his feet up on his desk, and dreams for 12 hours; the person who arrives at 5 A.M. and works for 16 hours, never once stopping to dream; and the person who puts his feet up, dreams for one hour, then does something about those dreams."[122] The organizational term used for a dream that challenges and energizes a company is strategic intent.[123]

Strategists have opportunities to dream and to act, and the most effective ones provide a vision (strategic intent) to effectively elicit the help of others in creating a firm's competitive advantage.

THE STRATEGIC MANAGEMENT PROCESS

The pursuit of competitiveness is at the heart of strategic management and the choices made when designing and using the strategic management process. Firms are in competition with one another—to gain access to the resources needed to earn above-average returns and to provide superior satisfaction of stakeholders' needs. Effective use of the interdependent parts of the strategic management process results in selecting the direction the firm will pursue and its choices to achieve the desired outcomes of strategic competitiveness and above-average returns.

As suggested by Figure 1.1, the strategic management process is intended to be a rational approach to help a firm respond effectively to the challenges of the new competitive landscape. This process calls for a firm to study its external (Chapter 2) and internal (Chapter 3) environments to identify its marketplace opportunities and threats and determine how to use its core competencies in the pursuit of desired strategic outcomes. With this knowledge, the firm forms its strategic intent so it can leverage its resources, capabilities, and core competencies and win battles in the global economy. Flowing from strategic intent, the strategic mission specifies, in writing, the products a firm intends to produce and the markets it will serve when leveraging its resources, capabilities, and competencies.

A firm's strategic inputs provide the foundation for its strategic actions to formulate and implement strategies. As strategic actions, both formulation and implementation are critical to achieving strategic competitiveness and earning above-average returns.

As suggested by the horizontal arrow linking the two types of strategic actions (see Figure 1.1), formulation and implementation must be integrated simultaneously. When formulating strategies, thought should be given to implementing them. During implementation, effective strategists seek feedback that allows improvement of the selected strategies. Thus, the separation of strategy formulation from strategy implementation in Figure 1.1 is for discussion purposes only. In reality, these two sets of actions allow the firm to achieve its desired strategic outcomes only when they are carefully integrated.

Figure 1.1 shows the topics we examine to study the interdependent parts of the strategic management process. In Part II of this book, actions related to the formulation of strategies are explained. The first set of actions studied is the formulation of strategies at the business-unit level (Chapter 4). A diversified firm, one competing in multiple product markets and businesses, has a business-level strategy for each distinct product market area. A company competing in a single product market has but one business-level strategy. In all instances, a business-level strategy describes a firm's actions designed to exploit its competitive advantage over rivals. But, as is explained in Chapter 5, business-level strategies are not formulated and implemented in isolation. Competitors respond to and try to anticipate each other's actions. Thus, the dynamics of competition are an important input to the formulation and implementation of all strategies, but especially to business-level strategies.

For the diversified firm, corporate-level strategy (Chapter 6) is concerned with determining the businesses in which the company intends to compete, how resources are to be allocated among those businesses, and how the different units are to be managed. Other topics vital to strategy formulation, particularly in the diversified firm, include the acquisition of other companies and, as appropriate, the restructuring of the firm's portfolio of businesses (Chapter 7) and the selection of an international strategy that is consistent with the firm's resources, capabilities, and core competencies and its external opportunities (Chapter 8). Chapter 9 examines cooperative strategies. Increasingly important in a global economy, firms use the strategies to gain competitive advantage by forming advantageous relationships with other companies.

To examine more direct actions taken to implement strategies successfully, we consider several topics in Part III of this book. First, the different mechanisms used to govern firms are considered (Chapter 10). With demands for improved corporate governance voiced by various stakeholders, organizations are challenged to manage in ways that will result in the satisfaction of stakeholders' interests and the attainment of desired strategic outcomes. Finally, the matters of organizational structure and actions needed to control a firm's operations (Chapter 11), the patterns of strategic leadership appropriate for today's firms and competitive environments (Chapter 12), and the link among corporate entrepreneurship, innovation, and strategic competitiveness (Chapter 13) are addressed.

As noted earlier, competition requires firms to make choices to survive and succeed. Some of these choices are strategic in nature, including those of selecting a firm's strategic intent and strategic mission, determining which strategies to implement to offer a firm's products to customers, choosing an appropriate level of corporate scope, designing governance and organization structures that will properly coordinate a firm's work, and, through strategic leadership, encouraging and nurturing organizational innovation.[124] When made successfully, choices in terms of any one of these sets of actions have the potential to result in a competitive advantage for a firm over its rivals.

Primarily because they are related to how a firm interacts with its stakeholders, almost all strategic decisions have ethical dimensions.[125] Organizational ethics are revealed by an organization's culture; that is to say, a firm's strategic decisions are a product of the core values that are shared by most or all of a company's managers and employees. Especially in the turbulent and often ambiguous new competitive landscape, those making strategic decisions are challenged to recognize that their decisions do affect capital market, product market, and organizational stakeholders differently and to evaluate the ethical implications of their decisions. Certainly, top executives at Columbia/HCA should have heeded this suggestion. In 1997, allegations of misconduct by top managers in Columbia/HCA affected shareholders and consumers alike. U.S. federal government officials issued indictments against several Columbia/HCA employees for alleged false statements regarding interest payments on debt that led to overpayments of Medicare and the Department of Defense insurance organization.[126] (Additional descriptions of actions taken in this firm are offered in other parts of the book.) Relationships between organizational ethics and particular strategic decisions are described in virtually all of the remaining chapters of this book.

As you will discover, the strategic management process examined in this text calls for disciplined approaches to the development of competitive advantages. These approaches provide the pathway through which firms will be able to achieve strategic competitiveness and earn above-average returns in the twenty-first century. Mastery of this strategic management process will effectively serve readers and the organizations for whom they choose to work.

SUMMARY

- Through their actions, firms seek strategic competitiveness and above-average returns. Strategic competitiveness is achieved when a firm has developed and learned how to implement a value-creating strategy successfully. Above-average returns—returns in excess of what investors expect to earn from other investments with similar lev-

els of risk—allow a firm to simultaneously satisfy all of its stakeholders.

- A new competitive landscape—one in which the fundamental nature of competition is changing—has emerged. This landscape challenges those responsible for making effective strategic decisions to adopt a new mind-set, one that is global in nature. Through this mind-set, firms learn how to compete in what are highly turbulent and chaotic environments that produce disorder and a great deal of uncertainty. The globalization of industries and their markets and rapid and significant technological changes are the two primary realities that have created the new competitive landscape. Globalization—the spread of economic innovations around the world and the political and cultural adjustments that accompany this diffusion—is likely to continue. Globalization also increases the standards of performance companies must meet or exceed to be strategically competitive in the new competitive landscape. Developing the ability to satisfy these global performance standards also helps firms compete effectively in their critical domestic markets.

■ There are two major models of what a firm should do to earn above-average returns. The I/O model argues that the external environment is the *primary* determinant of the firm's strategies. Above-average returns are earned when the firm locates an attractive industry and sucessfully implements the strategy dictated by the characteristics of that industry. The resource-based model assumes that each firm is a collection of unique resources and capabilities that determines a firm's strategy. In this model, above-average returns are earned when the firm uses its valuable, rare, costly to imitate, and nonsubstitutable resources and capabilities (i.e., core competencies) to establish a competitive advantage over its rivals.

■ Strategic intent and strategic mission are formed in light of the information and insights gained from studying a firm's internal and external environments. Strategic intent suggests how resources, capabilities, and core competencies will be leveraged to achieve desired outcomes in the competitive environment. The strategic mission is an application of strategic intent. The mission is used to specify the product markets and customers a firm intends to serve through the leveraging of its resources, capabilities, and competencies.

■ Stakeholders are those who can affect and are affected by a firm's strategic outcomes. Because a firm is dependent on the continuing support of stakeholders (shareholders, customers, suppliers, employees, host communities, etc.), they have enforceable claims on the company's performance. When earning above-average returns, a firm can adequately satisfy all stakeholders' interests. However, when earning only average returns, a firm's strategists must carefully manage all stakeholder groups in order to retain their support. A firm earning below-average returns must minimize the amount of support it loses from dissatisfied stakeholders.

■ Organizational strategists are responsible for the design and execution of an effective strategic management process. Today, the most effective of these processes are grounded in ethical intentions and conduct. Strategists themselves, people with opportunities to dream and to act, can be a source of competitive advantage. The strategist's work demands decision tradeoffs, often among attractive alternatives. Successful top-level managers work hard, conduct thorough analyses of situations, are brutally and consistently honest, and ask the right questions, of the right people, at the right time.

REVIEW QUESTIONS

1. What are strategic competitiveness, competitive advantage, and above-average returns? Why are these terms important to those responsible for an organization's performance?

2. What *is* the challenge of strategic management?

3. What are the two factors that have created the new competitive landscape? What meaning does this landscape have for those interested in starting a business firm in the near future?

4. According to the I/O model, what should a firm do to earn above-average returns?

5. What does the resource-based model suggest a firm should do to achieve strategic competitiveness and earn above-average returns?

6. What are the differences between strategic intent and strategic mission? What is the value of the strategic intent and mission for a firm's strategic management process?

7. What are stakeholders? Why can they influence organizations? Do stakeholders always have the same amount of influence over an organization? Why or why not?

8. How would you describe the work of organizational strategists?

9. What are the parts of the strategic management process? How are these parts interrelated?

APPLICATION DISCUSSION QUESTIONS

1. As suggested in the opening case, the outcomes in the telecommunications industry are uncertain. Go to your library to study WorldCom's current performance. Based on your reading, do you judge WorldCom to be a success? Why or why not?

2. Choose several firms in your local community with which you are familiar. Describe the new competitive landscape to them and ask for their feedback about how they anticipate the landscape will affect their operations during the next five years.

3. Select an organization (e.g., school, club, church) that is important to you. Describe the organization's stakeholders and the degree of influence you believe each has over the organization.

4. Are you a stakeholder at your university or college? If so, of what stakeholder group, or groups, are you a part?

5. Think of an industry in which you want to work. In your opinion, which of the three primary stakeholder groups is the most powerful in that industry today? Why?

6. Reject or agree with the following statement: "I think managers have little responsibility for the failure of business firms." Justify your view.

7. Do strategic intent and strategic mission have any meaning in your personal life? If so, describe it. Are your current actions being guided by an intent and mission? If not, why not?

ETHICS QUESTIONS

1. Can a firm achieve a competitive advantage and thereby strategic competitiveness without acting ethically? Explain.

2. What are a firm's ethical responsibilities if it earns above-average returns?

3. What are some of the critical ethical challenges to firms competing in the global economy?

4. How should ethical considerations be included in analyses of a firm's internal and external environments?

5. Can ethical issues be integrated into a firm's strategic intent and mission? Explain.

6. What is the relationship between ethics and stakeholders?

7. What is the importance of ethics for organizational strategists?

INTERNET EXERCISE

The following is a list of well-recognized American companies:

Exxon: **http://www.exxon.com**
Southwest Airlines: **http://www.iflyswa.com**
General Motors: **http://www.gm.com**
Wal-Mart: **http://www.wal-mart.com**
McDonald's: **http://www.mcdonalds.com**

Select two of these companies. For each company, use the Internet to collect sufficient information to compile a list of the company's major stakeholders. In what ways are the stakeholders of each company similar and in what ways are they different? In your research, did you find any evidence that the companies you studied are actively managing their stakeholder groups?

Strategic Surfing

Strategy & Business is a publication that prints a variety of thoughtful articles, interviews, and case studies focused on strategic management and general business issues. The on-line version of this publication can be accessed at the following website:

http://www.strategy-business.com

NOTES

1. J. B. Barney, 1994, Commentary: A hierarchy of corporate resources, in P. Shrivastava, A. Huff, and J. Dutton (eds.), *Advances in Strategic Management* 10A, (Greenwich, Conn.: JAI Press), 119.
2. J. B. Barney, 1991, Firm resources and sustained competitive advantage, *Journal of Management* 17: 99–120.
3. D. J. Collis and C. A. Montgomery, 1995, Competing on resources: Strategy in the 1990s, *Harvard Business Review* 73, no. 4: 118–128.
4. R. M. Grant, 1995, *Contemporary Strategy Analysis*, 2nd ed. (Cambridge, Mass.: Blackwell Business), 138–140.
5. R. A. D'Aveni, 1995, Coping with hypercompetition: Utilizing the new 7S's framework, *Academy of Management Executive* IX, no. 3: 54; D. Schendel, 1994, Introduction to the Summer 1994 special issue—Strategy: Search for new paradigms, *Strategic Mangement Journal* (Special Summer Issue) 15: 3.
6. P. Shrivastava, 1995, Ecocentric management for a risk society, *Academy of Management Review* 20: 119.
7. R. P. Rumelt, D. E. Schendel, and D. J. Teece (eds.), 1994, *Fundamental Issues in Strategy* (Boston: Harvard Business School Press), 527–530; A. D. Meyer, 1991, What is strategy's distinctive competence? *Journal of Management* 17: 821–883.
8. Schendel, Introduction to the Summer 1994 special issue, 1–3.
9. Rumelt, Schendel, and Teece, *Fundamental Issues in Strategy*, 534–547.
10. M. E. Porter, 1994, Toward a dynamic theory of strategy, in R. P. Rumelt, D. E. Schendel, and D. J. Teece (eds.), *Fundamental Issues in Strategy* (Boston: Harvard Business School Press), 423–425.
11. R. Teitelbaum, 1997, America's greatest wealth creators, *Fortune*, November 10, 265–276.
12. C. J. Loomis, 1993, Dinosaurs, *Fortune*, May 3, 36–42.
13. *The State of Small Business: A Report of the President*, 1994, Washington, D.C., 41–42.
14. Rumelt, Schendel, and Teece, *Fundamental Issues in Strategy*, 530.
15. Loomis, Dinosaurs, 36.
16. K. Naughton, E. Thorton, K. Kerwin and H. Dawley, 1997, Can Honda build a world car? *Business Week*, September 8, 100–108; M. Williams, 1997, The Limited tries to rebuild after losing some of its appeal, *Dallas Morning News*, November 2, H5.
17. D. Machalaba, 1997, Union Pacific battles problems as crashes continue to pile up, *Wall Street Journal Interactive Edition*, August 29, http://www.wsj.com.
18. A. Reinhardt, 1997, Paranoia, aggression, and other strengths, *Business Week*, October 13, 14; A. S. Grove, 1995, A high-tech CEO updates his views on managing and careers, *Fortune*, September 18, 229–230; S. Sherman, 1993, The secret to Intel's success, *Fortune*, February 8, 14.
19. This section is based largely on information featured in two sources: M. A. Hitt, B. W. Keats, and S. M. DeMarie, 1998, Navigating in the new competitive landscape: Building competitive advantage and strategic flexibility; in the 21st century, *Academy of Management Executive*, in press. R. A. Bettis and M. A. Hitt, 1995, The new competitive landscape, *Strategic Management Journal* (Special Summer Issue) 16: 7–19.
20. S. Kotha, 1995, Mass customization: Implementing the emerging paradigm for competitive advantage, *Strategic Management Journal* 16: 21–42.
21. Associated Press, 1995, Fox-TCI to challenge ESPN, *Dallas Morning News*, November 1, D1, D11.
22. C. K. Prahalad, 1995, forward in R. Ashkenas, D. Ulrich, T. Jick, and S. Kerr (eds.), *The Boundaryless Organization: Breaking the Chains of Organizational Structure*, (San Francisco: Jossey-Bass Publishers), xiii-xvii.
23. R. D. Ireland and M. A. Hitt, 1998, Achieving and maintaining strategic competitiveness in the 21st century: The role of strategic leadership, *Academy of Management Executive*, in press.
24. D'Aveni, Coping with hypercompetition, 46.
25. K. Ohmae, 1995, Letter from Japan, *Harvard Business Review* 73, no. 3: 154–163; P. Gyllenhammar, 1993, The global economy: Who will lead next? *Journal of Accountancy* 175: 61–67.
26. J. C. Madonna, 1992, If it's markets you need, look abroad, *New York Times Forum*, January 5, F13.
27. T. A. Stewart, 1993, The new face of American power, *Fortune*, July 26, 70–86.
28. L. C. Thurow, 1992, Who owns the twenty-first century? *Sloan Management Review* 33, no. 3: 5–17.
29. Whirlpool Corp., 1995, *Standard & Poor Stock Reports*, August 31, 2474; Whirlpool Corp., 1995, *Value Line*, June 16, 135; S. Tully, 1995, So, Mr. Bossidy, we know you can cut. Now show us how to grow, *Fortune*, August 21, 70–80.
30. The big picture, 1995, *Business Week*, November 13, 8.
31. G. Koretz, 1997, America's edge in capital goods, *Business Week*, September 22, 26.
32. P. Krugman, 1994, Location and competition: Notes on economic geography, in R. P. Rumelt, D. E. Schendel, and D. J. Teece (eds.), *Fundamental Issues in Strategy*, (Boston: Harvard Business School Press), 463–493; W. W. Lewis and M. Harris, 1992, Why globalization must prevail, *McKinsey Quarterly* 2: 114–131.
33. Crain News Service, 1995, Toyota plans to build T100 in U.S., boost plants' autonomy, *Dallas Morning News*, Octo-

38

ber 28, D39; M. G. Harvey, 1993, "Buy American": Economic concept or economic slogan? *Business Horizons* 36, no. 3: 40–46.

34. R. Narisetti, 1997, Bridgestone plans to build a factory for tires in U.S., *Wall Street Journal*, July 15, B12.

35. Lewis and Harris, Why globalization must prevail, 115; J. Newmith and E. Jaspin, 1993, Japan's patents pending no more, *Waco Tribune-Herald*, January 24, A1, A10.

36. R. M. Kanter, 1995, Thriving locally in the global economy, *Harvard Business Review* 73, no. 5: 151–160; M. E. Porter and C. van der Linde, 1995, Green and competitive: Ending the stalemate, *Harvard Business Review* 73, no. 5: 120–134.

37. S. Zaheer and E. Mosakowski, 1997, The dynamics of the liability of foreignness: A global study of survival in financial services, *Strategic Management Journal* 18: 439–464.

38. M. A. Hitt, R. E. Hoskisson, and H. Kim, 1997, International diversification: Effects on innovation and firm performance in product-diversified firms, *Academy of Management Journal* 40: 767–798.

39. R. W. Moxon and C. Bourassa-Shaw, 1997, The global free-trade dilemma: Can you control the personal gale of creative destruction? *Business* 18(Spring): 6–9.

40. W. Hopkins and S. A. Hopkins, 1997, Strategic planning-financial performance relationships in banks: A casual examination, *Strategic Management Journal* 18: 635–652.

41. H. J. Aaron, 1992, Comments included in a debate called "How real is America's decline?" *Harvard Business Review* 70, no. 5: 172.

42. *Business Week*, 1997, The rich ecosystem of Silicon Valley, August 25, 202.

43. Grove, A high-tech CEO, 229.

44. B. Morris, 1997, IBM really wants your E-business, *Fortune*, November 10, 36–38.

45. J. C. Ramo, 1997, How AOL lost the battles but won the war, *Time*, September 15, http//www.pathfinder.com.

46. A. L. Sprout, 1995, The Internet inside your company, *Fortune*, November 27, 161–168.

47. Liberation, courtesy of the Internet, 1995, *Business Week*, December 4, 136; Sprout, The Internet inside your company, 161–168.

48. A. Goldstein, 1995, Microsoft may not always be king of the hill, Gates says, *Dallas Morning News*, November 24, D4.

49. T. A. Stewart, 1995, Mapping corporate brainpower, *Fortune*, October 30, 209–212; T. A. Stewart, 1995, Trying to grasp the intangible, *Fortune*, October 2, 157–161; T. A. Stewart, 1995, The information wars: What you don't know will hurt you, *Fortune*, June 12, 119–121.

50. C. A. Bartlett and S. Ghoshal, 1995, Changing the role of top management: Beyond systems to people, *Harvard Business Review* 73, no. 3: 141.

51. T. A. Stewart, 1995, Getting real about brainpower, *Fortune*, November 27, 201–203.

52. R. Sanchez, 1995, Strategic flexibility in product competition, *Strategic Management Journal* (Special Summer Issue) 16: 135–159.

53. Kotha, Mass customization, 21.

54. J. L. C. Cheng and I. F. Kesner, 1997, Organizational slack and response to environmental shifts: The impact of resource allocation patterns, *Journal of Management* 23: 1–18.

55. V. L. Barker III and I. M. Duhaime, 1997, Strategic change

in the turnaround process: Theory and empirical evidence, *Strategic Management Journal* 18: 13–38.

56. W. Boeker, 1997, Strategic change: The influence of managerial characteristics and organizational growth, *Academy of Management Journal* 40: 152–170.

57. N. Rajagopalan and G. M. Spreitzer, 1997, Toward a theory of strategic change: A multi-lens perspective and integrative framework, *Academy of Management Review* 22: 48–79.

58. N. Deogun, 1997, Coca-Cola Enterprises uncaps a global bottling play, *Wall Street Journal*, October 29, B4.

59. Our discussion of the I/O model is informed by the following works: Barney, Firm resources, 99–120; A. A. Lado, N. G. Boyd, and P. Wright, 1992, A competency based model of sustainable competitive advantage: Toward a conceptual integration, *Journal of Management* 18: 77–91; R. M. Grant, 1991, The resource-based theory of competitive advantage: Implications for strategy formulation, *California Management Review* 33 (Spring): 114–135.

60. D. Schendel, 1994, Introduction to competitive organizational behavior: Toward an organizationally-based theory of competitive advantage, *Strategic Management Journal* (Special Winter Issue) 15: 2.

61. A. Seth and H. Thomas, 1994, Theories of the firm: Implications for strategy research, *Journal of Management Studies* 31: 165–191.

62. Seth and Thomas, Theories of the firm, 169–173.

63. Porter, Toward a dynamic theory of strategy, 428.

64. M. E. Porter, 1985, *Competitive Advantage* (New York: Free Press); M. E. Porter, 1980, *Competitive Strategy* (New York: Free Press).

65. C. Mulhern, 1997, Bagel boom: Rising star of food franchising takes the world by storm, *Entrepreneur Magazine Online*, June 3, entrepreneurmag.com.

66. A. M. McGahan and M. E. Porter, 1997, How much does industry matter, really? *Strategic Management Journal* 18 (Summer Special Issue): 15–30.

67. R. Henderson and W. Mitchell, 1997, The interactions of organizational and competitive influences on strategy and performance, *Strategic Management Journal* 18 (Summer Special Issue): 5–14; C. Oliver, 1997, Sustainable competitive advantage: Combining institutional and resource-based views, *Strategic Management Journal* 18: 697–713; J. L. Stimpert and I. M. Duhaime, 1997, Seeing the big picture: The influence of industry, diversification, and business strategy on performance, *Academy of Management Journal* 40: 560–583.

68. J. R. Williams, 1994, Strategy and the search for rents: The evolution of diversity among firms, in R. P. Rumelt, D. E. Schendel, and D. J. Teece (eds.), *Fundamental Issues in Strategy* (Boston: Harvard Business School Press), 229–246.

69. K. Cool and I. Dierickx, 1994, Commentary: Investments in strategic assets: Industry and firm-level perspectives, in P. Shrivastava, A. Huff, and J. Dutton (eds.), *Advances in Strategic Management* 10A (Greenwich, Conn.: JAI Press), 35–44; Rumelt, Schendel, and Teece, *Fundamental Issues in Strategy*, 553; R. Rumelt, 1991, How much does industry matter? *Strategic Management Journal* 12: 167–185.

70. Barney, Commentary, 113–125.

71. Barney, Firm resources; Grant, Resource-based theory; Meyer, What is strategy's distinctive competence?

72. Grant, Resource-based theory, 119–120.

39

73. Rumelt, Schendel, and Teece, *Fundamental Issues in Strategy*, 31.

74. P. J. H. Schoemaker and R. Amit, 1994, Investment in strategic assets: Industry and firm-level perspectives, in P. Shrivastava, A. Huff, and J. Dutton (eds.), *Advances in Strategic Management* 10A (Greenwich, Conn.: JAI Press), 9.

75. R. E. Stross, 1997, Why Barnes & Noble may crush Amazon, *Fortune*, September 13, pathfinder.com.

76. J. B. Barney, 1995, Looking inside for competitive advantage, *Academy of Management Executive* IX, no. 4: 56.

77. Barney, Firm resources.

78. Lado, Boyd, and Wright, A competency based model; Grant, Resource-based theory; M. A. Hitt and R. D. Ireland, 1986, Relationships among corporate level distinctive competencies, diversification strategy, corporate structure, and performance, *Journal of Management Studies* 23: 401–416.

79. A. Madhok, 1997, Cost, value and foreign market entry mode: The transaction and the firm, *Strategic Management Journal* 18: 39–61.

80. A. A. Lado, N. G. Boyd and S. C. Hanlon, 1997, Competition, cooperation, and the search for economic rents: A syncretic model, *Academy of Management Review* 22: 110–141.

81. A. Arora and A. Gambardella, 1997, Domestic markets and international competitiveness: Generic and product specific competencies in the engineering sector, *Strategic Management Journal* 18 (Summer Special Issue): 53–74.

82. D. J. Teece, G. Pisano and A. Shuen, 1997, Dynamic capabilities and strategic management, *Strategic Management Journal* 18: 509–533.

83. D Lei, M. A. Hitt and R. A. Bettis, 1996, Dynamic core competences through meta-learning and strategic context, *Journal of Management* 22: 547–567.

84. G. Hamel and C. K. Prahalad, 1989, Strategic intent, *Harvard Business Review* 67, no. 3: 63–76.

85. S. Sherman, 1995, Stretch goals: The dark side of asking for miracles, *Fortune*, November 13, 231–232; G. Hamel and C. K. Prahalad, 1994, *Competing for the Future* (Boston: Harvard Business School Press), 129–136.

86. Hamel and Prahalad, Strategic intent, 66.

87. S. Sherman, 1993, The secret to Intel's success, 14.

88. Unocal Corporation, 1994, *Annual Report*, 4; Phillips Petroleum Company, 1994, *Health, Environmental and Safety Report*, 4; Eli Lilly and Company, 1993, *Annual Report to Shareholders*, 1; M. Loeb, 1993, It's time to invest and build, *Fortune*, February 22, 4; S. Sherman, 1993, The new computer revolution, *Fortune*, June 14, 56–84; C. A. Bartlett and S. Ghoshal, 1995, Changing the role of top management: Beyond systems to people, *Harvard Business Review* 73, no. 3: 136–137; A. Taylor III, 1993, How to murder the competition, *Fortune*, February 22, 87–90; Z. Schiller, 1992, No more Mr. nice guy at P&G—not by a long shot, *Business Week*, February 3, 54–56; S. Tully, 1995, So, Mr. Bossidy, we know you can cut, 73; AlliedSignal, 1995, *Value Line*, August 11, 1357.

89. Reebok, 1992, *Annual Report*, 2–12.

90. Hamel and Prahalad, Strategic intent, 64.

91. M. A. Hitt, D. Park, C. Hardee, and B. B. Tyler, 1995, Understanding strategic intent in the global marketplace, *Academy of Management Executive* IX, no. 2: 12–19.

92. R. D. Ireland and M. A. Hitt, 1992, Mission statements: Importance, challenge, and recommendations for development, *Business Horizons* 35, no. 3: 34–42.

93. A. D. DuBrin and R. D. Ireland, 1993, *Management and Organization*, 2nd ed. (Cincinnati, Ohio: Southwestern), 140.

94. N. Rajagopalan, 1992, Strategic orientations, incentive plan adoptions, and firm performance: Evidence from electric utility firms, *Strategic Management Journal* 18: 761–785.

95. M. A. Geletkanycz, 1997, The salience of culture's consequences: The effects of cultural values on top executive commitment to the status quo, *Strategic Management Journal* 18: 615–634, M. A. Hitt, M. T. Dacin, B. B. Tyler and D. Park, 1997, Understanding the differences in Korean and U.S. Executives' strategic orientation, *Strategic Management Journal* 18: 159–167.

96. M. B. E. Clarkson, 1995, A stakeholder framework for analyzing and evaluating corporate social performance, *Academy of Management Review* 20: 92–117; T. Donaldson and L. E. Preston, 1995, The stakeholder theory of the corporation: Concepts, evidence, and implications, *Academy of Management Review* 20: 65–91; T. M. Jones, 1995, Instrumental stakeholder theory: A synthesis of ethics and economics, *Academy of Management Review* 20: 404–437.

97. Clarkson, A stakeholder framework; R. E. Freeman, 1984, *Strategic Management: A Stakeholder Approach* (Boston: Pitman), 53–54.

98. G. Donaldson and J. W. Lorsch, 1983, *Decision Making at the Top: The Shaping of Strategic Direction* (New York: Basic Books), 37–40.

99. Rumelt, Schendel, and Teece, *Fundamental Issues in Strategy*, 33.

100. Donaldson and Lorsch, *Decision Making at the Top*, 37.

101. M. J. Polonsky, 1995, Incorporating the natural environment in corporate strategy: A stakeholder approach, *Journal of Business Strategies* 12: 151–168.

102. R. K. Mitchell, B. R. Agle and D. J. Wood, 1997, Toward a theory of stakeholder identification and salience: Defining the principle of who and what really count, *Academy of Management Review* 22: 853–886.

103. Donaldson and Preston, The stakeholder theory of the corporation, citing a quote from *The Economist*, 1994, Corporate governance special section, September 11, 52–62.

104. Don't be an ugly-American manager, 1995, *Fortune*, October 16, 225.

105. T. Aeppel, 1997, Rubbermaid warns 3rd-quarter profit will come in far below expectations, *Wall Street Journal*, September 19, A4.

106. D. Kirkpatrick, 1993, Could AT&T rule the world? *Fortune*, May 17, 55–66.

107. T. Petzinger, Jr., 1997, Boyd overcame race barriers to build a market for Pepsi, *Wall Street Journal Interactive Edition*, August 29, http://www.wsj.com.

108. New paths to success, 1995, *Fortune*, June 12, 90–94; T. A. Stewart, 1995, Mapping corporate brainpower, 209–211; S. Lee, 1993, Peter Drucker's fuzzy future, *Fortune*, May 17, 136.

109. T. Schellhardt, 1997, Talent pool is shallow as corporations seek executives for top jobs, *Wall Street Journal*, June 26, A1, A10; T. Schellhardt, 1997, Want to be a manager? Many people say no, calling job miserable, *Wall Street Journal*, April 4, A1, A4.

110. J. O. Moller, 1991, The competitiveness of U.S. industry: A view from the outside, *Business Horizons* 34, no. 6: 27–34.

111. G. McNamara and P. Bromiley, 1997, Decision making in an organizational setting: Cognitive and organizational influences on risk assessment in commercial lending, *Academy of Management Journal* 40: 1063–1088.

112. L. Markoczy, 1997, Measuring beliefs: Accept no substitutes *Academy of Management Journal* 40: 1228–1242.

113. M. A. Hitt and R. E. Hoskisson, 1991, Strategic competitiveness, in L. W. Foster (ed.), *Advances in Applied Business Strategy* (Greenwich, Conn.: JAI Press), 1–36.

114. Bartlett and Ghoshal, Changing the role of top management, 139.

115. K. Weigelt and C. Camerer, 1988, Reputation and corporate strategy, *Strategic Management Journal* 9: 443–454; J. B. Barney, 1986, Organizational culture: Can it be a source of sustained competitive advantage? *Academy of Management Review* 11: 656–665.

116. R. D. Ireland, M. A. Hitt, and J. C. Williams, 1992, Self-confidence and decisiveness: Prerequisites for effective management in the 1990s, *Business Horizons* 35, no. 1: 36–43.

117. R. C. Mayer, J. H. Davis, and F. D. Schoorman, 1995, An integrative model of organizational trust, *Academy of Management Review* 20: 709–734, J. H. Davis, F. D. Schoorman, and R. C. Mayer, 1995, The trusted general manager and firm performance: Empirical evidence of a strategic advantage, paper presented at the Strategic Management Society conference; J. B. Barney and M. H. Hansen, 1994, Trustworthiness as a source of competitive advantage, *Strategic Management Journal* 15: 175–190.

118. G. Belis, 1993, Beware the touchy-feely business book, *Fortune*, June 28, 147; A. E. Pearson, 1988, Tough-minded ways to get innovative, *Harvard Business Review* 66, no. 3: 99–106.

119. J. S. Harris, 1995, Bill Dodson, *Dallas Morning News*, September 3, H1, H2; Tully, So, Mr. Bossidy, we know you can cut, 70–80; K. W. Chilton, M. E. Warren, and M. L. Weidenbaum (eds.), 1990, *American Manufacturing in a Global Market* (Boston: Kluwer Academic Publishers), 72.

120. A. Deutschman, 1993, Odd man out, *Fortune*, July 26, 42.

121. T. Leavitt, 1991, *Thinking About Management* (New York: Free Press), 9.

122. M. Loeb, 1993, Steven J. Ross, 1927–1992, *Fortune*, January 25, 4.

123. Hamel and Prahalad, *Competing for the Future*, 129.

124. Rumelt, Schendel, and Teece, *Fundamental Issues in Strategy*, 9–10.

125. Our discussion of ethics and the strategic management process, both here and in other chapters, is informed by materials appearing in J. S. Harrison and C. H. St. John, 1994, *Strategic Management of Organizations and Stakeholders: Theory and Cases* (St. Paul, Minn.: West Publishing Company).

126. M. Brockhaus, L. Haynes, J. Ogletree and D. Parcel, 1997, Columbia/HCA: One-stop shopping in the health care industry, working paper, University of Oklahoma.

The External Environment: Opportunities, Threats, Industry Competition, and Competitor Analysis

CHAPTER 2

Learning Objectives

After reading this chapter, you should be able to:

1. Explain the importance of studying and understanding the external environment.

2. Define the general and industry environments.

3. Discuss the four activities of the external environmental analysis process.

4. Name and describe the six segments of the general environment.

5. Identify the five competitive forces and explain how they determine an industry's profit potential.

6. Define strategic groups and describe how they influence a firm's competitive actions.

7. Describe what firms need to know about their competitors and different methods used to collect competitive intelligence.

Transformation of the Electric Utility Industry

The electric power industry in the United States is on the verge of a historic transformation. This $250 billion industry has in the past pursued a vertical integration strategy while operating in protected geographic but regulated markets. In the future, however, participants in the electric power marketplace will have many diverse core competencies and product offerings. Some will operate in narrow product markets while others will cross state and even national geographic boundaries to create business. There are conditions within three general environmental segments driving the changes that will radically restructure the competitive market segments in this industry.

Changes occurring in the *political/legal segment*, for example, are having a dramatic effect on the electric power industry. It is estimated that the amount spent on electric power by its customers could drop by 20 to 30 percent over the next five to ten years due to deregulation. The move toward deregulation in the United States began in the 1970s with oil shocks to the economy. Utilities, saddled with higher costs, sought to increase their rates considerably. But a public outcry pressured many states to force utilities to hold down rates, effectively halting the companies' ability to increase capacity. To deal with this concern, independent power producers were authorized through the Capital Public Utility Regulatory Policy Act of 1978 to create new alternative power suppliers to the market. This led to a new set of independent power producers focusing on cogeneration technology. Cogeneration is produced by independent producers as a byproduct from normal production

http://www.eia.doe.gov

processes. This allowed many manufacturers who use steam, hot water, hot gases, or electrical/mechanical sources of power to become independent power producers.

Furthermore, because some households geographically adjacent to these manufacturers were paying utility rates as much as 50 percent higher than their neighbors, there was an untenable political situation. As such, consumers have not allowed regulatory barriers to restrict their economic interests. In addition, many firms have threatened to move their multibillion dollar operations to other areas of the country where utility rates are lower. Thus, conditions in the *economic segment* are at work to foster the changes emerging in this industry. There have also been a number of mergers and acquisitions in the utility industry. Because producers have been limited in growth and are facing declining earning prospects, this type of competitive behavior is likely to continue. Therefore, electric utilities are preparing for brutal competition, similar to that experienced in other deregulated industries, such as airlines, trucking, and telecommunications.

Significant changes in the *technological segment* are also affecting the U.S. electric power industry. From 1949 to 1965, the cost of producing a kilowatt of power fell 37 percent as the size of the generators increased. Additionally, new generation technologies such as combined-cycle and cogeneration plants have been producing power at efficiency levels of 50 to 60 percent with advanced technology targeting an efficiency level of 70 percent or better for the use of fuels by the year 2005. This productivity compares to standard conventional power plant efficiency levels of 30 to 40 percent of fuel use. Furthermore, renewable sources of power such as wind and solar are making advancements. Also, information technology is emerging as a powerful force. It allows highly automated real-time meters and other gateways to home electrical use to market and sell electricity much more efficiently. This has allowed markets to merge and develop so that power can be traded as a commodity. Not only is this happening in the United States, but many power utility companies are expanding their reach to global markets including China, India, and Latin America.

It is also likely that the Internet will facilitate the trading of electrical power. There was a reported experiment between Northern Telecom (a Canadian firm) and United Utilities (a British utilities firm) to use power lines as an Internet provider. If the technology materializes, utilities firms with transmission capability may become the largest provider of telecommunications in the world.

These environmental changes are likely to realign the competition in the electric utilities industry into a number of different competitive arenas. First, it is likely that there will be generation companies that will become mega-generators, controlling perhaps 80 percent of the total generation capacity across all U.S. geographical markets. Second, there will also be large intelligent networks that will manage the transmission of power. Finally, there will be distribution companies or wire companies that own and maintain the wires through which the power is distributed to various markets.

Another set of competitors likely to emerge is energy service companies. First, there will be companies that will meter the energy and develop customer service relationships with consumers and businesses. Second, power markets probably will develop where power is exchanged as a commodity on stock exchanges. Finally, there are likely to be companies dealing in information technology products and services that will provide information and appliances to improve power use efficiency. Thus, it is highly probable that the entire context of competition in the industry will change. This will alter the nature of the customer and supplier relationships and allow for many new entrants as well as possible product substitutes. Because electric power can be a huge operating expense, a large savings in this category could result in above-average returns for firms. On the other hand, this may create significant competitive problems for utilities with inefficient generating plants. Thus, this change portends substantial opportunities and threats for electric power customers at large as well as threats to the management of the electric utility companies. Change will be the common theme and adaptation must follow.

SOURCE: AP-Dow Jones News Service, 1997, Electric utilities announces Internet access via power lines, http://www.interactive.wsj.com, October 8; B. O'Reilly, 1997, Transforming the power business, *Fortune*, September 29, 143–156; M. Weiner, N. Nohria, A. Hickman and H. Smith, 1997, Value networks—the future of the U.S. utility industry, *Sloan Management Review* 37, no. 4, 21–34; P. Navarro, 1996, Electric utilities: The argument for radical deregulation, *Harvard Business Review*, 75, no. 1, 112–125.

Research has shown that the external environment plays a significant role in the growth and profitability of firms,[1] as dramatically demonstrated in the case of significant changes taking place in certain segments of the general environment facing firms competing in the electric utilities industry. Which companies will succeed in the changing utilities industry will be determined largely by firms' reactions to the changes in their environment. This chapter focuses on how firms should analyze and understand their external environment, as shown in Figure 1.1 in Chapter 1.

As noted in the first chapter, the environmental conditions facing firms currently are different from those of past decades. Many companies now compete in global, rather than domestic, markets. Technological changes and the explosion in information gathering and processing capabilities demand more timely and effective competitive actions and responses.[2] The rapid sociological changes occurring in many countries affect labor practices and the nature of products demanded by increasingly diverse consumers. Governmental policies and laws affect where and how firms choose to compete. Deregulation and local government changes such as those emerging in the electric utilities industry illustrate the importance these changes are likely to have on the strategic direction and competitive environment of both foreign and domestic firms. Companies must be aware of and understand the implications of these environmental realities to compete effectively in the global economy.

In high-performing, strategically competitive organizations, managers seek patterns to help them understand their external environment, which may be different from what they expect.[3] It is vital for decision makers to have a precise and accurate understanding of their company's competitive position. For example, one of the first decisions Louis Gerstner, Jr., made when chosen as IBM's CEO from outside the firm was to visit with each member of IBM's senior management team. A key reason for these visits was to learn about each business area's competitive standing in the industry (or industries) in which it competed.[4] Strategic decision makers know that understanding their firm's external environment helps to improve a company's competitive position, increase operational efficiency, and win battles in the global economy.[5]

Through a variety of means, firms attempt to understand their external environments by gaining information about competitors, customers, and other stakeholders in the external environment. In particular, firms are attempting to gain information to build their own base of knowledge and capabilities.[6] These firms may attempt to imitate the capabilities of able competitors or even successful firms in other industries or build new knowledge and capabilities to develop a competitive advantage. Based on this new information, knowledge, and capabilities, firms may take actions to buffer environmental effects on them or to build relationships with stakeholders in that environment.[7] To build knowledge and firm capabilities and to take actions that buffer or build bridges to external stakeholders, organizations must effectively analyze their external environment.

In this chapter, we discuss the external environment. Through an integrated understanding of the external and the internal environments, firms gain the information needed to understand the present and predict the future.[8] As shown in Figure 2.1, a firm's external environment has three major components: the general, industry, and competitor environments.

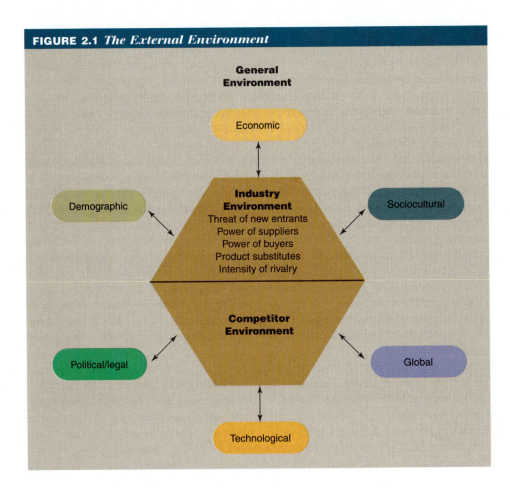

FIGURE 2.1 *The External Environment*

THE GENERAL, INDUSTRY, AND COMPETITOR ENVIRONMENTS

The **general environment** is composed of elements in the broader society that can influence an industry and the firms within it.[9] We group these elements into environmental *segments* called the demographic, economic, political/legal, sociocultural, technological, and global segments. Examples of *elements* analyzed in these six segments are shown in Table 2.1. Firms cannot directly control these elements. Instead, the strategic challenge is to understand each segment and its implications so appropriate strategies can be formulated and implemented.

The **industry environment** is the set of factors—the threat of new entrants, suppliers, buyers, product substitutes, and the intensity of rivalry among competitors—that directly influences a firm and its competitive actions and responses. In total, the interactions among these five factors determine an industry's profit potential. The challenge is to locate a position within an industry where a firm can favorably influence these factors or where it can successfully defend against their influence. The greater a firm's capacity to favorably influence its industry environment, the greater the likelihood that it will earn above-average returns.

We also discuss in this chapter how companies gather and interpret information about their competitors. Called *competitor analysis*, a firm's understanding of its current competitors complements the insights provided by study of the general and industry environments. In combination, the results of these three analyses influence the development of a firm's strategic intent, strategic mission, and strategic actions.

> The **general environment** is composed of elements in the broader society that can influence an industry and the firms within it.

> The **industry environment** is the set of factors—the threat of new entrants, suppliers, buyers, product substitutes, and the intensity of rivalry among competitors—that directly influences a company and its competitive actions and responses.

TABLE 2.1 *The General Environment: Segments and Elements*

Demographic Segment	■ Population size ■ Age structure ■ Geographic distribution	■ Ethnic mix ■ Income distribution
Economic Segment	■ Inflation rates ■ Interest rates ■ Trade deficits or surpluses ■ Budget deficits or surpluses	■ Personal savings rate ■ Business savings rates ■ Gross domestic product
Political/Legal Segment	■ Antitrust laws ■ Taxation laws ■ Deregulation philosophies	■ Labor training laws ■ Educational philosophies and policies
Sociocultural Segment	■ Women in the workforce ■ Workforce diversity ■ Attitudes about quality of work life	■ Concerns about the environment ■ Shifts in work and career preferences ■ Shifts in preferences regarding product and service characteristics
Technological Segment	■ Product innovations ■ Process innovations ■ Applications of knowledge	■ Focus of private and government-supported R&D expenditures ■ New communication technologies
Global Segment	■ Important political events ■ Critical global markets	■ Newly industrialized countries ■ Different cultural and institutional attributes

Analysis of the general environment is focused on the future; analysis of the industry environment is focused on understanding the factors and conditions influencing a firm's profitability; and, analysis of competitors is focused on predicting the dynamics of competitors' actions, responses, and intentions. Although each analysis is discussed separately, a firm's performance improves when the insights from analyses of the general environment, the industry environment, and the competitive environment are integrated.

The process of external environmental analysis is discussed next.

EXTERNAL ENVIRONMENTAL ANALYSIS

Most firms face external environments that are growing more turbulent, complex, and global, which makes them increasingly difficult to interpret.[10] To cope with what are often ambiguous and incomplete environmental data and to increase their understanding of the general environment, firms engage in a process called external environmental analysis. This process includes four activities: scanning, monitoring, forecasting, and assessing (see Table 2.2). It should be conducted on a continuous basis.[11]

An important objective of studying the general environment is identification of opportunities and threats. **Opportunities** are conditions in the general environment that may help a company achieve strategic competitiveness. **Threats** are conditions in the general environment that may hinder a company's efforts to achieve strategic competitiveness. In essence, external environmental opportunities represent *possibilities* while threats are potential *constraints*.

To analyze the general environment, several sources are used. Included among these are a wide variety of printed materials (e.g., trade publications, newspapers, business publications, the results of academic research and of public polls); attendance and participation in trade shows; the content of conversations with suppliers, customers, and employees of public-sector organizations; and, business-related "rumors" provided by many different people.[12] Additional sources of information and data include individuals in "boundary spanning" positions who interact with external constituents such as salespersons, purchasing managers, public relations directors, and human resource managers. Decision makers should verify the validity and reliability of the sources on which their environmental analyses are based.[13]

Opportunities are conditions in the general environment that may help a company achieve strategic competitiveness.

Threats are conditions in the general environment that may hinder a company's efforts to achieve strategic competitiveness.

TABLE 2.2 *Components of the External Analysis*	
Scanning	■ Identifying early signals of environmental changes and trends
Monitoring	■ Detecting meaning through ongoing observations of environmental change and trends
Forecasting	■ Developing projections of anticipated outcomes based on monitored changes and trends
Assessing	■ Determining the timing and importance of environmental changes and trends for firms' strategies and their management

Scanning

Scanning entails the study of all segments in the general environment. Through scanning, firms identify early signals of potential changes in the general environment and detect changes that are already under way.[14] When scanning, analysts typically deal with ambiguous, incomplete, and unconnected information and data. Environmental scanning has been found critically important for effective performance in firms that operate in highly volatile environments.[15] Additionally, scanning activity must be aligned with the organizational context; a scanning system designed for a volatile environment is inappropriate for a firm in a stable environment.[16]

In the 1990s, analysts in financial institutions are observing several changes in the general environment. First, some government officials and security analysts believe a combination of personal savings, private pensions, and Social Security income may be insufficient to support U.S. baby boomers' (those born between 1947 and 1964) retirement. It has even been suggested that financing baby boomers' retirement needs threatens the financial stability of most industrial nations, including the United States. The first of the baby boomer generation will retire in 2011. These retirements will push the total number of retirees from 25 million in 1991 to more than 33 million in 2011.[17] Changes in lifestyles and health care systems may result in longer average life spans for the baby boomers. By combining this information with data gleaned from scanning other environmental segments (e.g., the demographic, sociocultural, and political/legal segments), analysts can determine trends to monitor, forecast, and assess. Such analyses might result in an opportunity for financial institutions to serve effectively the baby boomers' retirement needs.

Monitoring

When *monitoring*, analysts observe environmental changes to see if, in fact, an important trend is emerging.[18] Critical to successful monitoring is an ability to detect meaning in different environmental events. For example, an emerging trend regarding education might be suggested by changes in federal and state funding for educational institutions, changes in high school graduation requirements, and changes in the content of high school courses. In this instance, analysts should determine whether these different events suggest an educational trend and, if so, whether other information and data should be studied to monitor it.

Forecasting

Scanning and monitoring are concerned with events in the general environment at a point in time. When *forecasting*, analysts develop feasible projections of what might happen, and how quickly, as a result of the changes and trends detected through scanning and monitoring.[19] For example, analysts might forecast the time that will be required for a new technology to reach the marketplace. Or they might forecast the length of time before different corporate training procedures are required to deal with anticipated changes in the composition of the workforce or how much time will elapse before changes in governmental taxation policies affect consumers' purchasing patterns. At Gillette, a recent forecast of slower sales and earnings growth led to a downturn in the firm's stock price. As this example shows, because markets respond so quickly, forecasts can lead to negative outcomes quickly.[20]

Assessing

The objective of *assessing* is to determine the timing and significance of the effects of environmental changes and trends on the strategic management of a firm.[21] Through scanning, monitoring, and forecasting, analysts are able to understand the general environment. Going a step further, the intent of assessment is to specify the implications of that understanding for the organization. Without assessment, analysts are left with data that are interesting but of unknown relevance.

Rubbermaid is an example of a firm that has learned to be careful about scanning, monitoring, forecasting, and assessing its external environment to avoid future problems with its customers and losing market share to emerging competitors. Rubbermaid has been ranked among the top 10 in *Fortune's* most admired companies list. During 1994 and 1995, it was ranked the number one company in corporate America. Recently, however, Rubbermaid experienced a number of problems. For example, it was confronted by several new competitors. In addition, Rubbermaid experienced major increases in the cost of resin (an important raw material in many of its products) and attempted to pass these costs to customers through large price increases. Wal-Mart was particularly angered by the large price increases because it is a huge customer of Rubbermaid. In response, Wal-Mart refused to stock a number of Rubbermaid products and deleted others from its promotional materials provided to customers. Instead, Wal-Mart featured Sterilite, one of Rubbermaid's prominent new competitors, in its promotional materials. Given that Wal-Mart is Rubbermaid's largest customer, accounting for more than 15 percent of Rubbermaid's total household-product sales, the discount store executives' anger seems well founded. Rubbermaid suffered from these forecasting errors and miscalculations. Expert competitive assessments in the future will contribute to Rubbermaid's efforts to avoid these types of difficulties.[22]

SEGMENTS OF THE GENERAL ENVIRONMENT

The general environment is composed of segments (and their individual elements) that are external to the firm (see Table 2.1). Although the degree of impact varies, these environmental segments affect each industry and its firms. The challenge is to scan, monitor, and assess those elements in each segment that are of the greatest importance to a firm. Results should include recognition of environmental changes, trends, opportunities, and threats. Opportunities are then matched with a firm's core competencies. When these matches are successful, the firm achieves strategic competitiveness and earns above-average returns.

The Demographic Segment

The **demographic segment** is concerned with a population's size, age, structure, geographic distribution, ethnic mix, and income distribution.[23] As noted previously, executives must analyze the demographics of the global areas potentially rel-

The **demographic segment** is concerned with a population's size, age, structure, geographic distribution, ethnic mix, and income distribution.

Demographic changes in populations are one of the key segments of the general environment. A few advanced countries have zero population growth; in others, such as the U.S., couples are having fewer than two children. In contrast, the populations of some developing nations are increasing, causing a depletion of resources and a reduction in the standard of living.

51

evant to their firms, rather than only those of the domestic population. In the following materials, each demographic element is discussed briefly.

Population Size Observing the demographic changes in populations highlights the importance of this environmental segment. For example, in some advanced nations, there is negative population growth (discounting the effects of immigration). In some countries, including the United States and several European nations, couples are averaging fewer than two children. Such a birth rate will produce a loss of population over time (even with the population living longer on average).[24] Population loss may require that a country increase immigration to have an adequate labor pool.

In contrast to advanced nations, the rapid growth rate in the populations of some Third World countries is depleting those nations' natural resources and reducing citizens' living standards. This rapid growth rate in the populations of some Third World countries may be a major challenge into the twenty-first century.

Age Structure In some countries, and certainly in the United States, the population's average age is increasing. In the U.S., for example, the percent of the population aged 55 and older is expected to increase from roughly 6 percent in 1995 to approximately 37.5 percent in 2019.[25] Contributing to this change are declining birth rates and increasing life expectancies. Among other outcomes, these changes create additional pressures on health care systems. Beyond this, these trends may suggest numerous opportunities for firms to develop goods and services to meet the needs of an increasingly older population.

It has been projected that some people alive today might live to the age of 200 or more. If such a life span becomes a reality, a host of interesting opportunities and problems will emerge. For example, the effect on individuals' pension plans will be significant and will create potential opportunities and threats for financial institutions.[26]

Geographic Distribution For several decades, the United States has experienced a population shift from the North and East to the West and South. Similarly, the trend of moving from metropolitan to nonmetropolitan areas continues. Among other effects, these trends have changed local and state governments' tax bases. In turn, the locations of business firms are influenced by the degree of support different taxing agencies offer.

The geographic distribution of populations throughout the world is being changed by the capabilities resulting from advances in communications technology. For example, through computer technologies, people can remain in their homes and communicate with others in remote locations to complete their work. In these instances, people can live where they prefer while being employed by a firm located in an unattractive location. Approximately 25 percent of U.S. employees may work out of their homes by the year 2000.[27]

Partially because of the advances in communication technology, approximately 29.5 percent of the more than 100 million employed workers in the United States in 1997 were contingency workers. Contingency workers include those who are part time, temporary, and on contract. As a result, these employees are more mobile. It is estimated that the number of contingency workers will continue to grow to as much as 50 percent of the U.S. workforce by the year 2000. This trend exists in other parts of the world as well, including Western Europe, Japan, Latin America, and Canada. Interestingly, the fastest growing segment of contingency workers is in the technical and professional area.[28]

Ethnic Mix The ethnic mix of countries' populations continues to change. Within the United States, the ethnicity of states, and of cities within the states, varies significantly. For business firms, the challenge is to be aware of and sensitive to these changes. Through careful study, firms can develop and market goods and services intended to satisfy the unique needs and interest of different ethnic groups.

Ethnic mix changes also affect a workforce's composition. In the United States, for example, by the mid-1990s, only 15 percent of the new workers entering the workforce were Caucasian males. The remainder of those entering the workforce during the 1990s were Caucasian, U.S.-born women (42 percent) and immigrants and U.S.-born minorities (43 percent).[29] The Hispanic population is predicted to be the fastest growing segment of the U.S. workforce in the 1990s. By 2000, Hispanics will account for 9.2 percent of the workforce, up from 7.8 percent in 1991. Because a labor force can be critical to competitive success, firms are challenged to work effectively with an increasingly diverse labor force.[30] Diversity in the workforce is also a sociocultural issue.

Effective management of a culturally diverse workforce can produce a competitive advantage. For example, heterogeneous work teams have been shown to produce more effective strategic analyses, more creativity and innovation, and higher quality decisions than homogeneous work teams.[31] Because of these potential outcomes, a number of companies promote cultural diversity in their workforce and facilitate effective management of such diversity through specialized management training. Among these companies are American Express, Northern States Power

Company, General Foods, US West, and British Petroleum. For example, all US West employees (more than 60,000) attend a diversity training program.[32]

Income Distribution Understanding how income is distributed within and across populations informs firms of different groups' purchasing power and discretionary income. Study of income distributions suggests that while living standards have improved over time, there are variances within and between nations.[33] Of interest to firms are the average incomes of households and individuals. For instance, a notable change is the increase of dual career couples. Although real income has been going down, dual career couples have increased their income. These figures yield strategically relevant information.

The Economic Segment

Clearly, the health of a nation's economy affects the performance of individual firms and industries. As a result, strategists study the economic environment to identify changes, trends, and their strategic implications.

The **economic environment** refers to the nature and direction of the economy in which a firm competes or may compete.[34] As shown in Table 2.1, indicators of an economy's health include inflation rates, interest rates, trade deficits or surpluses, budget deficits or surpluses, personal and business savings rates, and gross domestic product. However, because of the interconnectedness of the global financial community, analysts often must also scan, monitor, forecast, and assess the health of other countries' economies. For example, the economic status of nations with which the United States exchanges many products, such as Japan and Germany, can affect the overall health of the U.S. economy. In this regard, some worry that billions of dollars, yen, and deutsche marks move across national borders without much control by central banks. The delicately balanced global financial system permitting these easy transfers might contribute to an international economic crisis if the balance in the system were lost.[35]

Of course, some of these problems might be eliminated if European countries are able to achieve their goal of a single currency for all of Europe. European countries have set target dates for a European monetary union in which countries will agree on irrevocable exchange rates by 1999 and change completely to a new single currency by 2002. Some speculate that European countries will not be able to meet these target dates nor will they be able to establish a single currency. Alternatively, the single currency may begin with the union of several financially strong nations, such as Germany, Belgium, and France, allowing the others to join later as they are able to meet the requirements. The interrelatedness among different national economies is shown in ways other than currency exchange rates and similarities of their currencies.[36] Agreements to lower or eliminate trade barriers between nations, such as the North American Free Trade Agreement (NAFTA), have potentially significant economic consequences for the nations involved.

Economic issues can also have significant influences on political and legal issues. For example, some argue that the United States cannot afford to cancel favored-nation status for China, even though it has threatened to do so because of perceived human rights concerns. To take such action might have significant negative economic consequences for U.S. firms. The recent devaluation of multiple currencies in Asia shocked many fast paced economies into slow growth economies

The **economic environment** refers to the nature and direction of the economy in which a firm competes or may compete.

53

in the short term. For firms with significant assets in the Philippines, Thailand, Malaysia, and Indonesia, the devaluations had a significant negative effect. On the other hand, those who expect to build in these areas in the future may find significantly lower property and labor costs.[37]

The Political/Legal Segment

The **political/legal segment** is the arena in which organizations and interest groups compete for attention and resources and the body of laws and regulations guiding these interactions.

The **political/legal segment** is the arena in which organizations and interest groups compete for attention and resources and the body of laws and regulations guiding these interactions.[38] Essentially, this segment represents how organizations try to influence government and how government entities influence them. Constantly changing, this segment (see Table 2.1) influences the nature of competition. Because of this, firms must analyze carefully a new administration's business-related policies and philosophies. Antitrust laws, taxation laws, industries chosen for deregulation, labor training laws, and the degree of commitment to educational institutions are areas where an administration's policies can affect the operations and profitability of industries and individual firms.

As indicated in the opening case, deregulation in the electric power industry will force many firms to restructure their competitive practices. It is estimated that the $250 billion spent on electric power could decrease by 20 or 30 percent over the next five to ten years due to deregulation.[39] The electric power industry is the largest U.S. industry to be deregulated. "It's about twice the size of long-distance telephone service and dwarfs gas, airline, trucking, and railroad industries," states Kenneth Lay, CEO of Enron Corporation.[40] Because electric power can be such a huge operating expense, a large savings in this category could enhance corporate profitability substantially. Of course, this is the "great nightmare" for utilities with high-cost inefficient generating plants. Who will pay the cost of these stranded assets? Consumers? Electric utilities? These issues will be determined by the interactions occurring in the political/legal environment.

Viewpoints regarding government philosophies and policies (federal, state, and local), the most effective means of competition, and the ideal relationship between government and business can vary substantially. In addition to political perspectives, these viewpoints are affected by the nature of the industry in which a firm competes. As the 1990s come to a close, business firms across the globe are confronted by an interesting array of political/legal questions and issues. For example, the debate continues over trade policies. Some believe a nation should erect trade barriers to protect its domestic products. Others argue that free trade across nations serves the best interests of individual countries and their citizens. With the NAFTA and GATT agreements now in place, the trend seems to be toward free trade.

For instance, Central America, which was once a proving ground for guerrilla-warfare tactics, is joining most of the rest of Latin America as a proving ground for free-market reform.[41] Guatemala, for instance, is implementing one of the most aggressive telecommunication reform laws in Latin America. It is essentially opening its market to full competition in all segments; local, long-distance, paging, and cellular services. Motorola and 14 other foreign telecommunications companies are negotiating to provide these services. Furthermore, Guatemala has already privatized railroad, radio, and electrical utilities companies and has begun the process to privatize its telecommunications company, Guatel. Other Central American countries are taking similar if not identical actions. El Salvador ended 14 years of civil war and is reforming social security and tax collection systems. Nicaragua has attracted 19 factories to its free-trade zone and has slated its state phone company for sale.

In the United States, frequent debates occur over the appropriate amount of regulation of business. Many want less regulation; others, however, believe that more regulation is required to ensure appropriate business practices. Cases from both ends of the spectrum have been observed recently. For example, the Justice Department investigated Anheuser-Busch, Inc.'s sales practices to determine if it is abusing its dominant market position in its "100% share of mind program." Many microbrewers say the program is creating a situation where they have been dropped by Anheuser's distributors because of the incentive program. Often the distributor places them with Anheuser's microbrew label, Redhook.[42] At the other end of the spectrum, the Federal Communications Commission has been liberalizing its control over television networks and program ownership. This loosening of federal government controls over the entertainment industry has allowed the Disney Company to purchase Capital Cities/ABC. Outside of the fact that it involves well-known entertainment industry firms, the acquisition is interesting because it represents a vertical integration for Disney. It provides a means to distribute Disney products and thus is a related diversification move within the same industry (types of diversification are explained in Chapter 6). Certainly, it gives the Disney Company more power within the entertainment industry.[43]

The Sociocultural Segment

The **sociocultural segment** is concerned with different societies' social attitudes and cultural values. Because attitudes and values are a society's cornerstone, they often drive demographic, economic, political/legal, and technological changes. Firms are challenged to understand the meaning of attitudinal and cultural changes across global societies.

> The **sociocultural segment** is concerned with different societies' social attitudes and cultural values.

As mentioned earlier, a significant workforce trend in many countries concerns diversity. In the United States, for example, 76.3 million women are expected to participate in the labor force by 2011.[44] In addition, a large percentage of new entrants into the workforce will be ethnic minorities. As a result, the workforce will become increasingly diverse.

In the United States, approximately 46 percent of the workforce is composed of women. In Sweden, it's 50 percent, Japan, 41 percent, and Mexico, 37 percent. In the United States, 43 percent of the managerial jobs are held by women. In Sweden, 17 percent are held by women and in Japan, it is only 9.4 percent. In Japan, many women head businesses, but they are self-employed. The same is true in the United States, but approximately 17 percent of all U.S. businesses are headed by women, excluding those who are self-employed. In the United States, women are paid approximately 76 percent of the compensation paid to men. In Sweden, it's 77 percent, in Japan, 61.6 percent, and in Mexico, 68.2 percent. Thus, while women have experienced employment problems in the United States, the barriers to their participation in the workplace in many other countries seem to be greater.[45]

The influx of women and the increasing ethnic and cultural diversity in the workforce yield exciting challenges and significant opportunities.[46] Included among these are the needs to combine the best of both men's and women's leadership styles for a firm's benefit and to identify ways to facilitate all employees' contributions to their firms. An example of a firm attempting to do this is Avon. Four out of the eleven members of the board are women, and more than 40 percent of its global managers are women.[47] Some companies now provide training to nurture women's and ethnic minorities' leadership potential. Changes in organizational structure and management practices also often are required to eliminate subtle barriers that may exist. Learning to manage diversity in the domestic workforce can increase a firm's effectiveness in managing a globally diverse workforce, as it acquires more international operations. The results from these commitments to promote and manage diversity enhance a company's performance.[48]

Many women now choose to start their own businesses, as implied earlier, oftentimes because of frustration in dealing with the glass ceiling (a subtle barrier to the advancement of women and ethnic minorities in corporations). In 1982, there were 2.4 million female entrepreneurs in the United States; in 1991, that number exceeded 3 million. In 1994, women owned 7.7 million businesses, more than one-third of all U.S. firms. If this rate of start-ups continues, women will own one-half of U.S. businesses by the year 2000. The number of businesses owned by minority women continues to grow, increasing 153 percent between 1987 and 1996. The same trend has been observed in other countries such as Japan.[49]

The number of women in the corporate world who are relocating was up to 26 percent in 1996 from 16 percent in 1993. Many of these women relocate without their families and thereby lead complex lifestyles while trying to maintain their family life. Dorrit J. Bern, for example, is having a significant influence on the corporation she is leading. She is CEO of Charming Shoppes, Inc., which is headquartered in Philadelphia, but her family lives in Chicago. She didn't want to uproot her family, but the chance to turn around this business after being a successful executive with Sears was a significant opportunity. She maintains an apartment in Philadelphia Monday through Friday and a family life in Chicago on weekends. Her husband is a consultant and has more flexibility to manage the home and the lives of their three children.[50]

Moreover, the number of single fathers with custody of their children has increased dramatically to 1.86 million in 1996 from 393,000 in 1970. There are still more single mothers at 9.86 million, but single-father families have been growing by 10 percent annually. Demographers and marketers are noting this change.[51]

The Technological Segment

Pervasive and diversified in scope, technological changes affect many parts of societies. These effects occur primarily through new products, processes, and materials. The **technological segment** includes the institutions and activities involved with creating new knowledge and translating that knowledge into new outputs, products, processes, and materials.

Given the rapid pace of technological change, it is vital that firms carefully study different elements in the technological segment. For example, research has shown that early adopters of new technology often achieve higher market shares and earn higher returns. Thus, executives must continuously scan the environment to identify potential substitutes for their firm's technology as well as newly emerging technologies from which their firm could benefit. They need to identify the speed with

The **technological segment** includes the institutions and activities involved with creating new knowledge and translating that knowledge into new outputs, products, processes, and materials.

56

Research has shown that firms adopting new technology early often achieve greater market share and earn higher returns. The CAD system—a technological innovation—in the photo is being used to design cars.

57

which substitute technologies are likely to emerge and the timing of any major technological changes.[52]

A technology with important implications for business is the Internet, sometimes referred to as "the information superhighway." The Internet is a global web of more than 25,000 computer networks. It provides a quick, inexpensive means of global communication (i.e., with strategic alliance partners) and access to information. For example, GE engineers often use the Internet to communicate with their counterparts when doing development work for other companies. The Internet provides access to experts on such topics as chemical engineering and semiconductor manufacturing, to the Library of Congress, and even to satellite photographs. Other information available on the Internet includes Security and Exchange Commission (SEC) filings, Commerce Department data, Census Bureau information, new patent filings, and stock market updates.[53] Not only is the Internet an excellent source of data on a firm's external environment, there are a number of firms that provide Internet software that pushes data into customers' computers or other communication devices as soon as it happens. Tibco and Pointcast are two firms that specialize in products that keep their clients informed continuously about noteworthy news that is customized to the customers' interests.[54]

A number of firms have benefited from the popularity and use of the Internet. U.S. Robotics is one example. U.S. Robotics makes modems and other communications devices for computers and its sales are booming. Modems are important for connecting personal computers to phone lines that help gain access to the Internet. The technology in the manufacture of modems has advanced rapidly. Their speed may only be curtailed by the limits of conventional phone lines.[55] Encyclopedia Britannica Inc. is using the Internet to revive its business. For example, the firm now offers a free search engine with sites screened by its editors.[56] As Encyclopedia Britannica's actions demonstrate, the Internet can allow a firm to be both flexible and innovative with its product introductions.[57]

Microsoft is now changing its strategy not only to provide software for the Internet, but also to make sure that a new operating system does not displace its Windows business for PCs when a "Web lifestyle" emerges. As a result, Microsoft is working with phone companies and investing in cable companies Comcast and TCI. Similarly, Bill Gates has invested in WebTV Networks Inc. to obtain technology to deliver a high-speed digital stream that can be viewed—as movies, Web sites or advertising—on televisions with its equipment. Oracle Corporation, through its unit Network Computer, Inc. is developing a rival design for a cable box, which was given a significant boost by support from Intel.[58]

Another new technology that is gaining rapid popularity is satellite imaging. Several aerospace companies have invested up to $1 billion in corporate earth-imaging systems. For example, Space Imaging, Inc., a joint venture of Lockheed Martin, E-Systems, Mitsubishi Corporation, and Eastman Kodak Company, is a $500 million venture that provides images from an advanced satellite. Many expect this technology to compete in the global information trade industry and some anticipate that it will create a revolution. There are a number of uses for this technology. For example, Coldwell Banker Corporation uses it to offer real estate shoppers photographs from space of homes, neighborhoods, and traffic patterns. Television networks, such as ABC, use the technology to provide detailed images of battle zones for evening news broadcasts. Even urban planners are using the technology to update property tax rolls, while other firms may use it to plot new phone lines without using crews to study the terrain beforehand.[59]

Many firms are making significant revenues in the space-related businesses with demand for satellites the key driving factor.[60] For instance, the military now has a backpack-sized communicator called Manpack that gives the soldier on any battlefield in the world a direct satellite voice- and data-link. A soldier in a foxhole can talk directly with the Pentagon. Furthermore, the technology by ViaSat lets thousands of soldiers use one satellite simultaneously.[61] Spacehab is building research modules that could expand the amount of pressurized space on the shuttle and, thus, house more experiments. Demand for more space was created when the Challenger disaster created a backlog of 400 experiments with the suspension of space shuttle flights.

The Global Segment

The **global segment** includes relevant new global markets and existing ones that are changing, important international political events, and critical cultural and institutional characteristics of relevant global markets.

The **global segment** includes relevant new global markets and existing ones that are changing, important international political events, and critical cultural and institutional characteristics of relevant global markets. Although the previous segments should be analyzed in terms of their domestic and global implications, some additional specific global factors should be analyzed as well.

Firms must also attempt to identify critical new global markets and/or those that are changing. It is clear that many global markets are fast becoming borderless and integrated.[62] For example, firms may examine emerging markets such as those in South American countries or markets in newly industrialized countries such as in Asia (e.g., South Korea, Taiwan) for new opportunities. They should also be cognizant of the potential threats from these countries.

Newly industrialized countries, such as South Korea, have significant buying power but also have globally competitive firms. Based on significant support and economic planning from the government, the predominant goal of major South

Korean firms is growth. Thus, many South Korean firms place less emphasis on earning net profits and more on attaining major growth goals through their strategic actions.[63] An example of this is shown by Samsung's new venture into passenger-car production, partially because of executives' concerns at being ranked number two in size to Hyundai. Although Samsung is predicted to invest approximately $4.5 billion in developing its auto manufacturing venture, it also plans to invest up to $150 million in the development of a 100-seat jetliner, $3 billion to build semiconductor manufacturing plants in North America, Europe, and Southeast Asia, and $2 to $3 billion to establish a hypermedia city of offices, shops, entertainment centers, and housing in downtown Seoul by 2000. Recently, Samsung invested approximately $9.92 billion in expansion opportunities.[64]

Firms must also have a reasonable understanding of the different cultural and institutional attributes of global markets in which they operate or hope to operate. For example, a firm operating in South Korea must understand the value placed on hierarchical order, formality, self-control, and on duty rather than rights. Furthermore, Korean ideology places emphasis on communitarianism, a characteristic of many Asian countries. Korea's approach differs from that of Japan and China with its focus on *Inhwa* or harmony. *Inhwa* is based on a respect of hierarchical relationships and an obedience to authority. Alternatively, the approach in China is focused on *Guanxi* or personal relationships and in Japan on *Wa* or group harmony and social cohesion.[65] The institutional context of Korea suggests a major emphasis on centralized planning by the government. The emphasis placed on growth by many South Korean firms is the result of a government policy to promote economic growth in South Korea.[66]

The cultural and institutional contexts in which firms must operate in global markets can be critical. For example, in India there is a current nationalist campaign against multinational firms. This campaign led to the recent closing of a Kentucky Fried Chicken (KFC) restaurant in New Delhi. Although the official statement was that the KFC outlet was closed for health reasons after an inspection, executives of several U.S. food companies blamed political posturing related to an upcoming election. Also, those who oppose KFC's opening are often those who lobby against meat eating. KFC was one of the first major fast food giants to open a facility in India. Furthermore, it has been quite successful in Asia with more than 2,200 restaurants operating in that region of the world. Still, even a firm that has been as successful as KFC must carefully and thoroughly analyze the institutional and cultural environments of its global markets.[67]

As explained in the Strategic Focus on the takeover of Hong Kong, China offers potential opportunities but also threats to a number of firms with domestic headquarters outside its borders. Even more so with Hong Kong now a part of China, its growing economic prowess makes its firms potentially significant competitors, particularly in labor-intensive industries. As a result, firms operating in such industries worldwide must view the development of Chinese entrepreneurial operations as an environmental threat. Alternatively, firms that can invest in China may be able to take advantage of the low-cost labor; and, China also offers a huge and growing market for products, as evidenced by the success of Procter & Gamble's (P&G) products there.[68] P&G sells approximately 50 percent of the shampoo used in China, and its nationwide distribution system may be the best in that country. P&G owes its success to being an early mover in China, and its aggressiveness has paid dividends. It has been successful even though its prices are sometimes 300 percent greater than local brands. The development of the Chinese economy is one that must be analyzed carefully by firms operating in many industries, regardless of their home country.

STRATEGIC FOCUS

The Strategic Effect of the Chinese Takeover of Hong Kong

The Chinese takeover of Hong Kong was accomplished July 1, 1997. The effects of the environmental policy changes portend to be dramatic. There is now one country with two systems and a new economy for the capitalist hub of Asia, Hong Kong. It's not clear whether Hong Kong will become the cosmopolitan capital of Chinese capitalism or whether Chinese-style bureaucrats will change what has made it special. The economic environment that evolves will tell the ultimate outcome of the Chinese takeover of Hong Kong. Either of these scenarios may be inaccurate because China and Hong Kong are major investors in each other. Top officials in the special administrative region (SAR), which will be the official government of the Hong Kong territories, are determined to be more active than were the British. They use Singapore as an example of the type of policy to be implemented. Although Hong Kong will continue to be a standard setter in real estate and financial services, even more important is that it is likely to be the media and pop-culture hub for all of China. Although it will certainly be a financial and fashion hub, it may become too dependent on the Chinese economy. If it focuses too much on China, it may lose its standing as a regional center for all of Southeast Asia. If it is exposed to too many of the economic upheavals because of China's political and economic difficulties, Hong Kong may jeopardize its current standing.

As the change has been anticipated for some time, "red chip" companies—such as corporations controlled by mainland interests but listed in Hong Kong—are emerging as the new pillars of Hong Kong. They are restructuring the old order of local property developers and bankers who previously dominated the Hong Kong stock market. It is conceivable that many of the red chip companies will swallow major Hong Kong companies just as earlier Hong Kong entrepreneurs acquired British-owned companies in the 1980s. There is a question as to who will regulate the red chip companies. Will China be able to dictate who can list companies on the exchange or will this be determined solely by free market options?

Hong Kong has another concern. Because it does not have a strong manufacturing base, policy and administrative leaders are wondering if it will lose its central economic role as it competes with other economic coastal centers such as Shanghai. Because housing costs are so high in Hong Kong, some suggest that it will cost half as much to employ an engineer in California as in Hong Kong. Therefore, there is little incentive to invest in R&D and staff training in Hong Kong. Hong Kong companies rely on young laborers from China's interior who go home after a few years. These workers lack the technical skills required to manufacture more advanced products. Because costs are so high, manufacturers may simply shop for cheaper labor elsewhere in Asia. Thus, there is no clear evidence that Hong Kong will be able to maintain its financial and service center role without a strong manufacturing base such as that held by Shanghai.

Additionally, protecting the rule of law which has been the foundation of Hong Kong's economic success may be difficult if civil liberties erode under the Chinese system. There will be severe temptations by Chinese and/or Hong Kong firms to use their mainland connections to special advantage after the takeover. This can lead to corruption, which undermines the rule of law and the current economic success of Hong Kong. An additional factor is what the overseas Chinese, especially in Southeast Asia, will do with the Hong Kong takeover. The expatriate Chinese have kept their distance from the mainland politics. Their loyalties do not lie with the Chinese nation-state but rather with the returns that can be earned there. They have invested only in special economic zones that are protected and where they are free to move their capital. Many of them would not be willing to relinquish their foreign passport and go back to China. They will invest in China if that is where money can be earned, but if labor costs increase and productivity levels off, they are just as likely to turn to Vietnam to establish operations, or to other areas such as India, Bangladesh, Fiji, or Guatemala. If China attacks Taiwan or crushes the spirit and rule of law of Hong Kong, the overseas Chinese will not likely continue to invest in China. Loyalties to China will be overcome by economic pressures and fundamental loyalties to families.

How policy changes and ultimate government changes affect the economy will decide the nature of competition among firms and whether the Hong Kong takeover succeeds or fails. Potential demographic changes of foreign expatriate Chinese coming home or immigrants from the mainland will have an effect on these strategies. Certainly, politics and the rule of law will affect the nature of strategic exchange between firms. Thus, what happens in Hong Kong will have a strong influence on the strategic environment of the firms in Hong Kong and on the Chinese mainland, as well as all the multinational firms established there.

SOURCES: J. Barnathan, 1997, Hong Kong, *Business Week*, June 9, 45–49; M. Elliott and D. Elliott, 1997, Hong Kong: Why the world watches, *Newsweek*, May 19, 30–35; P. Engardio and J. Barnathan, 1997, Red chips rising, *Business Week*, June 9, 50–51; P. H. Kahn, 1997, Waiting for the shoe to drop in Hong Kong, *Wall Street Journal*, October 7, A18; P. Kwong, 1996, The Chinese Diaspora, *World Business* 2, no. 2: 26–31.

61

A key objective of analyzing the general environment is identification of anticipated significant changes and trends among external elements. With a focus on the future, the analysis of the general environment allows firms to identify opportunities and threats. Also critical to a firm's future operations is an understanding of its industry environment and its competitors, which are considered next.

INDUSTRY ENVIRONMENT ANALYSIS

An **industry** is a group of firms producing products that are close substitutes. In the course of competition, these firms influence one another. Typically, industries include a rich mix of competitive strategies that companies use in pursuing strategic competitiveness and above-average returns.[69]

An **industry** is a group of firms producing products that are close substitutes.

Compared to the general environment, the industry environment has a more direct effect on strategic competitiveness and above-average returns. The intensity of industry competition and an industry's profit potential (as measured by the long-run return on invested capital) are a function of five competitive forces: the threat of new entrants, suppliers, buyers, product substitutes, and the intensity of rivalry among competitors (see Figure 2.2).

Developed by Michael Porter, the five forces model of competition expands the arena for competitive analysis. Historically, when studying the competitive environment, firms concentrated on companies with which they competed directly. But

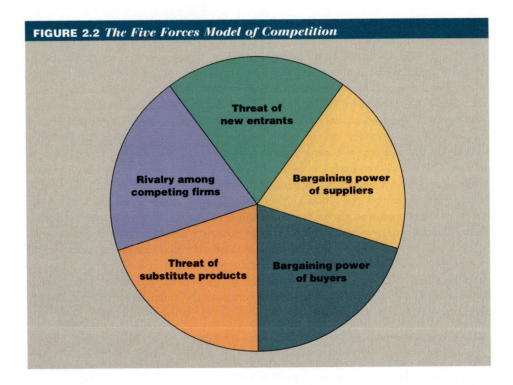

FIGURE 2.2 *The Five Forces Model of Competition*

today, competition is viewed as a grouping of alternative ways for customers to obtain the value they desire, rather than being limited to direct competitors. This is particularly important because in recent years industry boundaries have become blurred. For example, in the electrical utilities industry, as the opening case indicates, cogenerators, firms that also produce power, are competing for customers along with regional utility companies. Moreover, telecommunications companies now compete with broadcasters, software manufacturers also provide personal financial services, airlines now sell mutual funds, and automakers sell insurance and provide financing.[70] In addition to focusing on customers to define markets rather than specific industry boundaries, one should examine geographic boundaries as well. Research has shown that different geographic markets for the same product can have considerable differences in the competitive conditions.[71]

The five forces model recognizes that suppliers could become a firm's competitor (by integrating forward), as could buyers (by integrating backward). This is illustrated graphically in the pharmaceuticals industry where Merck & Company acquired Medco Containment Services, a mail-order pharmacy and prescription benefits management company. In so doing, Merck integrated forward and became a competitor of other pharmacies and prescription benefits management companies. Perhaps most importantly, Merck guaranteed a major source of distribution for its products. Shortly after Merck's acquisition, SmithKline Beecham and Eli Lilly announced plans to acquire similar companies and integrate forward as well.[72] Additionally, firms choosing to enter a new market and those producing products that are adequate substitutes could become competitors for an existing company.

Threat of New Entrants

New entrants to an industry can threaten existing competitors. New entrants bring additional production capacity. Unless product demand is increasing, additional capacity holds consumers' costs down, resulting in less sales revenue and lower returns for all firms in the industry. Often, new entrants have substantial resources and a keen interest in gaining a large market share. As such, new competitors may force existing firms to be more effective and efficient and to learn how to compete on new dimensions (e.g., computer-driven distribution channels). The likelihood that firms will enter an industry is a function of two factors: barriers to entry and the retaliation expected from current industry participants. When firms find entry into a new industry difficult or when firms are at a competitive disadvantage entering a new industry, entry barriers exist.

Barriers to Entry Existing competitors try to develop barriers to market entry. Alternatively, potential entrants seek markets where the entry barriers are relatively insignificant. The absence of entry barriers increases the probability a new entrant can operate profitably in an industry. There are several potentially significant entry barriers.

Economies of Scale. As the quantity of a product produced during a given time period increases, the costs of manufacturing each unit declines. These benefits are referred to as *economies of scale*.

Scale economies can be gained through most business functions (e.g., marketing, manufacturing, research and development, and purchasing). New entrants face a dilemma when existing competitors have scale economies. Small-scale entry places them at a cost disadvantage. However, large-scale entry, where the new entrant manufactures large volumes of a product to gain scale economies, risks strong reactions from established competitors.

Although still important in some industries (automobile manufacturing, for example), the competitive realities of the 1990s and the approaching twenty-first century may reduce the significance of scale economies as an entry barrier. Many companies now customize their products for large numbers of small customer groups. Customized products are not manufactured in the volumes necessary to achieve economies of scale. Customization is made possible by new flexible manufacturing systems. In fact, the new manufacturing technology facilitated by advanced computerization has allowed the development of mass customization in some industries. Mass customized products can be individualized to the customer in a very short period of time (e.g., within a day). Mass customization may become the norm in manufacturing products by the end of the 1990s.[73] Companies manufacturing customized products learn how to respond quickly to customers' desires, rather than developing scale economies.

Product Differentiation. Over time, customers may come to believe that an existing firm's product is unique. This belief can result from service to the customer, effective advertising campaigns, or the firm being the first to market a particular product. Many firms such as Coca-Cola and PepsiCo spend significant amounts of money on advertising to convince potential customers of the distinctiveness of their products. The belief that a firm's product is unique results in loyal customers

63

who have strong brand identification. Typically, new entrants must allocate significant resources over a long period of time to overcome existing customer loyalties. To combat the perception of uniqueness, new entrants frequently offer their products at lower prices. This can result, however, in lower profitability or even a loss for the new entrant.

Capital Requirements. Competing in a new industry requires resources to invest. In addition to physical facilities, capital is needed for inventories, marketing activities, and other critical business functions. Although competing in a new industry may appear attractive, the capital required for successful market entry may not be available.

Switching Costs. Switching costs are the one-time costs customers incur when buying from a different supplier. The costs of buying new ancillary equipment and of retraining employees and even the psychic costs of ending a relationship may be incurred in switching to a new supplier. In some cases, switching costs are low, such as switching soft drink brands, although cost may be higher for the bottler than the ultimate consumer. Sometimes larger companies help to pay the switching costs as Anheuser Busch is doing through an incentive program for beer distributors. At other times, switching costs are high even for the ultimate consumer; for instance, switching from cassette tapes to CDs as a music format. The consumer not only has to buy a CD player but CDs are more costly than cassettes. If switching costs are high, a new entrant must offer either a substantially lower price or a much better product to attract buyers. Usually, the more established the relationship, the greater the switching costs.

Access to Distribution Channels. Over time, industry participants can develop effective means of distributing products. Once developed, firms nurture their relationship with distributors. Such nurturing creates switching costs for distributors. Access to distribution channels can be a strong entry barrier for potential new entrants, particularly in consumer nondurable goods industries (e.g., in grocery stores, shelf space is limited). Thus, new entrants must persuade distributors to carry their products, either in addition to or in place of existing firms' products. Price breaks and cooperative advertising allowances may be used for this purpose, but their use reduces the new entrant's potential to earn above-average returns.

Cost Disadvantages Independent of Scale. In some instances, established competitors have cost advantages that new entrants cannot duplicate. Proprietary product technology, favorable access to raw materials, favorable locations, and government subsidies may provide such cost advantages. Successful competition requires new entrants to finds ways to reduce the strategic relevance of these factors. For example, the advantage of a favorable location can be reduced by offering direct delivery to the buyer (a number of food establishments, with unattractive locations, deliver goods directly to the consumer).

Government Policy. Through licensing and permit requirements, governments can control entry into an industry. Liquor retailing, banking, and trucking are examples of industries where government decisions and actions affect industry entry. Also, governments restrict entrance into some utility industries because of the need to provide quality service to all and the capital requirements necessary to do so.

Expected Retaliation Decision makers will also anticipate existing competitors' reactions to a new entrant. If retaliation is expected to be swift and vigorous, a decision could be reached against entry. Strong retaliation can be anticipated from firms with a major stake in an industry (e.g., having fixed assets with few, if any, alternative uses), from firms with substantial resources, and when industry growth is slow or constrained. Sometimes, a company will publicly announce its intentions.

The Cable News Network, better known as CNN and now part of Time Warner, has had a monopoly on the broadcast of 24-hour news. Capital Cities/ABC launched a 24-hour news service in 1997, using ABC News correspondents and anchors. Britain's BBC is also attempting to start a global news channel. GE's NBC has allied with Microsoft to initiate its national news network MSNBC. MSNBC also has a parallel Web site, allowing news and information to be distributed over the Internet. Time Warner intends to respond to these competitive actions by developing a parallel Web site called CityWeb. It will attempt to distribute programs to the main network affiliates (the local TV stations of ABC, NBC, Fox, and CBS) through the Internet and help them establish their own Web sites. The main networks do not have a Web site strategy. Fox indicated that the firm would eventually try to collaborate with its affiliates on co-branding and revenue sharing on Web traffic flowing in both directions. Thus, it will be interesting to see the outcome of both the 24-hour news market and how the Internet strategies evolve as competitors launch one initiative in response to other's actions.[74]

Firms can avoid entry barriers by searching out market niches that are not being served by the primary competition. Small entrepreneurial firms are generally best suited for searching out and serving these neglected market segments. A number of years ago when Honda entered the U.S. market, it concentrated on small engine motorcycles, a market that firms such as Harley-Davidson ignored. By targeting this neglected market segment, Honda avoided competition. After consolidating its position, however, Honda used its new strength to attack its rivals by

Honda sought a market niche by concentrating on small-engine motorcycles, which Harley-Davidson did not produce. Once it established itself in the small-engine niche, Honda was able to introduce larger motorcycles and compete in a broader market.

introducing larger motorcycles and competing in the broader market.[75] Competitive actions and responses are discussed in more detail in Chapter 5.

Bargaining Power of Suppliers

Increasing prices and reducing the quality of products sold are potential means through which suppliers can exert power over firms competing within an industry. If unable to recover cost increases through its pricing structure, a firm's profitability is reduced by the suppliers' actions. A supplier group is powerful when

- it is dominated by a few large companies and is more concentrated than the industry to which it sells;
- satisfactory substitute products are not available to industry firms;
- industry firms are not a significant customer for the supplier group;
- suppliers' goods are critical to buyers' marketplace success;
- the effectiveness of suppliers' products has created high switching costs for industry firms; and
- suppliers are a credible threat to integrate forward into the buyers' industry (e.g., a clothing manufacturer might choose to operate its own retail outlets). Credibility is enhanced when suppliers have substantial resources and provide the industry's firms with a highly differentiated product.

The Strategic Focus on Dell Computer Corporation illustrates how a supplier can use its power and save money for the ultimate consumer. Dell's strategy of selling directly to the corporate market is now being duplicated by Compaq and others. Dell has reduced its cost relative to other rivals and has increased its power relative to its buyers. Also, Dell is pursuing the direct consumer market.[76] Gateway 2000 sells directly to the consumer market and has now decided to pursue the corporate market by moving into larger servers.[77]

STRATEGIC FOCUS

Why Other Computer Firms Want to Imitate Dell Computer

Dell Computer Corporation's approach to selling PCs has focused on direct distribution using distributors or computer resellers. Because Dell's business model costs less to produce and distribute, the industry leaders, Compaq, IBM, Packard Bell, and Hewlett-Packard (HP) have tried to copy Dell's approach rather than use computer resellers to whom they have outsourced much of their business in this highly competitive industry.

The typical approach to distribution with the leading PC manufacturers is based on a forecast of demand. For instance, Compaq builds its machines based on this forecast. It test inspects and stores the PCs before sending them to a reseller's warehouse until customers purchase them. Often, the average time between inventory and purchase is six to eight weeks. Furthermore, the reseller's markup is generally between 7 and 9 percent. The reseller often unpacks the product, removes the computer, loads software and tests the whole thing before it is sold to the customer. The entire process is quite expensive because of packaging and repackaging as well as paying for the reseller's markup. In a fast-paced industry such as personal computers, time is money.

Compaq has unveiled recently an optimized-distribution model with much fanfare. The firm will not build a computer until it receives an order for one. Therefore, Compaq will begin to customize PCs in its own plants and ship them directly to the reseller. Similarly, HP has sought to reduce inventories and force reseller inventory down to two weeks. Compaq, IBM, and HP's advantage is that they can sell computers even through resellers; they have much broader computer lines and sell half of their product abroad. The international consumer base often does not buy computers over the phone or the Internet which is Dell's approach, but competition with Dell has required this firm's competitors to squeeze their resellers. The problem with squeezing the margins of the resellers is that there is no longer an incentive for resellers to provide the service to the larger producers.

For instance, both Compaq and HP have suggested that they will make a series of changes in reforming dealer relationships. Rather than shipping finished PCs, they would ship components, which dealers themselves would assemble into a finished unit.

One of the resellers, MicroAge, Inc., has dealt with this pressure by transforming itself into an assembler for the giants such as IBM, HP, Compaq, and Acer. MicroAge installs software and adds components requested by the customer. Furthermore, the firm collects fees for operating help desks for other companies and helps manage other companies' computer buying needs. Thus, MicroAge is searching for creative ways to increase its financial returns.

Except for Dell's approach, the buyer's power is increasing relative to seller's. Resellers are losing power and customers are gaining power and more customization. Competition is increasing dramatically among the PC producers. Dell's advantage is eroding as other computer companies and their resellers respond. Dell will struggle to maintain a competitive edge. It appears that without a direct selling advantage, the large firms will have to maintain an incentive for resellers, even though they sell a significant portion of their computers directly as well. Moreover, Dell is moving toward Gateway 2000's turf, the consumer or home market. Gateway 2000 also sells direct and has responded to Dell's actions by seeking to move to the corporate market. Dell is now trying to improve its inventory management system and has reduced its parts inventory to 12 days. This reduction in parts inventory improves Dell's efficiency and power over suppliers.

SOURCE: D. Darlin, 1997, Channel change, *Forbes*, August 25, 80; D. Kirkpatrick, 1997, Now everyone in PCs wants to be like Mike, *Fortune*, September 8, 91–92; A. Zipser, 1997, In search of greener pasters, Gateway moves on Dell's turf, *Barron's* Online, http://www.interactive.wsj.com, September 15; L. Zuckerman, 1997, Dell Computer taking aim at consumers, *New York Times* on the Web, http://www.nytimes.com, August 29; L. Zuckerman, 1997, Corporations betting that computers can buy productivity gains, *New York Times* on the Web, http://www.nytimes.com, January 2.

Bargaining Power of Buyers

Firms seek to maximize the return on their invested capital. Buyers (customers of the focal industry/firm) prefer to purchase products at the lowest possible price, at which the industry earns the lowest acceptable rate of return on its invested capital. To reduce their costs, buyers bargain for higher quality, greater levels of service, and lower prices. These outcomes can be achieved by encouraging competitive battles among firms in an industry. Customers (buyer groups) are powerful when

- they purchase a large portion of an industry's total output;
- the product being purchased from an industry accounts for a significant portion of the buyers' costs;

- they could switch to another product at little, if any, cost; and
- the industry's products are undifferentiated or standardized, and they pose a credible threat if they were to integrate backward into the sellers' industry.

Relations with customers and the service provided such customers have assumed significant meaning in recent years. For example, one study showed that a firm's value on the stock market increased with improvements in its customer service.[78] Poor relations with customers can also hurt a firm's performance. Without good relations, retail firms may give less shelf space to its products, similar to the action Wal-Mart took against Rubbermaid. In fact, this example is an excellent one where the buyer, Wal-Mart, has significant power over the seller, Rubbermaid. This is exemplified by the fact that Wal-Mart executives openly criticized Rubbermaid for the actions taken, but Rubbermaid only publicly stated positive comments about Wal-Mart. Of course, the differences in power are readily seen in the statistics showing Wal-Mart with $105 billion in 1997 sales compared to Rubbermaid's $2.35 billion.[79]

Just as Wal-Mart forced many of its suppliers into electronic data exchange (EDI), the Internet creates more power for the general consumer. For instance, *Amazon.com*, the largest book Internet seller, forced Barnes & Noble to create an Internet site. The ultimate result is a reduction in prices for the buyer. Thus, the Web may create a buyer-centric compared to a seller-centric environment shifting more power to buyers.[80] Rubbermaid is now searching for ways to deal with the power of retailers such as Wal-Mart.[81] Selling to specialty retailers and directly to consumers through direct-seller firms such as Amway and on the Internet is one way the company is trying to solve the problem. It may find, however, that the Internet creates more powerful consumers as well.

Threat of Substitute Products

Substitute products are different goods or services that can perform similar or the same functions as the focal product (functional substitute). Because it is available as an alternative or substitute, Nutrasweet places an upper limit on the prices sugar manufacturers can charge. Nutrasweet and sugar perform the same service but with different characteristics. Other product substitutes include fax machines instead of overnight delivery of correspondence, plastic containers instead of glass jars, paper versus plastic bags, and tea, with its lower caffeine content, as a healthier substitute for coffee.[82] Capable of satisfying similar customer needs, but with different characteristics, substitute products place an upper limit on the prices firms can charge. In general, the threat of substitute products is strong when customers face few, if any, switching costs and when the substitute product's price is lower and/or its quality and performance capabilities are equal to or greater than the industry's products. To reduce the attractiveness of substitute products, firms are challenged to differentiate their offerings along dimensions that are highly relevant to customers (e.g., price, product quality, service after the sale, and location).

Intensity of Rivalry among Competitors

In many industries, firms compete actively with one another to achieve strategic competitiveness and earn above-average returns. Competition among rivals is stimulated when one or more firms feel competitive pressure or when they identify an opportunity to improve their market position. Competition among rivals is often based on price, product innovation, and other actions to achieve product differentiation (such as extensive customer service, unique advertising campaigns, and extended product warranties).

Because firms in an industry are mutually dependent, one firm's actions often invite retaliation from competitors. An industry in which this pattern of action and reaction (competitive actions and responses) occurs repeatedly is the deregulated airline industry. Quick reactions to one firm's price cuts are normal in this industry. Similarly, reactions to the introduction of innovative products, such as frequent flyer programs, usually are swift. Originated by American Airlines, virtually all major airlines rapidly developed similar frequent flyer programs. Thus, in the airline industry, as in many industries, firms often *simultaneously* apply two or all three of the principal means of competition (price changes, product/service innovations, and different means of differentiation) used by rivals when trying to gain a favorable marketplace position. Robert Crandall, former CEO of American Airlines, stated that the airline "business is intensely, vigorously, bitterly, savagely competitive."[83] The *intensity* of competitive rivalry among firms is a function of several factors, as described next.

Numerous or Equally Balanced Competitors Industries populated by many participants tend to be characterized by intense rivalry. With many participants, often a few firms believe they can take actions without eliciting a response. Other firms generally notice these actions and choose to respond. Frequent patterns of actions and responses create intense rivalry. At the other extreme, industries with only a few firms of equivalent size and power also tend to have high degrees of competitive rivalry. The resource bases of these firms permit vigorous actions and responses. The marketplace battles between fast food chains and footwear companies (e.g., Nike versus Reebok) exemplify an intense rivalry between relatively equivalent competitors.

Slow Industry Growth When a market is growing, firms are challenged to use resources effectively to serve an expanding customer base. In this instance, fewer actions may be taken to attract competitors' customers. The situation changes, however, when market growth either slows or stops. Under these conditions, rivalry becomes much more intense; an increase in one firm's market share usually comes at the expense of competitors' shares.

To protect their market shares, firms engage in intense competitive battles. Such battles introduce market instability, often reducing industry profitability. Parts of the fast food industry are characterized by this situation. In contrast to years past, the market for these products is growing more slowly. To expand market share, many of these companies (e.g., McDonald's, Burger King, and Wendy's) are competing aggressively in terms of pricing strategies, product introductions, and product and service differentiation. These firms also search for new international markets to achieve their growth goals.[84]

High Fixed or Storage Costs When fixed costs account for a large part of total costs, companies are challenged to utilize most, if not all, of their productive capacity. Operating in this manner allows the costs to be spread across a larger volume of output. Such actions by many firms in an industry can result in excess supply. To reduce inventories, companies typically decrease product prices and offer product rebates as well as other special discounts. These practices often intensify rivalry among competitors. This same phenomenon is observed in industries with high storage costs. Perishable products, for example, lose their value rapidly with

69

the passage of time. When inventories grow, perishable goods producers often use pricing strategies to sell their products quickly.

Lack of Differentiation or Low Switching Costs Differentiated products engender buyer identification, preferences, and loyalty. Industries with large numbers of companies that have successfully differentiated their products have less rivalry. When buyers view products as commodities (i.e., as products with few differentiated features or capabilities), rivalry intensifies. In these instances, buyers' purchasing decisions are based primarily on price and service.

The effect of switching costs is identical to that described for differentiated products. The lower the buyers' switching costs, the easier it is for competitors to attract them (through pricing and service offerings). High switching costs, however, at least partially insulate firms from rivals' efforts to attract their customers.

Capacity Augmented in Large Increments In some industries, the realities of scale economies dictate that production capacity should be added only on a large scale (e.g., in the manufacture of vinyl chloride and chlorine). Additions of substantial capacity can be disruptive to a balance between supply and demand in the industry. Price cutting is used often to bring demand and supply back into balance. Achieving balance in this manner has, however, a negative effect on the firm's profitability.

Diverse Competitors Not all companies seek to accomplish the same goals, nor do they operate with identical cultures. These differences make it difficult to identify an industry's competitive rules. Moreover, with greater firm diversity, it becomes increasingly difficult to pinpoint a competing firm's strategic intent. Often firms engage in various competitive actions, in part to see how their competitors will respond. This type of competitive interaction can reduce industry profitability.

High Strategic Stakes Competitive rivalry becomes more intense when attaining success in a particular industry is critical to a large number of firms. For example, diversified firms' successes in one industry may be important to their effectiveness in other industries in which they compete. This is the case when firms follow a corporate strategy of related diversification (where the separate businesses are often interdependent. This strategy is explained in detail in Chapter 6).

High strategic stakes can also exist in terms of geographic locations. For example, Japanese automobile manufacturers are committed to a significant presence in the U.S. marketplace. Because of the stakes involved, for Japanese and U.S. manufacturers, rivalry in the automobile industry is quite intense.

High Exit Barriers Sometimes companies continue to compete in an industry even though the returns on their invested capital are low or even negative. Firms making this choice face high exit barriers. *Exit barriers* are economic, strategic, and emotional factors causing companies to remain in an industry even though the profitability of doing so may be in question. Common sources of exit barriers are

- specialized assets (assets with values linked to a particular business or location);
- fixed costs of exit (e.g., labor agreements);
- strategic interrelationships (mutual dependence relationships between one business and other parts of a company's operations, such as shared facilities and access to financial markets);

- emotional barriers (aversion to economically justified business decisions because of fear for one's own career, loyalty to employees, and so forth); and

- government and social restrictions (common outside the United States, restrictions often are based on government concerns for job losses and regional economic effects).

INTERPRETING INDUSTRY ANALYSES

Industry analyses can be challenging and are a product of careful study and interpretation of information and data from multiple sources. A wealth of industry-specific data is available for analyzing an industry. Because of the globalization described in Chapter 1, analysts must include international markets and rivalry in their analyses. In fact, research has shown that international variables are more important than domestic variables in the determination of competitiveness in some industries. Furthermore, because of the development of global markets, industry structures are no longer bounded by a country's borders; industry structures are often global.[85]

In general, the stronger the competitive forces, the lower the profit potential for firms in an industry. An *unattractive industry* has low entry barriers, suppliers and buyers with strong bargaining positions, strong competitive threats from product substitutes, and intense rivalry among competing firms. These industry attributes make it very difficult for firms to achieve strategic competitiveness and earn above-average returns. Alternatively, an attractive industry has high entry barriers, suppliers and buyers with little bargaining power, few competitive threats from product substitutes, and relatively moderate rivalry.[86]

A good example of global rivalry is that between Kimberly-Clark and Procter & Gamble. In 1995, Kimberly-Clark paid $7.36 billion to acquire Scott Paper Company and became the largest manufacturer of tissue products, greatly expanding its presence in Europe. This added strength was intended to help it compete more effectively in the global marketplace with P&G. In 1993 and 1994, Kimberly-Clark had to absorb losses from its European operations, which encountered difficulties in competing against P&G's aggressive promotion of its diapers and other paper products. In the United States, Kimberly-Clark is the dominant manufacturer of diapers with 40 percent of the market, compared to P&G's 36 percent. However, in Europe, P&G has a substantial market share with 68 percent of the British diaper market and up to 55 percent of the French diaper market. The Scott acquisition will accelerate Kimberly-Clark's expansion in Europe, to include the northern countries of Britain, Germany, and the Netherlands, and into southern countries, such as Spain and Italy.[87] Most recently the battle has begun to rage in emerging markets such as Brazil.[88] Both Kimberly-Clark and P&G are investing heavily in corporate R&D to develop and market new and more competitive products.

STRATEGIC GROUPS

More than 20 years ago, Michael Hunt studied the home appliance industry. He introduced the term *strategic group* to describe competitive patterns observed in that industry. Although he found differences in characteristics and strategies, Hunt

71

A **strategic group** is a group of firms in an industry following the same or a similar strategy along the same strategic dimensions.

also discovered that many firms were following similar strategies. He chose to label the groups following similar strategies strategic groups.[89] Formally, a **strategic group** is "a group of firms in an industry following the same or a similar strategy along the [same] strategic dimensions."[90] Examples of strategic dimensions include the extent of technological leadership, the degree of product quality, pricing policies, the choice of distribution channels, and the degree and type of customer service. Thus, membership in a particular strategic group defines the essential characteristics of a firm's strategy.[91] While the strategies of firms within a group are similar, they are different from the strategies being implemented by firms in other strategic groups.

The notion of strategic groups is popular for analyzing an industry's competitive structure.[92] Contributing to its popularity is the assertion that strategic group analysis is a basic framework that should be used in diagnosing competition, positioning, and the profitability of firms within an industry.[93]

Use of strategic groups for analyzing industry structure requires that dimensions relevant to the firms' performances within an industry (e.g., price and image) be selected. Plotting firms in terms of these dimensions helps to identify groups of firms competing in similar ways. For example, Dodge, Chevrolet, and Toyota form a strategic group, as do Mercedes and BMW. The products in each of these groups are similar in price and image (within the group).

There are several implications of strategic groups. First, a firm's major competitors are those within its strategic group. Because firms within a group are selling similar products to the same customers, the competitive rivalry among them can be intense. The more intense the rivalry, the greater the threat to each firm's profitability. Second, the strengths of the five competitive forces differ across strategic groups. As a result, firms within the various strategic groups have different pricing policies. Third, the closer the strategic groups in terms of strategies followed and dimensions emphasized, the greater the likelihood of competitive rivalry between the groups. For example, Nissan and Pontiac are more likely competitors for Dodge than for Mercedes and Porsche. In contrast, strategic groups that differ significantly in terms of strategic dimensions and strategies do not compete directly.

The Value of Strategic Group Analysis

Opinions vary about the value of strategic group analysis for understanding industry dynamics and structure. Some argue that there is no convincing evidence that strategic groups exist or that a firm's performance depends on membership in a particular group.[94] Another criticism of strategic groups is that the variances in many firms' product lines make it difficult to capture the nature of a company's outputs through study of a few strategic dimensions. For example, automobile companies manufacture many products with varying attributes. Dodge, for instance, manufactures some relatively inexpensive cars with a family orientation. However, the firm also sells the Dodge Viper, a sports car that is expensive and not family oriented.

These criticisms notwithstanding, strategic group analysis yields benefits. It helps in the selection and partial understanding of an industry's structural characteristics, competitive dynamics, evolution, and strategies that historically have allowed companies to be successful within an industry.[95] As is always the case, a tool's strengths and limitations should be known before it is used.

COMPETITOR ANALYSIS

Having an understanding of the general environment, the industry environment, and strategic groups, the final activity in the study of the external environment is competitor analysis. Competitor analysis focuses on each company with which a firm competes directly. Although important in all industry settings, competitor analysis is especially critical for firms facing one or a few powerful competitors.[96] For example, Nike and Reebok are keenly interested in understanding each other's objectives, strategies, assumptions, and capabilities. In successful companies, the process of competitor analysis is used to determine:

- what drives the competitor as shown by its *future objectives*;
- what the competitor is doing and can do as revealed by its *current strategy*;
- what the competitor believes about itself and the industry as shown by its *assumptions*; and
- what the competitor's capabilities are as shown by its *capabilities*.[97]

Information on these four issues helps strategists prepare an anticipated response profile for each competitor (see Figure 2.3). Thus, the results of an effective com-

73

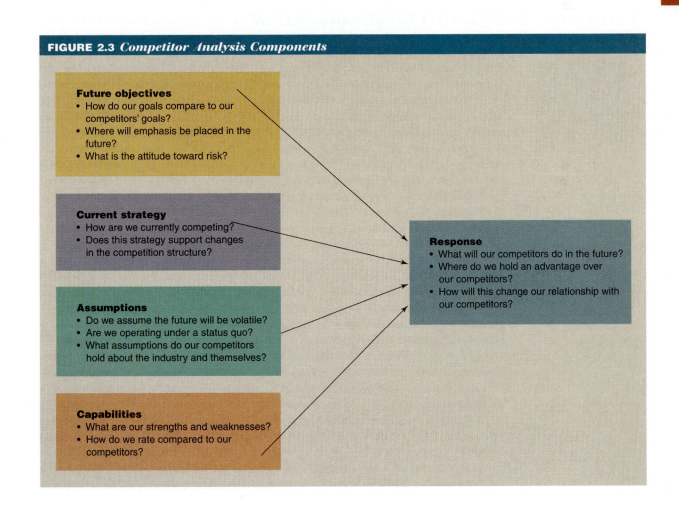

FIGURE 2.3 *Competitor Analysis Components*

Future objectives
- How do our goals compare to our competitors' goals?
- Where will emphasis be placed in the future?
- What is the attitude toward risk?

Current strategy
- How are we currently competing?
- Does this strategy support changes in the competition structure?

Assumptions
- Do we assume the future will be volatile?
- Are we operating under a status quo?
- What assumptions do our competitors hold about the industry and themselves?

Capabilities
- What are our strengths and weaknesses?
- How do we rate compared to our competitors?

Response
- What will our competitors do in the future?
- Where do we hold an advantage over our competitors?
- How will this change our relationship with our competitors?

petitor analysis help a firm understand, interpret, and predict its competitors' actions and initiatives.[98]

Critical to effective competitor analysis is the gathering of needed information and data, referred to as *competitor intelligence*. Analysts are challenged to obtain information and data ethically that inform them about competitors' objectives, strategies, assumptions, and capabilities. Intelligence gathering techniques commonly considered to be both legal and ethical include (1) obtaining publicly available information (e.g., court records, competitors' help-wanted advertisements, annual reports, financial reports of publicly held corporations, and Uniform Commercial Code filings, and (2) attending trade fairs and shows to obtain competitors' brochures, view their exhibits, and listen to discussions about their products.

However, as the Strategic Focus on corporate spying indicates, many firms are not being ethical in the way they pursue competitive intelligence. In fact, much of the spying is being supported by government agencies that formerly were focused on political causes. Economics, it appears, is becoming more prominent as the main impetus for state supported intelligence gathering.

STRATEGIC FOCUS

A New Law Safeguards Corporate Secrets

The Economic Espionage Act of 1996 (EEA) for the first time makes theft of trade secrets a federal offense. Since the end of the cold war, the FBI reports that spying did not stop but merely changed its focus. Foreign spies, who might otherwise be out of work, are focusing on corporations. Louis Freeh, FBI Director, suggests that more than $24 billion in proprietary information is being stolen each year. The FBI estimates that its economic espionage caseload jumped to 800 in 1995 from 400 in 1994. Because computer technology is so powerful and makes it much easier to copy and transmit information, intangible assets can be expropriated more easily without arousing immediate suspicion. Nothing is missing when computer files are copied and the originals remain in place. The victim only finds out later when his or her strategic advantage evaporates. Congress listened and responded with the Economic Espionage Act. EEA prescribes prison sentences of up to 15 years and fines of up to $500,000 for individuals. Furthermore, prosecutors can seize property used in commission of the crime. Several examples of spying are given below.

In January of 1997, a chemical engineer at Avery-Dennison Corporation crept into a colleague's office at the labelmaker's plant, clicked off the lights and, wearing gloves, began rifling confidential plans for expansion in the Far East. In fact, the engineer, Dr. Lee, had been stealing Avery secrets since 1989. Trained in the U.S. with three advanced degrees, he began to work for Avery in 1986. He had been selling secrets to P.Y. Yang, chairman of the Taiwanese Adhesive-Tapemaker Four-Pillars Enterprise Co. Mr. Yang offered Dr. Lee periodic payments of $10,000 to $15,000 for Avery trade secrets. The thefts became so common that Dr. Lee kept pre-addressed labels to Mr. Yang in Taiwan. Prosecutors estimated that he provided more than $15 million of secrets in return for a total of $150,000 paid to a Taiwan account controlled by his mother-in-law.

At one point, the head of office supply retailer Staples had his wife seek and receive a position working for Office Depot. She investigated Office Depot's delivery system work, how many people were in the operation, and how it trained employees. Under the current law, this type of competitor intelligence would be illegal. A company could violate the law by hiring an employee who brings a Rolodex from his past employer. The contacts on that

Rolodex would be considered trade secrets. In the past, there was an informal agreement among employers that companies would not sue each other in exchanging employees. More recently, there have been several lawsuits based on the theory that information inevitably will be disclosed as one company hires another's executives.

In January 1997, Volkswagen settled a dispute with General Motors Corp. GM's German Opal A.G. unit accused Volkswagen of industrial espionage, related to the hiring of VW purchasing and production manager Jose Ignacio Lopez de Arriortua. Volkswagen paid GM and Opal $100 million and agreed to purchase $1 billion worth of parts over a 7-year period.

A number of companies have developed significant business to protect corporate secrets. Sensormatic, for example, is working on technology with Sigma Circuits to develop a program that will embed security labels into circuit boards of computers during the initial manufacturing process. Theoretically, any information transferred from one machine to another would have this embedded label in the data processed on the individual computer. Many corporations, seeking to maintain their competitive advantage, are putting in state-of-the-art security systems. The American Society for Industrial Security (ASIS) annual meeting attracts more than 15,000 security practitioners, suppliers, and consultants from around the world. Thus, competitive intelligence is an important consideration in protecting one's trade secrets and competitive advantage in an era where spying has moved from political to economic espionage.

SOURCE: D. Starkman, 1997, Secrets and lies: The dual career of a corporate spy, *Wall Street Journal*, October 23, B1, B12; A. Farnham, 1997, How safe are your secrets?, *Fortune*, September 8, 114–120; M. G. Gotschall, 1997, Corporate security goes high tech: Protecting your people and assets makes good business sense, Special Advertising Section, *Fortune*, September 8, S1–S8.

Interestingly, a report by Deloitte & Touche suggests that 42 percent of major companies do not have a competitor intelligence system. In other words, they do not have a formal process for gathering and analyzing information about competitors. Undoubtedly, many of these firms have informal and less systematic means of gathering information about competitors. For example, 87 percent of these firms obtain information about competitor activities and 82 percent obtain information about changing market structures. Seventy-six percent of the firms also felt that they needed better information on competitor activities and 67 percent felt a need for better information on changing market structures. Nearly all of the firms felt that competitors had used intelligence techniques to gather information on their activities. Thus, firms understand the need for competitor information and gather it, even though in some firms the process may not be systematic.[99]

Competitor analysis has grown more important as a new competitive landscape has evolved. The following statements by major firm executives and investors suggest the reality of the new competitive landscape:

I don't believe in friendly competition. I want to put them out of business.
—Mitchell Leibovitz, CEO of Pepboys

Major sustainable competitive advantages are almost nonexistent in the field of financial services.
—Warren Buffett, investor[100]

Therefore, firms need to develop a more systematic means of capturing knowledge about a firm's competitive context. In effect, employees have substantial knowledge about their firms and about external constituencies and stakeholders, but few companies are able to transform this particular knowledge into a company-wide asset. Firms that are able to do so refer to this as *structural intellectual capital*. Companies such as Monsanto are attempting to link key individuals (e.g., sales representatives) across the globe to share information they obtain about competitors and other important external stakeholders. Some refer to these as knowledge networks and linking employees through networks can provide a breadth of knowledge representing a sum of employees' collective experiences and information. Furthermore, the sharing of information helps pass on organizational learning and thus becomes a true organizational asset.[101]

Obtaining competitor information is important, particularly given the statements noted earlier about significant competition and the competitive battlefield. Of course, because of systematic competitor intelligence systems, some firms have trouble maintaining critical secrets about their products, technology, or other operations. Sometimes, competitors steal information by using insiders (employees of the focal company) as illustrated in the Strategic Focus. For example, one study showed that about 75 percent of the Fortune 1000 companies believed that information they desired to remain secret was stolen from them or at least there were attempted thefts within the past five years. Thus, significant pressures can lead to the use of questionable practices to obtain desired information about competitors.[102]

Also, to deal with this situation, some firms communicate misinformation. For instance, Dell Computer Corporation set out to secretly produce a monitor for its PCs that was nearly the size of a big screen television. The purpose was to allow corporations as well as individual consumers to open many work-areas on one screen without overlap, thereby increasing their productivity. After much research and analysis, it was decided that this type of monitor was inefficient and uneconomical. Researchers decided that it would be more economical for consumers to purchase multiple small monitors and load each with whatever they needed. The top-secret plan was scrapped totally.

Immediately after the plan was eliminated, Dell allowed its secret to leak out in hopes that one of its main competitors (e.g., Gateway) would undertake the project. Gateway has often been a second-mover to Dell. After it learned of Dell's secret monitor, Gateway announced publicly that the firm would build a monitor the size of a television, and they would be the first in the industry to do so. Without much research or analysis, the monitor, named Destination, was produced and sold. From the beginning, sales were extremely slow, and constant problems existed with the few monitors that were sold. The project was a complete failure. Approximately 52 percent of all units sold were returned for repair. It wasn't long after this failure that Gateway realized that it had been set up by Dell. Dell knew that Gateway longed to be a 'first mover" and would seize the opportunity quickly. Of course, Michael Dell states that he has no idea how Gateway obtained the information, but found it quite amusing. Industry analysts referred to this action by Dell as "a corporate headfake." Sometimes in an intensely competitive industry the leader can act as if it intends to make a competitive move, when in reality it is only trying to get the followers to react, wasting both time and money.[103]

Certain techniques, eavesdropping, trespassing, blackmail, and the theft of drawings, samples, or documents, are unethical and considered to be illegal.[104] While a number of intelligence gathering techniques are legal, decision makers must determine if their use is ethical. In highly competitive environments, employees may feel greater pressure to rely on these techniques. Interestingly, evidence suggests that most business people believe their competitors use questionable intelligence gathering techniques far more frequently than they do.[105] Perhaps an appropriate guideline is to use intelligence gathering techniques that respect the principles of common morality and the right of competitors not to reveal certain information about their products, operations, and strategic intentions.[106]

As with analysis of the general environment, analyses of the industry and competitor environments should result in the identification of opportunities and threats for the focal firm. A procedure for identification of opportunities and threats is explained in the "Introduction to Preparing an Effective Case Analysis" (beginning of Part IV).

SUMMARY

- Firms' external environments are often challenging and complex. Because of their effect on performance, firms must develop the skills required to identify opportunities and threats existing in their external environments.

- The external environment has three major parts: the general environment (elements in the broader society that affect industries and their firms), the industry environment (factors that influence a firm and its competitive actions and responses—the threat of entry, suppliers, buyers, product substitutes, and the intensity of rivalry among competitors), and specific analyses of each major competitor.

- Environmental analyses often must assume a nationless and borderless business environment.

- The external environmental analysis process includes four steps: scanning, monitoring, forecasting, and assessing. Analysis of the external environment leads to the identification of opportunities and threats.

- The general environment includes six segments: demographic, economic, political/legal, sociocultural, technological, and global. For each, the objective is to identify and study the strategic relevance of different changes and trends.

- As compared to the general environment, the industry environment has a more direct effect on a firm's efforts to achieve strategic competitiveness and earn above-average returns.

- The five forces model of competition includes characteristics that determine the industry's profit potential. Through study of the five forces, firms select a position in the industry in which they can match their core competencies with an opportunity to achieve strategic competitiveness and earn above-average returns.

- Different strategic groups exist within industries (a strategic group is a collection of firms that follow similar strategies). The competition within each strategic group is more intense than is the competition between strategic groups.

- Competitor analysis informs a firm about the objectives, strategies, assumptions, and capabilities of the companies with which it competes.

- Different techniques are available for gathering the intelligence (information and data) needed to understand competitors' actions and intentions. Analysts must determine the appropriate and ethical techniques for use in their firm.

REVIEW QUESTIONS

1. Why is it important for firms to study and understand the external environment?
2. What are the differences between the general environment and the industry environment? Why are these differences important?
3. What is the environmental analysis process? What do analysts try to learn as they scan, monitor, forecast, and assess?
4. What are the six segments of the general environment? Explain the differences among them.

5. Using information in the chapter, can you justify accepting the following statement: "There are five competitive forces that determine an industry's profit potential." Explain.

6. What is a strategic group? Of what value is the strategic group concept in choosing a firm's strategy?

7. Why do firms seek information about competitors and how is that information best collected?

APPLICATION DISCUSSION QUESTIONS

1. Given the importance of understanding an external environment, why do some managers, and their firms, fail to do so? Provide an example of a firm that understood poorly its external environment and discuss the implications.

2. Select a firm and describe how you characterize the nature of the external environment facing it. As someone who will soon enter the business world, how do you react to these environmental conditions? Why?

3. Describe how it would be possible for one firm to think of a condition in the general environment as an opportunity, whereas a second firm would see that condition as a threat. Provide an example of an environmental characteristic that could be perceived this way.

4. Choose a firm in your local community. Explain the course of action you would follow and the materials you would read to understand its industry environment.

5. Select an industry and describe what firms could do to create barriers to entry in this industry.

6. What conditions would cause a firm to retaliate aggressively against a new entrant in the airline industry?

7. Is it possible for an industry to exist with only a single strategic group? If so, how? Please provide an example of such an industry.

ETHICS QUESTIONS

1. How can a firm apply its "code of ethics" in the study of its external environment?

2. What ethical issues, if any, may be relevant in a firm's monitoring of its external environment?

3. For each segment of the general environment, identify an ethical issue to which companies should be sensitive.

4. What is the importance of ethical practices between a firm and its suppliers and distributors? Explain.

5. In an intense rivalry, especially one that involves competition in the global marketplace, how can a firm undertake ethical practices and yet maintain its competitiveness? Discuss.

6. While differences in strategies may exist between strategic groups, should commonly accepted ethical values/practices be the same across strategic groups within an industry? Explain.

7. What are the primary ethical issues associated with competitor intelligence practices?

INTERNET EXERCISE

Go to Boeing's home page at:

http://www.boeing.com

Familiarize yourself with Boeing's current products, services, and worldwide operations. Also, using one of the popular search engines such as Yahoo or Excite, search the Internet for other timely information about Boeing. After you have completed your search, make a list of the issues affecting Boeing in its external environment. Organize your list into the different segments of the external environment shown in Figure 2.1.

Strategic Surfing

There are many on-line periodicals available that can help firms remain abreast of their external environment. Some examples include:

Business Week: **http://www.businessweek.com**
Fortune: **http://pathfinder.com/fortune**
Forbes: **http://www.forbes.com**
Inc.: **http://www.inc.com**

NOTES

1. J. A. Wagner and R. Z. Gooding, 1997, Equivocal information and attribution: An investigation of patterns of managerial sensemaking, *Strategic Management Journal* 18: 275–286; S. Kotha and A. P. Nair, 1995, Strategy and environment as determinants of performance: Evidence from the Japanese machine tool industry, *Strategic Management Journal* 16: 497–518.

2. C. M. Grimm and K. G. Smith, 1997, *Strategy As Action: Industry Rivalry and Coordination* (Cincinnati: Southwestern); C. J. Fombrun, 1992, *Turning Point: Creating Strategic Change in Organizations*, (New York: McGraw-Hill), 13.

3. K. E. Weick, 1995, *Sensemaking in Organizations* (Thousand Oaks: Sage).

4. Lou Gerstner's first 30 days, 1993, *Fortune*, May 31, 57–62.

5. Fombrun, *Turning Points*, 16–18.

6. M. Farjoun and L. Lei, 1997, Similarity judgments in strategy formulation: Role, process, and implications, *Strategic Management Journal* 18: 255–273; U. Zander and B. Kogut, 1995, Knowledge and the speed of the transfer and imitation of organizational capabilities: An empirical test, *Organization Science* 6: 76–92.

7. M. B. Meznar and D. Nigh, 1995, Buffer or bridge? Environmental and organizational determinants of public affairs activities in American firms, *Academy of Management Journal* 38: 975–996.

8. D. J. Teece, G. Pisano, and A. Shuen, 1997, Dynamic capabilities and strategic management, *Strategic Management Journal* 18: 509–533.

9. L. Fahey and V. K. Narayanan, 1986, *Macroenvironmental Analysis for Strategic Management* (St. Paul: West Publishing Company), 49–50.

10. M. A. Hitt, B. W. Keats, and S. M. DeMarie, 1998, Navigating in the new competitive landscape: Building strategic flexibility and competitive advantage in the 21st century, *Academy of Management Executive*, in press.

11. J. F. Preble, 1992, Environmental scanning for strategic control, *Journal of Managerial Issues* 4: 254–268; K. Gronhaug and J. S. Falkenberg, 1989, Exploring strategy perceptions in changing environments, *Journal of Management Studies* 26: 349–359.

12. Fombrun, *Turning Points*, 77; Gronhaug and Falkenberg, Exploring strategy perceptions, 350.

13. H. Courtney, J. Kirkland, and P. Visuerie, 1997, Strategy under uncertainty, *Harvard Business Review* 75, no. 6: 66–79; L. S. Richman, 1993, Why the economic data misleads us, *Fortune*, March 8, 108–114.

14. D. S. Elenkov, 1997, Strategic uncertainty and environmental scanning: The case for institutional influences on scanning behavior, *Strategic Management Journal* 18: 287–302.

15. I. Goll and A. M. A. Rasheed, 1997, Rational decision-making and firm performance: The moderating role of environment, *Strategic Management Journal* 18: 583–591; R. L. Priem, A. M. A. Rasheed, and A. G. Kotulic, 1995, Rationality in strategic decision processes, environmental dynamism and firm performance, *Journal of Management* 21: 913–929.

16. M. Yasai-Ardekani and P. C. Nystrom, 1996, Designs for environmental scanning systems: Tests of contingency theory, *Management Science* 42: 187–204.

17. R. Dodge, 1997, Summit turns attention to economics of aging, *Dallas Morning News*, June 21, F1, F2; S. Shepard, 1993, Baby boom could bust retirement system, *WacoTribune-Herald*, May 23, A1; How America will change over the next 30 years, 1993, *Fortune*, May 2, 12.

18. Fahey and Narayanan, *Macroenvironmental Analysis*, 39.

19. Ibid., 41.

20. M. Maremont, 1997, Gillette tries to soothe analyst fears on profit growth, *Wall Street Journal*, September 24, B1.

21. Fahey and Narayanan, *Macroenvironmental Analysis*, 42.

22. T. Aeppel, 1997, Rubbermaid warns 3rd-quarter profits will come in far below expectations, *Wall Street Journal*, September 19, A4; A. B. Fisher, 1996, Corporate reputations, *Fortune*, March 6, 90–93; L. Smith, 1995, Rubbermaid goes thump, *Fortune*, October 2, 90–104.

23. Fahey and Narayanan, *Macroenvironmental Analysis*, 58.

24. E. Cornish, 1990, Issues of the '90s, *Fortune*, February 11, 136–141.

25. R. Stodghill II, 1997, The coming job bottleneck, *Business Week*, March 24, 184–185.

26. G. Colvin, 1997, How to beat the boomer rush, *Fortune*, August 18, 59–63.

27. D. Kunde, 1997, Well connected, *Dallas Morning News*, October 22, D1, D2; Associated Press, 1997, Telecommuters say they'd walk before going back to the office, *Dallas Morning News*, October 21, D1.

28. R. Dodge, 1997, Labor complications, *Dallas Morning News*, September 1, D1, D2; M. N. Martinez, 1995, Contingency workers shed the bad rap, *HR Magazine* 40, no. 4: 16–18.

29. M. McLaughlin, 1989, A change of mind, *New England Business*, April, 42–53.

30. J. R. W. Joplin and C. S. Daus, 1997, Challenges of leading a diverse workforce, *Academy of Management Executive* XI, no. 3: 32–47; G. Robinson and K. Dechant, 1997, Building a business case for diversity, *Academy of Management Executive* IX, no. 3: 21–31.

31. S. Finkelstein and D. C. Hambrick, 1996, *Strategic Leadership: Top Executives and Their Effect on Organizations* (Minneapolis: West); T. Cox and S. Blake, 1991, Managing cultural diversity: Implications for international competitiveness, *Academy of Management Executive V*, no. 3: 45–46.

32. J. P. Fernandez, 1993, *The Diversity Advantage* (New York: Lexington Books).

33. J. Landers, 1997, Incomes rising around world, *Dallas Morning News*, September 15, D1, D4.

34. Fahey and Narayanan, *Macroenvironmental Analysis*, 105.

35. J. Landers, 1997, High labor costs slow investment in German economy, *Dallas Morning News*, October 27, D1, D4; New York Times Service, 1997, U.S. deficit at its lowest in 23 years, *Dallas Morning News*, October 27, D1, D3.

36. R. Norton, 1995, There go these Eurocrats again, *Fortune*, September 18, 51.

37. R. Henkoff, 1997, Asia: Why business is still bullish, *Fortune*, October 27, 139–142.

38. Fahey and Narayanan, *Macroenvironmental Analysis*, 139–157.

39. B. O'Reilly, 1997, Transforming the power business, *Fortune*, September 29, 143–156.

40. Ibid., 143.

41. T. Vogel, 1997, Central America goes from war zone to enterprise zone, *Wall Street Journal*, September 25, A18.

42. J. R. Wike and B. Ortega, 1997, Anheuser's sales practices under probe, *Wall Street Journal*, October 3, A3.

43. K. Harris, 1995, Lights! Camera! Regulation! *Fortune*, September 4, 83–86.

44. How America will change over the next 30 years, 12.

45. P. Thomas, 1995, Success at a huge personal cost: Comparing women around the world, *Wall Street Journal*, July 26, B1.

46. J. B. Roesner, 1991, Ways women lead, *Harvard Business Review* 69, no. 3: 119–125.

47. B. Morris, 1997, If women ran the world it would look a lot like Avon, *Fortune*, July 21, 74–79.

48. F. N. Schwartz, 1992, Women as a business imperative, *Harvard Business Review* 70, no. 2: 105–113; C. Torres and M. Bruxelles, 1992, Capitalizing on global diversity, *HR Magazine*, December, 30–33; B. Geber, 1990, Managing diversity, *Training*, July, 23–30.

49. E. H. Buttner and D. P. Moore, 1997, Women's organizational exodus to entrepreneurship: Self-reported motivations and correlations with success, *Journal of Small Business Management* 35, no. 1: 34–46; *USA Today*, 1997, More minority owners, June 27, B10; J. Files, 1996, Texas 2nd in women-owned businesses, *Dallas Morning News*, January 30, D5.

50. J. S. Lublin, 1997, How one CEO juggles a job and a family miles apart, *Wall Street Journal*, October 8, B1, B15.

51. D. Milbank, 1997, More dads raise families without mom, *Wall Street Journal*, October 3, B1, B2.

52. B. L. Dos Santos and K. Peffers, 1995, Rewards to investor in innovative information technology applications: First movers and early followers in ATMs, *Organization Science* 6: 241–259; S. A. Zahra, S. Nash, and D. J. Bickford, 1995, Transforming technological pioneering into competitive advantage, *Academy of Management Executive* IX, no. 1: 17–31.

53. R. Tetzeli, 1994, The Internet and your business, *Fortune*, March 7, 89–96.

54. E. W. Desmond, 1997, How data may soon seek you out, *Fortune*, September 8, 149–150.

55. S. McCartney, 1995, U.S. Robotics dials up dollars in market for modems, *Wall Street Journal*, July 27, B8.

56. R. A. Melcher, 1997, Dusting off the Britannica, *Business Week*, October 20, 143–146.

57. M. Iansiti and A. MacCormack, 1997, Developing products on Internet time, *Harvard Business Review* 75, no. 5: 108–117.

58. D. Bank, 1997, Microsoft's talks with TCI are part of a broader strategy, http://www.interactive.wsj.com, October 16; D. Bank, 1997, Microsoft claims digital breakthrough, *Wall Street Journal*, September 16, B14.

59. J. Cole, 1995, New satellite imaging could soon transform the face of the earth, *Wall Street Journal*, November 30, A1, A5.

60. E. Schonfeld, 1997, The space business heats up, *Fortune*, November 24, 142–152.

61. S. Woolley, 1997, ViaSat: Slow and steady does it, *Forbes*, November 3, 178–180.

62. J. Birkinshaw, A. Morrison, and J. Hulland, 1995, Structural and competitive determinants of a global integration strategy, *Strategic Management Journal* 16: 637–655.

63. G. R. Ungson, R. M. Steers, and S.H. Park, 1997, *Korean Enterprise: The Quest for Globalization* (Boston: Harvard Business School Press).

64. S. Glain, 1995, Going for growth: Korea's Samsung plans very rapid expansion into autos, other lines, *Wall Street Journal*, March 2, A1, A6; L. Nakarmi and R. Neff, 1994, Samsung's radical shakeup, *Business Week*, February 28, 74–76.

65. J. P. Alston, 1989, Wa, guanxi, and inhwa: Managerial principals in Japan, China and Korea, *Business Horizons*, March-April, 26–31.

66. M. A. Hitt, M. T. Dacin, B. B. Tyler, and D. Park, 1997, Understanding the differences in Korean and U.S. executives' strategic orientations, *Strategic Management Journal* 18: 159–167; S. Yoo and S. M. Lee, 1987, Management style and practice of Korean chaebols, *California Management Review* 29, Summer: 95–110.

67. K. Singh, 1996, Fried chicken's fearsome foes, *Far Eastern Economic Review*, January 25, 30; M. Jordan, 1995, U.S. food firms head for cover in India, *Wall Street Journal*, November 21, A14.

68. J. Kahn, 1995, P&G viewed China as a national market and is conquering it, *Wall Street Journal*, September 12, A1, A6.

69. S. M. Oster, 1994, *Modern Competitive Analysis*, 2nd edition (New York: Oxford University Press).

70. R. A. Bettis and M. A. Hitt, 1995, The new competitive landscape, *Strategic Management Journal* 16 (Special Summer Issue): 7–19.

71. G. R. Brooks, 1995, Defining market boundaries, *Strategic Management Journal* 16: 535–549.

72. A. M. McGahan, 1994, Industry structure and competitive advantage, *Harvard Business Review* 72, no. 5: 115–124.

73. J. H. Gilmore and B. J. Pine, II, 1997, The four faces of mass customization, *Harvard Business Review*, 75, no. 1: 91–101; S. Kotha, 1995, Mass customization: Implementing the emerging paradigm for competitive advantage, *Strategic Management Journal* 16 (Special Summer Issue): 21–42; B. Pine, 1993, *Mass Customization* (Boston: Harvard Business School Press); B. Pine, B. Victore, and A. C. Boynton, 1993, Making mass customization work, *Harvard Business Review* 71, no. 5: 108–119.

74. R. E. Calem, 1997, Time Warner goes after affiliates of TV networks. New York Times on the Web, http://www.nytimes.com, January 16; E. Jensen and J. Lippman, 1995, New competition may mean bad news for CNN, *Wall Street Journal*, December 6, B1, B4.

75. Take on the giants, 1996, *Success*, January/February, 30.

76. L. Zuckerman, 1997, Dell Computer taking aim at consumers, New York Times on the Web, http://www.nytimes.com, August 29.

77. A. Zipser, 1997, In search of greener pastures, Gateway moves on Dell's turf, Barron's Online, http://www.interactive.wsj.com, September 15.

78. P. R. Nayyar, 1995, Stock market reactions to customer service changes, *Strategic Management Journal* 16: 39–53.

79. Briefing Book, 1997, http://www.interactive.wsj.com, November 15; L. Smith, 1995, Rubbermaid goes thump, *Fortune*, October 2, 90–104.

80. J. W. Gurley, 1997, Seller, beware: The buyers rule e-commerce, *Fortune*, November 10, 234–236.

81. Aeppel, Rubbermaid warns 3rd-quarter profits will come in far below expectations, A4.

82. S. Browder, 1997, Tea is bagging a bigger crowd, *Business Week*, August 25, 6.

83. R. A. D'Aveni, 1995, Coping with hypercompetition: Utilizing the new 7S's framework, *Academy of Management Executive* IX, no. 3: 45.

84. R. Gibson, 1997, Burger wars sizzle as McDonald's clones the Whopper, *Wall Street Journal*, September 17, B1.

85. H. J. Moon and K. C. Lee, 1995, Testing the diamond model: Competitiveness of U.S. software firms, *Journal of International Management* 1: 373–387.

86. Much of the preceding discussion of competitive forces is based on Porter, *Competitive Strategy*.

87. H. S. Bryne, 1996, Global war: Beefed-up Kimberly-Clark prepares to battle P&G, *Barron's*, April 22, 17; P. Thomas, 1995, Kimberly-Clark and P&G face global warfare, *Wall Street Journal*, July 18, B1, B6.

88. R. Narisetti and J. Friedland, 1997, Diaper wars of P&G and Kimberly-Clark now heat up in Brazil, *Wall Street Journal*, June 4, A1, A10.

89. M. S. Hunt, 1972, Competition in the major home appliance industry, 1960–1970 (doctoral dissertation, Harvard University).

90. Porter, *Competitive Strategy*, 129.

91. R. K. Reger and A. S. Huff, 1993, Strategic groups: A cognitive perspective, *Strategic Management Journal* 14: 103–123; J. McGee and H. Thomas, 1986, Strategic groups: A useful linkage between industry structure and strategic management, *Strategic Management Journal* 7: 141–160.

92. J. B. Barney and R. E. Hoskisson, 1990, Strategic groups: Untested assertions and research proposals, *Managerial and Decision Economics* 11: 198–208.

93. M. Peteraf and M. Shanley, 1997, Getting to know you: A theory of strategic group identity, *Strategic Management Journal* 18 (Special Issue), 165–186; R. M. Grant, 1995, *Contemporary Strategy Analysis*, 2nd ed. (Cambridge, MA: Blackwell Publishers), 98.

94. D. Nath and T. Gruca, 1997, Covergence across alternatives for forming strategic groups, *Strategic Management Journal* 18: 745–760; Barney and Hoskisson, Strategic groups, 202.

95. K. G. Smith, C. M. Crimm, and S. Wally, 1997, Strategic groups and rivalrous firm behavior: Towards a reconciliation, *Strategic Management Journal* 18: 149–157.

96. S. Ghoshal and D. E. Westney, 1991, Organizing competitor analysis systems, *Strategic Management Journal* 12: 17–31.

97. Porter, *Competitive Strategy*, 49.

98. S. A. Zahra and S. S. Shaples, 1993, Blind spots in competitive analysis, *Academy of Management Executive* VII, no. 2: 7–28.

99. U.S. companies slow to develop business intelligence, 1995, *Deloitte & Touche Review*, October 16, 1–2.

100. D'Aveni, Coping with hypercompetition, 45.

101. T. A. Stewart, 1995, Getting real about brain power, *Fortune*, November 27, 201–203; T. A. Stewart, 1995, Mapping corporate brain power, *Fortune*, October 30, 209–211.

102. M. Geyelin, 1995, Why many businesses can't keep their secrets, *Wall Street Journal*, November 20, B1, B3.

103. A. Zipser, 1997, In search of greener pastures, Gateway moves on Dell's turf, Barron's Online, http://www.interactive.wsj.com, September 15.

104. K. A. Rehbeing, S. A. Morris, R. L. Armacost, and J. C. Hosseini, 1992, The CEO's view of questionable competitor intelligence gathering practices, *Journal of Managerial Issues* 4: 590–603.

105. S. A. Zahra, 1994, Unethical practices in competitive analysis: Patterns, causes, and effects, *Journal of Business Ethics* 13: 53–62; W. Cohen and H. Czepiec, 1988, The role of ethics in gathering corporate intelligence, *Journal of Business Ethics* 7: 199–203.

106. J. H. Hallaq and K. Steinhorst, 1994, Business intelligence methods—How ethical?, *Journal of Business Ethics* 13: 787–794; L. S. Paine, 1991, Corporate police and the ethics of competitor intelligence gathering, *Journal of Business Ethics* 10: 423–436.

The Internal Environment: Resources, Capabilities, and Core Competencies

CHAPTER 3

Learning Objectives

After reading this chapter, you should be able to:

1. Explain the importance of studying and understanding the internal environment.

2. Define value and discuss its importance.

3. Describe the differences between tangible and intangible resources.

4. Define capabilities and discuss how they are developed.

5. Describe four criteria used to determine if a firm's resources and capabilities are core competencies.

6. Explain how value chain analysis is used to identify and evaluate a firm's resources and capabilities.

7. Define outsourcing and discuss the reasons for its use.

8. Discuss the importance of preventing a firm's core competencies from becoming core rigidities.

9. Explain the relationship between a firm's strategic inputs and its strategic actions.

People as a Source of Competitive Advantage

In a *Fortune* survey featuring the most admired corporations worldwide, a critical theme emerged. Although no one strength was judged sufficient to place a company on top of the global list of most admired firms, a capability for finding, nurturing, and keeping intelligent and talented employees was most strongly related to a company's overall score. For instance, Disney received the highest score for being the most innovative company. Michael Eisner indicated that "we create a new product—a book, a movie, something—every five minutes and each one has to be superb. Our goal is to do it better every time out. But our real product is managing talent. That's what we really do here, and we never lose sight of that—because without that, what have you got?" Similarly, Jack Welch, GE's CEO, says, "All we can do is bet on the people who we pick. So my whole job is picking the right people." In fact, Welch personally interviews candidates for the top five hundred jobs at GE. Most companies in the survey found that the ability to attract and hold talented employees was the single most reliable predictor of excellence.

http://www.disney.com
http://www.ge.com
http://www.saic.com
http://www.levi.com
http://www.microsoft.com

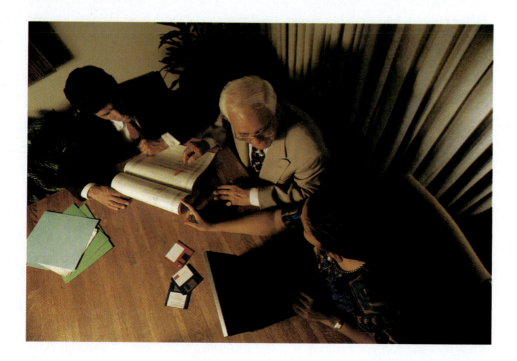

The Hay Group that conducted the survey for *Fortune* found that seven basic themes contribute to corporate excellence in hiring and career development practices:

1. Top managers at the most admired companies take their firm's mission statements seriously and expect everyone else to do likewise.
2. Success attracts the best people and the best people sustain success.
3. Top companies know precisely what they're looking for, often through intense psychological testing.
4. They see career development as an investment, not a chore.
5. Whenever possible, they promote from within.
6. They reward performance.
7. They measure workforce satisfaction.

In essence, the most admired firms in the survey are experts at managing human resources.

A number of private companies also take managing human resources seriously. Robert Beyster, the chief executive officer and founder of Science Applications International Corp. (SAIC), built a scientific consulting firm starting with twelve employees in 1969 to a 25,000-employee high-tech research and engineering firm. SAIC recently bought Bellcore, the former research arm of the Bell operating companies and improved its ranking to the forty-first largest private firm in *Forbes*'s ranking of the five hundred largest private companies. At SAIC, employees own 90 percent of the company and the other 10 percent is held by consultants or employees who left the company before SAIC required that departing employee owners were required to sell their shares back to the firm. Although Beyster has 1.5 percent of the $2 billion net worth of the firm instead of owning 100 percent, his philosophy has turned employees into committed and motivated stakeholders. The firm has four different employee-ownership programs that are among the most sophisticated in the country. As Narri Cooper indicates, "When I'm making a decision, I don't just make it as an information technology manager, I make it as an owner." Furthermore, nine employees sit on the twenty-two-person board alongside such luminaries as U.S. Navy Admiral B. R. Inman.

Because private firms compete with public companies for star talent, private companies have had to take actions such as those initiated by SAIC to attract the most qualified personnel. In a 1997 study, consultants found that 30 percent of the largest U.S. companies have stock option plans for more than half their employees. Although SAIC is exemplary, most private companies have yet to deal with the problem of the incentives that public companies are offering. To compete more effectively, Levi Strauss & Co., a privately owned firm that completed a leveraged buyout, has sought to revamp its profit sharing plan. It replaced its ESOP because it benefited mostly middle managers and because workers located outside the U.S. could not participate. The new plan rewards all 37,000 employees with a cash payment equal to their 1996 salaries if the company meets a cash flow target of $7.6 billion by the year 2001. In essence, the plan makes Levi Strauss employees implicit owners of the company.

Microsoft views human resources as an organizational capability. Microsoft has sought to make large new product teams work as efficiently as small teams. Although small teams of talented people may be the most desired way to develop new products, this is impossible when the product is complex and short deadlines are required to be competitive. As a result, firms such as Microsoft find it necessary to manage large teams (perhaps hundreds) of talented engineers to develop new complex software products. Because of this reality, Microsoft has developed innovative ways of managing teams of talented people. These managerial approaches help Microsoft produce innovative products.

In summary, human resources are critical. Developing the ability to hire, manage, motivate, and orchestrate people is an important capability that adds to a firm's core competence. If it can effectively manage this critical capability, the company may become one of the top firms on *Fortune*'s most admired corporations list or be highlighted in *Forbes*'s examples of outstanding private companies.

SOURCE: M.A. Cusumano, 1997, How Microsoft makes large teams work like small teams, *Sloan Management Review* 39, no. 1: 9–20; A. Fisher, The world's most admired companies, *Fortune*, October 27, 220–240; C.T. Geer, 1997, Turning employees into stakeholders, *Forbes*, December 1, 155–157; C.T. Geer, 1997, Sharing the wealth, capitalist-style, *Forbes*, December 1, 158–160; M.A. Huselid, S.E. Jackson and R.S. Schuler, 1997, Technical and strategic human resource management effectiveness as determinants of firm performance, *Academy of Management Journal* 40: 171–188; P. Cappelli and A. Crocker-Hefter, 1996, Distinctive human resources are firms' core competencies, *Organizational Dynamics* 24, no. 3: 7–22.

Disney, GE, Science Applications International Corp. and Microsoft have developed capabilities to manage their human resources. Each of these firms is interested in developing a *sustainable competitive advantage*. A sustainable competitive advantage is achieved when firms implement a value-creating strategy that is grounded in their own unique resources, capabilities, and core competencies (terms defined in Chapter 1). Firms achieve strategic competitiveness and earn above-average returns when their unique core competencies are leveraged effectively to take advantage of opportunities in the external environment. As the opening case indicates, one way to develop competitive advantage is through people, the firm's employees.[1]

Over time, the benefits of every firm's value-creating strategy can be duplicated. In other words, all competitive advantages have a limited life.[2] The question of duplication is not *if* it will happen, but *when*. During the 1980s, for example, the competitive advantage of brand names began to dissipate. Among the factors causing a temporary erosion of the competitive advantage yielded by brand names for some firms was a technological development—the checkout scanner. Studying data available to them from scanners allowed retailers (such as grocery stores) to determine quickly how price promotions on various products affected their sales volume. In the words of one analyst, this new technology "gave retailers tremendous new muscle over the brandmakers, and with all the increased emphasis on discounts and promotions, consumers learned how to bargain."[3]

Effective duplication by competitors may have contributed to Home Depot's performance difficulties. "Home Depot isn't such a nimble category killer anymore," says a business writer. Competitors such as Lowe's and Eagle Hardware have built hangar-size warehouses that offer an array of goods similar to that available from Home Depot. Moreover, these competitors' actions have reduced the service gap between them and Home Depot.[4] Although in Chapter 4 we describe actions Home Depot is taking to counteract this duplication, competitors' actions have contributed to Home Depot's reduced performance.

In general, the sustainability of a competitive advantage is a function of three factors: (1) the rate of core competence obsolescence due to environmental changes, (2) the availability of substitutes for the core competence, and (3) the imitability of the core competence.[5] The challenge for strategists in all firms—a challenge that can be met through proper use of the strategic management process—is to manage current core competencies effectively while simultaneously developing new ones to use when the competitive advantage derived from application of current ones has been eroded.[6] Only when firms develop a continuous stream of competitive advantages (as explained further in Chapter 5) do they achieve strategic competitiveness, earn above-average returns, and remain ahead of competitors. Intel and Microsoft continuously make investments that are intended to enhance their current sources of competitive advantage and simultaneously spur the creation of new ones.[7] These investments appear to contribute significantly to these firms' ability to achieve and maintain strategic competitiveness.

In Chapter 2, we examined the general environment, the industry environment, and rivalry among competing firms. Armed with knowledge about their firm's environments, managers have a better understanding of the marketplace opportunities and the products necessary to pursue them.

In this chapter, we focus on the firm. Through an analysis of the internal environment, a firm determines *what it can do*—that is, the actions permitted by its unique resources, capabilities, and core competencies. As discussed in Chapter 1, core competencies are a firm's source of competitive advantage. The magnitude of that competitive advantage is a function primarily of its uniqueness compared to competitors' competencies.[8] The proper matching of what a firm *can do* with what it *might do* allows the development of strategic intent, a strategic mission, and the formulation of strategies. When implemented effectively, a value-creating strategy is the pathway to strategic competitiveness and above-average returns. Outcomes resulting from internal and external environmental analyses are shown in Figure 3.1.

Several topics are examined in this chapter. First, the importance and the challenge of studying a firm's internal environment are addressed. We then discuss the roles that resources, capabilities, and core competencies play in the development of sustainable competitive advantage. Included in these discussions are descriptions

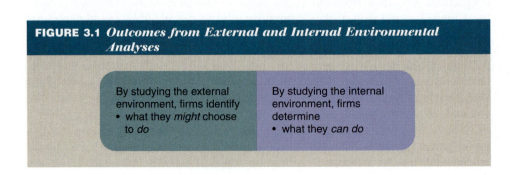

FIGURE 3.1 *Outcomes from External and Internal Environmental Analyses*

By studying the external environment, firms identify
• what they *might* choose to *do*

By studying the internal environment, firms determine
• what they *can do*

of the techniques used to identify and evaluate resources and capabilities and the criteria used to select the firm's core competencies from among its resources and capabilities. While studying these materials, it is important to recall that resources, capabilities, and core competencies are not valuable alone; they have value only because they allow the firm to perform certain activities that result in a competitive advantage. To have sustained competitive advantage these activities must be unique.[9]

As shown in Figure 1.1 in Chapter 1, strategic intent and strategic mission, coupled with insights gained through analyses of the internal and external environments, determine the strategies a firm will select and the actions it will take to implement them successfully. In the final part of the chapter, we describe briefly the relationship between intent and mission and a firm's strategy formulation and implementation actions.

THE IMPORTANCE OF INTERNAL ANALYSIS

In the new competitive landscape, traditional conditions and factors, such as labor costs, access to financial resources and raw materials, and protected or regulated markets, can still provide competitive advantage but to a lesser degree now than in the past.[10] A key reason for this decline is that the advantages created by these sources can be overcome through an international strategy (international strategies are discussed in Chapter 8). As a result, overcapacity is the norm in a host of industries, increasing the difficulty of forming competitive advantages. In this challenging competitive environment, few firms are able to make consistently the right strategic decisions. Additionally, less job security for individual employees is an inevitable consequence of operating in this more challenging competitive environment. It is interesting, for example, that a number of firms, including Kodak, Citicorp, Levi Strauss, Whirlpool, Apple, and Kimberly-Clark among others, announced layoffs in 1997 and early 1998, at a time when the economy was very strong.[11]

The demands of the new competitive landscape make it necessary for top-level managers to rethink the concept of the corporation. Although corporations are difficult to change, earning strategic competitiveness in the 1990s and into the twenty-first century requires development and use of a different managerial mind-set.[12] Most top-level managers recognize the need to change their mind-sets but many hesitate to do so. In the words of a European CEO of a major U.S. company, "It is more reassuring for all of us to stay as we are, even though we know the result will be certain failure . . . than to jump into a new way of working when we cannot be sure it will succeed."[13]

Critical to the managerial mind-set required is the view that a firm is a *bundle* of heterogeneous resources, capabilities, and core competencies that can be used to create an exclusive market position.[14] This view suggests that individual firms possess at least some resources and capabilities that other companies do not have, at least not in the same combination. Resources are the source of capabilities, some of which lead to the development of a firm's core competencies. By using their core competencies, firms are able to perform activities *better* than competitors or that competitors are unable to duplicate. Essentially, the mind-set required in the new competitive landscape defines its strategy in terms of unique competitive position rather than in terms of operational effectiveness. For instance, Michael Porter argues that quest for productivity, quality, and speed from a number of management techniques (total quality management, benchmarking, time-based competition, reengineering) have resulted in operational efficiency but not strong sustainable strategy.[15]

Increasingly, managers are being evaluated in terms of their ability to identify, nurture, and exploit their firm's unique core competencies.[16] By emphasizing competence acquisition and development, organizations learn how to learn—a skill that is linked with the development of competitive advantage. As a process, learning how to learn requires commitment, time, and the active support of top-level executives. At Deere & Co., managers have created an "in-house Yellow Pages" to help them find an expert inside or outside the firm.[17] The system is quite inexpensive, about the cost of one engineer to operate it, but it has paid for itself annually, at least six times over, especially when there is a crisis, say in production, and an expert is needed to solve it. In the final analysis, a corporate-wide obsession with the development and use of knowledge and core competencies more broadly may characterize companies able to compete effectively on a global basis in the twenty-first century.[18]

By exploiting their core competencies and meeting the demanding standards of global competition, firms create value for their customers. **Value** consists of the performance characteristics and attributes provided by companies in the form of goods or services for which customers are willing to pay. Ultimately, customer value is the source of a firm's potential to earn average or above-average returns. In Chapter 4, we note that value is provided to customers by a product's low cost, by its highly differentiated features, or by a combination of low cost and high differentiation, as compared to competitors' offerings. Core competencies, then, are actually a value-creating system through which a company seeks strategic competitiveness and above-average returns (these relationships are shown in Figure 3.2). In the new competitive landscape, managers need to determine if their firm's core competencies continue to create value for customers.[19]

During the last several decades, the strategic management process was concerned largely with understanding the characteristics of the industry in which a firm was competing and, in light of those characteristics, determining how the firm should position itself relative to competitors. The emphasis on industry characteristics and competitive strategy may have understated the role of organizational resources and capabilities in developing competitive advantage. A firm's core competencies, in addition to the results of an analysis of its general, industry, and competitive environments, should drive the selection of strategies. In this regard, core competencies, in combination with product-market positions or tactics, are the most important sources of competitive advantage in the new competitive landscape. Emphasizing core competencies when formulating strategies causes companies to learn how to compete primarily on the basis of firm-specific differences rather than seeking competitive advantage solely on the structural characteristics of their industries.[20]

Value consists of the performance characteristics and attributes provided by companies in the form of goods or services for which customers are willing to pay.

The Challenge of Internal Analysis

The decisions managers make in terms of resources, capabilities, and core competencies have a significant influence on a firm's ability to develop competitive advantages and earn above-average returns.[21] Making these decisions—that is, identifying, developing, protecting, and deploying resources, capabilities, and core

FIGURE 3.2 *Components of Internal Analysis Leading to Competitive Advantage and Strategic Competitiveness*

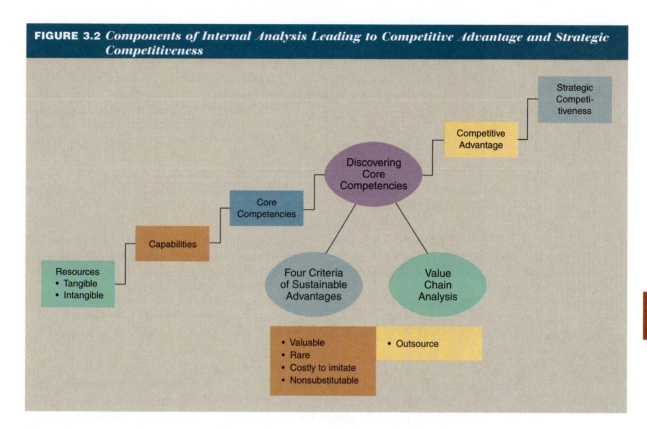

competencies—may appear to be relatively easy tasks. In fact, this work is as challenging and difficult as any other with which managers are involved; and, it is becoming increasingly internationalized and linked with the firm's success.[22]

Sometimes mistakes are made when conducting an internal analysis. Managers might, for example, select resources and capabilities as a firm's core competencies that do not, in fact, yield a competitive advantage. When this occurs, strategists must have the confidence to admit the mistake and take corrective actions. Firm growth can occur through well-intended errors. Indeed, learning generated by making and correcting mistakes can be important to the creation of new competitive advantages.[23]

To manage the development and use of core competencies, managers must have courage, self-confidence, integrity, the capacity to deal with uncertainty and complexity, and a willingness to hold people accountable for their work.[24] Successful strategists also seek to create an organizational environment in which operating units feel empowered to use the identified core competencies to pursue marketplace opportunities.

Difficult managerial decisions concerning resources, capabilities, and core competencies are characterized by three conditions: uncertainty, complexity, and intraorganizational conflicts (see Figure 3.3).

Managers face *uncertainty* in terms of the emergence of new proprietary technologies, rapidly changing economic and political trends, changes in societal values, and shifts in customer demands. Such environmental uncertainty increases the *complexity* and the range of issues managers examine when studying the internal

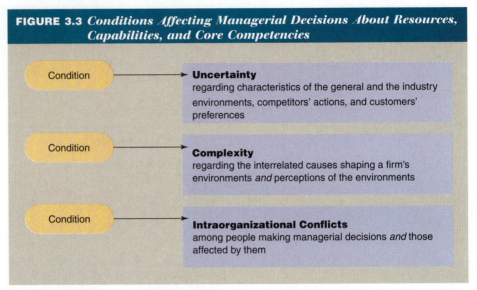

FIGURE 3.3 *Conditions Affecting Managerial Decisions About Resources, Capabilities, and Core Competencies*

Condition → **Uncertainty**
regarding characteristics of the general and the industry environments, competitors' actions, and customers' preferences

Condition → **Complexity**
regarding the interrelated causes shaping a firm's environments *and* perceptions of the environments

Condition → **Intraorganizational Conflicts**
among people making managerial decisions *and* those affected by them

Source: Adapted from R. Amit and P. J. H. Schoemaker, 1993, Strategic assets and organizational rent, *Strategic Management Journal* 14: 33.

environment. Managerial biases about how to cope with uncertainty affect decisions about the resources and capabilities that will become the foundation of the firm's competitive advantage. Finally, *intraorganizational conflict* surfaces when decisions are made about core competencies that are to be nurtured and about how the nurturing is to take place.

When making decisions affected by these three conditions, managers should use their judgment. *Judgment* is a capacity for making successful decisions when no obviously correct model or rule is available or when relevant data are unreliable or incomplete.[25] In this situation one must be aware of possible cognitive biases. For instance, one must compare internal firm resources and make a judgment whether a resource is a strength or a weakness. When exercising judgment, the strategist demonstrates a willingness to take intelligent risks in a timely manner. In the new competitive landscape, executive judgment can be a particularly important source of competitive advantage. One reason judgment can result in a competitive advantage is that over time, effective judgment allows a firm to retain the loyalty of stakeholders whose support is linked to above-average returns.[26]

Significant changes in the value-creating potential of a firm's resources and capabilities can occur in a rapidly changing global economy. Because these changes affect a company's power and social structure, inertia or resistance to change may surface. Firms should not deny the changes needed to assure strategic competitiveness; nonetheless, managers sometimes deny the need for organizational and/or personal change. *Denial* is an unconscious coping mechanism used to block out and not initiate painful changes.[27] Occasionally, an entire industry is accused of being in denial. Some analysts recently cited the automobile manufacturing industry as an example of this. In light of saturation in some major markets (such as the United States), automakers have had to increase incentives. The alternative is to reduce production, a difficult decision.[28] GE's CEO, Jack Welch, believes that top-level executives must demonstrate unflinching candor when making strategic decisions. Part of this candor demands that decision makers cause their firms and their people to face reality as it is—not as it once was or as they want it to be.[29] Successful strategists have learned that involving many people in decisions about changes reduces denial and intraorganizational conflict.

RESOURCES, CAPABILITIES, AND CORE COMPETENCIES

Our attention now turns to a description of resources, capabilities, and core competencies—characteristics that are the foundation of competitive advantage. As shown in Figure 3.2, some combination of resources and capabilities can be managed to create core competencies. This subsection defines and provides examples of these internal aspects.

Resources

Defined in Chapter 1, *resources* are inputs into a firm's production process such as capital equipment, the skills of individual employees, patents, finance, and talented managers. Broad in scope, resources cover a spectrum of individual, social, and organizational phenomena.[30] Resources alone do not typically yield a competitive advantage. A professional football team may benefit from employing the league's most talented running back, but it is only when the running back integrates his running style with the blocking schemes of the offensive linemen and the team's offensive strategy that a competitive advantage may develop. Similarly, a firm's production technology, if not protected by patents or other constraints, can be purchased or imitated by competitors, but when that production technology is in-

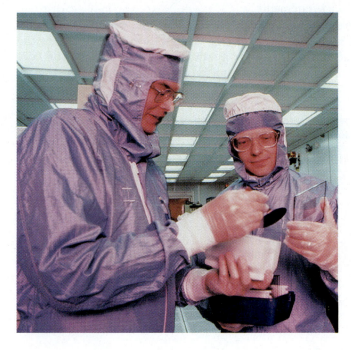

If a firm does not protect its technology with patents or other constraints, it can be purchased or imitated by competitors.

91

tegrated with other resources to form a capability, a core competence may develop that results in competitive advantage. Thus, a competitive advantage can be created through the *unique bundling of several resources*.[31] Physical assets alone usually cannot provide a firm with a sustainable competitive advantage.[32]

Tangible resources are assets that can be seen and quantified.

Intangible resources range from the intellectual property rights of patents, trademarks, and copyrights to the people-dependent or subjective resources of know-how, networks, organizational culture, and a firm's reputation for its goods or services and the ways it interacts with people (e.g., employees, suppliers, and customers).

92

Some of a firm's resources are tangible; others are intangible. **Tangible resources** are assets that can be seen and quantified. **Intangible resources** range from the intellectual property rights of patents, trademarks, and copyrights to the people-dependent or subjective resources of know-how, networks, organizational culture, and a firm's reputation for its goods or services and the ways it interacts with people (e.g., employees, suppliers, and customers).[33]

Reputation is viewed as an intangible resource that can endow companies with a competitive advantage. Some equate reputation to "what accountants call goodwill and marketers call brand equity."[34] Among other competitive benefits, a positive reputation allows the firm to charge premium prices for its goods or services and to reduce its marketing costs.[35] Harley-Davidson is a brand that may drive sales on any two-wheeled vehicle. Using the Harley-Davidson brand, GT Bicycles has been licensed to offer the Velo Glide for $1700. GT sold 1,000 Limited Edition Bicycles for $2,500 each in 1996 that were snapped up quickly by collectors. These bikes have real Harley paint jobs, a fake gas tank, and chrome fenders similar to a Harley soft-tail motorcycle.[36]

The four types of tangible resources are financial, physical, human, and organizational (see Table 3.1). The three types of intangible resources (*technological* and those resulting from the firm's *innovation* and *reputation*) are shown in Table 3.2.

Tangible Resources As tangible resources, a firm's borrowing capacity and the status of its plant and equipment are visible to all. The value of many tangible resources can be established through financial statements, but these statements do not account for the value of all of a firm's assets in that they disregard some intangible resources.[37] As such, sources of a firm's competitive advantage often are not reflected on its financial statements.

Managers are challenged to understand fully the strategic value of their firm's tangible and intangible resources. The *strategic value of resources* is indicated by the degree to which they can contribute to the development of capabilities and core competencies and, ultimately, a competitive advantage. For example, as a tangible

TABLE 3.1 *Tangible Resources*	
Financial Resources	■ The firm's borrowing capacity
	■ The firm's ability to generate internal funds
Physical Resources	■ Sophistication and location of a firm's plant and equipment
	■ Access to raw materials
Human Resources	■ The training, experience, judgment, intelligence, insights, adaptability, commitment, and loyalty of a firm's individual managers and workers
Organizational Resources	■ The firm's formal reporting structure and its formal planning, controlling, and coordinating systems

Source: Adapted from J.B. Barney, 1991, Firm resources and sustained competitive advantage, *Journal of Management* 17: 101; R.M. Grant, 1991, *Contemporary Strategy Analysis* (Cambridge, England: Blackwell Business), 100–102.

TABLE 3.2 *Intangible Resources*

Technological Resources	■ Stock of technology such as patents, trademarks, copyrights, and trade secrets
	■ Knowledge required to apply it successfully
Resources for Innovation	■ Technical employees
	■ Research facilities
Reputation	■ Reputation with customers
	■ Brand name
	■ Perceptions of product quality, durability, and reliability
	■ Reputation with suppliers
	■ For efficient, effective, supportive, and mutually beneficial interactions and relationships

Source: Adapted from R. Hall, 1992, The strategic analysis of intangible resources, *Strategic Management Journal* 13: 136–139; R.M. Grant, 1991, *Contemporary Strategy Analysis* (Cambridge, England: Blackwell Business), 101–104.

resource, a distribution facility will be assigned a monetary value on the firm's balance sheet. The real value of the facility as a resource, however, is grounded in other factors such as its proximity to raw materials and customers and the manner in which workers integrate their actions internally and with other stakeholders such as suppliers and customers.[38]

As shown in Figure 3.2, resources are the source of a firm's capabilities. Capabilities are the source of a firm's core competencies, which are the basis of competitive advantages. Intangible resources, as compared to tangible resources, are a superior and more potent source of core competencies.[39] In fact, in today's competitive environment, ". . . the success of a corporation lies more in its intellectual and systems capabilities than in its physical assets. [Moreover], the capacity to manage human intellect—and to convert it into useful products and services—is fast becoming the critical executive skill of the age."[40] Some evidence also suggests that the value of intangible assets is growing as a proportion of a firm's total shareholder value. In a recent 10-year period, for example, one study's results indicate that the relationship between tangible assets (defined as property, plant, and equipment in this study) and total market value for U.S. mining and manufacturing companies declined from 62 to 38 percent.[41]

Intangible Resources Because they are less visible and more difficult for competitors to understand, purchase, imitate, or substitute, managers prefer to use intangible resources as the foundation for a firm's capabilities and core competencies. In fact, it may be that the more unobservable (that is, intangible) a resource is, the more sustainable will be the competitive advantage based on it.[42]

Brand names are an intangible resource that helps to create a firm's reputation and are recognized widely as an important source of competitive advantage for many companies, especially for those manufacturing and selling consumer goods and services.[43] When effective, brand names inform customers of a product's performance characteristics and attributes. When products with strong brand names provide value across time, customers become very loyal by refusing to buy competitors' offerings, including private-label generic products.

When a brand name yields a competitive advantage, companies sometimes strive to find additional ways to exploit it in the marketplace as the earlier example of Harley-Davidson using its brand name to sell bicycles demonstrates. Century 21 Real Estate seeks to use its brand name to offer and sign up customers for a wide range of discounted home services.[44] Disney has used its brand name to offer clothes representing Disney figures. Currently, Disney is entering the restaurant business through a chain of sport theme restaurants based on its ESPN cable sports network brand. Disney has also launched ESPN merchandise stores.[45]

One way brand-name products are supported is through advertising. Advertising is considered one of the best ways to build brand equity, as suggested by the fact that spending on advertising continues to increase and exceeded $182 billion in the United States in 1997.[46] Consumer products giant Procter & Gamble was the largest advertiser in the United States in 1995, spending a total of $1.51 billion to advertise Crest toothpaste, Tide detergent, and its other well-known consumer goods. Close behind P&G in advertising spending in 1995 were General Motors, $1.5 billion, and Philip Morris, $1.4 billion. Nevertheless, the ad dollar is becoming diffused over many more alternative providers. For instance, advertising revenue on the Web reached $217 million through the first six months of 1997, which is more than triple the $61 million spent in the first six months of 1996.[47]

As a source of capabilities, tangible and intangible resources are a critical part of the pathway to the development of competitive advantage (see Figure 3.2). As discussed previously, resources' strategic value is increased when they are integrated or combined. Defined formally in Chapter 1, *capability* is the capacity for a set of resources to integratively perform a task or activity. Capabilities are unique combinations of the firm's information-based tangible resources (see Table 3.1) and/or intangible resources (see Table 3.2) and are what the firm is able to do as a result of teams of resources working together.

Capabilities

As just explained, capabilities represent the firm's capacity to deploy resources that have been purposely *integrated* to achieve a desired end state. As the glue that binds an organization together, capabilities emerge over time through complex interactions between and among tangible and intangible resources. As explained in the opening case, they are often based on developing, carrying, and exchanging information and knowledge through the firm's human capital. Thus, the firm's knowledge base is embedded in and reflected by its capabilities and is a key source of advantage in the new competitive landscape.[48] Because a knowledge base is grounded in organizational actions that may not be understood explicitly by all employees, the firm's capabilities become stronger and more valuable strategically through repetition and practice.

As illustrated in Figure 3.4, the primary base for the firm's capabilities is the skills and knowledge of its employees and often their functional expertise. As such, the value of human capital in the development and use of capabilities and, ultimately, core competencies cannot be overstated. Microsoft, for example, believes that its best asset is the "intellectual horsepower" of its employees. To assure continued development of this capability and the core competence that follows, the firm strives continuously to hire people who are more talented than the current set of employees.[49]

FIGURE 3.4 *Capabilities*

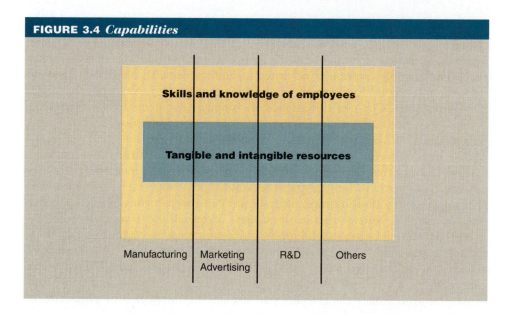

Some believe that the knowledge possessed by the firm's human capital is among the most significant of an organization's capabilities and may ultimately be at the root of all competitive advantages. In the words of one business analyst, "Companies have come to understand that one of the strongest competitive advantages is absolute knowledge."[50] Some even view knowledge as "the sum of everything everybody in [a] company knows that gives [the firm] a competitive edge in the marketplace."[51] Moreover, the *rate* at which firms acquire new knowledge and develop the skills necessary to apply it in the marketplace is a key source of competitive advantage.[52] To facilitate knowledge acquisition, development, and application, some firms (such as Coca-Cola, GE, and General Motors) have created a new top management team (this term is discussed in Chapter 12) position—the chief knowledge officer or the chief learning officer (CLO). Regardless of the title, the task for these strategists is primarily to help the firm become a learning organization that is open to making the changes required to establish and exploit competitive advantages.

Some evidence suggests that workforces throughout the global economy may lack the skills and knowledge firms require to exploit them as a source of competitive advantage. For instance, a National Association of Manufacturers study indicated that, "nearly nine out of 10 U.S. manufacturers are reporting shortages of qualified workers, and a growing gap has emerged between job requirements in the high technology economy and the skills available."[53] One manager has noted that "high tech is exploding. . . . And the only thing stopping growth from being even stronger is the lack of qualified high-tech professionals."[54] In particular, this concern, which exists across all types of industries, is directed toward the future. "These concerns are not about the existing workforce so much as about the people coming into the workforce."[55] The shortage is not only being felt by large firms. The report, *The Survey of Small and Mid-Sized Businesses*, prepared by the 63,000-member National Small Business United and Arthur Andersen Enterprise Group showed a similar concern. The survey reported that the single most important challenge was labor quality. When confronted with a possible shortage of skilled workers, companies desiring to develop their knowledge as a source of competitive advantage sometimes scan the global economy to find the required labor skills. For example, a number of firms, including Siemens, Motorola, Hewlett-Packard, and Digital Equipment, employed computer engineers from the city of Bangalore, India. The city's thousands of computer engineers have signaled that Bangalore is an important global source of information technology and workforce capabilities.[56]

The importance of human capital and knowledge to the firm's strategic competitiveness and the need to provide continuous learning opportunities for employees, particularly in light of the forecasted skilled labor force shortages, have been suggested by both business analysts and key government officials. One analyst, for example, believes that in all business organizations (especially those providing services) ". . . learning and productivity grow from the cumulative decision-making experiences of employees in long-term relationships with customers, vendors and fellow employees."[57] It has also been argued that the United States' competitiveness in the global economy and its ability to increase the standard of living of individual citizens is influenced strongly by the degree to which the nation's human capital is nourished and increased.[58]

As illustrated in Figure 3.4 and Table 3.3, capabilities are often developed in specific functional areas (e.g., manufacturing, R&D, marketing, etc.) or in a part (e.g., advertising) of a functional area. Research results suggest a relationship between distinctive competencies (or capabilities) developed in particular functional areas and the firm's financial performance at both the corporate and business-unit levels.[59] Thus, firms should seek to develop functional area distinctive competencies or capabilities in individual business units and at the corporate level (in the case of diversified firms). Table 3.3 shows a grouping of organizational functions and the capabilities certain companies are thought to possess in terms of all or parts of those functions.

As mentioned in the opening case, Science Applications International Corp, Levi Strauss, and Microsoft are respected for their different functional abilities to develop their human resources. In particular, Microsoft has a creative ability to make large new product teams work as efficiently as small teams.[60]

Armed with knowledge about resources and capabilities, managers are prepared to identify their firm's core competencies. As defined in Chapter 1, *core competencies* are resources and capabilities that serve as a source of competitive advantage for a firm over its rival.

Core Competencies

As the source of competitive advantage for a firm, core competencies distinguish a company competitively and reflect its personality. Core competencies emerge over time through an organizational process of accumulating and learning how to deploy different resources and capabilities. As a capacity to take action, core competencies ". . . are the essence of what makes an organization unique in its ability to provide value to customers over a long period of time."[61]

Not all of a firm's resources and capabilities are strategic assets—that is, assets that have competitive value and the potential to serve as a source of competitive advantage.[62] Some resources and capabilities may result in incompetence because they represent competitive areas in which the firm is weak compared to competitors. Thus, some resources or capabilities may stifle or prevent the development

TABLE 3.3 *Examples of Firms' Capabilities*

Functional Areas	Capabilities	Firm Examples
Distribution	Effective use of logistics management techniques	Wal-Mart
Human resources	Motivating, empowering, and retaining employees	AEROJET
Management information systems	Effective and efficient control of inventories through point-of-purchase data collection methods	Wal-Mart
Marketing	Effective promotion of brand-name products	Gillette
		Ralph Lauren Clothing
		McKinsey & Co.
	Effective customer service	Nordstrom
		Norwest
		Solectron Corporation
		Norrell Corporation
	Innovative merchandising	Crate & Barrel
Management	Effective execution of managerial tasks	Hewlett-Packard
	Ability to envision the future of clothing	The Gap
	Effective organizational structure	PepsiCo
Manufacturing	Design and production skills yielding reliable products	Komatsu
	Product and design quality	The Gap
	Production of technologically sophisticated automobile engines	Mazda
	Miniaturization of components and products	Sony
Research & development	Exceptional technological capability	Corning
	Development of sophisticated engineered elevator control solutions	Motion Control Engineering Inc.
	Rapid transformation of technology into new products and processes	Chaparral Steel
	Deep knowledge of silver-halide materials	Kodak
	Digital technology	Thomson Consumer Electronics

97

of a core competence. Firms with insufficient financial capital, for example, may be unable to purchase facilities or hire the skilled workers required to manufacture products that yield customer value. In this situation, financial capital (a tangible resource) would be a weakness. Armed with in-depth understandings of their firm's resources and capabilities, strategic managers are challenged to find external environmental opportunities that can be exploited through the firm's capabilities while avoiding competition in areas of weakness.

Additionally, an important question is: How many core competencies are required for the firm to have a competitive advantage? Responses to this question vary. McKinsey & Co. recommends that clients identify three or four competencies around which their strategic actions can be framed.[63] Note the consistency of Rolls-Royce's decisions with this advice to focus on only four competencies. The company has outsourced a number of peripheral activities such as making car bodies and fasteners so it can concentrate "on its core competencies—engines, paint, leather, (and) wood."[64] Trying to support and nurture more than four core competencies may prevent the firm from developing the focus it needs to exploit fully its competencies in the marketplace.

From an impoverished city in southern Italy called Santeramo Del Colle, Pasquale Natuzzi has taken his firm Industrie Natuzzi SpA from selling 100 leather sofas to Macy's in 1982 to having an estimated 25 percent of the U.S. leather furniture market.[65] Because his clients in Italy were pressuring him to send two or three sofas but only bill them for one or two to avoid taxes, he decided to begin selling his furniture overseas. He has focused his firm's competencies on design flair and quality leathers, highly skilled craftsmen, each with a computer to maintain efficient operations, and low labor costs with strong worker incentives. Because of Natuzzi's focus on a few critical core competencies, his furniture has maintained attractive designs that meet the needs of this fashion conscious industry at a price that is 20 percent less than what Macy's paid in 1982.

Not all resources and capabilities are core competencies. The following section discusses two approaches for identifying core competencies.

BUILDING CORE COMPETENCIES

Two conceptual tools can help to identify and build competencies and the achievement of competitive advantage. First, we discuss four specific criteria to determine which of a firm's resources and capabilities are core competencies. Because they have satisfied the four criteria of sustainable competitive advantage, the capabilities shown in Table 3.3 are core competencies for the firms processing them. Following this discussion, we describe value chain analysis for deciding what value-creating competencies should be maintained, upgraded, or developed and which activities should be outsourced.

Criteria of Sustainable Competitive Advantage

As shown in Table 3.4, capabilities that are valuable, rare, costly to imitate, and nonsubstitutable are strategic capabilities and a source of competitive advantage.[66] Capabilities failing to satisfy these criteria are not core competencies. Thus, as shown in Figure 3.5, every core competence is a capability, but every capability is not a core competence.

A sustained competitive advantage is achieved only when competitors have tried, without success, to duplicate the benefits of a firm's strategy or when competitors lack the confidence to attempt imitation. For some period of time, a firm may earn a competitive advantage through the use of capabilities that are, for example, valu-

TABLE 3.4 *Four Criteria for Determining Strategic Capabilities*	
Valuable Capabilities	■ Help a firm neutralize threats or exploit opportunities
Rare Capabilities	■ Are not possessed by many others
Costly to Imitate Capabilities	■ Historical: A unique and a valuable organizational culture or brand name
	■ Ambiguous cause: The causes and uses of a competence are unclear
	■ Social complexity: Interpersonal relationships, trust and friendship among managers, suppliers, and customers
Nonsubstitutable Capabilities	■ No strategic equivalent

FIGURE 3.5 *Core Competence as a Strategic Capability*

able and rare,[67] but are imitable. In such an instance, the length of time a firm can expect to retain its competitive advantage is a function of how quickly competitors can successfully imitate a good, service, or process. It is only through the combination of conditions represented by all four criteria that a firm's capabilities have the potential to create a sustained competitive advantage.

Valuable **Valuable capabilities** are those that create value for a firm by exploiting opportunities and/or neutralize threats in its external environment. Valuable capabilities enable a firm to formulate and implement strategies that create value for specific customers. Sony Corp. has used its valuable capabilities dealing with the designing, manufacturing, and selling of miniaturized electronic technology to exploit a range of marketplace opportunities, including those for portable disc players and easy-to-hold 8mm video cameras.[68]

Rare **Rare capabilities** are those possessed by few, if any, current or potential competitors. A key question managers seek to answer when evaluating this criterion is "How many rival firms possess these valuable capabilities?" Capabilities possessed by many rival firms are unlikely to be a source of competitive advantage for any one of them. Instead, valuable but common (i.e., not rare) resources and capabilities are sources of competitive parity.[69] Competitive advantage results only when firms develop and exploit capabilities that differ from those they share with competitors.

Costly to Imitate **Costly to imitate capabilities** are those that other firms cannot develop easily. Capabilities that are costly to imitate can occur because of one or a combination of three reasons (see Table 3.4).

First, a firm sometimes is able to develop capabilities because of *unique historical conditions*. "As firms evolve, they pick up skills, abilities, and resources that are unique to them, reflecting their particular path through history."[70] A firm with a

Valuable capabilities are those that create value for a firm by exploiting opportunities and/or neutralize threats in its external environment.

Rare capabilities are those possessed by a few, if any, current or potential competitors.

Costly to imitate capabilities are those that other firms cannot develop easily.

Sony Corp. used its valuable capabilities to design, manufacture, and sell its hand-held digital camcorders.

unique and valuable organizational culture that emerged in the early stages of the company's history "... may have an imperfectly imitable advantage over firms founded in another historical period"[71]—a period of time in which less valuable values and beliefs strongly influence the development of a firm's culture. This may be the case for the consulting firm McKinsey & Co.

McKinsey's culture is thought by competitors, clients, and analysts alike to be a primary source of competitive advantage. As testimony to the intangibility of culture, even to some of those familiar with it, consider the following description of culture as McKinsey's source of advantage: "It is that culture, unique to McKinsey and eccentric, which sets the firm apart from virtually any other business organization and which often mystifies even those who engage (its) services." The historical foundation for McKinsey's culture was established by Marvin Bower, the company's founding father. In fact, "much of what McKinsey is today harks back to the early 1930s" when Bower entered the consulting business. Bower's concept of how his consulting firm would operate was that it should provide advice about effective managerial practices to top-level executives. As guidance for McKinsey's consultants, Bower developed a set of principles. Cited frequently and with intensity, these principles actually define what McKinsey was and is today. As such, they are the backbone of the company's unique, and what some think is an enigmatic, culture. According to Bower's principles, a McKinsey consultant should (1) put the interests of the client ahead of increasing the company's revenues, (2) remain silent about the client's business operations, (3) be truthful and not fear challenging a client's opinion, and (4) perform only work that s/he believes is in the client's best interests and is something McKinsey can do well.[72]

A second condition of being costly to imitate occurs when the link between the firm's competencies and its competitive advantage is *causally ambiguous*.[73] In these instances, competitors are unable to understand clearly how a firm uses its competencies as the foundation for competitive advantage. As a result, competitors are uncertain about the competencies they should develop to duplicate the benefits of a competitor's value-creating strategy. Gordon Forward, CEO of Chaparral Steel, allows competitors to tour his firm's facilities. In Forward's words, competitors can be shown almost ". . . everything and we will be giving away nothing because they can't take it home with them."[74]

Social complexity is the third reason that capabilities can be costly to imitate. Social complexity means that at least some, and frequently many, of the firm's capabilities are the product of complex social phenomena. Examples of socially complex capabilities include interpersonal relationships, trust and friendships among managers, and a firm's reputation with suppliers and customers. Hewlett-Packard's culture is recognized widely as socially complex and as a source of competitive advantage. Socially complex capabilities resulting from this culture include the nurturing of innovation across divisional boundaries and the effective use of cross-functional work teams. Recently this culture provided the capability HP needed to develop work processes through which the firm was able to improve operations dramatically in its North American distribution organization. Designed by a cross-functional work team of 35 people from HP and two other companies, the distribution center's new work processes reduced the number of days required to deliver products to customers from 26 to 8.[75]

Nonsubstitutable **Nonsubstitutable capabilities** are those that do not have strategic equivalents. This final requirement for a capability to be a source of competitive advantage ". . . is that there must be no strategically equivalent valuable resources that are themselves either not rare or imitable. Two valuable firm resources (or two bundles of firm resources) are strategically equivalent when they each can be exploited separately to implement the same strategies."[76] In general the strategic value of capabilities increases the more difficult they are to substitute.[77] The more invisible capabilities are, the more difficult it is for firms to find substitutes and the greater the challenge is to competitors trying to imitate a firm's value-creating strategy. Firm-specific knowledge and trust-based working relationships between managers and nonmanagerial personnel are examples of capabilities that are difficult to identify and for which finding substitutes is challenging.

To summarize this discussion, we reiterate that sustainable competitive advantage results only through the use of capabilities that are valuable, rare, costly to imitate, and nonsubstitutable. Table 3.5 shows the competitive consequences and performance implications resulting from combinations of the four criteria of sustainability. The analysis suggested by the contents of the table helps managers determine the strategic value of the firm's capabilities. Resources and capabilities falling into the first row in the table (that is, resources and capabilities that aren't valuable or rare and that are imitable and for which strategic substitutes exist) are ones the firm should not emphasize to formulate and implement strategies. Capabilities yielding competitive parity and either temporary or sustainable competitive advantage, however, will be supported. Large competitors such as Coca-Cola and PepsiCo may have capabilities that can yield only competitive parity. In such cases, the firms will nurture these capabilities while simultaneously emphasizing those that can yield either a temporary or sustainable competitive advantage.

Nonsubstitutable capabilities are those that do not have strategic equivalents.

101

TABLE 3.5 *Outcomes from Combinations of the Criteria for Sustainable Competitive Advantage*

Is the Resource or Capability Valuable?	Is the Resource or Capability Rare?	Is the Resource or Capability Costly to Imitate?	Is the Resource or Capability Nonsubstitutable?	Competitive Consequences	Performance Implications
No	No	No	No	Competitive disadvantage	Below-average returns
Yes	No	No	Yes/no	Competitive parity	Average returns
Yes	Yes	No	Yes/no	Temporary competitive advantage	Above-average returns to average returns
Yes	Yes	Yes	Yes	Sustainable competitive advantage	Above-average returns

What about Toyota's advantage in new product development and production systems in the Strategic Focus? First, its strategy appears to create value because is has been successful with selling its designs at a low cost. Its production systems and new product development capabilities are obviously rare. Others have had difficulty reproducing this system even though many competitor executives have visited Toyota plants. Although the techniques may not be causally ambiguous, Toyota's system is socially complex. Furthermore, the firm continues to learn and maintain its early advantage in efficient production systems and new product development. Establishing early advantage and maintaining that advantage will be discussed more fully in Chapter 5. Also, because of the complexity and idiosyncrasy of Toyota's production system, the system is nonsubstitutable. In fact, Toyota has had trouble transferring its production system to other locations such as the Georgetown facility in Kentucky. Therefore, Toyota appears to have a sustainable competitive advantage.

STRATEGIC FOCUS

Toyota's New Product Development and Production Systems Are Difficult to Copy

Toyota's secret of competitive success has been its new product development and production systems. Toyota has a large manufacturing complex in Georgetown, Kentucky. Two days a month, more than 50 auto executives and engineers travel to this complex and participate in five hour tours. The tours include an intensive question and answer session for visiting executives of competing car companies. Even though Toyota shows competitors how it makes cars, no other company has succeeded in beating Toyota as the most efficient auto company in the world. Mercedes-Benz has sophisticated engineering; Honda has excellent engine technology; and Chrysler is excellent in styling. But Toyota sets the standard in efficiency, quality, and productivity.

Furthermore, although it has been considered conservative and slow-moving, the firm's new CEO, Hiroshi Okuda, seeks to make Toyota even more efficient. Speed is becoming more important as the twenty-first century approaches. Additionally, Okuda intends to not only increase Toyota's global market share but also to improve its operating margins. In Japan, Toyota has set a 40 percent market share as its goal while its closest rival, Nissan, currently has 22 percent. Furthermore, Toyota has 21 percent of the market in Southeast Asia. Additionally, Toyota ranks fourth in unit sales behind the Big Three in the U.S. with an 8 percent share. Okuda has set a 10 percent goal of market share in the United States.

Competitors understand the techniques and practices Toyota uses but cannot reproduce the firm's production system. Although the principles of Toyota's productivity are not complicated, its implementation and coordination require "an incredible amount of detail, planning, discipline, hard work and painstaking attention to detail." Therefore, although it is not causally ambiguous, it is highly socially complex. What makes imitation of the production system even more difficult is that Toyota continues to improve its own system.

Some believe that Toyota's exceptional strength lies in its ability to learn. Its employees are always problem-conscious and strongly customer-oriented. It has a simple ability to learn from its mistakes and improve continually. Although the 1997 Previa was an engineering marvel, it was powered by a small engine and buyers found it sluggish and too expensive at $30,000. In 1998, the Sienna XLE may not be an engineering marvel, but it has a larger engine, inventive technology, and a $22,000 price tag.

Toyota's new product development is unrivaled in the industry. The firm produces a new car in eighteen months. Some U.S. competitors are down to 30 months. Besides its speed at producing a new model, Toyota now develops similar models simultaneously. The industry approach is to develop a sedan and then follow sequentially with a coupe or some other variety. Toyota's approach is to develop these products simultaneously. Through this method, Toyota has doubled its engineering output over the past four years while increasing its budget by only 20 percent.

Toyota is also excelling as the first automobile maker to sell a mass production vehicle with a hybrid engine. A hybrid engine combines gasoline engine technology with an electric motor that receives electricity both from a battery pack and from the car's movement. Using this technology, the Prius, the first hybrid technology model car, gets 66 miles per gallon and generates half the normal amount of carbon dioxide. Toyota hopes to produce a thousand cars a month even though the Prius won't be profitable because it costs twice as much to make as its $17,900 price tag.

Toyota has also provided a breakthrough in engine design. It has designed a 120-horsepower engine for its 1998 Corolla, which uses 25 percent fewer parts, making it 10 percent lighter and 10 percent more fuel-efficient. This has allowed Toyota to slash the price of its '98 Corolla by $1,500 compared to its 1997 model. Toyota realizes that it is also dependent on its suppliers. As such, "it has consciously institutionalized a set of practices for transferring knowledge between itself and the suppliers, so that the whole group learns faster." On average, Toyota's independent suppliers are 59 miles away from its assembly plants. By comparison, GM's supplier average is 425 miles from the plants they serve. This results in a larger inventory for both the supplier and General Motors' plants.

Although Toyota is unexcelled in productivity as the above factors denote, the firm has had difficulty establishing its systems for production and product development outside of Japan. Therefore, Toyota remains Japan-centric. In the long run, this is likely to be a strong hindrance to future growth. In its Georgetown complex, decisions are often referred back to Tokyo. This has created a problem of relatively high turnover at the Georgetown complex. Toyota realizes that with the Japanese market quite saturated, growth will have to come in international markets; therefore, the company is pursing foreign direct investment. As such, production in Japan has dipped from the peak of four million in 1991 to 3.4 million in 1996. Notwithstanding the difficulties, no one has been able to determine how to duplicate Toyota's product development and production systems.

SOURCE: A. Taylor III, 1997, How Toyota defies gravity, *Fortune*, December 8, 100–108; A. Pollack, 1997, At Toyota, ten percent share is viewed as a start, http://www.nytimes.com, October 24; M. Krebs, 1997, Toyota ahead of pack on hybrid production, http://www.nytimes.com, July 25; B. Bremner, L. Armstrong, K. Kerwin, and K. Naughton, 1997, Toyota's crusade, *Business Week*, http://www.businessweek.com, April 7.

The Gap, a specialty retailer, operates more than 1,600 company outlets under the store names The Gap, GapKids, Banana Republic, and Old Navy. Through the presentation of dressed-down clothes at affordable prices, the firm is thought to have revolutionized the casual-apparel market for women, men, and children. The firm relied on various capabilities to develop competitive advantages in terms of its attention to quality and design and the use of clever advertising slogans and campaigns. To exploit what it saw as an opportunity to serve customers interested in dressed-down clothes but unable to afford The Gap's goods, the firm decided to use its capabilities and competencies to establish Old Navy stores.[78]

What type of advantage, if any, results from the use of some of The Gap's capabilities such as product design and quality, creative advertising, and store design and layout to develop the Old Navy format? It seems that the capabilities being used in this new retailing format are valuable and rare, but at least with respect to The Gap's major competitors, these capabilities can be imitated. For example, The Gap's CEO suggested that ". . . there are no secrets in retailing. The minute something new—a store or a look—is created in this industry, it is instantly visible, there for all the world to examine and replicate."[79] Strategic equivalents for these capabilities may or may not exist. Thus, an analysis of these capabilities suggests that The Gap has established a temporary competitive advantage with its Old Navy stores (see Table 3.5). In terms of the performance implications, the firm should earn above-average returns until competitors learn how to duplicate the value Old Navy stores creates through exploitation of The Gap's.

In the next section, we discuss another framework firms use to examine their resources and capabilities to discover core competencies. Value chain analysis allows the firm to understand the parts of its operations (see Figure 3.2) that create value and those that do not. Understanding these issues is important because the firm earns above-average returns only when the value it creates is greater than the costs incurred to create that value.[80]

Value Chain Analysis

The value chain is a template that firms use to understand their cost position and to identify the multiple means that might be used to facilitate the implementation of their business-level strategy.[81] As shown in Figure 3.6, a firm's value chain can be segmented into primary and support activities. **Primary activities** are involved with a product's physical creation, its sale and distribution to buyers, and its service after the sale. **Support activities** provide the support necessary for the pri-

Primary activities are involved with a product's physical creation, its sale and distribution to buyers, and its service after the sale.

Support activities provide the support necessary for the primary activities to take place.

FIGURE 3.6 *The Basic Value Chain*

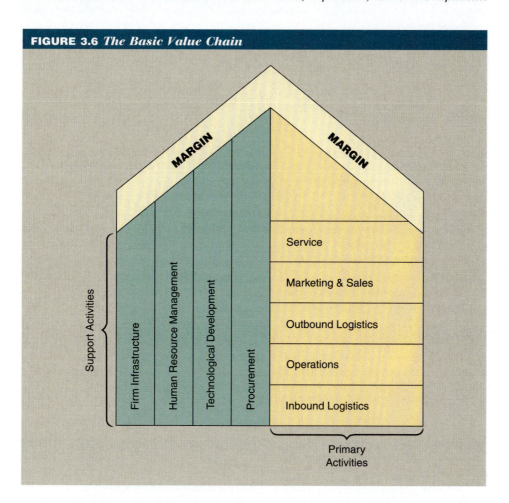

mary activities to take place. The value chain shows how a product moves from the raw material stage to the final customer. For individual firms, the essential idea of the value chain ". . . is to add as much value as possible as cheaply as possible, and, most important, to capture that value." In a globally competitive economy, ". . . the most valuable links on the chain tend to belong to people who own knowledge—particularly about customers."[82]

Table 3.6 lists the items to be studied to assess the value-creating potential of primary activities. In Table 3.7, the items to consider when studying support activities are shown. As with the analysis of primary activities, the intent in examining these items is to determine areas where the firm has potential to create and capture value. All items included in both tables are to be evaluated with competitors' capabilities in mind. To be a source of competitive advantage, a resource or capability must allow a firm to (1) perform an activity in a manner that is superior to competitors' performances or (2) perform a value-creating activity that competitors cannot complete. Only under these conditions does a firm create value for customers and have opportunities to capture that value. Sometimes, this requires firms to reconfigure or recombine parts of the value chain in unique ways. As shown in Figure 3.7, Federal Express (FedEx) changed the nature of the delivery

TABLE 3.6 *Examining the Value–Creating Potential of Primary Activities*

Inbound Logistics

Activities, such as materials handling, warehousing, and inventory control, used to receive, store, and disseminate inputs to a product.

Operations

Activities necessary to convert the inputs provided by inbound logistics into final product form. Machining, packaging, assembly, and equipment maintenance are examples of operations activities.

Outbound Logistics

Activities involved with collecting, storing, and physically distributing the final product to customers. Examples of these activities include finished goods warehousing, materials handling, and order processing.

Marketing and Sales

Activities completed to provide means through which customers can purchase products and to induce them to do so. To effectively market and sell products, firms develop advertising and promotional campaigns, select appropriate distribution channels, and select, develop, and support their sales force.

Service

Activities designed to enhance or maintain a product's value. Firms engage in a range of service-related activities, including installation, repair, training, and adjustment.

Each activity should be examined relative to competitors' abilities. Accordingly, firms rate each activity as *superior, equivalent,* or *inferior.*

Source: Adapted with the permission of The Free Press, a division of Simon & Schuster from *Competitive Advantage: Creating and Sustaining Superior Performance* by Michael E. Porter, pp. 39–40, Copyright © 1985 by Michael E. Porter.

TABLE 3.7 *Examining the Value–Creating Potential of Support Activities*

Procurement

Activities completed to *purchase* the inputs needed to produce a firm's products. Purchased inputs include items fully consumed during the manufacture of products (e.g., raw materials and supplies as well as fixed assets—machinery, laboratory equipment, office equipment, and buildings).

Technological Development

Activities completed to improve a firm's product and the processes used to manufacture it. Technology development takes many forms, such as process equipment, design, both basic research and product design, and servicing procedures.

Human Resource Management

Activities involved with recruiting, hiring, training, developing, and compensating all personnel.

Firm Infrastructure

Firm infrastructure includes activities such as general management, planning, finance, accounting, legal support, and governmental relations that are required to support the work of the entire value chain. Through its infrastructure, the firm strives to effectively and consistently identify external opportunities and threats, identify resources and capabilities, and support core competencies.

Each activity should be examined relative to competitors' abilities. Accordingly, firms rate each activity as *superior, equivalent,* or *inferior.*

Source: Adapted with the permission of The Free Press, a division of Simon & Schuster from *Competitive Advantage: Creating and Sustaining Superior Performance* by Michael E. Porter, pp. 40–43, Copyright © 1985 by Michael E. Porter.

FIGURE 3.7 *Increased Value in Human Resource Management and Outbound Logistics Created a Core Competency for Federal Express*

business by reconfiguring both its outbound logistics (primary activity) and human resource management (support activity) to originate the overnight delivery business, creating value for itself in the process of doing so.

In combination with Federal Express, Calyx and Corolla launched a mail-order flower service in 1989. Through the inventiveness of Ruth M. Owades, Calyx and Corolla changed radically the way flowers are distributed. Through this firm, flowers are shipped directly from growers to customers. Prices are reduced because middlemen are cut out and the flowers are fresher, creating better value for the customer.[83] The opportunity to purchase automobiles through on-line computer networks is another example of firms' efforts to reconfigure the value chain, especially in terms of primary activities. Companies such as Auto-By-Tel use the capabilities of the Internet to sell cars in cyberspace. Companies providing opportunities for customers to buy computers through the Internet also appear to have reconfigured the value chain in a way that allows them to create and capture value.[84]

Rating a firm's capacities to execute the primary and support activities is challenging. Earlier in the chapter, we noted that identifying and assessing the value of a firm's resources and capabilities requires judgment. Judgment is equally necessary when using value chain analysis. The reason for this is that there is no obviously correct model or rule available to help in this process. Moreover, most data available for these evaluations are largely anecdotal, sometimes unreliable, or difficult to interpret.

An effective value chain analysis results in the identification of new ways to perform activities to create value. In the Strategic Focus on Costco, we see that a firm has been able to focus on appropriate aspects of the value chain. This concentration has created significant value for customers and shareholders alike. Because the innovations employed at Costco are firm specific—that is, they are grounded in a company's unique way of combining its resources and capabilities—they are difficult for competitors to recognize, understand, and imitate. The greater the time necessary for competitors to understand how a firm is creating and capturing value through its execution of primary and support activities, the more sustainable is the competitive advantage gained by the innovating company.

STRATEGIC FOCUS

Costco Companies Inc.: The Retail Warehouse Store Revolution

Although Sam's Club (affiliated with Wal-Mart) has approximately 42 percent more members than Costco and 70 percent more stores, Costco's 1997 sales were $1 billion more than Sam's Club. Accordingly, the average Costco store outsells Sam's Clubs by an almost two-to-one margin. Because Wal-Mart has such a strong reputation in retailing, it seems almost counterintuitive to find a set of stores that can out-merchandise Wal-Mart. Even in such an unattractive, low margin business as warehouse retailing, there is room for strong competence and competitive advantage, as evidenced by the Costco approach.

Costco operates an international chain of Costco and Price Club warehouse membership stores. The company seeks to carry quality brand name merchandise at substantially lower prices than found at other conventional warehouse and retail outlets. Although Costco's warehouse approach offers one of the largest product category selections found under a single roof, it only has about 4,000 stock-keeping units (SKUs). Comparatively, a typical supermarket such as Safeway will carry 30,000 units while stores such as Kmart and

Wal-Mart will carry 40,000 to 60,000 and Fred Myers has as many as 200,000. Therefore, Costco's approach focuses on stocking a few branded items in each category such that, in essence, it has done the comparison shopping for its customer. Costco demands the best prices from the vendors and passes these savings on to customers through very low margins. Costco's gross margins were about 12.5 percent in 1997. Its closest competitor is Wal-Mart at 21.5 percent. Fred Myers' gross margins range as high as 32.5 percent, and comparatively, Home Depot, a category killer or competitor focused on home improvement and hardware, is at 29 percent.

Costco's approach also entails picking high priced items that are priced competitively and trying to create repeat business. Furthermore, its vendors largely finance Costco's inventory. For instance, Costco's accounts payable is only 80 percent of its inventory, while at Wal-Mart the ratio is 48 percent. Thus, relative to Wal-Mart, Costco requires little working capital.

In addition to well-regarded brand-name items, Costco stocks over 200 private-label items that account for 11 percent of sales. It also sells top-quality products using its Kirkland signature brand. Kirkland, Washington, is the former hometown of the now Issaquah, Washington, headquartered firm.

Costco also seeks to build customer trust through its Signature label. For instance, it sells a superior Procter & Gamble paper towel because the private-label brand was an inferior product. It does not offer extended service warranties or service contracts on appliances because "In our view, those programs are a rip-off." In addition, as James D. Sinegal, the current CEO, indicates, they also try to give before they get. "One way or another, the vendor is going to cheat you if you take too much out of his hide." Therefore, Costco managers try to cooperate with vendors to help them reduce the margins and offer valuable suggestions for increasing product value and reducing manufacturing cost.

Costco also promotes from within. Sinegal is an example, having started in the warehouse working under Sol Price, who founded the Price Club chain in 1976. There are very few formal meetings and virtually no bureaucracy. For instance, there is no press or investor relations staff. Virtually all the firm's energy is dedicated to the value chain activities of buying and merchandising products. Costco also has a line of periphery stores that provides pharmaceutical, optical, gasoline pumps, and even a business center that competes with Kinko's in some areas.

As a result of Costco's strategic approach, even with very low margins, it earned an 11.5 percent return on capital, which is near the same level as Wal-Mart's 13 percent. Costco's membership renewal rate is 97 percent among active small businesses. That type of loyalty is more than the average patient's loyalty to physicians. Costco also seeks to screen members (a support activity) to reduce bad checks and shrinkage (loss to pilferage), which is only 2 percent of sales. This level is one-tenth of that of many supermarkets and is a significant way to hold down overhead costs. Costco can drive down margins so low relative to its competitors that it creates significant and cascading amounts of value for its customers.

SOURCE: T.W. Ferguson, 1997, A revolution that has a long way to go, *Forbes*, August 11, 106–112; Costco Companies Inc. home page, 1997, http://www.pricecostco.com, December 5; Costco companies on the Forbes 500, 1997, http://www.forbes.com, December 11.

What should a firm do with respect to primary and support activities in which its resources and capabilities are not a source of competence and competitive advantage? For instance, if Costco moves too far from its competencies with its periphery stores, it may consider using subcontractors. In these instances, as discussed next, firms should study the possibility of outsourcing the work associated with primary and support activities in which they cannot create and capture value.

OUTSOURCING

Outsourcing is the purchase of a value-creating activity from an external supplier. In the view of one consultant, "outsourcing is a strategic concept—a way to add value to the business that converts an in-house cost center into a customer-focused service operation."[85] Sometimes, virtually all firms within an industry seek the strategic value that can be captured through effective outsourcing. The automobile manufacturing industry is an example of this. Based on an observation of the outsourcing trend in this industry an analyst concluded that the "whole strategy worldwide now in the auto industry is to get down to your core vehicle-producing operations. . . . That means shedding everything but stamping, powertrains and final assembly . . . and getting rid of everything that doesn't contribute to those areas."[86]

Several statistics demonstrate the increasing scope of outsourcing. For example, Dun and Bradstreet estimated that global outsourcing would increase to $180 billion in 1998; a 23 percent increase from $146 billion in 1997. Approximately two-thirds of this amount was to come from North American companies.[87] U.S. corporations spent more than $38 billion on information technology outsourcing alone in 1995. This amount represented a full 8 percent of total expenditures by U.S. firms on information technology during that year. In fact, approximately 20 percent of the largest U.S. companies use some form of information technology outsourcing.[88] Similar growth rates in outsourcing activities are expected in other fields, including health care, customer service, and human resources. This has been one of the trends that has increased the importance of cooperative strategy (e.g., the more frequent use of strategic alliances, as described in Chapter 9).

Perhaps the major reason outsourcing is being used prominently is that few, if any, firms possess the resources and capabilities required to achieve competitive superiority in all primary and support activities. With respect to technologies, for example, research suggests that few companies can afford to develop internally all the technologies that might lead to competitive advantage in the future. By nurturing a few core competencies, the firm increases its probability of developing a competitive advantage. Additionally, by outsourcing activities in which it lacks capabilities, the firm can concentrate fully on those areas in which it can create value.[89]

Universities are outsourcing food service and bookstore management. For instance, Marriott and Aramark have license agreements with Burger King, Blimpies, and other franchises to establish restaurants on university campuses. More than half of the 3,500 U.S. campuses now have at least one national brand restaurant. Similarly, Follett College Stores and Barnes & Noble bookstores operate 550 and 360 university bookstores, respectively.[90] Also, universities are turning to private firms to run dorms. Because on-campus housing is costly to build and universities are unsure about continued enrollments, there is reluctance to build new dorms. In Texas more than a dozen institutions have made arrangements with private developers to build space for about 6,500 students. The largest managers are American Campus Lifestyles, Camden Property Trust, and Century Development.[91] University administrators are trying to focus on their core mission—education.

Outsourcing is the purchase of a value-creating activity from an external supplier.

Boeing Co. has decided to expand its outsourcing program. To increase efficiency and eventually save an estimated $600 million annually, the firm has elected to buy more aircraft components and parts from outside suppliers instead of making them. Airplane doors, landing gear components, interiors, and control surfaces are examples of products Boeing decided to outsource. Core products such as engine struts and wings will still be manufactured in house. With these outsourcing decisions, the firm now manufactures approximately 52 percent of the components that comprise its airplanes, outside of engines. Of the remaining 48 percent, 34 percent is purchased from American suppliers with 14 percent coming from suppliers in other nations. Although some workers reacted negatively to Boeing's decision to outsource more of its work, the company felt that these actions were necessary to help it remain the largest aerospace manufacturer in the world. A review of the firm's choices suggests that no work was being outsourced in which the company's capabilities yielded a core competence that was a source of competitive advantage.[92]

When outsourcing, a firm seeks the greatest value. In other words, a company wants to outsource only to firms possessing a core competence in terms of performing the primary or support activity that is being outsourced. For companies to whom others outsource, being able to create value is the pathway through which they achieve strategic competitiveness and earn above-average returns.

When evaluating resources and capabilities, firms must be careful not to decide to outsource activities in which they can create and capture value. Additionally, companies should not outsource primary and support activities that are used to neutralize environmental threats or complete necessary ongoing organizational tasks. Called a "nonstrategic team of resources" in Figure 3.5, firms must verify that they do not outsource capabilities that are critical to their success, even though the capabilities are not actual sources of competitive advantage.

Another risk that is part of outsourcing concerns the firm's knowledge base. As discussed earlier in the chapter, knowledge continues to increase in importance as a source of competence and competitive advantage for firms in the new competitive landscape. In part, organizations learn through a continuous and integrated sharing of experiences employees have as they perform primary and support activities. One reason for the success of a learning organization is that with continuous and integrated sharing of experiences, it is able to evaluate thoroughly the ongoing validity of the key assumptions it holds about the nature and future of its business operations. Outsourcing activities in which the firm cannot create value can have an unintended consequence of damaging the firm's potential to continuously evaluate its key assumptions, learn, and create new capabilities and core competencies. Therefore, managers should verify that the firm does not outsource activities that stimulate the development of new capabilities and competencies.[93]

Occasionally, a firm discovers that areas in which it could perhaps develop a competence can and should be outsourced. For example, many believe that banks should develop a core competence in the area of information technology (IT). Following careful analysis of its resources and capabilities, however, managers at Continental Bank concluded that the bank lacked the skills required to develop a core competence in the IT area. As a result, the managers decided to outsource the firm's IT activities so the bank could "focus on its true core competencies—intimate knowledge of customers' needs and relationships with customers."[94]

In the next section, important cautions about core competencies are discussed.

CORE COMPETENCIES–CAUTIONS AND REMINDERS

An attractive attribute of a firm's core competencies is that, unlike physical assets, they tend to become more valuable through additional use. A key reason for this is that they are largely knowledge based.[95] Sharing knowledge across people, jobs, and organizational functions often results in an expansion of that knowledge in competitively relevant ways.[96] At Chaparral Steel, for example, the CEO believes that one of his firm's ". . . core competencies is the rapid realization of new technology into steel products."[97] As a learning organization, Chaparral extends significant efforts to verify that learning is shared across the entire firm. Thus, in a manner that is consistent with the most effective learning organizations, it seems that Chaparral Steel has a healthy disrespect for the status quo. Resulting from this "disrespect" is a commitment to constant self-examination and experimentation.[98]

Evidence and company experiences show that the value of core competencies as sources of competitive advantage should never be taken for granted. Moreover, the ability of any particular core competence to provide competitive advantage on a permanent basis should not be assumed. The reason for these cautions is due to the central dilemma that is associated with the use of core competencies as sources of competitive advantage. This dilemma is that all core capabilities simultaneously have the potential to be *core rigidities*. All capabilities, then, are both a strength and a weakness. They are strengths because they are the source of competitive advantage and, hence, strategic competitiveness; they are a weakness because if emphasized when they are no longer competitively relevant, they can be the seeds of organizational inertia.[99] Additionally, as explained in the Strategic Focus concerned with Toyota, some capabilities may be difficult to transfer even within the firm.[100] Toyota has had difficulties in transferring its productions systems to a U.S. environment.

Events occurring in the firm's external environment create conditions through which core competencies can become core rigidities and create inertia. "Often the flip side, the dark side, of core capabilities is revealed due to external events when new competitors figure out a better way to serve the firm's customers, when new technologies emerge, or when political or social events shift the ground underneath."[101] It really isn't changes in the external environment that cause core capabilities to become core rigidities; rather, it is strategic myopia and inflexibility on the part of a firm's managers that results in core competencies being emphasized to the point that strategic inertia strangles the firm's ability to grow and to adapt to environmental changes.[102] The experiences at Silicone Graphics, as described in the Strategic Focus, demonstrate these relationships.

STRATEGIC FOCUS

Silicone Graphics: Disappearing Core Competence

In 1997, Silicone Graphics (SGI) announced a layoff of up to 1,000 of its 10,500 employees. Furthermore, Edward R. McCracken, chairman and chief executive officer, stepped down after thirteen years at the helm. Additionally, SGI took a $50 million restructuring charge in 1997. Besides these internal difficulties, disgruntled shareholders filed a lawsuit against the firm. The plaintiffs alleged that SGI officers made "false and misleading comments" to "artificially inflate" the stock price while the company proceeded with a convertible debt transaction. Following the debt transaction and insider selling, the stock price fell from a high of $30 to $14 per share.

Silicone Graphics, Inc., has focused on making unique computers that manipulate three-dimensional graphics better than any other workstation. The dinosaurs on *Jurassic Park* were created on SGI machines. These machines are also used to design jets for Boeing and model cars for companies such as Ford. SGI's core strategy was to control the design of the microprocessor chips used in its computers. Although its products are scalable, which allows buyers to choose their entry point and then grow to larger systems, this focus may have turned out to be myopic. Until recently, this strategy has worked quite well for SGI. It allowed the firm to have close association between the microprocessor hardware and software development that could track the hardware chip design quite closely. It also facilitated its leadership in three-dimensional graphics and powerful Web servers. Having its core competence focus intertwined between both hardware and software became problematic as the Wintel standard (the combination of Intel chips and Microsoft software) began to increase in power and graphics capabilities. Furthermore, Microsoft's Windows NT seems to be approaching the de facto standard for corporate workstations. This is giving companies such as Dell Computer an advantage on servers using the Wintel standard. Because there is opportunity for software producers to make more money from a standard platform, these software makers inevitably write code for the Windows NT standard first, instead of closed platform producers such as SGI. For instance, Hewlett-Packard announced a machine to be used as a server that linked up to eight Pentium Pro Intel microprocessors running at two hundred megahertz each. The next version of Windows NT will enable up to eight microprocessors to work together. This type of "symmetric multi-processing" has been a standard practice in the Unix-based servers produced by Sun Microsystems and Silicone Graphics. Thus, the Hewlett-Packard and soon-to-follow products by Compaq and others are climbing the performance ladder and providing significant competition for the previous leaders in the workstation market.

Recognizing these difficulties, SGI sought to maintain its strategy by moving further up the performance ladder as well. In February 1996, the firm announced a planned acquisition of Cray Computer, the supercomputer maker. This would make SGI the number one high-performance computer company in the world. However, not only was the strategic value of the acquisition fuzzy, it added significant risk because Cray's research culture was much different than the fast paced one at Silicone Graphics. Thus, the acquisition of Cray Computer seemed to add to Silicone Graphic's woes rather than relieve them.

It may have been better for SGI to pursue software for the Wintel standard and manage its hardware business as a mature or even declining business. Focusing on software would allow SGI to take advantage of the Wintel standard and sell its graphics packages to those companies using this more high-volume approach. Of course, it is very difficult to change the strategic direction of a company when its core competence is built on high margin machines with proprietary operating system software and chips (hardware). Switching to a focus on market share from a focus on profit margin is also difficult when the core competence is built to create profit margins rather than market share.

SOURCE: Dow Jones Newswire, 1997, Shareholders file lawsuit against Silicone Graphics: *Wall Street Journal Interactive Edition*, http//www.wsj.com, December 3; L. Gomes, 1997, Hewlett-Packard to unveil computer with eight Pentium chips, *Wall Street Journal Interactive Edition*, http://www.wsj.com, December 1; R.D. Hof, I. Sager, and L. Himelstein, 1997, The sad saga of Silicone Graphics, *Business Week*, August 4, 67–68; R. Liu, 1997, SGI cuts jobs, CEO to leave, *CNN Financial News*, http://www.cnnfn.com, October 29; D. Darlin, 1996, The core problem, *Forbes*, February 26, 48.

FIGURE 3.8 *Declining Competitive Advantage*

Core Competence → is outdated by environmental change.

Core Competence → is replaced by substitution.

Core Competence → is imitated.

As evidenced by the Strategic Focus, managers operating in the new competitive landscape must remember that core competencies that are allowed to become core rigidities prevent the firm from changing when necessary. Firms that have achieved strategic competitiveness and earned above-average returns for extended periods of time are sometimes hesitant to change what they are doing. Capabilities are competencies only when they are strategically relevant; that is, when their use permits exploitation of opportunities in the external environment. Rapid and significant changes in the global economy prevent firms from permanently exploiting the same competencies. Firms failing to recognize this reality may quickly find themselves at a competitive disadvantage. Thus, executives must seek to strike a balance between nurturing and supporting existing core competencies while simultaneously encouraging the type of forthright appraisals that will cause the development of *new* competencies.

Figure 3.8 summarizes how competitive advantage declines. A firm may not adapt well to changes in the external environment, its core competence may be substituted by other firms and/or it may be imitated by competitors. All three of these things happened to Silicone Graphics. If it had been able to adapt and create a new competence, however, it may have retained its position.

STRATEGIC INPUTS AND STRATEGIC ACTIONS

Shown in Figure 1.1 in Chapter 1, the results gained through analyses of the external and internal environments provide the strategic inputs a firm needs to develop its strategic intent and strategic mission. The value of intent and mission is that they describe what a firm seeks to achieve in light of its internal competencies and external opportunities.

To close our discussion of strategic inputs, we offer a few final comments about intent and mission. Defined in Chapter 1, *strategic intent* is the leveraging of a firm's resources, capabilities, and core competencies (hereafter called capabilities for the purpose of this discussion) to accomplish the firm's goals in the competitive environment.[103] Recent evidence suggests that, indeed, successful companies competing in the global economy have learned how to leverage their capabilities to reach challenging goals.[104] For instance, Chaparral Steel's strategic intent may be captured by the following statement: "... the goal for every hour, the criterion for every person's activity, is crystal clear: make ever more steel, increasingly better than anyone else."[105] Other firms such as Silicone Graphics and Apple Computer may have overextended the firms' resources and capabilities. Apple, traditionally a niche player in education and publishing, sought to extend its capabilities into the business market, but because the company continued to focus on profit margins of its proprietary system rather than market share through an open systems approach, it was displaced by industry PC leaders such as Compaq and Dell.[106]

Strategic managers are challenged to stimulate the formation of stretch goals for each employee, even when some may not understand the importance of doing so. Individual stretch goals must be consistent with the objective embedded within the firm's strategic intent. When employees are motivated by a well-articulated strategic intent, properly established stretch goals leverage all of a firm's competencies and may create future success for both individual employees and their firm.[107] Moreover, when handled correctly, pursuing accomplishment of a firm's strategic intent "... causes employees to perform in ways they never imagined possible."[108]

The thoughts of an assistant brand manager at Procter & Gamble's location in Rotterdam, Netherlands, describe positive outcomes from the application of strategic intent. When first exposed to the firm's strategic intent, this employee thought to himself, "You've got to be kidding!" However, after working toward his personal stretch goals that were consistent with the firm's strategic intent, he concluded that the concept works! Describing his view about intent, the employee

115

Apple Computer, which had a niche in the education and publishing markets, may have overextended its resources and capabilities by trying to enter the business market.

stated that "Even though I might not reach a specific goal, I do get near it, and that is a greater achievement than I would ever have expected."[109]

Andersen Consulting is a firm stretching its capabilities to reach its strategic intent. Viewing itself as the "world's premier business and technology consultancy," the firm intends to become the world's first and foremost full-service consulting emporium, capable of serving clients by rewiring computer systems, recrafting strategies, reeducating employees, and reengineering work processes. Already earning more than 51 percent of its revenues from outside the United States, Andersen's work in 46 countries reflects its commitment to remain what some believe is the leading global consulting firm.[110] The capabilities Andersen is using to achieve its strategic intent include its knowledge, skills, and experiences in terms of logistics and operations strategies, total supply chain management processes, and information and technology strategies.[111] Challenging as it should be, this strategic intent may be reached through effective use of Andersen Consulting's capabilities and core competencies.

Strategic intent defines the framework for a firm's strategic mission. The strategic mission is a statement of a firm's unique purpose and the scope of its operations in product and market terms.[112] Because it specifies the products a firm will offer in particular markets, and presents a framework within which the firm will work, the strategic mission is an application of strategic intent.[113] In a small private school, for example, the strategic intent is the vigorous pursuit of excellence. The strategic mission flowing from this intent is to serve intellectually gifted or highly motivated students from a six-county region seeking a college preparatory educational experience.

In the case of all firms and organizations, once formulated, the strategic intent and strategic mission are the basis for the development of business-level, corporate-level, acquisition, restructuring, international, and cooperative strategies (see Chapter 4 and Chapters 6 through 9). The first of these strategy types—business-level strategy—is discussed in the next chapter.

SUMMARY

- In the new competitive landscape, traditional conditions and factors, including labor costs and effective access to financial resources and raw materials, can still provide a competitive advantage but to a lesser degree. In this new landscape, a firm's internal environment (that is, its resources, capabilities, and core competencies) may have a stronger influence on the development of competitive advantage and the formulation and implementation of strategies than do the characteristics and conditions of the external environment. But, no competitive advantage lasts forever. Over time, the benefits provided by all competitive advantages can be duplicated. Because of this, firms are challenged to exploit their current competitive advantage while simultaneously using their resources, capabilities, and core competencies to de-

velop advantages that will be relevant in the future.

- Effective management of core competencies requires careful analysis of a firm's resources (inputs to the production process) and capabilities (capacities for teams of resources to perform a task or activity integratively). To complete these analyses successfully, strategic managers must be self-confident, courageous, and willing to hold people accountable for their work.

- Individually, resources are typically not sources of competitive advantage. Capabilities, which result from groupings of both tangible and intangible resources, are more likely to yield an advantage. A key reason for this is that how the firm forms, nurtures, and exploits core competencies that are grounded in capabilities is less visible to competitors and, hence, more difficult to understand and costly to imitate.

- The skills and knowledge of the firm's human capital may be the primary basis for all of its capabilities. Capabilities of this type emerge by developing human capital and sharing information regarding how tangible and intangible resources can be combined in strategically relevant ways.

- Not all of the firm's capabilities are core competencies. Only capabilities that are valuable, rare, costly to imitate, and nonsubstitutable are sources of competitive advantage and, as such, can be selected as core competencies. Over time, core competencies must be supported and nurtured, but they cannot be allowed to become core rigidities. Competencies result in competitive advantage over the firm's rivals only when they allow the firm to create value by exploiting external environmental opportunities. When this is no longer the case, the firm's attention must be shifted to other capabilities that do satisfy the four criteria of sustainable competitive advantage.

- Value chain analysis is used to identify and evaluate a firm's resources and capabilities. By studying their primary and support activities, firms better understand their cost structure and the activities in which they can create and capture value.

- In the cases of primary and support activities that must be performed, but for which the firm lacks the resources and capabilities required to create value, outsourcing is considered. Used frequently in the new competitive landscape, outsourcing is the purchase of a value-creating activity from an external supplier. The firm should outsource only to companies that possess a competitive advantage in terms of the primary or support activity being outsourced. Strategic managers must verify that their firm does not outsource activities in which it can create and capture value. Additionally, firms must avoid outsourcing nonstrategic capabilities that are not a source of competitive advantage, yet are important to the firm's ongoing efforts to develop continuously value-adding knowledge.

- Strategic intent and strategic mission are grounded in the results obtained through analyses of the firm's external and internal environments. Taken together, the results of environmental analyses and the formation of the firm's strategic intent and mission provide the information needed to formulate and implement an array of strategies, including business-level, corporate-level, acquisition, restructuring, international, and cooperative.

REVIEW QUESTIONS

1. Why is it important for firms to study and gain an understanding of their internal environment?
2. What is value? How do firms earn value and why is it important that they be able to do so?
3. What are the differences between tangible and intangible resources? Which of these two categories of resources typically contributes more to the development of competitive advantage, and why?
4. What are capabilities? How are capabilities developed?
5. What are the four criteria used to determine which of a firm's resources and capabilities are its core competencies? Why is it important for strategic managers to use these criteria?
6. How is value chain analysis used in organizations? What knowledge can strategic managers gain by using value chain analysis?
7. What is outsourcing? Why is it so valuable to companies competing in the new competitive landscape?
8. Why is it important for firms to prevent their core competencies from becoming core rigidities?
9. What is the relationship between strategic inputs and strategic actions?

APPLICATION DISCUSSION QUESTIONS

1. Several companies are discussed in the opening case. Which of these companies are likely to have a sustainable competitive advantage based on their human resource management capability?

2. Select a store in your local community from which you purchase items. Ask one of the store's strategic managers to describe the value the firm provides to its customers. Do you agree with the strategic manager's assessment? Did the manager describe the value for which you pay when purchasing goods or services from this store? If not, what might account for the difference in opinions?

3. For an organization or club in which you are a member, prepare a list of what you think are its tangible and intangible resources. Using the categories shown in Tables 3.1 and 3.2, group the resources you identified. Show your list to other members of your organization and ask for their assessment. Did they agree with your groupings? If not, why not?

4. Refer to the third question. Was it easier for you to list the tangible or intangible resources? Why?

5. What competitive advantage does your college or university possess? On what core competencies is this advantage based? What evidence can you provide to support your opinions?

6. Discuss how Silicone Graphics, as described in a Strategic Focus, could have overcome the change in its competitive environment and its potential loss of core competence. Please obtain information from business sources to support your assessment.

ETHICS QUESTIONS

1. Can an emphasis on developing a competitive advantage result in unethical practices such as the use of questionable techniques to gather information about competitors? If so, do you believe these unethical practices occur frequently? Please provide evidence to support your opinion.

2. Can ethical practices facilitate development of a brand name and a corporate reputation? If so, explain how.

3. What is the difference between exploiting human capital and nurturing human capital to arrive at a competitive advantage? Can exploitation of human capital lead to a competitive advantage? If so, how?

4. Ethically, are strategic managers challenged to use their firm's resources to help train members of their society to reduce the shortage of skilled workers in their country? Why or why not?

5. What, if any, ethical dilemmas are associated with the use of outsourcing? How should strategic managers deal with them?

6. What ethical issues do strategic managers face when they conclude that their firm cannot earn above-average returns if thousands of employees are not laid off?

INTERNET EXERCISE

Go to Coca-Cola's home page at:

http://www.coca-cola.com

Search the Internet for information on the Coca-Cola Corporation. After you have completed your search, make a list of the company's tangible and intangible resources (see Tables 3.1 and 3.2). How do both sets of resources contribute to Coca-Cola's sustained competitive advantage?

Strategic Surfing

An increasing number of companies are establishing "internal" or "corporate" universities to facilitate their training needs and help build core competencies. Corporations are using this innovative concept to strengthen their internal environments. Following are several examples of corporate universities:

Motorola University:

http://www.mot.com/MU

Sears University:

http://www.sears.com/company/hr/suniv.html

Iams University:

http://www.iams.com/employ/universi.html

Dell University:

http://www.dell.com/dell/careers/benefits/dellu.htm

Intel University:

http://wiche.edu/telecom/membership/Sharing/forms/techintel.html

NOTES

1. M. A. Huselid, S. E. Jackson, and R. S. Schuler, Technical and strategic human resource management effectiveness as determinants of firm performance, *Academy of Management Journal* 40: 171–188.

2. D. J. Teece, G. Pisano, and A. Shuen, 1997, Dynamic capabilities and strategic management, *Strategic Management Journal* 18: 509–534; R. G. McGrath, I. C. MacMillan, and S. Venkataraman, 1995, Defining and developing competence: A strategic process paradigm, *Strategic Management Journal* 16: 251–275.

3. B. Morris, 1996, The brand's the thing, *Fortune*, March 4, 72–80.

4. P. Sellers, 1996, Can Home Depot fix its sagging stock? *Fortune*, March 4, 139–146.

5. P. C. Godfrey and C. W. L. Hill, 1995, The problem of unobservables in strategic management research, *Strategic Management Journal* 16: 519–533.

6. D. Leonard-Barton, 1995, *Wellsprings of Knowledge: Building and Sustaining the Sources of Innovation* (Boston: Harvard Business School Press); McGrath, MacMillan, and Venkataraman, 1995, Defining and developing competence, 253.

7. A. Reinhardt, I. Sager, and P. Burrows, 1997, Can Andy Grow keep profits up in an era of cheap PCs?, *Business Week*, December 22, 70–77; R. E. Stross, 1997, Mr. Gates builds his brain trust, *Fortune*, December 8, 84–98.

8. Godfrey and Hill, 1995, The problem of unobservables, 522.

9. J. B. Barney, 1996, The resource-based theory of the firm, *Organization Science* 7: 469–480; M. E. Porter, 1996, What is strategy? *Harvard Business Review* 74, no. 6: 61–78.

10. A. Mehra, 1996, Resource and market based determinants of performance in the U.S. banking industry, *Strategic Management Journal* 17: 307–322; J. Pfeffer, 1994, *Competitive Advantage Through People: Unleashing the Power of the Work Force* (Boston: Harvard Business School Press), 6–14.

11. F. R. Bleakley, 1997, New round of layoffs may be beginning, *Wall Street Journal*, November 13, A2.

12. R. Henderson and W. Mitchell, 1997, The interaction of organizational and competitive influences on strategy and performance, *Strategic Management Journal* 18 (Summer Special Issue), 5–14; A. A. Lado, N. G. Boyd, and S. C. Hanlon, 1997, Competition, cooperation and the search for economic rents: A syncretic model, *Academy of Management Review* 22: 110–141; Porter, 1996, What is strategy?; J. B. Barney, 1995, Looking inside for competitive advantage, *Academy of Management Journal Executive* IX, no. 4: 59–60.

13. S. Ghoshal and C. A. Bartlett, 1995, Changing the role of top management: Beyond structure to processes, *Harvard Business Review* 73, no. 1: 96.

14. Barney, 1996, Resource-based theory; Porter, 1996, What is strategy?; M. A. Peteraf, 1993, The cornerstones of competitive strategy: A resource-based view, *Strategic Management Journal* 14: 179–191.

15. Porter, 1996, What is strategy?, 61.

16. K. E. Marino, 1996, Developing consensus on firm competencies and capabilities, *Academy of Management Executive* X, no. 3: 40–51.

17. T. A. Stewart, 1997, Does anyone around here know. . . ?, *Fortune*, September 29, 279.

18. C. E. Helfat, 1997, Know-how and asset complementarity and dynamic capability accumulation: The case of R&D, *Strategic Management Journal* 18: 339–360; C. M. Christensen, 1997, Making strategy: Learning by doing, *Harvard Business Review* 75, no. 6: 141–156; R. M. Grant, 1996, Prospering in dynamically-competitive environments: Organizational capability as knowledge integration, *Organization Science* 7: 375–387; D. Lei, M. A. Hitt, and R. Bettis, 1996, Dynamic core competencies through metalearning and strategic context, *Journal of Management* 22: 247–267; H. Rheem, 1995, The learning organization, *Harvard Business Review* 73, no. 2: 10; G. Hamel and C. K. Prahalad, 1994, *Competing for the Future* (Boston: Harvard Business School Press).

19. A. Campbell and M. Alexander, 1997, What's wrong with strategy? *Harvard Business Review* 75, no. 6: 42–51.

20. C. Oliver, 1997, Sustainable competitive advantage: Combining institutional and resource-based views, *Strategic Management Journal* 18: 697–713; D. J. Collis and C. A. Montgomery, 1995, Competing on resources: Strategy in the 1990s, *Harvard Business Review* 73, no. 4: 118–128; B. Wernerfelt, 1995, The resource-based view of the firm: Ten years after, *Strategic Management Journal* 16: 171–174; J. B. Barney, 1994, Commentary; A hierarchy of corporate resources, *Advances in Strategic Management* 10A, 113–125.

21. J. H. Dyer, 1996, Specialized supplier networks as a source of competitive advantage: Evidence from the auto industry, *Strategic Management Journal* 17: 271–291; R. L. Priem and D. A. Harrison, 1994, Exploring strategic judgment: Methods for testing the assumptions of prescriptive contingency theories, *Strategic Management Journal* 15: 311–324; R. Amit and P. J. H. Schoemaker, 1993, Strategic assets and organizational rent, *Strategic Management Journal* 14: 33–46.

22. W. Boeker, 1997, Executive migration and strategic change: The effect of top manager movement on product-market entry, *Administrative Science Quarterly* 42: 213–236; C. R. Schwenk, 1995, Strategic decision making, *Journal of Management* 21: 471–493.

23. H. W. Jenkins, 1996, 40,000 job cuts! Where does he get off? *Wall Street Journal*, March 5, A15; McGrath, MacMillan, and Venkataraman, 1995, Defining and developing competence, 253.

24. D. Kunde, 1996, Self-control guru, *Dallas Morning News*, February 5, D1, D4; T. A. Stewart, 1996, Looking out for number 1, *Fortune*, January 15, 33–48.

25. M. Farjoun and L. Lai, 1997, Similarity judgments in strategy formulation: Role, process and implications, *Strategic Management Journal* 18: 255–273.

26. H. W. Vroman, 1996, The loyalty effect: The hidden force behind growth, profits, and lasting value (book review), *Academy of Management Executive* X, no. 1: 88–90.

27. W. Kiechel, 1993, Facing up to denial, *Fortune*, October 18, 163–165.

28. H. Ha, 1997, GM seen needing to cut production or raise

119

incentives, *Wall Street Journal Interactive Edition*, http://www.interactive.wsj.com, December 8.

29. P. Sellers, 1996, What exactly is charisma? *Fortune*, January 15, 68–75.

30. Teece, Pisano, and Shuen, 1997, Dynamic capabilities, 513–514; Barney, 1995, Looking inside for competitive advantage, 50.

31. McGrath, MacMillan, and Venkataraman, 1995, Defining and developing competence, 252.

32. T. Chi, 1994, Trading in strategic resources: Necessary conditions, transaction cost problems, and choice of exchange structure, *Strategic Management Journal* 15: 271–290; R. Reed and R. DeFillippi, 1990, Causal ambiguity, barriers to imitation, and sustainable competitive advantage, *Academy of Management Review* 15: 88–102.

33. R. Hall, 1991, The contribution of intangible resources to business success, *Journal of General Management* 16, no. 4: 41–52.

34. N. E. Grund, 1996, Reputation: Realizing value from the corporate image, *Academy of Management Executive* (book review section) X, no. 1: 100.

35. C. J. Fombrun, 1996, *Reputation: Realizing Value from the Corporate Image* (Boston: Harvard Business School Press).

36. R. Furchgott, 1997, Rebel without an engine, *Business Week*, September 15, 8.

37. T. A. Stewart, 1996, Coins in a knowledge bank, *Fortune*, February 19, 230–233.

38. S. Sherman, 1996, Secrets of HP's "muddled team," *Fortune*, March 18, 116–120.

39. McGrath, MacMillan, and Venkataraman, 1995, Defining and developing competence, 252; Porter, 1996, What is strategy?

40. J. B. Quinn, P. Anderson, and S. Finkelstein, 1996, Making the most of the best, *Harvard Business Review* 74, no. 2: 71–80.

41. T. A. Stewart, 1995, Trying to grasp the intangible, *Fortune*, October 2, 157–161.

42. Godfrey and Hill, 1995, The problem of inobservables, 522–523.

43. D. A. Aaker, 1996, *Building Strong Brands* (New York: Free Press).

44. S. Woolley, 1996, I want my Century 21! *Business Week*, January 15, 72–73.

45. B. Orwell, 1997, Disney is to enter restaurant business, and chain will sport an ESPN theme, *Wall Street Journal*, October 15, B6.

46. Fortune, 1996, Top stories for Monday, December 9, http://www.fortune.com.

47. A. R. Sorkin, 1997, Ad revenue on Web rises in first six months of 1997, *The New York Times* on the Web, http://www.nytimes.com, August 4.

48. Grant, 1996, Prospering in dynamically-competitive environments; Lei, Hitt, and Bettis, 1996, Dynamic core competencies; J. B. Quinn, 1994, *The Intelligent Enterprise* (New York: Free Press).

49. Stross, 1997, Mr. Gates builds his brain trust; E. M. Davies, 1996, Wired for hiring: Microsoft's slick recruiting machine, *Fortune*, February 5, 123–124.

50. D. Kunde, 1996, Corporations thinking ahead with chief knowledge officers, *Dallas Morning News*, January 14, D1.

51. T. A. Stewart, 1991, Brainpower, *Fortune*, June 3, 44.

52. Helfat, 1997, Know-how and asset complementarity; Lei, Hitt, and Bettis, 1996, Dynamic core competencies.

53. N. Dunne, 1997, US manufacturers see huge skill shortage, *Financial Times*, November 11, 4.

54. S. Kaufman, 1996, Firm offers essential high-tech component: People, *Dallas Morning News*, January 22, D2.

55. R. C. Monson, 1995, Firms worry about finding skilled workers, survey shows, *Dallas Morning News*, December 15, D10.

56. J. Landers, 1995, New jewel in the crown! *Dallas Morning News*, December 17, H1, H2.

57. F. F. Reichheld, 1996, Solving the productivity puzzle, *Wall Street Journal*, March 2, A1, A4.

58. R. Lowenstein, 1996, Why primary voters are so angry, *Wall Street Journal*, February 22, C1.

59. M. A. Hitt and R. D. Ireland, 1986, Relationships among corporate level distinctive competencies, diversification strategy, corporate structure, and performance, *Journal of Management Studies* 23: 401–416; M. A. Hitt and R. D. Ireland, 1985, Corporate distinctive competence, strategy, industry, and performance, *Strategic Management Journal* 6: 273–293; M. A. Hitt, R. D. Ireland, and K. A. Palia, 1982, Industrial firms' grand strategy and functional importance, *Academy of Management Journal* 25: 265–298; M. A. Hitt, R. D. Ireland, and G. Stadter, 1982, Functional importance and company performance: Moderating effects of grand strategy and industry type, *Strategic Management Journal* 3: 315–330; C. C. Snow and E. G. Hrebiniak, 1980, Strategy, distinctive competence, and organizational performance, *Administrative Science Quarterly* 25: 317–336.

60. M. A. Cusumano, 1997, How Microsoft makes large teams work like small teams, *Sloan Management Review* 39, no. 1: 9–20.

61. D. Leonard-Barton, H. K. Bowen, K. B. Clark, C. A. Holloway, and S. C. Wheelwright, 1994, How to integrate work and deepen expertise, *Harvard Business Review* 72, no. 5: 123.

62. Chi, 1994, Trading in strategic resources, 272; Porter, 1996, What is strategy?

63. C. Ames, 1995, Sales soft? Profits flat? It's time to rethink your business, *Fortune*, June 26, 142–146; S. Fatsis, 1993, Bigger is not necessarily better, *Waco Tribune-Herald*, January 17, B1, B6.

64. A. Taylor, III, 1993, Shaking up Jaguar, *Fortune*, September 6, 66.

65. R. C. Morais, 1997, A methodical man, *Forbes*, August 11, 70–72.

66. This section is drawn primarily from two sources: Barney, 1995, Looking inside for competitive advantage, J. B. Barney, 1991, Firm resources and sustained competitive advantage, *Journal of Mangement* 17: 99–120.

67. Barney, 1995, Looking inside for competitive advantage, 53.

68. Ibid., 50.

69. Ibid., 52.

70. Ibid., 53.

71. Barney, 1991, Firm resources, 108.

72. J. Huey, 1993, How McKinsey does it, *Fortune*, November 1, 56–81.

73. R. Reed and R. J. DeFillippi, 1990, Causal ambiguity, barriers to imitation, and sustainable competitive advantage, 88–102.

74. Leonard-Barton, 1995, *Wellsprings of Knowledge*, 7.

75. Sherman, 1996, Secrets of HP's "muddled team."

76. Barney, 1991, Firm resources, 111.

77. Amit and Schoemaker, 1993, Strategic assets, 39.

78. S. Caminiti, 1996, Will Old Navy fill the Gap? *Fortune*, March 18, 59–62.

79. Ibid., 60.

80. M. E. Porter, 1985, *Competitive Advantage* (New York: Free Press), 33–61.

81. G. G. Dess, A. Gupta, J-F. Hennart, and C. W. L. Hill, 1995, Conducting and integrating strategy research at the international, corporate, and business levels: Issues and directions, *Journal of Management* 21: 376; Porter, 1996, What is strategy?

82. T. A. Stewart, 1995, The information wars: What you don't know will you hurt you, *Fortune*, June 12, 119–121.

83. Calyx & Corolla home page, 1997, http://www.calyxandcorolla.com; Computerworld, 1994, Being the leader of the pack in the mail-order catalog industries doesn't require cutting-edge technology—just smart use of existing technology, *Computerworld*, March 7, 79.

84. D. Darlin, 1997, Channel change, *Forbes*, August 25, 80; D. Kirkpatrick, 1997, Now everyone in PC's wants to be like Mike, *Fortune*, September 8, 91–92.

85. Outsourcing: How industry leaders are reshaping the American corporation, 1996, *Fortune*, Special Advertising Section.

86. T. Box, 1996, Outsourcing to cut jobs in Arlington, *Dallas Morning News*, March 23, F1, F11.

87. M. R. Ozanne, 1997, Outsourcing: Managing strategic partnerships for the virtual enterprise, *Fortune*, Special Advertising Section, September 29, S1–S48.

88. J. W. Verity, 1996, Let's order out for technology, *Business Week*, May 13, 47.

89. H. W. Chesbrough and D. J. Teece, 1996, When is virtual virtuous? Organizing for innovation, *Harvard Business Review* 74, no. 1: 70.

90. M. Halkias, 1997, Fast-food firms, book sellers become big trend on campus, *Dallas Morning News*, September 8, D1, D8.

91. M. Totty, 1997, Flooded by students, colleges turn to private firms to manage dorms, *Wall Street Journal*, August 20, T1, T4.

92. J. Haley, 1995, Boeing strategy angers workers, *Daily Herald*, July 14, H2.

93. N. A. Wishart, J. J. Elam, and D. Robey, 1996, Redrawing the portrait of a learning organization: Inside Knight-Ridder, Inc., *Academy of Management Executive* X, no. 1: 7–20; D. Lei and M. A. Hitt, 1995, Strategic restructuring and outsourcing: The effect of mergers and acquisitions and LBOs on building firm skills and capabilities, *Journal of Management* 21: 835–859.

94. R. L. Huber, 1993, How Continental Bank outsourced its "crown jewels," *Harvard Business Review* 71, no. 2: 128.

95. J. C. Spender and R. M. Grant, 1996, Knowledge and the firm: Overview, *Strategic Management Journal* 17 (Winter Special Issue): 5–10.

96. Lei, Hitt, and Bettis, 1996, Dynamic core competences; Leonard-Barton, 1995, *Wellsprings of Knowledge*, 59–89.

97. Leonard-Barton, 1995, *Wellsprings of Knowledge*, 7.

98. Wishart, Elam, and Robey, 1996, Redrawing the portrait, 8.

99. M. Hannan and J. Freeman, 1977, The population ecology of organizations, *American Journal of Sociology* 82: 929–964.

100. G. Szulanski, 1996, Exploring internal stickiness: Impediments to the transfer of best practices within the firm, *Strategic Managment Journal* 17 (Winter Special Issue): 27–44.

101. Leonard-Barton, 1995, *Wellsprings of Knowledge*, 30–31.

102. R. Sanchez and J. T. Mahoney, 1996, Modularity, flexibility, and knowledge management in procut and organization design, *Strategic Management Journal* 17 (Winter Special Issue): 63–76; C. A. Bartlett and S. Ghoshal, 1994. Changing the role of top management. Beyond strategy to purpose. *Harvard Business Review* 72, no. 6: 79–88

103. G. Hamel and C. K. Prahalad, 1989, Strategic intent, *Harvard Business Review* 67, no. 3: 63–76.

104. P. Almeida, 1996, Knowledge sourcing by foreign multinationals: Patent citation analysis in the U.S. semiconductor industry, *Strategic Management Journal* 17 (Winter Special Issue): 155–165.

105. Leonard-Barton, 1995, *Wellsprings of Knowledge*, 8.

106. J. Heilemann, 1997, The perceptionist: How Steve Jobs took back Apple, *The New Yorker*, September 8, 34–41.

107. M. S. S. El-Namaki, 1992, Creating a corporate vision, *Long Range Planning* 25, no. 2: 119–121.

108. S. Sherman, 1995, Stretch goals: The dark side of asking for miracles, *Fortune*, November 13, 231–232.

109. H. W. Mentink, 1996, An employee's goals, *Fortune*, February 5, 26.

110. J A. Byrne, 1995, Hired guns packing high powered knowhow, *Business Week*, September 18, 92–96.

111. 1996, Andersen Consulting advertisement appearing in *Wall Street Journal*, February 6; R. Henkoff, 1993, Inside Andersen's army of advice, *Fortune*, October 4, 78–86.

112. R. D. Ireland and M. A. Hitt, 1992, Mission statements: Importance, challenge and recommendations for development, *Business Horizons* 35, no. 3: 34–42.

113. C. Marshall, 1996, A sense of mission, *The Strategist* 7, no. 4: 14–16.

Strategic Actions: Strategy Formulation

Chapters

4 Business-Level Strategy

5 Competitive Dynamics

6 Corporate-Level Strategy

7 Acquisition and Restructuring Strategies

8 International Strategy

9 Cooperative Strategy

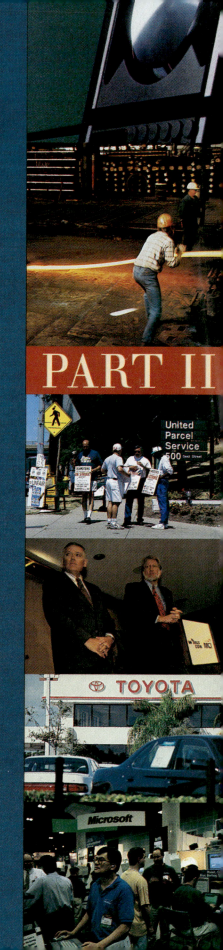

PART II

Business-Level Strategy

CHAPTER 4

Learning Objectives

After reading this chapter, you should be able to:

1. Define strategy and explain business-level strategies.

2. Describe the relationship between customers and business-level strategies.

3. Discuss the issues firms consider when evaluating customers in terms of *who*, *what*, and *how*.

4. Define the integrated low-cost/differentiation strategy and discuss its increasing importance in the new competitive landscape.

5. Describe the capabilities necessary to develop competitive advantage through the cost leadership, differentiation, focused low-cost, focused differentiation, and the integrated low-cost/differentiation business-level strategies.

6. Explain the risks associated with each of the five business-level strategies.

Strategic Actions: Strategy Formulation

Chapters

Focus Strategies: Achieving Strategic Competitiveness by Serving Narrow Market Segments

A Danish company Bang & Olufsen manufactures upscale electronics products. Using its core competencies in product design and manufacturing, the firm produces an array of what have been labeled as "fantastic-looking" luxury items. Among its offerings are $1,800 to $5,000 stereo speakers, and $15,000 television sets. Striving deliberately for high style and quality, the firm's top-of-the-line products are targeted to audiophiles and video buffs that are willing to pay premium prices. In describing the company's product design, Ole Bek, director of Bang & Olufsen's international distribution center, noted that he learns much more by window shopping at Louis Vuitton in Paris than by looking at consumer electronics outlets.

http://
http://www.snapon.com
http://www.iamsco.com

To highlight more clearly and consistently the uniqueness of its products and to better serve the specialized interests and needs of its target customers, the firm decided recently to launch a string of impeccably designed stores that sell only its own products. Simultaneously, Bang & Olufsen discontinued the practice of distributing its products through what it considered to be "downscale" shops. The practice of concentrating on its own dedicated shops as the primary means of product distribution is consistent with actions taken by other companies that serve upscale customer needs. Louis Vuitton, for example, sells its bags only in its own boutiques. Cartier International Inc. and Guicci Group have pulled their products from the shelves of hundreds of stores in the United States. The key reason for these withdrawals was to eliminate markdowns in the prices of their products. Moreover, selling products through its own retailing outlets allows Bang & Olufsen to move even further upscale. Doing this, the firm's executives believe, will allow the company to avoid having to compete against other electronics manufacturers on the basis of price. Bang & Olufsen recognized the disasters that have befallen other European companies (including Grundig, Ferguson, Brion Vega, and Telefunken) that tried and failed to compete successfully against primarily Asian manufacturers on the price dimension. This recognition solidified Bang & Olufsen's strategic decision to focus on the upscale, highly differentiated part of the electronics market.

Snap-on Tools also serves the needs of a particular customer segment. This firm's high-quality and high-priced tools are targeted to mechanics and other professionals who are deeply passionate about their tools, but have little time to shop for them. To deal with the time constraint faced by this customer group, the founders of Snap-on Tools developed a system through which the firm's products are delivered to customers on the same day of every week. In commenting about this strategy, one analyst noted, "Snap-on found a way to reach a group of customers who weren't being served and created a way to make its high-quality products affordable." Very successful, the firm's sales volume has grown from approximately $670 million in 1986 to an expected $1.8 billion in 1998. Snap-on Tools has exported its strategy of serving the unique needs of a particular market segment to other countries, such as Germany.

The Iams Company is another firm with a strategy that is built around serving the unique needs of certain customer groups. When this company was established in Dayton, Ohio, in 1946, pet food was relatively inexpensive, not very nutritious, and sold exclusively in supermarkets and some feed stores. Convinced that premium foods that could serve pets' nutritional needs would appeal to certain groups, Paul Iams, the firm's founder and an animal nutritionist, decided to bypass what had been the traditional distribution channels for pet foods. Instead of selling to supermarkets and feed stores, Iams went directly to veterinarians, breeders, and pet stores. Annual sales at this firm have grown from $16 million in 1982 to over $500 million. Study of the firm's success caused one analyst to observe, "In hindsight, I find it amazing that Ralston Purina and others didn't spot this market, but none of them did. A couple of guys in Dayton outsmarted a whole bunch of sophisticated marketers." Today, this firm continues to be guided by its mission: "To enhance the well-being of dogs and cats by providing world-class quality foods."

SOURCE: T. Brophy, 1997, Snap-on Tools Inc., *Value Line*, August 8, 1334; E. Davies, 1997, Selling sex and cat food, *Fortune*, June 9, 36; W. Echikson, Bang & Olufsen's class act gets classier, *Business Week*, October 20, 142F; The Iams Company, 1997, *The Iams Company Home Page*, October 20, http://www.iams.com.

The three firms mentioned in the opening case implement strategies that are intended to serve customers' unique needs. For this service and the high quality of the products being purchased, these companies' customers are willing to pay premium prices. Callaway Golf Company also strives to serve the unique needs of a particular group of customers. Offering products with exceptional performance capabilities, the essence of the firm's strategic intent and strategy is suggested by the following statements:

Callaway Golf Company designs, manufactures, and markets high quality, innovative golf clubs. The Company's basic objective is to design and manufacture its clubs in such a way that they are demonstrably superior to, and pleasingly different from, competitors' golf clubs. The Company's golf clubs are sold at premium prices to both average and skilled golfers on the basis of performance, ease of use and appearance.[1]

To achieve strategic competitiveness and earn above-average returns, as Callaway Golf Company has done, a company analyzes its external environment, identifies opportunities in that environment, determines which of its internal resources and capabilities are core competencies, and selects an appropriate strategy to implement.[2] A **strategy** is an integrated and coordinated set of commitments and actions designed to exploit core competencies and gain a competitive advantage. In this sense, strategies are purposeful and precede the taking of actions to which they apply.[3] An effectively formulated strategy marshals, integrates, and allocates a firm's resources, capabilities, and competencies so it can cope successfully with its external environment.[4] Such a strategy also rationalizes a firm's strategic intent and strategic mission and what will be done to achieve them.[5] Information about a host of variables, including markets, customers, technology, worldwide finance, and the changing world economy[6] must be collected and analyzed to formulate and implement strategies properly. In the final analysis, the test of a strategy's effectiveness is its ability to allow the firm to offer a good or service to customers that provides greater value relative to the value provided by competitors' products.[7]

Recall from Chapters 1 and 3 that *core competencies* are resources and capabilities that serve as a source of competitive advantage for a firm over its rivals. Strategic competitiveness and the earning of above-average returns hinge on a firm's ability to develop and exploit new core competencies faster than competitors can mimic the competitive advantages yielded by the current ones.[8] When focused on the continuous need to develop new core competencies, firms are able to drive competition in the future as well as the present.[9] Thus, especially in the new competitive landscape, with its continuing globalization and rapid technological changes, only firms with the capacity to improve, innovate, and upgrade their competitive advantages over time can expect to achieve long-term success.[10]

A **strategy** is an integrated and coordinated set of commitments and actions designed to exploit core competencies and gain a competitive advantage.

127

As explained in this chapter, successful firms use their core competencies to satisfy customers' needs. The relationship between appropriate strategic actions and the achievement of strategic competitiveness is increasingly important in today's turbulent and competitive environment.[11] These relationships are shown in Figure 1.1 in Chapter 1. As displayed in that figure, a firm's *strategic inputs* (gained through study of the external and internal environments) are used to select the *strategic actions* (the formulation and implementation of value-creating strategies) that will yield desired *strategic outcomes.*

Actions taken at The Iams Company exemplify these relationships. Through an examination of the general, industry, and competitor external environments, Paul Iams envisioned an opportunity to serve a particular segment of the pet food market—people interested in providing their pets with high-quality and nutritionally sound food products. Today, The Iams Company is recognized as a world leader in dog and cat nutrition. Through work completed at the Paul F. Iams Technical Center and Animal Care Facility, the firm is able to continuously discover new ways to improve its products, and in doing so, the health of its customers' pets.[12] As is the case with Bang & Olufsen and Snap-on Tools, focused differentiation is the business-level strategy (defined and discussed later in the chapter) The Iams Company chose to implement to achieve strategic competitiveness and above-average returns.

The initial environmental opportunity pursued by The Iams Company was identified through careful study. Opportunities to continue implementing a chosen business-level strategy can also surface somewhat unexpectedly for established firms. For example, Anheuser-Busch's initial announcement of its intention to sell the Eagle Snacks unit so it could refocus on its world-leading beer business provided an opportunity for Frito-Lay (a division of PepsiCo) to expand its already dominant share of the salty snack market.[13] Similarly, in light of major competitors' financial woes (identified through study of the firm's industry environment), Luby's Cafeterias decided to aggressively build additional units in one of its key Southwest locations. Because of its superior financial position (a source of competitive advantage), Luby's CEO concluded that "The stagnation of our competitors from the standpoint of expansion has allowed us a unique opportunity to continue to expand. . . ."[14] The August 1997 shutdown of United Parcel Service Inc. (UPS) resulted in a decrease of 5 percent in the firm's shipping volume. Estimates are that the Teamsters' strike cost UPS at least $700 million in lost revenue. Feeling emboldened by the UPS customers they serviced during the strike, UPS competitors, including FedEx and the U.S. Postal Service, are aggressively seeking to take additional customers from UPS. Through its acquisition of Caliber System Inc., FedEx is attacking UPS on its home turf—nonexpress ground delivery. To gain business from UPS, the U.S. Postal Service is offering cheaper rates and invested $270 million in advertising in 1998 to inform people about its overnight and parcel services.[15] Additional information about UPS is presented in Chapter 6's opening case.

At a broader level, companies committed to the importance of competing successfully in the global economy constantly study developments in the world's markets to identify emerging opportunities to exploit their competitive advantages. The breakup of the former Soviet Union in 1991, for example, has resulted in numerous commercial opportunities, especially for consumer goods companies. To succeed in the Russian consumer revolution, companies are advised to ". . . quickly seize opportunities to position themselves, and then prepare for keener competi-

128

tion."[16] Firms must exercise caution, however, when entering emerging markets such as Russia. Although they are, indeed, the new frontier for many of the world's companies, emerging markets come with a mix of opportunity and risk. Companies should be aware of this reality. In general, firms that establish deep local roots and align their strategies with the long-term goals of the host country have the greatest likelihood of being successful.[17]

Rapid development of Poland is yielding opportunities that are somewhat unexpected for many types of companies. Some observers of the Polish business environment feel that Poland "is emerging as Europe's star performer" following a difficult beginning. Reasons for this emergence include a commitment among Polish firms to benchmark their operations against the world's best performers and the restructuring of state-owned corporations. Foreign investment in Poland is on the rise "because foreign companies see the potential of Poland's domestic market and its attractiveness as a supply base for both West and East." In light of the country's extensive infrastructure needs and the projects already on its books, Asea Brown Boveri (ABB) expects annual sales of $1 billion in Poland by 2000. (ABB's sales in Poland were only $260 million in 1994.) Korea's Daewoo Motor Co. selected Poland as its center for automobile production in Europe. In addition, "a number of French and German retail chains have also been quietly positioning themselves to supply Poland's rising middle class."[18]

Business-level strategy, the focus of this chapter, is an integrated and coordinated set of commitments and actions designed to provide value to customers and gain a competitive advantage by exploiting core competencies in specific, individual product markets.[19] Thus, a business-level strategy reflects a firm's belief about where and how it has an advantage over its rivals.[20]

Customers are the foundation of successful business-level strategies. In the words of one CEO, "When you get people focused on customers, it has a very remarkable effect" on the firm's performance outcomes.[21] Because of their strategic importance, we begin this chapter with a discussion of customers. Three issues are considered in this analysis. Each firm determines (1) *who* it will serve, (2) *what* needs target customers have that it will satisfy, and (3) *how* those needs will be satisfied through implementation of a chosen strategy. For Bang & Olufsen, *who* the firm serves is audiophiles and video buffs; the *what* (or customer need) the company satisfies is for premium top-of-the-line electronics components; and, *how* these customer needs are satisfied is through use of Bang & Olufsen's competitive advantages in product design and manufacturing.

Following the discussion on customers, we describe four generic business-level strategies. These strategies are called *generic* because they can be implemented in both manufacturing and service industries.[22] Our analysis of the generic strategies includes descriptions of how each one allows a firm to address the five competitive forces discussed in Chapter 2. In addition, we use the value chain (see Chapter 3) to show examples of primary and support activities necessary to implement each generic strategy successfully. Risks associated with each generic strategy are also presented in this chapter. Organizational structures and controls required for the successful implementation of business-level strategies are explained in Chapter 11.

A fifth business-level strategy that both manufacturing and service firms are implementing more frequently is considered in the chapter's final section. Some believe that this integrated strategy (a combination of attributes of the cost leadership and differentiation strategies) is essential to establishing and exploiting competitive advantages in the global economy.[23]

129

A **business-level strategy** is an integrated and coordinated set of commitments and actions designed to provide value to customers and gain a competitive advantage by exploiting core competencies in specific, individual product markets.

CUSTOMERS: WHO, WHAT, AND HOW

Organizations must satisfy some group of customers' needs to be successful. *Needs* refer to the benefits and features of a good or service that customers want to purchase.[24] A basic need of all customers is to buy products that provide value.

A key reason that firms must be able to satisfy customers' needs is that in the final analysis, returns earned from relationships with customers are the lifeblood of all organizations.[25] Relationships with customers are strengthened when the firm is committed to providing *superior* value to those it serves. Superior value is often created when a firm's product helps a customer enhance the business's own competitive advantage.[26]

The challenge of identifying and determining how to satisfy the needs of what some business analysts believe are increasingly sophisticated, knowledgeable, and fickle customers is difficult.[27] Moreover, it is only through *total* satisfaction of their needs that customers develop the type of firm-specific loyalty companies seek. The belief of the president and chief operating officer (COO) of the Ritz-Carlton® Hotel Company describes the relationship between total need satisfaction and customer loyalty: "Unless you have 100 percent customer satisfaction—and I don't mean that they are just satisfied, I mean that they are excited about what you are doing—you have to improve."[28] Although difficult to earn, the estimate that "raising customer retention rates by five percentage points increases the value of an average customer by 25 percent to 100 percent"[29] is another indicator of the value of loyal customers. Increasingly, databases are linked with customer retention rates. Among other useful outcomes, information gleaned from these databases allows a firm to tailor its offerings more precisely to satisfy individualized customer needs.[30]

Strategically competitive organizations in the latter part of the 1990s and into the twenty-first century will (1) think continuously about who their customers are, (2) maintain close and frequent contacts with their customers, (3) determine how to use their core competencies in ways that competitors cannot imitate, and (4) design their strategies to allow them to satisfy customers' current, anticipated, and even unanticipated needs.[31] The chairman of AlliedSignal, a manufacturer of aerospace equipment, automobile parts, and a range of engineered materials, observes that there is a near unanimous opinion in his firm that its businesses should be run primarily by customer-oriented processes[32] such as the four mentioned here. Companies study their corporate memory (research stored documents) to enhance their understanding of product attributes that may appeal to current customers. Through these efforts, it might be discovered, for example, that a product being evaluated for possible introduction to the marketplace is quite similar to one the firm produced and sold previously. By analyzing customer reactions to the earlier product, the firm may be able to enhance the value that the new, yet similar product can offer to customers.[33]

Who: Determining the Customers to Serve

Customers can be divided into groups based on differences in their needs. Doing this is more effective than deciding that the firm will serve the needs of the "average customer." Averages sometimes do not provide in-depth insights about an issue that is relevant to decision makers. Shown in Table 4.1 are characteristics of the average American, the average woman, and the average man. Although inter-

TABLE 4.1 *Characteristics of the Average American*

The Average American

- Watches television seven hours daily, makes 1,029 telephone calls annually and eats 198 meals out a year.
- Wastes 150 hours a year sifting through clutter searching for things.
- Receives 49,060 pieces of mail in a lifetime. A third of it is junk.
- Charges $2,750 a year on credit cards.
- Owns 16 denim items, including seven pairs of jeans.
- Laughs 15 times daily. The average adult cusses once every eight words at leisure and every 29 words at work.
- Eats 11,113 M&M's in a lifetime.
- Has 40 hours of leisure a week. In an average week, the average American parent spends six hours shopping and 40 minutes playing with the kids.

Average Woman

- Lives 78.6 years.
- Has a body with 28 percent fat.
- Owns 30 pairs of shoes.
- Tries on 16 pairs of jeans to find a perfect fit.
- Spends 15.7 minutes on her hair each morning.

Average Man

- Lives 71.6 years
- Has a body with 15 percent fat.
- Owns 15 dress shirts, six pairs of slacks, six sport shirts, five knit shirts and three sweaters.
- Spends four hours a year tying his tie.
- Devotes 3,350 hours to shaving during his lifetime.

Sources: Columbus Dispatch; *In an Average Lifetime* and *On an Average Day* (Fawcett Columbine) by Tom Heymann; *Your Vital Statistics* (Citadel) by Gyles Brandreth; *American Averages* (Doubleday) *by Mike Feinsilber and William B. Mead; The Statistical Abstract of the United States.*

esting, these descriptors are of less value to a company seeking to target customers than attributes and needs associated with *specific* and *identifiable* customer segments.

Almost any identifiable human or organizational characteristic can be used to subdivide a large potential market into segments that differ from one another in terms of that characteristic.[34] Common characteristics on which customers' needs vary include (1) demographic variables (e.g., age, gender, income, occupation, education, race, nationality, and social class), (2) geographic segmentation (e.g., regions, countries, states, counties, cities, and towns), (3) lifestyle choices (lifestyle refers to a set of values or tastes exhibited by a group of customers, especially as they are reflected in consumption patterns[35]), (4) individual personality traits, (5) consumption patterns (e.g., usage rate and brand loyalty), (6) industry structural characteristics, and (7) organizational size.[36]

Recent experiences at Kmart demonstrate the importance of continuously focusing on the needs of a firm's target customer group. Kmart's core U.S. customer is over 55 years of age with an average income of under $20,000 and no children at home. Wal-Mart's average customer is under 44 and has an annual income of slightly under $40,000. These data suggest that compared to competitor Wal-Mart, Kmart's core customer seeks to purchase discounted products. Recent surveys also show that only 19 percent of Kmart shoppers are loyal to the chain. In comparison, 46 percent of Wal-Mart's customers are considered to be loyal (recall our earlier discussion about the positive effects of customer loyalty).

Even though women in the 25–44 age group are an important customer group for Kmart, the firm continues to experience weak results in women's apparel. Analysts believe that the primary reason for this weakness is that Kmart's women's apparel has become geared for a crowd that is younger than the 25- to 44-year-old group. The failure to serve effectively the needs of its target customers may be contributing to the lack of productivity at Kmart's stores as compared to Wal-Mart and Target. Kmart averages $195 in sales per square foot, as compared to $350 at Wal-Mart and $240 at Target. In late 1997, Kmart, one of the world's largest mass merchandise retailers, announced that it was offering early retirement to 28,500 hourly employees, or 11 percent of its workforce. This decision was made to reduce its high operating costs, but analysts have concluded that Kmart will not be able to return its core stores to healthy profitability until the core merchandising problems are solved.[37]

Increasing Segmentation of Markets In the new competitive landscape, many firms have become adept at identifying precise differences among customers' needs. Armed with these understandings, companies segment customers into *competitively relevant groups*—groups of customers with unique needs. As shown by the following statement, General Motors believes that four of its automobile product groups serve the unique needs of four competitively relevant groups: "The Chevy is squarely aimed at people shopping for a low price. The Pontiac targets performance enthusiasts. The Olds is for upscale buyers who might normally shop for import sport sedans, and the Buick will appeal to older buyers who want premium cars with conservative styling and room for six riders."[38] Named after a piece of legislation that was passed in the United States in 1972, Title 9 Sports sells athletic products to women of all ages. The firm's offerings are intended to support women's efforts to reach their personal fitness goals.[39]

In the United States, estimates are that at least 62 distinct classes of citizens exist, each with its own beliefs, aspirations, tastes, and needs. Some believe that, if anything, the trend toward fragmentation into smaller classes and subgroups is accelerating in the United States and throughout the world's markets.[40]

Nevertheless, companies' efforts to create a huge set of goods and services that is intended to satisfy unique needs may be confusing for some customers. This confusion can result from the sheer number of products available to consumers, particularly those in the United States. In fact, Americans today face by far the widest array of options they have ever confronted. The average number of items in a grocery store grew from 24,531 to over 30,000 between 1987 and 1997. During this time period, new products emerged on grocers' shelves at incredible rates, resulting in a peak of over 22,000 introductions in 1995. Of these introductions, nearly 70 percent fail. Given these realities, companies are challenged to provide sufficient detail to their target customers regarding the superiority of their product relative to competitors' offerings.[41]

U.S. teenagers represent a large but competitively relevant group whose purchasing power continues to expand (some of the spending patterns of this group are shown in Table 4.2). Teenagers are the target customer at Gadzooks, a successful specialty retailer of clothing and accessories. Just because individuals are 15 years old, says a Gadzooks store manager, doesn't mean they don't deserve good service.[42] JCPenney Co. uses its competitive advantage of private brands to design, manufacture, and sell its Arizona jeans. Launched in 1989, this brand is targeted to and driven by teens. In only five years, sales from the brand's tops, jeans, and

American consumers are confronted with over 30,000 products in the grocery store. In 1995, over 22,000 products were introduced, with approximately 70 percent doomed to failure.

jackets exceeded $500 million. In discussing reasons for the Arizona brand's success, a Penney's spokeswoman observed that teenagers identify with the brand, ". . . and even have given the brand their own pet name. They're calling it Zonez—with a 'z' at the end."[43]

Evidence suggests, though, that teenagers can be fickle customers. For example, during a recent spring season, Gadzooks carried a full stock of "retro" wear such as lizard-skin bell bottoms. Unfortunately for the firm, young shoppers failed to materialize as buyers for these items. After trying on a pair of the lizard-skin bell bottoms, a 15-year-old noted that while the clothing item was "cool," she had no interest in wearing it. In evaluating this situation, Gadzook's CEO observed

TABLE 4.2 *Spending Patterns of United States' Teenagers*

- They eat a lot, spending an average of $2,648.36 a year on food. As a group that is $64.48 billion a year, not including what parents purchase on weekly shopping trips to the supermarket.
- They read little. They spend an average of $13.82 a year on books for a total of $120.7 million.
- They like music, spending an average of $17.40 on compact disks and $12.96 on cassette tapes a year. Annual tab: $195.4 million on CDs and $129.6 million on tapes.
- Teens fork over an average of $62.10 a year of their own money for jeans or about $1 billion as a group.
- Teens spend an average of $95.35 of their own money each year for sneakers and athletic shoes. That represents about $1.4 billion a year.

Source: Simmons Market Research Bureau Inc. as reported in M. Halkias, 1995, To buy for—at least today, *Dallas Morning News,* October 14, F1, F2.

that his firm is in the business of trends and that, this time, it simply missed on its prediction about the popularity of retro wear.[44] Similarly, Guess clothing items appear to be losing some of their appeal to teenagers. By late 1997, the brand that teenagers judged third in "coolness" only two years earlier had fallen to number 23. Some analysts feel that the firm's products are no longer as innovative as they were in the 1980s. During a recent shopping trip, one teenager, for example, was observed to pass by Guess's low-waist, deep-blue-rinse jeans (priced at $48 per pair) in favor of a $39 pair of Levi's. When asked what drove her decision, the teen said simply, "Levi's are much cooler than Guess."[45]

What: Determining the Customer Needs to Satisfy

As a firm decides who it will serve, it must simultaneously identify the needs of the chosen customer group that its goods or services can satisfy. Top-level managers play a critical role in efforts to recognize and understand customers' needs. Their capacity to gain valuable insights from listening to and studying customers influences product, technology, and distribution decisions.

At Staples, which is the second-largest office supply superstore chain in the United States, top-level managers spend significant amounts of time analyzing reports about their customers' buying habits and solving customer problems. Spending executive time in this manner sends a strong signal to all employees that "Staples cares deeply, very deeply, about [understanding and] pleasing customers."[46] These efforts by top-level managers may contribute meaningfully to the firm's superior performance. Annual sales in 1998 were expected to increase by approximately 30 percent as compared to 1997. This rapid sales growth is four times faster than the overall North American office-supply-distribution industry. To further fuel its growth, Staples intends to continue with an aggressive store-opening program and to spend additional time seeking success in European markets.[47] Thus, in firms that achieve strategic competitiveness, such as Staples, customer contact is a key responsibility for top-level managers as well as marketing and sales personnel.[48]

An additional competitive advantage accrues to firms capable of anticipating and then satisfying needs that were unknown to target customers. Firms able to do this provide customers with unexpected value—that is, a product performance capability or characteristic they did not request, yet do value.[49] Moreover, anticipating customers' needs yields opportunities for firms to shape their industry's future and gain an early competitive advantage (an early competitive advantage is called a *first mover advantage* and is discussed in Chapter 5). For example, Sprint, a diversified telecommunications company, believes that it "set the standard in long distance with its fiber optic network." In terms of the future, the firm also believes that "by joining with our cable partners in a revolutionary venture, we will be setting the standard once again. We're creating the blueprint that other communications companies will have to follow: a new kind of company that delivers the entire interconnected world of globe-spanning voice, video and data—all from a single source."[50]

How: Determining Core Competencies Necessary to Satisfy Customers' Needs

Firms use their core competencies to implement value-creating strategies and satisfy customers' needs. One of the strategic imperatives at IBM is to more quickly convert the firm's technological competence into commercial products that customers value. IBM's intensive knowledge of its customers' businesses helps the firm accomplish this objective.[51] Honda's motorcycle, car, lawn mower, and generator businesses are all based on the company's core competence in engines and power trains. Honda continues to bolster its commitment to research and development to strengthen this core competence.[52] At Canon, core competencies in optics, imaging, and microprocessor controls provide the foundation to satisfy customer needs in a range of product markets including copiers, laser printers, cameras, and image scanners. One of the most solid and trusted suppliers in the electronics and computer industries, Hewlett-Packard uses its engineering core competence to manufacture products that are renowned for their quality.[53]

Next, we discuss the business-level strategies firms implement in the pursuit of strategic competitiveness and above-average returns.

TYPES OF BUSINESS-LEVEL STRATEGY

Business-level strategies are concerned with a firm's industry position relative to competitors.[54] Companies that have established favorable industry positions are better able to cope with the five forces of competition (see Chapter 2). To position itself, a firm must decide if its intended actions will allow it to perform activities differently or to perform different activities than its rivals.[55] Thus, favorably positioned firms may have a competitive advantage over their industry rivals. This is important in that the universal objective of all companies is to develop and sustain competitive advantages.[56]

Originally, it was determined that firms choose from among four generic business-level strategies to establish and exploit a competitive advantage within a particular competitive scope: *cost leadership, differentiation, focused low cost,* and *focused differentiation* (see Figure 4.1). A fifth generic business-level strategy, the integrated low-cost/differentiation strategy, has evolved through firms' efforts to find the most effective ways to exploit their competitive advantages.

When selecting a business-level strategy, firms evaluate two types of competitive advantage: "lower cost than rivals, or the ability to differentiate and command a premium price that exceeds the extra cost of doing so."[57] Having lower cost than rivals denotes the firm's ability to perform activities differently than rivals; being able to differentiate indicates a capacity to perform different activities.[58] Competitive advantage is achieved within some scope. Scope has several dimensions, including the group of product and customer segments served and the array of geographic markets in which a firm competes. Competitive advantage is sought by competing in many customer segments when implementing either the cost leadership or the differentiation strategy. In contrast, through implementation of focus strategies, firms seek either a cost advantage or a differentiation advantage in a *narrow competitive scope* or *segment*. With focus strategies, the firm "selects a segment or group of segments in the industry and tailors its strategy to serving them to the exclusion of others."[59]

None of the five business-level strategies is inherently or universally superior to the others.[60] The effectiveness of each strategy is contingent on the opportunities and threats in a firm's external environment *and* the possibilities permitted by the firm's unique resources, capabilities, and core competencies. It is critical, therefore, for the firm to select a strategy that is appropriate in light of its com-

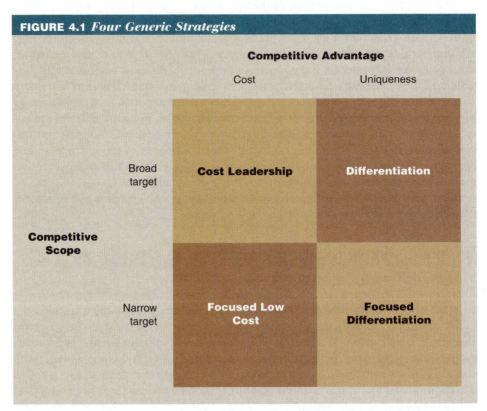

FIGURE 4.1 *Four Generic Strategies*

Source: Adapted with the permission of The Free Press, a division of Simon & Schuster from COMPETITIVE ADVANTAGE: Creating and Sustaining Superior Performance by Michael E. Porter, Fig. 1-3, 12. Copyright © 1985 by Michael E. Porter.

petencies and environmental opportunities; once selected, the strategy should be implemented carefully and consistently. Recently some criticized the Volkswagen group for what they saw as the firm's failure in terms of these strategic requirements. Indecision regarding the exact segments of the automobile industry in which the firm wanted to compete and how it intended to compete within chosen segments caused at least a temporary setback in the value of the firm's stock.[61]

Cost Leadership Strategy

A **cost leadership strategy** is an integrated set of actions designed to produce products at the lowest cost, relative to competitors, with features that are acceptable to customers. A **differentiation strategy** is an integrated set of actions designed to produce products that customers perceive as being different in ways that are important to them.[62] The differentiation strategy calls for firms to sell non-standardized products to customers with unique needs. The cost leadership strategy should achieve low cost relative to competitors while not ignoring means of differentiation that customers value. Alternatively, the differentiation strategy should consistently upgrade a product's differentiated features that customers value without ignoring costs to customers. Thus, although their nature differs, firms can create value (recall that value is defined in Chapter 3 as the product's set of char-

A **cost leadership strategy** is an integrated set of actions designed to produce products at the lowest cost, relative to competitors, with features that are acceptable to customers.

A **differentiation strategy** is an integrated set of actions designed to produce products that customers perceive as being different in ways that are important to them.

acteristics and attributes for which customers are willing to pay) through either cost leadership or the differentiation strategy.[63]

Firms seeking competitive advantage by implementing the cost leadership strategy often sell no-frills, standardized products to the most typical customers in the industry. In the new competitive landscape, it is increasingly difficult for firms implementing this type of strategy to differentiate between product features that are standard and those providing benefits that exceed the price the company's target customers are willing to pay.[64]

Successful implementation of the cost leadership strategy requires a consistent focus on driving costs lower, relative to competitors' costs. Firms often drive their costs lower through investments in efficient-scale facilities, tight cost and overhead control, and cost minimizations in such areas as service, sales force, and R&D. For example, Unifi Inc., one of the world's largest texturizers of filament polyester and nylon fiber, makes significant investments in its manufacturing technologies to drive its costs lower in an environment of upward pressure on prices of raw materials and packaging supplies. Already one of the most efficient producers in its industry, the company recently completed a modernization program for texturing polyester. Unifi also intends to modernize and expand its nylon, covered yarn, and dyed yarn operations. Combined, these actions are expected to increase the firm's technological lead over its rivals and further reduce its production costs.[65] Similarly, Nova Corp.'s chemical business is the low-cost leader in the manufacture of ethylene and polyethylene. To foster profitable growth as the twenty-first century begins, the firm intends to use its superior cost position to add pipeline miles in Canada and other locations in North America.[66]

Emerson Electric Co., a U.S. manufacturer that has earned above-average returns during both favorable and unfavorable economic climates, bases its operations on several principles—continuous cost reduction, use of state-of-the-art equipment, and open communications. The firm's adherence to these principles has resulted in impressive outcomes; "Adjusted for inflation, Emerson Electric's revenues have barely increased in the past half-dozen years. Yet in that period its earnings, cash flow and dividends per share have all increased by about 50 percent."[67]

As described in the Strategic Focus, the cost leadership strategy is being used in one of Dana Corp.'s business groups. While reading this Strategic Focus, notice the actions taken in one of the business group's plants to drive costs lower.

STRATEGIC FOCUS

Manufacturing a Truck Chassis: Dana Corp.'s Efforts to Continuously Reduce Its Production Costs

Dana Corp. is a global leader in the engineering, manufacture, and distribution of products and systems for the vehicular, off-highway, and industrial markets. A diversified firm (diversification strategies are explained in Chapter 6), Dana is organized into seven core business groups. With facilities in approximately 20 countries and over one-half of sales revenues earned outside the United States, Drivetrain components is the most global of Dana's business groups. Technological skills are the core competence on which this group's actions and growth objectives are based. Use of this competence recently helped the group develop the ability to build a complete rolling chassis for trucks and off-highway vehicles.

137

Less expensive on a per-unit basis, being able to purchase this type of chassis is important to automobile manufacturers as they seek ways to reduce parts and labor costs in their assembly plants.

Since 1995, Dana's plant in Stockton, California (a plant that is part of the Drivetrain components group) has been manufacturing truck chassis for a single customer: Toyota Motor Corp. Critical to Toyota's selection of this particular supplier was Dana's agreement to strive for a 2 percent price cut in the cost of its product. This reduction, which was to be reached by 1997, created a need for the Dana facility to find ways to drive its costs still lower. Reaching this objective has proved to be difficult, however. In 1995, the Stockton plant was already producing its products at world-class efficiency levels. Moreover, the fact that this plant essentially serves as a link in a transcontinental assembly line constrains its flexibility in terms of seeking ways to drive its costs lower. Approximately every 90 minutes, the plant receives steel parts from a Toyota facility located in Japan. With roughly 180 parts and 115 feet of welding involved, Dana builds a truck chassis that weighs roughly 300 pounds. At regular intervals, completed chassis are sent to a Toyota assembly plant that is located 63 miles from Stockton.

To find ways to drive costs lower in what was already a world-class manufacturing facility, the plant manager decided that the only hope was to create a culture of inventiveness—a culture in which every worker was challenged to find more efficient ways to produce the truck chassis. Believing that no change was too small, the manager insisted that every worker learn each job in the plant (to understand how each part fits into the whole) and that no person be given a permanent assignment (to maintain a fresh supply of perspectives). Challenged to question absolutely every activity completed in the facility, even down to the sequencing of individual welds, workers were required to submit two ideas in writing each month. Always oriented to actions that would increase efficiency and reduce costs, 81 percent of these ideas proved to be worth implementing during the facility's first two years of operation. One employee alone developed 180 ideas in a single year. Included among these were the installation of backup welding guns and the use of an electronic eye to assist in placing a cross-member.

Continuous feedback about plant productivity is provided to employees through use of electronic signs, similar to gymnasium scoreboards. The reaching of every efficiency goal, no matter how small, is celebrated openly. Multiple reinforcements, including free sodas for a day, the hosting of a family barbecue, and financial rewards, are used to acknowledge workers' achievements.

In late 1996, the plant reached an aggressive and long-sought threshold goal of producing 33 units hourly. As soon as it was reached, a new goal of manufacturing 36 chassis per hour was set. Developing the efficiencies required to reach this goal would reduce costs further and contribute to achievement of the 2 percent price-cut objective. Although not yet reached (Dana cut Toyota's price by .84 percent in early 1997), the facility continues to seek ways to increase its efficiencies and reduce its costs.

SOURCE: Dana Corp., 1997, Dana Corp. Home Page, December 7, http://www.dana.com; J.W. Milner, 1997, Dana Corp., *Value Line*, October 10, 814; T. Petzinger, Jr., 1997, A plant manager keeps reinventing his production line, *Wall Street Journal*, September 19, B1.

As described in Chapter 3, a firm's value chain determines which parts of its operations create value and which do not. Primary and support activities that allow a firm to create value through a cost leadership strategy are shown in Figure 4.2. Companies that cannot link the activities included in this figure lack the re-

FIGURE 4.2 *Examples of Value-Creating Activities Associated with the Cost Leadership Strategy*

MARGIN

MARGIN

Firm Infrastructure

Cost-effective management information systems.

Relatively few managerial layers in order to reduce overhead costs.

Simplified planning practices to reduce planning costs.

Human Resource Management

Consistent policies to reduce turnover costs.

Intense and effective training programs to improve worker efficiency and effectiveness.

Technology Development

Easy-to-use manufacturing technologies.

Investments in technologies in order to reduce costs associated with a firm's manufacturing processes.

Procurement

Systems and procedures to find the lowest cost (with acceptable quality) products to purchase as raw materials.

Frequent evaluation processes to monitor suppliers' performances.

Inbound Logistics

Highly efficient systems to link suppliers' products with the firm's production processes.

Operations

Use of economies of scale to reduce production costs.

Construction of efficient-scale production facilities.

Outbound Logistics

A delivery schedule that reduces costs.

Selection of low-cost transportation carriers.

Marketing and Sales

A small, highly trained sales force.

Products priced so as to generate significant sales volume.

Service

Efficient and proper product installations in order to reduce the frequency and severity of recalls.

Source: Adapted with the permission of The Free Press, a division of Simon & Schuster from *Competitive Advantage: Creating and Sustaining Superior Performance* by Michael E. Porter. Copyright © 1985 by Michael E. Porter.

sources and capabilities (and hence the core competencies) required to implement the cost leadership strategy successfully.

When implementing the cost leadership strategy, firms must be careful not to ignore completely sources of differentiation (e.g., innovative designs, service after the sale, product quality, etc.) that customers value. Emerson Electric Co. implements what it calls a best-cost producer strategy—"achieving the lowest cost consistent with quality."[68] Thus, the firm's products provide customers with a level of quality that at least meets, and often exceeds, their expectations relative to the purchase price.

Recently some worldwide travelers expressed dissatisfaction with the value they received from budget-priced hotels. In the words of one customer in response to her stay in a budget-priced Paris hotel, "Budget to me means clean, comfortable service for a good rate. But what I ended up getting was mediocre for a high price."[69] This feedback shows that customers evaluate a cost leader's product in terms of its cost, relative to the benefits its features provide.

As explained next, effective implementation of a cost leadership strategy allows a firm to earn above-average returns in spite of the presence of strong competitive forces.

Rivalry with Existing Competitors Having the low-cost position serves as a valuable defense against rivals. Because of the cost leader's advantageous position, rivals hesitate to compete on the basis of price. Instead, rivals try to compete against cost leaders through some means of differentiation. In South America, for example, top-level executives at Disco SA concluded that they could not compete against giant retailers Wal-Mart and Carrefour of France on the basis of price alone. Offering products at prices nearly as low as its largest competitors, Disco believes that it provides more convenience and service to customers. Carrying a wide range of brands and perishables, Disco stores offer home delivery, telephone ordering, and child care. Strategically, the firm's executives believe customers will accept a slight increase in product cost in return for the store's conveniences and services.[70] However, if rivals do challenge the firm to compete on the basis of price, the low-cost firm can still earn at least average returns after its competitors have lost theirs through competitive rivalry.[71]

Bargaining Power of Buyers (Customers) Powerful customers can force the low-cost leader to reduce its prices, but price will not be driven below the level at which the next-most-efficient industry competitor can earn average returns. Although powerful customers could force the low-cost leader to reduce prices even below this level, they probably would not choose to do so. Still lower prices would prevent the next-most-efficient competitor from earning average returns, resulting in its exit from the market and leaving the low-cost leader in a stronger position. Customers lose their power, and pay higher prices, when forced to buy from a firm operating in an industry without rivals.

Occasionally, a firm's bargaining power allows it to transfer increased costs to customers. Recently, for example, Unifi incurred substantially higher costs for raw materials and packaging products, but because it is a dominant supplier in many of its markets (up to a 70 percent share in some), Unifi was able to pass through higher costs to customers.[72]

Bargaining Power of Suppliers A firm in the low-cost position operates with margins greater than those of its competitors. Recently, for example, Emerson Elec-

140

tric Co. earned a net profit margin of 9 cents per sales dollar, a figure "... that's far higher than the industry average."[73] Moreover, analysts' expectations are that the firm's margins should continue to expand, especially in light of its efforts aimed at productivity gains and lower payroll costs (gained partly by directing production to low-wage regions).[74]

Among other benefits, higher margins relative to competitors make it possible for the low-cost firm to absorb price increases from suppliers. When an industry is faced with substantial increases in the cost of its supplies, the low-cost leader may be the only one able to pay the higher prices and continue to earn either average or above-average returns. Alternatively, powerful low-cost leaders may be able to force suppliers to hold down their prices, reducing their margins in the process.

Potential Entrants Through continuous efforts to reduce costs to levels below those of competitors, low-cost leaders become very efficient. Because they enhance profit margins, ever-improving levels of efficiency serve as a significant entry barrier to an industry for potential entrants. New entrants must be willing to accept no better than average returns until they gain the experience required to approach the efficiency of the low-cost leader. To earn even average returns, new entrants must have the competencies required to match the cost levels of other competitors.

The low-cost leader's low profit margins (relative to the margins earned by firms implementing the differentiation strategy) make it necessary for the firm to sell large volumes of its product to earn above-average returns. At Acer, the firm's CEO notes that the margins on his company's products, including its personal computers, are "shell-thin." "But sell enough of them," he believes, "and a formula emerges: Low margins and high turnover can be a recipe for success."[75] The cost leadership strategy, and the resulting emphasis on high volume and low margins, are the foundation for the firm's 20-plus-year effort to become Taiwan's first global brand-name powerhouse, similar to IBM or Sony Corp.[76] However, firms striving to be the low-cost leader must avoid pricing their products at a level that precludes them from earning above-average returns and encourages new industry entrants. Another computer manufacturer, Packard Bell, is sometimes thought to price its products too low in efforts to gain volume. "A favorite with first-time PC buyers seeking the latest multimedia features at rock-bottom prices," Packard Bell is challenged to sell its products at prices that permit the earning of at least average returns.[77]

Product Substitutes As compared to its industry rivals, the low-cost leader holds an attractive position in terms of product substitutes. When faced with the possibility of a substitute, the low-cost leader has more flexibility than its competitors. To retain customers, the low-cost leader can reduce its product's price. With still lower prices and features of acceptable quality, the low-cost leader increases the probability that customers will prefer its product, rather than a substitute.

Competitive Risks of the Cost Leadership Strategy

The cost leadership strategy is not without risks. One risk is that the low-cost leader's manufacturing equipment could become obsolete because of competitors' technological innovations. These innovations may allow rivals to produce at costs lower than those of the original cost leader.

141

A second risk is too much focus. Because of their focus on continuously driving costs lower, firms implementing a cost leadership strategy sometimes fail to detect significant changes in customers' needs or in competitors' efforts to differentiate what has traditionally been an undifferentiated, commodity-like product.

Before Orville Redenbacher and Charles Bowman launched Orville Redenbacher's Gourmet Popping Corn, for example, popcorn was thought to be a humble, commodity-like product. Convinced that people would pay more for high-quality popcorn, Orville Redenbacher developed a popcorn hybrid that produced fuller popping corn. He also perfected harvesting and packaging techniques that minimized kernel damage. In a tribute to Mr. Redenbacher, who died recently at the age of 88, the executive director of The Popcorn Institute observed that "He pioneered the gourmet popcorn niche. He promoted it very effectively and helped bring popcorn to a new level of acceptance."[78]

A final risk of the cost leadership strategy concerns imitation. Competitors sometimes learn how to imitate the low-cost leader's strategy successfully. When this occurs, the low-cost leader is challenged to find ways to increase the value provided by its good or service. Usually, value is increased by selling the current product at an even lower price or by adding features customers value while maintaining price. Even low-cost leaders must be careful when reducing prices to a still lower level. If the firm prices its good or service at an unrealistically low level (a level at which it will be difficult to retain satisfactory margins), customers' expectations about what they envision to be a reasonable price become difficult to reverse.[79]

Differentiation Strategy

With the differentiation strategy, the *unique* attributes and characteristics of a firm's product (other than cost) provide value to customers. Because a differentiated product satisfies customers' unique needs, firms implementing the differentiation strategy charge premium prices. To do this successfully, a "firm must truly be unique at something or be perceived as unique."[80] It is the ability to sell its differentiated product at a price that exceeds what was spent to create it that allows the firm to outperform its rivals and earn above-average returns.

Rather than costs, the focus of the differentiation strategy is on continuously investing in and developing features that differentiate products in ways that customers value. Overall, a firm using the differentiation strategy seeks to be different from its competitors along as many dimensions as possible. The less similarity between a firm's goods or services and those of competitors, the more buffered the firm is from rivals' actions. Commonly recognized differentiated products include Toyota's Lexus ("the relentless pursuit of perfection"), Ralph Lauren's and Tommy Hilfiger's clothing lines (image), Caterpillar (a heavy equipment and manufacturing firm committed to providing rapid delivery of spare parts to any location in the world), Maytag appliances (product reliability), McKinsey & Co. (the highest priced and most prestigious consulting firm in the world), and Rolex watches (prestige and image).

A product can be differentiated in an almost endless number of ways. Unusual features, responsive customer service, rapid product innovations and technological leadership, perceived prestige and status, different tastes, and engineering design and performance are examples of approaches to differentiation. In fact, virtually anything a firm can do to create real or perceived value for customers is a basis for differentiation. The challenge is to determine which features create value for the customer.

Starbucks Coffee Co., for example, believes that listening—a vital component of customer service—is one way the firm creates value. A company spokesperson notes, "We expect our employees to listen to customers." Catering to customers who value being able to "travel the world without leaving home," the ResidentSea cruise ship has only 250 apartments. These units range from 1,105 to 2,700 square feet, including penthouses and duplexes. Prices began at $1.2 million for the smallest units and peak at $5.4 million for the largest ones. Each apartment is equipped with a private terrace and whirlpool, home entertainment center, and three separate phone lines for phone, fax, and Internet access. Shapiro Marketing provides value through its Tie Protector. This product uses a little screen that retracts from a tie clip, shielding the customer's tie from damage that can result from spills.[81]

A leading manufacturer of integrated circuits, Intel Corp. creates value through implementation of the differentiation strategy. Intended to meet the needs of current and future sophisticated software applications, speed, innovation, and manufacturing expertise are core competencies Intel uses to differentiate its products from competitors' offerings. Additional information about Intel and its differentiation strategy are presented in the Strategic Focus.

STRATEGIC FOCUS

Intel Corp.: Achieving Strategic Competitiveness Through the Differentiation Strategy

Market share is one indicator of the success Intel has achieved through implementation of its differentiation strategy. With nearly 90 percent of new PCs using its chips, Intel's annual sales exceeded $25 billion in 1997. Some analysts believe that the firm's sales volume may reach $50 billion by 2000.

To maintain and enhance the differentiated features of its chips, Intel allocates significant financial resources to research and development (approximately 8.7 percent of sales) and capital improvements. Through these allocations and investments, Intel has developed an ability to convert more rapidly to new process technologies it is using to manufacture higher speed microprocessors. At least in part because of these investments, Intel's 1996 gross margin was 56 percent.

Impressive innovations that result in greater differentiation between Intel's products and those of its competitors continue to flow. In late 1997, for example, Intel announced that it had discovered how to double the amount of information that can be placed onto a transistor. This innovation overcomes a fundamental barrier in the design of integrated circuits. Initially, Intel intended to use this breakthrough to create more powerful memory chips for an array of products, including cellular phones, networking equipment, video arcade games, and other consumer electronics items. With this technology, a digital answering machine could have twice as much room to store messages. At the time of its announced discovery, this technology was good only for flash memory—chips that retain information even after the products in which they reside are turned off. As such, it could not be used for regular computer memory or for microprocessors such as Intel's Pentiums.

A more stunning innovation was also made known to the public in late 1997. Considered to be Intel's next-generation microprocessor, the firm developed the capability of producing a chip that can process 64 bits of information at a time. This compares to the simultaneous processing of 32 bits of information that Intel's most recent chip can handle. Industry experts estimated that the new chip, with Merced as its code name, will operate at 900 megahertz rather than the 300-megahertz capability of Intel's then-faster chip, the Pentium II. Moreover, the Merced will have approximately four times the 7.5 million transistors included on the Pentium II chip. The Merced's novel design features a change in the fundamental instructions that tell microprocessors what to do. Intel intends to use the new chip in high-end computers in 1999. Current plans call for the Merced to appear in desktop machines sometime after 2003.

Because of the chip's complexity, Intel's competitors such as Advanced Micro Devices (AMD) and Cyrix Corp. will find it difficult to duplicate the Merced and its capabilities. Thus, the chip, and the technology on which it is based, may serve to differentiate Intel's products for a reasonable period of time into the future.

Competing aggressively against AMD and Cyrix is consistent with Intel's objective of retaining its dominant market position. Because of the proliferation of computers costing less than $1,000, and some PC manufacturers' decisions to buy chips for these machines from AMD and Cyrix, Intel has had to cut the prices of its Pentium chips at a faster and steeper rate than usual. In commenting about this, an analyst stated that "back in the 486 era, Intel very satisfactorily thwarted the bid by AMD for a share of the CPU market. It then was able to maintain a clear technology lead as well as margins, despite price reductions that made the rival's offerings obsolescent. Now, however, AMD claims parity in performance, and so does a new entrant, Cyrix." Even in spite of these competitive challenges, the general consensus was that Intel's strengths would allow it to continue differentiating its products and to earn above-average returns as a result of doing so, even after sharing some of its markets with others.

SOURCE: *Bloomberg News*, 1997, Intel to give chip details, *Dallas Morning News*, October 13, D3; Intel Corp., 1997, *Intel Corp. Home Page*, http://www.intel.com; *San Francisco Chronicle*, Intel says it can double data storage on transistors, *Dallas Morning News*, September 17, D2; E. B. Swort, 1997, Advanced Micro, *Value Line*, October 24, 1053; E. B. Swort, 1997, Intel, *Value Line*, October 24, 1061; D. Takahashi, 1997, Intel's chip innovations could scramble PC industry, *Wall Street Journal*, October 21, B4.

A firm's value chain can also be used to determine if it can link the activities required to create value through implementation of the differentiation strategy. Examples of primary and support activities that are used commonly to differentiate a good or service are shown in Figure 4.3. Companies without the core competencies needed to link these activities cannot expect to implement the differentiation strategy successfully.

As explained next, successful implementation of the differentiation strategy allows a firm to earn above-average returns in spite of the presence of strong competitive forces.

Rivalry with Existing Competitors Customers tend to be loyal purchasers of products that are differentiated in ways meaningful to them. As their loyalty to a brand increases, their sensitivity to price increases lessens. This relationship between brand loyalty and price sensitivity insulates a firm from competitive rivalry. Thus, McKinsey & Co. is insulated from its competitors, even on the basis of price, as long as it continues to satisfy the differentiated needs of what appears to be a loyal customer group. The same outcome is true for Tommy Hilfiger, as long as its "classic preppy . . . with a twist" clothes[82] continue to satisfy the needs of "America's multicultural society" for garments with unique features.[83]

FIGURE 4.3 *Examples of Value-Creating Activities Associated with the Differentiation Strategy*

Firm Infrastructure: Highly developed information systems to better understand customers' purchasing preferences. A company-wide emphasis on the importance of producing high-quality products.

Human Resource Management: Compensation programs intended to encourage worker creativity and productivity. Somewhat extensive use of subjective rather than objective performance measures. Superior personnel training.

Technology Development: Strong capability in basic research. Investments in technologies that will allow the firm to produce highly differentiated products.

Procurement: Systems and procedures used to find the highest quality raw materials. Purchase of highest quality replacement parts.

MARGIN

Inbound Logistics: Superior handling of incoming raw materials so as to minimize damage and improve the quality of the final product.

Operations: Consistent manufacturing of attractive products. Rapid responses to customers' unique manufacturing specifications.

Outbound Logistics: Accurate and responsive order-processing procedures. Rapid and timely product deliveries to customers.

Marketing and Sales: Extensive granting of credit buying arrangements for customers. Extensive personal relationships with buyers and suppliers.

Service: Extensive buyer training to assure high-quality product installations. Complete field stocking of replacement parts.

145

Source: Adapted with the permission of The Free Press, a division of Simon & Schuster from *Competitive Advantage: Creating and Sustaining Superior Performance* by Michael E. Porter, Fig 4-1, 122. Copyright © 1985 by Michael E. Porter.

Bargaining Power of Buyers (Customers) The *uniqueness* of differentiated goods or services insulates the firm from competitive rivalry and reduces customers' sensitivity to price increases. Based on a combination of unique materials and brand image, Ralph Lauren's clothes satisfy certain customers' unique needs better than do competitors' offerings. A key reason that some buyers are willing to pay a premium price for this firm's clothing items is that for them, other products do not offer a comparable combination of features and cost. The lack of perceived acceptable alternatives increases the firm's power relative to its customers.

Bargaining Power of Suppliers Because a firm implementing the differentiation strategy charges a premium price for its products, suppliers must provide it with high-quality parts. However, the high margins the firm earns when selling effectively differentiated products partially insulate it from the influence of suppliers. Higher supplier costs can be paid through these margins. Alternatively, because of buyers' relative insensitivity to price increases, the differentiated firm might choose to pass the additional cost of supplies on to the customer by raising the price of its unique product.

Potential Entrants Customer loyalty and the need to overcome the uniqueness of a differentiated product are substantial entry barriers faced by potential entrants. Entering an industry under these conditions typically demands significant investments of resources and a willingness to be patient while seeking the loyalty of customers.

Product Substitutes Firms selling brand-name goods and services to loyal customers are positioned effectively against product substitutes. In contrast, companies without brand loyalty are more subject to their customers switching either to products that offer differentiated features that serve the same function as the current product, particularly if the substitute has a lower price, or to products that offer more features that perform more attractive functions.

As our discussion shows, firms can gain competitive advantage through successful implementation of the differentiation strategy. Nonetheless, several risks are associated with this strategy.

Competitive Risks of the Differentiation Strategy

One risk of the differentiation strategy is that customers might decide that the price differential between the differentiator's and the low-cost leader's product is too significant. In this instance, a firm may be providing differentiated features that exceed customers' needs. When this happens, the firm is vulnerable to competitors that are able to offer customers a combination of features and price that is more consistent with their needs.

Another risk of the differentiation strategy is that a firm's means of differentiation no longer provide value for which customers are willing to pay. Upscale retailer Bloomingdale's discovered that its focus on "glitz" as a means of differentiation no longer provided value to at least some of its customers, especially those shopping in the store's new locations. A review of the firm's situation resulted in one analyst concluding that "The mystique of the store hasn't been transferable" from New York City. Moreover, the analyst felt that the stores were "either too avant-garde or too humdrum. And in many cases, their prices were too high." In response to its situation, Bloomingdale's decided to emphasize comfort—a means of differentiation the firm thought would provide customer value—rather than glitz. Among other actions taken to focus on comfort was renovation of the chain's stores to provide customers with user-friendly designs.[84]

A third risk of the differentiation strategy is that learning can narrow customers' perceptions of the value of a firm's differentiated features. The value of the IBM name on personal computers was a differentiated feature for which some customers were willing to pay a premium price as the product emerged. However, as customers familiarized themselves with the standard features and as a host of PC clones entered the market, IBM brand loyalty began to fail. Clones offered customers features similar to those of the IBM product at a substantially lower price, reducing the attractiveness of IBM's product. Even currently, IBM's relatively new Aptiva line is failing to meet company expectations. In assessing the situation, one dealer observed that while the Aptiva is a "cool" machine, it simply costs too much for the features that it provides relative to the combination of features and price of products from competitors such as Compaq and Hewlett-Packard.[85]

Focus Strategies

In contrast to the cost leadership and differentiation strategies, a company implementing a focus strategy seeks to use its core competencies to serve the needs of a certain industry segment (e.g., a particular buyer group, segment of the product line, or geographic market).[86] A **focus strategy** is an integrated set of actions designed to produce products that serve the needs of a particular competitive segment. Although the breadth of a target is clearly a matter of degree, the essence of the focus strategy "is the exploitation of a narrow target's differences from the balance of the industry."[87] For example, the Dallas, Garland & Northeastern (DGNO) railroad firm runs from central Dallas, to Garland, and on to Greenville, Texas. Only a 92-mile line, the firm serves a segment (large firms including Kraft Foods and Sherwin-Williams) that is in need of rail transportation in a constrained geographic area.[88] Through successful implementation of a focus strategy, a company can gain a competitive advantage in its chosen target segments even though it does not possess an industry-wide competitive advantage.[89]

The foundation of focus strategies is that a firm can serve a particular segment of an industry more effectively or efficiently than can industry-wide competitors. Success with a focus strategy rests on a firm's ability either to find segments where unique needs are so specialized that broad-based competitors choose not to serve them or locate a segment being served poorly by the broad-based competitors.[90] When AT&T was in the process of selecting C. Michael Armstrong to replace then current CEO Robert Allen, smaller competitors began to move quickly to steal customers from the telecommunications giant. Behind these attempts was the belief that AT&T, as a broad-based competitor, was, at least at a point in time, poorly serving the needs of some segments.[91]

Value can be provided to customers through two types of focus strategies: focused low cost and focused differentiation.

Focused Low-Cost Strategy Using a double-drive-through format, Rally's Hamburgers Inc. implements the focused low-cost strategy. At the end of a recent year, Rally's had approximately 500 restaurants operating in 20 U.S. states.[92] These restaurants have limited menus and no indoor seating. According to the firm's CEO,

A **focus strategy** is an integrated set of actions designed to produce products that serve the needs of a particular competitive segment.

Rally's serves "the little-spare-time-or-cash crowd that McDonald's and Burger King have all but abandoned." Concentrating on the value-adding dimensions of price and speed, the firm recently sold and delivered to customers in 45 seconds a "fully-dressed burger, a 16-ounce soft drink and a good-sized fries for $1.97."[93]

No longer an independent entity, AST Research Inc., a maker of personal computers, is a wholly owned subsidiary of South Korea's Samsung Electronics Co., Ltd. This firm continues to struggle as it loses market share to larger rivals. To respond to its competitive challenges, AST decided, in December of 1997, to slash its worldwide workforce by over 1,100 jobs (about 37 percent of all employees). Additionally, executives concluded that AST could no longer compete effectively on an industry-wide basis. Now committed to implementing the focused low-cost strategy, AST is positioning itself as a company that can serve better the specialized needs of small- and medium-size businesses than can industry-wide competitors. Analysts, however, were not particularly optimistic, noting that "other leading PC makers are already pursuing that niche and that AST would be hard-pressed to separate itself from the rest of the pack."[94]

Focused Differentiation Strategy Other firms (such as Bang & Olufsen, Snap-on Tools, and The Iams Company, the firms described in the opening case) implement the focused differentiation strategy. The number of ways products can be differentiated to serve the unique needs of particular competitive segments is virtually endless. Consider the following examples.

Located in strip shopping centers that are accessible to the public, Sally Beauty Supply stores stock more than 4,000 hair, skin, and nail care products and salon equipment. Some of the chain's sales are to the general public, but the majority of its business is selling to professional hair and nail stylists. Because of its target customer, Sally Beauty Supply competes mainly with wholesalers rather than retailers. The key to the firm's success appears to be its ability to locate and offer new and "hot" products to a group of professionals that is interested in purchasing and using cutting-edge products. One analyst has suggested that the firm has "found a niche that others haven't tried to exploit."[95]

Other firms also implement the focused differentiation strategy, including Security Passions, located in Ciudad Juarez, Mexico. For less than $2,000, the firm will line a customer's favorite mink coat or leather jacket with material that is designed to deflect bullets from large-calibre handguns. Security Passions developed this product because its town is home to one of Mexico's most notorious drug cartels. Especially in the state of Texas in the United States, log homes are becoming popular. Aimed at middle-age professionals seeking upscale simulations of rugged living, technological advances are being used to build what are thought to be comfortable, yet unique dwellings. A fourth-generation bread baker is delighting customers throughout Europe with a variety of unique (and pricey) breads. Among the items he bakes are 10 different Bavarian and French loaves, two types of plaited Israeli cholla, loaves baked in a tin especially important from Australia to give a slice worthy of a sandwich, and a loaf with very expensive Italian sun-dried onions. Using its competitive advantages of unimpeachable quality and brand recognition, Patek Philippe, a family business, manufactures only 18,000 watches annually. Prices range from $7,000 for a plain wind-it-yourself Patek to $250,000 for a top-of-the-line model. In part, these watches are marketed as investments, which they seem to be. A 1989 limited edition that sold for $9,150 recently fetched $26,000 at an auction.[96]

Firms must be able to complete various primary and support activities in a competitively superior manner to achieve strategic competitiveness and earn above-average returns when implementing a focus strategy. The activities that must be completed to implement the focused low-cost and the focused differentiation strategies are virtually identical to those shown in Figures 4.2 and 4.3, respectively. Similarly, the manners in which the two focus strategies allow a firm to deal successfully with the five competitive forces parallel those described with respect to the cost leadership and the differentiation strategies. The only difference is that the competitive scope changes from industry wide to a narrow competitive segment of the industry. Thus, a review of Figures 4.2 and 4.3 and the text regarding the five competitive forces yields a description of the relationship between each of the two focus strategies and competitive advantage.

Competitive Risks of Focus Strategies

When implementing either type of focus strategy, a firm faces the same general risks as does the company pursuing the cost leadership or the differentiation strategy on an industry-wide basis. However, focus strategies have three additional risks beyond these general ones. First, a competitor may be able to focus on a more narrowly defined competitive segment and "outfocus" the focuser. For example, a firm might decide that it can better serve the specialized needs of one or the other of Sally Beauty Supply's two key customer groups—professional hair stylists and nail stylists. Second, a firm competing on an industry-wide basis may decide that the market segment being served by the focus-strategy firm is attractive and worthy of competitive pursuit. No longer content with its traditional customer group only, Home Depot now has plans to concentrate on more narrow segments that it has not tried to serve previously, such as people who make large-ticket home renovations. In addition, the firm has entered the institutional maintenance and cleaning business with its purchase of Maintenance Warehouse America Corp.[97] Because of its size and capabilities, firms now competing in focused market segments may be threatened by Home Depot's entrance into their market domains. The third risk of a focus strategy is that the needs of customers within a narrow competitive segment may become more similar to those of customers as a whole. When this occurs, the advantages of a focus strategy are either reduced or eliminated.

Next, we describe a business-level strategy that is being used more prominently in the new competitive landscape. A key reason for this is the requirements of global competition.

Integrated Low-Cost/Differentiation Strategy

Particularly in global markets, a firm's ability to blend the low-cost and the differentiation approaches may be critical to sustaining competitive advantages. Compared to firms relying on one dominant generic strategy for their success, a company capable of successfully implementing an integrated low-cost/differentiation strategy should be in a better position to adapt quickly to environmental changes, learn new skills and technologies more quickly, and effectively leverage its core competencies across business units and product lines.

A growing body of evidence supports the relationship between implementation of an integrated strategy and the earning of above-average returns.[98] Some time ago, for example, a researcher found that the most successful firms competing in low-profit potential industries were able to effectively combine the low-cost and differentiation strategies.[99] In a more recent comprehensive study, it was discovered that "businesses which combined multiple forms of competitive advantage outperformed businesses that only were identified with a single form."[100] Other research found that the highest performing companies in the Korean electronics industry were those combining both the differentiation and cost leadership strategies, suggesting the viability of the integrated strategy in different nations.[101]

A key reason firms capable of successfully implementing the integrated strategy can earn above-average returns is that the benefits of this strategy are additive: "differentiation leads to premium prices at the same time that cost leadership implies lower costs."[102] Thus, the integrated strategy allows firms to gain competitive advantage by offering two types of value to customers—some differentiated features (but often fewer than those provided by the product-differentiated firm) and relatively low cost (but not as low as the products of the low-cost leader).

Mabuchi Motor, a Japanese company, implements the integrated low-cost/differentiation strategy. This firm manufacturers the small electric motors that power compact disk players, toy airplanes, and car windows. Mabuchi's focus is singular and consistent. The firm's objective is to produce "high-quality products at low prices, but in limited variety." Approximately 99 percent of revenues are earned from the sales of motors. Costs are kept low by the firm's decision to design and manufacture a limited variety of its products. The company produces 4.9 million motors daily, but fills 55 percent of its orders with just 10 different models. These products are differentiated through the firm's "obsession" with its miniature devices. At a modern technical center, Mabuchi scientists constantly research ways to differentiate their firm's products from competitors' offerings, seeking ways to make their motors "lighter, quieter, hardier and cheaper." Indicators of Mabuchi's strategic competitiveness include control of more than one-half of the world's market for small motors and routine double-digit operating margins.[103]

Firms must be strategically flexible to implement successfully the integrated low-cost/differentiation strategy. Discussed next are three approaches to organizational work that can increase the strategic flexibility that is associated with implementation of this strategy.

Flexible Manufacturing Systems Made possible largely as a result of the increasing capabilities of modern information technologies, flexible manufacturing systems increase the "flexibilities of human, physical and information resources"[104] that are integrated to create differentiated products at low costs. A *flexible manufacturing system* (FMS) is a computer-controlled process used to produce a variety of products in moderate, flexible quantities with a minimum of manual intervention.[105]

The goal of FMS is to eliminate the low-cost versus product-variety trade-off inherent in traditional manufacturing technologies. The flexibility provided by an FMS allows a plant to "change nimbly from making one product to making another."[106] When used properly, an FMS can help a firm become more flexible in response to changes in its customers' needs, while retaining low-cost advantages and consistent product quality. Because an FMS reduces the lot size needed to manufacture a product efficiently, a firm's capacity to serve the unique needs of a narrow competitive scope is increased. Thus, FMS technology is a significant technological advance that allows firms to produce a large variety of products at a low cost. Levi Strauss, for example, uses an FMS to make jeans for women that meet their exact measurements. Andersen Windows lets customers design their own windows through use of proprietary software the firm has developed. Motorola successfully uses an FMS to customize pagers in different colors, sizes, and shapes.[107]

Effective use of an FMS is linked with a firm's ability to understand constraints these systems may create (in terms of materials handling and the flow of supporting resources in scheduling, for example) and to design an effective mix of machines, computer systems, and people.[108] As a result, this type of manufacturing technology facilitates the implementation of complex competitive strategies such as the integrated low-cost/differentiation strategy that lead to strategic competitiveness in global markets.[109]

Incorporated into firms' processes somewhat slowly at first, the number of companies anticipating their use of FMSs in the near future is substantial. For example, among U.S. firms with more than 10,000 employees, "68 percent of electrical equipment manufacturers, 78 percent of machinery producers, 93 percent of automobile makers, and 100 percent of aerospace companies expect to have some form of FMS by the year 2000.[110] Although these expressed intentions are impressive, it is interesting to note that according to a researcher's results, "the bulk of the major firms in Japan, Western Europe and the United States will have begun using FMS by (2000), but the percentage will still be higher in Japan than in the United States or Western Europe."[111] Contributing to the slower rate of adoption of FMSs in the United States is the reality that U.S. firms, as compared to European and especially Japanese companies, tend to require higher rates of return to justify investments in these systems.[112] Moreover, evidence to date suggests that Japanese manufacturing firms have derived greater benefits from investments in FMSs as compared to their U.S. counterparts. The cause of this outcome may be that FMSs are managed less effectively in U.S. firms.[113]

Information Networks Across Firms New information networks linking manufacturers with their suppliers, distributors, and customers are another technological development that increases a firm's strategic flexibility and responsiveness.[114] Recent changes in a range of information technologies facilitated the development of competitively valuable information networks. Examples of these technologies include CADD (computer-assisted design and development) systems, CIM (computer-integrated manufacturing) systems, and EDI (electronic data integration). Ford Motor Co., Allen Bradley, Hitachi, Motorola, and Boeing are but a few of the many companies using information networks to coordinate the development, production, distribution, and marketing of their products. Among many benefits, these computer-based information links substantially reduce the time needed to design and test new products and allow a firm to compete on the basis of fast delivery (a differentiated feature) and low cost.[115]

Total Quality Management Systems Although difficult to implement,[116] many firms have established total quality management (TQM) systems (also see Chapter 5). Important objectives sought through use of TQM systems include increases in the quality of a firm's product and the productivity levels of the entire organization.[117] Enhanced quality focuses customers' attention on improvements in product performance, feature utility, and reliability. This allows a firm to achieve differentiation and ultimately higher prices and market share. An emphasis on quality in production techniques lowers manufacturing and service costs through savings in rework, scrap, and warranty expenses. These savings can result in a competitive

151

CADD systems are an example of a competitively valuable information network. These computer-based links substantially reduce the time needed to design and test new products, such as the Airbus plane shown in the photograph. Firms with CADD systems are better able to compete on the basis of fast delivery and lower costs.

advantage for a firm over its rivals. Thus, TQM programs integrate aspects of the differentiation and cost leadership strategies.

Four key assumptions are the foundation of TQM systems. The first assumption is that "the costs of poor quality (such as inspection, rework, lost customers and so on) are far greater than the costs of developing processes that produce high-quality products and services."[118] The second assumption is that employees naturally care about their work and will take initiatives to improve it. These initiatives are taken only when the firm provides employees with the tools and training they need to improve quality and when managers pay attention to their ideas. The third assumption is that "organizations are systems of highly interdependent parts."[119] Problems encountered in such systems often cross traditional functional (e.g., marketing, manufacturing, finance, etc.) lines. Solving interdependent problems requires integrated decision processes with participation from all affected functional areas. The fourth assumption is that the responsibility for an effective TQM system rests squarely on the shoulders of upper-level managers. These people must openly and totally support use of a TQM system and accept the responsibility for an organizational design that allows employees to work effectively.

As with the other business-level strategies, there are risks associated with use of the integrated low-cost/differentiation strategy.

Competitive Risks of the Integrated Low-Cost/Differentiation Strategy

The potential of the integrated strategy, in terms of above-average returns, is significant, but this potential comes with substantial risk. Selecting a business-level strategy calls for firms to make choices about how they intend to compete. Achieving the low-cost position in an industry, or a segment of an industry (e.g., a focus strategy), demands that the firm be able to reduce its costs consistently relative to competitors. Use of the differentiation strategy, with either an industry-wide or a focused competitive scope (see Figure 4.1), results in above-average returns only when the firm provides customers with differentiated products they value and for which they are willing to pay a premium price.

The firm failing to establish a leadership position in its chosen competitive scope, as the low-cost producer or as a differentiator, risks becoming "*stuck-in-the-middle.*"[120] Being stuck in the middle prevents firms from dealing successfully with the five competitive forces and from earning above-average returns. Indeed, some research results show that the lowest performing businesses are those lacking a distinguishable competitive advantage. Not having a clear and identifiable competitive advantage results from a firm being stuck in the middle.[121] Such firms can earn average returns only when an industry's structure is highly favorable or when the firm is competing against others that are in the same position.[122]

Midsize accounting firms (those with as many as 50 partners and 300 employees) appear to be stuck in the middle. These companies lack the size and resources to offer the wide array of services available from the Big Six giants; at the same time, their overhead rates prevent them from matching the low prices charged by small accounting firms and solo practitioners. Thus, these firms' services seem to be too expensive to compete with the low-cost small firms and too undifferentiated to provide the value offered by the large, differentiated accounting firms. In an accounting firm consultant's opinion, these conditions suggest that by the year 2000, middle size accounting firms may be "as extinct as the dodo."[123]

As explained in the Strategic Focus, some firms competing in the specialty coffee business also face the possibility of becoming stuck-in-the-middle. If it materializes, this outcome would be a product primarily of the dynamics of competition within this industry.

STRATEGIC FOCUS

Efforts to Avoid Becoming Stuck in the Middle in the Specialty Coffee Business

Evidence suggests that some firms competing in the coffee-bar business may be stuck in the middle. The leader in this industry is Starbucks Corp. As shown by the following comments, the founder and CEO, Howard Schultz, has always wanted this firm to be more than a profitable enterprise: "We had a mission, to educate consumers everywhere about fine coffee. We had a vision, to create an atmosphere in our stores that drew people in and gave them a sense of wonder and romance in the midst of their harried lives."

Vertically integrated (the firm controls operations for its coffee sourcing, roasting, packaging, and distribution), Starbucks continues to expand rapidly. With approximately 1,250 units at the beginning of 1998, the company planned to add more than 400 stores in 1998 alone; 2,000 total units are expected by 2000. To better serve its customers, including the growing number of teenagers who see coffee houses as an alternative to the movies or the mall, Starbucks has introduced larger units in select markets. With 50 or more seats rather than the standard seating capacity of 20 to 25, these larger locations permit expanded menus and live entertainment.

Based in part on the prediction that sales in the specialty coffee industry will reach $3 billion in 1999 (up from only $44 million in 1969), an explosive growth is anticipated in the total number of coffee bars in the United States. This growth, through which the number of total units will likely double between 1996 and 2000, will lead to an industry shakeout. One analyst noted that the intensity of competition in this industry makes it highly improbable that all players in the business will survive. Even more directly, Michael Bergman, CEO of a coffee-bar business called Second Cup, believes that as a result of events occurring in the industry, "You will have the strong, big players and the small, well-run chains that really understand their particular customer. The victims are going to be marginal players in the middle."

Aware of these industry realities, some firms are taking actions in an effort to avoid become stuck in the middle. Timothy's World Coffee operates the bulk of its 28 U.S. stores in what is known to be a brutally competitive market in New York City. To differentiate itself and to serve the needs of a narrow customer group, the firm established Timothy's World-News Café. At these locations, customers can buy coffee as well as purchase and read their favorite magazines while in the store.

Chock Full O'Nuts roasts, packs, and markets regular, instant, decaffeinated, and specialty coffees and teas. The firm's products are sold to retail, foodservice, and private-label customers. Because of competitive difficulties, the company discontinued its Chock Full O'Nuts cafés in October 1996. In an effort to avoid being stuck in the middle in the coffee specialty business, Chock Full O'Nuts then decided to expand its Quikava coffee chain as the foundation of a focused differentiation strategy. Each Quikava unit is a tiny, double-drive-through that sells coffee, road-ready sandwiches, and baked goods. Because these units continue to operate in the red, analysts believe that the company will likely have to do more than double its number of stores to reach break even (an outcome that is not expected until at least fiscal 1999). Thus, at least in terms of the short run, Chock Full O'Nuts may not have developed a successful specialty coffee business concept—one that will allow it to remain a viable participant in an industry that may experience a shakeout in the near future.

SOURCE: *Bloomberg News*, 1997, Upscale coffee chains show signs of overheating, *Dallas Morning News*, August 3, H3; R. Coleman, 1997, Java Juniors, *Dallas Morning News*, June 9, D1, D4; R. M. Greene, 1997, Chock Full O'Nuts, *Value Line*, August 15, 1467; Starbucks: Making values pay, 1997, *Fortune*, September 29, 261–272; D. Vlassis, 1997, Starbucks Corp., *Value Line*, August 22, 1747; S. Caminiti, 1995, Coffee chains are getting the jitters, *Fortune*, November 27, 42, 44.

Once a firm has selected its business-level strategy, it must both anticipate and be prepared to respond to competitors' actions and responses. Recently, for example, Coffee Station, Inc., initiated competitive actions that have the potential to affect Starbucks. In a bid to become the number-two operator of specialty coffee outlets, the firm purchased the 61-store Pasqua Inc. chain. Some analysts suggested that Coffee Station might be seeking to gain the size required to compete against Starbucks. Because of the high visibility of Coffee Station and Pasqua outlets in New York City, San Francisco, and Los Angeles, respectively, it is possible that Coffee Station's attempt to consolidate part of the specialty coffee market will enhance the firm's strategic competitiveness. Increasing success by competitors will elicit competitive responses from Starbucks and other industry participants.[124] Competitive dynamics such as these that occur as firms implement their strategies are examined in the next chapter. These dynamics take place with respect to all types of strategies (see Chapters 6 through 9), but the majority of competitive actions and competitive responses are initiated in efforts to implement a firm's business-level strategy.

SUMMARY

- A business-level strategy is an integrated and co-ordinated set of commitments and actions designed to provide value to customers and gain a competitive advantage by exploiting core competencies in specific, individual product markets. Five business-level strategies are examined in this chapter. Strategic competitiveness is enhanced when a firm is able to develop and exploit new core competencies faster than competitors can mimic the competitive advantages yielded by its current competencies.

- Customers are the foundation of successful business-level strategies. When considering customers, firms simultaneously examine three issues: *who*, *what*, and *how*. Respectively, these issues cause the firm to determine the customer groups it will serve, the needs those customers have that it seeks to satisfy, and the core competencies it possesses that can be used to satisfy customers' needs. The increasing segmentation of markets occurring throughout the world creates multiple opportunities for firms to identify unique customer needs.

- Firms seeking competitive advantage through the cost leadership strategy often produce no-frills, standardized products for an industry's typical customer. Above-average returns are earned when firms continuously drive their costs lower than those of their competitors while providing customers with products that have low prices and acceptable levels of differentiated features.

- Competitive risks associated with the cost leadership strategy include (1) a loss of competitive advantage to newer technologies, (2) a failure to detect changes in customers' needs, and (3) the ability of competitors to imitate the low-cost leader's competitive advantage through their own unique strategic actions.

- Through implementation of the differentiation strategy, firms provide customers with products that have different (and valued) features. Because of their uniqueness, differentiated products are sold at a premium price. Products can be differentiated along any dimension that is valued by some group of customers. Firms using this strategy seek to differentiate their products from competitors' goods or services along as many dimensions as possible. The less similarity with competitors' products, the more buffered a firm is from competition with its rivals.

- Risks associated with the differentiation strategy include (1) a customer group's decision that the differences between the differentiated product and the low-cost leader's product are no longer worth a premium price, (2) the inability of a differentiated product to create the type of value for which customers are willing to pay a premium price, and (3) the ability of competitors to provide customers with products that have features similar to those associated with the differentiated product, but at a lower cost.

- Through the low-cost and the differentiated focus strategies, firms serve the needs of a narrow competitive segment (e.g., buyer group, product segment, or geographic area). This strategy is successful when firms have the core competencies required to provide value to a narrow competitive segment that exceeds the value available from firms serving customers on an industry-wide basis.

- The competitive risks of focus strategies include (1) a competitor's ability to use its core competencies to "outfocus" the focuser by serving an even more narrowly defined competitive segment, (2) decisions by industry-wide competitors to serve a customer group's specialized needs that the focuser has been serving, and (3) a reduction in differences of the needs between customers in a narrow competitive segment and the industry-wide market.

- Firms using the integrated low-cost/differentiation strategy strive to provide customers with relatively low-cost products that have some valued differentiated features. The primary risk of this strategy is that a firm might produce products that do not offer sufficient value—in terms of either low cost or differentiation. When this occurs, the company is "stuck in the middle." Firms stuck in the middle compete at a disadvantage.

155

REVIEW QUESTIONS

1. What is a strategy and what are business-level strategies?
2. What is the relationship between a firm's customers and its business-level strategy? Why is this relationship important?
3. When studying customers in terms of *who*, *what*, and *how*, what questions are firms trying to answer?
4. What is the integrated low-cost/differentiation strategy? Why is this strategy becoming more important to firms?
5. How is competitive advantage achieved through successful implementation of the cost leadership strategy? The differentiation strategy? The focused low-cost strategy? The focused differentiation strategy? The integrated low-cost/differentiation strategy?
6. What are the risks associated with selecting and implementing each of the five strategies mentioned in question 5?

APPLICATION DISCUSSION QUESTIONS

1. You are a customer of your university or college. What actions does your school take to understand *what* your needs are? Be prepared to discuss your views.
2. Choose a firm in your local community that is of interest to you. Based on interactions with this company, which business-level strategy do you believe the firm is implementing? What evidence can you provide to support your belief?
3. Assume that you have decided to establish and operate a restaurant in your local community. *Who* are the customers you would serve? *What* needs do these customers have that you could satisfy with your restaurant? *How* would you satisfy those needs? Be prepared to discuss your responses.
4. What business-level strategy is your school implementing? What core competencies are being used to implement this strategy?
5. Assume you overheard the following comment: "It is impossible for a firm to produce a low-cost, highly differentiated product." Accept or reject this statement and be prepared to defend your position.

ETHICS QUESTIONS

1. Can a commitment to ethical conduct on issues such as the environment, product quality, and fulfilling contractual agreements affect competitive advantage? If so, how?
2. Is there more incentive for differentiators or low-cost leaders to pursue stronger ethical conduct? Think of an example to support your answer.
3. Can an overemphasis on low-cost leadership or differentiation lead to ethical problems (such as poor product design and manufacturing) that create costly problems (e.g., product liability lawsuits)?
4. Reexamine the assumptions about effective TQM systems presented in this chapter. Do these assumptions urge top-level managers to maintain higher ethical standards? If so, how?
5. A brand image is one way a firm can differentiate its good or service. However, many questions are now being raised about the effect brand images have on consumer behavior. For example, considerable concern has arisen about brand images that are managed by tobacco firms and their effect on teenage smoking habits. Should firms be concerned about how they form and use brand images? Why or why not?

INTERNET EXERCISE

Go to Dayton Hudson's home page at:

http://www.shop-at.com

The Dayton Hudson Corporation owns a family of retail stores including Dayton's, Hudson's, Marshall Field's, Target, and Mervyn's. Dayton Hudson is unusual in that some of its stores pursue a low-cost strategy and some pursue a differentiation strategy. Visit Dayton Hudson's Web site and the Web sites of each of the individual chains of stores. Which of the stores pursue a low-cost strategy and which stores pursue a differentiation strategy? Provide examples of how each of the stores supports its respective strategy.

Strategic Surfing

Hoover's Online provides free access to information and current news stories about American companies. This re-

source is valuable to managers and students who are interested in learning more about the background, performance, and strategies of U.S. companies.

http://www.hoovers.com/

NOTES

1. Callaway Golf Company, 1997, *Annual Report*, 1.

2. A. Campbell and M. Alexander, 1997, What's wrong with strategy? *Harvard Business Review* 75, no. 6: 42–51; D. J. Collis and C. A. Montgomery, 1995, Competing on resources: Strategy in the 1990s, *Harvard Business Review* 73, no. 4: 118–128.

3. This particular view of strategy is mentioned in D. P. Slevin and J. G. Covin, 1997, Strategy formation patterns, performance, and the significance of context, *Journal of Management* 23: 189–209.

4. C. E. Helfat, 1997, Know-how and asset complementarity and dynamic capability accumulation: The case of R&D, *Strategic Management Journal* 18: 339–360; A. Seth and H. Thomas, 1994, Theories of the firm: Implications for strategy research, *Journal of Management Studies* 31: 167.

5. N. Rajagopalan and G. M. Spreitzer, 1997, Toward a theory of strategic change: A multi-lens perspective and integrative framework, *Academy of Management Journal* 22: 48–79; R. R. Nelson, 1994, Why do firms differ, and how does it matter? in R. P. Rumelt, D. E. Schendel, and D. J. Teece (eds.), *Fundamental Issues in Strategy* (Boston: Harvard Business School Press), 247–269.

6. H. Courtney, J. Kirkland, and P. Viguerie, 1997, Strategy under uncertainty, *Harvard Business Review* 75, no. 6: 67–79; P. F. Drucker, 1997, The future that has already happened, *Harvard Business Review* 75, no. 5: 20–24.

7. G. S. Day and D. J. Reibstein, 1997, *Wharton on Dynamic Competitive Strategy* (New York: John Wiley & Sons), 3.

8. G. S. Day, 1997, Maintaining the competitive edge: Creating and sustaining advantages in dynamic competitive environments, in G. S. Day and D. J. Reibstein (eds.), 1997, *Wharton on Dynamic Competitive Strategy* (New York: John Wiley & Sons), 48–75; D. Leonard-Barton, 1995, *Wellsprings of Knowledge* (Boston: Harvard Business School Press).

9. C. Oliver, 1997, Sustainable competitive advantage: Combining institutional and resource-based views, *Strategic Management Journal* 18: 697–713.

10. T. T. Baldwin, C. Danielson, and W. Wiggenhorn, 1997, The evolution of learning strategies in organizations: From employee development to business redefinition, *Academy of Management Executive* XI, no. 4: 47–58; D. Lei, M. A. Hitt, and R. Bettis, 1996, Dynamic core competences through meta-learning and strategic context, *Journal of Management* 22: 549–569.

11. C. M. Christensen, 1997, Making strategy: Learning by doing, *Harvard Business Review* 75, no. 6: 141–156.

12. The Iams Company, 1997, *The Iams Company Home Page*, October 20, http://www.iams.com.

13. M. Zimmerman, 1995, Frito-Lay stands to gain from rival's exit, *Dallas Morning News*, October 26, D1, D10.

14. M. Zimmerman, 1995, Luby's adds units as rivals face troubles, *Dallas Morning News*, November 6, D1, D4.

15. N. Harris, 1997, UPS puts its back into it, *Business Week*, October 27, 50.

16. J. Jenk, C. H. Michel, and V. Margotin-Roze, 1995, The Russian consumer revolution, *The McKinsey Quarterly*, no. 2: 35–46.

17. J. E. Garten, 1997, Troubles ahead in emerging markets, *Harvard Business Review* 75, no. 3: 38–50.

18. K. L. Miller, F. J. Comes, and P. Simpson, 1995, Poland: Rising star of Europe, *Business Week*, December 4, 64–70.

19. G. G. Dess, A. Gupta, J.-F. Hennart, and C. W. L. Hill, 1995, Conducting and integrating strategy research at the international, corporate, and business levels: Issues and directions, *Journal of Management* 21: 357–393.

20. Day and Reibstein (eds.), *Wharton on Dynamic Competitive Strategy*, 20.

21. B. Saporito, 1993, How to revive a fading firm, *Fortune*, March 22, 80.

22. M. E. Porter, 1980, *Competitive Strategy* (New York: The Free Press).

23. Lei, Hitt, and Bettis, Dynamic core competencies.

24. A. J. Slywotzky, 1996, *Value Migration* (Boston: Harvard Business School Press), 13.

25. A. W. H. Grant and L. A. Schlesinger, 1995, Realize your customers' full profit potential, *Harvard Business Review* 73, no. 5: 59–72.

26. Freightliner: Growing through innovation and agility, 1997, *Fortune*, December 8, S10.

27. T. A. Stewart, 1997, A satisfied customer isn't enough, *Fortune*, July 21, 112–113.

28. T. O. Jones and W. E. Sasser, Jr., 1995, Why satisfied customers defect, *Harvard Business Review* 73, no. 6: 88–99.

29. T. A. Stewart, 1995, After all you've done for your customers, why are they still not happy? *Fortune*, December 11, 182.

30. J. Hagel, III and J. F. Rayport, 1997, The coming battle for customer information, *Harvard Business Review* 75, no. 1: 53–65.

31. Slywotzky, *Value Migration*, 13; R. McKenna, 1995, Real-time marketing, *Harvard Business Review* 73, no. 4: 87–95; S. F. Wiggins, 1995, New ways to create lifetime bonds with your customers, *Fortune*, October 30, 115.

32. A master class in radical change, 1993, *Fortune*, December 13, 82–90.

33. V. Griffith, 1997, Treasures in the corporate memory, *The Financial Times*, November 10, 14.

34. T. C. Kinnear, K. L. Bernhardt, and K. A. Krentler, 1995, *Principles of Marketing*, 4th ed. (New York: HarperCollins), 149–150.

35. Ibid., 153.

36. Ibid., 149–161; D. F. Abell, 1980, *Defining the Business: The Starting Point of Strategic Planning* (Englewood Cliffs, NJ: Prentice-Hall).

37. R. Berner, 1997, Kmart makes early-retirement offer to 28,500, *Wall Street Journal*, November 14, B4; M. H. Gerstein, 1997, Kmart Corp., *Value Line*, August 22, 1654; K. Naughton, 1995, Bright lights, big city won't cut it for Kmart, *Business Week*, May 26, 57.

38. Associated Press, 1996, Automakers rolling out new models, *Dallas Morning News*, January 4, D2.

39. Title 9 Sports, 1997, *General Merchandise Catalog*, December, 12.

40. K. Labich, 1994, Class in America, *Fortune*, February 7, 114–126.

41. E. Osnos, 1997, Cornucopia of choices proves confusing for today's consumer, *Dallas Morning News*, September 29, D1, D5.

42. Strong holiday sales enable Gadzooks to expand, 1996, *Dallas Morning News*, January 4, D11; M. Halkias, 1995, To buy for—at least today, *Dallas Morning News*, October 14, F1, F2.

43. Halkias, To buy for, F2.

44. R. Coleman, 1997, Slow teen sales force Gadzooks to trim forecast, *Dallas Morning News*, July 22, D1, D5.

45. F. Rose and J. R. Emshwiller, 1997, Guess, "coolness" fading, plans sultry ads, *Wall Street Journal*, November 19, B4.

46. R. Jacob, 1995, How one red-hot retailer wins customer loyalty, *Fortune*, July 10, 72–79.

47. D. R. Cohen, 1997, Staples, *Value Line*, October 24, 1135.

48. R. McKenna, Real-time marketing; F. J. Gouillart and F. D. Sturdivant, 1994, Spend a day in the life of your customers, *Harvard Business Review* 72, no. 1: 116–125.

49. The future for strategy: An interview with Gary Hamel, 1993, *European Management Journal* 14: 179–191.

50. Sprint, 1994, *1994 Annual Report to Shareholders*, 1.

51. G. A. Niemond, 1997, International Business Machines, *Value Line*, October 24, 1099.

52. Honda Motor Company, 1997, *Honda Motor Company Home Page*, December 6, http://www.honda.com.

53. Trendy yet traditional, 1997, *The Financial Times*, November 14, 19.

54. M. E. Porter, 1985, *Competitive Advantage* (New York: The Free Press), 26.

55. M. E. Porter, 1996, What is strategy? *Harvard Business Review* 74, no. 6: 61–78.

56. Campbell and Alexander, What's wrong with strategy? 43; G. Colvin, 1997, The changing art of becoming unbeatable, *Fortune*, November 24, 299–300.

57. M. E. Porter, 1994, Toward a dynamic theory of strategy, in R. P. Rumelt, D. E. Schendel, and D. J. Teece (eds.), *Fundamental Issues in Strategy* (Boston: Harvard Business School Press), 423–461.

58. Porter, What is strategy? 62.

59. Porter, *Competitive Advantage*, 15.

60. P. M. Wright, D. L. Smart, and G. C. McMahan, 1995, Matches between human resources and strategy among NCAA basketball teams, *Academy of Management Journal* 38: 1502–1074; Porter, Toward a dynamic theory, 434.

61. G. Bowley and H. Simonian, 1997, Volkswagen makes series of U-turns, *The Financial Times*, November 21, 19.

62. Porter, *Competitive Strategy*, 35–40.

63. Campbell and Alexander, What's wrong with strategy? 42.

64. J. C. Anderson and J. A. Narus, 1995, Capturing the value of supplementary services, *Harvard Business Review* 73, no. 1: 75–83.

65. C. Sirois, 1997, Unifi, Inc., *Value Line*, August 22, 1640.

66. J. Arbitman, 1997, Nova Corp., *Value Line*, September 26, 439.

67. S. Lubove, 1994, It ain't broke, but fix it anyway, *Forbes*, August 1, 56–60.

68. Ibid., 56.

69. J. Simmons, 1995, Budget hotels aren't bargains abroad, *Wall Street Journal*, November 17, B1, B4.

70. J. Friedland, 1997, Latin American retailer fights giants, *Wall Street Journal*, September 19, A10.

71. Porter, *Competitive Strategy*, 36.

72. Sirois, Unifi, Inc., 1640.

73. Lubove, It ain't broke, 57.

74. P. M. Seligman, 1997, Emerson Electric, *Value Line*, October 24, 1007.

75. L. Kraar, 1995, Acer's edge: PCs to go, *Fortune*, October 30, 192.

76. J. Moore and P. Burrows, 1997, A new attack plan for Acer America, *Business Week*, December 8, 82–83.

77. Intel filing suggests trouble at PC maker Packard Bell, 1995, *Dallas Morning News*, November 28, D6.

78. T. Zorn, 1995, Orville Redenbacher leaves premium legacy, *Dallas Morning News*, September 24, H5.

79. Day and Reibstein (eds.), *Wharton on Dynamic Competitive Strategy*, 10.

80. Porter, *Competitive Advantage*, 14.

81. C. Crossen, 1997, The crucial question for these noisy times may just be: "Huh?" *Wall Street Journal*, July 10, A1, A6; A. Faircloth, 1997, Ultra-Lux condos of the high seas, *Fortune*, November 10, 40; M. J. McCarthy, 1997, New maneuvers in the necktie-spot war, *Wall Street Journal*, July 13, B1.

82. It's Tommy's world, 1996, *Vanity Fair*, February, 110.

83. F. Rice, 1995, Hilfiger's bipartisan fashions are hot, *Fortune*, October 30, 32.

84. S. Chandler and A. T. Palmer, 1995, Bloomie's tries losing the attitude, *Business Week*, November 13, 52.

85. I. Sager and P. Burrows, 1997, I'm not gonna pay a lot for this Aptiva, *Business Week*, October 13, 59.

86. Porter, *Competitive Strategy*, 38.

87. Porter, *Competitive Advantage*, 15.

88. T. Maxon, 1997, General manager works her way up the line at RailTex, *Dallas Morning News*, July 20, H2.

89. Porter, *Competitive Advantage*, 15.

90. Ibid., 15–16.

91. New York Times News Service, 1997, AT&T may name chief today, *Dallas Morning News*, October 20, D1, D4.

92. Rally's Hamburgers Inc., 1995, *Wall Street Journal*, December 6, B8.

93. N. J. Perry, 1992, Hit'em where they used to be, *Fortune*, October 19, 112–113.

94. A. Goldstein, 1997, PC maker cutting staff 37%, *Dallas Morning News*, December 4, D1, D12.

95. M. Halkias, 1995, Blush is on at Sally Beauty, *Dallas Morning News*, October 23, D1, D4.

96. L. Crawford, 1997, The bullet-proof fashions to die for on wild frontier of Mexico's drug war, *The Financial Times*, November 15, 132; A. Dworkin, 1997, Hewing a housing trend, *Dallas Morning News*, July 21, D1, D4; *The Financial Times*, 1997, A cosmopolitan crust, November 23, II; D. Weisgall, 1997, Buying time, *Fortune*, September 8, 192.

97. N. Harris, 1997, Home Depot: Beyond do-it-yourselfers, *Business Week*, June 30, 86–88; B. Sharav, 1997, Home Depot, *Value Line*, October 17, 888.

98. Insights presented in this section are drawn primarily from Dess, Gupta, Hennart and Hill, Conducting and integrating strategy research, 376–379.

99. W. K. Hall, 1980, Survival strategies in a hostile environment, *Harvard Business Review* 58, no. 5: 75–87.

100. Dess, Gupta, Hennart, and Hill, Conducting and integrating strategy research, 377.

101. L. Kim and Y. Lim, 1988, Environment, generic strategies, and performance in a rapidly developing country: A taxonomic approach, *Academy of Management Journal* 31: 802–827.

102. Porter, *Competitive Advantage*, 18.

103. R. Henkoff, 1995, New management secrets from Japan—really, *Fortune*, November 27, 135–146.

104. R. Sanchez, 1995, Strategic flexibility in product competition, *Strategic Management Journal* 16 (Special Summer Issue): 140.

105. Ibid., 105.

106. D. M. Upton, 1995, What really makes factories flexible? *Harvard Business Review* 73, no. 4: 74–84.

107. J. Martin, 1997, Give 'em exactly what they want, *Fortune*, November 10, 283–85.

108. R. S. Russell and B. W. Taylor, III, 1998, *Operations Management*, Second Edition (Upper Saddle River, NJ: Prentice-Hall), 255–257; S. W. Flanders and W. J. Davis, 1995, Scheduling a flexible manufacturing system with tooling constraints: An actual case study, *Interfaces* 25, no. 2: 42–54.

109. D. Lei, M. A. Hitt, and J. D. Goldhar, 1996, Advanced manufacturing technology, organization design and strategic flexibility, *Organization Studies* 17: 501–523.

110. E. Mansfield, 1993, The diffusion of flexible manufacturing systems in Japan, Europe and the United States, *Management Science* 39: 149–159 as quoted in Sanchez, Strategic flexibility in product competition, 141.

111. Mansfield, The diffusion of flexible manufacturing systems, 153–154.

112. Ibid., 158.

113. R. Garud and S. Kotha, 1994, Using the brain as a metaphor to model flexible production systems, *Academy of Management Review* 19: 671–698.

114. S. A. Melnyk and D. R. Denzler, 1996, *Operations Management: A Value-Driven Approach* (Chicago: Irwin).

115. A. Baxter, 1997, Designs for survival, *The Financial Times*, November 20, 14.

116. T. Y. Choi and O. C. Behling, 1992, Top managers and TQM success: One more look after all these years, *Academy of Management Executive* XI, no. 1: 37–47; R. K. Reger, L. T. Gustafson, S. M. DeMarie, and J. V. Mullane, 1994, Reframing the organization: Why implementing total quality is easier said than done, *Academy of Management Review* 19: 565–584.

117. J. D. Westphal, R. Gulati, and S. M. Shortell, 1997, Customization or conformity? An institutional and network perspective on the content and consequences of TQM adoption, *Administrative Science Quarterly* 42: 366–394.

118. J. R. Hackman and R. Wagemen, 1995, Total quality management: Empirical, conceptual, and practical issues, *Administrative Science Quarterly* 40: 310.

119. Ibid., 311.

120. Porter, *Competitive Advantage*, 16.

121. A. Miller and G. G. Dess, 1993, Assessing Porter's (1980) model in terms of its generalizability, accuracy and simplicity, *Journal of Management Studies* 30: 553–585.

122. Porter, *Competitive Advantage*, 17.

123. L. Berton, 1995, Midsize accountants lose clients to firms both large and small, *Wall Street Journal*, November 15, A1, A4.

124. D. Clark, 1997, Coffee Station, Inc. to acquire Pasqua, a specialty chain, *Wall Street Journal*, June 13, A6.

Competitive Dynamics

CHAPTER 5

Learning Objectives

After reading this chapter, you should be able to:

1. Define the conditions for undertaking competitive actions.

2. Identify and explain factors affecting the probability that a competitor will initiate a response to competitive actions.

3. Describe first, second, and late movers and the advantages and disadvantages of each.

4. Understand the factors that contribute to the likelihood of a response to a competitive action.

5. Explain the effects of firm size, speed of strategic decision making and implementation, innovation, and quality on a firm's ability to take competitive action.

6. Understand three basic market situations as outcomes of competitive dynamics.

7. Discuss the types of competitive actions most relevant for each of the three stages of an industry evolution.

Global Competitive Dynamics among Steel Manufacturers

Global market conditions are changing rapidly for steel manufacturing companies. Facilities that were previously government owned in some countries are being privatized. Once privatized, these companies often develop an active export strategy. Minimills, once dismissed as minor players, are increasing their share of various domestic markets, especially in the United States. Relying on highly efficient technologies, minimills typically remelt scrap metal to make rough products. New technology is allowing them to make finer steel products, which traditionally were manufactured solely by vertically integrated steel companies. Additionally, the trend of following customers to other countries continues. In the 1980s, this competitive action was quite visible in the United States. As Japanese automobile manufacturers built U.S. facilities, many of their suppliers, including steel companies, followed. The practice of following one's customer to provide superior service has expanded to other industry settings. Producers of appliances, heavy equipment, and machine tools are globalizing their operations and challenging suppliers to accompany them or risk losing business. Whirlpool Corporation, for example, has manufacturing facilities in 13 countries and recently built a second plant in India to produce frost-free refrigerators.

http://www.nsc.co.jp

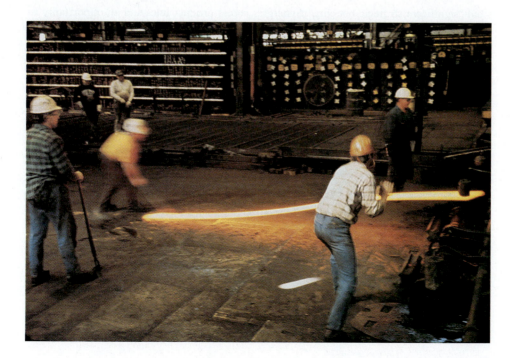

Steel companies with plants close to Whirlpool's operations increase the probability that they will earn the firm's business. The result of changes in global market conditions such as the ones cited here has increased rivalry among competitors.

In combination, this array of competitive actions and competitive responses is forcing steel manufacturers to globalize rapidly. Toward the end of the 1980s, for example, French steelmaker Usinor (the world's fourth largest manufacturer of crude steel and the largest supplier of steel to the European automobile manufacturing industry) decided to increase its global presence. Largely European-oriented at the time of this decision, Usinor chose to focus mainly on partnerships with local companies in the pursuit of globalization. Recently Usinor formed a relationship with Dofasco of Canada to build a galvanizing facility in Hamilton, Ontario. This effort will allow Usinor to supply galvanized sheet metal (one of the firm's most competitive products) for the first time to General Motors, Ford, and Chrysler on their home turf. The firm's chairman described this cooperative relationship as a "significant demonstration of the company's strategy of trying to globalize (its) strong points."

Large, vertically integrated steelmakers such as Bethlehem Steel are also taking strategic actions in response to the changing nature of the world's steel industry (the vertical integration strategy is discussed in Chapter 6). The second largest U.S. steelmaker, Bethlehem recently acquired Lukens. Analysts saw this acquisition as a reflection of the pressure on traditional integrated steelmakers to cut costs and close inefficient plants in the face of mounting competition from competitors located all over the world as well as from U.S. minimills. Bethlehem officials believed that ownership of Lukens, which was a leading North American specialty steel manufacturer producing stainless, alloy, and carbon products, would yield "significant strategic benefits." Synergies across product lines and an opportunity to reduce costs were the major anticipated benefits. For example, immediate plans called for closing one of Bethlehem's two steel plate mills and one of Lukens' in order to reduce costs and integrate product offerings.

Nippon Steel, Japan's largest steelmaker, also is making competitive decisions that are intended to enhance its global presence. Nippon has entered into a joint venture with Brazilian steel manufacturer Usiminas to produce steel for vehicle bodies. This venture (with 60 percent ownership by Usiminas and 40 percent by Nippon), is aimed at supplying a growing number of vehicle makers in South America, particularly Brazil, with high-grade steel products. Affected adversely by declining demand in its home markets and in other Asian markets as the 1990s came to a close, Nippon Steel remains interested in establishing other global operations to enhance its competitiveness.

Other firms competing in the world's increasingly globalized steel industry are also initiating competitive actions in light of environmental changes and the resulting competitive challenges that are facing them. For instance, British Steel PLC agreed to merge its production of large-diameter pipes into Europipe GmbH, which is the pipe-producing joint venture between German steel conglomerate Mannesmann AG and Usinor. Company officials indicated that this merger would help the firms cover a wider market spectrum, allowing Europipe to supply large-diameter pipes across the entire range of qualities and sizes.

Viewed collectively, the array of competitive actions being taken by steelmakers is likely to increase dramatically the rivalrous actions among these companies throughout the world.

SOURCE: M. Marshall, 1998, British Steel to merge unit into Europipe, *Wall Street Journal*, January 20, A14; N. Tait, 1998, Bethlehem increases bid for Lukens, *Financial Times*, January 6, 14; *Lukens Home Page*, 1998, January 21, http://www.lukens.com; *Usinor Home Page*, 1998, January 21, http://www.usinor.com; C. Adams, 1997, Steelmakers scramble in a race to become global powerhouse, *Wall Street Journal*, August 26, A1, A10; M. Nakamoto, 1997, Nippon Steel move in Brazil, *Financial Times*, December 15, 20; D. Owen and S. Wagstyl, 1997, French steel company targets US car industry, *Financial Times*, December 18, 13; R. Waters, 1997, Bethlehem pays $400m for Lukens, *Financial Times*, December 16, 20.

Characteristics and conditions associated with the global steel industry demonstrate the type of competitive landscape facing most firms as the twenty-first century nears. More volatile and unpredictable, companies competing in this landscape must learn how to cope successfully with the challenges presented by discontinuous environmental changes, the increasing globalization of their industries, and the array of competitive actions and competitive responses that are being taken by aggressive competitors.[1] In addition, top-level managers must be willing to make the type of difficult decisions that are called for by the nature of competitors' actions and responses. In fact, some believe that one of the most important skills that will be linked to strategic competitiveness in the twenty-first century will be managers' willingness and perhaps even eagerness to make significant, and sometimes painful decisions. Many of these decisions will be necessitated by the competitive dynamics affecting the firm's operations.[2]

As explained in the opening case, Bethlehem Steel's recent competitive actions are being influenced by the efforts of competitors to exploit their individual and unique competitive advantages in the pursuit of strategic competitiveness. The importance of Bethlehem's intention to reduce its overall costs, at least partially through the acquisition of Lukens, is supported by the competitive actions being considered by two minimill competitors.

In 1998's first calendar quarter, U.S.-based Nucor Corp. and Regina, Saskatchewan's, Ipsco Inc. were strongly considering building new mills to roll steel plate. Interestingly, both steelmakers acknowledged that the steel plate market was not expected to grow much and that the boost in manufacturing capability created by the new mills would result in production overcapacity on an industry-wide basis. To describe the reason for this competitive action, an Ipsco executive stated the following: "We assume steel is mature. We'd build because we think we'd be low-cost and high-quality and somebody would be knocked out of the market. We think we can take over a share of the market somebody else has." The "somebody else" could be Bethlehem Steel. Both new plants would be built in the eastern or southern United States, locations that would put the plants in approximately the same geographic market as Bethlehem's plate mill in Sparrows Point, Maryland. Already recognized as an inefficient facility, some analysts believed that Bethlehem would close the Sparrows Point plant if Nucor and Ipsco were to build their new facilities.[3]

INCREASED RIVALRY IN THE NEW COMPETITIVE LANDSCAPE

Conditions in the new competitive landscape are increasing competitive rivalry and require many companies (including steelmakers, as described previously) to compete differently to achieve strategic competitiveness and earn above-average returns. For instance, the current nature of competition for bus manufacturers (such as Daimler-Benz, Volvo, Scania, Fiat, Iveco, and Renault) is quite different from the past. One of the last big manufacturing industries to experience the worldwide changes of modernization and industry rationalization, some bus manufacturers are buying market share through acquisitions. Volvo, for example, purchased Carrus, which had been the largest independent manufacturer of bus bodies in the Nordic region. Renault now sells buses to price-sensitive European buyers from Karossa, the Czech bus and coachmaker, in which it purchased a controlling interest. Another competitive action being taken in the global bus industry is to scour international markets for customers to compensate for tougher conditions in the firm's domestic market. Mercedes-Benz, for instance, views Turkey as an important market as well as an export base for eastern Europe and the former Soviet Union.[4]

In the entertainment industry, megaplex theaters are changing the nature of competition. Transforming the way customers pick and watch movies, companies are scrambling to build theaters with as many as 30 screens. With each megaplex costing up to $30 million to build, movie entertainment at the local theater is becoming a capital-intensive business. The chairman of Regal Cinemas Inc., the fifth largest chain in the United States, believes that "middle-tier companies with limited resources have to wonder how they are going to play" in what the entertainment industry is becoming. Competitive actions being taken in this industry are as tactical as increasing individual ticket prices and as strategic as consolidation. (Regal, for example, recently purchased Cobb Theaters to gain control of the firm's 643 screens.) Other actions being considered by companies trying to differentiate themselves from competitors include building units with amenities such as babysitting services and cappuccino bars in addition to a still larger number of screens.[5]

Several reasons account for the changes in competition taking place in many industries.[6] First, in most industries, an emphasis on a single domestic market is decreasing; in its place is an increasing emphasis on international and global markets. This is certainly the outcome being witnessed among the world's automobile manufacturers. Thought to be a brutally competitive industry, the share of the U.S. market held by that nation's Big Three auto companies (General Motors, Ford, and Chrysler) continues to decline. In fact, these companies' combined share of car sales in the United States fell from 74 percent in 1985 to 61 percent at the end of 1997. Some analysts predicted that without successful competitive responses and innovative competitive actions, the Big Three's market share could decline another five percentage points by the end of 2002.[7]

Contributing partially to the decline in domestic market share held by the U.S. Big Three auto companies were ineffective decisions regarding the nature of competitive practices and the interests of consumers with respect to several product lines, including small cars.[8] However, a global managerial mind-set (see Chapter 1) that calls for an emphasis on international markets also accounts for some of this decline in market share. Toyota executives appear to operate from such a mind-set.

Currently the third largest auto manufacturer in the world, Toyota is initiating a series of competitive actions that is intended to result in the firm replacing Ford Motor Company as the world's second largest car company. Viewing the world as its marketplace, the firm wants to supply 65 percent of its sales in large markets such as the United States and Europe from local sources rather than from Japan. To reach this goal, Toyota is engaged in what has been labeled "breakneck" expansion plans in both the United States and Europe. As a result, Toyota will be able to produce more than one million units in its North American plants by 1999.[9] Furthermore, Toyota believes that its current competitive actions will allow it to increase its European market share to 5 percent (from its current 3 percent share) in the near future. (Toyota holds 10 percent of the U.S. market and between 20 percent and 30 percent of Asian markets.)[10]

As these examples demonstrate, once the firm begins to look outside its domestic market to enhance its strategic competitiveness, the effective managerial mind-set expands quickly to include consideration of the need to compete in multiple global markets. This seems to be the case for Mahindra & Mahindra, India's largest manufacturer of utility vehicles and tractors. With 70 percent and 27 percent domestic market shares, respectfully, this firm intends to establish a global presence within five to six years. Following initial introductions of some of its products to the southern parts of the United States, Mahindra & Mahindra plans to move into African, South American, and eventually, European markets.[11]

Significant advances in communications technologies that allow more effective coordination across operations in multiple markets and faster decision making and competitive responses are the second reason for the changes taking place in many industries' competitive landscapes.[12] Third, new technology and innovations, particularly in the information technology and computer industries, have changed competitive landscapes in ways that facilitate small and medium-sized businesses' efforts to compete more effectively. Finally, the increasing number of agreements to allow free trade across country borders (such as the 1993 North American Free Trade Agreement, NAFTA) is facilitating a growing cross-border focus.[13]

The changing competitive landscape even has former competitors cooperating in such areas as new technology development and forming strategic alliances to compete against other competitors (as discussed in Chapter 9).[14] For example, a set of companies has formed two major alliances to battle for a Latin American pay television audience that is estimated to be as many as 45 million homes. Composed of Rupert Murdoch's News Corporation, Mexico's Grupo Televisa, and Brazil's Organizacoes Globo, Sky Latin America is the larger of the two alliances. Competing against this cooperative arrangement is Galaxy Latin America, a combination of the Cisneros group of Venezuela, Grupo Abril of Brazil, and Multivison, a family-run Mexican media company, and Hughes Electronics.[15] Global alliances have also been formed among many of the world's telephone companies to pursue business in Europe.[16] (Additional information about some of these telecommunications alliances is presented in a Strategic Focus in Chapter 9.) Increasingly, cooperative R&D arrangements are also being developed in the new competitive landscape. These arrangements are vehicles through which firms overcome their resource constraints by acquiring skills and capabilities from alliance partners.[17]

This chapter focuses on competitive dynamics. The essence of this important topic is that a firm's strategies and their implementation (see Figure 1.1) are dynamic in nature. Actions taken by one firm often elicit responses from competi-

165

tors. These responses, in turn, typically result in responses from the firm that acted originally as illustrated by the opening case concerned with the competitive actions begin taken by some of the world's steel manufacturers. The series of competitive actions and competitive responses among firms competing within a particular industry creates **competitive dynamics**. Such dynamic competitive interaction often shapes the competitive position of firms undertaking the business-level strategies described in the previous chapter and to some extent, corporate strategies (product diversification, international diversification, and cooperative strategies) described in later chapters. Thus, because of the reality of competitive dynamics, the effectiveness of any type of strategy is determined not only by the initial move, but also by how well the firm "anticipates and addresses the moves and countermoves of competitors and shifts in customer demands over time."[18]

> **Competitive dynamics** results from a series of competitive actions and competitive responses among firms competing within a particular industry.

To discuss the part of the strategic management process called competitive dynamics, we introduce a model (see later discussion of Figure 5.1) of competitive dynamics; the remainder of the chapter describes it. Firms able to understand and deal successfully with competitive dynamics increase the probability of avoiding US Airways' recent situation. Caught in a competitive squeeze between lower-cost regional carriers, which were picking off the firm's best routes, and larger carriers with national and global route structures, US Airways lacked the resources to match, the company's executives were committed to finding a more attractive competitive position for their firm.[19]

After the overall model is introduced, we examine the factors that lead to competitive attack and potential response. This is followed by a discussion of the incentives of market leadership (first-mover advantages) and its disadvantages. We also discuss the advantages and disadvantages of followership (second or late movers). Once a competitive action is taken, a number of factors help determine the potential response. These factors are discussed next. We then examine firms' capabilities for attack and response, including firm size, speed of decision making, innovation, and product and process quality. Following these descriptions is a discussion of three different types of market competition (defined later as slow cycle, standard cycle, and fast cycle) that result from competitive interaction. In particular, we explore the nature of rivalry and propose strategies for competition in fast-cycle markets where competitive rivalry has escalated to an intense level and where the new competitive landscape is probably the most evident. This discussion examines the strategy of competitive disruption, in which firms capitalize on temporary compared to sustained competitive advantage by cannibalizing their past new product entry to introduce the next product or process innovation. Finally, we describe competitive rivalry outcomes as industries move through the emerging, growth, and maturity stages.

MODEL OF COMPETITIVE DYNAMICS AND RIVALRY

> **Competitive rivalry** exists when two or more firms jockey with one another in the pursuit of an advantageous market position.

Over time, firms competing in an industry are involved with a number of competitive actions and competitive responses.[20] **Competitive rivalry** exists when two or more firms jockey with one another in the pursuit of an advantageous market position. Competitive rivalry takes place between and among firms because one or more competitors feel pressure or see opportunities to improve their market position. Rivalry is possible because of competitive asymmetry. The principle of individual differences, competitive asymmetry exists when firms differ from one another in terms of their resources, capabilities, and core competencies (see Chapter 3) and in terms of the opportunities and threats in their industry and competitive environments (see Chapter 2). Strategies, and, especially business-level strategies, are formed to exploit the asymmetric relationships existing among competitors.[21]

In most industries, a firm's competitive actions have observable effects on its competitors and typically cause responses designed to counter the action.[22] In early 1998, for instance, Renault, France's largest car and truck manufacturer, announced plans to increase its output by 500,000 units a year through 2002. In addition, the carmaker indicated that it was committed to improving the efficiency of its manufacturing operations to reduce its overall costs. Renault's competitive decisions were made partly in response to Toyota's previously announced intention to build a new small-car manufacturing plant in France. Even in light of chronic overcapacity in the world's automobile manufacturing industry, Renault officials believed that the firm's response was required for it to become more competitive in its home market and to prevent Renault from falling behind more efficient rivals such as Toyota.[23]

As the example of competitive actions and competitive responses among the world's steel manufacturers demonstrates, firms are mutually interdependent with their competitors.[24]

Mutual interdependence among firms means that strategic competitiveness and above-average returns result only when companies recognize that their strategies are not implemented in isolation from their competitors' actions and responses. Eastman Kodak Co. and Fuji Photo Film Co., for example, continue to engage in a series of competitive actions and responses in efforts to establish competitive advantages. Competition in the United States with Fuji has affected Kodak's performance. To reduce the decline in its domestic market share, Kodak priced its film products aggressively during the 1997 Christmas season. Company officials indicated that this pricing decision boosted the firm's U.S. film sales 2 percent during the year's last quarter. Ted McGrath, president of Fuji's U.S. photo imaging operations, said, "Fuji is evaluating its 1998 strategy. We're not going to sit back and be submissive, but we're not going to do anything alarming."[25] Thus, because it affects strategic competitiveness and returns, firms are concerned about the pattern of competitive dynamics and the rivalry it creates.[26]

Figure 5.1 illustrates a summary model of interfirm rivalry and the likelihood of attack and response. As can be seen from the model, competitor analysis begins with analyzing competitor awareness and motivation to attack and respond to competitive action. *Awareness* refers to whether or not the attacking or responding firm is aware of the competitive market characteristics such as the market commonality and the resource similarity of a potential attacker or respondent (these terms are defined in a subsequent section).[27] Managers may have "blind spots" in their industry and competitor analyses due to underestimation or an inability to analyze these factors.[28] This may be the case in the U.S. blue-jeans market. Levi Strauss & Co.'s failure to pay close attention to changes in teenagers' interests appears to have contributed to the decline in the firm's share of its core market. In 1990, Levi had 30.9 percent of the U.S. blue jeans market; at the end of 1997, this percentage had declined to 18.7. During this time period, competition in this part of the clothing fashion industry intensified considerably, affecting Levi Strauss in the

167

Mutual interdependence among firms means that strategic competitiveness and above-average returns result only when companies recognize that their strategies are not implemented in isolation from their competitors' actions and responses.

FIGURE 5.1 *A Summary Model of Interfirm Rivalry: The Likelihood of Attack and Response*

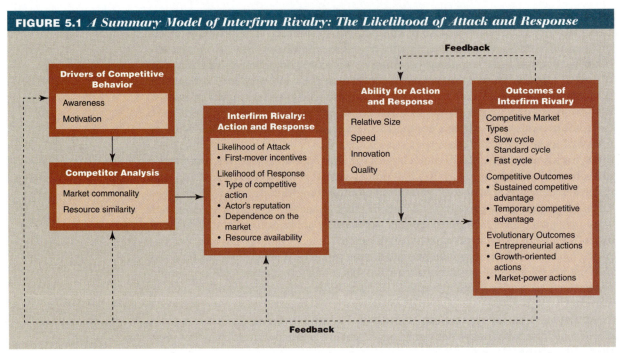

Source: Adapted from M. J. Chen, 1996, Competitor analysis and interfirm rivalry: Toward a theoretical integration, *Academy of Management Review* 21: 100–134.

process: "Top-end designers such as Tommy Hilfiger and Ralph Lauren have squeezed Levi on one end, while private labels sold by low-priced retailers such as J.C. Penney Co. and Sears Roebuck and Co. have come on strong from the other direction.[29] This lack of awareness may lead to such things as industry overcapacity and excessive competition.[30] *Motivation* relates to the incentives a firm has to attack and respond if attacked. A firm may perceive advantages to moving first, given the potential for interaction.

As Figure 5.1 suggests, both market commonality and resource similarity mediate the awareness and motivation to undertake actions and responses. The likelihood of action and response will result in the competitive outcomes. These outcomes, however, will be moderated by a firm's ability to undertake strategic actions and responses. Furthermore, Figure 5.1 illustrates that feedback from the nature of rivalry will also influence the nature of a competitor's view of the previous exchange and may change the nature of awareness and motivation.

Market Commonality

Many firms, for example, those in the airlines, chemical, pharmaceutical, breakfast cereals, and electronics industries, compete in the same multiple markets. In the brewery industry, many beer producers compete in the same regional markets.[31] Regional competition is also evident in international markets through "triad" competition or the necessity for multinational corporations to have businesses in Asia (traditionally Japan), Europe, and North America.[32] When multimarket overlap exists between firms, this presents opportunities for **multipoint competition**, a situation in which firms compete against each other simultaneously in several product or geographic markets.[33] In the airline industry for instance, there are opportunities for multipoint competition. The three largest U.S. airlines, United, American, and Delta, have substantial market overlap and therefore substantial awareness and motivation to respond to competitive actions. Research has shown that such commonality reduces the likelihood of competitive interaction in the industry.[34] Because these three airlines operate in many common markets, competitive peace will reign until one firm makes a competitive move, then the competitive response will be swift.[35]

There are many other examples of firms whose competitive actions involve them in situations of multipoint competition. For example, Bayerische Motoren Werke (BMW) and Honda Motor Company engage in multipoint competition as they both manufacture and sell cars and motorcycles. Hoechst AG and DuPont compete against each other in the specialty chemicals and plastic markets. Compaq, IBM, and Dell encounter multipoint competition as they compete in the home and business personal computer markets and the expanding server market.[36]

Resource Similarity

The intensity of competitive rivalry often is based on a potential response and is of great concern for an attacker. An attacker may not be motivated to target a rival that seems likely to retaliate. This is especially true for firms with strategic resources similar to those of a potential attacker.[37] (Resource similarity refers to the extent of resource overlap between two firms.)[38] In addition, resource dissimilarity likely plays a vital role in a competitor's motivation to attack or respond. In fact, "the greater is the resource imbalance between the acting firm and competitors or potential responders, the greater will be the delay in response."[39] Although the degree of market commonality is quite visible to the strategists of both firms, strategic resources, because of their possible indeterminable nature (due to, for example, causal ambiguity and social complexity as described in Chapter 3), tend to be much less identifiable. The difficulty in identifying and understanding relationships among the competing firms' resources (including its capabilities and core competencies) also contributes to response delays, especially in instances of resource dissimilarity.

Coca-Cola and Pepsi's decisions to compete in the bottled water market demonstrate an imbalance in resources between the acting firms (Coke and Pepsi) and the potential responding companies (Perrier Group, Suntory International, McKesson, Great Brands of Europe, and Crystal Geyser). Attracted by the then-current size ($3.6 billion in 1997) and rapid growth (8 percent annually) of the bottled water market, Coke and Pepsi decided to engage the industry's incumbents in competitive battle. Seeking to become the nation's number-one bottled water company, Pepsi introduced Aquafina in 1997. In addition to the several bottled waters it sells outside the United States, Coca-Cola intended to introduce such products in the U.S. market no later than 1998. In response to these intended competitive actions, an industry analyst observed, "Anytime Coke and Pepsi get into the market, they're going to shake things up." Indications are that executives at the Perrier Group are preparing their firm's competitive responses to the two giant firms' market entries. Kim Jeffery, president of the Perrier Group, suggested that "no one's going to dethrone us. The competition will only make us better."

multipoint competition occurs when firms compete against each other simultaneously in several product or geographic markets.

169

However, the resource dissimilarity between the Perrier Group and Coca-Cola and Pepsi may delay initiation of the competitive responses the company will take to protect its key bottled water brands—Arrowhead, Poland Spring, and Great Bear.[40]

LIKELIHOOD OF ATTACK

A **competitive action** is a significant competitive move taken by a firm that is designed to gain a competitive advantage in a market.

Although awareness and motivation to respond are derived largely from competitor analysis of market commonality and resource similarity, there are strong incentives to be the first mover in a competitor battle if the attacking firm believes it has potential to win. A **competitive action** is a significant competitive move taken by a firm that is designed to gain a competitive advantage in a market.[41] Some competitive actions are large and significant; others are small and designed to help fine-tune or implement a strategy. The first mover in a competitive interaction may be able to gain above-average returns while competitors consider potential countermoves. Furthermore, the first mover may be able to deter counterattack if given enough time. Therefore, there are significant incentives to be a first mover and the order of each competitive action and response influences an industry's competitive dynamics. Of greatest importance are first movers, second movers, and late movers.

First, Second, and Late Movers

A **first mover** is a firm that takes an initial competitive action.

A **first mover** is a firm that takes an initial competitive action. The concept of first movers has been influenced by economist Joseph Schumpeter. In particular, he believed that firms achieve competitive advantage through entrepreneurial discovery and innovative competitive action.[42] In general, first movers "allocate funds for product innovation and development, aggressive advertising, and advanced research and development."[43] Through competitive actions such as these, first movers hope to gain a competitive advantage. For example, Mitsubishi Consumer Electronics America Inc. decided to discontinue selling tube-based television sets in the United States in the latter part of 1998. Seeking to "stake out a leading role in digital TV," Mitsubishi intended to concentrate all of its technological skills on the development of advanced sets.[44] The merger between Renaissance Capital Group, a Western-operated investment bank, and Russia's International Co. for Finance & Investment (ICFI) resulted in Russia's largest investment bank. Combining Renaissance's access to global capital with ICFI's extensive domestic operations made the bank the first in Russia to compete on an international scale. The merged unit was hopeful that its operational capacities would result in first mover advantages.[45]

Several competitive advantages can accrue to the firm that is first to initiate a competitive action. Successful actions allow a firm to earn above-average returns until other competitors are able to respond effectively. In addition, first movers have the opportunity to gain customer loyalty, thereby making it difficult for responding firms to capture customers. For instance, Harley-Davidson has been able to maintain a competitive lead in large motorcycles due to intense customer loyalty. Across time, though, the competitive advantage of a first mover begins to erode (recall from discussions in Chapter 1 that every competitive advantage can be imitated eventually). Consider Harley-Davidson's situation as an example. Since its turnaround in the early 1980s, Harley-Davidson has set the standard for loud,

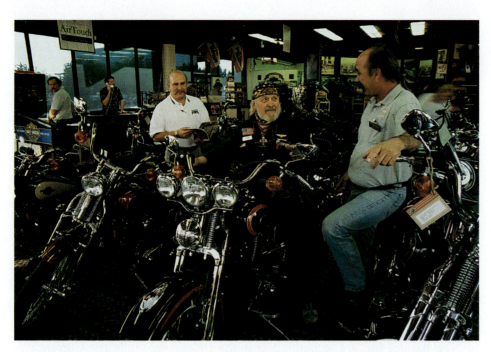

Harley-Davidson has been able to maintain a competitive lead in large motorcycles because of intense customer loyalty.

171

low-riding, heavyweight V-twin cruisers. For most of the past 20 years, the firm has derived competitive benefits from being the first mover in its market segment and as a result of emphasizing its reputation and brand name as competitive advantages. Recently, however, competitors are achieving some success in competing against Harley. Big Dog Motorcycles is one of several new U.S. motorcycle manufacturers trying to produce products that emulate the characteristics and performance attributes of Harley's cruisers. For the most part, these competitors seek to offer customers a product that is of quality similar to Harley's, but at a lower price.[46]

The advantages and their duration vary by type of competitive action and industry. First-mover advantages also vary based on the ease with which competitors can imitate the action. The more difficult and costly an action is to imitate, the longer a firm may receive the benefits of being a first mover. When core competencies are the foundation of a competitive action, first-mover advantages tend to last for a longer period of time. Core competence-based competitive actions have a high probability of resulting in a sustained competitive advantage.

However, potential disadvantages may result from being the first firm to initiate a competitive action. Chief among these is the degree of risk taken by first movers. Risk is high because it is not easy to predict the amount of success a particular competitive action will produce prior to its initiation.[47] Oftentimes, first movers have high development costs. Second movers can avoid these costs through reverse engineering (taking apart a new product and then reassembling it to learn how it works). Another potential disadvantage of being a first mover may exist if the market in which the firm is competing is dynamic and uncertain. In other words, the extent and range of marketplace competition heighten the potential risk. In fact, in a highly uncertain market, it may be more appropriate to be a second or late mover.

A **second mover** is a firm that responds to a first mover's competitive action, often through imitation or a move designed to counter the effects of the action.

A **second mover** is a firm that responds to a first mover's competitive action, often through imitation or a move designed to counter the effects of the action.

When the second mover responds quickly to a first mover's competitive action, it may earn some of the first-mover advantages without experiencing the potential disadvantages. For example, a fast second mover may gain some of the returns and obtain a portion of the initial customers and thereby customer loyalty, while avoiding some of the risks encountered by the first mover. The firm taking a second action as a competitive response to the first mover can do so after evaluating customers' reactions to the first mover's action.[48] To be a successful first or fast second mover, a company must be able to analyze its markets and identify critical strategic issues.[49]

In some instances, it may not be possible to move quickly in response to a first mover's action. For example, if the first mover introduces a sophisticated new product and competitors have not undertaken similar research and development, considerable time may be required to respond effectively. Therefore, there are some risks involved in being a follower, as opposed to a leader, in the market. There are no blueprints for first-mover success. Followers may be able to respond without significant market development costs by learning from a first mover's successes and mistakes. Thus, the actions and outcomes of the first firm to initiate a competitive action may provide a more effective blueprint for second and later movers.[50] Table 5.1 provides a list of classic cases where imitators were able to overcome the pioneers' early entries.

New Balance Inc. is a second mover in the athletic shoe industry. Currently, it spends only $4 million annually to advertise its products. Mark Coogan, a marathoner who placed forty-first in the 1996 Olympics in his event, is the firm's best-known endorser. In contrast, Nike spent $1 billion on sponsored endorsements and advertising during 1997; in the same year for the same purposes, Reebok spent over $400 million.[51] Unlike Nike and Reebok, New Balance's market share is increasing rapidly. In fact, while the industry's sales increased 3 percent in 1997, New Balance recorded a sales gain of 16 percent.

Accounting for New Balance's success as a second mover is its ability to satisfy baby boomers' needs. The firm's target market is demonstrated by customers' average ages—Nike (25), Reebok (33), and New Balance (42). As a second mover, the firm's shoes are not particularly innovative as compared to industry leader Nike. In contrast to many competitors that introduce new models roughly every six weeks, New Balance introduces a new one approximately every 17 weeks. New Balance's competitive success as a second mover appears to be based on its ability to offer high-quality products at moderate prices but in multiple-sized widths. Unlike most companies, which produce shoes in two widths—medium and wide—New Balance offers customers five choices, ranging from a narrow AA to an expansive EEEE. The varying widths is a valued competitive feature, in that about 20 to 30 percent of the U.S. population has narrower, or wider, than average feet.[52]

A **late mover** is a firm that responds to a competitive action, but only after considerable time has elapsed after the first mover's action and the second mover's response. Although some type of competitive response may be more effective than no response, late movers tend to be poorer performers and often are weak competitors.

LIKELIHOOD OF RESPONSE

Once firms take competitive action, the success of the particular action will often be determined by the likelihood and nature of response. A **competitive response**

TABLE 5.1 *Cases Where Second/Late Movers Surpassed First Movers*

Product	First Movers	Second/Late Movers	Comments
35mm cameras	Leica (1925) Contrax (1932) Exacta (1936)	Canon (1934) Nikon (1946) Nikon SLR (1959)	The German pioneers were the technology and market leader for decades until the Japanese copied their technology, improved on it, and lowered prices. The pioneers then failed to react and ended up as incidental players.
Ballpoint pens	Reynolds (1945) Eversharp (1946)	Parker "Jotter" (1954) Bic (1960)	The pioneers disappeared when the fad first ended in the late 1940s. Parker entered eight years later. Bic entered last and sold pens as cheap disposables.
Caffeine-free soft drinks	Canada Dry's "Sport" (1967) Royal Crown's RC1000 (1980)	Pepsi Free (1982) Caffeine-free Coke, Tab (1983)	The pioneers had a three-year head start on Coke and Pepsi but could not hope to match the distribution and promotional advantages of the giants.
CAT scanners (computed axial tomography)	EMI (1972)	Pfizer (1974) Technicare (1975) GE (1976) Johnson & Johnson (1978)	The pioneers had no experience in the medical equipment industry. Imitators ignored its patents and drove the pioneer out of business with marketing, distribution, and financial advantages, as well as extensive industry experience.
Commercial jet aircraft	deHavilland Comet 1 (1952)	Boeing 707 (1954) Douglas DC-8 (1955)	The British pioneer rushed to market with a jet that crashed frequently. Boeing followed with safer, larger, and more powerful jets unsullied by tragic crashes.
Diet soft drinks	Kirsch's No-Cal (1952) Royal Crown's Diet Rite Cola (1962)	Pepsi's Patio Cola (1963) Coke's Tab (1963) Diet Pepsi (1964) Diet Coke (1982)	The pioneers could not match the distribution advantages of Coke and Pepsi. Nor did they have the money needed for massive promotional campaigns.
Dry beer	Asahi (1987)	Kirin, Sapporo, and Suntory in Japan (1988) Michelob Dry (1988) Bud Dry (1989)	The Japanese pioneer could not match Anheuser-Busch's financial, marketing, and distribution advantages in the U.S. market.
Light beer	Rheingold's Gablinger's (1966) Meister Brau Lite (1967)	Miller Lite (1975) Natural Light (1977) Coors Light (1978) Bud Light (1982)	The pioneers entered nine years before Miller and sixteen years before Bud Light, but financial problems drove both out of business. Marketing and distribution determined the outcome. Costly legal battles were commonplace.
MRI (magnetic resonance imaging)	Fonar (1978)	Johnson & Johnson's Technicare (1981) General Electric (1982)	The tiny pioneer faced the huge medical equipment suppliers, who easily expanded into the MRI arena. The pioneer could not hope to match their tremendous market power.
Operating systems personal computers	CP/M (1974)	MS-DOS (1981) Microsoft Windows (1985)	The pioneer created the early standard but did not upgrade for the IBM-PC. Microsoft bought an imitative upgrade and became the new standard. Windows entered later and borrowed heavily from predecessors, then emerged as the leading interface.
Personal computers	MITS Altair 8800 (1975) Apple II (1977) Radio Shack (1977)	IBM-PC (1981) Compaq (1982) Dell (1984) Gateway (1985)	The pioneers created computers for hobbyists, but when the market turned to business uses, IBM entered and quickly dominated, using its reputation and its marketing and distribution skills. The second movers then copied IBM's standard and sold at lower prices.
Pocket calculators	Bowmar (1971)	Texas Instruments (1972)	The pioneer assembled calculators using TI's integrated circuits. TI controlled Bowmar's costs, which rose as calculator prices fell. Vertical integration was the key.

173

Source: S. P. Schnaars, 1994, *Managing Imitation Strategies: How Later Entrants Seize Markets from Pioneers* (New York: The Free Press).

A **late mover** is a firm that responds to a competitive action, but only after considerable time has elapsed after the first mover's action and the second mover's response.

A **competitive response** is a move taken to counter the effects of an action by a competitor.

is a move taken to counter the effects of an action by a competitor. Firms considering offensive action need to be cognizant of the potential response from competition. An offensive action may escalate rivalry to a point where action becomes self-defeating and an alternative strategy may be necessary. A *deescalation strategy* is an attempt to reduce overly heated competition that has become self-defeating. As Figure 5.1 shows, the probability of a competitor response to a competitive action is based on the type of action, the reputation of the competitor taking the action, the competitor's dependence on the market, and competitor resource availability.

Type of Competitive Action

A **strategic action** represents a significant commitment of specific and distinctive organization resources; it is difficult to implement and to reverse.

The two types of competitive actions are strategic and tactical.[53] A **strategic action** represents a significant commitment of specific and distinctive organizational resources; it is difficult to implement and to reverse. The introduction of an innovative product to a market, Compaq Computer's purchase of Digital Equipment Corporation, and the recent decision by some high-tech companies to allocate significant financial resources to build brand names for their products are all examples of strategic actions.

Manufacturers of the hardware and software that drive computer networks are becoming powerful global competitors, but few of these companies are known outside of the business markets in which their products are sold. Recently three of the largest firms in the network-computing business (Cisco Systems, Oracle, and Sun Microsystems) concluded that their future success requires recognition and admiration by a wider public. Expensive in nature (analysts estimate that the three firms collectively will spend billions of dollars), each company's newly developed long-term marketing campaign is intended to promote its image with the general public.

The effort to build a brand name for its products was inspired by the success of the "Intel Inside" campaign. Market research results suggest that for many PC buyers, the Intel Inside logo that is positioned on computer manufacturers' products has become a "trustmark"—a trademark on which a significant part of the purchase decision is based. Cisco, Oracle, and Sun hope to duplicate Intel's brand-image accomplishment among buyers of computer networks. Oracle, for example, which is the world's second largest software firm, chose the slogan "Oracle—Enabling the Information Age" for its advertising campaign. Initially, Sun used the logo "100% Pure Java" to support its brand-building efforts; Cisco coined the Cisco Powered Network (CPN) logo for the same purpose.[54] Because of the expense and the commitment being made to the marketplace, each firm's decision to enter into brand-building marketing campaigns is an example of a strategic competitive action.

A **tactical action** is taken to fine-tune a strategy; it involves fewer and more general organizational resources and is relatively easy to implement and reverse.

In contrast to strategic actions, a **tactical action** is taken to fine-tune a strategy; it involves fewer and more general organizational resources and is relatively easy to implement and reverse. A price increase in a particular market (e.g., in airfares) is an example of a tactical action. This action involves few organizational resources (e.g., communicating new prices/changing prices on products), its implementation is relatively easy, and it can be reversed (through a price reduction, for example) in a relatively short period of time.

174

Responses to a strategic action, as compared to a tactical action, are more difficult because they require more organizational resources and are more time consuming. As compared to strategic actions, tactical actions usually have more immediate effects. The announcement of a price increase in a price-sensitive market such as airlines could have immediate effects on competitors. As such, it is not uncommon to find airlines responding quickly to a competitor's price change, particularly if the announced change represents a price decrease because without a response other airlines may lose market share.[55]

Airline companies also respond quickly to tactical actions taken regarding frequent flier programs. For example, American Airline's recent creation of an Executive Platinum level of service for the "ultra frequent flyer" was imitated quickly by Trans World Airlines.[56] Rapid competitive responses are often initiated in low-cost goods and services markets. Cash flow is critical to firms (such as airline companies) competing in these markets, and consumers are price-sensitive because there is relatively little differentiation in the services provided. Moreover, attempted differentiated efforts tend to be imitated rapidly. In addition to imitations of frequent flyer program changes, those competing in the airline industry in the latter part of the 1990s imitated actions being taken to (1) refurbish airplanes, (2) set aside the best seats for the firm's best customers, (3) add food to more flights and increase the amount of food on flights currently receiving such service, and (4) assure on-time arrivals and effective and safe handling of luggage.[57]

Not all competitive actions will elicit or require a response from competitors. On the whole, there are more competitive responses to tactical than to strategic actions.[58] It is usually easier to respond to tactical than to strategic actions and sometimes more necessary, at least in the short term. For example, responding to changes in a competitor's frequent flier program is much easier and requires far fewer resources as compared to responding to a major competitor's decision to upgrade its fleet of jets and to form strategic alliances to enter new markets.

Actor's Reputation

An action (either strategic or tactical) taken by a market leader is likely to serve as a catalyst to a larger number of and faster responses from competitors and to a higher probability of imitation of the action. In other words, firms are more likely to imitate the actions of a competitor that is a market leader. For instance, Anheuser-Busch's decision to deepen its ties with Mexican brewer Grupo Modelo is a competitive action that may elicit rapid and imitative actions. By increasing its ownership position in Modelo to 37 percent, U.S. market leader Anheuser-Busch signaled to competitors its renewed commitment to broaden its profit base and to establish Budweiser as a global brand.[59] Similarly, FedEx's merger with Caliber System is the type of competitive action that will be evaluated carefully by the firm's competitors. With Caliber System's RPS subsidiary now in its fold, analysts thought that FedEx would be able to grow more rapidly than it could have alone. Using RPS's fleet of 13,500 trucks, FedEx enhanced its ability to compete against United Parcel Service, "because both companies move nonexpress parcels primarily by ground when they don't absolutely, positively have to arrive by the next day"[60] (additional information about UPS appears in Chapter 6).

175

Firms also often react quickly to imitate successful competitor actions. An example is the personal computer market, where IBM quickly dominated the market as a second mover but was also imitated by Compaq, Dell, and Gateway (see Table 5.1). Alternatively, firms that have a history as strategic players that take risky, complex, and unpredictable actions are less likely to solicit responses to and imitation of their actions.[61] Finally, firms that are known to be price predators (frequently cutting prices to hurt competitors and obtain market share, only to raise prices later) also do not elicit a large number of responses or imitation. In fact, there is less imitation and a much slower response to price predators than to either of the other two types of firms (market leader and strategic player).[62]

Dependence on the Market

Firms with a high dependency on a market in which a competitive action is taken are more likely to respond to that action. For example, firms with a large amount of total sales from one industry are more likely to respond to a particular competitive action taken in their primary industry than is a firm with businesses in multiple industries (e.g., conglomerate). Thus, if the type of action taken has a major effect on them, firms are likely to respond, regardless of whether it is a strategic or a tactical action. A pattern of competitive actions and competitive responses occurring between two firms that are highly dependent on their core market is described in the Strategic Focus about Burger King and McDonald's.

STRATEGIC FOCUS

Burger King and McDonald's: The Battle of Burgers and Fries

Burger King and McDonald's are both completely dependent on sales in the fast food industry. As such, it is not surprising that the firms monitor each other's strategic and tactical actions quite carefully. Moreover, competitive actions taken by one of these companies, whether strategic or tactical, almost certainly will result in a competitive response. Following are examples of such competitive actions and responses.

McDonald's is much larger than its counterpart. In the United States, McDonald's had almost 12,500 units at the beginning of 1998, compared to Burger King's total of about 7,500 in the same market at the same time. Burger King has 2,000-plus units outside the United States, which is substantially fewer than the over 10,000 units that bear the McDonald's name. But, recent experiences may suggest that being the biggest does not assure recording the best performance. In fact, difficulties at McDonald's in the latter part of the 1990s contributed to Burger King's willingness to engage in a series of competitive actions and competitive responses with McDonald's. Examples of McDonald's end-of-the-1990s woes include the following: (1) a low-fat hamburger that was launched in 1991 and abandoned in 1996, (2) the Arch Deluxe that was introduced in 1996 and whose future was in doubt in 1998 (the company even conceded that in consumer taste tests, the Arch Deluxe was not seen, at least by some survey participants, as delivering value versus Burger King's Whopper), and (3) the ineffectiveness of 1997's 55-cent promotion program. (Consumers were annoyed that 55-cent burgers, including the Big Mac, at one point, were available only when other full-priced food items were purchased simultaneously.)

Sensing that the firm might be more vulnerable to competitive attack as a result of these difficulties, Burger King took several actions. On August 28, 1997, the company launched the Big King. A direct competitor of McDonald's Big Mac, this was Burger King's first new sandwich offering since introducing the BK Broiler in 1990. A Big Mac lookalike, the Big King had 75 percent more beef and considerably less bread than the Big Mac. Describing the initial success of the product's introduction, Burger King officials suggested that the "personality" of the Big King would allow it to compete well in direct competition with the Big Mac. "Get ready for the taste that beats the Big Mac" was the advertising slogan accompanying the Big King's introduction.

McDonald's did not take Burger King's decision to attack its 30-year-old core product lightly, especially because customer's initial reaction to the Big King was positive. In fact, less than one month after the Big King was introduced, McDonald's launched its lookalike challenge to the Whopper, which is Burger King's flagship sandwich. Called "The Big 'n Tasty," analysts observed the remarkable similarity between this product and the Whopper, "right down to the 4.5-inch diameter of its sesame-seed bun."

Also, the competitive battle between these two firms escalated beyond burgers to fries. Because fries had long been acknowledged as one of McDonald's competitive advantages, Burger King's decision to fight McDonald's in terms of this particular product was significant. Burger King used another slogan that attacked McDonald's product directly—"The taste that beat McDonald's fries"—to introduce its new fries to the marketplace. As suggested by the following statement, a different production process is what Burger King believes creates its superior product: "The new fries are made with a process in which fresh-cut potatoes are sprayed with a potato-based coating before they are frozen, shipped and then cooked, as before, in vegetable oil. The result is fries that are tastier, crispier, and stay hot longer." To promote the new product, Burger King declared Friday, December 26, 1997, Free FryDay in the United States. On this day, anyone could visit a Burger King unit and receive a free bag of french fries. Company officials indicated that about 15 million bags were handed out through this promotion.

Burger King executives interpreted the results of blind french fry taste tests positively. In these tests, 57 percent of consumers preferred Burger King's new fries against 35 percent preferring McDonald's, with the 8 remaining percent expressing no opinion. The history of competitive dynamics between these two firms suggests that each firm should expect a rapid competitive response to the competitive actions it has taken in regard to both burgers and french fries.

SOURCE: R. Tomkins, 1998, Burger King fires harder, *The Financial Times*, January 5, 19; Associated Press, 1997, Frying in the face of McDonald's, *Dallas Morning News*, December 11, D1; E. S. Browning and R. Gibson, 1997, McDonald's arches lose golden luster, *Wall Street Journal*, September 3, C1, C2; G. DeGeorge, 1997, Can it make hash out of Big Mac? *Business Week*, September 8, 42; M. H. Gerstein, 1997, McDonald's Corp., *Value Line*, September 19, 321; R. Gibson, 1997, Burger wars sizzle as McDonald's clones the Whopper, *Wall Street Journal*, September 17, B1.

Competitor Resource Availability

A competitive response to a strategic or tactical action also requires organizational resources. Firms with fewer resources are more likely to respond to tactical actions than to strategic ones because responses to tactical actions require fewer resources and are easier to implement. In addition, firm resources may dictate the type of response. For example, local video stores have relatively limited resources to respond to competitive actions taken by Blockbuster, one of the large retail chains competing in the video business and the industry's dominant firm. Typically, a local store cannot imitate a Blockbuster strategic action to establish multiple units within a particular geographic area in the pursuit of blanket market coverage. In contrast, the smaller local firm is far more likely to respond to a Blockbuster tactical action of reduced prices. However, because of its lower volume and lack of purchasing power, relative to the large chains, initiating a competitive response in the form of a tactical price reduction can also be difficult for the local store. To compete against Blockbuster, the local video store often relies on personalized customer service and a concentration on being willing to stock or search for hard-to-find videos as the sources of its competitive advantage. A focus on mass availability of the most popular titles and a desire to hold operating costs as low as possible suggest that a large video chain such as Blockbuster will not necessarily respond to the local store's service-oriented competitive actions, even though it has the resources to do so.[63]

As this example suggests, small firms can respond effectively to their larger counterparts' competitive actions. In the toy industry, some small, localized competitors are initiating an array of competitive responses to the big toy store chains' (e.g., Toys "R" Us and Kay-Bee Toys) promotions, discount prices, and enormous merchandise variety. Children's General Store, for example, seeks to carry specialized products that the chains don't stock. Sullivan's Toy Store in Washington, D.C., expects its clerks to spend as much as a half-hour helping customers find the "perfect" gift. The store's owners believe that such personalized service is of significant value to customers. Located in Essex Junction, Vermont, Timeless Toys Inc. specializes in what it considers to be "beautiful dolls." Janet's Thingamajigs focuses on classic, second-hand toys. This store seems to benefit competitively from the enjoyment some parents derive from watching their children play with toys they used during their youth. Thus, even without the level and types of resources required to imitate larger firms' competitive actions, small companies can achieve success when their competitive responses allow them to use their unique resources to create value for a specialized customer segment.[64]

FIRMS' ABILITIES TO TAKE ACTION AND RESPOND

As indicated earlier, resource availability and ability to respond affect the probability of a company's response to a competing firm's competitive actions. Firms' abilities therefore moderate the relationship between interfirm rivalry and the competitive outcomes (see Figure 5.1). There are four general firm abilities to take action that influence competitive interaction within a market or industry: (1) relative firm size within a market or industry, (2) the speed at which competitive actions and responses are made, (3) the extent of innovation by firms in the market or industry, and (4) product quality.

Relative Firm Size

The *size* of a firm can have two important, but opposite, effects on an industry's competitive dynamics. First, the larger a firm, the greater its market power. Of course, the extent of any firm's market power is relative to the power of its competitors. Boeing Company (with roughly a 65 percent share of the world's commercial aircraft market) and Airbus Industrie (with approximately a 33 percent market share) both have substantial market power. Relatively, however, Boeing's market power exceeds that of Airbus.[65] In the U.S. automobile manufacturing industry, all three major competitors are large; as such, no individual firm has relative and critical market power over the others. Nonetheless, it is difficult for small firms to enter the market because the sheer size of the Big Three creates substantial entry barriers to the industry. On a global level, Toyota continues to increase its market power as a result of its growth. This power will increase again if it is able to reach the objective discussed earlier in the chapter—namely, replacing Ford Motor Company as the world's second largest car and truck manufacturer.

Another example of market power is shown by Sega's recent problems. A Japanese maker of video games and the equipment on which the games are played, Sega encounters stiff competition throughout the world. In particular, Sony's PlayStation recently was able to outpace sales of Sega's Saturn machine. Following analysis of the competitive situation, Sega decided not to pursue sales of the Saturn because of the belief that to do so would result in further damage to the firm's profitability. Also contributing to this decision was Sony's market signal to Sega that the PlayStation would be priced even more competitively. Relative to Sega, Sony has a much stronger resource base to support this tactical competitive action. Because of declining volume and Sony's market power, Sega executives concluded that it could not continue to compete primarily on the basis of price with its more powerful competitor. Instead of selling the Saturn machine, Sega decided to focus on software sales where the firm's profit margins were more attractive.[66]

Problems created by firm size are demonstrated by events—both historical and current—in the computer industry. Although the giant in the industry, IBM, was highly successful, it did not invent or first introduce the microcomputer, which is the primary basis of the industry today. It took entrepreneurial ventures, such as Apple Computer, Dell Computer, and Compaq, to introduce the innovations in goods and services that revolutionized the industry. Small firms often do this by fostering what Joseph Schumpeter referred to as creative destruction.[67] As Steven Jobs and his partner Steve Wozniak revolutionized the computer industry, Michael Dell, who was in high school when Apple introduced its computers, revolutionized the way computers were produced and distributed.

Some believe that the success of the revolution credited to Dell Computer Corp. is demonstrated by the view that the firm had become the driving force in the PC business as the 1990s came to a close. In suggesting this perspective, one business writer noted, "In just a few years the company has gone from a compelling sideshow in the industry to a fast-charging threat to big boys like Compaq and IBM. Thanks to a low-cost, direct-sales model . . . Dell's global-market-share rank has climbed to a virtual tie for No. 3, from No. 8"[68] at the beginning of 1997.

Dell's superior marketplace performance quickly attracted a host of competitors. PC makers Hewlett-Packard, Compaq, and IBM, as well as retailers CompUSA, OfficeMax, and Computer City, all announced in 1997 that they were entering Dell's stronghold—the build-to-order (BTO) business. Some of these firms, CompUSA, for example, reported initial success with their direct sales approach.[69] As another indicator of the potential challenge to Dell's success, Compaq's CEO Eckhard Pfeiffer noted that his firm had been able to quickly erase Dell's cost advantages through the methods it was using in its newly created BTO business.[70] After surveying the late 1990s competitive landscape, Compaq's Pfeiffer suggested, "The future belongs to whichever company provides the right bundle of products, technology, solutions, and services with the lowest cost of ownership to customers."[71] History suggests that entrepreneurial ventures may be the ones to first discover ways to satisfy what CEO Pfeiffer sees as his industry's competitive challenges. On the other hand, Compaq's acquisition of Digital Equipment Corp. in 1998 and its selection as the sole provider of PCs to be sold in Tandy Corp.'s Radio Shack stores in the same year suggested that the firm was making progress toward its goal of becoming a full-service company with a solutions-oriented approach for customers.[72]

A quote attributed to Herbert Kelleher, co-founder and CEO of Southwest Airlines, best describes the approach needed by large firms. In Kelleher's words, "Think and act big and we'll get smaller. Think and act small and we'll get bigger."[73] This suggests that large firms should use their size to build market power, but that they must think and act like a small firm (e.g., move quickly and be innovative) in order to achieve strategic competitiveness and earn above-average returns over the long run. A commitment to the value of each employee and to the use of organizational structures that encourage individuals to demonstrate initiative appear to facilitate large firms' efforts to act entrepreneurially.[74] Thermo Electron, 3M, GTE, and Xerox are examples of large companies that are following these prescriptions to overcome the liabilities of size through the creation and support of entrepreneurship.[75]

Speed of Competitive Actions and Competitive Responses

Our world is one in which time and speed are important. We go to fast food restaurants and use microwave ovens. We regularly use e-mail, overnight express mail (public and private), and fax machines. The same is true with competition. The

"Think and act big and we'll get smaller. Think and act small and we'll get bigger," says Herb Kelleher, co-founder and CEO of Southwest Airlines.

speed with which a firm can initiate competitive actions and competitive responses may determine its success. In the global economy, speed in developing a new product and moving it to the marketplace is becoming critical to a firm's efforts to establish a sustainable competitive advantage and earn above-average returns.[76]

Executives at British Telecommunications (BT) have consciously increased the speed at which competitive decisions are made within the firm. Top-level managers considered the ability to make decisions more rapidly as vital if BT were to be able to take advantage of opportunities produced by various market liberalization policies. Making swift decisions, BT moved into new product territories, including advanced media services, as the twenty-first century approached. To compete successfully in this particular product area, BT formed an alliance, called British Interactive Broadcasting, with BskyB, Matsushita, and HSBC Midland. BT also created a 50–50 joint venture with the industrial group Viag to compete in Germany, which is Europe's largest telecommunications market. In France, BT has become a partner with Compagnie Generale des Eaux in Cegetel. Analysts expected this union to become the chief competitor to France Telecom. Through a series of alliances and partnerships such as these, BT has rapidly extended its influence outside of its home market. Some analysts believe that BT's decision-making speed and the competitive actions resulting from it indicate that the firm "can claim European leadership in moves to exploit market liberalisation."[77]

Speed to the marketplace is one of the problems U.S. automobile manufacturers have experienced in competing with Japanese firms. Some time ago, Japanese auto companies were able to design a new product and introduce it to the market within three years. In comparison, U.S. firms required between five and eight years to complete these activities. This time differential made it possible for Japanese firms to design and move to the market two or three new automobiles in the same time it took a U.S. automaker to do one.

In a global economy, although time is a critical source of competitive advantage, managing for speed requires more than attempting to have employees work faster. Essentially, it requires working smarter, using different types of organizational structures, and having the time required for completion as a primary work-related goal.[78] Research has shown that the pace of strategic decision making may be affected by an executive's cognitive ability, use of intuition, tolerance for risk, and propensity to act.[79] Executives who use intuition and have a greater tolerance for risk are predisposed to make faster strategic decisions than do those without such characteristics. It is also known that decisions are likely to occur faster in centralized organizations because they will not have to go through as many levels or get approval from as many people. More formalized and bureaucratic organizations, however, may find it difficult to make fast strategic decisions[80] because they require more layers of approval.

Jack Welch, chairman and CEO of General Electric, states that speed is the ability sought by all of today's organizations.[81] He suggests that companies are striving to develop products faster, speed up production cycles in moving them to the market, and improve response time to customers. In Welch's opinion, having faster communications and moving with agility are critical to competitive success.

Innovation

A third general factor, innovation, has long been known in some industries, such as pharmaceuticals and computers, to have a strong influence on firm perfor-

181

mance.[82] The strategic importance of innovation is explored further in Chapter 13. In today's global economy, research suggests that innovation (both product innovation and process innovation) is becoming linked with above-average returns in a growing number of industries.[83] One study, for example, found that companies with the highest performance also invested the most in research and development. In 1960, U.S. firms held more than two-thirds of the world market in 10 of the top 15 major industries. By 1970, the United States continued to dominate 9 of those 15 industries. However, by 1980, U.S. domination was limited to only 3 of the 15 industries. The study found that this was due largely to changes in innovation. Firms from other countries were move innovative than U.S. firms in many of the industries.[84] In fact, a contributing factor to the productivity and technology problems experienced by U.S. firms has been managers' unwillingness to bear the costs and risks of long-term development of product and process innovations.[85]

In general, the dynamics of competition among firms competing in high-tech industries encourage significant allocations to each company's research and development function.[86] This is the case of Taiwan's Thunder Tiger, one of the world's leading manufacturers of radio-controlled model aircraft. Between 1987 and 1996, Thunder Tiger spent between 5 and 7 percent of its sales revenue on R&D. These allocations contributed to the firm's development of high-quality precision engineering skills as well as rigorous quality control techniques. These core competencies were the ones on which Thunder Tiger relied to develop and manufacture innovative, high-quality products over the years.

In 1997, the firm allocated 15 percent of revenues to R&D; similar if not identical allocations are expected in future years. Thunder Tiger's executives believe that the additional resources for R&D will support the company's new contract with the Taiwanese government that calls for it to develop an innovative prototype thrust engine for military and industrial purposes. The military will use Thunder Tiger's engine for remote-controlled decoy aircraft; in the industrial field, the engine will be used in turbine generators. In commenting about the nature of this contract, the firm's founder, Aling Lai, observed the following: "From toys to aerospace—sounds crazy, doesn't it? But, we see a lot of opportunities in the aerospace field and our R&D team is capable of developing advanced technology products."[87] Thus, innovation skills can be a great equalizer for small firms competing against large companies (see Chapter 13).

Firms competing in industries in which the pattern of competitive dynamics calls for innovation-related abilities should recognize that implementing innovations effectively can be difficult. Some researchers believe that implementation failure, not innovation failure, increasingly is the cause of a firm's inability to derive adequate competitive benefits from its product and process innovations.[88] Among other capabilities, a firm requires executives who are able to integrate its innovation strategy with other strategies (such as the business-level strategies discussed in Chapter 4) and an ability to recruit and select high-tech workers to successfully implement innovations.[89]

Our discussion of factors influencing an industry's competitive dynamics suggests that large firms with significant market power that act like small firms—making strategic decisions and implementing them with speed—and that are innovative are strong competitors and are likely to earn above-average returns. However, no matter how large, fast, and innovative an organization is, product quality also affects an industry's competitive dynamics and influences a firm's ability to achieve strategic competitiveness in domestic and global markets.

Quality

Product quality has become a universal theme in the global economy and continues to shape the competitive dynamics in many industries.[90] Today product quality is important in all industry settings and is a necessary, but not sufficient, condition to successful strategy implementation. Without quality goods or services, strategic competitiveness cannot be achieved. Quality alone, however, does not guarantee that a firm will achieve strategic competitiveness or earn above-average returns. In the words of the president of the National Center for Manufacturing Sciences, a nonprofit research consortium, "Quality used to be a competitive issue out there, but now it's just the basic denominator to being in the market."[91]

This is the case in the café-bakery business, for example. Accepting product quality as a given, executives heading competitors La Madeleine and Corner Bakery believe that their products are more than simply food. They suggest that their establishments and products contribute to a way of life for those interested in purchasing items from neighborhood bakeries with a family atmosphere.[92]

Quality involves meeting or exceeding customer expectations in the goods and/or services offered.[93] The quality dimensions of goods and services are shown in Table 5.2. As a competitive dimension, quality is as important in the service sector as it is in the manufacturing sector.[94]

Quality begins at the top of the organization. Top management must create values for quality that permeate the entire organization.[95] These values should be built into strategies that reflect long-term commitments to customers, stockholders, and other important stakeholders.[96]

183

Quality involves meeting or exceeding customer expectations in the goods and/or services offered.

TABLE 5.2 *Quality Dimensions of Goods and Services*

Product Quality Dimensions	Service Quality Dimensions
1. *Performance*—Operating characteristics	1. *Timeliness*—Performed in promised time period
2. *Features*—Important special characteristics	2. *Courtesy*—Performed cheerfully
3. *Flexibility*—Meeting operating specifications over some time period	3. *Consistency*—All customers have similar experiences each time
4. *Durability*—Amount of use before performance deteriorates	4. *Convenience*—Accessible to customers
5. *Conformance*—Match with preestablished standards	5. *Completeness*—Fully serviced, as required
6. *Serviceability*—Ease and speed of repair or normal service	6. *Accuracy*—Performed correctly each time
7. *Aesthetics*—How a product looks and feels	
8. *Perceived quality*—Subjective assessment of characteristics (product image)	

Source: Adapted from J.W. Dean, Jr., and J.R. Evans, 1994, *Total Quality: Management, Organization and Society* (St. Paul, Minn.: West Publishing Company); H.V. Roberts and B.F. Sergesketter, 1993, *Quality Is Personal* (New York: The Free Press); D. Garvin, 1988, *Managed Quality: The Strategic and Competitive Edge* (New York: The Free Press).

Recent actions taken by Michael Dell demonstrate top managerial support for product quality. Although Dell Computer products have long had some of the highest quality ratings in the PC industry, Dell himself remains obsessed with the need for continuous quality improvements. To reduce the already relatively low failure rate of Dell's PCs, Dell became convinced that it was necessary to find a way to reduce the number of times a computer's hard drive—the most sensitive part of the PC—was handled during the assembly process. Based on this conviction, he insisted "that the number of touches be dramatically reduced from an existing level of more than 30 per drive." By revamping production lines, Dell employees were able to cut the number of touches by 50 percent. The results from this particular quality-based activity are impressive. After eliminating one-half of the hard drive touches, "the rate of rejected hard drives fell by 40 percent, and the overall failure rate for the company's PC dropped by 20 percent."[97] When top-level managers emphasize product quality in the manner demonstrated by Michael Dell, a process of total quality management pervades the firm in all activities and processes.

Quality and total quality management are closely associated with the philosophies and teachings of W. Edwards Deming (and, to a lesser extent, Armand Feigenbaum and Joseph Juran).[98] These individuals' contributions to the practice of management are based on a simple, yet powerful, insight; the understanding that it costs less to make quality products than defect-ridden ones.

Total quality management (TQM) is a "managerial innovation that emphasizes an organization's total commitment to the customer and to continuous improvement of every process through the use of data-driven, problem-solving approaches based on empowerment of employee groups and teams."[99] Actually a philosophy about how to manage, TQM "combines the teachings of Deming and Juran on statistical process control and group problem-solving processes with Japanese values concerned with quality and continuous improvement."[100] Statistical process control (SPC) is a technique used to upgrade continually the quality of the goods or services a firm produces. SPC benefits the firm through the detection and elimination of variations in processes used to manufacture a good or service.[101]

Although there are skeptics, when applied properly, the principles of total quality management can help firms achieve strategic competitiveness and earn above-average returns.[102] Three principal goals sought when practicing total quality management are boosting customer satisfaction, reducing product introduction time, and cutting costs. As discussed in this chapter, achievement of these goals can be expected to have a positive effect on a firm's performance. To reach these goals, firms must provide their employees and leaders with effective TQM training.[103]

Ironically, Deming's and Juran's ideas on quality and continuous improvement were adapted and implemented by Japanese firms long before many U.S. firms acknowledged their importance. For this reason, a host of Japanese firms developed a competitive advantage in product quality that has been difficult for U.S. firms to overcome.[104] Deming's 14 points for managing and achieving quality (see Table 5.3) have become a watchword in many businesses globally.

Embedded within Deming's 14 points for management is the importance of striving continuously to improve how a firm operates and the quality of its goods or services. In fact, Deming did not support use of the TQM term, arguing that he did not know what total quality was and that it is impossible for firms to reach a goal of "total quality." The pursuit of quality improvements, Deming believed, should be a never-ending process.

Total quality management is managerial innovation that emphasizes an organization's total commitment to the customer and to continuous improvement of every process through the use of data-driven, problem-solving approaches based on empowerment of employee groups and teams.

TABLE 5.3 *Deming's 14 Points for Management*

1. Create and publish to all employees a statement of the aims and purposes of the company or other organization. The management must demonstrate constantly their commitment to this statement.
2. Learn the new philosophy, top management and everybody.
3. Understand the purpose of inspection, for improvement of processes and reduction of costs.
4. End the practice of awarding business on the basis of price tag alone.
5. Improve constantly and forever the system of production and service.
6. Institute training.
7. Teach and institute leadership.
8. Drive out fear. Create trust. Create a climate for innovation.
9. Optimize toward the aims and purposes of the company—the efforts of teams, groups, staff areas.
10. Eliminate exhortations for the workforce.
11. (a) Eliminate numerical quotas for production. Instead, learn and institute methods for improvement. (b) Eliminate management by objective. Instead, learn the capabilities of processes and how to improve them.
12. Remove barriers that rob people of pride of workmanship.
13. Encourage education and self-improvement for everyone.
14. Take action to accomplish the transformation.

Source: Reprinted from *Out of the Crisis* by W. Edwards Deming by permission of MIT and The W. Edwards Deming Institute. Published by MIT, Center for Advanced Engineering Study, Cambridge, MA 02139. Copyright © 1986 by W. Edwards Deming.

Newer methods of TQM use benchmarking and emphasize organizational learning.[105] Benchmarking facilitates TQM by developing information on the best practices of other organizations and industries. This information is often used to establish goals for the firm's own TQM efforts. Benchmarking provides a process from which a firm can learn from the outcomes of other firms.[106] Because of the importance of product (both goods and service) quality in achieving competitive parity or a competitive advantage, many firms in the United States and around the world are emphasizing total quality management and integrating it with their strategies.

As our discussions have indicated, relationships between each of the four general abilities (size, speed, innovation, and quality) influence a firm's competitive actions and outcomes. Those responsible for selecting a firm's strategy should understand these relationships and anticipate that competitors will take competitive actions and competitive responses designed to exploit the positive relationships depicted in Figure 5.2. In the next section, we describe the different outcomes of competitive dynamics.

OUTCOMES OF INTERFIRM RIVALRY

Figure 5.1 illustrates potential outcomes of interfirm rivalry. In some competitive environments, sustainable competitive advantage may be more likely. As discussed in Chapter 3, one of the key determinants of sustainability is whether a firm's prod-

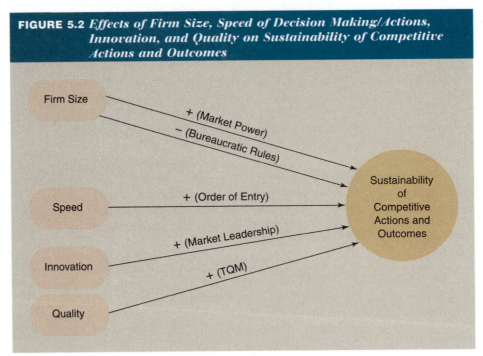

FIGURE 5.2 *Effects of Firm Size, Speed of Decision Making/Actions, Innovation, and Quality on Sustainability of Competitive Actions and Outcomes*

*Plus and minus signs indicate effects on performance.

ucts are costly to imitate. A sustainability framework, therefore, might focus on different market types where product imitability is largely or partially shielded.[107] All major markets have seen their foreign rivals make inroads into what had been their domestic markets. However, even with strong rivalry and increasing potential for imitability, some markets have been shielded from such competition. These markets are described as slow-cycle or sheltered markets. In other markets, product imitability is moderate. As such, they are labeled standard-cycle markets, often described as oligopolistic. In still other markets, firms are in rapid, dynamic, and often entrepreneurial environments where changes are identified as fast cycle.[108]

Competitive Market Outcomes

Products in **slow-cycle markets** reflect strongly shielded resource positions where competitive pressures do not readily penetrate a firm's sources of strategic competitiveness.

Products in **slow-cycle markets** reflect strongly shielded resource positions where competitive pressures do not readily penetrate the firm's sources of strategic competitiveness. This is often characterized in economics as a monopoly position. A firm that has a unique set of product attributes or an effective product design may dominate its markets for decades as did IBM with large mainframe computers. This type of competitive position can be established even in markets where there is significant technological change, such as Microsoft's position with difficult to imitate, complex software systems. Drug manufacturers often have established such a position legally under patent laws. Shielded advantages may be geographic; as such, the opening of huge emerging markets in Eastern Europe, Russia, China, and India offers strong motivation for firms to pursue such opportunities.

Although the idea of a monopoly, which has a single seller, restricted output, and high prices, is not likely to be attained in the United States because of government policy restrictions, subtle and more complex variations are possible with a local monopoly approach. This is what Wal-Mart did in its early years. It established a local monopoly in rural areas in the southwest United States, especially when coupled with efficient distribution systems. Many airlines also seek to establish a shielded advantage by the innovation of hub control at airports. Examples included American Airlines' dominance in Dallas and Delta's hubs in Atlanta and Salt Lake City.

Effective product designs may be able to dominate their markets for many years. For example, the McIlhenny family of Louisiana has dominated the hot sauce industry for 125 years with a singe product unchanged since its inception: Tabasco sauce.[109] These firms may be closely associated with the main idea of the resource-based view of the firm because their resources and capabilities are difficult to imitate. The sustainability of competitive action associated with a slow-cycle market is depicted in Figure 5.3.

Standard-cycle markets may be more closely associated with the industrial organization economics approach following Porter's five force model on competitive strategy. In these organizations, strategy and organization are designed to serve high-volume or mass markets. The focus is on coordination and market control as in automobile and appliance industries.[110] These organizations, even though they may be able to sustain world-class products for decades (e.g., Kellogg, Coca-Cola), may experience severe competitive pressures. Extended dominance and, in fact, world leadership is possible through continuing capital investment and superior learning as is the case with Coca-Cola. This contrasts with protected markets because there is not such a high rate of ongoing investment into the production of Tabasco sauce. Although it may be difficult to enter standard-cycle markets because of the competitive intensity, if successful and if duplicated by competitors, more intense competitive pressures can be brought to bear. More intense competition may be similar to that found in fast-cycle markets.[111]

Products in **standard-cycle markets** reflect moderately shielded resource positions where competitive interaction penetrates a firm's sources of strategic competitiveness; but with improvement of its capabilities, the firm may be able to sustain a competitive advantage.

187

FIGURE 5.3 *Gradual Erosion of a Sustained Competitive Advantage*

Source: Adapted from I.C. MacMillan, 1988, Controlling competitive dynamics by taking strategic initiative, *Academy of Management Executive* II, no. 2: 111–118.

Although Coca-Cola has been able to sustain world-class products for decades, it is still under pressure from competitors. Through continued capital investment and superior learning, the firm is able to maintain world dominance.

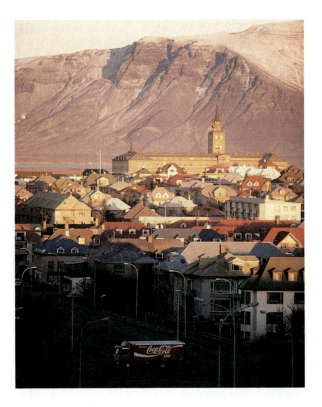

Competitive pressures facing Procter & Gamble (P&G) and Whirlpool Corp. are described in the Strategic Focus. Both of these firms have long held dominant positions while serving mass markets on a global basis, but as discussed in the Strategic Focus, competitors continue to challenge their positions through aggressive competitive actions. Thus, these two firms are experiencing significant competitive pressures while competing in standard-cycle markets.

STRATEGIC FOCUS

Of Toothpaste and Home Appliances: Competitive Dynamics in Standard-Cycle Markets

Competing in mature, slow-growth markets that tend to be overrun with products, Colgate-Palmolive (C-P) is being credited with revitalizing its North American operations in toothpaste, detergent, and personal care products.

Although New York-based, C-P generates almost 70 percent of its sales revenue from outside the United States and Canada. Nonetheless, the lack of a growth focus in the North American market was of deep concern to top-level executives for several years. To correct its deficiencies in this market, the firm recently closed inefficient facilities, revamped production processes, and invested heavily in new products. The results of these efforts were impressive for the 1997 fiscal year: North American sales increased 23 percent, gross margins expanded 5 percentage points (from 50 percent to 55 percent), and operating profits grew by 73 percent.

Toothpaste is one of the products that is of keen interest to C-P, primarily because oral care accounts for roughly one-third of the firm's revenues. For the first time, C-P's toothpaste market share in the United States now exceeds Procter & Gamble's. This accomplishment is impressive in that P&G held the top spot in this market for 35 consecutive years before being unseated by C-P in 1997.

To stimulate toothpaste sales even further, C-P recently introduced Total toothpaste into the United States (the product is also sold in 103 other countries). Analysts see Total as a potential blockbuster for C-P in terms of revenue and profit growth. It is the first oral pharmaceutical ever approved by the Food and Drug Administration. Total contains Triclosan, which is a broad-spectrum antibiotic that helps heal gingivitis. Gingivitis is a bleeding-gum disease that is afflicting an increasing number of aging baby boomers. To promote Total, C-P intended to spend $100 million in 1998 on an advertising campaign. None of C-P's rivals were even close to launching a similarly effective gum-disease-fighting toothpaste at the time Total was introduced. Having studied C-P's recent performance and intended future competitive actions, one analyst suggested that while Colgate-Palmolive was an underdog to P&G in the past, it is now "sucker-punching" the company through product and process innovations.

Whirlpool is the world's largest manufacturer of home appliances. To be competitive, the firm has taken a number of actions over the years, including investing in three appliance companies in Brazil and one in Canada and forming joint ventures with companies in Mexico, India, Taiwan, and China. Whirlpool now faces an attack from long-time rival General Electric (GE).

Under Jack Welch's leadership, GE seeks the number-one market position in businesses in which it competes. But, for all of its efforts, GE has never been able to unseat Whirlpool from its position as the largest appliance maker in the United States. As an indicator of the intensity of the rivalry between these two firms, consider the fact that based on its 35 percent share of the U.S. market as compared to GE's 32 percent, Whirlpool referred to GE in one of its recent annual reports as the "number-two company."

GE is redoubling its commitment to gain the top market share position from Whirlpool. The company spent approximately $100 million to develop what it sees as an innovative plastic basket for its new clothes washer. It is this basket on which GE is grounding its competitive attacks. GE claims that the clothes basket in Whirlpool's machines is made of steel covered with porcelain and that the porcelain chips. When told of this view, Whirlpool's CEO David Whitwam said, "You'd have to throw a brick in there to make it chip."

Of course, Whirlpool and GE face additional competitors. Haier Group, for example, is the number-one consumer electronics company in China. This firm accounts for almost 40 percent of China's refrigerator sales and a third of the country's washing machine and air-conditioner sales. Committed to aggressive growth, Haier's president wants his company to become an export powerhouse and achieve status as a global brand name. More aggressive pressure from other global competitors such as Haier Group suggests that Whirlpool and GE must continue to examine the full range of competitors when making decisions about how to compete in what historically has been a standard-cycle market.

SOURCE: L. Grant, 1998, Outmarketing P&G, *Fortune*, January 12, 150–162; W. M. Carley, 1997, GE, no. 2 in appliances, is agitating to grab share from Whirlpool, *Wall Street Journal*, July 2, A1, A6; K. Chen, 1997, Would America buy a refrigerator labeled "made in Qingdao"? *Wall Street Journal*, September 17, A1, A14; M. Moffett, 1997, Brasmotor's success draws competitors, *Wall Street Journal*, July 11, A10; C. Quintanilla and J. Carlton, 1997, Whirlpool unveils global restructuring effort, *Wall Street Journal*, September 19, A3, A6; P. H. Roth, 1997, Whirlpool Corp., *Value Line*, September 12, 134.

In **fast-cycle markets**, a competitive advantage cannot be sustained; firms attempt to gain temporary competitive advantages by strategically disrupting the market.

In **fast-cycle markets**, such as cellular telephones and DRAM computer chips, it does not appear that a first-mover advantage yields sustained competitive advantage. One way to examine the intensity of dynamics in these industries is to study the long-run pricing patterns of some products. For instance, in 1988, the cost per megabyte of DRAM computer chips was $378. Three years later, the market price for a one-megabyte chip had dropped to $35.[112] When cellular phones were introduced, they were priced at around $3,500, but five years later the price dropped below $100 and now cellular phone equipment is often given away if you subscribe to a cellular system service. Perpetual innovation and shorter product cycles dominate this market class. Standard-cycle markets are scale oriented, whereas fast-cycle markets are idea driven.

Competing in Fast-Cycle Markets

To this point in the chapter, the focus has been on trying to obtain a sustained competitive advantage. Sustained competitive advantage is possible in slow- and standard-cycle markets. Figure 5.3 focuses on this type of competitive advantage. Usually there is an entrepreneurial launch stage of the strategy, a period of exploitation, and, ultimately, a period of counterattack where the competitive advantage erodes. In fast-cycle markets, a sustained competitive advantage may be a goal that creates inertia and exposes one to aggressive global competitors. Even though GM and IBM have economies of scale, huge advertising budgets, the best distribution systems in their industry, cutting edge R&D, and deep pockets, many of their advantages have been eroded by global competitors in Europe, Japan, and now Korea.

A new competitive advantage paradigm is emerging where a firm seizes the initiative through a small series of steps as illustrated in Figure 5.4. As you can see from this figure, the idea is to create a counterattack before the advantage is eroded.

FIGURE 5.4 *Obtaining Temporary Advantages to Create Sustained Advantage*

Source: Adapted from I. C. MacMillan, 1988, Controlling competitive dynamics by taking strategic initiative, *Academy of Management Executive* II, no. 2: 111–118.

This actually leads to cannibalizing your own products through the next stage of product evolution and entry.[113] Thus, the focus of this new paradigm is competitive disruption.[114] In this competitive approach, one can escalate competition in an arena such as price and quality only so far, then the dominant competitor should seek to jump to another level of competition such as speed and know-how or innovation. As explained in the Strategic Focus, this is the approach that Komatsu took in competing with Caterpillar and that Caterpillar is now taking to compete against Komatsu.

STRATEGIC FOCUS

Fast-Cycle Competition between Caterpillar and Komatsu

In the early to middle part of the 1980s, Komatsu initiated a series of successful competitive actions against Caterpillar. First, Komatsu developed a line of effective products that it priced competitively. When Caterpillar responded in a similar fashion, Komatsu, in turn, used process innovations to enhance the value of its products and then introduced them into niche markets. Additionally, Komatsu entered emerging markets where Caterpillar was not strong.

However, competition between these two firms today may be even more rivalrous as compared to a decade ago; and, as a result of a series of seemingly effective competitive actions and responses, Caterpillar is now a stronger competitor. Some of its current strength is a product of the firm's decade-long program of cost cutting, targeted investments, and market-based reorganizations.

Caterpillar has long been the world's largest manufacturer of construction and mining equipment, natural gas engines and industrial gas turbines, and remains a leading global supplier of diesel engines. The firm's major markets include road building, mining, logging, agriculture, petroleum, and general construction. Coupled with the firm's size is a vast array of knowledge and capabilities that are being used as the foundation for its competitive rivalry with Komatsu.

It is generally acknowledged that Caterpillar has beaten off the challenge to its dominant position in the large-scale equipment market. Critical to Caterpillar's ability to counterattack Komatsu's invasion to its dominance in the large-scale equipment market were the firm's innovation skills and well-developed dealer network. Called the firm's single largest strategic weapon by its chairman Donald Fites, Caterpillar has 192 dealers serving customers in nearly 200 countries. For the last ten-plus years, extensive efforts have been completed to cement the links between Caterpillar and its dealer network. A technologically sophisticated worldwide computer network that provides instant information about parts availability and new machines to all dealers is one example of what the firm does to derive competitive advantages from the links with its dealers.

Caterpillar is also initiating competitive actions that will allow it to attack Komatsu in markets that traditionally have been strongholds for that firm. For example, through the results of a $100 million investment, Caterpillar launched a family of "compact" building equipment in 1998. (This attack parallels in nature the one Komatsu launched against Caterpillar in the large-scale equipment market.) The compact building equipment line features products that are targeted to the mini-excavators' field. At the time of the launch, this market was dominated by Komatsu, although two other Japanese manufacturers, Yanmar and Kubota, also held significant shares of this market. Producing its new machines in the United

Kingdom, United States, and Japan, Caterpillar's goal was to gain quickly one-fifth of the $3.5 billion a year market for compact equipment.

Caterpillar's current competitive actions include geographic as well as product launches. When Komatsu initiated its competitive attacks, Caterpillar was not strong in the world's emerging markets (as noted previously). Today, however, Caterpillar is pushing intensely into China and other developing countries where rapid growth for construction equipment is expected. In fact, Caterpillar is committed deeply to extending its global presence in the pursuit of strategic competitiveness: "Mr. Fites envisages domestic sales will fall from roughly half total revenues this year (1997) to 25 percent within the next two decades. The company is expecting particularly large returns from China, where it is half way through a $90 million investment programme and where annual sales are projected to climb from about $200 million to up to $1 billion by early next century."

SOURCE: Caterpillar Home Page, 1998, January 27, http://www.caterpillar.com; D. Weimer, 1998, A new Cat on the hot seat, *Business Week*, March 9, 56–61; J. Beisler, 1997, Caterpillar, *Value Line*, November 7, 1310; P. Marsh and S. Wagstyl, 1997, The hungry Caterpillar, *Financial Times*, December 2, 22.

The array of competitive actions and competitive responses occurring between Caterpillar and Komatsu described in the Strategic Focus demonstrate the four strategic steps shown in Table 5.4. At different times and in terms of different products and markets, each of these firms has been able to (1) identify a competitive opportunity that disrupted the status quo, (2) create a temporary advantage that was eroded through aggressive responses by its competitor, (3) seize the initiative from its competitor through effective competitive actions, and (4) sustain its momentum by continually offering new products and entering new markets. As this example about Caterpillar and Komatsu shows, firms must exhibit strategic flexibility if they are to be successful while competing in fast-cycle markets. Thus, when facing these market conditions, firms must learn how to respond quickly to technological change and market opportunities by offering more new products, broader product lines, and product upgrades more rapidly.[115]

Competitive Dynamics and Industry Evolution Outcomes

Because industries and markets evolve over time, so do the competitive dynamics between firms in the industry. We have examined how firms interact in a short span of time using an action–reaction framework, but we have not yet considered how competitive interaction evolves over longer periods of time. Three general stages of industry evolution are relevant to our study of competitive dynamics: emerging entrepreneurial, larger growth-oriented, and mature firms. These are shown in Figure 5.5.

Firms entering emerging industries attempt to establish a niche or an initial form of beginning dominance within an industry. Competitive rivalry for the loyalty of customers is serious. In these industries, depending on the types of products, firms often attempt to establish product quality, technology, and/or advantageous relationships with suppliers in order to develop a competitive advantage in the pursuit of strategic competitiveness. These firms are striving to build their reputation. As a result, a variety of different competitive strategies may be employed in such an industry. This diversity can be beneficial to many of the firms

TABLE 5.4 *Strategic Steps for Seizing the Initiative in Fast-Cycle Markets*

1. *Disrupting the status quo.*	Competitors disrupt the status quo by identifying new opportunities to serve the customer and by shifting the rules of competition. These moves end the old pattern of competitive interaction between rivals. This requires speed and variety in approach.
2. *Create temporary advantage.*	Disruption creates temporary advantages. These advantages are based on better knowledge of customers, technology, and the future. They are derived from customer orientation and employee empowerment throughout the entire organization. These advantages are short lived and eroded by fierce competition.
3. *Seizing the initiative.*	By moving aggressively into new areas of competition, acting to create a new advantage or undermine a competitor's old advantage, the company seizes the initiative. This throws the opponent off balance and puts it at a disadvantage for a while. The opponent is forced to play catch up, reacting rather than shaping the future with its own actions to seize the initiative. The initiator is proactive, whereas competitors are forced to be reactive.
4. *Sustaining the momentum.*	Several actions in a row are taken to seize the intiative and create momentum. The company continues to develop new advantages and does not wait for competitors to undermine them before launching the next initiative. This succession of actions sustains the momentum. Continually offering new initiatives is the only source of sustainable competitive advantage in fast-cycle environments.

Source: Adapted from R.A. D'Aveni, 1995, Coping with hypercompetition: Utilizing the new 7's framework, *Academy of Management Executive* IX, no. 3: 45–60.

FIGURE 5.5 *An Action–Based Model of the Industry Life Cycle*

Source: Adapted from C.M. Grimm and K.G. Smith, 1997, *Strategy as Action: Industry Rivalry and Coordination* (St. Paul, MN: West Publishing Co.).

in the industry. The diversity of competitive strategies may avoid direct competition and help firms gain dominance in market niches.[116] Although speed is important in new emerging industries, access to capital is often the critical issue. Therefore, it is not uncommon to have strategic alliances develop between a new firm entering the market and a more established firm that wishes to gain a foothold in the new industry.[117]

These firms often rely on top management to develop market opportunities. Stephen Jobs and Bill Gates were able to foresee the future possibilities of the microcomputer and the standardized microcomputer operating system. Their vision of an uncertain environment gave rise to both Apple Computer and Microsoft. Thus, firms in the emerging stage take *entrepreneurial actions* which focus on entrepreneurial discovery in uncertain environments.

Growth-oriented firms are the survivors from the emerging industry stage. In the growth stage, *growth-oriented actions* are emphasized, which tend to create product standardization as consumer demand creates a mass market with growth potential. Thus, many of these firms are more established, but no less competitive. In fact, as the industry begins to mature, the variety of strategies being implemented tends to decrease.[118] As such, entrepreneurial actions are still taking place but there is more emphasis on growth-oriented actions. Oftentimes, groups of firms will follow a similar strategy and thus become directly competitive. However, the rivalry between groups may be more indirect.[119] In industries where there is considerable within-strategic-group rivalry and competitive rivalry between firms in separate strategic groups, firms frequently earn below-average returns.[120]

Some of these industries may also be fragmented. Fragmented markets, such as fast food restaurants, tend to offer standardized facilities and products, but decentralized decision making to the local units. The standardization allows for low-cost competition. The primary value added comes from services provided. These markets offer a prime opportunity for franchising because of the ability to standardize facilities, operations, and products.[121]

In nonfragmented industries, the speed of new product development and introduction to the marketplace becomes an important competitive weapon. Consumers tend to be more sophisticated and expect not only quality products, but also product designs that meet their needs. Firms that can move new products that better meet consumers' needs to the market more quickly than competitors are likely to gain a competitive advantage.

In mature industries, there are usually fewer surviving competitors. Those that do survive tend to be larger with dominant market share positions. Therefore, firms in the mature stage emphasize *market-power actions* which focus the firm's attention on offering product lines that are profitable and producing those products in an efficient manner. New product innovation or entrepreneurial actions continue but are greatly deemphasized. Process innovations are emphasized more because they maintain dominance through cost efficiencies and the quality of the product manufactured and provided to customers.[122] Finally, firms in industries in the mature stage frequently seek international expansion or an increasing emphasis on their international operations and sales, a move that often extends a product's life. Thus, growth-oriented actions also continue even though the primary emphasis is on market-power actions.

In summary, once mature firms have a dominant market share, they seek to exploit their market power and extensive resources and capabilities in an attempt to maintain dominance. In a study examining the 1950–1972 period, market leaders

Kellogg, General Mills, General Foods, and Quaker Oats introduced more than 80 new brands without significant product innovation in an attempt to fill all niches and deter entry.[123] This strategy was very successful until the private-label producers grew powerful enough to counter this strategy.

This chapter concludes our emphasis on business-level strategy, although some business-level issues are discussed in future Chapters (e.g., Chapters 8, 9 and 11). The next chapter begins our discussion of corporate-level strategy.

SUMMARY

- Competitive rivalry entails actions and responses to competitive actions taken by other firms. Competitive attack and response are more likely when awareness, motivation, and abilities to attack or respond are present.

- Market commonality, as determined by multimarket contact in such industries as airlines, is likely to lead to dampening of a potential attack. However, if an offensive action is taken, a response is more likely in the presence of market commonality.

- Awareness of competitors' ability to attack or respond is facilitated by resource similarity among competitors. Those with similar resources are more likely to attack and respond than are those with fewer resources.

- First movers can gain a competitive advantage and customer loyalty by being the first in the market. First movers also take more risks. However, first movers often are higher performers. Second movers, particularly those that are larger and faster, can also gain a competitive advantage and/or earn at least average returns because they imitate, but do not take some of the risk that first movers do. The longer the time required to respond, the higher the probability that the first mover will enjoy strong performance gains. Late movers (those that respond a long time after the original action was taken) tend to be lower performers and much less effective.

- The probability of a response by a competitor to a competitive action is based partially on the extent to which the competitor is dependent on the particular market in which the action was taken. In addition, the probability of response is based on the type of action, the reputation of the firm taking the strategic action (the expectation of suc-

cess), and the resources available to the competitor contemplating response.

- The two types of competitive actions are strategic and tactical. Strategic actions are more long term in nature, require many specific resources, and are difficult to reverse. Alternatively, tactical actions tend to be more short term in orientation, require fewer and more general resources, and can be more easily reversed. More tactical, rather than strategic, actions are taken and more responses are made to tactical than to strategic actions. It is easier to respond to a tactical action, partly because it requires fewer resources. In addition, a tactical action is likely to have a shorter term effect than a strategic action. Responses to strategic actions are more difficult, require more resources, and require a longer-term investment.

- When competitors are highly dependent on a market in which competitive actions are taken, there is a high probability that they will respond to such actions. However, firms that are more diversified across markets are less likely to respond to a particular action that affects only one of the markets in which they compete.

- The highest probability of a response comes when an action is taken by a market leader. Furthermore, when an action is taken by a market leader, it is more likely that a competitor will imitate the action taken. Alternatively, if the firm has a reputation as a strategic player (a firm that takes more complex and risky actions), there is a lower probability of response. A price predator is also less likely to elicit a response from competitors.

- Those with more resources are more likely to respond to strategic actions than are those with fewer resources. Furthermore, the probability of response is determined not only by the amount of resources, but by the ability to use those resources in taking competitive action.

- Abilities needed to engage in competitive actions and responses include the relative size of the acting and responding firms, the function of speed in the market or industry, the importance of innovation in competitive moves, and product quality.

- Large firms often have strong market power. Alternatively, as firms grow larger, they often institute bureaucratic rules, procedures, and structures. These have the effect of reducing the probability that a firm will take actions and respond to others' actions. In addition, they reduce the speed with which a firm may be able to implement an action or respond to competitors' actions.

- Speed is becoming increasingly important in many industries in order to gain and hold a competitive advantage. In fact, many large firms must act like small firms (flexible and agile) to be competitive. This may require that they decentralize many responsibilities and decisions and that they create cross-functional teams in order to speed multiple processes (e.g., the innovation process).

- Both product and process innovation are becoming more important in the competitive posture of many industries. Some research has shown that firms that invest more in R&D and that are more innovative tend to have higher performance in multiple industries. Product innovation tends to be more important in emerging and growth industries, while mature industries may emphasize process innovation.

- Product quality has become critical in order to maintain competitive parity in most industries. Total quality management must be infused throughout the organization by top management and integrated with firm strategies. Benchmarking is used to help make comparative judgments about quality relative to other firms' best practices.

- There are three basic market outcomes from interfirm rivalry. Slow-cycle markets allow a firm to establish competitive advantage in a near monopoly situation. Until recently, many utility firms were in this position. Standard-cycle markets allow market situations where sustainability is possible. Firms that have multimarket contact may dampen competition somewhat. Fast-cycle markets create a situation where only temporary competitive advantage is possible such as in the electronics and pharmaceutical industries.

- In fast-cycle markets, a new paradigm of competitive action may be necessary, competitive disruption. This usually involves cannibalization of a previous product entry through decreasing prices, while establishing the new innovative product at the high end of the market, with increased product performance at a premium price.

- Industry evolution is important in determining the type of competition and the type of competitive actions that are emphasized. For example, firms in an emerging stage attempt to establish a reputation and develop a market niche in technology or quality of products provided. The main task is to establish an entrepreneurial action, usually in an uncertain environment. In growth firms, special emphasis may be placed on innovation to increase economies of scale. Speed of competitive actions taken is also important. The key task is to pursue growth-oriented actions by exploiting factors of production to increase dominance. In mature industries with fewer competitors, special emphasis is placed on market-power actions designed to defend the most profitable product lines and processes in order to produce and distribute those products with the greatest efficiency (lowest cost). However, entrepreneurial, growth-oriented, and market-power actions are taken at all stages, although the emphasis is different at each stage.

REVIEW QUESTIONS

1. What two factors contribute to awareness, motivation, and ability in competitor analysis?
2. What are the advantages and disadvantages of being a first, second, or late mover?
3. On what four factors is the likelihood of a response to a competitive action based?

4. What is the likelihood of response to a tactical action, a strategic action, and actions taken by market leaders? Explain why.
5. What are the advantages and the disadvantages of size regarding strategic actions and responses thereto?
6. Why is speed important in many industries? What can

firms do to increase the speed at which they make and implement strategic decisions?

7. In what types of industries is innovation important for competitive advantage? Explain the importance of different types of innovation (product and process) for success in different industries.

8. Describe three types of markets and the nature of rivalry in each.

9. How does industry evolution affect interfirm rivalry? Identify three stages of industry evolution, and briefly explain the types of competitive actions emphasized in those stages.

APPLICATION DISCUSSION QUESTIONS

1. Read the popular business press (e.g., *Business Week*, *Fortune*) and identify a strategic action and a tactical action taken by firms approximately two years ago. Next, read the popular business press to see if, and how, competitors responded to those actions. Explain the actions and the responses, linking your findings to the discussion in this chapter.

2. Why would a firm regularly choose to be a second-mover? Likewise, why would a firm purposefully be a late mover?

3. Explain how Sun Microsystems' strategic actions af-

fected its primary competitors (e.g., IBM, DEC, HP, Silicone Graphics).

4. Choose a large firm and examine the popular business press to identify how its size, speed of actions, level of innovation, and quality of goods or services have affected its competitive position in its industry. Explain your findings.

5. Identify a firm in a fast-cycle market and trace why its strategy was successful or unsuccessful over several strategic actions.

ETHICS QUESTIONS

1. In your opinion, are some industries known for ethical practices, while others are not? If so, name industries thought to be ethical and those that are evaluated less favorably in terms of ethics. How might the competitive actions and competitive responses differ between an "ethical" and an "unethical" industry?

2. When engaging in competitive rivalry, firms jockey for a market position that is advantageous, relative to competitors. In this jockeying, what kind of competitor intelligence gathering approaches are ethical?

3. A second mover is a firm that responds to a first mover's competitive actions, often through imitation. Is there

anything unethical about how a second mover engages in competition? Why or why not?

4. Standards for competitive rivalry differ in countries throughout the world. What should firms do to cope with these differences?

5. Is it possible that total quality management practices could result in firms operating more ethically than before such practices were implemented? If this is possible, what might account for an increase in the ethical behavior of a firm when using TQM principles?

6. What ethical issues are involved in fast-cycle markets?

INTERNET EXERCISE

The following companies are past winners of the Malcolm Baldrige National Quality Award:

ADAC Laboratories: **http://www.adaclabs.com**
Ames Rubber Corporation: **http://www.amesrubber.com**
Eastman Chemical: **http://www.eastman.com**

Federal Express: **http://www.fedex.com**
Motorola: **http://www.mot.com**
Trident Precision: **http://www.tridentprecision.com**

The Malcolm Baldrige National Quality Award, which is administered by the National Institute of Standards and

Technology and the U.S. Commerce Department, recognizes U.S. firms for excellence in quality management. Select one of the past winners of this award. Use the Internet to find information that enables you to write a short critique of how this company uses an emphasis on quality management to enhance its competitiveness.

Strategic Surfing

DePaul University maintains a Web site that provides links to a variety of Web sites that focus on quality management issues.

http://condor.depaul.edu/~mgt/om_sub11.html

NOTES

1. J. Kurtzman, 1998, An interview with C. K. Prahalad, in J. Kurtzman (ed.), *Thought Leaders* (San Francisco: Jossey-Bass), 40–51; C. M. Grimm and K. G. Smith, 1997, *Strategy as Action: Industry Rivalry and Coordination* (Cincinnati: South-Western College Publishing); A. Y. Illinitch and R. A. D'Aveni, 1996, New organizational forms and strategies for managing in hypercompetitive environments, *Organization Science* 7: 211–220.

2. G. Colvin, 1997, The most valuable quality in a manager, *Fortune*, December 29, 279–280.

3. C. Adams, 1998, Two steelmakers may build new mills, *Wall Street Journal*, January 7, A2.

4. H. Simonian, 1997, No stopping them, *Financial Times*, November 7, 15.

5. R. Grover, 1997, Now playing on screen 29 . . . , *Business Week*, July 7, 46.

6. K. Nobeoka and M. A. Cusumano, 1997, Multiproject strategy and sales growth: The benefits of rapid design transfer in new product development, *Strategic Management Journal* 18: 169–186; R. A. Bettis and M. A. Hitt, 1995, The new competitive landscape, *Strategic Management Journal* 16 (Special Summer Issue), 7–19.

7. K. Kerwin and K. Naughton, 1997, Can Detroit make cars that baby boomers like? *Business Week*, December 1, 134–148.

8. B. Vlasic and K. Naughton, 1997, The small-car wars are back, *Business Week*, September 22, 40–42.

9. T. Box, 1997, Toyota steers a solid course of growth, *Dallas Morning News*, November 30, H1, H2; H. Simonian, 1997, A steady drive around the world, *Financial Times*, December 5, 14.

10. M. Nakamoto, 1998, Japan carmakers renew their European offensive, *The Financial Times*, January 15, 7; M. Nakamoto, 1997, Toyota targets European sales, *Financial Times*, November 20, 21.

11. J. Kurtzman, 1998, An interview with Keshub Mahindra, in J. Kurtzman (ed.), *Thought Leaders* (San Francisco: Jossey-Bass), 29–39.

12. E. K. Clemons, 1997, Technology-driven environmental shifts and the sustainable competitive disadvantage of previously dominant companies, in G. S. Day and D. J. Reibstein (eds.), *Wharton on Dynamic Competitive Strategy* (New York: John Wiley & Sons), 99–126.

13. B. S. Silverman, J. A. Nickerson, and J. Freeman, 1997, Profitability, transactional alignment, and organizational mortality in the U.S. trucking industry, *Strategic Management Journal* 18 (Special Summer Issue), 31–52.

14. A. C. Inkpen and P. W. Beamish, 1997, Knowledge, bargaining power, and the instability of international joint ventures, *Academy of Management Review* 22: 177–202; J. Stiles, 1995, Collaboration for competitive advantage: The changing world of alliances and partnerships, *Long Range Planning* 28: 109–112.

15. S. Fidler, 1997, Big guns target a sky wars victory, *Financial Times*, December 19, 5.

16. E. Tucker, 1997, Euro-regulator spectre hovers backstage, *Financial Times*, December 19, 3.

17. M. Sakakibara, 1997, Heterogeneity of firm capabilities and cooperative research and development: An empirical examination of motives, *Strategic Management Journal* 18 (Special Summer Issue), 143–164.

18. G. S. Day and D. J. Reibstein, 1997, The dynamic challenges for theory and practice, in G. S. Day and D. J. Reibstein (eds.), *Wharton on Competitive Strategy* (New York: John Wiley & Sons) 2.

19. D. Foust and W. Zellner, 1997, US Airways: Not much room to maneuver, *Business Week*, October 13, 40.

20. S. J. Marsh, 1998, Creating barriers for foreign competitors: A study of the impact of anti-dumping actions on the performance of U.S. firms, *Strategic Management Journal* 19: 25–37; K. G. Smith, C. M. Grimm, and S. Wally, 1997, Strategic groups and rivalrous firm behavior: Towards a reconciliation, *Strategic Management Journal* 18: 149–157.

21. R. A. Klavans, C. A. Di Benedetto, and J. J. Prudom, 1997, Understanding competitive interactions: The U.S. commercial aircraft market, *Journal of Managerial Issues* IX, no. 1: 13–36.

22. Day and Reibstein, *Wharton on Competitive Strategy*; M. E. Porter, 1980, *Competitive Strategy* (New York: The Free Press), 17.

23. H. Simonian, 1998, Renault expands horizons, *Financial Times*, January 2, 10.

24. Porter, *Competitive Strategy*.

25. L. Johannes, 1998, Kodak reports loss of $744 million including big restructuring charge, *Wall Street Journal*, January 16, A4.

26. C. R. Henderson and W. Mitchell, 1997, The interactions of organizational and competitive influences on strategy and performance, *Strategic Management Journal* 18 (Special Summer Issue), 5–14.

27. W. Ocasio, 1997, Towards an attention-based view of the firm, *Strategic Management Journal* 18 (Special Summer Issue), 187–206.

28. Grimm and Smith, *Strategy as Action*, 75–102.

29. L. Himelstein, 1997, Levi's is hiking up its pants, *Business Week*, December 1, 70–75.

30. G. P. Hodgkinson and G. Johnson, 1994, Exploring the mental models of competitive strategists: The case for a processual approach, *Journal of Management Studies* 31: 525–551; J. F. Porac and H. Thomas, 1994, Cognitive categorization and subjective rivalry among retailers in a small city, *Journal of Applied Psychology* 79: 54–66.

31. N. Houthoofd and A. Heene, 1997, Strategic groups as subsets of strategic scope groups in the Belgian brewing industry, *Strategic Management Journal* 18: 653–666; G. P. Carroll and A. Swaminathan, 1992, The organizational ecology of strategic groups in the American brewing industry from 1975–1988, *Industrial and Corporate Change* 1: 65–97.

32. K. Ohmae, 1985, *Triad Power* (New York: The Free Press).

33. Grimm and Smith, *Strategy as Action*, 84; f. i. smith and R. L. Wilson, 1995, The predictive validity of the Karnani and Wernerfelt model of multipoint competition, *Strategic Management Journal* 16: 143–160.

34. J. Gimeno and C. Y. Woo, 1996, Hypercompetition in multimarket environment: The role of strategic similarity and multimarket contact in competitive deescalation, *Organization Science* 7: 322–344; W. N. Evans and I. N. Kessides, 1994, Living by the "golden rule": Multimarket contact in the U.S. airline industry, *Quarterly Journal of Economics* 109: 341–366.

35. M. J. Chen, 1996, Competitor analysis and interfirm rivalry: Toward a theoretical integration, *Academy of Management Review* 21: 100–134.

36. L. Kehoe and P. Taylor, 1998, Compaq achieves goal of joining top three ahead of time, *Financial Times*, January 25, 5; Hoechst, 1996, *Annual Report*.

37. M. A. Peteraf, 1993, Intraindustry structure and response toward rivals, *Journal of Managerial Decision Economics* 14: 519–528.

38. Grimm and Smith, *Strategy as Action*, 84; Chen, Competitor analysis.

39. Grimm and Smith, *Strategy as Action*, 125.

40. B. Horovitz, 1997, Coca-Cola, Pepsi tap bottled water market, *USA Today*, August 27, B10.

41. Smith and Grimm, *Strategy as Action*, 53–74.

42. A. A. Lado, N. G. Boyd, and S. C. Hanlon, 1997, Competition, cooperation, and the search for economic rents: A syncretic model, *Academy of Management Review* 22: 110–141.

43. J. L. C. Cheng and I. F. Kesner, 1997, Organizational slack and response to environmental shifts: The impact of resource allocation patterns, *Journal of Management* 23: 1–18.

44. E. Ramstad, 1998, Mitsubishi unit bets big on digital TV, to end sales of standard sets in U.S., *Wall Street Journal*, January 19, B10.

45. B. McKay, 1997, Merger to create Russia's largest investment bank, *Wall Street Journal*, July 10, A12.

46. K. Stevens and K. Kurschner, 1997, That vroom! you hear may not be a Harley, *Business Week*, October 20, 159–160.

47. M. B. Lieberman and D. B. Montgomery, 1988, First-mover advantages, *Strategic Management Journal* 9: 41–58.

48. K. G. Smith, C. M. Grimm, and M. J. Gannon, 1992, *Dynamics of Competitive Strategy* (Newberry Park, CA: Sage).

49. A. Ginsberg and N. Venkatraman, 1992, Investing in new information technology: The role of competitive posture and issue diagnosis, *Strategic Management Journal* 13 (Special Summer Issue): 37–53.

50. Smith, Grimm, and Gannon, *Dynamics of Competitive Strategy*.

51. V. Griffith, 1998, Reebok to cut sponsorships, *Financial Times*, January 15, 15.

52. I. Pereira, 1998, Sneaker company tags out-of-breath baby boomers, *Wall Street Journal*, January 16, B1, B2.

53. G. S. Day, 1997, Assessing competitive arenas: Who are your competitors? In G. S. Day and D. J. Reibstein, *Wharton on Competitive Strategy* (New York: John Wiley & Sons) 25–26.

54. *The Economist*, 1997, Soap power, with added logic, December 7, 68–73.

55. K. Labich, 1994, Air wars over Asia, *Fortune*, April 4, 93–98.

56. T. Maxon, 1998, American to bolster flier plan, *Dallas Morning News*, January 22, D3.

57. T. Maxon, 1997, Return trip, *Dallas Morning News*, June 10, D1, D14.

58. Grimm and Smith, *Strategy as Action*, 134.

59. E. Malkin and R. A. Melcher, 1997, On the prowl for more suds, *Business Week*, October 6, 154D–154F.

60. L. Grant, 1997, Why FedEx is flying high, *Fortune*, November 10, 156–160.

61. Smith, Grimm, and Gannon, *Dynamics of Competitive Strategy*.

62. Ibid.

63. B. Pinsker, 1997, Rental block, *Dallas Morning News*, June 14, C5, C8.

64. H. Stout, 1997, Tiny toy stores scramble for ways to lure customers, *Wall Street Journal*, December 9, B2.

65. M. Skapinker, 1998, Airbus boasts year of record orders, *Financial Times*, January 8, 6.

66. M. Nakamoto, 1997, Sega sales suffer as competition bites, *Financial Times*, November 21, 17.

67. J. A. Schumpeter, 1961, *Theory of Economic Development* (New York: Oxford University Press).

68. A. E. Serwer, 1997, Michael Dell turns the PC world inside out, *Fortune*, September 8, 76–86.

69. M. Halkias, 1998, CompUSA Inc., *Dallas Morning News*, January 29, D10; S. A. Forest and P. Burrows, 1997, And give me an extra-fast modem with that, please, *Business Week*, September 29, 38; K. Lyons, 1997, CompUSA to offer built-to-order PCs, *Dallas Morning News*, July 16, D1, D12.

70. A. Goldstein, 1997, Dell surpasses analyst expectations as profits soar 71% in third quarter, *Dallas Morning News*, November 25, D7.

71. A. Goldstein, 1997, Compaq CEO sees industry consolidation, *Dallas Morning News*, November 18, D6.

72. Bloomberg News, 1998, Radio Shack to sell only Compaq PCs, *Dallas Morning News*, January 29, D2; A. Goldstein, 1998, Compaq to buy Digital, *Dallas Morning News*, January 27, D1, D6.

73. R. A. Melcher, 1993, How Goliaths can act like Davids, *Business Week* (Special Issue), 193.

74. J. Kurtzman, 1998, An interview with Charles Handy, in J. Kurtzman (ed.), *Thoughts Leaders* (San Francisco: Jossey-Bass), 4–15; J. Birkinshaw, 1997, Entrepreneurship in multinational corporations: The characteristics of subsidiary initiatives, *Strategic Management Journal* 18: 207–229.

75. Harvard Business Review Perspectives, 1995, How can big companies keep the entrepreneurial spirit alive? *Harvard Business Review* 73, no. 6: 183–192.

199

76. E. H. Kessler and A. K. Chakrabarti, 1996, Innovation speed: A conceptual model of context, antecedents, and outcomes, *Academy of Management Review* 21: 1143–1191; S. L. Brown and K. M. Eisenhardt, 1995, Product development: Past research, present findings, and future directions, *Academy of Management Review* 20: 343–378; K. M. Eisenhardt and B. N. Tabrizi, 1995, Accelerating adaptive processes: Product innovation in the global computer industry, *Administrative Science Quarterly* 40: 84–110.

77. A. Cane, 1997, Long-distance visionary, *Financial Times*, December 19, 3.

78. R. R. Nayyar and K. A. Bantel, 1994, Competitive agility: A source of competitive advantage based on speed and variety, *Advances in Strategic Management* 10A, 193–222.

79. S. Wally and J. R. Baum, 1994, Personal and structural determinants of the pace of strategic decision-making, *Academy of Management Journal* 37: 932–956.

80. Ibid.

81. T. Smart and J. H. Dobrzynski, 1993, Jack Welch on the art of thinking small, *Business Week*, (Special Enterprise Issue), 212–216.

82. J. Kurtzman, 1998, An interview with Gary Hamel, in J. Kurtzman (ed.), *Thought Leaders* (San Francisco: Jossey-Bass), 134–149; J. Wind, 1997, Preemptive strategies, in G. S. Day and D. J. Reibstein, *Wharton on Dynamic Competitive Strategy* (New York: John Wiley & Sons), 256–276; S. C. Wheelwright and K. B. Clark, 1995, *Leading Product Development* (New York: The Free Press).

83. B. N. Dickie, 1998, Foreword, in J. Kurtzman (ed.), *Thought Leaders* (San Francisco: Jossey-Bass), xi–xvii; J. Kurtzman, 1998, An interview with Paul M. Romer, in J. Kurtzman (ed.), *Thought Leaders* (San Francisco: Jossey-Bass), 66–83.

84. L. G. Franko, 1989, Global corporate competition: Who's winning, who's losing, and the R&D factor as one reason why, *Strategic Management Journal* 10: 449–474.

85. R. E. Hoskisson and M. A. Hitt, 1994, *Downscoping: How to Tame the Diversified Firm* (New York: Oxford University Press).

86. K. J. Klein and J. S. Sorra, 1996, The challenge of innovation implementation, *Academy of Management Review* 21: 1055–1080.

87. L. Tyson, 1997, Model Taiwan company becomes a high flyer, *Financial Times*, December 18, 16.

88. Klein and Sorra, The challenge of innovation implementation.

89. N. Dunne, 1998, American goldmine for high-tech workers, *Financial Times*, January 15, 4; V. Griffith, 1998, Learning to wear two hats, *Financial Times*, January 5, 20; N. Timmins, 1998, Manufacturers face skills shortfall, *Financial Times*, January 9, 4.

90. J. W. Dean, Jr., and D. E. Bowen, 1994, Management theory and total quality: Improving research and practice through theory development, *Academy of Management Review* 19: 392–419.

91. J. Aley, 1994, Manufacturers grade themselves, *Fortune*, March 21, 26.

92. M. Halkias, 1997, Rising competition, *Dallas Morning News*, November 13, D1, D12.

93. J. Heizer and B. Render, 1996, *Production and Operations Management*, 4th ed. (Upper Saddle River, NJ: Prentice-Hall), 75–106.

94. M. van Biema and B. Greenwald, 1997, Managing our way to higher service-sector productivity, *Harvard Business Review* 75, no. 4: 87–95.

95. S. Chatterjee and M. Yilmaz, 1993, Quality confusion: Too many gurus, not enough disciples, *Business Horizons* 36, no. 3: 15–18.

96. B. Render and J. Heizer, 1997, *Principles of Operations Management*, 2nd ed. (Upper Saddle River, NJ: Prentice Hall), 89–113.

97. Serwer, Michael Dell.

98. W. S. Sherman and M. A. Hitt, 1996, Creating corporate value: Integrating quality and innovation programs, in D. Fedor and S. Ghoshal (eds.), *Advances in the Management of Organizational Quality* (Greenwich, CT: JAI Press), 221–244.

99. J. D. Westphal, R. Gulati, and S. M. Shortell, 1997, Customization or conformity: An institutional and network perspective on the content and consequences of TQM adoption, *Administrative Science Quarterly* 42: 366–394.

100. E. E. Lawler, III, 1994, Total quality management and employee involvement: Are they compatible? *Academy of Management Executive* VIII, no. 1: 68.

101. R. S. Russell and B. W. Taylor, III, 1998, *Operations Management*, 2nd ed. (Upper Saddle River, NJ: Prentice Hall), 130–165.

102. A. M. Schneiderman, 1998, Are there limits to total quality management?, *Strategy Business* 11, second quarter, 35–45; R. Krishnan, A. B. Shani, and G. R. Baer, 1993, In search of quality improvement: Problems of design and implementation, *Academy of Management Executive* VII, no. 3: 7–20.

103. R. Blackburn and B. Rosen, 1993, Total quality and human resources management: Lessons learned from Baldridge award-winning companies, *Academy of Management Executive* VII, no. 3: 49–66.

104. H. V. Roberts and B. F. Sergesketter, 1993, *Quality Is Personal* (New York: The Free Press).

105. S. B. Sitkin, K. M. Sutcliffe, and R. G. Schroeder, 1994, Distinguishing control from learning in total quality management: A contingency perspective, *Academy of Management Review* 19: 537–564.

106. J. R. Hackman and R. Wageman, 1995, Total quality management: Empirical, conceptualization and practical issues, *Administrative Science Quarterly* 40: 309–342.

107. J. R. Williams, 1992, How sustainable is your competitive advantage? *California Management Review* 34 (Spring): 29–51.

108. G. S. Day, 1997, Maintaining the competitive edge: Creating and sustaining advantages in dynamic competitive environments, in G. S. Day and D. J. Reibstein, *Wharton on Dynamic Competitive Strategy* (New York: John Wiley & Sons) 48–75.

109. J. H. Perser, 1993, McIlhenny used shrewd marketing to keep Tabasco a hot export product, *Traffic World*, April 5, 15–16.

110. A. D. Chandler, 1990, The enduring logic of industrial success, *Harvard Business Review* 68, no. 2: 130–140.

111. J. L. Bower and T. M. Hout, 1988, Fast-cycle capability for competitive power, *Harvard Business Review* 66, no. 6: 110–118.

112. Williams, How sustainable is your competitive advantage?

113. K. R. Conner, 1995, Obtaining strategic advantage from being imitated: When can encouraging "clones" pay? *Management Science* 41: 209–225; K. R. Connor, 1988, Strategies for product cannibalism, *Strategic Management Journal* 9 (Special Summer Issue), 135–159.

114. R. A. D'Aveni, 1995, Coping with hypercompetition: Utilizing the new 7's framework, *Academy of Management Executive* IX, no. 3: 45–60.

115. R. Sanchez, 1995, Strategic flexibility in product competition, *Strategic Management Journal* 16 (Special Summer Issue), 9–26.

116. M. A. Hitt, B. B. Tyler, C. Hardee, and D. Park, 1994, Understanding strategic intent in the global marketplace, *Academy of Management Executive* IX, no. 2: 12–19.

117. G. Miles, C. Snow, and M. P. Sharfman, 1993, Industry variety and performance, *Strategic Management Journal* 14: 163–177.

118. D. Lei, 1989, Strategies for global competition, *Long-Range Planning* 22: 102–109.

119. Miles, Snow, and Sharfman, Industry variety.

120. K. Cool and I. Dierickx, 1993, Rivalry, strategic groups and firm profitability, *Strategic Management Journal* 14: 47–59.

121. S. A. Shane, 1996, Hybrid organizational arrangements and their implications for firm growth and survival: A study of new franchisors, *Academy of Management Journal* 39: 216–234.

122. D. M. Schroeder, 1990, A dynamic perspective on the impact of process innovation upon competitive strategies, *Strategic Management Journal* 11: 25–41.

123. R. Schmalensee, 1978, Entry deterrence in the ready-to-eat breakfast cereal industry, *Bell Journal of Economics* 9: 305–328.

Corporate-Level Strategy

CHAPTER 6

Learning Objectives

After reading this chapter, you should be able to:

1. Define corporate-level strategy and discuss its importance to the diversified firm.

2. Describe the advantages and disadvantages of single-business and dominant-business strategies.

3. Explain three primary reasons why firms move from single-business and dominant-business strategies to more diversified strategies.

4. Describe how related-diversified firms use activity sharing and the transfer of core competencies to create value.

5. Discuss the two ways an unrelated diversification strategy can create value.

6. Discuss the incentives and resources that encourage diversification.

7. Describe motives that can encourage managers to further diversify a firm.

The Diversification of United Parcel Service

Founded in 1970 in Seattle, Washington, United Parcel Service (UPS) is the world's largest package distribution company, transporting over 3.1 billion parcels and documents annually. UPS offers its services in over 200 countries through the efforts of approximately 340,000 employees. To improve both effectiveness and efficiency, the firm's package operations are grouped into five geographic sections to handle deliveries outside the United States—Asia Pacific, Canada, Europe, Latin America/Caribbean, and Middle East/Africa. UPS utilizes more than 500 aircraft, 147,000 vehicles, and 2,400 facilities to deliver packages. In fact, UPS believes that it operates the world's largest airline. As the twenty-first century approaches, company leaders suggest that the firm's commitment to learning how to continuously increase its competitiveness in global markets represents the cornerstone of the future for UPS.

http://www.ups.com

During August 1997, the operational capacities of UPS were damaged severely by a two-week strike that was called by the firm's unionized personnel. The strike resulted in a loss of over $600 million in sales revenue and highlighted the company's dependence on the core part of its business operations. This dependence is illustrated by the fact that at the

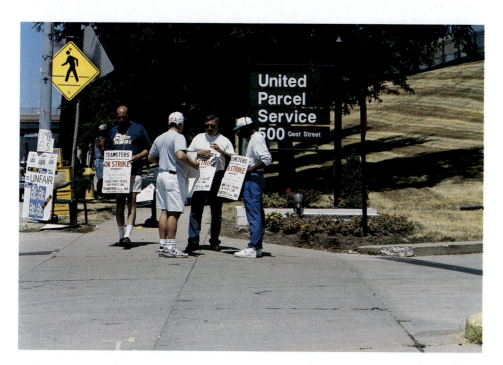

end of 1997, roughly 97.8 percent of UPS's sales revenue was generated through the delivery of parcels and documents. The remaining 2.2 percent of revenue was earned by a wholly owned, independently managed subsidiary called UPS Worldwide Logistics.

Established in 1991, UPS Worldwide Logistics is a third-party provider of global supply-chain management solutions, including transportation management, warehouse operations, inventory management, documentation for import and export, and network optimization practices, among other services. In essence, as a group to whom others outsource their need for a service, UPS Worldwide Logistics has the ability required "to partner with its customers to move goods from the source of raw materials through to the end consumer, meeting every need in the distribution chain along the way."

The 1997 strike's effect on sales revenues created a renewed interest among UPS executives to derive additional sales revenue from the diversification represented by the firm's Worldwide Logistics unit. Focused on logistics management, which is the science of moving and storing products, UPS top-level managers believe that the Logistics unit can grow sevenfold in only six years. If this objective is reached, the revenues generated by the Logistics unit through the early part of the twenty-first century would approximate 13 percent of UPS's total sales revenue.

Predicted growth in the market for the outsourcing of logistics to companies such as UPS Worldwide Logistics and Electronic Data Systems Corp. (one of UPS's major competitors in the logistics business) encourages the belief among UPS executives that its diversification effort will benefit the entire company. In 1997, U.S. firms spent approximately $10 billion on outsourced logistics services; this figure is expected to increase to over $50 billion by 2000. By transferring its distribution system core competence from the major part of UPS to the Worldwide Logistics unit, the firm believes it possesses a competitive advantage that will allow it to succeed in the burgeoning logistics business.

Currently, the Logistics unit offers a variety of transportation-related services. For example, to provide a batch of independent components to Dell Computer Corp.'s customers simultaneously, various portions of computer shipments from different distributors are collected and then combined into a single shipment for the Round Rock, Texas-based firm. To expand its operations, the unit intends to offer more services. Data handling and "electronic commerce," such as taking care of billing for customers, are examples of services being planned for the future. Committed to the global marketplace in providing its services, UPS Worldwide Logistics has warehouse and distribution centers in Singapore; Cologne, Germany; and Best, Netherlands, as well as a facility in Louisville, Kentucky.

SOURCE: C. Batchelor, 1998, UPS sets up rail service in Germany, *Financial Times*, March 17, 27; Associated Press, 1998, UPS, pilots reach tentative labor deal, *Dallas Morning News*, January 20, D2; A. Dworkin, 1997, Delivering the goods, *Dallas Morning News*, September 14, H1, H6; UPS Home Page, 1998, January 12, http://www.ups.com.

As indicated in the opening case, top-level managers at UPS decided that their firm should become more diversified. This decision also indicates that a change is being made in the firm's corporate-level strategy. The company had been implementing what is called a *single-business* corporate-level strategy (see Figure 6.1). With a low level of diversification (recall that in 1997, approximately 2.2 percent of revenue was earned outside its core business), UPS sought strategic competitiveness and above-average returns by concentrating on the distribution of packages and documents. For many years, this strategy was successful. Based on the competitive advantage yielded by the firm's core competency in distribution, UPS became the world's largest package distribution company. The sales revenue and financial returns that UPS has earned historically suggest that this firm has achieved a position of strategic competitiveness.

However, 1997 proved to be the year in which UPS's almost total reliance on the package distribution business for its revenue and profitability became an issue. As explained previously, a strike by the firm's unionized personnel resulted in a loss of approximately $600 million in sales revenue in a two-month period. This situation caused some UPS customers to consider the wisdom of relying on a single source for distribution of their products. Similarly, UPS executives concluded that some diversification away from its core business would benefit their company.

The focal point of the interest in additional diversification quickly became the firm's own Worldwide Logistics unit. Convinced that it can be a "big player" in the logistics management field, UPS executives established an ambitious set of sales revenue goals for this subsidiary. Revenues of roughly $700 million in 1997 (up from $500 million in 1996) were expected to reach $1 billion in 1998 and increase by $700 or $800 million annually through 2003. If achieved, this pace of growth will exceed the expected 8 percent annual growth rate in the firm's core parcel-shipping business.

205

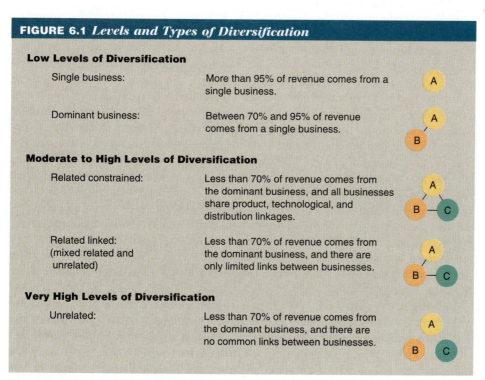

FIGURE 6.1 *Levels and Types of Diversification*

Low Levels of Diversification

| Single business: | More than 95% of revenue comes from a single business. |

| Dominant business: | Between 70% and 95% of revenue comes from a single business. |

Moderate to High Levels of Diversification

| Related constrained: | Less than 70% of revenue comes from the dominant business, and all businesses share product, technological, and distribution linkages. |

| Related linked: (mixed related and unrelated) | Less than 70% of revenue comes from the dominant business, and there are only limited links between businesses. |

Very High Levels of Diversification

| Unrelated: | Less than 70% of revenue comes from the dominant business, and there are no common links between businesses. |

Source: Adapted from R. P. Rumelt, 1974, *Strategy, Structure and Economic Performance* (Boston: Harvard Business School).

Although aggressive in nature, some analysts believe these revenue goals are attainable. The CEO of Armstrong & Associates Inc., a logistics analysis company, noted that he had "been expecting great things from UPS Logistics for a long time." Moreover, in this analyst's view, "UPS has got so many resources, they ought to be able to build a worldwide logistics operation that could force others out of business."[1] If this type of success is achieved, and the firm is able to earn 13 percent or more of sales revenue from the operations of its Worldwide Logistics unit, UPS's corporate-level strategy will have changed from *single business* to *dominant business* (see Figure 6.1). The success of UPS's additional diversification is not assured, however. Diversification strategies are difficult to manage.[2] Nonetheless, the risk UPS executives believed their firm would face by failing to become more diversified exceeded the risk associated with learning how to effectively manage a more diversified corporation. Beyond the matter of risk, UPS executives were convinced that the firm's financial returns would increase through proper management of a greater amount of diversification.

In Chapters 4 and 5, our discussions focused on the selection and use of business-level strategies.[3] Our discussions of different business-level strategies (Chapter 4) and the competitive dynamics associated with their use (Chapter 5) were focused primarily on firms competing in a single industry or product market.

When a firm chooses to diversify its operations beyond a single industry and to operate businesses in several industries, it is pursuing a corporate-level strategy of diversification. As is the case with business-level strategies, a corporate-level strategy of diversification allows a firm to adapt to conditions in its external environment.[4] An influential strategic choice in firms, diversification strategies play a major role in the behavior of large firms.[5] Strategic choices regarding diversification are, however, fraught with uncertainty.[6]

A diversified company has two levels of strategy: a business-level (or competitive) strategy and a corporate-level (or company-wide) strategy.[7] In diversified firms, each business unit chooses a business-level strategy to implement to achieve strategic competitiveness and earn above-average returns. But diversified firms must also choose a strategy that is concerned with the selection and management of its businesses. Defined formally, a **corporate-level strategy** is action taken to gain a competitive advantage through the selection and management of a mix of businesses competing in several industries or product markets. In essence, a corporate-level strategy is what makes "the corporate whole add up to more than the sum of its business unit parts."[8] Corporate-level strategy is concerned with two key questions: what businesses the firm should be in and how the corporate office should manage its group of businesses.[9] Roberto Goizueta, former CEO of Coca-Cola, captured the essence of these two questions by suggesting that top-level executives were responsible for verifying that the firm could develop effective strategies across time and knew how to allocate capital effectively and efficiently.[10] In the current complex global environment, top-level managers should view their firm's businesses as a portfolio of core competencies when seeking answers to these critical questions.[11]

Relating back to Figure 1.1 in Chapter 1, our focus herein is on the formulation of corporate-level strategy. The corporate-level strategy should evolve from the firm's strategic intent and mission. Also, as with business-level strategies, corporate-level strategies are expected to help the firm earn above-average returns (create value).[12] Some have suggested that few corporate-level strategies actually create value.[13] In the final analysis, the value of a corporate-level strategy "must be that the

A **corporate-level strategy** is action taken to gain a competitive advantage through the selection and management of a mix of businesses competing in several industries or product markets.

businesses in the portfolio are worth more under the management of the company in question than they would be under any other ownership."[14] Thus, the corporate-level strategy should be expected to contribute a given amount to the returns of all business units that exceeds what those returns would be without the implementation of such a strategy.[15] When managed effectively, corporate-level strategies enhance a firm's strategic competitiveness and contribute to its ability to earn above-average returns.[16] In the latter part of the 1990s and into the twenty-first century, corporate-level strategies will be managed in a global business environment characterized by high degrees of risk, complexity, uncertainty, and ambiguity.[17]

A primary approach to corporate-level strategy is diversification, which requires corporate-level executives to craft a multibusiness strategy. One reason for the use of a diversification strategy is that managers of diversified firms possess unique, general management skills that can be used to develop multibusiness strategies and enhance a firm's strategic competitiveness.[18] To derive the greatest benefit from their skills, managers must focus their energies on the tasks associated with managing a diversification strategy.[19] The prevailing theory of diversification suggests that firms should diversify when they have excess resources, capabilities, and core competencies that have multiple uses.[20] Multibusiness strategies often encompass many different industry environments, and, as discussed in Chapter 11, these strategies require unique organizational structures.

This chapter begins by addressing the history of diversification. Included in this discussion are descriptions of the advantages and disadvantages of single-business and dominant-business strategies. We next describe different levels of diversification (from low to high) and reasons firms pursue a corporate-level strategy of diversification. Two types of diversification strategies that denote moderate to very high levels of diversification—related and unrelated—are then examined.

Large diversified firms often compete against each other in several markets. This is called *multipoint competition*. For instance, RJR Nabisco competes against Philip Morris in both cigarettes and consumer foods. Svenska Aeroplan Aktiebolaget (Saab) and Daimler-Benz AG compete against one another in both automobiles and aircraft engines. Vertical integration strategies designed to exploit market share and gain power over competitors are also explored. Closing the chapter is a brief discussion of questions firms should consider when examining the possiblility of becoming a diversified company. For the already-diversified firm, these questions can be used to determine if additional levels of diversification should be pursued.

Of course, there are alternatives to diversification. These options entail long-term contracts, such as strategic alliances and franchising, discussed in Chapter 9, and expanding into new geographic markets such as international diversification, discussed in Chapter 8.

HISTORY OF DIVERSIFICATION

In 1950, only 38.1 percent of the *Fortune* 500 U.S. industrial companies generated more than 25 percent of their revenues from diversified activities. By 1974, this figure had risen to 63 percent. In 1950, then, more than 60 percent of the largest *Fortune* 500 industrial companies were either single-business or dominant-business firms; by 1974, this had dropped to 37 percent.[21]

Beginning in the late 1970s, and especially through the middle part of the 1980s, a significant trend toward refocusing and divestiture of business units unrelated to core business activities took place in many firms. In fact, approximately 50 percent of the *Fortune* 500 companies refocused on their core businesses from 1981–1987.[22] As a result, by 1988, the percentage of single- or dominant-business firms on the *Fortune* 500 list of industrial companies had increased to 53 percent.[23] Although many diversified firms have become more focused, this is somewhat masked because extensive market and international diversification (compared to product diversification) has occurred that is not included in these statistics. As Chapter 8's discussion reveals, international strategy has been increasing in importance and has led to greater financial performance relative to product diversification.[24]

The trend toward product diversification of business organizations has been most significant among U.S. firms. Nonetheless, large business organizations in Europe, Asia, and other parts of the industrialized world have also implemented diversification strategies. In the United Kingdom, the number of single- or dominant-business firms fell from 60 percent in 1960 to 37 percent in 1980. A similar, yet less dramatic trend toward more diversification occurred in Japan. Among the largest Japanese firms, 60 percent were dominant- or single-business firms in 1958, although this percentage fell only to 53 percent in 1973.

These trends toward more diversification, which have been partially reversed due to restructuring (see Chapter 7), indicate that learning has taken place regarding corporate diversification strategies. The main lesson learned is that firms performing well in their dominant business may not want to diversify. Moreover, firms that diversify should do so cautiously, choosing to focus on a relatively few, rather than many, businesses.[25]

Deciding to become more diversified in terms of both product offerings and geographic locations appears to have contributed to Cott Corporation's recent difficulties. Originally, Cott produced and sold (at discount prices) an array of private-label beverages including soft drinks, New Age beverages, iced teas, juice drinks, sport drinks, and bottled water. Cott's customers were large retail chains such as Wal-Mart and Safeway. Through effective implementation of its strategy, this Toronto, Canada, company grew, in less than 10 years, from a small family business to a multinational corporation with annual sales of over $1 billion. This growth resulted in the firm becoming the leading worldwide supplier of premium retailer branded beverages and the world's fourth largest soft drink company. The company believes that product innovation, employee creativity, high-quality products, and world-class packaging are its core competencies.

As one analyst observed recently, the firm followed its initial success with expansions "into things it had no business expanding into, such as the Canadian beer market and faraway countries." In addition to these product and geographic forays, Cott also planned, but did not execute, a strategy that called for it to pattern a major line of private-label foods after the approach it used to sell its private-label soft drinks. Given the problems created by ill-advised diversification efforts, Cott Corporation sold its beer business and reorganized its international operations to cut costs.[26]

Thus, for Cott Corporation, diversification outside its core business area did not result in additional financial returns. Sometimes, however, the failure to pursue appropriate types of diversification may have a negative effect on the firm's strategic competitiveness. Some analysts believe that this may have been the case recently for AT&T. During the time AT&T was searching for a new CEO, its competitors, such as WorldCom, GTE, and MCI Communications, completed transactions to achieve dominant market positions in different segments of the telecommunications industry. Inactive during the search for its new CEO, AT&T may have lost some opportunities to buy assets required to do battle (see the opening case in Chapter 10). As a result, AT&T may find itself competing against a raft of fortified new rivals. The breadth of its rivals' strengths suggests that AT&T is facing the "fight of its life" in everything from local phone services to the Internet as the twenty-first century approaches. Calling for the firm to pursue a strategy of related diversification, some proposed that AT&T should have been adding to its communications assets at the same time competitors were adding to theirs. AT&T pursued related diversification earlier (in the mid-1990s) when it filled a hole in its wireless services capabilities through the purchase of McCaw Cellular Communications for more than $12 billion.[27]

As these examples about Cott and AT&T suggest, strategic competitiveness can be increased when the firm pursues a level of diversification that is appropriate for its resources (especially financial resources) and core competencies and the opportunities and threats that exist in its external environment. For some companies, however, the match between competencies and external environmental conditions indicates that they can flourish by focusing on single or highly related businesses. Two prominent examples include Wal-Mart and Coca-Cola. In fact, when he became Coca-Cola's CEO, Roberto Goizueta went against then-current wisdom when he decided to change the firm from a highly diversified company to one that was focused tightly on its core products. Goizueta explained, "There's a perception in this country that you're better off if you're in two lousy businesses than if you're in a good one—that you're spreading the risk. It's crazy."[28]

Another example of a firm that achieves success through highly focused operations is Mabuchi Motor, a midsize but highly successful Japanese firm. Ninety-nine percent of its annual revenue comes from the sale of motors. The focus on motors allows company scientists to continuously examine ways to improve the motors, such as making them lighter, quieter, more enduring, and cheaper.[29]

LEVELS OF DIVERSIFICATION

Diversified firms vary according to the level of diversification and connection between and among their businesses. Figure 6.1 lists and defines five categories of businesses according to increasing levels of diversification. Besides single- and dominant-business categories, more fully diversified firms are classified into related and unrelated categories. A firm is related through its diversification when there are several links between business units; for example, units share products or services, technologies, and/or distribution channels. The more links among businesses, the more "constrained" the relatedness of diversification. Unrelatedness refers to a lack of direct links between businesses.

Low Levels of Diversification

A firm pursing a low level of diversification focuses its efforts on a single or a dominant business. The Wm. Wrigley Jr. Company is an example of a firm with little diversification. Its primary focus is on the chewing gum market.[30] A firm is classified as a single business when revenue generated by the dominant business is greater than 95 percent of the total sales.[31] Dominant businesses are firms that generate between 70 percent and 95 percent of their total sales within a single category. Because of the sales it generates from breakfast cereals, Kellogg is an example of a dominant business firm.

Hershey Foods Corp. (the largest U.S. producer of chocolate and nonchocolate confectionery items) is another dominant business firm. Although Hershey manufactures some food products (principally San Giorgio, American Beauty, Delmonico, Skinner, and Ronzoni pastas), the bulk of the firm's revenue is earned through the selling of its confectionery items. To generate interest in its candies across time, the company introduces new products carefully and deliberately. Commenting about this approach, an analyst suggested the following: "Announcing that a new candy is on the way, then keeping it under wraps until it is ready increases sales and sparks a general feeling of enthusiasm for Hershey stock."[32]

As a result of recent decisions to become less diversified, Volvo AB now follows the dominant business corporate-level strategy. Although still diversified, with varied business interests including its agricultural equipment, the car and heavy-truck units are the firm's core businesses. Together, these units account for 70 percent of sales revenue and 50 percent of profits. To enhance its competitiveness in these units, Volvo embarked on a three-year strategic drive in late 1997 that was intended to "cut purchasing costs, slim management and lift productivity by 5 percent a year."[33] Often dominant business firms have some level of vertical integration. Many firms (such as Texaco) started as single businesses and evolved to use a dominant-business strategy involving vertical integration.

Moderate and High Levels of Diversification

When a firm earns more than 30 percent of its sales volume outside a dominant business, and when its businesses are related to each other in some manner, the company is classified as a related-diversified firm. With more direct links between the businesses, the firm is defined as related constrained. Examples of related-constrained firms include Campbell Soup, Procter & Gamble, Xerox, and Merck & Company. If there are only a few links between businesses, the firm is defined as a mix related and unrelated business, or a related-linked firm, (see Figure 6.1). Johnson & Johnson, Westinghouse, General Electric, and Schlumberger are examples of related-linked firms. Related-constrained firms share a number of resources and activities between businesses. Related-linked firms have less sharing of actual resources and assets and relatively more transfers of knowledge and competencies between businesses. Highly diversified firms, which have no relationships between businesses, are called unrelated-diversified firms. Examples of firms pursuing an unrelated diversification strategy include Dart Group, Tenneco, Textron, and Thailand's Charoen Pokphand (with department stores and business units operating in the petrochemicals and telecommunications industries, this firm's annual sales revenue approximates $8 billion).[34]

In general, there are more unrelated-diversified firms in the United States than in other (e.g., European) countries. In Latin America and other emerging economies such as Korea and India, conglomerates (firms following the unrelated diversification strategy) continue to dominate the private sector.[35] For example, typically family controlled, these corporations account for more than two-thirds of the 33 largest private business groups in Brazil. Similarly, the largest business groups in Mexico, Argentina, and Colombia are family-owned, diversified enterprises.[36]

Consistent with a global trend of refocusing, some companies decide to become less diversified. As indicated in the Strategic Focus, less diversification allows the firm to concentrate on fewer business lines. A decision to refocus could be a product of an inability to effectively manage greater levels of diversification or recognition of the fact that a lower level of diversification would permit a superior match between the firm's core competencies and its environmental opportunities and threats.

STRATEGIC FOCUS

Changes in Diversification Strategies at Hanson PLC, Terex, and Westinghouse

Cited historically as perhaps the world's most successful follower of the unrelated diversification strategy, Hanson PLC nonetheless decided in the mid-1990s to become less diversified and to streamline its operations. Thus, Hanson either sold or spun off a number of its operating businesses; those remaining were structured into four independent business units. Spinning off 34 operating companies created one of these new business units, U.S. Industries. After completing all of its streamlining actions, top-level executives were convinced that the firm's newly created ability to concentrate on its core holdings would lead to increased financial returns. Also contributing to an anticipated enhancement of the firm's strategic competitiveness was the elimination of $1.4 billion of debt through the spin-offs and divestitures.

Terex was also once more diversified than it is today. After divestitures, the firm is now focused more tightly on its related constrained diversification strategy (roughly 33 percent of revenue comes from the Terex Trucks unit; the remaining 67 percent is generated by Terex Cranes). Terex implements the cost leadership strategy in both its truck and crane business units. Emphasizing efficiency, the company uses streamlined assembly lines to produce simple, standardized equipment that is priced 10 to 15 percent lower than competitors' offerings.

Terex's former chairman and CEO relied on high-yield debt to finance an acquisition strategy during the late 1980s and early 1990s. Among the acquisitions were truck trailer manufacturer Fruehauf Trailer Corp. and forklift maker Clark Material Handling Company. Related to the firm's other units, Terex was, nonetheless, unable to successfully implement the cost leadership strategy to manufacture truck trailers and forklifts. Although substantial progress was made by the firm's new CEO to reduce costs and increase efficiencies at Clark Material (a $20 million profit in 1996 was a significant improvement over a $30 million loss in 1993), Terex sold Clark in 1996. This transaction followed the finalization of the divestment of the Fruehauf unit in January 1995. Selling these units has allowed Terex to refocus on the core truck and crane businesses rather than allocating its energies and resources across four units that shared some commonalties.

As a 100-year-plus-old industrial manufacturer, Westinghouse Electric Corp. implemented the related-linked diversification strategy for many years. The significant reduction in the amount of this firm's diversification began with the August 1995 acquisition of CBS for $5.4 billion in cash. Convinced that the firm's future was in broadcasting, CEO Michael H. Jordan initiated a process that culminated in the official changing of the firm's name to CBS Corporation. To create its broadcasting focus, two business units were sold in 1997 (Thermo King and Westinghouse Power Generation). Jordan intended to complete the sales of the remaining major business units—energy systems, process control, and government operations—by mid-1998.

211

During these divestitures, CBS Corp. acquired American Radio Systems' radio broadcasting operations. Calling this transaction "strategically attractive," a top-level CBS executive stated, "This investment will significantly strengthen CBS's position in the fast growing radio industry. It will enable CBS Radio to expand into new top 50 markets and increase its position in its existing markets." Thus, to expand its single product line of broadcasting, a line that includes CBS Network, CBS radio, the TV station group, cable, and "other" broadcasting, CBS Corp. was committed to making selective acquisitions.

SOURCE: *CBS Corporation Home Page*, 1998, January 13, http://www.cbs.com; *Terex Corporation Home Page*, 1998, January 13, http://www.terex.com; *The Economist*, 1997, Westinghouse RIP, November 29, 63–65; T. Aeppel, 1997, How Westinghouse's famous name simply faded away, *Wall Street Journal*, November 20, B4; G. Fairclough, 1997, Terex's fortunes improve after tough cost-cutting, *Wall Street Journal*, September 30, B4; L. L. Brownlee and J. R. Dorfman, 1995, Birth of U.S. industries isn't without complications, *Wall Street Journal*, May 18, B4.

REASONS FOR DIVERSIFICATION

Firms implement a diversification strategy as their corporate-level strategy for many reasons. A partial list of these is shown in Table 6.1. These reasons are discussed throughout the remainder of this chapter in relationship to specific diversification strategies.

Most firms implement a diversification strategy to enhance the strategic competitiveness of the entire company. This is the case at UPS, as explained in the

---

TABLE 6.1 *Motives, Incentives, and Resources for Diversification*

Motives to Enhance Strategic Competitiveness

- Economies of scope (related diversification)
  Sharing activities
  Transferring core competencies
- Market power (related diversification)
  Blocking competitors through multipoint competition
  Vertical integration
- Financial economies (unrelated diversification)
  Efficient internal capital allocation
  Business restructuring

Incentives and Resources with Neutral Effects on Strategic Competitiveness

- Antitrust regulation
- Tax laws
- Low performance
- Uncertain future cash flows
- Firm risk reduction
- Tangible resources
- Intangible resources

Managerial Motives (Value Reduction)

- Diversifying managerial employment risk
- Increasing managerial compensation

opening case, and for Saab and Daimler-Benz as well. With headquarters in Brussels, this is also true for the Solvay Group. In pursuit of above-average returns, Solvay concentrates on diversified activities in five sectors—alkalis, peroxygens, plastics, processing, and health.[37] When a diversification strategy does enhance strategic competitiveness, the firm's total value is increased. Value is created through either related diversification or unrelated diversification when those strategies allow a company's business units to increase revenues and/or reduce costs while implementing their business-level strategies.

Another reason for diversification is to gain market power relative to competitors. To increase its market power by building a national home-care network, Integrated Health Services, Inc. purchased RoTech Medical Corp. for $615 million in stock. Integrated Health officials suggested that the additional diversification this transaction created would enable the firm to provide a broad spectrum of home health services, from nursing to respiratory care to intravenous medication and nutrition. Similarly, the purchase of a Cleveland-based retail real estate brokerage firm by Trammel Crow Co., a prominent Dallas-based industrial real estate company, was intended to increase quickly the firm's retail penetration on a national scale. In commenting about the purchase, a Trammel Crow executive observed, "We think that this acquisition advances our progress by a number of years."[38] In the instance of both Integrated Health and Trammel Crow, additional diversification was expected to help each firm gain a competitive advantage over its rivals.

Other reasons for implementing diversification may not enhance strategic competitiveness; in fact, diversification could have neutral effects or actually increase costs or reduce a firm's revenues. These reasons include diversification (1) to neutralize a competitor's market power (e.g., to neutralize the advantage of another firm by acquiring a distribution outlet similar to those of the competitors) or (2) to expand a firm's portfolio to reduce managerial employment risk (e.g., if a single business fails, a top-level manager remains employed in a diversified firm). Because diversification can increase firm size and thus managerial compensation, managers may have motives to diversify a firm. This type of diversification may reduce the firm's value.

RELATED DIVERSIFICATION

As suggested earlier in the chapter, related diversification is a strategy through which the firm intends to build upon or extend its existing resources, capabilities, and core competencies in the pursuit of strategic competitiveness.[39] Thus, firms that have selected related diversification as their corporate-level strategy seek to exploit economies of scope between business units. Available to firms operating in multiple industries or product markets,[40] **economies of scope** are cost savings attributed to transferring the capabilities and competencies developed in one business to a new business without significant additional costs.

Firms seek to create value from economies of scope through two basic kinds of operational economies: sharing activities and transferring core competencies. The difference between sharing activities and transferring competencies is based on how separate resources are used jointly to create economies of scope. Tangible resources, such as plant and equipment or other business-unit physical assets, often must be shared to create economies of scope. Less tangible resources, such as sales forces, also can be shared. However, when know-how is transferred between sep-

Economies of scope are cost savings attributed to transferring the capabilities and competencies developed in one business to a new business without significant additional costs.

213

arate activities and there is no physical or tangible resource involved, a core competence has been transferred as opposed to sharing activities.

Sharing Activities

Activity sharing is quite common, especially among related-constrained firms. At Procter & Gamble, a paper towels business and a baby diapers business both use paper products as a primary input to the manufacturing process. Having a joint paper production plant that produces inputs for both divisions is an example of a shared activity. In addition, these businesses are likely to share distribution sales networks because they both produce consumer products.

In Chapter 3, primary and support value chain activities were discussed. In general, primary activities, such as inbound logistics, operations, and outbound logistics, might have multiple shared activities. Through efficient sharing of these activities, firms may be able to create core competencies. In terms of inbound logistics, the business units may share common inventory delivery systems, warehousing facilities, and quality assurance practices. Operations might share common assembly facilities, quality control systems, or maintenance operations. With respect to outbound logistics, two business units might share a common sales force and sales service desk. Support activities could include the sharing of procurement and technology development efforts. The sharing of activities occurring at Honeywell and TRW is described in the Strategic Focus.

STRATEGIC FOCUS

The Sharing of Activities to Create Value

Implementing the related-constrained diversification strategy, Honeywell has a single product focus—controls. A worldwide manufacturer and marketer of control systems and components, the firm has three major business units—home and building controls, industrial controls, and space and aviation controls. These units account for approximately 45 percent, 31 percent, and 22 percent of total sales revenue, respectively. (The remaining 2 percent is earned by what the firm classifies as "other" businesses.) Controls for homes and buildings are intended to create comfortable, safe, efficient environments. The firm's industrial control systems and components are designed to improve productivity, optimize the use of raw materials, help companies comply with environmental regulations, ensure plant safety, and enhance overall competitiveness. The space and aviation controls unit is the world's leading supplier of avionics systems for commercial, military, and space markets.

Seeking total sales revenue of $10 billion by 2000 (revenues were expected to reach $8.8 billion in 1998), Honeywell established a new division to reach this goal and to increase its financial returns. Called Consumer Goods, this division's creation was stimulated by results generated through market research. To Honeywell's surprise, recent market research indicated that the firm's name is recognized widely by the public. In fact, researchers "discovered that although consumers knew little about most Honeywell products, they had seen its name on about 140 million central heating and air conditioning controls installed in the U.S. and Europe."

Honeywell is now using the technology and manufacturing core competencies that were developed in its three major business units to produce consumer goods such as fans, humidifiers, dehumidifiers, and air cleaners. Offered initially in the United States, Honeywell executives believe that Europe and East Asia are promising markets for its consumer goods. By sharing some of the activities required to manufacture high-quality controls among its major units, and through an emphasis on the value provided by Honeywell's reputation as a manufacturer of high-quality products, the firm hopes to achieve sales of $1 billion in its Consumer Goods division by 2002.

In September 1996, TRW sold its information services business. With two business units remaining (automotive components, generating 66 percent of sales revenue, and space and defense, accounting for the remaining 34 percent), TRW is following the related-linked diversification strategy. Several divisions exist within each of the two units to serve different customer groups' unique needs. Nonetheless, the firm is now less diversified than it was before the information services unit was sold.

In early 1998, TRW formed a new division in its space and defense unit. Called Telecommunications, this division uses technologies TRW developed originally to manufacture components for use in top-secret military satellites. The firm's objective was for this division to achieve sales revenues of up to $4 billion annually by 2008. The technologies committed to this new division via internal transfers are used to manufacture a range of hardware aimed at operators of commercial telecommunication satellites and suppliers of ground-based communication equipment.

Analysts had a favorable view of TRW's attempt to share some of its activities and skills. One reason for this reaction could be TRW's success in early efforts to use military technologies in the commercial sector. For example, the firm learned how to produce ultra-fast semiconductor chips for use in mobile telephone handsets such as those manufactured by Motorola and Ericsson. These commercial chips are based on "gallium arsenide that [TRW had] developed for digital processing jobs on defense satellites, such as the Pentagon's Milstar telecoms spacecraft."

Over time, top-level executives want activities to be shared between TRW's two major units as well as within the divisions of each unit. Learning how to share activities between the major units could result in dramatic successes in the marketplace. Although important to the firm's future success, this objective will not be achieved easily. In fact, TRW's president and chief operating officer observed recently that one of his company's biggest challenges is to find ways of transferring military-related technologies from the company's space division to the automotive sector.

SOURCE: Honeywell Inc. Home Page, 1998, January 14, http://www.honeywell.com; TRW Inc. Home Page, 1998, January 14, http://www.trw.com; T. Brophy, 1997, TRW Inc., *Value Line*, November 7, 1381; P. Marsh, 1997, TRW to form new telecoms division, *Financial Times*, December 15, 19; P. M. Seligman, 1997, Honeywell, *Value Line*, October 24, 1013; S. Wagstyl, 1997, Honeywell bows to consuming passions, *Financial Times*, November 28, 23.

As explained in the Strategic Focus, firms expect the sharing of activities across units to result in increased strategic competitiveness and financial returns. Other matters affect the degree to which these outcomes will be achieved through activity sharing. For example, firms should recognize that sharing activities requires sharing business-unit strategic control. Moreover, one business-unit manager may feel that another business-unit manager is receiving more benefit from the activity sharing. Such a perception could create conflicts between division managers. Activity sharing is also risky because business-unit ties create links between outcomes. If demand for the product of one business is reduced, there may not be sufficient revenues to cover the fixed costs of running the joint plant. Shared activities create interrelationships that affect the ability of both businesses to achieve strategic competitiveness. Activity sharing may be ineffective if these costs are not taken into consideration.

The costs of activity sharing notwithstanding, research shows that the sharing of activities and resources across businesses within a firm can increase the firm's value. For example, recent research examining acquisitions of firms in the same industry (referred to as horizontal acquisitions) such as in the banking industry, has found that sharing resources and activities (thereby creating economies of scope) contributed to postacquisition performance increases and higher returns to shareholders.[41] Additionally, research suggests that firms selling off related units where resource sharing is a possible source of economies of scope produced lower returns than selling off businesses unrelated to the firm's core business.[42] Still other research found that firms with more related units had lower risk.[43] These results suggest that gaining economies of scope by sharing activities and resources across businesses within a firm may be important to reduce risk and gain positive returns from diversification efforts.

Transferring of Core Competencies

Over time, a strategically competitive firm's intangible resources, such as know-how, become the foundation for competitively valuable capabilities and core competencies. Thus, in diversified firms, core competencies are complex sets of resources and capabilities that link different businesses primarily through managerial and technological knowledge, experience, and expertise.[44]

Marketing expertise is an example of a core competence that could be used this way. Because the expense of developing such a competence has already been incurred, and because competencies based on intangible resources are less visible and more difficult for competitors to understand and imitate, transferring these types of competencies from an original business unit to another one may reduce costs and enhance an entire firm's strategic competitiveness.[45] A key reason Philip Morris decided to acquire Miller Brewing Company was that it believed that a competitive advantage could be achieved by transferring its marketing core competence to Miller.

As a cigarette company, Philip Morris developed a particular expertise in marketing. When Philip Morris purchased Miller Brewing, the beer industry had efficient operations, but no firm in the industry had established marketing competence as a source of competitive advantage. The marketing competence transferred from Philip Morris to Miller resulted in the introduction of improved marketing practices to the brewing industry. These practices, especially in terms of advertising, proved to be the source of competitive advantage that allowed Miller Brewing to earn above-average returns for a period of time. In fact, several years passed before Anheuser-Busch, the largest firm in the brewing industry, developed the capabilities required to duplicate the benefits of Miller's strategy. A strong competitive response from Anheuser-Busch was predictable, however, in that beer is the firm's core business.

Some firms discover that they either are unable to transfer competencies or they transfer competencies that do not help a business unit establish a competitive advantage. One way managers facilitate the transfer of competencies is to move key people into new management positions. Although Philip Morris accomplished competence transfer to Miller Brewing in this way, a business-unit manager of an older division may be reluctant to transfer key people who have accumulated the knowledge and experience necessary to transfer the competencies. Thus, managers with the ability to facilitate the transfer of a core competence may come at a premium or may not want to transfer, and the top-level managers from the transferring division may not want them to be transferred to a new division to fulfill a diversification objective.

Market Power

Related diversification can also be used to gain market power. **Market power** exists when a firm is able to sell its products above the existing competitive level or reduce the costs of its primary and support activities below the competitive level, or both.[46]

One approach to gaining market power through diversification is multipoint competition. *Multipoint competition* exists when two or more diversified firms compete in the same product areas or geographic markets.[47] For example, when Philip Morris moved into foods by buying General Foods and Kraft, RJR's competitive response was the acquisition of another foods company, Nabisco. The competitive rivalry between these two companies is an example of multipoint competition.

If these firms compete head to head in each market, multipoint competition will not create potential gains; instead, it will generate excessive competitive activity. Over time, if these firms refrain from competition and in effect realize mutual forbearance, this may be classified as a form of related diversification that creates value for each firm through less competitive activity (see discussion in Chapter 5). *Mutual forbearance* is a relationship between two or more firms in which excessive competition leads to a situation where all firms in the competitive set see that such competition is self-destructive and, without formal agreement, cease the self-destructive competitive actions and responses.

Walt Disney and Time Warner operate in similar businesses—theme parks, movie and television production, and broadcasting activities. Disney has spent considerable amounts of money advertising its theme parks in Time Warner magazines. Time Warner, however, began an aggressive advertising campaign aimed at taking Disney's theme park customers. Disney retaliated by canceling its advertising in Time Warner's publications. Time Warner responded by canceling corporate meetings in Florida at a Disney resort. Disney responded by canceling Time Warner advertisements of its theme parks on a Los Angeles television station owned by Disney.[48] This illustrates the potential negative side of multipoint competition. Disney's actions represents a counterattack mode, argued to be a prominent strategic action when multipoint competition exists.[49] Counterattacks are not common where multipoint competition exists because the threat of a counterattack may prevent strategic actions from being taken or, more likely, firms may retract their strategic actions with the threat of counterattack.[50]

Another approach to creating value by gaining market power is the strategy of vertical integration. **Vertical integration** exists when a company is producing its own inputs (backward integration) or owns its own source of distribution of outputs (forward integration). It is also possible to have partial vertical integration where some inputs and outputs are sold by company units, while other inputs and outputs are produced or sold by outside firms.

A company pursuing vertical integration is usually motivated to strengthen its position in its core business by gaining market power over competitors. This is done through savings on operations costs, avoidance of market costs, better control to establish quality, and, possibly, protection of technology.

In response to prominent threats in their external environment (such as changes in environmental regulations and third-party reimbursement practices) in the early

Market power exists when a firm is able to sell its products above the existing competitive level or reduce the costs of its primary and support activities below the competitive level, or both.

Vertical integration exists when a company is producing its own inputs (backward integration) or owns its own source of distribution of outputs (forward integration).

to mid-1990s, some firms competing in the pharmaceutical industry pursued a strategy of vertical integration. In November 1993, for example, Merck & Company, at the time the world's largest prescription drug manufacturer, paid $6.6 billion to acquire Medco Containment Services Inc. (one of the largest mail-order pharmacy and managed care companies at the time of its purchase). With Medco, Merck controls a dominant supplier of its products. Further contributing to an increase in Merck's market power as a result of pursuing vertical integration was its opportunity to have detailed and immediate access to information regarding customers' marketing-related needs. In identical fashion, SmithKline Beecham PLC attempted to increase its market power through the forward vertical integration purchase of United HealthCare's pharmacy-benefit services unit, Diversified Pharmaceutical Services Inc.; Eli Lilly & Company's purchase of McKesson's PCS Health Systems unit was completed for the same strategic reason.[51] Important benefits accruing to Merck & Company, SmithKline Beechman, and Eli Lilly as a result of the decision to vertically integrate in a forward direction include reductions in market transaction costs and some additional protection of proprietary technologies.

Of course, there are limits to vertical integration. For example, an outside supplier may produce the product at a lower cost. As a result, internal transactions from vertical integration may be expensive and reduce profitability. Also, bureaucratic costs are incurred when implementing this strategy. Because it can require that substantial sums of capital be invested in specific technologies, vertical integration may be problematic when technology changes quickly. Changes in demand also create capacity balance and coordination problems. If one division is building a part for another internal division, but achieving economies of scale requires the division to build it at a scale beyond the capacity of the internal buyer to absorb demand, sales outside the company would be necessary. However, if demand slackens, an overcapacity would result because the internal users cannot absorb total demand. Thus, although vertical integration can create value and contribute to strategic competitiveness, especially in gaining market power over competitors, it is not without risks and costs.

UNRELATED DIVERSIFICATION

Financial economies are cost savings realized through improved allocations of financial resources based on investments inside or outside the firm.

An unrelated diversification strategy can create value through two types of financial economies. **Financial economies** are cost savings realized through improved allocations of financial resources based on investments inside or outside the firm.[52]

The first type of financial economy involves efficient internal capital allocations. This type also seeks to reduce risks among the firm's business units. This can be achieved, for example, through development of a portfolio of businesses with different risk profiles, thereby reducing business risk for the total corporation. A second approach of financial economies is concerned with purchasing other corporations and restructuring their assets. This approach allows a firm to buy and sell businesses in the external market with the intent of increasing its total value.

Efficient Internal Capital Market Allocation

Capital allocation is usually distributed efficiently in a market economy by capital markets. Efficient distribution of capital is induced because investors seek to purchase shares of firm equity (ownership) that have high future cash-flow values.

Capital is allocated not only through equity, but also through debt, where shareholders and debtholders seek to improve the value of their investment by investing in businesses with high growth prospects. In large diversified firms, however, the corporate office distributes capital to divisions to create value for the overall company. Such an approach may provide potential gains from internal capital market allocation, relative to the external capital market.[53] The corporate office, through managing a particular set of businesses, may have access to more detailed and accurate information as well as actual business and performance prospects.

Compared to corporate office personnel, investors would have relatively limited access to internal information and can only estimate actual divisional performance and future business prospects. Although businesses seeking capital must provide information to capital providers (e.g., banks, insurance firms), firms with internal capital markets may have at least two informational advantages. First, information provided to capital markets through annual reports and other sources may not include negative information, but rather only positive prospects and outcomes. External sources of capital have limited ability to know *specifically* what is taking place inside large organizations. Although owners have access to information, they have no guarantee of full and complete disclosure.[54]

Second, although a firm must disseminate information, this information becomes available to potential competitors simultaneously. With insights gained by studying this information, competitors might attempt to duplicate a firm's competitive advantage. Without having to reveal internal information, a firm may protect its competitive advantage through an internal capital market.

If intervention from outside the firm is required to make corrections, only significant changes are possible, such as forcing the firm into bankruptcy or changing the dominant leadership coalition (e.g., the top-management team described in Chapter 12). Alternatively, in an internal capital market, the corporate office may choose to adjust managerial incentives or suggest strategic changes in the division to make fine-tuned corrections. Thus, capital allocation can be adjusted according to more specific criteria than is possible with external market allocation. The external capital market may fail to allocate resources adequately to high-potential investments, compared to corporate office investments, because it has less accurate information. The head office of a diversified company can more effectively perform such tasks as disciplining underperforming management teams and allocating resources.[55]

Intensely devoted to the unrelated diversification strategy, Harold Geneen is recognized by some for his ability to organize what was, for a certain period of time, a highly effective corporate office—an office that disciplined operating units through the imposition of strict financial controls. As CEO of then highly diversified ITT, Geneen based his leadership practices on the belief "that sound financial management could be applied successfully to any business, from rental cars to bakeries to insurance."[56] Known also for his unshakable commitment to "facts" that were generated through detailed quantitative analyses, Geneen expected long hours and unquestionable loyalty from those working with and for him. At the height of his success, perhaps no other corporate leader exceeded Geneen's ability to guide a firm following the unrelated diversification strategy.[57]

Although ITT no longer follows the unrelated diversification strategy, other firms do. One of Europe's oldest and most powerful industrial dynasties, Ifil is rapidly becoming more diversified. Historically, this Italian firm's major holding has been its 30 percent ownership of Fiat. Since 1986, however, Ifil has diversified aggressively and extensively through entries into food, cement, tourism, and retailing. Current plans include a possible acquisition-based movement into the telecommunications industry. As a result of becoming more diversified, Ifil's holdings in Fiat now represent less than 45 percent of its $4.1 billion in net assets.[58] In this firm, the primary function of the corporate office is the efficient allocation and management of resources. As such, financial economies are critical to attempts to earn above-average returns at Ifil. However, such risk reduction strategies may not be valuable to all firms' stakeholders. Shareholders and debtholders have lower cost ways of reducing their risk through diversification of their own investment portfolios. Successful implementation of an unrelated diversification strategy requires that a firm incur fewer costs to reduce an individual investor's risks as compared to the costs that investor would experience to diversify his or her own portfolio.[59]

Restructuring

Another alternative, similar to the internal capital market approach, focuses exclusively on buying and selling other firm assets in the external market. It is similar to the real estate business, where profits are earned by buying assets low, restructuring them, and selling them as high as possible. The restructuring approach usually entails buying the firm, selling off assets such as corporate headquarters, and terminating corporate staff members.

Selling underperforming divisions and placing the remaining divisions under the discipline of rigorous financial controls are other often used restructuring actions. Rigorous controls require divisions to follow strict budgets and account regularly for cash inflows and outflows to corporate headquarters. A firm pursuing this approach may have to use hostile takeovers or tender offers. Hostile takeovers have the potential to increase the resistance of the target firm's top-level managers. In these cases, corporate-level managers often are dismissed, while division managers are retained.

Creating financial economies through the purchase of other companies and the restructuring of their assets requires an understanding of significant trade-offs. First, success usually calls for a focus on mature, low-technology businesses. Otherwise, resource allocation decisions become too complex because the uncertainty of demand for high-technology products requires information-processing capacities beyond the smaller corporate staffs of unrelated-restructuring firms. Service businesses are also difficult to buy and sell in this way because of their client or sales orientation. Sales staffs of service businesses are more mobile than those of manufacturing-oriented businesses and may seek jobs with a competitor, taking their clients with them. This is true in professional service businesses such as accounting, law, advertising, and investment banking. As such, these businesses probably would not create value if acquired by an unrelated-restructuring firm.

DIVERSIFICATION: INCENTIVES AND RESOURCES

The economic reasons given in the last section summarize the conditions under which diversification strategies increase a firm's value. Diversification, however, is often undertaken with the expectation that doing so will prevent a firm from reducing its value. Thus, there are reasons to diversify that are value neutral. As we explain next, several incentives may lead a firm to pursue further diversification.[60]

Incentives to Diversify

Incentives provide reasons to diversify; they come from both the external environment and a firm's internal environment. The term *incentive* implies that managers have some choice whether to pursue the incentive or not. Incentives external to the firm include antitrust regulation and tax laws. Internal firm incentives include low performance, uncertain future cash flows, and overall firm risk reduction.

Antitrust Regulation and Tax Laws Government antitrust policies and tax laws provided incentives for U.S. firms to diversify in the 1960s and 1970s. Applications of antitrust laws regarding mergers that create increased market power (vertical and horizontal integration) were stringent in the 1960s and 1970s.[61] As a result, many of the mergers during this time were unrelated—that is, they involved companies pursuing different lines of business. Thus, the merger wave of the 1960s was "conglomerate" in character. Merger activity leading to conglomerate diversification was encouraged primarily by the Celler-Kefauver Act (which discouraged horizontal and vertical mergers). For example, in the 1973–1977 period, 79.1 percent of all mergers were conglomerate.[62]

The mergers of the 1980s, however, were different. Antitrust enforcement ebbed, permitting more and larger horizontal mergers (acquisition of the same line of business, such as a merger between two oil firms).[63] In addition, investment bankers became more freewheeling in the kinds of mergers they would try to facilitate; as a consequence, hostile takeovers increased to unprecedented numbers.[64] The conglomerates or highly diversified firms of the 1960s and 1970s became more "focused" in the 1980s and 1990s as merger constraints were relaxed and restructuring implemented.[65]

Tax effects on diversification stem not only from individual tax rates but also from corporate tax changes. Some companies (especially mature companies) may have activities that generate more cash than they can reinvest profitably. Michael Jensen, a prominent financial economist, believes that such *free cash flows* (liquid financial assets for which investments in current businesses are no longer economically viable) should be redistributed to shareholders in the form of dividends.[66] However, in the 1960s and 1970s, dividends were taxed more heavily than ordinary personal income. As a result, in the pre-1980s, shareholders preferred that companies retain these funds for use in buying and building companies in high-performance industries. If the stock value appreciated over the long term, shareholders might receive a better return for these funds than through dividends because they would be taxed more lightly under capital gains rules.

In 1986, however, the top ordinary individual income tax rate was reduced from 50 percent to 28 percent, and the special capital gains tax was changed, causing capital gains to be treated as ordinary income. These changes suggested that shareholders would no longer encourage firms to retain funds for purposes of diversification. Moreover, the elimination of personal interest deductions, as well as the lower attractiveness of retained earnings to shareholders, has prompted the use of more leverage by firms (interest expense is tax deductible for firms). These tax law changes also influenced an increase in divestitures of unrelated business units after 1984. Thus, individual tax rates for capital gains and dividends may have created a shareholder incentive for increased diversification before 1986, but an incentive for reduced diversification after 1986, unless funded by tax-deductible debt.

Regarding corporate taxation, acquisitions typically increase a firm's depreciable asset allowances. Increased depreciation (non–cash-flow expense) produces lower taxable income, thereby providing additional incentive for acquisitions. Before 1986, acquisitions may have been the most attractive means for securing tax benefits.[67] The tax incentives are particularly important because acquisitions represent the primary means of firm diversification, but the 1986 Tax Reform Act reduced some of the corporate tax advantages of diversification.[68]

As this discussion notes, across different time periods, U.S. government policy has provided incentives for both increased and reduced levels of diversification. Recently, a loosening of federal regulations, coupled with a desire to expand their product offerings to hold onto and build upon their existing franchises, have provided incentives for large U.S. banks to become more diversified through the pursuit of related diversification. By acquiring securities firms, investment banks, and other financial services companies, some large banks have diversified their revenue streams considerably. Banc One, for example, paid $7.3 billion to purchase credit-card issuer First USA. Similarly, NationsBank acquired the investment firm Montgomery Securities for $1.2 billion.[69] Commenting favorably about this acquisition, NationsBank's chief financial officer suggested that the acquisition enabled his firm "to provide [its] clients true 'one-stop-shopping' capabilities." Moreover, the CFO observed, "The combination of our businesses will give all our clients access to the financial products and services they need to reach their goals, from bank loans and bridge financings to debt and equity underwriting and risk management. Simply put, this new organization gives all of us more freedom to put creative solutions on the table for our clients."[70]

In addition to the external incentive to diversify that antitrust regulation and tax laws provide, there are incentives internal to the firm that increase the likelihood that diversification will be pursued.

Low Performance It has been proposed that "high performance eliminates the need for greater diversification,"[71] as in the example of the Wm. Wrigley Jr. Co. Conversely, low performance may provide an incentive for diversification. Firms

A loosening of federal regulations and a desire to expand their product offerings have given large U.S. banks the incentive to become more diversified through acquisitions. Banc One Corp. paid $7.3 billion for First USA Inc., a credit-card issuer.

plagued by poor performance often seek to take higher risks.[72] Interestingly, though, some researchers have found that low returns are related to greater levels of diversification.[73] Poor performance may lead to increased diversification, especially if resources exist to pursue additional diversification. Continued poor returns following additional diversification, however, may slow the pace of diversification and even lead to divestitures. Thus, an overall curvilinear relationship, as illustrated in Figure 6.2, may exist between diversification and performance.

Germany's Daimler-Benz provides an example of poor performance fueled by diversification. Under its former CEO, Edzard Reuter, Daimler-Benz diversified to become a manufacturer of jets, helicopters, trains, and electronics in addition to its core automotive and truck businesses. The purpose of this diversification was to transform the firm into an "integrated technology company."[74]

Unfortunately, the acquisitions were less than sterling; furthermore, attempts to integrate the various businesses that had been acquired faltered. In 1993 and in 1995, Daimler-Benz had substantial net losses, largely attributed to the new businesses added in previous years. Its core business, Mercedes-Benz Automotive and Truck Division, continued to be profitable during this time period. The CEO following Reuter, Juergen Schrempp, was under increasing pressure to reverse the diversification strategy begun by Reuter.[75]

Recent evidence suggests that Juergen Schrempp is dealing successfully with the challenges that were created partly by the firm's failed diversifications. Since assuming leadership control for the firm in May 1995, Schrempp has taken decisive actions.[76] Money-losing operations, including the firm's electronics business and its 24 percent stake in Cap Gemini, the French software-services company, were sold. Fokker, the Dutch airplane manufacturer, was liquidated (interestingly, when serving as head of Daimler-Benz's aerospace division, Schrempp himself orches-

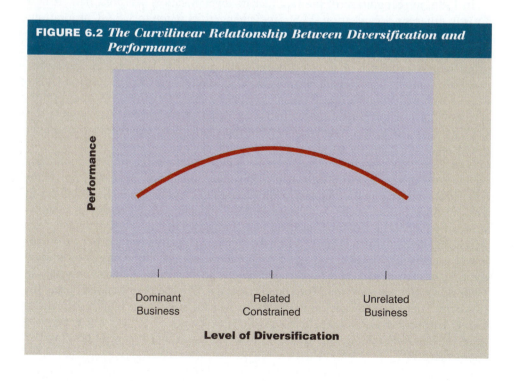

FIGURE 6.2 *The Curvilinear Relationship Between Diversification and Performance*

trated the acquisition of Fokker).[77] In addition, Schrempp eliminated a layer of upper-level executives and is trying to instill a culture of responsibility and entrepreneurship. Thought of as a cultural revolution, one in which each of Daimler's 23 remaining business units is expected to earn at least 12 percent on its invested capital, innovation is the driving force being used to create the new culture. Cross-disciplinary project teams, called function groups, represent one technique created to stimulate process and product innovations.[78] The fact that 1997 sales revenue and earnings exceeded those of 1996 (revenues, for example, increased almost 20 percent) suggests the possibility that the poor performance that was stimulated by Daimler-Benz's diversification efforts is being reversed.

Uncertain Future Cash Flows As a firm's product line matures and/or is threatened, diversification may be perceived as an important defensive strategy. Firms in mature or maturing industries sometimes find it necessary to diversify to survive over the long term.[79] Certainly, this has been one of the dominant reasons for diversification among railroad firms during the 1960s and 1970s. Railroads diversified primarily because the trucking industry was perceived to have significant negative effects on the demand for rail transportation. Uncertainty, however, can be derived from both supply and demand sources.

Diversification because of uncertainty also pertains to firms in industries where foreign competitors with lower average costs have penetrated domestic markets. The diversification in the steel industry in the 1970s exemplifies this type of supply-side uncertainty as an incentive. To reduce its dependence on steel, U.S. Steel bought Marathon Oil and Texas Oil and Gas. This competitive action was taken because international integrated steel makers (such as Nippon Steel) were able to produce steel at a lower cost due to lower labor costs and newer, more efficient production facilities.

In 1986, in recognition of the fact that its diversification decisions had created a vastly different organization, U.S. Steel changed its name to USX Corporation. Today, with three independent business units (Marathon, U.S. Steel, and Delhi Groups), this firm "is a major worldwide producer of oil and natural gas, the nation's largest producer of steel products and one of the largest U.S. gatherers, processors, and transporters of natural gas. USX today is really three separate businesses, each with its own management, yet operating under the USX board of directors."[80] Once the world's dominant steel manufacturer, sales revenue from USX's U.S. Steel group now accounts for approximately 27 percent of total corporate sales.

The U.S. defense industry has downsized significantly in recent years and many of the firms in this industry have had to diversify to survive. An indicator of this downsized industry is the decline in the Pentagon's budget from $370 billion in 1987 to $259 billion in 1997.[81] Major defense industry diversification is demonstrated by General Dynamics' decision to sell all of its defense industry businesses so it could diversify into other product markets. At the same time, other firms followed a horizontal integration strategy in the pursuit of the market power they thought was required to remain competitive in the downsized defense industry. In 1997 alone, Boeing acquired McDonnell Douglas, Raytheon purchased Texas Instruments' defense business, and Lockheed Martin sought to acquire Northrop Grumman. Occurring among firms in the same lines of business, these acquisitions caused some to conclude that the entire defense industry would become less competitive.[82]

Thus, demand uncertainties about expected future cash flows have affected diversification strategy decisions in some defense firms and horizontal, market power-oriented integration strategies in others.[83] Because of evidence regarding the results of such actions, the effects of the decision to diversify into other businesses by a firm such as General Dynamics will be interesting to observe. In general, existing evidence indicates that although diversification may increase shareholder wealth and reduce the uncertainty of future cash flows in selected instances, these outcomes are achieved often at the expense of profitability.

Firm Risk Reduction Because diversified firms pursuing economies of scope often have investments that are too inflexible to realize synergy between business units, several potential problems exist. **Synergy** exists when the value created by business units working together exceeds the value those same units create when working independently. For example, as a firm increases its relatedness between business units, it increases its risk of corporate failure because synergy produces joint interdependence between business units and the firm's flexibility of response is constrained. This threat may force two basic decisions.

First, the firm may reduce the level of technological change by operating in more certain environments. This may make the firm risk averse and, thus, uninterested in pursuing new product lines that have potential but are not proven. Alternatively, the firm may constrain the level of activity sharing and forego the benefits of synergy. Either or both decisions may lead to further diversification. The former would lead to related diversification into industries where more certainty exists. The latter result may produce further, but unrelated, diversification.[84]

Synergy exists when the value created by business units working together exceeds the value those same units create when working independently.

225

Resources and Diversification

Although incentives to diversify may exist, a firm must possess the resources required to make diversification economically feasible. As mentioned earlier, tangible, intangible, and financial resources may facilitate diversification. Resources vary in their utility for value creation, however, because of differences in rarity and mobility; that is, some resources are easier for competitors to duplicate because they are not rare, valuable, costly to imitate, and nonsubstitutable. For instance, free cash flows may be used to diversify the firm. Because financial resources such as free cash flows are more flexible and common, they are less likely to create value as compared to other types of resources.[85] The diversification mentioned earlier for steel firms was facilitated significantly by the presence of free cash flows.

This is also likely true of the diversification efforts by Anheuser-Busch. Anheuser-Busch was a very profitable company and significant cash flows were created from the success of the brewery business. These resources were then used to purchase the St. Louis Cardinals, to invest almost $400 million in the development and operation of the Eagle snack food business, and to acquire the Campbell Taggart bakery business. The use of these resources, however, did not produce significant positive returns for Anheuser-Busch. As a result, the firm decided to spin off Campbell Taggart, sell the St. Louis Cardinals, and close the Eagle snacks business.[86] Still the world's largest brewing organization, Anheuser-Busch continues to use free cash flows to support its business interests in theme park operations, manufacturing and recycling aluminum beverage containers, rice milling, real estate development, turf farming, railcar repair and transportation, and paper label printing, among others.[87] It is the diversification created by this particular mix of businesses that the corporation's executives are able to manage in a way that creates value.

Tangible firm resources usually include the plant and equipment necessary to produce a product. Such assets may be less flexible. Any excess capacity of these resources (plant and equipment) often can be used only for very closely related products, especially those requiring highly similar manufacturing technologies. Excess capacity of other tangible resources, such as a sales force, can be used to diversify more easily. Again, excess capacity in a sales force would be more effective with related diversification because it may be utilized to sell similar products. The sales force would be more knowledgeable about related product characteristics, customers, and distribution channels. Tangible resources may create resource interrelationships in production, marketing, procurement, and technology, defined earlier as activity sharing.

Intangible resources would, of course, be more flexible than actual tangible physical assets in facilitating diversification. Although the sharing of tangible resources may induce diversification, intangible resources could encourage even more diversification. Clearly, there were some potential intangible resource synergies that could be achieved by Anheuser-Busch. For example, Anheuser-Busch's knowledge of yeast products may have been useful in the use of yeast within Campbell Taggart. This did not, however, produce significant positive synergies between the brewery and bakery businesses as hoped by Anheuser-Busch executives.[88] Apparently, there was little sharing of tangible or intangible resources; thus, little value was created.

Extent of Diversification

If a firm has incentives and resources to diversify, the extent of diversification will be greater than if it just has incentives or resources alone.[89] The more flexible, the more likely the resources will be used for unrelated diversifications; the less flexible, the more likely the resources will be used for related diversification. Thus, flexible resources (e.g., free cash flow) are likely to lead to relatively greater levels of diversification. Also, because related diversification requires more information processing to manage links between businesses, more unrelated units can be managed by a small corporate office.[90]

MANAGERIAL MOTIVES TO DIVERSIFY

Managerial motives for diversification may exist independent of incentives and resources. These motives include managerial risk reduction and a desire for increased compensation.[91] For instance, diversification may reduce top-level managers' *employment risk* (risk of job loss or income reduction). That is, corporate executives may diversify a firm in order to diversify their employment risk, as long as profitability does not suffer excessively.[92] Diversification also provides an additional benefit to managers that shareholders do not enjoy. Diversification and firm size are highly correlated and, as size increases, so does executive compensation.[93] Large firms are more complex and harder to manage and, thus, managers of larger firms are compensated more highly.[94] As a result, diversification provides an avenue for increased compensation and therefore may serve as a motive for managers to engage in greater diversification. Governance mechanisms, such as the board of directors, ownership monitoring, executive compensation, and the market for corporate control may limit managerial tendencies to overdiversify. These governance mechanisms are discussed in more detail in Chapter 10.

Governance mechanisms may not be strong and, in some instances, managers may diversify the firm to the point that it fails to earn even average returns.[95] Resources employed to pursue each diversification are most likely to include financial assets (e.g., free cash flows), but may also involve intangible assets. Thus, this type of diversification is not likely to lead to improved performance. The loss of adequate internal governance may result in poor relative performance, thereby triggering a threat of takeover. Although external controls, such as the threat of takeover, may create improved efficiency by replacing ineffective managerial teams, managers may avoid takeovers through defensive tactics (golden parachutes, poison pills, etc.) Therefore, an external governance threat, although having a restraining influence on managers, does not provide flawless control of managerial motives for diversification.[96]

Most of the large, publicly held firms are profitable because managers are positive agents and many of their strategic actions (e.g., diversification moves) contribute to this success. As mentioned, governance devices are designed to deal with exceptions to the norms of achieving strategic competitiveness and increasing shareholder wealth in the process. It is overly pessimistic to assume that managers will usually act in their own self-interest as opposed to their firm's interest.[97]

Managers may also be held in check by concerns for their reputation in the labor market. If reputation facilitates power, a poor reputation may also reduce power. Likewise, a market for managerial talent may constrain managerial abuse of power to pursue inappropriate diversification.[98] In addition, some diversified firms also provide policing of other diversified firms. These large, highly diversified firms seek out poorly managed diversified firms for acquisition to restructure the target firm's asset base. Knowing that their firms could be acquired if not managed successfully, managers are encouraged to find ways to achieve strategic competitiveness.

In summary, although managers may be motivated to increase diversification, governance mechanisms are in place to discourage such action merely for managerial gain. However, this governance is imperfect and may not always produce the intended consequences. Even when governance mechanisms cause managers to correct a problem of overdiversification, these moves are not without trade-offs. For instance, spinoff firms may not realize productivity gains, although it is in the best interest of the divesting firm.[99] As such, the assumption that managers need disciplining may not be entirely correct, and sometimes governance may create consequences that are worse than those resulting from overdiversification.[100]

Therefore, as this discussion suggests, the level of diversification the firm chooses should be based on the optimal levels that are indicated by market and strategic characteristics (resources) owned or available to each company. Optimality may be judged by the factors examined in this chapter: resources, managerial motives, and incentives.

As shown in Figure 6.3, the level of diversification that can be expected to have the greatest positive effect on performance (in terms of strategic competitiveness and the earning of above-average returns) is based partly on how the interaction of resources, managerial motives, and incentives affects the adoption of particular diversification strategies. As indicated earlier, the greater the incentives and the more flexible the resources, the higher the level of expected diversification. Financial resources (the most flexible) should have a stronger relationship to the extent of diversification than either tangible or intangible resources. Tangible resources (the most inflexible) would be useful primarily for related diversification.

The model suggests that implementation issues are important to whether diversification creates value or not (see Chapter 11). It also suggests that governance mechanisms are important to the level and type of diversification implemented (see Chapter 10).

As we have discussed, diversification strategies can enhance a firm's strategic competitiveness and allow it to increase its financial returns. This appears to be the case for Estee Lauder. One of the world's largest cosmetics companies with brands such as Clinque, Aramis, Origins, and Prescriptives, as well as its flagship Lauder products, this firm follows a long-term strategy of diversifying into niche

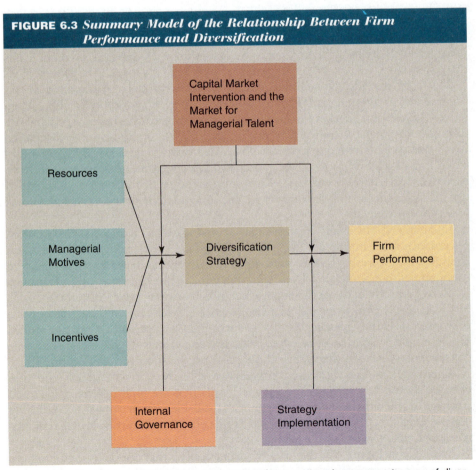

FIGURE 6.3 *Summary Model of the Relationship Between Firm Performance and Diversification*

Source: R. E. Hoskisson and M. A. Hitt, 1990, Antecedents and performance outcomes of diversification: A review and critique of theoretical perspectives, *Journal of Management* 16: 498.

areas of the beauty business. To diversify, Lauder purchases firms with high-profile brands and then uses its managerial and organizational skills to create value. Recently Lauder pursued still more related diversification through its acquisition of Aveda Corporation. Aveda's natural beauty products are made from flower and plant essences, using aromatherapy principles. Attracted to Aveda because of its unique market position and entrepreneurial management team, Lauder executives believed that Aveda's products would augment its existing portfolio by extending its presence in hair care and by introducing Lauder into a new distribution channel of specialist hair salons. (At the time of its acquisition, Aveda's products were sold in 30,000 salons worldwide.)[101]

Positive outcomes from diversification such as those experienced by Estee Lauder are achieved only when the company has pursued a proper amount of diversification. Presented in this chapter's final Strategic Focus is a set of questions that should be considered when deciding if the firm should diversify or, for the already diversified company, if additional levels of diversification should be pursued. Preparing forthright answers to these questions improves the probability that top-level managers will make an informed and effective decision regarding diversification. If the answers to these questions are in the direction opposite to that which suggests an ability to create value through diversification, then a decision not to become more diversified is required.

While reading this Strategic Focus, recall that any corporate-level diversification strategy will enhance a firm's strategic competitiveness and increase its financial returns only when it creates value. At the corporate level, value is created through the selection and management of a particular group of businesses that is worth more under the ownership of the company than it would be under any other ownership.[102]

229

Estee Lauder acquired Aveda Corporation, whose natural beauty products are based on aromatherapy principles. Aveda's products enhanced Lauder's portfolio by extending the firm's presence in hair care and giving it a presence in specialist hair care salons.

STRATEGIC FOCUS

Issues to Evaluate When Considering Diversification

As suggested in this chapter, decisions regarding diversification are among the most challenging a firm and its top-level managers face. More effective decisions can be reached through analysis of the following six questions.

- What resources, capabilities, and core competencies do we possess that would allow us to outperform competitors?

To create value across businesses from the corporate level, top-level managers must determine precisely what it has the capacity to do that would increase the competitiveness of an acquired company or that would allow it to move successfully into a new geographic market. (Geographic diversification, which is movement into different market areas, is discussed in detail in Chapter 8.) The work of creative employees, excellent distribution capabilities, and superior knowledge about the transfer of information are examples of competencies on which the firm could rely to create value when diversifying. Borders, one of North America's largest book and music retailers, opened its first European store in 1998 on London's Oxford Street. This store was the largest bookshop built in Britain in 50 years. The company intended to open at least three or four additional stores in 1998 (one in Leeds) and 1999. The value to be created through Borders' geographic diversification was the building of what some in the United Kingdom view as "cultural superstores"—stores with vast collections of CDs and computer games as well as the offering of coffees and cakes to those browsing through the firm's huge book collection. To create value in its new geographic locations, Borders intended to rely on its ability to determine the particular set of diverse and unique cultural products that would be of interest to customers. Once identified, additional value is created for customers by Borders' capacity to offer this array of products in a single site.

- What core competencies must we possess to succeed in a new product or geographic market?

To compete successfully, companies typically must own or have access to all competencies that are linked to the earning of above-average returns in a given market. Coca-Cola, for example, concluded that its superior distribution capabilities and marketing and branding expertise were sufficient to allow the firm to be successful through its diversification into the wine business, but because the company lacked intimate knowledge about the wine business, its diversification effort failed. Similarly, Tomkins, a United Kingdom conglomerate, divested its distribution operations. Although the firm has the competencies (including possession of the detailed knowledge about how to allocate capital effectively and efficiently across and within business units) that are necessary to add value to its food, automotive parts manufacturing, and building and industrial companies, it was not able to add value in the distribution business.

- Is it possible for us to leapfrog competitors?

If the firm lacks the competencies required to create value in an area into which it seeks to diversify, it can try to purchase the skill that it lacks or develop that skill inhouse. Additionally, the firm could use the competencies it does possess to redefine the rules of competition. To diversify from its core camera business into photocopiers, Canon rewrote the competitive rules in an industry dominated by Xerox. Relying on its photographic technology and dealer management skills, Canon targeted small businesses and the consumer market rather than large companies, sold its machines through a network of dealers rather than through a direct sales force, and focused on quality and price in the manufacturing of its products rather than speed.

- Will diversification break up capabilities and competencies that should be kept together?

Sometimes, the firm's strategic competitiveness is a product of the synergy that results from a unique combination of resources and capabilities. If those are broken apart so one or two skills can be transferred to a new setting, the diversification effort may fail. In Markides' words, "Too many companies mistakenly assume that they can break up clusters of competencies or skills that, in fact, work only because they are together, reinforcing one another in a particular competitive context. Such a misjudgment can doom a diversification move."

- Will we only be a player in the new product or geographic market or will we emerge as a winner?

Corporate-level capabilities and competencies create value through diversification efforts only when they are valuable, rare, costly to imitate, and nonsubstitutable (see Chapter 3). Thus, to earn above-average returns through diversification, firms must be able to create something that is unique.

- What can the firm learn through its diversification and is it organized properly to acquire such knowledge?

To create value on a long-term basis, the firm should view each diversification effort as an opportunity to learn. Acquired knowledge should then become the foundation upon which future diversification possibilities are evaluated.

SOURCE: A. Davis, 1998, Distribution sell-off likely at Tomkins, *Financial Times*, January 5, 27; A. Rawsthorn, 1998, US book chain to open first European store, *Financial Times*, January 7, 10; C. C. Markides, 1997, To diversify or not to diversify, *Harvard Business Review* 75, no. 6: 93–99; A. Roseno and C. Nokkentved, 1997, *Management Processes and Corporate-Level Strategy* (Copenhagen, Denmark: Management Process Institute).

SUMMARY

- Pursuing a single- or dominant-business corporate-level strategy may be preferable to a more diversified-business strategy, unless a corporation can develop economies of scope or financial economies between businesses, or obtain market power through additional levels of diversification. These economies and market power are the main sources of value creation for firm diversification.

- The primary reasons a firm pursues increased diversification are value creation through economies of scope, financial economies, or market power; actions because of government policy, performance problems, or uncertainties about future

cash flow; and managerial motivations (e.g., to increase their compensation).

- Managerial motives to diversify can lead to over-diversification. On the other hand, managers can also be good stewards of the firm's assets.

- The level of firm diversification is a function of the incentives, firm resources, and the managerial motives to diversify.

- Related diversification can create value by sharing activities or transferring core competencies.

- Activity sharing usually involves sharing tangible resources between businesses. Core competence transfer involves transferring the core competencies developed in one business to another business. It also may involve transferring competencies between the corporate office and a business unit.

■ Activity sharing is usually associated with related-constrained diversification. Activity sharing is

costly to implement and coordinate, may create unequal benefits for the divisions involved in sharing, and may lead to fewer risk-taking behaviors.

■ Successful unrelated diversification is accomplished by efficiently allocating resources or restructuring a target firm's assets and placing them under rigorous financial controls.

REVIEW QUESTIONS

1. What is corporate-level strategy? Why is it important to a diversified firm?
2. Identify the advantages and disadvantages of single- and dominant-business strategies as compared to firms with higher levels of diversification.
3. What are three reasons why firms choose to move from either a single- or a dominant-business position to a more diversified position?
4. How do firms share activities and transfer core compe-

tencies to obtain economics of scope, while pursuing a related diversification strategy?
5. What are the two ways to obtain financial economies when pursuing an unrelated diversification strategy?
6. What incentives and resources encourage diversification in firms?
7. What motives might encourage managers to engage a firm in more diversification?

APPLICATION DISCUSSION QUESTIONS

1. This chapter suggests that there is a curvilinear relationship between diversification and performance. How can this relationship be modified so that the negative relationship between performance and diversification is reduced and the downward curve has less slope or begins at a higher level of diversification?
2. The *Fortune* 500 industrial firms are very large, and many of them have significant product diversification. Are these large firms overdiversified currently and experiencing lower performance than they should? Explain.
3. What is the primary reason for overdiversification, industrial policies, such as taxes and antitrust regulation, or because managers pursue self-interest, increased compensation, and reduced risk of job loss? Why?

4. One rationale for pursuing related diversification is to obtain market power. In the United States, too much market power, however, may result in a challenge by the Justice Department (because it may be perceived as anticompetitive). Under what situations might related diversification be considered unfair competition?
5. Assume you have received two job offers—one from a dominant-business firm and one from an unrelated-diversified firm (the beginning salaries are virtually identical). Which offer would you accept and why?
6. By the year 2010, do you believe large firms will be more or less diversified than they are today? Why? Will the trends regarding diversification be identical in Europe, the United States, and Japan? Explain.

ETHICS QUESTIONS

1. Assume you overheard the following statement: "Those managing an unrelated-diversified firm face far more difficult ethical challenges than do those managing a dominant-business firm." Based on your reading of this chapter, do you accept or reject this statement? Why?
2. Is it ethical for managers to diversify a firm rather than return excess earnings to shareholders? Provide reasoning in support of your answer.

3. What unethical practices might occur when a firm restructures its operations? Explain.
4. Do you believe ethical managers are unaffected by the managerial motives to diversify discussed in this chapter? If so, why? In addition, do you believe ethical managers should help their peers learn how to avoid making diversification decisions on the basis of the managerial motives to diversify? Why or why not?

INTERNET EXERCISE

Go to the *Fortune* 500 List at:

http://www.pathfinder.com/fortune/fortune500/500list.html

Select three firms from the *Fortune* 500 and visit their Web sites. From their Web sites and other Internet resources, determine each firm's level of diversification (see Figure 6.1). For each firm, comment on the appropriateness of its level of corporate diversification given the overall nature of the firm.

Strategic Surfing

NewsPage-Company Lookup is a very helpful Web site for accessing current news stories about U.S. corporations. These stories, which are selected from major American periodicals, provide current insight into the corporate and business-level company strategies.

http://www.companylink.com

NOTES

1. A. Dworkin, 1997, Delivering the goods, *Dallas Morning News*, September 14, H1, H6.
2. D. D. Bergh, 1997, Predicting divestiture of unrelated acquisitions: An integrative model of *ex ante* conditions, *Strategic Management Journal* 18: 715–731; J. L. Stimpert and I. M. Duhaime, 1997, Seeing the big picture: The influence of industry, diversification, and business strategy on performance, *Academy of Management Journal* 40: 560–583.
3. M. E. Porter, 1980, *Competitive Strategy* (New York: The Free Press), xvi.
4. K. Ramaswamy, 1997, The performance impact of strategic similarity in horizontal mergers: Evidence from the U.S. banking industry, *Academy of Management Journal* 40: 697–715.
5. M. A. Hitt, R. E. Hoskisson, and H. Kim, 1997, International diversification: Effects on innovation and firm performance in product-diversified firms, *Academy of Management Journal* 40: 767–798; W. G. Rowe and P. M. Wright, 1997, Related and unrelated diversification and their effect on human resource management controls, *Strategic Management Journal* 18: 329–338.
6. W. Boeker, 1997, Executive migration and strategic change: The effect of top manager movement on product-market entry, *Administrative Science Quarterly* 42: 213–236; H. A. Haverman, 1993, Organizational size and change: Diversification in the savings and loan industry after deregulation, *Administrative Science Quarterly* 38: 20–50.
7. M. E. Porter, 1987, From competitive advantage to corporate strategy, *Harvard Business Review* 65, no. 3: 43–59.
8. Ibid., 43.
9. Boeker, Executive migration and strategic change; C. A. Montgomery, 1994, Corporate diversification, *Journal of Economic Perspectives* 8: 163–178.
10. J. Huey, 1997, In search of Roberto's secret formula, *Fortune*, December 29, 230–234.
11. J. Kurtzman, 1998, An interview with C. K. Prahalad, in J. Kurtzman (ed.), *Thought Leaders* (San Francisco: Jossey-Bass), 40–51; D. Lei, M. A. Hitt, and R. Bettis, 1996, Dynamic core competencies through meta-learning and strategic context, *Journal of Management* 22: 547–567.
12. C. C. Markides, 1997, To diversify or not to diversify, *Harvard Business Review* 75, no. 6: 93–99.
13. C. C. Markides and P. J. Williamson, 1996, Corporate diversification and organizational structure: A resource-based view, *Academy of Management Journal* 39: 340–367; M. Goold and K. Luchs, 1993, Why diversify? Four decades of management thinking, *Academy of Management Executive* VII, no. 3: 7–25.
14. A. Roseno and C. Nokkentved, 1997, *Management Processes and Corporate-Level Strategy* (Copenhagen, Denmark: Management Process Institute); A. Campbell, M. Goold, and M. Alexander, 1995, Corporate strategy: The question for parenting advantage, *Harvard Business Review* 73, no. 2: 120–132.
15. T. H. Brusch and P. Bromiley, 1997, What does a small corporate effect mean? A variance components simulation of corporate and business effects, *Strategic Management Journal* 18: 825–835.
16. J. B. Barney, 1997, *Gaining and Sustaining Competitive Advantage* (Reading, MA: Addison-Wesley).
17. M. A. Hitt, B. W. Keats, and S. DeMarie, 1998, Navigating in the new competitive landscape: Building strategic flexibility and competitive advantage in the 21st century, *Academy of Management Executive* (in press); T. Mroczkowski and M. Hanaoka, 1997, Effective rightsizing strategies in Japan and America: Is there a convergence of employment practices? *Academy of Management Executive* XI, no. 2: 57–67.
18. Campbell, Goold, and Alexander, Corporate strategy; Goold and Luchs, Why diversify?, 8.
19. R. Simons and A. Davila, 1998, How high is your return on management? *Harvard Business Review* 76, no. 1: 71–80.
20. D. Collis and C. A. Montgomery, 1995, Competing on resources: Strategy in the 1990s, *Harvard Business Review* 73, no. 4: 118–128; M. A. Peteraf, 1993, The cornerstones of competitive advantage: A resource-based view, *Strategic Management Journal* 14: 179–191.
21. R. P. Rumelt, 1974, *Strategy, Structure and Economic Performance* (Cambridge, MA: Harvard University Press).
22. C. C. Markides, 1995, Diversification, restructuring and economic performance, *Strategic Management Journal* 16: 101–118.
23. R. E. Hoskisson, M. A. Hitt, R. A. Johnson, and D. S. Moesel, 1993, Construct validity of an objective (entropy) categorical measure of diversification strategy, *Strategic Management Journal* 14: 215–235.

24. Hitt, Hoskisson, and Kim, International diversification; M. A. Hitt, R. E. Hoskisson, and R. D. Ireland, 1994, A midrange theory of the interactive effects of international and product diversification on innovation and performance, *Journal of Management* 20: 297–326.

25. W. M. Bulkeley, 1994, Conglomerates make a surprising comeback—with a '90s twist, *Wall Street Journal*, March 1, A1, A6.

26. M. Heinzl and N. Deogun, 1998, Cott loses sparkle due to price war, chairman's health, *Wall Street Journal*, January 6, B8; G. G. Marcial, Why Cott may bubble up, *Business Week*, March 2, 108; *Cott Corporation Home Page*, 1998, January 13, http://www.cott.com.

27. J. J. Keller, 1997, As AT&T seeks CEO, megadeals pass by, *Wall Street Journal*, October 17, A8.

28. J. Talton, 1997, Late Coke CEO built empire with quiet grace, *Dallas Morning News*, October 26, H3.

29. R. Henkoff, 1995, New management secrets from Japan—really, *Fortune*, November 27, 135–146.

30. *Value Line*, 1994, Edition 10 (February 18): 1494.

31. Rumelt, *Strategy, Structure, and Economic Performance*; L. Wrigley, 1970, Divisional autonomy and diversification (Ph.D. dissertation, Harvard Business School).

32. P. M. Seligman, 1997, Hershey Foods, *Value Line*, November 14, 1478; Associated Press, 1997, Psst! Hershey's up to something, *Dallas Morning News*, October 14, D1.

33. G. McIvor, 1997, Volvo unveils profit drive, *Financial Times*, December 9, 15; B. Mitchener, 1997, Volvo proves small players can perform, *Wall Street Journal*, October 22, A19.

34. B. Einhorn and S. Prasso, 1997, Thailand's anxious giant, *Business Week*, October 27, 70E4–70E16; P. J. Williamson, 1997, Asia's new competitive game, *Harvard Business Review* 75, no. 5: 55–67; *Business Week*, 1997, Corporate scoreboard, August 25, 163.

35. T. Khanna and K. Palepu, 1997, Why focused strategies may be wrong for emerging markets, *Harvard Business Review* 75, no. 4: 41–50.

36. *The Economist*, 1997, Inside story, December 6, 7–9.

37. M. Smith, 1998, Solvay thaws 15% advance, *Financial Times*, February 6, 16; Solvay Group, 1996, *Annual Report*, 2.

38. S. Brown, 1997, Crow signals expansion into retail, *Dallas Morning News*, August 27, D3; R. Winslow, 1997, Integrated Health to buy RoTech for $615 million, *Wall Street Journal*, July 8, A3, A8.

39. D. J. Teece, G. Pisano, and A. Shuen, 1997, Dynamic capabilities and strategic management, *Strategic Management Journal* 18: 509–533.

40. M. E. Porter, 1985, *Competitive Advantage* (New York: The Free Press), 328.

41. T. H. Brusch, 1996, Predicted change in operational synergy and post-acquisition performance of acquired businesses, *Strategic Management Journal* 17: 1–24; H. Zhang, 1995, Wealth effects of U.S. bank takeovers, *Applied Financial Economics* 5: 329–336.

42. D. D. Bergh, 1995, Size and relatedness of units sold: An agency theory and resource-based perspective, *Strategic Management Journal* 16: 221–239.

43. M. Lubatkin and S. Chatterjee, 1994, Extending modern portfolio theory into the domain of corporate diversification: Does it apply? *Academy of Management Journal* 37: 109–136.

44. Barney, *Gaining and Sustaining Competitive Advantage*, 367; A. Mehra, 1996, Resource and market based determinants of performance in the U.S. banking industry, *Strategic Management Journal* 17: 307–322; S. Chatterjee and B. Wernerfelt, 1991, The link between resources and type of diversification: Theory and evidence, *Strategic Management Journal* 12: 33–48.

45. N. Argyres, 1996, Capabilities, technological diversification and divisionalization, *Strategic Management Journal* 17: 395–410.

46. W. G. Shepherd, 1986, On the core concepts of industrial economics, in H. W. deJong and W. G. Shepherd (eds.), *Mainstreams in Industrial Organization* (Boston: Kluwer Publications).

47. K. Hughes and C. Oughton, 1993, Diversification, multimarket contact and profitability, *Economica* 60: 203–224.

48. L. Landro, P. M. Reilly, and R. Turney, 1993, Disney relationship with Time Warner is a strained one, *Wall Street Journal*, April 14, A1, A9.

49. A. Karnani and B. Wernerfelt, 1985, Multipoint competition, *Strategic Management Journal* 6: 87–96.

50. f. i. smith and R. L. Wilson, 1995, The predictive validity of the Karnani and Wernerfelt model of multipoint competition, *Strategic Management Journal* 16: 143–160.

51. E. Karrer-Rueedi, 1997, Adaptation to change: Vertical and horizontal integration in the drug industry, *European Management Journal* 15: 461–469.

52. Bergh, Predicting divestiture of unrelated acquisitions; C. W. L. Hill, 1994, Diversification and economic performance: Bringing structure and corporate management back into the picture, in R. P. Rumelt, D. E. Schendel, and D. J. Teece (eds.), *Fundamental Issues in Strategy* (Boston: Harvard Business School Press), 297–321.

53. O. E. Williamson, 1975, *Markets and Hierarchies: Analysis and Antitrust Implications* (New York: Macmillan Free Press).

54. R. Kochhar and M. A. Hitt, 1998, Linking corporate strategy to capital structure: Diversification strategy, type, and source of financing, *Strategic Management Journal* (in press).

55. Ibid.; P. Taylor and J. Lowe, 1995, A note on corporate strategy and capital structure, *Strategic Management Journal* 16: 411–414.

56. *The Economist*, 1997, Harold Geneen, December 6, 99.

57. Ibid., 99.

58. J. Rossant, 1997, When the Agnellis go shopping, they really go shopping, *Business Week*, October 27, 70E28–70E30.

59. R. Amit and J. Livnat, 1998, A concept of conglomerate diversification, *Journal of Management* 14: 593–604.

60. M. Lubatkin, H. Merchant, and M. Srinivasan, 1997, Merger strategies and shareholder value during times of relaxed antitrust enforcement: The case of large mergers during the 1980s, *Journal of Management* 23: 61–81.

61. D. L. Smart and M. A. Hitt, 1998, A test of the agency theory perspective of corporate restructuring, working paper, Texas A&M University.

62. R. M. Scherer and D. Ross, 1990, *Industrial Market Structure and Economic Performance* (Boston: Houghton Mifflin).

63. A. Shleifer and R. W. Vishny, 1994, Takeovers in the 1960s and 1980s: Evidence and implications, in R. P. Rumelt, D. E. Schendel, and D. J. Teece (eds.), *Fundamental Issues in Strategy* (Boston: Harvard Business School Press), 403–422.

64. Lubatkin, Merchant, and Srinivasan, Merger strategies and shareholder value; D. J. Ravenscraft and R. M. Scherer,

234

1987, *Mergers, Sell-Offs and Economic Efficiency* (Washington, DC: Brookings Institution), 22.

65. P. L. Zweig, J. P. Kline, S. A. Forest, and K. Gudridge, 1995, The case against mergers, *Business Week*, October 30, 122–130; J. R. Williams, B. L. Paez, and L. Sanders, 1988, Conglomerates revisited, *Strategic Management Journal* 9: 403–414.

66. M. C. Jensen, 1986, Agency costs of free cash flow, corporate finance, and takeovers, *American Economic Review* 76: 323–329.

67. R. Gilson, M. Scholes, and M. Wolfson, 1988, Taxation and the dynamics of corporate control: The uncertain case for tax motivated acquisitions, in J. C. Coffee, L. Lowenstein, and S. Rose-Ackerman (eds.), *Knights, Raiders, and Targets: The Impact of the Hostile Takeover* (New York: Oxford University Press), 271–299.

68. C. Steindel, 1986, Tax reform and the merger and acquisition market: The repeal of the general utilities, *Federal Reserve Bank of New York Quarterly Review* 11, no. 3: 31–35.

69. M. Murray, 1997, Banks look afield to satisfy appetite for expansion, *Wall Street Journal*, July 9, B4.

70. PR Newswire Association, Inc., 1997, NationsBank completes acquisition of Montgomery Securities, October 1.

71. Rumelt, *Strategy, Structure and Economic Performance*, 125.

72. E. H. Bowman, 1982, Risk seeking by troubled firms, *Sloan Management Review* 23: 33–42.

73. Y. Chang and H. Thomas, 1989, The impact of diversification strategy on risk-return performance, *Strategic Management Journal* 10: 271–284; R. M. Grant, A. P. Jammine, and H. Thomas, 1988, Diversity, diversification, and profitability among British manufacturing companies, 1972–1984, *Academy of Management Journal* 31: 771–801.

74. A. Taylor, III, 1997, Revolution at Daimler-Benz, *Fortune*, November 10, 144–152.

75. J. Templeman, 1995, The shocks for Daimler's new driver, *Business Week*, August 21, 38–39.

76. Daimler-Benz Home Page, 1998, January 15, http://www.Daimler-Benz.com.

77. Taylor, Revolution at Daimler-Benz, 147.

78. B. Mitchener, 1997, Daimler's Alabama M-class experiment gives a transatlantic jolt to Stuttgart, *Wall Street Journal*, October 17, A18.

79. C. G. Smith and A. C. Cooper, 1988, Established companies diversifying into young industries: A comparison of firms with different levels of performance, *Strategic Management Journal* 9: 111–121.

80. USX Corporation Home Page, 1998, January 15, http://www.usx.com.

81. L. Smith, 1997, Air power, *Fortune*, July, 134–136.

82. A. Dworkin, 1997, Defense mergers raise fears, *Dallas Morning News*, July 5, F1, F9.

83. S. Crock, 1997, Can this farm boy keep Lockheed in orbit? *Business Week*, October 27, 103–115; J. Dial and K. J. Murphy, 1995, Incentives, downsizing, and value creation at General Dynamics, *Journal of Financial Economics* 37: 261–314.

84. N. M. Kay and A. Diamantopoulos, 1987, Uncertainty and synergy: Towards a formal model of corporate strategy, *Managerial and Decision Economics* 8: 121–130.

85. Jensen, Agency costs.

86. R. A. Melchor and G. Burns, 1996, How Eagle became extinct, *Business Week*, March 4, 68–69.

87. Anheuser-Busch Companies, Inc. Home Page, 1998, January 15, http://www.anheuser-busch.com.

88. R. Gibson, 1995, Anheuser-Busch will sell snacks unit, Cardinals, and the club's home stadium, *Wall Street Journal*, October 26, A3, A5; M. Quint, 1995, Cardinals and snack unit are put on block by Busch, *New York Times*, October 26, D2.

89. R. E. Hoskisson and M. A. Hitt, 1990, Antecedents and performance outcomes of diversification: Review and critique of theoretical perspectives, *Journal of Management* 16: 461–509.

90. C. W. L. Hill and R. E. Hoskisson, 1987, Strategy and structure in the multiproduct firm, *Academy of Management Review* 12: 331–341.

91. A. A. Cannella, Jr., and M. J. Monroe, 1997, Contrasting perspectives on strategic leaders: Toward a more realistic view of top managers, *Journal of Management* 23: 213–237; S. Finkelstein and D. C. Hambrick, 1996, *Strategic Leadership: Top Executives and Their Effects on Organizations* (St. Paul, MN: West Publishing Company).

92. D. L. May, 1995, Do managerial motives influence firm risk reduction strategies? *Journal of Finance* 50: 1291–1308; Y. Amihud and B. Lev, 1981, Risk reduction as a managerial motive for conglomerate mergers, *Bell Journal of Economics* 12: 605–617.

93. S. R. Gray and A. A. Cannella, Jr., 1997, The role of risk in executive compensation, *Journal of Management* 23: 517–540; H. Tosi and L. Gomez-Mejia, 1989, The decoupling of CEO pay and performance: An agency theory perspective, *Administrative Science Quarterly* 34: 169–189.

94. S. Finkelstein and R. A. D'Aveni, 1994, CEO duality as a double-edged sword: How boards of directors balance entrenchment avoidance and unity of command, *Academy of Management Journal* 37: 1070–1108.

95. R. E. Hoskisson and T. Turk, 1990, Corporate restructuring: Governance and control limits of the internal market, *Academy of Management Review* 15: 459–477.

96. J. K. Seward and J. P. Walsh, 1996, The governance and control of voluntary corporate spin offs, *Strategic Management Journal* 17: 25–39; J. P. Walsh and J. K. Seward, 1990, On the efficiency of internal and external corporate control mechanisms, *Academy of Management Review* 15: 421–458.

97. Finkelstein and D'Aveni, CEO duality as a double-edged sword.

98. E. F. Fama, 1980, Agency problems and the theory of the firm, *Journal of Political Economy* 88: 288–307.

99. R. A. Johnson, 1996, Antecedents and outcomes of corporate refocusing, *Journal of Management* 22: 439–483; C. Y. Woo, G. E. Willard, and U. S. Dallenbach, 1992, Spin-off performance: A case of overstated expectations, *Strategic Management Journal* 13: 433–448.

100. H. Kim and R. E. Hoskisson, 1996, Japanese governance systems: A critical review, in S. B. Prasad (ed.), *Advances in International Comparative Management* (Greenwich, CT: JAI Press), 165–189.

101. A. Rawsthorn, 1997, Estee Lauder agrees to buy Aveda for $300m, *Financial Times*, November 20, 25.

102. D. J. Collis and C. A. Montgomery, 1998, Creating corporate advantage, *Harvard Business Review* 76, no. 3: 71–83.

235

Acquisition and Restructuring Strategies

CHAPTER 7

Learning Objectives

After reading this chapter, you should be able to:

1. Describe why acquisitions have been a popular strategy.

2. List and explain the reasons why firms make acquisitions.

3. Describe seven problems that work against developing a competitive advantage when making acquisitions.

4. Name and describe the attributes of acquisitions that help make them successful.

5. Define restructuring and distinguish among its common forms.

6. Describe how a firm can achieve successful outcomes from a restructuring strategy.

Today MCI, Tomorrow the World for WorldCom?

The 1998 WorldCom acquisition of MCI has been one of the largest to date. The two firms initially agreed to a price of $37 billion, $9 billion more than the second largest bid made by GTE. Originally, British Telecom (BT) and MCI had agreed to an acquisition, but BT later decided to reduce its offer, making it worth approximately $18 billion. Analysts have said that BT may have made a large error in reducing the amount of its offer and driving MCI into the arms of a different suitor. Due to stock price changes the acquisition is worth approximately $42 billion.

WorldCom is the product of a brash entrepreneur, Bernard J. Ebbers. The fact that WorldCom is smaller than MCI does not bother Ebbers. Over the last ten years, WorldCom has been built through over 50 acquisitions. Included among these acquisitions have been several billion dollar deals. The MCI deal is worth approximately four times the budget of the state of Mississippi, where WorldCom's headquarters is located.

http://www.mci.com
http://www.worldcom.com

WorldCom's acquisition of MCI makes it the third largest telecommunications firm behind AT&T. The combined firm controls over 60 percent of the traffic on the global computer network in the United States. The newly combined firm controls four of the six largest Internet service providers. Furthermore, WorldCom is now the only telecommunications company to provide nationwide local phone service and long distance service for both business and residential customers. WorldCom is saving considerable money partly because it owns local networks and thus no longer has to pay a 45 percent tariff on long distance revenues to the Baby Bells as MCI did. It also is saving about $700 million annually because the newly combined firm has the needed infrastructure.

The new company's name, MCI WorldCom, created some debate, but when the dust settled, analysts and investors alike gave the acquisition a positive review. Its ultimate success, however, may depend on what other telecommunications firms do in response. For example, some analysts are speculating that this huge acquisition may pave the way for AT&T to make an acquisition (and SBC) that will not be rejected by the Justice Department. Because the telecommunications market is global, there could be other actions in Europe in response to this acquisition.

SOURCE: D. A. Blackmon, 1997, WorldCom's massive bid shakes up little town, *Wall Street Journal*, October 13, B1, B9; P. Elstrom, C. Yang, and S. Jackson, 1997, WorldCom + MCI: How it all adds up, *Business Week*, November 4, 44; J. Files, 1997, GTE offers $28 billion for MCI in all-cash deal, *Dallas Morning News*, October 16, A1, A20; H. Goldblatt and N. D. Schwartz, 1997, Telecom in play, *Fortune*, November 10, 83–88; S. Pulliam, 1997, WorldCom bid for MCI raises question: Who's next? *Wall Street Journal*, October 2, C1, C2; WorldCom and MCI engaged, 1997, *The Economist*, November 15, 69–70; WorldCom bid to alter telecom industry, 1997, *Wall Street Journal*, October 2, A1, A10; T. E. Weber and R. Quick, 1997, Would WorldCom-MCI deal lift tolls on net? *Wall Street Journal*, October 2, B1, B2; S. Young, 1997, MCI merger could smooth the way for AT&T deal. *WSJ Interactive Edition*, http://www.interactive.wsj.com/edition.

Chapter 6 examined corporate-level strategy and, in particular, discussed types and levels of product diversification that can build core competencies. The dominant means for fashioning a diversification strategy is through acquisitions. Although acquisitions have been a popular strategy among U.S. firms for many years, the decade of the 1980s was labeled by some as "merger mania." In fact, depending on whether only whole-firm acquisitions or partial (ownership) acquisitions are included, the number of acquisitions completed in the United States during the 1980s varies from slightly over 31,000 to as many as 55,000. The total value of these acquisitions exceeded $1.3 trillion.[1]

While these numbers are impressive, they are small compared to the current "merger mania." The total value of mergers and acquisitions during 1997 was $1.6 trillion, more than the total amount for the whole decade of the 1980s. Furthermore, there were more than 22,000 transactions in 1997, 40 percent of the total number of transactions in the decade of the 1980s. The 40 percent increase in total value of the transactions over 1996 is due mostly to the large deals, exemplified by the WorldCom acquisition of MCI. The large acquisitions are primarily because of the need to consolidate for market power to be competitive in global markets. Also, deregulation, low interest rates, and growing stock values in 1997 fueled the large increase in activity. Another trend is also evident, the growing number of cross-border acquisitions.[2]

With the large number of acquisitions in the 1980s and 1990s and the substantial capital investment required to support this activity, one would expect that it was driven by strong positive returns to shareholders of the acquiring firms. However, the outcomes do not fully support this expectation. For example, research has shown that *shareholders of acquired firms* often earn above-average returns from the acquisition, but that *shareholders of acquiring firms* are less likely to gain such returns. The average returns earned by shareholders of acquiring firms was close to zero.[3] The significant negative returns earned from some acquisition activity and the overdiversification of some firms (see Chapter 6) have produced a need for restructuring strategies. Restructuring involves acquiring and divesting businesses or assets to position a firm's operations strategically and develop effective core competencies.[4] Furthermore, many firms including AT&T, ITT, Hanson PLC, 3M, Melville, W. R. Grace, Sprint, Tenneco, Sears, Roebuck and Company, and General Motors have been spinning off or breaking up their diversified portfolios to create greater returns for shareholders. Often these firms reduce employment levels in corporate headquarters where highly integrated corporate structures exist.[5]

The purpose of this chapter is to explore the reasons for acquisitions and the potential problems firms encounter in attempting to achieve strategic competitiveness through an acquisition strategy (see Figure 1.1). As the opening case illustrates, the WorldCom acquisition of MCI positions the newly combined firm as a major presence in the telecommunications market. It is third in size only to AT&T and the complementary resources provide special synergies. An example is the access to long distance customers provided by MCI and the local phone networks provided by WorldCom. These features alone will save the new firm millions of dollars in tariff fees that MCI had to pay to the Baby Bells in the past. However, merging and integrating two large firms will be no easy task. Effective integration will be required to realize the expected synergies. We also describe acquisitions that have been disastrous because efforts to merge the two firms effectively were not successful. The primary reasons for the lack of strategic competitiveness among acquiring firms, along with the attributes of acquisitions that create competitive advantage, are discussed next. Thereafter, we explore the phenomenon of restructuring, the reasons for its use, and the restructuring alternatives that create strategic competitiveness. Finally, we explain how a few unique firms are able to create a competitive advantage through unrelated diversification. These firms may obtain a core competence of continually acquiring other firms, restructuring them, and retaining certain firm assets, while divesting others.

MERGERS AND ACQUISITIONS

A **merger** is a transaction in which two firms agree to integrate their operations on a relatively coequal basis because they have resources and capabilities that together may create a stronger competitive advantage. The transaction between Reading & Bates and Falcon Drilling is an example of a merger with a new ten-member board of directors composed of five members from each company. This merger created a firm with major market power in deep-water oil and gas drilling.[6] Alternatively, an **acquisition** is a transaction in which one firm buys controlling or 100 percent interest in another firm with the intent of more effectively using a core competence by making the acquired firm a subsidiary business within its portfolio. Usually, the management of the acquired firm reports to the management

239

A **merger** is a transaction in which two firms agree to integrate their operations on a relatively coequal basis because they have resources and capabilities that together may create a stronger competitive advantage.

An **acquisition** is a transaction in which one firm buys controlling or 100 percent interest in another firm with the intent of more effectively using a core competence by making the acquired firm a subsidiary business within its portfolio.

A **takeover** is an acquisition in which the target firm did not solicit the bid of the acquiring firm.

of the acquiring firm. Most mergers represent friendly agreements between the two firms, whereas acquisitions include unfriendly takeovers. A **takeover** is an acquisition in which the target firm did not solicit the bid of the acquiring firm. Only a small minority of these transactions are mergers; most are acquisitions. Therefore, the primary focus in this chapter is on acquisitions.

Reasons for Acquisitions

Firms follow an acquisition strategy and/or make selected acquisitions for several potential reasons.[7] Among them are achieving a competitive advantage through greater market power, overcoming barriers to entry, increasing the speed of market entry, the significant costs involved in developing new products, avoiding the risks of new product development, achieving diversification (either related or unrelated), and, finally, avoiding competition.[8] These reasons are described more fully in the following sections.

Increased Market Power A primary reason for acquisitions is to achieve greater market power. Many firms may have core competencies but lack the size to exercise their resources and capabilities. Market power usually is derived from the size of the firm and the firm's resources and capabilities to compete in the marketplace. Therefore, most acquisitions designed to achieve greater market power entail buying a competitor, supplier or distributor, or a business in a highly related industry to allow exercise of a core competence and gain competitive advantage in the acquiring firm's primary market. Acquisition of a competing firm is referred to as a *horizontal acquisition*. A *vertical acquisition* refers to a firm acquiring a supplier or distributor of its good or service. Acquisition of a firm in a highly related industry is referred to as a *related acquisition*. Recent research suggests that horizontal acquisitions of firms with similar characteristics result in higher performance than when firms with dissimilar characteristics are acquired. Similar characteristics of importance include strategy, managerial styles, and resource allocation patterns. Similarities in these characteristics makes the integration of the two firms proceed more smoothly.[9] An example of a horizontal acquisition between firms with similar characteristics was Ernst & Young's acquisition of KPMG Peat Marwick. The Chairman and Chief Executive Officer of Ernst & Young, Philip Laskawy, stated, "we concluded that our global practices, our personality and our chemistry matched perfectly." This acquisition was driven by the need for market power because of the requirement to provide global full-service operations.[10]

The opportunity to make horizontal and vertical acquisitions was enhanced by changes in the interpretation and enforcement of U.S. antitrust laws in the early 1980s (see Chapter 10).[11] Prior to that time, very few acquisitions of direct competitors were allowed by the U.S. government. Of course, this action by the federal government represented a major impetus to an acquisition strategy. Firms that gain greater share and/or have more resources for gaining competitive advantage have more power to use against competitors in their markets.[12]

Market power dominance was probably the driving force behind many mergers in the drug industry such as Merck's vertical acquisition of Medco Containment Services, Inc., a drug distribution company. Other pharmaceutical companies such as Eli Lilly and SmithKline Beecham PLC have made similar vertical acquisitions to ensure distribution of their drug product lines by managing prescription plans.[13] Sandoz AG's acquisition of Gerber Products, however, was a related acquisition. Many of these pharmaceutical mergers—vertical, horizontal, and related—are directed at increased market power because managed-care and potential regulatory changes in the health care industry challenged the traditional power of pharmaceutical firms. The trade-off for pharmaceutical firms, however, is that they will likely reduce spending on R&D and new product development as they invest money in acquisitions and the transaction costs associated with them.[14]

Overcome Entry Barriers Barriers to entry (introduced in Chapter 2) represent factors associated with the market and/or firms currently operating in the market that make it more expensive and difficult for a new firm to enter that market. For example, it may be difficult to develop a new venture in a market because large and established competitors may already occupy the niche of interest. Such an entry may require substantial investments in a large manufacturing facility and substantial advertising and promotion to produce adequate sales for the manufacturer to achieve economies of scale and offer products at a competitive price. Market entry also requires a firm to have an efficient distribution system and outlets to reach the consumer. If consumers have loyalty to existing brands already in the market, even these actions may not be adequate to produce a successful new venture. In this case, a firm may find it easier to enter the market by acquiring an established company. Although the acquisition can be costly, the acquiring firm can achieve immediate access to the market and can do so with an established product that may have consumer loyalty. In fact, the higher the barriers to entry are, the more likely it is that acquisitions will be used to enter a particular market.

In 1997, Caterpillar acquired the Perkins Engine unit from Lucas Varity to gain a presence in the small engine market. This acquisition provided entry for Caterpillar into a fast growing market and simultaneously allowed the firm to gain control over a major supplier. This acquisition will also help Caterpillar build the capability to manufacture and market smaller-scale construction equipment that is growing in popularity. There were no overlaps in the two businesses (thus, an entry into a new market), but there are substantial opportunities for synergy.[15] Caterpillar's acquisition of Perkins Engine represents related diversification (see Chapter 6). Computer Services' acquisition of Continuum also represents related diversification. Computer Services provides computer services such as information systems integration and outsourcing with its main competitors being IBM and Electronic Data Systems. Continuum, on the other hand, provides supplies and support software to the insurance and banking industry. This acquisition allowed Computer Services to enter the market for computer and other support services for these two important and related industries. In particular, the strategic action moves Computer Services into a new and lucrative market of software services for the financial sector.[16]

Acquisitions are used commonly to enter new international markets as explained in Chapter 8. For example, cross-border acquisitions currently acount for approximately 30 percent of all acquisitions in Europe. Acquisitions are a popular means of entering new international markets because they are perhaps the fastest way to enter new markets, and they enable the acquirer to achieve a critical mass (presence) in a market and more control over foreign operations (compared to strategic alliances with a foreign partner, for example).[17] Because of this control, an acquiring firm can also make changes in the acquired firm if desired or use its resources and capabilities to make changes in the acquired firm's operations. The emphasis on cross-border acquisitions is particularly evident in the telecommunications industry as described in the opening case in Chapter 1.[18] This recent surge in international acquisitions is also exemplified in the Strategic Focus on cross-border acquisitions.

STRATEGIC FOCUS

The Flood of Cross-Border Acquisitions

Merger mania has now reached Europe and is spreading globally. Of particular importance is the increasing number of cross-border acquisitions that help firms either enter a new regional market or increase their market power in that region of the world. For example, in 1997 there were a number of large cross-border acquisitions in Europe. Among those were the largest hostile takeover attempt in French history with Assicurazioni General (Italy) acquiring Assurances Generales de France (AGF) and the British based Reed Elsevier PLC's acquisition of Wolters Kluwer to form one of the world's largest publishing firms. Interestingly, Germany's Allianz outbid Italy's Generali and acquired AGF. Part of the incentives for these acquisitions is the need to reduce costs and to develop market power. To compete with other international firms, European companies must have a global or at least a European presence. Some of the acquisitions are needed to attain critical mass to compete with U.S. and Asian firms in certain markets.

The merger mania extends well beyond Europe to other parts of the world. For example, Mexico's Cemex has embarked on a worldwide expansion strategy, primarily using acquisitions to expand into new markets. Cemex made its first move into Asia paying $70 million for a 30 percent stake in Rizal, a Philippine cement firm. Since 1989, Cemex has grown through acquisitions to become the third largest cement maker globally. Its primary operations outside of Mexico are in the United States, Spain, Central America, South America, and the Caribbean. Acquisitions are also increasing in other Latin American countries such as Brazil, an attractive market for acquisitions for foreign firms. Brazilian companies in the financial and retail sectors particularly have suffered recently and are thus good buys. Examples include England's BBA Group PLC's acquisition of Brazil's polyester manufacturer, Bidim Ltda and Swiss Bank Group's acquisition of Banco Omega Group S.A., a bank headquartered in Rio de Janeiro.

Surging growth in Shiseido, a Japanese cosmetics firm, has been fueled by acquisitions. In 1997 Shiseido bought the Japanese division of Helene Curtis from Unilever, a large European firm. The union between B.A.T. Industries PLC, headquartered in London and Zurich Insurance of Switzerland also represent this major trend toward cross-border acquisitions. The integration of the two firms financial services businesses exemplifies a global trend toward consolidation in this field. Consolidation provides market power and the cross-border acquisition provides an increased global presence.

This merger trend, however, is being observed closely for antitrust actions by European governments. Several of the transactions noted above were scrutinized closely by the respective governments of the countries involved. For example, the B.A.T. and Zurich insurance union was reviewed carefully by antitrust officials in the European Union. The compelling need for market power and more global presence in order to be competitive in international markets makes it less likely that these acquisitions will be disapproved. The trend toward global merger mania probably will continue for years to come.

SOURCE: C. Adams, 1997, Cemex firm paves expansionary path, *Houston Chronicle*, December 26, C1, C4; E. Beck, 1997, B.A.T., Zurich Insurance discuss merger, *Wall Street Journal*, October 13, A3, A10; B. Coleman, 1997, EU antitrust officials brace themselves for merger wave, *Wall Street Journal Inter-*

active, October 15, http://www.wsj.com; B. Coleman, 1997, Giant European mergers facing review, *Wall Street Journal*, October 15, A17; P. Druckerman, 1997, Mergers still hot in Brazil despite jitters, *Wall Street Journal*, November 17, A20, A22; T. Kamm and R. Frank, 1997, Eurodeal day: Four bids, pacts hop borders, *Wall Street Journal*, October 14, A16, A19; B. Hutton, 1997, Acquisitions behind surge at Shiseido, *Financial Times*, November 12, 17; J. Rossant, 1997, Why merger mania is rocking the continent, *Business Week*, October 27, 64.

Cost of New Product Development Oftentimes, the development of new products internally and the start-up of new ventures can be quite costly and require significant time to develop the products and achieve a profitable return. For example, new ventures require an average of 8 years to achieve profitability and 12 years to generate adequate cash flows.[19] In addition, it has been estimated that almost 88 percent of innovations fail to achieve adequate returns on investment.[20] Furthermore, about 60 percent of innovations are effectively imitated within 4 years after patents are obtained. Therefore, internal development is often perceived by managers as entailing high risk.[21] The basic problem is that the costs of developing and bringing a new product to market can be substantial.[22] As a result, managers may prefer other means of market entry that are much quicker and less risky. This is an important strategy in the pharmaceutical industry, for example. Acquiring an established firm, although sometimes costly, is less risky than a new venture because there is a track record on which that firm can be evaluated. Furthermore, an acquisition offers immediate access to the market with an established sales volume and customer base.[23] Alternatively, new ventures often have to build their sales volume over time, working hard to develop a relationship with customers. One of the reasons Johnson & Johnson acquired Cordis was to more fully establish its name among doctors and hospitals who were worrying about the cost of its stent device to open clogged arteries. Cordis also provides devices that facilitate the opening of clogged arteries. This built credibility for Johnson & Johnson's stent device and resulted in reduced R&D and distribution costs.[24] Therefore, acquisition of an established firm provides a significant presence in the market and can provide profitability in the short term. Thus, reduced cost compared to new product development can be one reason why acquisitions have been a popular strategy.

Increased Speed to Market Firms can increase their speed to market by pursuing an acquisition rather than new product development.[25] Compaq Computer bought Tandem Computers for $3 billion to expand its product line into larger computers for the business market, for example. Tandem is a manufacturer of large, powerful computers that are targeted for the banking, financial, retail, and telecommunications industries. It would have taken Compaq a substantial amount of time to develop the computers of the size and power that Tandem manufactures and then to establish a presence in the business market. One analyst remarked that, "with one signature on the checkbook, all of Compaq's research and development gets compressed into a one-day event." This action also gives Compaq a more complete product line allowing it to provide one-stop shopping for business customers.[26]

Lucent Technologies, the technologically advanced telecommunications manufacturer spun off from AT&T, purchased Octel Communications to fill a void in its product line. While Lucent has the technological capabilities to develop products such as voice mail systems manufactured by Octel, it is much faster and possibly cheaper when all costs are considered over time to acquire a firm already established in the market. Lucent executives believe that by offering a more complete product line, the firm will experience greater sales even of its established product lines.[27]

Firms use acquisitions to enter foreign markets more quickly as well. Acquiring a company with established operations and relations in a new foreign market is a much faster way to enter these markets than to try to establish a new facility and new relationships with stakeholders in the new country. For example, Merrill Lynch purchased Mercury Asset Management, a London based money manager, in the largest international acquisition by a U.S. securities firm. The purchase gave Merrill a greater global presence that would have taken years for the company to develop on its own. In fact, the acquisition made Merrill the fourth largest asset manager in the world.[28]

There has been a record number of bank mergers and acquisitions recently and an increasing number in the insurance industry as well. These are representative of attempts to reduce costs available through technological change and increase market power in the banking and insurance industry rapidly as regulations have been relaxed to allow entry into new markets.

244

Lower Risk Compared to Developing New Products Internally developed new ventures can be quite risky. New ventures have high failure rates and take longer to achieve adequate cash flows and profitability. Alternatively, acquisitions provide outcomes that are more certain and can be estimated more accurately. This is because the target firms (e.g., Octel) have a track record that can be carefully analyzed, and forecasts of future revenues and costs can be based on historical records.[29] No such records exist for newly developed products such as Johnson & Johnson's coronary stent innovation.

It has been suggested that acquisitions have become a common means of avoiding risky internal ventures (and therefore risky R&D investments). In fact, acquisition may become a substitute for innovation.[30] Firms also may use acquisitions to avoid internal ventures because constraints on their resources and capabilities require decisions on whether to invest their scarce resources in developing new products or in making acquisitions. Of course, acquisitions are not riskless ventures. The risks of making an acquisition are discussed later in the chapter.

Increased Diversification A firm may find it easier to develop new products and new ventures within its current market because its managers better understand the products and the market. However, it is often more difficult for a firm to develop new products that are quite different from its existing set of products and to enter new markets because its managers may have less understanding of such markets. Thus, it is uncommon for a firm to develop new products and ventures internally as a means of diversifying its product line.[31] Instead, a firm usually opts to diversify through acquisition.

Research shows that acquisitions are a common means of diversification. Acquisitions provide the fastest and perhaps the easiest way to change a firm's portfolio of businesses.[32] Acquisitions are used often by firms to reduce dependence on a provider of resources or major supplier of parts or other items necessary to conduct business. Caterpillar's acquisition of Perkins Engine involved the purchase of a major supplier. Such acquisitions provide more control and reduce a firm's dependence on an external organization.[33] Nevertheless, acquisitions that diversify a firm's product lines must be undertaken after careful study and evaluation. Research shows that horizontal acquisitions usually are more successful than diversifying acquisitions. The difference in performance can be even greater when an acquired firm operates in highly diverse markets from those of the acquiring firm.[34]

In addition, as mentioned earlier, until the early 1980s, the U.S. government did not favor horizontal acquisitions and often precluded them through the enforcement of antitrust laws. As noted in Chapter 6, changes in the interpretation and enforcement of such laws led to a substantial number of horizontal acquisitions within the same market and acquisitions of firms in related businesses. Therefore, acquisitions have become a popular means of expanding market share and/or moving into related markets (and thus, achieving related diversification) as well as making unrelated diversification moves.

Avoiding Excessive Competition Firms sometimes use acquisitions to move into related and unrelated markets to decrease dependence on markets with substantial competitive pressure, frequently from foreign firms. In the 1980s, U.S. firms in many industries experienced problems maintaining their competitiveness in markets where Japanese, German, and other foreign firms had a strong presence. This is probably best exemplified by the U.S. automobile market. At the start of the 1980s, General Motors had approximately a 50 percent share of the U.S. automobile market. By the early 1990s, GM's share of the U.S. market fell to near 30 percent. Much of the lost market share was captured by Japanese and German and later South Korean firms. During the mid-1980s, General Motors acquired Electronic Data Systems (EDS) and Hughes Aerospace, possibly to avoid competition with the Japanese. Now, U.S. firms are becoming more competitive and GM sold its stakes in these two businesses to refocus on the automobile market.

U.S. Steel's acquisitions of Marathon Oil and Texas Oil and Gas were, in part, an attempt to avoid competition with imported steel from Japan. The Japanese do not have a strong industrial sector in petroleum and natural gas. Therefore, many U.S. firms attempted to spread their risks and diversify into other industries because of significant foreign competition. This has not been an effective strategy because it did not help U.S. firms gain strategic competitiveness or earn above-average returns, although, in some cases, it prevented below-average returns.

The Japanese have been much less active in acquisitions than have U.S. firms, and many of the earlier acquisitions in Japan, such as the merger to create Nippon Steel, were designed primarily to increase the market power of firms within Japanese markets.[35] Sony's acquisition of CBS Records and Bridgestone's acquisition of Firestone Tire and Rubber, on the other hand, illustrate that the Japanese were becoming important players in the international market for acquisitions in the 1980s. The increase in Japanese acquisitions at this time was partly motivated by the lower value of the dollar relative to the yen; as the yen appreciates in value relative to the dollar, U.S. assets can be bought with yen that are worth more dollars.

There were multiple reasons for these acquisitions. In both the Sony and the Bridgestone cases, the acquisitions provided the acquiring firms with significant footholds in the market. Sony's acquisition of CBS Records and Columbia Pictures provided vertical integration and outlets for some of Sony's new technology and products. For instance, despite poor performance of this business, Sony's president, Noboyuki Idei, refused to sell the firm's entertainment division (previously CBS Records and Columbia Pictures) in order to help standardize the digital video disk (DVD) format on which Sony and other consumer electronic producers have temporarily agreed.[36] After the final standard emerges, Sony's entertainment unit will provide the firm with an important distribution presence to market its products. (Matsushita, on the other hand, sold its film producer, MCA, to Seagram's and took a significant charge on its earnings because of competitive pressure.) Also, these acquisitions helped both Sony and Bridgestone overcome significant barriers to entry in U.S. markets, were completed rapidly, and seemed to entail less risk because of the known markets and past performance of each firm.

The Bridgestone acquisition of Firestone Tire and Rubber was a horizontal acquisition. Therefore, while it did not represent product diversification, it did represent international diversification, an important topic covered in Chapter 8. Alternatively, Sony's acquisitions of CBS Records and Columbia Pictures represented related diversification moves. As such, neither seemed to entail significant risk because of potential increased capabilities for market power and synergies from these acquisitions. These and other primary reasons for making acquisitions are summarized in Figure 7.1.

Although advantages can be gained from acquisitions, potentially significant problems can also accrue. Sometimes, these problems may equal or exceed the benefits gained. As a result, the average returns on acquisitions have varied closely around zero, as noted earlier in this chapter. Next, we examine some of these potential problems.

Problems in Achieving Acquisition Success

Among the potential problems of an acquisition strategy are difficulties integrating the acquired firm into the acquiring firm, inadequate analysis of target firm and managerial hubris, the large or extraordinary debt assumed to complete the acquisition, an inability to achieve synergy (no complementarities), too much diversification, managers who are overly focused on acquisitions, and acquiring firms that become too large.[37] These problems are also shown in Figure 7.1.

Integration Difficulties Integrating two companies after an acquisition can be quite difficult.[38] Among the problems that can arise are melding two disparate corporate cultures,[39] linking different financial and control systems, building effective working relationships (particularly when management styles differ), and resolving problems regarding the status of acquired firm executives.[40]

PhyCor acquired its major rival, MedPartners, in 1997. The newly combined company operates in 50 states and has 35,000 physicians affiliated with it. Although some analysts predicted the union would produce the "tiger" in the industry, others questioned whether their previous rivalry and two significantly different cultures and operating styles would allow an effective integration. PhyCor has a slow and deliberate style of operating while MedPartners is much more aggressive. Because of the different styles, PhyCor grew at a steady pace by acquisitions but MedPartners' growth was more rapid and erratic. The differences in style are similar to the childrens' story about the race between the tortoise and the hare. There is concern that MedPartners was built too fast and not well developed. As such, it may cause PhyCor indigestion when integration is attempted. That is the reason that PhyCor's stock suffered when the acquisition was announced. Prior to the acquisition, PhyCor's stock price declined because of investors' concerns. PhyCor has 53 well-established group practice clinics, while MedPartners had a more di-

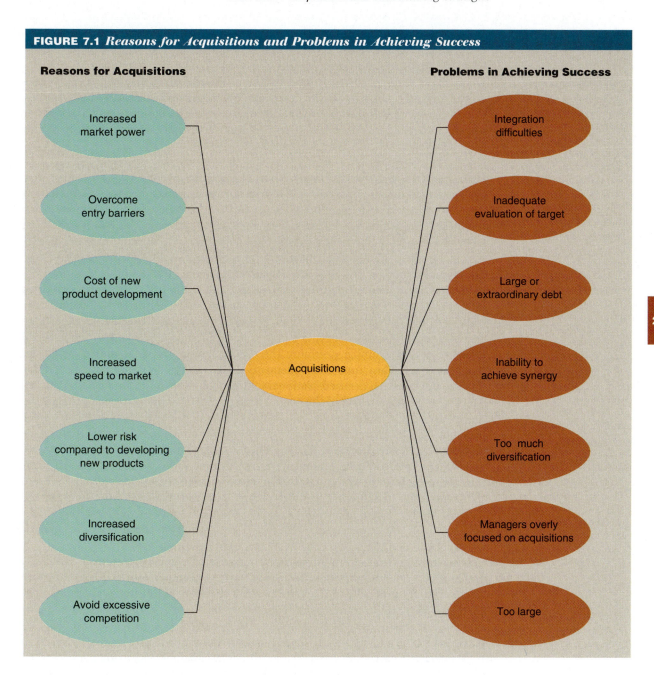

FIGURE 7.1 *Reasons for Acquisitions and Problems in Achieving Success*

Reasons for Acquisitions

- Increased market power
- Overcome entry barriers
- Cost of new product development
- Increased speed to market
- Lower risk compared to developing new products
- Increased diversification
- Avoid excessive competition

Acquisitions

Problems in Achieving Success

- Integration difficulties
- Inadequate evaluation of target
- Large or extraordinary debt
- Inability to achieve synergy
- Too much diversification
- Managers overly focused on acquisitions
- Too large

verse and fragmented physician base. The CEO of MedPartners was offered a position on the Board of the combined company but was not offered a management position. Time will tell whether the two companies can be integrated effectively. PhyCor management has its share of challenges to regain the confidence of investors.[41] One of the biggest challenges for the acquiring company after the acquisition is how to effectively integrate the two firms so that they operate as one.[42]

Robert Frankenberg, the CEO of Novell, Inc., which at one point was the second largest personal computer software company next to Microsoft, took over for Raymond Noorda. Novell became smaller when Frankenberg divested WordPerfect software and other application programming assets. Frankenberg found it necessary to sell WordPerfect for $124 million, compared to a purchase price of $855 million, in part, due to fierce competition from Microsoft. There was an extraordinary clash between the staffs of Novell and WordPerfect that crippled the integration after the acquisition and compounded management errors. Thus, the culture clash added significantly to the decreased value in the company and further necessitated selling WordPerfect. As the next section discusses, Novell may also have paid too much for WordPerfect.[43]

Inadequate Evaluation of Target Another potential problem is that a firm may pay too much for an acquisition. If a firm does not thoroughly analyze the target and fails to develop adequate knowledge of its market value, too much money may be offered to acquire it. In addition, current shareholders in the target firm must be enticed to sell their stock. To do so, they often require a premium over the current stock price. The bank acquisitions are requiring significant premiums. These premiums frequently are between 40 and 60 percent. For example, late in 1997 National City agreed to acquire First of America Bank for $6.78 billion. This price is approximately 3.8 times the book value of First of America and 22.9 times the bank's estimated 1998 earnings. The CEO of National City, David Daberko, stated that he knew his bank was paying a premium for First of America, but that it would have had to pay a similar premium three or four years ago. Of course, having to pay a premium at any time is not adequate justification and investors suggested this because the price paid caused National City's stock price to decline by 5.9 percent. Analysts were also critical of the acquisition, particularly the price paid, suggesting that National City's aggressive cost cutting plans may not be realistic.[44] A similar problem may be encountered by First Union, which acquired CoreStates Financial at a cost of $16.3 billion. The CEO of First Union, Edward Crutchfield, previously had vowed to reject acquisition targets that could not contribute to earnings within 18 months of the acquisition. However, the acquisition price is 5.3 times the book value of CoreStates, much larger than that paid for First of America. Thus, there is concern about the price paid in this instance as well. While Crutchfield has been largely successful with the 75 acquisitions in the last decade, analysts are skeptical about this one because of the high premium paid.[45]

The seemingly large premiums paid for banks pale in comparison to what Federated Department Stores paid for Broadway Department Stores. Federated paid a huge premium of $8 per share for a stock that was selling for less than $2 per share in a $1.6 billion transaction. In fact, between 1994 and 1996, Federated made two huge acquisitions of R.H. Macy's (centered in New York City) with 123 department stores and Broadway (based in Los Angeles) with 82 stores.[46]

Managerial hubris has been blamed for overpayment and inadequate rational evaluation of many targets.[47] Raymond Noorda may have also been influenced by hubris when he was CEO of Novell before Robert Frankenberg. Noorda completed the failed acquisition of WordPerfect. Ex-employees indicate that Noorda may have been overly obsessed with William Gates, Microsoft's chairman, causing Noorda to jump at the chance to acquire WordPerfect and Borland International's Quattro Pro spreadsheet software.[48]

Large or Extraordinary Debt Many of the acquisitions completed in the 1980s and 1990s were financed with significant debt. In fact, the 1980s produced an innovation called *junk bonds*.[49] Junk bonds represented a new financing option in which risky acquisitions were financed with money (debt) that provided a high return to the lenders (often referred to as the bondholders). Some of the interest rates on junk bonds were as high as 18 and 20 percent because they are unsecured (not tied to specific assets as collateral) and thus, are risky. Furthermore, firms were encouraged to take on significant debt because it was believed to positively discipline managerial actions. Some well-known finance scholars argued that debt disciplines managers not to misuse funds and, therefore, executives were often encouraged to utilize significant leverage to complete large acquisitions.[50] However, there are dramatic and unfortunate examples of the significant costs entailed in financing acquisitions. Federated Department Stores took on substantial debt to buy Macy's and Broadway. The debt and other transaction expenses resulted in a $62 million loss on Federated's 1995 $43 billion annual sales. A study by Stern Stewart, a consulting firm that tracks market value created in the last decade, indicated that Federated had destroyed $2.6 billion in capital. This performance ranked close to the bottom of the 1,000 firms tracked in the study.[51] A great deal of the number and dollar value of bankruptcies has been attributed to the use of excess leverage, the cost of such debt, and the reduced managerial flexibility resulting from high leverage.[52]

Some of the use of leverage was fueled by the sale of junk bonds, described earlier, and by the notion that the use of high levels of debt constrains managers from taking opportunistic actions in their own interest and forces them to act more in shareholders' interests.[53] Although this is an accurate characterization of the effects of debt, it fails to recognize the potential trade-offs that firms may have to make when large amounts of debt are used, particularly when the costs of debt are high. Obviously, resources are finite, and when payments for interest and principal on the debt are high, those dollars cannot be invested in other opportunities. A substantial amount of evidence suggests that when a firm has significant debt, managers forego investments that are likely to have long-term payoffs. These investments may include research and development and capital equipment. In both cases, these types of investments appear to be important for long-term firm competitiveness.[54]

Therefore, we conclude that the use of debt has both positive and negative effects. On the one hand, leverage can be a positive force in the development of a firm, allowing it to take advantage of attractive expansion opportunities. However, the use of too much leverage (e.g., extraordinary debt) can lead to negative outcomes, such as postponing or eliminating investments necessary to maintain strategic competitiveness. As such, many acquisitions in the 1990s are using more equity offerings instead of debt.[55] For instance, the acquisition of First of America by National City, mentioned earlier, used a tax-free stock swap to accomplish the transaction.

Inability to Achieve Synergy Another significant problem in achieving success with acquisitions is assessing the potential synergy involved and/or the benefits of such synergy. To achieve a competitive advantage through an acquisition, a firm must realize private synergy and core competence that cannot be imitated easily by competitors. Private synergy refers to the benefit from merging the acquiring and target firms that is due to a unique resource or a capability (set of resources) that is complementary between the two firms and not available among other potential bidders for that target firm.[56] Unfortunately, private synergy that is not easily imitated by competitors is uncommon. Perhaps this is one of the primary reasons that acquisitions rarely provide significant positive returns to acquiring firms' shareholders.

Early in 1996, Anheuser-Busch, the largest brewer in the United States, admitted defeat in two of its acquired businesses, snack foods and bread. It bought Eagle Snacks in 1979 because it saw that it could not only distribute beer but also salty snacks on regular beer routes to taverns and supermarkets. Anheuser also bought Campbell Taggart, a bakery unit. In doing so, Anheuser felt that because one of beer's main ingredients is yeast, it could also use this expertise in bread making. Furthermore, it could use its distribution process and network associated with its other products. Eagle boosted quality and began expanding from peanuts and pretzels to potato and tortilla chips. This created a significant strategic response from Frito-Lay. Frito launched an array of new products and upgraded its distribution while cutting costs. Frito's market share jumped to around 50 percent from 40, while Anheuser's never topped 6 percent and poor returns were realized year after year. As competition increased in Anheuser's main market, beer, these added businesses were distractions and diverted top managers' attention. This led to delays in new brand rollouts and the need to rebuild beer momentum. Instead of focusing on product diversification as it did earlier, Anheuser-Busch is now focusing on international markets where synergies are more likely to be realized in their dominant beer market.[57]

Synergy is not necessarily easy to achieve as described in the Strategic Focus regarding the purchase of Southern Pacific Rail by Union Pacific for $3.9 billion. After Union Pacific acquired Southern Pacific, numerous problems ensued including substantial railroad congestion. In short, Union Pacific had significant problems in merging the two companies and the firm's performance deteriorated. One could speculate that Union Pacific has actually achieved negative synergy. Because of the poor performance caused by the acquisition, customers that use the railroad are suffering and are expected to lose as much as $1.3 billion.

Synergy between two firms is not always easy to achieve. Union Pacific may have achieved negative synergy by acquiring Southern Pacific. Union Pacific's performance deteriorated after the acquisition.

Acquisitions entail many indirect costs, often referred to as transaction costs.[58] There are many costs involved in selecting acquisition targets and negotiating the acquisition. There are direct costs such as legal fees and fees of investment bankers in addition to those charged by consultants. There are also indirect costs such as the time of managers and staff evaluating proposals and in negotiating the deal. After the acquisition is consummated, there is considerable time spent evaluating the assets and employees of the acquiring firm and deciding how to integrate them into the acquiring firm's operations. Another indirect cost is the loss of key managers and employees after the acquisition.[59] Sometimes the acquiring firm lays off employees from the acquiring firm who work in redundant activities; this reduces costs. In other cases, the managers and employees experience a loss of autonomy after the merger and look for new jobs in other companies that give them more autonomy.[60] Interestingly, research shows that acquisitions of foreign firms results in higher turnover of acquired firm employees.[61] The differences in national culture and general means of operation may exacerbate other differences that normally exist in acquisitions. These costs, particularly the indirect ones, are often underestimated when considering the potential synergies.

251

STRATEGIC FOCUS

Chaos on the Railroads After Acquisition

Union Pacific acquired Southern Pacific Rail for $3.9 billion in September 1996. In early 1997, it began experiencing significant problems as it tried to integrate Southern Pacific's operations into its own. The problems continued throughout 1997 and into 1998. Union Pacific expected to obtain large returns from the acquisition through reduced costs and promised to improve delivery times by 20 percent after the acquisition. Unfortunately, neither of these benefits materialized.

Union Pacific faced substantial challenges because Southern Pacific Rail was a weak and ineffectively managed company. It had suffered from inadequate investment and performed poorly. Union Pacific underestimated the crews and locomotives needed to staff the trains and to transport the freight. The consequences of Union Pacific's miscalculations were significant traffic snarls and delays, along with mishaps such as derailments and equipment breakdowns. Furthermore, because Union Pacific encouraged many key Southern Pacific personnel to leave, there was a substantial loss of institutional knowledge. These same key personnel kept the Southern railroad operating under bad conditions. With these people gone, there was no one to help solve the problems when they occurred. At times, more than 10,000 railroad cars were stuck in limbo on the Union Pacific rails.

The logjam created many hardships for Union Pacific customers that depended on the railroad to move their goods to market. One Union Pacific customer suggested that the problems were similar to a cancer that spread to affect at least 20 percent of the railroad's system. Many customers could not get their goods to their customers. For example, the chemical companies using the railroad lost millions of dollars in sales and had to absorb extra costs, such as inventory costs and higher shipping fees from alternative shippers. As some firms discovered, using trucks for shipping can cost as much as 20 percent more with bulky orders, and trucks were not always available causing substantial delays in some cases. The costs were estimated to be as much as $1.3 billion. This does not include the lost business and goodwill suffered by Union Pacific. Clearly, Union Pacific was not able to achieve synergy through its acquisition of Southern Pacific Rail.

SOURCE: C. Boisseau, 1998, Union Pacific reports progress on slowdown, *Houston Chronicle*, January 14, C2; Big railroad merger quickly goes awry, 1997, *Wall Street Journal*, October 2, A1, A8; C. Boisseau, 1997, Rail customers want end to delays, *Houston Chronicle*, August 30, C1, C3; D. Machalaba and A. W. Mathews, 1997, Union Pacific tie-ups reach across economy, *Wall Street Journal*, October 8, B1, B10; Logjam costs $762 million, professor says, 1997, *Bryan-College Station Eagle*, November 27, A22.

Too Much Diversification An outcome of the trend toward acquisitions over the 1960s, 1970s, and 1980s was that firms often became overdiversified. Research suggests that the long-term performance of many acquisitions is not positive. It is not uncommon for prior acquisitions to be divested several years thereafter, primarily because of poor performance.[62] As noted earlier, acquisition has been used as a primary means of diversifying a firm's product line. When a firm becomes overdiversified, it is difficult to manage effectively. The level at which a firm becomes overdiversified differs for each firm. This is because each firm's type of diversification and managerial expertise determine when a firm reaches a point of diversification that is too complex and unmanageable. Because related diversification requires more information processing than unrelated diversification, overdiversification is reached with fewer business units than with unrelated diversification.[63] When overdiversification occurs, firm performance usually suffers.[64]

In addition, high diversification often is accompanied by other attributes that can produce lower long-term performance. For example, when a firm becomes more diversified, top-level executives often emphasize financial controls over strategic controls in the evaluation of divisional performance.[65] Defined and explained more extensively in Chapters 11 and 12, strategic control in the diversified firm refers to top executive understanding of business unit strategy and operations, whereas financial control refers to objective evaluation (e.g., ROI) criteria of business unit performance. The change in emphasis comes about because the top executives do not have adequate knowledge of the various businesses to evaluate effectively the strategies and strategic actions taken by division general managers. As a result, the division general managers become short-term oriented because strategic controls do not balance the risk that is shifted to them. Oftentimes, their compensation is tied to the achievement of certain financial outcomes. As a result, they may reduce long-term investments (e.g., R&D, capital investment) that entail some risk in order to boost short-term profits.[66] When they do so, long-term performance may suffer.

Too much diversification through acquisition creates significant problems for the management of the firm. Top-level managers may not effectively manage each of the businesses and maintain strategic competitiveness. Over time, this may result in lower innovation in those businesses.[67]

Firms following an acquisition strategy may begin to use acquisitions as a substitute for innovation. They become locked into a self-reinforcing cycle. They make several acquisitions that produce less innovation over time. As they encounter significantly stronger competition and lose their competitive advantage in certain markets, they may seek to acquire firms in other markets. This reinforces the cycle. As a result, if firms use acquisitions as a substitute for innovation, eventually they are likely to encounter performance problems.[68]

Managers Overly Focused on Acquisitions An active acquisition strategy often requires much managerial time and energy. For example, the process of making acquisitions requires extensive preparation and sometimes lengthy negotiations. Searches for viable acquisition candidates must be conducted that involve extensive data gathering and analyses. Although executives are rarely involved in the data gathering and analyses, they must review the results and select the best candidate from the alternatives. After selecting the acquisition candidate, an effective acquisition strategy must be formulated and implemented. Negotiations with target firm representatives can consume considerable time, particularly if the acquisition is an unfriendly takeover. Therefore, because the process involves much time and energy, executives may become overly focused on the process. Such focused energy can divert managerial attention from other important matters within the firm, particularly those that are long term in nature and require significant time and attention.[69] Furthermore, these negotiations often do not consider potential postmerger integration problems.[70]

Target firm executives also may spend substantial amounts of time and energy on the acquisition. Operations in target firms being pursued for acquisition have been described as being in a state of virtual suspended animation.[71] While day-to-day operations continue, albeit sometimes at a slower pace, most target firm executives are unwilling to make long-term commitments. Long-term decisions are frequently postponed until the negotiation process has been completed. Therefore, the acquisition process can create a short-term perspective and greater risk aversion among top-level executives in the target firm.[72]

Besides creating a short-term perspective and greater risk aversion among top-level managers, acquisitions and change of ownership can foster neglect of the firm's core business. For instance, in the 1980s and early 1990s, car rental companies neglected their core business because of many changes of ownership through acquisitions. Since its start-up in the 1940s, Avis has been owned by 12 different parents, including ITT, Beatrice Companies, and Wesray Capital. In 1990, GM owned a small stake in Avis and in National Car Rental System, which is also now independent. Ford controlled Budget and part of Hertz. Chrysler owned Snappy, Dollar, and Thrifty rental car companies. In the early 1990s, the car rental companies were receiving so many incentives to take new cars from the Detroit Big Three that they made more money buying and selling cars than they did in the rental business. However, between 1992 and 1996, the cash incentives to rental car companies were eliminated. During this period, many of the rental car companies lost the focus of their business, did not update technology and reservation systems, ended up with too many cars, and did not have consistent brand identities. For instance, Alamo pioneered the off-airport rental plaza but now is in more airport locations. To improve performance, these firms must refocus on their core business, car rentals. It is hoped that the employee ownership programs at Avis and National will help facilitate an improved focus on their core business.[73]

Additionally, it is not unusual for significant layoffs to occur after acquisitions, particularly in the acquired business. For example, when Ciba-Geigy and Sandoz merged to form Novartis AG, they laid off about 12,000 employees.[74] Given the large amount of turnover in the executive ranks of acquired firms, it is not surprising that many executives are reluctant to make major decisions for fear that they may be evaluated negatively by acquiring firm executives and laid off after the acquisition is completed.[75] This loss of managerial personnel can be problematic. In addition to losing significant managerial experience and expertise, those championing new products may leave and, therefore, the development and transfer of those new products to the market may be postponed or eliminated.[76]

253

Too Large Most acquisitions create a larger firm. In theory, increased size should help the firm gain economies of scale and therefore develop more efficient operations. This would be true, for example, in research and development operations and, thus, larger firms should over time produce greater amounts of innovation. However, it has been found that increases in size create efficiencies only when the acquiring firm is not too large. After reaching some level of size, the problems created by large size outweigh the benefits gained from increased size. For example, larger firms can become unwieldy to manage. If too many levels of managers exist, approval for the development and implementation of innovations can become lengthy and burdensome. Furthermore, to manage the larger size, firms often use more bureaucratic controls. **Bureaucratic controls** are formalized supervisory and behavioral rules and policies that are designed to ensure consistency of decisions and actions across different units. Although these more formalized rules and policies can be beneficial to the organization, they sometimes produce more rigid and standardized behavior among managers.

It is not uncommon for the acquiring firm to adopt and implement centralized controls within the acquired firm in order to facilitate integration. This reduces flexibility and, in the long run, may produce less innovation and less creative decision making, thus harming long-term firm performance.[77]

The preceding discussion provides reasons to pursue acquisitions and delineates the problems in realizing success. Next, we summarize the characteristics of effective acquisitions.

EFFECTIVE ACQUISITIONS

As noted, evidence suggests acquisition strategies rarely produce positive returns for the acquiring firm's shareholders. However, an acquisition strategy can have positive outcomes. Some of the specific attributes of acquisitions are more likely than others to produce positive outcomes and therefore may require the careful attention of top executives considering an acquisitions strategy.

Recent research identified some potentially important attributes of successful and unsuccessful acquisitions.[78] The research indicated that successful acquisitions entailed target firms that had complementary assets or resources for the acquiring firm. As a result, when the acquired firm was integrated into the acquiring firm, positive synergy and capability were created. In fact, the integration of the two firms frequently produced unique resources, a requirement to build strategic competitiveness, as described earlier.[79] Thus, the acquisitions were generally highly related to the acquiring firm's businesses. In fact, the acquiring firm maintained its focus on core businesses and leveraged those core businesses with the complementary assets and resources from the acquired firm. Oftentimes targets were selected and "groomed" by establishing a working relationship sometime prior to the acquisition (e.g., through strategic alliances).[80]

In addition, friendly acquisitions normally facilitate integration of the two firms. The two parties work together to find ways to integrate their firms and achieve positive synergy. In hostile takeovers, animosity often results between the two top management teams, which can permeate the new joint organization. As a result, more key personnel in the acquired firm may be lost, and those who remain may resist the changes necessary to integrate the two firms and create synergy.[81] With effort, cultural clashes can be overcome, and fewer key managers and employees

Bureaucratic controls are formalized supervisory and behavioral rules and policies that are designed to ensure consistency of decisions and actions across different units.

will become discouraged and leave.[82] Thus, successful acquisitions tend to be friendly, although there are exceptions.

Research suggests that successful acquirers often conduct a deliberate and careful selection of target firms and also consider the ensuing negotiations. In addition, the acquiring and frequently the target firms have considerable financial slack in the form of cash and/or debt capacity. A significant attribute is that the merged firm continues to maintain a low or moderate debt position, even if a substantial amount of leverage is used to finance the acquisition. Where substantial debt is used to finance the acquisition, it is reduced quickly by selling off assets from the acquired firm. Often the assets sold are not complementary to the acquiring firm's businesses or are performing poorly. Also, the acquiring firm may sell its own lower performing businesses after making an acquisition. In this way, high debt and debt costs are avoided. Therefore, the debt cost does not prevent long-term investments such as R&D, and managerial discretion in the use of cash flow is relatively flexible.

Another characteristic of firms that launch successful acquisitions is that they emphasize innovation and continue to invest in R&D as part of their overall strategy. As a result, they maintain a high managerial commitment to innovation. This is clearly evidenced in the case of Johnson & Johnson that has made a number of acquisitions over the years. Nonetheless, it continues to focus on creating internal innovation as well. Although the firm recently developed a new R&D lab, it has continued to make excellent acquisitions that are complementary to its various product lines, such as the Cordis acquisition, which aligns with Johnson & Johnson's coronary stent.[83] Johnson & Johnson also maintains its manufacturing skills and improves the operations of its acquired firms.

The final two characteristics of successful acquisitions are flexibility and adaptation skills. When both the acquiring and the target firms have experience in managing change, they will be more skilled at adapting their capabilities to new environments. As a result, they are more adept at integrating the two organizations, which is particularly important when disparate cultures are encountered. Adaptation skills allow the two firms to integrate more quickly, efficiently, and effectively both firms' assets. As a result, the merged firm begins to produce the positive synergy and capabilities envisioned more quickly.

The attributes of a successful acquisition and their results are summarized in Table 7.1. Although some acquisitions have been successful, the majority of acquisitions completed during the last three decades have not been highly successful. Because of their lack of success and the growth of some firms to unmanageable sizes with too much diversity, a number of firms, in the United States and internationally, have restructured.

RESTRUCTURING

A significant wave of restructuring began in the late 1980s and increased in the 1990s that changed the composition of many U.S. and international firms.[84] Although restructuring was a common strategy among many U.S. firms during this period, it has spread internationally to countries such as Japan, Germany, and South Korea. **Restructuring** refers to changes in the composition of a firm's set of businesses and/or financial structure.[85] Much restructuring has entailed downsizing and the divestiture of businesses.[86] During this restructuring, a significant reduction in the number of acquisitions occurred, as firms attempted to "get their houses in or-

Restructuring refers to changes in the composition of a firm's set of businesses and/or financial structure.

TABLE 7.1 *Attributes of Successful Acquisitions*

Attributes	Results
1. Acquired firm has assets and/or resources that are complementary to the acquiring firm's core business	High probability of positive synergy and competitive advantage by maintaining strengths
2. Friendly acquisition	Faster and more effective integration; possibly lower premiums
3. Careful and deliberate selection of target firms and conduct of negotiations	Acquire firms with strongest complementarities and avoid overpayment
4. Financial slack (cash and/or favorable debt position)	Financing (debt or equity) easier to obtain and less costly
5. Merged firm maintains low-to-moderate debt position	Lower financing cost, lower risk (e.g., of bankruptcy and avoids trade-offs associated with high debt)
6. Has experience with change and is flexible and adaptable	Faster and more effective integration; facilitates achievement of synergy
7. Sustained and consistent emphasis on R&D and innovation	Maintain long-term competitive advantage in markets

256

der." The primary impetus for restructuring was poor performance, along with correction of overdiversification.[87] For example, International Paper announced plans to sell $1 billion of its noncore assets to refocus the firm and improve financial performance. In particular, it will sell businesses that have failed to achieve market share and profitability goals. The announcement came after posting a loss equal to $1.39 a share. Businesses expected to be sold include the imaging business and those marketing printing supplies. In addition to the divestitures, other restructuring actions were announced. Among those was a planned layoff of more than 40 percent of International Paper's work force or about 9,000 employees. The intent is to refocus on its core businesses and to substantially improve performance.[88]

Although restructuring has been a worldwide phenomenon, some of the most significant restructuring has taken place in U.S. firms. Next, we examine some common means of restructuring—downsizing, downscoping, and leveraged buyouts.

Downsizing

One of the most common means of making changes within U.S. firms is that of downsizing. **Downsizing** is a reduction in the number of employees, and sometimes in the number of operating units, but it may or may not change the composition of businesses in the corporation's portfolio. The late 1980s and 1990s evidenced the loss of thousands of jobs in private and public organizations throughout the United States. There have been significant workforce reductions at General Motors, IBM, Kodak, Procter & Gamble, TRW, Unisys, and Xerox, among many others. In fact, one study estimates that 85 percent of the *Fortune* 1000 firms have implemented some downsizing.[89] The intent of these downsizings was to become "lean and mean."[90] However, results of a survey published in the *Wall Street Journal* suggest that many of the firms that downsized did not meet their goals. Eighty-nine percent of the firms surveyed suggested that the downsizing had a goal of reducing expenses, but only 46 percent achieved this goal. Another 71 percent suggested that their goal was to improve productivity, but only 22 percent of the respondents said that they met their goal for increasing productivity. Finally, 67

Downsizing is a reduction in the number of employees, and sometimes in the number of operating units, but it may or may not change the composition of businesses in the corporation's portfolio.

percent stated a goal of increasing competitive advantage, but only 19 percent noted that this goal was achieved.[91] These results have been confirmed in a study sponsored by the American Management Association and by other studies as well.[92]

Recent research shows that firms from both the United States and Japan received lower returns after downsizing. In effect, the stock markets in the respective countries evaluated the downsizings negatively (i.e., they evaluated that the downsizings would have negative outcomes for the firms over the long term). The researcher concluded that downsizing is not a panacea for problems that firms have and that they must take positive actions to deal with the problems directly and strategically. Normally, downsizing occurs because of other problems the firm is experiencing.[93]

When overcapacity exists, as in the defense industry, downsizing can produce above-average returns as it did for General Dynamics as the first mover to reduce the overcapacity.[94] Thus, although downsizing can be successful, it has not generally been as successful as intended. Furthermore, it has other unintended and potentially negative consequences. For instance, it is often problematic because corporations do not have total control over which employees stay and which seek new positions elsewhere. Often the best employees take advantage of separation payments during layoffs because they have other employment options. Research has shown that downsizing improves shareholder wealth when it is done for strategic purposes as in the General Dynamics case.[95] This has also been confirmed in other studies where the term *rightsizing* is used to mean that when downsizing is necessary firms should make certain that cuts are not done too deeply so that the changes to the firm's human capital do not affect strategic competitiveness.[96]

Despite the problems, downsizing continues in many large firms in the United States and worldwide. Many of the downsizings occur because of poor performance such as the case with International Paper, as discussed earlier. The downsizings announced in 1997 by Kodak and Ericsson were also due to poor performance. Kodak was suffering market share losses and thus stock price reductions because Fuji, a Japanese firm, was substantially undercutting its price for film. Kodak had to cut costs to reduce the price of its film to combat Fuji.[97] Similar to Kodak, Ericsson announced a 10,000 employee reduction in its Infocom business because of declining profits due to margin and price reductions.[98] Kimberly Clark announced a layoff of 5,000 employees because of a profit shortfall in 1997 and to reduce its overcapacity.[99] Even in these cases, care must be taken not to cut too many employees and to try to keep the most talented ones, both of which can be a significant challenge.

Downscoping

Other firms have downscoped and met more success.[100] **Downscoping** refers to divestiture, spin-offs, or some other means of eliminating businesses that are unrelated to a firm's core businesses. This is often referred to as strategically refocusing on the firm's core businesses. A firm that downscopes often also downsizes as noted in the example of International Paper described earlier.[101] However, it does not eliminate key employees from its primary businesses, which could lead to loss of core competence. The firm reduces its size by reducing the diversity of businesses in its portfolio. When accomplished, the top management team can more effectively manage the firm. This is because the firm becomes less diversified, and the top management team can better understand and manage the remaining businesses, primarily the core and other related businesses.[102] (Strategic leadership exercised by the top management team is the focus of Chapter 12.)

Downscoping refers to divestiture, spin-offs, or some other means of eliminating businesses that are unrelated to a firm's core businesses.

257

Rather than downscoping, some firms are spinning off businesses. PepsiCo chose to spin off KFC, Pizza Hut, and Taco Bell; the three fast-food businesses are known as Tricon. PepsiCo spun off the three businesses in part because of their poor performance.

258

A number of very large spin-offs have been undertaken in recent times. EDS was successfully spun off from General Motors. The EDS spin-off created the largest independent computer services company. EDS has grown with the outsourcing of computer systems, but it is now designing software and selecting hardware and training clients to use the software and hardware. EDS also operates one of the world's top six management consulting practices.[103]

Several other recent spin-offs are described in the Strategic Focus. These include spin-offs by PepsiCo of its fast-food businesses, by U.S. West, and by Cordiant. The spin-off by PepsiCo is dissimilar from the spin-off of EDS by GM in that the fast-food businesses have been underperforming PepsiCo's core business. The opposite was true at GM. In both cases, however, the spin-offs allowed the firms to focus on their core businesses. Thus, this strategic move can be considered a form of downscoping for both firms. Thus, while many of the firms, both the parent and the spin-off, increase shareholder value and accounting performance, some do not (see the Strategic Focus).[104]

STRATEGIC FOCUS

Cast Out, Orphaned, or Spun Off?

Through divestitures of various businesses, many firms have downscoped or refocused on their core businesses. However, in recent years, the trend has been to spin off businesses rather than to sell them to new owners. In many cases, this approach has been more lucrative for shareholders and allows the firm to refocus on its core business. The popularity of this approach is seen in recent announcements of spin-offs by PepsiCo and U.S. West in the United States and by Cordiant, a London-based advertising holding company.

PepsiCo decided to spin off its three fast-food businesses, KFC, Pizza Hut, and Taco Bell, while U.S. West and Cordiant chose to split theirs into two separate businesses. The new PepsiCo spin-off is known as Tricon for the three icons. In 1997, both KFC and Taco

Bell increased their sales over the previous year. This represents a trend for KFC but is the first increase in recent years for Taco Bell. Alternatively, Pizza Hut's sales declined during both 1996 and 1997. Thus, part of the reason that PepsiCo decided to spin off these businesses was their performance. They did not meet PepsiCo's criterion. Some analysts suggest that the new firm, Tricon, will have a challenge in handling its $4.7 billion debt, 10 times the businesses' cash flow, and a negative $740 million shareholder equity. On the other hand, Tricon managers expect these businesses to be more innovative without "big brother" PepsiCo looking over their shoulders. Already several fast food innovations are planned for both Pizza Hut and Taco Bell. There are also positive feelings about the top two executives for Tricon, David Novak, who turned around the performance of KFC, and Andrall Pearson, former president of PepsiCo. That said, the hypercompetition in the fast-food industry makes it difficult for any firm to succeed. Even the perennial market leader, McDonald's, has encountered problems in recent years (as explained in a Strategic Focus in Chapter 5).

One common reason for spin-offs is poor performance as in the case with PepsiCo. In others, it may be a lack of synergy, as in the case of U.S. West and Cordiant. U.S. West was the only Baby Bell to move into the cable business to take advantage of the expected synergy between the cable and communications businesses. Unfortunately, this synergy never materialized. Communications companies no longer expect to use cable systems as a means to carry communications into homes. Such plans changed with new Internet technology and with growing knowledge of the expense of using a universal cable communications system. Because of these changes, there has been little interaction between the two separate businesses at U.S. West. Therefore, the top executive felt that spinning them off into two separate companies would allow each to focus on its business without distractions. At Cordiant, the two separate advertising businesses did not mix well, possibly because of differing cultures when they were merged. Thus, the two new firms, Saatchi & Saatchi and Cordiant Communications Group, are reestablishing separate identities. Saatchi & Saatchi was considered the much stronger of the two originally and thus, is expected to flourish alone.

It should be noted that spin-offs are not a cure-all for performance problems. For example, AT&T's spin-off of Lucent Technologies and NCR did not improve NCR's performance. Similarly, AT&T has not performed as well as hoped after the spin-off. Actually, because of the highly disappointing performance of NCR within AT&T, many referred to the change as a cast-off. Lucent Technologies is the only one of the three businesses that seems to have benefited from the separation. Analysts also question whether the spin-offs and divestitures planned by the poorly performing Tele-Communications Inc. (TCI) will improve its performance. Thus, the popular new trend seems to have some benefits but cannot cure all the ills of companies with multiple businesses.

SOURCE: P. Galuska, 1997, Still waiting for the new NCR, *Business Week*, December 15, 142–146; R. Gibson, 1997, Fast-food spin-off enters Pepsi-free era, *Wall Street Journal*, B1, B10; R. Grover, 1997, The dismantling of an empire, *Business Week*, June 30, 94–95; S. Lipin, 1997, U.S. West to split into two companies, *Wall Street Journal*, October 27, A3; Y. Ono, 1997, Cordiant breakup fails to impress market, *Wall Street Journal*, December 16, B10; S. Pulliam, 1997, Pepsi's fast-food spin-off may cause some indigestion, *Wall Street Journal*, September 17, C1, C2; P. Sellers, 1997, Pepsi's eateries go it alone, *Fortune*, August 4, 27–30.

Probably one of the best known cases of downscoping outside of AT&T is Hanson PLC. Hanson was a British conglomerate well known for its strategy of acquiring unrelated businesses often operating in declining markets that were poor performers and undervalued. Hanson would immediately implement actions designed to increase efficiency, reduce costs, and improve profits. Oftentimes after these actions were accomplished and successful, Hanson would sell the firm for a

259

profit. For years, this strategy seemed to work well for Hanson. However, as the global environment for business changed and the markets became increasingly competitive, Hanson management was unable to adapt. As a result, the firm's performance declined.[105] Hanson managers decided that the way to deal with these problems was to downscope by splitting the firm into four separate businesses. It began the process in 1995 by spinning off a set of unrelated businesses located in the United States. It finished the process in 1996 by spinning off three more businesses, Energy, Imperial Tobacco, and Millenium Chemicals. Thus, while Hanson referred to this as a separation into four businesses, it actually split into five separate businesses with the original Hanson firm remaining after spinning off four groups of businesses. The U.S. businesses spin-off, USI, was successful as its stock price increased 55 percent within one year after the action. The performance of Hanson after the spin-offs in 1996 was mixed.[106] There are a number of other firms that have downscoped or are currently in the process of downscoping in hopes of improving performance. Among these is Campbell Soup. This company announced that it was spinning off seven of its noncore businesses, which generate annual revenues of $1.4 billion, in order to refocus.[107] Thus, downscoping appears to be a major restructuring strategy in the 1990s.

Leveraged Buyouts

A **leveraged buyout (LBO)** is a restructuring action whereby the managers of the firm and/or an external party buys all of the assets of the business, largely financed with debt, and takes the firm private.

Although downscoping is a prominent and generally successful restructuring strategy, another restructuring strategy, leveraged buyouts, has received significant attention in the popular press. A **leveraged buyout (LBO)** is a restructuring action whereby the managers of the firm and/or an external party buys all of the assets of the business, largely financed with debt, and takes the firm private. The firm is bought by a few owners often in partnership associations, such as Kolberg, Kravis and Roberts (KKR), primarily by obtaining significant amounts of debt. Through this action, the stock of the firm is no longer traded publicly. This form of restructuring was predicted by a prominent finance scholar to be the corporate form of the future.[108] Oftentimes the new owners of the LBO firm also sell a significant number of assets after the purchase and, in so doing, downscope the firm.[109] Some of these assets are sold to help reduce the significant debt costs. In addition, it is frequently the intent of the new owners to increase the efficiency of the firm and sell it within a period of five to eight years. It is interesting to note, however, that recent research suggests that increased efficiency does not come from pressures of debt. Researchers have found that managerial ownership creates more effective incentives in the buyout than debt.[110] This is supported by anecdotal evidence at Clayton, Dubilier & Rice, Inc., a firm that facilitates leveraged buyouts.[111] This firm reports that managers who received ownership incentives help implement performance improvements. It is the equity incentive rather than the fear of not making debt payments that creates improvement.

The three types of leveraged buyouts are (1) management buyouts (MBO), (2) employee buyouts (EBO), and (3) an LBO in which another firm or partnership such as KKR buys the whole firm, as opposed to a part of the firm, and takes it private. MBOs have been found to lead to downscoping, increased strategic focus, and improved performance.[112] As part of CBS, Fender Musical Instruments was a poor performer. In 1981, William Schultz was brought in to fix it, but ended up putting together an MBO in 1985. Fender's independence proved Schultz's strategy to be correct. It began with $11 in debt for every $1 in equity, but the brand name was strong. In 1995, Fender's sales were $300 million with nearly 50 percent of the guitar market share. Recent evaluation has seen the equity of Schultz's group grow to more than $100 million compared to an initial investment of $500,000.[113]

Improvements at UAL (parent of United Airlines) and Avis Rent-A-Car are attributed to EBOs at these firms. The UAL arrangement appears to be working better than the situation at Avis. At UAL there has been more of a cooperative spirit with gains in market share and above-average returns.[114] At Avis and other EBOs, difficulties have arisen between management and employees. Furthermore, few employee owners have been requested to sit on boards.[115] These problems are very similar to the problems of the employee buyouts experienced in Russia. Needed restructuring is hard to accomplish because of employee job security fears.[116] When change is needed, more problems usually occur between managers and employees.

Whole-firm LBOs, on the other hand, see improvements through downsizing and retrenchment. This approach was illustrated through a buyout at Dr Pepper by Forsmann Little, a leveraged buyout specialist like KKR. Dr Pepper was successful enough to receive a new infusion of capital through an initial public offering. It subsequently was bought out by Cadbury Schweppes PLC.[117]

While LBOs have been hailed as a significant innovation in the financial restructuring of firms, there are potentially negative trade-offs. First, the large debt increases the financial risk of the firm, as evidenced by the number of LBO firms that have had to file for bankruptcy in the 1990s. The intent of owners to increase the efficiency of the LBO firm and sell it within five to eight years sometimes creates a short-term and risk-averse managerial focus. As a result, many of these firms fail to invest in R&D or take other major actions designed to maintain or improve the core competence of the firm.[118]

Most scholars believe LBOs occur because of poor corporate governance (discussed in Chapter 10). The poor governance allows managers to take actions that

261

Employee buyouts (EBOs) do not always have a positive effect on a firm. At Avis, for example, there have been problems between management and employees.

are not in the best interests of the firm but from which the managers may profit. Thus, many scholars argue the LBO occurs to correct the inefficiencies created by this environment. Because the managerial actions often entail acquiring businesses that do not create value for the firm, LBOs lead frequently to divestitures of these businesses. Some research supports this explanation of LBOs.[119] Others argue that the problems are not due to weaknesses in corporate governance but rather to managerial mistakes.[120] There is research to support this view as well.[121] We conclude that in reality there may be several reasons that LBOs are undertaken.

Restructuring Outcomes

The restructuring alternatives, along with typical short- and long-term outcomes, are presented in Figure 7.2. As shown in the figure, the most successful restructuring actions are those that help top management regain strategic control of the firm's operations. Thus, downscoping has been the most successful because it refocuses the firm on its core business(es). Executives can control the strategic actions of the businesses because they are fewer, less diverse, and deal with operations with which top management is more knowledgeable.

Jack Welch, CEO of General Electric, has created significant wealth for GE shareholders. He has done so largely by restructuring the firm to create greater efficiencies and by developing an excellent management team. In 1997, Welch again decided that GE needed to restructure one more time before he retired. His intent was to increase the efficiencies in GE's industrial businesses. He believed this was necessary if these businesses were to compete effectively in global mar-

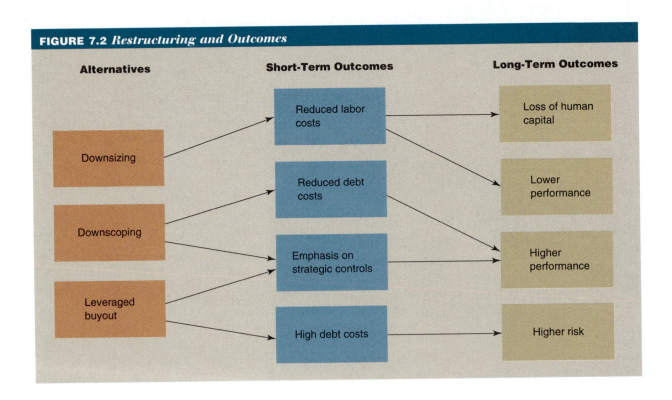

FIGURE 7.2 *Restructuring and Outcomes*

kets. By increasing efficiencies, he intended to improve these businesses' profitability. The restructuring was aimed at reducing costs and increasing productivity. Most expect him to be successful because of his past performance.[122]

Lastly, takeover bids and managerial resistance have been found to affect performance of an acquisition. For example, research has shown that hostile takeover bids often do not produce the outcomes expected. The raiders in hostile bids argue the takeover is the result of an entrenched management that has not acted in the best interests of the shareholders. This kind of acquisition, however, produces problems in integrating the two firms. The target firm managers often leave or are forced out and the remaining employees may be resentful. Sometimes, losing key people means a loss of knowledge and experience that could be helpful in making the acquired business productive for the acquiring firm. One study found no instances where acquisitions involving hostile bids were effective. Only friendly acquisitions produced high performance after the merger of the two firms.[123] Also, hostile bids induce managerial resistance. Research has shown that managerial resistance increases the acquisition offer which enhances the market value for the target firm shareholders.[124] Therefore, acquirers should carefully consider the situation before making a hostile bid for a target firm.

263

SUMMARY

- Acquisition has been a popular strategy for many years, but the number and the size of acquisitions increased greatly during the 1980s and 1990s. The popularity of acquisitions was facilitated by a change in the interpretation of U.S. antitrust laws and innovations in the financing of large acquisitions (i.e., junk bonds).

- Firms might make acquisitions for several reasons. Among these are increasing their market power, overcoming barriers to entry, avoiding the costs involved in developing new products internally and bringing them to market, increasing the speed at which the firm can enter a new business, reducing the risk of entering a new business, diversifying the firm more easily, and avoiding severe competition, often from foreign firms.

- Acquisitions produce their share of problems for the acquiring firm as well. It is often difficult to achieve effective integration between the acquiring and the acquired firms. Firms sometimes inadequately evaluate the target firm because of the bidding process. In addition, firms can overestimate the potential capabilities and synergy that can be created between the acquiring and the acquired firms. The costs of acquisition can be significant. These include the costs of obtaining financing and arranging for the acquisition of

another firm. When a firm takes on large or extraordinary levels of debt to complete an acquisition, problems can arise. Other firms have been unsuccessful because the acquiring firm became too diversified. Managers have also become overly focused on making acquisitions, which may lead to inappropriate managerial oversight over other firm operations. Finally, a firm may become too large in size through acquisition, which makes the firm more difficult to manage.

- However, acquisitions can be successful. Successful acquisitions often require deliberate and careful selection of the target and firm negotiations. In addition, both the acquiring and the target firms in successful mergers frequently have considerable slack in the form of cash and/or debt capacity. Successful acquiring firms often maintain a low or moderate debt position. Even if significant leverage is used to finance the acquisition, the firm quickly reduces the debt and debt costs by selling off portions of the acquired firm or some of its own lower performing businesses. Successful acquisitions involve firms with complementary assets/resources, and those complementary resources are used to leverage the core competence of the joint firm. Related to this point, friendly acquisitions often lead to more success. Acquisitions also tend to be more successful when both the acquiring and the target firms have experience in adapting to change and therefore are better able to achieve effective integration. Finally, many of the successful acquiring firms maintain an emphasis on innovation and R&D as a part of their overall strategy.

- In the late 1980s and 1990s, restructuring became a common and important strategic action. Oftentimes this restructuring is undertaken to downsize the firm. The approach requires employee layoffs and also seeks to reduce the number of hierarchical levels in an organization. Although it does reduce formal behavioral controls, it is problematic because corporations do not have total control of which employees stay and which seek new positions elsewhere. Therefore, a firm may lose many high-performing employees.

- Another approach to restructuring is downscoping. The goal of downscoping is to reduce the level of a firm's diversification. This form of restructuring is often accomplished by divesting unrelated businesses, whereby the firm's top executives can strategically refocus on the firm's core business. It is often accompanied by downsizing as well. This approach has been more successful than downsizing alone.

- Another popular form of restructuring is known as the leveraged buyout (LBO). In a leveraged buyout, the management or an external party buys 100 percent of the firm's stock, largely financed with debt, and takes the firm private. The three types of LBOs are management buyouts (MBOs), employee buyouts (EBOs), and whole-firm LBOs. MBOs have functioned best because they provide clear incentives for managers. EBOs provide the potential for improved cooperation, but power struggles can occur between managers and workers if significant change is required. In general, LBOs have met with mixed success. Oftentimes, the intent is to improve the firm's efficiency and performance and to sell the firm (or take it public) within five to eight years after the leveraged buyout. Some LBO firms have been successful because of improved incentives for managers, but in recent years some have experienced performance problems, primarily because of the high debt and debt costs.

- The main goal of corporate restructuring, in most cases, is to gain or regain strategic control of the firm. Downscoping and strategic refocusing on core businesses reduce the pressure for processing information to manage a wider diversity of businesses and allow the top executives to control the businesses by evaluating strategic actions, as opposed to placing an emphasis on financial outcomes. This generally produces higher performance and achieves strategic competitiveness over the long term.

REVIEW QUESTIONS

1. Why have acquisitions been a popular strategy?
2. For what reasons might firms follow an acquisition strategy?
3. What problems might be encountered by firms following an acquisition strategy?
4. What are some of the approaches that firms employ to complete an acquisition strategy successfully?
5. What are the common forms of restructuring and their goals?
6. How can a firm successfully implement a restructuring strategy?

APPLICATION DISCUSSION QUESTIONS

1. Given the evidence that the shareholders of many acquiring firms gain little or nothing in value from acquisitions, why do so many firms follow such a strategy?
2. Of the reasons for following an acquisition strategy described in the chapter, which are positive, and which are more negative and likely to create performance problems over the long term?

264

3. After reading popular press accounts of large acquisitions, choose a recent one and detail the important characteristics of the acquiring and the acquired firms. Based on these characteristics and other information, do you think this acquisition will succeed in achieving high performance? Explain why or why not.

4. Search popular press accounts to find an acquisition that has the attributes necessary for success. Why do you feel this acquisition has a high probability of success over the long term?

5. What is meant by the term *synergy?* Explain how the merger of two separate businesses can create synergy.

How can firms create private synergy that cannot be imitated easily by other companies?

6. How can top executives in a firm determine the most appropriate level of diversification and thereby avoid becoming overdiversified? How can they determine the appropriate level of debt/leverage to utilize?

7. Why have LBOs not become the organization of the future, as proposed by a prominent finance scholar? Why have MBOs been more successful than EBOs?

8. In comparing acquiring a business with developing a new product/business internally, what are the advantages and disadvantages of each?

ETHICS QUESTIONS

1. If there is a relationship between the size of the firm and a top executive's compensation, is there an inducement for top executives to engage in mergers and acquisitions in order to increase their compensation? What is the board of directors' role in maintaining the integrity of the compensation system?

2. When a manager seeks to restructure (acquire or divest firm assets), are there incentives to do it in a way that builds the manager's power relative to shareholders or other stakeholders such as employees, rather than the firm's power relative to the market in order to achieve strategic competitiveness? Could this motive be related to the lack of success among acquiring firms?

3. If shareholders increase their wealth through a downsizing, does this come at the expense of employees who have invested a considerable portion of their life in the firm or at the expense of whole communities dependent on employment from the downsizing firm?

4. Do "corporate raiders" always target firms that are performing poorly and thus have a rational reason for pursuing the restructuring due to mismanagement, or is there also an incentive to pursue firms that have resources to "buy off" hostile suitors ("green mail")?

5. When a leveraged buyout is attempted, shareholders often increase their wealth (e.g., stock price increases), but debtholders may find their investment at risk because bond ratings are often downgraded. Are there any ethical issues associated with the transfer of wealth from debtholders to shareholders?

6. Before an LBO, should a manager reveal information about planned new products that might bring personal gain (e.g., when the manager becomes an owner through the LBO) rather than gain to public shareholders, once the firm is private?

INTERNET EXERCISE

Go to M&A Marketplace at:

http://www.mergernetwork.com/default.html

At the Web site, go to "News Headlines" and select the link that provides access to recent announcements of corporate mergers. Select one of the mergers and visit the Web sites of the companies involved. From what you learn about the companies, speculate on the reason for the merger. Does the merger make sense to you? Why or why not?

Strategic Surfing

Of the many sites on the Internet that provide merger-related information, two are particularly useful. The first site, Pointers to the World of Mergers and Acquisitions, provides links to other merger-related Web sites and newsgroups. The second site, Securities Data Company, provides a broad array of merger-related information, news, and data.

http://www.gwdg.de/~ifbg/mergers.html

http://www.secdata.com

NOTES

1. M. A. Hitt, R. E. Hoskisson, R. D. Ireland, and J. S. Harrison, 1991, Effects of acquisitions on R&D inputs and outputs, *Academy of Management Journal* 34: 693–706; M. Sikora, 1990, The M&A bonanza of the '80s and its legacy, *Mergers and Acquisitions*, March/April, 90–95; J. F. Weston and K. S. Chung, 1990, Takeovers and corporate restructuring: An overview, *Business Economics* 25, no. 2: 6–11.

2. S. R. Curry, 1997, First: The year of the very big deals, *Fortune*, November 24, 36–38; Mergers, acquisitions up record 40%, 1997, *Dallas Morning News*, January 3, F11; The business of travel, 1997, *Financial Times*, November 20, 1.

3. M. C. Jensen, 1988, Takeovers: Their causes and consequences, *Journal of Economic Perspectives* 1, no. 2: 21–48.

4. D. Lei and M. A. Hitt, 1995, Strategic restructuring and outsourcing: The effect of mergers and acquisitions and LBOs on building firm skills and capabilities, *Journal of Management* 21: 835–860.

5. J. S. Lublin, 1995, Spinoffs may establish new companies but they often spell the end of jobs, *Wall Street Journal*, November 21, B1, B8.

6. S. Lipin and P. Fritsch, 1997, Falcon Drilling to merge with Reading & Bates, *Wall Street Journal Interactive Edition*, July 15, http://www.wsj.com.

7. P. C. Haspeslagh and D. B. Jemison, 1991, *Managing Acquisitions: Creating Value Through Corporate Renewal* (New York: The Free Press).

8. D. K. Datta, G. E. Pinches, and V. K. Naravyanan, 1992, Factors influencing wealth creation from mergers and acquisitions: A metaanalysis, *Strategic Management Journal* 13: 67–84; G. F. Davis and S. K. Stout, 1992, Organization theory and the market for corporate control: A dynamic analysis of the characteristics of large takeover targets, 1980–1990, *Administrative Science Quarterly* 37: 605–633; W. B. Carper, 1990, Corporate acquisitions and shareholder wealth: A review and exploratory analysis, *Journal of Management* 16: 807–823.

9. K. Ramaswamy, 1997, The performance impact of strategic similarity in horizontal mergers: Evidence from the U.S. banking industry, *Academy of Management Journal* 40: 697–715.

10. E. MacDonald, 1997, Ernst & Young to merge with KPMG, *Wall Street Journal*, October 20, A3, A13.

11. A. Shleifer and R. W. Vishny, 1991, Takeovers in the '60s and the '80s: Evidence and implications, *Strategic Management Journal* 12 (Special Winter Issue): 51–59.

12. M. Lubatkin, N. Srinivasan, and H. Merchant, 1997, Merger strategies and shareholder value during times of relaxed antitrust enforcement: The case of large mergers during the 1980s, *Journal of Management* 23: 59–81.

13. J. Wyatt, 1995, Drug stocks—where M&A pays off, *Fortune*, October 30, 222.

14. E. Tanouye and G. Anders, 1995, Drug industry takeovers mean more cost-cutting, less research spending, *Wall Street Journal*, February 1, B1, B4.

15. C. Quintanilla, 1997, Caterpillar to buy small-engine maker, Lucas Varity's Perkins, for $1.33 billion, *Wall Street Journal*, December 12, A3, A4.

16. L. Bannon, 1997, Computer Services to buy Continuum, *Wall Street Journal*, April 30, A3, A5.

17. D. Angwin and B. Savill, 1997, Strategic perspectives on European cross-border acquisitions: A view from the top European executives, *European Management Review* 15: 423–435.

18. L. Capron and W. Mitchell, 1997, Outcomes of international telecommunications acquisitions: Analysis of four cases with implications for acquisitions theory, *European Management Review*, 15: 237–251.

19. R. Biggadike, 1979, The risky business of diversification, *Harvard Business Review* 57, no. 3: 103–111.

20. E. Mansfield, 1969, *Industrial Research and Technological Innovation* (New York: Norton).

21. L. H. Clark, Jr., and A. L. Malabre, Jr., 1988, Slow rise in outlays for research imperils U.S. competitive edge, *Wall Street Journal*, November 16, A1, A5; E. Mansfield, M. Schwartz, and S. Wagner, 1981, Imitation costs and patents: An empirical study, *Economic Journal* 91: 907–918.

22. J. K. Shank and V. Govindarajan, 1992, Strategic cost analysis of technological investments, *Sloan Management Review* 34 (Fall): 39–51.

23. M. A. Hitt, R. E. Hoskisson, R. A. Johnson, and D. D. Moesel, 1996, The market for corporate control and firm innovation, *Academy of Management Journal* 39: 1084–1119.

24. E. Tanouye and S. Lipin, 1995, Cordis agrees to be acquired by J&J in a stockswap valued at $1.8 billion, *Wall Street Journal*, November 7, B6; R. Winslow, 1995, Going for flow: Simple device to prop clogged arteries open changes coronary care: Johnson & Johnson's 'stent' is a hit, but the cost is worrying hospitals, *Wall Street Journal*, October A1, A8.

25. K. F. McCardle and S. Viswanathan, 1994, The direct entry versus takeover decision and stock price performance around takeovers, *Journal of Business* 67: 1–43.

26. D. Silverman, 1997, Compaq to acquire Tandem, *Houston Chronicle*, June 24, C1, C8.

27. T. Weber, 1997, Lucent to acquire Octel for $1.8 billion, *Wall Street Journal*, July 18, A3, A4.

28. A. Raghavan and S. Callan, 1997, Merrill's $5.3 billion global bet, *Wall Street Journal*, November 20, C1, C22.

29. M. A. Hitt, R. E. Hoskisson, and R. D. Ireland, 1990, Mergers and acquisitions and managerial commitment to innovation in M-form firms, *Strategic Management Journal* 11 (Special Summer Issue): 29–47.

30. Hitt et al., The market for corporate control and innovation; J. Constable, 1986, Diversification as a factor in U.K. industrial strategy, *Long Range Planning* 19: 52–60.

31. Hitt et al., Effects of acquisitions; Hitt, Hoskisson, and Ireland, Mergers and acquisitions.

32. D. D. Bergh, 1997, Predicting divestiture of unrelated acquisitions: An integrative model of *ex ante* conditions, *Strategic Management Journal* 18: 715–731.

33. S. Finkelstein, 1997, Interindustry merger patterns and resource dependence: A replication and extension of Pfeffer (1972), *Strategic Management Journal* 18: 787–810.

34. J. Anand and H. Singh, 1997, Asset redeployment, acquisitions and corporate strategy in declining industries, *Strategic Management Journal*, 18 (Special Summer Issue): 99–118.

35. W. C. Kester, 1991, *Japanese Takeovers: The Global Contest for Corporate Control* (Boston: Harvard Business School Press), 94–95.

36. P. Newcomb, 1996, Video games, *Forbes*, May 6, 45.

37. M. A. Hitt, J. S. Harrison, R. D. Ireland, and A. Best, 1998, Attributes of successful and unsuccessful acquisitions of U.S. firms, *British Journal of Management*, in press.

38. D. K. Datta, 1991, Organizational fit and acquisition performance: Effects of post-acquisition integration, *Strategic Management Journal* 12: 281–297; J. Kitching, 1967, Why do mergers miscarry? *Harvard Business Review* 45, no. 6: 84–101.

39. H. Aaron, 1994, A poisoning of the atmosphere, *Wall Street Journal*, August 29, A10; P. M. Elsass and J. F. Veiga, 1994, Acculturation in acquired organizations: A force field perspective, *Human Relations* 47: 453–471.

40. A. F. Buono and J. L. Bowditch, 1989, *The Human Side of Mergers and Acquisitions* (San Francisco: Jossey-Bass).

41. A. Bianco, 1997, Will these blood types mix? *Business Week*, November 24, 82–83; PhyCor to purchase rival MedPartners, 1997, *Houston Chronicle*, C3.

42. D. B. Jemison and S. B. Sitkin, 1986, Corporate acquisitions: A process perspective, *Academy of Management Review* 11: 145–163.

43. R. Tamburri and D. Clark, 1996, Technology: Corel to acquire Novell's WordPerfect for $124 million in cash and stock, *Wall Street Journal*, February 1, B5; D. Clark, 1996, Software firm fights to remake business after ill-fated merger, *Wall Street Journal*, January 12, A1, A6.

44. M. Murray, 1997, National City to acquire First of America in a stock swap valued at $6.78 billion, *Wall Street Journal*, December 2, A3, A8.

45. D. Greising and N. Harris, 1997, You paid how much for that bank? *Business Week*, December 1, 152; S. Lipin and S. E. Frank, 1997, First Union to acquire CoreStates for stock valued at $16.3 billion, *Wall Street Journal*, November 19, A3, A4.

46. L. Grant, 1996, Miracle or mirage on 34th Street? *Fortune*, February 5, 84–90.

47. R. Roll, 1986, The hubris hypothesis of corporate takeovers, *Journal of Business* 59: 197–216.

48. Clark, Software firm fights.

49. G. Yago, 1991, *Junk Bonds: How High Yield Securities Restructured Corporate America* (New York: Oxford University Press), 146–148.

50. M. C. Jensen, 1987, A helping hand for entrenched managers, *Wall Street Journal*, November 4, A6; M. C. Jensen, 1986, Agency costs of free cash flow, corporate finance, and takeovers, *American Economic Review* 76: 323–329.

51. Grant, Miracle or mirage on 34th Street?, 85.

52. M. A. Hitt and D. L. Smart, 1994, Debt: A disciplining force for managers or a debilitating force for organizations? *Journal of Management Inquiry* 3: 144–152.

53. M. C. Jensen, 1989, Is leverage an invitation to bankruptcy? On the contrary—it keeps shaky firms out of court, *Wall Street Journal*, February 1, A14; Jensen, A helping hand.

54. B. H. Hall, 1990, The impact of corporate restructuring on industrial research and development, in M. N. Baily and C. Winston (eds.), *Brookings Papers on Economic Activity* 3: 85–135; B. Baysinger and R. E. Hoskisson, 1989, Diversifi-

cation strategy and R&D intensity in multi-product firms, *Academy of Management Journal* 32: 310–332.

55. L. Grant, 1993, Corporate connections: Mergers are on the rise, but unlike deals of the 80s they aren't debt laden, *U.S. News & World Report*, August 2, 46–49.

56. Hitt et al., Effects of acquisitions; J. B. Barney, 1988, Returns to bidding firms in mergers and acquisitions: Reconsidering the relatedness hypothesis, *Strategic Management Journal* 9 (Special Summer Issue): 71–78.

57. R. Gibson, 1996, Anheuser-Busch plans to spin off baking unit, ending costly foray, *Wall Street Journal*, February 29, B3; R. A. Melcher and G. Burns, 1996, How Eagle became extinct: Anheuser saw synergies in beer and snacks, *Business Week*, March 4, 68–69.

58. J-F. Hennart and S. Reddy, 1997, The choice between mergers/acquisitions and joint ventures: The case of Japanese investors in the United States, *Strategic Management Journal* 18: 1–12.

59. Hitt, Hoskisson, Johnson, and Moesel, The Market for Corporate Control.

60. P. Very, M. Lubatkin, R. Calori, and J. Veiga, 1997, Relative standing and the performance of recently acquired European firms, *Strategic Management Journal* 18: 593–614.

61. J. A. Krug and H. Hegarty, 1997, Post-acquisition turnover among U.S. top management teams: An analysis of the effects of foreign vs domestic acquisitions of U.S. targets, *Strategic Management Journal* 18: 667–675.

62. M. E. Porter, 1987, From competitive advantage to corporate strategy, *Harvard Business Review* 65, no. 3: 43–59; D. J. Ravenscraft and R. M. Scherer, 1987, *Mergers, Sell Offs and Economic Efficiency* (Washington, D.C.: Brookings Institute).

63. C. W. L. Hill and R. E. Hoskisson, 1987, Strategy and structure in the multiproduct firm, *Academy of Management Review* 12: 331–341.

64. R. A. Johnson, R. E. Hoskisson, and M. A. Hitt, 1993, Board of director involvement in restructuring: The effects of board versus managerial controls and characteristics, *Strategic Management Journal* 14 (Special Issue): 33–50; C. C. Markides, 1992, Consequences of corporate refocusing: *Ex ante* evidence, *Academy of Management Journal* 35: 398–412.

65. R. E. Hoskisson and M. A. Hitt, 1988, Strategic control systems and relative R&D investment in large multiproduct firms, *Strategic Management Journal* 9: 605–621.

66. Hitt, Hoskisson, and Ireland, Mergers and acquisitions.

67. Hitt et al., The market for corporate control and innovation.

68. Hitt, Hoskisson, and Ireland, Mergers and acquisitions.

69. Ibid.

70. Jemison and Sitkin, Corporate acquisitions.

71. Hitt et al., Effects of acquisitions.

72. R. E. Hoskisson, M. A. Hitt, and R. D. Ireland, 1994, The effects of acquisitions and restructuring (strategic refocusing) strategies on innovation, in G. von Krogh, A. Sinatra, and H. Singh (eds.), *Managing Corporate Acquisitions* (London: Macmillan Press), 144–169.

73. L. Miller and G. Stern, 1996, Car rental companies neglect core business, often skid into losses, *Wall Street Journal*, February 15, A1, A8.

74. M. R. Sesit and G. Steinmetz, 1997, UBS, Swiss Bank are expected to merge, *Wall Street Journal*, December 2, A3, A4.

75. J. P. Walsh, 1988, Top management team turnover following mergers and acquisitions, *Strategic Management Journal* 9: 173–183.

76. M. A. Hitt, R. E. Hoskisson, R. D. Ireland, and J. Harrison, 1991, Are acquisitions a poison pill for innovation?, *Academy of Management Executive* V, no. 4: 22–34.

77. Hitt, Hoskisson, and Ireland, Mergers and acquisitions.

78. Hitt et al., Attributes of successful and unsuccessful.

79. J. S. Harrison, M. A. Hitt, R. E. Hoskisson, and R. D. Ireland, 1991, Synergies and post acquisition performance: Differences versus similarities in resource allocations, *Journal of Management* 17: 173–190; Barney, Returns to bidding firms.

80. M. A. Lubatkin and P. J. Lane, 1996, Psst . . . The merger mavens still have it wrong! *Academy of Management Executive* X, no. 1: 21–39.

81. J. P. Walsh, 1989, Doing a deal: Merger and acquisition negotiations and their impact upon target company top management turnover, *Strategic Management Journal* 10: 307–322.

82. L. S. Lublin, 1995, Strategies for preventing post-takeover defections, *Wall Street Journal*, April 28, B1, B8.

83. Tanouye and Lipin, Cordis agrees to be acquired by J&J; G. P. Pisano and S. C. Wheelwright, 1995, The new logic of R&D, *Harvard Business Review* 73, no. 5: 93–105.

84. R. A. Johnson, 1996, Antecedents and outcomes of corporate refocusing, *Journal of Management* 22: 437–481.

85. J. E. Bethel and J. Liebeskind, 1993, The effects of ownership structure on corporate restructuring, *Strategic Management Journal* 14 (Special Summer Issue): 15–31.

86. E. Bowman and H. Singh, 1990, Overview of corporate restructuring: Trends and consequences, in L. Rock and R. H. Rock (eds.), *Corporate Restructuring* (New York: McGraw-Hill).

87. R. E. Hoskisson, R. A. Johnson, and D. D. Moesel, 1994, Divestment intensity of restructuring firms: Effects of governance, strategy and performance, *Academy of Management Journal* 37: 1207–1251.

88. J. Welch, 1997, International Paper to cut work force and sell $1 billion of noncore assets, *Wall Street Journal*, July 4, A4.

89. W. McKinley, C. M. Sanchez, and A. G. Schick, 1995, Organizational downsizing: Constraining, cloning, learning, *Academy of Management Executive* IX, no. 3: 32–44.

90. R. E. Hoskisson and M. A. Hitt, 1994, *Downscoping: How to Tame the Diversified Firm* (New York: Oxford University Press).

91. A. Bennet, 1991, Downsizing doesn't necessarily bring an upswing in corporate profitability, *Wall Street Journal*, June 4, B1, B4.

92. K. S. Cameron, S. J. Freeman, and A. K. Mishra, 1991, Best practices in white-collar downsizing: Managing contradictions, *Academy of Management Executive* V, no. 3: 57–73.

93. P. M. Lee, 1997, A comparative analysis of layoff announcements and stock price reactions in the United States and Japan, *Strategic Management Journal* 18: 879–894.

94. J. Dial and K. J. Murphy, 1995, Incentives, downsizing and value creation at General Dynamics, *Journal of Financial Economics* 37: 261–314.

95. D. L. Worrell, W. M. Davidson, and V. M. Sharma, 1991, Layoff announcements and stockholder wealth, *Academy of Management Journal* 34: 662–678.

96. M. A. Hitt, B. W. Keats, H. F. Harback, and R. D. Nixon, 1994, Rightsizing: Building and maintaining strategic leadership and long-term competitiveness, *Organizational Dynamics* 23 (Autumn), 18–32; J. S. Lublin, 1994, Don't stop cutting staff, study suggests, *Wall Street Journal*, September 27, B1.

97. R. Waters, 1997, Eastman Kodak to cut 10,000 jobs, *Financial Times*, November 12, 13.

98. T. Burt, 1997, Ericsson plans to cut 10,000 jobs, *Financial Times*, December 3, 17.

99. J. Kirkpatrick, 1997, Kimberly-Clark to slash up to 5,000 jobs, *Dallas Morning News*, November 22, F1, F11; R. Langreth, 1997, Kimberly-Clark's sweeping cutbacks should ease overcapacity, analysts say, *Wall Street Journal*, November 24, A3.

100. Hoskisson and Hitt, *Downscoping*.

101. J. Kose, H. P. Lang, and J. Nitter, 1992, The voluntary restructuring of large firms in response to performance decline, *Journal of Finance* 47: 891–917; J. S. Lublin, 1995, Spin offs may establish new companies, but they often spell the end of jobs, *Wall Street Journal*, November 21, B1, B8.

102. Johnson, Hoskisson, and Hitt, Board of directors involvement; R. E. Hoskisson and M. A. Hitt, 1990, Antecedents and performance outcomes of diversification: A review and critique of theoretical perspectives, *Journal of Management* 16: 461–509.

103. N. Templin, 1996, Under Alberthal, EDS is out of limelight but triples revenue, *Wall Street Journal*, February 21, A1, A6.

104. Johnson, Antecedents and outcomes.

105. P. Stonham, 1997, Demergers and the Hanson experience. Part one: The prelude, *European Management Journal* 15: 266–274.

106. P. Stonham, 1997, Demergers and the Hanson experience. Part two: Demerger tactics, *European Management Journal* 15: 413–422.

107. Campbell's higher-margin diet, 1997, *Business Week*, September 22, 43; E. Jensen, 1997, Campbell Soup may shed some noncore soup lines, *Wall Street Journal*, July 14, A4.

108. M. C. Jensen, 1989, Eclipse of the public corporation, *Harvard Business Review* 67, no. 5: 61–74.

109. M. F. Wiersema and J. P. Liebeskind, 1995, The effects of leveraged buyouts on corporate growth and diversification in large firms, *Strategic Management Journal* 16: 447–460.

110. P. H. Phan and C. W. L. Hill, 1995, Organizational restructuring and economic performance in leveraged buyouts: An ex-post study, *Academy of Management Journal* 38: 704–739.

111. W. C. Kester and T. A. Luehrman, 1995, Rehabilitating the leveraged buyout, *Harvard Business Review* 73, no. 3: 119–130.

112. A. Seth and J. Easterwood, 1995, Strategic redirection in large management buyouts: The evidence from post-buyout restructuring activity, *Strategic Management Journal* 14: 251–274.

113. M. Matzer, 1996, Playing solo, *Forbes*, March 25, 80–81.

114. S. Chandler, 1996, United we own, *Business Week*, March 18, 96–100.

115. A. Bernstein, 1996, Why ESOP deals have slowed to a crawl, *Business Week*, March 18, 101–102.

116. I. Filatochev, R. E. Hoskisson, T. Buck, and M. Wright, 1996, Corporate restructuring in Russian privatizations:

Implications for US investors, *California Management Review* 38, no. 2: 87–105.

117. B. Ortega, 1995, Cadbury seeking a new king of pop to oversee no. 3 soft-drink business, *Wall Street Journal*, January 30, B2.

118. W. F. Long and D. J. Ravenscraft, 1993, LBOs, debt, and R&D intensity, *Strategic Management Journal* 14 (Special Issue, Summer): 119–135.

119. D. D. Bergh and G. F. Holbein, 1997, Assessment and redirection of longitudinal analysis: Demonstration with a study of the diversification and divestiture relationship, *Strategic Management Journal* 18: 557–571.

120. C. Markides and H. Singh, 1997, Corporate restructuring:

A symptom of poor governance or a solution to past managerial mistakes? *European Management Journal* 15: 213–219.

121. D. L. Smart and M. A. Hitt, 1997, A test of the agency theory perspective of corporate restructuring, working paper, University of Nebraska.

122. A. Bernstein, S. Jackson, and J. Byrne, 1997, Jack cracks the whip again, *Business Week*, December 15, 34–35.

123. Hitt, Harrison, Ireland, and Best, Attributes of successful and unsuccessful acquisitions.

124. P. Holl and D. Kyriazis, 1997, Wealth creation and bid resistance in U.K. takeover bids, *Strategic Management Journal* 18: 483–498.

International Strategy

CHAPTER 8

Learning Objectives

After reading this chapter, you should be able to:

1. Explain traditional and emerging motives for firms to pursue international diversification.

2. Explore the four factors that lead to a basis for international business-level strategies.

3. Name and define generic international business-level strategies.

4. Define the three international corporate-level strategies: multidomestic, global, and transnational.

5. Discuss the environmental trends affecting international strategy.

6. Name and describe the five alternative modes for entering international markets.

7. Explain the effects of international diversification on firm returns and innovation.

8. Name and describe two major risks of international diversification.

9. Explain why the positive outcomes from international expansion are limited.

Globalization: The Driving Force of International Strategy

Introduced in Chapter 1, globalization is a reality around which our study of the strategic management process is framed. An increasingly globalized world is dramatically changing today's economic landscape from that of only 20 years ago. Moreover, the pace of global economic expansion will increase, perhaps significantly so, in the next 20 years.

Defined earlier as the spread of economic innovations around the world and the political and cultural adjustments that accompany this diffusion, globalization can be viewed through different lenses that represent specific levels of analysis. At a *worldwide level*, globalization concerns the increasing economic interdependence among countries. This growth in interdependence is demonstrated by increases in the cross-border flow of goods, services, capital, and knowledge. Public policy analysts focus on *country-level* globalization, which is the extent of interlinkages between their country's economy and those of the rest of the world. The *industry level* of globalization refers to the degree to

http://
http://www.nike.com
http://www.reebok.com
http://www.adidas.com
http://www.toyota.co.jp
http://www.sony.com
http://www.hoechst.com

which a firm's competitive position within a particular industry is interdependent with its position in another country. The pharmaceutical industry is an example of one that is highly globalized. In globalized industries, markets across the world tend to be dominated by the same companies. Nike, Reebok, and Adidas, for example, are dominant in the athletic footwear industry. For the *individual firm*, globalization refers to the extent to which the company has expanded its revenue and asset base across countries and the degree to which it engages in cross-border flows of capital, goods, services, and knowledge across subsidiaries.

Toyota is an example of a highly globalized company (Toyota's effective use of its core competencies is described in a Strategic Focus in Chapter 3; its innovation ability is explained in a Strategic Focus in Chapter 13). Approximately 35 percent of the firm's global output is generated from wholly or partially owned affiliates in over 25 countries in Europe, Asia, and the Americas. Furthermore, "Toyota exported 38 percent of its domestic production from Japan to foreign markets and engaged in significant intra-firm flows among its affiliates. For example, within its Southeast Asian regional network, Toyota exported diesel engines from Thailand, transmissions from the Philippines, steering gears from Malaysia and engines from Indonesia." With over $20 billion in cash, Toyota has allocated $13.5 billion to global expansion through the year 2000. The intent of these investments is to create the automobile manufacturing industry's first truly globally organized company.

Toyota follows the multidomestic international strategy (discussed in this chapter) at the corporate level and the integrated/low-cost differentiation strategy at the business unit level (see Chapter 4). Through the multidomestic strategy, Toyota seeks to use its vast manufacturing clout to customize vehicles for regional markets. Manufacturing hubs in Asia, North America, and Europe rely on locally based suppliers and design teams to tailor vehicles to local tastes. Through its integrated supplier networks, world-standard setting manufacturing efficiencies, and superior product development skills, Toyota is able to reduce costs continuously relative to competitors while simultaneously offering differentiated features (e.g., product quality and reliability) to customers that create value for them.

Sony Corporation is another example of a highly globalized and successful company. Sony's better-than-expected year-end 1997 profits were in sharp contrast to many of its rivals, especially its Japanese counterparts. In light of results such as these, some analysts believe that "Sony has built a competitive advantage that is sustainable; its strategy is very well defined and [is] absolutely right."

In recognition of the increasingly globalized nature of the world's markets and the industries in which it competes, Hoechst AG is becoming a globalized firm rather than a German company. The company's CEO indicates that the change processes required for Hoechst to become a globalized company were initiated some 15 or 20 years ago. Although Hoechst is not yet truly an international company, neither is it still a typical German company. Following a significant reorganization, Hoechst is a widely diversified corporation with operations in pharmaceuticals, animal health, polyester products, industrial gases, paints and coatings, agribusiness, and basic chemicals and cellulose acetate. In light of this reorganization, one in which decision making responsibility has been decentralized to those managing the strategic business units, the firm's top-level managers are making decisions regarding Hoechst's strategic positioning for the next 10 to 20 years. This is a time period in which Hoechst executives believe the world's economies will become more interdependent. The decision areas the executives are examining include choices about the company's portfolio of businesses and how capital will be allocated among those divisions (recall that these are corporate-level strategy issues). Within individual strategic business units, decisions must be made regarding products to be offered and in which global markets, the pace at which the business will globalize, and the methods for entering different global markets, among others. Thus, to achieve strategic competitiveness in the global economy, Hoechst AG must choose and implement international strategies at both the corporate and business unit levels. The international strategy choices available to firms, such as Hoechst AG, that have decided to internationalize their operations are the focus of this chapter.

SOURCE: V. Govindarajan and A. Gupta, 1998, Setting a course for the new global landscape, in Part One of As business goes global, *Financial Times*, February 10–11, 3–5; M. Nakamoto, 1998, Sony posts 45% rise as games beat rivals, *Financial Times*, January 30, 13; T. Box, 1997, Toyota steers a solid course of growth, *Dallas Morning News*, November 30, H1, H6; B. Bremner, L. Armstrong, K. Kerwin, and K. Naughton, 1997, Toyota's crusade, *Business Week*, April 7, 104–114; C. Cookson, Interview with Jurgen Dormann, 1997, *Fortune* (Special edition), November 10, 106E6–106E26; M. Nakamoto, 1997, Toyota targets European sales, *Financial Times*, November 20, 21; H. Simonian, 1997, A steady drive around the world, *Financial Times*, December 5, 14.

273

In the 1980s, the dramatic success of Japanese firms and products, such as Toyota and Sony, in the United States and other international markets provided a powerful jolt to U.S. managers and awakened them to the importance of international competition and global markets. In the 1990s, Russia and China represent potential major international market opportunities for firms from many countries, including the United States, Japan, Korea, and European nations. They also represent formidable competitors, particularly China in low-technology manufacturing industries. There is some debate, however, regarding the relative attractiveness of the Russian and Chinese markets for companies competing in the global marketplace. Some believe that for at least a period of time, foreign investors will continue to favor China. The reason for this preference is that China is more orderly while Russia remains full of risks. Moreover, it may be that Russia's movement to more of a free-market economy could depend on homegrown developments instead of foreign direct investments (FDI) and other modes firms use to internationalize their operations.[1]

Thus, the international arena features both opportunities and threats for firms seeking strategic competitiveness in global markets. This chapter examines opportunities facing firms as they seek to develop and exploit core competencies by diversifying into global markets. In addition, we discuss different problems and complexities that can be associated with implementation of the firm's chosen international strategies.[2] The importance of learning how to respond successfully to these opportunities and threats should not be underestimated. Some executives, for example, believe that goods and services may be imitated somewhat easily by effective global competitors, but it is much more difficult to duplicate the competitive benefits resulting from a firm's ability to become a truly global corporation. Selecting and implementing appropriate international strategies allows the firm to become a global corporation.[3]

FIGURE 8.1 *Opportunities and Outcomes of International Strategy*

In this chapter, as illustrated in Figure 1.1 in Chapter 1, we discuss the importance of international strategy as a source of strategic competitiveness and above-average returns. The chapter focuses first on the incentives to internationalize. Once the firm decides to compete internationally, it must select its strategy and choose a mode of entry. It may enter international markets by exporting from domestic-based operations, licensing, forming joint ventures with international partners, acquiring a foreign-based firm, or establishing a new subsidiary. Such international diversification can extend product life cycles, provide incentives for more innovation, and produce above-average returns. These benefits are tempered by political and economic risks and the problems of managing a complex international firm with operations in multiple countries. Figure 8.1 provides an overview of these choices and outcomes. The relationships among international opportunities, exploration of resources and capabilities that result in strategies and modes of entry that are based on core competencies are explored in this chapter.

IDENTIFYING INTERNATIONAL OPPORTUNITIES: THE INCENTIVE TO PURSUE AN INTERNATIONAL STRATEGY

An **international strategy** refers to the selling of products in markets outside the firm's domestic market.[4] One of the primary reasons for implementing an international strategy (as opposed to a strategy focused on the domestic market) is that international markets yield potential new opportunities. Raymond Vernon captured the classic rationale for international diversification.[5] He suggested that typically a firm discovers an innovation in its home country market, especially in an advanced economy such as that found in the United States. Some demand for the

An **international strategy** refers to the selling of products in markets outside the firm's domestic market.

product may develop in other countries and, thus, exports are provided by domestic operations. Increased demand in foreign countries justifies direct foreign investment in production capacity abroad, especially as foreign competitors also organize to meet increasing demand. As the product becomes standardized, the firm may rationalize its operations by moving production to a region where manufacturing costs are low. Vernon, therefore, suggests that firms pursue international diversification to extend a product's life cycle.

Another traditional motive for firms to become multinational is to secure key resources. Key supplies of raw material, especially minerals and energy, are important in some industries. For instance, aluminum producers need a supply of bauxite, tire firms need rubber, and oil companies scour the world to find new petroleum reserves.

Others seek to secure access to low-cost factors of production. Clothing, electronics, watchmaking, and many other industries have moved portions of their operations to foreign locations in pursuit of lower costs. To enhance its cost competitiveness in the deflationary environment at the end of the 1990s, GE continued to shift some of its appliance manufacturing operations to various locations throughout the world. All of the firm's gas ranges are now made in San Luis Potosi, Mexico, through the firm's joint venture with Mabe, a Mexican company. In total, GE employs over 24,000 people in Mexico, primarily to manufacture appliances.[6]

Ireland's low labor costs and its use of the English language have helped make it the fastest growing telesales location in the European Union. To date, over 50 international companies have established telephone-based operations in Ireland. In American Airlines' Dublin office, now responsible for all of the firm's European reservations, approximately 300 Irish telephone operators complete the work that was handled previously by eight separate reservation centers scattered across Europe.[7]

Turkey's wage rates are among the lowest in Europe. In fact, the nation's hourly rates average one-half of those in Portugal, the poorest country in the European Union. Moreover, wages are lower than in some eastern European countries and

275

GE moved some of its appliance manufacturing operations to other locations around the world to enhance its cost competitiveness in the deflationary environment of the late 1990s. All of GE's gas ranges are now made in Mexico through a joint venture with Mabe, a Mexican company.

many developing nations. Because of these wage rates, coupled with the fact that workers' productivity is increasing by 3.6 percent annually, compared to the OECD average of 2.8 percent, many multinational companies are establishing operations in Turkey. In fact, these investments have caused Turkey's economy to grow at a rate that has actually created labor shortages.[8]

Low cost production factors are sometimes influenced by government actions. For example, Alabama outbid North and South Carolina for the first U.S. Mercedes-Benz car plant.[9] The state provided land and training wages for new workers and made commitments that government agencies and utilities would buy large quantities of the four-wheel-drive recreational vehicles the plant will produce.

Although these traditional motives continue to exist, as the Mercedes example illustrates, other emerging motivations have been driving international expansion (see Chapter 1). For instance, pressure has increased for global integration of operations, mostly driven by more universal product demand. As nations industrialize, demand for commodity products appears to become more similar.[10] This nationless or borderless demand for products may be due to lifestyle similarities in developed nations. Also, increases in global communication media facilitate the ability of people in different countries to visualize and model lifestyles in disparate cultures.[11]

In some industries, technology is driving globalization because economies of scale necessary to reduce costs to the lowest level often require efficient scale investment greater than that needed to meet domestic market demand.[12] There is also pressure for cost reductions in purchasing from the lowest cost global suppliers. For instance, R&D expertise for a new emerging business start-up may not be found in the domestic market.[13]

New large-scale markets, such as Russia, China, and India, also provide a strong incentive because of potential demand. And, because of currency fluctuations, firms may desire to have their operations distributed across many countries to reduce the risk of currency devaluation in one country.[14] This desire notwithstanding, the unique nature of countries such as China and Russia should not be overlooked. China, for example, differs from Western countries on many contextual variables, including culture, politics, and the precepts of its economic system.[15] The serious challenges these differences pose for Western competitive paradigms emphasize the need for global competitors to possess the skills to manage financial, economic, and political risks. Moreover, the vast percentage of U.S.-based companies' overseas business is in European markets. In addition, 60 percent of U.S. firms' assets that are located outside the domestic market are in Europe; and, two-thirds of all foreign R&D spending by U.S. affiliates takes place in Europe.[16] Therefore, companies seeking to internationalize their operations should also be aware of increased pressure for local country or regional responsiveness, especially where goods or services require customization because of cultural differences.[17] For example, with operations in 104 nations, McDonald's tailors its food products from country to country. In India, the McMaharajah, a mutton-based sandwich, replaces the Big Mac. Bolivian units sell McSaltenas as well as the standard U.S.-style offerings. The McSaltenas is a typical Andean dish of beef, potatoes, peas, and hot peppers, all encased in pastry.[18]

The frequent need for local repair and service is another factor influencing an increased desire for local country responsiveness. This localization may even affect industries that are seen as needing more global economies of scale such as white goods (e.g., refrigerators and other appliances.)[19] For large products, such as heavy earthmoving equipment, transportation costs become significant. Employment contracts and labor forces differ significantly. It is more difficult to negotiate employee layoffs in Europe than in the United States because of employment contract differences. Often host governments demand joint ownership, which allows the entering firm to avoid tariffs. Also, host governments frequently require a high percentage of local procurements, manufacturing, and R&D. These issues increase the need for local investment and responsiveness compared to seeking global economies of scale.

Given the traditional and emerging motivations for expanding into international markets, firms may achieve four basic opportunities through international diversification: increased market size; greater returns on major capital investments and/or investments in new product and process developments; greater economies of scale, scope, and/or learning; and/or a competitive advantage through location (e.g., access to low-cost labor, critical resources, or customers). These potential opportunities to enhance the firm's strategic competitiveness are examined relative to the costs incurred to pursue them and the managerial challenges that accompany both product and geographic international diversification decisions. Higher coordination expenses, a lack of familiarity with local cultures, and a lack of full access to knowledge about political influences in the host country are examples of costs firms incur when pursuing international diversification.[20]

Increased Market Size

Firms can expand the size of their potential market, sometimes dramatically, by moving into international markets. As part of its expansion efforts, Tupperware chose to market its storage containers in Russia. Sold initially in St. Petersburg, this strategic decision was based on market research indicating that the company's products appealed to Russian consumers. A company spokesperson noted, "With the large number of households and significant underemployment in Russia, we see this country as a great market opportunity and are investing time and training to build a strong sales force."[21]

To expand the size of its markets, Friday's Hospitality Worldwide Inc. is establishing its Friday's American Bar concept in major urban settings and airports throughout Europe and Asia. Geographic diversification is expected to be a major part of the company's growth. The company's CEO noted that his firm's different concepts, including the flagship TGI Friday's units, are very successful in countries outside the United States.[22] Frito-Lay plans to continue pursuing international growth opportunities through strategic acquisitions. Recently the firm purchased several snack food operations from United Biscuits Holdings PLC (this company is headquartered in the United Kingdom). Frito-Lay officials indicated that this acquisition improved the firm's European market position by giving it much needed production capacity.[23]

Following an international strategy is a particularly attractive option to firms competing in domestic markets that have limited growth opportunities. For example, the U.S. soft drink industry is relatively saturated. Most changes in market share for any single firm must come at the expense of competitors' share. Given this competitive reality, the two major soft drink manufacturers, Coca-Cola and PepsiCo, decided to enter international markets to take advantage of growth opportunities. Pepsi moved into the former Soviet Union years ago; later, Coke entered China. Originally, each firm obtained an exclusive franchise in those countries; today however, markets in Russia and China are more open. Coke has gained competitive parity and has now surpassed Pepsi in Russia. Beyond this, Coke's volume exceeds Pepsi's in Europe, Latin America, and Asia. In terms of overall volume, Coke outsells Pepsi almost three to one outside the United States. To combat this challenge and to increase its international market size, Pepsi is pushing hard in developing markets such as India and Indonesia where Coke is not entrenched completely. In an effort to use its resources wisely, Pepsi is lowering its market share expectations in Brazil and Japan, two countries in which Coke holds strong market positions. In discussing this decision, an analyst noted, "Pepsi is saying we'll be a profitable no. 2 in these two large markets."[24]

Across time, the competitive battle between these two giants seeking to increase the size of their served markets will continue to expand into product areas other than traditional soft drinks. Coke, for example, recently purchased the Orangina brand from Pernod Ricard of France. This acquisition gives Coke a new sparkling orange drink. A leading brand in France, Orangina had limited exposure in other European countries and small sales in the United States at the time of Coke's purchase. Coke executives believed that their company's global distribution system would result in significant sales increases for Orangina in Europe and other markets as well.[25] This acquisition demonstrates the belief of Coke's top-level managers that product and geographic diversification can enhance their firm's strategic competitiveness.

Return on Investment

Large markets may be crucial for earning a return on significant investments, such as plant and capital equipment and/or R&D. Therefore, most R&D-intensive industries are international. For example, the aerospace industry requires heavy investments to develop new aircraft. To recoup investments, aerospace firms may need to sell new aircraft in both domestic and international markets. This is the case for Boeing and Airbus Industrie. International sales are critical to the ability of each firm to earn satisfactory returns on its invested capital. In light of this reality, Boeing and Airbus are deciding how to allocate their production capacities to satisfy the major portion of demand projected for commercial jets between 1997 and 2006. During this time period, it is estimated that 2,460 jets can be sold in North America, 2,070 in Europe, 1,750 in the Asia/Pacific area, and another 1,100 in other countries throughout the world.[26] As these projected deliveries of commercial jets suggest, international sales are linked strongly to the strategic competitiveness of both Boeing and Airbus.

In addition to the need for a large market to recoup heavy investment in R&D, the development pace for new technology is increasing. As a result, new product obsolescence occurs more rapidly. Therefore, investments need to be recouped more quickly. Beyond this, firms' abilities to develop new technologies are expanding, and because of different patent laws across country borders, competitor imitation is more likely. Through reverse engineering, competitors are able to take apart a competitive product, learn the new technology, and develop a similar product that imitates the new technology (see Chapters 5 and 13). Because of competitors' abilities to do this relatively quickly, the need to recoup new product development costs rapidly is increasing. Therefore, the larger markets provided by international expansion are particularly attractive in many industries (e.g., computer hardware) because they expand the opportunity to recoup large capital investment and large-scale R&D expenditures.[27]

Economies of Scale and Learning

When firms expand their markets, they may be able to enjoy economies of scale, particularly in their manufacturing operations. Thus, to the extent that firms are able to standardize products across country borders and use the same or similar production facilities, coordinating critical resource functions, they are likely to achieve more optimal economic scale.[28] This is the goal of many firms in Europe as the common market continues to evolve. Sweden's Volvo, for example, has reduced its car manufacturing platforms from three to two. This action eliminated a costly indulgence for a relatively small manufacturer, and lowered the firm's break-even point through economies of scale.[29]

This is the case, too, for Korean automobile companies. By 2002, current plans call for Korea's five care manufacturers to increase their worldwide vehicle-making capacity by 60 percent. Other global automobile manufacturers criticized this expansionary decision. The essence of this criticism was that additional output by Korean car companies would contribute to an emerging glut in worldwide manufacturing capacity. In response, Korean automobile manufacturing executives indicated that they intended to develop additional capacity to gain the economies of scale required to compete effectively in the global marketplace.[30]

Firms may also be able to exploit core competencies across international markets. This allows resource and knowledge sharing between units across country borders.[31] It generates synergy and helps the firm produce higher quality goods or services at lower cost.

Location Advantages

Firms may locate facilities in other countries to lower the basic costs of the goods and/or services provided.[32] For example, they may have easier access to lower cost labor, energy, and other natural resources. Other location advantages include access to critical supplies/resources and to customers. Once positioned favorably through an attractive location, firms must manage their facilities effectively to gain the full benefit of a location advantage.[33]

Toyota, for example, may use one of its European facilities (in either Britain or France) to produce a new sporty car that is replacing the Tercel. Saying that the firm's goal is to "... get a car that gives young people goosebumps," Toyota executives indicated that the company would not abandon the entry-level youth market in spite of the seriousness of the competitive challenge from rival Honda's Civic line. A key location advantage associated with either one of these European sites is that Toyota could hold down the flow of imports to Europe from its Japanese facilities.[34] Ford Motor Company believes the initial success of its joint venture with Jiangling Motors in China gives it a location advantage relative to General Motors. Through this venture, Ford was the first of the two giant firms to actually produce a minibus in China. Ford executives are hopeful that first-mover advantages will result from this achievement.[35]

We have explored why international strategies may be important and some of their advantages. Next, we describe the types and content of international strategies that might be formulated and then implemented.

279

INTERNATIONAL STRATEGIES

An international strategy may be one of two basic types, business or corporate level. At the business level, firms follow generic strategy types: low cost, differentiation, focused low cost, focused differentiation, or integrated low cost/differentiation. At the corporate level, firms can formulate three types: multidomestic, global, or transnational (a combination of multidomestic and global). However, to create competitive advantage, each of these strategies must realize a core competence based on difficult to duplicate resources and capabilities.[36] As discussed in Chapters 4 and 6, the firm expects to create value through the implementation of a business-level and a corporate-level strategy.[37]

International Business-Level Strategy

Each business must develop a competitive strategy focused on its own domestic market. We discussed business-level generic strategies in Chapter 4 and competitive dynamics in Chapter 5. However, international business-level strategies have some unique features. In pursuing an international business-level strategy, the home country of operation is often the most important source of competitive advantage.[38] The resources and capabilities established in the home country often allow the firm to pursue the strategy beyond the national boundary. Michael Porter developed a model that describes the factors contributing to the advantage of firms in a dominant global industry and associated with a specific country or regional environment.[39] His model is illustrated in Figure 8.2.

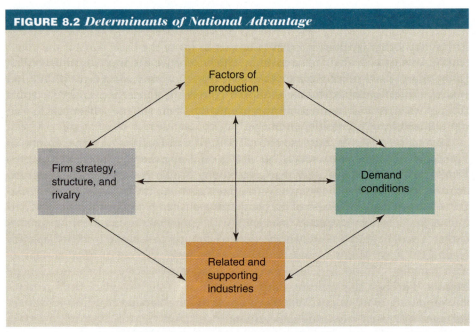

FIGURE 8.2 *Determinants of National Advantage*

Source: Adapted and reprinted with the permission of The Free Press, an imprint of Simon & Schuster from *The Competitive Advantages of Nations* by Michael E. Porter, p. 72. Copyright © by Michael E. Porter.

The first dimension in the model, *factors of production*, refers to the inputs necessary to compete in any industry, such as labor, land, natural resources, capital, and infrastructure (e.g., highway, postal, and communication systems). Of course, there are basic (e.g, natural and labor resources) and advanced (e.g., digital communication systems and highly educated workforces) factors. There are also generalized (highway systems, supply of debt capital) and specialized factors (skilled personnel in a specific industry, such as a port that specializes in handling bulk chemicals). If a country has both advanced and specialized production factors, it is likely that this will serve an industry well in spawning strong home-country competitors that can become successful global competitors. Ironically, countries often develop advanced and specialized factor capabilities because they lack critical basic resources. Some Asian countries, such as Korea, lack abundant natural resources, but the strong work ethic, the large number of engineers, and the systems of large firms have created an expertise in manufacturing. Germany developed a strong chemical industry, partially because Hoechst and BASF spent years developing a synthetic indigo dye to reduce their dependence on imports. This was not the case in Britain because large supplies of natural indigo were available in the colonies.[40]

The second dimension, *demand conditions*, is characterized by the nature and size of the buyers' needs in the home market for the industry's goods or services. The sheer size of a sales segment could produce the demand necessary to create scale-efficient facilities. This efficiency could also lead to domination of the industry in other countries. However, specialized demand may also create opportunities beyond national boundaries. For example, Swiss firms have long led the world in tunneling equipment because of the need to tunnel through mountains for rail and highway passage. Japanese firms have created a niche market for compact, quiet air conditioner units. Small, but quiet units are required in Japan because homes are often small and packed together tightly. Under these conditions, large, noisy units would be unacceptable.[41]

Related and supporting industries is the third dimension in the model. Italy has become the leader in the shoe industry because of related and supporting industries. The leather supplies necessary to build shoes are furnished by a well-established industry in leather processing. Also, many people travel to Italy to purchase leather goods. Thus, there is support in distribution. In addition, supporting industries in leather-working machinery and design services contribute to the success of the shoe industry. In fact, the design services industry supports many related industries, such as ski boots, fashion apparel, and furniture. In Japan, cameras and copiers have been related industries. In Denmark, the dairy products industry is related to an industry focused on food enzymes.

Firm strategy, structure, and rivalry, the final country dimension, also fosters the growth of certain industries. The pattern of firm strategy, structure, and rivalry among firms varies greatly from nation to nation. Earlier, much attention was placed on examining U.S. enterprise managers; more recently, the Japanese have been scrutinized and emulated. In Germany, because of the excellent technical training system, there is a strong inclination toward methodological product and process improvement. In Japan, unusual cooperative and competitive systems have facilitated cross-functional management of complex assembly operations. In Italy, the national pride of its designers has spawned strong industries in sports cars, fashion apparel, and furniture. In the United States, competition among computer manufacturers and software producers has favored the development of these industries.

The four basic dimensions of the "diamond" model shown in Figure 8.2 emphasize the environmental or structural attributes of a national economy that may contribute to national advantage. One could therefore conclude that chance or luck has led to the competitive advantage of individual firms in these industries. To a degree this is true, but government policy also had contributed to the success and failure of firms and industries. This is certainly the case in Japan, where the Ministry of International Trade and Investment (MITI) has contributed significantly to the corporate strategies followed. Nevertheless, each firm must create its own success. Not all firms have survived to become global competitors, given the same country factors that spawned the successful firms. Therefore, the actual strategic choices managers make may be the most compelling reason for success or failure. The factors illustrated in Figure 8.2, therefore, are likely to lead to competitive advantages for a firm only when an appropriate strategy is applied, taking advantage of distinct country factors. We therefore reiterate examples of the low-cost, differentiation, focused low-cost, focused differentiation, and integrated low-cost/differentiation generic strategies that are discussed in Chapter 4.

International Low-Cost Strategy The international low-cost strategy is likely to develop in a country with a large demand. Usually the operations of such an industry are centralized in a home country, and obtaining economies of scale is the primary goal. Outsourcing of low value-added operations may take place, but high value-added operations are retained in the home country. As such, products are often exported from the home country.

As explained in the Strategic Focus, certain global air carriers are seeking strategic competitiveness through use of the international low-cost strategy. Through a variety of entry modes (entry modes are discussed in detail later in the chapter), Wal-Mart, too, follows this strategy as it continues to globalize its operations.

STRATEGIC FOCUS

Air Service and Discount Retailing: Achieving Strategic Competitiveness by Using the International Low-Cost Strategy

EasyJet is a London-based low-cost airline that was founded after the liberalization of the European Union (EU) aviation market. The market's liberalization permits European airlines to begin services anywhere in the EU without obtaining government permission. This company has modeled its operations after U.S. low-fare carriers such as Southwest Airlines. Along with others using the international low-cost strategy, including Ryanair and Debonair, EasyJet's business practices have resulted in lower airfares in the United Kingdom and Ireland. One reason for the companies' initial success is the inducement their low fares create for previous nonflyers to use their services. Brussels-based Virgin Express, a part of Richard Branson's group, is achieving the same outcomes in continental Europe.

The low-cost airlines claim that a large percentage of their customers are business travelers. The fares offered to these people are enticing. Recently, for example, Ryanair sold tickets for a one-way trip from London to Glasgow for nine pounds (before tax). Customers are promised safe passage, but little else is provided. Most do not serve meals. Passengers wanting something to drink must pay for the product. These practices, as well as others, are followed to drive costs lower.

To reduce its costs of servicing a plane once it is on the ground and to turn units around quicker for departures, Ryanair discontinued carrying cargo. With less loading and unloading to complete, aircraft are now turned around in 20 minutes. Ryanair offers no frills and a single class of seating. The essence of the firm's low-cost strategy is captured by the following statement by Michael O'Leary, the firm's CEO: "We said that we're not going to feed you or put you up in hotels or give you frequent flyer points or any of that rubbish." To reduce its maintenance and staff costs, Ryanair flies only one type of aircraft— the Boeing 737-200. Moreover, the firm operates from secondary airports. In London, for example, it uses Stansted and Luton rather than Gatwick or Heathrow. To reduce yet another cost, Ryanair's CEO informed travel agents that his firm would pay a seven and one-half percent commission instead of the industry standard of 9 percent. Ryanair is expanding its market coverage. It now offers flights between the British Isles and continental Europe, Dublin and Paris and Dublin and Brussels, and from London to Stockholm and to Oslo. The firm is also negotiating with airports in eight additional European countries to establish more routes.

The essence of Wal-Mart's international low-cost strategy is demonstrated by founder Sam Walton's words: "We'll lower the cost of living for everyone, not just in America." One of the keys to implementing its low-cost strategy, both domestically and internationally, is the firm's advanced retail technology. This technology enables Wal-Mart to have the correct quantities of goods in the appropriate place at the right time while minimizing inventory costs. The latest variation of this sophisticated system has employees carrying hand-held computers that allow them to reorder merchandise. Simultaneously, backroom computers link each store with a sophisticated satellite system.

Wal-Mart started to internationalize its operations in 1991. Since then, the firm has already become the largest retailer in Canada (144 stores) and Mexico (396 stores). Wal-Mart also operates eight stores in Argentina, two in Brazil, three in China, and two in Indonesia through joint ventures. To continue diversifying internationally, Wal-Mart decided to enter the European market. This process was started with the purchase of the Wertkauf hypermarket company from Germany's Mann family. Suggesting that no German retailer was capable of matching Wal-Mart's logistics core competency, analysts viewed Wal-Mart's movement into Germany positively. The challenge to Wal-Mart in Germany is to gain quickly the volume it requires for its international low-cost strategy to be effective. Combining its volume with the firm's logistics skills and merchandising savvy may yield the combination required for Wal-Mart to achieve strategic competitiveness in Germany and perhaps the European market in general.

SOURCE: L. Lee, 1998, Wal-Mart net rose 17% in quarter, fueling optimism, *Wall Street Journal*, February 19, B2; M. Skapinker, 1997, Cut to the bone . . . fares, service and turnaround, *Financial Times*, November 20, VII; M. Skapinker, 1997, No-frills airlines travelling on a wing and a fear, *Financial Times*, November 20, VI; Sam's Travels, 1997, *Financial Times*, December 19, 13; R. Tomkins, 1997, Wal-Mart comes shopping in Europe, *Financial Times*, December 21, 23; R. Tomkins, 1997, Wal-Mart enters Europe, *Financial Times*, December 19, 15.

As the Strategic Focus discussion suggests, using the international low-cost strategy to diversify their operations may be reasonable strategic choices for several of Europe's no-frills airlines and for Wal-Mart. In fact, some analysts do believe Wal-Mart should aggressively pursue international growth opportunities using its low-cost strategy to further enhance its strategic competitiveness.[42]

For all of these firms, there are risks associated with implementing the international low-cost strategy. The airline companies, for example, may face competition from their larger and better-resourced competitors. Recently EasyJet found itself engaged in a pricing battle with KLM, the Dutch airline. This competition evolved when EasyJet starting flying from its base at Luton airport, near London, to Shiphol airport in Amsterdam. British Airways and Germany's Lufthansa are both considering starting their own low-cost companies to compete against Debonair and Ryanair.[43]

A major risk for Wal-Mart is that it may not learn quickly how to compete successfully in what is seen to be Europe's unique retailing environment. Does Wal-Mart have the confidence it needs to make small adjustments to satisfy local tastes while maintaining the discipline required to drive costs lower on a continuous basis? Will first German and then other European retailers retain their customers by learning how to create value either through differentiation strategies or by driving their costs lower relative to Wal-Mart's? These issues pose strategic challenges to Wal-Mart's executives; but, the fact that the company hopes to generate one-third of its profit growth annually through international sales suggests its intentions in Europe and other world markets.[44]

International Differentiation Strategy A country with advanced and specialized factor endowments is likely to develop an international differentiation strategy. Germany has a number of world-class chemical firms. The differentiation strategy followed by many of these firms to develop specialized chemicals was possible because of the factor conditions surrounding the development of this industry. The Kaiser Wilhelm (late Max Planck) Institutes and university chemistry programs were superior in research and produced the best chemistry education in the world. Also, Germany's emphasis on vocational education fostered strong apprenticeship programs for workers.[45] Today, German companies competing in retailing consumer goods are learning how to improve their service to battle against competitors (e.g., Lands' End and Marks & Spencer) who are implementing their international differentiation strategies in Germany.[46]

The Japanese capabilities in consumer electronics have given them an advantage in memory chips and integrated circuits, the basic components in this industry. However, differentiation by Sharp Corporation, a Japanese electronics firm, has given it the lead in liquid crystal displays (LCDs), which are used with laptop computer and camcorders.[47] Alternatively, the United States is the leader in logic chips, the main components of computers, telecommunications equipment, and defense electronics. Intel is the world's leading producer of computer logic chips, and its products are differentiated worldwide by the slogan "Intel inside."

International Focus Strategies Many firms remain focused on small market niches as they pursue international focus strategies.[48] The ceramic tile industry in Italy contains a number of medium and small fragmented firms that produce approximately 50 percent of the world's tile.[49] These tile firms, clustered in the Sassuolo area of Italy, have formed a number of different focus strategies. Firms such as Marazzi, Iris, Cisa-Cerdisa, and Flor Gres invest heavily in technology to improve product quality, aesthetics, and productivity. These firms have close relationships with equipment manufacturers. They tend to emphasize the focused low-cost strategy, while maintaining a quality image. Another group, including Piemme and Atlas Concorde, attempts to compete more on image and design. Firms in this group invest heavily in advertising and showroom expositions. Because they try to appeal to selected customer tastes, they emphasize the focused differentiation strategy.[50]

Other uses of the international focus strategy are described in the Strategic Focus. While reading these materials, notice each firm's intent to serve exceptionally well a particular need of a particular market segment.

STRATEGIC FOCUS

Focusing Internationally on Specific Market Segments

285

Volvo earns 70 percent of its sales revenue from manufacturing and selling cars and trucks (other businesses include construction equipment and marine engines). To reverse the firm's recent declines, the CEO initiated a new product development drive to put cars on a more stable footing and to expand trucks globally. The two competitive advantages on which Volvo's automobiles have been sold are product security (safety) and reliability.

New cars are being manufactured for what the firms calls "niche customers." Two new models were introduced in 1998. Sharing a common platform, one product introduction was a replacement for the aging 900 series; the second was a smaller successor to the S70 and V70 cars. In describing the firm's new design philosophy, the CEO explained, "We are defining lifestyle segments and trying to shoot off sharply designed products based on a few basic platforms." Aware of the global challenge facing his small firm, the CEO notes that Volvo is interested in following a niche strategy that allows it to capture 10 percent to 15 percent of its chosen markets.

The efficiency of the highly capitalized domestic institutions, coupled with their large branch networks and use of high quality, sophisticated technologies, creates a retail banking environment in Spain in which it is difficult for foreign firms to compete successfully. Because of the domestic banks' competitive advantages, foreign rivals now concentrate on niche activities. Chase Manhattan, for example, focuses on a range of niches including corporate finance, capital markets and derivatives businesses, and peseta clearing activities. Chase's recent performance based on its international focus strategy in Spain is impressive—a return on earnings of 23 percent and a return on assets of 5.9 percent.

Because of what they envision as significant growth potential in terms of mutual and pension funds, U.K.-based Barclays and U.S.-based Citibank are focusing on the private banking sector. Citibank has converted the 83 branches it operates in Spain into product advisory centers. In each location, customers have access to computer systems that help them determine their desired risk levels; once known, a set of investment alternatives is recommended. As is the case for Citibank, Barclays has ". . . scaled back its retail operations in Spain, concentrated on the big cities and focused on asset management of medium to big private accounts according to a carefully elaborated segmentation of potential clients." Barclays operates 180 branches as it competes against Citibank and others to serve the unique needs of the private banking market segment.

Denizli, Turkey, has a long history as a town with multiple textiles manufacturing facilities. The town and its new factories are an example of the success being achieved as a result of recent Turkish industrial modernization efforts.

Denizli's factories specialize in the manufacture of towels, sheets, and garments. In the past, however, these facilities concentrated on selling their output to domestic markets. Now, many of the town's textile companies are looking abroad to sell goods to the lucrative but demanding consumer outlets of Western Europe and the United States. This expansion into global markets with niche textile products is being helped by bank support and state encouragement.

Nesa Textiles is one of Denizli's factories that is striving to compete globally. Through a substantial investment program, Nesa has acquired high technology machinery that it uses to weave, dye, and prepare bath towels and gowns—the firm's primary products. Nesa's focus is on the manufacture of products that are targeted to the high quality, high value market segment. The firm's modern technology permits the focus. Nesa's marketing manager believes that the success of Denizli's textile factories make it impossible for them to compete on a low-cost basis with countries, such as Pakistan and Indonesia, where manufacturing expenses, including labor costs, are much lower. (As mentioned earlier in this chapter, Turkey's overall wage rates are quite low, but in Denizli's textile factories the wage rates exceed the country's average by quite a margin.) With an MBA from Izmir University and fluency in three foreign languages, Nesa's marketing manager is confident of his firm's success as well as the success of other Turkish firms. This confidence is suggested by the following comment: "You in Western Europe will have to watch out, the Anatolian tiger is coming."

In 1990, Western companies such as Smirnoff's owner Diageo PLC of Britain and Absolut's V&S Vin & Spirit AB of Sweden expressed high hopes for the success of their vodka products in Russia. With famous brand names and well-honed marketing skills, these firms anticipated being able to sell their products to a consumer segment that was willing to pay for a product that was differentiated from local vodkas. Thus, these companies intended to follow the international focused differentiation strategy to compete in the Russian market.

To date, these firms' performances are disappointing. With a combined market share of less than 1 percent, they are discovering that the segment of the market willing to trade up to Western brands and to pay a higher price for the opportunity to do so is apparently quite small. Moreover, Russia's private and state vodka producers are challenging Western producers' differentiation strategy as they introduce new niche brands into the market and hawk them with clever, eye-catching packaging and advertising campaigns.

SOURCE: E. Beck, 1998, Why foreign distillers find it so hard to sell vodka to the Russians, *Wall Street Journal*, January 15, A1, A9; T. Burns, 1997, Niche goals bring away results, *Financial Times*, November 17, II; H. Simonian, 1997, Volvo's lights burn brighter, *Financial Times*, December 9, 17; R. Taylor, 1997, Global markets beckon for old weaving centre, *Financial Times*, December 12, VI.

International Integrated Low-Cost/Differentiation Strategy The integrated strategy has become more popular because of flexible manufacturing systems, improved information networks within and across firms, and total quality management systems (see Chapter 4). Because of the wide diversity of markets and competitors, following an integrated strategy may be the most effective in global markets.[51] Therefore, competing in global markets requires sophisticated and effective management.[52] Komatsu illustrates a classic case where this strategy was well executed. Komatsu was able to gain on a strong competitor, Caterpillar, by pursuing the integrated low-cost/differentiation strategy. Caterpillar had a very strong brand image in world markets, but Komatsu was able to overcome this differentiation advantage by improving its image and reducing its costs. It was initially able to do this because of lower labor costs and steel prices. Furthermore, in the 1970s, the dollar was strong, and this allowed a successful export strategy. Although Komatsu has remained very competitive, it faces critical challenges today due to the competitive actions being taken by Caterpillar.[53] Some of the competitive actions and competitive responses occurring between Caterpillar and Komatsu were considered in a Strategic Focus in Chapter 5.

International Corporate-Level Strategy

The business-level strategies discussed previously depend, to a degree, on the type of international corporate-level strategy the firm is following. Some corporate strategies give individual country units the authority to develop their own strategies; other corporate strategies require that country business-level strategies be compromised because of dictates from the home office to accomplish standardization of products and sharing of resources across countries. International corporate-level strategy is distinguished from international business-level strategy by the scope of the operations in both product and geographic diversification. International corporate-level strategy is required when the level of product complexity increases to multiple industries and multiple countries or regions.[54] Corporate strategy is guided by headquarters, rather than by business or country managers. The three international corporate-level strategies are shown in Figure 8.3.

Multidomestic Strategy A **multidomestic strategy** is one in which strategic and operating decisions are decentralized to the strategic business unit in each country in order to tailor products to the local market.[55] A multidomestic strategy focuses on competition within each country. It assumes that the markets differ and

A **multidomestic strategy** is one in which strategic and operating decisions are decentralized to the strategic business unit in each country in order to tailor products to the local market.

287

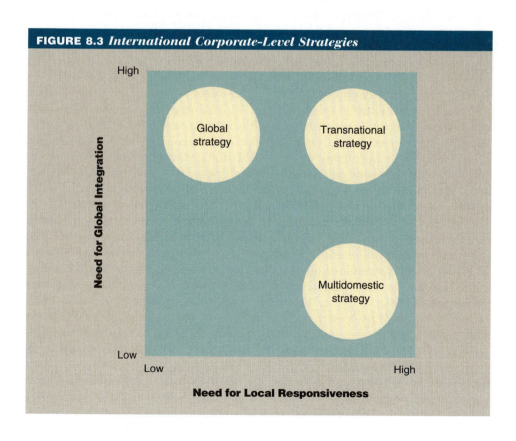

FIGURE 8.3 *International Corporate-Level Strategies*

A **global strategy** is one in which standardized products are offered across country markets and competitive strategy is dictated by the home office.

therefore are segmented by country boundaries. In other words, consumer needs and desires, industry conditions (e.g., number and type of competitors), political and legal structures, and social norms vary by country. Multidomestic strategies allow for the customization of products to meet the specific needs and preferences of local customers. Therefore, they should be able to maximize competitive response to the idiosyncratic requirements of each market. However, multidomestic strategies do not allow for the achievement of economies of scale and thus can be more costly. As a result, firms employing a multidomestic strategy decentralize strategic and operating decisions to the business units operating in each country. The multidomestic strategy has been more prominent among European multinational firms because of the varieties of cultures and markets found in Europe.

Owning some of the world's best known food brands (e.g., Knorr soups and sauces, Hellmann's salad dressings, Skippy peanut butter, and Entenmann's baked goods), Bestfoods follows the multidomestic strategy. The company is organized around three worldwide businesses. To implement the multidomestic strategy, Bestfoods' managers are given a great deal of autonomy to adapt products to local tastes. This is necessary, says the firm's CEO, because food brands have geographical limitations. An example of these limitations is suggested by the following comment from the CEO: "The day I teach Americans to eat Marmite will be the day I teach the French to eat peanut butter."[56] (Marmite is a thick, dark, spread that is a staple of the national diet in Britain).

Global Strategy Alternatively, a global strategy assumes more standardization of products across country markets.[57] As a result, competitive strategy is centralized and controlled by the home office. The strategic business units operating in each country are assumed to be interdependent, and the home office attempts to achieve integration across these businesses. Therefore, a **global strategy** is one in which standardized products are offered across country markets and competitive strategy is dictated by the home office. Thus, a global strategy emphasizes economies of scale and offers greater opportunities to utilize innovations developed at the home office or in one country in other markets. A global strategy, however, often lacks responsiveness to local markets and is difficult to manage because of the need to coordinate strategies and operating decisions across country borders. Therefore, achieving efficient operations with a global strategy requires the sharing of resources and an emphasis on coordination and cooperation across country boundaries. This requires more centralization and central headquarters control. The Japanese have often pursued this strategy with success.[58]

CMS Energy is the fourth largest integrated utility in the United States. Over the last several years, CMS has spent approximately $3 billion to become involved in projects outside its domestic market (current projects include ones in Argentina and Morocco). As a result of these investments, 25 percent of the firm's earnings come from international operations. The CEO wants this percentage to be at least 50 percent by 2002. Active in the entire energy chain, from wellhead to the end-user, CMS controls its operations from its Detroit, Michigan, home office. Across time, CMS hopes to operate in a total of between six and nine countries as it provides standardized products through implementation of the global strategy.[59]

Transnational Strategy A **transnational strategy** is a corporate-level strategy that seeks to achieve both global efficiency and local responsiveness. Realizing the diverse goals of the transnational strategy is difficult because one goal requires close global coordination, while the other requires local flexibility. Thus, "flexible coordination" is required to implement the transnational strategy.[60] It requires building a shared vision and individual commitment through an integrated network. In reality, it is difficult to achieve a pure transnational strategy because of the conflicting goals.

Examples of firms following the transnational strategy are presented in the Strategic Focus. Notice that each of these firms is attempting the difficult task of simultaneously achieving the benefits of global efficiency and local responsiveness.

A **transnational strategy** is a corporate-level strategy that seeks to achieve both global efficiency and local responsiveness.

STRATEGIC FOCUS

Using the Transnational Strategy as a Pathway to Strategic Competitiveness

289

Headquartered in Switzerland, Nestlé is the world's largest food company. Well over two-thirds of the firm's sales revenue is earned outside its domestic market. Nestlé operates almost 500 factories and employs approximately 225,000 people worldwide. The company produces more than 8,500 products that are sold in more than 100 countries. Decentralization is important to how Nestlé's conducts business. In fact, the firm notes that its policy is ". . . to adapt as much as possible to local customs and circumstances while allowing decisions about products, marketing and personnel to be made at the local level." Simultaneously, however, efforts are undertaken at the corporate office to introduce as many efficiencies as possible across Nestlé's widely dispersed product operations.

Shiseido is Japan's largest cosmetics maker. Committed to the importance of thinking locally and acting globally, Shiseido established several regional offices. To coordinate activities in the Americas, an office was placed in New Jersey; similarly, a European regional headquarters was established in France. The charge to personnel in these offices is to improve operational efficiencies within their assigned geographic territories. Shiseido also continues to create a local focus by opening new outlets in Vietnam, Colombia, and Eastern Europe. Through use of the transnational strategy, Shiseido seeks to become the world's largest cosmetics company by 2000.

GE is using what it calls a "smart bomb" strategy to design, manufacture, and sell appliances. In essence, this strategy, one that GE top-level managers believe allows them to manage markets rather than factories, proceeds as follows: "GE executives examine each country's idiosyncrasies microscopically, then tailor a mix of products, brands, manufacturing facilities, marketing, and retail approaches to wring the best performance from each. They measure factors such as the quality and strength of local competitors, the market's growth potential, and the availability of skilled labor. Their unyielding goal: to generate the handsomest returns possible on the smallest investment possible." Complementing the efforts to satisfy unique local needs is a commitment to derive the greatest number of economies of scale as possible from the firm's various manufacturing facilities. Additionally, once discovered, innovations are applied across GE's various Asian factories.

Results obtained in Asia from these actions continue to be impressive. For example, appliance sales are growing at a 12 percent annual rate. Although used initially in GE's appliance businesses in Asia, smart bombing is now sweeping across all of GE's other business units. Thus, GE appears to be moving toward use of the transnational strategy in many if not all of its strategic business units as it seeks to become even more competitive internationally.

The Thomson Corporation is widely diversified in terms of both products and geographic areas. The company is involved in over 350 businesses or product lines; its products are sold in over 200 countries. Thomson's principal business focus, however, is specialized information and publishing. These activities are directed at participants in its core markets of regulatory, financial services, higher education, scientific, technical and medical/healthcare, and reference.

In the pursuit of strategic competitiveness and above-average returns, Thomson remains committed to a decentralized organizational structure. This structure, executives believe, allows business unit decision makers to offer customers products that satisfy their unique tastes. Accompanying this structure, however, are rigorous financial controls and operating criteria. Thomson's headquarters personnel use these controls to increase the efficiency of each operating unit. The performance criteria influence the selection of businesses to add to the firm's corporate portfolio (Thomson pursues growth and diversification through an acquisition strategy) and determine when an individual unit's performance warrants divestiture. Thus, Thomson also uses the transnational strategy to achieve both global efficiency and local responsiveness.

SOURCE: S. P. Khu, 1998, Thomson plans $2.5bn listing for travel arm, *Financial Times*, March 19, 15; Nestlé Home Page, 1998, February 8, http://www.nestle.com; The Thomson Corporation Home Page, 1998, February 8, http://www.thomcorp.com; L. Grant, 1997, GE's 'smart bomb' strategy, *Fortune*, July 21, 109–110; Shiseido to launch new brand, *Financial Times*, February 20, 29; Shiseido, 1997, *Fortune* (Special Advertising Section), August 4, S–39.

ENVIRONMENTAL TRENDS

Although the transnational strategy is difficult to implement, emphasis on the need for global efficiency is increasing as more industries begin to experience global competition as well as an increased emphasis on local requirements. Moreover, as discussion in the Strategic Focus suggested, global goods and services often require some customization to meet government regulations within particular countries or to fit customer tastes and preferences. In addition, most multinational firms desire to achieve some coordination and sharing of resources across country markets to hold down costs. Furthermore, some products and industries may be better suited for standardization across country borders than others. As a result, most large multinational firms with diverse products may employ a partial multidomestic strategy with certain product lines and global strategies with others. This may be the case with GE's smart bomb strategy. Because the strategy is intended to satisfy the unique appliance needs of different groups of Asian customers, it possesses some of the characteristics of a multidomestic strategy. In addition, though, central headquarters personnel are establishing operational guidelines to pursue economies of scale and a limited degree of standardization across products.

Regionalization

Regionalization in world markets is becoming more common. Location can affect a firm's strategic competitiveness.[61] Firms must decide whether to compete in all (or many) world markets or to focus on a particular region(s).[62] The advantage of attempting to compete in all markets relates to the economies that can be achieved because of the combined market size. However, if the firm is competing in industries where the international markets differ greatly (e.g., it must employ a multidomestic strategy), it may wish to narrow its focus to a particular region of the world. In so doing, it can better understand the cultures, legal and social norms, and other factors important for effective competition in those markets. Therefore, a firm may focus on Far East markets only, rather than attempting to compete in the Middle East, Europe, and the Far East. It may choose a region of the world where the markets are more similar and thus some coordination and sharing of resources would be possible. In this way, the firm may be able not only to understand the markets better, but also to achieve some economies, even though it may have to employ a multidomestic strategy.

Sometimes, however, regional opportunities surface unexpectedly for companies carefully analyzing their external environments (see Chapter 2). Based in Houston, Texas, Service Corporation International (SCI) is the world's largest undertaker (annual revenues exceed $2.3 billion). Recently the firm identified an opportunity in Germany's funeral industry. Specifically, SCI observed that approximately 95 percent of Germany's 4,500 undertakers are small, family-run businesses (discussed further in Chapter 9, Germany's business economy has long been dominated by small family firms). Because of size constraints, these companies typically do not offer services such as helping relatives arrange for flowers and the purchase of a headstone and a cemetery plot. In contrast, SCI provides customers with a one-stop shopping option, flexible hours, and amenities (e.g., an optional photographer). Even with these additional services, SCI's prices are competitive with the average $5,000 cost of a German funeral. SCI entered the German market in 1995 to pursue this opportunity. To date, the firm has purchased all or parts of 15 funeral homes located in major German cities. With sales exceeding $8 million annually, SCI is committed to further extending its operations in Germany.[63] Seeking to be competitive on a global basis, SCI also has operations in Britain, Canada, and France.

Regional strategies may be promoted by countries that develop trade agreements to increase the economic power of a region. The European Community (EC) and the Organization of American States (OAS, South America) are collections of countries that developed trade agreements to promote the flow of trade across country boundaries within the region.[64] For example, many European firms have been acquiring and integrating their businesses in Europe to better rationalize pan-European brands as the EC creates more unity in European markets. The North American Free Trade Agreement (NAFTA), signed by the United States, Canada, and Mexico, is designed to facilitate free trade across country borders in North America and may be expanded to include other countries in South America, such as Argentina, Brazil, and Chile.[65] These agreements loosen restrictions on international strategies within a region and provide greater opportunity to realize the advantages of international strategies. NAFTA does not exist for the sole purpose of U.S. businesses going north and south. Bernardo Dominguez, a Mexican businessman, arranged to purchase Westin Hotels Group in North America, South America, and Europe for $708 million for Aoki Corp. of Japan.[66] Also, Cementos de Mexico (CEMEX), the largest cement company in Mexico, has been buying cement makers in Spain and Venezuela as well as in the southwestern United States to extend its market share after the NAFTA agreement was confirmed. Anticipating entry by foreign competitors into Mexico, CEMEX is readying itself to compete globally, especially in emerging markets. For instance, it is stepping up exports to Asia. It received orders for 2 million tons of cement in 1995 from Taiwan, Thailand, and Indonesia.[67]

NAFTA, signed by the United States, Canada, and Mexico, was designed to facilitate free trade across North American borders. It gives firms the opportunity to realize the advantages of international strategies, as evidenced by Pennzoil's automotive business in Guadalajara, Mexico.

After firms decide on their international strategies and whether to employ them in regional or world markets, they must decide how to accomplish such international expansion.[68] Therefore, the next section discusses how to enter new international markets.

CHOICE OF INTERNATIONAL ENTRY MODE

International expansion is accomplished through exporting, licensing, strategic alliances, acquisitions, and establishing new wholly owned subsidiaries. These means of entering international markets and their characteristics are shown in Table 8.1. Each has its advantages and disadvantages as described in the following subsections.

TABLE 8.1 *Global Market Entry: Choice of Entry Mode*

Type of Entry	Characteristics
Exporting	high cost, low control
Licensing	low cost, low risk, little control, low returns
Strategic alliances	Shared costs, shared resources, shared risks, problems of integration (e.g., two corporate cultures)
Acquisition	Quick access to new market, high cost, complex negotiations, problems of merging with domestic operations
New wholly owned subsidiary	Complex, often costly, time consuming, high risk, maximum control, potential above-average returns

Exporting

Many industrial firms initially begin international expansion by exporting their goods or services to other countries.[69] Exporting does not require the expense of establishing operations in the host countries, but exporters must establish some means of marketing and distributing their products. In so doing, exporting firms must develop contractual arrangements with host country firms. Its disadvantages include the often high costs of transportation and possible tariffs placed on incoming goods. Furthermore, the exporter has less control over the marketing and distribution of its products in the host country and must pay the distributor and/or allow the distributor to add to the price to recoup its costs and make a profit. As a result, it may be difficult to market a competitive product through exporting or to provide a product that is customized to each international market through exporting.

Historically, Japanese firms have succesfully used exporting as an international entry mode. This is the case for Canon, a world leader in imaging and information technology. The firm began in 1937 as a producer of high-quality cameras. At that time, Canon's products were relatively expensive for consumers in its domestic market. This situation, according to current president Fujio Mitarai, forced the firm to learn how to compete internationally. Thus, almost from its founding, Canon has used exporting as a mode of entry to multiple global markets.[70]

As the 1990s come to a close, the number of Japanese firms interested in exporting their products to different countries, but especially to the United States, is increasing. Declining domestic demand is significantly influencing this interest, as is the devaluation of Japan's currency. For instance, Rheon Automatic Machinery, a manufacturer of pastry-making machines, seeks to triple exports to the United States by 2000. Suffering from a softening in demand for its products in Japan, the firm's general manager also observes that the "U.S. market is huge and we can't afford not to be there." The managers at plastics producer Iris Ohyama felt that they faced a simple choice in 1994—export or die. Increased domestic competition, coupled with the nation's then-weakened economy, caused company executives to conclude that additional sales of its flower pots, storage containers, and garbage bins in Japan, its only market, were problematic. A decision was reached to export extensively, particularly to North America. Building on the success of its exporting entry mode, the firm soon established two American factories. These facilities now generate all of the company's U.S. sales, which today, account for 10 percent of total revenue.[71]

Licensing

A licensing arrangement allows a foreign firm to purchase the right to manufacture and sell the firm's products within a host country or set of countries.[72] The licenser is normally paid a royalty on each unit produced and sold. The licensee takes the risks and makes the monetary investments in facilities for manufacturing, marketing, and distributing the goods or services. As a result, licensing is possibly the least costly form of international expansion.

Licensing is also a way to expand returns based on previous innovations. For instance, Sony and Philips codesigned the audio CD. In 1994, makers of CDs and CD-ROM players and disks generated $50 billion in revenues. Sony and Philips collected 5 cents for every CD sold.[73] As the Sony–Philips example demonstrates, many firms can stand on the shoulders of their past innovations. Continual focus

293

on research and patent licensing allows a firm to gain strong returns from its innovations for many years in the future.[74]

Today, however, the returns to Sony and Philips from CD sales are threatened somewhat. Knockoff disks, which are cheap counterfeits of original products, are a growth business. Sales of counterfeit disks in China alone are estimated to exceed $1 billion annually. Interestingly, technological advances are contributing to the severity of the problem. In fact, innovation makes it easier for counterfeiters to improvise. Pressing machinery used to manufacture disks is so advanced and compact in size that it can be operated in the smallest of quarters. Located commonly in housing tenements, it is difficult for officials to find counterfeiters' production lines. Corporations are seeking legal remedies to their situation but with limited success to date.[75]

Of course, licensing has its disadvantages. For example, this approach to international expansion provides the firm very little control over the manufacture and marketing of its products in other countries. In addition, licensing provides the least potential returns because returns must be shared between the licenser and the licensee. The international firm may learn the technology and, after the license expires, produce and sell a similar competitive product. Komatsu, for example, first licensed much of its technology from U.S. companies International Harvester, Bucyrus-Erie, and Cummins Engine to enter the earthmoving equipment business to compete against Caterpillar. It subsequently dropped these licenses and developed its own products using the technology it gained from the U.S. companies.[76]

Strategic Alliances

Strategic alliances have enjoyed popularity in recent years as a primary means of international expansion.[77] Strategic alliances allow firms to share the risks and the resources required to enter international markets.[78] Moreover, alliances can facilitate the development of new core competencies that can contribute to the firm's future strategic competitiveness.[79] In addition, most strategic alliances are with a host country firm that has knowledge of the competitive conditions, legal and social norms, and cultural idiosyncrasies that should help the firm manufacture and market a competitive product. Alternatively, the host firm may find access to technology and new products attractive. Therefore, each partner in an alliance brings knowledge and/or resources to the partnership.[80]

Ford Motor Company has joined an alliance that existed previously between Germany's Daimler-Benz AG and Canada's Ballard Power Systems. This new and larger alliance, between two manufacturers and an alternative energy company, was organized so the three companies could work together to develop automotive engines and drive trains that produce power more efficiently and cleanly compared to products used currently. By participating in this alliance, Ford and Daimler-Benz are showing their support for the concept of electric cars that do not need batteries but can create their own electricity with a device called a fuel cell. Ballard's knowledge as a leader in fuel-cell technology is critical to the work to be completed through the formation of the alliance. In addition to their knowledge regarding electric vehicles, Ford and Daimler-Benz are committing significant amounts of financial resources ($420 million from Ford alone) to this alliance. Thus, the three partners to this alliance are contributing in ways that are intended to result in the alliance's success.[81] Strategic alliances are discussed in more depth in Chapter 9.

Acquisitions

Cross-border acquisitions have been increasing significantly with free trade in global markets.[82] They have also been increasing among Japanese and German firms because the value of the dollar has fallen relative to their home countries' currencies.[83] As explained in Chapter 7, acquisitions can provide quick access to a new market. In fact, acquisitions may provide the fastest and often the largest initial international expansion of any of the alternatives. This was the case with BMW's acquisition of Rover Cars in order to enter the sport utility vehicle market. Although acquisitions have become a popular mode of entering international markets, they are not without their costs. International acquisitions carry some of the same disadvantages that exist for domestic acquisitions, as discussed in Chapter 7. In addition, they can be expensive and often require debt financing (which also carries an extra cost). International negotiations for acquisitions can be exceedingly complex—generally more complicated than in domestic acquisitions. Dealing with the legal and regulatory requirements in the foreign host country of the target firm and obtaining appropriate information for effective negotiation of the agreement frequently present significant problems. Finally, the problems of merging the new firm into the acquiring firm often are more complex than for domestic acquisitions. The acquiring firm must deal not only with different corporate cultures, but also with potentially different social cultures and practices. Therefore, while international acquisitions have been popular because of the rapid access to new markets they provide, they also carry with them important costs and multiple risks.

Some analysts believe that South Korea may be a country targeted by companies seeking to expand internationally through acquisitions. Chase Manhattan, General Motors, and GE were considering such acquisitions early in 1998. In part, these interests were being fueled by the requirement for the South Korean government to open its nation's economy as part of a $60 billion international bailout. In concert with Robert Bosch GmbH and Sachs AG, General Motors is examining the possibility of acquiring Mando Machinery, a large but ailing auto parts company. GE's approach to South Korea's economic crises was expressed by a company spokesperson who explained that "sometimes when there are situations with uncertainty, it can create acquisition opportunities for us."[84]

Forestry company UPM-Kymmene also uses acquisitions as an entry mode into global markets. This Finnish firm was created in 1996 through a merger of two rivals. A string of strategic acquisitions has allowed UPM-Kymmene to establish itself "as one of the few genuinely transcontinental producers in a traditionally fragmented industry." Now the world's largest pulp and paper producer after U.S.-based International Paper, some analysts see UPM-Kymmene's actions as setting a cross-border consolidation trend in its industry. Collectively, the company's acquisitions have created a worldwide producer and a worldwide seller. Although the firm is currently concentrating on integrating its acquisitions into its existing operations, the CEO does not rule out the possibility of further acquisitions if attractive opportunities were to surface.[85]

The world's largest retailer, Wal-Mart, is using several entry modes to globalize its operations. For example, in China, the firm used a joint venture mode of entry. To begin the firm's foray into Germany, an acquisition was completed. In all likelihood, the same entry mode will be used to establish Wal-Mart's presence in Japan. The head of Wal-Mart's international operations describes the reason-

Wal-Mart is planning to use a combination of entry modes into the Japanese market. Some areas of Japanese industry are open to greenfied start-ups and others are more conducive to acquisitions.

ing for this decision: In Japan, "there may be isolated pockets where you could do greenfield start-ups, but Japan has a very sophisticated, well-developed retail industry. When you have that situation, critical mass is more difficult to obtain, so acquisitions are a more appropriate first step."[86]

New, Wholly Owned Subsidiary

A **greenfield venture** is one in which a new, wholly owned subsidiary is established.

The establishment of a new, wholly owned subsidiary is referred to as a **greenfield venture**. This is often a complex and potentially costly process. This alternative has the advantage of providing maximum control for the firm and, therefore, if successful, has the most potential to provide above-average returns. The risks are also great because of the costs involved in establishing a new business operation in a new country. The firm may have to acquire the knowledge and expertise of the existing market by hiring host country nationals, possibly from competitive firms, and/or consultants (which can be costly). It maintains control over the technology, marketing, and distribution of its products through this process. Alternatively, it must build new manufacturing facilities, establish distribution networks, and learn and implement appropriate marketing strategies to compete in the new market.

Dynamics of Mode of Entry

Choice of mode of entry is determined by a number of factors.[87] Initial market entry will often be through export because this requires no foreign manufacturing expertise and investment only in distribution. Licensing can also facilitate the product improvement necessary to enter foreign markets, as in the Komatsu example. Strategic alliances have been popular because they allow partnering with an experienced player already in the targeted market. Strategic alliances also reduce risk through the sharing of costs. These modes therefore are best for early market development tactics.

To secure a stronger presence, acquisitions or greenfield ventures may be required. Many Japanese automobile manufacturers, such as Honda, Nissan, and Toyota, have gained presence in the United States through a greenfield venture in addition to joint ventures. Both acquisitions and greenfield ventures are likely to come at later stages in the development of an international diversification strategy.

Thus, there are multiple means of entering new global markets. As is the case with Wal-Mart, firms select the entry mode that is suited best to the situation at hand. In some instances, these options will be followed sequentially, beginning with exporting and ending with greenfield ventures. In other cases, the firm may use several but not all of the different entry modes. The decision regarding the entry mode to use is primarily a result of the industry's competitive conditions, the country's situation and government policies, and the firm's unique set of resources, capabilities, and core competencies.

STRATEGIC COMPETITIVENESS OUTCOMES

Once the strategy and mode of entry have been selected, firms need to be concerned about overall success. International expansion can be risky and may not result in a competitive advantage. The following strategic competitiveness issues are discussed, as suggested in Figure 8.1.

International Diversification and Returns

International diversification is the primary international corporate-level strategy. In Chapter 6, we discussed the corporate-level strategy of product diversification. Through this strategy, the firm engages in the manufacture and sale of multiple diverse products. **International diversification** is a strategy through which a firm expands the sale of its goods or services across the borders of global regions and countries into different geographic locations or markets. The number of different markets in which it operates and their importance shows the degree to which a firm is diversified internationally. The percentage of total sales is often used to measure a region's or country's importance to the firm.[88]

As noted earlier, multiple reasons exist for firms to diversify internationally. Because of its potential advantages, international diversification should be related positively to firm returns. Research has shown that as international diversification increases, firm returns increase, whereas domestic product diversification is often related negatively to firm returns.[89] There are many reasons for the positive effects of international diversification, such as the potential economies of scale and experience, location advantages, increased market size, and potential to stabilize returns. The stabilization of returns helps reduce a firm's overall risk.[90]

Firms in the Japanese automobile industry have found that international diversification may allow a company to better exploit its core competencies. Therefore, the sharing of knowledge resources can produce synergy among the operations in different countries/international markets as it has among Japanese automakers.[91]

International diversification is a strategy through which a firm expands the sales of its goods or services across the borders of global regions and countries into different geographic locations or markets.

On the other hand, firm returns may affect international diversification. For example, poor returns in a domestic market may encourage a firm to expand internationally to enhance its profit potential. In addition, internationally diversified firms may, in turn, have access to more flexible labor markets, as the Japanese do in the United States, and benefit from global scanning for competition and market opportunities.[92] As a result, multinational firms with efficient and competitive operations are more likely to produce above-average returns for their investors and better products for their customers than are solely domestic firms.[93] However, as explained later, international diversification can be carried too far.

International Diversification and Innovation

In Chapter 1, we noted that the development of new technology is at the heart of strategic competitiveness. Michael Porter stated that a nation's competitiveness depends on the capacity of its industry to innovate and suggested that firms achieve competitive advantage in international markets through innovation. Competitors eventually and inevitably outperform firms that fail to innovate and improve their operations and products. Therefore, the only way to sustain a competitive advantage is to upgrade it continually.[94]

International diversification provides the potential for firms to achieve greater returns on their innovations (through larger and/or more numerous markets) and thus lowers the often substantial risks of R&D investments. Therefore, international diversification provides incentives for firms to innovate. In addition, international diversification may be necessary to generate the resources required to sustain a large-scale R&D operation. An environment of rapid technological obsolescence makes it difficult to invest in new technology and the capital-intensive operations required to take advantage of it. Firms operating solely in domestic markets may find such investments difficult because of the length of time required to recoup the original investment. Furthermore, if the time is extended, it may not be possible to recover the investment before the technology becomes obsolete.[95] As a result, international diversification improves the firm's ability to appropriate additional and necessary returns from innovation before competitors can overcome the initial competitive advantage created by the innovation.

The relationship among international diversification, innovation, and returns is complex. Some level of performance is necessary to provide the resources to generate international diversification. International diversification provides incentives and resources to invest in research and development. Research and development, if done appropriately, should enhance the returns of the firm, which, in turn, provides more resources for continued international diversification and investment in R&D.

Because of the potential positive effects of international diversification on performance and innovation, some have argued that such diversification may even enhance returns in product diversified firms. International diversification would increase market potential in each of the product lines, but the complexity of managing a product diversified and internationally diversified firm is significant. Therefore, it is likely that international diversification can enhance the returns of a firm that is highly product diversified, but only when it is managed well.

Asea Brown Boveri (ABB) may demonstrate these relationships. This firm's operations involve high levels of both product and international diversification; yet, ABB's performance is quite strong. Some believe that the firm's ability to effec-

298

tively implement the transnational strategy contributes to its strategic competitiveness. To manage itself, ABB assembles culturally diverse corporate and divisional management teams. These teams are used to facilitate simultaneous achievement of global integration and local responsiveness. Evidence suggests that more culturally diverse top management teams often have a greater knowledge of international markets and idiosyncrasies.[96] (Top management teams are discussed further in Chapter 12.) Moreover, an in-depth understanding of diverse markets among top-level managers facilitates intra-firm coordination and the use of long-term, strategically relevant criteria to evaluate the performance of managers and their units. In turn, this approach facilitates improved innovation and performance.[97]

Complexity of Managing Multinational Firms

Although many potential benefits can be realized by implementing an international strategy, problems and complexities can also arise. For example, multiple risks are involved when operating in several different countries. Firms can become only so large and diverse before becoming unmanageable or the costs of managing them exceed their benefits. Other complexities include the highly competitive nature of global markets, multiple cultural environments, potentially rapid shifts in the value of different currencies, and the possible instability of some national governments.

299

Political risks are related to instability in national governments and to war, civil or international.

RISKS IN AN INTERNATIONAL ENVIRONMENT

International diversification carries with it multiple risks. International expansion is difficult to implement and manage after implementation because of these risks. Primary among these are the political and economic risks. Because of these risks, highly diversified firms are accustomed to market conditions yielding competitive situations that differ from what was predicted. Sometimes, these situations contribute positively to the firm's efforts to enhance its strategic competitiveness; on other occasions, they have a negative effect on the firm's efforts.[98] Specific examples of political and economic risks are shown in Figure 8.4.

Political Risks

Political risks are related to instability in national governments and to war, civil or international. Instability in a national government creates multiple problems. Among these are economic risks and the uncertainty created in terms of government regulation, many legal authorities, and potential nationalization of private assets. For example, foreign firms that are investing in Russia may have concerns about the stability of the national government and what might happen to their investments/assets in Russia should there be a major change in government.

Different concerns exist for foreign firms investing in China. They are less worried about the potential for major changes in China's national government than about the uncertainty of China's regulation of foreign business investments. Tensions among Hong Kong, Taiwan, and China create concern about investment in the region. Taiwan is the second largest investor in China behind Hong Kong. Much of the tension is political: Taiwan and Hong Kong have been a laboratory in which capitalism was tested against socialism in China.[99]

FIGURE 8.4 *Risks in the International Environment*

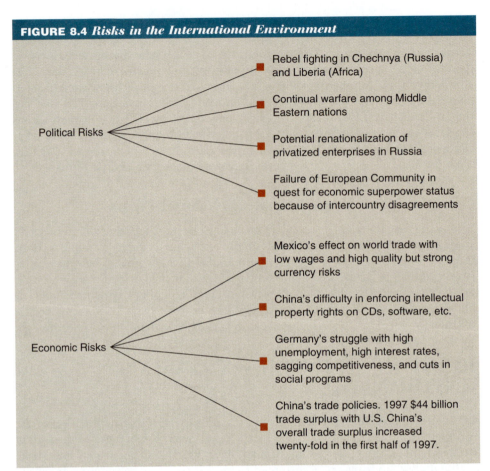

Political Risks
- Rebel fighting in Chechnya (Russia) and Liberia (Africa)
- Continual warfare among Middle Eastern nations
- Potential renationalization of privatized enterprises in Russia
- Failure of European Community in quest for economic superpower status because of intercountry disagreements

Economic Risks
- Mexico's effect on world trade with low wages and high quality but strong currency risks
- China's difficulty in enforcing intellectual property rights on CDs, software, etc.
- Germany's struggle with high unemployment, high interest rates, sagging competitiveness, and cuts in social programs
- China's trade policies. 1997 $44 billion trade surplus with U.S. China's overall trade surplus increased twenty-fold in the first half of 1997.

Source: N. Banerjee, 1996, Russia's many regions work to attract funds from foreign investors, *Wall Street Journal,* April 30, A1, A8; P. Engardio and D. Roberts, 1996, Rethinking China, *Business Week,* March 4, 57–64; R.S. Greenberger, 1996, U.S. sharply attacks China over intellectual property, *Wall Street Journal,* May 1, A3, A4; A.D. Marcus, 1996, Israel seems to target Lebanon economy, *Wall Street Journal,* April 17, A16; C. Rosett, 1996, Russian Communists target privatizers, *Wall Street Journal,* February 13, A11; P. Stein, 1996, Hong Kong feels heavy hand of China, *Wall Street Journal,* April 17, A16; J. Templeman, 1996, The economy that fell to earth, *Business Week,* January 15, 46.

Economic Risks

Economic risks are interdependent with political risks, as noted earlier. However, there are other economic risks associated with international diversification. Chief among these are the differences and fluctuations in the value of different currencies. For example, with U.S. firms, the value of the dollar relative to other currencies determines the value of their international assets and earnings. An increase in the value of the dollar can reduce the value of U.S. multinational firms' international assets and earnings in other countries. Furthermore, the value of different currencies can, at times, dramatically affect a firm's competitiveness in global markets because of its effect on the prices of goods manufactured in different countries. For example, an increase in the value of the dollar can harm U.S. firms' exports to international markets because of the price differential of the products.

Miller Brewing Company's recent experience with a joint venture demonstrates how political and economic risks are interwoven. Formed with Brazil's Cia, Cervejaria Brahma SA, Miller held a 50 percent ownership in this alliance. Brazil's Administrative Council of Economic Defense (Cade) ruled that the alliance between Miller and Brahma, both among the largest brewers in the world, deprived consumers of the benefits of head-to-head competition between the two giants. The agency allowed Miller 24 months to sell its stake in the alliance. Analysts suggested that this decision cast a cloud over efforts by multinational corporations to penetrate fast-growing Brazilian markets. Thus, this decision raised the possibility that other companies seeking to expand their operations through entry into Brazil's markets via cooperative arrangements such as a joint venture would either delay or cancel such expansion plans. The following comment from a lawyer representing the two brewers suggests this as well as the possibility that a different market entry mode may be appropriate for use in Brazil: "This decision is a yellow light, which says that if foreign companies wish to come into Brazil, they should not joint venture with Brazilian companies but should come in and make investments themselves."[100]

Limits to International Expansion: Management Problems

Research has shown that there are positive returns to early international diversification, but they tend to level off and become negative as the diversification increases past some point.[101] There are multiple reasons for the limits to the positive effects of international diversification. For example, greater geographic dispersion across country borders increases the costs of coordination between units and the distribution of products. Additionally, trade barriers, logistical costs, cultural diversity, and other differences by country (e.g., access to raw materials, different employee skill levels) greatly complicate the implementation of international diversification.[102]

Institutional and cultural factors often represent strong barriers to the transfer of a firm's competitive advantages from one country to another. Marketing programs often have to be redesigned and new distribution networks established when firms expand into new countries. In addition, they may encounter different labor costs and capital charges. Therefore, it is difficult to effectively implement, manage, and control international operations.[103]

Amway Corporation's recent experiences in South Korea demonstrate the managerial challenges in international diversification. Long committed to the relationship between international diversification and financial returns, Amway competes extensively in what it calls the Asian-Pacific region. Countries into which Amway has expanded in this region include Japan, South Korea, Taiwan, Thailand, Australia, China, Hong Kong, and New Zealand. The importance of South Korea to Amway is indicated by the fact that this country is the firm's third largest market on a worldwide basis. As a result of attacks by local consumer groups and environmental activities and competitive actions taken by South Korea's domestic competitors, Amway's sales in this important market plunged recently by 64 percent. Contributing to this precipitous decline was the decision by approximately 70,000 of the firm's 140,000 distributors to discontinue working for the company. Following a study of the situation, an analyst suggested that "Amway's continuing woes in Korea . . . underscore how cultural land mines and informal trade barriers still make it tough for many foreign companies to make it in this market."

At the center of Amway's problem was a detergent called Dish Drops. To express their concerns, 82 consumer and environmental groups formed an Anti-Amway Committee. These groups alleged that Amway was misleading consumers by advertising that Dish Drops was an environmentally friendly product. Moreover, the groups asserted that Amway was overcharging consumers by a factor of two or three relative to the costs of local manufacturers' detergents. In light of these claims, some of the consumer groups suggested that "Amway is not a moral company; and, they have the wrong attitude in marketing their products." To publicize these allegations, the Korea Soap and Detergent Association, a trade group for local manufacturers, sponsored advertisements.

Brian Chalmers, the president of Amway's Korean operation, responded to these allegations. For example, Amway asserted that the tests used to determine that Dish Drops was not an environmentally friendly product were flawed. Instead of complying with the international standard of eight days or more of testing to determine a detergent's biodegradability, Amway officials noted that the Dish Drops product was studied in only one and two days of testing. Furthermore, Chalmers denied that Amway was overcharging customers. He explained that Dish Drops is economical if the customer dilutes the concentrated soap as directed on the package. Chalmers suggested that because consumer groups refuse to accept Amway's guidelines for using the concentrate, they mistakenly concluded that the product is too expensive.

In spite of these difficulties, Chalmers remains positive about Amway's market potential in South Korea. To explain his decision to expand the firm's product line in South Korea, Chalmers said, "The opportunity this market provides is still absolutely unbounded."[104]

The amount of international diversification that can be managed will vary by firm and the abilities of the managers. The problems of central coordination and integration are reduced if the firm diversifies into more friendly countries that have similar cultures. In so doing, there are fewer trade barriers, a better understanding of the laws and customs, and the product is easier to adapt for local markets. For example, U.S. firms may find it less difficult to expand their operations into Canada and Western European countries (e.g., Great Britain, France) than into Asian countries (e.g., Japan, Korea).[105] The difficulties Amway is having in South Korea appear to support the contention that U.S. firms may find entry into Asian markets more challenging as compared to entries into more culturally similar markets.

Other Management Problems

One critical concern is that the global marketplace is highly competitive. Firms accustomed to a highly competitive domestic market experience more complexities in international markets. That is caused not only by the number of competitors encountered, but also by the differences of those competitors. A U.S. firm expanding operations into a European country may encounter competitors not only from Great Britain, Germany, France, and Spain, but also from countries outside of Europe, such as Hong Kong, Japan, Korea, Taiwan, Canada, and possibly even South America. Firms from each of these countries may enjoy different competitive advantages. Some may have low labor costs, others may have easy access to financing and low capital costs, and still others may have access to new high technology. Finally, attempting to understand the strategic intent of a competitor is more complex because of the different cultures and mind-sets.[106]

Another problem focuses on the relationships between the host government and the multinational corporation. For example, while Japanese firms face few trade barriers in competing in U.S. markets, U.S. firms often encounter many barriers to selling their products and operating in Japanese markets.[107] These regulations have traditionally kept the yen high relative to the dollar by keeping out imports and reducing the value of Japanese exports. This increases the price of Japanese products abroad. As noted earlier, the problem has been reversing itself somewhat, but much more remains to be done to reduce entry barriers. Many firms, such as Toyota and General Motors, are turning to strategic alliances to overcome entry barriers.

The nature of managerial complexity not only in international markets, but in domestic ones as well, has led managers to seek help in meeting this challenge. The next chapter focuses on how firms are cooperating with each other to meet some of their management challenges.

SUMMARY

- International diversification is increasing not only because of traditional motivations, but also for emerging reasons. Traditional motives include extending the product life cycle, securing key resources, and having access to low-cost labor. Emerging motivations focus on increased pressure for global integration as the demand for commodity products becomes borderless, and yet pressure for local country responsiveness is increasing.

- An international strategy usually attempts to capitalize on four important opportunities: potential increased market size; opportunity to earn a return on large investments, such as plant and capital equipment and/or research and development; economies of scale and learning; and potential location advantages.

- International business-level strategies are similar to the generic business-level strategy types: international low cost, international differentiation, international focus, and international integrated low cost/differentiation. However, each of these strategies is usually grounded in some home country advantage, as Porter's diamond model suggests. The diamond model emphasizes four determinants: factors of production; demand conditions; related and supporting industries; and patterns of firm strategy, structure, and rivalry.

- International corporate-level strategies are classified into three types. A multidomestic strategy focuses on competition within each country in which the firm operates. Firms employing a multidomestic strategy decentralize strategic and operating decisions to the strategic business units operating in each country so each can tailor its goods and services to the local market. A global strategy assumes more standardization of products across country boundaries. Therefore, competitive strategy is centralized and controlled by the home office. A transnational strategy seeks to combine aspects of both multidomestic and global strategies in order to emphasize both local responsiveness and global integration and coordination. The strategy is difficult to implement, requiring an integrated network and a culture of individual commitment.

- Although the transnational strategy is difficult to implement, environmental trends are causing many multinational firms to consider the needs for both global efficiencies and local responsiveness. Most large multinational firms, particularly those with many diverse products, may use a multidomestic strategy with some product lines and a global strategy with others.

- Some firms decide to compete only in certain regions of the world, as opposed to viewing all markets in the world as potential opportunities. Competing in regional markets allows firms and managers to focus their learning on specific markets, cultures, location resources, etc.

- Firms may enter international markets in one of several different ways, including exporting, licensing, forming strategic alliances, making acquisitions, and establishing new, wholly owned subsidiaries, often referred to as greenfield ventures. Most firms begin with exporting and/or licensing because of their lower costs and risks, but later may expand to strategic alliances and acquisitions. The most expensive and risky means of entering a new international market is through the establishment of a new, wholly owned subsidiary. Alternatively, it provides the advantages of maximum control for the firm and, if successful, potentially the greatest returns as well.

■ International diversification facilitates innovation in the firm. It provides a larger market to gain more and faster returns from investments in innovation. In addition, international diversification may generate the resources necessary to sustain a large-scale R&D program.

■ In general, international diversification is related to above-average returns, but this assumes effective implementation of international diversifica-

tion and management of international operations. International diversification provides greater economies of scope and learning. These, along with the greater innovation, help produce above-average returns.

■ Several risks are involved with managing multinational operations. Among these are political risks (e.g., instability of national governments) and economic risks (e.g., currency value fluctuations).

■ There are also limits to the ability to manage international expansion effectively. International diversification increases coordination and distribution costs, and management problems are exacerbated by trade barriers, logistical costs, and cultural diversity, among other factors.

■ Additionally, international markets are highly competitive and firms must maintain an effective working relationship with the host government.

REVIEW QUESTIONS

1. What are the traditional and emerging motives that are causing firms to expand internationally?
2. What four factors are a basis for international business-level strategies?
3. What are the generic international business-level strategies? How do they differ from each other?
4. What are the differences among the following corporate-level international strategies: multidomestic, global, and transnational?
5. What environmental trends are affecting international strategy?

6. What five modes of international expansion are available, and what is the normal sequence of their use?
7. What is the relationship between international diversification and innovation? How does international diversification affect innovation? What is the effect of international diversification on firm returns?
8. What are the risks involved in expanding internationally and managing multinational firms?
9. What are the factors that create limits to the positive outcomes of international expansion?

APPLICATION DISCUSSION QUESTIONS

1. Given the advantages of international diversification, why do some firms choose not to expand internationally?
2. How do firms choose among the alternative modes for expanding internationally and moving into new markets (e.g., forming a strategic alliance versus establishing a wholly owned subsidiary)?
3. Does international diversification affect innovation similarly in all industries? Why or why not?

4. What is an example of political risk in expanding operations into China or Russia?
5. Why do some firms gain competitive advantages in international markets? Explain.
6. Why is it important to understand the strategic intent of strategic alliance partners and competitors in international markets?
7. What are the challenges associated with pursuing the transnational strategy? Explain.

ETHICS QUESTIONS

1. As firms attempt to internationalize, there may be a temptation to locate where product liability laws are lax to test new products. Are there examples where this motivation is the driving force behind international expansion?

2. Regulation and laws regarding the sale and distribution of tobacco products are stringent in the U.S. market. Undertake a study of selected U.S. tobacco firms to see if sales are increasing in foreign markets compared to domestic markets. In what countries are sales increasing and why? What is your assessment of this practice?

3. Some firms may outsource production to foreign countries. Although the presumed rationale for such outsourcing is to reduce labor costs, examine the liberality of labor laws (for instance, the strictness of child labor laws) and laws on environmental protection in another country to evaluate the ethics of this action.

4. Are there markets that the U.S. government protects through subsidy and tariff? If so, which ones and why?

5. Should the United States seek to impose trade sanctions on other countries such as China because of human rights violations?

6. Latin America has been experiencing a significant change in both political orientation and economic development. Describe these changes. What strategies should foreign international businesses implement, if any, to influence government policy in these countries? Is there a chance these political changes will reverse? How would business strategy change if Latin American politics reverses its current course?

305

INTERNET EXERCISE

Go to International Business Resources at:

http://www.ciber.bus.msu.edu/busres.html

This Web site is an award-winning site maintained by the Center for International Business and Research at Michigan State University. The site contains numerous links to other international business sites. Put yourself in the place of the manager of a firm that is thinking about exporting for the first time. Which links on the above site would be valuable to you as a first-time exporter? Explain the merits of each of the links that you feel would be helpful.

STRATEGIC SURFING

To help U.S. businesses understand foreign markets, the U.S. Central Intelligence Agency and the U.S. State Department produce "country profiles" that are available to the public free of charge. These profiles are available at the following Web sites:

CIA World Factbook:

http://www.odci.gov/cia/publications/nsolo/wfb-all.html

U.S. State Department Country Reports on Economic Policy and Trade Practices:

http://www.state.gov/www/issues/economic/trade_reports/index.html

NOTES

1. G. Mellon, 1997, Which has the brightest future, China or Russia? *Wall Street Journal*, August 29, A19.
2. B. L. Kirkman and D. L. Shapiro, 1997, The impact of cultural values on employee resistance to teams: Toward a model of globalized self-managing work team effectiveness, *Academy of Management Review* 22: 730–757.
3. P. Martin, 1997, A future depending on choice, *Financial Times*, November 7, 12.
4. C. W. L. Hill, 1998, *Global Business Today* (Boston: Irwin/McGraw Hill), 336; B. J. Punnett and D. A. Ricks, 1997, *International Business*, second edition, (Cambridge, MA: Blackwell Publishers), 8.

5. R. Vernon, 1996, International investment and international trade in the product cycle, *Quarterly Journal of Economics* 80: 190–207.
6. A. Bernstein, S. Jackson, and J. Byrne, 1997, Jack cracks the whip again, *Business Week*, December 15, 34–35.
7. J. M. Brown, 1997, World eyes Ireland for telesales growth, *Financial Times*, November 7, 2.
8. *Financial Times*, 1997, Flexible and cheap, December 12, II.
9. D. Woodruff and K. L. Miller, 1995, Mercedes' maverick in Alabama, *Business Week*, September 11, 64–65.
10. J. N. Kapferer, 1998, Making brands work around the world,

in Part One of As business goes global, *Financial Times*, February 12–13.

11. Punnett and Ricks, *International Business*, 334–337.

12. S. Batholomew, 1997, National systems of biotechnology innovation: Complex interdependencies in the global system, *Journal of International Business Studies* 28: 241–266; A. Madhok, 1997, Cost, value and foreign market entry mode: The transaction and the firm, *Strategic Management Journal* 18: 39–61.

13. W. Kuemmerle, 1997, Building effective R&D capabilities abroad, *Harvard Business Review* 75, no. 2: 61–70; B. J. Oviatt and P. P. McDougall, 1995, Global start-ups: Entrepreneurs on a worldwide stage, *Academy of Management Executive* IX, no. 2: 30–44.

14. J. J. Choi and M. Rajan, 1997, A joint test of market segmentation and exchange risk factor in international capital markets, *Journal of International Business Studies* 28: 29–49.

15. J. L. Xie, 1996, Karasek's model in the People's Republic of China: Effects of job demands, control, and individual differences, *Academy of Management Journal* 39: 1594–1618.

16. J. P. Quinlan, 1998, Europe, not Asia, is corporate America's key market, *Wall Street Journal*, January 12, A20.

17. M. A. Hitt, M. T. Dacin, B. B. Tyler, and D. Park, 1997, Understanding the differences in Korean and U.S. executives' strategic orientations, *Strategic Management Journal* 18: 159–167.

18. McDonald's adapts Mac attack to foreign tastes with expansion, 1997, *Dallas Morning News*, December 7, H3.

19. Berstein, Jackson, and Byrne, Jack cracks the whip again.

20. S. Zaheer and E. Mosakowski, 1997, The dynamics of the liability of foreignness: A global study of survival in financial services, *Strategic Management Journal* 18: 439–464.

21. Tupperware snaps at chance to sell in Russia, 1997, *Dallas Morning News*, November 25, D4.

22. M. Halkias, 1997, Friday's outlines growth, *Dallas Morning News*, December 3, D1, D10.

23. M. Halkias, 1997, Frito-Lay to buy snack brands abroad, *Dallas Morning News*, November 18, D1, D7.

24. N. Harris, 1997, If you can't beat 'em, copy 'em, *Business Week*, November 17, 50.

25. R. Tomkins and A. Jack, 1997, Coca-Cola to buy Orangina for $840 million, *Financial Times*, December 23, 15.

26. M. Skapinker, 1998, Airbus boasts year of record orders, *Financial Times*, January 7, 6; F. M. Biddle, 1997, Boeing's effort to cushion itself from cycle backfires, *Wall Street Journal*, October 24, B4; C. Goldsmith, 1997, Airbus plans to spend $2.9 billion on jets to compete with Boeing, *Wall Street Journal*, December 9, B4.

27. W. Shan and J. Song, 1997, Foreign direct investment and the sourcing of technological advantage: Evidence from the biotechnology industry, *Journal of International Business Studies* 28: 267–284.

28. A. J. Venables, 1995, Economic integration and the location of firms, *The American Economic Review* 85: 296–300.

29. H. Simonian, 1997, Volvo's lights burn brighter, *Financial Times*, December 9, 17.

30. M. Schuman and V. Reitman, 1997, A world-wide glut doesn't sway Samsung from auto business, *Wall Street Journal*, August 25, A1, A11.

31. J. Birkinshaw, 1997, Entrepreneurship in multinational corporations: The characteristics of subsidiary initiatives, *Strategic Management Journal* 18: 207–229.

32. S. Makino and A. Delios, 1996, Local knowledge transfer and performance: Implications for alliance formation in Asia, *Journal of International Business Studies* 27 (Special Issue), 905–927.

33. K. Ferdows, 1997, Making the most of foreign factories, *Harvard Business Review* 75, no. 2: 73–88.

34. V. Reitman, 1998, Toyota plans new lost-cost car to replace its struggling Tercel, *Wall Street Journal*, January 9, B4.

35. Ford beats GM to be first to make cars in China, 1997, *Wall Street Journal*, December 2, A17.

36. D. J. Teece, G. Pisano, and A. Shuen, 1997, Dynamic capabilities and strategic management, *Strategic Management Journal* 18: 509–533.

37. A. Campbell and M. Alexander, 1997, What's wrong with strategy? *Harvard Business Review* 75, no. 6: 42–51.

38. A. Rugman, 1998, Multinationals as regional flagships, in Part One of As business goes global, *Financial Times*, February 10–11, 6–9.

39. M. E. Porter, 1990, *The Competitive Advantage of Nations* (New York: The Free Press).

40. Ibid., 84.

41. Ibid., 89.

42. N. D. Schwartz, 1998, Why Wall Street's buying Wal-Mart again, *Fortune*, February 16, 92–94.

43. R. B. Lieber, 1997, Flying high, going global, *Fortune*, July 7, 195–197; M. Skapinker, 1997, No-frills airlines travelling on a wing and a fear, *Financial Times*, November 20, VI.

44. Schwartz, Why Wall Street's buying Wal-Mart again, 94; Sam's travels, 1997, *Financial Times*, December 19, 13.

45. Porter, *Competitive Advantage*, 133.

46. D. Woodruff, 1997, Service with a what? *Business Week*, September 8, 130F–130H.

47. J. Friedland, 1994, Sharp's edge: Prowess in LCD screens puts it ahead of Sony, *Far Eastern Economic Review*, July 28, 74–76.

48. T. Burns, 1997, Niche goals bring away results, *Financial Times*, November 17, II; Oviatt and McDougall, Global start-ups.

49. Porter, *Competitive Advantage*, 210–225.

50. M. J. Enright and P. Tenti, 1990, How the diamond works: The Italian ceramic tile industry, *Harvard Business Review* 68, no. 2: 90–91.

51. D. Lei, M. A. Hitt, and J. D. Goldhar, 1996, Advanced manufacturing technology: The impact on organization design and strategic flexibility, *Organization Studies* 17: 501–523.

52. R. D. Ireland and M. A. Hitt, 1998, Achieving and maintaining strategic competitiveness in the 21st century: The role of strategic leadership, *Academy of Management Executive* (in press).

53. D. Weimer, 1998, A new Cat on the hot seat, *Business Week*, March 9, 56–61; A. E. Johnson, 1997, Caterpillar pays $1.3 billion for Varity Perkins, *Financial Times*, December 12, 1; P. Marsh and S. Wagstyl, 1997, The hungry Caterpillar, *Financial Times*, December 2, 22.

54. M. A. Hitt, R. E. Hoskisson, and R. D. Ireland, 1994, A midrange theory of the interactive effects of international and product diversification on innovation and performance, *Journal of Management* 20: 297–326.

55. S. Ghoshal, 1987, Global strategy: An organizing framework, *Strategic Management Journal* 8: 425–440.

56. R. Tomkins, 1998, US market benefits from Knorr know-how, *Financial Times*, January 20, 19.

57. Ghoshal, Global strategy.

58. J. K. Johaansson and G. S. Yip, 1994, Exploiting globalization potential: U.S. and Japanese strategies, *Strategic Management Journal* 15: 579–601.

59. N. Tait, 1998, CMS pumps up its power across the world, *Financial Times*, January 8, 17.

60. C. A. Bartlett and S. Ghoshal, 1989, *Managing Across Borders: The Transnational Solution* (Boston: Harvard Business School Press).

61. Govindarajan and Gupta, Setting a course; A. Saxenian, 1994, *Regional Advantage: Culture and Competition in Silicon Valley and Route 128* (Cambridge, MA: Harvard University Press).

62. Rugman, Multinationals as regional flagships, 6.

63. Woodruff, Service with a what?

64. L. Allen and C. Pantzalis, 1996, Valuation of the operating flexibility of multinational corporations, *Journal of International Business Studies* 27: 633–653.

65. J. I. Martinez, J. A. Quelch, and J. Ganitsky, 1992, Don't forget Latin America, *Sloan Management Review* 33 (Winter): 78–92.

66. P. B. Carroll, 1994, Buyer of Westin deal may represent new breed of Mexican businessman, *Wall Street Journal*, March 1, A15.

67. G. Smith and J. Person, 1996, CEMEX: Solid as Mexico sinks, *Business Week* February 27, 58–59.

68. V. Govindarajan and A. Gupta, 1998, How to build a global presence, in Part One of As business goes global, *Financial Times*, February 10–11; Madhok, Cost, value and foreign market entry mode, 41.

69. Punnett and Ricks, *International Business*, 249–250; G. M. Naidu and V. K. Prasad, 1994, Predictors of export strategy and performance of small- and medium-sized firms, *Journal of Business Research* 31: 107–115.

70. Canon: Sixty Years of Progress, 1998, *Fortune* (Special Advertising Section), August 4, S-5.

71. S. Glain, 1997, A whole new wave of Japanese exports is headed westward, *Wall Street Journal*, November 14, A1, A6.

72. Hill, *Global Business Today*, 361–363.

73. B. Schlender, 1995, Sony on the brink, *Fortune*, June 12, 66.

74. J. R. Green and S. Schotchmer, 1995, On the division of profit in sequential innovation, *The Rand Journal of Economics* 26: 20–33.

75. B. Einhorn, 1997, China's CD pirates find a new hangout, *Business Week*, December 15, 138F.

76. C. A. Bartlett and S. Rangan, 1992, Komatsu limited, in C. A. Bartlett and S. Ghoshal (eds.), *Transnational Management: Text, Cases and Readings in Cross-Border Management* (Homewood, IL: Irwin), 311–326.

77. A. C. Inkpen and P. W. Beamish, 1997, Knowledge, bargaining power, and the instability of international joint ventures, *Academy of Management Review* 22: 177–202; S. H. Park and G. R. Ungson, 1997, The effect of national culture, organizational complementarity, and economic motivation on joint venture dissolution, *Academy of Management Journal* 40: 279–307.

78. Y. Pan and D. K. Tse, 1996, Cooperative strategies between foreign firms in an overseas country, *Journal of International Business Studies* 27 (Special Issue): 929–946.

79. M. A. Hitt, B. W. Keats, and S. M. DeMarie, 1998, Navigating in the new competitive landscape: Building strategic flexibility and competitive advantage in the 21st century, *Academy of Management Executive* (in press).

80. M. A. Lyles and J. E. Salk, 1996, Knowledge acquisition from foreign parents in international joint ventures: An empirical examination in the Hungarian context, *Journal of International Business Studies* 27 (Special Issue): 877–903.

81. Ford joins global alliance on electric cars, *Dallas Morning News*, December 16, D6.

82. M. A. Hitt, R. E. Hoskisson, and H. Kim, 1997, International diversification: Effects on innovation and firm performance in product-diversified firms, *Academy of Management Journal* 40: 767–798.

83. J. F. Hennart and S. Reddy, 1997, The choice between mergers/acquisitions and joint ventures: The case of Japanese investors in the United States, *Strategic Management Journal* 18: 1–12.

84. U.S. firms consider growth into S. Korea, 1997, *Dallas Morning News*, December 27, F1, F3.

85. G. McIvor, 1998, Paper-maker unwraps global aims, *Financial Times*, January 6, 16.

86. R. Tomkins, 1997, Wal-Mart on the prowl for retail acquisitions in Europe and Japan, *Financial Times*, December 23, 15.

87. W. C. Kim and P. Hwang, 1992, Global strategy and multinationals' entry mode choice, *Journal of International Business Studies* 23: 29–53.

88. Hitt, Hoskisson, and Kim, International diversification, 767.

89. R. Buhner, 1987, Assessing international diversification of West German corporations, *Strategic Management Journal* 8: 25–37.

90. J. M. Geringer, P. W. Beamish, and R. C. daCosta, 1989, Diversification strategy and internationalization: Implications for MNE performance, *Strategic Management Journal* 10: 109–119; R. E. Caves, 1982, *Multinational Enterprise and Economic Analysis* (Cambridge, MA: Cambridge University Press).

91. B. Bremner, L. Armstrong, K. Kerwin, and K. Naughton, 1997, Toyota's crusade, *Business Week*, April 7, 104–114.

92. S. J. Kobrin, 1991, An empirical analysis of the determinants of global integration, *Strategic Management Journal* 12 (Special Issue): 17–37.

93. M. Kotabe, 1989, Hollowing-out of U.S. multinationals and their global competitiveness, *Journal of Business Research* 19: 1–15.

94. Porter, *Competitive Advantage*.

95. M. Kotabe, 1990, The relationship between off-shore sourcing and innovativeness of U.S. multinational firms: An empirical investigation, *Journal of International Business Studies* 21: 623–638.

96. S. Finkelstein and D. C. Hambrick, 1996, *Strategic Leadership: Top Executives and Their Effects on Organizations* (St. Paul, MN: West Publishing Company).

97. Hitt, Hoskisson, and Kim, International diversification, 790.

98. A lorry-load of trouble in Asia, 1997, *The Economist*, December 6, 65–66.

99. A. Tanzer, 1996, How Taiwan is invading China, *Forbes*, April 8, 86–91.

100. M. Moffett, 1997, Miller Brewing is ordered to sell its stake in Brazilian joint venture, *Wall Street Journal*, June 13, A14.

101. Hitt, Hoskisson, and Kim, International diversification; S. Tallman and J. Li, 1996, Effects of international diversity and product diversity on the performance of multinational firms, *Academy of Management Journal* 39: 179–196; Hitt, Hoskisson, and Ireland, A mid-range theory of interactive effects; Geringer, Beamish, and daCosta, Diversification strategy.

102. Porter, *Competitive Advantage*.

103. Hitt, Hoskisson, and Kim, International diversification.

104. M. Schuman, 1997, Amway finds itself washed over in a South Korean soap drama, *Wall Street Journal*, October 22, A16.

105. Hitt, Dacin, Tyler, and Park, Understanding the differences.

106. M. A. Hitt, B. B. Tyler, and C. Hardee, 1996, Understanding strategic intent in the global marketplace, *Academy of Management Executive* IX, no. 2: 12–19.

107. D. P. Hamilton, M. Williams, and N. Shirouzu, 1995, Japan's big problem: Freeing its economy from over regulation, *Wall Street Journal*, April 25, A1, A6.

Cooperative Strategy

CHAPTER 9

Learning Objectives

After reading this chapter, you should be able to:

1. Identify and define different types of cooperative strategy.

2. Explain the rationale for a cooperative strategy in three types of competitive situations: slow-cycle, standard-cycle, and fast-cycle markets.

3. Understand competitive advantages and disadvantages and competitive dynamics of cooperative strategies at the business level.

4. Describe uses of cooperative strategies at the corporate level.

5. Identify appropriate applications of cooperative strategies when pursuing international strategies.

6. Distinguish the competitive risks of cooperative strategies.

7. Understand the nature of trust as a strategic asset in forming cooperative strategies.

8. Describe the two basic management approaches for managing strategic alliances.

Increasing Numbers of Small and Large Firms Are Collaborating to Compete

Trends in both large firms such as multinational enterprises and small entrepreneurial firms have begun to emphasize a cooperative strategy or partnering with other companies. As explained in Chapter 8, large multinational enterprises have formed to exploit firm-specific advantages on a worldwide basis. However, many of these large firms have found their potential profits dissipating because internal governance and organizational structure costs outweigh their benefits. To improve this situation, many large multinationals are spinning off businesses they own and forming partnerships with other companies. These firms have moved away from a wholly-owned approach toward managing a business network of partners. Some of the better known of these networks or firms have been created by the Japanese. Often known as *vertical keiretsus* (a flagship firm with associated suppliers and distributors as partners), these networks have succeeded in forming strong global competitive positions in such diverse fields as consumer electronics (Sony, Matsushita), automobiles (Toyota, Nissan), and computers (NEC, Toshiba).

http://www.microsoft.com

Microsoft is an example of a firm that has a large system of partnerships with smaller software producers. Nowhere is this more evident than at the Comdex trade show where Microsoft's partner pavilion exhibits the nearly three hundred firms that eagerly show their relationship to the giant company. As the industry consolidates around Microsoft's Windows operating system, many firms are finding considerable momentum selling into this mass market. Because of their investment decisions, even IBM's global services division found its customers asking for software supporting the Windows NT operating system.

With the convergence of technologies, however, Microsoft is worried that if the Internet web moves to the television screen, the market may change to a direction that is not compatible with the software standard it has pursued. As a result, the company has been interested in developing a partnership or ownership stake in the cable TV industry. For instance, it has talked with Tele-Communications, Inc. (TCI), one of the largest cable television operators. TCI pays a large amount for digital cable boxes that have the capability of providing high-speed Internet access, besides hundreds of digital cable channels. Microsoft has been trying to influence the design of these new set-top boxes that will help bring the Internet into living rooms through cable wires by pressuring computer desktop manufacturers to adopt CE Windows (Microsoft's operating system for apparatus other than computers). It would be impossible for even Microsoft to purchase subsidiaries in all the areas of technology where the Internet will be established; therefore, it must forge these relationships through partnering or at the very most, partial ownership.

For small firms, forming cooperative relationships with other small companies as well as large ones is becoming a necessity. Although advances in technology, communications, and transportation have created many opportunities for growing small companies, it is almost impossible for single, entrepreneurial firms to exploit them on their own. Market pressures force small companies to work together in cooperative relationships. Today, large companies (e.g., those in the automobile industry) are winnowing their base and focusing on "tier one" suppliers (those who handle multiple parts and often supervise other subcontracting suppliers). These actions force smaller firms farther down the supply chain in two opposite directions—specialization and comprehensiveness. Quality is forcing more specialization, while suppliers are expected to provide all-encompassing or "do-it-all" solutions. This forces the smaller companies into cooperation with other firms, even former competitors. Such small-firm networks are being used in Italy and Denmark as well as other places throughout the world.

In the United States, for example, Harry Brown bought a Rust Belt company, Erie Bolt, now EBC Industries and transformed it by building alliances with many of his former competitors. Brown works with a machine shop to produce metal studs because both companies can produce a higher quality product for their customers. Brown and his former competitors, numbering about fifty, jointly market their capabilities to create business that they couldn't generate as individual firms. Furthermore, they share information about quality systems, consult with each other before investing in machinery, use each other's sales reps, and refer customers to each other. They can now offer a far more comprehensive product and a single point of contact for a variety of products. These alliances are not without their drawbacks. Harry Brown has had to take on the nearly full-time job of coordinating the group's efforts.

Other businesses form hybrid trade associations or work through an umbrella organization such as the Center for Advanced Fiber Optics Applications. This center is comprised of 12 companies that formed a separate non-profit entity to help them market separate new business opportunities. Usually with each network, you will find a leader behind it (and a strategic-center firm as explained later in the chapter) that champions the network firms. Although a particular CEO of a company, such as Brown, can be the champion, a third party can also offer an outside perspective needed to plant the seed necessary to develop the network. Often network brokers, whose very existence is a testimony to the trend, have a flair for getting overburdened CEOs to see the picture of the usefulness of such business network strategies.

SOURCE: S. Hamm, A. Cortese, and S.B. Garland, 1998, Microsoft's future, *Business Week*, January 19, 58–69; D. Fenn, 1997, Sleeping with the enemy, INC Online, http://www.inc.com, November; A. Rugman and J. D'Cruz, 1997, The theory of the flagship firm, *European Management Journal* 15: 403–412; D. Bank, 1997, Microsoft emphasizes its role as a partner at Comdex, *Wall Street Journal*, November 19, B4; E. Shapiro, 1997, TCI may get investment by Microsoft, *Wall Street Journal*, October 15, A3, A4; S.E. Human and K.G. Provan, 1997, An emergent theory of structure and outcomes in small-firm strategic manufacturing networks, *Academy of Management Journal* 40: 368–404.

Cooperative strategies have become increasingly popular since the mid-1980s. For example, the number of petitions to the U.S. Department of Justice for clearance of joint ventures increased by 423 percent during the 1986–1995 time period. Some have referred to this new trend as "coopetition" in that major competitors are now forming cooperative alliances to fend off other competition, oftentimes from foreign firms.[1] For instance, two U.S.-based competitors, Nucor Corporation and USX Corporation, formed an alliance to take advantage of each firm's unique competencies. USX researchers developed the idea for a revolutionary new steel-making process that eliminates the use of blast furnaces and coke batteries. They estimated this new process would reduce the cost of steel production by 20 to 25 percent.[2] As in the USX-Nucor partnership, alliances help firms obtain new technology rapidly and reduce the investment necessary to develop and introduce new products, to enter new markets, or to survive in their current ones. Also, as the opening case shows, cooperative strategies help firms overcome managerial and size limits to growth.[3] An increasing number of small and medium-sized companies, such as EBC Industries in the opening case, are engaging in cooperative strategies.[4] A Coopers and Lybrand survey of small companies found that such firms participating in alliances increased their revenues faster by generating 23 percent more goods and services than those not involved in them.[5] Alliances have become even more popular in international markets (between firms with headquarters in different countries) in recent years as the Japanese keiretsus mentioned in the opening case demonstrate.[6] Chrysler and other auto firms have been seeking to develop keiretsu type networks among their suppliers.[7]

Although strategic alliances, a prominent cooperative strategy, can serve a number of purposes and many are successful, managing them can be difficult.[8] The failure rate for alliances is notably high.[9] A study on the airline industry, for example, found that less than 30 percent of the alliances between international carriers have been successful.[10] As discussed in this chapter, firms must be careful when selecting alliance partners. They need to understand their potential partner's strategic intent and should attempt to develop trust among the partners to facilitate a more effective operation.[11] Because of the high failure rate, top executives who are considering entering into an alliance must develop a good understanding of the appropriate cooperative strategy to use and how to best implement it.

To this point in the book, competition among firms has been our focus. The previous chapters facilitate understanding of competitive advantage and strategic competitiveness through strong positions against external challenges, maximizing of core competencies, and minimizing of weaknesses. This chapter focuses on gaining competitive advantage through cooperation with other firms.[12]

TYPES OF COOPERATIVE STRATEGIES

Strategic alliances are a primary cooperative strategy. **Strategic alliances** are partnerships between firms whereby their resources, capabilities, and core competencies are combined to pursue mutual interests in developing, manufacturing, or distributing goods or services. Strategic alliances are explicit forms of relationships between firms. They come in three basic types.

One type of strategic alliance is a **joint ventures** in which two or more firms create an independent company. For instance, Dow Corning and Owens Corning were joint ventures created by Corning (formerly Corning Glass) with Dow Chemical Corporation and Owens Corporation, respectively. In joint ventures, each partner typically owns 50 percent of the equity.

A second type of strategic alliance is an **equity strategic alliance**, in which the partners own different percentages of equity in the new venture such as 60 and 40 percent. Many foreign direct investments are completed through equity strategic alliances such as those by Japanese and U.S. companies in China.[13] Unisource is an equity strategic alliance among three European telecommunication companies: Netherland's Koninklijke PTT, Sweden's Telia, and Swiss Telecom PTT. Chrysler Corporation and Mitsubishi Motors and Ford Motor Company and Mazda Motor Corporation have also formed significant equity strategic alliances. Equity strategic alliances are considered better at transferring know-how between firms because they are closer to hierarchical control than nonequity alliances.[14]

Finally, **nonequity strategic alliances** are formed through contract agreements given to a company to supply, produce, or distribute a firm's goods or services without equity sharing. Chrysler's network of supplier partners was mentioned earlier. This firm's approach to suppliers used to be based on a supplier's ability to build components at the lowest possible cost. There were no consultations concerning product design or the supplier's profit margins. Today, Chrysler's suppliers are involved deeply such that each partner works closely with Chrysler engineers. As a result, these mostly nonequity alliances have created $1.7 billion in annual savings for Chrysler; the supplier-partner's profits have increased as well.[15] Other types of cooperative contractual arrangements concern marketing and in-

Strategic alliances are partnerships between firms whereby their resources, capabilities, and core competencies are combined to pursue mutual interests in developing, manufacturing, or distributing goods or services.

A **joint venture** is when two or more firms create an independent company, with each of the partners typically owning equal shares in the new enterprise.

An **equity strategic alliance** consists of partners who own different percentages of equity in the new venture.

Nonequity strategic alliances are formed through contact agreements given to a company to supply, produce, or distribute a firm's goods or services without equity sharing.

formation sharing. Airlines, for example, use flight code sharing arrangements. Many of these additional relationships demonstrate nonequity strategic alliances.

Although this chapter focuses primarily on the explicit forms of strategic alliances as noted above, there are also implicit cooperative arrangements. One is called tacit collusion. **Tacit collusion** exists when several firms in an industry cooperate tacitly in reducing industry output below the potential competitive level, thereby increasing prices above the competitive level.[16] Most strategic alliances, however, exist not to reduce industry output but to increase learning, facilitate growth, or increase returns and strategic competitiveness.[17]

Cooperative agreements may also be explicitly collusive, which is illegal in the United States unless regulated by the government as was the case in the telecommunications industries until recent deregulation. *Mutual forbearance* (another term for tacit collusion) is tacit recognition of interdependence, but it has the same effect as explicit collusion in that it reduces output and increases prices. (Mutual forbearance is defined and explained in Chapter 6.)

The following sections explain strategic alliances in depth. We first discuss reasons for engaging in strategic alliances. This is followed by examining strategic alliances at the business-unit level, then at the corporate and international levels. Additionally, we describe network strategies where the cooperative relations among firms produce multiple alliances, including large consortia and different types of business networks. As such, we discuss how strategies among multiple alliance partnerships differ from those with two partner alliances. The major risks of pursuing the various types of alliances are considered. Finally, we discuss the importance of trust as a strategic asset to foster cooperative strategies that create competitive advantage and endure over time.

Reasons for Alliances

A number of different rationales support participation in strategic alliances.[18] The reasons for cooperation differ based on three types of basic market situations: slow-cycle, standard-cycle, and fast-cycle.[19] These three market situations were introduced in Chapter 5. As noted earlier, *slow-cycle* markets refer to markets that are sheltered or near monopolies such as railroads and, historically, telecommunications companies and utilities. Often, these companies cooperate to develop standards (e.g., to regulate air or train traffic), but because they can also collude to reduce competition, the government usually provides significant regulation to avoid consumer price discrimination. *Standard-cycle* market cooperation can result from firms trying to avoid overcapacity rather than attempting to increase their opportunities. As such, these cooperative arrangements are often focused on obtaining market power. *Fast-cycle* markets frequently involve entrepreneurial firms offering new goods or services with short life cycles that are imitated quickly. In these markets, a cooperative strategy is used to increase the speed of product development or market entry as well as to gain strategic competitiveness. The reasons for strategic alliances in each of these markets are listed in Table 9.1.

Firms in slow-cycle markets tend to seek entry into markets that are restricted or try to establish franchises in new markets. For instance, many firms in slow-cycle markets consider cooperative strategic alliances in emerging markets that usually have restricted entry. In emerging markets in Eastern Europe, Russia, Latin America, India, China, and elsewhere, utility firms from developed countries are strongly motivated to form strategic alliances with local partners. For example, as

Tacit collusion exists when several firms in an industry cooperate tacitly in reducing industry output below the potential competitive level, thereby increasing prices above the competitive level.

TABLE 9.1 *Reasons for Strategic Alliances by Market Type*

Market	Reason
Slow Cycle	■ Gain access to a restricted market
	■ Establish a franchise in a new market
	■ Maintain market stability (e.g., establishing standards)
Standard Cycle	■ Gain market power (reduce industry overcapacity)
	■ Gain access to complementary resources
	■ Overcome trade barriers
	■ Meet competitive challenge from other competitors
	■ Pool resources for very large capital projects
	■ Learn new business techniques
Fast Cycle	■ Speed up new goods or service entry
	■ Speed up new market entry
	■ Maintain market leadership
	■ Form an industry technology standard
	■ Share risky R&D expenses
	■ Overcome uncertainty

deregulation occurs in the United States, U.S. telecommunications firms have the opportunity to share in establishing a near-monopoly franchise in these emerging markets. Firms operating in emerging markets desire these alliances because they need the expertise and technological know-how that can be provided by firms from developed countries. France's Alcatel has established a strong market position through joint ventures with local partners in Mexico and China.[20] It is also a leading telecommunications equipment supplier in South Africa and other emerging markets.[21] Unisource, itself a joint venture among three national telecommunication monopolies (from the Netherlands, Sweden, and Switzerland), is launching a venture in Hungary. The partners, previously state monopolies, are Hungarian oil and gas company MOL rt. (21 percent), Hungarian railways MAV rt. (25 percent), and a technological research institute KFKI (5 percent). Called MKM-Tel, this venture "hopes to blanket the country with a fiber optic network by the end of 1999," initially providing telecom services to businesses.[22] This approach has also been used by utility firms participating in energy, electricity, and gas pipeline projects such as one in India arranged by Enron Corporation.

Cooperation, however, may be difficult to establish in slow-cycle markets. Near monopolies usually seek to be self-sustaining rather than be maintained jointly by partners. For example, as competition for telecommunication services emerges in Europe, a number of telecommunication firms that were previously state monopolies have sought to cooperate and form strategic alliances. The Global One Alliance, formed by France Telecom and Deutsche Telekom, which is also allied with Sprint, has had difficulties. In this joint venture, the two original partners often compete with one another and thereby pull in opposite directions. These partners have significantly different corporate cultures and technical infrastructures and are scrutinized frequently by government agencies. Both the Unisource alliance mention above and the now defunct British Telecom (BT) and MCI alliance have had similar difficulties.[23] On the other hand, deregulation and privatization (e.g., in Russia) create opportunities for establishing monopoly franchises in emerging market countries; slow-cycle market firms often seek to take advantage of these opportunities.

In standard-cycle markets, which are often large and oriented toward economies of scale (e.g., automobile and commercial aerospace), alliances are more likely to be between partners with complementary resources, capabilities, and core competencies (see Table 9.1). In these markets where economies of scale are important for competitive advantage or parity, large international alliances are useful because national markets may be too small to support the scale-efficient nature of the businesses. Therefore, the increasing globalization of markets presents opportunities to combine resources, capabilities, and competencies. This is a primary reason for alliances between automobile firms such as Ford and Mazda.

A new venture, Teledesic, based in Seattle, Washington, is a partnership between Craig McCaw and Bill Gates. McCaw and Gates want to circle the globe with 288 satellites supplying high-speed Internet access around the world. Other competing companies also see the potential of this service. Although the network speed is not as great as that proposed by Teledesic, Motorola has launched 5 of its intended 66 satellites for its Iridium system. Alcatel's network called SkyBridge is another threat to Teledesic because the company's subsidiary has experience in launching satellites. To counter this competition, Teledesic is partnering with Boeing, granting it the rights to launch Teledesic's satellites. Boeing is also conveniently headquartered in Seattle as is Gate's Microsoft. Teledesic's plan to resell the service through local country telephone companies to overcome regulatory barriers may also give it a competitive edge.[24]

Firms also may cooperate in standard-cycle markets to reduce industry overcapacity and pool resources to meet capital needs. Although mergers can help to overcome overcapacity, such as in the defense industry (e.g., between Martin Marietta and Lockheed to form Lockheed Martin), they are not forms of cooperative strategy (this is because merged firms do not remain independent). The European alliances in aerospace, for instance Airbus Industrie, have been designed to help the partners become more competitive with U.S. aerospace firms. Airbus aircraft are manufactured under a consortium composed of France's Aerospatiale and Germany's Daimler-Benz Aerospace, each with 37.9 percent of the business; British Aerospace, with 20 percent, and Spain's Construcciones Aeronauticas, with 4.2 percent.[25] Because most aerospace projects require huge capital outlays, pooling resources is often a rational step. Also, when a firm has a project that requires significant R&D investment, as in a new casting approach for a steel mill, it may be necessary to seek a partner to share in these outlays.[26] Finally, firms in standard-cycle markets also may form alliances to overcome trade barriers (see Chapter 8) and to learn new business techniques.

Fast-cycle markets, which have short product cycles, such as those among electronics firms, create incentives for cooperation because development, manufacture, and distribution of a new product can happen more quickly. Furthermore, cooperation can lead to the development of standard products in a high-technology market.[27] For instance, Sematech, a cooperative strategic alliance among multiple electronic and semiconductor firms, was quite important in establishing the adoption of the UNIX standard operating system for workstation computer producers.[28] Intel and Hewlett-Packard (HP) are collaborating to offer a new chip that would process data in 64-bit chunks instead of Intel's Pentium standard 32 bits. The chip would be able to run today's Window's software as well as programs written for HP's version of UNIX, without modification. This innovation portends to take the microprocessor revolution to a level that will allow competition with mainframes; Intel will be able to compete across the full spectrum of computing. This vision is reminiscent of the great expectations for the Power PC, a joint venture among IBM, Motorola, and Apple that was to propel the companies into a leadership position by combining the best of the PC with the best of Apple. The Power PC, however, failed to meet the expectations the partnering firms had of it.[29]

Uncertainty is also a rationale for increased cooperation among fast-cycle market firms. Cable television firms are collaborating on moving interactive television and Internet service through cable systems. As discussed in the opening case, Microsoft is trying to influence this movement's direction. The ultimate cable set-top box is likely to be the outcome of this activity. This device may bring together digital TV channels, interactive TV, and Internet access. Because the technology is still uncertain as to how to combine these technologies and because the expertise for each technology is held by a different company, strategic alliances are the preferred approach until a standard emerges. An amalgam of microprocessor and chip companies (Intel, Motorola, SGS Thompson, LSI Logic, and others), operating system and Internet software firms (Microsoft, Oracle, and Netscape), set-top manufacturers (NextLevel Systems, Scientific-Atlantic, Sony, and others), and cable and Internet service providers (AtHome Corp., America Online, TCI, NBC, and AT&T) are joining forces to establish this market.[30] This example suggests the uncertain and competitive nature of fast-cycle markets. As such, alliances between firms in fast-cycle markets also may be formed to share risky R&D investments, maintain market leadership, and develop an industry technology standard.[31]

These rationales are used to pursue strategy at different levels. The next section describes business-level cooperative strategies.

BUSINESS-LEVEL COOPERATIVE STRATEGIES

In this section, we explain four types of business-level cooperative strategies: complementary strategies, competition reduction strategies, competition response strategies, and uncertainty reduction strategies (see Figure 9.1). Following our dis-

FIGURE 9.1 *Types of Business- and Corporate-Level Strategic Alliances*

cussion of these four general types of business-level cooperative strategies is an assessment of the potential competitive advantages associated with each one.

Complementary Alliances

Complementary strategic alliances are designed to take advantage of market opportunities by combining partner firm assets in complementary ways to create new value.[32] As the race toward a standard in cable TV set-top boxes suggests, firms often form alliances because they lack certain resources or competencies held by other companies. As Figure 9.2 illustrates, there are two types of complementary strategic alliances, vertical and horizontal. The vertical complementary strategic alliance involves distribution, supplier, and outsourcing functions that are at different stages in the value chain. Benetton and Marks and Spencer are successful clothing firms that use alliances for suppliers and distributors of their products.

Many large U.S. firms have adopted a supply partnership approach that does not entail ownership positions. Traditionally large U.S. firms have preferred vertical integration (ownership of the supply source). This has been especially true in the U.S. automobile industry. In comparison, Japanese auto manufacturers use supply partnerships in a system of cooperation and competition between partner suppliers.[33] Performance of supply partnerships suggests that they provide an effective substitute for vertical integration.[34] Chrysler, as mentioned earlier, has been developing a keiretsu-type network of partners among its suppliers.[35] Just-in-time inventory systems for the suppliers and distributors require significant amounts of cooperation between partnering firms. Such systems can reduce costs for both parties and increase the solidarity of the relationship between manufacturers and their suppliers and distributors.

Outsourcing (discussed in Chapter 3) has been an important means of reducing costs and the basis for an increasing number of strategic alliances. For instance, many large firms such as Xerox, Delta Air Lines, and Kodak outsource their information technology (IT) function.[36] Sears, Ameritech, Lucent Technologies (an AT&T spin-off), and J.P. Morgan have outsourced their data and computer support as well.[37] For instance, J.P. Morgan has not only outsourced to reduce costs, but also to maintain currency. It outsourced its IT function to Pinnacle Alliance, a consortium of Andersen Consulting, AT&T Solutions, Computer Sciences Corporation, and Bell Atlantic Network Integration. J.P. Morgan's chairman, Douglas A. Warner III, explained, "Technology is critical to J.P. Morgan's success—so critical, and on so many specialized fronts, that no one firm can be a leader in all of them.... Teaming up with these firms will [increase] our ability to exploit new technologies, manage costs, and create competitive advantage."[38]

A growing number of traditional consulting firms have added managing outsourced functions such as IT because of their ability in these functional areas. For example, in addition to EDS, Andersen Consulting performs outsourced IT operations along with IT consulting. Magna International has increased its revenues by performing outsourced manufacturing and design work for the Big Three U.S. automakers.[39] Although Magna faces increased competition, it possesses the capabilities not only to manufacture goods effectively, but also to design high value-added goods. In fact, Magna can perform initial design, engineering, and development of whole vehicles and thus, has become a strong supplier. Significant outsourcing such as this might be of concern to traditional automakers because it could give their suppliers more power, resulting in in-

Complementary strategic alliances are designed to take advantage of market opportunities by combining partner firms assets in complementary ways to create new value.

319

FIGURE 9.2 *Vertical and Horizontal Complementary Strategic Alliances*

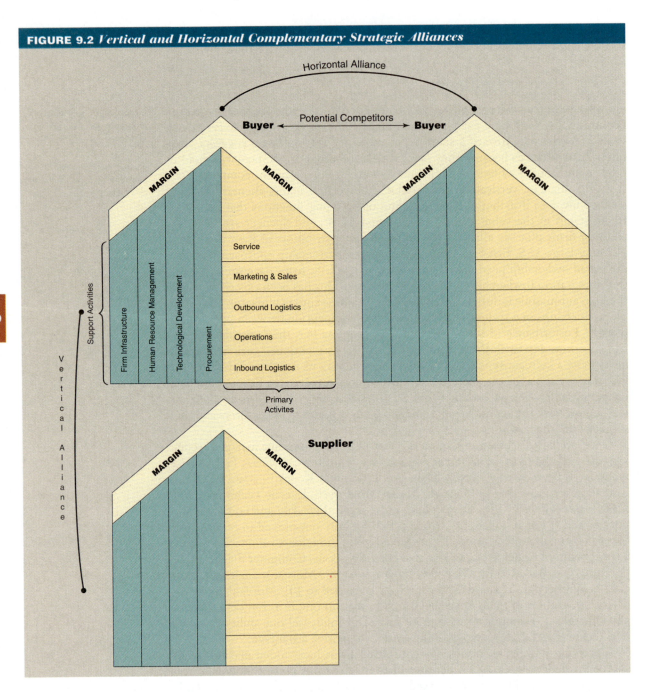

creased costs. As Chapter 3 indicates, outsourcing critical resources and capabilities can also harm the development and maintenance of a firm's core competence. A firm needs to ensure that critical functions are not outsourced in order to maintain its core competencies.[40] Also, partnerships with firms completing work that is outsourced may not be necessary when the purchase is nonstrategic. Because partnerships can be expensive, it may be better to manage the relationship using a free market approach.[41] Therefore, a balanced approach is required. A firm does not want to outsource a strategic competence nor enter into a costly partnership, so selectively choosing partners where they are critical to complement capabilities in suppliers is important.

Some firms that have market power use it in detrimental ways. Manufacturing suppliers and retailers, for example, have traditionally seen each other as adversaries. Wal-Mart's power over Rubbermaid may not be the most effective approach to foster a relationship with a supplier. If the balance of power changes, use of power can come back to haunt a company. Victims will seek ways to resist as Rubbermaid did in its relationship with Wal-Mart (see Chapter 2). Working together often encourages partners to provide greater value to customers than when they try to exploit their power. Understanding this dynamic has been the key to Marks and Spencer's success.[42] Research also shows that such "soft" relationship aspects are important to the long-term success of foreign exporters.[43]

Horizontal complementary strategic alliances (partners at the same stage in the value chain) are often used to increase the strategic competitiveness of the partners involved. Although horizontal chain alliances usually focus on long-term product and service technology development,[44] many competitors also form joint marketing agreements. Some of these agreements not only reduce costs but increase revenues and market power. As described in the Strategic Focus, European airlines have formed many joint marketing agreements inside and outside of Europe. For example, Lufthansa and Scandinavian Airlines have outlined a strategic alliance in Europe and extended their reach internationally.[45] Their Star Alliance system contains Lufthansa, UAL's United Airlines, Scandinavian Airlines, Air Canada and Thai Airways International. Similarly, Delta has extended its agreements with SwissAir, Sabena World, and Austrian Airlines in Europe.[46] Since these partnerships can increase market power substantially and reduce competition, there have been calls to regulate the international airline links and route allocations.[47]

STRATEGIC FOCUS

The Star Alliance System: An Example of a Horizontal Airline Alliance

In May 1997 Lufthansa Airlines announced its Star Alliance with UAL's United Airlines, Scandinavian Airlines, Air Canada, and Thai Airways International. More recently, the Star Alliance announced an attempt to broaden its bilateral agreements through negotiations with Asian Airlines Systems, Singapore Airlines, and Cathay Pacific Airways. This alliance has the potential to offer "seamless global service," and would be a competitive threat to the alliance sought by British Airways (BA) and AMR Corp.'s American Airlines. The BA/AMR alliance was unveiled a year before Star's system but to date, has failed to win regulatory approval.

The Star Alliance also threatens the established Global Alliance system composed of Delta, Swissair, Sabena, Austrian Airlines, and Singapore Airlines. Because Singapore Airlines is a part of the Swissair-Delta team, Global's network would be disrupted. Swissair has taken a 30 percent ownership position in Italian airline AirOne, Alitalia's leading Italian competitor. But this still leaves Delta without access to a major hub in Europe (major hubs include Rome, London, Amsterdam, and Frankfurt). If Global can establish an alliance with Air France, which is pending, then it may get entry to Paris.

Northwest and KLM Royal Dutch Airlines also have a competing network airline system. Although Alitalia had been pressured by some government factions to choose Air France because both airlines remain state run, it chose to link with KLM as a strategic partner and plans to have European hubs in Milan's Malpensa, Rome's Fiumicino, and Amsterdam's Schiphol airports. It will also allow Alitalia to have better global links and may lead to a three-way link with KLM and Northwest, which could save the airline partners several hundred million dollars within two years. The cooperative agreement could facilitate privatization of Alitalia, which the government scheduled for 1998. However, the agreement likely will cause Alitalia to renegotiate its alliance with Continental Airlines of the U.S. because of KLM's agreement with Northwest. Continental and Northwest have been in joint discussions for a potential partnership as well.

The instability among these alliances may cause partners to rethink their alliance plans. For instance, prior to the attempted agreement between American Airlines and British Airways, British Airways had a relationship with USAir. To form the British Air-American alliance, the former alliance with USAir had to be broken. If Singapore Air joins the Star Alliance, it likely will have to break its alliance with Swissair and Delta. As with the USAir alliance with BA, the changeover to the Star Alliance may create mistrust of forming future alliances with competitors. Similarly, Alitalia may have to renegotiate its alliance agreement with Continental. Another concern is the possibility of these alliances creating monopolistic power. This potential has been the reason the British Air-American Airlines alliance has been unable, to date, to win regulators' approval. Regulators have demanded that the two carriers give away, rather than sell, 350 valuable slots a week, mostly at the all-important London Heathrow hub. Although American may have to retreat to a simple co-sharing agreement rather than a more comprehensive alliance system, the firm probably will execute an alliance that is allowable under the current regulations.

SOURCE: T.Y. Jones, 1998, Musical chairs, *Forbes*, January 12, 60–63; AP-Dow Jones News Service, 1997, Swissair to take 30% stake in Italy's AirOne, *Wall Street Journal* Interactive edition, http://www.wsj.com, December 30; D. Ball, 1997, Alitalia may be ready for takeoff, profit, KLM link signal rebound, *Wall Street Journal* Interactive edition, http://www.wsj.com, December 22; AP-Dow Jones News Service, 1997, Alitalia/Continental–2: Few $100M Saving in two years, *Wall Street Journal* Interactive edition, http://www.wsj.com, December 19; C. Goldsmith, 1997, Lufthansa looks to broaden its alliances, *Wall Street Journal*, September 15, A18; H. Banks, 1997, Trans-Atlantic headache, *Forbes*, September 8, 165.

A few observations may be useful about horizontal versus vertical alliance situations. The perception of partner trustworthiness may be different in horizontal alliances where the potential partners are competitors and vertical alliances where the partners are buyers and suppliers. For example, the relationship that Chrysler is developing with its supplier network may be built on trustworthiness that has evolved through previous business transactions.

Horizontal alliances, formed among competitors, may have less of a basis for trust. For example, as mentioned earlier, although Nucor Steel and USX Corporation formed an alliance to produce a new steel-making process, the perceptions of trustworthiness may be relatively low in the relationship because the two companies are former competitors. Similarly, the level of trust among airlines may be quite low because they continue to compete, even with current partners, on many routes. It is not likely that horizontal alliances, therefore, will prove long lasting. This seems to be clear in the airline alliance systems discussed in the Strategic Focus. The airline partnerships appear to be quite tenuous and opportunistic. Such alliances, although they do provide scale advantages, do not appear to be fertile ground for trust and long-standing partnerships.

Competition Reduction Strategies

In the heat of rivalry, many firms may seek to avoid destructive or excessive competition. One means of avoiding such competition is tacit collusion or mutual forbearance (see Chapter 6). This may be accomplished in some markets through cartels such as OPEC that seek to manage the price and output of companies (e.g., oil companies in member countries) in a specific industry.

In the mid-1990s, Russia had a huge surplus of aluminum. When these aluminum manufacturing firms were privatized, they began to export the metal in large quantities, which caused the world price to drop precipitously. These Russian producers undercut the western price by as much as 50 percent. The Aluminum Association, a trade association of aluminum manufacturers, met and called for the United States to file anti-dumping trade charges, claiming that Russia was "dumping" aluminum below market rates. The Russians argued that they needed foreign hard currency to deal with a difficult transitional economy; to cut them off from foreign markets would create a difficult political problem. As a result, there was a meeting by government and industry officials in Brussels in 1994 that resulted in a government pact calling for "voluntary" cuts in production. Although the politicians claimed this was not a cartel, it had the same result: production cuts to sustain a world price.[48] Aluminum prices in the late 1990s increased. Prices rose from near 50 cents per pound to 65 in 1996 and 72 in 1997.[49]

Japan's economy entails a number of entrenched cartels and significant collusion. Even though economic and political forces have been working against cartels and collusion, approximately 50 percent of the manufacturing industries in Japan engage in some form of price fixing. Because some cartels date back to the 1600s, such anticompetitive activity in Japan is accepted and tolerated, which makes it difficult to change cartels and collusive practices. Although the situation is complex, Eastman Kodak argues that cartels and collusion have given Japanese competitors excessive returns against which it is difficult for international firms to compete.[50] More recently, some have argued that problems suffered by Asian economies such as South Korea have resulted because large Korean chaebols, industrial groups mentioned in Chapters 5 and 7, have followed collusive practices similar to the Japanese keiretsus. The basic problem is that cartels have restricted output, while governments restrict imports, and as a result, the countries' currencies have been devalued. The cartels have proven to be problematic for country competitiveness in a global economy.[51]

There is an opposing view. Some claim Japan's firms are less profitable because domestically they are hypercompetitive against each other.[52] For instance, Japan has 10 car firms compared to three competing in the United States. These firms engage in intense competitive battles. If, however, this is harmful, why do the 10 auto firms continue to survive? In the United States, they would have been forced into bankruptcy. Part of the answer lies in Japan's industrial policies, such as lifetime employment.

Even more telling is the comparison between South Korea and Taiwan, two "Asian tigers." Industrial policy in South Korea has placed economic development in the hands of the large family-dominated conglomerates or chaebols. In Taiwan, investment decisions are more decentralized because small and medium-sized firms dominate economic development. Although the large chaebols have developed economies of scale and scope in manufacturing, and even moved into more complex and technologically sophisticated industries such as auto, steel, and semi-conductors, their image is not that of leading edge technology firms.[53] Taiwan, on the other hand, has many small firms that often collaborate with one another such as in electronic components, computer peripherals, and machine tools. In the recent downturn among Asian tigers, Taiwan's approach to economic development appears to have faired much better than South Korea's. The close chaebol-government ties may have led Korean companies to make less effective investments because of government guarantees. More capital was in the hands of a larger number of investors in Taiwan, resulting in less collusion and superior investment decisions. For instance, as with Japan, Korea has too many automobile firms; it has five offerings through the chaebols when its economy can really only support two, even with an export-oriented strategy.[54] The bottom line also provides impetus for this interpretation; the average return on equity was 14 percent in Taiwan versus 4 percent in South Korea in 1996.[55]

Reduction of competition also can be accomplished through industry trade organizations or government policy that is designed to reduce excessive competition, as the aluminum example illustrates above.[56] Some firms follow pricing rules that have developed without direct coordination among competitors. For instance, banks have set rules for lowering or raising mortgage or prime interest rates. This keeps the pricing system for interest rates coordinated among competitors.

Sometimes firms use direct collusion. Consider the ADM example where managers were accused of trying to fix prices on farm commodities with other competitors.[57] Similarly, Toys 'R' Us, the dominant toy retailer, was found to be in violation of federal trade laws by colluding with toy manufacturers to not sell popular toy lines to its chief competitors, warehouse clubs such as Price/Costco or Sam's Club. By getting toy manufacturers to refuse to sell their products to these large powerful retailers, the price could be higher for toy manufacturers and Toys

Toys 'R' Us was found to be in violation of federal trade laws because it was alleged to be in collusion with toy manufacturers to prevent them from selling popular toys to its competitors—primarily warehouse clubs. By keeping manufacturers from selling to other retailers, Toys 'R' Us could charge higher prices.

'R' Us, even though Toys 'R' Us argued that they have to sell toys year round and not just during hot selling cycles.[58]

Competition Response Strategies

As Chapter 5 suggests, some firms enter into strategic alliances to respond to competitors' major strategic actions. For example, as competition for telecommunications services in emerging markets has mushroomed, alliance formation in these areas has increased. Mexico is a country in which these developments are being witnessed. When MCI formed an alliance in Mexico with Grupo Financiero Banamex in January 1994, it was followed by other strategic alliances among competitors to battle for this emerging market. Specifically, AT&T and Grupo Alpha and Sprint and Texmex formed partnerships in November and December 1994, respectively.[59] The airline alliances mentioned in the Strategic Focus are generally complementary, but may also be considered competition response alliances. Susan Snider, director of international alliances for Delta Air Lines, said: "Alliances are not an option anymore. The only way you can fill in the voids is through global partnerships."[60] As businesses go global, travelers are demanding more seamless travel. If one airline can provide it through an alliance system, others are forced to form similar alliances.

DirecTV, a unit of General Motor's Hughes Electronics subsidiary, is the dominant provider of direct satellite broadcasting with 3 million subscribers. Primestar Partners, a joint venture among a consortium of cable television operators, has approximately 2 million subscribers. EchoStar Communications is in the third position with 1 million subscribers, but it is the fastest growing. This competition has forced the price of satellite receiver systems down from $699 to $199, with some discounting even as low as $100, through offers of free installation ($100 value), free pay-per-view movie coupons or do-it-yourself installation kits. Since DirecTV's breakup with AT&T, it has tried to deal with its competitors by following two strategies. First, the firm is trying to offer exclusive programming to its subscribers by forming partnership agreements with media producers. For instance, it has an agreement with Time Warner to produce a weekly music series, resembling MTV programming, exclusively for DirecTV subscribers. Second, the firm is exploring alliances with Bell firms to continue to expand its subscriber base. For instance, SBC, a San Antonio based Bell system, now owns Pacific Telesis Group and thereby has access to the Southern California market. An alliance between DirecTV and SBC would give SBC an entry into the video market, which it has been hesitant to enter. Alternatively, an alliance with Bell Atlantic would support Chairman Raymond Smith's ardent strategy for the video market. Also, Bell Atlantic recently increased its market power through the acquisition of Nynex Corp.[61]

Uncertainty Reduction Strategies

Strategic alliances also can be used to hedge against risk and uncertainty.[62] For instance, the recent changes in regulation of the telecommunications industry have led to a significant number of alliances. Although President Clinton signed the 1996 Telecommunications Act into law in February, the Federal Communications Commission did not set up its rules implementing the law until August. A New Year's Eve ruling in 1997 struck down the telecommunication industries' rules of competition in a ruling by a U.S. judge in Texas. The result came from a suit filed by GTE and the local Bell system contesting pricing and especially the restriction on offering long-distance service in their home territories.[63] This legislation and subsequent court battles have created significant uncertainty for the firms involved.

Similarly, in Europe, a law implementing deregulation went into effect on January 1, 1998. The law dismantled inefficient state monopolies and opened a $130 billion market for competition. To deal with the uncertainty involved, a number of firms formed alliances in the United States, Europe, and throughout the world. Examples of these alliances are explored in the Strategic Focus.

STRATEGIC FOCUS

Alliances in Both the U.S. and Europe Help Firms Overcome Uncertainty in the Telecommunications Industry

AT&T recently announced its intended acquisition of Teleport for approximately $11.3 billion. This strategic action is a way of dealing with the uncertainty associated with telecommunication deregulation and subsequent regulatory court battles. Robert Annunziata helped to create Teleport Communications when he left AT&T in 1983. He went to work for Merrill Lynch as an internal satellite communications manager, but he eventually told his new employer to abandon its satellite strategy and instead build a fiber-optic network to bypass the Bell monopolies and save a significant amount on their phone bills. This advice was followed, and the effort ultimately evolved into Teleport, a provider of telecommunications services to business customers. Teleport recruited the United Nations and several large banking firms as its first major business customers. In the early 1990s, cable companies realized that they could partnership with Teleport using their cable systems to install fiber-optic cable.

In 1992, Comcast, Continental Cablevision, Cox Communications, and Tele-communications joined in a partnership to acquire Teleport. Later, Continental Cablevision, which had been acquired by U.S. West, sold its Teleport shares to get federal approval for the accord. Teleport has now become the nation's largest independent, competitive local carrier. Because laying fiber-optic and developing a local business is very capital-intensive, AT&T chose to make this acquisition as an entry into the local market.

Teleport's cable partners originally entered this market as a strategic option because it was unclear what would happen with their businesses with deregulation pending. Various cable companies have found it difficult and costly to enter the telephone business. For instance, Teleport's cable partners also have a separate wireless-phone partnership with Sprint. Maintaining the relationship with AT&T and Sprint will allow Teleport's partners to watch what happens in the industry from the sidelines. It also gives them the option of returning to the telecommunications industry more aggressively when cable upgrades allow transmission of an array of voice, data, and video services to consumers nationwide.

Teleport's partners are not only dealing with the uncertainty of the regulatory environment, but also with technological uncertainty. At some point, cable lines will have greater capability for two-way communications, which is less flawed and expensive. Furthermore, the Bell firms and long distance companies such as AT&T and MCI have more to lose in the telecommunications business. They can let the telecommunications giant AT&T determine how to handle the local phone service and then enter at a later date when there is less uncertainty.

In Europe, the large telecommunication monopolies have been confronting the uncertainty of the regulatory change with alliances as well. As of January 1, 1998, a competitor from any country in the Common Market could offer traditional phone services to all customers in any other country. It could do this by either renting part of the country monopoly provider's network or by building its own new network. In anticipation of this, several giant telecommunication monopoly providers formed alliances as mentioned earlier in the chapter. Unisource is an alliance between the Netherlands' Koninklijke PTT, Sweden's Telia, and Swiss Telecom PTT. British Telecom and MCI had allied prior to the MCI acquisition by WorldCom. WorldCom's international arm has planned to sink $3 billion into building a pan-European network. Although Spain won the opportunity to postpone deregulation until 1999, it recently changed its mind and is offering some alternatives to Telefonica de Espana's monopoly. Retevision SA is the second firm offering international and interprovincial telephone service in Spain. A third operator's license has been approved by the Spanish government. The Global One alliance of Deutsche Telekom, France Telecom, and Sprint has expressed an interest as has Cable Europa, a cable company controlled by General Electric, Capital Bank of America, and Callahan Associates. Furthermore, the Retevision enterprise is supported by a consortium led by the Spanish Utility Empresa Nationalde Electricidad and Telecom Italia, which outbid Global One. The Spanish utility and Italian telecom consortium acquired 70 percent of the Retevision franchise.

SOURCE: L. Cauley, 1998, AT&T deal offers three cable giants some wiggle room, *Wall Street Journal*, January 9, B1, B16; S. N. Mehta, 1998, Why Ma Bell called Teleport CEO, *Wall Street Journal*, January 9, B1, B7; K. Pope and E. Ramstead, 1998, HDTV sets: Too pricey too late? *Wall Street Journal*, January 7, B1, B11; In the shark pond, 1998, *The Economist*, January 3, 59–60; J. R. Wilke and S. N. Mehta, 1998, U.S. plans immediate appeal of Telecom ruling, *Wall Street Journal*, January 2, 3; C. Vitzthum, 1997, Retevision will offer services charging Telefonica's might, *Wall Street Journal* Interactive Edition, http://www.wsj.com, December 31; G. Naik, 1997, Firms vie to ring in new year in Europe, *Wall Street Journal*, December 18, A18; J. Brinkley, 1997, U.S. and Europe in battle over digital TV, *The New York Times* on the Web, http://www.nytimes.com, August 25.

Although much of the uncertainty leading to the formation of these alliances has been caused by deregulation in the United States and Europe, technology and anxiety regarding potential demand also leads to multiple alliances. The technical standards for high definition TV (HDTV), which will use digital technology, have not been set. A number of alliance systems have been created to establish and market technological standards. Furthermore, broadcasters and TV set manufacturers are unsure of the demand for digital transmission programming.

A number of alliances have been formed to share the risk and uncertainty associated with the market potential of HDTV. The Grand Alliance system was formed in the United States. by AT&T, General Instruments, the Massachusetts Institute of Technology, Thompson Consumer Electronics, and the Sarnoff Research Center and others to help create a standard to deal with the technological uncertainty. Realizing that, ultimately, digital television is expected to be worth billions of dollars in sales to broadcasters and consumers around the world, European firms have also formed an alliance called Digital Video Broadcast (DVB). Although the U.S. alliance system was created before the European one, the Europeans have completed their work and marketing started about the same time that the deployment of the Grand Alliance system was set to begin marketing. Even though neither system is set completely, both alliances are competing in the world marketplace for countries seeking to establish digital television broadcast systems and equipment.[64]

Another uncertainty concerns the broadcasters who haven't decided when to offer high-definition programs, which require special digital transmitters and eventually upgraded cameras. It is a chicken and egg problem. Broadcasters simply don't know how many viewers will have the necessary receiving equipment, and TV makers haven't decided when to launch the sets, uncertain as to when programming will begin. Hitachi and Thompson Consumer Electronics have jointly produced a real projection HDTV that can transmit digital video. Samsung, Sony, and Zenith all are demonstrating different types of receiving and broadcasting equipment, most through partnership arrangements.

In summary, uncertainty can come from a number of sources: regulatory, technological, and demand. Regardless of the source of uncertainty, it leads to firms working together to manage the uncertainty in a collaborative way through strategic alliances. These systems of alliances, however, are often short lived once the uncertainty disappears.

Assessment of Competitive Advantage

Although all alliances are undertaken for strategic purposes, it does not mean that they will realize complementary assets, achieve strategic competitiveness, and earn above-average returns. For instance, alliances to reduce competition are more likely to achieve competitive parity than competitive advantage. In fact, they are usually undertaken to blunt or slow other competitive strategic or tactical moves, which more than likely results in only average returns. An alliance that is formed by a firm lagging behind its competitors for the purpose of improving its capabilities is also likely to achieve no more than competitive parity.

Complementary alliances, however, are more likely to create competitive advantage, achieve strategic competitiveness, and earn above-average returns. When potential complementary capabilities between two firms are realized, there is usually a cost saving advantage or creation of new capabilities or both, which enhances performance. Furthermore, when a firm is able to enter a market quicker through alliance activities than it could otherwise, it may gain at least a short-term competitive advantage. Many supplier and distributor agreements are of this nature.

Uncertainty reduction strategies, however, are likely to realize only average returns because they attempt to buffer uncertainty and rely, to some degree, on luck. This type of alliance increases the number of options a firm has and thus increases its flexibility and ultimate survival.[65] As such, these alliances are important because without them, a firm may experience below-average returns. For example, earlier entrants into the market have established relationships with key firms and, thus, may create stronger barriers to the entry of new competitors.

CORPORATE-LEVEL COOPERATIVE STRATEGIES

Strategic alliances designed to facilitate product and/or market diversification are called **corporate-level cooperative strategies**.

Diversifying strategic alliances allow a firm to expand into new product or market areas without an acquisition.

Strategic alliances designed to facilitate product and/or market diversification (see Chapter 6) are called **corporate-level cooperative strategies**. The three types of corporate-level cooperative strategies are diversifying, synergistic, and franchising (see Figure 9.1).

Diversifying strategic alliances allow a firm to expand into new product or market areas without an acquisition. Large diversified firms generally seek growth through mergers and acquisitions, as explained in Chapters 6 and 7. However, two firms that do not want to merge can still achieve diversified growth by forming a strategic alliance.[66]

South Korea's Samsung Group is a large conglomerate or chaebol that uses strategic alliances to expand into new markets first. Currently, Samsung is investing $4.5 billion to develop cars with Nissan. Samsung Aerospace is also heading a strategic alliance with the Chinese government and aerospace contractors to develop a 100-seat jetliner by the end of the decade. Additionally, Samsung negotiated with Boeing and Airbus Industrie of Europe to buy three 100- to 200-seat commercial jetliners. Some speculate that it is trying to create a domestic airline that would compete with Korean Air and Asiana Airlines. Samsung is also a part owner of movie producer DreamWorks SKG and has had discussions with Disney about a possible multimedia alliance.[67] The late 1990s' financial crisis throughout much of Asia, however, has Samsung pondering the wisdom of such far flung investments.[68] Further analyses may cause Samsung to change some of its investment plans.

Joint ventures have some similar strategic characteristics to mergers and acquisitions. In the United States, legal restrictions can constrain the ability of firms to make major acquisitions. Historically, the U.S. government has tried to prevent horizontal acquisitions that created excessive market power. Such acquisitions may be prohibited because they are viewed as fostering explicit collusion. Acquisitions lack the flexibility that is accommodated by strategic alliances. As mentioned earlier, strategic alliances are similar to financial options that create flexibility and reduce risk when moving into uncertain markets.[69] Large diversified firms may adopt diversifying strategic alliances to increase flexibility and reduce risk. Firms also may use a strategic alliance as an experimental step prior to acquisition.[70] If the alliance proves successful, the firm can then acquire its alliance partner.

If potential business partners have unique resources or capabilities that cannot be imitated easily by competitors, strategic alliances may be more efficient than acquisitions. These characteristics may be lost in the acquisition process. To buy them on the open market may be very expensive because of their unique qualities and value.[71]

Additionally, some firms are using alliances as a preliminary step to ease the difficulty of other forms of restructuring.[72] For instance, Daimler-Benz Aerospace (DASA) has had significant performance problems, given the downturn of the defense industry. DASA and Thomson CSF, a French missile component and armament sales firm, formed a joint venture known as TDA. This alliance, along with others, will allow DASA and Thomson to circumvent local politics in both countries. It will provide more flexibility to consolidate operations and alleviate excess capacity in the defense and aerospace industries.[73]

Synergistic strategic alliances create joint economies of scope between two or more firms. They are similar to horizontal strategic alliances at the business level, but they create synergy across multiple functions or multiple businesses between partner firms. Two firms might, for example, create joint research and manufacturing facilities that they both use to their advantage and thus attain economies of scope without a merger. Sony Corporation shares its know-how through strategic alliances with multiple small firms. A key reason Sony forms these strategic alliances is to acquire commercially useful economies of scope without incurring the costs of acquisitions.[74]

As mentioned in the opening case, the main corporate strategy of Microsoft historically has been its strategic use of partnerships. Microsoft got its start through

Synergistic strategic alliances create joint economies of scope between two or more firms.

329

a strategic alliance with IBM, which had been reluctant through the 1970s to use collaboration. In launching its entry into personal computers, IBM again began to rely on outside partners: Intel for logic chips, Microsoft for operating system software, Epson for peripherals, and a number of Asian vendors for other components.[75] Its success with the IBM partnership allowed Microsoft to improve its competition with Apple. With Windows and Windows 95, it achieved a strong market reliance on PC manufacturer partnerships. Although a collaboration to develop OS/2, an alternative operating system, with IBM failed, Microsoft's collaborations with PC producers succeeded; Windows 95 and soon Windows 98 is the operating system sold with virtually every new PC. It also has used collaboration to establish its Internet browser, Explorer, and to pursue a multimedia strategy with a joint venture with NBC called MSNBC, along with other strategic alliances (e.g., DreamWorks SKG). The centerpiece of Bill Gates' strategy is to take large chunks of the corporate market by dominating the server and mainframe world through Windows NT and BackOffice software.

Windows NT is directed at running the corporate network to which the desktop is connected. BackOffice is the suite of applications that runs on NT. Most client server networks have been run on UNIX, an operating system invented at AT&T's Bell Labs. Microsoft approached Bell Labs about developing and jointly standardizing the operating system, but Bell Labs chose to go it alone. As a result, sales of UNIX-based machines have been replaced by NT-based machines. Also, the dominant network software firm, Novell, faces stiff competition as well because NT incorporates the networking software as part of the operating system. This has been possible because Intel has produced chips (e.g., Pentium Pro chips) that are competitive with chips that run servers produced by competitor firms. This has allowed traditional PC partners such as Compaq and Hewlett-Packard to produce NT-based machines. The acceptance of NT has contributed to precipitous declines for some firms such as Silicone Graphics (see the Strategic Focus in Chapter 3).

In part, NT has been more profitable than Windows 95 because it is being sold by larger computer firms, which have higher margins, in partnership with Microsoft. Digital Equipment has also developed a strategic partnership with Microsoft. Even though Digital has had difficulties, Microsoft signed the deal because it needs large firms to serve corporate clientele. Often when a large server network system is sold, the selling corporation leaves a representative on site to serve the client. Microsoft, coming from the PC market, has no extensive sales service capability. It needs Digital even with its problems. It has HP. It could use the help of IBM. Although IBM is working with Microsoft because of the potential business it might lose otherwise, it is reluctant to form a strategic partnership because IBM sells competing software, Notes (former Lotus Notes, e-mail and networking software) and DB2 (database software). Sun, at this point, continues to focus on high-end UNIX-based servers, although it has an entry level machine that competes strongly with Intel-based machines running Windows NT.[76]

Besides microcomputers and servers, Microsoft has created Windows CE, an operating system for smaller systems such as hand-held computers or palmtops. It can also be used in a number of mobile communicators and other gadgets. For instance, Microsoft is hoping to have Windows CE become the standard system for TV set-top boxes to bring the Internet to the television. To achieve this, Microsoft has purchased part ownership in Comcast, the fourth-largest cable company, for $1 billion. In addition, as mentioned earlier, Microsoft has also attempted to form an alliance with TCI. Alternatively, Microsoft has acquired WebTV for $425 million, which delivers interactive content to ordinary television sets. Thus, a small $299 box will allow a television to be used to view and interact with Internet Web sites.[77]

Small firms also partner with Microsoft because such partnerships bring market credibility. Commerce One announced a "strategic relationship" with Microsoft in electronic commerce, that is, business-to-business electronic commerce software. Once SAP, a popular network software producer, understood that the relationship with Microsoft was clear, Commerce One got an equity investment from SAP.[78]

Microsoft's successes at partnerships have brought inordinate market power to the firm and Bill Gates in particular. There is concern that Microsoft will dominate the industry as well as exert political influence. Although Gates hired nine lobbying and law firms with offices in Washington, D.C., Microsoft recently lost its battle to have Internet Explorer bundled with Windows 95.[79] Daniel Goodhope, a special assistant in the Texas Attorney General's office, likened Microsoft's form of collaboration as similar to the fictional Star Trek race called the Borg. Part flesh and part machine, the Borg beings prowl the universe conquering other races. Goodhope uses the Borg as a metaphor for Microsoft: "Resistance is futile. You will be assimilated."[80] Gates' claim is that being a software company, he simply wants to move into every business where software matters.

Microsoft has a corporate strategy of strategic alliances with partnerships across many businesses and functions. However, its dominant partnerships in operating systems are synergistic across all its businesses and functions. While this strategy has given Microsoft extraordinary market power that it shares with its partners, it has also brought on the scrutiny of the U.S. government, spurred by other industry participants.

Franchising is another alternative to diversification that may be considered a cooperative strategy based on contracting.[81] Franchising provides an alternative to vertical integration and has been a popular strategy.[82] It allows relatively strong centralized control and facilitates knowledge transfer without significant capital investment.[83] Approximately one-third of all retail sales in the United States and Canada are made through franchised outlets.[84] Firms often diversify because focus on a single business is risky (i.e., potential for loss of demand for goods and services without counterbalancing demand from other markets). Service firms may diversify some of their business and financial risk by creating franchises. Many hotels and fast food restaurants (e.g., Hilton Hotels and McDonald's) use this cooperative alternative to diversify into new markets. Real estate firms, such as Century 21, also create nationwide chains through franchising. Examples of other firms that pursue franchising include Charles Schwab in financial services, HCA/Columbia in hospitals, and Service Corporation International in mortuaries. Franchising reduces financial risk because franchisers invest their own capital to expand the service. This capital investment motivates franchisers to perform well by perpetuating the quality, standards, and reputation of the original business. As such, franchising may provide growth at less risk than diversification. Of course, the franchising firm loses some control, but the franchise contract usually provides for performance and quality audits.

In real estate many of the large referral networks, which have served as referral services for local brokers, are losing market share to firms that are wholly owned or that have strong national or international alliance systems. As corporations have

331

Franchising is another alternative to diversification that may be considered a cooperative strategy based on contracting.

downsized and outsourced, there is a stronger demand for property management services and also a stronger relationship with client companies. As firms expand globally, there is also a need to offer services in more international areas such as Hong Kong. Thus, national chains with strong affiliations both domestically and internationally are providing a broader range of service than has been offered traditionally by national or international networks. Strong relationships are being created as the local independent company broker systems appear to be breaking down. The networks of affiliate independent brokers can work, but they need to assume the appearance of a corporation. Colliers International Property Consultants has developed such as system. It can offer broker partners a 12-person research department that a purely local firm could not support.[85]

Motives for Corporate-Level Cooperative Strategies

Because corporate-level cooperative strategies involve not only motives for obtaining competitive advantage but also for reducing risk, assessment of the effects of these motives is essential (for a related discussion, see motives for diversification in Chapter 6). Managers have incentives to increase sales when performance is low as well as to increase their salaries by expanding the size of the business. Alliances can help managers achieve both of these objectives similar to diversification. For example, they can expand the size of the business and thus increase their compensation. Unless a corporation has strong corporate governance to guard against managers using strategic alliances inappropriately (see Chapter 10 regarding governance mechanisms), they may be used for purposes that do not enhance a firm's strategic competitiveness. Managers, for example, may use the intricacy of alliance networks to enrich their own position in the firm. Alliances built on a CEO's contacts and relationships may be lost if that person leaves the company. He or she may be the only one who effectively understands the complex web of relationships existing in the corporate network of alliance partners.[86] These understandings can entrench the manager, making dismissal difficult.

Alternatively, the capability to manage a large number of strategic alliances may exist in very few firms and may be difficult for competitors to imitate. In this light, managing a cooperative network may result in another competitive advantage for the firm. Research shows that firms capable of learning from their collaborations develop know-how that can be distinguished from mere experience with strategic alliances.[87] Although networks of alliances can be used to diversify the firm, to create competitive advantage, and possibly to enrich managers' positions, the cost and difficulty of managing them should not be underestimated. Monitoring these relationships and maintaining cordial and trusting relations require time and effort. Such costs should be considered before entering into numerous strategic alliances.[88]

INTERNATIONAL COOPERATIVE STRATEGIES

In general, multinational corporations have achieved higher performance than firms operating domestically.[89] Also, as domestic economics have grown more global, the importance of international cooperative strategies has increased.[90] Often, firms that develop distinct resources and capabilities in their home markets may be able to leverage them by making direct investments in international markets as opposed to licensing or exporting their products. Cooperative strategies (e.g., international strategic alliances) are a common mode for making such investments in international markets.

Firms can create more corporate flexibility and extend or leverage their core competencies in new geographic regions by developing international strategic alliances.[91] However, such alliances are more complex and risky than domestic ones. For example, there is a higher failure rate for international joint ventures than for international greenfield ventures (establishing a wholly owned subsidiary).[92] Although strategic alliances allow partner firms to share risks, and thus are less risky for each individual partner than a greenfield venture, they are difficult to manage. The need to coordinate and cooperate to share skills and knowledge requires significant processing of information on the part of all partner managers.[93] Where significant demands are placed on partners' managers to achieve quick returns, there is less alliance success. Thus, while international cooperative strategies can have significant positive outcomes, care must be taken when choosing the particular partners, managers, and ventures to ensure success.[94]

As indicated in Chapter 8, some countries regard local ownership as an important national policy objective. In general, western governments, though nervous about foreign ownership in some industries, are less concerned than many other governments. India, on the other hand, strongly prefers to license local companies as opposed to foreign ownership and joint ventures with a local firm or wholly foreign-owned subsidiaries. Another example is South Korea, whose government increased the ceiling on foreign investment in South Korean firms from 15 to 18 percent in 1996.[95] Accordingly, in some countries, managers may not have the full range of entry mode choices discussed in Chapter 8. Investment by foreign firms may only be allowed through cooperative agreements such as a joint venture. This is often true in newly industrialized and developing countries with emerging markets. Joint ventures can be helpful to foreign partners because the local partner can provide information about local markets, capital sources, and management skills.

As trade agreements have proliferated globally, the rules of competition have changed and, therefore, cooperative strategies have likewise changed. More than 100 countries are signatories to the World Trade Organization (WTO) and the International Monetary Fund (IMF). With other treaties, such as the North American Free Trade Agreement (NAFTA), only two or three countries are involved. Accordingly, the strategies have changed to adjust to these agreements. In the European Union, for instance, firms have increased their direct control over subsidiaries and use Pan-European strategies rather than individual country strategies. In other words, these firms establish a strategy for all of their operations in Europe as opposed to a different strategy for each European country. However, in general, the trade agreements spawned more cooperative ventures between partners from those countries that were a party to the agreement. These trade agreements promote freer trade and therefore increase the opportunity for more foreign direct investment, at least from firms headquartered in countries covered by the agreement. As illustrated by the Strategic Focus on telecommunication firms, this trend is occurring in the European Union and in North America and also in Asia through the Asia-Pacific Economic Cooperation Forum (APEC).

As mentioned earlier, joint ventures are more prominent in emerging markets. For instance, international joint ventures represent 52 percent of the value of new manufacturing ventures in China.[96] Additionally, since 1985, alliances between U.S. and international firms have been growing at a 27 percent annual rate across all industries.[97] This growth occurs even though many alliances are eventually replaced by mergers or acquisitions.[98]

Strategic Intent of Partner

With the increased number of international cooperative strategies comes a greater variance in the partner's strategic intent. For example, a partner may intend to learn a technology and use it later to become a competitor. Thus, it is important to assess potential partners' strategic intent in forming cooperative relationships.[99]

Emerging economies, such as Russia's, have a distinct need for foreign investment and technology transfer. Although approximately 75 percent of the Russian economy has been privatized, there has been no large influx of capital. The Russian process was intended more to establish private property rights. As the nature of the Russian economy changes, there is a dire need for new investment, but the Russians are wary of foreign investment in their country.[100] They are quite sensitive about the strategic intent of foreign partners who want to establish cooperative agreements and operations in their country, although this is beginning to change with more market-oriented and entrepreneurial managers.[101]

A recent partnership, for example, between Khanty-Mansiyskneftegazgeologia (KMNNG), a privatized Russian oil exploration company, and UPC, a private Delaware-based oil exploration and production company, could be an example for other international alliances between Russian and western partners. The interests of each partner have been better aligned than most typical 50/50 Russian joint ventures. In previous oil industry joint ventures, the Russian partner desires quick cash and the foreign partner wants ownership of reserves to bolster its balance sheet. Russian partners do not want to cede control and the foreign partner does not want to bankroll them. In contrast, UPC and KMNGG fused themselves into a complicated cash and stock transaction. Technically, KMNGG is an 86 percent owned subsidiary of UPC named KMOC. With this structure, it was possible to win a $55 million private placement investment. Gerard de Geer, a Swedish businessman who founded a Moscow-based Brunswick investment bank, which is a large shareholder, has become the chairman of KMOC. He has the deciding vote on all business deals. This arrangement was a key in winning foreign investment. Perhaps the deal would not have taken place if it were in the hands of tradition-bound oil industry executives from both sides.[102]

Some countries, and the firms within them, have distinct needs for the transfer of technology to facilitate their economic development. Oftentimes, companies in these countries, especially in Asia, have an organizational culture that promotes and facilitates learning. These firms then have the strategic intent in cooperative arrangements of learning from their partner(s). Firms that have different strategic intents may realize a loss of the competitive advantage of their core competence if their alliance partner learns it; therefore, technology and knowledge transfer must be controlled carefully.[103]

On the other hand, Texas Instruments (TI) and Hitachi began conducting joint research in 1988 and incrementally expanded their relationship. During the early part of the relationship, managers from the two firms had to bridge cultural differences. For example, there were significant differences in decision-making processes. TI used a common American approach in which managers held a meeting to discuss an issue, then spent time brainstorming, followed by a decision. Hitachi executives, on the other hand, more commonly held informal discussions and came to a decision prior to the meeting. The actual meeting was used to ratify the final decision. Over time, the two companies learned to work together effectively and eventually developed a joint venture to produce memory chips. Although it took almost six months of negotiations, it was decided that the new venture would sell its chips to both companies at the same time and Hitachi and TI would then be free to sell the chips in competition with each other. TI's executives suggest that it intends to provide better services for its customers to differentiate itself from Hitachi.[104]

NETWORK STRATEGIES

To this point, the focus has been on the cooperative relations between two (or a very few) firms, such as joint ventures or contractual arrangements.[105] However, networks are an important complement to other forms of cooperative strategy. Often networks of smaller firms work together because they are located in geographic industrial districts such as Silicon Valley. Networks such as these are described in the Strategic Focus.

STRATEGIC FOCUS

Cooperative Strategy Often Develops in Economic Districts

Cooperative strategy has been fostered widely in the Silicon Valley of California where many electronic, computer, and biotech firms create innovation and cooperative relationships between large and startup firms. The "Cambridge phenomenon" was a phrase coined more than a decade ago as Britain tried to create its own Silicon Valley. The Cambridge area of Britain has a network of technologically able and entrepreneurial people. Some 1,200 "knowledge-based" companies are located here, employing 30,000 people and generating more than three billion pounds of sales. About 85 percent of the startup companies in the area survive beyond five years, which is well above the British norm of 50 percent. Cambridge University has been a magnet for technological developments. It boasts 50 Nobel prize winners and has many research institutes such as the Laboratory for Molecular Biology where Watson and Crick first discovered the structure of DNA.

The seemingly tranquil lifestyle of this small community will be difficult to maintain as fast growing companies locate in the area. For example, in the summer of 1997, Microsoft announced plans to build a £50 million research laboratory, the first such facility for Microsoft outside of the United States. Additionally, Bill Gates donated $20 million toward a new computer studies building at Cambridge. He is also helping to develop a £30 million venture capital pool, managed by Amadeus Fund Management Group.

Throughout Italy, a number of cooperative districts can be found focusing on specific industry groups. In northeast Lombardy, the small town of Lumezzane is the world leader in silverware, faucet, and valve production with more than two thousand small companies manufacturing these items. In this town of 24,000, most companies have 20 or fewer employees with each worker specializing in particular crafts, such as shaping forks, sculpting their edges, and polishing the specific piece of silverware.

There is a tight network among family, friends and colleagues in Lumezzane. For example, when a business is threatened with bankruptcy, a set of phone calls usually yields a group of six to eight unofficial "trustees" who help bring the company safely back into the black. Townspeople are fiercely loyal to Lumezzane. They usually don't sell their businesses to outsiders, and they stick to the geographic area even though better housing prices are available in nearby Brescia.

There are a number of districts such as these throughout the world where cooperative strategy is often developed among smaller and larger companies. For instance, Dalton, Georgia, is the center for carpet manufacturers. Similar clothes design districts are found in New York City and vicinity. These areas frequently foster significant interrelationships between networks of firms that are often competitors but also collaborators.

SOURCE: T. Mueller, 1997, A town where cooperation is king, *Business Week*, December 15, 155; T. Buerkle, 1997, Cambridge: Britain's I-technology hotbed, *International Herald-Tribune*, October 8, 13; R. Pouder and C.H. St. John, 1996, Hot spots and blind spots: Geographical clusters of firms and innovation, *Academy of Management Review* 21: 1192–1225.

A **network strategy** involves a group of interrelated firms that works for the common good of all.

Although clustered groups of firms often form cooperative networks, it does not mean that the firms in the district are more competitive.[106] A **network strategy** involves a group of interrelated firms that works for the common good of all. The intent of the network strategy is to increase performance of a network of firms.[107] The relationships may be formal or informal. Examples of such networks include Japanese keiretsus and U.S. R&D consortia.

In the 1950s, the emphasis was on larger and stronger firms as product diversification grew popular and larger firms expanded into new product and geographic markets. Similarly, in the multinational and matrix organizations of the 1970s, a combination of functional and divisional structures was used to create large firms of enormous strength and complexity. More recently, however, a newer type of strategy known as a network has emerged. The structural characteristics of a network organization are discussed in Chapter 11. Herein, we outline the strategic approach of these networks. There are three types of networks: stable, dynamic, and internal.[108]

Stable networks often appear in mature industries with largely predictable market cycles and demand. In Japan, these relationships usually include some shared ownership among the network firms as part of a keiretsu.[109] Among U.S. firms, ties have grown stronger and, thus, stable relationships are more common. For example, in the athletic footwear and apparel business, Nike has long established relationships with a network of suppliers and distributors throughout the world.

Dynamic networks often emerge in industries where rapid technological innovations are introduced, frequently because of the short life cycles of products. Apple Computer employed a dynamic network with its innovative Newton, a personal digital assistant. Although the product was developed by Apple, Newtons are manufactured almost entirely by Sharp Corporation. Apple is also involved in an alliance with Motorola and IBM to develop a new microprocessor. Along with this relationship, Apple provided its partners, suppliers, dealers, and consultants with access to its internal electronic mail system, which greatly reduced the boundaries across these organizations.[110] Unfortunately, Apple's network of alliances has not proven very successful.

Internal networks can also be implemented to facilitate firm operations. For example, the global electric products firm, Asea Brown Boveri (ABB), buys and sells a multitude of products across many country boundaries using an internal network for coordination. Benetton, serving as a chief broker among many independent specialist suppliers and distributors, has an external network similar to ABB's internal network.[111]

Each of these network types has a focal **strategic center** or firm that manages the network. The main bank is the strategic center in *horizontal Japanese keiretsus* that entail loosely coupled, diverse businesses. The primary relationship among these diverse businesses is common ownership and arrangements with the same bank or set of banks. In *vertical keiretsus*, such as Toyota and Nissan automobile manufacturers, a dominant firm manages a supplier network.[112] Firms such as Nike, Nintendo, Benetton, Apple, Sun Microsystems, and IKEA (a Swedish furniture maker) are strategic centers associated with network structures. These companies are not "virtual firms" where all central competence is outsourced;[113] instead, they have capabilities and core competencies that allow them to shift important activities to other companies which creates value when these companies are better able to perform such activities.[114]

Strategic center refers to the firm that manages a network.

Monorail is a small company that produces personal computers under $1,000 that fit into a FedEx optimal-size shipping box. These computers now account for approximately one-third of the computers sold. Douglas Johns, a former Compaq employee, started the company. He decided that the computer was becoming a commodity where superior logistics would become the main competitive advantage. He hired designers and managers and contracted for everything else, including manufacturing and shipping through FedEx. Although the company has had significant success and has garnered retail support through CompUSA, the largest computer superstore chain in the United States, its strategy is easily copied. Compaq and IBM have added low-priced computers and Power Computing, recently purchased by Apple, is designing a PC company with product designers but no factory. Also, Dell and Gateway 2000, who ship directly to the customer, are still more efficient than Monorail. When it introduces a new product, Monorail will stick with proven technology and try to keep inventory and other logistic costs low.[115]

Douglas Johns, a former Compaq employee, started Monorail because he felt that superior logistics would become a major competitive advantage in the PC industry. Monorail computers sell for under $1,000 and fit into FedEx shipping boxes.

337

As with Monorail, virtual companies go beyond alliances and depend totally on their network to sustain performance. For instance, when a Monorail contractor's die used for stamping out steel computer cases broke, it took five days for a subcontractor to build a new one. By the time the system was back on line, store shelves were empty of Monorail products. Thus, while a virtual company is the ultimate form of network and can be powerful, it also is vulnerable to its network partners. If the partners do not perform well, the virtual company may fail.[116]

R&D Consortia and Other Network Strategies

R&D consortia represent a form of a network strategy where there is a strong need for cooperation among firms (often direct competitors) in an industry.[117] The U.S. National Cooperative Research Act of 1984 allowed the formation of joint venture and research consortia among domestic competitors fostering the development and realization of R&D objectives for industrial progress. These network organizations have been in existence for some time in Japan, Korea, and more recently in the European Union.[118] For example, the Japanese government's industrial policy and the Japanese Machine Tool Building Association (a trade group) have fostered the successful development of the machine tool industry in Japan.[119] The Japanese machine tool industry accounted for less than 1 percent of world production in 1955; in 1991 it accounted for 28 percent of world output. In contrast, the American share of world machine tool production declined from about 40 percent in 1955 to 6.6 percent in 1991.

In high-technology industries, where there is significant uncertainty, coalitions among firms are likely to form to develop an industry technological standard, thereby reducing consumer uncertainty. The videotape VHS Alliance, coordinated by Matsushita to sponsor video recorder standards and the Technical Workstation Alliance created in 1988 to develop and sponsor the UNIX operating system standards, are two examples of this phenomenon.[120] Such alliances may be developed by a sponsoring firm that offers a technology license at a low cost to induce other firms to adopt its technology. In these cases, there is an incentive to make the consortium as large as possible so that there is broad acceptance of the standard across firms using the technology. However, these firms still often compete with one another. Participating firms are concerned with potential disproportionate gains by rival firms. This is most likely when alternative standards are being proposed. The firms proposing a standard try to make it as functionally equivalent to their prealliance technology as possible. Interestingly, the alliance partners frequently compete in similar market segments. This is illustrated by the nine computer companies that participated in two different alliances sponsoring competing UNIX operating systems standards in 1988.[121] Therefore, R&D consortia tend to develop naturally as competition evolves.

Sematech is one of the successful examples of a major research consortium headquartered in the United States.[122] Its goal was to help the U.S. semiconductor industry regain its competitiveness by increasing the number of usable chips that could be manufactured from each wafer of silicon and make each chip capable of being more productive. Because the U.S. semiconductor industry has rebounded and is currently very strong, several critics have argued that Sematech has accomplished its goals. Currently, Sematech's corporate members include 10 of the largest semiconductor manufacturers in the United States. These companies invest in Sematech to hedge their risks for operating in this industry. Its predecessor, Microelectronics Computer Cooperation (MCC), was not as successful in transferring R&D technology products to the marketplace as Sematech. MCC's top management concluded that its main value was in the collaboration and shared technology generated by the industry cooperation. The cooperation among industry competitors has probably generated many intangible benefits as well. Although there are multiple potential benefits from the use of cooperative strategies, there continues to be some significant competitive risks.

COMPETITIVE RISKS WITH COOPERATIVE STRATEGIES

Even as companies attempt to cooperate, they also compete, both with firms in and outside their alliances. As such, there are significant risks with a cooperative strategy, including such actions or outcomes as poor contract development, misrepresentation of partner firms' competencies, failure of partners to make complementary resources available, being held hostage through specific investments associated with the alliance or the partner, and misunderstanding of a partner's strategic intent.

While there are incentives to cooperate in strategic alliances, there are also incentives to act opportunistically. If a poor contract is developed, the partnership is likely to dissolve in time. The strategic intent of the parties forming an alliance should be identified and incorporated into the contract to guard against potential opportunistic behaviors.

Some partnerships may dissolve because firms misrepresent their potential competencies to partners. Such misrepresentation is more likely when a partner offers intangible resources such as "knowledge of local conditions." Some partnerships may fail because partners refuse to allow their complementary resources to be available to the venturing firm. Contractual arrangements can sometimes discourage this form of adverse behavior, but once a firm makes an investment, in a joint venture for example, the local partner may hold those assets hostage if foreign countries do not have laws protecting them.

An alliance between Foote, Cone & Belding (FCB) of Chicago and Publicis of Paris, two premiere advertising agencies, suited the needs of each partner. FCB needed help to support its international clients, while Publicis could use FCB's experience in North and South America. However, the trust between the two chief executives who formed the alliance began to dissolve soon after the deal was struck. The divorce came in 1997 after many aspersions were cast on both sides; but, that did not end the fight. Publicis made a hostile takeover for the parent of FCB, True North Communications. Both companies, but especially FCB, are worse off than before the alliance was established.[123]

In addition to the moral hazards (potential cheating by partner firms), there are other risks. One of those risks is having the ability to form and manage a joint venture effectively. Prior experience may not be adequate for collaborative strategies to endure. Another risk is having the ability to collaborate. Alternatively, it may be difficult to identify trustworthy partners with which to collaborate.

Substitutes for alliances include mergers and acquisitions or internal development of new products. To the extent that there are reasonable substitutes (e.g., acquisitions) and significant risks, such cooperative strategies may lose their attractiveness. The increasing number of strategic alliances suggests that they may be

339

FIGURE 9.3 *Managing Competitive Risks in Cooperative Strategies*

imitated easily by competitors. Many firms form alliances with other companies because their competitors have done so. The different risks and means of managing them in strategic alliances are shown in Figure 9.3.

TRUSTWORTHINESS AS A STRATEGIC ASSET

A component critical to the success of alliances is trust between partners.[124] The fact that there are incentives to pursue cooperative strategies does not mean that partnering firms have the capability to manage such cooperative relationships and maintain them. Corning, over time, has developed a strong reputation for collaborative venturing. Because of Corning's reputation, potential partners know that a strategic alliance is likely to be successful because it has a reputation for being trustworthy. If a firm takes advantage of other firms in cooperative relationships, it will develop a reputation that will prevent future cooperative opportunities; the firm will be considered untrustworthy by potential partners.[125] Trustworthiness is a strategic asset in cooperative relations because it can be rare. Because all aspects of a cooperative relationship cannot be specified in a contract, trustworthiness is an important attribute. As previously mentioned, horizontal strategic alliances have been found to be successful in developing and bringing new products to the market. However, because this form of cooperation often occurs between competitors, trust is critical to its success. Over time, collaborators gain knowledge about the reliability of partner firms as well as knowledge about partner capabilities.[126]

Frito-Lay and Sara Lee formed a new strategic alliance to produce a product line of sweet snack items for sale in convenience stores, vending machines, and supermarkets. Frito-Lay, a unit of PepsiCo, has approximately $5 billion in annual sales and controls more than 50 percent of the U.S. market for salty snacks such as pretzels and potato chips. Sara Lee is an $18 billion consumer products firm that has other food businesses such as Jimmy Dean and Hillshire Farm as well as consumer businesses such as Playtex, Hanes, and L'Eggs. While not competitors, both Sara Lee and Frito-Lay have strong reputations in the food business. The products from the new alliance will be made in Sara Lee bakeries and marketed under the brand name BreakAways carrying the Sara Lee logo. The products will be distributed by Frito-Lay, which has one of the best distribution systems in the food industry. This new product line will provide both firms their first entry into the $914 million a year snack cake market. Some analysts have estimated that the joint venture could eventually generate as much as $500 million in annual sales. While each firm brings distinct and important capabilities to the alliance, the need to work together closely will require a significant degree of trust. For example, the new snacks will be produced in Sara Lee bakeries but with help from Frito-Lay technical teams. The manufacture and distribution of these goods will require careful coordination between the two parent firms. The alliance will have to fend off a powerful competitor who also just entered the market, Nabisco. Thus, time will tell whether this alliance between two highly successful snack food producers and marketers will lead to the success predicted.[127]

STRATEGIC APPROACHES TO MANAGING ALLIANCES

Two basic approaches to managing assets and liabilities are associated with cooperative strategies (see Figure 9.3).[128] One approach, based on minimizing alliance costs, requires that firms develop capabilities to create effective partner contracts and to monitor such contracts. The other approach, focused on maximizing value-creation opportunities, requires trustworthy partners with complementary assets and emphasizes trusting relationships. The first approach may produce successful joint ventures, but it is costly to write protective contracts and to develop effective monitoring systems. Furthermore, protective contracts and monitoring systems shield parts of the organization from both participating partners. Although monitoring systems can largely prevent opportunism and cheating among partner firms, they also preclude spontaneous opportunities that might develop between cooperating partners. Thus, they may preclude both firms from realizing the venture's full potential.

If trust can be used as a strategic asset in choosing partners, monitoring costs will be lower and opportunities between collaborating firms can be maximized. This second approach to governance is referred to as *opportunity maximizing* because partners in such alliances are able to pursue potential rent-generating opportunities that would simply be unavailable to partners in more contractually restricted alliances.[129] It is important, then, for firms to consider both the assets and liabilities of monitoring systems that will be used to manage the alliance.[130] For example, AT&T entered an alliance with a much smaller credit card technology firm to develop a new credit card service. To ensure secrecy so that the alliance could maintain a critical lead in the industry, no contract was used for the first several months of this relationship. During this time the firms worked collaboratively, sharing information and resources, while relying on the character and goodwill of each other to guide the relationship. In examining this relationship, AT&T was more concerned with maximizing the opportunities of the alliance than with the minimization of potential opportunism within the alliance.[131]

In summary, trust is not required for cooperation between two parties, but without it, monitoring costs will be higher. Furthermore, trust will increase risk-taking behavior between partners to take advantage of opportunities.[132] Trust has distinct advantages, but it also has increased liabilities associated with the risks of cooperative strategies.

Our focus in the next major section of the book is the strategic actions taken to implement formulated strategies. The first topic examined is corporate governance: how firms align managers' interests with those of the shareholders and control their operations to affect their strategic competitiveness.

SUMMARY

- Strategic alliances are partnerships between firms whereby resources, capabilities, and core competencies are combined to pursue mutual interests. Usually, firms' complementary assets are combined in strategic alliances. Strategic alliances have three basic varieties: joint ventures, equity strategic alliances, and nonequity strategic alliances.

- Other types of cooperative strategies are usually implicit rather than explicit. These include mutual forbearance or tacit collusion, in which firms in an industry tacitly cooperate to reduce industry output below the potential competitive output level and thereby raise prices above the competitive level. Firms might also explicitly collude, which is an illegal practice unless it is sanctioned through government regulations such as in the case of electric and telecommunications utilities.

- Cooperative strategies are often used at the business-unit level. We identified four types of business-level strategic alliances. Complementary strategic alliances are firm partnerships created to take advantage of market opportunities that combine assets between partner firms in ways that create value. Often, vertical complementary strategic alliances are organized in a way to facilitate supply or distribution. Outsourcing strategies are also of this type when complementarities are possible. Highly visible examples of outsourcing are shown in large firms such as Xerox, Delta Air Lines, and Kodak, which have outsourced their information technology functions.

- Horizontal complementary strategic alliances facilitate business-level strategies. These alliances include marketing agreements and joint product development between competitors and other complementary firms (e.g., domestic and international airlines).

- Competition reduction and response alliances are formed to respond to competitive interactions be-

tween firms. Competition reduction alliances are proposed to avoid excessive competition and are used to respond to competitors' actions.

- Uncertainty also fosters the use of strategic alliances. Strategic alliances can be used to hedge against risks if there is significant uncertainty about performance or new technologies.

- All business-level strategic alliances may not result in strategic competitiveness and above-average returns. Complementary alliances are most likely to create strategic competitiveness, whereas competition reduction and competitive response alliances are more likely to achieve competitive parity. Uncertainty reduction alliances may prevent a firm from experiencing below-average returns.

- Strategic alliances also can be used at the corporate level. Corporate-level diversifying strategic alliances reduce risk but, at the same time, can be highly complex. Strategic alliances may also help to avoid government prohibitions against horizontal mergers. Furthermore, strategic alliances may be used as an experimental step before acquisition.

- Corporate-level synergistic alliances create economies of scope between two firms. Such alliances facilitate achievement of synergy across multiple businesses and functions at the corporate level.

- Franchising is an additional corporate-level cooperative strategy that provides an alternative to diversification. Firms following a franchising strategy can diversify their risk associated with a single business (even those in many markets) without adding new products. McDonald's has used this strategy extensively.

- A number of international cooperative strategies exist. Many firms pursue cooperative international strategies because some countries regard local ownership as an important national policy objective. Furthermore, the new trade agreements (e.g., World Trade Organization, NAFTA, etc.) have facilitated an increased number of cooperative ventures as firms are allowed to participate in more foreign investments. This is especially true in emerging markets where foreign partners are often essential. International strategic alliances can be risky. One of the most serious errors managers make in forming foreign ventures is not understanding the strategic intent of the partner.

- Adding to the number of cooperative strategies is the network organization. Network organizations are associations of firms with formal or informal relationships that work for the common good of all. These networks can be one of three types: stable, dynamic, or internal.

- Stable networks appear in mature industries with predictable cycles and market demands. The Japanese horizontal keiretsu is an example of this type of network.

- Dynamic networks produce rapid techonological innovations, where product life cycles are short and shifts in consumer tastes alter frequently. Often, these networks are formed to create more stability and facilitate adoption of a new industry

technology standard such as the VHS format in video recorders.

- Internal networks occur in firms that have established entities across countries that facilitate coordination between headquarters and subsidiary organizations. ABB and Benetton are examples of firms with significant internal networks.

- A number of competitive risks are associated with cooperative strategies. If a contract is not developed appropriately or if a potential partner firm misrepresents its competencies or fails to make available promised complementary resources, failure is likely. Furthermore, a firm may be held hostage through asset-specific investments made in conjunction with a partner, which may be exploited.

- Trust is an important asset in many strategic alliances. Firms recognize other firms that have a reputation for trustworthiness in cooperative strategic relations. This suggests that firms pursuing cooperative relations may have two competing objective functions, one fostering strong governance and contract development capabilities and another focusing on selecting trustworthy partners where complementary assets exist.

REVIEW QUESTIONS

1. What are the three types of cooperative strategies?
2. What are the different rationales for cooperative strategies in slow-cycle, standard-cycle, and fast-cycle markets?
3. What are the advantages and disadvantages of the four different types of cooperative strategies at the business level?
4. How are cooperative strategies used at the corporate level of strategic analysis? When would these strategy types be used and what are the potential problems associated with each one?

5. How are cooperative strategies applied in international operations?
6. What are the four competitive risks of engaging in cooperative strategies?
7. Why is trust important in cooperative strategies?
8. How is the cost minimization approach different from the opportunity maximization approach to managing strategic alliances?

APPLICATION DISCUSSION QUESTIONS

1. Select an issue of the *Wall Street Journal* and identify all of the articles that focus on cooperative strategies. Classify the particular type of cooperative strategy and identify the strategic objective of the cooperative venture for each.
2. Find two articles describing a cooperative strategy, one where trust is being used as a strategic asset and another

where contracts and monitoring are being emphasized. Examine the differences between the management approaches and describe advantages and disadvantages of each approach.
3. Choose a *Fortune* 500 firm that has a significant need to outsource some aspect of its business such as its information technology function. Describe the potential

343

outsourcing opportunities available and explain the approach you would use to achieve the outsourcing objective.

4. Find an example of a research consortia and examine its organization and strategic approaches. Provide an alternative strategy using the network organization that you think would be equivalent in performance.

5. How can corporate-level cooperative strategies help achieve a boundaryless organization? Describe the advantages and disadvantages to such an organization.

ETHICS QUESTIONS

1. Think about the idea of asset-specific investment and hostage taking in cooperative relations. Is hostage taking, as described in the chapter, a central problem in strategic alliances or is it more of a problem in vertical relationships between firms (e.g., suppliers, distributors)? Please explain.

2. "A contract is necessary because most firms cannot be trusted to act ethically in a cooperative venture such as a strategic alliance." Please explain whether you think this statement is true or false.

3. Ventures in foreign countries without strong contract law are more risky because managers are subject to bribery and lack of commitment once assets have been invested in the country. How can managers deal with these problems?

4. Monopoly firms are regulated in the United States. However, a monopoly enterprise is often considered unethical if it seeks to enter an emerging country. Please explain why.

5. Firms with a reputation for ethical behavior in strategic alliances are likely to have more legitimate venture opportunities than firms without this reputation for good character. How do firms develop such positive reputations?

INTERNET EXERCISE

The following companies have information about their business alliances on their Web sites:

British Airways: **http://www.british-airways.com**

First Virtual: **http://www.firstvirtual.com**

Unisys: **http://www.unisys.com**

General Magic: **http://www.genmagic.com**

Select two of these companies. For each company, go to its Web site and locate the section that discusses the company's business alliances. Then write a critique of how an involvement in business alliances helps each of these companies achieve its business objectives.

STRATEGIC SURFING

The *Alliance Analyst* is the only management publication dedicated solely to the topic of strategic alliances. Although it is not available on-line, the *Alliance Analyst* does maintain a Web site that features past articles and other alliance-related information.

http://www.allianceanalyst.com/

NOTES

1. A. N. Brandenburger and B. J. Nalebuff, 1996, *Co-opetition* (New York: Doubleday).

2. N. Templin, 1995, Strange bedfellows: More and more firms enter joint ventures with big competitors, *Wall Street Journal*, November 1, Al, A12.

3. D. Fenn, 1997, Sleeping with the enemy, INC Online, http://www.inc.com, November; S.A. Shane, 1996, Hybrid organizational arrangements and their implications for firm growth and survival: A study of new franchisers, *Academy of Management Journal* 39: 216–234.

4. S. E. Human and K. G. Provan, 1997, An emergent theory of structure and outcomes in small-firm strategic manufacturing networks, *Academy of Management Journal* 40: 368–404.

5. S. Gruner, 1996, Benchmark: Partnering for products, INC online, http://www.inc.com, February.

6. S. H. Park and G. R. Ungson, 1997, The effect of national culture, organizational complementarity, and economic motivation on joint venture dissolution, *Academy of Management Journal* 40: 279–307; A. Rugman and J. D'Cruz, 1997, The theory of the flagship firm, *European Management Journal* 15: 403–412.

7. J. H. Dyer, 1996, How Chrysler created an American keiretsu, *Harvard Business Review* 74, no. 4: 42–56.

344

8. D. Fenn and S. Greco, 1997, Details, details, details, INC homepage, http://www.inc.com, July.

9. S. H. Park and M. Russo, 1996, When cooperation eclipses competition: An event history analysis of joint venture failures, *Management Science* 42: 875–890.

10. Airline alliances: Flying in formation, 1995, *The Economist*, July 22, 59.

11. T. Saxton, 1997, The effects of partner and relationship characteristics, *Academy of Management Journal* 40: 443–462; Park and Ungson, The effect of national culture, organizational complementarity and economic motivation on joint venture dissolution.

12. B. Gomes Casseres, 1996, *The Alliance Revolution: The New Shape of Business Rivalry* (Cambridge, MA: Harvard University Press).

13. Y. Pan, 1997, The formation of Japanese and U.S. equity joint ventures in China, *Strategic Management Journal* 18: 247–254.

14. D. C. Mowery, J. E. Oxley, and B. S. Silverman, 1996, Strategic alliances and interfirm knowledge transfer, *Strategic Management Journal* 17 (Special Winter Issue): 77–92.

15. Dyer, How Chrysler created an American keiretsu.

16. J. B. Barney, 1997, *Gaining and Sustaining Competitive Advantage* (Reading, MA: Addison Wesley), 255.

17. B. Kogut, 1988, Joint ventures: Theoretical and empirical perspectives, *Strategic Management Journal* 9: 319–332.

18. A. A. Lado, N. G. Boyd, and S. C. Hanlon, 1997, Competition, cooperation, and the search for rents: A syncretic model, *Academy of Management Review* 22: 110–141; F. J. Contractor and P. Lorange, 1988, Why should firms cooperate? The strategic and economic bases for cooperative strategy, in F. J. Contractor and P. Lorange (eds.), *Cooperative Strategies in International Business* (Lexington, MA: Lexington Books).

19. E. E. Bailey and W. Shan, 1995, Sustainable competitive advantage through alliances, in E. Bowman and B. Kogut (eds.), *Redesigning the Firm* (New York: Oxford University Press); J. R. Williams, 1992, How sustainable is your competitive advantage? *California Management Review* 34, no. 2: 29–51.

20. J. Kahn, 1996, Alcatel's local call paying off in China, *Wall Street Journal*, January 15, A5.

21. J. C. Huertas and J. P. Chapon, 1997, Alcatel awarded major contract in South Africa, Alcatel home page, http://www.alcatel.com, press release, July 23.

22. M. Feher, 1997, Unisource to invest $250 Mln in Hungary Telecoms Co., *Wall Street Journal* Interactive Edition, http://www.wsj.com, December 22.

23. J. L. Schenker and J. Pressley, 1997, Feared French-German telecom venture poses little threat so far, *Wall Street Journal* Interactive Edition, http://www.wsj.com, December 23.

24. P. Wayner, 1997, Sky-high dreams for the Internet, *The New York Times* on the Web, http://www.nyt.com, May 22.

25. J. Tagliabue, 1997, Airbus partners agree to form independent corporation. *The New York Times* on the Web, http://www.nyt.com, January 14.

26. Templin, Strange bedfellows: More and more firms enter joint ventures.

27. C. W. L. Hill, 1997, Establishing a standard: Competitive strategy and technological standards in winner-take-all industries, *Academy of Management Executive* XI, no. 2: 7–25.

28. R. Axelrod, W. Mitchell, R.E. Thomas, D.S. Bennett, and E. Bruderer, 1995, Coalition formation in standard-setting alliances, *Management Science* 41: 1493–1508; L. D. Browning, J. M. Beyer, and J. C. Shetler, 1995, Building cooperation in a competitive industry: Sematech and the semiconductor industry, *Academy of Management Journal* 38: 113–151.

29. B. Schlender and A. H. Moore, 1997, Killer chip, *Fortune*, http://www.pathfinder.com/fortune, November 10.

30. D. Bank, 1997, TCI uses hi-tech "layer cake" to ward off Microsoft, *Wall Street Journal*, December 16, B4.

31. Hill, Establishing a standard.

32. Park and Ungson, The effect of national culture, organizational compementarity, and economic motivation on joint venture dissolution; R. Johnston and P. Lawrence, 1988, Beyond vertical integration—The rise of the value adding partnership, *Harvard Business Review* 66, no. 4: 94–101.

33. X. Martin, W. Mitchell, and A. Swaminathan, 1995, Recreating and extending Japanese automobile buyer-supplier links in North America, *Strategic Management Journal* 16: 589–619; J. Dyer and W. S. Ouchi, 1993, Japanese style partnerships: Giving companies a competitive edge, *Sloan Management Review* 35, no. 1: 51–63; B. Asanuma, 1989, Manufacturer-supplier relationships in Japan and the concept of relation-specific skill, *Journal of the Japanese and International Economies* 3: 1–30.

34. J. H. Dyer, 1996, Specialized supplier networks as a source of competitive advantage: Evidence from the auto industry, *Strategic Management Journal* 17: 271–291; J. T. Mahoney, 1992, The choice of organizational form: Vertical financial ownership versus other methods of vertical integration, *Strategic Management Journal* 13: 559–584.

35. J. H. Dyer, How Chrysler created an American keiretsu.

36. L. Willcocks and C. J. Choi, 1995, Cooperative partnership and "total" IT outsourcing: From contractual obligation to strategic alliance? *European Management Journal* 13, no. 1: 67–78.

37. J. W Verity, 1996, Let's order out for technology, *Business Week*, May 13, 47.

38. As quoted in P. Hapaaniemi, 1997, Side by side, *Chief Executive*, June, S4–S10.

39. M. Heinzl, 1995, Magna International profits on big three outsourcing, *Wall Street Journal*, August 24, B5.

40. R. A. Bettis, S. R Bradley, and G. Hamel, 1992, Outsourcing and industrial decline, *Academy of Management Executive* VI, no. 1: 7–22.

41. V. Kapoor and A. Gupta, 1997, Aggressive sourcing: A free-market approach, *Sloan Management Review* 39, no. 1: 21–31.

42. K. Nirmalya, 1996, The power of trust in manufacturing-retailer relationships, *Harvard Business Review* 74, no. 6: 92–106.

43. N. F. Piercy, C. S. Katsikeas, and D. W. Cravens, 1997, Examining the role of buyer-seller relationships in export performance, *Journal of World Business* 32, no. 1: 73–86.

44. M. Kotabe and K. S. Swan, 1995, The role of strategic alliances in high technology new product development, *Strategic Management Journal* 16: 621–636.

45. B. Coleman, 1995, Lufthansa and Scandinavian Airlines unveil plans for a strategic alliance, *Wall Street Journal*, May 12, A9.

46. E. McDowell, 1995, Delta seeks to expand its tie with three airlines in Europe, *New York Times*, September 9, 34.

345

47. M. Brannigan, 1995, Airlines' "code sharing" helps them, hinders travelers, *Wall Street Journal*, October 13, B1; T.H. Oum and A.J. Taylor, 1995, Emerging patterns in intercontinental air linkages and implications for international route allocation policy, *Transportation Journal* 34 (Summer): 5–27.

48. E. Norton and M. DuBois, 1994, Foiled competition: Don't call it a cartel, but world aluminum has forged a new order, *Wall Street Journal*, June 9, A1, A6.

49. C. Adams, 1998, Aluminum companies earnings increased in the fourth quarter, *Wall Street Journal* Interactive Edition, http://www.wsj.com, January 8.

50. D. P. Hamilton and N. Shirouzu, 1995, Japan's business cartels are starting to erode, but change is slow, *Wall Street Journal*, December 4, Al, A6.

51. G. Melloan, 1997, This year's economic lesson: Japan's model failed, *Wall Street Journal*, December 30, A11.

52. H. Tezuka, 1997, Success as the source of failure? Competition and cooperation in the Japanese economy, *Sloan Management Review* 39, no. 2: 83–93.

53. G. R. Ungson, R. M. Steers and S. H. Park, 1997, *Korean Enterprise: The Quest for Globalization* (Cambridge, MA: Harvard Business School Press), 163.

54. M. Ihlwan and B. Bremner, 1998, Korea Inc. balks, *Business Week*, January 19, 44–46.

55. A. Tanzer, 1998, Tight little island, *Forbes*, January 12, 52–53.

56. R. Brahm, 1995, National targeting policies, high technology industries, and excessive competition, *Strategic Management Journal* 16 (Special Issue, Summer): 71–92.

57. H. S. Bryne, 1995, Damage control at ADM, *Barrons*, October 23, 14.

58. J. M. Broder, 1997, Toys 'R' Us led price collusion, judge rules in upholding F.T.C., *The New York Times* on the Web, http://www.nytimes.com, October 1.

59. C. Torres, 1996, Mexican phone competition heats up, *Wall Street Journal*, April 23, Al5.

60. As quoted in T.Y. Jones, 1998, Musical chairs, *Forbes*, January 12, 60–63.

61. F. M Biddle and L. Cauley, 1997, DirecTV seeks new partners, fresh programs, *Wall Street Journal*, December 17, B1, B3.

62. R. G. McGrath, 1997, A real options logic for initiating technological positioning investments, *Academy of Management Review* 22: 974–996; B. Kogut, 1991, Joint ventures and the option to expand and acquire, *Management Science* 37: 19–33.

63. J. R. Wilke and S. N. Mehta, 1998, U.S. plans immediate appeal of telecom ruling, *Wall Street Journal*, January 2, A3.

64. J. Brinkley, 1997, U.S. and Europe in battle over digital TV, *The New York Times* on the Web, http://www.nytimes.com, August 25; D. Caruso, In debate on advanced TV, FCC can be assertive, *The New York Times* on the Web, http://www.nytimes.com, June 17.

65. K. Singh, 1997, The impact of technolgical complexity and interfirm cooperation on business survival, *Academy of Management Journal* 40: 339–367.

66. J.-F. Hennart and S. Ready, 1997, The choice between mergers/acquisitions and joint ventures in the United States, *Strategic Management Journal* 18: 1–12.

67. S. Glain, 1995, Korea's Samsung plans very rapid expansion into autos, other lines, *Wall Street Journal*, March 2, A1, A11.

68. Ihlwan and Bremner, Korea Inc. balks.

69. H. Ingham and S. Thompson, 1994, Wholly owned versus collaborative ventures in diversifying financial services, *Strategic Management Journal* 15: 325–334.

70. J. Bleeke and D. Ernst, 1995, Is your alliance really a sale? *Harvard Business Review* 73, no. 1: 97–105.

71. J. B. Barney, 1988, Returns to bidding firms in mergers and acquisitions: Reconsidering the relatedness hypothesis, *Strategic Management Journal* 9 (Special Summer Issue): 71–78.

72. A. Nanda and P.J, Williamson, 1995, Use joint ventures to ease the pain of restructuring, *Harvard Business Review* 73, no. 6: 119–128.

73. C. Covault, 1995, German, French firms merge armaments units, *Aviation Week & Space Technology*, January 30, 25.

74. U. Gupta, 1991, Sony adopts strategy to broaden ties with small firms, *Wall Street Journal*, February 28, B2.

75. M. J. Yoshino and U. S. Rangan, 1995, *Strategic Alliances: An Entrepreneurial Approach to Globalization* (Cambridge, MA: Harvard Business School Press).

76. D. Kirkpatrick, 1997, Gates wants all your business—and he's starting to get it, *Fortune*, May 26, 58–68.

77. Windows on the whole world, 1997, *The Economist*, November 29, 68; Set-top boxing, 1997, *The Economist*, November 29, 67–68.

78. D. Kirkpatrick, 1998, These days, everybody needs a Microsoft strategy, *Fortune*, January 12, 134–135.

79. J. H. Birnbaum, 1998, D.C.'s anti-Gates lobby, *Fortune*, January 12, 135.

80. S. Hamm, A. Cortese, and S.B. Garland, 1998, Microsoft's future, *Business Week*, January 19, 58.

81. Shane, Hybrid organizational arrangements and their implications for firm growth and survival.

82. R. Martin and R. Justis, 1993, Franchising, liquidity constraints and entry, *Applied Economics* 25: 1269–1277; S. W. Norton, 1988, Franchising, brand name capital, and the entrepreneurial capacity problem, *Strategic Management Journal* 9 (Special Summer Issue): 105–114.

83. P. Ingram and J.A.C. Baum, 1997, Opportunity and constraint: Organizations' learning from the operating and competitive experience of industries, *Strategic Management Journal*, 18 (Special Summer Issue): 75–98.

84. G. F. Mathewson and R. H. Winter, 1985, The economies of franchise contracts, *Journal of Law and Economics* 28: 503–526.

85. J. Holusha, 1997, As industry changes, networks feel a ripple, *The New York Times* on the Web, http://www.nyt.com, January 26.

86. R. E. Hoskisson, W. P. Wan and M. H. Hansen, 1998, Strategic alliance formation and market evaluation: Effects of parent firm's governance structure, in M. A. Hitt, J. Ricart and R.D. Nixon (eds.), Managing Strategically in an Interconnected World (London: John Wiley & Sons), in press.

87. B. L. Simonin, 1997, The importance of collaborative know-how: An empirical test of the learning organization, *Academy of Management Journal* 40: 1150–1174.

88. P. J. Buckley and M. Casson, 1996, An economic model of international joint venture strategy, *Journal of International Business Studies* 27: 849–876; J. E. McGee, M. J. Dowling, and W. L. Megginson, 1995, Cooperative strategy and new ven-

ture performance: The role of business strategy and management experience, *Strategic Management Journal* 16: 565–580.

89. M. A. Hitt, R. E. Hoskisson, and H. Kim, 1997, International diversification: Effects on innovation and firm performance in product diversified firms, *Academy of Management Journal* 40: 767–798; R. Morck and B. Yeung, 1991, Why investors value multinationality, *Journal of Business* 64, no. 2: 165–187.

90. L. K. Mytelka, 1991, *Strategic Partnerships and the World Economy* (London: Pinter Publishers).

91. J. Hagedoorn, 1995, A note on international market leaders and networks of strategic technology partnering, *Strategic Management Journal* 16: 241–250.

92. J. Li, 1995, Foreign entry and survival: Effects of strategic choices on performance in international markets, *Strategic Management Journal* 16: 333–351.

93. R. Madhavan and J. E. Prescott, 1995, Market value impact of joint ventures: The effect of industry information-processing load, *Academy of Management Journal* 38: 900–915.

94. J. L. Johnson, J. B. Cullen, and T. Sakano, 1996, Setting the stage for trust and strategic integration in Japanese-U.S. cooperative alliances, *Journal of International Business Studies* 27: 981–1004; J.M. Geringer, 1991, Measuring performance of international joint ventures, *Journal of International Business Studies* 22, no. 2: 249–263.

95. M. Schuman, 1996, South Korea raises limit to 18% on foreign investment in firms, *Wall Street Journal*, February 27, A12.

96. *The Bulletin of the Ministry of Foreign Trade and Economic Cooperation of the People's Republic of China*, 1995, issues no. 1 and no. 2.

97. J. Blecke and W. Ernst, 1992, The way to win in cross-border alliances, *Harvard Business Review* 70, no. 6: 475–481.

98. J. J. Reuer and K. D. Miller, 1997, Agency costs and the performance implications of international joint venture internalization, *Strategic Management Journal* 18: 425–438.

99. M. T. Dacin, M. A. Hitt, and E. Levitas, 1997, Selecting partners for successful international alliances: Examinations of U.S. and Korean firms, *Journal of World Business* 32, no. 1: 3–16; M. A. Hitt, M. T. Dacin, B. B. Tyler, and D. Park, 1997, Understanding the differences in Korean and U.S. executives strategic orientations, *Strategic Management Journal* 18: 159–168.

100. M. Wright, R. E. Hoskisson, I. Filatochev, and T. Buck, 1998, Revitalizing privatized Russian enterprises, *Academy of Management Executive*, in press; I. Filatochev, R.E. Hoskisson, T. Buck, and M. Wright, 1996, Corporate restructuring in Russian privatizations: Implications for U.S. investors, *California Management Review* 38, no. 2: 87–105.

101. S. M. Puffer, D. J. McCarthy, and A. I. Naumov, 1997, Russian managers' beliefs about work: Beyond the stereotypes, *Journal of World Business* 32, no. 2: 258–275.

102. J. Thornhill, 1997, Prospects for partnership, *Financial Times*, December 1, 10.

103. G. Hamel, 1991, Competition for competence and interpartner learning with international strategic alliances, *Strategic Management Journal* 12: 83–103.

104. Dacin, Hitt, and Levitas, Selecting partners for successful international alliances; Templin, 1995, Strange bedfellows: More and more firms enter joint ventures.

105. C. Jones, W. S. Hesterly, and S. P. Borgatti, 1997, A general theory of network governance: Exchange conditions and social mechanisms, *Academy of Management Review* 22: 911–945; T. J. Rowley, 1997, Moving beyond dyadic ties: A network theory of stakeholder influences, *Academy of Management Review* 22: 887–910.

106. R. Pouder and C. H. St. John, 1996, Hot spots and blind spots: Geographical clusters of firms and innovation, *Academy of Management Review* 21: 1192–1225.

107. Rugman and D'Cruz, 1997, The theory of the flagship firm; D.B. Holm, K. Eriksson and J. Johanson, 1996, Business networks and cooperation in international business relationships, *Journal of International Business Studies* 27: 1033–1053.

108. R. Miles and C. C. Snow, 1994, *Fit, Failure and the Hall of Fame: How Companies Succeed or Fail* (New York: The Free Press).

109. M. L. Gerlach, 1992, *Alliance Capitalism: The Social Organization of Japanese Business* (Berkeley, CA: University of California Press).

110. H. Bahrami, 1992, The emerging flexible organization: Perspectives from Silicon Valley, *California Management Review* 34, no. 3: 33–52.

111. J. Levine, 1996, Even when you fail, you learn a lot, *Forbes*, March 11, 58–62.

112. T. Nishiguchi and J. Brookfield, 1997, The evolution of Japanese subcontracting, *Sloan Management Review* 39, no. 1: 89–101; T. Nishiguchi, 1994, *Strategic Industrial Sourcing* (New York: Oxford University Press).

113. W. Davidow and M. Malone, 1992, *A Virtual Corporation: Structuring and Revitalizing the Corporation of the 21st Century* (New York: Harper Business).

114. G. Lorenzoni and C. Baden-Fuller, 1995, Creating a strategic center to manage a web of partners, *California Management Review* 37, no. 3: 146–163.

115. E. Ramstad, 1997, A PC maker's low-tech formula: Start with the box, *Wall Street Journal*, December 29, B1, B6.

116. H. W Chesbrough and D. J. Teece, 1996, When is virtual virtuous? Organizing for innovation, *Harvard Business Review* 74, no. 1: 65–73.

117. P. Olk and C. Young, 1997, Why members stay in or leave an R&D consortium: Performance and conditions of membership as determinants of continuity, *Strategic Management Journal* 18: 855–877; M. Sakakibara, 1997, Hetergeneity of firm capabilities and cooperative research and development: An empirical examination of motives, *Strategic Management Journal* 18 (Special Summer Issue): 143–164.

118. Brahm, National targeting policies.

119. S. Kotha and A. Nair, 1995, Strategy and environment as determinants of performance: Evidence from the Japanese machine tool industry, *Strategic Management Journal* 16: 497–518.

120. G. Saloner, 1990, Economic issues in computer interface standardization, *Economic Innovation and New Technology* 1: 135–156.

121. Axelrod, Mitchell, Thomas, Bennett, and Bruderer, Coalition formation in standard-setting alliances.

122. L. D. Browning, J. M. Beyer, and J. C. Shetler, 1995, Building cooperation in a competitive industry: Sematech and the semiconductor industry, *Academy of Management Journal* 38: 113–151.

347

123. R. A. Melcher and G. Edmundson, 1997, A marriage made in hell, *Business Week*, December 22, 40–42.

124. J. B. Barney and M. H. Hansen, 1994, Trustworthiness: Can it be a source of competitive advantage? *Strategic Management Journal* 15 (Special Winter Issue): 175–203.

125. M. J. Dollinger, P. A. Golden, and T. Saxton, 1997, The effect of reputation on the decision to joint venture, *Strategic Management Journal* 18: 127–140; C. W. L. Hill, 1990, Cooperation, opportunism, and the invisible hand: Implications for transaction cost theory, *Academy of Management Review* 15: 500–513.

126. R. Gulati, 1996, Social structure and alliance formation patterns: A longitudinal analysis, *Administrative Science Quarterly* 40: 619–652.

127. M. Zimmerman, 1996, A BreakAway success? *Dallas Morning News*, January 8, Dl, D4.

128. J. H. Dyer, 1997, Effective interfirm collaboration: How firms minimize transaction costs and maximize transaction value, *Strategic Management Journal* 18: 535–556; M. Hansen, R. E. Hoskisson, and J. B. Barney, 1997, Trustworthiness in strategic alliances: Opportunism minimization versus opportunity maximization, Working paper, Brigham Young University.

129. P. Moran and S. Ghoshal, 1996, Theories of economic organization: The case for realism and balance, *Academy of Management Review* 21: 58–72.

130. A. Parke, 1993, Strategic alliance structuring: A game theoretic and transaction cost examination of interfirm cooperation, *Academy of Management Journal* 36: 794–829.

131. C. S. Sankar, W. R. Boulton, N. W. Davidson, C. A. Snyder, and R. W. Ussery, 1995, Building a world-class alliance: The universal card—TSYS case, *Academy of Management Executive* IX, no. 2: 20–29.

132. R. C. Mayer, J. H. Davis, and F. D. Schoorman, 1995, An integrative model of organizational trust, *Academy of Management Review* 20: 709–734.

Strategic Actions: Strategy Implementation

PART III

Chapters

Corporate Governance

CHAPTER 10

Learning Objectives

After reading this chapter, you should be able to:

1. Define corporate governance and explain why it is used to monitor and control managers' strategic decisions.

2. Explain how ownership came to be separated from managerial control in the modern corporation.

3. Define an agency relationship and managerial opportunism and describe their strategic and organizational implications.

4. Explain how four internal corporate governance mechanisms—ownership concentration, board of directors, executive compensation, and the multidivisional (M-form) structure—are used to monitor and control managerial decisions.

5. Discuss trends among the three types of compensation executives receive and their effects on strategic decisions.

6. Describe how the external corporate governance mechanism—the market for corporate control—acts as a restraint on top-level managers' strategic decisions.

7. Discuss the use of corporate governance in Germany and Japan.

8. Describe how corporate governance mechanisms can foster ethical strategic decisions and behaviors on the part of top-level executives.

AT&T's Board Overcomes Difficulties in Choosing a New CEO

A *Business Week* special report classified AT&T's board of directors as one of the worst in the country. AT&T suffered through a year-long CEO succession fiasco because, some feel, the board failed to exercise effective control over its previous CEO, Robert E. Allen. AT&T recently hired C. Michael Armstrong, former CEO of Hughes Electronics. The board had considered hiring Armstrong but was then sidetracked by Allen who recommended John Walter to ultimately succeed him. Walter, the former CEO of printing leader R.R. Donnelley & Sons, left eight months after coming to AT&T. In fact, Walter quit, seemingly a victim of behind-the-scenes lobbying by Allen to deny him the CEO job. Apparently, it was difficult for Allen to actually terminate his position as AT&T's CEO.

http://www.att.com

Four out of ten money managers and governance experts who responded to the *Business Week* survey said that AT&T's board was among the worst in corporate America. They accused it of harmful acquisitions (e.g., the acquisition of NCR), a number of costly write-offs including the NCR acquisition, and layoffs and spin-offs where AT&T lost a significant amount of its human capital, including personnel working at Bell Labs.

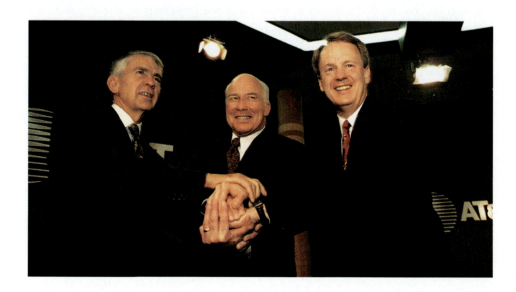

351

John D. Zeglis, who sought to succeed the outgoing Allen before Armstrong was nominated, has become the number two man and likely heir apparent to Armstrong when he retires. When Armstrong took over as CEO, he required Allen, who had been in trouble even before the Walter debacle, to step down from all his positions within the company. Zeglis matches well with Armstrong, and as a lawyer, he understands the institutional network of key legislators and regulators including knowledge of the Federal Communications Commission. As their first move, Armstrong and Zeglis announced the acquisition of Teleport Communications, a local carrier based in New York City. AT&T's competitiveness declined during its leadership crises. WorldCom took over MCI and many other acquisitions occurred, which put AT&T behind in possible strategic moves that it could have taken (see the discussion in Chapter 6).

Many expect significant changes in AT&T's board of directors. Over the last two years, outside directors who are CEOs from Eastman Kodak, Johnson & Johnson, Chevron, and Caterpillar have joined the board. Some outside directors have come on with significant commitment as shareholders. For instance, George M.C. Fisher, Kodak's CEO, bought nearly five thousand shares a month before coming on the board. Other directors who collectively own ten thousand shares may not have as great a commitment. These are former CBS CEO Thomas H. Wyman, Columbia University ex-president Michael I. Sovern, and consultants Donald F. McHenry and Kathryn Eickhoff. Because AT&T's reputation has been tarnished with major institutional investors, it sought to employ its directors in an effort to rebuild the company's image.

Campbell Soup Company, on the other hand, won the honors in the *Business Week* survey for the best board of directors for the second year in a row. Chairman David W. Johnson has sought to build the reputation of its board as a progressive governance pioneer. Outside directors took control of the search for the new CEO and therefore created a new role for boards in management succession. Furthermore, Campbell has initiated performance evaluations for board members, making individual members more concerned with self-improvement and more attuned to creating effective processes. Typically, boards are packed with trusted friends and colleagues who rarely challenge the CEO's policies and directives. This has given a country club atmosphere to the perception of many boards. Campbell's board members have been trained to focus on one purpose: acting in the shareholders' best interest.

The emphasis of institutional investors, such as the California Public Employees' Retirement System (CalPERS), has fueled pressures for stronger corporate governance practices. Pfizer, for instance, has a new innovative position, vice president for corporate governance. A critical characteristic of board members, from the investor viewpoint, is that they should be independent of the CEO. That does not mean that board members should micromanage or circumvent the CEO; rather, they should provide strong oversight without rubber-stamping the CEO's plans. This suggests that all strategic plans should be scrutinized rigorously and managers should be evaluated against high performance standards.

Furthermore, as the Campbell example illustrates, board members are taking more control of the leadership succession process. Outside directors are becoming more free of all ties to either the CEO or the company. Many suggest a minimum of inside managers and no consultants who work with the firm should be on the board. Also of concern is the idea of interlocking directorships, where CEOs serve on each other's boards.

More firms are now insisting directors own significant stock in the company for which they provide oversight. Although some CEOs argue that board governance doesn't matter as much as shareholder value, a critical goal of many boards today is the prevention of future problems. If problems do occur with the CEO's leadership, a proactive board of independent directors who own shares has more of an incentive to spot problems in advance and act swiftly than a board packed with management loyalists.

However, some see boards as having overcorrected for the years when rubber-stamping was the norm. Their basic fear is that if a board receives unfair criticism, this will make directors hesitant to take strategic risks. Often, a firm's wrong-headedness is an honest strategic mistake and not a substantive governance problem.

The size of the board can also change its group dynamics. Smaller boards may be more effective than larger boards. Smaller boards are likely to have informal but in-depth communication. In contrast, larger boards are likely to have more ceremonial presentations and be more formalized and thereby go into less depth when making strategic decisions.

Boards of directors, owners, and the decisions they make in governing the corporation have a strong influence on a firm's strategic direction. Corporate governance is an important issue in examining the implementation of a firm's strategies.

SOURCES: A. Bryant, 1998, How the mighty have fallen and managed to profit handsomely, *The New York Times* on the Web, http://www.nytimes.com, January 5; S. Lipin, 1998, AT&T to buy Teleport for $11.3 billion, *Wall Street Journal*, January 9, A3, A6; T. Elstrom, 1997, Honeymoon in Jersey, *Business Week*, December 15, 40; J. A. Byrne, R. Grover, and R. A. Melcher, 1997, The best and worst boards: Our special report on corporate governance, *Business Week*, December 8, 91–98; J. J. Keller, 1997, AT&T's board faces many twists and turns in search for new CEO, *Wall Street Journal*, October 13, A1, A6; J. A. Byrne, 1997, AT&T: How to turn a dud into a dynamo, *Business Week*, December 8, 95; K. Day, 1997, Big investors say Walter's exit is latest sign that directors are unequal to their task, *Washington Post*, July 18, G1.

A s the opening case illustrates, corporate governance is increasingly important as a part of the strategic management process.[1] If the board makes the wrong decision in selecting the firm's strategic leader, the CEO, the whole firm suffers as well as its shareholders. This may have been the case at AT&T. On the other hand, solid governance procedures can create credibility for the firm and its strategy as in the instance of Campbell Soup.[2]

Corporate governance is a relationship among stakeholders that is used to determine and control the strategic direction and performance of organizations.[3] At its core, corporate governance is concerned with identifying ways to ensure that strategic decisions are made effectively.[4] Additionally, governance can be thought of as a means used in corporations to establish order between parties (the firm's

Corporate governance is a relationship among stakeholders that is used to determine and control the strategic direction and performance of organizations.

owners and its top-level managers) whose interests may be in conflict.[5] In modern corporations, especially those in the United States and the United Kingdom, a primary objective of corporate governance is to ensure that the interests of top-level managers are aligned with shareholders' interests. Corporate governance involves oversight in areas where owners, managers, and members of boards of directors may have conflicts of interest. These areas include the election of directors, general supervision of CEO pay and more focused supervision of director pay, and the corporation's overall structure and strategic direction.[6]

Effective governance of the modern organization is of interest to shareholder activists, businesspeople, business writers, and academic scholars. One reason for this interest is the belief held by some that corporate governance mechanisms have failed to adequately monitor and control top-level managers' strategic decisions.[7] Although perhaps more frequently associated with firms in the United States and the United Kingdom, this perspective is causing changes in governance mechanisms in corporations throughout the world, especially with respect to efforts intended to improve the performance of boards of directors.[8] This attention and interest, however, are understandable for a second and more positive reason; namely, evidence suggests that a well-functioning corporate governance and control system can result in a competitive advantage for an individual firm.[9] For example, with respect to one governance mechanism—the board of directors—it has been suggested that the board's role is rapidly evolving into a major strategic force in U.S. business firms.[10] Thus, in this first chapter describing strategic actions used to implement strategies, we describe monitoring and controlling mechanisms that, when used properly, ensure that top-level managerial decisions and actions contribute to the firm's strategic competitiveness and its ability to earn above-average returns.

Effective corporate governance is also of interest to nations. As stated by a researcher, "Every country wants the firms that operate within its borders to flourish and grow in such ways as to provide employment, wealth, and satisfaction, not only to improve standards of living materially but also to enhance social cohesion. These aspirations cannot be met unless those firms are competitive internationally in a sustained way, and it is this medium- and long-term perspective that makes good corporate governance so vital."[11] Thus, in many individual corporations, shareholders are striving to hold top-level managers more accountable for their decisions and the results they generate. As with individual firms and their boards, nations that govern their corporations effectively may gain a competitive advantage over rival countries.

In a range of countries, but especially in the United States and the United Kingdom, the fundamental goal of business organizations is to maximize shareholder value.[12] Traditionally, shareholders are treated as the firm's key stakeholder because they are the company's legal owners. The firm's owners expect top-level managers and others influencing the corporation's actions (e.g., the board of directors) to make decisions that will result in the maximization of the company's value and, hence, of their own wealth.

In this chapter's first section, we describe the relationship that is the foundation on which the modern corporation is built. For the most part, this relationship provides an understanding of how U.S. firms operate. The majority of this chapter is then devoted to an explanation of various mechanisms owners use to govern managers and ensure that they comply with their responsibility to maximize shareholder value.

In many corporations, shareholders expect top-level managers to make decisions that result in the maximization of the company's value—and of their own wealth.

Four internal governance mechanisms and a single external one are used in the modern corporation (see Table 10.1). The four internal governance mechanisms examined here are (1) ownership concentration, as represented by types of shareholders and their different incentives to monitor managers, (2) the board of directors, (3) executive compensation, and (4) the multidivisional (M-form) organizational structure. (As explained in Chapter 11, in addition to governing managers'

TABLE 10.1 *Corporate Governance Mechanisms*

Internal Governance Mechanisms

Ownership Concentration
- Relative amounts of stock owned by individual shareholders and institutional investors

Board of Directors
- Individuals responsible for representing the firm's owners by monitoring top-level managers' strategic decisions

Executive Compensation
- Use of salary, bonuses, and long-term incentives to align managers' interests with shareholders' interests

Multidivisional Structure
- Creation of individual business divisions to closely monitor top-level managers' strategic decisions

External Governance Mechanism

Market for Corporate Control
- The purchase of a firm that is underperforming relative to industry rivals in order to improve its strategic competitiveness

decisions, the M-form structure is the one required to implement successfully different types of related and unrelated corporate-level diversification strategies.)

We next consider the market for corporate control, an external corporate governance mechanism. Essentially, the market for corporate control is a set of potential owners seeking to "raid" undervalued firms and earn above-average returns on their investments by replacing ineffective top-level management teams.[13] The chapter's focus then shifts to the issue of international corporate governance. We briefly describe governance approaches used in German and Japanese firms whose traditional governance structures are being affected by the realities of competing in the global economy. In part, this discussion suggests the possibility that the structures used to govern global companies in many different countries, including Germany, Japan, the United Kingdom, and the United States, are becoming more, rather than less, similar. Closing our analysis of corporate governance is a consideration of the need for these control mechanisms to encourage and support ethical behavior in organizations.

Before we begin, we need to highlight two matters related to corporate governance. First, research results suggest that the mechanisms explained in this chapter have the potential to influence positively the governance of the modern corporation. This evidence is important, because the development of the modern corporation has placed significant responsibility and authority in the hands of top-level managers. The most effective of these managers hold themselves accountable for their firm's performance and respond positively to the demands of the corporate governance mechanisms explained in this chapter.[14] Second, it is the appropriate use of a variety of mechanisms that results in the effective governance of a corporation. The firm's owners should not expect any single mechanism to govern the company effectively across time. It is through the proper use of several mechanisms that owners are able to govern the corporation in ways that maximize strategic competitiveness and increase the financial value of their firm.[15]

SEPARATION OF OWNERSHIP AND MANAGERIAL CONTROL

Historically, U.S. firms were managed by their founder-owners and their descendants. In these cases, corporate ownership and control resided in the same person(s). As firms grew larger, ". . . the managerial revolution led to a separation of ownership and control in most large corporations, where control of the firm shifted from entrepreneurs to professional managers while ownership became dispersed among thousands of unorganized stockholders who were removed from the day-to-day management of the firm."[16] These changes created the modern public corporation, which is based on the efficient separation of ownership and managerial control. A basic legal premise supporting this efficient separation is that the primary objective of a firm's activities should be to increase the corporation's profit and the financial gains of the owners, that is, the shareholders.[17]

The separation of ownership and managerial control allows shareholders to purchase stock, which entitles them to income (residual returns) from firm operations after expenses have been paid. This right, however, requires they also take a risk that the firm's expenses may exceed its revenues. To manage this investment risk, shareholders seek to maintain a diversified portfolio by investing in several companies to reduce their overall risk.

In small firms, managers often are the owners, so there is no separation between ownership and managerial control, but as firms grow and become more complex, owners/managers may contract with managerial specialists. These managers oversee decision making in the owner's firm and are compensated on the basis of their decision-making skills. Managers, then, operate a corporation through use of their decision-making skills and are viewed as agents of the firm's owners.[18] In terms of the strategic management process (see Figure 1.1 in Chapter 1), managers are expected to form a firm's strategic intent and strategic mission and then formulate and implement the strategies that realize them. Thus, in the modern public corporation, top-level managers, especially the CEO, have primary responsibility for initiating and implementing an array of strategic decisions.

As shareholders diversify their investments over a number of corporations, their risk declines (the poor performance or failure of any one firm in which they invest has less overall effect). Shareholders thus specialize in managing their investment risk; managers specialize in decision making. Without management specialization in decision making and owner specialization in risk bearing, a firm probably would be limited by the abilities of its owners to manage and make effective strategic decisions. Therefore, the separation and specialization of ownership (risk bearing) and managerial control (decision making) is theoretically economically efficient.

357

Agency Relationships

The separation between owners and managers creates an agency relationship. An **agency relationship** exists when one or more persons (the principal or principals) hire another person or persons (the agent or agents) as decision-making specialists to perform a service.[19] Thus, an agency relationship exists when one party delegates decision-making responsibility to a second party for compensation (see Figure 10.1).[20] In addition to shareholders and top-level managers, other examples of agency relationships include consultants and clients and insured and insurer. Moreover, within organizations, an agency relationship exists between managers and their employees as well as between top-level executives and the firm's owners.[21] In the modern corporation, managers must understand the links between these relationships and the firm's effectiveness.[22] Although the agency relationship between managers and their employees is important, this chapter focuses on the agency relationship between the firm's owners (the principals) and top-level managers (the principals' agents) because this relationship is related directly to the strategies implemented by managers.

The separation between ownership and managerial control can be problematic. Research evidence documents a variety of agency problems in the modern corporation.[23] Problems can surface because divergent interests exist between the principal and the agent, or because shareholders often lack direct control of large publicly traded corporations. Problems arise when an agent makes decisions that result in the pursuit of goals that conflict with those of the principals. Thus, when ownership and control are separated, a relationship is formed that *potentially* allows divergent interests (between principals and agents) to surface, which can lead to managerial opportunism.[24] **Managerial opportunism** is the seeking of self-interest with guile (cunning, deceit).[25] Opportunism is both an attitude (e.g., an inclination or proclivity) and a set of behaviors (i.e., specific acts of self-interest that are sought with guile).[26] Although few agents act opportunistically, the inclination and proclivity to engage in opportunistic behaviors varies among individuals and across cultures.[27] The prob-

An **agency relationship** exists when one or more persons (the principal or principals) hire another person or persons (the agent or agents) as decision-making specialists to perform a service.

Managerial opportunism is the seeking of self-interest with guile.

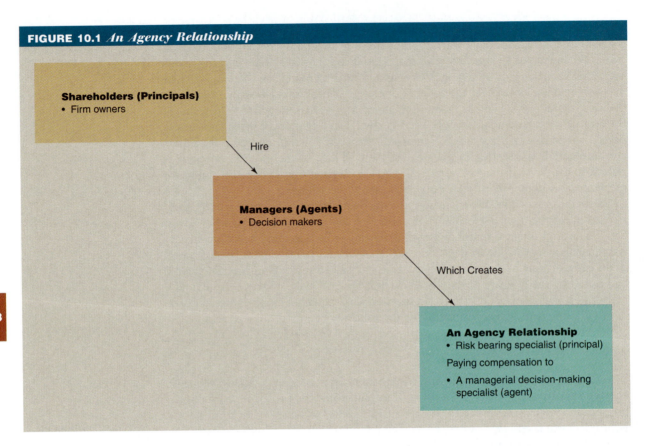

FIGURE 10.1 *An Agency Relationship*

lem for principals, however, is that it is impossible to know beforehand which agents will or will not engage in opportunistic behavior. Because a top-level manager's reputation is an imperfect guide to future behavior, and because opportunistic behavior cannot be observed until it has taken place, principals establish governance and control mechanisms on the assumption that some agents might act opportunistically.[28] Thus, the principals' delegation of decision-making responsibilities to agents creates the opportunity for conflicts of interest to surface. Top-level managers, for example, may make strategic decisions that maximize their personal welfare and minimize their personal risk.[29] Decisions such as these prevent the maximization of shareholder wealth. Decisions regarding product diversification demonstrate these possibilities.

Product Diversification as an Example of an Agency Problem

As explained in Chapter 6, corporate-level strategies involving product diversification can enhance a firm's strategic competitiveness and increase its returns, both of which serve the interests of shareholders and top-level managers. However, because product diversification can provide two benefits to managers that shareholders do not enjoy, top-level executives sometimes prefer more product diversification than do shareholders.[30]

The first managerial benefit occurs because of the positive relationships between diversification and firm size and between firm size and executive compensation. Thus, increased product diversification provides an opportunity for higher compensation for top-level managers through growth in firm size.[31]

The second managerial benefit is that product diversification and the resulting diversification of the firm's portfolio of businesses can reduce top-level managers' employment risk.[32] *Managerial employment risk* is the risk of job loss, loss of compensation, and loss of managerial reputation. These risks are reduced with increased diversification because a firm and its upper-level managers are less vulnerable to the reduction in demand associated with a single or a limited number of product lines or businesses. Furthermore, the firm may have free cash flows over which top-level managers have discretion. *Free cash flows* are resources generated after investment in all projects that have positive net present values within the firm's current product lines.[33] In anticipation of positive returns, managers may decide to use these funds to invest in products that are not associated with the current lines of business, even if the investments increase the firm's level of diversification. The managerial decision to consume free cash flows to increase the firm's diversification inefficiently is an example of self-serving and opportunistic managerial behavior. In contrast to managers, shareholders may prefer that free cash flows be returned as dividends so they will have control over reinvestment decisions.[34]

Curve S in Figure 10.2 depicts shareholders' optimal level of diversification. Owners seek the level of diversification that reduces the risk of the firm's total failure while simultaneously increasing the company's value through the development of economies of scale and scope (see Chapter 6). Of the four corporate-level diversification strategies shown in Figure 10.2, shareholders might prefer the diver-

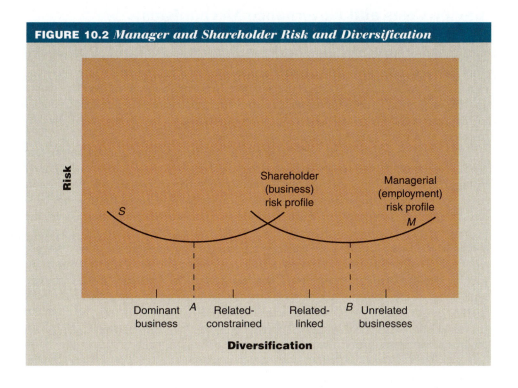

FIGURE 10.2 *Manager and Shareholder Risk and Diversification*

sified position noted by point A on curve S—a position that is located between the dominant business and related-constrained diversification strategies. Of course, the optimum level of diversification sought by owners varies from firm to firm. Factors that affect shareholders' preferences include the firm's primary industry, the intensity of rivalry among competitors in that industry, and the top management team's experience with implementing diversification strategies.

As with principals, upper-level executives—as agents—seek what they perceive to be an optimal level of diversification. Declining performance resulting from too much product diversification increases the probability that a firm will be acquired through the market for corporate control. Once acquired, the employment risk for the firm's top-level managers increases substantially. Furthermore, a manager's employment opportunities in the external managerial labor market (discussed in Chapter 12) are affected negatively by a firm's poor performance. Therefore, top-level managers prefer diversification, but not to a point that it increases their employment risk and reduces their employment opportunities.

Curve M (in Figure 10.2) shows that executives prefer higher levels of product diversification than shareholders. Top-level managers might prefer the level of diversification shown by point B on curve M. In general, shareholders prefer riskier strategies with more focused diversification and reduce their risk through holding a diversified portfolio of equity investments. Alternatively, managers cannot work for a diverse portfolio of firms to balance their employment risk. As such, top-level managers may prefer more diversification in order to maximize firm size and executive compensation and reduce employment risk. Product diversification, therefore, is a potential agency problem that could result in principals incurring costs to control their agents' behaviors.

Agency Costs and Governance Mechanisms

The potential conflict illustrated in Figure 10.2, coupled with the fact that principals do not know which managers might act opportunistically, demonstrates why principals establish governance mechanisms. But establishing and using the governance mechanisms discussed in this chapter is not without costs. **Agency costs** are the sum of incentive, monitoring, enforcement costs, and individual financial losses incurred by principals because it is impossible to use governance mechanisms to guarantee total compliance by the agent.[35]

Agency costs are the sum of incentive, monitoring, enforcement costs, and individual financial losses incurred by principals because it is impossible to use governance mechanisms to guarantee total compliance by the agent.

In general, managerial interests may prevail when governance mechanisms are weak. For example, the firm's level of diversification will move closer to curve M in Figure 10.2 when governance mechanisms allow managers a significant amount of autonomy in making strategic decisions. If, however, the board of directors controls managerial autonomy, or if other strong governance mechanisms are used, the firm's diversification level will approach that desired by shareholders (see curve S).

In the following sections, we explain the effects of various means of governance on managerial decisions to formulate and implement the firm's different strategies, especially corporate-level diversification strategies. We focus on this strategy type because the relationship between principals and agents, developed through the use of governance mechanisms, is observed easily. Moreover, this relationship is critical in diversified firms. The failure to govern strategic decisions properly in companies implementing diversification results in significant negative effects on the firm's performance as measured by strategic competitiveness and financial returns.[36]

OWNERSHIP CONCENTRATION

Ownership concentration is defined by both the number of large-block shareholders and the total percentage of shares they own. **Large-block shareholders** typically own at least five percent of a corporation's issued shares. Ownership concentration as a governance mechanism has been researched extensively.[37] One reason for this level of interest and analysis is that large-block shareholders are increasingly active in their demands that corporations adopt effective governance mechanisms to control the decisions of their managerial agents.[38]

In general, *diffuse ownership* (a large number of shareholders with small holdings and few if any large-block shareholders) produces weak monitoring of managerial decisions. Among other problems, diffuse ownership makes it difficult for owners to coordinate their actions effectively. An outcome of weak monitoring might be diversification of the firm's product lines beyond the shareholders' optimum level. Higher levels of monitoring could encourage managers to avoid levels of diversification that exceed shareholders' preferences. Such monitoring could also disallow excessive compensation paid to managers by holding down diversification and thereby the size of the firm. In fact, research evidence shows that ownership concentration is associated with lower levels of firm diversification.[39] Thus, with high degrees of ownership concentration, the probability is greater that managers' strategic decisions will be intended to maximize shareholder value.

Typically, shareholders monitor managerial decisions and firm actions through the board of directors. Shareholders elect members to their firm's board. Elected members are expected to oversee managerial agents and to ensure that the corporation is operated in ways that will maximize shareholders' wealth.

The Growing Influence of Institutional Owners as Large-Block Shareholders

A classic work published in the 1930s argued that the "modern" corporation had become characterized by a separation of ownership and control.[40] This change occurred as firm growth prevented founders-owners from maintaining their dual positions as owners and managers of their corporations. More recently, another shift has occurred. Ownership of many modern corporations is now concentrated in the hands of institutional investors rather than individual shareholders.[41]

Institutional owners are financial institutions such as stock mutual funds and pension funds that control large-block shareholder positions. Because of their prominent ownership positions, institutional owners, as large-block shareholders, are a powerful governance mechanism.[42] Institutions of these types now own more than 50 percent of the stock in large U.S. corporations. Of the top 1,000 corporations, they own on average 59 percent of the stock.[43] Pension funds alone are expected to control at least one-half of corporate equity by 2000.[44] Thus, as these ownership percentages suggest, institutional owners have both the size and incentive to discipline ineffective top-level managers and are able to influence significantly a firm's choice of strategies and overall strategic decisions.[45]

Ownership concentration is defined by both the number of large-block shareholders and the total percentage of shares they own.

Large-block shareholders typically own at least five percent of a corporation's issued shares.

Institutional owners are financial institutions such as stock mutual funds and pension funds that control large-block shareholder positions.

361

Research evidence indicates that institutional and other large-block shareholders are becoming more active in efforts to influence a corporation's strategic decisions. Initially, the focus seemed to be on the accountability of CEOs. After focusing on the performance of many CEOs, which has contributed to the ouster of a number of them, shareholder activists and institutional investors are targeting what they perceive as ineffective boards of directors (see AT&T opening case example).

Anthony J.F. O'Reilly, former CEO of H.J. Heinz, Inc., was the target of activist shareholders, even though his corporation had earned above-average returns. Both Teachers Insurance and Annuity Association—College Retirement Equities Fund (TIAA-CREF) and California Public Employees' Retirement System (CalPERS) believed that Heinz's board of directors was an example of what a board should not be: "a cozy club of loyalists headed by a powerful and charismatic chieftain."[46] O'Reilly held lavish parties for company officials and analysts. Activists believe that a stronger board would have reined in such costly events. O'Reilly fought such board reforms because Heinz had performed well. However, as the opening case illustrates, Campbell Soup, a rival of Heinz, has found that higher accountability for the board of directors is paying dividends. Recall that Campbell placed first in the *Business Week* survey of corporate governance two years in a row.[47]

CalPERS provides retirement and health coverage to more than one million current and retired public employees.[48] It is the largest public employee pension fund in the United States, with a portfolio approximating $135 billion invested in more than 1,200 companies. As an active institutional owner, the organization's actions have earned it a reputation for bullying some U.S. companies into adopting its recommendations. CalPERS is generally thought to act aggressively to promote decisions and actions that it believes will enhance shareholder value in companies in which it invests. To pressure boards of directors to make what it believes are needed changes, CalPERS annually issues a target list of companies in which it owns stock that it believes are underachieving. This list is based on corporations' relative rates of shareholder return, their degree of responsiveness to CalPERS' inquiries, labor practices, and the percentage of shares owned by CalPERS. Once published, CalPERS usually demands meetings with top-level managers from companies included on the list and is known to flex its muscle to oust directors when its requests are denied.[49] According to CalPERS officials, the intent of these sessions is to persuade corporate boards to force management to initiate appropriate strategic changes inside the targeted company. Based on inputs from this institutional investor, some believe that top-level executives at various companies, including GM, IBM, and Kodak, have lost their jobs.

Public pension funds such as CalPERS also must achieve strategic success through their operations, but research results suggest that the activism of large public pension funds such as CalPERS has not been universally successful. These findings indicate that activists' proposals to top-level managers that are not focused on firm performance issues can have a negative effect on the company's efforts to earn above-average returns. Thus, questions exist regarding the practice of shareholder activists and the long-term performance effects of their actions on targeted firms.[50]

The Strategic Focus discusses CalPERS recent change in its strategic approach to pursue increased investments in international companies. As CalPERS and other pension funds begin to invest overseas, they are actively trying to change corporate governance procedures. Also, as pointed out in the Strategic Focus, institutional investors may consider taking board seats on firms in which they are invested heavily.

STRATEGIC FOCUS

CalPERS Initiates New Shareholder Activist Approaches

Many of the rules of corporate governance have changed because of activist shareholders such as public pension funds like the California Public Employees' Retirement System (CalPERS). Historically, CalPERS has been proud of its intolerance of poor corporate performance. The policies of institutional activists such as CalPERS have changed the way most boards are structured and managed: boards are not overly large now so that they can have more effective group processes. Most board members are composed of outside directors who are non-employees and independent. Outside directors chair key committees such as the audit and compensation committees. Furthermore, new proxy rules have been required by the Security and Exchange Commission because activist investors such as CalPERS have pushed for more accurate information on those who perform the corporate governance role (e.g., board members and large stockholders).

U.S.-style shareholder activism is now being adopted in other areas of the world. For instance, in Europe, the International Corporate Governance Network drew 35 people to an inaugural meeting in London in 1996. Its second meeting in Paris in the summer of 1997 drew 125 people. The French Business Council was addressed by Richard Koppes, the former general council of CalPERS. The top managers of French firms were concerned about governance issues because U.S. institutions already own 25 to 40 percent of the shares of many French companies. Many of these top managers expect to be majority owned by U.S. institutional investors within the next few years. Although many union and civil service employee funds limit investments in non-U.S. companies, others have been increasing the size of their international portfolios. CalPERS, for instance, invests more than $25 billion overseas. This suggests that the organization's fiduciary duty should also challenge it to be more active in overseas governance matters.

Recent actions indicate that CalPERS is, in fact, beginning to flex its muscles overseas. In 1997, it established corporate governance principles for investments in Britain and France. It is now developing similar principles for Germany and Japan. It does not rule out giving foreign companies the same treatment that it has given to U.S. companies in its annual list of underperforming management teams. CalPERS funds invested in foreign shares have risen from $8 billion at the end of 1993 to over $25 billion. CalPERS decided to address corporate governance issues in Britain, France, Germany and Japan because these are the countries where it has the largest holdings.

Britain has a set of guidelines aimed at developing more effective board structures and has improved on the disclosure of compensation. France has also been improving. However, Germany and Japan have large bank ownership stakes and in Japan, cross ownership between companies is common. Therefore, CalPERS is concerned about companies' ability to appoint independent directors, one of its key principles, in these countries. After a significant bear market in Japan, CalPERS expects the Japanese to be more responsive to advice on corporate governance related issues.

Domestically, CalPERS is also considering a new initiative. Until recently, it did not seek direct board seats as a way to further evangelize its principles of corporate governance. Recently, however, trustees of the organization have approved a draft policy that could end the longstanding practice of avoiding directorships. If CalPERS pursues board memberships because of increasing ownership positions, other influential activist funds may follow its lead. The Council of Institutional Investors, a 110-member pension fund group, which holds more than $1 trillion in assets, suggests that the potential implications for such a move would be substantial.

There are concerns about such a move. Terence J. Gallagher, corporate-governance vice president at Pfizer, observed, "You'd be getting sort of a contingency director, which is generally not considered to be good corporate governance. It could lead to friction on the board." It also could lead to micromanagement of the corporation, something that CalPERS has said it opposes. Micromanagement could lead to managers being risk-averse when significant strategic decisions are at issue. As CalPERS and other institutional investors become more proactive, not only in their own domestic economies but also toward international companies, they must avoid taking actions that could reduce a firm's competitiveness.

SOURCE: CalPERS Home Page, 1998, http://www.calpers.ca.gov.may; J. S. Lublin, 1997, CalPERS considers seeking board seats, *Wall Street Journal*, A3, A4; T. A. Stewart, 1997, A visitor from the dark side, The Pathfinder Network, http://www.fortune.com, November 10; S. Webb, 1997, CalPERS sets its sight overseas, *Wall Street Journal*, October 20, C1, C18; S. S. Hemmerick, 1997, CalPERS lends muscle to governance effort, *Pensions & Investments*, March 31, 20.

Shareholder Activism: How Much Is Possible?

The U.S. Securities and Exchange Commission (SEC) has issued several rulings that support shareholder involvement and control of managerial decisions. One such action is the easing of the rule regarding communications among shareholders. Historically, shareholders could communicate among themselves only through what had proved to be a cumbersome and expensive filing process. With a simple notification to the SEC of the intended meeting, shareholders can now meet to discuss a corporation's strategic direction. If a consensus on an issue exists, shareholders can vote as a block. For example, the 20 largest shareholders of Philip Morris own approximately 25 percent of the firm's stock. Coalescing around a position and voting as a block would send a powerful message to Philip Morris' top-level managers and its board of directors. This voting capability has been referred to as *shareholder empowerment*.

Others argue that even greater latitude should be extended to those managing the funds of large institutional investor groups. Allowing these individuals to hold positions on the boards of directors of corporations in which their organization has significant investments might allow fund managers to better represent the interests of those they serve.[51] As the Strategic Focus indicates, CalPERS is considering this because it would enable institutional investors to influence corporations' strategic decisions more effectively. Additionally, this capability would foster more direct disciplining of poor performing or dissident top-level managers when needed.

The type of shareholder and board of director activism we have described sometimes provokes reactions from top-level managers. Unintended and not always anticipated, these reactions require still further attention by those monitoring the decisions being made by the firm's agents. A reaction articulated by one corporate CEO demonstrates this issue. When asked to evaluate results achieved through shareholder activism, the CEO believed that at least some of the actions requested by shareholder activists exceed the roles specified by the separation of ownership and managerial control. When this occurs, the CEO argued, owners and directors begin to micromanage the corporation, which is not their job. Faced with this situation, executives may reduce their managerial employment risk. Implementing strategies with greater diversification, as explained earlier, is one path top-level managers can pursue to achieve this objective. O'Reilly, for instance, did not increase Heinz's diversification, but he held ownership positions and board responsibilities in a number of other enterprises.[52] Of course, such a course reduces the time he was able to spend on Heinz strategic issues.

For this reason, a number of CEOs are deciding to decline to be outside directors on other firms' boards. CEOs that are on too many boards have been criticized. The National Association of Corporate Directors (NACD) has urged that CEOs hold no more than three directorships in publicly held firms. Gordon Bethune of Continental Airlines asks, "How much time do I want to spend doing somebody else's work?" Instead of serving on other firms' boards, top-level managers, such as those at Continental Airlines, increasingly desire to spend time improving their own firm's performance. Improved performance reduces the likelihood that a firm will become a takeover candidate.[53]

Executives may protect themselves against employment risks when institutional investors have major investments in their firm. Besides the offensive protection of doing a better job, they may seek defensive protection from a possible acquisition. Evidence suggests that the number of executives receiving such protection is increasing. In mid-1996, 57 percent of U.S. public companies offered severance packages to top-level executives in case a firm changed hands. The percentage of firms engaging in these practices in 1987 was only 35 percent.[54] A *golden parachute*, a type of managerial protection that pays a guaranteed salary for a specified period of time in the event of a takeover and the loss of one's job, is sought by many top-level managers, particularly the CEO. There are a number of other anti-takeover provisions that allow a firm to defend itself if a takeover is attempted.[55] A more recently developed protection is called "the golden goodbye." A golden goodbye provides automatic payments to top-level executives if their contracts are not renewed, regardless of the reason for nonrenewal. Michael Ovitz, former president

Many top-level executives seek a golden parachute, which will guarantee a salary for a specified period of time in the event of a takeover or loss of a job.

365

of Walt Disney, had a five-year contract that included a $10 million golden good-bye. However, when he stepped down after only one year on the job, he was able to collect $93 million in cash and stock options.[56] Similarly, John R. Walter received a severance package valued at $26 million after working at AT&T for only eight months. In theory, the golden goodbye arrangement protects top-level managers working at corporations whose long-term prospects are uncertain.

In general, though, the degree to which institutional investors can actively monitor the decisions being made in all of the companies in which they are invested is questionable. CalPERS, for instance, targets 12 companies at a time. The New York Teachers Retirement Fund, another activist institutional investor, focuses on 25 of the 1,300 plus companies in its portfolio. Given limited resources, even large-block shareholders tend to concentrate on corporations in which they have significant investments. Thus, although shareholder activism has increased, institutional investors face barriers to the amount of active governance they can realistically employ.[57]

Next, we examine boards of directors—another governance mechanism used to control managerial decisions and align owners' and managers' interests.

BOARDS OF DIRECTORS

As we have described, the practices of large institutional investors have resulted in an increase in ownership concentration in U.S. firms. Nonetheless, diffuse ownership still describes the status of most U.S. firms,[58] which means that monitoring and control of managers by individual shareholders is limited in large corporations. Furthermore, large financial institutions, such as banks, are prevented from directly owning firms and from having representatives on boards of directors. These conditions highlight the importance of the board of directors for corporate governance. Our analysis of the board of directors shows that, although they are imperfect, there is a respected body of thought and research supporting the view that boards of directors can positively influence both managers and the companies they serve.

The **board of directors** is a group of elected individuals whose primary responsibility is to act in the owners' interests by formally monitoring and controlling the corporation's top-level executives.[59] This responsibility is a product of the American legal system, which ". . . confers broad powers on corporate boards to direct the affairs of the organization, punish and reward managers, and protect the rights and interests of shareholders."[60] Thus, an appropriately structured and effective board of directors protects owners from managerial opportunism.

Generally, board members (often called directors) are classified in one of three groups (see Table 10.2). *Insiders* are active top-level managers in the corporation who are elected to the board because they are a source of information about the firm's day-to-day operations.[61] *Related outsiders* have some relationship with the firm—contractual or otherwise—that may create questions about their independence, but these individuals are not involved with the corporation's day-to-day activities. *Outsiders* are individuals elected to the board to provide independent counsel to the firm and may hold top-level managerial positions in another company or have been elected to the board prior to the beginning of the current CEO's tenure.[62]

Some argue that many boards are not effectively fulfilling their primary fiduciary duty to protect shareholders. Among other possibilities, it may be that boards are a managerial tool—a tool that largely rubber stamps managers' self-serving ini-

The **board of directors** is a group of elected individuals whose primary responsibility is to act in the owners' interests by formally monitoring and controlling the corporation's top-level executives.

TABLE 10.2 *Classifications of Boards of Directors' Members*

Insiders
- The firm's CEO and other top-level managers

Related outsiders
- Individuals not involved with the firm's day-to-day operations, but who have a relationship with the company

Outsiders
- Individuals who are independent of the firm—in terms of day-to-day operations and other relationships

tiatives.[63] In general, those critical of boards as a governance device believe that inside managers dominate boards and exploit their personal ties with them. A widely accepted view is that a board with a significant percentage of its membership from the firm's top-level executives tends to result in relatively weak monitoring and control of managerial decisions.[64] Board critics advocate reforms to ensure that independent outside directors represent a significant majority of the total board's membership.[65] Practitioners and academics, however, disagree over the most appropriate role of outside directors in a firm's strategic decision-making process.[66]

Because of external pressures, board reforms have been initiated. To date, these reforms have generally called for an increase in the number of outside directors, relative to insiders, serving on a corporation's board. For example, in 1984, the New York Stock Exchange started requiring that listed firms have board audit committees composed solely of outside directors.[67] As a result of external pressures, more boards of large corporations are now dominated by outsiders. But with fewer insiders and related outsiders on a firm's board, legitimate managerial concerns may not be adequately represented. Thus, there are potential strategic implications associated with the movement toward having corporate boards dominated by outsiders.

Outsiders do not have contact with the firm's day-to-day operations. This lack of contact precludes easy access to the rich information about managers and their skills that is required to evaluate managerial decisions and initiatives effectively. Valuable information may be obtained through frequent interactions with insiders during board meetings. Insiders possess such information by virtue of their organizational positions. Thus, boards with a critical mass of insiders can be informed more effectively about intended strategic initiatives—both in terms of the reasons for them and the outcomes expected through their accomplishments.[68] Without this type of information, outsider-dominated boards may emphasize financial, as opposed to strategic, evaluations. Such evaluations shift risk to top-level managers, who, in turn, may make decisions to maximize their interests and reduce their employment risk. Reductions in R&D investments, additional diversification of the firm, and pursuit of greater levels of compensation are examples of decisions managers could make to achieve these objectives.

Enhancing the Effectiveness of the Board of Directors as a Governance Mechanism

Our discussion has suggested that the board of directors is an important source of control and governance in the modern corporation. Because of this importance, and as a result of increased scrutiny from shareholders, particularly large institutional investors, the performances of individual board members and of entire boards are being evaluated more formally and with greater intensity.[69] Some believe that directors increase the probability of fulfilling their responsibilities effectively when they are honest and act with prudence and integrity for the good of the entire firm and are committed to reaching independent judgments on an informed basis rather than rubber stamping management proposals.[70]

Given the demand for greater accountability and improved performance, many boards of directors have initiated voluntary changes. Among these changes are (1) increases in the diversity of board members' backgrounds (e.g., a greater number of directors are being selected from public service, academic, and scientific settings; the percentage of boards with ethnic minorities has increased; and more U.S. boards now have members from different countries), (2) the strengthening of internal management and accounting control systems, and (3) the establishment and consistent use of formal processes to evaluate the board's performance. The result of changes such as these should be enhancements in the effectiveness of the board of directors as a means of control.

The following Strategic Focus also indicates that other innovative board approaches are being pursued. Managers are becoming more interested and aggressive in putting outside directors on their company's boards. One reason for this is that CEOs are finding that including a top-notch outside director can increase a firm's stock price. McKinsey & Co., in a hypothetical survey, found that when companies in which outsiders constitute a majority of the board, owned significant amounts of stock, were subjected to formal evaluation, and were not personally tied to top management, institutional shareholders were willing to pay up to 11 percent more for their shares.[71] Also, top boards, its seems, are becoming smaller, especially in high-technology firms, such as many found in Silicon Valley. Increasingly, outside directors are being required to hold significant equity stakes as a prerequisite to holding a board position. A recent study also suggests that inside director performance increases if they hold an equity position. The announcement of an inside director with less than 5 percent ownership decreases shareholder wealth, but an insider with ownership between 5 percent and 25 percent increases shareholder wealth. Therefore, an inside director's knowledge of the firm can be used appropriately. Finally, an inside director's relationship to the CEO does not necessarily lead to CEO entrenchment if the inside director has a strong ownership position.[72]

STRATEGIC FOCUS

Examples of Board of Directors Reforms

Shareholder activism has pressured many boards to undertake significant reforms. Many CEOs are also seeking to use the board as a way to improve strategy and corporate performance. The Business Roundtable, which includes 200 CEOs of the largest U.S. companies, has openly endorsed ideas on corporate governance once considered radical. The Roundtable is endorsing that the utmost duty of both management and corporate boards is to ensure that shareholder wealth is created.

During the time that Louis E. Platt has been CEO at Hewlett-Packard (HP), he indicates that he has benefited significantly from his board and the right level of independence. He suggests that there needs to be an effective balance between collaboration and independence to function appropriately. HP's board emphasizes three fundamental elements that create effective governance. First, there is an emphasis on performance. If the firm is not performing well, the board is not likely to perform well either. This is the foundational governance principle. The second element is to make sure that each board member is an effective representative of the company's shareholders. Board service then is not just supplemental income for board members. They must realize that if something goes wrong, shareholders expect accountability from not only the company managers but also board members for not performing well as their representatives. Finally, they seek to have a culture of openness between the CEO and board members. If the company stumbles and the board struggles to deal effectively with its poor performance, the board may have been kept in the dark about the real issues facing the company.

HP's board, in coordination with the CEO, has developed a set of guidelines and duties for directors that has been approved by CalPERS. In addition, the board has established the following mission statement: "The mission of the board of directors of Hewlett-Packard Company is to monitor and support management in creating long term value for its shareholders, customers and employees in an ethically and socially responsible manner while maintaining the standard of excellence that has become associated with Hewlett-Packard."

Although the board's approach has improved governance substantially and HP's performance is exemplary, Albert Dunlap, the former CEO of Sunbeam, pursued a more radical approach to board reform. When he came to Sunbeam, the first thing he did was pay the board 100 percent in stock. Additionally, he had them buy stock in the firm as a condition of being on the board. He also did this at Scott Paper, and it was considered to be revolutionary. He has even undertaken to put governance activists on his boards. For instance, Charles Elson, a professor at Stetson University of Law, and a noted writer and theorist on the role of the board and the value of shareholder activism, was put on Sunbeam's board. As a legal academic, buying five thousand shares at $23 per share was a significant commitment. He indicated that the investment was significantly more than he had equity in his home. He obviously had to put his money where his mouth was since he had been writing about governance activism for some time. Dunlap has also suggested board term limits of five years.

Interestingly, Dunlap believes that the CEO should also be the chairperson. This view is contrary to many of the governance views held by institutional investors such as CalPERS. In support of this belief, he says the following: "The professional chairman comes to that meeting, and although these are capable, well-meaning people, they don't have enough background in the company to raise the important issues. They are not conversant enough with what's going on. The board meeting becomes highly inefficient and many times misses the most important points." However, he also suggests that he needs a strong board: "If you don't have a strong board, you will fail. I need people who will stand up and say, 'That's nonsense.'"

He also suggests that a board should never have more than ten people. In fact, the ideal board would probably have eight people, according to Dunlap. One other insider would be useful on the board, the chief financial officer, because he or she has to be so intimately involved in board communications. He would also seek to have a board with a variety of backgrounds to help a company deal with international, marketing, and financial market issues. Dunlap has criticized the typical board as "a group of CEOs who have failed miserably running companies, and yet they are on a multiplicity of other boards."

Although Al Dunlap has run large companies, his approach is similar to that of smaller more entrepreneurial firms such as those found in Silicon Valley. Because today's firms are intensely competitive, the role of the board of directors has become a lot less ceremonial and more proactive in the oversight and actual running of the corporation. The high-tech-

369

nology sector, which accounts for approximately one quarter of U.S. wage growth, has an approach that may be useful in creating more successful boards. For most Silicon Valley boards, their role is to be active in the strategic direction of the company. Rather than sheer oversight, each director brings to the board some specialized skill in specific areas (sales and marketing, legal, technical, financial, etc.). The board helps the CEO by asking hard questions to ensure that the strategic direction is sound and viable. The boards that are able to do this have several characteristics in common.

These boards have far fewer members than most boards of comparable companies outside the technology industry. For instance, Sun Microsystems, Seagate, Oracle, and Cisco each have fewer than 10 directors on their boards. Smaller and faster growing successful companies often have as few as five directors where traditional companies will have a dozen or more such board members. Large boards create communication difficulties, which tend to make boards less efficient. Some view small boards as too cohesive, thus stifling dissent. Experience shows, however, that smaller group dynamics allows for freer exchange of views because dissent in a smaller group is less imposing than being an outcast in a larger group. Also, small boards put a premium on the effectiveness of individual directors. "Glamour" directors who do not have specific knowledge or expertise relevant to the company are not justifiable. In contrast, effective boards feature people who are familiar with the company, including its venture capitalists, lawyers, and consultants. Although these people are considered outsiders, they have a closer relationship with the company and understand internal operations better than those who would be recommended under traditional governance theory. The best Silicon Valley directors are quite independent, but they also have a large equity stake in the firms they run. Meetings are more frequent and informal exchange of information takes place on a regular basis. Usually firms' boards meet every eight weeks and more frequently in a crisis situation.

The high ownership position is particularly true of venture capitalists and early advisers and investors in high-technology companies. High-technology companies usually also make sure that management teams have large equity stakes and therefore a common interest with shareholders. The large equity ownership of officers, directors and employees ensures common interest among all stakeholders. Although boards of high-technology companies have instituted practices that don't necessarily fit with current governance procedures, they may be worth considering as a model because of the success of many of these firms.

SOURCES: J. A. Byrne, 1997, Governance: CEOs catch up with shareholder activists, *Business Week*, September 22, 36; J. A. Byrne, 1997, The CEO and the board, *Business Week*, September 15, 106–116; Reforming the Board, 1997, *The Economist*, August 9, 16–17; A. Dunlap, 1997, On "Dunlapping" the Board, *Corporate Board*, January-February, 102–108; D. J. Berger, 1997, The Silicon Valley board, *Corporate Board*, July-August, 105–110; L. E. Platt, 1997, Governance the H-P Way, *Directors & Boards*, 21; no. 4: 20–25; Charles Elson: The board outsider goes inside, 1997, *Corporate Board*, March-April, 32.

Besides the board reforms mentioned in the Strategic Focus, a number of analysts have suggested that more women need to be represented on boards. Approximately 10.6 percent of board seats are held by women.[73] Korn/Ferry International, an executive search firm, reports that 71 percent of boards surveyed had at least one woman on the board, up from 46 percent a decade ago. Catalyst, a nonprofit group that studies women in business, notes that among the *Fortune* 500, 84 percent have at least one woman on their board. However, the increase in 1997 was only 3 percent, following jumps of 9 percent and 7 percent the previous two years; thus, among *Fortune* 500 firms the rate of inclusion is slowing.[74] However, Korn/Ferry's survey found that 36 percent of companies reported that at least one other woman has joined after the first woman or women were put on a board. The survey, however, reported that although their influence was increasing, female board members believed their opinions were weighed less heavily in executive succession and compensation decisions. Thus, it appears that more board reform is necessary in regard to diversity and board functioning.[75]

Next, we discuss a highly visible corporate governance mechanism—executive compensation.

EXECUTIVE COMPENSATION

A reading of the business press shows that the compensation of top-level managers, and especially of CEOs, generates a great deal of interest and strongly held opinions. What factors account for this level of visibility and interest? In response to the issues suggested by this question, two researchers observed that while "widespread interest in CEO pay can be traced to a natural curiosity about extremes and excesses . . . it also stems from a more substantive reason. Namely, to observe CEO pay is to observe in an indirect but very tangible way the fundamental governance processes in large corporations. Who has power? What are the bases of power? How and when do owners and managers exert their relative preferences? How vigilant are boards? Who is taking advantage of whom?"[76]

The purpose of executive compensation is to improve the alignment of management and shareholder interests and reward managers for effort rendered.[77] The board of directors is responsible for determining the extent to which the firm's executive compensation structure provides incentives to top-level managers to act in the owners' best interests.[78]

Executive compensation is a governance mechanism that seeks to align managers' and owners' interests through salary, bonuses, and long-term incentive compensation such as stock options. Stock options are a mechanism used to link executives' performance to the performance of their company's stock.[79] Increasingly, long-term incentive plans are becoming a critical part of compensation packages in U.S. firms.[80] At Baxter International, for example, more than 70 senior-level managers were extended an opportunity to take out personal loans from a bank to buy up to several times their annual compensation in the company's common stock.[81] This decision is supported by the conviction of many board directors that linking more of top-level management's overall compensation to the corporation's financial performance is a superior way to align managers' and owners' interests.

Using executive compensation effectively as a governance mechanism is particularly challenging in firms implementing international strategies. For example, preliminary evidence suggests that the interests of owners of multinational corporations are served best when there is less uniformity among the firm's foreign subsidiaries' compensation plans rather than more.[82] Developing an array of unique compensation plans requires additional monitoring and increases the firm's agency costs. For instance, this study also found that the cultural distance between the headquarters country and the foreign subsidiary country (e.g., U.S. headquarters is more culturally distant from a subsidiary in Japan than one in the U.K.) increases the agency problem. Pay must, therefore, align correctly with the situation.

371

Executive compensation is a governance mechanism that seeks to align managers' and owners' interests through salary, bonuses, and long-term incentive compensation such as stock options.

A Complicated Governance Mechanism

For several reasons, executive compensation, especially long-term incentive compensation, is complicated. First, the strategic decisions made by top-level managers are typically complex and nonroutine; as such, direct supervision of executives is inappropriate for judging the quality of their decisions. Because of this, there is a tendency to link the compensation of top-level managers to measurable outcomes such as financial performance. Second, an executive's decision often affects a firm's financial outcome over an extended period of time, making it difficult to assess the effect of current decisions on the corporation's performance. In fact, strategic decisions are more likely to have long-term, rather than short-term, effects on a company's strategic outcomes. Third, a number of variables intervene between top-level managerial decisions and behavior and firm performance. Unpredictable economic, social, or legal changes (see Chapter 2) make it difficult before implementation to discern the effects of strategic decisions. Thus, although performance-based compensation may provide incentives to managers to make decisions that best serve shareholders' interests, such compensation plans alone are imperfect in their ability to monitor and control managers.

Although incentive compensation plans may increase firm value in line with shareholder expectations, they are subject to managerial manipulation. For instance, annual bonuses may provide incentives to pursue short-run objectives at the expense of the firm's long-term interests. Supporting this conclusion, some research has found that bonuses based on annual performance were negatively related to investments in R&D, which may affect the firm's long-term strategic competitiveness.[83] Although long-term performance-based incentives may reduce the temptation to underinvest in the short run, they increase executive exposure to risks associated with uncontrollable events, such as market fluctuations and industry decline.[84] The longer the focus of incentive compensation, the greater the long-term risks borne by top-level managers.

The Effectiveness of Executive Compensation

In recent times, many stakeholders, including shareholders, have been angered by the compensation received by some top-level managers, especially CEOs. CEOs have a different perspective. George Fisher, chairman and CEO of Eastman Kodak, stated that "We all should be compensated based on competitive issues. If you want a world-class shortstop, you pay. The good news is that many CEOs are getting well-compensated for really good performances."[85] Indeed, it is the rare CEO who does not sincerely believe that she or he has earned a reward.[86] Thus, some executives argue that they are being rewarded for effectively making critical decisions that affect their firm's performance in the highly competitive global economy.[87]

The level and intensity of the dissatisfaction with executive compensation appears to be influenced by layoffs announced by a host of corporations in the United States and across the world.[88] Some of those critical of executive compensation as a means of corporate governance cited the experiences of AT&T's workers and the firm's CEO.[89] During 1996, the year in which AT&T decided to lay off as many as 40,000 employees, then current CEO Robert E. Allen received $16.2 million in salary and stock payouts. As an indication of the complexity of achieving strategic competitiveness in the global economy, AT&T expected to hire as many as 15,000 new employees during 1996 while laying off thousands of others in order to restructure the businesses in its diversified portfolio.[90] At the beginning of 1998, the new CEO of AT&T, C. Michael Armstrong, suggested that AT&T might lay off as many as 18,000 plus 7,000 announced earlier. Although in the short run the stock fell 5.8 percent, Armstrong's compensation package will be based on future performance.[91]

In general, it may be that organizational employees, a key stakeholder, are feeling disenfranchised, discouraged, and angry in a time period of significant downsizings, stagnant wages, and ever more burdensome work loads for layoff survivors.[92] Contributing to these feelings is the fact that during 1996, the average salary and bonus for CEOs increased by 39 percent. When stock options are included total compensation rose 54 percent. This increase compares to an average gain of 3.2 percent for white-collar professionals and of 3 percent for factory employees during the same year.[93] Moreover, the spread between the pay of the typical worker and CEOs concerns employees. In the 1960s the ratio between a worker's pay and that of the CEO was 30-to-1; by the end of 1995 it was 100-to-1.[94]

Among several challenges facing board directors striving to use executive compensation to align managers' interests with shareholders' interests is the determination of what represents "fair" compensation for top-level managers. As guidance for making this decision, board directors should remember that the most important criterion to consider is shareholder wealth creation. This is necessary because the economic principles on which executive compensation is based are concerned not with fairness but with productivity.[95] At least at a point in time, the situation at Green Tree Financial demonstrated the effectiveness of linking an executive's compensation with her or his performance.

At Green Tree, the CEO, Lawrence M. Coss, received a $65.1 million bonus during 1995 and a $102.4 million bonus in 1996.[96] Based in St. Paul, Minnesota, this company finances manufactured housing and home improvement loans. Green Tree had been one of the best performing stocks on the New York Stock Exchange. Between 1991 and 1996, its stock had compounded annual returns of 53 percent. As a result of the creation of wealth for shareholders at a point in time, "... Green Tree isn't getting gripes from stockholders about Mr. Coss's compensation," said John Dolphin, Green Tree's vice president for investor relations. Dolphin further noted that Coss's contract was entirely performance based and that shareholders were thrilled with his work and the corporation's financial performance.[97] His compensation was 2.5 percent of pretax earnings paid in shares pegged to the 1991 value of $3 per share. When the stock soared above $45 dollars per share, so did his compensation.

Somewhat similarly, GE's CEO Jack Welch saw his salary and bonus increase 22.3 percent between 1994 and 1995 and 18 percent between 1995 and 1996. Welch was also awarded stock-appreciation rights valued at a potential $12.9 and $21.3 million at the close of the firm's 1995 and 1996 fiscal years, respectively. In 1996, GE's compensation committee observed that Welch's compensation was appropriate in light of the corporation's financial performance and the CEO's decisive management of both operational and strategic issues.[98] The amount of shareholder wealth created at GE during Welch's tenure as CEO appears to support the compensation committee's position.

However, in *Business Week*'s special report on executive pay for 1996, both these executives were criticized because the size of the compensation was so great relative to the actual shareholder value created.[99] In regard to Green Tree, although most shareholders have not complained, Mr. Coss and Green Tree's board have been sued by several small pension funds for excessive compensation. When Green Tree reported a charge to fourth quarter 1997 earnings due to the high rate of refinancing among its clientele, its stock price began to fall. When Green Tree restated its earnings, Coss was asked to repay part of his compensation. Also, because the company had been overly aggressive in its accounting for earnings, it changed its procedure. Furthermore, Coss's compensation was changed to a more standard plan where he received stock options instead of stock as a percentage of earnings. In 1998, Green Tree was acquired by Conseco, partly because its stock price was low.[100]

As the example of Green Tree seems to suggest, executive compensation is an imperfect means of corporate governance. (Individually, each governance mechanism discussed in this chapter is imperfect.) The dissatisfaction with executive compensation being expressed by shareholders and other stakeholders as well may have surfaced because of the mechanism's imperfection and/or ineffective use. Specifically, there is criticism of excessive stock option packages such as that of Michael Eisner at Disney.[101] It is possible that members of corporate boards of directors have not been effective in their use of this governance mechanism. If executive compensation plans are not aligning top-level managers' interests with the interests of other stakeholders, especially those of shareholders, appropriate changes must be made. For instance, one proposal is that, to be awarded the intended stock option, the executive must outperform peer companies. Alternatively, boards may be rewarding mediocre performance when the stock market is going up in general and executives are able to take advantage of the increased value without appropriate accountability.

Thus, the proactive positions concerning executive compensation taken by institutional investors and individual shareholders have been effective. Input from these stakeholders should result in modifications to executive compensation that will improve its value as a means of corporate governance.

Many stakeholders are dissatisfied with executive compensation as a means of corporate governance. The excessive stock option package commanded by Michael Eisner at Disney, for example, has been severely criticized.

374

A company's organizational structure also influences the alignment of principals' and agents' interests. As indicated in the next section, structure can be an especially valuable governance mechanism in diversified firms.

THE MULTIDIVISIONAL STRUCTURE

Oliver Williamson, an economist, argues that organizational structure, particularly the multidivisional (M-form) structure, serves as an internal governance mechanism in that it controls managerial opportunism.[102] The corporate office that is a part of the M-form structure, along with the firm's board of directors, closely monitors the strategic decisions of managers responsible for the performance of the different business units or divisions that are a part of the diversified corporation's operations. Active monitoring of an individual unit's performance suggests a keen managerial interest in making decisions that will maximize shareholders' wealth. Williamson believes that the M-form structure brings forth a greater managerial interest in wealth maximization than do other organizational structures such as the variations of the functional structure (another type of structure that is discussed in Chapter 11).

To improve his firm's financial performance, Domenico Cempella, CEO of the Italian flag carrier Alitalia SpA, announced a restructuring plan that calls for use of the M-form structure. To provide managerial incentives and controls so Alitalia could better compete in what was to become a deregulated European market after 1998, the CEO intended to split the company into two separate, highly competitive carriers—one for long routes and one for medium and short routes—as well as other operating divisions.[103] Recently GE, another corporation using a multidivisional organizational structure, allocated $200 million to a program (called Six Sigma, which refers in statistical terms to a very high level of quality) that was designed to sharply improve the quality of the firm's vast array of products. At the time of the announced allocation, GE generated approximately 35,000 defects per million products. The objective of the program was to reduce defects to less than 4 per million. To align the interests of division managers with those of the CEO and the program being implemented to enhance shareholder wealth, CEO Jack Welch decided that GE would weight 40 percent of bonus compensation on the intensity of managers' efforts and progress being made toward achieving Six Sigma quality.[104]

While the M-form may limit division managers' opportunistic behaviors, it may not limit corporate-level managers' self-serving actions. For example, research evidence suggests that diversified firms organized through the M-form structure are likely to implement corporate-level strategies that cause them to become even more diversified.[105] In fact, one of the potential problems with the divisionalization that is a part of the M-form structure is that it will be used too aggressively.[106] As discussed in Chapters 6 and 10, beyond some point, diversification serves managers' interests more than it serves shareholders' interests.

In addition, a depth-for-breadth trade-off often occurs in an extensively diversified firm with an M-form structure. Because of the diversification of product lines (breadth of businesses), top-level executives do not have adequate information to evaluate the strategic decisions and actions of divisional managers (depth). To complete their evaluations, they must wait to observe the financial results achieved by individual business units. In the interim period, division managers may be able to act opportunistically.

Where internal controls are limited because of extensive diversification, the external market for corporate control and the external managerial labor market may be the primary controls on managers' decisions and actions, such as pursuing acquisitions to increase the size of their firm and their compensation.[107] Because external markets lack access to relevant information inside the firm, they tend to be less efficient than internal governance mechanisms for monitoring top-level managers' decisions and performance. Therefore, in diversified firms, corporate executive decisions can be controlled effectively only when other strong internal governance mechanisms (e.g., the board of directors) are used in combination with the M-form structure. When used as a single governance mechanism, the M-form structure may actually facilitate overdiversification and inappropriately high compensation for corporate executives.[108]

MARKET FOR CORPORATE CONTROL

The **market for corporate control** is composed of individuals and firms that buy ownership positions in (or take over) potentially undervalued corporations so they can form new divisions in established diversified companies or merge two previously separate firms.

The market for corporate control is an external governance mechanism that becomes active when a firm's internal controls fail.[109] The **market for corporate control** is composed of individuals and firms that buy ownership positions in (or take over) potentially undervalued corporations so they can form new divisions in established diversified companies or merge two previously separate firms. Because they are assumed to be the party responsible for formulating and implementing the strategy that led to poor performance, the top management team of the purchased corporation is usually replaced. Thus, when operating effectively, the market for corporate control ensures that managerial incompetence is disciplined.[110] This governance mechanism should be activated by a firm's poor performance relative to industry competitors. A firm's poor performance, often demonstrated by the earning of below-average returns, is an indicator that internal governance mechanisms have failed—that is, their use did not result in managerial decisions that maximized shareholder value.

Michael Price is a participant in the market for corporate control. He is head of Franklin Mutual which oversees $28 billion in assets. Known by various terms, including value investor and corporate raider, individuals such as Price purchase shares of an underperforming company's stock. Through their ownership position, such individuals pressure firms to maximize shareholder value by breaking up assets or selling out. He has recently tried to put Dow Jones, a publishing company, into play. His plan was to merge assets of Dow Jones with the Washington Post. Dow Jones has good potential capabilities, but has been underperforming lately. Price has also been involved in forcing out management teams, directly or indirectly at Sunbeam, Dial, and Chase Manhattan. For instance, partly as a result of his pressure, Chemical Bank bought Chase Manhattan.[111]

Managerial Defense Tactics

Historically, the increased use of the market for corporate control has enhanced the sophistication and variety of managerial defense tactics that are used to reduce the influence of this governance mechanism. The market for corporate control tends to increase risk for managers. As a result, managerial pay is often increased indirectly through *golden parachutes* (where a CEO can receive up to three years' salary if his or her firm is taken over). Among other outcomes, takeover defenses increase the costs of mounting a takeover and can entrench incumbent management while reducing the chances of introducing a new management team.[112] Some defense tactics require the type of asset restructuring that results from divesting one or more divisions in the diversified firm's portfolio. Others necessitate only financial structure changes such as repurchasing shares of the firm's outstanding stock.[113] Some tactics (e.g., a change in the state of incorporation) require shareholder approval, but the greenmail tactic (wherein money is used to repurchase stock from a corporate raider to avoid the takeover of the firm) does not.

A potential problem with the market for corporate control is that it may not be totally efficient. A study of several of the most active corporate raiders in the 1980s showed that approximately 50 percent of their takeover attempts targeted firms with above-average performance in their industry—corporations that were neither undervalued nor poorly managed.[114] The targeting of high-performance businesses may lead to acquisitions at premium prices and to decisions by target firm managers to establish what may prove to be costly takeover defense tactics to protect their corporate positions.

Although the market for corporate control lacks the precision possible with internal governance mechanisms, the fear of acquisition and influence by corporate raiders is an effective constraint on the managerial growth motive.[115] The market for corporate control has been responsible for significant changes in many firms' strategies and has, when used appropriately, served the best interests of corporate owners—the shareholders. For instance, the announcement of Compaq's purchase of Digital Equipment shares lifted the Digital share price by 25 percent.[116] Although unthinkable a few years ago, Digital has been performing poorly recently, and the link with Compaq appears to be a positive result for Digital shareholders.

Next, we address the topic of international corporate governance primarily through a description of governance structures used in Germany and Japan.

INTERNATIONAL CORPORATE GOVERNANCE

Comparisons of corporate governance structures used in other economic systems with the one used in the United Kingdom and the United States are interesting.[117] In this section, we describe the governance structures used in Germany and Japan among others. Our brief discussion of the governance of German and Japanese corporations shows that the nature of corporate governance in these two nations is being affected by the realities of the global economy and the competitive challenges that are a part of it.[118] Thus, while the stability associated with German and Japanese governance structures has been viewed historically as an asset, some believe that it may now be a burden.[119]

We chose to examine Germany and Japan here because of their prominent positions in the global economy. Furthermore, their governance structures contrast with those of the United States and the United Kingdom. The strategic management process should be used to study governance processes throughout the world to increase understanding.

Corporate Governance in Germany

In many private German firms, the owner and manager are still the same individual. In these instances, there is no agency problem. Even in publicly traded corporations, there is often a dominant shareholder.

Historically, banks have been at the center of the German corporate governance structure, which is the case in many continental European countries such as Italy and France. As lenders, banks become major shareholders when companies they had financed earlier seek funding on the stock market or default on loans. Although stakes are usually under 10 percent, there is no legal limit on how much of a firm's stock banks can hold (except that a single ownership position cannot exceed 15 percent of the bank's capital). Today, various types of specialized institutions—savings banks, mortgage banks, savings and loan associations, leasing firms, and insurance companies—are also important sources of corporate funds.

Through their own shareholdings and by casting proxy votes for individual shareholders who retain their shares with the banks, three banks in particular—Deutsche, Dresdner, and Commerzbank—exercise significant power. Although individual shareholders can tell the banks how to vote their ownership position, they generally elect not to do so. A combination of their own holdings with their proxies results in majority positions for these three banks in many German companies. These banks, as well as others, monitor and control managers both as lenders and as shareholders by electing representatives to supervisory boards.

German firms with more than 2,000 employees are required to have a two-tier board structure. Through this structure, the supervision of management is separated from other duties normally assigned to a board of directors, especially the nomination of new board members. Thus, Germany's two-tiered system places the responsibility to monitor and control managerial (or supervisory) decisions and actions in the hands of a separate group.[120] One of the reasons underlying this division is that the stronger management is the less safe it is to assume that its interests coincide with those of the owners of the business. The application of this principle is to place all the functions of direction and management in the hands of the management board—the Vorstand—except appointment to the Vorstand itself, which is the responsibility of the supervisory tier—the Aufsichtsrat. Employees, union members, and shareholders appoint members to the Aufsichtsrat.

As implied by our discussion of the importance of banks in Germany's corporate governance structure, private shareholders do not have major ownership positions in their country's firms. Historically, continental Europeans have held the belief that the control of large corporations is too important an asset to be left only to the discretion of public shareholders.[121] Large institutional investors such as pension funds and insurance companies are also relatively insignificant owners of corporate stock. Thus, at least historically, top-level managers in German corporations generally have not been dedicated to the proposition that their decisions and actions should result in maximization of shareholder value. This lack of emphasis on shareholder value is changing in some German firms.

At Veba AG, a diversified industrial giant that builds shopping malls, runs a cable-television system, and is Germany's largest operator of gasoline stations, CEO Ulrich Hartmann has taken actions that are quite different from those observed normally in German firms. To become less vulnerable to a takeover and to create shareholder value, Hartmann evaluated and changed Veba's portfolio. Veba exited the coal-trading business, reduced the workforce by 12,000 in its chemical operations, closed its tire-rubber business, and sold its synthetic-rubber operation. In addition, it initiated an investor relations program where it explained its actions to key investors. As a result, its stock price doubled between 1991 and 1995, and it has consistently outperformed the German stock market in recent years. Many German companies such as Veba are listing on stock exchanges outside of Germany, which often require more transparency and accounting disclosure.[122] As this practice continues, German firms will likely move toward a greater emphasis on creating shareholder value.

Corporate Governance in Japan

Attitudes toward corporate governance in Japan are affected by the concepts of obligation, family, and consensus. In Japan, obligation does not result from broad general principles; rather, it is a product of specific causes or events. In this context, an obligation "... may be to return a service for one rendered or it may derive from a more general relationship, for example, to one's family or old alumni, or one's company (or Ministry), or the country. This sense of particular obligation is common elsewhere but it feels stronger in Japan."[123] As part of a company family, individuals are members of a unit that envelops their lives to an unusual degree. Families command the attention and allegiance of parties from the top to the bottom in corporations. Moreover, a keiretsu (defined in Chapter 9) is more than an economic concept—it, too, is a family. Consensus, the most important influence on the Japanese corporate governance structure, calls for the expenditure of significant amounts of energy to win the hearts and minds of people when possible as opposed to proceeding by edict of top-level managers. Consensus is highly valued, even when a firm's commitment to it results in a slow and cumbersome decision-making process.

As in Germany, banks play a more important role in financing and monitoring large public firms in Japan. The bank owning the largest share of stocks and largest amount of debt, the main bank, has the closest relationship with the company's top-level managers. The main bank not only provides financial advice to the firm, but also is responsible for closely monitoring managerial agents. Thus, Japan has a bank-based financial and corporate governance structure while the United States has a market-based financial and governance structure.

Aside from lending money (debt), a Japanese bank can hold up to 5 percent of a firm's total stock; a group of related financial institutions can hold up to 40 percent. In many cases, main-bank relationships are part of a horizontal keiretsu (see Chapter 9). A horizontal keiretsu is a group of firms tied together by cross-shareholdings. Thus, firms in such a keiretsu develop interrelationships and are interdependent. A keiretsu firm usually owns less than 2 percent of any other member firm; however, each company typically has a stake of that size in every firm in the keiretsu. As a result, somewhere between 30 percent and 90 percent of a firm is owned by other members of the keiretsu. Thus, a keiretsu is a system of relationship investments.

Other characteristics of Japan's corporate governance structure include (1) powerful government intervention (the Japanese Ministry of Finance maintains strong regulatory control of all of Japan's businesses), (2) close relationships between corporations and government sectors, (3) passive and stable shareholders (individuals and groups who exercise little monitoring and control of managerial agents), and (4) the virtual absence of an external market for corporate control, although mergers are common.

As is the case in Germany and the United States, Japan's corporate governance structure is changing. For example, because of their continuing development as economic organizations, the role of banks in the monitoring and control of managerial behavior and firm outcomes is less significant than it has been.[124] As with

German firms, the availability of global capital increases the sources of funds for Japanese corporations. Additionally, the business arrangements resulting from keiretsus and relationships between companies and government agencies are being studied. Some observers of Japan's corporate governance structure suggest that significant competition from global rivals and the strong yen are among factors stimulating efforts to study governance practices that may not be as effective as they have been historically.[125] Also, some noticeable changes are taking place in annual shareholder meetings. Executives are lengthening meetings and listening carefully to shareholder complaints.[126]

Other Global Governance Reforms

As our explanation of governance structures suggests, it is possible that the new competitive landscape (see Chapters 1 and 5) and the global economy that is a critical part of it will foster the creation of a relatively uniform governance structure that will be used by firms throughout the world.[127] As markets become more global and customer demands become more similar, shareholders are becoming the focus of managerial agents' efforts in an increasing number of companies. This is true of German and Japanese systems that are becoming more shareholder oriented. In turn, however, U.S. firms are becoming increasingly tied to financial institutions with higher debt levels and increased institutional investor activism. Thus, regardless of their national origin, the structures used to govern corporations will tend to become more similar than is the case today.

This is illustrated in the Strategic Focus about corporate governance reforms taking place in companies around the world. The Japanese model of corporate governance that has been followed by Korean chaebols, large conglomerate firms, is being questioned and reforms in governance are expected. European countries such as France and Italy, which have bank-centered governance approaches, are moving to more shared ownership. In Italy and other western European countries, much of this increased focus on equity markets is coming through privatization of large previously state-owned enterprises. The privatization process has also fostered much of the increases in equity in Russia and Eastern Europe as well. It is interesting to note that research has found that privatization has not led to decreases in employment as was previously feared by countries that had initiated the privatization process.[128] China is also undertaking reforms that have affected corporate governance. Although China has not truly privatized, except through the joint venture process, it has decentralized its system to provide much more local control.

STRATEGIC FOCUS

Reforms in International Corporate Governance

In both developed and developing economies, corporate governance is being reformed. For several decades, intellectuals and policymakers worried that the U.S. financial system was forcing businesses to pursue short-term profits at the expense of long-term investment. In fact, there was a national commission headed by Professor Michael Porter of Harvard Business School that recommended significant changes to the U.S. approach to capitalism. Many looked to the Japanese and German systems and found that the capital was more "patient" in those economies. Therefore, it was suggested that the U.S. system of corporate governance become more relationship oriented as was the case with the financial systems in Japan and Germany.

However, the financial systems across Asia, many of which are based on the Japanese-style approach, such as the Korean model, had serious difficulties in 1997 and into 1998. Many of the Asian and continental European economies are bank and debt based. A World Bank study found that total bank loans in the U.S. equal 50 percent of the nation's gross domestic product. This compares with 100 percent in Malaysia, 150 percent in Japan, and 170 percent in Germany. The bond market, on the other hand, totals 100 percent of annual U.S. gross domestic product, compared with 90 percent in Germany, 75 percent in Japan, 50 percent in Korea, and less than 10 percent in Thailand and Indonesia. Therefore, in most of Asia and a significant part of Europe, banks are at the center of providing capital. Additionally, in many of these economies, banks can hold equity, unlike the U.S. economy where the Glass Stegall Act prevents banks from having equity holdings. For this reason, the Germanic and Japanese approaches have been credited with providing patient and long-term oriented capital to corporations.

Lately, a number of countries have been questioning whether this is true. The chaebols of Korea, for instance, have been accused of being unresponsive and pursuing "wrong-headed" long-term investments. For instance, Chapter 9 discusses Samsung's investment into the car industry that continued even when there was significant overcapacity in the global auto industry.

France, as well as Italy, has significant bank-oriented financial systems. France, for instance, has been undergoing gradual but significant changes as demands for increasing shareholder value have become more important. As with Italy, France's system has been based on cross-shareholdings and reciprocal board memberships. However, with the large numbers of mergers, privatizations and restructurings taking place, shareholders are becoming more influential in the governance of large corporations. One active investor in France, G. Guy Wyser-Pratte, suggests, "France is a banana republic when it comes to corporate governance." It is difficult for shareholder power to prosper in a country such as France. The Paris Bourse lists only 681 stocks of French companies, compared with more than 2,100 on the London Stock Exchange and more than 7,700 on the New York and NAS-DAQ exchanges combined. Italy's stock market is even smaller compared to Germany, France, and Spain. Italy's system of corporate governance also includes significant amounts of cross-shareholdings and reciprocal board arrangements between and among companies.

Of course, some systems of corporate governance are built to focus not solely on shareholder concerns. For instance, in the Netherlands and Germany, a two-tiered system of corporate governance is at work. German corporations have a supervisory board with half the members representing shareholders and the other half representing employees. Shareholders have the ultimate control over the supervisory board and thus have the ability to influence decisions. The chairman is one of the shareholder representatives and in cases where voting results in a deadlock, he or she can cast an additional vote to break the logjam. However, there have been some recent challenges to the two-tiered board system. The argument by corporate officials is that the constant search for social consensus among workers and managers has led to a compromise of Germany's competitive edge in world markets. This lack of competitiveness creates large levels of unemployment, not only in Germany but also in other countries such as France where corporate governance has not been incisive.

Board reforms have also been taking place in emerging economies such as Russia and China. In Russia, privatization of numerous banks combined with broad licensing rules has allowed the Russian bank industry to become 75 percent private. Furthermore, privatized firms have wrestled control from "red directors" (former Communist managers who were previously managers of state-owned enterprises) as investment companies. Such concentrated ownership after the privatization process has allowed many Russian firms to be more rapidly revitalized than would have been the case under less diffused ownership.

Although there are significant differences between the Russian approach and the Chinese approach, China is adopting a corporate governance restructuring scheme as well. The China approach has decentralized operations by giving local control to previously centralized state enterprises. This is a separation of ownership approach—one that requires accountability in terms of spending and debt payment by these local managers over financial resources. Improvements could be made by providing performance-based incentives for managers, better private financial institutions, and a stronger application of bankruptcy law for poor performance. These issues, as well as stronger private enterprises, would ensure more effective corporate governance.

SOURCES: "More consensus" in Germany, 1997, *Financial Times*, December 18, 11; Italian governance, 1997, *Financial Times*, December 15, 18; A. Murray, 1997, New economic models fail while America Inc. keeps rolling, *Wall Street Journal*, September 8, A1, A13; Comic opera: Italy's stock exchange, 1997, *The Economist*, August 30, 54–55; S. Douma, 1997, The two-tier system of corporate governance, *Long Range Planning* 30, no. 4: 612–615; S. Li and T. Zhu, 1997, Put onus on managers in China, *Asian Wall Street Journal Weekly*, July 21, 12; A. Osterland, 1997, France is a banana republic: Corporate governance is changing in France ... slowly, *Financial World*, July-August, 40–43; Co-termination, 1997, *Industry Week*, July 21, 54; A. Jack, 1997, New tricks for old dog, *Financial Times*, June 26, 29; J. S. Abarbanell and A. Meyendorff, 1997, Bank privatization in post-Communist Russia: The case of Zhilsotsbank, *Journal of Comparative Economics* 25: 62–97; S. Liesman, 1997, Outsiders at Russia's Rao Gazpron vie for crucial first seat on firm's board, *Wall Street Journal*, June 25, A18.

GOVERNANCE MECHANISMS AND ETHICAL BEHAVIOR

In this chapter's final section, we discuss the need for governance mechanisms to support ethical behaviors. The governance mechanisms described in this chapter are designed to ensure that the agents of the firm's owners—that is, the corporation's top-level managers—make strategic decisions that best serve the interests of the entire group of stakeholders as described in Chapter 1. In the United States at least, shareholders are recognized as a company's most significant stakeholder. As such, the focus of governance mechanisms is on the control of managerial decisions to increase the probability that shareholders' interests will be served, but product market stakeholders (e.g., customers, suppliers, and host communities) and organizational stakeholders (e.g., managerial and nonmanagerial employees) are important as well.[129] In this regard, at least the minimal interests or needs of all stakeholders must be satisfied by outcomes achieved through the firm's actions. Without satisfaction of at least minimal interests, stakeholders will decide to withdraw their support or contribution to one firm and provide it to another (e.g., customers will purchase products from a supplier offering an acceptable substitute).

John Smale, an outside member of General Motors' board of directors, believes that all large capitalist enterprises must be concerned with goals in addition to serving shareholders. In Smale's opinion, "A corporation is a human, living enterprise. It's not just a bunch of assets. The obligation of management is to perpetuate the corporation, and that precedes their obligation to shareholders."[130] The argument, then, is that the firm's strategic competitiveness is enhanced when its governance mechanisms are designed and implemented in ways that take into consideration the interests of all stakeholders. Although subject to debate, some believe that ethically responsible companies design and use governance mechanisms that serve all stakeholders' interests. There is, however, a more critical relationship between ethical behavior and corporate governance mechanisms.

Evidence demonstrates that all companies are vulnerable to a display of unethical behaviors by their employees, including, of course, top-level managers. For example, in March 1997, federal agents raided Columbia/HCA facilities in El Paso, Texas. In July, they took documents from 35 different hospitals. The probe involved 700 governance agents and sent Columbia/HCA stock price plummeting. Several executives were indicted on charges of Medicaid fraud. Thomas Frist, Jr., started HCA, which was later sold to a smaller partner, Columbia. Richard L. Scott took over and started an aggressive plan to increase returns, which had slowed. Scott pushed to transform the traditional arm's-length distance between doctors and hospitals. He wanted doctors to hold equity in Columbia/HCA hospitals. However, federal law prohibits doctors from referring patients to laboratories and certain other health-care facilities in which they have ownership. The exception is in rural areas, where hospitals might not exist if doctors couldn't invest in them. Columbia/HCA made the most of this exception to increase performance. Scott also pushed cost-cutting efforts, which created an incentive to squeeze as much revenue as possible from patients. This created an incentive for hospital administrators to push beyond ethical limits. It is clear that for the federal probe, the main administrators stepped over the line. Scott spent little time forging a strong board and, therefore, little oversight was provided. Although the board pushed Scott out and brought back Frist, the board, including Frist, must take some responsibility for the failure and try to restore the company's image and improve its performance.[131] (Additional information about this firm appears in Chapter 12.)

The decisions and actions of a corporation's board of directors can be an effective deterrent to unethical behaviors. In fact, some believe that the most effective boards participate actively in setting boundaries for business ethics and values.[132] Once formulated, the board's expectations related to ethical decisions and actions by all of the firm's stakeholders must be communicated clearly to top-level managers. Moreover, these managers should be made to understand that the board will hold them fully accountable for the development and support of an organizational culture that results in only ethical decisions and behaviors. As explained in Chapter 12, CEOs can be positive role models for ethical behavior.

It is only when the proper controls of governance mechanisms are in place that strategies are formulated and implemented in ways that result in strategic competitiveness and above-average returns. As this chapter's discussion suggests, corporate governance mechanisms are a vital, yet imperfect part of firms' efforts to implement strategies successfully.

SUMMARY

- Corporate governance is a relationship among stakeholders that is used to determine the firm's direction and control its performance. How firms monitor and control top-level managers' decisions and actions, as called for by governance mechanisms, affects the implementation of strategies.

Effective governance that aligns managers' interests with shareholders' interests can result in a competitive advantage for the firm.

- In the modern corporation, there are four internal governance mechanisms—ownership concen-

383

tration, board of directors, executive compensation, and the multidivisional structure—and one external—the market for corporate control.

- Ownership is separated from control in the modern corporation. Owners (principals) hire managers (agents) to make decisions that will maximize the value of their firm. As risk specialists, owners diversify their risk by investing in an array of corporations. As decision-making specialists, top-level managers are expected by owners to make decisions that will result in the earning of above-average returns. Thus, modern corporations are characterized by an agency relationship that is created when one party (the firm's owners) hires and pays another party (top-level managers) because of their decision-making skills.

- Separation of ownership and control creates an agency problem when an agent pursues goals that are in conflict with the principals' goals. Principals establish and use governance mechanisms to control this problem.

- Ownership concentration, an internal governance mechanism, is defined by the number of large-block shareholders and the percentage of shares they own. With significant ownership percentages such as those held by large mutual funds and pension funds, institutional investors often are able to influence top-level managers' strategic decisions and actions. Thus, unlike diffuse ownership, which tends to bring about relatively weak monitoring and control of managerial decisions, concentrated ownership results in more active and effective monitoring of top-level managers. An increasingly powerful force in corporate America, institutional owners are actively using their positions of concentrated ownership in individual companies to force managers and boards of directors to make decisions that maximize a firm's value. These owners (e.g., CalPERS) have caused executives in prominent companies to lose their jobs because of their failure to serve shareholders' interests effectively.

- In the United States and the United Kingdom, the board of directors, composed of insiders, related outsiders, and outsiders, is a governance mechanism shareholders expect to represent their collective interests, especially because ownership is diffuse. The percentage of outside directors on most boards now exceeds the percentage of insider directors. This relative percentage of outsiders seems appropriate. These individuals are expected to be more independent of a firm's top-level managers than are those selected from inside the firm.

- A highly visible and often criticized governance mechanism is executive compensation. Through the use of salary, bonuses, and long-term incentives, the mechanism is intended to strengthen the alignment of managers' and shareholders' interests. A strong emphasis on executive incentives has widened the gap between the pay of the typical worker and CEOs. A firm's board of directors has the responsibility of determining the degree to which executive compensation is succeeding as a governance mechanism and to initiate all appropriate corrective actions when required.

- As an internal governance mechanism, the multidivisional (M-form) structure is intended to reduce managerial opportunism and to align principals' and agents' interests as a result. The M-form makes it possible for the corporate office to monitor and control managerial decisions in the individual divisions in diversified firms. However, at the corporate level, the M-form may actually stimulate managerial opportunism, resulting in top-level executives overdiversifying.

- In general, evidence suggests that shareholders and board directors have become more vigilant in their control of managerial decisions. Nonetheless, these mechanisms are insufficient to govern the diversification of many large companies. As such, the market for corporate control is an important governance mechanism. Although it, too, is imperfect, the market for corporate control has been effective in causing corporations to downscope and reduce their degree of inefficient diversification.

- Corporate governance structures used in Germany and Japan differ from each other and from the one used in the United States. Historically, the U.S. governance structure has focused on maximizing shareholder value. In Germany, employees, as a stakeholder group, have a more prominent role in governance than is the case in the United States. Until recently, Japanese shareholders played virtually no role in the monitoring and control of top-level managers. However, these

384

systems are becoming more similar as are many governance systems in both developed countries such as France and Italy and developing countries such as Russia and China.

■ Effective governance mechanisms ensure that the interests of all stakeholders are served. Thus, long-term strategic success results when firms are governed in ways that permit at least minimal satisfaction of capital market stakeholders (e.g., shareholders), product market stakeholders (e.g., customers and suppliers), and organizational stakeholders (managerial and nonmanagerial employees). Moreover, effective governance causes the establishment and consistent use of ethical behavior as the firm formulates and implements its strategies.

REVIEW QUESTIONS

1. What is corporate governance? What factors account for the considerable amount of attention corporate governance receives from several parties, including shareholder activists, business press writers, and academic scholars? Why are governance mechanisms used to control managerial decisions?

2. What does it mean to say that ownership is separated from control in the modern corporation? What brought about this separation?

3. What is an agency relationship? What is managerial opportunism? What assumptions do owners of modern corporations make about managerial agents? What are the strategic implications of these assumptions?

4. How are the four internal governance mechanisms—ownership concentration, boards of directors, executive compensation, and the multidivisional (M-form) structure—used to align the interests of managerial agents with those of the firm's owners?

5. What trends exist in terms of executive compensation? What is the effect of increased use of long-term incentives on executives' strategic decisions?

6. What is the market for corporate control? What conditions generally cause this external governance mechanism to become active? How does this mechanism constrain top-level managers' decisions?

7. What is the nature of corporate governance mechanisms used in Germany and Japan?

8. How can corporate governance mechanisms foster ethical strategic decisions and behaviors on the part of managerial agents?

385

APPLICATION DISCUSSION QUESTIONS

1. The roles and responsibilities of top-level managers and members of a corporation's board of directors are different. Traditionally, executives have been responsible for determining the firm's strategic direction and implementing strategies to achieve it, whereas the board has been responsible for monitoring and controlling managerial decisions and actions. Some argue that boards should become more involved with the formulation of a firm's strategies. In your opinion, how would the board's increased involvement in the selection of strategies affect a firm's strategic competitiveness? What evidence can you offer to support your position?

2. Do you believe that large U.S. firms have been overgoverned by some corporate governance mechanisms and undergoverned by others? Provide an example of a business firm to support your belief.

3. How can corporate governance mechanisms create conditions that allow top-level managers to develop a competitive advantage and focus on long-term performance? Search the business press to find an example of a firm in which this occurred and prepare a description of it.

4. Some believe that the market for corporate control is not an effective governance mechanism. If this is an accurate view, what factors might account for the ineffectiveness of this method of monitoring and controlling managerial decisions?

5. Assume that you overheard the following comments: "As a top-level manager, the only agency relationship I am concerned about is the one between myself and the firm's owners. I think that it would be a waste of my time and energy to worry about any other agency relationship." How would you respond to this person? Do you accept or reject this view? Be prepared to support your position.

ETHICS QUESTIONS

1. As explained in this chapter, the use of corporate governance mechanisms should establish order between parties whose interests may be in conflict. Do firm owners have any ethical responsibilities to managers when using governance mechanisms to establish order? If so, what are they?

2. Is it ethical for a firm owner to assume that agents (managers hired to make decisions that are in the owner's best interests) are averse to work and risk? Why or why not?

3. What are the responsibilities of the board of directors to stakeholders other than shareholders?

4. What ethical issues are involved with executive compensation? How can we determine if top-level executives are paid too much?

5. Is it ethical for firms involved in the market for corporate control to target companies performing at levels exceeding the industry average? Why or why not?

6. What ethical issues, if any, do top-level managers face when asking their firm to provide them with either a golden parachute or a golden goodbye?

7. How can governance mechanisms be designed to ensure against managerial opportunism, ineffectiveness, and unethical behaviors?

INTERNET EXERCISE

Go to CalPERS at:

http://www.calpers.ca.gov

To ensure an acceptable return on their investment, the major stockholders of public corporations are becoming increasingly involved in corporate governance issues. The California Public Employees Retirement Fund, which is referred to as CalPERS, exemplifies this trend. CalPERS is the largest public pension system in America, with more than $128 billion in assets. In recent years, CalPERS has become very aggressive in terms of applying pressure on low-performing companies to improve their governance practices. With this in mind, visit the CalPERS Web site. From this site and other Internet resources, make a list of the activities that CalPERS has engaged in to try to influence the governance practices of the companies in which it invests.

Strategic Surfing

Corporate Governance is a Web site that is dedicated solely to corporate governance issues. The site is very extensive and contains information pertaining to a broad spectrum of corporate governance issues. Executive Paywatch is another site of interest to observers of corporate governance issues. This site is sponsored by the AFL-CIO and monitors the compensation packages of the CEOs of major American corporations.

http://www.corpgov.net
http://www.aflcio.paywatch.org/ceopay

NOTES

1. R. D. Ward, 1997, *21st Century Corporate Board* (New York: John Wiley & Sons).

2. J. A. Byrne, R. Grover, and R. A. Melcher, 1997, The best and worst boards: Our special report on corporate governance, *Business Week*, December 8, 91–98.

3. R. K. Mitchell, B. R. Agle, and D. J. Wood, 1997, Toward a theory of stakeholder identification and salience: Defining the principle of who and what really counts, *Academy of Management Review* 22: 853–886.

4. J. H. Davis, F. D. Schoorman, and L. Donaldson, 1997, Toward a stewardship theory of management, *Academy of Management Review* 22: 20–47.

5. O. E. Williamson, 1996, Economic organization: The case for candor, *Academy of Management Review* 21: 48–57.

6. E. F. Fama and M. C. Jensen, 1983, Separation of ownership and control, *Journal of Law and Economics* 26: 301–325.

7. Ward, *21st Century Corporate Board*, 3–144.

8. C. Arnold and K. Breen, 1997, Investor activism goes worldwide, *Corporate Board* 18, no. 2: 7–12.

9. M. Kroll, P. Wright, L. Toombs, and H. Leavell, 1997, Form of control: A critical determinant of acquisition performance and CEO rewards, *Strategic Management Journal* 18: 85–96; J. K. Seward and J. P. Walsh, 1996, The governance and control of voluntary corporate spinoffs, *Strategic Management Journal* 17: 25–39.

10. J. D. Westphal and E. J. Zajac, 1997, Defections from the inner circle: Social exchange, reciprocity and diffusion of board independence in U.S. corporations, *Administrative*

Science Quarterly 42: 161–212; Ward, *21st Century Corporate Board.*

11. J. Charkham, 1994, *Keeping Good Company: A Study of Corporate Governance in Five Countries* (New York: Oxford University Press), 1.

12. Cadbury Committee, 1992, *Report of the Cadbury Committee on the Financial Aspects of Corporate Governance* (London: Gee).

13. M. A. Hitt, R. E. Hoskisson, R. A. Johnson, and D. D. Moesel, 1996, The market for corporate control and firm innovation, *Academy of Management Journal* 39: 1084–1119; J. P. Walsh and R. Kosnik, 1993, Corporate raiders and their disciplinary role in the market for corporate control, *Academy of Management Journal* 36: 671–700.

14. Davis, Schoorman, and Donaldson, Toward a stewardship theory of management.

15. C. Sundaramurthy, J. M. Mahoney, and J. T. Mahoney, 1997, Board structure, antitakeover provisions, and stockholder wealth, *Strategic Management Journal* 18: 231–246; K. J. Rediker and A. Seth, 1995, Boards of directors and substitution effects of alternative governance mechanisms, *Strategic Management Journal* 16: 85–99.

16. G. E. Davis and T. A. Thompson, 1994, A social movement perspective on corporate control, *Administrative Science Quarterly* 39: 141–173.

17. M. A. Eisenberg, 1989, The structure of corporation law, *Columbia Law Review* 89, no. 7: 1461 as cited in R. A. G. Monks and N. Minow, 1995, *Corporate Governance* (Cambridge, MA: Blackwell Business), 7.

18. E. E. Fama, 1980, Agency problems and the theory of the firm, *Journal of Political Economy* 88: 288–307.

19. M. Jensen and W. Meckling, 1976, Theory of the firm: Managerial behavior, agency costs, and ownership structure, *Journal of Financial Economics* 11: 305–360.

20. H. C. Tosi, J. Katz, and L. R. Gomez-Mejia, 1997, Disaggregating the agency contract: The effects of monitoring, incentive alignment, and term in office on agent decision making, *Academy of Management Journal* 40: 584–602; P. C. Godfrey and C. W. L. Hill, 1995, The problem of unobservables in strategic management research, *Strategic Management Journal* 16: 519–533.

21. P. Wright and S. P. Ferris, 1997, Agency conflict and corporate strategy: The effect of divestment on corporate strategy, *Strategic Management Journal* 18: 77–83.

22. T. M. Welbourne and L. R. Gomez Meiia, 1995, Gainsharing: A critical review and a future research agenda, *Journal of Management* 21: 577.

23. P. Wright, S. P. Ferris, A. Sarin, and V. Awasthi, 1996, Impact of corporate insider, blockholder, and institutional equity ownership on firm risk taking, *Academy of Management Journal* 39: 441–463.

24. P. B. Firstenberg and B. G. Malkiel, 1994, The twenty-first century boardroom: Who will be in charge? *Sloan Management Review*, Fall, 27–35, as cited in C. M. Daily, 1996, Governance patterns in bankruptcy reorganizations, *Strategic Management Journal* 17: 355–375.

25. O. E. Williamson, 1996, *The Mechanisms of Governance* (New York: Oxford University Press), 6; O. E. Williamson, 1993, Opportunism and its critics, *Managerial and Decision Economics* 14: 97–107.

26. S. Ghoshal and P. Moran, 1996, Bad for practice: A critique of the transaction cost theory, *Academy of Management Review* 21: 13–47.

27. Williamson, Economic organization, 50.

28. Godfrey and Hill, The problem of unobservables in strategic management research.

29. Y. Amihud and B. Lev, 1981, Risk reduction as a managerial motive for conglomerate mergers, *Bell Journal of Economics* 12: 605–617.

30. R. E. Hoskisson and T. A. Turk, 1990, Corporate restructuring: Governance and control limits of the internal market, *Academy of Management Review* 15: 459–477.

31. S. Finkelstein and D. C. Hambrick, 1989, Chief executive compensation: A study of the intersection of markets and political processes, *Strategic Management Journal* 16: 221 239; H. C. Tosi and L. R. Gomez-Mejia, 1989, The decoupling of CEO pay and performance: An agency theory perspective, *Administrative Science Quarterly* 34: 169–189.

32. Hoskisson and Turk, 1990, Corporate restructuring.

33. M. S. Jensen, 1986, Agency costs of free cash flow, corporate finance, and takeovers, *American Economic Review* 76: 323–329.

34. C. W. L. Hill and S. A. Snell, 1988, External control, corporate strategy, and firm performance in research intensive industries, *Strategic Management Journal* 9: 577–590.

35. A. Sharma, 1997, Professional as agent: Knowledge asymmetry in agency exchange, *Academy of Management Review* 22: 758–798.

36. R. Comment and G. Jarrell, 1995, Corporate focus and stock returns, *Journal of Financial Economics* 37: 67–87.

37. A. Shleifer and R. W. Vishny, 1986, Large shareholders and corporate control, *Journal of Political Economy* 94: 461–488.

38. J. A. Byrne, 1997, The CEO and the board, *Business Week*, September 15, 107–116.

39. R. E. Hoskisson, R. A. Johnson, and D. D. Moesel, 1994, Corporate divestiture intensity in restructuring firms: Effects of governance, strategy, and performance, *Academy of Management Journal* 37: 1207–1251.

40. A. Berle and G. Means, 1932, *The Modern Corporation and Private Property* (New York: Macmillan).

41. M. P. Smith, 1996, Shareholder activism by institutional investors: Evidence from CalPERS, *Journal of Finance* 51: 227–252.

42. J. D. Bogert, 1996, Explaining variance in the performance of long-term corporate blockholders, *Strategic Management Journal* 17: 243–249.

43. M. Useem, 1998, Corporate leadership in a globalizing equity market, *Academy of Management Executive* XII, in press.

44. C. M. Dailey, 1996, Governance patterns in bankruptcy reorganizations, *Strategic Management Journal* 17: 355–375.

45. Useem, Corporate leadership in a globalizing equity market; R. E. Hoskisson and M. A. Hitt, 1994, *Downscoping: How to Tame the Diversified Firm* (New York: Oxford University Press).

46. Byrne, The CEO and the board, 109.

47. Byrne, Grover, and Melcher, The best and worst boards.

48. E. Schine, 1997, CalPERS' grand inquisitor, *Business Week*, February 24, 120.

49. CalPERS highlights retailers in its list of underperformers, 1996, *Wall Street Journal*, February 7, Cl8.

387

50. B. Rehfeld, 1997, Low-cal CalPERS, *Institutional Investor*, March 31, 4–12; Smith, Shareholder activism.

51. M. J. Roe, 1993, Mutual funds in the boardroom, *Journal of Applied Corporate Finance* 5, no. 4: 56–61.

52. Byrne, The CEO and the board, 114.

53. J. S. Lublin, 1997, More CEOs decide: No time for seats, *Wall Street Journal*, October 28, A2.

54. *Bloomberg Business News*, 1996, More companies add severance package for execs, survey says, *Dallas Morning News*, July 6, F3.

55. Sundaramurthy, Mahoney, and Mahoney, Board structure, antitakeover provisions, and stockholder wealth; C. Sundaramurthy, 1996, Corporate governance within the context of antitakeover provisions, *Strategic Management Journal* 17: 377–394.

56. R. Grover and E. Schine, 1997, At Disney, Grumpy isn't just a dwarf, *Business Week*, February 24, 38.

57. B. S. Black, 1992, Agents watching agents: The promise of institutional investors voice, *UCLA Law Review* 39: 871–893.

58. Rediker and Seth, Boards of directors, 85.

59. J. K. Seward and J. P Walsh, 1996, The governance and control of voluntary corporate spinoffs, *Strategic Management Journal* 17: 25–39.

60. P. Mallete and R. L. Hogler, 1995, Board composition, stock ownership, and the exemption of directors from liability, *Journal of Management* 21: 861–878.

61. B. D. Baysinger and R. E. Hoskisson, 1990, The composition of boards of directors and strategic control: Effects on corporate strategy, *Academy of Management Review* 15: 72–87.

62. E. J. Zajac and J. D. Westphal, 1996, Director reputation, CEO-board power, and the dynamics of board interlocks, *Administrative Science Quarterly* 41: 507–529.

63. J. D. Westphal and E. J. Zajac, 1995, Who shall govern? CEO/board power, demographic similarity, and new director selection, *Administrative Science Quarterly* 40: 60–83.

64. R. P. Beatty and E. J. Zajac, 1994, Managerial incentives, monitoring, and risk bearing: A study of executive compensation, ownership, and board structure in initial public offerings, *Administrative Science Quarterly* 39: 313–335.

65. A. Bryant, 1997, CalPERS draws a blueprint for its concept of an ideal board, *New York Times*, June 17, C1.

66. I. M. Millstein, 1997, Red herring over independent boards, *New York Times*, April 6, F10; W. Q. Judge, Jr., and G. H. Dobbins, 1995, Antecedents and effects of outside directors' awareness of CEO decision style, *Journal of Management* 21: 43–64.

67. I. E. Kesner, 1988, Director characteristics in committee membership: An investigation of type, occupation, tenure and gender, *Academy of Management Journal* 31: 66–84.

68. S. Zahra, 1998, Governance, ownership and corporate entrepreneurship among the *Fortune* 500: The moderating impact of industry technological opportunity, *Academy of Management Journal* 41: in press.

69. J. A. Conger, D. Finegold, and E. E. Lawler III, 1998, Appraising boardroom performance, *Harvard Business Review* 76, no. 1: 136–148; J. A. Byrne and L. Brown, 1997, Directors in the hot seat, *Business Week*, December 8, 100–104.

70. H. Kaback, 1996, A director's guide to board behavior, *Wall Street Journal*, April 1, A14.

71. J. A. Byrne, 1997, Putting more stock in good governance, *Business Week*, September 15, 116; A. Bianco and J. A. Byrne, 1997, The rush to quality on corporate boards, *Business Week*, March 3, 34–35.

72. S. Rosenstein and J. G. Wyatt, 1997, Inside directors, board effectiveness, and shareholder wealth, *Journal of Financial Economics* 44: 229–250.

73. E. Cetera, 1997, *Business Week*, October 13, 44.

74. It's lonely at the top: Women's progress in gaining company directorships slows to crawl, 1997, *Dallas Morning News*, October 2, D11.

75. A boardroom gender gap, *Business Week*, November 24, 1997, 32.

76. D. C. Hambrick and S. Finkelstein, 1995, The effects of ownership structure on conditions at the top: The case of CEO pay raises, *Strategic Management Journal* 16: 175.

77. L. R. Gomez-Mejia and R. Wiseman, 1997, Reframing executive compensation: An assessment and review, *Journal of Management* 23: 291–374.

78. D. Bilimoria, 1997, Perspectives on corporate control: Implications for CEO compensation, *Human Relations* 50: 829–858; S. Werner and H. L. Tosi, 1995, Other people's money: The effects of ownership on compensation strategy and managerial pay, *Academy of Management Journal* 38: 1672–1691.

79. S. Finkelstein and B. K. Boyd, 1998, How much does the CEO matter?: The role of managerial discretion in the setting of CEO compensation, *Academy of Management Journal* 41: 179–199; I. Kristol, 1996, What is a CEO worth? *Wall Street Journal*, June 5, A14.

80. L. Wines, 1996, Compensation plans that support strategy, *Journal of Business Strategy* 17, no. 4: 17–20.

81. V. R. Loucks, Jr., 1995, An equity cure for managers, *Wall Street Journal*, September 26, A19.

82. K. Roth and S. O'Donnell, 1996, Foreign subsidiary compensation: An agency theory perspective, *Academy of Management Journal* 39: 678–703.

83. R. E. Hoskisson, M. A. Hitt, and C. W. L. Hill, 1993, Managerial incentives and investment in R&D in large multiproduct firms, *Organization Science* 4: 325–341.

84. K. A. Merchant, 1989, *Rewarding Results: Motivating Profit Center Managers* (Cambridge, MA: Harvard Business School Press); J. Eaton and H. Rosen, 1983, Agency, delayed compensation, and the structure of executive remuneration, *Journal of Finance* 38: 1489–1505.

85. C. Duff, 1996, Top executives ponder high pay, decide they're worth every cent, *Wall Street Journal*, May 15, B1.

86. Kristol, What is a CEO worth?

87. L. Uchitelle, 1996, Performance pay made 1995 bonus year for executives, *Houston Chronicle*, March 30, C3.

88. R. E. Yates, 1995, Restless in the ranks, *Dallas Morning News*, October 12, D1, D10.

89. S. Puri, 1997, The problem with stock options: Pay for underperformance, *Fortune*, December 8, 52–56.

90. Associated Press, 1996, Downsized firms start adding staff, *Dallas Morning News*, May 29, D2.

91. J. J. Keller, 1998, AT&T revamping to trim 18,000 jobs, *Wall Street Journal*, January 27, A3.

92. Special Report, 1996, How high can CEO pay go? *Business Week*, April 22, 100–121.

93. J. Reingold, 1997, Executive pay: Special report, *Business Week*, April 21, 58–64.

94. Uchitelle, Performance pay.

95. D. Machan, 1996, The last article you will ever have to read on executive pay? No way! *Forbes*, May 20, 176–234.

96. Reingold, Executive pay: Special report, 60.

97. Associated Press, 1996, Low-profile exec gets high-profile bonus, *Dallas Morning News*, April 11, D2.

98. GE chief's salary, bonus rose 22.3% to $5.32 million in '95, 1996, *Wall Street Journal*, March 13, B5.

99. Reingold, Executive pay: Special report, 60.

100. J. Bailey, 1998, Conseco agrees to acquire Green Tree, *Wall Street Journal*, April 8, A2, A6; J. Bailey, 1998, Green Tree's Coss must repay part of '96 bonus, *Wall Street Journal*, January 28, A3, A11; A. Osterland, 1997, How Green Tree got pruned, *Business Week*, December 1, 37.

101. J. Reingold, 1997, The folly of jumbo stock options, *Business Week*, December 22, 36–37.

102. O. E. Williamson, 1985, *The Economic Institutions of Capitalism: Firms, Markets and Relational Contracting* (New York: Macmillan Free Press).

103. New CEO presents plan for restructuring airline, 1996, *Wall Street Journal*, May 17, B8.

104. W. M. Carley, 1996, GE implements $200 million program to slash number of defects per product, *Wall Street Journal*, April 25, A4.

105. B. W. Keats and M. A. Hitt, 1988, A causal model of linkages among environmental dimensions, macro organizational characteristics, and performance, *Academy of Management Journal* 31: 570–598.

106. O. E. Williamson, 1994, Strategizing, economizing, and economic organization, in R. P. Rumelt, D. E. Schendel, and D. J. Teece (eds.), *Fundamental Issues in Strategy* (Cambridge, MA: Harvard Business School Press), 380.

107. Hoskisson and Turk, Corporate restructuring: Governance and control limits of the internal market.

108. M. A. Hitt, R. E. Hoskisson, and R. D. Ireland, 1990, Mergers and acquisitions and managerial commitment to innovation in M-form firms, *Strategic Management Journal* 11 (Special Summer Issue): 29–47.

109. Hitt, Hoskisson, Johnson, and Moesel, The market for corporate control and firm innovation; Walsh and Kosnik, Corporate raiders.

110. Mallette and Hogier, Board composition, 864.

111. A. E. Serwer, 1997, Michael Price has a plan for Dow Jones, *Fortune*, November 10, 137–140.

112. Sundaramurthy, Mahoney and Mahoney, Board structure, antitakeover provisions, and stockholder wealth.

113. R. A. Johnson, R. E. Hoskisson, and M. A. Hitt, 1998, The effects of environmental uncertainty on the mode of corporate restructuring, working paper University of Missouri.

114. Walsh and Kosnik, Corporate raiders.

115. S. Johnston, 1995, Managerial dominance of Japan's major corporations, *Journal of Management* 21: 191–209.

116. E. Ramstad and J. G. Auerback, 1998, Compaq buys Digital, an unthinkable event just a few years ago, *Wall Street Journal*, January 28, A1, A14.

117. Useem, Corporate leadership in a globalizing equity market.

118. Our discussion of corporate governance structures in Germany and Japan is drawn from Monks and Minow, *Corporate Governance*, 271–299; Charkham, *Keeping Good Company*, 6–118.

119. H. Kim and R. E. Hoskisson, 1996, Japanese governance systems: A critical review, in B. Prasad (ed.), *Advances in International Comparative Management* (Greenwich, CT: JAI Press), 165–189.

120. S. Douma, 1997, The two-tier system of corporate governance, *Long Range Planning* 30, no. 4: 612–615.

121. A. Osterland, 1997, France is a banana republic; corporate governance is changing in France . . . slowly, *Financial World*, July-August, 40–43; B. Riley, 1996, French leave for shareholders, *Financial Times*, June 23, XX.

122. Shake it up, 1997, *Wall Street Journal*, July 15, A18; G. Steinmetz, 1996, Satisfying shareholders is a hot new concept at some German firms, *Wall Street Journal*, March 6, A1, A6.

123. Charkham, *Keeping Good Company*, 70.

124. Williamson, *The Mechanisms*, 320.

125. D. P. Hamilton and N. Shirouau, 1996, Japan's business cartels are starting to erode, but change is slow, *Wall Street Journal*, December 4, A1, A6.

126. Japanese firms change meeting format, invite shareholder questions, 1997, *Dallas Morning News*, June 28, F2.

127. M. E. Porter, 1992, Capital disadvantages: America's failing capital investment system, *Harvard Business Review* 70, no. 5: 65–82.

128. W. L. Megginson, R. C. Nash, and M. van Randenborgh, 1994, The financial and operating performance of newly privatized firms: An international empirical analysis, *Journal of Finance* 49: 403–452.

129. E. Freeman and J. Liedtka, 1997, Stakeholder capitalism and the value chain, *European Management Journal* 15, no. 3: 286–295.

130. A. Taylor, III, 1996, GM: Why they might break up America's biggest company, *Fortune*, April 29, 84.

131. L. Lagnado, A. Sharpe, and G. Jaffe, 1997, Doctors' orders: How Columbia/HCA changed health care, for better or worse, *Wall Street Journal*, August 1, A1, A4.

132. R. F. Felton, A. Hudnut, and V. Witt, 1995, Building a stronger board, *McKinsey Quarterly 1995*, no. 2: 169.

Organizational Structure and Controls

CHAPTER 11

Learning Objectives

After reading this chapter, you should be able to:

1. Explain the importance of integrating strategy implementation and strategy formulation.

2. Describe the dominant path of evolution from strategy to structure to strategy again.

3. Identify and describe the organizational structures used to implement different business-level strategies.

4. Discuss organizational structures used to implement different corporate-level strategies.

5. Identify and distinguish among the organizational structures used to implement three international strategies.

6. Describe organizational structures used to implement cooperative strategies.

Changes in Organizational Structure at Raytheon Company

A diversified company, Raytheon follows the related-linked corporate-level strategy (see Figure 6.1 in Chapter 6). The firm's newly created size (close to $21 billion in sales revenue), expansive product focus, and geographic diversity (the company has customers in more than 80 countries) call for the use of a particular type of the multi-divisional organizational structure (this structural type is explained fully later in the chapter) to implement its chosen corporate-level strategy of related-linked diversification. The organizational structure now in place at this firm and actions being taken to use it effectively are the focus of this opening case.

Strategic decisions made recently at the corporate level have influenced Raytheon's organizational structure. In 1997, the firm completed two acquisitions to increase its competitiveness in the defense businesses. In July, Texas

http://www.raytheon.com

Instruments' defense lines were bought at a price of $2.9 billion; in December, $9.5 billion was spent to acquire Hughes Electronics' defense business from General Motors Corporation. Combining these acquisitions with the firm's existing operations created the third largest defense company in the United States and spurred changes in Raytheon's organizational structure.

To exploit fully the competitive advantage corporate executives believed these acquisitions provided their firm, Raytheon Systems was created as a division or strategic business unit, with five operating segments. As shown below, the company's other three strategic business units are Raytheon Electronics, Raytheon Aircraft Co., and Raytheon Engineers & Constructors. Believing that the combination of this business unit's products creates a "defense powerhouse," the company stated, "With products that cover air, land and sea, Raytheon brings together a unique set of skills, experience, and state-of-the-art technologies to provide total defense systems solutions to the U.S. and its allies around the world."

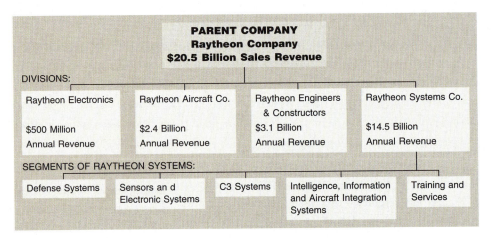

The structure shown above is an example of the strategic business unit (SBU) form of the multidivisional structure. Discussed fully in this chapter, this structure is appropriate for use by firms following a corporate-level strategy of related-linked diversification. This structure allows each of the business units to operate independently which means interactions between and among these units are infrequent. The reason for this is that relatively few product and geographic market relationships exist across the strategic business units. Within each unit, however, segments are related by products manufactured and/or geographic markets served. For example, while Raytheon Electronics and Raytheon Engineers & Constructors are not related, the five segments that have been grouped to form Raytheon Systems produce similar products and/or serve similar markets.

The SBU structural form calls for mechanisms to be used to integrate activities among a business unit's segments when doing so can enhance the unit's overall performance. Product similarities, for example, sometimes allow the sharing of a segment's resources and capabilities to produce components that are common to products being manufactured in more than one segment.

At Raytheon Systems, Centers of Excellence are used as an integrating mechanism. These "centers of excellence are cross-functional organizations that design and manufacture key components and subassemblies. The Centers of Excellence allow a focus on best-of-class engineering and manufacturing practices; maximize design efficiency and standardization; eliminate duplication of work and underutilization of facilities; and provide productivity through a reduced number of processes." One Center of Excellence is called Printed Wiring Board Fabrication. Located in Austin, Texas, this cross-functional unit combines work that had been completed previously at six different facilities. Two or more of Raytheon Systems' five segments share some of the products produced by this Center.

Corporate executives were optimistic about the potential of the Raytheon Systems' unit. As a result of strategic and structural changes made at the corporate level, the firm's top-level managers suggested that the System's strategic business unit could grow 10 percent annually. Some analysts concurred with this assessment, noting that ". . . Raytheon Systems was poised to dominate the defense electronics business, which is the main growth area of defense spending." Challenges to the business unit's potential include well-positioned competitors such as Lockheed Martin and the significant amount of debt the firm incurred to acquire Hughes Electronics and Texas Instruments' defense lines. To enhance the efficiency of its newly created Raytheon Systems business unit and to reduce its corporate debt, the company announced a reduction of 8,500 employees in early 1998. To have an even more positive effect on the corporation's operational efficiency, another 1,000 jobs in Raytheon Engineers & Constructors' unit were eliminated at the same time.

SOURCE: J. G. Auerbach, 1998, Raytheon expects to post charge of $500 million for revamping, *Wall Street Journal*, January 26, B4; A. Dworkin, 1998, Raytheon cuts may herald industry changes, *Dallas Morning News*, January 24, F1, F2; V. Griffith, 1998, Raytheon set to axe 9,700 jobs, *Financial Times*, January 26, 17; L. Johannes, 1998, Raytheon has loss following charges, but sales rise 18 percent, *Wall Street Journal*, January 27, B4; Raytheon Company Home Page, 1998, February 3, http://www.raytheon.com; A. Dworkin, 1997, Raytheon Systems unveiled, *Dallas Morning News*, December 19, D1, D11; T. A. Schwartzman, 1997, Raytheon, *Value Line*, October 3, 567.

In the previous chapter, we described mechanisms companies use to govern their operations and to align various parties' interests, especially the interests of top-level executives, with those of the firm's owners. Governance mechanisms can influence a company's ability to implement formulated strategies successfully and thereby facilitate competitive advantage.[1]

In this chapter, our focus is on the organizational structures and controls used to implement the strategies discussed previously (e.g., business-level, Chapter 4; corporate-level, Chapter 6; international, Chapter 8; and cooperative, Chapter 9). Moreover, as the discussion about actions taken at Raytheon Company suggests, the proper use of an organizational structure and its accompanying integrating mechanisms and controls can contribute to the firm's strategic competitiveness.[2] In fact, the most productive global competitors are those with effective product innovation skills and an organizational structure in place that facilitates successful and timely applications of internal capabilities and core competencies.[3] Thus, organizational structure influences managerial work and the decisions made by top-level managers.[4]

Organizational structure alone, however, does not create a competitive advantage;[5] rather, a competitive advantage is created when there is a proper match between strategy and structure. For example, it may be that what makes 3M's competitive advantage somewhat sustainable ". . . is its unique blend of practices, values, autonomous structures, funding processes, rewards, and selection and development of product champions."[6] Similarly, the Acer Group, manufacturer of Acer personal computers, is known as an innovative competitor. Some analysts believe that a unique organizational structure (which the CEO labels "global brand, local touch") contributes significantly to the firm's strategic competitiveness.[7] On the other hand, ineffective strategy/structure matches may result in firm rigidity and failure given the complexity and need for rapid changes in the new competitive landscape.[8] Thus, effective strategic leaders (see Chapter 12) seek to develop an organizational structure and accompanying controls that are superior to those of their competitors.[9] Using competitively superior structures and controls explains in part why some firms survive and succeed while others do not.[10] Executives at Bayerische Motoren Werke AG (BMW), for example, believe that the recently created process-oriented organizational structure will contribute to the firm's future success. The objective of this structure is to enable BMW to strengthen its focus on customers and markets and to improve further the efficiency of its manufacturing operations.[11] As with the other parts of the strategic management process, top-level managers bear the final responsibility to make choices about organizational structures that will enhance firm performance.[12] Following its acquisition of Digital Equipment Corporation (DEC), Compaq Computer Corporation executives, for example, must make structural decisions that will facilitate a successful integration of DEC's businesses into their own. Although generally optimistic, analysts see developing an organizational structure that could integrate what had been two different businesses operating within the guidelines of two different cost structures to be challenging.[13]

Selecting the organizational structure and controls that result in effective implementation of chosen strategies is a fundamental challenge for managers, especially top-level managers. A key reason is that in the global economy, firms must be flexible, innovative, and creative to exploit their core competencies in the pursuit of marketplace opportunities.[14] They also require a certain degree of stability in their structures so that day-to-day tasks can be completed efficiently. Accessible and reliable information is required for executives to reach decisions regarding the selection of a structure that can provide the desired levels of flexibility and stability. By helping executives improve their decision making, useful information contributes to the formation and use of effective structures and controls.[15]

Executives at Barclays, the United Kingdom banking group, recently made decisions regarding the firm's strategy and organizational structure. Information flows from investor groups and a desire to improve its stock market rating were instrumental in stimulating the executives' strategic and structural decisions. To bring its retail financial services to the forefront, Barclays' CEO decided to regroup the company's operations into four business units: retail financial services, asset management, investment banking, and business banking. The purpose of this structural reorganization was to split personal and business banking, which the firm believes have different managerial requirements, risk profiles, and cost structures. The largest of the four units is the newly created retail financial services. This unit includes personal banking in the United Kingdom and Europe, private banking, the African and Caribbean banks, mutual funds, and Barclay Trust. By concentrating on the retail financial services division, as permitted by changes to the firm's organizational structure, Barclays' top-level managers hope to reduce the volatility of the company's earnings flow that a focus on corporate banking had engendered.[16]

To examine organizational structure and controls, this chapter first describes a pattern of growth and accompanying changes in organizational structure experienced by strategically competitive firms. This pattern is one in which structural change follows strategic growth and success. In turn, structural adjustments can affect future formulations of strategies.

The chapter's second major section discusses organizational structures and controls that are used to implement different business-level strategies. The dominant structures and control characteristics that contribute to the effective implementation of each of the business-level strategies described in Chapter 4 are explained in this part of the chapter.

Corporate-level strategy implementation is then described. The transition from the functional to the multidivisional structure is highlighted in this section. This major structural innovation took place in several firms during the 1920s, including DuPont. In fact, noted business historian Alfred Chandler cites DuPont as the innovator in both the strategy of diversification and the multidivisional structure.[17] Specific variations of the multidivisional structure are discussed in terms of their relationship with effective implementation of related and unrelated diversification strategies.

Next, we describe structures that are used to implement different international strategies. Because of the increasing globalization of many industries, the number of firms implementing international strategies continues to grow. As noted in previous chapters, the trend toward globalization is significant and pervasive.[18] In the words of Joe Gorman, CEO of TRW, a large diversified firm with operations in defense, auto parts, and data, "There's no question in my mind that a great transformational change is occurring. It's a change from regional economies and industries to truly global ones."[19] Almost identically, a business historian believes that the "global restructuring of industries and work [that is occurring today] is the most significant economic change in 100 years."[20] Having observed conditions such as these, GE's CEO and chairman, Jack Welch, suggested that the speed at which the future is approaching the firm creates a discontinuous set of environmental conditions.[21] To cope successfully with the strategic challenges associated with discontinuous changes, the firm must develop and use organizational structures that facilitate meaningful conversations among all stakeholders regarding opportunities and threats facing the company at different points in time.[22] To examine the use of structure to implement international strategies effectively, we first describe the structure and control characteristics of the multidomestic strategy. This section is followed by a similar discussion of the global strategy. The transnational strategy is examined next, along with the variations in structure that are required to implement it. In the chapter's final two sections, we discuss the use of organizational structures to implement cooperative strategies and a few issues concerning organizational forms that should be of interest to those responsible for effective use of a firm's strategic management process.

EVOLUTIONARY PATTERNS OF STRATEGY AND ORGANIZATIONAL STRUCTURE

All firms require some form of organizational structure to implement their strategies. In this section, we describe how organizational structures have evolved in response to managerial and organizational needs.

Principally, structures are changed when they no longer provide the coordination, control, and direction managers and organizations require to implement strategies successfully.[23] The ineffectiveness of a structure typically results from increases in a firm's revenues and levels of diversification. In particular, the formulation of strategies involving greater levels of diversification (see Chapter 6) demands structural change to match the strategy. Some structures become elaborate while others become focused on financial rather than strategic control.

Organizational structure is a firm's formal role configuration, procedures, governance and control mechanisms, and authority and decision-making processes.[24] Influenced by situational factors including company size and age, organizational structure reflects managers' determination of *what* the firm does and *how* it completes that work given its chosen strategies.[25] Strategic competitiveness can be attained only when the firm's selected structure is congruent with its formulated strategy.[26] As such, a strategy's potential to create value is reached only when the firm configures itself in ways that allow the strategy to be implemented effectively. Thus, as firms evolve and change their strategies, new structural arrangements are required. Additionally, existing structures influence the future selection of strategies. Accordingly, the two key strategic actions of strategy formulation and strategy implementation continuously interact to influence managerial choices about strategy and structure.

Figure 11.1 shows the growth pattern many firms experience. This pattern results in changes in the relationships between the firm's formulated strategies and the organizational structures used to support and facilitate their implementation.

Simple Structure

A **simple structure** is an organizational form in which the owner-manager makes all major decisions directly and monitors all activities, while the staff serves as an extension of the manager's supervisory authority. This structure involves little specialization of tasks, few rules, and limited formalization. Although important, information systems are relatively unsophisticated, and owner-managers participate directly in the firm's day-to-day operations. Typically, this structure is used by firms offering a single product line in a single geographic market. Because of the small organization size, the simple structure is used frequently in firms implementing either the focused low-cost or focused differentiation strategy. Restaurants, repair businesses, and other specialized enterprises are examples of firms whose limited complexity calls for the use of the simple structure. In this structure, communication is frequent and direct, and new products tend to be introduced to the market quickly, which can result in a competitive advantage. Because of these characteristics, few of the coordination problems that are common in larger organizations exist.

The simple structure, the operations it supports, and the strategies being implemented in these companies play important roles in the success of various economies. Job creation data are one indicator of this importance. In the United States, for example, companies with between 100 and 500 employees have become the largest job creators.[27] These small firms created approximately 85 percent of the new jobs in the United States between 1991 and 1996. The value of small firms to the United Kingdom's economy has also been recognized. In the U.K., some analysts believe that the simple organizational structure may result in competitive advantages for some small firms relative to their larger counterparts. A broad-based openness to innovation, greater structural flexibility, and an ability to respond more rapidly to environmental changes are examples of these potential competitive ad-

Organizational structure is a firm's formal role configuration, procedures, governance and control mechanisms, and authority and decision-making processes.

A **simple structure** is an organizational form in which the owner-manager makes all major decisions directly and monitors all activities, while the staff serves as an extension of the manager's supervisory authority.

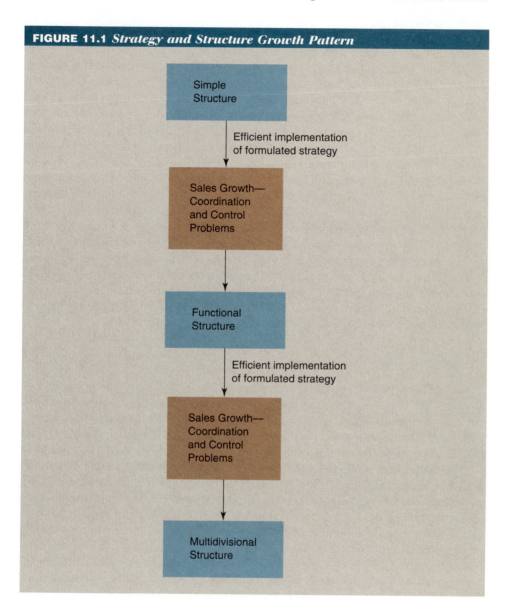

FIGURE 11.1 *Strategy and Structure Growth Pattern*

Simple Structure

↓ Efficient implementation of formulated strategy

Sales Growth—Coordination and Control Problems

↓

Functional Structure

↓ Efficient implementation of formulated strategy

Sales Growth—Coordination and Control Problems

↓

Multidivisional Structure

vantages.[28] Thus, although large corporations are indeed vital to the health of the world's economies, the importance of small firms should not be overlooked. The simple organizational structure properly supports the implementation of the focused strategies that are chosen most often by small firms (see Chapter 4).

However, as the small firm grows larger and more complex, managerial and structural challenges emerge. For example, the amount of competitively relevant information requiring analysis increases substantially. These more complicated information processing needs place significant pressures on the simple structure and the owner-manager. Commonly, owner-managers lack the organizational skills and experiences required to manage effectively the specialized and complex tasks involved with multiple organizational functions. Owner-managers or the top-level managers employed by the small firm's owner bear the responsibility to recognize the inadequacy of the firm's current organizational structure and the need to change to one that is consistent with the firm's strategy.[29]

The experiences of Yo! provide a useful illustration. Established as a sushi restaurant in London, this company achieved immediate success. In its first year of operation, Yo! grew by adding products related directly to its restaurant business such as a London-wide sushi delivery service and an event catering service. After its first year of operation, the company's founder announced ambitious plans to move the Yo! name into new areas including supermarkets and hotels. The objective was to establish Yo! as a mass-market youth brand. Initial product line expansions included clothing for young adults and children and toys. A more contemporary style of hotel—to be called Yotel—was also planned. Beyond this, the founder also believed that there was ". . . an opportunity for Yo! at the convenience-store level, providing a new retail environment involving home delivery and Internet shopping."[30] These ambitious growth objectives, however, create significant pressures on Yo!'s managers and its simple organizational structure. As the firm's product lines become more diverse (recall that increased product diversity signals a change in strategy), an appropriate response to the pressures the firm and its top-level managers face includes movement to a functional organizational structure or perhaps even one of the forms of the multidivisional structure.

398

The **functional structure** consists of a chief executive officer and limited corporate staff, with functional line managers in dominant organizational areas such as production, accounting, marketing, R&D, engineering, and human resources.

Functional Structure

To coordinate more complex organizational functions, firms such as Yo! should abandon the simple structure in favor of the functional structure. The functional structure is used by larger firms implementing one of the business-level strategies and by firms with low levels of diversification (for instance, companies implementing either the single- or dominant-business corporate-level strategy).

The **functional structure** consists of a chief executive officer and limited corporate staff, with functional line managers in dominant organizational areas such as production, accounting, marketing, R&D, engineering, and human resources. This structure allows for functional specialization, thereby facilitating knowledge sharing and idea development.[31] Because the differences in orientation among organizational functions can impede communication and coordination, the central task of the CEO is to integrate the decisions and actions of individual business functions for the benefit of the entire corporation.[32] This organizational form also facilitates career paths and professional development in specialized functional areas.

An unintended negative consequence of the functional structure is the tendency for functional-area managers to focus on local versus overall company strategic issues. Such emphases cause specialized managers to lose sight of the firm's overall strategic intent and strategic mission. When this situation emerges, the multidivisional structure often is implemented to overcome this difficulty.

Another condition that encourages a change from the functional to the multidivisional structure is greater diversification. Strategic success often leads to growth and diversification. Deciding to offer the same products in different markets (market diversification) and/or choosing to offer additional products (product diversification) creates control problems. The multidivisional structure provides the controls required to deal effectively with additional levels of diversification. In fact, the firm's returns may suffer when increased diversification is not accompanied by a change to the multidivisional structure.

Multidivisional Structure

The chief executive's limited ability to process increasing quantities of strategic information, the focus of functional managers on local issues, and increased diversification are primary causes of the decision to change from the functional to the multidivisional (M-form) structure. According to Alfred Chandler, "The M-form came into being when senior managers operating through existing centralized, functionally departmentalized . . . structures realized they had neither the time nor the necessary information to coordinate and monitor day-to-day operations, or to devise and implement long-term plans for the various product lines. The administrative overload had become simply too great."[33]

The **multidivisional (M-form) structure** is composed of operating divisions where each division represents a separate business or profit center and the top corporate officer delegates responsibilities for day-to-day operations and business-unit strategy to division managers. Because the diversified corporation is the dominant form of business in the industrialized world, the M-form is being used in most of the corporations competing in the global economy.[34] However, only effectively designed M-forms enhance a firm's performance. Thus, for all companies, and perhaps especially for diversified firms, performance is a function of the goodness of fit between strategy and structure.[35]

Chandler's examination of the strategies and structures of large American firms documented the M-form's development.[36] Chandler viewed the M-form as an innovative response to coordination and control problems that surfaced during the 1920s in the functional structures being used by large firms such as DuPont and General Motors.[37] Among other benefits, the M-form allowed firms to greatly expand their operations.[38]

Use of the Multidivisional Structure at DuPont and General Motors Chandler's studies showed that firms such as DuPont began to record significant revenue growth through the manufacture and distribution of diversified products while using the functional structure. Functional departments such as sales and production, however, found it difficult to coordinate the conflicting priorities of the firm's new and different products and markets. Moreover, the functional structures being used allocated costs to organizational functions rather than to individual businesses and products. This allocation method made it virtually impossible for top-level managers to determine the contributions of separate product lines to the firm's return on its investments. Even more damaging for large firms trying to implement newly formulated diversification strategies through use of a functional structure that was appropriate for small companies and for those needing proprietary expertise and scale[39] was the increasing allocation of top-level managers' time and energies to short-term administrative problems. Focusing their efforts on these issues caused executives to neglect the long-term strategic issues that were their primary responsibility.

To cope with similar problems, General Motors CEO Alfred Sloan, Jr., proposed a reorganization.[40] Sloan conceptualized separate divisions, each representing a distinct business, that would be self-contained and have its own functional hierarchy. Implemented in 1925, Sloan's structure delegated day-to-day operating responsibilities to division managers. The small staff at the corporate level was responsible for determining the firm's long-term strategic direction and for exercising overall financial control of semiautonomous divisions. Each division was to

The **multidivisional (M-form) structure** is composed of operating divisions where each division represents a separate business or profit center and the top corporate officer delegates responsibility for day-to-day operations and business-unit strategy to division managers.

make its own business-level strategic decisions, but because the corporate office's focus was on the outcomes achieved by the entire corporation rather than the performance of separate units, decisions made by division heads could be superseded by corporate office personnel. Sloan's structural innovation had three important outcomes: "(1) it enabled corporate officers to more accurately monitor the performance of each business, which simplified the problem of control; (2) it facilitated comparisons between divisions, which improved the resource allocation process; and (3) it stimulated managers of poor performing divisions to look for ways of improving performance."[41]

The Use of Internal Controls in the Multidivisional Structure The M-form structure holds top-level managers responsible for formulating and implementing overall corporate strategies; that is, they are responsible for the corporate-level acquisition and restructuring, international, and cooperative strategies that we examined in Chapters 6 through 9.

Strategic and financial controls are the two major types of internal controls used to support implementation of strategies in larger firms.[42] Properly designed organizational controls provide clear insights to employees regarding behaviors that enhance the firm's competitiveness and overall performance.[43] Effective implementation of diversification strategies results when firms appropriately use both types of controls. For example, when Ford Motor Company increased its ownership in Mazda Motor Corp. to a controlling interest of approximately 33 percent, top-level managers acknowledged the need to use strategic controls when evaluating the performance of all Ford units. Simultaneously, however, the appointment of Ford executive Henry D. G. Wallace as Mazda's new president (Wallace was the first foreigner to head a Japanese automaker) was a partial signal of the need for financial controls to manage Mazda's extensive product line and base of supplier costs.[44] Similarly, top-level managers at CKS Group, a leader in Internet-related advertising, concluded recently through the use of strategic controls that the firm should reduce its roster of businesses from 10 operating units to four. Additionally, the need for financial controls was emphasized as demonstrated by realignments in reporting relationships between units and managers and the stated need for costs to be reduced on a company-wide basis.[45]

Strategic control entails the use of long-term and strategically relevant criteria by corporate-level managers to evaluate the performance of division managers and their units.

Strategic control entails the use of long-term and strategically relevant criteria by corporate-level managers to evaluate the performance of division managers and their units. Strategic control emphasizes largely subjective judgments and may involve intuitive evaluation criteria. Behavioral in nature, strategic controls typically require high levels of cognitive diversity among top-level managers. Cognitive diversity captures the differences in beliefs about cause-effect relationships and desired outcomes among top-level managers' preferences.[46] Corporate-level managers rely on strategic control to gain an operational understanding of the strategies being implemented in the firm's separate divisions or business units. Because strategic control allows a corporate-level evaluation of the full array of strategic actions—those concerned with both the formulation and implementation of a business-unit strategy—corporate-level managers must have a deep understanding of a division's or business unit's operations and markets.[47] The use of strategic controls also demands rich information exchanges between corporate and divisional managers. These exchanges take place through both formal and informal (i.e., unplanned) face-to-face meetings.[48] As diversification increases, strategic control can be strained.[49] Sometimes, this strain results in a commitment to reduce the firm's level of diversification. For example, Black & Decker's top-level managers decided recently to divest some divisions to reduce the firm's overall level of diversification. Units sold were the household products division in North America, Latin America, and Australia; Emhart Glass (a maker of equipment for the manufacture of glass containers); and True Temper Sports (a manufacturer of golf club shafts). Difficulties encountered when attempting to use strategic controls to evaluate the performance of these units and those managing them may have contributed to the divestment decisions. These divestments, coupled with a workforce reduction of 3,000 jobs (10 percent of the firm's workforce), were expected to generate annual savings of more than $100 million.[50]

Financial control entails objective criteria (e.g., return on investment) that corporate-level managers use to evaluate the returns being earned by individual business units and the managers responsible for their performance. Because they are oriented to financial outcomes, an emphasis on financial controls requires divisional performance to be largely independent of other divisions.[51] As such, when the firm chooses to implement a strategy calling for interdependence among the firm's different businesses, such as the related-constrained corporate-level strategy, the ability of financial control to add value to strategy implementation efforts is reduced.[52]

Next, we discuss the organizational structures and controls that are used to implement different business-level strategies.

Financial control entails objective criteria (e.g., return on investment) that corporate-level managers use to evaluate the returns being earned by individual business units and the managers responsible for their performance.

401

IMPLEMENTING BUSINESS-LEVEL STRATEGIES: ORGANIZATIONAL STRUCTURE AND CONTROLS

As discussed in Chapter 4, business-level strategies establish a particular type of competitive advantage (typically either low cost or differentiation) in a particular competitive scope (either an entire industry or a narrow segment of it). Effective implementation of the cost leadership, differentiation, and integrated low-cost/differentiation strategies occurs when certain modifications are made to the characteristics of the functional structure based on the unique attributes of the individual business-level strategies.

Using the Functional Structure to Implement the Cost Leadership Strategy

The structural characteristics of specialization, centralization, and formalization play important roles in the successful implementation of the cost leadership strategy. *Specialization* refers to the type and numbers of job specialties that are required to perform the firm's work.[53] For the cost leadership strategy, managers divide the firm's work into homogeneous subgroups. The basis for these subgroups is usually functional areas, products being produced, or clients served. By dividing and grouping work tasks into specialties, firms reduce their costs through the efficiencies achieved by employees specializing in a particular and often narrow set of activities.

Centralization is the degree to which decison-making authority is retained at higher managerial levels. Today, the trend in organizations is toward decentralization—the movement of decision-making authority down to people in the firm who have the most direct and frequent contact with customers. However, to coordinate activities carefully across organizational functions, the structure used to implement the cost leadership strategy calls for centralization. Thus, when designing this particular type of functional structure, managers strive to push some decision-making authority lower in the organization while remaining focused on the more general need for activities to be coordinated and integrated through the efforts of a centralized staff.

Because the cost leadership strategy is often chosen by firms producing relatively standardized products in large quantities, formalization is necessary. *Formalization* is the degree to which formal rules and procedures govern organizational activities.[54] To foster more efficient operations, R&D efforts emphasize improvements in the manufacturing process.

As summarized in Figure 11.2, successful implementation of the cost leadership strategy requires an organizational structure featuring strong task specialization, centralization of decision-making authority, and formalization of work rules and procedures. This type of functional structure encourages the emergence of a low-cost culture—a culture in which all employees seek to find ways to drive their firm's or unit's costs lower than rivals' costs. Using highly specialized work tasks, low-cost leader Southwest Airlines strives continuously to increase the efficiency of its

FIGURE 11.2 *Functional Structure for Implementation of a Cost Leadership Strategy*

Notes:
- Operations is the main function
- Process engineering is emphasized rather than new product R&D
- Relatively large centralized staff coordinates functions
- Formalized procedures allow for emergence of a low-cost culture
- Overall structure is mechanical; job roles are very structured

production and distribution systems. For example, Southwest was one of the first carriers to sell tickets on the Internet. A travel industry consultant concluded that Southwest's simple fares and schedule make it easy to sell travel directly to consumers on the Internet.[55] Similarly, some European carriers that are preparing for privatization, including Air France, TAP Air Portugal, Alitalia, and LOT off Poland, are seeking to develop a low-cost culture that may prove to be critical to their success as deregulated firms competing in the global marketplace.[56]

Using the Functional Structure to Implement the Differentiation Strategy

Successful implementation of the differentiation strategy occurs when a functional structure is used in which decision-making authority is decentralized. Unlike the cost leadership strategy, where coordination and integration of organizational function activities occurs through centralization of decision-making authority, the functional structure used to implement the differentiation strategy demands that people throughout the firm learn how to coordinate and integrate their activities effectively. This is the expectation at Nordstrom, the successful retailer. This firm's structure calls for individual stores to employ buyers who specialize in purchasing products that will satisfy the unique tastes of customers in different geographic locales.[57]

The marketing and R&D functions are often emphasized in the differentiation strategy's functional structure. For example, because of its commitment to continuous product innovation across all of its operations, R&D is emphasized in several of FAG Kugelfischer's business units to facilitate implementation of the differentiation strategy in those individual units. This emphasis is suggested by the following comment: "All our efforts in the R&D field have only one objective—improving the performance parameters of our products for the benefit of our customers in such a way that new machinery equipped with them constitutes a clear advance in terms of purchasing costs, service, and maintenance."[58] As in the case at FAG, an emphasis on R&D in firms implementing the differentiation strategy typically is focused on those activities required to develop new products. Centralized staffs make certain that the efforts of those working in these two critical functions are integrated successfully. To properly control new product development, a centralized research facility may be established, and to maintain efficiency, the manufacturing facility also may be partially centralized. This allows integration of new products quickly while maintaining the highest possible efficiency.[59] Alternatively, many firms use decentralized cross-functional teams composed of representatives from marketing, R&D, and manufacturing to integrate these functions for new product design, manufacturing, and introduction to the marketplace.

Finally, to capitalize on emerging trends in key markets, the firm implementing the differentiation strategy often makes rapid changes based on ambiguous and incomplete information. Such rapid changes demand that the firm use a relatively flat organizational structure to group its work activities (in a relatively flat structure, workers are likely to have a number of tasks included in their job descriptions). The implementation of the differentiation strategy is affected negatively when the firm has extensive centralization and formalization, especially in a rapidly changing environment. Thus, the overall organizational structure needs to be flexible and job roles less structured. Additional characteristics of the form of the functional structure used to implement the differentiation strategy are shown in Figure 11.3.

403

FIGURE 11.3 *Functional Structure for Implementation of a Differentiation Strategy*

Notes:
- Marketing is the main function for keeping track of new product ideas
- New product R&D is emphasized
- Most functions are decentralized, but R&D and marketing may have centralized staffs that work closely with each other
- Formalization is limited so that new product ideas can emerge easily and change is more readily accomplished
- Overall structure is organic, job roles are less structured

Using the Functional Structure to Implement the Integrated Low-Cost/Differentiation Strategy

To implement the integrated low-cost/differentiation strategy, companies seek to provide value that differs from that offered by the low cost and the differentiated firm—low cost, relative to the cost of the differentiated firm's product, and valuable differentiated features, relative to the features offered by the low-cost firm's product.

The integrated low-cost/differentiation strategy is being formulated more frequently, especially by global firms, but it is difficult to implement. The primary reason for this is that the strategic and tactical actions required to implement the low-cost and the differentiation strategies are not the same. For example, to achieve the low-cost position, relative to rivals, emphasis is placed on production and manufacturing process engineering, with infrequent product changes. In contrast, to achieve a differentiated position, marketing and new product R&D are emphasized. But, as explained earlier, the structural characteristics used to emphasize new product development differ from those needed to emphasize process engineering. To implement this strategy successfully, managers are challenged to form an organizational structure that allows the development of differentiated product features while costs, relative to rivals' costs, are reduced. Often the functional structure has to be supplemented by horizontal coordination, such as cross-functional teams and a strong organizational culture to implement this strategy effectively.

Recent decisions made by top-level managers at Peugeot-Citroen, the French car manufacturer, and Japan's Nissan Motor Company suggest an interest on the part of both firms to use the functional structure to implement the integrated low-cost/differentiation strategy. Although committed to continuous product innovation and to launching new models more rapidly, these two companies want simultaneously to reduce their costs. At the heart of the cost control efforts are reconfigurations of the firms' assembly plants. Nissan plans to shift to five platforms from the current total of 24. Executives believe that this cost-reducing decision will also allow the firm to quickly offer nine new models to the marketplace and shorten overall product development times to a mere 12 months. Similarly, officials at Peugeot-Citroen seek to prune the number of its car platforms from seven to three. Both companies also announced organizational structural changes that were intended to facilitate implementation of their car manufacturing strategies.[60]

Using the Simple Structure to Implement Focused Strategies

As noted earlier, many focused strategies—strategies through which a firm concentrates on serving the unique needs of a narrow part or scope of the industry—are implemented most effectively through the simple structure. At some point, however, the increased sales revenues resulting from success necessitate changing from a simple to a functional structure. The challenge for managers is to recognize when a structural change is required to coordinate and control effectively the firm's increasingly complex operations.

The intent of companies manufacturing regional soft drinks is to serve the needs of a narrow group of customers better than do giants Coca-Cola and PepsiCo. People targeted by the regional manufacturers are those with individualized tastes for soft drinks. To describe these firms and their products, an analyst noted that "... obscure soft drinks like Cheerwine are thriving in local markets across the country. These regional or 'cult' brands—with down-home names like Moxie, Big Red, Sun-drop, and Kickapoo Joy Juice—grew up in mostly rural areas. Many es-

405

To attain its goals of continuous product innovation and cost reduction, Nissan Motor Company is planning to reconfigure its assembly plants with 5 platforms instead of 24.

chew marketing, relying on the appeal of long histories, local pride and wild formulas, including one derived from a Russian cake-icing recipe and another that sprang from a failed pharmaceutical experiment."[61] Revolving around flexible production functions, these manufacturers have low levels of specialization and formalization. Additionally, as demonstrated by the nature of their marketing efforts, the regional soft drink companies centralize few of the decisions about the activities of different organizational functions.

Regional or "cult" brand colas, such as Moxie, Big Red, and Sun-drop, serve a narrow group of customers with individualized tastes for soft drinks.

Service Performance Corporation (SPC) also uses the simple organizational structure. Serving approximately 100 customers, SPC provides janitorial and facilities services in office buildings, malls, airports, laboratories, and manufacturing facilities. The firm's founder and CEO believes that service is his company's only product. To describe the character of SPC's organizational structure, the CEO noted that his nine-year-old company had retained its "aversion to bureaucracy." The simple structure is used to help all employees focus on what is believed to be the firm's competitive advantage—superior customer service.[62]

Movement to the Multidivisional Structure

The above-average returns gained through successful implementation of a business-level strategy often result in diversification of the firm's operations. This diversification can take the form of offering different products (product diversification) and/or offering the same or additional products in other markets (market diversification). As explained in Chapter 6, increased product and/or market diversification demands that firms formulate a corporate-level strategy as well as business-level strategies for individual units or divisions (see Figure 6.1 to review the different corporate-level strategies and their respective levels of diversification). With greater diversification, the simple and functional structures must be discarded in favor of the more complex, yet increasingly necessary multidivisional structure.

IMPLEMENTING CORPORATE-LEVEL STRATEGIES: ORGANIZATIONAL STRUCTURE AND CONTROLS

Effective use of the multidivisional structure helps firms implement their corporate-level strategy (diversification). In this section, we describe three M-form variations (see Figure 11.4) that are required to implement the related-constrained, related-linked, and unrelated diversification strategies.

Using the Cooperative Form to Implement the Related-Constrained Strategy

The **cooperative form** (of the multidivisional structure) is an organizational structure that uses many integration devices and horizontal human resource practices to foster cooperation and integration among the firm's divisions.

To implement the related-constrained strategy, firms use the cooperative form of the multidivisional structure. The **cooperative form** is an organizational structure that uses many integration devices and horizontal human resource practices to foster cooperation and integration among the firm's divisions. The cooperative form (see Figure 11.5) emphasizes horizontal links and relationships more than the two

FIGURE 11.4 *Three Variations of the Multidivisional Structure*

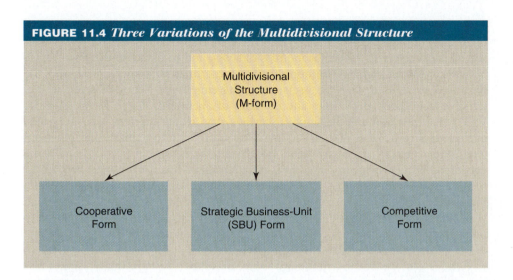

FIGURE 11.5 *Cooperative Form of the Multidivisional Structure for Implementation of a Related–Constrained Strategy*

Notes:
- Structural integration devices create tight links among all divisions
- Corporate office emphasizes centralized strategic planning, human resources, and marketing to foster cooperation between divisions
- R&D is likely to be centralized
- Rewards are subjective and tend to emphasize overall corporate performance in addition to divisional performance
- Culture emphasizes cooperative sharing

other variations of the multidivisional structure described later in the chapter. Cooperation among divisions that are formed around either products or markets served is necessary to realize economies of scope and to facilitate the transferring of skills.[63] Increasingly, it is important for these links to allow and support the sharing of a range of strategic assets, including employees' "know-how" as well as tangible assets such as facilities and methods of operations.[64]

To facilitate cooperation among divisions that are either vertically integrated or related through the sharing of strategic assets, some organizational functions (e.g., human resource management, R&D, and marketing) are centralized at the corporate level. Work completed in these centralized functions is managed by the firm's central administrative, or headquarters, office. When the central office's efforts allow exploitation of commonalties among the firm's divisions in ways that yield a cost or differentiation advantage (or both) in the divisions as compared to undiversified rivals, the cooperative form of the multidivisional structure is a source of competitive advantage for the diversified firm.[65]

Besides centralization, a number of structural integration links are used to foster cooperation among divisions in firms implementing the related-constrained diversification strategy. Frequent direct contact between division managers encourages and supports cooperation and the sharing of strategic assets. Sometimes, liaison roles are established in each division to reduce the amount of time division managers spend facilitating the integration and coordination of their units' work. Temporary teams or task forces may also be formed around projects and may require the efforts of many people from separate divisions to achieve desired levels of divisional coordination. Formal integration departments might be formed in firms requiring the work of temporary teams or task forces on a continuous basis. Ultimately, a matrix organization evolves in firms implementing the related-constrained strategy. A *matrix organization* is an organizational structure in which there is a dual structure combining both functional specialization and business product or project specialization.[66] Although complicated, effective matrix structures can lead to improved coordination among a firm's various divisions.[67]

As implied by the horizontal procedures used for coordination that we described earlier, information processing must increase dramatically to implement the related-constrained diversification strategy successfully. But, because cooperation among divisions implies a loss of managerial autonomy, division managers may not readily commit themselves to the type of integrative information processing activities demanded by this organizational structure. Moreover, coordination among divisions sometimes results in an unequal flow of positive outcomes to divisional managers. In other words, when managerial rewards are based at least in part on the performance of individual divisions, the manager of the division able to derive the greatest marketplace benefit from the sharing of the firm's strategic assets might be viewed as receiving relative gains at others' expense. In these instances, performance evaluations are emphasized to facilitate sharing of strategic assets. Furthermore, using reward systems that emphasize overall company performance besides outcomes achieved by individual divisions helps overcome problems associated with the cooperative form.

The use of the cooperative form of the multidivisional structure in three companies is described in the Strategic Focus. Notice that each firm is implementing the related-constrained diversification strategy, which, it seems, results in a match between strategy and structure within these companies.

STRATEGIC FOCUS

Using the Cooperative Form of the Multidivisional Structure to Achieve Strategic Competitiveness in the Transportation, Information and Entertainment, and Financial Services Industries

Montreal-based Bombardier is a worldwide manufacturer of transportation-related equipment. It has production facilities in eight countries in addition to Canada. The firm's corporate organizational structure features four product divisions—transportation, recreational products, aerospace, and services. Shared across the four product divisions is the firm's set of technological capabilities and competencies. As a source of competitive advantage, these capabilities and competencies allow Bombardier to introduce innovative products continuously and rapidly. To describe the factors contributing to his firm's strategic competitiveness, Bombardier's CEO observed, "We're selling technology, and we're selling new products. That's what makes us a success."

Bombardier has recently introduced a stream of innovative products. In the aerospace division, for example, the firm is offering the Learjet 45. A midsize plane that is priced like a light jet, the Learjet 45 is capable of nonstop transcontinental flights. In great demand, Bombardier has booked orders that will keep its factories busy through at least 2000. In 2000, the aerospace division will introduce a plane that analysts believe will yield even greater results for Bombardier. With a capacity of 70 seats, the Canadair Regional Jet Series 700 already has received an order from American Eagle, the commuter division of American Airlines. The transportation division is building 680 highly automated New York City subway cars for nearly $1 billion. Another project (yielding $419 million in sales revenue) is the manufacture of Amtrak's first high-speed trains. These trains will be providing service on Amtrak's Boston-Washington route by 1999. The recreational products division is introducing an entirely new product called the Neighborhood Vehicle (NV). Essentially a "souped-up golf cart," the NV is directed to those living in retirement or gated communities. Bombardier Services was created in 1996 so the firm could develop a stronger presence in the growing worldwide market for support, maintenance, and training services related to commercial aircraft and defense products.

To increase its strategic competitiveness, E. W. Scripps engaged in a year-long strategic realignment of its assets. Operations that were divested include book publishing and a cable-TV distribution system. The firm's corporate-level strategy now calls for it "... to be a provider of information and entertainment to particular consumer categories." To implement this strategy, three product divisions have been formed—publishing, broadcast, and entertainment. Personnel in the three divisions cooperate with one another to integrate and coordinate their operations when doing so increases the firm's competitive ability. Facilitating these integration and coordination attempts is Scripps' targeting of particular geographic locations in all three product divisions. Essentially, the firm seeks to cluster its media operations in midsize, high-growth Sun Belt markets such as Florida and Texas.

As a reflection of changes in financial markets and its own rapid growth, Morgan Stanley & Co. recently reorganized itself into two main product divisions—securities and asset management. Corporate executives viewed this structural change as a logical extension of the company's drive to build value in a rapidly changing environment. A key objective of this structural change was for the firm's investment bankers and securities salespeople and traders to work together more closely. Moreover, Morgan Stanley wanted to simplify the way it conducts business with its major corporate clients. Through use of the cooperative form of the multidivisional structure, Morgan Stanley was able to combine its various securities and investment-banking skills that previously were divided among three departments. These departments had offered separate debt, equity, and investment-banking strategies to corporate clients. According to company documents, "Morgan Stanley has improved efficiencies and established a position to provide a more effective, integrated approach to client services" as a result of changing its organizational structure.

Morgan Stanley's top-level managers suggested that their company was the first big Wall Street firm to integrate its securities businesses so closely. Analysts, however, argued that structural changes completed by Merrill Lynch in 1995 resulted in a similar outcome. To enhance its competitiveness, Merrill brought all of its investment-banking and capital-markets businesses into one group under one manager. Thus, both of these firms initiated changes that were designed to align more closely their organizational structures with their corporate level strategies. In commenting about the results of his firm's efforts, one Morgan Stanley employee noted that the structural changes would compel individuals to work together more closely.

SOURCES: Bombardier Home Page, 1998, February 4, http://www.bombardier.com; E. W. Scripps Home Page, 1998, February 4, http://www.scripps.com; Morgan Stanley Home Page, 1998, February 4, http://www.ms.com; J. Weber, W. Zellner, and G. Smith, 1998, Loud noises at Bombardier, *Business Week*, January 26, 94–95; J. P. Miller, 1997, E. W. Scripps turns page, and spots new opportunities, *Wall Street Journal*, September 23, B4; Morgan Stanley forms 2 big divisions, following industry trends, 1997, *The New York Times* on the Web, http://www.nytimes.com, December 16.

When there are fewer and/or less constrained links among the firm's divisions, the related-linked diversification strategy should be implemented. As explained next, this strategy can be implemented successfully through use of the SBU form of the multidivisional structure.

Using the SBU Form to Implement the Related-Linked Strategy

The **strategic business unit (SBU) form** of the multidivisional structure consists of at least three levels, with the top level being corporate headquarters; the next level, SBU groups; and the final level, divisions grouped by relatedness (either product or geographic market) within each SBU (see Figure 11.6). The firm's business portfolio is organized into those related to one another within a SBU group and those unrelated in other SBU groups. Thus, divisions within groups are related, but groups are largely unrelated to each other. Within the SBU structure, divisions with similar products or technologies are organized to achieve synergy. Each SBU is a profit center that is controlled by the firm's headquarters office. An important benefit of this structural form is that individual decision makers, within their strategic business unit, look to SBU executives rather than headquarters personnel for strategic guidance. Recall from the opening case that Raytheon Company also uses the SBU multidivisional structural form. Divisions within the firm's four strategic business units are related, but the business units are largely unrelated to one another.

Scotts is another company that uses the SBU form of the multidivisional structure. A producer and marketer of products for do-it-yourself lawn care, profes-

The **strategic business unit (SBU) form** of the multidivisional structure consists of at least three levels, with the top level being corporate headquarters; the next level, SBU groups; and the final level, divisions grouped by relatedness (either product or geographic market) within each SBU.

FIGURE 11.6 *SBU Form of the Multidivisional Structure for Implementation of a Related-Linked Strategy*

Notes:
- Structural integration among divisions within SBUs but independence across SBUs
- Strategic planning may be the most prominent function in headquarters to manage the strategic planning approval process of SBUs for the president
- Each SBU may have its own budget for staff to foster integration
- Corporate headquarters staff serve as consultants to SBUs and divisions, rather than having direct input to product strategy as in the cooperative form

411

sional turf care, and horticulture, the firm seeks $1 billion in sales revenues by 2000 (revenues were $606 million in 1994).[68] Recently Scotts revamped its organizational structure to help the company reach its sales revenues goal. The company is now organized into four main business units: consumer lawn (its mainstay fertilizers and other home products); consumer garden (primarily consisting of Stern's Miracle-Gro Products); professional (includes commercial applications such as golf courses); and international.[69]

The organizational structure for large diversified firms such as Scotts and Raytheon can be complex. This complexity is a reflection of the size and diversity of a diversified firm's operations. Consider the case of General Electric (GE). Implementing the related-linked corporate-level strategy, this firm's structure calls for integration among divisions within SBUs but independence between the SBUs. GE managers expect to be able to "walk, think, and talk" like a small firm and to make decisions and introduce innovative products at a pace that is equivalent to its smaller competitors.[70]

Recently GE's SBU structure featured 13 major strategic business units. GE Power Systems is one of these. Other units include GE Aircraft Engines (the world's

GE Information Services is one of the firm's 13 SBUs. The unit provides business-to-business electronic commerce solutions and manages the world's largest electronic trading company.

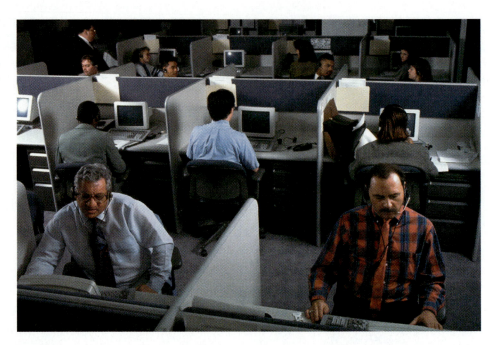

largest manufacturer of military and commercial aircraft jet engines), GE Information Services (a leading provider of business-to-business electronic commerce solutions, managing the world's largest electronic trading community of more than 40,000 trading partners), and GE Medical Systems (a world leader in medical diagnostic imaging technology). GE Power Systems serves those who are supplying the world's need for reliable, highly efficient electricity. Gas Turbines is one of at least 15 divisions within the Power Systems portfolio. Other divisions with which Gas Turbines is integrated to varying degrees include Steam Turbines, Hydro Turbines and Generators, Boiling Water Reactor Services, and Advanced Nuclear Reactor Systems. Featuring the broadest line of gas turbines in the industry today, GE is the acknowledged world leader with more than 5,000 units installed and more than 4,600 combustion turbines operating successfully around the globe.[71]

As noted above, GE's organizational structure is expected to enable the firm to act quickly and effectively. Thus, even for firms as large as GE, structural flexibility is as important as strategic flexibility (recall the discussion in Chapter 5 indicating that today's challenging competitive dynamics have created a need for the firm to have strategic flexibility). Through a combination of strategic and structural flexibility, GE is able to respond rapidly to opportunities as they emerge throughout the world. An example of this is GE's commitment to pursue investment and growth opportunities that senior-level executives envisioned during Asia's late 1990's economic crisis.[72]

Using the Competitive Form to Implement the Unrelated Diversification Strategy

Firms implementing the unrelated diversification strategy seek to create value through efficient internal capital allocations or by restructuring, buying, and selling businesses.[73] The competitive form of the multidivisional structure is used to implement the unrelated diversification strategy. The **competitive form** is an organizational structure in which the controls used emphasize competition between separate (usually unrelated) divisions for corporate capital. To realize benefits from efficient resource allocations, divisions must have separate, identifiable profit performance and must be held accountable for such performance. The internal capital market requires organizational arrangements that emphasize *competition* rather than *cooperation* between divisions.[74]

To emphasize competitiveness among divisions, the headquarters office maintains an arms-length relationship and does not intervene in divisional affairs except to audit operations and discipline managers whose divisions perform poorly. In this situation, the headquarters office sets rate-of-return targets and monitors the outcomes of divisional performance.[75] It allocates cash flow on a competitive basis, rather than automatically returning cash to the division that produced it. The competitive form of the multidivisional structure is illustrated in Figure 11.7.

A diversified supplier of hardware items to U.S. discount retailers, Newell Company uses the competitive form of the multidivisional structure to implement its unrelated diversification strategy. Committed to growth by acquisition, product lines added across time to the firm's independent divisions share no common characteristics. Supplying primarily large firms such as Wal-Mart, Newell sells an array of products, including pots and pans, paint brushes, and curtain rods. Newell's competitive advantage is created at the corporate level. Using a small corporate

The **competitive form** is an organizational structure in which the controls used emphasize competition between separate (usually unrelated) divisions for corporate capital.

413

FIGURE 11.7 *Competitive Form of the Multidivisional Structure for Implementation of an Unrelated Strategy*

Notes:
- Corporate headquarters has a small staff
- Finance and auditing are the most prominent functions in the headquarters to manage cash flow and ensure accuracy of performance data coming from divisions
- The legal affairs function becomes important when acquiring and divesting assets
- Divisions are independent and separate for financial evaluation purposes
- Divisions retain strategic control, but cash is managed by the corporate office
- Divisions compete for corporate resources

TABLE 11.1 *Characteristics of the Structures Necessary to Implement the Related-Constrained, Related-Linked, and Unrelated Diversification Strategies*

	Overall Structural Form		
Structural Characteristics	**Cooperative M-form (Related-Constrained Strategy[a])**	**SBU M-form (Related-Linked Strategy[a])**	**Competitive M-form (Unrelated Diversification Strategy[a])**
Centralization of operation	Centralized at corporate office	Partially centralized (in SBUs)	Decentralized to division
Use of integrating mechanisms	Extensive	Moderate	Nonexistent
Divisional performance appraisal	Emphasizes subjective criteria	Uses a mixture of subjective and objective criteria	Emphasizes objective (financial or ROI) criteria
Divisional incentive compensation	Linked to overall corporate performance	Mixed linkage to corporate, SBU, and divisional performance	Linked to divisional performance

[a]Strategy implemented with structural form.

headquarters staff, the firm has developed a sophisticated electronic, logistical system. Allocated to each of its divisions, this system is used as the basis for each division's logistics with its customers. Although not related to each other, each of Newell's divisions creates value "from the lower cost and improved customer relations provided by the Newell system."[76]

In summary, our discussion describes three major forms of the multidivisional structure and the relationship of the individual forms with particular corporate-level strategies. Table 11.1 shows the characteristics of these structures. As shown in the table, differences are seen in the degree of centralization, the focus of performance appraisal, the horizontal structures (integrating mechanisms), and the incentive compensation schemes necessary to implement the three corporate-level strategies of related-constrained, related-linked, and unrelated diversification successfully. The most centralized and most costly organizational form is the cooperative structure. The least centralized, with the lowest bureaucratic costs, is the competitive structure. The SBU structure requires partial centralization and involves some of the mechanisms necessary to implement the relatedness between divisions. Also, the divisional incentive compensation awards are allocated according to both SBU and corporate performance. In the competitive structure, the most important criterion is divisional performance.

Earlier in the chapter, we indicated that, once formed, an organizational structure can influence a firm's efforts to implement its current strategy and the selection of future strategies. Using the multidivisional structure as the foundation for the discussion, the explanation in the next section exemplifies the relationship between structure and strategy.

THE EFFECT OF STRUCTURE ON STRATEGY

As explained earlier, the M-form is a structural innovation intended to help managers deal with the coordination and control problems created by increasing product and market variety. Once established, however, the M-form structure has the potential to positively influence the firm's diversification strategy.[77] Strong and appropriate incentives, ones that encourage managers to pursue additional marketplace opportunities, coupled with improved accountability and superior internal resource allocations from the corporate office, may stimulate additional diversification. Furthermore, these additional levels of diversification can result in greater returns on the firm's investments.[78] Eventually, however, there is a tendency for the M-form to encourage inefficient levels of diversification. Following a comprehensive review of research evidence, some researchers noted that there is a growing body of evidence which suggests that adoption of the M-form structure facilitates the pursuit of inefficient diversification.[79] Again, this cause/effect relationship—that is, the influence of the M-form on a firm's pursuit of additional diversification—is not inherently negative. The complicating factor is that at some point, the additional amounts of diversification stimulated by the M-form become inefficient, thereby reducing the firm's strategic competitiveness and its returns.

Other theory and research suggests that once the M-form influences the pursuit of more diversification that yields inefficient strategic outcomes, the relationship between structure and strategy may reverse in direction.[80] In other words, firms that become inefficiently diversified implement strategies that result in less efficient levels of diversification. One researcher found, for example, that half of the diversified acquisitions made by unrelated diversified firms were later divested.[81] Another discovered that a decrease in the diversified scope of M-form firms was associated with an improvement in shareholder wealth. This finding, too, suggests that these firms' diversification had become inefficient.[82] An example of a firm that recently changed its diversification strategy to increase its efficiency and strategic competitiveness is described in the Strategic Focus. Sara Lee Corporation intends to reduce substantially its level of diversification by the year 2000. To achieve all of the potential gains from this corporate-level decision, the firm will also need to change its organizational structure to facilitate implementation of a less diversified strategy.

Sara Lee's commitment to lower levels of diversification parallels what appears to be a 1990's trend in some countries. In the United States and the United Kingdom, for example, the 1990s is a time period in which "pure plays" are in and diversified companies are out. This preference results in decisions in firms ranging from AT&T to ITT to split up into separately traded companies that focus on their core businesses.[83] The trend toward focus is not as apparent among German firms yet, but recent evidence suggests it may increase in Germany if pressure to reduce costs and improve efficiency gains strength in the near future.[84]

STRATEGIC FOCUS

Deverticalization: Sara Lee's Path to Lower Levels of Diversification

Founded by a Canadian entrepreneur, Sara Lee Corporation became a global manufacturer and marketer of high-quality, brand name products for consumers throughout the world. In 1997, the firm had operations in more than 40 countries and sold its products in over 140 nations. Using the SBU form of the multidivisional structure to implement the related-linked diversification strategy, Sara Lee was organized into four separate businesses: packaged meats and bakery (39 percent of sales revenue), coffee and grocery (14 percent), household and body care (9 percent), and personal products (38 percent). Famous brand names included in Sara Lee's portfolio of businesses were Hanes, Hanes Her Way, L'eggs, Bali, Champion, Hillshire Farm, Jimmy Dean, Sanex, and Kiwi, among others. For many years, the company's growth was fueled by what its leaders viewed to be strategic acquisitions.

Although generating record profits in 1997, the corporation's stock was languishing on Wall Street. Sara Lee's CEO and chairman, John Bryan, described the firm's status with the financial community as follows: "We were pretty boring to Wall Street, and there was a clamor to do something." The "something" Bryan and other Sara Lee top-level managers decided upon was to "deverticalize" their corporation. Through deverticalization, Sara Lee's level of diversification will be reduced substantially. In fact, this restructuring program was intended to fundamentally reshape Sara Lee in a manner that executives believed better prepared their firm to compete in the twenty-first century.

On September 15, 1997, Bryan announced formally Sara Lee's plan to deverticalize. The conglomerate intended to sell $3 billion of its assets, including entire divisions and multiple manufacturing operations. According to Bryan, the firm's ". . . deverticalization program was designed to enable us to focus our energies and talents on the greatest value-creating activities in our business, which are building and managing leadership brands. Minimizing the degree to which our business is vertically integrated reduces the capital demands on our company while enhancing our competitiveness." As a less diversified corporation, the intention was for Sara Lee to become a company similar to Nike, Coca-Cola, and Polo/Ralph Lauren. Each of these firms allocates significant amounts of its resources to marketing and to outsourcing manufacturing. Thus, the intent was for Sara Lee to move away from manufacturing the brand name goods it was selling. Executives believed that the deverticalization program would generate as much as $3 billion within a three-year period (culminating by the year 2000).

To reach its objective of building branded leadership positions through deverticalization, Sara Lee intended to divest substantial portions of its U.S. yarn and textile operations. This is a significant decision given that Sara Lee Knit Products held the number one U.S. market share position in men's and boys' and women's and girls' underwear garments. The first of the divestments in this product line was announced on January 5, 1998. On this date, National Textiles agreed to purchase nine of Sara Lee's yarn and textile operations. The yield to Sara Lee from this transaction was expected to approximate $600 million over a three-year period. Other divestments were planned for some of the company's food and nonfood businesses by 2000.

The results of these divestments and of the less diversified strategy that Sara Lee will follow at the corporate level demand a different organizational structure. Possible structural choices include the cooperative form of the multidivisional structure and even the functional structure (if Sara Lee's final set of divestments results in a highly focused firm—one with low levels of diversification).

Wall Street's initial reaction to Sara Lee's deverticalization program was positive. On September 15, 1997, the day of the program's announcement, the company's stock rose 14 percent.

SOURCES: Sara Lee Corporation Home Page, 1998, http://www.saralee.com; *The Economist*, 1997, Separate and fit, September 20, 69; R. Lowenstein, 1997, Remember when companies made things? *Wall Street Journal*, September 18, C1; R. Melcher, 1997, A finger in fewer pies, *Business Week*, September 29, 44; J. P. Miller, 1997, Sara Lee to retreat from manufacturing, *Wall Street Journal*, September 16, A3, A10.

Our discussion now turns to an explanation of organizational structures used to implement the three international strategies explained in Chapter 8.

IMPLEMENTING INTERNATIONAL STRATEGIES: ORGANIZATIONAL STRUCTURE AND CONTROLS

Increasingly, a firm's ability to achieve strategic competitiveness is a function of its competitive success in the global marketplace.[85] Although important for many firms, competing successfully in global markets is perhaps especially critical for large companies. General Motors CEO Jack Smith, for example, intends for his company to expand sales outside the United States, Canada, and Mexico to 4.5 million vehicles by 2006. Critical to accomplishing this objective is the successful implementation of GM's international strategy. Included as parts of this strategy are the manufacture of (1) an inexpensive family car in Poland, (2) Chevrolet Blazers in Russia, (3) Chevrolet Corsicas in Argentina, and (4) Buick sedans in China.[86] Supporting implementation of GM's international and domestic strategies are newly formed organizational structures designed to integrate effectively the work of engineers and manufacturing and marketing personnel.[87] As explained in this section of the chapter, international strategies such as those chosen by GM's top-level executives cannot be implemented successfully without use of the proper organizational structure.[88] As the decade closes, results from implementation of GM's international strategy through its new organizational structure are encouraging. Fueled by continuing cost-cutting efforts and stronger-than-expected factory sales, GM posted record earnings in the fourth quarter of 1997.[89]

417

Using the Worldwide Geographic Area Structure to Implement the Multidomestic Strategy

The *multidomestic strategy* is a strategy in which strategic and operating decisions are decentralized to business units in each country to facilitate tailoring of products to local markets. Through this strategy, Campbell Soup customizes its products to local tastes. For example, the firm's cream of pumpkin soup is Australia's largest selling canned soup. In Hong Kong, Campbell sells watercress-and-duck-gizzard soup.[90] However, it is sometimes difficult for firms to know how local their products should or can become. Lands' End, for example, is one of the U.S. mail-order firms being lured by the promise of the European market for its products and services. Interested in adapting to local preferences, the firm's director of international operations observed that the most difficult part of achieving this objective is to know in which areas to be local.[91]

Firms implementing the multidomestic strategy often attempt to isolate themselves from global competitive forces by establishing protected market positions or by competing in industry segments that are most affected by differences among local countries. The worldwide geographic area structure (see Figure 11.8) is used to implement the multidomestic strategy. The **worldwide geographic area structure** emphasizes national interests and facilitates managers' efforts to satisfy local or cultural differences.

Recently, Coca-Cola shed the management structure it had been using to implement the firm's strategy with its core soft drink business. Previously, soft drinks had been divided into two units—North America and International. "But given that some of [the firm's] individual operating groups outside of North America now generate income equal to that of our entire company in the mid-1980s,

The **worldwide geographic area structure** emphasizes national interests and facilitates managers' efforts to satisfy local or cultural differences.

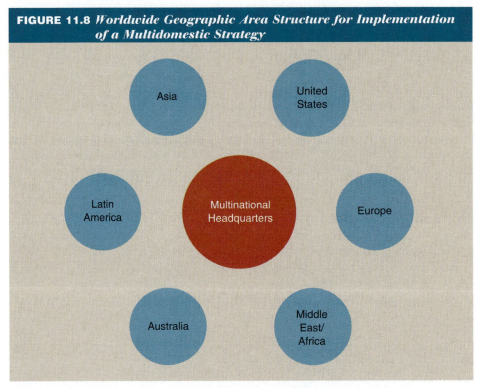

FIGURE 11.8 *Worldwide Geographic Area Structure for Implementation of a Multidomestic Strategy*

Notes:
- Blue shaded perimeter circles indicate decentralization of operations
- Emphasis is on differentiation by local demand to fit an area or country culture
- Corporate headquarters coordinates financial resources among independent subsidiaries
- The organization is like a decentralized federation

bundling those units under the title of 'International' had become artificial and impractical." Today, Coca-Cola's worldwide soft drink operations are divided into five groups, with North America but one of the five newly formed units. Forming this worldwide geographic area structure will likely enhance the firm's ability to manage its soft drink business globally.[92]

Because implementing the multidomestic strategy requires little coordination between different country markets, there is no need for integrating mechanisms among divisions in the worldwide geographic area structure. As such, formalization is low and coordination among units in a firm's worldwide geographic area structure is often informal. Because each European country has a distinct culture, the multidomestic strategy and the associated worldwide geographic structure were a natural outgrowth of the multicultural marketplace. This type of structure often was developed originally by friends and family members of the main business who were sent as expatriates into foreign countries to develop the independent country subsidiary. The relationship to corporate headquarters by divisions took place through informal communication among "family members."[93]

The primary disadvantage of the multidomestic strategy and worldwide geographic area structure combination is the inability to create global efficiency. As the emphasis on lower cost products has increased in international markets, the need to pursue worldwide economies of scale and scope has increased. These changes have fostered use of the global strategy.

Using the Worldwide Product Divisional Structure to Implement the Global Strategy

The *global strategy* is a strategy in which standardized products are offered across country markets and where competitive strategy is dictated by the firm's home office. International scale and scope economies are sought and emphasized when implementing this international strategy. Because of the important relationship between scale and scope economies and successful implementation of the global strategy, some activities of the firm's organizational functions are sourced to the most effective worldwide providers.

The worldwide product divisional structure (see Figure 11.9) is used to implement the global strategy. The **worldwide product divisional structure** is an organizational form in which decision-making authority is centralized in the worldwide division headquarters to coordinate and integrate decisions and actions among disparate divisional business units. This form is the organizational structure of choice for rapidly growing firms seeking to manage their diversified product lines effectively.[94] Integrating mechanisms also create effective coordination through mutual adjustments in personal interactions. Such integrating mechanisms include direct contact between managers, liaison roles between departments, temporary task forces or permanent teams, and integrating roles. As managers participate in

The **worldwide product divisional structure** is an organizational form in which decision-making authority is centralized in the worldwide division headquarters to coordinate and integrate decisions and actions among disparate divisional business units.

419

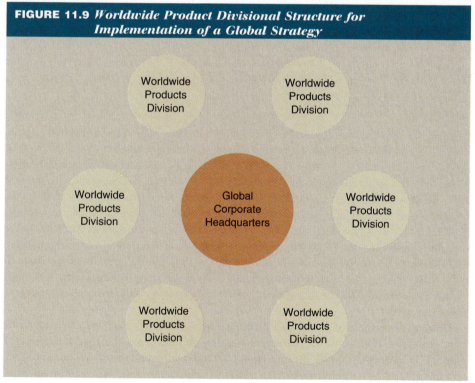

FIGURE 11.9 *Worldwide Product Divisional Structure for Implementation of a Global Strategy*

Notes:
- Orange shaded headquarters circle indicates centralization to coordinate information flow among worldwide products
- Corporate headquarters uses many intercoordination devices to facilitate global economies of scale and scope
- Corporate headquarters also allocates financial resources in a cooperative way
- The organization is like a centralized federation

cross-country transfers, they are socialized in the philosophy of managing an integrated strategy through a worldwide product divisional structure. A shared vision of the firm's strategy and structure is developed through standardized policies and procedures (formalization) that facilitate implementation of this organizational form.

Two primary disadvantages of the global strategy and its accompanying worldwide product divisional structure are the difficulty involved with coordinating decisions and actions across country borders and the inability to respond quickly and effectively to local needs and preferences. For example, Federal Express was reported to have encountered difficulties with its expansion into Asia, an area of international growth the company believed had significant potential. One problem the firm experienced concerned attempts to establish hub systems. The hub system is vital to FedEx's ability to achieve required levels of coordination across country borders. As an analyst noted, "The hub system is critical; it positions Federal Express to simultaneously pursue two massive markets—trans-Pacific and intra-Asian—at lower costs. The same planes that carry freight to the hub destined for the U.S. and Japan can also provide regular overnight delivery between cities on the continent."[95]

As explained in the Strategic Focus, H. J. Heinz uses the worldwide product divisional structure to implement the global strategy. Notice that this structure is expected to contribute to the firm's efforts to improve its international operations.

STRATEGIC FOCUS

Using the Worldwide Product Divisional Structure as a Means of Increased Internationalization

Headquartered in Pittsburgh, Pennsylvania, H. J. Heinz Company is a worldwide food producer. Perhaps known best for its ubiquitous ketchup, the firm also sells infant foods, condiments, pet foods, tuna, and is involved with weight-control products and programs as well. Heinz has a strong international presence, deriving 45 percent of sales revenue from operations outside the United States. However, the firm's newly appointed CEO, William R. Johnson, believes that Heinz has yet to derive full strategic benefit from efforts to internationalize its business (Johnson's tenure as Heinz's CEO began formally in April 1998). As such, he is convinced that Heinz can improve its overall corporate performance through renewed efforts to compete successfully outside the firm's domestic U.S. markets. Committed to the global strategy rather than the multidomestic strategy, organizational structure plays a key role in the strategic actions Johnson is taking to enhance Heinz's strategic competitiveness.

Under the leadership of Anthony O'Reilly, Johnson's predecessor, Heinz used the worldwide geographic area structure to implement the multidomestic international strategy. Through this structure, decisions were decentralized to business units in various countries or regions to facilitate the tailoring of the company's products to local tastes. Johnson, however, is organizing Heinz in terms of product categories rather than geographic areas. In this manner, "... tuna managers in Europe will work with tuna managers in Asia, Latin America, and other regions, allowing the best brand manager to advise all the countries." Through the operations supported by this structure, Heinz seeks to create additional value by emphasizing its brand names.

One indicator of the new organizational structure was the establishment of a new worldwide products division. Created in February of 1998, the Specialty Pet Food division was given the responsibility of marketing Heinz's specialty pet foods on a global basis. In particular, marketing efforts were to be focused on introducing Heinz's specialty pet food brands (e.g., Nature's Recipe, Vet's Choice, and Martin Pet Foods) to Europe and other developing pet food markets such as South America, Asia, Australia, and South Africa. In commenting about this new division, then-current CEO O'Reilly suggested that Specialty Pet Foods was an example of Heinz's commitment to reorganize its corporate structure to support the firm's growth initiatives and its desire to continue building international operations.

Johnson has other strategic actions that he wants Heinz to initiate. Implementation of these actions, too, will be supported by use of the worldwide product divisional structure. For example, he wants his firm to continue test-marketing products that have been successful in one country in other locations. Frozen tuna filets and flavored tuna, which have sold well in Europe, were tested recently in the United States. In fact, attempts to cross-sell products among different nations are an important component to Heinz's desire to exploit the value of its brand names internationally.

Another decision that has been made concerns performance assessments. To evaluate more effectively the performance of individual worldwide products divisions, personnel at Heinz's headquarters have assumed a more prominent role. One result of these evaluations is the decision to consider selling Weight Watchers, the weight-control business that makes frozen foods and offers classes. Although successful in the United Kingdom, the program has been a disappointment in the United States. Thus, decision making within this firm is becoming more centralized in order to identify and then group appropriately the products that can contribute to Heinz's attempts to improve its international operations.

SOURCES: Infoseek, 1998, Heinz makes appointments at three international affiliates; Announces formation of Specialty Pet Food unit, February 4, http://www.infoseek.com; R. Balu, 1997, Heinz's Johnson to divest operations, scrap management of firm by regions, *Wall Street Journal*, December 8, B22; *The Economist*, 1997, Separate and fit, September 20, 69.

Using the Combination Structure to Implement the Transnational Strategy

The *transnational strategy* is an international strategy through which a firm seeks to provide the local responsiveness that is the focus of the multidomestic strategy *and* to achieve the global efficiency that is the focus of the global strategy. The **combination structure** has characteristics and structural mechanisms that result in an emphasis on both geographic and product structures. Unilever Group uses the combination structure. The firm's operations are divided into 14 business groups. Some of the groups are framed around emerging markets; others are framed around the company's European food and drink businesses.[96] Thus, this structure has the multidomestic strategy's geographic area focus and the global strategy's product focus. The following company statements show the approach this structure supports:

The **combination structure** has characteristics and structural mechanisms that result in an emphasis on both geographic and product structures.

> Unilever describes itself as international, not global, because it does not attempt to enter all markets with the same product. Half of Unilever's business is in food, where it is often essential to take a local view. Only a few products—like ice cream, tea, and olive oil—successfully cross national or regional borders.

Similarly, in detergents, the formulation Unilever sells in South Africa will differ from the one in France because washing habits, machines, clothes, and water quality are all different. Personal wash products, on the other hand, need to vary less, so there are strong international brands like *Lux* and *Dove*. The Unilever portfolio includes a balanced mix of local, regional and international brands which take account of the differences as well as the similarities in consumer needs.[97]

The fits between the multidomestic strategy and the worldwide geographic area structure and the global strategy and the worldwide product divisional structure are apparent. However, when a firm seeks to implement both the multidomestic and global strategies simultaneously through a combination structure, the appropriate integrating mechanisms for the two structures are less obvious. The structure used to implement the transnational strategy must be simultaneously centralized and decentralized, integrated and nonintegrated, and formalized and nonformalized. These seemingly opposing structural characteristics must be managed by a structure that is capable of encouraging all employees to understand the effects of cultural diversity on a firm's operations. Moreover, the combination structure should allow the firm to learn how to gain competitive benefits in local economies by adapting capabilities and core competencies that often have been developed and nurtured in less culturally diverse competitive environments.

In the next section, we focus on implementation of the dominant forms of the cooperative strategies that were discussed in Chapter 9.

IMPLEMENTING COOPERATIVE STRATEGIES: ORGANIZATIONAL STRUCTURE AND CONTROLS

Increasingly, companies develop multiple rather than single joint ventures or strategic alliances to implement cooperative strategies. Furthermore, the global marketplace accommodates many interconnected relationships among firms. Resulting from these relationships are networks of firms competing through an array of cooperative arrangements or alliances.[98] When managed effectively, cooperative arrangements can contribute positively to each partner's ability to achieve strategic competitiveness and earn above-average returns.

To facilitate the effectiveness of a *strategic network*—a grouping of organizations that has been formed to create value through participation in an array of cooperative arrangements such as a strategic alliance—a strategic center firm may be necessary. A *strategic center firm* facilitates management of a strategic network. Through its management, the central firm creates incentives that reduce the probability of any company taking actions that could harm its network partners, and it identifies actions that increase the opportunity for each firm to achieve competitive success through its participation in the network.[99] Illustrated in Figure 11.10, the strategic center firm is vital to the ability of companies to create value and increase their strategic competitiveness. The four critical aspects of the strategic center firm's function are

Strategic outsourcing: The strategic center firm outsources and partners with more firms than do the other network members. Nonetheless, the strategic center

FIGURE 11.10 *A Strategic Network*

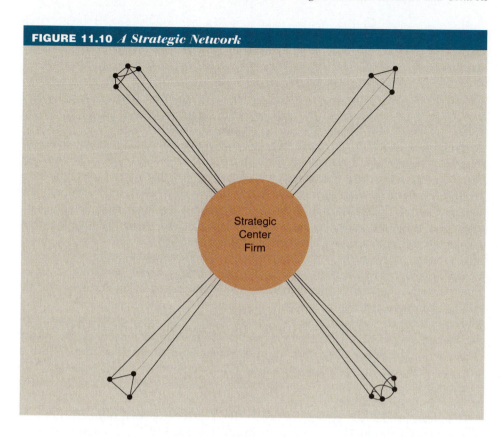

firm requires partners to be more than contractors. Partners are expected to solve problems and to initiate competitive courses of action that can be pursued by the network.

Capability: The strategic center firm has core competencies that are not shared with all network partners. To increase the network's effectiveness, the central firm attempts to develop each partner's core competencies and provides incentives for network firms to share their capabilities and competencies with partners.

Technology: The strategic center firm manages the development and sharing of technology-based ideas among network partners.

Race to learn: The strategic center firm emphasizes to partners that the principal dimension of competition in competitive environments is between value chains and networks of value chains. As a result, a strategic network is as strong as its weakest value chain link. As a value chain link, a strategic network seeks to develop a competitive advantage in a primary or support activity (see Chapter 3). The need for each firm to be strong for the benefit of the entire network encourages positive rivalry among partners to learn rapidly and effectively.[100] The most effective strategic center firms learn how to manage learning processes occurring among network members.

The dominant problem in single venture cooperative arrangements is the lack of ability to control innovation and learning. However, a well-managed strategic network can overcome this problem. Therefore, as explained in the following discussions, the managerial role of the strategic center firm is critical to the successful implementation of business-level, corporate-level, and international cooperative strategies.

Implementing Business-Level Cooperative Strategies

As noted in Chapter 9, there are two types of complementary assets at the business level—vertical and horizontal. Vertical complementary strategic alliances are formed more frequently than horizontal alliances. Focused on buyer-supplier relationships, vertical strategic networks usually have a clear strategic center firm. Japanese vertical keiretsus such as those developed by Toyota Motor Company are structured this way. Acting as the strategic center firm, Toyota fashioned its lean production system around a network of supplier firms.

A strategic network of vertical relationships in Japan such as the network between Toyota and its suppliers often includes the following implementation issues. First, the strategic center firm encourages subcontractors to modernize their facilities and provides them with technical and financial assistance if necessary. Second, it reduces its transaction costs by promoting longer term contracts with subcontractors so that supplying partners increase their long-term productivity, rather than continually negotiating short-term contracts based on unit pricing. Third, it provides engineers in upstream companies (suppliers) better communication with contractees. Thus, the contractees and center firms become more interdependent and less independent.[101]

The lean production system pioneered by Toyota has been diffused throughout the Japanese and U.S. automobile industries. However, no automobile producer is able to duplicate the effectiveness and efficiency Toyota derives from use of this manufacturing system.[102] A key factor accounting for Toyota's ability to derive a competitive advantage from this system is the cost to imitate the structural form used to support its application. In other words, Toyota's largely proprietary actions as the strategic center firm in the network it created are ones that competitors are unable to duplicate.

In vertical complementary strategic alliances, such as the one between Toyota and its suppliers, the company that should function as the strategic center firm is obvious. However, this is not always the case with horizontal complementary strategic alliances, as the following example demonstrates.

A jet engine joint venture formed between rivals GE and United Technologies' Pratt and Whitney unit promised significant returns for both firms.[103] However, other cooperative arrangements between jet engine manufacturers have not yielded anticipated results. Previously, for example, GE and Rolls-Royce's jet engine division formed a joint venture to manufacture engines for Boeing's 777 commercial jet. Bitter disputes between the partners led to the breakup of this venture. Similarly, an earlier venture among Pratt, Rolls-Royce, and other small contractors to build smaller jet engines failed. A problem common to all of these ventures was the difficulty of selecting the strategic center firm. The distrust that had formed among the joint venture companies through years of aggressive competition prevented agreements regarding the firm that should function as the strategic center of a network. Thus, because the dominant strategic center firm is evident, vertical complementary strategic alliances tend to be far more stable than horizontal complementary strategic alliances.

Joint ventures between jet engine manufacturers have not always been successful. Because the companies involved often were aggressive competitors, it is difficult for them to agree on which firm should serve as the strategic center.

Implementing Corporate-Level Cooperative Strategies

Although corporate-level cooperative strategy partnerships should select a strategic center firm to operate the network of alliances effectively, it is more difficult to choose a strategic center firm in some types of corporate-level cooperative strategies. It is easier, for example, for a strategic center firm to emerge in a centralized franchise network than in a decentralized set of diversified strategic alliances. This situation is demonstrated by McDonald's.

McDonald's has formed a centralized strategic network in which its corporate office serves as the strategic center for its franchisees. Recently, McDonald's decided that the firm should use its core competencies to better serve the adult market. Long a favorite of children, many parents of adolescents do not share their offsprings' excitement about eating at McDonald's. Developed through the strategic center's centralized R&D function, a new product, aimed at adults, was introduced in mid-1996. Called the Arch Deluxe, this food item was pitched as "the burger with a grownup taste." However, this was not a successful product introduction (see the Strategic Focus in Chapter 5). This result, coupled with other issues, caused one analyst to suggest that McDonald's was a brand in need of "radical surgery."

To cope with its problems, McDonald's, as a strategic center firm, initiated a series of actions. Framed around the need to improve the quality of its products and speed up their delivery, the company developed its "just-in-time kitchen" concept for use by franchisees. This new production system is designed to move made-to-order sandwiches to customers without increasing the preparation time. As part of this system, a computer-monitored machine dumps frozen fries into a basket that in turn is dunked into hot oil for cooking. The machine then shakes the fries and dumps them into bins for serving. Simultaneously, robot machines prepare drinks quickly as ordered by the customer. Preventing full use of this system's capabilities, however, was the delay in supplying all franchisees with the equipment.

Thus, as the strategic center firm in its centralized franchise network, McDonald's still faces significant challenges.[104]

Unlike McDonald's, Corning's corporate-level cooperative strategy has resulted in the implementation of a system of diversified strategic alliances. This has required Corning to implement a decentralized network of joint ventures and strategic alliances in which it is more difficult to form a strategic center firm among network partners. Over time, Corning has focused on intangible resources, such as a reliable reputation for being a trustworthy and committed partner, to develop competitively successful strategic networks. In these situations, the strategic network has loose connections between joint ventures or multiple centers, although Corning is typically the principal center. However, the joint ventures are less dependent on the strategic center firm and, as such, require less managerial attention from it.[105]

Implementing International Cooperative Strategies

Competing in multiple countries increases dramatically the complexity associated with attempts to manage successful strategic networks formed through international cooperative strategies.[106] A key reason for this increased complexity is the differences among countries' regulatory environments. These differences are especially apparent in regulated industries such as telecommunications and air travel.

As shown in Figure 11.11, many large, multinational firms form distributed strategic networks with multiple regional strategic centers to manage their array

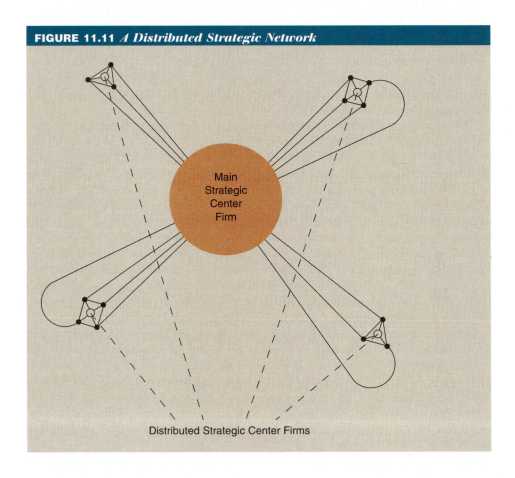

FIGURE 11.11 *A Distributed Strategic Network*

Main Strategic Center Firm

Distributed Strategic Center Firms

of cooperative arrangements with partner firms.[107] These networks are illustrated by several large multinational firms. Swedish firms such as Ericsson (telecommunications exchange equipment) and Electrolux (white goods, washing machines) have strategic centers located in countries throughout the world instead of only in Sweden where they are headquartered. Ericsson, for example, is active in more than 100 countries and employs over 85,000. Divided into five business areas (public telecommunications, radio communications, business networks, components, and microwave systems), the firm has cooperative agreements with companies throughout the world.

A world leader in electrical engineering, Asea Brown Boveri Group (ABB) is involved with a significant number of distributed strategic networks. Organized into four key business segments (power generation, power transmission and distribution, industrial and building systems, and financial services), ABB features 1,000 companies and 36 separate business areas. With a new, global 11-member board of directors representing seven nationalities, ABB considers itself a truly global company—one without a single country home. The firm has formed strategic networks in its key world areas of the Americas, Europe (including the former Soviet Union), the Middle East and North Africa, sub-Sahara Africa, and Asia Pacific.[108]

427

CONTEMPORARY ORGANIZATIONAL STRUCTURES: A CAUTIONARY NOTE

Contemporary organizational structures such as those used to implement international cooperative strategies emerge typically in response to social and technological advances.[109] However, the redesign of organizations throughout the society—indeed globally—necessarily entails losses as well as gains.[110] For example, DuPont, the world's largest chemicals concern, decided recently to scrap most of its central support groups. Primarily, these groups provided information technology, communications, and other services to the company's main operating divisions. The gains expected from this decision included elimination of some corporate bureaucracy and reductions in the amount of time required for production innovations to reach the marketplace. The primary loss associated with these gains concerned personnel. While some workers were to be transferred to other positions, many lost their jobs.[111]

With new organizational forms, many workers become deskilled—that is, their abilities are not sufficient to perform sucessfully in a new structure that often demands constant innovation and adaptation. This may describe the situation for some of the workers that are to be assigned to new positions within DuPont. The learning organization that is a part of new organizational forms requires that each worker become a self-motivated, continuous learner.[112] At least in the short run, a number of employees lack the level of confidence necessary to participate actively in organizationally sponsored learning experiences. Moreover, the flatter organizational structures that accompany contemporary structures can seem intrusive as a result of their demand for more intense and personal interactions with internal and external stakeholders. Combined, these conditions may create stress for many.

These realities do not call for managers to abandon efforts to adopt organizational structures that have the greatest probability of facilitating sucessful implementation of a firm's strategies. The challenge for those responsible for effective use of the strategic management process depicted in Figure 1.1 of Chapter 1 is to respond to various issues associated with the development and use of new organizational structures in ways that will enhance the productivity of individuals and the firm.[113] As explained in the next chapter, this responsibility belongs to strategic leaders.

SUMMARY

- Organizational structure is a formal configuration that largely determines *what* a firm will do and *how* the firm will complete its work. Different structures are required to implement different strategies. A firm's performance increases when strategy and structure are matched properly.

- Business-level strategies are usually implemented through the functional structure. The cost leadership strategy requires a centralized functional structure—one in which manufacturing efficiency and process engineering are emphasized. The differentiation strategy's functional structure decentralizes implementation-related decisions, especially those concerned with marketing, to those involved with individual organizational functions. Focus strategies, used in small firms, require a simple structure until such time that a firm begins to compete in multiple markets and/or sells multiple products.

- The evolution from the functional structure to the three types of the multidivisional structure (M-form) occurred from the 1920s to the early 1970s. The cooperative M-form, used to implement the related-constrained corporate-level strategy, has a centralized corporate office and extensive integrating mechanisms. Divisional incentives are linked to overall corporate performance. The related-linked SBU M-form structure establishes separate profit centers within the diversified firm. Each profit center may have divisions offering similar products, but the centers are unrelated to each other. The competitive M-form structure, used to implement the unrelated diversification strategy, is highly decentralized, integrating mechanisms are nonexistent, and objective financial criteria are used to evaluate each unit's performance.

- Initially, an organizational structure is chosen in light of support required to implement a firm's strategy. Once established, however, structure influences strategy. This is observed most prominently in the M-form structure stimulating additional diversification in the diversified firm.

- The multidomestic strategy, implemented through the worldwide geographic area structure, emphasizes decentralization and locates all functional activities in the country or geographic area. The worldwide product divisional structure is used to implement the global strategy. This structure is centralized to coordinate and integrate different functions' activities to gain global economies of scope and scale. Decision-making authority is centralized in the firm's worldwide division headquarters. The transnational strategy—a strategy through which the firm seeks the local responsiveness of the multidomestic strategy *and* the global efficiency of the global strategy—is implemented through the combination structure. Because it must be simultaneously centralized and decentralized, integrated and nonintegrated, and formalized and nonformalized, the combination structure is difficult to organize and manage successfully.

- Increasingly important to competitive success, cooperative strategies are implemented through organizational structures framed around strategic networks.

REVIEW QUESTIONS

1. Why is it important that the strategic actions of strategy implementation and strategy formulation be integrated carefully?

2. What is the meaning of the following statement? "In organizations, there is a consistent path of structure following strategy and then strategy following structure."

428

3. What organizational structures are used to implement the cost leadership, differentiation, integrated low-cost/differentiation, and focused business-level strategies?
4. What organizational structures are used to implement the related-constrained, related-linked, and unrelated corporate-level diversification strategies?
5. What organizational structures should be used to implement the multidomestic, global, and transnational international strategies?
6. What is a strategic network? What is a strategic center firm? What roles do they play in organizational structures used to implement cooperative strategies?

APPLICATION DISCUSSION QUESTIONS

1. Why do firms experience evolutionary cycles where there is a fit between strategy and structure punctuated with periods in which strategy and structure are reshaped? Provide examples of prominent U.S. firms that have experienced this pattern.
2. Select an organization (for example, an employer, a social club, or a nonprofit agency) in which you currently hold membership. What is this organization's structure? Do you believe this organization is using the structure that is appropriate, given its strategy? If not, what structure should be used?
3. Examine the popular business press to find a firm using the multidivisional structure. Which form of the multidivisional structure is the firm using? What is there about the firm that makes it appropriate for the M-form to be in use?
4. Through reading of the business press, locate one firm implementing the global strategy and one implementing the multidomestic strategy. What organizational structure is being used in each firm? Are these structures allowing each firm's strategy to be implemented successfully? Why or why not?
5. Identify a businessperson in your local community. Provide definitions to the person of strategic and financial controls. Ask that the businessperson describe to you the use of each type of control in his or her business. In which type of control does the businessperson have the greatest confidence, and why?

ETHICS QUESTIONS

1. When a firm changes from the functional structure to the multidivisional structure, what responsibilities do you believe it has to current employees?
2. Are there ethical issues associated with the use of strategic controls? With the use of financial controls? If so, what are they?
3. Are there ethical issues involved in implementing the cooperative and competitive M-form structures? If so, what are they? As a top-level manager, how would you deal with them?
4. Global and multidomestic strategies call for different competitive approaches. What ethical concerns might surface when firms attempt to market standardized products globally or when they develop different products/approaches for each local market?
5. What ethical issues are associated with the view that the "redesign of organizations throughout the society—indeed globally—necessarily entails losses as well as gains"?

INTERNET EXERCISE

Go to Eastman Kodak's Home Page at:

http://www.kodak.com

Use the Internet to conduct research on Eastman Kodak Corporation. How would you describe Kodak's organizational structure? Does Kodak's structure appropriately complement its competitive strategies?

Strategic Surfing

The Economist is a high-quality British magazine that is available on-line. The magazine publishes thoughtful articles on economics, politics, international business, management, and other issues.

http://www.economist.com

NOTES

1. M. Kroll, P. Wright, L. Toombs, and H. Leavell, 1997, Form of control: A critical determinant of acquisition performance, *Strategic Management Journal* 18: 85–96.

2. D. J. Teece, G. Pisano, and A. Shuen, 1997, Dynamic capabilities and strategic management, *Strategic Management Journal* 18: 509–533.

3. C. Hales and Z. Tamangani, 1996, An investigation of the relationship between organizational structure, managerial role expectations and managers' work activities, *Journal of Management Studies* 33: 731–756.

4. S. E. Human and K. Provan, 1997, An emergent theory of structure and outcomes in small-firm strategic manufacturing networks, *Academy of Management Journal* 40: 368–403.

5. M. H. Overholt, 1997, Flexible organizations: Using organizational design as a competitive advantage, *Human Resource Planning* 20, no. 1: 22–32.

6. J. R. Galbraith, 1995, *Designing Organizations* (San Francisco: Jossey-Bass), 6.

7. J. Kurtzman, 1998, An interview with Stan Shih, in J. Kurtzman (ed.), *Thought Leaders* (San Francisco: Jossey-Bass), 85–93.

8. A. Y. Ilinitch, R. A. D'Aveni, and A. Y. Lewin, 1996, New organizational forms and strategies for managing in hypercompetitive environments, *Organization Science* 7: 211–220.

9. D. A. Nadler and M. L. Tushman, 1997, *Competing by Design: The Power of Organizational Architecture* (New York: Oxford University Press).

10. E. F. Suarez and J. M. Utterback, 1995, Dominant designs and the survival of firms, *Strategic Management Journal* 16: 415–430.

11. *PR Newswire*, 1998, BMW prepares for the future with a process-oriented organizational structure, January 16, 116.

12. R. A. Heifetz and D. L. Laurie, 1997, The work of leadership, *Harvard Business Review* 75, no. 1: 124–134; R. H. Hall, 1996, *Organizations: Structures, Processes, and Outcomes* (6th ed.) (Englewood Cliffs, NJ: Prentice-Hall), 106–107.

13. L. Kehoe, 1998, Compaq will pay $9.6 billion in cash and stock for Digital, *Financial Times*, January 27, 22.

14. H. W. Volberda, 1996, Toward the flexible form: How to remain vital in hypercompetitive environments, *Organization Science* 7: 359–374.

15. T. R. Kayworth and R. D. Ireland, 1998, The use of information technology (IT) standards as a means of implementing the cost leadership strategy, working paper, Baylor University; Nadler and Tushman, *Competing by Design*, 9.

16. G. Graham and J. Kibazo, 1998, Barclays plans internal reorganisation, *Financial Times*, January 20, 21.

17. Suarez and Utterback, Dominant designs and the survival of firms.

17. A. D. Chandler, Jr., 1990, *Scale and Scope: The Dynamics of Industrial Capitalism* (Cambridge: The Belknap Press of Harvard University Press), 182–183.

18. F. R. Bleakly, 1996, The future of the global marketplace, *Wall Street Journal*, May 15, A13; J. Janssen-Bauer and C. C. Snow, 1996, Responding to hypercompetition: The structure and processes of a regional learning network organization, *Organization Science* 7: 413–427.

19. G. P. Zachary, 1995, Behind stocks' surge is an economy in which big U.S. firms thrive, *Wall Street Journal*, November 22, A1, A3.

20. Ibid., A1.

21. R. M. Hodgetts, 1996, A conversation with Steve Kerr, *Organizational Dynamics*, Spring, 74.

22. G. Hamel, 1997, Killer strategies, *Fortune*, June 23, 82.

23. S. Singhal, 1994, *Senior Management—The Dynamics of Effectiveness* (New Delhi: Sage Publications), 48.

24. Ibid., 48; Galbraith, *Designing Organizations*, 13; R. R. Nelson, 1994, Why do firms differ, and how does it matter? in R. P. Rumelt, D. E. Schendel, and D. J. Teece (eds.), *Fundamental Issues in Strategy* (Cambridge, MA: Harvard Business School Press), 259.

25. L. Donaldson, 1997, A positivist alternative to the structure-action approach, *Organization Studies* 18: 77–92; Hales and Tamangani, An investigation of the relationship, 738; Nelson, Why do firms? 259.

26. B. C. Esty, 1997, A case study of organizational form and risk shifting in the savings and loan industry, *Journal of Financial Economics* 44: 57–76; C. W. L. Hill, 1994, Diversification and economics performance: Bringing structure and corporate management back into the picture, in R. P. Rumelt, D. E. Schendel, and D. J. Teece (eds.), *Fundamental Issues in Strategy* (Cambridge, MA: Harvard Business School Press), 297–321.

27. R. Waters, 1997, Return of the downsizers, *Financial Times*, December 19, 13.

28. V. Griffith, 1997, Lumbering giants, *Financial Times*, December 15, 10.

29. H. M. O'Neill, R. W. Pouder, and A. K. Buchholtz, 1998, Patterns in the diffusion of strategies across organizations: Insights from the innovation diffusion literature, *Academy of Management Review* 23: 98–114.

30. M. Carter, 1998, The world according to Yo!, *Financial Times*, January 26, 11.

31. Galbraith, *Designing Organizations*, 25.

32. P. Lawrence and J. W. Lorsch, 1967, *Organization and Environment* (Cambridge, MA: Harvard Business School Press).

33. A. D. Chandler, 1994, The functions of the HQ unit in the multibusiness firm, in R. P. Rumelt, D. E. Schendel, and D. J. Teece (eds.), *Fundamental Issues in Strategy* (Cambridge, MA: Harvard Business School Press), 327.

34. W. G. Rowe and P. M. Wright, 1997, Related and unrelated diversification and their effect on human resource management controls, *Strategic Management Journal* 18: 329–338; D. C. Galunic and K. M. Eisenhardt, 1996, The evolution of intracorporate domains: Divisional charter losses in high-technology, multidivisional corporations, *Organization Science* 7: 255–282.

35. G. G. Dess, A. Gupta, J.-F. Hennart, and C. W. L. Hill, 1995, Conducting and integrating strategy research at the international, corporate, and business levels: Issues and directions, *Journal of Management* 21: 357–393.

36. A. D. Chandler, 1962, *Strategy and Structure: Chapters in the History of the American Industrial Enterprise* (Cambridge, MA: The MIT Press).

37. O. E. Williamson, 1994, Strategizing, economizing, and economic organization, in R. P. Rumelt, D. E. Schendel, and D. J. Teece (eds.), *Fundamental Issues in Strategy* (Cambridge, MA: Harvard Business School Press), 361–401.

38. Rowe and Wright, Related and unrelated diversification; S. Ghoshal and C. A. Bartlett, 1995, Changing the role of top management: Beyond structure to processes, *Harvard Business Review* 73, no. 1: 87–88.

39. Galbraith, *Designing Organizations*, 27.

40. Nadler and Tushman, *Competing by Design*, 206.

41. R. E. Hoskisson, C. W. L. Hill, and H. Kim, 1993, The multidivisional structure: Organizational fossil or source of value? *Journal of Management* 19: 269–298.

42. Rowe and Wright, Related and unrelated diversification.

43. C. M. Farkas and S. Wetlaufer, 1996, The ways chief executive officers lead, *Harvard Business Review* 74, no. 3: 110–122.

44. Associated Press, 1996, Trouble-shooter aims to galvanize Mazda, Ford, *Dallas Morning News*, April 13, F2; V. Reitman, 1996, Japan is aghast as foreigner takes the wheel at Mazda, *Wall Street Journal*, April 15, A11.

45. S. G. Beatty, 1998, CKS Group will reduce its businesses to 4 from 10 and revamp management, *Wall Street Journal*, January 20, B8.

46. C. C. Miller, L. M. Burke, and W. H. Glick, 1998, Cognitive diversity among upper-echelon executives: Implications for strategic decision processes, *Strategic Management Journal* 19: 39–58; D. J. Collis, 1996, Corporate strategy in multibusiness firms, *Long Range Planning* 29: 416–418.

47. M. A. Hitt, R. E. Hoskisson, R. A. Johnson, and D. D. Moesel, 1996, The market for corporate control and firm innovation, *Academy of Management Journal* 39: 1084–1119.

48. R. E. Hoskisson, M. A. Hitt, and R. D. Ireland, 1994, The effects of acquisitions and restructuring (strategic refocusing) strategies on innovation, in G. von Krogh, A. Sinatra, and H. Singh (eds.), *Managing Corporate Acquisitions* (London: Macmillan Press), 144–169.

49. R. E. Hoskisson and M. A. Hitt, 1988, Strategic control and relative R&D investment in large multiproduct firms, *Strategic Management Journal* 9: 605–621.

50. R. Tomkins, 1998, Black & Decker plans to cut 3,000 jobs, *Financial Times*, January 28, 15.

51. Collis, Corporate strategy, 417.

52. M. A. Hitt, R. E. Hoskisson, and R. D. Ireland, 1990, Mergers and acquisitions and managerial commitment to innovation in M-form firms, *Strategic Management Journal* 11 (Special Summer Issue): 29–47.

53. S. Baiman, D. F. Larcker, and M. V. Rajan, 1995, Organizational design for business units, *Journal of Accounting Research* 33: 205–229; Hall, *Organizations*, 13.

54. Ibid., Hall, 64–75.

55. T. Maxon, 1996, Southwest to let surfers use 'Net to arrange flights, *Dallas Morning News*, April 30, D1.

56. V. Boland, 1998, Airlines prepare to hit runway to privatisation, *Financial Times*, January 26, 17.

57. M. Halkias, 1996, Changing the retail landscape, *Dallas Morning News*, March 17, H1, H2.

58. FAG Kugelfischer, 1996, *Annual Report*, 22.

59. V. Govindarajan, 1988, A contingency approach to strategy implementation at the business-unit level: Integrating administrative mechanisms with strategy, *Academy of Management Journal* 31: 828–853.

60. D. Owen, 1998, Peugeot-Citroen unveils revamp, *Financial Times*, January 22, 19; Motor moves, 1998, *Financial Times*, January 28, 13; Nissan, 1998, *Financial Times*, January 28, 14.

61. R. Frank, 1996, Moxie, Big Red, other cult drinks thrive on being hometown heroes, *Wall Street Journal*, May 6, B1, B5.

62. Service Performance Corporation, 1998, *Fortune*, Special Advertising Section, February 2, S2.

63. C. C. Markides and P. J. Williamson, 1996, Corporate diversification and organizational structure: A resource-based view, *Academy of Management Journal* 39: 340–367; C. W. L. Hill, M. A. Hitt, and R. E. Hoskisson, 1992, Cooperative versus competitive structures in related and unrelated diversified firms, *Organization Science* 3: 501–521.

64. J. Robins and M. E. Wiersema, 1995, A resource-based approach to the multibusiness firm: Empirical analysis of portfolio interrelationships and corporate financial performance, *Strategic Management Journal* 16: 277–299.

65. C. C. Markides, 1997, To diversify or not to diversify, *Harvard Business Review* 75, no. 6: 93–99.

66. Nadler and Tushman, *Competing by Design*, 99.

67. Hall, Organizations, 186; J. G. March, 1994, *A Primer on Decision Making: How Decisions Happen* (New York: The Free Press), 117–118.

68. Master Entrepreneur Award, 1996, Netscape, May 12, http://www.sddt.com.

69. M. Murray, 1996, Massive restructuring at Scotts to include cuts in spending, staff, *Wall Street Journal*, April 3, B4.

70. P. J. Frost, 1997, Bridging academia and business: A conversation with Steve Kerr, *Organization Science* 8: 335.

71. GE Home Page, 1998, February 4, http://www.ge.com.

72. R. Waters, General Electric sees Asian opportunity, 1998, *Financial Times*, January 23, 19.

73. R. E. Hoskisson and M. A. Hitt, 1990, Antecedents and performance outcomes of diversification: A review and critique of theoretical perspectives, *Journal of Management* 16: 461–509.

74. C. W. L. Hill, M. A. Hitt, and R. E. Hoskisson, 1992, Cooperative versus competitive structures in related and unrelated diversified firms, *Organization Science* 3: 501–521.

75. J. B. Barney, 1997, *Gaining and Sustaining Competitive Advantage* (Reading, MA: Addison-Wesley), 420–433.

76. Collis, *Corporate strategy*, 418.

77. Williamson, Strategizing, economizing, 373.

78. B. W. Keats and M. A. Hitt, 1988, A causal model of linkages among environmental dimensions, macro organizational characteristics, and performance, *Academy of Management Journal* 31: 570–598.

79. Hoskisson, Hill, and Kim, The multidivisional structure, 276.

80. R. E. Hoskisson, R. A. Johnson, and D. D. Moesel, 1994, Corporate divestiture intensity: Effects of governance strategy and performance, *Academy of Management Journal* 37:1207–1251; R. E. Hoskisson and T. Turk, 1990, Corporate restructuring, governance and control limits of the internal capital market, *Academy of Management Review* 15: 459–471.

81. M. E. Porter, 1987, From competitive advantage to corporate strategy, *Harvard Business Review* 65, no. 3: 43–59.

82. C. C. Markides, 1992, Consequences of corporate refocusing: Ex ante evidence, *Academy of Management Journal* 35: 398–412.

83. S. Lipin, 1998. Cognizant, a D&B spin-off, to split in two, *Wall Street Journal*, January 15, A3.

84. V. Houlder, 1997, Fashion, focus and frontiers, *Financial Times*, December 19, 9.

85. R. D. Ireland, M. A. Hitt, and K. Artz, 1998, The effects of competitive strategies, cooperative strategies, and core competencies on superior financial performance in small manufacturing firms, working paper, Baylor University; M. A. Hitt, R. E. Hoskisson, and R. D. Ireland, 1994, A mid-range theory of the interactive effects of international and product diversification on innovation and performance, *Journal of Management* 20: 297–326.

86. Wire Reports, 1996, GM to focus on global sales market, *Dallas Morning News*, May 25, F1, F3.

87. K. Naughton and K. Kerwin, 1995, At GM, two heads may be worse than one, *Business Week*, August 14, 46.

88. M. A. Hitt, M. T. Dacin, B. B. Tyler, and D. Park, 1997, Understanding the differences in Korean and U.S. executives' strategic orientations, *Strategic Management Journal* 18: 159–167.

89. R. Blumenstein, 1998, GM doubles net on strong factory sales, *Wall Street Journal*, January 27, A3, A8.

90. L. Grant, 1996, Stirring it up at Campbell, *Fortune*, May 13, 80–86.

91. C. Rahweddeer, 1998, U.S. mail-order firms shake up Europe, *Wall Street Journal*, January 6, A15.

92. Coca-Cola Home Page, 1998, February 4, http://www.cocacola.com; G. Collins, 1996, Coke changes its recipe for administration, *Austin-American Statesman*, January 13, C1, C2; C. A. Bartlett and S. Ghoshal, 1989, *Managing Across Borders: The Transnational Solution* (Cambridge, MA: Harvard Business School Press).

93. Bartlett and Ghoshal, *Managing Across Borders*.

94. Ibid.

95. D. A. Blackmon, 1996, Fedex swings from confidence abroad to a tightrope, *Wall Street Journal*, March 15, B4.

96. C. Rohwedder, 1996, Unilever reorganizes its management as a first step in broad restructuring, *Wall Street Journal*, March 14, A11.

97. Unilever Home Page, 1998, February 5, http://www.unilever.com.

98. B. Gomes-Casseres, 1994, Group versus group: How alliance networks compete, *Harvard Business Review* 72, no. 4: 62–74.

99. G. R. Jones, 1998, *Organizational Theory* (Reading, MA: Addison-Wesley), 163–165.

100. G. Lorenzoni and C. Baden-Fuller, 1995, Creating a strategic center to manage a web of partners, *California Management Review* 37, no. 3: 146–163.

101. T. Nishiguchi, 1994, *Strategic Industrial Sourcing: The Japanese Advantage* (New York: Oxford University Press).

102. W. M. Fruin, 1992, *The Japanese Enterprise System* (New York: Oxford University Press).

103. W. M. Carley, 1996, GE–Pratt venture, like others before it, faces hurdles, *Wall Street Journal*, May 10, B3.

104. S. Branch, 1997, What's eating McDonald's? *Fortune*, October 13, 122–125; C. Edwards, 1997, Putting the fast in food, *Dallas Morning News*, July 21, D4; R. Gibson and M. Moffett, 1997, Why you won't find any egg McMuffins for breakfast in Brazil, *Wall Street Journal*, October 23, A1, A12.

105. Corning Home Page, 1998, February 5, http://www.corning.com; J. R. Houghton, 1990, Corning cultivates joint ventures that endure, *Planning Review* 18, no. 5: 15–17.

106. C. Jones, W. S. Hesterly, and S. P. Borgatti, 1997, A general theory of network governance: Exchange conditions and social mechanisms, *Academy of Management Review* 22: 911–945.

107. R. E. Miles, C. C. Snow, J. A. Mathews, G. Miles, and J. J. Coleman, Jr., 1997, Organizing in the knowledge age: Anticipating the cellular form, *Academy of Management Executive* XI, no. 4: 7–20.

108. ABB Home Page, 1998, February 5, http://www.abb.com; Nadler and Tushman, *Competing by Design*, 89.

109. Chandler, *Scale and Scope*.

110. B. Victor and C. Stephens, 1994, The dark side of the new organizational forms: An editorial essay, *Organization Science* 5: 479–482.

111. R. Waters, 1998, New DuPont shake-up to slash bureaucracy, *Financial Times*, January 8, 3; A. Barrett, 1997, At DuPont, time to both sow and reap, *Business Week*, September 29, 107–108.

112. M. A. Hitt, B. W. Keats, and S. M. DeMarie, 1998, Navigating in the new competitive landscape: Building competitive advantage and strategic flexibility in the 21st century, *Academy of Management Executive* (in press).

113. R. D. Ireland and M. A. Hitt, 1998, Achieving and maintaining strategic competitiveness in the 21st century: The role of strategic leadership, *Academy of Management Executive* (in press).

Strategic Leadership

CHAPTER 12

Learning Objectives

After reading this chapter, you should be able to:

1. Define strategic leadership and describe the importance of top-level managers as an organizational resource.

2. Define top management teams and explain their effects on the firm's performance and its ability to innovate and make appropriate strategic changes.

3. Describe the internal and external managerial labor markets and their effects on the development and implementation of firm strategy.

4. Discuss the value of strategic leadership for determining the firm's strategic direction.

5. Explain the role of strategic leaders in exploiting and maintaining core competencies.

6. Describe the importance of strategic leaders in developing a firm's human capital.

7. Define organizational culture and explain the importance of what must be done to sustain an effective culture.

8. Describe what strategic leaders can do to establish and emphasize ethical practices in their firms.

9. Discuss the importance and use of organizational controls.

Strategic Leadership in the Twenty-First Century

Given changes toward a new competitive landscape mentioned in this book (see in particular Chapters 1, 2, and 5), the role of strategic leaders is changing accordingly. Because of changes in competition and technology and an increased emphasis on customer satisfaction as well as globalization of industries, organizations face significant adaptive challenges. As a result, leaders must manage this change process in a way that facilitates competitive success. This takes more than just providing a well-designed solution. It requires an effective implementation process and commitment from people throughout the organization. It takes the collective intelligence of employees at all levels who need to use each other as resources. Working across internal and external organizational boundaries, employees must learn to work together to find solutions. Employees may look to the strategic leader for relief from stress in times of change, but rather than protecting them from outside threats, it is the role of a leader to stimulate his or her employees to adapt. Instead of maintaining norms, leaders encourage employees to change the way business is done from seemingly immutable practices bound by cultural heritage and history.

http://www.pathfinder.com

In light of the adaptive challenge to make transformation toward the twenty-first century, a number of firms are choosing CEOs who come from not only outside the firm but often outside the industry. Therefore, many CEOs are following a track outside of an individual firm rather than pursuing internal promotion and lifetime careers in one organization. Many of these CEOs are considered portable, not because they know a specific business, but because they have the emotional stature to facilitate change in an organization. One study, for instance, found that more than a third of the CEOs hired by 369 major corporations in the 1990s came from outside the company. These include some of the largest and best-known companies in the United States, such as Eastman Kodak Co., IBM Corporation, and AT&T Corporation. The experiences of these companies have influenced other boards to go outside their company to look for their executives, particularly when the company is in trouble. Despite this trend, some companies continue to groom and pick insiders, such as the succession of M. Douglas Ivester at Coca-Cola after the death of Roberto Goizueta.

As Chapter 10 suggests, boards have grown more powerful and are taking charge of managerial succession. They are concerned about signals to investors and workers. Sometimes a new outside CEO is like a professional athlete, "a free agent," who is dynamic and charismatic and may be able to send a signal that will improve company performance, both in terms of morale and the stock price. However, there are significant risks with this approach. Consider, for example, AT&T's mistake discussed in Chapter 10. John R. Walter, who was appointed president and was the heir apparent for the CEO position, lost credibility after Robert Allen decided that he was not capable of filling the job. AT&T lost eight months between the time Walter came to the company and when he left. It was time overly focused on leadership succession and not on strategic success.

Some executives have become temporary CEOs who focus on rescuing firms in crises. Steve Miller, the temporary CEO of Waste Management Corporation, has also had a similar job at Olympia & York Developments Ltd., Morrison Knudsen Corporation, and Federal-Mogul Corporation. This role started before he left Chrysler and, ever since, has been one of coming into companies in crisis, reassuring workers and investors, and then seeking to change things to stabilize the firm. Subsequently, he leaves or takes a position on the board as they seek and hire a more permanent CEO. Gerard Roche, chairman of Heidrick & Struggles, Inc., says "I wish I had ten Steve Millers—who'd take the job."

Miller began this phase of his career at Chrysler in 1980 during negotiations for a loan bailout to rescue the firm from liquidation. When he was unable to get the CEO position at Chrysler (Lee Iacocca was the CEO at the time), he moved to help rescue the real estate giant Olympia & York. This firm had a significant $12 million debt load. Although he could not save Olympia & York because banks were able to seize individual properties and wouldn't forbear, he did oversee the organization's orderly collapse. Subsequently, he became an outside director to Sun River. That position lasted only one year because he was called on to rescue Morrison Knudsen after William Agee was dismissed. Agee had pushed the engineering construction company into a disastrous expansion program and nearly into bankruptcy. Miller held the banks off until the company could dispose of some assets. The firm was finally acquired by Washington Construction Group in 1996. Miller also served as the interim CEO at Federal-Mogul, another company that had expanded beyond its basic businesses and engaged in aggressive accounting. It failed to live up to Wall Street earnings estimates and was in a crisis. He administered a rapid and dramatic turnaround and facilitated the acquisition of Federal-Mogul by British auto parts maker T & N PLC. In the spring of 1997, Miller joined Waste Management's board. Because of some succession difficulties, Waste Management began to look for a new CEO. Miller persuaded Ronald T. LeMay, the number two executive at Spring Corporation, to take the position. After a short period on the job, LeMay quit suddenly and stock analysts expected the worst. As a result, the board asked Miller to step in and fill the role until someone more permanent could be found.

Although competitive trends are forcing firms to adapt, and outside leaders are often brought in to facilitate change to meet competitive challenges, significant changes require special leadership skills. Leaders are needed who take an interest in employees and develop a firm's human capital. Some feel that the "slash and burn" CEO who pursues significant downsizing such as Al Dunlap at Sunbeam and Robert Allen at AT&T is giving way to a new, less autocratic type of boss. For instance, Ronald W. Allen, recently hired by Delta Airlines, was chosen to help rebuild employee morale and reduce customer complaints. The board decided on a CEO who was a great listener and could capture the imagination of Delta employees. People skills and the ability to build human capital were very important to their search. John F. Welch, Jr., the renowned CEO of General Electric, is celebrated as one of the nation's most effective CEOs because of his stress on quality and customer service. He's also seeking to create the "borderless" company with better relationships among inside units and between inside and outside constituents. Henry Schacht, the CEO of Lucent Technologies, is excellent at sharing power and helping employees to feel involved.

Another leader, Alex Trotman, CEO at Ford Motor Company, keeps employees informed about both desirable and less desirable events. Some CEOs can focus on both getting the job done and facilitating employee development and relationships. Robert Crandall, American Airlines former CEO, Jack Welch at General Electric, and Andrew S. Grove, Intel's former CEO, have been considered to be strong simultaneously on task and on relationships. Because change is an essential and ongoing process, successful strategic managers will be able to make tough decisions such as downsizing and be sensitive to employee relationships.

In summary, strategic leaders are now required to be transformational managers who not only can help firms operate efficiently, but can provide visionary leadership, which empowers not only managers with good product ideas but motivates people to make the necessary changes as well.

SOURCES: J. Helyar and J. S. Lublin, 1998, Do you need an expert on widgets to head a widget company?, *Wall Street Journal*, January 21, A1, A10; J. Bailey, 1997, Steve Miller thrives in his second career: Corporate salvage, *Wall Street Journal*, December 16, A1, A9; A. A. Cannella, Jr. and M. J. Monroe, 1997, Contrasting perspectives on strategic leaders: Toward a more realistic view of top managers, *Journal of Management* 23: 213–237; S. Walsh, 1997, Captains Courteous: Era of the brutal boss may be giving way to a new sensitivity at the top, Inside Washington Post, http://www.washingtonpost.com, August 31; R. A. Heifetz and D. L. Laurie, 1997, The work of leadership, *Harvard Business Review* 75, no. 1: 124–134.

The examples of significant strategic changes with which CEOs are confronted in the opening case emphasize the importance and outcomes of effective strategic leadership. As this chapter makes clear, it is through effective strategic leadership that firms are able to use the strategic management process successfully (see Figure 1.1). Thus, as strategic leaders, top-level managers must guide the firm in ways that result in the formation of strategic intent and strategic mission. This may lead to goals that stretch everyone in the organization to improve their performance.[1] Moreover, strategic leaders are then challenged to facilitate the development of appropriate strategic actions and determine how to implement them, culminating in strategic competitiveness and above-average returns[2] (see Figure 12.1).

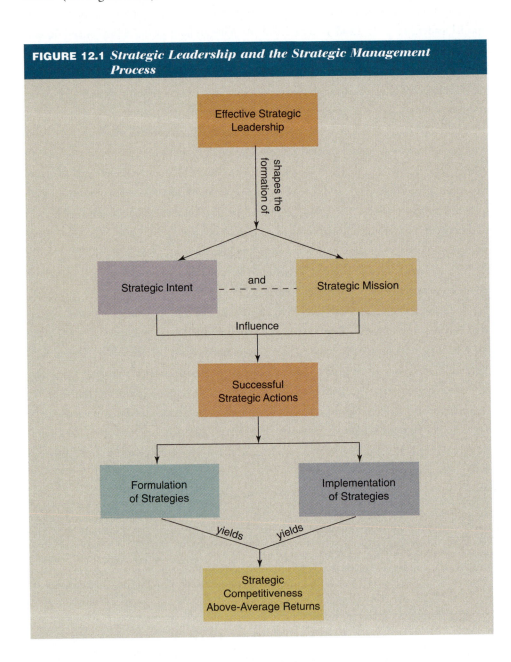

FIGURE 12.1 *Strategic Leadership and the Strategic Management Process*

This chapter begins with a definition of strategic leadership and its importance as a potential source of competitive advantage. Next, we examine top management teams and their effects on firm innovation, strategic change, and performance. Following this discussion is an analysis of the internal and external managerial labor markets from which strategic leaders are selected. Closing the chapter are descriptions of the six key components of effective strategic leadership: determining strategic direction, exploiting and maintaining core competencies, developing human capital, sustaining an effective organizational culture, emphasizing ethical practices, and establishing balanced organizational control systems.

There is an evident consistency between many of the strategic leadership characteristics just mentioned and the actions taken by Eckhard Pfeiffer as Compaq Computer's CEO. By providing the vision for strategic intent, Pfeiffer has determined the firm's strategic direction. In 1997, not only did Compaq maintain its leading share of the PC business market and servers, it recaptured the second place position in notebook computers and was one of the top two sellers of home PCs. In addition, Compaq pushed further in the large computer business through the acquisition of Tandem Computers.[3] In early 1998, Compaq rocked the larger computer world by making a tender offer for Digital Equipment Corporation. Existing core competencies and those acquired through merger partners (e.g., brand name and distribution channels) are being used to implement the firm's new strategies in larger machines.[4] Efforts are also taken to develop and support the firm's human capital and to maintain what seems to be an effective organizational culture. This evidence suggests that Compaq Computer's CEO is an effective strategic leader.[5]

439

STRATEGIC LEADERSHIP

Strategic leadership is the ability to anticipate, envision, maintain flexibility, and empower others to create strategic change as necessary. Multifunctional in nature, strategic leadership involves managing through others, managing an entire enterprise rather than a functional subunit, and coping with change that seems to be increasing exponentially in today's new competitive landscape. Because of the complexity and global nature of this new landscape, strategic leaders must learn how to influence human behavior effectively in an uncertain environment. By word and/or personal example and through their ability to dream pragmatically, effective strategic leaders meaningfully influence the behaviors, thoughts, and feelings of those with whom they work.[6] The ability to manage human capital may be the most critical of the strategic leader's skills.[7] In the opinion of a well-known leadership observer, the key to competitive advantage in the 1990s and beyond "... will be the capacity of top leadership to create the social architecture capable of generating intellectual capital. . . . By intellectual capital, I mean know-how, expertise, brainpower, innovation (and) ideas."[8] Competent strategic leaders also establish the context through which stakeholders (e.g., employees, customers, and suppliers) are able to perform at peak efficiency.[9]

In the twenty-first century, many managers, who work in nations throughout the world, will be challenged to change their frames of reference to cope with the rapid and complex changes occurring in the global economy. A **managerial frame of reference** is the set of assumptions, premises, and accepted wisdom that bounds—or *frames*—a manager's understanding of the firm, the industry(ies) in which it competes, and the core competencies it uses in the pursuit of strategic

Strategic leadership is the ability to anticipate, envision, maintain flexibility, and empower others to create strategic change as necessary.

A **managerial frame of reference** is the set of assumptions, premises, and accepted wisdom that bounds—or *frames*—a manager's understanding of the firm, the industry(ies) in which it competes, and the core competencies it uses in the pursuit of strategic competitiveness.

competitiveness. A frame of reference is the foundation on which a manager's mind-set is built (see Chapter 3).

A firm's ability to achieve strategic competitiveness and earn above-average returns is compromised when strategic leaders fail to respond appropriately and quickly to mind-set-related changes that an increasingly complex and global competitive environment demands. Research suggests that a firm's "long-term competitiveness depends on managers' willingness to challenge continually their managerial frames" and that global competition is more than product versus product or company versus company—it is also a case of "mind-set versus mind-set, managerial frame versus managerial frame."[10] Competing on the basis of mind-set demands that strategic leaders learn how to deal with diverse and cognitively complex competitive situations. One of the most challenging mind-set changes is overcoming one's own successful mind-set when change is required. For instance, it was a particular mind-set that led to Wal-Mart's low-pricing strategy win over Sears. Being able to successfully complete challenging assignments that are linked to achieving strategic competitiveness early and frequently in one's career appears to improve a manager's ability to make appropriate changes to his or her mind-set.[11]

Effective strategic leaders are willing to make candid, courageous, yet pragmatic, decisions—decisions that may be difficult yet necessary in light of internal and external conditions facing the firm.[12] Effective strategic leaders solicit corrective feedback from their peers, superiors, and employees about the value of their difficult decisions. Often, this feedback is sought through face-to-face communications. The unwillingness to accept feedback may be a key reason talented executives fail, highlighting the need for strategic leaders to solicit feedback consistently from those affected by their decisions.[13]

The primary responsibility for effective strategic leadership rests at the top—in particular, with the CEO, but other commonly recognized strategic leaders include members of the board of directors, the top management team, and division general managers. Regardless of title and organizational function, strategic leaders have substantial decision-making responsibilities that cannot be delegated.[14]

Strategic leadership is an extremely complex but critical form of leadership. Strategies cannot be formulated and implemented to achieve above-average returns without effective strategic leaders. Because it is a requirement of strategic success, and because organizations may be poorly led and overmanaged, firms competing in the new competitive landscape are challenged to develop effective strategic leaders.[15] Wayne Calloway, PepsiCo's former CEO, has suggested that ". . . most of the companies that are in life-or-death battles got into that kind of trouble because they didn't pay enough attention to developing their leaders."[16]

MANAGERS AS AN ORGANIZATIONAL RESOURCE

As the introductory discussion suggests, top-level managers are an important resource for firms seeking to effectively formulate and implement strategies.[17] A key reason for this is that the strategic decisions made by top managers influence how the firm is designed and whether performance outcomes will be achieved. Thus, a critical element of organizational success is having a top management team that has superior managerial skills.[18]

Managers often use their discretion (or latitude of action) when making strategic decisions, including those concerned with the effective implementation of strategies.[19] Managerial discretion differs significantly across industries. The primary factors that determine the amount of a manager's (especially a top-level manager's) decision discretion include (1) external environmental sources (e.g., industry structure, rate of market growth in the firm's primary industry, and the degree to which products can be differentiated), (2) characteristics of the organization (e.g., size, age, resource availability, and culture), and (3) characteristics of the manager (e.g., commitment to the firm and its strategic outcomes, tolerance for ambiguity, skills to work with different people, and aspiration level) (see Figure 12.2). Because strategic leaders' decisions are intended to help the firm gain a

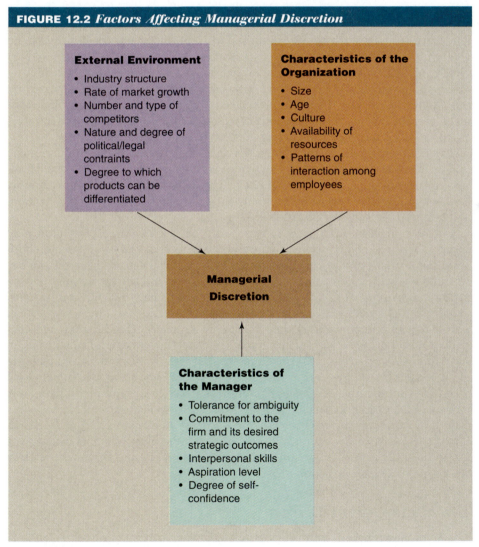

FIGURE 12.2 *Factors Affecting Managerial Discretion*

External Environment
- Industry structure
- Rate of market growth
- Number and type of competitors
- Nature and degree of political/legal contraints
- Degree to which products can be differentiated

Characteristics of the Organization
- Size
- Age
- Culture
- Availability of resources
- Patterns of interaction among employees

Managerial Discretion

Characteristics of the Manager
- Tolerance for ambiguity
- Commitment to the firm and its desired strategic outcomes
- Interpersonal skills
- Aspiration level
- Degree of self-confidence

Source: Adapted from S. Finkelstein and D. C. Hambrick, 1996, *Strategic Leadership: Top Executives and Their Effects on Organizations* (St. Paul, Minn: West Publishing Co.).

441

competitive advantage, the way in which managers exercise discretion when determining appropriate strategic actions is critical to the firm's success.[20]

In addition to determining new strategic initiatives, top-level managers also develop the appropriate organizational structure and reward systems of a firm. (In Chapter 11, we described how organizational structure and reward systems affect strategic actions taken to implement different types of strategies.) Furthermore, top-level managers have a major effect on a firm's culture. Evidence suggests that managers' values are critical in shaping a firm's cultural values.[21] As this discussion shows, top-level managers have an important effect on organizational activities and performance.[22] The significance of this effect should not be underestimated.

The degree to which top-level managers influence a firm's performance is observed by financial markets. For example, when Eric Schmidt, chief technology officer at Sun Microsystems, was hired to be Novell's chairman of the board and CEO after a seven-month search, Novell's stock price gained 9 percent. In reaction, Sun's stock price declined $2\frac{1}{2}$ percent. The market's reaction may have been due in part to Schmidt's broad experience with the Internet. Novell may also be able, with Schmidt's help, to establish important alliances with companies such as Oracle, Netscape Communications, and Sun to foster sales for Novell networking software. Novell should have been a stronger player in Internet services and has been losing business to Microsoft.[23] Thus, a strategic leader's experience and judgment, and the quality of the decisions based on them, is oftentimes of keen interest to various stakeholders, including current and potential shareholders.[24]

As the following discussion shows, the decisions and actions of some strategic leaders result in their becoming a source of competitive advantage for their firm. Consistent with the criteria of sustainability discussed in Chapter 3, strategic leaders can be a source of competitive advantage only when their work is valuable, rare, costly to imitate, and nonsubstitutable.

Effective strategic leaders focus their work on the key issues that ultimately shape the firm's ability to earn above-average returns. For example, Helmut Maucher at Nestlé and Michael Dell at Dell Computer focus their energies on determining how their companies can be market leaders and then structure their organizations to support this focus.[25] CEOs such as Maucher and Dell take actions to gain desired results. They delegate day-to-day operations to others so they can ask "big picture" questions of their managers, suppliers, shareholders, and customers. The most effective strategic leaders also travel to other companies to study successful work processes, and they build time into their schedules to think. One of the most important issues effective strategic leaders think about is the source of their firm's competitive advantage. Finding ways to release employees' brainpower influences the degree to which the firm's expertise is applied throughout the company in a competitively relevant fashion.[26] Robert Buckman, CEO of Buckman Laboratories, a specialty chemical maker, says that the most powerful incentives a CEO has are salary increases and promotions. He makes sure that these rewards are given based on how people share and borrow ideas.[27]

Top Management Teams

The **top management team** is composed of the key managers who are responsible for formulating and implementing the organization's strategies. Typically, the

The **top management team** is composed of the key managers who are responsible for formulating and implementing the organization's strategies.

top management team includes the officers of the corporation as defined by the title of vice president and above and/or by service as a member of the board of directors.[28] The quality of the strategic decisions made by a top management team affects the firm's ability to innovate and engage in effective strategic change.[29]

Top Management Team, Firm Performance, and Strategic Change The job of top-level executives is complex and requires a broad knowledge of firm operations, as well as the three key parts of the firm's external environment. Therefore, firms try to form a top management team that has the appropriate knowledge and expertise to operate the internal organization, yet also deal with external stakeholders. This normally requires a heterogeneous top management team. A **heterogeneous top management team** is composed of individuals with different functional backgrounds, experiences, and education. The more heterogeneous a top management team is, with varied expertise and knowledge, the more capacity it has to provide effective strategic leadership in terms of strategy *formulation*. Members of a heterogeneous top management team benefit from discussing the different perspectives advanced by separate team members. In many cases, these discussions increase the quality of the top management team's decisions, especially when a synthesis emerges from the contesting of diverse perspectives that is generally superior to the individual perspectives.[30] For example, heterogeneous top management teams in the airline industry have the propensity to take stronger competitive actions and reactions.[31] The net benefit of these actions was positive in terms of market share and above-average returns.

A **heterogeneous top management team** is composed of individuals with different functional backgrounds, experiences, and education.

It is also important that the top management team members function cohesively. For example, some believe that an apparent inability to work together as a board affected the selection process for the new CEO at AT&T.[32] In general, the more heterogeneous and larger the top management team is, the harder it is for the team to *implement* strategies effectively.[33] The research finding that comprehensive and long-term strategic plans can be inhibited by communication difficulties when top managers of a firm come from different backgrounds and have different cognitive skills may account for these implementation-related difficulties.[34] Having members who have substantive expertise in the firm's core functions and businesses is also important to the effectiveness of a top management team. In a high-technology industry, it may be critical for a firm to have R&D knowledge and expertise included on the top management team, particularly when growth strategies are being implemented.[35]

The characteristics of top management teams are related to innovation and strategic change.[36] For example, more heterogeneous top management teams are associated positively with innovation and strategic change. Thus, firms that need to change their strategies are more likely to do so if they have top management teams with diverse backgrounds and expertise. A top management team with various areas of expertise is more likely to identify environmental changes (opportunities and threats) or changes within the firm that require a different strategic direction.[37] This fact may explain CEO Louis Gerstner's decision to change IBM's top management team. Relying more extensively on hiring from outside the company, Gerstner chose top-level managers that he believed had the skills required to help IBM better exploit the firm's core competencies.[38] The outsider approach, however, may only be temporary. Despite a significant turnaround since 1993, Gerstner suggests that the next leader may be an insider.[39]

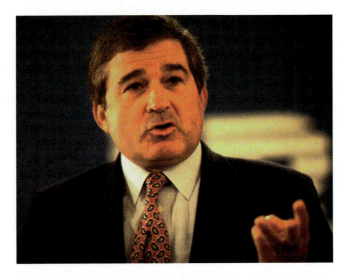

Louis Gerstner, IBM's CEO, hired top-level managers from outside the firm whose skills would help IBM take advantage of its core competencies. Although the outsider approach led to a significant turnaround since 1993, IBM's next leader may come from within the firm.

CEO and Top Management Team Power As suggested in Chapter 10, the board of directors is an important mechanism for monitoring a firm's strategic direction and for representing the interests of stakeholders, especially those of shareholders. In fact, higher performance normally is achieved when the board of directors is involved more directly in shaping a firm's strategic direction.[40]

Boards of directors, however, may find it difficult to direct the strategic actions of powerful CEOs and top management teams. It is not uncommon for a powerful CEO to appoint a number of sympathetic outside board members, or have inside board members who are on the top management team and report to the CEO. Therefore, the CEO may have significant control over the board's actions. "A central question is whether boards are an effective management control mechanism . . . or whether they are a 'management tool,'. . . a rubber stamp for management initiatives . . . and often surrender to management their major domain of decision-making authority, which includes the right to hire, fire, and compensate top management."[41]

CEOs and top management team members can also achieve power in other ways. Holding the titles of chairperson of the board *and* chief executive officer usually gives a CEO more power than the one who is not simultaneously serving as chair of the firm's board.[42] Although the practice of CEO duality (i.e., when the CEO and the chairperson of the board are the same) has become more common in U.S. businesses, it ". . . has recently come under heavy criticism—duality has been blamed for poor performance and slow response to change in firms such as General Motors, Digital Equipment Corporation, and Goodyear Tire and Rubber."[43] Although it varies among industries, duality occurs most commonly in the largest firms. Increased shareholder activism, however, has brought CEO duality under increased scrutiny and attack in European firms as well. Historically, an independent board leadership structure in which the positions of CEO and chair were not held by one person was believed to enhance a board's ability to monitor top-level managers' decisions and actions, particularly in terms of the firm's financial performance.[44] Stewardship theory, on the other hand, suggests that CEO duality facilitates effective decisions and actions. In these instances, the increased effectiveness gained through CEO duality accrues from the individual who wants to perform effectively and desires to be the best possible steward of the firm's assets. Because of this person's positive orientations and actions, extra governance and the coordination costs resulting from an independent board leadership structure would be unnecessary.[45]

To date, the question of the effect of duality on the firm's strategic outcomes is unresolved. In a study of the relationship between duality and firm performance, researchers found that (1) the stock market is indifferent to changes in a company's duality status, (2) changes in a company's duality status has a negligible effect on its financial performance, and (3) "there is only weak evidence that duality status affects long-term performance, after controlling for other factors that might impact that performance."[46] Thus, it may be that, in general, the potential for managerial abuse created through CEO duality is unrealized in many firms.

Top management team members and CEOs who have long tenures—on the team and in the organization—have an increased ability to influence board decisions.[47] Moreover, long tenure is known to restrict the breadth of an executive's knowledge base. With the limited perspective associated with a restricted knowledge base, long-tenured top-level managers typically develop fewer alternatives to evaluate when making strategic decisions.[48] Long tenure and a restricted knowledge base increase an executive's ability to forestall or avoid board involvement in strategic decisions. However, managers of long tenure also may be able to exercise more effective strategic control, thereby obviating the need for board of director involvement because effective strategic control generally produces higher performance.[49]

In the final analysis, boards of directors should develop an effective relationship with the firm's top management team. The relative degrees of power to be held by the board and top management team members should be examined in light of an individual firm's situation. For example, the abundance of resources in a firm's external environment and the volatility of that environment may affect the ideal balance of power between boards and top management teams.[50] Through the development of effective working relationships, boards, CEOs and other top management team members are able to serve the best interests of the firm's stakeholders.

MANAGERIAL LABOR MARKET

The choice of top-level managers, especially CEOs, is a critical organizational decision with important implications for firm performance.[51] Moreover, selection of new members for a top management team represents an opportunity for the firm to adapt to changes occurring in its external environment, that is, in its general, industry, and competitive environments (see Chapter 2).

Successful companies develop screening systems to identify those with managerial and strategic leadership potential. The most effective of these systems evaluates people within the firm and gains valuable information about the capabilities of other firms' managers, particularly their strategic leaders. Screening systems are vital, in that just because a person shares the firm's values ". . . doesn't mean he or she is leadership material."[52] For current managers, training and development programs are provided to preselect and attempt to shape the skills of people who may become tomorrow's leaders.

There are two types of managerial labor markets—internal and external—from which organizations select managers and strategic leaders. An **internal mana-**

445

An **internal managerial labor market** consists of the opportunities for managerial positions within a firm.

An **external managerial labor market** is the collection of career opportunities for managers in organizations outside of the one for which they work currently.

gerial labor market consists of the opportunities for managerial positions within a firm. As the Opening Case illustrates, an **external managerial labor market** is the collection of career opportunities for managers in organizations outside of the one for which they work currently. Given this chapter's topic of strategic leadership, our discussion focuses on how managerial labor markets are used to select CEOs.

Several benefits are thought to accrue to a firm when the internal labor market is used to select a new CEO. Because of their experience with the firm and the industry environment in which it competes, insiders are familiar with company products, markets, technologies, and standard operating procedures. Additionally, internal hiring results in less turnover among existing personnel, many of whom possess valuable firm-specific knowledge.

It is not unusual for employees to have a strong preference for using the internal managerial labor market to select top management team members and the CEO. For example, the initial reaction among employees to the choice of outsider Ronald Zarrella as the head of all of General Motors' marketing efforts was negative. With previous executive experience at Playtex and Bausch Lomb, employees felt that Zarrella lacked the skills and background to understand the intricacies of selling cars. However, after a relatively brief time in his new position, his style and decisions earned him the respect and acceptance of many, including Jack Smith, GM's internally appointed CEO.[53]

The selection of insiders to fill top-level management positions reflects a desire for continuity and a continuing commitment to the firm's current strategic intent, strategic mission, and chosen strategies. Because of the potential importance and perceived desirability of organizational continuity, internal candidates tend to be valued over external candidates[54] when selecting a firm's CEO and other top-level managers. In fact, outside succession to the CEO position "is an extraordinary event for business firms [and] is usually seen as a stark indicator that the board of directors wants change,"[55] but as the opening case illustrates, outsiders are increasingly being used to succeed insiders.

Valid reasons exist for a firm to select an outsider as its new CEO. For example, research evidence suggests that executives who have spent their entire career with a particular firm may become "stale in the saddle."[56] Long tenure with a firm seems to reduce the number of innovative ideas top-level managers are able to develop to cope with conditions facing their firm. Given the importance of innovation for firm success in the new competitive landscape (see Chapter 13), an inability to innovate and/or to create conditions that stimulate innovation throughout the firm is a liability for a strategic leader. In contrast to insiders, CEOs selected from outside the firm may have broader, less limiting perspectives. As such, they usually encourage innovation and strategic change. Nevertheless, CEOs selected from outside the firm and even the firm's industry are sometimes disadvantaged by a lack of firm-specific knowledge and industry experience. For example, although credited with strategic leadership success at ConAgra Inc., Charles Harper's tenure as CEO of RJR Nabisco Holdings Corporation disappointed many stakeholders, including board members, employees, and financial investors. Among reasons cited for Harper 's inability to boost RJR's struggling stock price was his lack of experience running a cigarette company.[57]

Subsequently, RJR was spun off from Nabisco and an initial public offering was completed in 1995. Commencing his work as Nabisco's new CEO in 1998, James M. Kilts, a former Phillip Morris executive at Kraft Foods, has been bringing in other outsiders as well. He brought in Richard H. Lenny, who was also an executive with Philip Morris and a former president of the U.S. Business of Pillsbury Corporation, a business unit of DAIGO PLC. Lenny was brought in to run the beleagured biscuit business unit at Nabisco. Apparently, in trying to meet ambitious earnings targets promised through the initial public offering, Nabisco let its overall spending on merchandising and advertising lag behind its rivals. Nabisco spends only 2.5 percent of its sales on advertising compared with 6 percent for the average company in the food industry. Thus, significant changes need to take place to turn the flat sales and earnings around in Nabisco's basic product lines such as Oreo cookies.[58]

Figure 12.3 shows how the composition of the top management team and CEO succession (managerial labor market) may interact to affect strategy. For example, when the top management team is homogeneous (e.g., members have similar functional experiences and educational backgrounds) and a new CEO is selected from inside the firm, the firm's current strategy is unlikely to change. On the other hand, when a new CEO is selected from outside the firm and the top management team is heterogeneous, there is a high probability of a change in strategy. When the new CEO is from inside the firm, the strategy may not change, but with a heterogeneous top management team, innovation is likely to continue. An external CEO succession with a homogeneous team creates a more ambiguous situation.

As noted earlier, the type of strategic leadership that results in successful implementation of strategies is exemplified by several key actions. The most critical of these are shown in Figure 12.4. The remainder of this chapter is devoted to explaining each action. Note that many of these actions interact with each other. For example, developing human capital through executive training contributes to establishing a strategic direction, fostering an effective culture, exploiting core competencies, using effective organizational control systems, and establishing ethical practices.

447

FIGURE 12.3 *Effects of CEO Succession and Top Management Team Composition on Strategy*

FIGURE 12.4 *Exercise of Effective Strategic Leadership*

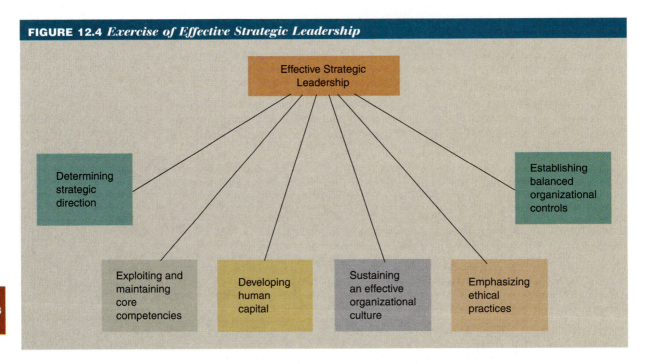

Determining the strategic direction of a firm refers to the development of a long-term vision of a firm's strategic intent.

DETERMINING STRATEGIC DIRECTION

Determining the strategic direction of a firm refers to the development of a long-term vision of a firm's strategic intent. A long-term vision normally looks at least 5 to 10 years into the future. A philosophy with goals, a long-term vision is the ideal image and character the firm seeks.[59] The ideal long-term vision has two parts, core ideology and envisioned future. While the core ideology motivates employees through the company's heritage (e.g., the "HP way" at Hewlett-Packard), the envisioned future encourages employees to stretch beyond their expectations of accomplishment and requires significant change and progress to attain.[60] The envisioned future serves as a guide to many aspects of a firm's strategy implementation process, including motivation, leadership, employee empowerment, and organizational design. For firms competing in many different industries, evidence suggests that the most effective long-term vision is one that has been accepted by those affected by it.[61]

To determine the firm's long-term vision, managers must take a sufficient amount of time to think about how it should be framed. Areas requiring executive thought include an analysis of the firm's external and internal environments and its current performance levels. Most top-level managers ask people with a range of skills to help them analyze various aspects of the firm's operations. Macroeconomists, for example, through their study of trends in the global economy, often provide insights to strategic leaders.[62]

Once the vision is determined, CEOs must motivate employees to achieve them. Some, but not all, top-level managers are thought to be charismatic strategic leaders. Theory suggests that charisma comes through interactions between leaders and followers. These interactions have been studied by examining impression management where framing, scripting, staging, and performing by the strategic leader relate to attribution of charisma by followers.[63] Although charisma is perceived as helpful, it is not a requirement for strategic leadership success. Noncharismatic people often have other skills and traits—intelligence, vision, ambition, and toughness, for example—that provide benefits similar to those gained when one is thought to be charismatic.[64] In certain situations, charismatic CEOs might facilitate better performance; in others, it might reduce leadership credibility. Jack Welch, General Electric's CEO, combines outrageous self-confidence, high-strung passion for ideas he unabashedly borrows, and unforgiving candor and appears to have charisma.[65] Tony O'Reilly, H. J. Heinz's former CEO, is a charming, pretentious Renaissance man. Although extra-curricular activities (he owns newspapers in his native Ireland) diverted his attention, until recently his star power enchanted Heinz investors. However, during his final days as Heinz's CEO, his regal ways soured institutional investors, and he came to represent the type of CEO the corporate governance advocates love to hate (see discussion in Chapter 10).[66]

Other CEOs who are typically not described as charismatic include Wal-Mart's David Glass. Though a fierce competitor, this earnest boss stands no chance in a personality contest with the larger-than-life Sam Walton. To inspire associates, Glass wisely milks the late founder's legacy. General Motors' Jack Smith is thought by some to be as charismatic as his name. He eschews TV cameras and the press. A pragmatic consensus builder, he accumulates power by giving it away. He has made GM shine even though he doesn't. Despite his lack of charisma, Smith is considered to be an effective strategic leader. Actions dedicated to enhancing one's skills (as discussed earlier) contribute positively to a strategic leader's efforts to help her or his firm reach its desired strategic outcomes.

A charismatic CEO may help gain employees' commitment to a new vision and strategic direction. Nonetheless, for all firms, it is important not to lose sight of the strengths of the organization when making changes required by a new strategic direction. Achieving this objective demands the balancing of a firm's short-term needs to adjust to a new vision while maintaining its long-term survival by emphasizing its current and valuable core competencies.

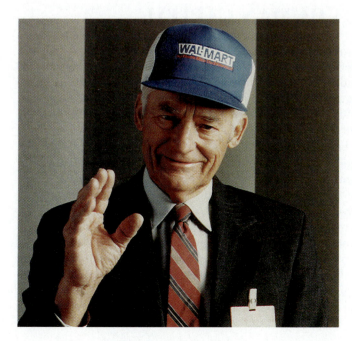

Although charisma may help a CEO motivate employees to achieve a corporate vision, it is not a requirement for strategic leadership success. Wal-Mart's former CEO Sam Walton was renowned for his larger-than-life personality, whereas his successor, David Glass, is a fierce competitor who lacks charisma.

449

EXPLOITING AND MAINTAINING CORE COMPETENCIES

Examined in Chapters 1 and 3, *core competencies* are resources and capabilities that serve as a source of competitive advantage for a firm over its rivals. Typically, core competencies relate to an organization's functional skills, such as manufacturing, finance, marketing, and research and development. As shown by the following descriptions, firms develop and exploit core competencies in many different functional areas in order to implement their strategies. Strategic leaders must verify that the firm's competencies are emphasized in strategy implementation efforts. Hewlett-Packard and Intel, for example, have core competencies in terms of competitive agility (an ability to act in a variety of competitively relevant ways) and competitive speed (an ability to act quickly when facing environmental and competitive pressures).[67]

In many large firms, and certainly in related diversified ones, core competencies are exploited effectively when they are developed and applied across different organizational units (see Chapter 6). Philip Morris demonstrates this by applying its marketing and promotion competencies across multiple businesses. The company's rejuvenation of Miller Beer is a classic example. Whirlpool also has well-known competencies that are emphasized to create value across country borders.[68] Some argue that the development, nurturing, and application of core competencies within multinational firms facilitates management of the complex relationships across businesses operating in different international markets.[69] Because GE Capital, a large business unit of General Electric, has made a number of acquisitions, its managers have become skilled at integrating the new businesses into GE Capital's operating culture. In the process, they have developed a new management position, that of integration manager.[70] Core competencies, however, cannot be developed or exploited effectively without appropriate human capital.

DEVELOPING HUMAN CAPITAL

Human capital refers to the knowledge and skills of the firm's entire workforce.

Human capital refers to the knowledge and skills of the firm's entire workforce. Employees, from this perspective, are viewed as a capital resource that requires investment. Much of the development of U.S. industry can be attributed to the effectiveness of its human capital. One-third of the growth in the U.S. gross national product from 1948 to 1982 was attributed to increases in the education level of the workforce. Fifty percent of this growth resulted from technical innovations and knowledge that also are based strongly on education. Only 15 percent of the growth of the gross national product during this time was attributed to investment in capital equipment.[71] Outcomes such as these support the position, as discussed in Chapter 3, that "... as the dynamics of competition accelerate, people are perhaps the only truly sustainable source of competitive advantage."[72] This suggests that the role of human resource management should be increasing in importance.[73] In turn, the effective development and management of the firm's human capital—that is, of all of the firm's managerial and nonmanagerial personnel—may be the primary determinant of a firm's ability to formulate and implement strategies successfully.[74]

As the Strategic Focus suggests, a significant problem is the lack of adequate human capital to run an organization effectively. Because of this, many firms are

450

turning to temporary employees, while others are employing better recruiting techniques. Solving the problem, however, requires more than just hiring temporary employees; indeed, building effective commitment to organizational goals is also required. Hiring star players is also insufficient. A strategic leader needs to build an effective organizational team committed to achieving the company's vision and goals.

STRATEGIC FOCUS

Human Resource Shortages: Temporary Workers Versus Creative Recruiting and Building Commitment

The Information Technology Association of America says that about 10 percent of U.S. technical jobs remain vacant because there are no qualified workers. There has been a shortage of talent because U.S. colleges have been graduating fewer computer science and electrical and computer engineering graduates throughout the 1990s. The falling graduation rate is due partly to the decline in baby boomers of college age. The lack of sufficient numbers of workers is not only a high-tech phenomenon. The American Trucking Association reported that 400,000 truck drivers were needed in 1997. The association also suggests that 50,000 drivers leave the industry each year, while another 300,000 switch trucking jobs, hoping to find better pay and conditions. Werner Enterprises Inc., a major firm in Omaha, Nebraska, replaced 65 percent of its drivers in one year, primarily due to turnover. Demand for drivers is correlated with the expected growth for handling freight, which is projected to increase 100 millions tons a year through 2004. The United States also faces a shortage of tool-and-die workers. According to the National Tooling and Machining Association, orders of machine tools rose significantly in 1997 while at the same time there was an estimated 24,000 vacancies for tool-and-die makers.

Companies throughout the world are creatively seeking ways to overcome the shortages. For instance, the number of part-time workers is growing significantly. The *Washington Post* reported that part-time arrangements affect 57 percent of workers. Part-time workers are also being seen in areas where unemployment is high. In Japan, for instance, nearly 20 percent of the country's 10 million workers are temporary part-time employees. Almost half of Japanese companies employ part-time workers. Similarly, in Germany, part-time workers are used increasingly because of the high unemployment rate. The use of temporary workers has increased in Europe because it helps to overcome inflexible labor market regulations. Milwaukee-based Manpower Inc., which supplies temporary workers, has been opening offices across Europe. Many multinationals, especially those headquarters in the U.S., have been sensitive to Europe's high labor costs and are leading the drive to outsource some business activities to temporary workers. However, European-based multinationals are not far behind. Phillips Electronics, for instance, employs 17,000 temporary workers, nearly 7 percent of its workforce.

With significant shortages in some markets and unemployment in others, how can a company develop its human resource? Cisco Systems, a networking company in Silicon Valley, has sought to develop ways to hire top talent and maintain its high performing employees. Its recruiting team identifies exactly the kind of people the company should hire, then plans a job-hunting strategy and provides innovative hiring processes to attract new employees. Cisco has a goal of hiring the top 10–15 percent of people in its industry. CEO John Chambers says: "Our philosophy is very simple. If you get the best people in the industry to fit into your culture and you motivate them properly, then you're going to be an industry leader." Cisco has an unusual and creative technique of infiltrating art fairs and microbrewery festivals as well as home and garden shows. At these events, Cisco recruiters work the crowd, collect business cards from prospects and speak informally with them about their careers and aspirations. They also have a "friends" referral program to help them pick out those who would like to work at Cisco. Employees receive a generous referral fee, starting at $500 for those prospects who are ultimately hired. Cisco also has a Web site that allows potential employees to fill out a profile by answering a handful of questions on an applicant's background.

Besides trying to hire talented people, Cisco makes acquisitions based on the quality of the engineering and R&D talent at potential target companies. Although many companies may be able to copy Cisco's hiring efforts, the firm continues to develop additional innovative ways to recruit the industry's best employees. It was rated the top firm in a *Forbes ASAP* ranking of the one hundred top dynamic companies.

In a survey completed by *Fortune* magazine about companies that employees love to work for, three characteristics became apparent. First, the best companies to work for had inspiring leadership. As one worker from Southwest Airlines, which was at the top of *Fortune*'s list of 100 best companies to work for, said: "Working here is truly an unbelievable experience. They treat you with respect, pay you well, and empower you. They use your ideas to solve problems. They encourage you to be yourself. I love going to work!!" Effective leaders not only inspire employees to work hard and succeed, but they also expect everyone to become a mini-version of top leadership and inspire employees that work for them. Second, employees value impressive corporate facilities. For instance, at USAA, a San Antonio-based insurance and financial services company, the corporate amenities include an exceptionally well-developed child care center. If you can't drive to work, the company sponsors a van pool. USAA also provides athletic facilities where employees enjoy breaks from their tasks during the work week. Finally, employees desire to have a strong sense of purpose. For example, at Merck, a pharmaceutical and health-care company, number nine on the list of well-respected companies, workers derive satisfaction from their jobs because they feel they are producing products that help restore people's lives. Therefore, besides seeking to build shareholder value, many firms seek to create value in the human capital by motivating employees through a broader sense of purpose.

Firms are seeking not only to have excellent human capital but to build the commitment of employees to work as a team and focus their intellectual skills and energies on company goals. As suggested above, managers can buy, build, or borrow talent. Furthermore, they may get rid of those individuals who are not contributing and seek to retain employees or bind those who they want to keep by treating them properly. However, recruiting competent individual talent should not be the only focus. It can be like buying the best talent and putting those people on an All-Star team. While the individual players may be talented, they may not perform as a team. Building commitment involves gauging employees' emotional energy and attention. If employees feel overwhelmed because demands on their time and emotional energy are too high, then they are likely to become discouraged. Furthermore, if demands are high but resources to do the work are inadequate, this is likely to lead to a lack of commitment as well. Therefore, there needs to be a good balance between available resources and appropriate levels of demand on workers' time.

Tools for developing commitment include enabling employees to control decisions on how they do their work and providing employees with vision and direction. These tools create an incentive for working hard. Challenging work, which allows stimulation and development of new skills, also is motivational. At Southwest Airlines, having a fun work culture where work is done in teams and gains are shared has also instilled superior commitment.

Candid communication and concern for the people involved provides better commitment as well. Adequate training and providing employees with appropriate technology to make their work easier is motivational, too. Thus, facing the challenges of finding competent people is not enough. Developing a team spirit and treating employees appropriately is also essential to garnering employee commitment in the pursuit of organizational objectives.

SOURCES: M. Aguilera-Hellweg, 1998, The ASAP dynamic 100: Cisco's CEO John Chambers, *Forbes ASAP*, February 23, 51–52; D. Ulrich, 1998, Intellectual Capital = Competence × Commitment, *Sloan Management Review* 39, no. 2: 15–26; R. B. Lieber, 1998, Why employees love these companies, *Fortune*, January 12, 72–74; L. Grant, 1998, Happy workers, high returns, *Fortune*, January 12, 81; R. Levering and M. Moskowitz, 1998, The 100 best companies to work for in America, *Fortune*, January 12, 85–95; D. Kunde, 1997, Companies go to great lengths to fill plethora of jobs, *Dallas Morning News*, December 9, D1, D15; Number of part-timers grows, 1997, *Dallas Morning News*, December 2, D4; G. Edmondson, A tidal wave of temps in Europe, *Business Week*, December 1, 164; E. Thornton, 1997, Moral cracks in the social contract, *Business Week*, October 27, 70; P. Nakache, 1997, Cisco's recruiting edge, *Fortune*, September 29, 275–276; A. W. Mathews, Wanted: 400,000 Long-distance truck drivers, *Wall Street Journal*, September 11, B1, B6; Associated Press, 1997, U.S. faces shortage of tool-and-die workers, *Dallas Morning News*, August 11, D4.

For individuals, active participation in company-sponsored programs to develop their abilities is highly desirable, in that being able to upgrade one's skills continuously leads to more job and economic security.[75] Increasingly, part of the development required to be selected as a strategic leader is international experience. As a business analyst noted, "With nearly every industry targeting fast-growing foreign markets, more companies are requiring foreign experience for top management positions."[76] Thus, companies committed to the importance of competing successfully in the global economy provide opportunities for their future strategic leaders to work in locations other than their home nation. Also, because foreign sources of management capabilities are becoming important, managing inpatriation (the process of transferring host-country or third-country national managers into the home/domestic market of multinational firms) is becoming more important to build global core competencies.[77]

Through participation in effective training and development programs, the probability increases that a manager will be a successful strategic leader. Among other outcomes, these programs build skills, inculcate a common set of core values, and give a systematic view of the organization, thus promoting the firm's strategic vision and organizational cohesion. Furthermore, they help strategic leaders improve skills that are critical to completing other tasks associated with effective strategic leadership (e.g., determining the firm's strategic direction, exploiting and maintaining core competencies, and developing an organizational culture that supports ethical practices).

The efforts at PepsiCo demonstrate an emphasis on shaping strategic leaders so that they in turn can develop human capital in their areas of responsibility.[78] This is an important challenge, given that most strategic leaders need to enhance their human resource management abilities. When human capital investments are successful, the result is a workforce capable of learning continuously. Being able to learn continuously and to leverage the firm's expanding knowledge base is linked with strategic success in the new competitive landscape. When asked to name what accounts for Johnson & Johnson's competitive success, the firm's CEO answered that his company is ". . . not in the product business. [It] is in the knowledge business."[79]

Programs that gain outstanding results in the training of future strategic leaders become a competitive advantage for a firm. General Electric's system of training and development of future strategic leaders is comprehensive and thought to be among the best.[80] As such, this training system may be a source of competitive advantage for the firm. Similarly, Avon as been particularly effective at hiring, training, and promoting women managers. Four of its eight top officers are women and 95 percent of its sales come from Avon Ladies. Performance at the cosmetics, toiletries, and fragrance company shows that this has been not only good for diversity, but has also helped improve returns substantially.[81]

As discussed in Chapter 7, millions of managers, strategic leaders, and non-managerial personnel have lost jobs in recent years through the restructuring and downsizing in many companies. In the mid-1980s, IBM employed 405,000 workers; today, the firm employs around 225,000. During the 1990s, Sears shed 50,000 people; in 1996, AT&T announced its intended layoffs of up to 40,000 employees. The view of AT&T's former CEO, Robert Allen, about his firm's job reductions captures the sentiment of many strategic leaders facing this reality: "My company had to make the necessary, even painful changes today or forfeit the future."[82] Almost identically, Robert Eaton, Chrysler's CEO, believes, "Downsizing and layoffs are part of the price of becoming more competitive. The price for not doing it, however, is much higher in both economic and human terms."[83] A number of firms, including Kodak, Citicorp, Levi Strauss, Whirlpool, Apple, and Kimberly-Clark, among others, announced layoffs in 1997 and 1998, at a time when the economy was very strong.[84]

Regardless of the cause, layoffs can result in a significant loss of knowledge that is possessed by a firm's human capital. Although it is also not uncommon for restructuring firms to reduce their expenditures/investments in training and development programs, restructuring may be an important time to *increase* investment in such development. These firms have less slack and cannot absorb as many errors; moreover, many employees may be placed into positions without all of the skills or knowledge necessary to perform required tasks effectively.[85] In the final analysis, a view of employees as a resource to be maximized rather than a cost to be minimized facilitates successful implementation of a firm's strategies. The effectiveness of implementation processes also increases when strategic leaders approach layoffs in a manner that employees believe is fair and equitable.[86]

As described next, human capital is an important part of the firm's ability to develop and sustain an effective organizational culture.

SUSTAINING AN EFFECTIVE ORGANIZATIONAL CULTURE

An **organizational culture** consists of a complex set of ideologies, symbols, and core values that is shared throughout the firm and influences the way it conducts business. Evidence suggests that a firm can develop core competencies both in terms of the capabilities it possesses and the way the capabilities are used to produce strategic actions. In other words, because it influences how the firm conducts its business and helps regulate and control employee behavior, organizational culture can be a source of competitive advantage.[87] Thus, shaping the context within which the firm formulates and implements its strategies—that is, shaping the organizational culture—is a central task of strategic leaders.[88]

An **organizational culture** consists of a complex set of ideologies, symbols, and core values that is shared throughout the firm and influences the way it conducts business.

Hewlett-Packard provides an example of the potential power of culture. The core values of this firm's culture are in the basic belief that "men and women want to do a good job, a creative job, and that if they are provided the proper environment, they will do so."[89] An effective organizational culture encourages and supports an entrepreneurial orientation.

Entrepreneurial Orientation

Organizational culture often encourages (or discourages) the pursuit of entrepreneurial opportunities, especially in large firms.[90] At Thermo Electron, George N. Hatsopoulous, chair and CEO, has fostered an entrepreneurial spirit by offering to spin off businesses that become successful. This is opposite of conventional wisdom; when a company divests, it usually does so with its less successful businesses. Thermo Electron has completed twelve spin-offs over the years. For employees and managers involved in these spin-offs, it has provided a vehicle for ownership and significant incentive to increase value. John Hatsopoulous, the company's president, adds, "We found that the only way we could sustain the process of creating new businesses was to be able to maintain the benefits of a small company while preserving the advantages of a big company."[91]

Successful outcomes derived through employees' pursuit of entrepreneurial opportunities are a major source of growth and innovation for firms competing in today's complex, globalized environment.[92] Innovation, and a CEO that has nurtured a culture that fosters it, may account for Bombardier's recent successful innovations. As noted in Chapter 11, Laurent Beaudoin, the 59-year-old chief executive of Montreal-based Bombardier Inc., has moved ahead with a number of product innovations over the last several years. Although Bombardier has had performance difficulties, the CEO is counting on a number of new products to increase returns. He has sought to foster innovation in three of the firm's diversified businesses—aerospace, transportation, and recreational products. In 1998, Bombardier offered the Learjet 45, a mid-sized plane priced like a light jet but capable of nonstop transcontinental flights. A number of regional jet airlines such as Canada Air and American Eagle have placed orders for the plane. Its Global Express, a top of the line executive jet, has also presold a number of planes. It has also redesigned its subway cars and has a $1 billion contract for New York City featuring automatic announcements and electronic information signs. Its American Flyer high-speed rail trains will be carrying Amtrak passengers from Boston to Washington at 150 miles per hour starting in 1999. It has moved into jetskis as an offshoot from its snowmobile business. Similarly, it has developed a new two-passenger golf cart featuring an electronic motor capable of 25 miles per hour. It expects to establish a strong market share in this $33 million dollar market. The product can also be used as a neighborhood vehicle in gated or retirement communities. Bombardier also expects to introduce a new sporty all-terrain recreational vehicle to compete with models sold by Honda and Yamaha. Even though quite diversified, Bombardier is resolute in selling new technology and products in all of its product lines.[93]

Five dimensions characterize a firm's entrepreneurial orientation (EO).[94] In combination, these dimensions influence the activities a firm uses in efforts to be innovative and to launch new ventures. Discussed in Chapter 13, one of the key ways new ventures are launched in large firms is through internal corporate entrepreneurship. Particularly for firms seeking first-mover advantages (see Chapter 5), an entrepreneurial orientation among employees is critical.

455

Autonomy is the first of an EO's five dimensions. Autonomy is an active part of a firm's culture when employees are able to take actions that are free of stifling organizational constraints. Generally, autonomy allows individuals and groups to be self-directed. The second dimension, *innovativeness*, "reflects a firm's tendency to engage in and support new ideas, novelty, experimentation, and creative processes that may result in new products, services, or technological processes."[95] Cultures with a tendency toward innovativeness encourage employees to think beyond existing knowledge, technologies, and parameters in efforts to find creative ways to add value. *Risk taking* reflects a willingness by employees and their firm to accept risks in the pursuit of marketplace opportunities. These risks can include assuming significant levels of debt and allocating large amounts of other resources (e.g., people) to uncertain projects. Often, these risks are accepted to seize marketplace opportunities that can substantially increase the firm's strategic competitiveness and its returns. The fourth EO dimension, *proactiveness*, describes a firm's ability to be a market leader rather than a follower. Proactive organizational cultures constantly use processes to anticipate future market needs and to satisfy them before competitors learn how to do so. Finally, *competitive aggressiveness* is a firm's propensity to take actions that allow it to outperform its rivals consistently and substantially. Thus, the key dimensions that characterize an EO include autonomy, a willingness to innovate and take risks, and a tendency to be aggressive toward competitors and proactive relative to marketplace opportunities.[96]

These attributes are illustrated in the Strategic Focus about Fastenal, a service-oriented business focusing on selling fasteners to industrial companies (such as specialized nuts and bolts). Bob Kierlin, the CEO, has developed an entrepreneurial culture in the firm that provides a commonplace set of products in a way that creates value for its customers. Additional information about this firm's ability to innovate is provided in a Strategic Focus in Chapter 13 (see page 493).

STRATEGIC FOCUS

Fastenal's Culture for Selling Nuts and Bolts

Bob Kierlin founded Fastenal Company in 1967 in Winona, Minnesota. It has become the largest fastener distributor in the nation through a service-oriented business network. In addition to an in-house manufacturing division and a quality assurance department, Fastenal has a strategic system of distribution centers and a fleet of over 60 owned semi trucks and trailers with 660 branches in 48 states, Canada, and Puerto Rico. Fastenal has been on the *Forbes'* 200 Best Small Companies list for the last 10 years. When it first made the list in 1988, the company had annual sales of $22.5 million. In 1997, its sales were $339 million; almost enough to remove it from the small company list. Notwithstanding this phenomenal growth, its average return on equity has been 26.6 percent over the last five years, and 28.5 percent in 1997.

When Kierlin, current CEO of Fastenal, is asked to describe the reasons for this success, he says, "Just believe in people, give them a chance to make decisions, take risks, and work hard." Furthermore, he suggests, "We could have made this work selling cabbages." In essence, Kierlin and his top officers have facilitated an entrepreneurial culture that stimulates the kind of growth and returns experienced by Fastenal. This success apparently has nothing to do with his salary. Kierlin is paid $120,000 annually, an amount which has remained constant for the past ten years. He receives no options, bonuses, or long-term incentives. He admits, however, that his net worth is tied to the stock price, which has provided better shareholder returns than Coca-Cola or General Electric. Total returns to shareholders over the past five years have been 39.3 percent annually. This performance has come through selling nuts and bolts—49,000 different kinds of fasteners, from grade eight hex nuts to weld studs to pin bold drive anchors—in 620 stores across the United States and Canada. Furthermore, Fastenal's gross margins are 53 percent, approximately 15 percentage points higher than rivals.

Kierlin fosters a culture of decentralized decision making. Fastenal's branches can bypass the company's central purchasing department. In fact, this happens in 42 percent of purchases. Often, management-level decision making is pushed down to entry level positions. One branch decided that it required improved deliveries to increase sales. To insure that it was stocked properly, deliveries were received daily. The main focus is to furnish customers with exemplary service and charge them premiums for the value that is created by having the product available on time. The premium price works primarily because Fastenal's sales are focused on replacement parts for industrial and other kinds of machines. The company has successfully implemented a focused differentiation strategy (see Chapter 4). When something breaks, Fastenal employees provide the necessary parts in a timely manner. Rich Schmidt of Machinery Services, says, "As far as Fastenal goes, we never get told no." Of course, this kind of service builds loyalty and allows Fastenal to charge its premium price. Usually, a large factory is not likely to quibble over a three dollar bolt when its machine is down.

Many construction and equipment manufacturers outsource their inventory function to Fastenal, which means it can move to its secret weapon of cutting and machining or molding virtually any fastener or other product that it has in inventory or available from suppliers. Although such custom purchases account for only 4 percent of revenues, it is an effective sales tool and builds customer loyalty.

To foster the significant growth of Fastenal, Kierlin has kept the organizational structure very flat. There are only three management levels between branch managers and Fastenal's president, Will Oberton, who is thirty-nine years old. Often new employees work as few as six months before being given their own store to manage. Compensation for sales people after three years is likely to be split between bonus and base salary. There is no stock option, 401(K), or other pension plan available. Kierlin believes that employees should be responsible for their own retirement.

Some on Wall Street have been concerned about Fastenal's exceedingly strong growth rate and expect the fastener market to be saturated soon. Kierlin responds that he thought the smallest population that would justify a Fastenal store's presence was 25,000, but with new product lines that have similar margins to nuts and bolts, Kierlin feels that his firm can enter communities as small as 8,000 people. Accordingly, Fastenal has begun to sell power tools, saws, drills, and sanders under the FastTool brand. Although people like to comparison shop for tools that cost $150 and up, they are less likely to haggle over accessories such as drill bits, saw blades, sandpaper, and safety accessories. The margins for these replacement products rival those of fastener lines. Kierlin also suggests that its oldest stores are its most profitable ones; and, as such, sales continue to grow in already established stores. Therefore, with new lines it appears Fastenal may be able to maintain its high growth level.

Although the new locations and product lines give potential for the new growth, Kierlin is quick to remind analysts that it's not the new stores and products lines that allow for success; it's the way people are treated. Fastenal gives people a chance to make decisions and take risks and provides incentives to work hard. In essence, it's the entrepreneurial culture that Kierlin has created at Fastenal that is its true cause of underlying success.

SOURCES: B. Pappas and R. Boone, Jr., 1997, The best of the best, Forbes magazine online, http://www.forbes.com, November 3; Fastenal Company homepage, http://www.fastenal.com; R. Teitelbaum, 1997, Who is Bob Kierlin—and why is he so successful?, *Fortune*, December 8, 254–258.

Changing Organizational Culture and Business Reengineering

Changing organizational culture is more difficult than maintaining it, but effective strategic leaders recognize when change is needed. Incremental changes to the firm's culture typically are used to implement strategies. However, more significant and sometimes even radical changes to organizational culture are designed to support the selection of strategies that differ from the ones the firm has implemented historically. Regardless of the reasons for change, shaping and reinforcing a new culture requires effective communication and problem solving, along with the selection of the right people (those who have the values managers wish to infuse throughout the organization), effective performance appraisals (establishing goals and measuring individual performance toward those goals that fit with the new core values), and appropriate reward systems (rewarding the desired behaviors that reflect the new core values).[97]

Evidence suggests that cultural changes succeed only when they are supported actively by the firm's CEO, other key top management team members, and middle-level managers.[98] In fact, for large-scale changes, approximately one-third of middle-level managers need to be effective change agents. These change agents "... have a nice balance of capabilities: They are technically skilled people who are also very capable in personal relationships. They're an odd combination. On the one hand, they're tough decision-makers who are highly disciplined about performance results. But they also know how to get lots of people energized and aligned in the same direction."[99]

One catalyst for change in organizational culture, particularly for critical changes, is the selection of new top management team members from outside the corporation. Company founder and CEO Michael Dell of Dell Computer, who pioneered the direct marketing of computers to customers, recruited executives from companies such as Motorola, Hewlett-Packard, and Apple Computer to deal with problems the firm encountered in late 1993 and early 1994.[100] Interestingly,

Michael Dell, founder and CEO of Dell Computer, recruited top managers from Motorola, Hewlett-Packard, and Apple in the early 1990s. Market analysts wondered if Dell had the skills to compete in the PC industry, but record sales in 1996 and 1997 proved that he was more than up to the task.

Dell is 10 years younger than the next youngest member of the newly formed top management team.[101]

A key member of Dell's new team is Mort Topfer, a former Motorola executive. As vice chair, Topfer has changed Dell Computer's organizational culture. Prior to his arrival, relatively few control systems were in place. For example, the company lacked a clear understanding of the "relationships between costs and revenues and profits and losses within the different lines of business."[102] Relying on discipline and planning, Topfer designed a number of strategic and financial control systems that affect both the selection and implementation of Dell Computer's strategies. Michael Dell believes that Topfer's contributions have helped his firm change from being relatively undisciplined to one that is more focused on sustained performance and market momentum.[103] Working together effectively, Dell Computer's top management team has collectively accepted the responsibility for running the firm successfully and for initiating required changes to its organizational culture.[104] The market wondered whether Dell really had the skills to guide the company in a highly competitive industry, but huge sales increases in 1996, 1997, and early 1998 show that the direct market approach was larger than analysts anticipated and that Michael Dell was more than up to the task of getting the job done.[105]

Business reengineering is the fundamental rethinking and radical redesign of business processes to achieve dramatic improvements in performance in such areas as cost, quality, service, and speed.[106] It is a technique used by companies to survive and succeed in the new competitive landscape. Business reengineering is of significant benefit to strategic leaders seeking ways to implement chosen strategies more effectively and perhaps change the organization's culture in the process. By focusing on the activities necessary to transform materials into goods or services that are valuable to customers, business reengineering challenges firms to find ways to increase dramatically the effectiveness and efficiency of their organizational culture. For a differentiation business-level strategy (see Chapter 4), reengineering efforts are directed at finding ways to more sharply and meaningfully differentiate the firm's products from competitors' offerings. Similarly, firms implementing a cost leadership business-level strategy (see Chapter 4) use business reengineering to drive their costs lower than competitors'.

The benefits of reengineering are attained through the efforts of dedicated employees. Business reengineering success is maximized when employees believe that (1) every job in the company is essential and important, (2) all employees must create value through their work, (3) constant learning is a vital part of every person's job, (4) teamwork is essential to implementation success, and (5) problems are solved only when teams accept the responsibility for their solution.[107] These beliefs and commitments appear to exist at British Petroleum PLC (BP). In 1992, BP was forced to undergo an intense cost-cutting and restructuring plan. The company discovered that downsizing alone wasn't enough to compete in the oil-related business. For decades, BP had a corporate culture that was very traditional, formal, and predictable. The 1992 crisis was so severe that the reorganization led to making middle managers accountable for their own results and giving them a financial stake in their performance. The underlying management structure was reordered into networks or groups of employees who do similar work but are located in different countries or even different continents. The reorganization facilitated a much more decentralized structure where, although it seemed uncomfortable at first, created a much more loyal workforce. Formal titles have given way to looser roles where initiative, not conformity, is valued.[108]

EMPHASIZING ETHICAL PRACTICES

The effectiveness of strategy implementation processes increases when they are based on ethical practices. Ethical companies encourage and enable people at all organizational levels to exercise ethical judgment. Alternately, if unethical practices evolve in an organization, they become like a contagious disease.[109] To properly influence employee judgment and behavior, ethical practices must shape the firm's decision-making process and be an integral part of an organization's culture. Once accepted, ethical practices serve as a moral filter through which potential courses of action are evaluated.[110]

As discussed in Chapter 10, *managerial opportunism* occurs when managers take actions that are in their own best interests but not in the firm's best interests. In other words, managers take advantage of their positions and therefore make decisions that benefit them to the detriment of the owners (shareholders).[111] An implicit assumption of the agency model described in the discussion of corporate governance in Chapter 10 is that top-level managers may act as opportunistic agents who will capitalize on every chance to maximize personal welfare at the expense of shareholders. Individual opportunism is well documented by Wall Street insider trading scandals and other actions taken by those who financed large leveraged buyouts and acquisitions.[112] Other potential problems that have been documented include questionable hiring practices and a willingness to commit fraud by understating write-offs that reduce corporate returns.[113] It is possible, too, that very high CEO compensation is a sign of opportunism being pursued by those in the upper echelons of management.[114]

Another set of studies sheds light on these issues. Research examining managers' ethical values and beliefs in the mid-1980s and again in the early 1990s showed little change. At both times, managers emphasized utilitarian goals, that is, the achievement of economic gains for the organization's stakeholders. In fact, the earlier survey found that one of the primary reasons managers emphasized ethical practices was to achieve greater profits. Some argue that the managerial and organizational gains are mutually beneficial. In other words, firms that establish and maintain ethical practices are more likely to achieve strategic competitiveness and earn above-average returns. A key reason for this is that a reputation for ethical practices attracts loyal customers.[115]

On the other hand, recent evidence suggests that at least some individuals from different groups—including top-level executives and business students—may be willing to commit either illegal actions (e.g., fraud) or actions that many think are unethical. In one study, researchers found that 47 percent of upper-level executives, 41 percent of controllers, and 76 percent of graduate-level business students expressed a willingness to commit fraud (as measured by a subject's willingness to misrepresent his/her company's financial statements). Moreover, these researchers discovered that 87 percent of the managers made at least one fraudulent decision out of a total of seven situations requiring a decision. Another finding is that the more an individual valued a comfortable life and/or pleasure, and the less he or she valued self-respect, the greater was the probability that a fraudulent decision would be made.[116]

Another study's results appear to have important implications for organizations and those who manage them.[117] The study found that although cheating was observed, there was reluctance to report it. An unwillingness to report wrongdoing calls for the development of comprehensive organizational control systems to assure that individuals' behaviors are consistent with the firm's needs and expectations.

Thus, the findings from these studies seem to support the need for firms to employ ethical strategic leaders—ones who include ethical practices as part of their long-term vision for the firm, who desire to do the right thing, and for whom honesty, trust, and integrity are important.[118] Strategic leaders who consistently display these qualities inspire employees as they work with others to develop and support an organizational culture in which ethical practices are the expected behavioral norms.

As our discussion suggests, strategic leaders are challenged to take actions that increase the probability that an ethical culture will exist in their organization. When these efforts are successful, the practices associated with an ethical culture become institutionalized in the firm; that is, they become the set of behavioral commitments and actions accepted by most of the firm's employees and other stakeholders with whom employees interact. Actions that strategic leaders can take to develop an ethical organizational culture include (1) establishing and communicating specific goals to describe the firm's ethical standards (e.g., developing and disseminating a code of conduct), (2) continuously revising and updating the code of conduct, based on inputs from people throughout the firm and from other stakeholders (e.g., customers and suppliers), (3) disseminating the code of conduct to all stakeholders to inform them of the firm's ethical standards and practices, (4) developing and implementing methods and procedures to use in achieving the firm's ethical standards (e.g., use of internal auditing practices that are consistent with the standards), (5) creating and using explicit reward systems that recognize acts of courage (e.g., rewarding those who use proper channels and procedures to report observed wrongdoings), and (6) creating a work environment in which all people are treated with dignity.[119] The effectiveness of these actions increases when they are undertaken simultaneously since the six major actions are mutually supportive. A failure to develop and engage in all six actions reduces the likelihood that the firm can establish an ethical culture. Moreover, when strategic leaders engage successfully in these actions they serve as moral role models for the firm's employees and other stakeholders.

When ethical practices are not firmly established, trouble can emerge. For example, Columbia/HCA Health Care Corporation has been accused of wrongdoing and is under federal investigation. Although the top officers have not been charged with any crime, a number of hospital managers within the corporation have been. The main problem has been a culture that encourages managers to be overly aggressive in regard to performance, stimulates too much growth, and a weak board of directors that did not provide appropriate oversight. The system created incentives for hospital administrators to charge too much on Medicare and engage in other improper billing for services.[120] To overcome these difficulties, Columbia/HCA has appointed special ethics and compliance officers at each of its 338 hospitals. This move was spearheaded by its new ethics vice president, Alan Yuspeh, in an effort to extricate Columbia from the massive federal Medicare-fraud investigation. In most cases, Columbia is hiring external people to fill these slots. In addition, Columbia's board is forming a new committee of compliance and ethical issues headed by Judith A. Karam. This case highlights the importance of establishing ethical practices and control systems that foster strong ethics among managers and employees.[121]

As the Columbia/HCA example illustrates, organizational control systems can help to foster ethical practices and other areas important for the exercise of strategic leadership.

461

ESTABLISHING BALANCED ORGANIZATIONAL CONTROLS

Organizational controls have long been viewed as an important part of strategy implementation processes. Controls are necessary to help ensure that firms achieve their desired outcomes of strategic competitiveness and above-average returns.[122] Defined as the ". . . formal, information-based . . . procedures used by managers to maintain or alter patterns in organizational activities," controls help strategic leaders build credibility, demonstrate the value of strategies to the firm's stakeholders, and promote and support strategic change.[123] Most critically, controls provide the parameters within which strategies are to be implemented as well as corrective actions to be taken when implementation-related adjustments are required. In this chapter, we focus on two organizational controls—strategic and financial—that were introduced in Chapter 11. Our discussion of organizational controls in this chapter emphasizes strategic and financial controls because strategic leaders are responsible for their development and effective use.

Although critical to the firm's success, evidence suggests that organizational controls are imperfect. Consider the example of Columbia/HCA as discussed above where the wrong incentive structure has brought the largest hospital operator to its knees over a broad federal fraud investigation. Control failures such as this have a negative effect on the firm's reputation and divert managerial attention from actions necessary to use the strategic management process effectively.

As explained in Chapter 11, financial controls are often emphasized in large corporations. Financial controls focus on short-term financial outcomes. In contrast, strategic control focuses on the *content* of strategic actions, rather than their *outcomes*. Some strategic actions can be correct but poor financial outcomes may still result because of external conditions such as recessionary economic problems, unexpected domestic or foreign government actions, or natural disasters.[124] Therefore, an emphasis on financial control often produces more short-term and risk-averse managerial decisions because financial outcomes may be due to events beyond managers' direct control. Alternatively, strategic controls encourage lower level managers to make decisions that incorporate moderate and acceptable levels of risk because outcomes are shared between the business-level executives making strategic proposals and the corporate-level executives evaluating them.

Successful strategic leaders balance strategic control and financial control (they do not eliminate financial control) with the intent of achieving more positive long-term returns.[125] In fact, most corporate restructuring is designed to refocus the firm on its core businesses, thereby allowing top-level executives to reestablish strategic control of their separate business units.[126]

Effective use of strategic control by top-level managers is integrated frequently with appropriate autonomy for the various subunits so they can gain a competitive advantage in their respective markets. Strategic control can be used to promote the sharing of both tangible and intangible resources among interdependent businesses within a firm's portfolio. In addition, the autonomy provided allows the flexibility necessary to take advantage of specific marketplace opportunities. As a result, strategic leadership promotes the simultaneous use of strategic control and autonomy.[127]

The Strategic Focus on diversified business groups suggests how important it is that diversified firms maintain a balanced control orientation. Because large diversified business groups have not maintained this balance, many throughout the world are having to restructure their operations. For instance, those in South Korea have had significant problems as the currency crisis in Southeast Asia has revealed problems in their diversification strategies.

STRATEGIC FOCUS

Balancing Controls in Large, Diversified Business Groups

Large, diversified business groups are diversified across a wide range of businesses. They often have practical financial interlocks among their holdings, and, in many cases, family ownership and control. These diversified business groups dominate private-sector industrial and service activities in many of the world economies. Even in the United States, family ownership is quite prevalent. It is estimated that over a third of the *Fortune* 500 companies are family-owned or dominated. As for the world economy as a whole, the number is certainly over 50 percent. Many diversified business groups (unrelated diversified firms or conglomerates) in the United States have been refocusing because of the market for corporate control and the ability of large investors to buy diffuse equity holdings and keep firms from overdiversifying into too many product markets.

In some developing markets, diversified business groups have provided advantages that allow them to exist more prominently throughout the world. Usually in these emerging markets, equity markets are illiquid and most financing is provided by banks, some of which are nationalized. Also, large business groups provide a significant training ground for managers in economies with few business schools where talent is usually developed. Crossholding among business groups also facilitates contract enforcement where contract laws are often unpredictable. Thus, many economies have diversified business groups such as the chaebols in South Korea and the large diversified business groups in India and throughout Southeast Asia. Furthermore, many developed economies throughout Europe such as Italy, France, and Sweden have large diversified business groups.

Strategic leaders are seeing that the control systems they have implemented to manage large diversified business groups are becoming critical as economies become more liberal (regarding trade policies) and experience currency shocks such as those in Southeast Asia. In South Korea, many strategic leaders of the chaebols have been reorganizing to refocus on core businesses and also maintain a better balance between strategic and financial controls. For example, the Hyundai Group has indicated during the financial crises that it would scrap plans to build a $5 billion steel mill and would relinquish management of its money-losing newspaper operation. It also indicated that it would sell or merge unprofitable affiliates that can operate independently. Hyundai has 58 affiliates and sales of over $50 billion. It did not specify which of its 58 affiliates would be affected by the restructuring. Likewise, LG Group said it would cut 90 business lines worth $1.48 billion. Samsung also suggested that it will restructure as well. As with Hyundai and LG, Samsung promised that by 1999, it would adopt consolidated financial statements and eliminate cross-guarantees between affiliates for loans. This measure would provide greater transparency for the group's accounting procedures. Samsung plans to focus on three or four core industries but again, like the others, declined to name them. Because the chaebols are largely family-owned, it has been difficult to understand their operation, governance, and control procedures.

Ssangyong's restructuring has been defying the usual convention of diversified business groups in South Korea. Although it has one of the largest chaebols, Kim Suk Joon has taken his company through a long but painful restructuring that included selling its prized automobile company to a rival. Many chaebols have been too proud to scale back and often delay unveiling restructuring plans until days before declaring default. Six of the largest chaebols sought court protection from creditors in 1997. Ssangyong, in 1997, sold off its profitable paper company to Procter & Gamble for $46.7 million and sold a California cement company, Riverside Cement, to Texas Industries. Although Ssangyong's restructuring gives it an advantage because it readily undertook the restructuring process relative to other chaebols, the lesson is still the same; they have all overexpanded and overdiversified because their strategic leaders did not have adequate strategic controls in place.

Ahlstrom Corporation, a large Finnish conglomerate, restructured its governance and control systems as it confronted more competitive markets. As with many Asian firms, the Finnish conglomerate was controlled mostly by over 200 family owners. To manage the operation professionally and yet include family involvement, the Ahlstrom owners formed a family assembly that allowed them to have formal communications between family members and the board and the CEO. Furthermore, family assemblies often served as an informal sounding board for the CEO and board of directors. For instance, the family council drafted a document—the Ahlstrom Family Values and Policies—that was extensively discussed and serves as a constitution for the corporation. Ahlstrom ultimately reorganized its diversified holdings into more focused business groups after downscoping by selling off some holdings. Once the holdings were sold off and organized into four groups, the family restructured the operation so that each business group has its own board. There is an industrial holding company above the four business groups, and above that is a main board. This structure has provided much better corporate governance that is closer to the operations and allows each business group with its own subsidiaries and divisions to run more efficiently with better balance between financial controls and strategic controls, as well as better governance of management. Therefore, from a strategic leadership point of view, this structure allows for more family members to be involved and to ensure that the company is running according to the family constitution.

Many of the business groups in Southeast Asia are run by family-owned companies of expatriate Chinese. Traditionally, these firms have been in consumer industries that are nontechnical, such as shipping, commodity trading, hotel, real estate and financial services, and other light industries. As these firms seek to move into high-tech industries, such as chemicals and electronics, they have had to move away from the family-managed business concept to more professional managerial techniques. This adjustment is partly due to the change in capital markets where more transparency is required and where contracting law is becoming more prominent. Business operations, before these economic shocks, were run by their strategic leaders, mostly based on relationships between family members and friends. They are now being forced to implement better and more professional control systems as have other diversified business groups throughout the world.

Diversified business operations have also been found in India. Many Indian groups have also been restructuring, as have those in Southeast Asia such as the chaebols in Korea and in Western Europe such as the Ahlstrom Group. Their strategic leaders are seeking to develop a better balance between financial controls and strategic controls as their economies have become more liberalized and open to foreign competition.

SOURCES: P. Ghemawat and T. Khanna, 1998, The nature of diversified business groups: A research design and two case studies, *Journal of Industrial Economics*, in press; J. Magretta, 1998, Governing the family-owned enterprise: An interview with Finland's Krister Ahlstrom, *Harvard Business Review* 76, no. 1: 112–123; M. Cho, 1998, Samsung to sell units, focus on core industries, *Wall Street Journal*, January 22, A15; M. Schuman, 1998, Samsung weighs retreat on auto output, *Wall Street Journal*, January 21, A7; M. Cho, 1998, Hyundai, LG Groups to trim operations, *Wall Street Journal*, January 20, A14; M. Schuman, 1997, Seoul survivor: A giant resists the crisis, *Wall Street Journal*, December 24, A8; T. Khanna and K. Palepu, 1997, Why focused strategies may be wrong for emerging markets, *Harvard Business Review* 75, no. 4: 41–50; M. Weidenbaum, 1996, The Chinese family business enterprise, *California Management Review* 38, no. 4: 141–156.

As our discussion suggests, organizational controls establish an integrated set of analyses and actions that reinforce one another. Through effective use of strategic controls, strategic leaders increase the probability that their firms will gain the benefits of carefully formulated strategies but not at the expense of the financial control that is a critical part of the strategy implementation process. Effective organizational controls provide an underlying logic for strategic leadership, focus attention on critical strategic issues, support a competitive culture, and provide a forum that builds commitment to strategic intent.

SUMMARY

- Effective strategic leadership is required to use the strategic management process successfully, including the strategic actions associated with the implementation of strategies. Strategic leadership entails the ability to anticipate, envision, maintain flexibility, and empower others to create strategic change.

- Top-level managers are an important resource requirement for firms to develop and exploit competitive advantages. In addition, strategic leaders can be a source of competitive advantage. Top executives exercise discretion in making critical strategic decisions.

- The top management team is composed of key managers who formulate and implement strategies. Generally, they are officers of the corporation and/or members of the board of directors.

- There is a relationship among top management team characteristics, firm strategy, and performance. For example, a top management team that has significant marketing and R&D knowledge often enhances the firm's effectiveness as the team steers the firm toward implementation of growth strategies. Overall, most top management teams are more effective when they have diverse and heterogeneous skills.

- When boards of directors are involved in shaping strategic direction, firms generally improve their strategic competitiveness. Alternatively, boards may be less involved in strategic decisions about strategy formulation and strategy implementation when CEOs have more power. CEOs obtain power when they appoint people to the board and when they simultaneously serve the firm as its CEO and board chair.

- Strategic leaders are selected from either the internal or the external managerial labor market. Because of their effect on firm performance, the selection of strategic leaders from these markets

has implications for a firm's effectiveness. Valid reasons exist to use both labor markets when selecting strategic leaders and managers with the potential to become strategic leaders. The internal market is used in the majority of cases to select the firm's CEO. Outsiders are selected to initiate needed change.

- Effective strategic leadership has six components: determining the firm's strategic direction, exploiting and maintaining core competencies, developing human capital, sustaining an effective organizational culture, emphasizing ethical practices, and establishing balanced organizational controls.

- Often requiring a significant amount of thinking and time to form, determining strategic direction refers to the development of a long-term vision of the firm's strategic intent. A charismatic leader can help achieve strategic intent.

- Strategic leaders must verify that their firm exploits its core competencies, which are used to create and deliver products that create value for customers, to implement strategies. In related diversified and large firms, in particular, core competencies are exploited effectively when they are shared across units and products.

- A critical element of strategic leadership and effective strategy implementation processes is the ability to develop the firm's human capital. Effective strategic leaders and firms view human capital as a resource to be maximized rather than as a cost to be minimized. Resulting from this perspective is the use of programs intended to train current and future strategic leaders so they will have the skills needed to nurture and develop the rest of the firm's human capital.

- Shaping the firm's culture is a central task of effective strategic leadership. In the new competitive landscape, an appropriate organizational culture encourages the development of an entrepreneurial orientation among employees and an ability to change the culture as necessary. Reengineering can facilitate this process.

■ In ethical organizations, employees are encouraged to exercise ethical judgment and to display only ethical practices. Ethical practices can be promoted through several actions, including those of setting specific goals to describe the firm's ethical standards, using a code of conduct, rewarding eth-

ical behaviors, and creating a work environment in which all people are treated with dignity.

■ The final component of effective strategic leadership is the development and use of effective organizational controls. It is through organizational controls that strategic leaders provide the direction the firm requires to flexibly, yet appropriately, use its core competencies in the pursuit of marketplace opportunities. Best results are obtained when there is a balance between strategic and financial controls.

REVIEW QUESTIONS

1. What is strategic leadership? In what ways are top-level managers considered important resources for an organization?
2. What is a top management team and how does it affect a firm's performance and its abilities to innovate and make appropriate strategic changes?
3. What are the differences between the internal and external managerial labor markets? What are the effects of each labor market type on the formulation and implementation of firm strategy?
4. How does strategic leadership affect determination of the firm's strategic direction?
5. Why is it important for strategic leaders to make cer-

tain that their firm exploits its core competencies in the pursuit of strategic competitiveness and above-average returns?
6. What is the importance of human capital and its development for strategic competitiveness?
7. What is organizational culture? What must strategic leaders do to sustain an effective organizational culture?
8. As a strategic leader, what actions could you take to establish and emphasize ethical practices in your firm?
9. What are organizational controls? Why are strategic controls and financial controls, two types of organizational controls, an important part of the strategic management process?

APPLICATION DISCUSSION QUESTIONS

1. Choose a CEO of a prominent firm you believe exemplifies the positive aspects of strategic leadership. What actions does this CEO take that demonstrate effective strategic leadership? What are the effects of these actions on the firm's performance?
2. Select a CEO of a prominent firm you believe does not exemplify the positive aspects of strategic leadership. What actions does this CEO take that are inconsistent with effective strategic leadership? How have these ineffective actions affected the firm's performance?
3. What are managerial resources? What is the relationship between managerial resources and a firm's strategic competitiveness?
4. By examining popular press articles, select an organization that has recently gone through a significant strategic change. While reading these articles, collect as much information as you can about the organization's top management team. Does your analysis suggest that

there is a relationship between the top management team's characteristics and the type of change the organization experienced? If so, what is the nature and outcome of that relationship?
5. Through a reading of popular press articles, identify two new CEOs, one chosen from the internal managerial labor market and one from the external labor market. Based on your reading, why do you think these individuals were chosen? What do they bring to the job and what strategy do you think they will implement in the future?
6. In light of your reading of this chapter and popular press accounts, select a CEO you feel has exhibited vision. Has the CEO's vision been realized? If so, what have the effects been of its realization? If it has not been realized, why not?
7. Identify a firm in which you believe strategic leaders have emphasized and developed human capital. What

466

do you believe are the effects of this emphasis and development on the firm's performance?

8. Select an organization you think has a unique organizational culture. What characteristics of that culture make it unique? Has the culture had a significant effect on the organization's performance? If so, what is that effect?

9. Why is the strategic control exercised by a firm's strategic leaders important for long-term competitiveness? How do strategic controls differ from financial controls?

ETHICS QUESTIONS

1. As discussed in this chapter, effective strategic leadership occasionally requires managers to make difficult decisions. In your opinion, is it ethical for managers to make these types of decisions without being willing to receive feedback from employees about the effects of those decisions? Be prepared to justify your response.

2. As an employee with less than one year of experience in a firm, what actions would you pursue if you encountered unethical practices by a strategic leader?

3. In your opinion, are firms obligated ethically to promote from within, rather than relying on the external labor market to select strategic leaders? What reasoning supports your position?

4. What are the ethical issues involved, if any, with the firm's ability to develop and exploit a core competence in the manufacture of goods that may be harmful to consumers (e.g., cigarettes)? Be prepared to discuss the reasons for your response.

5. As a strategic leader, would you feel ethically responsible to develop your firm's human capital? Why or why not? Do you believe your position is consistent with the majority or minority of today's strategic leaders?

6. Select an organization, social group, or volunteer agency in which you hold membership that you believe has an ethical culture. What factors caused this culture to be ethical? Are there events that could occur that would cause this culture to become less ethical? If so, what are they?

467

INTERNET EXERCISE

Go to *Fortune* magazine's Ten Most Admired Companies in America at:

http://www.pathfinder.com/fortune/mostadmired/ topone.html

Each year *Fortune* magazine administers a survey to top executives, outside directors, and securities analysts to determine the most admired companies in America. The results of this survey are closely watched and have been the subject of countless news articles and board-room conversations. The above Web site lists the top 10 companies from the 1997 survey. Select three of these companies and research the attributes of their CEOs using the *Fortune* Web site as a starting point. It what ways do these CEOs exemplify strategic leadership? Do the CEOs of these "most admired companies" have attributes in common? Explain your answer.

Strategic Surfing
CEO Express is a Web site designed specifically for busy executives. The site contains a menu of links to sites that appeal to CEOs and other business leaders. A similar site is referred to as The CEO Homepage. This site contains links to on-line versions of business publications valuable to CEOs and other top managers.

http://www.ceoexpress.com
http://ceohomepage.com/bizpubs.html

NOTES

1. K. R. Thompson, W. A. Hochwarter, and N. J. Mathys, 1997, Stretch targets: What makes them effective? *Academy of Management Executive* XI, no. 3: 48–59.
2. R. D. Ireland and M. A. Hitt, 1998, Achieving and maintaining strategic competitiveness in the 21st century: The role of strategic leadership, *Academy of Management Executive* XII, in press; D. Lei, M. A. Hitt, and R. Bettis, 1996, Dynamic core competencies through meta-learning and strategic context, *Journal of Management* 22: 547–567.
3. E. Ramstad, 1998, Compaq CEO takes tricky curves fast, *Wall Street Journal*, January 5, B4.
4. G. McWilliams, I. Sager, P. C. Judge, and P. Burrows, 1998,

Power play: How the Compaq-Digital deal will reshape the entire world of computers, *Business Week*, February 9, 90–97.

5. Special Report: The 25 top managers of the year, 1998, *Business Week*, January 12, 54–68.

6. H. Gardner, 1995, *Leading Minds: An Anatomy of Leadership* (New York: Basic Books); S. Sherman, 1995, How tomorrow's best leaders are learning their stuff, *Fortune*, November 27, 90–102.

7. J. B. Quinn, P. Anderson, and S. Finkelstein, 1996, Managing professional intellect: Making the most of the best, *Harvard Business Review* 74, no. 2: 71–80.

8. M. Loeb, 1994, Where leaders come from, *Fortune*, September 19, 241–242.

9. M. F. R. Kets de Vries, 1995, *Life and Death in the Executive Fast Lane* (San Francisco: Jossey-Bass).

10. G. Hamel and C. K. Prahalad, 1993, Strategy as stretch and leverage, *Harvard Business Review* 71, no. 2: 75–84.

11. Sherman, How tomorrow's best, 99; R. Calori, G. Johnson, and P. Sarnin, 1994, CEOs' cognitive maps and the scope of the organization, *Strategic Management Journal* 15: 437–457.

12. Loeb, Where leaders come from, 241; N. Nohria and J. D. Berkley, 1994, Whatever happened to the take-charge manager?, *Harvard Business Review* 72, no. 1: 128–137.

13. M. Hammer and S. A. Stanton, 1997, The power of reflection, *Fortune*, November 24, 291–296.

14. S. Finkelstein and D. C. Hambrick, 1996, *Strategic Leadership: Top Executives and Their Effects on Organizations* (St. Paul, Minn.: West Publishing Company), 2.

15. J. A. Byrne and J. Reingold, 1997, Wanted: A few good CEOs, *Business Week*, August 11, 64–70.

16. Sherman, How tomorrow's best, 102.

17. H. P. Gunz and R. M. Jalland, 1996, Managerial careers and business strategy, *Academy of Management Review* 21: 718–756.

18. C. M. Christensen, 1997, Making strategy: Learning by doing, *Harvard Business Review* 75, no. 6: 141–156; M. A. Hitt, B. W. Keats, H. E. Harback, and R. D. Nixon, 1994, Rightsizing: Building and maintaining strategic leadership and long-term competitiveness, *Organizational Dynamics* 23: 18–32; R. L. Priem and D. A. Harrison, 1994, Exploring strategic judgment: Methods for testing the assumptions of prescriptive contingency theories, *Strategic Management Journal* 15: 311–324.

19. M. J. Waller, G. P. Huber, and W. H. Glick, 1995, Functional background as a determinant of executives' selective perception, *Academy of Management Journal* 38: 943–974; N. Rajagopalan, A. M. Rasheed, and D. K. Datta, 1993, Strategic decision processes: Critical review and future directions, *Journal of Management* 19: 349–384.

20. Finkelstein and Hambrick, *Strategic Leadership*, 26–34; D. C. Hambrick and E. Abrahamson, 1995, Assessing managerial discretion across industries: A multimethod approach, *Academy of Management Journal* 38: 1427–1441; D. C. Hambrick and S. Finkelstein, 1987, Managerial discretion: A bridge between polar views of organizational outcomes, in B. Staw and L. L. Cummings (eds.), *Research in Organizational Behavior* (Greenwich, CT: JAI Press), 369–406.

21. R. C. Mayer, J. H. Davis, and F. D. Schoorman, 1995, An integrative model of organizational trust, *Academy of Management Review* 20: 709–734.

22. N. Rajagopalan and D. K. Datta, 1996, CEO characteristics:

Does industry matter?, *Academy of Management Journal* 39: 197–215.

23. L. M. Fisher, 1997, Novell selects Internet guru to lead company, *The New York Times* on the Web, http://www.nytimes.com, March 19.

24. A. C. Amason, 1996, Distinguishing the effects of functional and dysfunctional conflict on strategic decision making: Resolving a paradox for top management teams, *Academy of Management Journal* 39: 123–148; Priem and Harrison, Exploring strategic judgment, 311.

25. C. M. Farkas and P. De Backer, 1996, There are only five ways to lead, *Fortune*, January 15, 109–112.

26. R. E. Stross, 1997, Mr. Gates builds his brain trust, *Fortune*, December 8, 84–98.

27. T. A. Stewart, 1997, Why dumb things happen to smart companies, *Fortune*, June 23, 159–160.

28. H. A. Krishnan, 1997, Diversification and top management team complementarity: Is performance improved by merging similar or dissimilar teams?, *Strategic Management Journal* 18: 361–374; J. G. Michel and D. C. Hambrick, 1992, Diversification posture and top management team characteristics, *Academy of Management Journal* 35: 9–37.

29. A. L. Iaquito and J. W. Fredrickson, 1997, Top management team agreement about the strategic decision process: A test of some of its determinants and consequences, *Strategic Management Journal* 18: 63–75; K. G. Smith, D. A. Smith, J. D. Olian, H. P. Sims, Jr., D. P. O'Bannon, and J. A. Scully, 1994, Top management team demography and process: The role of social integration and communication, *Administrative Science Quarterly* 39: 412–438.

30. Amason, Distinguishing the effects, 127.

31. D. C. Hambrick, T. S. Cho, and M. J. Chen, 1996, The influence of top management team heterogeneity on firms' competitive moves, *Administrative Science Quarterly* 41: 659–684.

32. J. J. Keller, 1997, AT&T's board faces many twists and turns in search for new CEO, *Wall Street Journal*, October 13, A1, A6.

33. Finkelstein and Hambrick, *Strategic Leadership*, 148.

34. C. C. Miller, L. M. Burke, and W. H. Glick, 1998, Cognitive diversity among upper-echelon executives: Implications for strategic decision processes, *Strategic Management Journal* 19: 39–58.

35. D. K. Datta and J. P. Guthrie, 1994, Executive succession: Organizational antecedents of CEO characteristics, *Strategic Management Journal* 15: 569–577; M. A. Hitt and R. D. Ireland, 1986, Relationships among corporate-level distinctive competencies, diversification strategy, corporate structure, and performance, *Journal of Management Studies* 23: 401–416; M. A. Hitt and R. D. Ireland, 1985, Corporate distinctive competence, strategy, industry, and performance, *Strategic Management Journal* 6: 273–293.

36. W. Boeker, 1997, Strategic change: The influence of managerial characteristics and organizational growth, *Academy of Management Journal* 40: 152–170; W. Boeker, 1997, Executive migration and strategic change: The effect of top manager movement on product-market entry, *Administrative Science Quarterly* 42: 213–236.

37. M. E. Wiersema and K. Bantel, 1992, Top management team demography and corporate strategic change, *Academy of Management Journal* 35: 91–121; K. Bantel and S. Jackson,

1989, Top management and innovations in banking: Does the composition of the top team make a difference? *Strategic Management Journal* 10: 107–124.

38. I. Sager and A. Cortese, 1995, At IBM, the great shrink-down may be over, *Business Week*, September 25, 58.

39. R. Narisetti, 1997, IBM's Gerstner to stay five more years, *Wall Street Journal*, November 27, A3, A14.

40. W. Q. Judge, Jr. and C. P. Zeithaml, 1992, Institutional and strategic choice perspectives on board involvement in the strategic decision process, *Academy of Management Journal* 35: 766–794; J. A. Pearce II and S. A. Zahra, 1991, The relative power of CEOs and boards of directors: Associations with corporate performance, *Strategic Management Journal* 12: 135–154.

41. J. D. Westphal and E. J. Zajac, 1995, Who shall govern? CEO/board power, demographic similarity, and new director selection, *Administrative Science Quarterly* 40: 60.

42. Ibid., 66; E. J. Zajac and J. D. Westphal, 1995, Accounting for the explanations of CEO compensation: Substance and symbolism, *Administrative Science Quarterly* 40: 283–308.

43. B. K. Boyd, 1995, CEO duality and firm performance: A contingency model, *Strategic Management Journal* 16: 301.

44. C. M. Daily and D. R. Dalton, 1995, CEO and director turnover in failing firms: An illusion of change? *Strategic Management Journal* 16: 393–400.

45. R. Albanese, M. T. Dacin, and I. C. Harris, 1997, Agents as stewards, *Academy of Management Review* 22: 609–611; J. H. Davis, F. D. Schoorman, and L. Donaldson, 1997, Toward a stewardship theory of management, *Academy of Management Review* 22: 20–47.

46. B. R. Baliga and R. C. Moyer, 1996, CEO duality and firm performance: What's the fuss? *Strategic Management Journal* 17: 41–53.

47. J. D. Westphal and E. J. Zajac, 1997, Defections from the inner circle: Social exchange, reciprocity and diffusion of board independence in U.S. corporations, *Administrative Science Quarterly* 161–183; A. K. Buchholtz and B. A. Ribbens, 1994, Role of chief executive officers in takeover resistance: Effects of CEO incentives and individual characteristics, *Academy of Management Journal* 37: 554–579.

48. Rajagopalan and Datta, CEO characteristics, 201.

49. R. A. Johnson, R. E. Hoskisson, and M. A. Hitt, 1993, Board involvement in restructuring: The effect of board versus managerial controls and characteristics, *Strategic Management Journal* 14 (Special Summer Issue): 33–50.

50. B. K. Boyd, 1995, CEO duality and firm performance: A contingency model, *Strategic Management Journal* 16: 301–312.

51. T. A. Stewart, 1998, Why leadership matters, *Fortune*, March 2, 71–82.

52. Sherman, How tomorrow's best, 92.

53. D. Woodruff and M. Maremont, 1995, GM learns to love an outsider, *Business Week*, July 3, 32.

54. Datta and Guthrie, Executive succession, 570.

55. Finkelstein and Hambrick, *Strategic Leadership*, 180–181.

56. D. Miller, 1991, Stale in the saddle: CEO tenure and the match between organization and environment, *Management Science* 37: 34–52.

57. S. L. Hwang, 1995, RJR's CEO Harper quits his position, *Wall Street Journal*, December 6, A3, A4.

58. S. L. Hwang, 1998, At Nabisco, the new chief walks into a hot kitchen, *Wall Street Journal*, February 5, B1, B2.

59. J. E. Ettlie, 1996, Review of *The Perpetual Enterprise Machine: Seven Keys to Corporate Renewal through Successful Product and Process Development*, E. Bowman (ed.), (New York: Oxford University Press), appearing in *Academy of Management Review* 21: 294–298; Hitt et al., Rightsizing, 20.

60. J. C. Collins and J. I. Porras, 1996, Building your company's vision, *Harvard Business Review* 74, no. 5: 65–77.

61. C. M. Falbe, M. P. Kriger, and P. Miesing, 1995, Structure and meaning of organizational vision, *Academy of Management Journal* 39: 740–769.

62. B. Wysocki, Jr., 1995, As firms downsize, business economists find jobs dwindling, *Wall Street Journal*, October 9, Al, A8.

63. W. L. Gardner and B. J. Avolio, 1998, The charismatic relationship: A dramaturgical perspective, *Academy of Management Review* 23: 32–58.

64. Finkelstein and Hambrick, 1996, *Strategic Leadership*, 69–72; P. Sellers, 1996, What exactly is charisma? *Fortune*, January 15, 68–75.

65. T. Smart, 1996, Jack Welch's encore, *Business Week*, October 28, 154–160.

66. J. A. Byrne, 1997, The CEO and the board, *Business Week*, September 15, 107–116.

67. P. R. Nayyar and K. A. Bantel, 1994, Competitive agility: A source of competitive advantage based on speed and variety, in P. Shrivastava, A. Huff, and J. Dutton (eds.), *Advances in Strategic Management* 10A, (Greenwich, CT: JAI Press), 193–222.

68. R. F. Maruca, 1994, The right way to go global: An interview with Whirlpool CEO David Whitwam, *Harvard Business Review* 72, no. 2: 136.

69. Lei, Hitt, and Bettis, Dynamic core competencies.

70. R. N. Askenas, L. J. DeMonaco, and S. C. Francis, 1998, Making the deal real: How GE Capital integrates acquisitions, *Harvard Business Review* 76, no. 1: 165–178.

71. B. Nussbaum, 1988, Needed: Human capital, *Business Week*, September 19, 100–102.

72. S. A. Snell and M. A. Youndt, 1995, Human resource management and firm performance: Testing a contingency model of executive controls, *Journal of Management* 21: 711–737.

73. D. Ulrich, 1998, A new mandate for human resources, *Harvard Business Review* 76, no. 1: 124–134.

74. Snell and Youndt, Human resource, 711; K. Chilton, 1994, *The Global Challenge of American Manufacturers* (St. Louis, MO: Washington University, Center for the Study of American Business); J. Pfeffer, 1994, *Competitive Advantage Through People* (Cambridge, MA: Harvard Business School Press), 4.

75. H. W. Jenkins, Jr., 1996, What price job security?, *Wall Street Journal*, March 26, Al9.

76. J. S. Lublin, 1996, An overseas stint can be a ticket to the top, *Wall Street Journal*, January 29, Bl, B2.

77. M. G. Harvey and M. R. Buckley, 1997, Managing inpatriates: Building a global core competency, *Journal of World Business* 32, no. 1: 35–52.

78. R. Frank, 1996, Enrico to lead new generation at top of Pepsi, *Wall Street Journal*, February 23, B2, B5.

469

79. H. Rudnitsky, 1996, One hundred sixty companies for the price of one, *Forbes*, February 26, 56–62.

80. L. Grant, 1995, GE: The envelope, please, *Fortune*, June 26, 89–90.

81. B. Morris, 1997, If women ran the world it would look a lot like Avon, *Fortune*, July 21, 74–79.

82. J. Nocera, 1996, Living with layoffs, *Fortune*, April 1, 69–71.

83. Chrysler CEO calls downsizing the price of competitiveness, 1996, *Dallas Morning News*, March 19, D8.

84. F. R. Bleakley, 1997, New round of layoffs may be beginning, *Wall Street Journal*, November 13, A2.

85. M. A. Hitt, R. E. Hoskisson, J. S. Harrison, and B. Summers, 1994, Human capital and strategic competitiveness in the 1990s, *Journal of Management Development* 13, no. 1: 35–46; C. R. Greer and T. C. Ireland, 1992, Organizational and financial correlates of a contrarian human resource investment strategy, *Academy of Management Journal* 35: 956–984.

86. C. L. Martin, C. K. Parsons, and N. Bennett, 1995, The influence of employee involvement program membership during downsizing: Attitudes toward the employer and the union, *Journal of Management* 21: 879–890.

87. C. M. Fiol, 1991, Managing culture as a competitive resource: An identity-based view of sustainable competitive advantage, *Journal of Management* 17: 191–211; J. B. Barney, 1986, Organizational culture: Can it be a source of sustained competitive advantage?, *Academy of Management Review* 11: 656–665.

88. S. Ghoshal and C. A. Bartlett, 1994, Linking organizational context and managerial action: The dimensions of quality of management, *Strategic Management Journal* 15: 91–112.

89. Sherman, How tomorrow's best, 102.

90. How can big companies keep the entrepreneurial spirit alive?, 1995, *Harvard Business Review* 73, no. 6: 183–192; S. G. Scott and R. A. Bruce, 1994, Determinants of innovative behavior: A path model of individual innovation in the workplace, *Academy of Management Journal* 37: 580–607.

91. Thermo Electron home page, 1998, http://www.thermo.com, company history.

92. C. A. Bartlett and S. Goshal, 1997, The myth of the generic manager: New personal competencies for new managerial roles, *California Management Review* 40, no. 1: 92–116.

93. J. Webber, W. Zellner, and G. Smith, 1998, Loud noises at Bombardier, *Business Week*, January 26, 94–95.

94. G. T. Lumpkin and G. G. Dess, 1996, Clarifying the entrepreneurial orientation construct and linking it to performance, *Academy of Management Review* 21: 135–172.

95. Ibid., 142.

96. Ibid., 137.

97. Ireland and Hitt, Achieving and maintaining strategic competitiveness in the 21st century.

98. J. E. Dutton, S. J. Ashford, R. M. O'Neill, E. Hayes, and E. E. Wierba, 1997, Reading the wind: How middle managers assess the context for selling issues to top managers, *Strategic Management Journal* 18: 407–425.

99. S. Sherman, 1995, Wanted: Company change agents, *Fortune*, December 11, 197–198.

100. A. E. Serwer, 1997, Michael Dell turns the PC world inside out, *Fortune*, September 8, 76–86.

101. R. Jacob, 1995, The resurrection of Michael Dell, *Fortune*, September 18, 117.

102. Ibid., 118.

103. A. Goldstein, 1995, Dell powers up, *Dallas Morning News*, September 19, D1, D4.

104. T. M. Hour and J. C. Carter, 1995, Getting it done: New roles for senior executives, *Harvard Business Review* 73, no. 6: 133–145.

105. Serwer, Michael Dell turns the PC world inside out, 84.

106. M. Hammer and J. Champy, 1995, *Reengineering the Corporation* (New York: HarperCollins).

107. Ibid.

108. S. Murray, 1997, BP alters atmosphere amid turnaround, *Wall Street Journal*, September 17, A19.

109. D. J. Brass, K. D. Butterfield, and B. C. Skaggs, 1998, Relationships and unethical behavior: A social network perspective, *Academy of Management Review* 23: 14–31.

110. J. M. Lozano, 1996, Ethics and management: A controversial issue, *Journal of Business Ethics* 15: 227–236; J. Mitchell, 1996, Professor leads attack on big business, *Dallas Morning News*, March 17, H6; J. Milton-Smith, 1995, Ethics as excellence: A strategic management perspective, *Journal of Business Ethics* 14: 683–693.

111. C. W. L. Hill, 1990, Cooperation, opportunism, and the invisible hand: Implications for transaction cost theory, *Academy of Management Review* 15: 500–513.

112. M. Zey, 1993, *Banking on Fraud* (New York: Aldine De Gruyter).

113. D. Blalock, 1996, Study shows many execs are quick to write off ethics, *Wall Street Journal*, March 26, Cl, C3; A. P. Brief, J. M. Dukerich, P. R. Brown, and J. F. Brett, 1996, What's wrong with the Treadway Commission Report? Experimental analysis of the effects of personal values and codes of conduct on fraudulent financial reporting, *Journal of Business Ethics* 15: 183–198; G. Miles, 1993, In search of ethical profits: Insights from strategic management, *Journal of Business Ethics* 12: 219–225.

114. Zajac and Westphal, Accounting for the explanations of CEO compensation.

115. S. R. Premeaux and R. W. Mondy, 1993, Linking management behavior to ethical philosophy, *Journal of Business Ethics* 12: 219–225.

116. Brief et al., What's wrong?

117. B. K. Burton and J. P. Near, 1995, Estimating the incidence of wrongdoing and whistle-blowing: Results of a study using randomized response technique, *Journal of Business Ethics* 14: 17–30.

118. Milton-Smith, Ethics as excellence, 685.

119. Brief et al., What's wrong?, 194; P. E. Murphy, 1995, Corporate ethics statements: Current status and future prospects, *Journal of Business Ethics* 14: 727–740.

120. L. Lagnado, E. M. Rodriguez, and G. Jaffe, 1997, How 'out of a loop' was Dr. Frist during Columbia's expansion?, *Wall Street Journal*, September 4, A1, A6.

121. L. Lagnado, 1997, Columbia wants hospitals to name ethics officers, *Wall Street Journal*, December 12, B7.

122. L. J. Kirsch, 1996, The management of complex tasks in organizations: Controlling the systems development process, *Organization Science* 7: 1–21.

123. R. Simons, 1994, How new top managers use control systems as levers of strategic renewal, *Strategic Management Journal* 15: 170–171.

124. K. J. Laverty, 1996, Economic "short-termism": The debate, the unresolved issues, and the implications for management practice and research, *Academy of Management Review* 21: 825–860.

125. M. A. Hitt, R. E. Hoskisson, and R. D. Ireland, 1990, Mergers and acquisitions and managerial commitment to innovation in M-form firms, *Strategic Management Journal* 11 (Special Summer Issue): 29–47.

126. R. A. Johnson, Antecedents and outcomes of corporate refocusing, *Journal of Management* 22: 437–481; R. E. Hoskisson and M. A. Hitt, 1994, *Downscoping: How to Tame the Diversified Firm* (New York: Oxford University Press).

127. Ireland and Hitt, Achieving and maintaining strategic competitiveness in the 21st century.

Corporate Entrepreneurship and Innovation

CHAPTER 13

Learning Objectives

After reading this chapter, you should be able to:

1. Describe three strategic approaches used to produce and manage innovation.

2. Discuss the two sources of internal corporate venturing: autonomous strategic behavior and induced strategic behavior.

3. Define three types of innovation.

4. Discuss how the capability to manage cross-functional teams can facilitate implementation of internal corporate ventures and innovation efforts.

5. Explain how strategic alliances can be used to produce innovation.

6. Discuss how a firm can create value by acquiring another company to gain access to its innovations or innovative capabilities.

7. Explain how large firms use venture capital to increase the effectiveness of their innovation efforts.

8. Describe the resources, capabilities, and core competencies of small versus large firms in producing innovation.

Killer Chips, Wimps, and Other Things

Intel and Hewlett-Packard are collaborating to develop a new super chip called the Merced. The project began in 1994 with the purpose of developing a more powerful chip to replace the Pentium, today's ultimate chip. The Merced, due for entry into the market in 1999, entails a new chip design. Predictions are that the Merced will be three times faster than the top Pentium. The Merced's speed and parallel processing capabilities should allow the top personal computers to handle tasks now reserved for the larger mainframe computers. If the chip works as planned, it should solidify Intel's hold on the market, eliminating any serious competition. Intel currently has about 80 percent of the microprocessor market for personal computers. Some analysts have predicted that the Merced will ensure that Intel dominates the microprocessor market for at least another 50 years. Hewlett-Packard expects to be considered one of the technology pioneers, which should boost its presence in the personal computer market.

http://www.intel.com
http://www.hp.com

Intel competitors are preparing for the Merced with their own strategic moves. For example, in a move that seems to suggest that microprocessors are for wimps, Motorola is abandoning the market for the primary microprocessor chips for personal computers. Motorola will now emphasize customized highly integrated circuits. It will focus on the system chip or microcontroller. This action suggests that Motorola no longer will try to compete with Intel. However, other chip makers, including Intel, are also entering new markets. For example, Texas Instruments, SJS-Thomson Electronics, and National Semiconductor are all entering specialty markets although different ones from Motorola. These firms are planning to build chips that fit into small devices such as tiny cell phones with Web access, e-mail access in automobiles, and PCs that will fit into a wallet. Some of these firms, such as SJS-Thomson Electronics, have already been successful in the system chip business. Thus, Motorola will be competing in a crowd.

Because of the expected doubling of demand, 35 new chip fabrication plants are planned by the year 2002. These plants represent a major effort. They normally require about 600,000 square feet of space, with access to an amount of water equivalent to the needs of a city with 80,000 residents. Such an undertaking may require as many as 2,000 construction workers. Within the last decade IBM took three years to complete a fabrication plant. However, in 1997, a fabrication plant was completed in half the time by a joint venture between IBM and Toshiba. Samsung built a new plant in Austin, Texas, in about the same amount of time. Thus, speed is of the essence not only in the development of new products as argued in Chapter 1 but also in the development of the plants to manufacture the new products.

Intel is not stopping with the Merced. It is also entering the market to provide support for broadcasters on digital television. In 1997, Intel announced it was investing $100 million in alliances with several other firms to develop content to be broadcast over digital TV. While still closely aligned with Microsoft and Compaq to set standards for personal computers, this action represents a break from Microsoft and Compaq's position that they would only support digital TV formats. Intel is leading the charge to ensure that interactive programs will be able to run on any delivery platform (e.g., satellite TV, cable TV) as well as digital broadcasts. Thus, Intel is not only a large and powerful company, it is also entrepreneurial. In fact, one of the main reasons that it has maintained its dominant position in the market is because of its entrepreneurial efforts.

SOURCES: D. Kirkpatrick, 1998, Three promising (non-Intel) chipmakers, *Fortune*, http://www. pathfinder.com/fortune/digitalwatch; J. Markoff, 1998, Inside Intel, the future is riding on a new chip, *The New York Times*, April 5, section 3, 1 and 6; P. Siekman, 1998, The race to build and staff America's chip plants, *Fortune*, http://www.pathfinder.com/fortune/1997; G. McWilliams, 1997, Microprocessors are for wimps, *Business Week*, December 15, 134–135; B. Schlender, 1997, Killer chip, *Fortune*, http://www.pathfinder.com/fortune/1997; D. Takahashi, 1997, Intel to support broadcasters on digital TV, *Wall Street Journal*, December 5, B3.

The opening case illustrates the importance of entrepreneurial activities for large firms, long thought the purview only of small firms. Intel is developing a new product that is likely to help it continue to dominate the microprocessor chip market. In fact, Intel's entrepreneurial capabilities have helped it develop and maintain its current dominance with the Pentium chip. The effect of Intel's entrepreneurship is substantial. One analyst predicts that its new chip, the Merced, will help it maintain its dominance in the market for another 50 years. Evidence of this possibility is shown by such large competitors as Motorola moving out of the microprocessor chip market to avoiding trying to compete directly with Intel.

Entrepreneurship is important for both large and small firms. Regardless of their size, firms in most industries have to be innovative to survive in global markets. Thus, the development of new products and new processes along with innovation in other areas of the business may be required for survival in competitive global markets. Being entrepreneurial entails risk and with risk there will be failure. Interestingly, the new competitive landscape described in Chapter 1 requires that firms take risks. Firms must take chances to align with a changing landscape. The Chinese word for crisis has two characters. The first represents danger and the other represents opportunity.[1] This is similar to entrepreneurship; it represents both risk and opportunity. Because of the clear need, many firms are increasing their entrepreneurial efforts. New businesses are being formed, by large and small firms and individuals regularly. In fact, it is estimated that approximately 3.5 million businesses are formed annually in the U.S.[2]

Relating back to Figure 1.1 in Chapter 1, our focus herein is on a critical element for implementing strategy—producing and managing innovation. (Innovation may also provide feedback for the formulation of new strategies; see the feedback loop in Figure 1.1.) In addition to the general need for innovation for a firm to be competitive, innovation is a direct requirement of specific strategies such as differentiation (product innovation) and cost leadership (process innovation). Additionally, innovation is an important capability associated with competitive dynamics (see Chapter 5). This chapter examines the resources and skills required to produce and manage innovation. Although this chapter emphasizes innovation in large companies, evidence shows that they are not the sole generators of product and process innovations. Many small and medium-sized firms are also effective innovators. Moreover, large companies often develop relationships and alliances with smaller firms to help them produce innovations. Because of the importance of their innovative abilities, the chapter's final section addresses the different capabilities of small firms that produce and manage innovation.

INNOVATION AND CORPORATE ENTREPRENEURSHIP

Some evidence suggests that effective innovation results in a sustainable competitive advantage. More specifically, innovations that are (1) difficult for competitors to imitate, (2) able to provide significant value to customers, (3) timely, and (4) capable of being exploited commercially through existing core competencies help firms develop competitive advantages.[3] Because of the link between the development of competitive advantages and the earning of above-average returns, many companies, especially those active in the global marketplace, are interested in producing innovations and in effectively managing the innovation process.

Need for Innovation and Entrepreneurship

The technological revolution and greater competition in international markets have increased the competitive importance of innovation.[4] Research has shown that firms competing in global industries that invest more in innovation also achieve the highest returns.[5] In fact, investors often react positively to new product introductions, thereby increasing the price of a firm's stock. Thus, entrepreneurship is an essential feature of high-performance firms.[6] William R. Howell, chairman of the JCPenney Company, noted that you can never "rest on your laurels. Rather, you have to try to stay ahead of the curve since competitors tend to pick up on your successes."[7]

Entrepreneurship and Innovation Defined

Entrepreneurs seek to create the future. To do so, they must take risks and be aggressive, proactive, and innovative.[8] Furthermore, they must identify anomalies in markets or opportunities where no current market exists.[9] Another important feature of entrepreneurship is growth. In fact, some authors suggest that growth is a primary differentiator of entrepreneurial firms from small businesses. Thus, effective entrepreneurial firms are fast-growth businesses. These fast-growth firms create new businesses.[10]

Corporate entrepreneurship is the set of capabilities possessed by a firm to produce or acquire new goods or services and manage the innovation process.

Corporate entrepreneurship includes the commitments, mind-sets, and actions firms take to develop and manage innovations. Formally, **corporate entrepreneurship** is the set of capabilities possessed by a firm to produce or acquire new goods or services and manage the innovation process.[11] Corporate entrepreneurship is based on effective product design and successful commercialization. Because it is a set of capabilities that results in the effective *and* efficient design and manufacture of products, corporate entrepreneurship can be a basis for strategic competitiveness.

In U.S. companies, the role of corporate entrepreneurship in both effectiveness and efficiency has been recognized only somewhat recently. After World War II, for example, U.S. manufacturers sought to satisfy worldwide demand for their goods and services by focusing on mass-production techniques that allowed them to produce products in large quantities. This focus resulted in an opportunity for other producers (e.g., those in Japan and what was then West Germany) to use a different set of strategic actions.[12] The focus of U.S. firms on quantity allowed inefficiencies, which the Japanese and the Germans exploited commercially with high levels of product quality. By the 1970s, Japanese manufacturers were more competitive than their U.S. rivals as a result of the development and use of a host of product, process, and managerial innovations. Workers in Japanese factories, for example, exercised a degree of responsibility not allowed in U.S. factories. In Japanese factories, the activities of everyone—from top-level managers to line workers to suppliers—were combined into a tightly integrated whole. Firms committed to these methods set their sights on perfection: "continually declining costs, zero defects, zero inventories, and endless product variety."[13] More has been learned about operating a manufacturing enterprise in the 1980s and 1990s than in all of the rest of the century. Regional dominance no longer exists. Global markets and competition dominate the new competitive landscape. Thus, innovations in both manufacturing and service companies are necessary for survival in a highly competitive world.[14]

Invention is the act of creating or developing a new product or process idea.

Innovation is the process of creating a commercial product from invention.

Imitation is adoption of the innovation by similar firms.

Joseph Schumpeter's classic work on management of the innovation process suggests that firms engage in three types of innovative activity.[15] **Invention** is the act of creating or developing a new product or process idea. **Innovation** is the process of creating a commercial product from invention. Finally, **imitation** is adoption of the innovation by similar firms. Imitation usually leads to product or process standardization. In the United States in particular, the most critical of these activities has been innovation. Many firms are able to create ideas that lead to in-

476

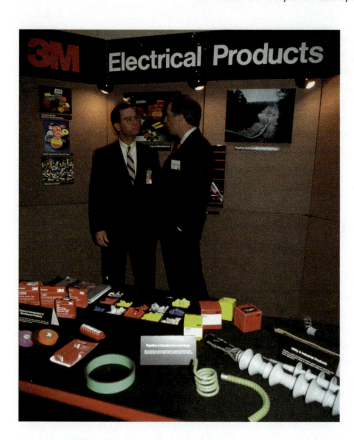

3M has been very successful at commercializing inventions. Thus, the firm is known to be highly innovative.

477

vention, but commercializing those inventions through innovation has, at times, proved to be difficult.

Strategic leaders, managers, and entrepreneurs all have roles that are critical to effective corporate entrepreneurship.[16] Especially with regard to corporate entrepreneurship, the strategic leader's role is to inspire an organization's members to work cooperatively in the pursuit of meaningful outcomes. Leaders and their words assume symbolic value to inspire organizational members to accomplish a firm's strategic intent and strategic mission. Strategic leaders have emphasized innovation at 3M for years. This company has introduced over 50,000 new products. George Allen, retired vice president of research and development at 3M, states, "3M innovates for the same reason that cows eat grass. It is a part of our DNA to do so."[17] Firms such as 3M use innovation to build a competitive advantage. Corporate entrepreneurship that produces innovation can provide a platform on which industry leadership can be built.[18]

Middle- and lower-level managers are promoters and caretakers of organizational efficiency. Their work is especially important once a product idea has been commercialized and the organization necessary to support and promote it has been formed.[19] Middle- and lower-level managers are critical to creating and implementing (commercializing) innovations at 3M.

Entrepreneurs are people who are the first to see an economic opportunity and seek to take advantage of it.[20] Often, entrepreneurs' commercial insights are not initially shared by others, forcing them to live with the social burden of not being accepted until the economic value of their insights is confirmed.

The most effective entrepreneurs are often those who work against existing product standards by behaving as if they do not exist. This mind-set seems to facilitate creativity and innovation. Within large organizations, however, effective corporate entrepreneurship can be difficult to establish and support. In large organizations, people engaged in entrepreneurial practices must fully understand the corporate culture and mind-set (see Chapter 1) that drive the firm's innovation process and the attributes of the structure, controls, and reward systems within which organizational work is completed.

STRATEGIC FOCUS

The Razor's Edge: An Innovation Machine

478

Gillette worked for six years to create the successor to its highly popular razor, the Sensor. The Sensor is the world's most successful razor, helping Gillette to maintain double digit growth over a period of years. In 1996 alone, Gillette achieved an increase in sales of almost 43 percent. The firm has been able to grow at phenomenal rates, particularly for a company operating in consumer goods industries, largely because of its innovation. In fact, it has been labeled an innovation machine.

Currently, about 41 percent of sales come from products introduced in the last five years. The CEO's goal is to increase that to 50 percent. Essentially, Gillette invests heavily to be the market technology leader and produce innovative products that can be sold at premium prices. This approach has paid off for Gillette. A recent study of the top 50 consumer goods companies showed that only 17 earned above the industry average growth in sales and profits for 1985–1990. Only seven of the seventeen earned above the industry average for the 1990–1995 period. Gillette was one of these seven companies. To continue significant growth in sales and profits, Gillette invests over $200 million in R&D. This annual allocation to R&D is approximately twice the average for consumer goods firms.

Its R&D is rigorous in testing newly developed products. To select the best Sensor razor design, the firm produced seven different versions and tested each one. The one design that was selected incorporated many of the best features of the other six before it was taken to the market. There were over 15,000 tests of this razor before it was placed on the market. Gillette also invests money in process innovation. It is expert at designing ways to produce its products cheaper. Thus, Gillette integrates both process and product innovation, something that few other firms are able to do.

While Gillette is best known for razors and blades, it is also a market leader in batteries (Duracell), dental care products (Oral-B), toiletries (Right Guard, White Rain), small appliances (Braun), and writing products (Parker Pen, Liquid Paper). In addition, Gillette receives over 60 percent of its revenue from outside the United States. It has significant sales of its products in Europe (particularly the United Kingdom) and Asia (particularly Japan). Its sales are also growing in South America. Gillette sells its products in more than 200 countries and has manufacturing facilities in 27 different countries. Gillette is clearly a firm that is well prepared to enter the twenty-first century.

SOURCES: W. C. Symonds and C. Matlack, 1998, Gillette's Edge: The secret of a great innovation machine? Never relax, *Business Week*, January 10, http://www.businessweek.com.premium; The Gillette Company, February 1, 1998, http://www.bigmouth.pathfinder.com/mon...vers/profiles/byid; The Gillette Company, February 1, 1998, http://www.oakland.co.uk/gilbert; The Gillette Company, February 1, 1998, *Hoovers Online*, http://www.hoovers.com.cgi-bin/brand_wp_mlist.cgi.

As described in the Strategic Focus, the Gillette Company is an excellent example of corporate entrepreneurship. It is a highly innovative company and is able to bring new products successfully to the market. It is a technology leader in all of the industries in which it competes and earns a significant amount of its annual revenue from new products introduced to the market in the last five years. The results of the firm's emphasis on innovation is also clear. Gillette has been one of the highest performing consumer goods firms for more than a decade. Its growth in sales and profits have averaged more than 17 percent annually for the last 10 years. Thus, we can conclude that corporate entrepreneurship is alive and well and, at least in some firms, such as Gillette, leads to strategic competitiveness.

While innovativeness in Japanese firms has received some attention during the last two decades, U.S. firms continue to be perceived as the most innovative. However, corporate entrepreneurship and innovation are not limited to the United States and Japan.

International Entrepreneurship

In the late 1970s, Chinese economic reforms began to allow more autonomy to market forces and legalized private entrepreneurship. Many Chinese people have more disposable income, are better informed, and have more personal freedom than at any time since 1949 when the Communists took control of the country. The outcomes are primarily the result of the reforms unleashing the entrepreneurial spirit of the Chinese people. In fact, considerable entrepreneurship is currently being exhibited in the People's Republic of China.[21] Some significant tension has arisen between the need for individualism to promote entrepreneurship and the more traditional Chinese cultural characteristics of collectivism. Individualism, a dominant characteristic in U.S. society, is important to the creativity needed for entrepreneurial behavior. Furthermore, research has shown that entrepreneurship declines as collectivism is emphasized. The same research, however, shows that exceptionally high levels of individualism can be dysfunctional for entrepreneurship as well. Thus, a balance is needed between individual initiative and the spirit of cooperation and group ownership of innovation. For firms to achieve corporate entrepreneurship, they must provide appropriate autonomy and incentives for individual initiative to surface, but also promote cooperation and group ownership of an innovation if it is to be implemented successfully. Thus, corporate entrepreneurship often requires teams of people with unique skills and resources.[22]

The importance of balancing individualism and collectivism for entrepreneurship is perhaps best exemplified by the success of Asian entrepreneurs in North America. Some have argued that the success of those of Chinese and Korean origin in North America was due to their industriousness, perseverance, frugality, and emphasis on family. Research shows, however, that there are other traits that promote their success. In North America, these individuals are allowed the autonomy necessary for creativity and entrepreneurial behavior. However, their cultural background emphasizes collectivism, which helps them promote cooperation and group ownership of innovation.[23]

Interestingly, Chinese entrepreneurs operating in China have several character traits that are similar to those of U.S. entrepreneurs, for example, achievement, independence, and self-determination. But the two sets of entrepreneurs also have different characteristics, particularly those most influenced by Confucian social philosophy.[24] Entrepreneurs of Chinese and Korean descent who operate in the

U.S. exhibit differences from all other entrepreneurs in the U.S. For example, U.S. Chinese and Korean entrepreneurs invest more equity, obtain more capital from family and friends, and receive fewer loans from financial institutions. Furthermore, they achieve higher profits than their non-Asian counterparts.[25] In contrast, a study of Israeli women showed that industry experience, business skills, and achievement were related to their performance much like other entrepreneurs in the U.S. and Europe. But, unlike others, affiliation with a network for support and advice was positively related to the success of Israeli women entrepreneurs. When they were affiliated with multiple networks, their performance suffered, possibly because of too much and potentially conflicting advice.[26]

There are other dimensions of international entrepreneurship in addition to cross cultural and ethnic comparisons. International entrepreneurship is new with activities that cross national boundaries and have the goal of creating value for the firm.[27] This definition applies to large and small firms alike. Both large and small firms are expanding their operations into new international markets and different countries. For example, in the early 1990s about 20 percent of small firms in the United States were involved in international markets. Today over 50 percent of small firms in the United States are involved in international markets.[28] Research suggests that expanding into international markets can produce higher innovation and firm performance.[29] Research also suggests that high performance firms should be first or second movers (see Chapter 5) in those markets. Order of entry (timing) is even more important than the size of the entry.[30]

INTERNAL CORPORATE VENTURING

Internal corporate venturing is the set of activities used to create inventions and innovations within a single organization.

Composed of two processes, **internal corporate venturing** is the set of activities used to create inventions and innovations within a single organization.[31] The two processes in internal corporate venturing are shown in Figure 13.1. The first in-

FIGURE 13.1 *Model of Internal Corporate Venturing*

Source: Adapted from R. A. Burgelman, 1983, A model of the interactions of strategic behavior, corporate context, and the concept of strategy, *Academy of Management Review* 8: 65.

volves a bottom-up approach to the creation of product and process innovations. **Autonomous strategic behavior** is a bottom-up process in which product champions pursue new product ideas, often through a political process, whereby they develop and coordinate the commercialization of a new good or service until it achieves marketplace success. A **product champion** is a member of an organization who has an entrepreneurial vision of a new good or service and seeks to create support for its commercialization. Autonomous strategic behavior is based on a firm's wellsprings of knowledge and resources that provide the sources of a firm's innovation. Thus, a firm's capabilities and competencies are the basis for new products and processes.[32]

Changing the concept of corporate-level strategy through autonomous strategic behavior results when product championing takes place within strategic and structural contexts (see Figure 13.1). The strategic context refers to the process used to arrive at strategic decisions (often requiring political processes to gain acceptance). The best firms may keep changing the strategic context and strategies because of the continuous changes in the new competitive landscape described in Chapter 1. In fact, well-known author and consultant, Gary Hamel, says that the best companies change the rules of the game. According to Hamel, they often reinvent their existing industry or develop a completely new one. For example, Nike dramatically changed the footwear industry by developing and marketing a premium-priced athletic shoe. In addition, Nike partially changed the game in the industry through a marketing blitz. In other words, firms in the industry could not

Autonomous strategic behavior is a bottom-up process in which product champions pursue new product ideas, often through a political process, whereby they develop and coordinate the commercialization of a new good or service until it achieves marketplace success.

A **product champion** is a member of an organization who has an entrepreneurial vision of a new good or service and seeks to create support for its commercialization.

481

Nike dramatically changed the footwear industry by developing and marketing a premium-priced athletic shoe. The change of rules was successful because it was accompanied by a marketing blitz.

Induced strategic behavior is a top-down process whereby the current strategy and structure foster product innovations that are associated closely with the current strategy and structure.

survive without doing the same thing. This strategy clearly worked for Nike. Since 1986, its stock price has increased by an average of 47 percent annually. Interestingly, there are only a few firms that try to change the rules. Most follow similar strategies because it seems less risky.[33]

Induced strategic behavior is a top-down process whereby the current strategy and structure foster product innovations that are associated closely with the current strategy and structure. In this situation, the strategy in place is filtered through a matching structural hierarchy.

An example of induced strategic behavior is shown by Sony's decision to develop and enter the market for smart portable sensors such as Sony's portable digital assistant, the Navicam. The Navicam is the first of a new product category, portables that can sense their environment. By the year 2000, these portable sensors will serve as personal guides to major museums and shopping malls. Essentially, Sony is developing context-sensitive friendly computers. For automobiles, Sony is developing small robots with mounted TV cameras that can recognize their environment and navigate on their own.[34]

Sony also is attempting to integrate digital technologies into multiple new products in addition to personal computers, including high-resolution television and multimedia eyeglasses. CEO Nobuyuki Idei's strategic intent for Sony is to become a "digital dream kid." Thus, the vision of the firm's new CEO is to integrate digital technologies into multiple new products.[35]

Although Sony has the vision and technical experience to accomplish its goals, large firms often encounter difficulties when striving to pursue internal corporate ventures effectively. The induced processes can dominate and create strategic and structural contexts that become barriers to change. Effective internal corporate venturing processes are established only when both internal political processes and strategic and structural contexts allow a new strategic mission to emerge.

Developing and implementing an entrepreneurial strategy is a highly complex task, partly because of the significant uncertainty in the environment.[36] Such a strategy requires firms to decide and deploy corporate resources to develop new technology and then decide which innovative ideas to pursue and bring to the market, often rapidly. Some researchers have arued that there are strategic windows of opportunity of which firms must take advantage. The windows may be open only for a short period of time; thus, it may not be possible to delay decisions to act.[37] Given the rapid changes and diffusion of technology, traditional valuation and budgeting techniques may not be useful to guide the decisions to invest and develop new technologies.[38] Thus, entrepreneurial strategies and technology investment decisions require a new managerial mind-set as discussed in Chapter 1.

While an important goal of R&D may be to create knowledge, the most successful R&D outputs (e.g., new product ideas) may lead to the development of an internal corporate venture.[39] Internal corporate ventures are often formed for radically new products, products that may not be marketed and distributed effectively by an existing business within the current corporate umbrella.[40] Also, corporate ventures emphasize different resources than independent new ventures. For example, corporate ventures emphasize internal capital, development of proprietary knowledge, and building marketing expertise. Alternatively, independent ventures primarily emphasize external capital, building technical expertise, and development of brand identification. Most corporate ventures can use the corporate reputation and so brand name will be less important. Furthermore, the technical expertise exists, flowing from the larger corporate entity.[41]

Inventing and commercializing new products is becoming more critical in many industries as stated earlier. In addition to having an effective R&D unit to develop new product ideas, firms must have a process and structure that facilitates moving these new product ideas rapidly to the market. Companies such as 3M, Pfizer, and Intel have effective processes to implement new product ideas. For example, 3M introduced 500 new products to the market in 1996, and over 50,000 new products over the life of the firm. Developing and marketing innovative new products has been referred to as a style of corporate behavior. This style, often aggressive about new ideas, change, and risk, must permeate the organization. This style includes a passion for innovation in all that the firm does.[42] It is clear that this passion exists at Toyota as explained in the Strategic Focus. Toyota continues to be a market leader for introducing new products and doing it rapidly. It has introduced a new concept auto in 15 months from inception of its idea whereas U.S. firms require on average about 36 months to do the same.

STRATEGIC FOCUS

The Mean Innovative Machine

In the automobile industry, there is one firm that stands above the others when it comes to innovation, Toyota. Toyota is the industry leader in bringing new products to the market rapidly. It holds the industry mark for time, 15 months to develop a new concept car and introduce it to the market. Most other Japanese firms require about 24 months. The fastest U.S. firm can do this, on average, in about 36 months. The current president of Toyota, Hiroshi Okuda, has emphasized speed. In fact, one senior manager says that his message is speed, speed, speed.

Toyota is known for more than its speed of product development. In December 1997, the firm introduced a new automobile that is the first mass produced car with both electric and gasoline powered engines. This auto, called the Prius, produces significant economies over a traditional gasoline powered car. For example, it has an average fuel consumption of between 66 and 85 miles to the gallon. This auto also has lower emission levels than its traditional counterpart. The electric engine is used for starting and for running at low speeds. As the speed of the vehicle increases, the gasoline powered engine begins to operate. In this way, the auto has better fuel efficiency and lower emissions than traditional automobiles. The car contains a power split device to ensure that power is transmitted to the wheels continuously. While other rival automakers, Honda and Nissan, are also developing hybrid cars, Toyota was the first to the market and thus will enjoy the advantages of a first mover with respect to this particular product. Toyota has also developed a new engine that requires 25 percent fewer parts. Such an engine weighs less and is cheaper to build. This new 1.8 liter, four-cylinder engine has 560 parts compared to its predecessor with 741 parts. The engine weighs 64 pounds, about 10 percent less than its predecessor, and yet, it produces 15 percent more horsepower.

Analysts and knowledgeable industry sources believe that Toyota sets many of the standards in the industry. For example, many argue that it possesses superior skills in manufacturing, engineering, and marketing. It also manages its finances effectively. Toyota maintains $21 billion in cash and marketable securities. With this much cash available, it has the capability to move rapidly if an opportunity is identified that requires fast action to take advantage of it.

Certainly, other automakers are innovative. For example, Audi has become an aggressive innovator. Audi builds technologically innovative cars about which its customers are passionate. Also, these autos are cheaper than most of the direct competitors such as BMW, Lexus, Mercedes, Saab, and Volvo. Another example of an innovative automaker is Land Rover. This company produces vehicles not known for their fuel efficiency. Nonetheless, the firm won an energy efficiency award for energy-efficient power generation. The award was given by the Combined Heat & Power Association for Land Rover's cogeneration (combined heat and power generation) facilities at its assembly plant in Solihull, Birmingham, in the United Kingdom. Thus, Land Rover is a leading innovator in other areas of its business.

Although other auto innovations could be named, Toyota is the undisputed leader and will likely remain so for the foreseeable future. Toyota continues to invest heavily in the development of fuel cells and in producing a highly efficient, high powered electric vehicle. Many will take bets that Toyota will succeed and be the first to do so.

SOURCES: L. Boulton, 1997, Land Rover's energy drive takes a prize, *Financial Times*, November 2, 2; J. Griffiths, 1997, Global race for fuel efficiency, *Financial Times*, November 2, 8; V. Reitman, 1997, Toyota introduces new engine in the U.S. that is much lighter, cheaper to make, *Wall Street Journal*, October 8, B13; H. Simonian, 1997, Staying in the fast lane of innovation, *Financial Times*, November 7, 20; A. Taylor, III, 1997, How Toyota defies gravity, *Fortune*, December 8, 100–108; E. Thornton, K. Naughton, and D. Woodruff, 1997, Toyota's green machine, *Business Week*, December 15, 108–110; S. Zesiger, 1997, The most improved wheels, *Fortune*, November 24, 194–204.

Implementing Internal Corporate Ventures

The creation and commercialization of a new good or service is a complex process. The design and transfer of technology from engineering to manufacturing and ultimately to distribution and to the marketplace are critical. The design stage entails a high degree of integration among the various functions involved in the innovation process—from engineering to manufacturing and ultimately to market distribution. Initial design efforts that do not consider down-line aspects in the production process (manufacturing, testing, marketing, service, etc.) may result in high product costs and low product quality. Such cross-functional integration facilitates reciprocal information flows among the functions responsible for development, design, and implementation. Developing a capability to innovate rapidly using team processes, as Toyota has done, helps large firms overcome the difficulties they encounter when trying to be entrepreneurial. These matters are discussed in greater detail in the next subsection.

Implementing Product Development Teams and Facilitating Cross-Functional Integration

Horizontal organization refers to changes in organizational processes where managing across functional units becomes more critical than managing up and down functional hierarchies.

The importance of cross-functional integration has been recognized for some time, but it has not been practiced widely in industry until recently. However, because of an emerging emphasis on horizontal organization, firms are becoming more skilled at cross-functional integration. **Horizontal organization** refers to changes in organizational processes where managing across functional units becomes more critical than managing up and down functional hierarchies.[43] Therefore, instead of being built around vertical hierarchical functions or departments, the organization is built around core horizontal processes.

Evidence suggests that a key benefit that can be gained through successful application of horizontal organizational processes is effective utilization of sophisticated manufacturing technologies [e.g., the computer-aided design and manufacturing (CAD/CAM) system].[44] Thus, cross-functional integration can facilitate a firm's efforts to establish a competitive advantage.

Barriers to Integration

Barriers may exist that can stifle attempts to integrate functions effectively within an organization. For example, an emphasis on functional specialization may affect cross-functional integration. Such specialization creates distancing of divergent functions and characteristically different roles for engineering, manufacturing, and marketing. Functional departments have been found to be differentiated along four dimensions: time orientation, interpersonal orientation, goal orientation, and formality of structure.[45] Individuals from different functional departments that have different orientations understand separate aspects of product development in different ways. As such, they place emphasis on separate design characteristics and issues. For example, a design engineer may place strong importance on characteristics that make a product functional and workable. Alternatively, a person from the marketing function may place extreme importance on product characteristics that satisfy customer needs. These types of characteristics may overlap or they may differ. These different orientations can create barriers to effective communication across functions.[46] Although functional specialization may be damaging to the horizontal relationships necessary for implementing innovation, such specialization has an important purpose in creating an efficient organization. Therefore, eliminating such task specialization to overcome barriers to cross-functional integration may do more harm than good to the organization.

Another barrier to integration can be organizational politics. In some organizations, considerable political activity may center on resource allocations to the different functions. If different functions have to compete aggressively with each other to obtain adequate or needed resources, it can lead to conflict between the functions. Of course, dysfunctional conflict between functions creates a barrier to their integration.[47] Methods must be found through which cross-functional integration can be promoted without excessive concurrent political conflict and without concurrently changing the basic structural characteristics necessary for task specialization and efficiency.

Facilitating Integration

Firms can use four methods to achieve effective cross-functional integration. The first of these methods utilizes *shared values*.[48] Shared values, when linked clearly with a firm's strategic intent and mission, reduce political conflict and become the glue that promotes coupling among functional units. Hewlett-Packard has remained an accomplished technological leader because it has established the "HP way." In essence, the HP way refers to the firm's esteemed organizational culture that promotes unity and internal innovation.

Leadership is a second method of achieving cross-functional integration. Effective strategic leaders remind organizational members continuously of the value that product innovations create for the company (see Chapter 12). In the most desirable sit-

485

uations, this value-creating potential becomes the basis for the integration and management of functional department activities. At General Electric, Jack Welch frequently highlights the importance of integrated work, among both business units and different functions. To frame this message consistently, Welch has been instrumental in establishing and operating a managerial training center that focuses on these relationships among all levels of the company's management structure.

A third method of achieving cross-functional integration is concerned with *goals and budgets*. This method calls for firms to formulate goals and allocate the budgetary resources necessary to accomplish them. These goals are specific targets for the integrated design and production of new goods and services. Chrysler's reorganization to focus on platform teams, for example, effectively reinforced in employees' minds the importance of team processes.

A fourth means of facilitating cross-functional integration is an *effective communication system*. This may be achieved by developing a horizontal organization and emphasizing the use of cross-functional teams. More is often required, however, to overcome the barriers to integration noted earlier.[49] Shared values, effective leadership, appropriate resources to accomplish team tasks, and an information system that facilitates communications between team members and different functions contribute to an effective communication system within teams.[50] A network information system can facilitate communication among geographically dispersed team members, even those located in different countries. Because of the growing popularity of horizontal organizational structures, in particular cross-functional teams that may be geographically dispersed across international borders, firms such as IBM are emphasizing network-centered computing. According to Louis Gerstner, CEO of IBM, network-centered computing "will change the way we do business, the way we teach our children, how we communicate, how we interact as individuals."[51]

Appropriating (Extracting) Value from Innovation

Cross-functional integration, when implemented properly, may also facilitate reduced time to market, improve product quality, and create value for customers. For firms competing globally, increasing attention is being paid to the amount of time required to transfer products from the lab to the consumer.[52] A firm can gain a competitive advantage if it is able to develop a product idea and transfer it to the market sooner than competitors, especially in high-tech environments such as biotechnology.[53] If the product has wide consumer appeal, the first mover has an advantage.[54] Although there is inherent risk in being a pioneer, a first mover may be able to establish a dominant position from which to build future market share and earn above-average returns (see discussion in Chapter 5). Research evidence suggests that firms with long development cycles typically are outperformed by companies with short ones.[55] Although shorter time-to-market cycles can help firms appropriate value from their innovations, poor design can lead to expensive recalls, higher production costs, low product performance, and product liability exposure.

As noted earlier, speed has become a major factor on which firms such as Toyota compete.[56] In fact, Kim Sheridan, chairman of Avalon Software, Inc., stated that "it's not the big companies that eat the small; it's the fast that eat the slow."[57] A recent study showed that the competitive clock continues to tick while a firm delays adopting a new generation of technology. The sooner a firm innovates, the better it performs.[58] There is no single means of increasing a firm's speed. Clearly, integrating new technology into a firm's operations can increase the speed with which it accomplishes tasks. Many firms are attempting to accelerate product development and integration through cross-functional teams.[59]

Because product design teams often are composed of many different players, each of whom possesses critical knowledge and skills, cross-functional integration may reduce uncertainty and facilitate the successful introduction of innovative goods or services. In fact, the simultaneous evaluation of multiple alternatives, as is often the case with cross-functional teams, increases decision speed.[60] Hewlett-Packard, for example, is divided into global, cross-functional teams that are capable of making decisions quickly to deal with rapidly changing market conditions. However, it is essential that design teams be managed effectively. If implementation is not effective in a complex situation, uncertainty may be increased.[61]

In summary, the model presented in Figure 13.2 shows how value may be appropriated from internal innovation processes. As our discussion has indicated, the internal innovation process must be managed to facilitate cross-functional integration to appropriate the greatest amount of value from product design and commercialization efforts. Effective management of internal innovation processes can reduce both the time required to introduce innovations into the marketplace and the degree of decision uncertainty associated with the design of an innovative product and the demand for it.[62]

FIGURE 13.2 *Appropriating Value from Internal Firm Innovation*

Source: Adapted from M. A. Hitt, R. E. Hoskisson, and R. D. Nixon, 1993, A mid-range theory of interfunctional integration, its antecedents and outcomes, *Journal of Engineering and Technology Management* 10: 161–185.

STRATEGIC ALLIANCES: COOPERATING TO PRODUCE AND MANAGE INNOVATION

It is difficult for most firms to possess all the knowledge required to compete successfully in their product areas over the long term. Thus, internal innovation may contribute to the development of a sustainable competitive advantage when a firm possesses the core competencies required to innovate effectively and efficiently. But because the stock of human knowledge is large and increasing at an accelerating pace, many firms, regardless of their size, cannot keep up to date on this vast pool of knowledge. Complicating this matter is the fact that the knowledge base confronting today's organizations is not only vast, but also increasingly more specialized. As such, the knowledge needed to commercialize goods and services is frequently embedded within different corporations and countries that have the ability to create specialized products.

In Chapter 9, we discussed why and how firms use strategic alliances (*strategic alliances* are partnerships between firms whereby resources, capabilities, and core competencies are combined to pursue common interests and goals)[63] to gain either competitive parity or competitive advantage relative to rivals. Moreover, one of the specific reasons to enter into a strategic alliance is to introduce innovative goods or services. Strategic alliances are often used to innovate by sharing two or more firms' knowledge and skill bases.[64]

The dreams of many biotechnology firms of becoming the next Merck are being scaled back. Most of these firms are small and many have experienced failures of new drugs, a significant problem because of their lack of resources. Thus, survival is of key concern. To avoid failure and to obtain the needed resources to continue biotechnology research, many of these companies are seeking strategic alliances with larger resource-rich firms. Over a recent 12-month period, biotechnology companies entered into 246 alliances with larger pharmaceutical firms. It is expensive and quite risky for new startup firms to operate independently in this industry. The average cost of developing a new drug is approximately $300 million and only 10 percent of the experimental drugs used in human trials are further developed and brought to the market.[65]

Similarly, large pharmaceutical firms are eagerly shopping for opportunities to team with biotechnology firms. Some of them are using the small biotechnology companies to perform the early-stage research. As such, they can reduce their in-house research costs and some of the risks as well. Forming an alliance with these firms enables the pharmaceutical firms to convert some of their fixed research costs to variable costs and to diversify their risk. Thus, the pharmaceutical firms are attempting to reduce their risk and some of their fixed costs without reducing the probability of discovering and marketing new blockbuster drugs.[66]

In a more general sense, some argue that strategic alliances can be dangerous. Supporting this argument is the contention that they allow partner firms to gain knowledge and resources that make them stronger competitors, which, if true, could ultimately lower profitability for an industry's leading firms.[67] Perhaps the most important decision with regard to alliances occurs in the selection of a partner. Not only should a firm choose a partner with complementary skills, but also one that has compatible goals and strategic orientations.[68] Thus, organizations are challenged to evaluate carefully all the risks associated with strategic alliances that might be formed in the pursuit of strategic competitiveness and above-average returns.

Across time, strategic alliances can slowly reduce the skills of a partner that does not understand the inherent risks. Collaboration within alliances can lead to competition, both in learning new skills and in refining new capabilities and core competencies that can be used to design and produce other innovative products and processes.

Japanese corporations, for example, appear to be expert in learning new technologies through strategic alliances. This skill has been instrumental in helping these firms learn how to compete in markets where they were locked out previously. For instance, all electronics products sold under the Eastman Kodak, General Electric, RCA, Zenith, and Westinghouse brand names are made by their foreign alliance partners and imported into the United States.[69]

As our discussion has suggested, alliances can lead to a company's dependence on partners through outsourcing to obtain low-cost components and inexpensive assembly. Often manufacturing skills and knowledge related to upgrading precision manufacturing and testing are lost, whereas such skills are gained by the competitors to which the firm is outsourcing.[70] Ultimately, then, a firm may lose its core competence by participating in alliances if it is not careful.

In summary, building successful strategic alliances requires focusing on knowledge, identifying core competencies, and developing strong human resources to manage these core competencies. Expecting to gain financial benefits in the short run may lead to unintended consequences in the long run. Firms may view their collaboration with other firms as an indirect form of competition for knowledge.[71]

BUYING INNOVATION: ACQUISITIONS AND VENTURE CAPITAL

In this section, we focus on the third approach firms use to produce and manage innovation. The intent of this approach is to acquire innovation, and innovative capabilities, from outside the organization. For example, in addition to strategic alliances, some pharmaceutical firms are acquiring small biotechnology companies with promising new drugs. Ciba-Geigy Ltd. bought a 50 percent interest in Chiron Corp. for $2.1 billion. The pharmaceutical firms are buying biotechnology firms not only for their promising new drugs but also their research techniques using gene-based analysis and computerization. Some time-honored techniques for creating drugs are becoming obsolete. Thus, they are attempting to buy innovation and the skills to create more innovation.[72]

As approaches to producing and managing innovation, both strategic alliances and acquisitions appear to be increasing in popularity. One reason is that the innovation prowess of companies in other countries is growing at a rapid pace. A number of indicators suggest that Japanese firms, for instance, have progressed during the post-war period from borrowing, magnifying, and successfully commercializing foreign technologies to operating at the technological frontier, especially in process innovation. The National Science Foundation reported that Japanese firms accounted for the largest single share of foreign-origin patents.[73] Japanese companies are becoming skilled at transferring technologies from Japan into their global R&D networks. One way for companies from other nations to gain competitive parity or perhaps competitive advantage is to gain access to Japanese technology by acquiring companies that have such technology.

Acquisitions

Acquiring other firms as a method of producing and managing innovation is becoming more common and may be used as a substitute for internally developed innovation.[74] A key risk of this method is that a firm may substitute the ability to buy innovations for the ability to produce innovations internally. Research suggests this tradeoff has a negative effect on the processes a firm uses to produce innovations internally.[75]

Figure 13.3 shows that firms gaining access to innovations through the acquisition of other companies risk reductions in both R&D inputs (as measured by investments in R&D) and R&D outputs (as measured by the number of patents). Evidence in Figure 13.3 shows the R&D-to-sales ratio drops after acquisitions have been completed and that the patent-to-sales ratio drops significantly after companies have been involved with large acquisitions. Additional research shows that firms engaging in acquisitions introduce fewer new products to the market.[76] These relationships indicate that firms substitute acquisitions for their internal innovation process. This may result because firms lose strategic control and emphasize financial control of original, and especially of acquired, business units.[77] Although reduced innovation may not always result, managers in acquiring firms should be aware of this potential outcome.

Innovation can be obtained in a way other than acquiring a whole firm. For example, sometimes foreign firms can acquire a license from the home country patent

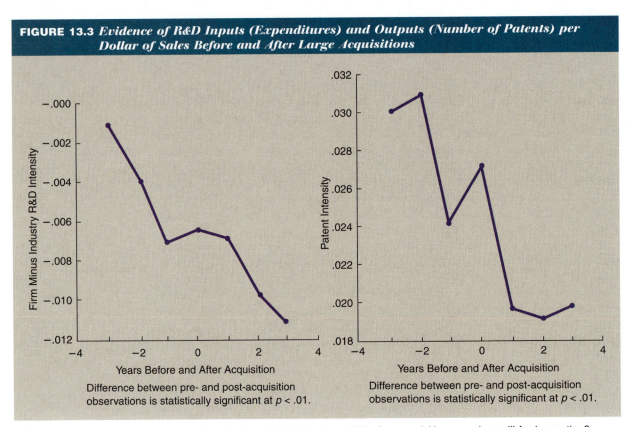

FIGURE 13.3 *Evidence of R&D Inputs (Expenditures) and Outputs (Number of Patents) per Dollar of Sales Before and After Large Acquisitions*

Years Before and After Acquisition

Difference between pre- and post-acquisition observations is statistically significant at $p < .01$.

Difference between pre- and post-acquisition observations is statistically significant at $p < .01$.

Source: M. A. Hitt, R. E. Hoskisson, R. D. Ireland, and J. S. Harrison, 1991, Are acquisitions a poison pill for innovation?, *Academy of Management Executive V*, no. 4: 24–25.

holder to use a technology. It may also buy the rights to the technology. This process is common among Indian firms. In India, most companies do not invest heavily in R&D and thus, they acquire technology and new products from firms in other countries. Interestingly, however, research shows that even modest amounts of R&D can be helpful to these firms in identifying sources of new technology.[78] Given the global marketplace and growing competition from foreign companies, firms are likely to become less willing to license or sell the rights to their technology to foreign firms. Indian firms may be forced, therefore, to invest more to develop their own technology to remain competitive.

Venture Capital

Another approach used to acquire innovations involves venture capital. Some firms choose to establish their own venture capital divisions. These divisions carefully evaluate other companies to identify those with innovations or innovative capabilities that could help the firm develop a sustainable competitive advantage. In other instances, firms decide to serve as an internal source of capital for innovative product ideas that can be spun off as independent or affiliate firms. New enterprises that are backed by venture capital provide an important source of innovation and new technology. Furthermore, they are a major source of new wealth creation in the United States. For example, these firms account annually for about one-third of all initial public offerings of stock. On average these venture capital backed new enterprises create approximately 230,000 new jobs and spend about $5 billion on R&D each year.[79]

Historically, the venture capital business has been associated primarily with independent venture capital firms, but both domestic and foreign corporations have discovered that investing in venture capital adds a new dimension to their corporate development strategies and can produce an attractive return on their investments.[80] The strategic benefits to a corporation include the ability to invest early and observe what happens to the new venture. This may lead to subsequent acquisitions, technology licensing, product marketing rights, and possibly the development of international opportunities. Large firms often view venture capital as a window on future technological development. Participation by corporations can take many forms, but usually begins with investment in several venture capital funds as a limited partner and evolves into direct investments in new business ventures. Many firms begin this strategy by forming a venture development division.

Disdain of large corporations by outside entrepreneurs can be a potential pitfall. Entrepreneurs may be wary of large corporations that seek to dominate fledgling companies. The syndication of venture funds to reduce risk may also be a factor limiting potential gains from venture capital investments. Other large firms may become part of the syndication and reduce the potential returns for the large corporate partner (through sharing of knowledge).[81] With corporate restructuring and downsizing continuing, executives seem willing to try more entrepreneurial ventures. Venture capital is apparently one way to participate and may be less risky than internal development.[82]

Larger and more experienced venture capitalists sometimes search to invest for entrepreneurs who have experience starting other ventures. These entrepreneurs have commercial experience, have knowledge about a particular industry or market sector, and ambition to succeed.[83] Alternatively some successful entrepreneurs become venture capitalists. Gary Reichling became a millionaire by selling his business to a larger corporation. In turn, he became a venture capitalist and provided capital to a small firm with little equity but a great product. Manufactured by Doumar Products, Inc., this product, un-du, is able to remove adhesives without ruining the surface product (e.g., labels, stickers, price tags, bumper stickers, etc.). Un-du can also make paper-based products temporarily transparent without harming them (e.g., making an envelope transparent to see if you signed the check sealed in it). Reichling was attracted to the product but was seriously concerned about the problems with the business plan. Eventually, Reichling took over the firm as its CEO, an unusual action for most venture capitalists, but perhaps not so unusual for former entrepreneurs.[84]

Up to this point, the focus of our discussion largely has been on corporate entrepreneurship in large firms, but small firms may even be better at producing revolutionary innovations. Although large firms often possess the significant financial resources and organizational capabilities necessary to more fully exploit innovative product opportunities, small firms may have more flexibility to produce innovations.

STRATEGIC FOCUS

492

Are Venture Capitalists and Entrepreneurs from the Same Mold?

Stewart Alsop is a venture capitalist and likes it because there is no ambiguity about what business he is in; he is in the business of earning money. In fact, Alsop says that he is in the business of earning lots of money. A venture capitalist who makes a small amount of money is not very good. Each year, Alsop estimates he listens to about 100 presentations and reads another 200 business plans. David Cowan is also a venture capitalist. He became interested in entrepreneurship while in college. As a freshman, he started a company that sold application software to private libraries. Later while he was a graduate student, he provided free consulting for Bessemer Ventures hoping to obtain a job with the company. He was successful. Cowan is now a partner in Bessemer Ventures and has the distinction of never losing money on one of his investments. Of course, given the risk involved, the likelihood that none of his investments will produce a negative return is very low. Recently, when Cisco Systems was sold to NetSys Technologies for $60 million, Bessemer received a 600 percent return on its investment in one year. Cowan is an aggressive investor to the point of relentlessly pursuing a person he has identified as a good CEO for a startup. If he cannot find investment opportunities fitting the appropriate criteria, he will start a company on his own, a practice that is becoming more common for venture capitalists. Thus, Cowan seems to have entrepreneurial acumen, and it would be difficult to separate him from other entrepreneurs (except that he now has equity capital).

Bob Kierlin is the highly successful CEO of Fastenal, a business selling literally nuts and bolts. His company has been providing better shareholder returns, though, than Coca-Cola or GE. Kierlin saves money in many ways. He never even thinks of flying first class and sometimes not coach either. In a recent trip from Minnesota to California, he used a company van and drove the 5,000 miles roundtrip. His salary is only $120,000 annually but his net worth is tied up in the stock. Over a recent five-year period, Fastenal produced an average 39.3 percent total return annually to shareholders. He uses what some refer to as commonsense entrepreneurship. Company policy allows branch managers to bypass company central purchasing of products if they can obtain a better deal. Branch managers bypass central purchasing 42 percent of the time. They provide exemplary service and charge premium prices. Kierlin says that the primary reason for his company's success is the philosophy that "just believe in people, give them the chance to make decisions, take risks, and work hard. We could have made this work selling cabbages."

Armando Conti is the founder of Expresso Armando, the premier manufacturer of domestic expresso machines. In 1993, Armando decided to build the world's best expresso coffee machine. This was his second entrepreneurial venture. He started his first business in 1987 and began to search for his next business in 1989. The idea for the expresso machine venture came when he purchased a $300 machine that did not produce quality expresso. He decided that there was a need for a better quality machine. With his technical skills, he designed a new expresso machine that he felt would brew superior expresso. His prototype brewed excellent coffee. It required one-and-one-half years to complete the commercial machine. The first machine was shipped to a Boston customer in December 1993. One of Armando's largest customers is Starbuck's, known throughout North America and now opening stores in Asia. In 1998, Armando's expects to sell 200 machines.

There are an increasing number of defectors from large corporations who are turning to entrepreneurship. These people often leave behind large salaries and nice offices to start or operate small new ventures. This was the case for two relatively young entrepreneurs, D. J. Edgerton and Paul Geczik. D. J. became bored with his job working in a big corporation, and Paul's employer closed his business. Paul received a piece of graphics software as severance pay and the two friends decided to use it to start a new design firm. They worked out of a run-down, rent-controlled apartment. They decided to reinvest their revenue back into their hardware and software rather than their surroundings. To establish themselves, they took almost any job, sometimes accepting last-minute jobs requiring that they work all night or all weekend to meet the deadline. One time Disney Adventure magazine needed an advertising supplement developed and completed over a weekend. No large firm could mobilize that fast so the marketing director took a chance on D. J. and Paul. They did a great job thereby winning a new customer. One of their suppliers moved back to his home in Ireland and started a new brewery. The owner wanted to establish a brand identity but had no money for a design firm to help. He proposed to give D. J. and Paul's business called Draw the Line a 5 percent stake for such work. They accepted the offer and provided about $50,000 in services. The brewery was a success, supplying dozens of pubs in Dublin. Draw the Line now has about $1 million in annual revenues with a highly successful Web-design business as a part of its portfolio and no debt.

Thus, when one examines the characteristics, it may be difficult to distinguish the entrepreneur from the venture capitalist. Many venture capitalists have prior experience as entrepreneurs and now even become involved in entrepreneurial ventures as active parties.

SOURCES: R. Teitelbaum, 1998, Who is Bob Kierlin—and why is he so successful? *Fortune*, January 10, http://www.pathfinder.com/fortune; J. Useem, 1998, The new entrepreneurial elite, *Inc. Online*, January 19, http://www.inc.com; Stewart Alsop, 1997, My secret life: The big ideas of a venture capitalist, *Fortune*, July 21, http://www.pathfinder.com/fortune; Expresso Armando, 1998, *The EM Launch Pad*, January 19, http://www.benlore.com; S. M. Mehta, 1997, The investor, *Wall Street Journal*, December 8, R28; T. Petzinger, Jr., 1997, These two young artists take tough jobs and big chances, *Wall Street Journal Interactive*, June 6, http://www.interactive6.wsj.com.

Venture capitalists and entrepreneurs play important roles in the United States and increasingly in the world economy. As noted in the Strategic Focus, they share many characteristics. In fact, it may be difficult to separate some of them as several play both roles. Clearly, entrepreneurs are important as catalysts for small businesses. Next we discuss entrepreneurship and small firms.

ENTREPRENEURSHIP AND THE SMALL FIRM

Research suggests that small firms, based in the United States and other nations throughout the world, are awarded a large number of U.S. patents.[85] Although 80 percent of the world's R&D activities in developing nations is concentrated in firms with 10,000 or more employees, these same large firms account for under half of the world's technological activity, as measured by U.S. patenting. These facts show that while large firms are important for technological advances, small firms and private individuals account for a significant share of the innovative activity and technological progress. There has been a substantial shift toward self-employment and entrepreneurial ventures in the United States.[86] Small entrepreneurial firms have become an important part of the mainstream economy and business activity in the United States.[87]

The lure of entrepreneurship is becoming far reaching. For example, women and minorities compose the largest portion of the increase in new firms. Women now own over one-third of all businesses in the United States. A majority of these firms were started in the last 10 years and may be classified as small businesses. The number of businesses owned by African Americans and Hispanic Americans has also increased dramatically in recent years.[88] One such business has thrived by providing nursing services to the inner city. Geric Home Health Care, started by an African American husband and wife team, not only serves inner city customers but also hires its employees from the inner city. Many of Geric's employees are single mothers receiving welfare. The owners found that employees assigned to the neighborhoods where they live are not afraid to work in the inner city, unlike many outsiders. To make this work, the Johnsons, who own Geric Home Health Care, had to establish a state-certified school for nursing aides. The turnover is low for this type of business, 25 percent annually. One employee explained the culture at Geric, "we're like Tom Sawyer lying in the grass dreaming about what we can do."[89]

Other entrepreneurs like Ludmila Rusakova and Jannifer Kramer, immigrants from Russia, are successful operators of a service firm. Their firm, called Master-Word Services, offers translations of documents into as many as 40 different languages. Rusakova, who is 26 and president of the firm, has nine full-time employees and 30 contractors, and the firm has revenue of approximately $2 million. The firm's customers include major oil and gas corporations, engineering companies, and law firms, and it provides services on call 24 hours a day. Currently, Rusakova is building contacts with thousands of interpreters around the world that can be hired to help on projects as needed.[90]

Even in some of the areas where large firms are effective innovators, individual entrepreneurs and small firms still make significant contributions. This relationship is demonstrated by the interactions between small and large firms operating in the electronics industry (especially among firms located in the Silicon Valley in the United States). For instance, the semiconductor industry benefited significantly by the development of new technology-based firms. Most of these firms were spin-offs created by former employees of large firms.[91] The complementarity of small and large firms in innovation is exemplified by the integration of biotechnology and pharmaceutical firms to produce innovative drugs as discussed earlier.

The balance of power between large and small companies appears to be shifting. In the United States, small and midsize companies have been responsible for nearly all of the new jobs created since 1987.[92] The Davids have what the Goliaths so desperately want: agility, resourcefulness, and flexibility. Computers and communications technologies have been great equalizers, giving individual entrepreneurs and small firms an enhanced ability to mobilize resources, hire qualified individuals, and market their goods and services (e.g., on the Internet).[93] Small firms have created most of the new jobs in the U.S. economy in the 1990s because of (1) the flexibility provided by desktop computers, (2) networks of small firms that have the ability to communicate with each other, (3) vast computerized information databases, and (4) computer-controlled machine tools that help small companies provide quality equal to that of large manufacturers.[94]

Although small firms do not have large safety nets and benefits for employees, there is a certain excitement in working for such firms. Employees feel a clear sense of purpose. Lines of communication are short and direct; often the boss walks around the facility several times a day. Employees who are dedicated and care are given serious responsibility. They are trained in numerous jobs and typically are rewarded in ways that encourage their allegiance to their employer.[95]

Interestingly, new entrepreneurial firms have tended to perform better and have a higher survival rate than franchised startup firms. Franchised firms often receive considerable support from the larger businesses from which they are franchised but also must adhere to many of the larger firms' corporate policies and procedures. As such, franchises have less flexibility and are less innovative. Research has shown that over a three-year period, the average net loss for retailing franchising was $4,000 plus, whereas cohort independent entrepreneurial retailing firms had an average net income for the same three-year period of more than $14,000. Similarly, franchise firms had a 45 percent failure rate, whereas young entrepreneurial independent retail firms had a slightly less than 24 percent failure rate for the same time period.[96]

Additionally, entrepreneurs who founded firms are significantly more innovative in their decisions than owners who did not initially establish the firm. These findings suggest that entrepreneurs who operate independent companies are likely to be more innovative and more successful than nonentrepreneurs, particularly those connected to larger firms and operating under their policies and procedures, like franchises.[97]

One of the reasons that entrepreneurs are more innovative than managers in large companies is that they tend to use more heuristics in making decisions. The use of heuristics has been found to be associated with more innovative decisions and outcomes, but the heavy reliance on it is probably why entrepreneurs rarely make effective managers as their firm grows.[98]

As entrepreneurial firms grow, entrepreneurs need to learn the following new skills to manage them well: (1) how to use cash flow to make decisions, (2) how to finance growth, (3) how to increase the value of the business, (4) how to compensate self and associates, (5) how to effectively hire, train, and motivate employees to achieve growth, (6) how to deal with a rapidly changing environment, (7) how to develop management succession, and (8) how to understand the problems of growth.[99] While many entrepreneurs do not seem to have the right skills or mindset to manage their firm after it has grown, Catherine Candland seems to be an exception. Ms. Candland is the founder, owner, and manager of Advantage Staffing Services, a temporary staffing firm. She started the firm in 1983 and now has 17 offices, 200 employees, and almost $70 million in annual revenue. Not only has she developed a successful business, but she also has had three children since founding Advantage.[100]

Successfully innovating and commercializing a new product idea outside large corporations is not an easy task. Putting together the funding, marketing plan, and production facilities, along with completing the regulatory paperwork, is a challenge for entrepreneurs seeking to start their own private company. Nonetheless, small new technology-based firms have fostered the growth of many industries, including semiconductors, CAD, and biotechnology. These examples illustrate the importance of entrepreneurs and small firms in the development of new products and the diffusion of innovation.

What can large firms do to act small and be innovative? First, many firms, through restructuring as described in Chapter 7, are being organized into more manageable units.[101] Accompanying these restructurings, firms are reengineering to reduce organizational processes to the essential functions, share risks with partners, and listen more fully and effectively to customers. Second, large companies are trying to offer attractive places to work and seek to bind employee interests to those of the company. This is accomplished through arrangements such as self-managed teams and customer-satisfaction bonuses. For example, Herbert Kelleher, CEO of Southwest Airlines, has sought to keep a small-firm culture by using traditional profit-sharing plans and a buddy system linking longtime and new employees.

Many large firms have handled decreasing competitiveness by laying off tens of thousands of employees. But downsizing has not realized the gains anticipated. Although head-count cuts happen fast and the stock market sometimes reacts favorably, research indicates that 50 percent or more of the firms end up worse after their downsizing.[102] Much to large firms' chagrin, massive layoffs can sometimes merely erode morale. Divestitures and spin-offs have produced much more favorable results.[103] In the long run, large firms must practice a delicate balancing act that allows autonomy at the lowest levels, while maintaining the advantages of size.

One of the ways large firms contribute to innovation is with the significant resources they can invest in R&D. Table 13.1 lists the top 10 firms throughout the world that have invested the most in R&D. While possibly not the most innovative, these firms should produce a substantial number of new ideas.[104] One way for large firms to make major strategic moves quickly is to link up with smaller, more agile firms. To do this, some large firms provide the venture capital for smaller

TABLE 13.1 *The Largest Investors in R&D in the World*

Company	Dollars Invested (in Billions)	R&D/Sales
1. General Motors (U.S.)	8.8	5.6%
2. Ford (U.S.)	6.8	5.8
3. Siemens (Germany)	4.6	7.7
4. Hitachi (Japan)	4.2	6.1
5. IBM (U.S.)	4.0	5.2
6. Daimler-Benz (Germany)	3.6	5.2
7. Matsushita (Japan)	3.4	5.9
8. Fujitsu (Japan)	3.0	9.2
9. NTT (Japan)	2.8	4.0
10. Novartis (Switzerland)	2.8	10.1

Source: C. Cookson, 1998, Financial community develops a taste for industrial research, *Financial Times,* January 20, 17.

firms to develop a good idea as noted earlier. Larger firms often have more efficient manufacturing and distribution systems as compared to smaller firms. A linkage with smaller firms can also be useful in implementing other strategic moves. This is being done by a number of large firms seeking to establish a presence in the Russian market. Because of their proximity, Finnish firms have operated in Russia for many years and have built a storehouse of knowledge about the Russian culture and markets. Importantly, they also have built numerous contacts. Thus, many large firms from other European and North American countries have established strategic alliances with Finnish firms to enter Russian markets ranging from oil and gas to computer hardware and software.[105]

Still, it seems that many new concepts for business come from small firms. For example, Wawa Inc. started as a family dairy but grew into a five-state chain of new concept convenience stores. In its 515 stores, customers have such upscale choices as kiwi, fresh tomatoes, mineral water, pasta salad, cappuccino, and yogurt. Wawa also serves Taco Bell burritos and Pizza Hut pizzas. The editor-in-chief of *Convenience Store News* states that, "They're on the cutting edge." These new concept convenience stores attract a new type of customer compared to the typical convenience store that sells more beer, gasoline, and tobacco than other products. Wawa founded its first store in 1985. Its current annual sales approximate $850 million.[106] There likely will be other new concepts in service industries in future years. For example, one author predicts that there will be a business and leisure hotel on the moon and other hotels in parts of the solar system. In the shorter term, new hotels are being built in South America, China, Eastern Europe, and lesser known parts of southeast Asia to fill a need for business and tourist travelers.[107]

Thus, large and small firms alike can be innovative. Oftentimes, cooperative efforts between large and small firms may produce the best opportunity to commercialize innovations. The small firms can develop the innovation and the large firms can best get it to the market. This type of cooperative endeavor may be a key link to the ability of both large and small firms to achieve strategic competitiveness and earn above-average returns.[108]

SUMMARY

- Three basic strategic approaches are used to produce and manage innovation. The first approach is called internal corporate venturing. This approach emphasizes the development of autonomous strategic behavior wherein product champions pursue new product ideas and executives help them manage the strategic context to commercialize the new products within a larger firm. Induced strategic behavior is a top-down process wherein incremental product changes and adjustments are made to the original product. This is a process driven by the organization's current corporate strategy, structure, and reward and control systems.

- The innovation process has three stages. Invention is the act of creating and developing a new product idea. The next stage, innovation, is the process of commercializing products from invention. Ultimately, other firms in the industry imitate the new product and diffuse the innovation. Imitation results in product standardization and market acceptance.

- In the past, internal innovation was done serially. Now, more parallel innovation is created through cross-functional teams. Facilitated by cross-functional teams, cross-functional integration can reduce the time a firm needs to introduce innovative products into the marketplace, improve product quality, and ultimately help a firm create value for its targeted customer. When innovations decrease the time to market (speed is a critical competitive factor) and create product quality and customer value, it is likely that a firm will be able to appropriate (or extract) value from the innovation process.

- A second approach used to produce and manage innovation is to obtain innovation through strategic alliances. Because knowledge is exploding and is often located in specialized firms, the only way a firm may be able to obtain the knowledge necessary to create new products is through strategic alliances and/or joint ventures.

- The third basic approach for large firms to produce and manage innovation is to acquire it. Innovation can be acquired either through direct acquisition or through indirect investment. An example of indirect investment is the formation of a wholly owned venture capital division and/or the use of private placement of venture capital. Buying innovation, however, may be risky and detrimental to a firm's internal innovation process.

- The best way to succeed with a wholly owned venture capital operation is to consider the venture capital as an investment and only secondarily as a strategy to acquire innovation. Alternatively, a firm may seek to invest venture capital directly in

small firms or to spin off firms into a network of affiliate companies.

- Small firms are particularly well suited for fostering innovation that does not require large amounts of capital (as semiconductors and chemicals do). Small firms have therefore become a vibrant part of industrialized nations, accounting for more job creation than large firms during the last decade. Where there are low-cost ways to invent, for example, through mechanical inventions, small firms are likely to have a higher innovation rate than large firms.

- Large firms are needed to foster innovation due to capital requirements. Small firms are often found to be better at creating specialty products and diffusing the innovation through spin-offs from large corporations. Large firms are seeking ways to think and act smaller in order to become more entrepreneurial. Often, however, the best way for both small and large firms to solve technological problems is to cooperate and collaborate.

REVIEW QUESTIONS

1. What are three strategic approaches firms use to produce and manage innovation?
2. What are the two processes used to engage in internal corporate venturing known as autonomous strategic behavior and induced strategic behavior?
3. What are three types of innovation that are developed in organizations?
4. Some believe that when managed successfully, cross-functional teams facilitate the implementation of internal corporate ventures and a firm's innovation efforts. How should cross-functional teams be managed to achieve these desirable outcomes?

5. Some firms use strategic alliances to contract for innovation. What are the actions taken to use strategic alliances for this purpose?
6. How can a firm create value when it acquires another company to gain access to its innovations and/or its ability to produce innovations?
7. How do large firms use venture capital to create innovations and to identify new product opportunities?
8. What are the differences in the resources, capabilities, and core competencies of large and small firms to produce and manage innovation?

APPLICATION DISCUSSION QUESTIONS

1. In the 1980s and 1990s, the number of acquisitions has accelerated. The number of dollars being spent as venture capital also increased. Discuss whether or not you think there is a relationship between the wave of acquisitions and the increase in venture capital funding.
2. In your opinion, is the term *corporate entrepreneurship* an oxymoron? In other words, is it a contradiction of terms? If so, why?
3. Discuss the reasons for using cross-functional teams as a popular approach to develop new product designs.

4. How would you suggest that developing countries with a tradition of centralized bureaucracy, such as China and Russia, begin to compete in a global economy that emphasizes product innovation? What should be emphasized in these countries to make firms and their countries more competitive on a global basis? Should they encourage entrepreneurial firms (as is the case in Taiwan)? Should they encourage large firms (as is the case in South Korea)? Should both types of firms be emphasized? Be prepared to justify your views.

5. The restructuring movement (e.g., acquisitions, divestitures, and downsizing) of the 1980s and 1990s has apparently made U.S. firms more *productive* (as measured by traditional output-per-employee ratios). But, in your opinion, are U.S. firms more innovative because of the restructuring and downsizing activity? Why or why not?

6. Are strategic alliances a way to increase existing technological capacity, or are strategic alliances used more by firms that are behind technologically and trying to catch up? In other words, are strategic alliances a tool of firms that have a technological advantage, or are they a tool of technologically disadvantaged companies? Please explain.

ETHICS QUESTIONS

1. Is it ethical for a company to purchase another firm in order to gain ownership of its innovative products? Why or why not?

2. Entrepreneurs are sometimes more effective when they work against existing product standards. How do entrepreneurs know when their new products might harm consumers? Should government agencies or trade associations establish guidelines to assist entrepreneurs on this issue? If so, what might some of those guidelines be?

3. Are there any ethical concerns surrounding the use of an internal venturing process to produce and manage innovation? Why or why not?

4. When participating in a strategic alliance, partner firms may legitimately seek to gain knowledge from each other. At what point does it become unethical for a firm to gain additional and competitively relevant knowledge from a strategic alliance partner? Is this point different when partnering with a domestic firm as opposed to a foreign firm? If so, why?

5. Small firms often have innovative products. When is it appropriate for a large firm to buy a small firm for its new products and new product ideas?

INTERNET EXERCISE

Go to Texas Instrument's History of Innovation at:

http://www.ti.com/corp/docs/history/tihistory.html

Texas Instruments (TI) has a rich history of innovation. For example, in 1954 the company produced the first transistor radio, in 1967 the first hand-held calculator, and in 1989, the first quantum-effect transistor. What is particularly striking about TI's legacy of innovation is the diverse set of management techniques that it has used to facilitate the innovation process. These techniques include acquisitions, joint ventures, strategic alliances, and other management initiatives designed to promote and expedite the innovation process.

Visit the Texas Instrument's History of Innovation Web site and make a list of the management techniques that TI has used over the years to facilitate the innovation process. Make special note of the techniques discussed in this chapter.

Strategic Surfing

A number of organizations maintain Web sites that focus on entrepreneurship and innovation. Several of the premier sites include:

EntreWorld, maintained by the Kauffman Foundation:

http://www.entreworld.org

Center for Entrepreneurial Studies at Babson College:

http://www.babson.edu/entrep

EGOPHER, maintained by St. Louis University:

http://www.slu.edu/eweb/egopher.html

Lets Talk Business Network:

http://www.ltbn.com

NOTES

1. H. Lancaster, 1997, A company crisis could be a chance to make your mark, *Wall Street Journal Interactive*, August 29, http://www.wsj.com/edition/current/articles.

2. The expert's corner, 1998, January 19, http://www.benlore.com/files/emexpert2.

3. C. A. Lengnick-Hall, 1992, Innovation and competitive ad-

vantage: What we know and what we need to learn, *Journal of Management* 18: 399–429.

4. M. A. Hitt, B. W. Keats, and S. M. DeMarie, 1998, Navigating in the new competitive landscape: Building strategic flexibility and competitive advantage in the 21st century, *Academy of Management Executive*, in press; R. A. Bettis and M. A. Hitt, 1995, The new competitive landscape, *Strategic Management Journal* 16 (Special Summer Issue): 7–19.

5. R. Price, 1996, Technology and strategic advantage, *California Management Review* 38, no. 3: 38–56; L. G. Franko, 1989, Global corporate competition: Who's winning, who's losing and the R&D factor as one reason why, *Strategic Management Journal* 10: 449–474.

6. G. T. Lumpkin and G. G. Dess, 1996, Clarifying the entrepreneurial orientation construct and linking it to performance, *Academy of Management Review* 21: 135–172; K. M. Kelm, V. K. Narayanan, and G. E. Pinches, 1995, Shareholder value creation during R&D innovation and commercialization stages, *Academy of Management Journal* 38: 770–786.

7. B. C. Reimann, 1995, Leading strategic change: Innovation, value, growth, *Planning Review* 23 (September/October): 6–9.

8. Lumpkin and Dess, Clarifying the entrepreneurial orientation construct.

9. R. C. Solomon, 1995, Marketing heidegger: Entrepreneurship and corporate practices, *Inquiry* 38: 75–81.

10. D. L. Sexton and R. W. Smilor, 1997, Growth strategies in D. L. Sexton and R. W. Smilor (eds.), *Entrepreneurship 2000* (Chicago: Upstart Publishing Company); M. B. Low and E. Abrahamson, 1997, Movements, bandwagons, and clones: Industry evolution and the entrepreneurial process, *Journal of Business Venturing* 12: 435–457.

11. J. M. Stopford and C. W. F. Baden-Fuller, 1994, Creating corporate entrepreneurship, *Strategic Management Journal* 15: 521–536.

12. C. Farrell, 1993, A wellspring of innovation: Factories have changed relentlessly from 18th century mills to today's worker-empowered auto plants, *Fortune* (Special Bonus Issue): 62.

13. J. P. Womack, D. T. Jones, and D. Roos, 1990, *The Machine That Changed the World* (New York: Rawson Associates), 14.

14. R. J. Schonberger, 1996, *World Class Manufacturing: The Next Decade* (New York: The Free Press).

15. J. Schumpeter, 1934, *The Theory of Economic Development* (Cambridge, MA: Harvard University Press).

16. B. Czarniawska-Joerges and R. Wolff, 1991, Leaders, managers, entrepreneurs on and off the organizational stage, *Organization Studies* 12: 529–546.

17. J. Bowles, 1997, Best practices: Driving growth through innovation, alliances, and stakeholder symbiosis, *Fortune*, November 14, S3–S24.

18. Stopford and Baden-Fuller, Creating corporate entrepreneurship.

19. J. P. Kotter, 1990, *A Force for Change* (New York: The Free Press); H. Mintzberg, 1971, Managerial work: Analysis from observation, *Management Science* 18, no. 2: 97–110.

20. R. W. Smilor, 1997, Entrepreneurship: Reflections on a subversive activity, *Journal of Business Venturing* 12: 341–346.

21. F. N. Pieke, 1995, Bureaucracy, friends and money: The growth of capital socialism in China, *Comparative Studies in Society and History* 37: 494–518.

22. M. H. Morris, D. L. Davis, and J. W. Allen, 1994, Fostering corporate entrepreneurship: Cross-cultural comparisons of the importance of individualism versus collectivism, *Journal of International Business Studies* 25: 65–89.

23. P. S. Li, 1993, Chinese investment and business in Canada: Ethnic entrepreneurship reconsidered, *Pacific Affairs* 66: 219–243.

24. D. H. Holt, 1997, A comparative study of values among Chinese and U.S. entrepreneurs: Pragmatic convergence between contrasting cultures, *Journal of Business Venturing* 12: 483–505.

25. T. Bates, 1997, Financing small business creation: The case of Chinese and Korean immigrant entrepreneurs, *Journal of Business Venturing* 12: 109–124.

26. M. Lerner, C. Brush, and R. Hisrich, 1997, Israeli women entrepreneurs: An examination of factors affecting performance, *Journal of Business Venturing* 12: 315–339.

27. P. P. McDougall and B. M. Oviatt, 1997, International entrepreneurship literature in the 1990s and directions for future research in D. L. Sexton and R. W. Smilor (eds.), *Entrepreneurship 2000* (Chicago: Upstart Publishing Co.), 291–321.

28. M. A. Hitt and B. B. Bartkus, 1997, International entrepreneurship in J. A. Katz and R. H. Brockhaus, Sr. (eds.), *Advances in Entrepreneurship, Firm Emergence and Growth* (Greenwich, CT: JAI Press), 7–30.

29. M. A. Hitt, R. E. Hoskisson, and H. Kim, 1997, International diversification: Effects on innovation and firm performance in product-diversified firms, *Academy of Management Journal* 40: 767–798.

30. B. Mascarenhas, 1997, The order and size of entry into international markets, *Journal of Business Venturing* 12: 287–299.

31. R. A. Burgelman, 1983, A model of the interaction of strategic behavior, corporate context, and the concept of strategy, *Academy of Management Review* 8: 61–70.

32. D. Leonard-Barton, 1995, *Wellsprings of Knowledge: Building and Sustaining the Sources of Innovation* (Cambridge, MA: Harvard Business School Press).

33. G. Hamel, 1997, Killer strategies that make shareholders rich, *Fortune*, June 23: 70–88.

34. S. V. Brull, 1997, Sony: A little sensor with a big future, *Business Week Interactive*, June 16, http://www.businessweek.com.

35. P. Coy and R. Grover, 1995, It's Nobuyuki Idei's Sony now, *Business Week*, December 18, 39.

36. G. G. Dess, G. T. Lumpkin, and J. G. Covin, 1997, Entrepreneurial strategy and firm performance: Tests of contingency and configurational models, *Strategic Management Journal* 18: 677–695.

37. L. C. Wright and R. W. Wright, 1997, Developing and deploying corporate resources in the technological race to market in H. Thomas, D. O'Neal, and M. Ghertman (eds.), *Strategy, Structure and Style* (Chichester, GB: John Wiley & Sons), 114–135.

38. R. G. McGrath, 1997, A real options logic for initiating technology positioning investments, *Academy of Management Review* 22: 974–996.

39. D. M. A. Rogers, 1996, The challenge of fifth generation R&D, *Research-Technology Management* July-August: 33–41.

40. B. L. David, 1994, How internal venture groups innovate, *Research-Technology Management* March–April: 38–43.

41. R. C. Shrader and M. Simon, 1997, Corporate versus independent new ventures: Resource, strategy, and performance differences, *Journal of Business Venturing* 12: 47–66.

42. B. O'Reilly, 1997, The secrets of America's most admired corporations: New ideas, new products, *Fortune*, March 3, 60–64.

43. J. A. Byrne, 1993, The horizontal corporation: It's about managing across, not up and down, *Business Week*, December 20, 76–81.

44. J. E. Ettlie, 1988, *Taking Charge of Manufacturing* (San Francisco: Jossey-Bass).

45. A. C. Amason, 1996, Distinguishing the effects of functional and dysfunctional conflict on strategic decision making: Resolving a paradox for top management teams, *Academy of Management Journal* 39: 123–148; P. R. Lawrence and J. W. Lorsch, 1969, *Organization and Environment* (Homewood, IL: Richard D. Irwin).

46. D. Dougherty, 1992, Interpretive barriers to successful product innovation in large firms, *Organization Science* 3: 179–202; D. Dougherty, 1990, Understanding new markets for new products, *Strategic Management Journal* 11 (Special Summer Issue): 59–78.

47. M. A. Hitt, R. D. Nixon, R. E. Hoskisson, and R. Kochhar, 1998, Corporate entrepreneurship and cross-functional fertilization: Activation, process and disintegration of a new product design team, *Entrepreneurship: Theory and Practice*, in press.

48. J. D. Orton and K. E. Weick, 1990, Loosely coupled systems: A reconsideration, *Academy of Management Review* 15: 203–223.

49. S. L. Brown and K. M. Eisenhardt, 1995, Product development: Past research, present findings and future directions, *Academy of Management Review* 20: 343–378.

50. A. Barua, C. H. S. Lee, and A. B. Whinston, 1995, Incentives and computing systems for team-based organizations, *Organization Science* 6: 487–504.

51. I. Sager, 1995, The view from IBM, *Business Week*, October 30, 142–150; IBM says it's ready for networking era, 1995, *Dallas Morning News*, November 14, D4.

52. K. M. Eisenhardt and S. L. Brown, 1998, Time pacing: Competing in markets that won't stand still, *Harvard Business Review* 76, no. 2: 59–69.

53. W. Q. Judge and A. Miller, 1991, Antecedents and outcomes of decision speed in different environmental contexts, *Academy of Management Journal* 34: 449–463.

54. M. B. Lieberman and D. B. Montgomery, 1988, First-mover advantages, *Strategic Management Journal* 9 (Special Summer Issue): 41–58.

55. W. Davidson, 1988, Technology, environments and organizational choice, paper presented at the conference on Managing the High-Tech Firm, Graduate School of Business, University of Colorado.

56. M. J. Chen and D. C. Hambrick, 1995, Speed, stealth and selective attack: How small firms differ from large firms in competitive behavior, *Academy of Management Journal* 38: 453–482.

57. W. M. Bulkeley, 1994, The latest big thing at many companies is speed, speed, speed, *Wall Street Journal*, December 23, A1, A5.

58. M. W. Lawless and P. C. Anderson, 1996, Generational technological change: The effects of innovation and local rivalry on performance, *Academy of Management Journal* 39: 1185–1217; U. Zander and B. Kogut, 1995, Knowledge and the speed of the transfer and imitation of organizational capabilities: An empirical test, *Organization Science* 6: 76–92.

59. K. M. Eisenhardt and B. N. Tabrizi, 1995, Accelerating adaptive processes: Product innovation in the global computer industry, *Administrative Science Quarterly* 40: 84–110.

60. Judge and Miller, Antecedents and outcomes.

61. Hitt, Nixon, Hoskisson, and Kochhar, Corporate entrepreneurship.

62. M. A. Hitt, R. E. Hoskisson, and R. D. Nixon, 1993, A midrange theory of interfunctional integration, its antecedents and outcomes, *Journal of Engineering Technology Management* 10: 161–185.

63. J. E. Forrest, 1992, Management aspects of strategic partnering, *Journal of General Management* 17, no. 4: 25–40; B. Borys and D. B. Jemison, 1989, Hybrid arrangements as strategic alliances: Theoretical issues in organizational combinations, *Academy of Management Review* 14: 234–249.

64. J. L. Badaracco, Jr., 1991, *The Knowledge Link: How Firms Compete Through Strategic Alliances* (Cambridge, MA: Harvard University School Press).

65. R. Langreth, 1995, Biotech companies abandon go-it-alone approach, *Wall Street Journal*, November 21, B4.

66. R. T. King, Jr., 1995, Pharmaceutical giants are eagerly shopping biotech bargain bin, *Wall Street Journal*, April 19, A1, A10.

67. G. Hamel, 1991, Competition for competence and interpartner learning within international strategic alliances, *Strategic Management Journal* 12: 83–103.

68. M. T. Dacin, M. A. Hitt, and E. Levitas, 1997, Selecting partners for successful international alliances: Examination of U.S. and Korean firms, *Journal of World Business*, 32, 1: 3–16; M. A. Hitt, M. T. Dacin, B. B. Tyler, and D. Park, 1997, Understanding the differences in Korean and U.S. Executive's strategic orientations, *Strategic Management Journal* 18: 159–167.

69. C. K. Prahalad and G. Hamel, 1990, The core competence of the corporation, *Harvard Business Review* 68, no. 3: 79–93.

70. D. Lei and M. A. Hitt, 1995, Strategic restructuring and outsourcing: The effect of mergers and acquisitions and LBOs on building firm skills and capabilities, *Journal of Management* 21: 835–860.

71. Hamel, Competition for competence.

72. King, Pharmaceutical giants are eagerly shopping.

73. D. C. Mowery and D. J. Teece, 1993, Japan's growing capabilities in industrial technology: Implications for U.S. managers and policy makers, *California Management Review* 35, no. 2: 9–34.

74. M. A. Hitt, R. E. Hoskisson, R. A. Johnson, and D. D. Moesel, 1996, The market for corporate control and firm innovation, *Academy of Management Journal* 39: 1084–1119.

75. M. A. Hitt, R. E. Hoskisson, R. D. Ireland, and J. S. Harrison, 1991, Effects of acquisitions on R&D inputs and outputs, *Academy of Management Journal* 34: 693–706.

76. Hitt et al., The market for corporate control and firm innovation.

77. M. A. Hitt, J. S. Harrison, R. D. Ireland, and A. Best, 1998, Attributes of successful and unsuccessful acquisitions of U.S. firms, *British Journal of Management*, in press; M. A. Hitt,

501

R. E. Hoskisson, and R. D. Ireland, 1990, Mergers and acquisitions and managerial commitment to innovation in M-form firms, *Strategic Management Journal* 11 (Special Summer Issue): 29–47.

78. B. L. Pandit and N. S. Siddharthan, 1998, Technological acquisition and investment: Lessons from recent Indian experience, *Journal of Business Venturing* 13: 43–55.

79. D. S. Cable and S. Shane, 1997, A prisoner's dilemma approach to entrepreneur-venture capitalist relationships, *Academy of Management Review* 22: 142–176.

80. T. E. Winters and D. L. Murfin, 1988, Venture capital investing for corporate development objectives, *Journal of Business Venturing* 3: 207–222.

81. G. F. Hardymon, M. J. DeNino, and M. S. Salter, 1983, When corporate venture capital doesn't work, *Harvard Business Review* 61, no. 3: 114–120.

82. U. Gupta, 1993, Venture capital investment soars, reversing four-year slide, *Wall Street Journal*, June 1, B2.

83. M. Wright, K. Robbie, and C. Ennew, 1997, Venture capitalists and serial entrepreneurs, *Journal of Business Venturing* 12: 227–249.

84. B. J. Feder, 1998, Good product, sound plans, no sure thing, *New York Times on the Web*, January 19, http://www.search.nytimes.com.

85. P. Patel and K. Pavitt, 1992, Large firms in the production of the world's technology: An important case of non-globalization in O. Granstrand, L. Hakanson, and S. Sjolander (eds.), *Technology Management and International Business: Internationalization of R&D and Technology* (New York: John Wiley & Sons), 53–74.

86. B. O'Reilly, 1994, The new face of small business, *Fortune*, May 2, 82–88.

87. Farrell et al., The boom in IPOs.

88. S. Chartrand, 1998, Women and minorities now account for biggest jump in startup companies, *New York Times* on the Web, January 19: http://www.search.nytimes.com.

89. T. Petzinger, Jr., 1997, Nurse agency thrives taking hard cases in the inner city, *Wall Street Journal* Interactive, October 19: http://www.interactive.wsj.com.

90. C. Boisseau, 1996, Young entrepreneurs finding themselves in good company, *Houston Chronicle*, March 26, C1, C6.

91. R. Rothwell, 1984, The role of small firms in the emergence of new technologies, *International Journal of Management Science* 12, no. 1: 19–29.

92. J. A. Byrne, 1993, Enterprise: Introduction, *Business Week* (Special Bonus Issue): 12; Hitt and Bartkus, International entrepreneurship.

93. G. McWilliams, 1995, Small fry goes on-line, *Business Week*, November 20, 158–164.

94. P. Coy, 1993, Start with some high-tech magic, *Business Week* (Special Bonus Issue): 24–28.

95. C. Burck, 1993, The real world of the entrepreneur, *Fortune*, April 5, 62–81.

96. T. Bates, 1995, Analysis of survival rates among franchise and independent small business startups, *Journal of Small Business Management* 33: 26–36.

97. J. S. Walsh and P. H. Anderson, 1995, Owner-manager adaptations/innovation preference and employment performance: A comparison of founders and non-founders in the Irish small firm sector, *Journal of Small Business Management* 33: 1–8.

98. L. W. Busenitz, 1997, Differences between entrepreneurs and managers in large organizations: Biases and heuristics in strategic decision making, *Journal of Business Venturing* 12: 9–30.

99. D. L. Sexton, N. B. Upton, L. E. Wacholtz, and P. P. McDougall, 1997, Learning needs of growth-oriented entrepreneurs, *Journal of Business Venturing* 12: 1–8.

100. Advantage staffing chief has found the right fit, 1997, *Wall Street Journal* Interactive, October 19: http://www.interactive.wsj.com.

101. R. A. Melcher, 1993, How Goliaths can act like Davids, *Business Week* (Special Bonus Issue): 192–201.

102. M. A. Hitt, B. W. Keats, H. F. Harback, and R. D. Nixon, 1994, Rightsizing: Building and maintaining strategic leadership and long-term competitiveness, *Organizational Dynamics* 23, no. 2: 18–32.

103. R. E. Hoskisson and M. A. Hitt, 1994, *Downscoping: Taming the Diversified Firm* (New York: Oxford University Press).

104. C. Cookson, 1998, Financial community develops a taste for industrial research, *Financial Times*, January 20, 17.

105. R. Routamo, 1998, Dragon as a playmate: Small businesses in Finland make big money in Russia, *The EM Global Perspective*, January 19: http://www.benlore.com.

106. A. Westfeldt, 1997, Convenience stores in the 90s: Wawa redefines an American institution, *Waco Tribune-Herald*, December 25, C5.

107. M. Thompson-Noel, 1997, Boldly venturing into virgin territories, *Financial Times*, November 20, 5.

108. Hitt, Keats, and DeMarie, Navigating in the new competitive landscape.

502

CASES

Contents

Preparing an Effective Case Analysis

In most strategic management courses, cases are used extensively as a teaching tool. A key reason is that cases allow opportunities to identify and solve organizational problems through use of the strategic management process. Thus, by analyzing cases and presenting the results, students learn how to effectively use the tools, techniques, and concepts that combine to form the strategic management process.

The cases that follow involve actual companies. Presented within them are problems and situations that managers must analyze and resolve. As you will see, a strategic management case can focus on an entire industry, a single organization, or a business unit of a large, diversified firm. The strategic management issues facing not-for-profit organizations also can be examined with the case analysis method.

Basically, the case analysis method calls for a careful diagnosis of an organization's current conditions (internal and external) so that appropriate strategic actions can be recommended. Appropriate actions not only allow a firm to survive in the long run, but also describe how it can develop and use core competencies to create sustainable competitive advantages and earn above-average returns. The case method has a rich heritage as a pedagogical approach to the study and understanding of managerial effectiveness.[1]

Critical to successful use of the case method is your *preparation*—that is, the preparation of the student or case analyst. Without careful study and analysis, you will lack the insights required to participate fully in the discussion of a firm's situation and the strategic actions that are appropriate.

Instructors adopt different approaches in their use of the case method. Some require their students to use a specific analytical procedure to examine an organization; others provide less structure, expecting students to learn by developing their own unique analytical method. Still other instructors believe that a moderately structured framework should be used to analyze a firm's situation and make appropriate recommendations. The specific approach you take will be determined by your professor. The approach we present to you here is a moderately structured framework.

Discussion of the case method is divided into four sections. First, it is important for you to understand why cases are used and what skills you can expect to learn through successful use of the case method. Second, a process-oriented framework is provided that can help you analyze cases and effectively discuss the results of your work. Using this framework in a classroom setting yields valuable experiences that can, in turn, help you successfully complete assignments received from your employer. Third, we describe briefly what you can expect to occur during in-class discussions of cases. As this description shows, the relationship and interactions between instructors and students during case discussions are different than they are during lectures. Finally, a moderately structured framework is offered for effective completion of in-depth oral and written presentations. Written and oral communication skills also are attributes valued highly in many organizational settings; hence, their development today can serve you well in the future.

USING THE CASE METHOD

The case method is based on a philosophy that combines knowledge acquisition with significant student involvement. In the words of Alfred North Whitehead, this philosophy "rejects the doctrine that students had first learned passively, and then, having learned should apply knowledge."[2] The case method, instead, is based on principles elaborated by John Dewey:

> Only by wrestling with the conditions of this problem at hand, seeking and finding his own way out, does [the student] think. . . . If he cannot devise his own solution (not, of course, in isolation, but in correspondence with the teacher and other pupils) and find his own way out he will not learn, not even if he can recite some correct answer with a hundred percent accuracy.[3]

The case method brings reality into the classroom. When developed and presented effectively, with rich and interesting detail, cases keep conceptual discus-

sions grounded in reality. Experience shows that simple fictional accounts of situations and collections of actual organizational data and articles from public sources are not as effective for learning as are fully developed cases. A comprehensive case presents you with a partial clinical study of a real-life situation that faced practicing managers. A case presented in narrative form provides motivation for involvement with and analysis of a specific situation. By framing alternative strategic actions and by confronting the complexity and ambiguity of the practical world, case analysis provides extraordinary power for your involvement with a personal learning experience. Some of the potential consequences of using the case method are summarized in Table 1.

As Table 1 suggests, the case method can help you develop your analytical and judgment skills. Case analysis also helps you learn how to ask the right questions—that is, the questions that focus on the core strategic issues included within a case. Students aspiring to be managers can improve their ability to identify underlying problems, rather than focusing on superficial symptoms, through development of the skills required to ask probing, yet appropriate, questions.

The particular set of cases your instructor chooses to assign the class can expose you to a wide variety of organizations and managerial situations. This approach vicariously broadens your experience base and provides insights into many types of managerial situations, tasks, and responsibilities. Such indirect experience can help you make a more informed career

---

TABLE 1 *Consequences of Student Involvement with the Case Method*

1. Case analysis requires students to practice important managerial skills—diagnosing, making decisions, observing, listening, and persuading—while preparing for a case discussion.
2. Cases require students to relate analysis and action, to develop realistic and concrete actions despite the complexity and partial knowledge characterizing the situation being studied.
3. Students must confront the *intractability of reality*—complete with absence of needed information, an imbalance between needs and available resources, and conflicts among competing objectives.
4. Students develop a general managerial point of view—where responsibility is sensitive to action in a diverse environmental context.

Source: C. C. Lundberg and C. Enz, 1993, A framework for student case preparation, *Case Research Journal* 13 (Summer): 134.

C-2

decision about the industry and managerial situation you believe will prove to be challenging and satisfying. Finally, experience in analyzing cases definitely enhances your problem-solving skills.

Furthermore, when your instructor requires oral and written presentations, your communication skills will be honed through use of the case method. Of course, these added skills depend on your preparation as well as your instructor's facilitation of learning. However, the primary responsibility for learning is yours. The quality of case discussion is generally acknowledged to require, at a minimum, a thorough mastery of case facts and some independent analysis of them. The case method therefore first requires that you read and think carefully about each case. Additional comments about the preparation you should complete to successfully discuss a case appear in the next section.

STUDENT PREPARATION FOR CASE DISCUSSION

If you are inexperienced with the case method, you may need to alter your study habits. A lecture-oriented course may not require you to do intensive preparation for *each* class period. In such a course, you have the latitude to work through assigned readings and review lecture notes according to your own schedule. However, an assigned case requires significant and conscientious *preparation before class*. Without it, you will be unable to contribute meaningfully to in-class discussion. Therefore, careful reading and thinking about case facts, as well as reasoned analyses and the development of alternative solutions to case problems, are essential. Recommended alternatives should flow logically from core problems identified through study of the case. Table 2 shows a set of steps that can help you develop familiarity with a case, identify problems, and propose strategic actions that increase the probability that a firm will achieve strategic competitiveness and earn above-average returns.

Gaining Familiarity

The first step of an effective case analysis process calls for you to become familiar with the facts featured in the case and the focal firm's situation. Initially, you should become familiar with the focal

firm's general situation (e.g., who, what, how, where, and when). Thorough familiarization demands appreciation of the nuances as well as the major issues in the case.

Gaining familiarity with a situation requires you to study several situational levels, including interactions between and among individuals within groups, business units, the corporate office, the local community, and the society at large. Recognizing relationships within and among levels facilitates a more thorough understanding of the specific case situation.

It is also important that you evaluate information on a continuum of certainty. Information that is verifiable by several sources and judged along similar dimensions can be classified as a *fact*. Information representing someone's perceptual judgment of a particular situation is referred to as an *inference*. Information gleaned from a situation that is not verifiable is classified as *speculation*. Finally, information that is independent of verifiable sources and arises through individual or group discussion is an *assumption*. Obviously, case analysts and organizational decision makers prefer having access to facts over inferences, speculations, and assumptions.

Personal feelings, judgments, and opinions evolve when you are analyzing a case. It is important to be aware of your own feelings about the case and to evaluate the accuracy of perceived "facts" to ensure that the objectivity of your work is maximized.

Recognizing Symptoms

Recognition of symptoms is the second step of an effective case analysis process. A symptom is an indication that something is not as you or someone else thinks it should be. You may be tempted to correct the symptoms instead of searching for true problems. True problems are the conditions or situations requiring solution before an organization's, unit's, or individual's performance can improve. Identifying and listing symptoms early in the case analysis process tends to reduce the temptation to label symptoms as problems. The focus of your analysis should be on the *actual causes* of a problem, rather than on its symptoms. It is important therefore to remember that symptoms are indicators of problems; subsequent work facilitates discovery of critical causes of problems that your case recommendations must address.

TABLE 2 *An Effective Case Analysis Process*

Step 1: Gaining Familiarity	a. In general—determine who, what, how, where, and when (the critical facts of the case). b. In detail—identify the places, persons, activities, and contexts of the situation. c. Recognize the degree of certainty/uncertainty of acquired information.
Step 2: Recognizing Symptoms	a. List all indicators (including stated "problems") that something is not as expected or as desired. b. Ensure that symptoms are not assumed to be the problem (symptoms should lead to identification of the problem).
Step 3: Identifying Goals	a. Identify critical statements by major parties (e.g., people, groups, the work unit, etc.). b. List all goals of the major parties that exist or can be reasonably inferred.
Step 4: Conducting the Analysis	a. Decide which ideas, models, and theories seem useful. b. Apply these conceptual tools to the situation. c. As new information is revealed, cycle back to substeps a and b.
Step 5: Making the Diagnosis	a. Identify predicaments (goal inconsistencies). b. Identify problems (discrepancies between goals and performance). c. Prioritize predicaments/problems regarding timing, importance, etc.
Step 6: Doing the Action Planning	a. Specify and prioritize the criteria used to choose action alternatives. b. Discover or invent feasible action alternatives. c. Examine the probable consequences of action alternatives. d. Select a course of action. e. Design an implementation plan/schedule. f. Create a plan for assessing the action to be implemented.

Source: C. C. Lundberg and C. Enz, 1993, A framework for student case preparation, *Case Research Journal* 13 (Summer): 144.

Identifying Goals

The third step of effective case analysis calls for you to identify the goals of the major organizations, units, and/or individuals in a case. As appropriate, you should also identify each firm's strategic intent and strategic mission. Typically, these direction-setting statements (goals, strategic intents, and strategic missions) are derived from comments of the central characters in the organization, business unit, or top management team described in the case and/or from public documents (e.g., an annual report).

Completing this step successfully sometimes can be difficult. Nonetheless, the outcomes you attain from this step are essential to an effective case analy-sis because identifying goals, intent, and mission helps you to clarify the major problems featured in a case and to evaluate alternative solutions to those problems. Direction-setting statements are not always stated publicly or prepared in written format. When this occurs, you must infer goals from other available factual data and information.

Conducting the Analysis

The fourth step of effective case analysis is concerned with acquiring a systematic understanding of a situation. Occasionally cases are analyzed in a less-than-thorough manner. Such analyses may be a product of a busy schedule or the difficulty and complexity of the issues described in a particular case. Sometimes you will face pressures on your limited amounts of time and may believe that you can understand the situation described in a case without systematic *analysis* of all the facts. However, experience shows that familiarity with a case's facts is a necessary, but insufficient, step to the development of effective solutions—solutions that can enhance a firm's strategic competitiveness. In fact, a less-than-thorough analysis typically results in an emphasis on symptoms, rather than problems and their causes. To analyze a case effectively, you should be skeptical of quick or easy approaches and answers.

A systematic analysis helps you understand a situation and determine what can work and probably what will not work. Key linkages and underlying causal networks based on the history of the firm become apparent. In this way, you can separate causal networks from symptoms.

Also, because the quality of a case analysis depends on applying appropriate tools, it is important that you use the ideas, models, and theories that seem to be useful for evaluating and solving individual and unique situations. As you consider facts and symptoms, a useful theory may become apparent. Of course, having familiarity with conceptual models may be important in the effective analysis of a situation. Successful students and successful organizational strategists add to their intellectual tool kits on a continual basis.

Making the Diagnosis

The fifth step of effective case analysis—diagnosis—is the process of identifying and clarifying the roots of the problems by comparing goals to facts. In this step, it is useful to search for predicaments. Predicaments are situations in which goals do not fit with known facts. When you evaluate the actual performance of an organization, business unit, or individual, you may identify over- or under achievement (relative to established goals). Of course, single-problem situations are rare. Accordingly, you should recognize that the case situations you study probably will be complex in nature.

Effective diagnosis requires you to determine the problems affecting longer-term performance and those requiring immediate handling. Understanding

these issues will aid your efforts to prioritize problems and predicaments, given available resources and existing constraints.

Doing the Action Planning

The final step of an effective case analysis process is called action planning. Action planning is the process of identifying appropriate alternative actions. Important in the action planning step is selection of the criteria you will use to evaluate the identified alternatives. You may derive these criteria from the analyses; typically, they are related to key strategic situations facing the focal organization. Furthermore, it is important that you prioritize these criteria to ensure a rational and effective evaluation of alternative courses of action.

Typically, managers "satisfice" when selecting courses of actions; that is, they find *acceptable* courses of action that meet most of the chosen evaluation criteria. A rule of thumb that has proved valuable to strategic decision makers is to select an alternative that leaves other plausible alternatives available if the one selected fails.

Once you have selected the best alternative, you must specify an implementation plan. Developing an implementation plan serves as a reality check on the feasibility of your alternatives. Thus, it is important that you give thoughtful consideration to all issues associated with the implementation of the selected alternatives.

WHAT TO EXPECT FROM IN-CLASS CASE DISCUSSIONS

Classroom discussions of cases differ significantly from lectures. The case method calls for instructors to guide the discussion, encourage student participation, and solicit alternative views. When alternative views are not forthcoming, instructors typically adopt one view so students can be challenged to respond thoughtfully to it. Often students' work is evaluated in terms of both the quantity and the quality of their contributions to in-class case discussions. Students benefit by having their views judged against those of their peers and by responding to challenges by other class members and/or the instructor.

During case discussions, instructors listen, question, and probe to extend the analysis of case issues. In the course of these actions, peers or the instructor may challenge an individual's views and the validity of alternative perspectives that have been expressed. These challenges are offered in a constructive manner; their intent is to help students develop their analytical and communication skills. Commonly instructors encourage students to be innovative and original in the development and presentation of their ideas. Over the course of an individual discussion, students can develop a more complex view of the case, benefiting from the diverse inputs of their peers and instructor. Among other benefits, experience with multiple case discussions should help students increase their knowledge of the advantages and disadvantages of group decision-making processes.

Comments that contribute to the discussion are valued by student peers as well as the instructor. To offer *relevant* contributions, you are encouraged to use independent thought and, through discussions with your peers outside of class, to refine your thinking. We also encourage you to avoid using "I think," "I believe," and "I feel" to discuss your inputs to a case analysis process. Instead, consider using a less emotion laden phrase, such as "My analysis shows. . . ." This highlights the logical nature of the approach you have taken to complete the six steps of an effective case analysis process.

When preparing for an in-class case discussion, you should plan to use the case data to explain your assessment of the situation. Assume that the case facts are known to your peers and instructor. In addition, it is good practice to prepare notes before class discussions and use them as you explain your view. Effective notes signal to classmates and the instructor that you are prepared to engage in a thorough discussion of a case. Moreover, thorough notes eliminate the need for you to memorize the facts and figures needed to discuss a case successfully.

The case analysis process described above can help you prepare to effectively discuss a case during class meetings. Adherence to this process results in consideration of the issues required to identify a focal firm's problems and to propose strategic actions through which the firm can increase the probability it will achieve strategic competitiveness.

In some instances, your instructor may ask you to prepare either an oral or a written analysis of a particular case. Typically, such an assignment demands even more thorough study and analysis of the case contents. At your instructor's discretion, oral and written analyses may be completed by individuals or by groups of two or more people. The information and insights gained through completing the six steps shown in Table 2 often are of value in the development of an oral or a written analysis. However, when preparing an oral or written presentation, you must consider the overall framework in which your information and inputs will be presented. Such a framework is the focus of the next section.

PREPARING AN ORAL/WRITTEN CASE PRESENTATION

Experience shows that two types of thinking are necessary to develop an effective oral or written presentation (see Figure 1). The upper part of the model in Figure 1 outlines the *analysis* of case preparation.

In the analysis stage, you should first analyze the general external environmental issues affecting the firm. Next your environmental analysis should focus on the particular industry (or industries, in the case of a diversified company) in which a firm operates. Finally, you should examine the competitive environment of the focal firm. Through study of the three levels of the external environment, you will be able to identify a firm's opportunities and threats. Following the external environmental analysis is the analysis of the firm's internal environment. This analysis results in the identification of the firm's strengths and weaknesses.

As noted in Figure 1, you must then change the focus from analysis to *synthesis*. Specifically, you must *synthesize* information gained from your analysis of the firm's internal and external environments. Synthesizing information allows you to generate alternatives that can resolve the significant problems or challenges facing the focal firm. Once you identify a best alternative, from an evaluation based on predetermined criteria and goals, you must explore implementation actions.

Table 3 outlines the sections that should be included in either an oral or a written presentation: introduction (strategic profile and purpose), situation analysis, statements of strengths/weaknesses and opportunities/threats, strategy formulation, and imple-

FIGURE 1 *Types of Thinking in Case Preparation: Analysis and Synthesis*

ANALYSIS

External environment

General environment
Industry environment
Competitive environment

Internal environment

Statements of
strengths,
weaknesses,
opportunities,
and threats

Alternatives
Evaluations of alternatives
Implementation

SYNTHESIS

C-7

mentation. These sections, which can be completed only through use of the two types of thinking featured in Figure 1, are described in the following discussion. Familiarity with the contents of your book's 13 chapters is helpful because the general outline for an oral or a written presentation shown in Table 3 is based on an understanding of the strategic management process detailed in those chapters.

Strategic Profile and Case Analysis Purpose

The strategic profile should state briefly the critical facts from the case that have affected the historical strategic direction and performance of the focal firm. The case facts should not be restated in the profile;

rather, these comments should show how the critical facts lead to a particular focus for your analysis. This primary focus should be emphasized in this section's conclusion. In addition, this section should state important assumptions about case facts on which the analyses may be based.

Situation Analysis

As shown in Table 3, a general starting place for completing a situation analysis is the general environment.

General Environmental Analysis First, your analysis of the general environment should consider the *effects of globalization* on the focal firm and its indus-

TABLE 3 *General Outline for an Oral or a Written Presentation*

I. Strategic Profile and Case Analysis Purpose

II. Situation Analysis

   A. General environmental analysis

   B. Industry analysis

   C. Competitive environmental analysis

   D. Internal analysis

III. Identification of Environmental Opportunities and Threats and Firm Strengths and Weaknesses (SWOT Analysis)

IV. Strategy Formulation

   A. Strategic alternatives

   B. Alternative evaluation

   C. Alternative choice

V. Strategic Alternative Implementation

   A. Action items

   B. Action plan

try. Following that evaluation, you should analyze general environmental trends. Table 4 lists a number of general environmental trends that, when studied, should yield valuable insights. Many of these issues are explained more fully in Chapter 2. These trends need to be evaluated for their impact on the focal firm's strategy and on the industry (or industries) in which it competes in the pursuit of strategic competitiveness.

Industry Analysis Once you analyze the general environmental trends, you should study their effect on the focal industry. Often the same environmental trend may have a significantly different impact on separate industries. Furthermore, the same trend may affect firms within the same industry differently. For instance, with deregulation of the airline industry, older, established airlines had a significant decrease in profitability, while many smaller airlines, with lower cost structures and greater flexibility, were able to aggressively enter new markets.

Porter's five force model is a useful tool for analyzing the specific industry (see Chapter 2). Careful study of how the five competitive forces (i.e., supplier power, buyer power, potential entrants, substitute products, and rivalry among competitors) affect firm strategy is important. These forces may create threats or opportunities relative to the specific business-level strategies (i.e., differentiation, low cost, focus) being implemented. Often a strategic group's analysis reveals how different environmental trends

are affecting industry competitors. Strategic group analysis is useful for understanding the industry's competitive structure and the profit possibilities within those structures.

Competitive Environmental Analysis
Firms also need to analyze each of their primary competitors. This analysis should identify competitors' current strategies, strategic intent, strategic mission, capabilities, core competencies, and a competitive response profile. This information is useful to the focal firm in formulating an appropriate strategy and in predicting competitors' probable responses. Sources that can be used to gather information about an industry and companies with whom the focal firm competes are listed in Appendix I. Included in this list is a wide range of publications, such as periodicals, newspapers, bibliographies, directories of companies, industry ratios, forecasts, rankings/ratings, and other valuable statistics.

Internal Analysis Assessing a firm's strengths and weaknesses through a value chain analysis facilitates moving from the external environment to the internal environment. Analysis of the primary and support activities of the value chain provides opportunities to understand how external environmental trends affect the specific activities of a firm. Such analysis helps highlight strengths and weaknesses (see Chapter 3 for an explanation of the value chain).

TABLE 4 *Sample General Environmental Categories*

Technology	■ Information technology continues to become cheaper and have more practical applications.
	■ Database technology allows organization of complex data and distribution of information.
	■ Telecommunications technology and networks increasingly provide fast transmission of all sources of data, including voice, written communications, and video information.
Demographic Trends	■ Computerized design and manufacturing technologies continue to facilitate quality and flexibility.
	■ Regional changes in population due to migration
	■ Changing ethnic composition of the population
	■ Aging of the population
	■ Aging of the "baby boom" generation
Economic Trends	■ Interest rates
	■ Inflation rates
	■ Savings rates
	■ Trade deficits
	■ Budget deficits
	■ Exchange rates
Political/Legal Environment	■ Anti-trust enforcement
	■ Tax policy changes
	■ Environmental protection laws
	■ Extent of regulation/deregulation
	■ Developing countries privatizing state monopolies
	■ State-owned industries
Sociocultural Environment	■ Increasing number of women in the work force
	■ Awareness of health and fitness issues
	■ Concern for the environment
	■ Concern for customers
Global Environment	■ Currency exchange rates
	■ Free trade agreements
	■ Trade deficits
	■ New or developing markets

C-9

For purposes of preparing an oral or a written presentation, it is important to note that strengths are internal resources and capabilities that have the potential to be core competencies. Weaknesses, on the other hand, are internal resources and capabilities that have the potential to place a firm at a competitive disadvantage relative to its rivals. Thus, some of a firm's resources and capabilities are strengths; others are weaknesses.

When evaluating the internal characteristics of the firm, your analysis of the functional activities emphasized is critical. For instance, if the strategy of the firm is primarily technology driven, it is important to evaluate the firm's R&D activities. If the strategy is market driven, marketing functional activities are of paramount importance. If a firm has financial difficulties, critical financial ratios would require careful evaluation. In fact, because of the importance of financial health, most cases require financial analyses. Appendix II lists and operationally defines several common financial ratios. Included are tables describing profitability, liquidity, leverage, activity, and shareholders' return ratios. Other firm characteristics that should be examined to study the internal environment effectively include leadership, organizational culture, structure, and control systems.

Identification of Environmental Opportunities and Threats and Firm Strengths and Weaknesses (SWOT Analysis)

The outcome of the situation analysis is the identification of a firm's strengths and weaknesses and its environmental threats and opportunities. The next step requires that you analyze the strengths and weaknesses and the opportunities and threats for configurations that benefit or do not benefit a firm's efforts to achieve strategic competitiveness. Case analysts, and organizational strategists as well, seek to match a firm's strengths with its external environmental opportunities. In addition, strengths are chosen to prevent any serious environmental threat from affecting negatively the firm's performance. The key objective of conducting a SWOT analysis is to determine how to position the firm so it can take advantage of opportunities, while simultaneously avoiding or minimizing environmental threats. Results from a SWOT analysis yield valuable insights into the selection of strategies a firm should implement to achieve strategic competitiveness.

The *analysis* of a case should not be overemphasized relative to the *synthesis* of results gained from your analytical efforts. There may be a temptation to spend most of your oral or written case analysis on results from the analysis. It is important, however, that you make an equal effort to develop and evaluate alternatives and to design implementation of the chosen strategy.

Strategy Formulation–Strategic Alternatives, Alternative Evaluation, and Alternative Choice

Developing alternatives is often one of the most difficult steps in preparing an oral or a written presentation. Development of three to four alternative strategies is common (see Chapter 4 for business-level strategy alternatives and Chapter 6 for corporate-level strategy alternatives). Each alternative should be feasible (i.e., it should match the firm's strengths, capabilities, and especially core competencies), and feasibility should be demonstrated. In

addition, you should show how each alternative takes advantage of the environmental opportunity or avoids/buffers against environmental threats. Developing carefully thought out alternatives requires synthesis of your analyses' results and creates greater credibility in oral and written case presentations.

Once you develop strong alternatives, you must evaluate the set to choose the best one. Your choice should be defensible and provide benefits over the other alternatives. Thus, it is important that both alternative development and evaluation of alternatives be thorough. The choice of the best alternative should be explained and defended.

Strategic Alternative Implementation– Action Items and Action Plan

After selecting the most appropriate strategy (that is, the strategy with the highest probability of enhancing a firm's strategic competitiveness), you must consider effective implementation. Effective synthesis is important to ensure that you have considered and evaluated all critical implementation issues. Issues you might consider include the structural changes necessary to implement the new strategy. In addition, leadership changes and new controls or incentives may be necessary to implement strategic actions. The implementation actions you recommend should be explicit and thoroughly explained. Occasionally, careful evaluation of implementation actions may show the strategy to be less favorable than you thought originally. A strategy is only as good as the firm's ability to implement it effectively. Therefore, effort to determine effective implementation is important.

Process Issues

You should ensure that your presentation (either oral or written) has logical consistency throughout. For example, if your presentation identifies one purpose, but your analysis focuses on issues that differ from the stated purpose, the logical inconsistency will be apparent. Likewise, your alternatives should flow from the configuration of strengths, weaknesses, opportunities, and threats you identified by the internal and external analyses.

Thoroughness and clarity also are critical to an effective presentation. Thoroughness is represented by the comprehensiveness of the analysis and alternative generation. Furthermore, clarity in the results of the analyses, selection of the best alternative strategy, and design of implementation actions are important. For example, your statement of the strengths and weaknesses should flow clearly and logically from the internal analyses presented.

Presentations (oral or written) that show logical consistency, thoroughness, and clarity of purpose, effective analyses, and feasible recommendations (strategy and implementation) are more effective and will receive more positive evaluations. Furthermore, developing the skills necessary to make such presentations will enhance your future job performance and career success.

APPENDIX I: SOURCES FOR INDUSTRY AND COMPETITOR ANALYSES

Abstracts and Indexes

Periodicals	ABI/Inform
	Business Periodicals Index
	InfoTrac (CD-ROM computer multidiscipline index)
	Investext (CD-ROM)
	Predicasts F&S Index United States
	Predicasts Overview of Markets and Technology (PROMT)
	Predicasts R&S Index Europe
	Predicasts R&S Index International
	Public Affairs Information Service Bulletin (PAIS)
	Reader's Guide to Periodical Literature
Newspapers	NewsBank
	Business NewsBank
	New York Times Index
	Wall Street Journal Index
	Wall Street Journal/Barron's Index
	Washington Post Index

Bibliographies

	Encyclopedia of Business Information Sources
	Handbook of Business Information

Directories

Companies—General	America's Corporate Families and International Affiliates
	Hoover's Handbook of American Business
	Hoover's Handbook of World Business
	Million Dollar Directory
	Standard & Poor's Corporation Records
	Standard & Poor's Register of Corporations, Directors, and Executives
	Ward's Business Directory
Companies—International	America's Corporate Families and International Affiliates
	Business Asia
	Business China
	Business Eastern Europe
	Business Europe
	Business International

	Business International Money Report
	Business Latin America
	Directory of American Firms Operating in Foreign Countries
	Directory of Foreign Firms Operating in the United States
	Hoover's Handbook of World Business
	International Directory of Company Histories
	Moody's Manuals, International (2 volumes)
	Who Owns Whom
Companies—Manufacturers	*Manufacturing USA: Industry Analyses, Statistics, and Leading Companies*
	Thomas Register of American Manufacturers
	U.S. Office of Management and Budget, Executive Office of the President, *Standard Industrial Classification Manual*
	U.S. Manufacturer's Directory
Companies—Private	*Million Dollar Directory*
	Ward's Directory
Companies—Public	Annual Reports and 10-K Reports
	Disclosure (corporate reports)
	Q-File
	Moody's Manuals:
	Moody's Bank and Finance Manual
	Moody's Industrial Manual
	Moody's International Manual
	Moody's Municipal and Government Manual
	Moody's OTC Industrial Manual
	Moody's OTC Unlisted Manual
	Moody's Public Utility Manual
	Moody's Transportation Manual
	Standard & Poor Corporation, *Standard Corporation Descriptions:*
	Standard & Poor's Handbook
	Standard & Poor's Industry Surveys
	Standard & Poor's Investment Advisory Service
	Standard & Poor's Outlook
	Standard & Poor's Statistical Service
Companies—Subsidiaries and Affiliates	*America's Corporate Families and International Affiliates*
	Ward's Directory
	Who Owns Whom
	Moody's Industry Review
	Standard & Poor's Analyst's Handbook
	Standard & Poor's Industry Report Service
	Standard & Poor's Industry Surveys (2 volumes)
	U.S. Department of Commerce, *U.S. Industrial Outlook*

Industry Ratios

Dun & Bradstreet, *Industry Norms and Key Business Ratios*
Robert Morris Associates Annual Statement Studies
Troy Almanac of Business and Industrial Financial Ratios

Industry Forecasts

International Trade Administration, *U.S. Industrial Outlook Predicasts Forecasts*

Rankings & Ratings

Annual Report on American Industry in *Forbes*
Business Rankings and Salaries
Business One Irwin Business and Investment Almanac
Corporate and Industry Research Reports (CIRR)
Dun's Business Rankings
Moody's Industrial Review
Rating Guide to Franchises
Standard & Poor's Industry Report Service
Value Line Investment Survey
Ward's Business Directory

Statistics

American Statistics Index (ASI) Bureau of the Census, U.S. Department of Commerce, *Economic Census Publications*

Bureau of the Census, U.S. Department of Commerce, *Statistical Abstract of the United States*

Bureau of Economic Analysis, U.S. Department of Commerce, *Survey of Current Business*

Internal Revenue Service, U.S. Treasury Department, *Statistics of Income: Corporation Income Tax Returns*

Statistical Reference Index (SRI)

C-13

APPENDIX II: FINANCIAL ANALYSIS IN CASE STUDIES

TABLE A.1 *Profitability Ratios*

Ratio	Formula	What it Shows
1. Return on total assets	$\dfrac{\text{Profits after taxes}}{\text{Total assets}}$	The net return on total investment of the firm
	or	or
	$\dfrac{\text{Profits after taxes} + \text{interest}}{\text{Total assets}}$	The return on both creditors' and shareholders' investments
2. Return on stockholders' equity (or return on net worth)	$\dfrac{\text{Profits after taxes}}{\text{Total stockholders' equity}}$	How effectively the company is utilizing shareholders' funds
3. Return on common equity	$\dfrac{\text{Profit after taxes} - \text{preferred stock dividends}}{\text{Total stockholders' equity} - \text{par value of preferred stock}}$	The net return to common stockholders
4. Operating profit margin (or return on sales)	$\dfrac{\text{Profits before taxes and before interest}}{\text{Sales}}$	The firm's profitability from regular operations
5. Net profit margin (or net return on sales)	$\dfrac{\text{Profits after taxes}}{\text{Sales}}$	The firm's net profit as a percentage of total sales

TABLE A.2 *Liquidity Ratios*

Ratio	Formula	What it Shows
1. Current ratio	$\dfrac{\text{Current assets}}{\text{Current liabilities}}$	The firm's ability to meet its current financial liabilities
2. Quick ratio (or acid-test ratio)	$\dfrac{\text{Current assets} - \text{inventory}}{\text{Current liabilities}}$	The firm's ability to pay off short-term obligations without relying on sales of inventory
3. Inventory to net working capital	$\dfrac{\text{Inventory}}{\text{Current assets} - \text{current liabilities}}$	The extent to which the firm's working capital is tied up in inventory

TABLE A.3 *Leverage Ratios*

Ratio	Formula	What it Shows
1. Debt-to-assets	$\dfrac{\text{Total debt}}{\text{Total assets}}$	Total borrowed funds as a percentage of total assets
2. Debt-to-equity	$\dfrac{\text{Total debt}}{\text{Total shareholders' equity}}$	Borrowed funds versus the funds provided by shareholders
3. Long-term debt-to-equity	$\dfrac{\text{Long-term debt}}{\text{Total shareholders' equity}}$	Leverage used by the firm
4. Times-interest-earned (or coverage ratio)	$\dfrac{\text{Profits before interest and taxes}}{\text{Total interest charges}}$	The firm's ability to meet all interest payments
5. Fixed charge coverage	$\dfrac{\text{Profits before taxes and interest} + \text{lease obligations}}{\text{Total interest charges} + \text{lease obligations}}$	The firm's ability to meet all fixed-charge obligations including lease payments

TABLE A.4 *Activity Ratios*

Ratio	Formula	What it Shows
1. Inventory turnover	$\dfrac{\text{Sales}}{\text{Inventory of finished goods}}$	The effectiveness of the firm in employing inventory
2. Fixed assets turnover	$\dfrac{\text{Sales}}{\text{Fixed assets}}$	The effectiveness of the firm in utilizing plant and equipment
3. Total assets turnover	$\dfrac{\text{Sales}}{\text{Total assets}}$	The effectiveness of the firm in utilizing total assets
4. Accounts receivable turnover	$\dfrac{\text{Annual credit sales}}{\text{Accounts receivable}}$	How many times the total receivables have been collected during the accounting period
5. Average collection period	$\dfrac{\text{Accounts receivable}}{\text{Average daily sales}}$	The average length of time the firm waits to collect payments after sales

TABLE A.5 *Shareholders' Return Ratios*

Ratio	Formula	What it Shows
1. Dividend yield on common stock	$\dfrac{\text{Annual dividends per share}}{\text{Current market price per share}}$	A measure of return to common stockholders in the form of dividends.
2. Price-earnings ratio	$\dfrac{\text{Current market price per share}}{\text{After-tax earnings per share}}$	An indication of market perception of the firm. Usually, the faster-growing or less risky firms tend to have higher PE ratios than the slower-growing or more risky firms.
3. Dividend payout ratio	$\dfrac{\text{Annual dividends per share}}{\text{After-tax earnings per share}}$	An indication of dividends paid out as a percentage of profits.
4. Cash flow per share	$\dfrac{\text{After-tax profits} + \text{depreciation}}{\text{Number of common shares outstanding}}$	A measure of total cash per share available for use by the firm.

NOTES

C-15

1. C. Christensen, 1989, *Teaching and the Case Method* (Boston: Harvard Business School Publishing Division); C. C. Lundberg, 1993, Introduction to the case method, in C. M. Vance (ed.), *Mastering Management Education* (Newbury Park, Calif.: Sage).

2. C. C. Lundberg and E. Enz, 1993, A framework for student case preparation, *Case Research Journal* 13 (Summer): 133.

3. J. Soltis, 1971, John Dewey, in L. E. Deighton (ed.), *Encyclopedia of Education* (New York: Macmillan and Free Press).

Amazon.com

Suresh Kotha
Emer Dooley

University of Washington

Amazon is the beginning of a completely new way to buy books. . . . It could increase book sales quite dramatically by making it easier for people to find the books they want.

—Alberto Vitale,
Chairman, Random House Inc.

It is projected that as many as 700 million people worldwide will be using the Internet by the year 2000. The typical Internet user in 1996 was young, affluent, and well educated. The potential size and affluence of this target market has led many observers to coin the phrase the "Internet Gold Rush." Not unlike the California gold rush of 1849 when prospectors lost everything, pickings in the Internet gold rush so far have been extremely limited. Most commercial Web sites—they number in the thousands—generate no revenue and cost upwards of $500,000 a year to maintain and operate. Losses by major corporations are so widespread that Don Logan, CEO of Time Warner, declared publicly that the Time Warner Web site, "Pathfinder," gave a "new definition to the term black hole." Although historically every gold rush has been a net loss, there have always been the successful few who buck the

trend and garner extraordinary rewards. This case explores the efforts of one such entrepreneur, Jeffrey Bezos, and his online bookstore—Amazon.com—on the World Wide Web.

Amazon.com provides a singular case in which the frequently hyped World Wide Web is actually changing how consumers buy products and services. Not content to just transplant the traditional book retailing format to the World Wide Web, Jeff Bezos, the founder behind Amazon.com, is attempting to transform it through technology that taps the interactive nature of the Internet. At Amazon.com like-minded bibliophiles can meet, discuss books, swap raves and pans, and, most importantly, spend money. Over the past two years, Bezos has quietly built a fast-growing business. His Web site (http://www.amazon.com) has become an underground sensation for thousands of book lovers around the world who spend hours perusing its vast electronic library, reading other customers' amusing online reviews, and ordering books. This case describes how Bezos has managed to build a rapidly growing business on the Internet and the challenges he currently faces as other firms attempt to imitate his model of competition.

COMPANY BACKGROUND

In 1994, Jeffrey Bezos, a computer science and electrical engineering graduate from Princeton Univer-

This case was prepared by Assistant Professor Suresh Kotha and Emer Dooley, as the basis for class discussion rather than to illustrate either effective or ineffective handling of an administrative situation. Copyright © Kotha and Dooley. All rights reserved.

sity, was the youngest senior vice president in the history of D. E. Shaw, a Wall Street-based investment bank. During the summer of that year, one statistic about the Internet caught his imagination—Internet usage was growing at 2,300 percent a year. His reaction: "Anything that's growing that fast is going to be ubiquitous very quickly. It was my wake-up call."

He left his job, drew up a list of 20 possible products that could be sold on the Internet, and quickly narrowed the prospects to music and books. Both had a potential advantage for online sale: far too many titles for a single store to stock. He chose books.

> There are so many of them! There are 1.5 million English-language books in print, 3 million books in all languages worldwide. This volume defined the opportunity. Consumers keep demonstrating that they value authoritative selection. The biggest phenomenon in retailing is the big-format store—the "category killer"—whether it's selling books, toys, or music. But the largest physical bookstore in the world has only 175,000 titles. . . . With some 4,200 U.S. publishers and the two biggest booksellers, Barnes & Noble and Borders Group Inc., accounting for less than 12 percent of total sales, there aren't any 800-pound gorillas in book selling.[1]

In contrast, the music industry had only six major record companies. Because these companies controlled the distribution of records and CDs, they had the potential to lock out a new business threatening the traditional record store format.

To start his new venture, Bezos left New York City to move west, either to Boulder, Seattle, or Portland. As he drove west, he refined and finetuned his thoughts and his business plan. In doing so, he concluded that Seattle was his final destination. Recalls Bezos:

> It sounds counterintuitive, but physical location is very important for the success of a virtual business. We could have started Amazon.com anywhere. We chose Seattle because it met a rigorous set of criteria. It had to be a place with lots of technical talent. It had to be near a place with large numbers of books. It had to be a nice place to live—great people won't work in places they don't want to live. Finally, it had to be in a small state. In the mail-order business, you have to charge sales tax to customers who live in any state where you have a business presence. It made no sense for us to be in California or New York. . . . Obviously Seattle has a great programming culture. And it's close to Roseburg, Oregon, which has one of the biggest book warehouses in the world.[2]

Renting a house in Bellevue, a Seattle suburb, Bezos started work out of his garage. Ironically, he held meetings with prospective employees and suppliers at a nearby Barnes & Noble superstore. He also raised several million dollars from private investors. Operating from a 400-square-foot office in Bellevue, he launched his venture, Amazon.com, on the Internet in July 1995.

At first Bezos was concerned that sales would be so slow he wouldn't be able to meet the 10-book minimum that distributors require. Improvising, he combed through a big distributor's catalog and found a book entry he suspected wasn't actually available—an obscure publication about lichen (a thallophytic plant). His plan was simple: if the firm needed three books, it would pad the order with seven copies of the lichen book.

As it happened this plan wasn't necessary, as word about the new venture spread quickly across the Internet and sales picked up rapidly. Six weeks after opening, Jeff moved his new firm to a 2,000-square-foot warehouse. Six months later, he moved once again to a 17,000-square-foot building in an industrial neighborhood in Seattle. Estimates for the first year of operations indicate that Amazon.com revenues were about $5 million. These revenues are comparable to a large Barnes & Noble superstore.

THE BOOK PUBLISHING INDUSTRY

The United States is the world's largest market for books, with retail sales accounting for about $25.5 billion in 1995. Book publishing traditionally has been one of the oldest and most fragmented industries in the United States, with over 2,500 publishers.[3] Exhibit 1 shows the structure of the U.S. publishing industry.

Publishers Books are sold on a consignment basis, and publishers assume all the risk. They accept returns on unsold books guaranteeing their distributors a 100 percent refund. They provide money and

EXHIBIT 1 *Book Publishing Market Structure*

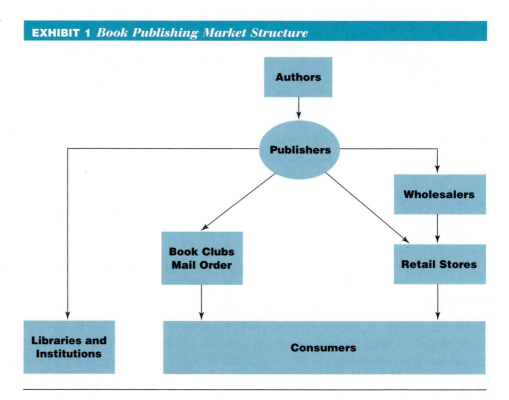

contracts to prospective authors and decide how many copies of the book to print. Typically a "first-run" print for a book can vary from 5,000 to 50,000 copies. However, best-selling authors' first-run prints are generally set at around 300,000 copies.

In practice, trade and paperback publishers print far more copies than will be sold. About 25 percent of all books distributed to wholesalers are returned and at times these percentages run as high as 40 percent for mass-market paperbacks. According to industry experts, 20–30 percent for hardcover books returns is considered acceptable, 30–50 percent is considered high, and anything above 50 percent is considered disastrous. Publishers drastically reduce the price after a certain period in a process known as *remaindering* (offering books to discount stores, jobbers, and other vendors). Apart from the material cost of returns and the lost revenue they represent, the industry spends millions of dollars each year transporting books back and forth. Profit margins in publishing are driven by book volume, which in turn hinges on the size of each print run. Book publishers generally depend on 10 percent of titles for profit, with 90 percent barely breaking even.[4]

The "big three"—Warner Books, Simon & Schuster, and Pearson—accounted for 21 percent of sales. The 20 largest book publishing companies in the United States commanded over 60 percent of all retail sales. Warner Books, a subsidiary of Time Warner, the U.S. entertainment giant, was the largest publisher, with sales of $3.7 billion in 1995. Simon & Schuster, a division of Viacom Corporation, ranked second with sales reaching $2.17 billion. These two leaders are followed by Pearson, a group that owns the *Financial Times*, which recorded sales revenues of $1.75 billion. Exhibit 2 illustrates the margins on a typical hard-cover book.

Wholesalers Books are distributed by wholesalers. Wholesalers take orders from independent booksellers and chains and consolidate them into lot-orders for publishers. Publishers supply wholesalers who in turn supply the thousands of retail bookstores located throughout the country. According to industry estimates, in 1996 wholesalers accounted for almost 30 percent of publishers' sales. Unlike publishing and retailing, wholesalers are highly concentrated with firms such as Ingram Book Co. com-

EXHIBIT 2 *Profit Margins for a "Typical" Book*

Book List Price	**$19.95**	
Revenue to publisher (i.e., price paid by wholesaler or bookstore)	$10.37	48% discount off suggested retail price
Manufacturing cost	$ 2.00	Printing, binding, jacket design, composition, typesetting, paper, ink
Publisher overhead	$ 3.00	Marketing, fulfillment
Returns and allowances	$ 3.00	
Author's royalties	$ 2.00	
Total publishing costs	$10.00	
Publisher's operating profit	$ 0.37	Returns amount for 3.7%

manding the major share (50 percent in 1995) of the market. Competition revolves around the speed of delivery and the number of titles stocked. Ingram, for instance, receives more than 70 percent of its orders electronically and offers one-day delivery to about 82 percent of its U.S. customers. In 1994, the average net profit for wholesalers was less than 1.5 percent. This figure was down from the traditional margins of about 2 percent a few years earlier.[5]

Technological advances have made warehouse operations more efficient and this in turn has made it possible for wholesalers to provide attractive discounts to retailers. Also, the types of books wholesalers are supplying to retailers are changing. Increasingly, bookstores are relying on wholesalers for fast-selling titles and less-popular backlist books.[6] However, with the emergence of superstores, the large retailers, such as Barnes & Noble and Borders Books & Music, are no longer using wholesalers for initial orders of major titles. In 1994, for example,

Borders Books & Music bought more than 95 percent of its titles directly from publishers.

Retail Book Stores Retail bookstores, independents, and general retailers accounted for 35 to 40 percent of industry revenues (Exhibit 3). Also 1995 marked the first year in which book store chains sold more books than independents.[7] From 1975 to 1995, the number of bookstores in the United States increased from 11,990 to 17,340, and these bookstores accounted for about 21 percent of the total retail book sales. The superstores, the new Goliaths of retailing, such as Barnes & Noble and Borders Books & Music accounted for about 15 percent of all retail sales. Estimates suggest that from 1992 through 1995, superstore bookstore sales grew at a compounded rate of 71 percent while nonsuperstore sales grew at a rate of 4 percent. According to Rick Vanzura of Borders Books & Music: "When one of our superstores opens up near one of our mall stores, the mall store tends

EXHIBIT 3 *Book Sales in 1994 by Various Distribution Channels*

Channel	% of Total Sales
Bookstore chains, independents, and general retailers	35–40%
Mail order and book clubs	21
Sales to college book stores	17
Schools	15
Libraries and other institutions	10

to lose 10 to 15 percent of its sales. But the superstore is doing a lot more business—say, seven times—what the mall store was doing."

Experts cautioned that in smaller markets a shakeout was inevitable.[8] Mr. Vlahos, a spokesman for the American Book Sellers Association, noted:

In the three years from 1993 to 1995, 150 to 200 independent-owned bookstores went out of business—50 to 60 in 1996 alone. . . . By contrast in the same period, approximately 450 retail superstore outlets opened, led by Barnes & Noble and the Borders Group, with 348 openings.[9]

Independent booksellers believe the growth of superstores may be reaching the saturation point. However, notes Leonard Riggio, the chairman of Barnes & Noble: "We are so far from reaching the saturation point [because] we are in the midst of one of the biggest rollouts in the history of retail." But even as Barnes & Noble and Borders entered city after city, as many as 142 U.S. metropolitan markets still did not have a book superstore. According to Amy Ryan, a Prudential Securities analyst, the current rate of expansion could continue at least through the year 2000. In her opinion, this is because the United States could support about 1,500 such large stores.[10]

Institutions and Libraries There are more than 29,000 private, public and academic libraries in the United States.[11] Because of its stability and size, this market is crucial to publishers. Because libraries order only what they want, this lowers the overhead costs associated with inventory and return processing, making this market a relatively profitable one for publishers. Moreover, as hardcover trade books have become relatively expensive, many readers are borrowing them from libraries rather than purchasing them outright. Industry experts observed that about 95 percent of general titles published in any year sold less than 20,000 copies; of that amount, about 55 percent is purchased by libraries. Libraries also frequently repurchase titles to replace worn-out and stolen books. By doing so, they kept the backlist sales healthy.

Mail Order and Book Clubs The year 1995 witnessed a significant drop in the mail-order book business. This drop in sales was attributed to the growth of large discount-sale retailers. Publishers' book club sales, on the other hand, rose steadily, gaining 9 per-

cent in 1994 and in early 1995. The strong growth in this segment was attributed to the increasing popularity of specialized book clubs which focused on favorite baby-boomer interests such as gardening and computers.

The industry sells a variety of books which include: trade, professional, mass market, El-Hi (elementary-high school) and college textbooks, and others. Each of these categories varied in terms of sales, competition, profitability, and volatility (see Exhibits 4 and 5).

A survey commissioned by American Booksellers Association found that some 106 million adults purchased about 456.9 million books in any given quarter. The survey, which looked at book-buying habits of consumers during the calendar year 1994, revealed that 6 in 10 American adults (60 percent) say they purchased at least one book in the last three months. Annually, that corresponds to 1.8 billion books sold, an average of 17 books per book-buying consumer a year. The average amount paid for the three most recent books purchased by consumers in the past 30 days was about $15.

Emergence of "Virtual" Bookstores

The two hardest challenges for book selling—physically distributing the right numbers of books to bookstores and getting the word about serious books out to potential readers—are getting a more than trivial assist from the new online technologies.

The rapid growth of Internet businesses was spreading to book publishing. According to Larry Daniels, director of information technologies for the National Association of College Stores:

Booksellers' concern revolves around the potential for publishers to deal directly with consumers and the media on the Internet. . . . The phenomenon could mean the elimination of middlemen such as bookstores.[12]

Moreover, Daniels notes that there is also the potential for publishers to be "disintermediated," because computer-literate writers can now publish and distribute their own works online.

However, the leading publishing houses are skeptical of electronic book-publishing capabilities and remain uncertain about the Internet's future in the sale of physical books. Despite such skepticism, selling online was a fast-growing phenomenon. A

EXHIBIT 4 *The Various Product Categories*

Trade Books. This segment includes general interest hardcover and paperback books sold to adults and juveniles. Trade books accounted for almost 30 percent of publishers' revenues in 1994. According to an industry group, books sold to adults increased by more than 30 percent between 1991 and 1995. Juvenile book sales, which showed a double-digit growth rate in the late 1980s and early 1990s, however, were much slower at 1.1 percent in 1994. This slow growth was attributed to a decline in the number of popular titles and increased spending by children on toys and games.

In 1995, Random House, Inc., Bantam Doubleday Dell, Simon & Schuster, HarperCollins, and Penguin were some of the leading firms that competed in this product category.

Professional Books. Over 165 million professional books were sold in 1995 accounting for $3.9 billion. Since 1991, professional book sales have grown at a compounded annual rate of 3.0 percent (in units). Legal publishing was the largest segment of the professional books category, with the scientific and technical category in second place. The long-term outlook for this category was good because employment in the medical, legal, scientific, and business professions was expected to grow significantly.

Thomson Corp. was the largest professional books publisher with sales of $1.99 billion. Professional book revenues comprised 3 percent of Thomson's total revenues. Reed Elsevier ranked second with 1994 sales of $1.63 billion and was followed by Wolters Kluwer and Times Mirror with $1.07 billion and $775 million in sales, respectively.

Mass-Market Books. These books are sold primarily through magazine wholesalers and outlets such as newsstands and drugstores. This category includes best-sellers that have shelf lives of about three to six weeks. Although the cost of acquiring the paperback rights to a best-selling hardcover title can cost millions of dollars, the per-unit fixed costs for printing are small because print runs were as large as 500,000. However, when return rates that typically exceed 40 percent are factored in, profit margins are typically less than 12 percent.

The largest mass-market publishers are Random House, Inc., Bantam Doubleday Dell, Simon & Schuster, and HarperCollins.

El-Hi Textbooks. El-Hi or Elementary-High school books accounted for 30 percent of all books sold in 1994. The El-Hi market is driven by state adoption and enrollment levels and the books are sold to school systems on a contract basis. The development of materials for schools is a capital-intensive process that typically takes up to five years for most new programs. Per pupil expenditures as well as the number of students are expected to grow through the year 2000. This implied moderately strong annual growth (about 3 to 4 percent) for El-Hi textbooks through the remainder of the decade.

The big publishers are owned by media conglomerates such as News Corp., Times Mirror, and Paramount. The largest El-Hi publisher is McGraw-Hill, followed by Paramount (the parent company of Prentice Hall and Silver Burdett), Harcourt Brace, and Houghton Mifflin.

College Textbooks. College publishing is the most profitable category. The cost of producing a college text is lower than in the El-Hi market because the texts are typically prepared by university faculty members and used individually. However, the unit sales tend to be small and used textbook sales generally accounted for 20 to 40 percent of total sales. The U.S. Department of Eduction was forecasting a decline in college enrollments for 1996, and slow growth thereafter. College textbook sales that grew by 4.4 percent in 1995 to 155 million books were expected to decline in the future.

Prentice Hall (owned by Viacom) is the largest college publisher, followed by HB College (owned by Harcourt General), International Thomson, McGraw-Hill, and Irwin (a division of Times Mirror).

plethora of bookstores are selling books on the Internet. Companies such as Amazon.com, Bookserver, Book Stacks Unlimited, Cbooks Express, Pandora's, and the Internet Bookstore are growing at the self-reported rates of 20 to 35 percent a month. Of the $518 million expected to be sold online in 1996 on the Internet, book sales are a small segment relegated to the "other" category. Total book sales online ac-

EXHIBIT 5 *Sales and Profit Margins by Product Category*

Product Category	1993 ($m)	1994 ($m)	Profit Margins in 1993, %
Trade books			
Hardcover books for adults	1,069.0	1,187.0	0.6%
Paperback books for adults	586.4	674.5	13.7
Books for juveniles	431.6	439.9	7.7
Bibles, hymnals, and prayer books	45.6	54.7	12.4
Mass-market paperbacks	998.7	1,202.8	3.1
Business, medical, scientific, and technical	813.5	891.6	8.0
El-Hi textbooks and materials	1,977.8	1,836.8	14.9
College textbooks and materials	1,586.7	1,611.3	15.8

Source: *Standard and Poor Industry Surveys*, July 20, 1995.

counted for less that 1 percent of overall book sales. However, because the amount of money Americans spend on books is projected to reach $31 billion by 2000, selling online is expected to grow further.

COMPETING ON THE WORLD WIDE WEB

A Virtual Bookstore

Unlike traditional bookstores, there are no bookshelves to browse at Amazon.com. All contact with the company is done either through its Web page (at http://www.amazon.com) or by e-mail. At the firm's Web site, customers can search for a specific book, topic, or author, or they can browse their way through a book catalog featuring 40 subjects. Visitors can also read book reviews from other customers, *The New York Times*, *Atlantic Monthly*, and Amazon.com's staff. Customers can browse, fill up a virtual shopping basket, and then complete the sale by entering their credit card information or by placing their order online and then phoning in their credit card information.[13] Customer orders are processed immediately. Books in stock (mostly bestsellers) are packaged and mailed the same day. When their order has been shipped, customers are notified immediately by e-mail. Orders for non-best-sellers are placed immediately with the appropriate book publisher by Amazon.com.

Shunning the elaborate graphics that clutter so many Web sites, Amazon.com instead loads up its customers with information (see Exhibit 6). For many featured books, it offers capsule descriptions, snippets of reviews, and "self-administered" interviews posted by authors. More importantly, the firm has found a way to use the technology to offer services that a traditional store or catalog can't match. Notes Bezos:

An Amazon customer can romp through a database of 1.1 million titles (five times the largest superstore's inventory), searching by subject or name. When you select a book, Amazon is programmed to flash other related titles you may also want to buy. If you tell Amazon about favorite authors and topics, it will send you by electronic mail a constant stream of recommendations. You want to know when a book comes out in paperback? Amazon will e-mail that too.[14]

Additionally, the firm offers space for readers to post their own reviews and then steps out of the way and lets its customers sell to each other. For example, recently a book called *Sponging: A Guide to Living Off Those You Love* drew a chorus of online raves from customers, one of whom remarked: "This gem is crazy! Flat Out. Hysterical. You'll have a good laugh, but wait! Let me let you in on a lil' secret— it's useful!" This book swiftly made it onto Amazon.com's own best-seller list. Notes Bezos:

We are trying to make the shopping experience just as fun as going to the bookstore, but there's some things we can't do. I'm not interested in retrofitting the physical bookstore experience in the virtual world. Every few weeks, someone

EXHIBIT 6 *Amazon.com's Web site as of October 1996*

Amazon.com Homepage

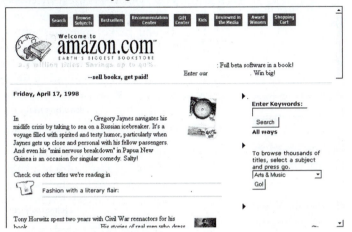

Amazon.com Search Page

around here asks, 'When are we going to do electronic book signings?' We still haven't done them. The experience of book signings works best in the real world.[15]

But he is fast to add:

There are so many things we can do online that can't be done in the real world. We want customers who enter Amazon.com to indicate whether they want to be "visible" or "invisible." If they choose "visible," then when they're in the science fiction section, other people will know they're there. People can ask for recommendations—"Read any good books lately?"—or recommend books to others. I'm an outgoing person, but I'd never go into a bookstore and ask a complete stranger to recommend a book. The semi-anonymity of the online environment makes people less inhibited.[16]

When asked why people come to the site, Bezos responds:

Bill Gates laid it out in a magazine interview. He said, "I buy all my books at Amazon.com because I'm busy and it's convenient. They have a big selection, and they've been reliable." Those are three of our four core value propositions: convenience, selection, service. The only one he left out is price: we are the broadest discounters in the world in any product category.... These value propositions are interrelated, and they all relate to the Web.[17]

At Amazon.com all books are discounted. Bestsellers are sold at a 30 percent discount and the other books at a 10 percent discount. Notes Bezos:

We discount because we have a lower cost structure than physical stores do. We turn our inventory 150 times a year. That's like selling bread in a supermarket. Physical bookstores turn their inventory only 3 or 4 times a year.[18]

The firm's small warehouse is used only to stock best-sellers and to consolidate and repack customer orders. Moreover, only after the firm receives a paid customer order does it ask the appropriate publisher to ship the book to Amazon.com. The firm then ships the book to the customer. The firm owns no expensive retail real estate and its operations are largely automated.

Industry observers note that although Amazon.com discounts most books, it levies a $3 service charge per order, plus 95 cents per book. And it can take Amazon a week to deliver a book that isn't a best-seller, and even longer for the most esoteric titles. Also, some people don't like providing their credit card number over the Internet.

Virtual Customer Service

According to the firm, about 44 percent of the book orders come from repeat customers.[19] To maintain customer interest in Amazon.com, the firm offers two forms of e-mail-based service to its registered customers. "Eyes" is a personal notification service in which customers can register their interests in a particular author or topic. Once registered, they are notified each time a new book by their favorite author or topic is published. "Editor's service" provides editorial comments about featured books via e-mail. Three full-time editors read book reviews, pore over customer orders, and survey current events to select the featured books. These and other freelance editors employed by the firm provide registered users with e-mail updates on the latest and greatest books they've been reading. These services are automated and are available free of charge.

According to Bezos, such services are vital for success on the Internet:

Customer service is a critical success factor in any retail business. But it's absolutely make-or-break online. If you make customers unhappy in the physical world, they might each tell 6 friends. If you make customers unhappy on the Internet, they can each tell 6,000 friends with one message to a newsgroup. If you make them really happy, they can tell 6,000 people about that. You want every customer to become an evangelist for you.[20]

Additionally, the firm's employees compile a weekly list of the 20 most obscure titles on order, and Bezos awards a prize for the most amusing. Recent entries include: *Training Goldfish Using Dolphin Training Techniques*, *How To Start Your Own Country*, and *Life Without Friends*. Amazon.com drums up all these orders through a mix of state-of-the-art software and old-fashioned salesmanship.

Associates Program

According to Leslie Koch, vice president of marketing at Amazon.com, the firm is currently growing at the rate of 20–30 percent a month. Part of the reason for this rapid growth is the firm's Associates Program. The program was designed to increase traffic to Amazon.com by creating a referral service from other Web sites to Amazon.com's 1.1 million book catalog. An associates Web site, such as Starchefs—which features cookbook authors—recommends books and makes a link from its Web page to Amazon's catalog page for the books. The associated Web site then earns referral fees for sales generated by these links. Partners receive quarterly referral fee statements and a check for the referral fees earned in that quarter. More than 1,800 sites have already signed up under this program and earn a commission of 8 percent of the value of books bought by the referred customer. Notes Bezos, "[The] Web technology has made it possible to set up microfranchises, and with zero overhead."[21]

Operating Philosophy

Unlike traditional bookstores, there are no salespeople at Amazon.com. Moreover, the firm is open for business 24 hours a day and has a global presence. Customers from 66 countries have purchased books from the firm. This list includes Bosnia, where more than 25 U.S. soldiers have placed orders. The firm is devoid of expensive furnishings, and money is spent sparingly. Notes Bezos:

> We made the first four desks we have here ourselves—all our desks are made out of doors and four-by-fours. . . . My monitor stand is a bunch of old phone books. We spend money on the things that matter to our customers and we don't spend money on anything else.[22]

According to Leslie Koch, although the firm advertises in print, it spends a substantial amount on Web advertising. According to Jupiter Communications, the firm spent over $340,000 for the first half of the 1996 and ranked 34th in Web ad spending. Because Amazon.com is an Internet-only retailer, Web advertising gives it a unique opportunity to track the success of an ad by the number of click-throughs to the store's Web site and the number of Internet surfers who actually purchase something. Industry analysts estimate that between 2 and 3 percent of people who see an ad on the Web will actually click through to see more. Advertising is done mainly in the large-circulation newspapers such as *The Wall Street Journal*, *The New York Times*, and *San Jose Mercury News*, and on Internet search-engine sites such as Yahoo! and Lycos, the Microsoft Network, and Microsoft's *Slate* magazine. Amazon.com keeps its banner ads simple, with just a few words and a Web address.[23] Recently, the firm has started advertising on CNN.

The decision to locate Amazon.com in Seattle appears to be paying off. The firm has been able to attract some Microsoft veterans; for instance, Leslie Koch is a six-year Microsoft veteran. The firm's business development manager, Scott Lipsky, is also from Microsoft, and so is the advertising manager, Jodie de Lyon. See Exhibit 7 for an illustration of how the firm is organized and a brief description the firm's management.

Amazon had 110 employees in October 1996. Of these, 14 employees manage customer support and seven employees attend to marketing. In addition, a few employees manage "content" on the firm's Web site, including such tasks as Web page updating and formatting book reviews for display. The vast majority of the remaining employees work on developing software tools for operating on the Internet. According to Julia King, an executive assistant in

marketing, "This is a very driven place. Hours are typically 8 to 8 and many people work weekends. Jeff spends every waking hour on this business." Bezos, for example, lives just a few minutes away, but keeps a sleeping bag in his office for all-nighters.

When asked to differentiate this firm from potential rivals, Bezos notes:

> People who just scratch the surface of Amazon.com say—"oh, you sell books on the Web,"—don't understand how hard it is to actually be an electronic merchant. We're not just putting up a Web site. We do 90 percent of our customer service by e-mail rather than by telephone. Fourteen of our 110 employees do nothing but answer e-mail from customers. There are very few off-the-shelf tools that help do what we're doing. We've had to develop lots of our own technologies. There are no companies selling software to manage e-mail centers. So we had to develop our own tools. In a way this is good news. There are lots of barriers to entry.[24]

In discussing the technical side of the business, Bezos explains:

> We have the best programmers, the best servers in the world. We use 64-bit Digital Alpha servers with 500 megabytes of RAM. It's worked very well for us. All of the stuff that actually matters to our customers, we buy the very best.[25]

Explosive Growth

Since July 1995 Amazon has doubled in size every 2.4 months.[26] By August 1996, sales were growing at 34 percent a month. Although estimates vary, the company's gross revenue is expected to be around $17 to $19 million for 1996. When the company was founded in 1995, the plan was to be profitable in five years. As of October 1996 the firm claims to have exceeded expectations and has made its business plan more aggressive. According to Bezos: "We're not focused on trying to make the company profitable. If we're profitable any time in the short term, it'll just be an accident."[27]

Regardless of the firm's profitability, interest in the new venture remains strong. The firm recently attracted $8 million from Kleiner, Perkins, Caufield & Byers, a venture-capital firm based in Silicon Valley that has funded firms such as Sun Microsystems and Netscape.

EXHIBIT 7 *Amazon.com's Organizational Structure and Top Management*

Jeff Bezos	Jeff Bezos founded Amazon.com in July 1994. Formerly at Bankers Trust Corp. and D.E. Shaw in New York, Bezos decided to form Amazon.com when the growth of the Internet caught his interest. Bezos is a summa cum laude, Phi Beta Kappa graduate of Princeton in electrical engineering and computer science.
Founder and CEO	
Rick Ayre	*Responsible for editorial content and design of Amazon.com web site.* Ayre joined Amazon.com from *PC Magazine,* a Ziff-Davis publication, where he was executive editor for technology. Ayre launched *PC Magazine* on the World Wide Web in March 1995. It quickly became one of the 20 most popular Web sites. He began his technology career as a Ph.D. student in psychiatric epidemiology, but quickly became a programmer and information technology specialist.
Vice President, Executive Editor	
Scott E. Lipsky	*Responsible for corporate expansion and development of new products and services.* Prior to joining Amazon.com, Lipsky was chief information officer in the superstore and college bookstore division of Barnes & Noble in New York. Before that he was founder and president of Omni Information Group, a Dallas-based software development and systems integration firm.
Vice President, Business Expansion	
Leslie Koch	*Responsible for marketing, including advertising and communications, strategic relationships, and customer programs.* Koch was at Microsoft Corporation for six years, where she was lead product manager for Word and then Excel. She was general manager for personal finance, with P&L responsibility, for Microsoft Money worldwide, and her investigation of the potential for electronic banking led to Microsoft's bid for Intuit.
Vice President, Marketing	

Bezos is focused on expanding Amazon.com: "In the year 2000, our goal is to be one of the world's leading bookstores. Since the world's leading bookstores are billion-dollar companies, people impute that [this figure is our target]."[28] But he quickly dismisses fears that his firm could ever spell the end of traditional bookstores.

Amazon.com is not going to put bookstores out of business. Barnes & Noble is opening a new superstore every four days. Borders is opening a new superstore every nine days. . . . I still buy half of my books at bookstores. Sometimes I want the book right now, not tomorrow. Sometimes I just like to get out of the office and go to a nice environment. What you're going to see—and it's happening already—is that physical bookstores will become ever-nicer places to be. They are going to have more sofas, better lattes, nicer people working there. Good bookstores are the community centers of the late 20th century. That's the basis on which they're going to compete. There is plenty of room for everyone.[29]

Adds Leslie Koch:

Book sales are stagnating, but we believe we're expanding the market for books. With this new way of selling books on the Web we can expose people to far more books than before. People buy books from us that they won't find in bookstores. And we're growing rapidly in this stagnant market.

CHALLENGES FACING AMAZON.COM

Bezos acknowledges that many strategic challenges remain. In particular, two challenges demand his immediate attention. His first concern is to find innovative ways to fruitfully use the massive database his firm has been accumulating about his customers without alienating them. The second more threatening development is the emerging copycat ventures offering books on the Internet.

The "Massive" Database

For the past year, Amazon.com has been building a detailed purchasing history and profile of its customers. Notes Alberto Vitale, chairman of Random House, Inc.: "Amazon is creating a database that doesn't exist anywhere else. Book publishers have never had much market data about readers, and some are already salivating for a peek into Amazon's files."[30] Yet customers who buy books from Amazon are assured of privacy by the Amazon Bill of Rights (see Exhibit 8).

Bezos is concerned that his customers might be outraged if he turns over this information to other marketers. To him the Web is the ultimate word-of-mouth medium. Still he is considering whether a plan to let publishers offer hand-picked Amazon customers books at discounted prices before their publication date should be implemented.

The Emerging Competition

More than half of the Internet's computers reside in the United States, with the rest spread out among connected networks in 100 other countries. Estimates of the number of Internet users (and more importantly the number of potential users) vary widely (see Exhibit 9). The number of businesses joining the Internet has risen dramatically over the past year, and growth hasn't been limited to large corporations (see Exhibit 10 for some leading sites on the Internet). From July 1994 to July 1995, the number of hosts on the Internet rose from 3.2 million to 6.6 million. By the end of the decade, 120 million machines are expected be linked to the Internet.[31]

Every day approximately 150 new businesses come onto the Net, and their total number is estimated to

C-27

EXHIBIT 8 *Amazon.com's Customer Bill of Rights*

Amazon Bill of Rights claims that as a customer there is:

1. **No obligation.** Eyes & Editors Personal Notification Services are provided free of charge, and you are under no obligation to buy anything.
2. **Unsubscribing.** You can unsubscribe or change your subscriptions at any time.
3. **Privacy.** We do not sell or rent information about our customers. If you would like to make sure we never sell or rent information about you to third parties, just send a blank e-mail message to never@amazon.com.

EXHIBIT 9 *Varying Estimates of Internet Users in 1996*

Source	Date	Definition	Users (millions)
Intelliquest	July 1996	U.S. Internet users	35.0
Louis Harris	May 1996	U.S. Internet users	29.0
International Data Corp.	May 1996	WWW surfers	23.5
Computer Intelligence	May 1996	Year-end 1995 (U.S. Internet users)	15.0
Hoffman/Novak	April 1996	U.S. Internet users	16.4
Wall Street Journal	March 1996	North American home/office users	17.6
Morgan Stanley	February 1996	1995 Net/Web users	9.0
Matrix	February 1996	1995 Worldwide Internet users	26.4
Find/SVP	January 1996	U.S. users who use any Internet service except e-mail	9.5

Source: *CyberAtlas,* August 1996.

be about 40,000. Most of these companies use the Web as a public relations tool to promote their products and services.[32] More than 35 million Americans now use the Internet—9 million of whom joined just this year. From a commercial perspective, the demographics of Internet and World Wide Web users makes them part of an extremely attractive market segment. The average age of computer users is 39, while the average age of a typical Internet user is 32. About 1 in 10 Internet users (more than 3 million)

is under 18 and uses the Internet from home or school. About 64 percent of the Internet users have at least a college degree with a median household income of $60,000.[33]

The global Internet market is expected to soar to $23 billion by 2000 (Exhibit 11). Estimates for 1996 indicate that the World Wide Web has attracted more than 100,000 retailers, with some spending more than $1 million each on eye-popping sites. Yet, worldwide retail sales on the Web amounted to only

EXHIBIT 10 *Leading Sites on World Wide Web*

In a June 1996 survey of 1,100 Web-based businesses, 31 percent claimed to be profitable and 28 percent said that they would be profitable in the next 12 to 24 months. Here are a few of the most prominent Web success stories:

- **Auto-by-Tel.** Founder Peter Ellis claims his car-buying service will turn a profit on $6.5 million in revenue this year.
- **CDnow.** Started in the basement of their parents' home, Jason and Matthew Olim expect to reach $6 million in sales in 1996, triple last year's revenue, while maintaining an 18 percent operating margin.
- **Netscape.** Netscape already sells $1.5 million worth of its products over the Net each month.
- **ONSALE.** This auction house, founded by Jerry Kaplan (of Go fame), is on a $45 million annual run rate.

Source: *ActivMedia,* May 1996, and *Business Week,* 1996.

EXHIBIT 11 *Internet Forecast by Market and Product Segments ($ Millions)*

Forecast by Market Segment*				1995	2000
Network services (ISPs)				300	5,000
Hardware (routers, modems, computer hardware)				500	2,500
Software (server, applications)				300	4,000
Enabling services (electronic commerce, directory services, Web tracking)				20	1,000
Expertise (system integrators, business consultants)				50	700
Content and activity (online entertainment, information, shopping)				500	10,000
Total market				1,170	23,200

Forecast by Product Segment**	1996	1997	1998	1999	2000
Computer products	$140	$323	$701	$1,228	$2,105
Travel	126	276	572	961	1,579
Entertainment	85	194	420	733	1,250
Apparel	46	89	163	234	322
Gifts/flowers	45	103	222	386	658
Food/drink	39	78	149	227	336
Other	37	75	144	221	329
Total ($M)	518	1,138	2,371	3,990	6,579

*Source: Hambrecht & Quist, December 1995.
**Source: Forrester Research, Inc., May 1996.

$324 million last year, which averages out to slightly more than $3,000 in sales per retailer.[34] In 1996 about 2.7 million people used the Internet for shopping or to obtain commercial services such as banking or travel information.

Recent forecasts suggest that while Internet merchants will sell about $518 million in goods in 1996, online retailing revenues are likely to grow to about $6.6 billion by the end of this century.[35] Notes Bezos:

We're by far the largest bookseller out there in terms of the number of titles we offer for sale and the services we provide. We are, for all intents and purposes, competing against a vacuum right now. That's not going to last.[36]

Bezos's concerns about potential competition are not farfetched. During mid-1996, we witnessed a plethora of virtual bookstores sprouting on the Internet. Exhibit 12 provides a partial list of virtual bookstores on the Internet. Not surprisingly, many of these new virtual bookstores are modeled after Amazon.com. For example, Bookserver was founded with a mere $20,000 by brothers David (26) and Michael

(23) Mason and originally operated from their family garage. This firm claims to offer more than a million book titles. Additionally, the firm specializes in finding books for customers. Books are offered in English, German, Dutch, and Spanish at discounts similar to Amazon.com and at half the shipping fees charged by Amazon.com. According to David, the store's sales have increased steadily by about 20 percent a month since founding. This growth has enabled the firm to shift operations from the family garage to a strip mall in Lavergne, Tennessee. Bezos was also concerned about the prospect of new competition from some of high-tech and retailing's mightiest players: a new joint venture between Wal-Mart Stores Inc. and Microsoft Corp., Amazon.com's neighbor in nearby Redmond, Washington.

Elliot Bay Books, a Seattle-based independent book store, had set up a Web site to establish an Internet presence. Further, a report in the *Seattle Times* indicated that both Barnes & Noble and Borders, the giants in the industry, expect to offer online services in 1997.[37]

In response Bezos is considering novel ways to attract new customers and, at the same time, maintain

EXHIBIT 12 *Partial List of Virtual Bookstores on Web in October 1996*

- **Bookserver.** This firm was founded by brothers David and Michael Mason from the family garage in Tennessee. Since its founding, the firm has moved to a mall in Lavergne, Tennessee.
- **CBooks Express.** This Internet startup specializes in technical books and computer-related materials.
- **Pandora's Books Ltd.** This firm features out-of-print science fiction and fantasy books to read when Star Trek reruns can't be found.
- **The Internet Book Shop.** This firm claims that it is the biggest online bookstore in the world with over 912,000 titles. The firm lets you track your order online.
- **MacMillan Information Superlibrary.** This Web site is an attempt to pull together MacMillan's various print, reference, and electronic publishing efforts. Its bookstore, however, carries only 6,000 titles.
- **The Cosmic Web.** This is a nonprofit book center dedicated to circulating "words of inspiration and evolutionary answers that awaken souls to the infinitude of our experience as planetary beings."
- **Dial-A-Book.** This venture focuses on selling books in a downloadable format.
- **Moe's Books.** This firm specializes in used books. The firm searches 1,500 affiliated stores to bring you the used books you're looking for. Customers specify the condition they would like the book to arrive in.

his existing customer base. One of the options under consideration is to customize offerings for each customer. Describes Bezos:

> We want to "redecorate the store" for every customer. We can let people describe their preferences, analyze their past buying patterns, and create a home page specifically for them. If you're a big mystery reader, we can show you the three hottest new mystery novels and highlight one from an author you've bought before. These interactive features are going to be incredibly powerful. And you can't reproduce them in the physical world.[38]

Yet, he is concerned and is searching for ways in which Amazon.com can stay ahead of this emerging competition. Although sales are increasing, he sees this as a continuing challenge:

Our customers are loyal right up to the point somebody offers them a better service. That's the dimension on which we compete. The goal of Amazon.com has to be to make sure that we are the preeminent brand name associated with online bookselling in the year 2000. I think we have a huge opportunity to build an interactive retailing company beyond books.[39]

Paul Hilts, technology editor of *Publishers Weekly*, remains guarded:

> It remains to be seen whether online bookselling will completely transform the industry. Their [Amazon.com] timing was exquisite, and they promoted the heck out of it. Everyone will have their eyes on them to see how it goes.[40]

NOTES

1. "Who's writing the book on web business?" *Fast Company*, October–November, 1996, pp. 132–133.
2. *Fast Company*, October–November, 1996.
3. U.S. Bureau of the Census, 1992.
4. "World book market 'faces further consolidation,'" *Financial Times*, October 2, 1996, p. 16.
5. *Publishers Weekly*, January 1, 1996.

6. Although the best-selling books get the bulk of the attention and marketing dollars, "backlist" books are considered the "bread and butter" of the industry. A backlist is the publishing company's catalog of books that have already appeared in print. Estimates indicated that as much as 25 to 30 percent of a publisher's revenues come from this source. Backlisted books have predictable sales with occasional bumps, such as when a

subject matter loses favor with the consumers or when an author dies. Since these books require no editing and little promotion, they are generally profitable. Moreover, print runs are easier to predict, resulting in fewer returns to publishers.

7. *Philadelphia Business Journal*, September 27, 1996.

8. *Publishers Weekly*, March 11, 1996. Superstores, originally confined to big metropolitan areas, were increasingly entering markets with populations of 150,000 or less. Industry estimates indicated that superstores had to make around $200 a square foot to turn a profit. A typical Barnes & Noble superstore needed, for example, $3 to $4 million in sales revenues to break even. Some industry observers questioned whether such cities can support one or more of these mammoth stores and whether superstores in these locations could sell enough books to turn a profit.

9. "A Nonchain Bookstore Bucks the Tide," *The New York Times*, September 8, 1996.

10. Compounding the competition from superstores, many independent booksellers claimed to be unfairly treated by publishers. They claimed that publishers offered book store chains better prices and greater promotional support than independents. In response, the American Book Sellers Association (ABA) brought an antitrust suit against six publishers, five of which have been settled favorably out of court. The only remaining ABA suit was against Random House, Inc.

11. *Standard and Poors Industry Surveys*, July 20, 1995.

12. *The Christian Science Monitor*, September 18, 1996.

13. When the company first started, only 50 percent of the people were prepared to enter their credit card number on Amazon's Web page. The other half phoned it in. However, within a year this ratio has changed to 80:20.

14. *The Wall Street Journal*, Thursday, May 16, 1996.

15. *Fast Company*, October–November, 1996.

16. *Fast Company*, October–November, 1996.

17. *Fast Company*, October–November, 1996.

18. *Fast Company*, October–November, 1996.

19. "Booked up on the Net," *Seattle Times*, January 5, 1997.

20. *Fast Company*, October–November, 1996.

21. "Amazon.com forges new sales channel," *Web Week*, August 19, 1996.

22. *Upside*, October 1996.

23. Web advertising is gaining increasing legitimacy. Revenue for advertising on the World Wide Web rose 83 percent to $46.4 million in the second quarter of 1996. The figure is expected to reach $312 million by the end of the year. This amount is still quite small in comparison to the $30 billion spent on television advertising each year.

24. *Fast Company*, October–November 1996.

25. *Upside*, October 1996.

26. *Financial Times*, October 7, 1996.

27. *Upside*, October 1996.

28. *Upside*, October 1996.

29. *Fast Company*, October–November 1996.

30. "Reading the market: How a Wall Street whiz found a niche selling books on the Internet," *The Wall Street Journal*, May 16, 1996.

31. Estimates provided by the *Internet Society*, 1996.

32. Statistics from *Internet World*, November 1995 and TDM Software and Consulting.

33. Nielsen Media Research, 1995.

34. Based on data from *International Data Corp. 1996*.

35. *Forrester Research Inc.*, May 1996.

36. *Upside*, October 1996.

37. *Seattle Times*, January 5, 1997.

38. *Fast Company*, October–November 1996.

39. *Seattle Times*, January 5, 1997.

40. *Seattle Times*, January 5, 1997.

Americast: A New Era in Home Entertainment

Dane Campbell
Amy Chapman
Katy Harper
Nanette Tello

INDUSTRY PROFILE

The United States has had a long love affair with television and the home entertainment possibilities it has provided. Since its inception, television has connected homes with the world through its programming. News, comedies, dramas, and sports are just a few of the offerings that television has given people. But what does the future hold for television? Currently, cable, satellite television, video rental services, and interactive television are substitute services competing directly or indirectly in this market. And, as advances in technology are made, the possibility exists for other industries, such as Internet providers, to enhance the home entertainment industry.

At the end of 1996, a revolutionary interactive entertainment product was launched into the home entertainment market under the name Americast. Americast, made up of entertainment giant Disney/ABC and five regional holding centers (RHCs), SBC Communications, BellSouth, Ameritech, GTE and Southern New England Telephone Co., offers traditional entertainment services to viewers, but has added features such as a proprietary program navigator that facilitates program location for users, video-on-demand, home shopping, and a variety of interactive services.

This case was prepared under the direction of Professor Robert E. Hoskisson. The case is intended to be used as the basis for class discussion rather than to illustrate effective or ineffective handling of an administrative situation.

As a result of the Telecommunications Act of 1996, the revolution promises to continue as more industries are enabled to enter the home entertainment industry. Rules governing infrastructure usage, as well as capacity limitations, have loosened for all companies pursuing telecommunication positions in this marketplace. This relaxation of a centralized government policy has opened opportunities for industries involved in telecommunications technology. The days when cable companies possessed monopoly powers over local television markets are gone. A new invasion of telecommunications players may shift market share away from local cable providers.

This has significantly shaped the environment for the home entertainment industry. Buyers are no longer tied to one product offering and are now in a better position to demand higher quality and lower prices from a multiple set of providers. As more companies enter this market, they will have to discover new ways to compete to gain market share and profits. This can prove to be a daunting task, given the variety of choices accessible to consumers. Finally, as technology continues to change, so will the faces of these competitors.

The competitive industries definitely create various barriers to entry for interactive television, but to what degree? Interactive television's main advantage over the competitors is its ability to be delivered through existing infrastructures. However, this scope is limited to satellite and coaxial cable. Additional investment is needed to upgrade fiber optic lines to levels that can adequately deliver interactive television programming. At this point, many telephone companies fail to see the benefits resulting in the upgrade cost, partly due to the lack of consumer demand for interactive television. Additionally, if companies that provide interactive television programming fail to respond to the distributors' concerns about costs, they may see their opportunity for market share decreased drastically. Another challenge facing interactive television is that consumers have not seen the differentiation between their programming and cable programming and therefore cannot justify the difference in price.

On a lighter note, the planned programming is broad in scope and integrated to satisfy a wide spectrum of consumer demand. At this point it is clear that satellite and cable stand as interactive television's greatest threats to market penetration. However, satellite technology possesses a greater geographic reach than interactive television. If interactive television fails to obtain distribution outlets that can substantially compete with and surpass the cable programmers, they may fall short of success. These issues make the emerging entertainment outlet uncertain at best. What will companies such as Americast need to do to lure customers from the traditional cable providers and win market share? Which technologies are the most promising and economical to pursue? Finally, what strategy should Americast and other alliances employ to access the capabilities and resources needed to compete in this industry?

THE BEGINNING OF A NEW ERA IN HOME ENTERTAINMENT

The Telecommunications Act of 1996

The heightened level of competition now found in the home entertainment market is, in large part, attributable to the federal government's intervention. On February 1, 1996, Congress passed the Telecommunications Act of 1996 that relaxed the rules governing cable and limited provision of video programming by telephone companies. This deregulation resulted in a "crossover" by many players in the areas of electricity, telephone, and television provision who now felt they could provide one-stop servicing for customers. In the home entertainment industry, the Act allowed the following changes to occur.[1]

1. Local telephone companies now can offer cable television services or carry video programming through radio waves, as a common carrier, or through open video systems.

2. Telephone companies will now be regulated as are cable companies.

3. State and local regulation of telecommunications services is altered and reduced.

4. Rate regulation is eliminated in telephone markets.

5. Rate regulation for all cable operators will be removed on March 31, 1999, except for the "basic tier" of over-the-air channels and public and educational channels.

6. Video programming providers in which any cable operator has a 5 percent or greater equity interest may not exercise price discrimination in the distribution of cable programming. They cannot obtain exclusive dealing contracts unless they can demonstrate to the Federal Communications Commission that such a contract is in the public interest.

With the passage of this Act, the U.S. government opened the home entertainment industry to competition. Cable companies were no longer allowed to hold exclusive rights to provide cable programming within an area. Now, telephone companies can use their resources to distribute video programming to consumers. Some of these resources, however, provide the opportunity to not only send data to the home, but also to receive it, allowing them to provide truly interactive television. This may make telephone companies more of a threat to the cable market.

The Americast Story

Americast's start-up activities are being funded jointly by the partners with $500 million invested over a 5-year period.[2] Disney, who spearheaded the venture, is in charge of delivering the Americast programming and content to its five telephone company partners, as well as providing Americast's national marketing plan. The partners, positioned in diverse locations nationwide, provide the networking system needed for transmitting the Americast programming on a national level.

The RHCs are not required to follow a standardized transmission system for program distribution.

For example, BellSouth has chosen a wireless alternative called the multichannel multipoint distribution system (MMDS); Ameritech, SNET, and GTE are choosing to build traditional hybrid fiber/coax (HFC) cable systems; and SBC is providing a more advanced transmission system through the switched digital technology (SDV) system. Whether this will cause problems for Americast's success down the road remains to be seen. Letting a partner choose how it wants to transmit programming allows flexibility in capital investment for each telephone company. On the other hand, these different transmission systems possess different capabilities of output, creating inconsistency in the quantity and quality of the Americast programming being distributed across the country. Americast's short-term goal is to accumulate sufficient programming for its launch in 1997. This is important because quantity and variety of programming offerings are what will draw customers away from other home entertainment suppliers in the market. It has aggressively licensed programming, leveraged the program access rules, and used its relationship with Disney/ABC to obtain specially made programming. Also, in exchange for the Disney-produced programming, the owners have agreed to offer the Disney Channel with their basic cable packages and forego the customary charge for premium service paid by subscribers.

In terms of programming distribution, Americast is competing mainly in the market by acquiring out-of-region cable properties and obtaining new franchises to compete with cable within its regions. Ameritech, one of the most aggressive Americast partners, has already succeeded in obtaining at least 13 new cable franchises in the Midwest. The major markets to be served initially include Chicago, Columbus, Detroit, Atlanta, Houston, Dallas, Cleveland, Miami, St. Louis, Tampa/St. Petersburg, Honolulu, Portland, Seattle, Raleigh/Durham, Los Angeles, and a large portion of southern California. To facilitate the transmission of programming to the home, Americast has signed an agreement with Zenith Corporation for $1 billion to produce at least three million set-top boxes. The Americast box is designed to receive MMDS wireless signals and can be configured for SDV and Hybrid fiber-coax transmission to work with all the Americast partners' networking systems.

While Americast has significant potential for success in the interactive market due to the strong rep-

utation and the "deep pockets" of Disney partners, the venture has not been without problems. For example, on December 6, 1996, Americast complained to the government that it was being charged discriminatory rates for cable-owned sports programming by Rainbow Programming Holdings, Inc. Rainbow, which has a history of resisting telcos that want its networks, including regional sports channels, American Movie Classics (AMC), and Bravo!, is accused of charging Americast more for its programming than other cable operators. Americast stated that the discriminatory rates for the programming were a "real economic and financial issue for the venture."[3] Americast has also experienced trouble in parts of Michigan where it has had to delay cable launches because it cannot obtain HBO due to an exclusive agreement between HBO and Continental Cablevision, Inc. that was signed prior to the deregulation of the Telecommunications Act.

Interactive Television

Interactive television is the newest service in the home entertainment industry. This service can be delivered by satellite, coaxial telephone, and terrestrial media, but the primary delivery system is through fiber optic lines. This is prompting telephone companies to invest heavily in fiber optic systems, and it is expected that the installation of fiber optic lines will grow from $100 million in 1996 to $4.5 billion in 2000.[4]

One issue affecting the interactive television market is customer enthusiasm for the product. Market trials of interactive television throughout the United States and Europe have shown little enthusiasm for what has been offered. The main issue affecting customer reception to interactive television is that many customers are choosing to spend their new media budgets on the Internet instead.[5] Also, interactive television turned out to be a lot more expensive than expected, and customers cannot justify the expense of having the product, given that there are substitute products of comparable quality. Cable, for example, has the strength of providing incredibly high penetration and wide bandwidth. Cable is currently accessible in 92 percent of U.S. households, and its bandwidth is essential to support truly interactive services.

Aside from the initial cool reception, it is still predicted that interactive television's benefits will allow for significantly improved penetration in the future.

Currently, it is estimated that 50,000 homes in the United States have access to interactive television. By 2000, that number is expected to grow to 22.5 million. By 2005, the number of homes with cable access to interactive television is supposed to reach 26.4 million.

Revenue potential for the market is also great. For 1997 alone, the market is expected to be worth an impressive $1 billion. This, of course, is not enough to earn positive overall returns for many companies. It is predicted that interactive television will not break even until 2001.[6]

There are several issues facing this industry. Interactive television may not currently be cost competitive given the many options consumers have available to them in the home entertainment market. Also, telephone companies have shown an unwillingness to pursue opportunities within this market because they have not been able to justify the investment required to upgrade their networks to the level necessary to support interactive television. This great investment expense becomes more difficult to justify as many telephone companies do not regard interactive television as the staple of their business and have little intention of increasing its presence in their businesses. Such issues of commitment are not faced by those already established and committed to this industry.

A SURVEY OF THE COMPETITORS

This section looks at the current providers in the home entertainment market, the threats to Americast's success: TELE-TV, a similar interactive alliance; cable, satellite, and video rental.

TELE-TV

TELE-TV is the other major competitor in the interactive market. TELE-TV is made up of telecommunications companies Pacific Telesis, NYNEX, and Bell Atlantic. This partnership differentiates itself by focusing on the programming rather than the network. This venture does not have the interactive capabilities that Americast is offering in some of its markets, but it still allows "gadget-oriented" interactive features such as game shows that viewers can participate in, movies where one can choose the end-

ing, and traditional pay-per-view programming.[7] Pacific Telesis, NYNEX, and Bell Atlantic each bring capabilities to the TELE-TV alliance.

Bell Atlantic currently operates in the businesses of local network services, wireless communications, video services, directory services, and information services. NYNEX's major businesses are in land-wire telecommunications, wireless communications, directory publishing, video entertainment, and information services. Pacific Telesis's operations include local wire telephone services, Internet access services, and video services. These three telecommunications companies created TELE-TV to develop programming and technology for wired interactive television systems.[8] The alliance will provide nationally branded traditional and interactive home entertainment, informational and educational programming over the companies' broadband and wireless networks.[9]

While both TELE-TV and Americast are competing for the interactive television market, the two alliances differ in several ways. First, the two ventures will cover different regions of the United States. TELE-TV covers most of the northeastern states and California and Nevada. Americast covers much of the midwestern and southern states as well as markets in the northwestern region. Second, TELE-TV plans to use the wireless communication known as MMDS that Bell Atlantic and NYNEX are bringing to the venture as its method of access. Americast is using varied methods depending on the capabilities of each partner. The third difference in the two alliances is the fact that TELE-TV faces the disadvantage of not having an entertainment-savvy company like Disney heading the venture and does not have the access to unique programming that Disney can provide Americast.

The progression of the two ventures has also differed greatly. Aside from a few hurdles, Americast has been progressing smoothly while TELE-TV has been floundering. TELE-TV was originally predicted to be the future in interactive television. Problems between the partners, however, are stalling the alliance's actions. The partners in the venture have begun to stray and focus their attention in different directions. The future structure of the alliance has come into question with the announcement of the possible acquisition of the NYNEX Corporation by Bell Atlantic Corporation. This development among two of TELE-TV's partners would greatly affect the structure and future of the TELE-TV alliance. The acquisition has faced some resistance, however. Approval has been delayed as the two sides determine how NYNEX customers will be compensated for the years of service problems encountered as well as lost income. State regulators are demanding hundreds of millions of dollars in lower rates and other concessions such as investments in the phone network. If granted New York regulators' approval, the deal is expected to close by April 1, 1997. These heavy concessions by Bell Atlantic could culminate in the demise of TELE-TV and pave the way for Americast to capture the interactive television market. The original partnership, consisting of three companies, could become an "organization folded into the Bell Atlantic/NYNEX merger."[10] The possibility of both of these developments becoming reality would have tremendous effects on both Americast and TELE-TV. Both alliances could face obstacles that will affect how they compete within the interactive television market. Their performance in this industry may also affect how interactive television competes in the home entertainment industry.

To add to the turmoil, Bell Atlantic and NYNEX have decided to dissolve plans to launch the TELE-TV programming, focusing on direct satellite instead. Amidst the roller coaster ride that the venture has become, Michael Ovitz and Howard Stringer, two key figures in the formation of the venture, have pulled out of the project, citing "rising costs, technical difficulties, and vast changes in the electronic marketplace."[11]

The Cable Television Market

The cable industry currently holds an 89 percent market share in the multichannel video market. This constitutes competitive advantages in distribution, logistics, marketing, and reputation. To defend its position as the leader in home entertainment, the cable industry has launched initiatives focusing on three areas of interest to the consumer: (1) "The Future Is on Cable," which focuses on utilizing the top technology available such as fiber optic lines for high quality and diverse programming and access to the Internet; (2) the On Time Customer Service Guarantee (OTC) to improve the devotion and responsiveness of cable companies toward meeting their customers' needs; and (3) "Cable in Focus," which strongly encourages all employees of cable providers to remain current on new technological advances applicable to the cable industry.[12]

It is clear that the cable industry intends to remain the leader in the home entertainment industry by proving to be proactive in such a competitive environment. The current infrastructures that cable has in place provide an access advantage to easily market Internet capabilities to the existing 45.2 million subscriber base.[13] Despite the market leader's position, the cable industry has been losing ground to a rising player, the satellite industry.

The Satellite Television Market

The cable industry slipped from 91 percent market share in 1995 to 89 percent in 1996, partly due to the increase in direct satellite service (DSS) usage.[14] DSS, a programming delivery service, was started by Thomson, the electronics giant, and DIRECTV, owned by Hughes Electronics Corporation. DSS packages entertainment programming and distributes it via digital satellite messaging. The signals are captured through a small satellite dish attached to the outside of a consumer's home. Thomson contributes production and sale of the dishes through RCA and its own label. Currently, households subscribing to DIRECTV enjoy network programs and premium channels.[15]

In addition to providing a greater number of channels for viewing, the quality of picture and sound was ranked first and second in programming satisfaction ratings.[16] The advantage that the capital-intensive satellite industry has over other telecommunications infrastructures is geographic reach. Currently, DSS is available from five providers: IntelSat, EutelSat, Orion, DIRECTV, and Echostar. Geographic reach extends throughout the United States, Latin America, Western Europe, Indonesia, some parts of China and Eastern Europe.[17] The government policies of these regions either restrict or welcome satellite broadcasting, and thus have an influence on the number of households permitted to receive access. DSS has the potential to reach the largest percentage of households worldwide, given government permission. As a result, the parties involved in satellite programming are exploring and designing improved satellite units to launch into orbit to extend geographic reach.

The Video Rental Industry

The growing inroads of new technology, such as advances made by cable, satellite, and interactive television, have caused the home video industry's market share to slip. This will most likely continue unless an aggressive strategy is implemented to ensure survival. This affects both the companies that rent the videos and the companies that produce the video tapes to resell through retailers. Specifically, this affects Viacom's Blockbuster Video, other video retailers, and the film companies that also produce videos, such as Time Warner. Two initiatives have been communicated and launched to achieve this goal: (1) communicating to consumers that video is the first window in the home entertainment environment and (2) lengthening home video's window of exclusivity.[18] Exclusivity permits the movie to be accessed only through the video tape medium for a specific length of time, as opposed to simultaneous pay-per-view or premium movie channel programming. Due to strong marketing campaigns from both the cable and satellite industries, people believe that cable and satellite can deliver the movies before the video distributors can; however, this is not the case. The video industry has developed the phrase, "First in Home Entertainment," and will continue to be marketed with that slogan to achieve the first initiative.[19] In addressing the second initiative, video distributors prefer to lengthen their exclusivity to the movie just as theater owners enjoy their window. Viewers will not be able to view the movies for three to four months and will therefore be influenced to rent the bigger hits, causing a boost in slipping rental revenues.

The strategies that the video industry have initiated are defensive in nature, given the threat of the cable and the substitution of other industries for the video rental market. Nonetheless, the video segment definitely serves as a competitor to the previously mentioned industries, especially with the exclusivity initiative. If consumers perceive that video is the "First in Home Entertainment," the video industry may regain lost ground in the fierce competition to be the home entertainment leader.

Pending Challenges

In such a highly competitive industry, including cable, satellite, video rental, and interactive television, the future of home entertainment faces eminent strategic issues as it continues to change. Immense capabilities and resources are needed to compete. However, the best strategy to access these capabilities and resources is uncertain. Americast was formed to answer this question with the creation of a joint venture. But as technologies and new trends continue to evolve, is this sort of commitment of pooled resources the right answer? Does the instability of alliances such as Americast and TELE-TV cause even more uncertainty, leading to the eventual failure of interactive television in the home entertainment market? Or will it fuel competition that may lead to an overwhelming success? And if success is in the future and growth seems inevitable, what strategies should telecommunication companies follow to ensure the continuation of this success?

C-37

NOTES

1. http://www.roscoe.law.harvard.edu/cour...course/sessions/Digital/sem_3.html.
2. http://www.sbc.com.swbell/investor_rels/disney2.html., press release, Los Angeles, Sept. 28, 1995.
3. Gibbons, K., "Americast Can't See Over the Rainbow," *Multichannel News*, December 23, 1996, p. 3.
4. "In the Emerging Interactive Television Industry Fiber Optics Line and Equipment Will See Explosive Growth," *Research Studies*, February 14, 1995.
5. "Interactive Television to Become Cash-Positive in the US By 2001, Europe a Year Later, OVUM Believes," *Computergram International*, January 24, 1996 (courtesy of Market Insite).
6. Ibid.
7. McCarthy, S., "Getting Back to Cable Basics," *Telephony*, September 23, 1996, 231(13): 22–23.
8. Gibbons, K., "TELE-TV End May Be Near," *Multichannel News*, December 9, 1996, p. 7.

9. "Bell Atlantic, NYNEX, PacTel Launch TELE-TV National Brand," *Telco Business Report*, May 22, 1995, p. 1.
10. Levine, S., "Cold Shoulder in California: Will TELE-TV Dissolution Leave PacTel Shivering?" *Telephony*, Feb. 3, 1997, p. 62.
11. "Baby Bell's Pulling the Plug on TELE-TV," *Media Daily*, December 6, 1996.
12. Collins, J., *Multichannel News*, Sept. 9, 1996, 126(35), p. 26.
13. McConnell, C., *Broadcasting & Cable*, August 19, 1996, 126(35), p. 26.
14. *Television Digest*, February 5, 1996, 36(6), p. 16.
15. "Thomson Hits 3,000,000 Mark," *Business Wire*, January 10, 1997, p. 1101238.
16. Ibid.
17. Blake, P., "Who's Going Interactive?" *Telephony*, January 13, 1997, p. 18 (courtesy of Market Insite).
18. Thorward, R., *Video Business*, November 8, 1996, 16(45), p. 12.
19. Ibid.

Anheuser-Busch and Redhook Create Froth in Craft Beers

Bruce Rishel
Jonathan Newton
Thomas D. Sigerstad

I don't know of any large brewer that does not appreciate and admire what small brewers have done to increase public appreciation for beer, and I don't know any large brewer that isn't working frantically to capture this market.[1]

—Bob Weinberg
President, R.S. Weinberg & Assoc.
(craft beer consulting group)

INTRODUCTION

With overall beer sales stagnant but the craft brew segment experiencing tremendous growth, large brewers, craft brewers, and distributors were anxious to understand and to capitalize on any potential remedy for flat sales. (Exhibit 1 provides the Institute for Brewing Studies' definition of *craft brewer*, and for the balance of this case, the terms *craft brew*, *microbrewery*, and *specialty brew* are used interchangeably.) As a key competitor, Anheuser-Busch (A-B) was on the outside of the fastest growing market segment in the industry. Within the growing segment, the Redhook Ale Brewery was experiencing rapid growth but, because of poor distribution capabilities, was confined to the Pacific Northwest. As the middlemen, Anheuser-Busch's distributors did not have a

craft-brewed beer to offer as a part of its product line. Given these challenges and the opportunity for increased profitability of each party, a new distribution alliance was inevitable.

Because a proposed alliance between A-B and Redhook would be the first between a major brewer and a smaller brewer, many uncertainties awaited the parties involved. A-B would be making a large capital investment in Redhook based on the recent growth of the craft beer market. A-B had no way of knowing whether these growth rates could be maintained, or if they would taper off in the near future. Furthermore, by investing in Redhook, A-B would be, if only symbolically, backing off from creating and heavily marketing its own craft beer lines. Redhook would be entering the alliance wanting access to A-B's distribution network but uncertain as to the implications of the alliance on its brand image. A-B's distributors would also be facing many unknowns as a result of the proposed alliance. On the one hand, distributors would be gaining access to the first-class, micro-brewed label they had been asking for; but on the other hand, they would be forced to deal with the added complexity of promoting competing labels in the same market.

BEER INDUSTRY TRENDS

The top 10 U.S. brewers sold over 180 million barrels of beer in 1995 (see Exhibit 2). The "Big Three"

This case was prepared under the direction of Professor Robert E. Hoskisson. The case is intended to be used as the basis for class discussion rather than to illustrate either effective or ineffective handling of an administrative situation.

EXHIBIT 1 *IBS Defines "Craft Brewer"*

According to the Institute for Brewing Studies, a craft brewer:

1. Possesses a Federal Brewer's Notice (or a Brewer's License under the Canadian Excise Tax).

2. Brews at least 90 percent of beer sold using no more than 10 percent corn, rice, or refined sugar adjunct, of any form (except in the case of some traditional Belgian-style strong ales, that can contain as much as 20 percent adjunct).

3. Does not use artificial colors, artificial flavors, or any processing aids that combine to become part of the final beer product.

4. Is not more than one-third owned (or the economic equivalent) by another company of greater than $50 million revenue that is not a craft brewer.

IBS Director David Edgar explains the reasoning behind the definition. The first point shows "a certain level of commitment or involvement in the brewing of the beer while still allowing for some contract brewing companies to be counted as 'craft brewers.'" The second point indicates that craft brewers generally brew all-malt beers, but leaves room for variations. The third point stipulates all natural ingredients while avoiding the strictness of the German beer purity law. The last point relates to independence, particularly from companies that are not in the craft brewing business. The IBS feels that such a company would affect the way a subordinate craft brewer does business.

Source: http://www.beerhunter.com/news/index25.html

brewers (Anheuser-Busch, Miller, and Coors) were responsible for 77 percent of that volume. Although the Big Three brewers had enjoyed increasing market share from the mid-1980s to the mid-1990s (see Exhibit 3), some individual brands started to experience share losses in the 1990s (see Exhibit 4). In addition, domestic sales for the industry were leveling off (see Exhibit 5). The lack of growth in volume for the large and traditional brewers was primarily the result of demographic changes in the U.S. market. For many years, the beer industry had the luxury of seeing the baby boom population produce

EXHIBIT 2 *The Top 10 U.S. Brewers and Their 1995 Market Share and Sales*

Brewer	1995 Market Share	1995 Sales
1 Anheuser-Busch	44.1%	87.5 million barrels
2 Miller*	22.7%	45.0 million barrels
3 Adolph Coors	10.2%	20.3 million barrels
4 Stroh**	5.4%	10.8 million barrels
5 Heileman	4.0%	7.9 million barrels
6 Pabst	3.2%	6.3 million barrels
7 Genesse	0.9%	1.8 million barrels
8 Latrobe	0.6%	1.2 million barrels
9 Boston Beer Co.	0.5%	1.0 million barrels
10 Pittsburgh	0.5%	0.9 million barrels

Source: Anheuser-Busch 1996–1997 Fact Book.
Note: A barrel contains 31 gallons.
*Includes Molson
**Excludes contract volume

EXHIBIT 3 *Domestic Market Share—1984, 1989, and 1994*

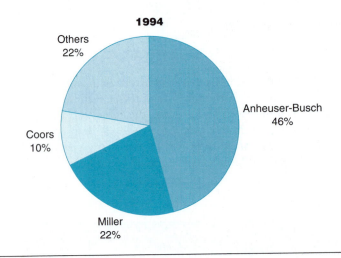

Source: *Modern Brewery Age.*

an annual set of newly legal drinking-age boomers. Beer consumption is largely signaled by demographics. "Younger consumers drink more beer, but younger consumers have been a dwindling resource."[2] The beer industry used to grow approximately 2 percent annually just from the number of people turning 21. Now the consumer base for the beer industry grows by only one-half of 1 percent annually as a result of newly legal consumers.[3] Adding to the dilemma, today's 21-year-olds are not imbibing as much as their counterparts in the past. This trend of moderation has also extended to the balance of the beer-drinking population, leaving in-

dustry forecasters pointing to a continuation of health consciousness as the U.S. population ages.

While the foam had subsided on the traditional brewers' growth, the craft brewers continued to enjoy heady and substantial gains. The craft brewing industry output is meager in comparison with traditional brewers. The top 15 craft brewers shipped a mere 2.3 million barrels in 1995 (see Exhibit 6), compared to the sales of over 180 million barrels of the major U.S. brewers. In 1996, the craft segment grew over 25 percent, reaching an annual dollar volume of almost $3 billion. But, the overall U.S. brewing industry annual dollar volume still eclipsed the craft

EXHIBIT 4 *Top 10 Beer Brands—1994 (ranked by unit sales)*

	Sales (million barrels)			Market Share, %		
Brand	1992	1993	1994	1992	1993	1994
1. Budweiser	45.4	42.8	41.5	24.1%	22.7%	22.1%
2. Bud Light	13.6	14.9	16.4	7.2	7.9	8.7
3. Miller Light	17.9	16.6	15.6	9.5	8.8	8.3
4. Coors Light	12.6	12.8	12.8	6.7	6.8	6.8
5. Busch	9.9	9.1	8.6	5.3	4.8	4.6
6. Miller Genuine Draft	6.9	7.4	7.0	3.7	3.9	3.7
7. Natural Light	5.3	6.9	6.9	2.8	3.7	3.7
8. Milwaukee's Best	6.0	6.5	5.7	3.2	3.5	3.0
9. Miller High Life	4.7	5.1	5.3	2.5	2.7	2.8
10. Old Milwaukee	5.2	5.4	5.0	2.8	2.9	2.7

Sources: *Modern Brewery Age* and *Beverage World*.

EXHIBIT 5 *U.S. Beer Sales (in thousands of barrels)*

Category	1990	1991	1992	1993	1994	% Change (93–94)
Domestic	184,473	181,446	180,807	180,875	179,700	(0.6)
Imports	8,783	7,926	8,323	9,247	10,490	13.4
Exports	4,208	4,611	5,471	5,304	7,000	32.0
Total	197,464	193,983	194,601	195,427	197,190	0.9

Source: *Modern Brewery Age*.

EXHIBIT 6 *Top 15 U.S. Craft Brewing Companies, 1995 (shipments rounded to nearest 100 barrels)*

Company	1995 Shipments	% Growth Over 1994	Market Share*	Share Change
Boston Beer**†	948,000	34	25.1	−3.1
Pete's Brewing**	347,800	91	9.2	+2.0
Sierra Nevada Brewing	200,000	28	5.3	−0.9
Redhook Brewing††	155,000	66	4.1	+0.4
Hart Brewing††	123,100	70	3.3	+0.4
Anchor Brewing	103,000	1	2.7	−1.4
Full Sail Brewing††	71,500	36	1.9	−0.2
Widmer Brewing††	69,200	40	1.8	−0.2
Portland Brewing††	62,000	68	1.6	−0.1
Spanish Peaks Brewing**	53,200	83	1.4	−0.2
Mass. Bay Brewing**	39,000	63	1.0	0.0
Nor'Wester Brewery	32,400	24	0.9	+0.2
Rockies Brewing	32,400	24	0.9	−0.1
New Belgium Brewing	31,800	68	0.8	0.0
Deschutes Brewery††	31,600	60	0.8	0.0

Source: *The New Brewer*, May-June 1996.
*Of total craft-brewing segment.
**All or partially contract-brewed by another company.
†Includes total of Oregon Ale and Beer subsidiary (35,000 barrels).
††More than one facility.

brewers with sales of approximately $50 billion.[4] In stark contrast to the stagnation of the beer industry in general, the craft brewing market segment achieved astounding growth (see Exhibit 7) from 1986 to 1995 ranging from 30 to over 70 percent. Craft brewers saw dramatic growth in sales dollar volume, climbing from $109 million in 1987 to over $2 billion in 1995 (see Exhibit 8).

The same changing demographics, which slowed growth in the Big Three's brands, were promising continued growth for the craft-brewing industry. The specialty beer consumer's demographic profile is considerably different than that of the traditional beer consumer (see Exhibit 9). It is important to note that while the number of younger beer drinkers is shrinking overall, the same younger market is causing the rapid growth of the craft beer segment. The specialty beer drinker profile is skewed toward the younger drinker, hinting of future loyal customers as they maintain their brand preferences in future years. The interest in specialty brews caused in part by this educated and higher-income group continues to af-

fect market demand characteristics as evidenced by the 1,250 microbreweries operating in 1997 as compared with only 4 that were in existence in the United States in 1980.[5]

Craft brewing quickly grew out of the micro-brewery stage of 15,000 barrels of beer per year.[6] Fueling this trend were several developments. Technology provided small-batch brewing equipment, legal changes allowed on-premises brewing as well as home brewing, and demographic changes provided the better educated and higher-income households that not only appreciated better-quality beer but could afford to pay a premium price for a premium beer.[7]

Understanding that consumers are drinking less but higher quality beer, and faced with their own declining sales, large brewers, including Anheuser-Busch, began studying the microbrew industry as a key component in the ongoing market share battle. One reason for the acceptance of craft brews and the resultant growth rates is the perception among the beer-drinking public that smaller brew-

C-42

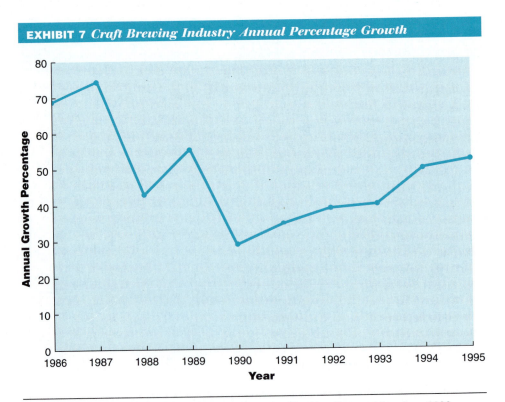

EXHIBIT 7 *Craft Brewing Industry Annual Percentage Growth*

Source: Compiled by the Institute for Brewing Studies, *The New Brewer*, May–June 1996.

EXHIBIT 8 *Craft Brewing Industry Annual Dollar Volume*

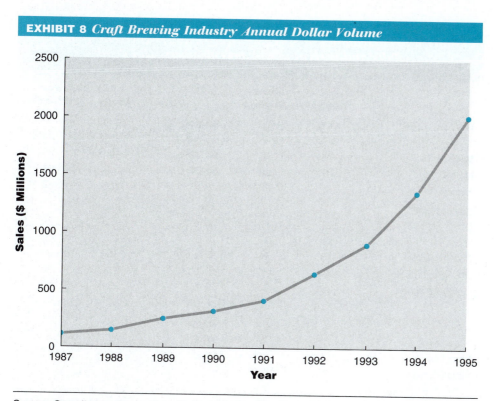

Source: Compiled by the Institute for Brewing Studies, *The New Brewer,* May–June 1996.

eries offer a more unique, higher-quality beer. This perception causes marketing problems for the large brewers. To compete in this market, the Big Three have created their own craft beer labels and tried to distance these labels from their mass-market brands. Miller has even created the separate Plank Road Brewery as a new venture. These various craft beer labels have met with mixed results as the craft beer segment has rocketed upwards.

Another option for entry into this market by the Big Three is to form alliances with small breweries already in the craft-brewing market. Commenting on this strategy, Pat Stokes, president of Anheuser-Busch, said:

Our way of involving ourselves in that kind of beer—if the notion is that it has to come from a small brewery, because one thing Anheuser-Busch will never be is a small brewery—is to invest in someone who is and let them take that forward.[8]

ANHEUSER-BUSCH HISTORY[9]

Founded in 1852 in St. Louis by George Schneider, today Anheuser-Busch is the world's largest brewer. Mr. Schneider sold his small brewery in 1860 to a group of St. Louis businessmen, one of whom would be the company's part namesake Eberhard Anheuser. The Bavarian Brewery was indeed small, ranking 29th of 40 breweries in St. Louis. Anheuser later bought out the other partners in the venture and became sole owner of the brewery. In 1861, Adolphus Busch married Lilly Anheuser and the long-running association between Anheuser and Busch began.

Budweiser Lager Beer was first introduced in 1876. Carl Conrad provided distribution and bottling and E. Anheuser Co.'s Brewing Association was the brewer. This agreement marked one of the first distribution associations in A-B's history. Production increased in the years before prohibition, from 8,000

EXHIBIT 9 *Demographics of Specialty Beer Drinkers (percent of all U.S. adults and percent of U.S. beer drinkers who drink microbrewed beers, 1994)*

	Adults	Beer Drinker		Adults	Beer Drinkers
U.S. Average	13%	25%	**Region**		
			Northwest	17%	29%
Sex			Midwest	14	25
Male	18	29	South	12	18
Female	8	20	West	20	32
Education			**Age**		
Some high school	5	10	18 to 24	14	26
High school graduate	8	17	25 to 34	23	36
Some college	15	26	35 to 44	15	27
College graduate	24	38	45 to 54	10	20
Graduate school	35	54	55 to 64	5	16
			65 and older	2	7
Income			**Race**		
No answer	5	27	White	15	27
Less than $20,000	11	20	Black	7	15
$20,000 to 29,999	7	18			
$30,000 to 49,999	11	21			
$50,000 to 74,999	19	30			
$75,000 or more	31	50			

Source: *American Demographics,* May 1995.

barrels in 1865 to 318,107 barrels in 1885. Anheuser's production passed the million-barrel mark in 1901, and by 1907 production hit 1,599,918 barrels, a record unbroken until 1937.

In 1919, Missouri became the 37th state to ratify the 18th Amendment—Prohibition. Later that year, Anheuser-Busch, Inc., adopted its new corporate name. In 1920, national Prohibition took effect and A-B found new ways to remain in business. Malt syrup, Budweiser near beer, and ice cream production all started in 1920. Later in the 1920s, Carcho, a chocolate beverage, was introduced and an A-B yeast production department opened. The ice cream business was good for A-B, exceeding 1 million gallons in 1926. A-B also manufactured truck and bus bodies during this period as well as refrigerated cabinets.

Prohibition ended in 1933 and beer sales that year totaled 607,511 barrels for A-B. Beer production took off for A-B in the years after Prohibition, hit-ting the 2 million-barrel mark by the end of 1938 and the 3 million-barrel mark by the end of 1941. New breweries opened in 1951, 1954, and 1959 to deal with steadily increasing sales, and by 1964 annual beer production had reached 10 million barrels. In each of the years, 1968, 1969, 1970, and 1972 new breweries came on line, and by 1974 Anheuser-Busch reached 30 million barrels for the year.

New offerings introduced throughout the 1970s and 1980s included Budweiser Malt Liquor, Michelob Classic Dark, Anheuser-Busch Natural Light, Michelob Light, Chelsea, Wurzburger-Hofbrau, Root 66, Budweiser Light, Anheuser-Busch Wines, King CobraMalt Liquor, LA, Baybry's Champagne Cooler, Dewey Stevens Wine Cooler, Zelter-Seltzer, Anheuser Marzen, Michelob Dry, Bud Dry, O'Doul's, and Busch Light Draft. While many of these products did not enjoy long lives, others remain among top brands today.

Along with diversifying through new products,

Anheuser-Busch signed a licensing agreement with Labatt Brewing in Canada to brew and sell Budweiser there in 1980, the year Budweiser was introduced to Japan. Budweiser was introduced in England, brewed by Watney, Mann, and Truman, in 1984 and in Denmark in 1985 by United Breweries Ltd. Later in the 1980s, A-B would continue its globalization drive through agreements with Oriental Brewing Co. Ltd. of South Korea, Guinness Ireland, Ltd., and the introduction of Budweiser to Mexico.

HISTORY OF REDHOOK BREWING COMPANY[10]

"Enlightened demand" was the idea behind the birth of the Redhook Brewing Company in Seattle, Washington. In the late 1970s, Paul Shipman (Redhook's current president) and Gordon Bowker (one of the founder's of Starbucks Coffee), hit on the idea that Seattle would support a locally made, European-style beer label. From this idea, the Independent Ale Brewery (later renamed Redhook Brewery) was born in May 1981 in an abandoned transmission shop.

From these beginnings, Redhook increased production from 1,000 barrels of beer in 1981 to 158,000 barrels in 1995. As a result of rapid growth, Redhook outgrew its first brewery and purchased the historic Fremont Car Barn in 1988. This building, built in 1908 to house the cars of the Seattle Electric Railway, has since become a "must-see" on Seattle's tour of brewing sites.

Many in the craft brewing industry, including the well-recognized Boston Beer Company, maker of Samuel Adams, and Pete's Brewing company, maker of Pete's Wicked Ale, act as marketing organizations, contracting their brewing operations to brewers that have excess capacity. Redhook Brewing chose a different strategy: to concentrate on making all of its own beers.

Faced with a 40 percent annual growth rate, Shipman realized that Redhook would meet its maximum production capacity by mid-1994. He convinced the board of directors to expand. This resulted in the construction of a new 200,000-barrel capacity brewery at Woodinville, Washington, to meet this rising demand. Redhook invested $5 million in a new bottling line to make Woodinville the most technologically advanced bottling line in America. As demand continued, Redhook announced plans in May 1995

to construct a 250,000-barrel capacity brewery in Portsmouth, New Hampshire, to service the eastern United States. Much of this capacity is to be used for expansion over the next three to four years. Keith Freising, Redhook's Texas sales manager, indicated that Redhook's production goal for 1997 was 350,000 barrels.[11] Construction of a brewery in Boulder, Colorado, to service the central states has also been mentioned.

In the 16 years since its inception, Redhook has expanded its product line from the original Redhook Ale to include Redhook ESB (Extra Special Bitter), Ballard Bitter India Pale Ale, Blackhook Porter, Winterhook (Redhook's seasonal beer), Redhook Hefe-Weizen, Wheathook, and Doubleblack Stout (a beer combining Redhook beer and Starbucks Coffee).

In an effort to increase its brewing operations and distribution, Redhook recently entered into an alliance with Anheuser-Busch.[12] The makers of Budweiser now hold 25 percent of Redhook stock. In addition to this massive cash infusion from A-B, Redhook has secured the use of A-B's countrywide distribution network.[13] As a result of the alliance, there are now over 400 A-B distributors across the country distributing Redhook Beer.[14]

ANHEUSER-BUSCH AND THE DISTRIBUTOR RELATIONSHIP

Anheuser-Busch operates within the three-tier system created by federal law in 1933. In this system, the brewer, distributor, and retailer have separate roles; it was designed to keep brewers from gaining "excessive market control" over the beer-drinking public.[15] The law was in response to the pre-Prohibition system where a few brewers had much control over the beer market. The 1933 law helped create over 3,000 distributors, typically small and mid-size businesses, that today still manage the $24 billion business of beer distribution.[16]

Today, the beer distributor is on the front lines in the war to gain market share and increase beer sales. In nearly every bar in the country, you can see the distributors at work. From chatting with bar owners to placing point-of-sale promotional materials such as banners, table tents, and posters around the bar, distributors are constantly battling for new customers.[17] According to industry insiders, good point-of-sale merchandising can produce results in the range of plus or minus two market share points.[18] Not only do distributors promote, but they also send out draft technicians to clean the bar's draft lines and to ensure that the bar has good, drinkable beer. They repair neon signs and work to make certain their beer has prime tap location and more tap handles than the competition's. If there are weekend events in store parking lots or at the local Elks Club, the distributor is the brewer's link to the customer.

Anheuser-Busch works closely with its distributors to coordinate the strategic and tactical battle plans for the market share war. In the early 1990s A-B decided it was time to focus on Texas, where one in ten beers in the United States is sold, and turn Texas to Bud.[19] Texas is a key state in A-B's market share battle. Home to a population of heavy beer drinkers, Texans consumed 16 million barrels of beer in 1995; only Californians consume more. While other states were experiencing a loss in beer sales growth, sales in Texas increased 2 percent in 1995.[20]

First in this fight was the goal to reform the role of Bud Light. Once a "Diet Bud," A-B changed its focus to take on Miller Lite. After placing a big "Lone Star" on the side of Bud Light, A-B set aside $20 million per year for the Texas campaign. Using this money, A-B attacked the competition using Texas-based TV commercials, promotions, billboards, and a Texas radio campaign. Anheuser-Busch's distributors took on the challenge by promoting Bud Light in bars and retailers across the state. Distributors worked to make displays in stores and convert the taps in bars to Bud Light.[21]

Budweiser's commitment to its distributors is illustrated by Chairman August Busch III's response to the A-B distributor in Houston, Texas, when asked for a beer to combat Shiner Bock produced by Spoetzl, the largest regional brewer in the Southwest. Shiner Bock was an increasing threat in Texas and distributors had begged for a beer to take back the market share being lost to Shiner. Within 30 days of August Busch III's arrival, A-B had produced the full-bodied amber lager, ZiegenBock. "It was the fastest I've seen Anheuser-Busch move in my entire life," says Laurie Watson, vice president of Brown Distributing Co., A-B's Austin distributor.[22] This Texas onslaught helped Anheuser-Busch not only in the battle with small breweries, but as of December 1996, A-B raised its market share to 44 percent, up from 37 percent in 1991, and has dethroned Miller Lite as the top beer in Texas.[23]

Anheuser-Busch's success can be traced to its close relationship with distributors. A-B is able to provide a wide range of large-scale marketing, training and promotion for the partnership. The distributor, on the other hand, brings its knowledge of the local market to the partnership. This association has allowed A-B to maintain economies of scale possible for a global brewer while local distributors provide a constant evaluation of the local market conditions. Each distributor is out in the bars and among the retailers maintaining relationships with the people who have the closest contact to the customer. This allows the distributor, and therefore the brewery, to closely monitor shifting conditions in the marketplace. A-B deems this front-line attack so important that it provides the distributor with personnel to help with marketing and promotions. These individuals, known as the CMTs (contemporary marketing teams), spend their weekends in the bars across the distributor's territory promoting Budweiser and its full line of beers.

In an interview with David Stinson, the Dallas general manager for Ben E. Keith Beers (one of the largest beer distributors in the country as well as A-B's largest distributor), Stinson was asked about the key to a successful relationship with Anheuser-Busch:

> Relationship management is the key to making the partnership successful; the association is really a balancing act. You have to be able to see the big picture. Not only must you understand the local market, but you have to be able to see circumstances from A-B's perspective.[24]

Troy LaGrone, president of Ben E. Keith Beers, notes, "You can only buy Budweiser from one company and that's Bud."[25] This statement highlights the need for the distributors to work closely in their relationship with A-B and understand the beer industry from all angles. The partnership must focus on a strategy that is good for the distributor and the brewery in the long term.

Response from the Competition

The alliance between A-B and Redhook was the first one between any of the Big Three breweries and a smaller regional brewery. The aftershocks from this alliance were felt not only by the other two Big Three breweries, Miller Brewing and Adolph Coors, but by Boston Beer Company, the country's leading craft brewery.

In 1995 Miller Brewing Company, a subsidiary of Philip Morris, responded by acquiring a majority interest in the Celis Brewery in Austin, Texas. Celis brews a very unique, fruity line of beers. The terms of the deal were not disclosed, but like the alliance between A-B and Redhook, Celis will remain independent. Unlike the A-B/Redhook alliance, however, the alliance between Miller and Celis is not based on distribution. Miller will not distribute Celis's line of beers, but it is expected to contribute its marketing, accounting, and purchasing expertise to Celis through the alliance.

Adolph Coors Company chose a different strategy for entering the craft brew market. Coors relied on the development of its own craft brew labels and distanced them from the Coors brand and image. To help with this strategy, Coors introduced a new marketing unit called Unibev Limited to develop boutique beers. Unibev utilized a grassroots marketing campaign stressing patience and allowing the beer to "percolate through the beer-drinking community," according to George Mansfield, brand manager with Unibev. To date, Unibev's most popular brand has been Killian's Irish Red with sales increasing 60 percent in 1994.[26]

Boston Beer is the company that stands to lose the most in competing against a successful A-B/Redhook alliance. Unlike Miller and Coors, Boston Beer does not have other successful brands and market share to rely on if the craft brew business becomes highly competitive. Boston Beer has built itself on the strength of the very popular and highly decorated Samuel Adams brand. Samuel Adams targets the same market as Redhook, but does not have the strength of A-B's distribution network. When asked to comment on the alliance, Jim Koch, founder of Boston Beer Co., said:

That was no press release. That was a declaration of war. What it means is that the cozy, fraternal days of the microbrewery business are over.... Redhook now has access to virtually unlimited capital to build breweries throughout the country. As it increases production, you can expect to see brutal competition for shelf space, accompanied by intense price wars. This is not going to be pretty.[27]

Concerns with the Alliance

The alliance poses a distribution concern for Redhook. Traditionally, Redhook relied on a sales team that was forced to act as educators as well as salespeople because Redhook did not have a mass-marketing campaign. Now, in most areas of the country, Redhook faces the problem of raising the beer consciousness of a sales force that it has no control over to meet the "enlightened demand" for its products. To combat this training problem, Redhook executives frequently visit local distributors to throw parties while educating the distributor's sales force about Redhook beers and the craft brew market.

Another concern facing Redhook is what critics of the alliance have labeled the "Budhook" debate. Other micro and regional breweries have been the biggest proponents of the Budhook debate, stating that Redhook will not be able to retain its brand image and quality because of the relationship with A-B. According to Pamela Hinckley, Redhook's vice president of marketing:

Many of our fans were horrified and terrified when they heard about Anheuser-Busch, because everyone assumed it would lead to the automatic decline of the quality of beer.... We were thrown out of some places (in Seattle). Retailers were so upset, they thought that we had betrayed them.[28]

This concern comes from the idea that A-B would choose to satisfy a greater number of beer drinkers by brewing a beer with a less distinct character.[29] In an effort to quell these fears, Paul Shipman, CEO of Redhook beer, said, "A-B has left the company alone, partly as an acknowledgment that it doesn't know anything about the microbrewery industry."[30] When asked about the reaction to the A-B investment in Redhook, Freising said the response was negative in the Seattle area at first but, as time went by, people realized that Redhook was not going to change the quality of its beers, and the customer reaction to A-B was understandable but unjustified.[31]

When Freising was asked about the nature of the A-B/Redhook partnership, he said, "The arrangement is strictly a distribution agreement along with a 25 percent investment in Redhook stock by A-B." When asked about the consequences of this distribution agreement, he said that it means Redhook provides all its own advertising and promotion.[32] As an integral part of the promotion, Redhook provides

C-47

the alliance personnel in the marketplace to help promote the Redhook product line. These personnel work out of the distributor's office but are paid by Redhook.

In actions that will probably complicate the relationship between Anheuser-Busch and its distributors, A-B is in the process of adding its own craft brew line under the Michelob label. These beers will include Michelob Hefe-Weizen, Pale Ale, Honey Lager, Amber Bock, and Golden Pilsner. Stinson was asked how Ben E. Keith manages the relationships between Redhook and A-B:

> It is rather complex. Budweiser wants you to sell their specialty beers and Redhook wants you to sell its beers to the same market. We have to sell the full product line. If a new bar opens, is looking for a craft beer and has only so many taps, we have to try to sell them on a specialty A-B beer as well as a Redhook product. The focus has to be on promoting the full line.[33]

Regarding the added complexity of the A-B/Redhook agreement, Stinson added:

> We have to do everything twice now; before we could negotiate with Budweiser but now we have to have meetings with Bud and the same meetings later with Redhook. The time commitment has been extended when it comes to maintaining our relationships with the breweries.[34]

Freising, commenting on the growing craft beer trend and how A-B felt about Redhook and their mutual customers, stated:

> People are moving toward craft beer; customers are starting to drink less beer but are looking for a premium beer and are willing to pay for it. If Redhook does not get this business, some other craft brewer will. Bud realizes this and it is part

of the reason for the investment in the Redhook breweries.[35]

CONCLUSION

The alliance between A-B and Redhook has raised many questions. One facing all three partners in the alliance—A-B, Redhook, and the distributors—is the legitimacy of the craft beer market. Is it simply a fad that will pass in the future? Anheuser-Busch is faced with the dilemma of whether to push its own microbrew labels or reserve the majority of the market niche for its new partner and concentrate on reviving the growth of its core brand labels. Now that Redhook is not confined to the Pacific Northwest, it must deal with the rapid expansion and increased demand that it will be facing as part of the A-B distribution network. Can Redhook become a nationally recognizable brand, yet retain the brand cachet and quality on which it was founded? For distributors once solely concerned with A-B products, how does the A-B/Redhook alliance reprioritize their local efforts? How do they promote competing products at the same time and in the same market? Should distributors focus on A-B's own microbrew labels, or should they push the Redhook brand now available to them?

In addition to the issues faced by the three main players in this case, the alliance between A-B and Redhook causes a great deal of uncertainty for the entire industry. Should the other two major breweries, Miller and Coors, develop further ties to the craft brew industry, or should they adopt a wait-and-see position? Should the hundreds of microbreweries around the country seek out large brewery partners or merge their efforts with other microbreweries? Can they rely on local brand loyalty as beers such as Redhook move into their home territory?

NOTES

1. Anonymous, 1996, Craft & specialty beer report: Taking the pulse of the specialty segment at the National Craftbrewers Conference & Trade Show, *Modern Brewery Age*, May, 47, no. 21, 7–15.

2. Anonymous, 1997, Year in Review: 1996, *Modern Brewery Age*, March, online, http://www.breweryage.com/stat97.html

3. Anonymous, 1995, Does might make right? If you're A-B, do you have to ask?, *Beverage World*, December 31, 114.

4. Anonymous, 1997, Craft-brewing industry fact sheet, September 25, Institute for Brewing Studies, http://www.beertown.org/IBS/ibs.html.

5. Anonymous, 1997, Beer with us, *U.S. News & World Report*, December 22, 123, (24): 16.

6. J. A. Tannenbaum, 1995, Enterprise: Small breweries slide one down the bar to Wall Street; Redhook IPO finds strong

demand as 'craft brewers' draw underwriters, *Wall Street Journal*, August 17, B2.

7. J. Student, 1995, True brew, *American Demographics*, May, 17, (5): 32–39.

8. Anonymous, Does might make right?, 114.

9. Anonymous, 1997, Budweiser through the years ... The company timeline: History of Anheuser-Busch, http://www.budweiser.com

10. Excerpted in part from: T. Forder, 1995, Redhook marches on, *Ale Street News*, August.

11. K. Freising, 1997, personal interview, March 15.

12. R. Gibson and M. Charlier, 1993, Marketing & Media: Anheuser-Busch plans beer-price cuts to help relieve its sales in California, *Wall Street Journal*, December 14, B6.

13. Tannenbaum, Enterprise: Small breweries slide.

14. P. J. Lim, 1996, Brewer's nationwide expansion on track, chief executive says, *Seattle Times*, May 22, D1.

15. P. Abercrombie, 1996, Tampa beer distributor drops Busch lawsuit, *Tampa Bay Business Journal*, December 13, 3; M. Charlier, 1993, Marketscan, Brewers' price cutting and promotions fail to put much of a head on beer sales, *Wall Street Journal*, July 15, B1.

16. M. Charlier, 1993, Beer brouhaha: Existing distributors are being squeezed by brewers, retailers; biggest discounters, chains seek ways to eliminate 'middlemen' wholesalers trend worries little guys, *Wall Street Journal*, November 22, A1.

17. Gibson and Charlier, Anheuser-Busch plans beer-price cuts.

18. M. Charlier, 1993, Corporate focus: Coors looks to local distributors for national growth; new president Kiely hopes in-

creased marketing boosts brewer's sales volume, *Wall Street Journal*, June 28, B4.

19. M. J. McCarthy, 1996, Bud fight: In Texas beer brawl, Anheuser and Miller aren't pulling punches; barroom blitzes, price wars are some of the tactics brewers use to conquer; staying king of the Bubbas, *Wall Street Journal*, December 5, A1.

20. Ibid.

21. Ibid.

22. Ibid.

23. Ibid.

24. D. Stinson and T. LaGrone, 1997, personal interview, March 15.

25. Ibid.

26. M. Charlier, 1994, Thinking small: Specialty beers' success prompts big brewers to try out the niche; Coors scores with Killian's by forgoing TV ads, using more local push; Anheuser sticks with Bud, *Wall Street Journal*, January 5, A1.

27. G. Gendron, 1994, Brewed Awakening, *INC.*, October 11, 11.

28. Forder, Redhook marches on.

29. M. S. Baker, 1996, Captain Redhook: Paul Shipman is the quiet force behind Redhook Ale Brewery's steady rise to the top, *Business Journal-Portland*, March 1, 1.

30. Gibson and Charlier, Anheuser-Busch plans beer-price cuts.

31. Freising, personal interview.

32. Ibid.

33. Stinson and LaGrone, personal interview.

34. Ibid.

35. Freising, personal interview.

The Australian Pineapple Industry: An Exporting Case Study

John Jackson

Central Queensland University

Whilst seemingly everyone else has jumped aboard such bandwagons as export, globalization, the Asia-Pacific Rim, APEC, ASEAN, WTO, and other exotic business objectives, the dilemma for the Australian Fresh Pineapple Industry in this regard seems problematic. The size, shape, and weight of the fruit are not conducive to export, nor is the distance to foreign consumer markets. Most Asian and North American markets have their needs apparently well met by local producers, in the former case at much lower costs. The Australian industry is not corporatized and capitalized (like some of these competitors) in any way that would readily enable pineapple production to be done by Australians in foreign countries. On the surface it would appear that this particular Australian industry is precluded from exporting.

INTRODUCTION

During the 1994–1995 season, it was clear to most participants and informed observers of the Australian fresh pineapple industry that all was not well. There

© 1995 John Jackson. The author acknowledges with thanks the help of the following: the Rural Industry Research Development Corporation (RIRDC) for funding and backing the project; the Faculty of Business CQU, Queensland Fruit and Vegetable Growers (QFVG), Nick MacLeod, Sam Henson and all those many people in the Pineapple Industry who cooperated.

was an oversupply of fruit on the market and profits were not being made. Quality levels and consistency issues were still not resolved. The industry was as fragmented as ever, with no new stable groupings of size on the horizon. A small number of growers flew to Japan on a government program to investigate the prospects for an up-market dried pineapple product, yet no commercial quantities of the dried fruit were being made or sold in Australia. Some wholesale merchants were predicting the demise or major "downsizing" of the central markets as some of the major supermarket chains bypassed them and bought direct from growers. At the same time the Cannery reduced the quantities it wanted due to increased levels of imported canned pineapples, amongst other reasons, thereby forcing more cannery-quality fresh product onto the fresh market. Concurrently it was apparent that, whilst many other sectors were experiencing similar difficulties, there was a definite improvement in the professionalism behind some conspicuously successful Australian and overseas fruit and vegetable operations. Many in the fresh pineapple industry knew that they could all do much better, but it was not clear to all what needed to be done.

THE HORTICULTURAL INDUSTRY

The total Queensland horticultural industry is valued at around $714 million per annum (Kingston

1994). Total pineapple production in Australia from 1991–1995 has averaged 130,000 tonnes, of which 30,000 tonnes are sold fresh. The annual value is approximately $37.9 million. The fresh sector of approximately 1.85 million cartons is valued at about $13 million (Swete-Kelly 1989). Pineapples are the major horticultural industry in Central Queensland, with $8 million in value and 40 percent of the nation's production volume (MacLeod and Higham 1994).

There is no limit to the production capacity of Australia for growing pineapples with the possible exception of water/rain supply. As a result there are big swings in production with huge oversupplies of pines resulting in the cannery closing its quota. All limits seem to be imposed by alternative uses of the land and by market opportunities for alternative crops.

THE PINEAPPLE BUSINESS

Pineapples are grown in four main growing districts: Central Queensland around Yeppoon, North Queensland around Rollingstone, Southern Queensland around Wamuran, and the Wide Bay area near Bundaberg. Trials have been made in the Ord River area of Western Australia but were not economical. A handful of Northern Territory and northern New South Wales growers met much of their local demand, but all other areas of the country are supplied out of Queensland. No whole imported pines are supplied.

In comparative terms, Australian products suffer from a significant wage rate differential. It is said that one day's labour cost for an Austrlian worker is equivalent to a full week in the Philippines. Some see this as an overwhelming obstacle and either talk about leaving or actually leave the industry. Others look for ways of compensating for this and ways to gain an edge. For example, a computerised package called "Pineman" is reputed to improve a grower's returns substantially by $75 per tonne (Newett 1994). Over recent years the industry has seen a decline in the number of commercial growers with a compensating rise in the size of each remaining farm.

It is common for cannery growers to put their excess fruit onto the fresh fruit market, and also to use the fresh market as cash flow while they wait for payment from the cannery.

During 1993 and 1994 there has been an over-

supply of fruit, and the general industry view is that this is likely to continue. At the present average price to the growers of $8 per carton, they are losing approximately 50 cents on each carton. Thus smaller, less committed, and inefficient producers are leaving the industry whilst the others are living off reserves from previous good years or other incomes and/or investments. Some of the latter admit that they have caused some of their own problems by buying more land and expanding production during good years when they had a "tax problem," rather than expanding the market demand or investing in value-added products.

"THE FRESH FOOD REVOLUTION"

Fresh food sales of all types in Australia have grown exponentially in recent times. For example, Woolworth's growth in this area is from $920 million in 1986–87 to $3.9 billion in 1993–94, and accounts for 40 percent of turnover in their supermarkets. Other retailers report a 30–35 percent of turnover level compared with less than 20 percent five years ago. A CSIRO survey found that 45 percent of men and 50 percent of women had increased their consumption of fruit and vegetables since 1991 (Shoebridge 1994).

The so-called "fresh-food revolution" that we are told started in the 1980s and accelerated into the 1990s, is attributed to a consumer search for healthy living, convenience needed due to the pace of modern life and more women in the work force, an increased insistence on natural taste, and the ready availability of an abundance of fresh food through improved technologies and distribution. It has obviously not been harmed by higher gross profit margins than dry and frozen goods at retail.

The fresh-food industry has also increased substantially in most modernized or rapidly modernizing export markets.

INDUSTRY TYPE

Like many other agri-food industries, the pineapple industry is not significantly corporatized and managed by specialist business professionals. Growers, whilst highly skilled in this task, are usually too busy or untrained to engage in major managerial activity.

Many growers will tell you that they are too physically tired at the end of the day to engage in business beyond the absolutely necessary. Besides the Cannery and a few of the central market agents, there are few groups or individuals of any great size or power. Thus, whilst many of their competitors are moving ahead with major strategic and other initiatives, the backbone of this industry remains relatively small and production oriented. Exporting is often seen as adding one extra complicating dimension to the task of earning a living from pines.

COMPETITION

Price competition is generally strong, whether against other fresh produce, the canned alternative, or others. Wholesale agents must satisfy both growers and retailers, thereby adding competitive pressures.

Competitors who have increased in importance are the supermarket chains, other multiples, buying and selling groups, the Cannery, and large multinationals such as Chiquita that have diversified.

Even less exciting foods are increasing their competitiveness. For example, in the United States, the carrot industry is offering mini whole peeled carrots, carrot stick snack packs, microwavable carrot packs, and packs in resealable bags and is developing hybrid carrot varieties, better flavours, better textures, and increased carotene content (Bundaberg Region Horticulture 1994). Consider also the case of apples. In 1992 about 50 different Australian entities exported 32,000 tonnes of apples whilst the New Zealand Apple and Pear Marketing Board exported 210,000 tonnes (and has invested in a major Chilean apple export company to provide access to low-cost Chilean product) (Horticultural Task Force 1994).

TARGETING, SEGMENTATION, AND POSITIONING

Because the fresh pineapple has traditionally been sold as an unbranded commodity to the end consumer, it has not undergone any detailed market assessment in terms of precise target marketing, segmentation, or market positioning.

BRANDING

At the consumer end, there is very little branding other than distinctive names, colours, and designs on boxes. Most fresh pineapples are sold with no brand identification whatsoever. This is in contrast to the United States where Dole and Del Monte tend to have branding name stickers on each fruit. The size of the market is the main reason given for not doing the same in Australia. Only three or four brands have been exported at various times to the New Zealand market, and none have had the volumes, frequency, or promotion to establish a brand identity.

THE CANNED PINEAPPLE MARKET

Canned pineapple is available all year round and is supplied either by the Golden Circle Cannery in Brisbane or as a generic brand by retailers sourcing mainly from Asian countries such as Thailand, Indonesia, Malaysia, and the Philippines. Because of its ready availability, demand for the fresh alternative is relatively stable. Generally a less sweet fruit is used in the canning operation because sugars can be easily added in the process. The imported canned fruit varies enormously in quality.

Imported canned pineapple is a problem. Retailers state that, on the one hand, they cater to the price-conscious segment, and on the other, that they need to buy imported product because the local cannery cannot supply them with sufficient volumes. With government deregulation economic policies, it is possible that more imported canned pineapples will appear on retail shelves. Emotion can run high. In 1993 a fringe group calling themselves, "Australian Products First," poisoned a supermarket line of imported Thai canned pineapples (Hiely 1994). The major supermarket chains have recently undertaken to only use imported pineapple in the canned house brands if no local product is available.

One grower believed that there was an irony in the prospect that major competitors were trained in Australia under Aid Programs. Canadian markets are also reported to have been strongly affected by Asian imports.

Golden Circle has stated that it is implementing World Best Practice procedures and believes the rest of the value chain and distribution system in Australia will need to do likewise to survive.

Pineapples from Hawaii and South Africa are exported by multinational corporations (e.g., Dole), as are bananas and other products from Chiquita. Some wonder what the role will be for similar companies with Australian pineapples.

CUSTOMERS

Customers in Australia (and probably in all potential export markets) include supermarket chains, greengrocers, fruit marts, grocers, corner stores, grocery wholesalers, salad manufacturers, the catering and fast food industry, and, of course, families and individuals.

Present consumption patterns of whole fresh fruit indicate that pineapples are mainly used for fruit bowl displays and fruit salads. Consumption as a result is heavily weighted toward warm weather. Winter consumption is generally very low. Practically all the fresh fruit, other than fruit salad and pineapple juice, is sold and consumed in a non-value-added form. Most purchasers are families.

Generally, consumer benefits sought are:

1. Consistent quality (sweetness, lack of disease like black heart).
2. Versatility in use with other products (fruit, meat, pizza, etc.).
3. Attractive in a fruit bowl display (the more golden the better—though this can often result in an overripe eating experience when it is eventually cut).

CUSTOMER EDUCATION

While some are reasonably well informed, it is clear that many Australian customers (both retail and end user) are not knowledgeable about pineapples. Many incorrectly believe, for example, that:

1. A pineapple gets sweeter the longer you keep it.
2. The brighter the (golden) colour, the sweeter the fruit.
3. You can tell ripeness by how easily a leaf can be pulled out from the head.

4. A green-coloured pineapple can never be sweet.
5. Pineapples can be displayed for long periods and then still eaten satisfactorily.
6. The fruit looks robust and thus can be roughly treated.

Main consumer dislikes include sourness or tartness, black heart and other diseases, overripeness, and the fruit's lack of convenience in handling, preparation, and eating. Supermarkets and grocers in Australia report a lack of consumer confidence that each pineapple they get will be of a high enough quality. No market research is available on overseas customers.

EXPORT MARKET RESEARCH

Research is important, if for no other reason than to overcome misunderstandings and misinformation. For example, paw paw research showed that most consumers wanted small paw paws for a breakfast item, yet wholesale fruit merchants had been telling growers to only grow large ones because customers wanted the convenience.

The Golden Circle Cannery, the Queensland Fruit and Vegetable Growers (QFVG), and a joint project by Tropical Pines and Freshmark have commissioned formal surveys of consumers. Some of the findings are reported elsewhere in the case study.

In addition, teams of growers have made trips to, for example, Hawaii, USA mainland, Indonesia, Thailand, Malaysia, and South Africa to study overseas trends.

New product R&D is being conducted and will need to be conducted into new varieties that meet different needs and conditions. Sugar content research involving floatation and near infrared light testing are being conducted, but no quick, easy, and cheap solution is obvious.

No market research has been conducted in prospective export markets other than preliminary observations (both desk and visits).

QUALITY CONTROL

Several of the major growers have implemented some sort of formal quality control system, but the marketplace is still experiencing too much product in bad condition. A number of meetings have been held with both growers and the QFVG, but progress is slow.

At present the most common form of sugar level testing is the brix test. While this is worth doing, it is an invasive test and thus cannot be done on every fruit. So far noninvasive tests have proved unreliable. Best-eating pineapples have a sugar content of 16–20 brix, yet most on the market have a brix level between 11–14. Because agents often demand long shelf-life product, pineapples are picked early (yet as mentioned earlier, they do not ripen/sweeten once picked). Like strawberries and mangoes, they need to be consumed within a limited number of days of harvesting (Swete-Kelly 1989).

Golden Circle's and the DPI's horticulturalists are charged with the task of reporting detected problems quickly back to growers. Unfortunately, some problems like black heart are not as easily detected, and not reported.

In 1994 the Agri-Food Council brought in the Food Quality Program and the Clean Food Export Program to assist (financially and otherwise) all sectors of any food chain in implementing formal quality assurance and quality management cultures.

However, problems certainly remain. It is not uncommon both in Australia and overseas to see over-ripe, spongy and "sweaty" pines on sale. Similarly, cut pineapples on sale as halves have been seen in several centres with either black heart or unacceptable brown markings. In some cases the entire offering is a disgrace.

There is some confusion or disagreement as to who bears ultimate responsibility for quality. One large grower, for example, has argued that wholesalers would need to double their prices to growers if they wanted the growers to sort out the product.

PRODUCT

There are two main varieties, the more common smooth-leaf (all year, but best November to February) and the less common rough-leaf (October to January), with some trial plantations of a "Hawaiian" variety. The Hawaiian Gold can last six weeks, but needs irrigation, which is hard for a grower who is not making money anyway. The rough-leaf has increased in popularity due to its more reliable sweetness, but these pineapples only grow well in the far north and are still a difficult crop to grow consistently well. Pineapples are high in vitamin C and

potassium and are reported to help some hayfever sufferers in tests.

Branding is commonly done on boxes but not individual fruit in Australia. (Dole and Del Monte do it in their export markets.) Consumers are not aware of brands and rely on the retailer. By comparison, Chiquita brand bananas achieve a 10–15 percent price advantage over unbranded alternatives. Generally, the chains prefer to use their own brand names (Shoebridge 1994).

PRODUCT MODIFICATIONS

The Australian value-added sector is reported to be the fastest growing sector of fresh food (Shoebridge 1994). The same is said of the United States in its entire retail sector (A$4–6 billion in 1993) and forecasted to double over the next three to four years (Bundaberg Regional Horticulture 1994).

No commercial operation of dried pineapple pieces is widely available in Australia. In Asia, several brands made in Thailand and the Philippines are commonly offered for sale. Some Australian dried pineapple pieces ("Golden Circle Northgate") sell well at Christmas, but for the rest of the year lower-quality white, dried product comes in from Thailand. A South Australian-made semidry glacé-coated alternative is available at almost double the price of the Northgate variety ($9.55 per kilo plus 11 percent sales tax in November 1993).

As regards cut-and-cored chilled pineapple slices and pieces, one Wamuran grower has been offering these for a few years, but sales have been modest. The Golden Circle Cannery also has launched a new offering in margarine-style containers, but it is too early to comment on consumer uptake. Both Woolworths and Coles are trialing (that is, pilot testing) these options in both diced and sliced.

A further product modification is MAP (modified atmosphere processing) pineapple pieces which can increase shelf life by between 100 and 500 percent (Shoebridge 1994). Quality and taste are still too unpredictable. Companies are also experimenting with microbe-controlling coatings in some other food sectors. Some industry players believe that Australians are conservative and prefer their fruit intact. Others say this has changed.

A major limiting factor with regard to new varieties, new product forms, and other new ventures is the lack of corporate funds, expertise, and drive that are not possible from a wide range of individual and small-group growers. Nevertheless, if the pineapple industry wishes to get into the rapidly growing and profitable convenience sector, what the Americans are calling "now food," the product will have to be looked at differently.

Pineapples used for jams, according to a local jam manufacturer, has considerable potential but at present the quality consistency is simply not good enough.

One further product modification use is as feed (silage or fresh) for cattle. Obviously, transport costs must be taken into account.

Greater access to peeler-and-corer machines amongst a wider range of firms and people (other than some chains, greengrocers and fruit juice operators) could increase the chances of newer product forms.

DISTRIBUTION

Freight to all the main southern and western markets from all four growing districts in Queensland is a significant factor, both cost-wise and time-wise. Larger growers and groups can attempt to negotiate differential rates and timing.

Like most other fruits, pineapples are picked early because of the need to get them to market at the best times. Unlike some other fruit, pineapples do not get noticeably sweeter once picked. Because of their perishable nature, reliable refrigerated transport networks are needed. For the Perth market, produce is on the road for a week before it reaches the central market. However, despite these factors, Perth is usually the best market for growers in terms of prices.

It is reported that 80 percent of air freight space out of Brisbane is taken up with perishable products, and thus space availability is still a problem. A possible new air cargo handling facility adjacent to the new Brisbane International Airport is being assessed due to the rising demands by exporters in general. There has also been increasing usage of sea freight out of Brisbane by horticultural exporters.

Prior to freightage, the product is first picked by casual labour and then graded and either put into cartons or bulk bins. Transport operators take the product mainly to the central markets of each major population centre, although some is bought by and delivered directly to the major supermarket chains.

The wholesalers receive the product early in the morning about three times a week and sell to retailers usually before 9:00 A.M. each day.

PRICING

Most industry participants see an opportunity for a premium quality product and a premium price at the consumer level. At this time, such an offering is seldom done as there is no new variety or major differential in quality and presentation amongst end consumers.

A two-tier price system operates at the Cannery, depending on the company's profitability. By way of contrast in 1991/92, Australian growers were paid $291 per tonne for No. 1 Pool pines and $232 per tonne for No. 2 pines, compared with $120 per tonne paid to Thai growers and $60 per tonne in Indonesia.

PROMOTION

Fruit displays, both at retail and in the home, are an integral part of many cultures and also a source of competitive edge. Pineapples are usually a feature in both locations.

Budgets for promotional campaigns inside Australia have been minuscule compared to most food competitors and even very low compared to banana and apple multimedia campaigns. The QFVG has a general levy on pineapple growers of approximately 1.75 cents (1992/93), of which 1 cent (of every one dollar gross amount realized on sales) is for sales promotions. Only $4.5 million was spent locally promoting *all* Queensland fruit and vegetable products during 1992/93, with only $34,000 on pineapples. Some individual growers and small-group packing sheds have done limited promotion for their brands. Practically no promotion has been done by individual exporters in any export market, including New Zealand, though group food promotions are increasingly done. For example, at the 1995 FOODEX Expo in Japan, six Queensland exporters, the Horticultural Export Council, and the Queensland Government Tokyo Office combined to promote, amongst other things, canned fruit, fruit drinks, macadamias, vapour-heated treated mangoes, frozen fruit, and other processed mangoes.

A GLOBAL ELECTRONIC MERCHANDISING AND MARKETING NETWORK

The IBM Corporation, together with Woolworths, has been offering their GEMMNET software package during 1995, and thus it is too early to ascertain its likely success. The system allows global traders (both buyers and sellers) to have on-line information and make decisions across the globe. The system covers any fresh produce category as well as potential suppliers, distributors, and so on. There are also e-mail and bulletin board facilities. It is hard to envisage at this stage which operators (other than the very biggest) would subscribe within the pineapple industry.

PEOPLE AND POLITICS

There has been difficulty getting the parties in this industry to work together on an ongoing basis. The QFVG's political wing, the Pineapple Sectional Committee, has made some progress, but especially with regard to cooperative quality and promotional measures, the going has been too slow.

At one stage, one marketing group of growers in Yeppoon had the most recognized brand in the country, a quality control program, 25 percent market share, and all year round supply. However, due to personality and philosophy differences, this group has split into two groups of roughly equal size but without the benefits obtained before. Philosophically the issue revolved mainly around whether the group should focus on its role as an efficient packing shed for CQ growers or whether it should merge with the northern growers and attempt to gain greater influence over the entire (local and export) market. Personality clashes and distrust were also a key factor. Many growers still believe the concept is very workable if given another chance, perhaps in a different form.

THE DOMESTIC FRUIT MARKET

Generally, the domestic markets for most fruit and vegetables in Australia are well supplied (MacLeod and Higham 1993). This has not resulted in any ma-

jor attention being given to fresh pineapple exports at this point in time.

EXPORT

Up to now, the only export market of any substance has been New Zealand, but this has involved irregular shipments and low volumes. For example, exports of fresh pineapples to New Zealand have declined from 2,300 tonnes in 1988/89 to 800 tonnes in 1992/93. Competitors there are mainly Indonesian and Malaysian.

Saudi Arabia was tried once by one grower, but was dropped when he experienced payment problems. This grower, and some others, maintain that the government should offer credit facilities for those trying to penetrate untried markets.

It has been argued that Australia's lack of commitment to export in this regard is largely because the domestic market is at present sufficiently large to support the industry. Whether this logic applies to other agricultural sectors, or other nations, is not clear. Most people agree that much of any growth in the industry would need to come from exports. Presently only about 10 percent of the national production of fruit and vegetables is exported (Armstrong 1994).

One exporter has complained that the charges imposed by the quarantine authorities have seriously reduced his profitability. He also points to some foreign governments helping their pineapple exporters with freight subsidies and lower-cost, nonunionized labour in both handling and transportation.

Golden Circle has stated that it is looking to become a major exporter of pineapple products. It has started to export special cuts of pineapple to Japan, with special attention being given to premium quality. They are also looking at ISO accreditation for the European market.

Australia has had no problems with chemical residues. Exported pineapple products could make use of the "Clean–Green" logo offered through Clean Food Marketing Australia.

Research by the multinational food company, Unilever, indicates that a country's per capita GDP needs to be above A$23,000 before it buys value-added fresh foods and A$14,000 for fresh foods (Shoebridge 1994). At present the value-added opportunities would then be restricted in Asia to Japan and Singapore, although the more affluent population sectors of the other rapidly growing "tiger economies" could not be omitted for too long.

Australia's export performance in horticulture, despite growth in recent years, is behind our growth in other sectors and also small relative to our Southern Hemisphere competitors. The opportunities in the Asia-Pacific region can readily be taken up by these and Asian competitors, thereby proving to be a relatively "short-term window of opportunity" (Horticultural Task Force 1994).

Despite barriers to entry into Asia's markets for fresh produce, their imports of value-added products are apparently growing at 22 percent per annum (Qld Government 1994).

SOME EXPORT STATISTICS

Total 1993/94 horticultural exports were valued at $433 million, with the government setting a target of $2 billion by the year 2000. The main fruits are oranges ($685 million), apples ($37.1 million), nuts ($39 mill.), grapes ($28.5 mill.), pears ($27.5 mill.), and other citrus ($16.9 mill.). FOB exports of pineapples were $360,000. Singapore is Australia's biggest market for fresh horticultural exports (21.4%), followed by Hong Kong (15.15%), Malaysia (13.74%), Japan (12.19%), and Indonesia (6.02%). Singapore was also the largest buyer of fruit ($92.8 mill.) (Suggett 1995).

Suggett also reports some comparative figures of concern by way of example. For instance, Sunkist spent 20 cents per carton on citrus promotion whilst the Australian industry spent 1.5 cents per carton (Suggett 1994). Also, Chile's fruit export trade begins the new year with approximately $12 million in government funding to help promote its fresh fruit exports to the world (Suggett 1995).

AUSTRALIA'S FRUIT EXPORTING TRACK RECORD

Minnis (1994, p. 17) provides the following brief scenario.

1990–91: Chile (14.1% share of world fruit trade); Australia (1% share).

1992: Australia earned less than 50 percent of what New Zealand did in both fresh and processed fruit and vegetables.

1991/1992: Australian horticulture exports represented by value less than 20 percent of the National Gross Value of Production.

1994–2004: Annual 4 percent increase expected in Asian food demand, with an unequivalent increase in their local food production.

EXPORT OPPORTUNITIES

Other than expanding whole fruit sales in New Zealand, the main export opportunities theoretically open to the Australian industry seem to be for dried and chilled pineapple snacks. It is generally acknowledged that these would need to be in the premium quality/higher-price sector, preferably with a clear "clean and green" differentiation positioning. For example, with dried pineapples there might need to be an emphasis on "sodium-free" in both processing and packaging.

AUSTRADE

Austrade, in its facilitating role, has Business Development Units to assist various industries in their export endeavours. Already there are groups for grain handling in China, sugar to Iran, and hay to Japan. There is a Tropical Agriculture Business Development Group established. The manager has emphasised that any significant growth in the industry would need to come from exporting.

GROUP EXPORT MARKETING

Fruit Marketing Groups during recent years have become a worldwide trend (Walker 1994, p. 21). These are done through various company or cooperative structures, and can be managed either by a full- or part-time manager or a consultant acting as a marketing coordinator (charging approximately 2 percent of gross sales). Group marketing for exporting to Asia can also be done through the government's Food Industries Networking for Asia (FINA) Exports

Program. Small operators are linked with complimentary producers, processors, specialist services, and the like.

THE GOLDEN CIRCLE CANNERY

The Cannery has indicated that it expects to become a major exporter of pineapple products, but that it can't do this without all stakeholders in the value-added chain having compatible objectives. Its biggest export market was New Zealand, but Indonesia and Malaysia were strong competitors there. Their Canadian market had been eroded by Asian suppliers. Recently, the Cannery had begun exporting special cuts of pineapple to Japan under very stringent quality checks. Similarly, the European market would require ISO accreditation.

GOVERNMENT EXPORT ASSISTANCE AND THE AQIS

In February 1995 the Queensland Government launched a $5.7 million package of subsidies and incentives to promote agribusiness exports. This was partly done to generally enhance export revenues and partly to minimise the real and perceived problems exporters were seeing in the Australian Quarantine and Inspection Service.

Exporters here complained, amongst other things, that charges by AQIS have reduced profitability unnecessarily. The $4.12 million Agribusiness Quality Assurance Scheme part of the package was developed by both the QDPI and the AQIS. Exporters can gain AQIS accreditation to undertake their own in-house certification of export shipments and eliminate the need for compulsory AQIS inspections. Firms can apply for up to $50,000 on a dollar-for-dollar basis to assist TQM implementation.

Other elements of the package include: $205,000 to boost existing federal government export assistance programmes; $690,000 to enhance Asian market databases; $50,000 for a major review of export skill courses; $630,000 to stage an annual Queensland Trade and Investment forum; establishment of a new Media Coverage of Export Achievements category in the Premier's Export Awards; and the improvement of Queensland school curriculum in terms of export awareness.

Overall the state government does have a Queensland Agribusiness Export Strategy, coordinated with the Queensland Horticultural Export Council.

AN EXPORTING LESSON— ORANGES TO NEW YORK

Austrade, the Australian Horticultural Corporation, the United States importer DNE World Fruit Sales, and South Australian fresh seedless navel orange growers combined together well for this example. The following characteristics of their campaign are worth considering for any possible lessons for fresh pineapple exporters:

1. Once the window of opportunity was spotted (free access in the United States off-season), an ambitious marketing campaign was designed to gain the attention of retailers, consumers, and the media.

2. The promotional campaign was linked into the regular trade-related marketing activities that had been done for three years already.

3. They realised that an aggressive campaign was necessary to generate enthusiasm for a product with a limited shelf life, and that it could not rely only on the retailer but needed to include the targeted consumer.

4. Besides stimulating a desire for the product, their aim was also to clearly develop an identity for the Australian product.

5. To guard against retaliation from local (Californian) growers, the Australian product was first launched in New York and distant parts of the country.

6. The promotional campaign involved a press release sent to 25,000 newspapers; a cooperative advertising incentive arrangement was used with supermarket chains; the editor of the leading trade journal was invited on a study tour to Australia; and use was made of local New York radio and the huge electronic billboard in Times Square. All this is very small compared to Sunkist and other competitors, but required the biggest impact for a reasonable cost in New York conditions.

7. The local importer played an active role with Austrade in the marketing campaign and also guided the Australian Horticultural Corporation through all the local U.S. rules and regulations.

8. They realised that only a particular level of quality would be acceptable and only that quality was allowed. Efforts were also directed toward ensuring that growers knew and supplied that quality from then on. (Derrick 1994)

SOME SUCCESSFUL AGRIBUSINESS PROGRAM CASE STUDIES

With the aid of consultants, business plans, export marketing skills training, market visits, and trade show participation funded by the DPIE, Mudgee winemakers started exporting to the United Kingdom, Queensland's Fresh Double Red Premium tomatoes entered Hong Kong, and persimmon growers established an export company and brand name in the face of looming domestic oversupply. The fresh pineapple industry has received similar funding for quality assurance, but as yet nothing for any major export initiatives.

DRIED PINEAPPLE FOR EXPORT

There already is a pre-existing consumption pattern in Asia for dried pineapple pieces sold in convenient snack packs. Manufacturing is done by firms in several of the main growing areas (Philippines, Thailand, and Malaysia), and distribution is achieved primarily through supermarkets and large convenience stores.

This established consumption practice, which is not found in Australia, has caused a number of participants in the Australian industry to look more closely at this option. For example, one local council and the local economic development body, with state government financial support, investigated the establishment of a local large-scale drying, processing, and packaging facility. Expertise in the drying of other fruits and vegetables was brought in from the southern states. The general conclusion was that it was technically possible but would rely largely on

local grower group commitment in terms of financing the venture, producing the right fruit, managing the process, and driving the exporting. At the time growers felt they had enough internal problems to solve, and their finances were being subjected to oversupply, low prices, and cost constraints. Many growers also expressed no real interest in export.

A further initiative was one termed "A Taste of the Tropics." In this one, three groups from the northern and central regions, together with QDPI and consultant help, began to investigate the prospect of exporting dried packaged pineapple fruit pieces into Japan. After some preliminary desk research, a group of the leading growers visited Japan, armed with attractive bilingual brochures and business cards, but at this stage no product samples. Their observations of the marketplace and discussions with prospective import agents were cautiously optimistic provided they both catered to Japanese tastes and distinguished themselves from the competition. There was a lack of clarity, however, as to whether (or how) the grower groups would actually work together. At the time of writing it would also appear that the venture is still a possibility.

SOME EXPORTING PROBLEMS

After visiting Japan, Taiwan, and Hong Kong in late 1994, Hodges identified the following major roadblocks yet to be overcome by Australian fruit and vegetable exporters (Hodges 1994, p. 8):

1. The relatively high cost and low efficiency and reliability of Australian shipping, and problems with the availability and usage of 40-foot containers.

2. Problems with producing a product that meets the requirements of a particular Asian market, and having sufficient volume of that product available with suitable packaging and brand identity to meet the demand.

3. Market access barriers in place, and the need to develop cost-effective disinfestation treatments.

4. Very strong competition from other exporting countries.

5. The need to minimise chemical residue levels and maintain our "clean and green" image.

6. In some markets Australian exporters are competing with each other and driving down prices and reputations.

7. The need to build more and better relationships with traders/importers (especially those linked to supermarkets) and to gain regular contractual or joint-venture access.

To this, Armstrong adds,

8. our inability to readily satisfy supermarkets who wish to source fruit directly because "there is not one single marketing group in Queensland which is currently capable of gaining major share of Asian markets" (Armstrong 1994, p. 18); and

9. "our easy-going manner does not give confidence to Asians who treat business in a serious manner with strict protocol."

CONCLUDING COMMENT

Industry figures are understandably unhappy. On the one hand, the industry faces all sorts of problems—profitability, politics, quality, consumer confusion, a lack of resources, and so on. On the other hand, they know they have a popular, versatile product in a massively attractive general fresh foods market that is the envy of most outsiders, and perhaps with enormous export potential. Whilst other fruits like mangoes go forward, the Australian pineapple industry hasn't even developed, at this point in time, the beginnings of an export culture.

BIBLIOGRAPHY

Armstrong, R. (1994), "QFVG Chairman's Report," QFVG Conference, March 1994, Townsville.

Armstrong, R. (1994), "Asian Markets Offer Queensland Industry Opportunities," *Queensland Fruit and Vegetable News*, Dec. 15, 1994, p. 18.

Boundy, B. (1994), "A Promotional Case Study—Bananas," QFVG Conference, March 1994, Townsville, p. 9.

Bundaberg and District Fruit and Vegetable Growers Association (1994), *Bundaberg Region Horticultural Magazine*, March 1994, p. 16.

Derrick, G. (1994), "Times Square Takes to Navel Gazing," BRW Sept. 26, 1994, pp. 74–76.

Fouras, D. (1994), "Householders' Purchasing Habits and Attitudes to Selected Fruit," Marketing Services Branch, Queensland Department of Primary Industries.

Hiely, M. (1994), "Who's Poisoning the Product?" *Marketing*, February 1994, pp. 18–23 & 57.

Hodges, H. (1994), "Opportunities for Fruit and Vegetable Exports for Asia, *Queensland Fruit and Vegetable News*, Dec. 15, 1994, p. 8.

Horticultural Policy Council (1992), "The Way Forward—Future Direction for Horticulture."

Horticultural Task Force (1994), "Strategies for Growth in Australian Horticulture," February 1994.

Kiel, G. (1994), "Consumer Driven Marketing of Fruit and Vegetables," QFVG Conference, March 1994.

Kingston, D. (1994), "Horticulture Industries Will Thrive in '94," *Townsville Bulletin*, March 25, 1994, p. 5.

MacLeod, W. N. B., and Higham, C. R. (1993), "Horticulture in Central Queensland," *CQ Journal of Regional Development*, March, pp. 21–26.

Marketshare Pty Ltd (1992), "A Qualitative Research Report— Exploratory Investigation into Tropical Pines Pineapples and MAP Packaging," prepared for Freshmark and Tropical Pines, April 1992, Brisbane.

Marketshare Pty Ltd (1994), "A Quantitative Research Report— Other Fruits," prepared for QFVG, April 1994, Brisbane.

Minnis, D. (1994), "Export," QFVG Conference, March 1994, Townsville, p. 517.

Newett, S. (1994), "Pineman: A Comparative Analysis Service for Pineapple Growers," QDPI.

Queensland Fruit and Vegetable Growers (1992), "QFVG Research Finds Most Consumers Unhappy with Quality of Fresh Produce," *QFVG News*, October 22, 1992, p. 1.

Queensland Govt (1994), "Exporting Queensland Primary Products."

Rippl, B. (1994), "Casey Moves Toward Simple Fruit Laws," *Business Queensland*, May 9, 1994, pp. 1 & 15.

Shepherd, D. (1981), "An Investigation of the Dynamics of Key Factors Affecting the Central Queensland Pineapple Industry and Their Impact on the Overall Industry in Queensland," Capricornia Institute of Advanced Education, Rockhampton.

Shoebridge, N. (1992), "Apple Ads Win with Crisp Fashion Image," *Business Review Weekly*, July 1992, pp. 72–73.

Shoebridge, N. (1994), "Fresh Food Boom Demands Quick Action," *Business Review Weekly*, July 18, 1994, pp. 40–44.

Suggett, R. (1994), "Leadership the Key to Success," *National Marketplace News*, Vol. 11, No. 116, July 1994, p. 22.

Suggett, R. (1995), "Fresh Exports Put on an $84 Million Burst," *National Marketplace News*, Vol. 12, No. 122, Feb. 1995, p. 2.

Swete-Kelly, D. (1989), "Growing Pineapples for the Fresh Market," Pineapple Industry Review Seminar.

Walker, M. (1994), "Group Marketing," QFVG Conference, March 1994, Townsville, p. 21.

Bank of America and the Carlsbad Highlands Foreclosure

Anne T. Lawrence
San Jose State University

Jim Jackson opened the file lying on his desk marked "Carlsbad Highlands." Recently appointed to the position of vice president, corporate real estate, in Bank of America's Costa Mesa office in Orange County, California, Jackson had the job—as he somewhat delicately put it—of converting bad loans into assets. Bank of America (B of A) was in the business of loaning money, not in the business of marketing real estate. But, when a developer was unable, for whatever reason, to meet payments on a loan, the bank often acquired the property in foreclosure. It was Jackson's job to find the best price he could for these properties and, if possible, prevent the bank from taking a loss on the loan. His job was to sell real estate—much of it unimproved or partially improved land where a developer's project had somehow gone bad.

The Carlsbad Highlands property did not look promising. The upper left-hand corner was stamped "In Foreclosure." He quickly skimmed the case file and appraiser's report forwarded to him by the bank's loan department. The story was plain enough, if painful in its details. The 263-acre property in the foothills north of San Diego had been acquired by a developer in the mid-1980s with a 5 percent downpayment and a $6.8 million loan from B of A. At the time of acquisition, the property had been approved for 740 single-family homes. The developer had been preparing to begin construction when, in 1989, the bubble burst in the Southern California housing market, lowering the probable market value of the homes.

Compounding the developer's problems, the City of Carlsbad, where the parcel was located, had imposed a requirement that the developer construct a two-mile extension to an existing road, Cannon Road. The developer had planned to share the construction costs with neighboring developments, but these had not proceeded as anticipated, leaving the entire road-building cost on his shoulders.

But the final blow to the project was not the market downturn or infrastructure requirements, but an environmental problem. In March 1993, the U.S. Fish and Wildlife Service (USFWS) listed the California gnatcatcher—a small, grayish bird with a call like a kitten's meow—as a "threatened" species under the Endangered Species Act of 1973. The gnatcatcher lived exclusively in the coastal sage scrub ecosystem—a mixture of sagebrush, cactus, and buckwheat that used to dominate much of coastal southern California. Under the pressure of relentless development, coastal sage scrub had dwindled to less than 400,000 fragmented acres between Los Ange-

Originally presented at the annual meeting of the Western Casewriters Association, March 1996. Research was supported in part by the San Jose State University College of Business. This case was written with the cooperation of the Bank of America and its officers and of federal, state, and regulatory agencies, solely for the purpose of stimulating student discussion. All persons and events are real. Copyright Anne T. Lawrence, 1996.

les and the Mexican border. The USFWS, under law, had authority to block development that encroached on gnatcatcher habitat. Unhappily for its would-be developer, Carlsbad Highlands was about 40 percent coastal sage scrub—and, moreover, connected two other parcels of prime gnatcatcher habitat, thus forming an ecologically significant corridor. Since the development plan had been approved 10 years earlier, it had not been designed to be sensitive to gnatcatcher habitat. Now, the U.S. Fish and Wildlife Service would surely not approve the necessary grading.

In July 1993, just two months after the gnatcatcher listing, the beleaguered developer had finally thrown in the towel on the project and walked away from the loan, and the bank was left holding the property.

Now, just days later, Jackson's eye scanned down the appraiser's report to the bottom line: APPRAISED VALUE: $112,000. One hundred and twelve thousand dollars on a loan of almost 7 million dollars! A native of San Diego, Jackson had had many years of experience as a land developer before coming to the bank, and he was all too familiar with the ups—and, more recently, downs—of the California land market. But the figures on Carlsbad Highlands were shocking even to his experienced eyes.

Within a few minutes, Jackson found himself in the car, driving south along the Pacific on Route 5, then turning up into the hills above the coastal city of Carlsbad. His route took him by several recent housing developments of the type planned for Carlsbad Highlands—compact communities of expensive, white stucco homes with red tile roofs, in the Mediterranean style favored by 1990s California home buyers.

About five miles up, Jackson got out of his car and started hiking across the property. Much of the land was covered with unprepossessing, low-lying, khaki-colored scrub—the kind preferred by the gnatcatcher, although Jackson could not see or hear any birds. Examining the land carefully as he walked, Jackson could see the remnants of an old irrigation system, installed by an earlier owner who had used part of the property for farming tomatoes. Up ahead, the land had been torn up by dirt bikers, who had left broken vegetation and tire marks in their wake. To the east, the property line was marked by new subdivision housing, lying just over the border in the City of Oceanside. Their utilities could be extended,

Jackson thought, if the cities would sign an agreement. To the west, the designated source of utilities, there was no development for a mile or more. Below and some five miles to the west, Pacific ocean swells broke against the shore.

"If I had $112,000 in my pocket, I'd buy this property myself," Jackson mused to himself as he walked back to his car. "This property has got to be worth more than that, even if all you wanted to do with it was build a single ranch house and keep some horses up here. The view alone is worth that much."

BANK OF AMERICA'S ENVIRONMENTAL STRATEGY

Bank of America, the reluctant owner of the Carlsbad Highlands property, was unusual in the financial services industry in its commitment to corporate social responsibility as well as its sensitivity to environmental issues. Founded in 1904 in San Francisco by A. G. Giannini, the Bank of Italy—as B of A was then known—was committed to serving the unmet banking needs of California's immigrants and working classes. Throughout its history, the bank had tended to seek out unconventional opportunities for growth. Richard M. Rosenberg, who became chairman and CEO in 1989, characterized the bank's philosophy as the belief that "conventional wisdom is just that—predictable at best . . . not very interesting . . . and frequently wrong." The most effective strategy, he stated, was one that met "the rising expectations among our larger universe of stakeholders who believe that business should actively address the social challenges of our time."[1]

In March 1990, Rosenberg formed an environmental task force comprised of 30 top officers, charged with developing an environmental strategy. In part, this initiative reflected the new CEO's own values. A committed environmentalist, Rosenberg had met with representatives of the Environmental Defense Fund shortly before taking office to share ideas about the bank's environmental stewardship. In part, it reflected the bank officers' perception of heightened stakeholder activism. The Exxon Valdez oil spill in 1989 had caused a public outcry, and shareholder activists had called on businesses to adopt a voluntary code of environmental responsibility, later known as the CERES (Coalition for Environmentally Responsible Economies) Principles. In late 1989, the corporate secretary had warned the CEO that the bank could become the target of a shareholder proxy election campaign, focused on environmental issues. Now, preparations for the 20th anniversay of Earth Day in April 1990 had once more cast a spotlight on "green" concerns.

Bank executives also clearly saw environmentalism as an opportunity for competitive advantage. Since the mid-1980s, courts had held lending institutions liable for environmentally contaminated property, increasing credit risk. In the late 1980s, B of A had begun systematic environmental risk assessment before approving credit applications. The bank had established and staffed an Environmental Services Department, charged with assessing possible environmental liabilities of assets or real estate pledged as collateral against proposed loans. The active work of this group had succeeded in reducing the number of loans with environmental problems.

Rosenberg's environmental task force, working with a consultant—SRI International—produced a set of nine principles. These principles (Exhibit 1) were approved by the Board of Directors in December 1990, making Bank of America the first major

U.S. financial institution to adopt an explicit policy on environmental issues. To implement these principles, the bank established a full-time unit, the Department of Environmental Policies and Programs (DEPP), headed by senior vice president Richard Morrison, a well-respected officer with 25 years of line experience. To support the work of the unit, the bank created a 14-person environmental "team" consisting of top bank officials who remained in their functional and geographic organizations, where they were responsible for implementation. "Environmentalism at Bank of America is not a central staff function," Morrison commented. "It is the responsibility of the major line and staff departments."[2]

The department immediately set about operationalizing the nine principles. Its first efforts, in Morrison's words, were "getting our own act together." The bank initiated internal programs to reduce consumption; recycle paper, plastic, and metals; and conserve water. Morrison's department staff worked with purchasing to buy recycled products when possible. They also worked with the Environmental Services Department to broaden preloan assessments to examine environmental benefits as well as costs. As Morrison put it, the objective was to "try harder to make an environmentally beneficial deal

C-63

EXHIBIT 1 *Bank of America's Environmental Principles*

Bank of America pledges to conduct business in a manner consistent with the following environmental principles:

1. Bank of America will follow responsible environmental practices in all of its operations and places of business.

2. Bank of America will make the environmental responsibility displayed by customers and suppliers a factor in all relevant business decisions.

3. Bank of America will solicit advice and technical expertise in the development and management of its environmental programs and practices.

4. Bank of America will make a special effort to identify businesses and organizations that are attempting to find solutions to environmental problems and provide appropriate support.

5. Bank of America will provide employees and retirees with information regarding environmental issues in order to help them make informed decisions.

6. Bank of America will expand its recycling, energy, and waste management programs.

7. Bank of America will recognize and reward employees for actions that support these principles.

8. Bank of America will periodically assess its performance in identifying and addressing environmental issues.

9. Bank of America is committed to improving the understanding of the full social impact of government and business actions that affect the environment and the economy.

C-64

bankable [as well as] deny . . . credit to borrowers who show a blatant disregard for the environment."[3]

By its third year of operation, 1993, Morrison's department had formulated four goals (Exhibit 2). On the first three—minimize environmental impact, enhance employee and public awareness, and establish standards for clean air and water—the bank had already made significant progress. However, the fourth goal—encourage economic activity that respects preservation of natural habitats and biological diversity—represented a new challenge.

The bank had begun to address this goal in its loans to companies in the forest products industry of the Pacific Northwest, where it had worked with a consultant to evaluate whether or not a company's practices were consistent with sustainable harvesting. Beyond this, however, Morrison's department had made little progress in operationalizing the fourth goal.

By the time the Carlsbad Highlands foreclosure landed on Jim Jackson's desk, the Bank of America had clearly established itself as the leading environmental activist among U.S. banks and had established a goal, in principle, of promoting habitat protection and biodiversity. Few people in the bank, however, had given much thought to how this lofty aim would be implemented, or what it might mean to troops in the field like Jackson.

THE ENDANGERED SPECIES ACT AND PROPERTY RIGHTS

The Endangered Species Act (ESA)—under which the California gnatcatcher had been listed—was passed by Congress in 1973 to conserve species of fish and wildlife threatened with extinction and the habitats on which they depended. Under the law, the Department of the Interior (through its subdivision, the USFWS) was required to make a list of threatened and endangered species, to designate critical habitat, and to devise plans for the species' recovery. Under the law's "taking" provision, it was illegal to "harass, harm, pursue, hunt, shoot, wound, kill, trap, capture, or collect" a threatened or endangered species, or "to attempt to engage in any such conduct." The term *taking* was interpreted to include modifying habitat in a way that would injure or harm a protected species. Violations of the law were subject to both civil and criminal penalties.

Two provisions of the Act gave the Department of the Interior broad powers to conserve land. The first, the "jeopardy clause," stated that federal agencies could not authorize, fund, or carry out any actions that would jeopardize an endangered or threatened species or modify critical habitat. In effect, this clause gave Interior power not only to limit the uses of public lands such as national forests, but also to cut off federal funding for projects, such as roads, dams, or military contracts, that would modify habitat. In an important 1978 decision, the Supreme Court blocked completion of the Tellico Dam (a Tennessee Valley Authority project) because it would flood a portion of the Little Tennessee River, the last remaining habitat of an endangered fish called the snail darter. The court ruled that the intent of the Endangered Species Act had been "to halt and reverse the trend toward species extinction, whatever the cost," and that the law did not include any mechanism for weighing the relative value of a particular species—in this case, the snail darter—against that of economic development—the dam. (Tellico was later completed, after Congress passed a special exemption for the project.)

EXHIBIT 2 *Bank of America's Environmental Goals*

Goal 1: Help generate sustainable economic prosperity with minimum adverse impact on the environment.

Goal 2: Enhance awareness among employees, customers, and the public about environmental issues.

Goal 3: Encourage economic activity that upholds high standards for clean air and water.

Goal 4: Encourage economic activity that respects preservation of natural habitats and biological diversity.

But the law had important significance for private landowners as well. The "taking" provision of the law was generally interpreted by Interior and by the courts as preventing private property owners from modifying their own land, if doing so would degrade habitat and disrupt important behavior patterns, such as nest building. The law often had the effect, therefore, of reducing the market value of land that included endangered species' habitat. Property owners with a sensitive species on their land had a perverse incentive to destroy habitat—or even to kill the species—*before* it was listed, so that the owner's use of the property would not be impaired. In the words of David Howard, an officer of a property rights group known as the Alliance for America, many landowners had come to the conclusion that "the answer is often SSS—short for 'shoot, shovel, and shut up.' "[4]

During the 1970s and 1980s, various mechanisms had evolved in other environmental protection laws to accommodate private landowners with impacted property. Most common was the practice of case-by-case mitigation. For example, under the Clean Water Act, development of wetlands was strictly controlled. But landowners could apply for "dredge-and-fill" permits. These were often granted, subject to the landowner's agreement to mitigate the impact—for example, by leaving some of the wetlands undeveloped, buying and setting aside wetlands somewhere else, or paying a fee to support conservation efforts.

Not all affected stakeholders, however, were pleased with this solution. Environmentalists were concerned that case-by-case mitigation tended to produce small, fragmented parcels of habitat where species would be vulnerable to predators and isolated from others of their kind. They preferred larger, contiguous preserves inhabited by larger populations that could be managed actively. For their part, developers were aggravated by delays, uncertainty, and contradictory rulings by different regulatory authorities. In some cases, developers were actually required to purchase property for mitigation—land they otherwise had no interest in owning. The system also burdened regulators, who confronted a stream of discrete permit requests without an overall plan to guide individual decisions.

In 1982, Congress amended the Endangered Species Act to address the emerging conflict between habitat conservation and land development. Section 10 established a new mechanism, the habitat conservation plan, or HCP. An HCP was intended to be a comprehensive, regional plan to conserve habitat for one or more listed species, negotiated in a collaborative process by a range of affected stakeholders, including developers, environmentalists, and regulators. If the U.S. Fish and Wildlife Service approved an HCP, the agency could issue an "incidental taking permit," allowing some development to proceed in an endangered species' habitat if part of a preapproved, areawide conservation plan. HCPs were praised for "adding flexibility . . . and promoting compromise and negotiated settlements between the development and environmental communities."[5] HCPs were also superior to the case-by-case mitigation used in wetlands regulation because they allowed, in principle at least, for regional conservation planning.

Despite their apparent advantages, few HCPs were negotiated during the 1980s. One successful application of the HCP process occurred near San Francisco, where landowners seeking to build on San Bruno Mountain—home to the federally listed mission blue butterfly—were able to negotiate with regulators a plan that allowed some development to proceed, while setting aside large sections of the property for butterfly habitat. Two other HCPs were approved in the 1980s, both also in California. Other habitat planning efforts were initiated, all in regions of the country that had both endangered species and strong real estate markets. In the "hill country" west of Austin, Texas; in the wetlands near Disney World in Orlando, Florida; and in the pine barrens of southeastern New Jersey, for example, stakeholders attempted to negotiate regional conservation plans. By 1992, however, none of these efforts had yet reached a successful conclusion. Some observers cited a lack of funding for habitat acquisition. Others pointed to a lack of support from the Reagan and Bush administrations, which some said "seemed to encourage conflicts as a means for building support from property owners, timber companies, and farmers to weaken the (endangered species) act."[6]

The Clinton administration, by contrast, moved aggressively to promote the habitat conservation plan model. In April 1993, barely three months after taking office, President Clinton convened a well-publicized "forest conference" in Portland, Oregon, at which he attempted to bring together adversaries in the long-simmering controversy over the spotted owl to

C-65

negotiate what was, in effect, a habitat conservation plan. Two weeks later, Clinton's Secretary of the Interior, Bruce Babbitt, seemed to signal the administration's intentions when he announced that the government had negotiated a plan with Georgia Pacific Corporation. The timber company had agreed to restrict logging on about 50,000 acres inhabited by the protected red-cockaded woodpecker; in exchange, the government had pledged not to use the ESA to curtail logging elsewhere on the company's timberlands in the southeastern states. This kind of negotiated settlement, Babbitt told the press, was the only way to avoid "the environmental and economic train wrecks we've seen in the past decade."[7]

DEVELOPMENT AND CONSERVATION PLANNING IN SAN DIEGO COUNTY

San Diego County, the site of Jim Jackson's problem, had all the ingredients of such a "train wreck." During the 1980s, the California population grew from 24 to 30 million—a growth rate of 25 percent, among the highest in the industrial world. Half the state's people lived in the corridor from Los Angeles south to the Mexican border. San Diego County itself had grown by 35 percent during this decade, adding 647,300 residents. More people created tremendous pressure for the conversion of open land. During the 1980s, the amount of developed land (housing, commercial, and industrial) in the urbanized coastal cordon, where most people lived, increased by 24 percent.

The San Diego region was also unusually rich in natural biological diversity, with many species pushed to the brink by relentless development. Its wide variety of topography, climate, and soils had created many unique habitats, including beaches and dunes, coastal sage scrub, oak woodlands, mountainous coniferous forest, and desert. By the early 1990s, the USFWS had listed over 70 species in southern California (including 24 in the San Diego region) as threatened or endangered and was considering adding over 300 more. In fact, a representative of the Nature Conservancy, writing in the early 1990s, called California the "epicenter of extinction in the continental United States."[8] Among the better-

known listed species in the San Diego area were the California gnatcatcher, the brown pelican, the golden eagle, and the mountain lion.

In 1991, California Governor Pete Wilson—a former mayor of San Diego who was familiar with the problems faced by developers there—had proposed a Natural Communities Conservation Program (NCCP) for the state. Intended as a kind of state version of the HCP, the NCCP aimed to develop habitat conservation plans that would simultaneously satisfy both the state's Department of Fish and Game (responsible for enforcing the state's own endangered species laws) and the USFWS. San Diego County's coastal scrub sage ecosystem was selected as the first pilot program.

Under the auspices of the NCCP, San Diego in 1991 initiated a multitiered regional planning process. The overall effort was directed by the San Diego Association of Governments (SANDAG), a regional agency. SANDAG began development of a comprehensive, regional multiple-species conservation plan and, subsumed under it, three subregional plans. One of these, the North County Multiple Habitat Conservation Program (MHCP), included the city of Carlsbad and the Carlsbad Highlands property. City of Carlsbad officials, like some other local jurisdictions, were also developing their own proposal, to be incorporated into the larger plans. The goal of this complex, multilayered process was to develop a habitat conservation plan for the entire region that would successfully balance economic and environmental objectives. Proponents hoped, moreover, that the effort would facilitate development by removing regulatory uncertainty and minimizing the likelihood of future endangered species listings.

The San Diego effort, not surprisingly, attracted Secretary Babbitt's attention as a potential model for the rest of the nation. In an interview in *Rolling Stone* in July 1993, Babbitt said of the NCCP:

> This experiment ... is breathtaking in its magnitude. ... The question is, can we invoke the land-use planning power of local communities, the enforcement power of the Endangered Species Act, and the framework of the state government to pull this off? ... I think it's going to work.[9]

By the summer of 1993, however, this "breathtaking experiment" was still in its early stages. In the northern part of San Diego County, the working group was still busy trying to inventory biological resources and to draft a map of a workable system of preserves, consisting of parcels of high-quality habitat and connecting corridors. There was still no good mechanism for paying for the preserves, and the plan was several years away from federal and state regulatory approval.

CONSIDERING THE OPTIONS

Over the next few days, Jackson began sketching out the bank's options for the Carlsbad Highlands property. The appraiser had been legally required to report a value on the land's "highest and best" use, which the appraiser judged to be speculation. Considering that the property's use for home development was compromised by the endangered species listing, the appraiser had assigned a rock-bottom estimate. The appraiser was probably right, Jackson thought, that the likelihood that the property would be approved for a big housing development any time soon was slim. However, a speculator might be willing to assume that risk or to buy at a low price and hold the land until it could be developed.

Considerable political uncertainty surrounded the Endangered Species Act and its enforcement. Clinton's Interior secretary strongly supported the ESA and the concept of habitat conservation planning, and the federal courts had generally supported this position. However, some property rights groups had clamored for repeal or revision of the Act, and they had the ear of important Republicans in congress. A political shift in Washington could change the risk equation significantly.

The land must have some conservation value, Jackson thought. But who would buy it? Was there a market for gnatcatcher habitat? Investigating further, Jackson learned that the 109 acres to the north of the property had been purchased within the past year by a developer as mitigation property. The buyer had paid a little over $1.4 million. However, this parcel had contained high-quality coastal sage scrub and several documented pairs of nesting California gnatcatchers. A survey of the Carlsbad Highlands property had turned up only one pair of birds. Jackson's property probably was not worth as much, even if he could find a willing buyer.

Working the phones, Jackson learned that Caltrans, the California state transportation agency, was building a freeway in the City of Oceanside, a project that impacted coastal sage scrub. The USFWS had required that the agency buy 83 acres of coastal scrub elsewhere as mitigation, under the terms of a permit Caltrans had negotiated. Jackson soon had Caltrans on the phone. He described the property in detail. Were they interested? The Caltrans officer sounded discouraged. The agency was actively shopping for coastal sage scrub for mitigation, but the USFWS was very particular about what was acceptable and what was not. "Of course we're interested. But I doubt the feds would approve the Carlsbad Highlands property," the official responded glumly. "It doesn't have enough birds."

Agricultural development was a final possibility. The property had most recently been used for farming tomatoes, and Jackson had observed a rudimentary irrigation system in place that could be repaired and brought back into service. A farmer might be willing to pay up to $8,000 an acre, Jackson figured. His initial inquiries generated some promising leads. Within a few weeks, one farmer had made a formal offer of $1 million for the property, contingent on obtaining a permit to build a ranch house. The City of Carlsbad seemed favorable, since sale to a farmer would provide an intermediate use for the property until housing development would again become feasible. Without housing on the property, the City would never be able to afford improvements to Cannon Road. The farmer's offer was the best one on the table, Jackson thought. Perhaps the bank ought to accept it.

C-67

NOTES

1. Rosenberg, Richard M., "Banking on the New America." Speech delivered at the University of California, Berkeley, December 14, 1994, p. 2.
2. Morrison, Richard, "Developing an Environmental Strategy in the Financial Services Industry." Speech delivered at the University of California, Irvine, Graduate School of Management, November 1, 1991, p. 10.
3. Ibid.
4. "Environmentalists Are On the Run," *Fortune*, September 19, 1994, p. 103.

5. Beatley, Timothy, "Preserving Biodiversity Through the Use of Habitat Conservation Plans." In Douglas R. Porter and David A. Salvesen, *Collaborative Planning for Wetlands and Wildlife*. Washington D.C.: Island Press, 1995, p. 57.

6. "Accord Is Reached to Aid Forest Bird," *New York Times*, April 16, 1993.

7. "Interior Secretary Is Pushing a New Way to Save Species," *New York Times*, February 17, 1993.

8. Sally W. Smith, "Wildlife and Endangered Species: In Precipitous Decline." In Tim Palmer, ed. *California's Threatened Environment: Restoring the Dream*. Washington D.C.: Island Press, 1993, p. 227.

9. Interview with Bruce Babbitt, *Rolling Stone*, July, 1993.

Birra Moretti

Arthur Sharplin

Institute for International Business Studies
Pordenone, Italy
and
Waltham Associates, Inc.
Austin, Texas

We want to keep momentum. Until we overtook Poretti we were pressing to be number three and had something to shoot at. It's a little harder now that we are third. Dreher is a long way away, and we need a share of about 18 percent of Italian production to get the breweries to true efficient scale. So we have to almost double sales again.

—Richard Beveridge,
February 1993

Key managers of Birra Moretti, Sp.A., met in Bologna, Italy, in February 1993 to develop their proposed FY 1994 (ending March 31) Comprehensive Business Plan. Birra Moretti had been acquired by Toronto's John Labatt Limited in June 1989 along with another Italian brewer, Prinz Brau Brewing Company. Prinz was merged into Moretti in the months after the acquisitions. The new Moretti's unit sales grew from a rate of about 800,000 hl/yr (hectoliters per year—a hectoliter is 100 liters, or 26.4 U.S. gallons) in late 1989 to 1.2 million in FY 1992 and a projected 1.4 million in FY 1993.

To continue its growth strategy in FY 1994, Moretti needed an estimated US$15 million from

Labatt. Such funding was hardly assured, as Labatt itself was retrenching and restructuring in Canada and the United States. Further, despite a similar infusion during FY 1993, Moretti's rate of growth in unit sales had slowed to 5 percent, down from 21 percent the previous year. And earnings before interest and taxes (EBIT) remained negative, as had been true since the 1989 acquisitions.

ITALY AND ITS BEER INDUSTRY

Foreign firms obtained control of most Italian brewers during the 1980s. The investments seemed promising at first, as Italians, like other southern Europeans, began to cut their consumption of wine and drink more beer. But beer sales in Italy stopped increasing in 1985. By 1988, every major Italian brewer was losing money. And political uncertainty along with worsening economic and demographic conditions suggested recovery would not occur soon.

Political and Economic Circumstances

Professor Franco Cazzola of the University of Florence described the worsening condition of the Ital-

Management assisted in the research for the case but exercised no editorial prerogative. The case was written for research purposes and to stimulate scholarly discussion. Special thanks go to Richard Beveridge, Yasmin Ferrari, Adam Humphries, William G. Bourne, Sidney M. Oland, and John Morgan as well as to the editor and anonymous referees for the *Case Research Journal*. Copyright © 1997 by the *Case Research Journal* and Arthur Sharplin.

ian government in early 1993, concluding, "An entire political system, faced with a crisis of legitimacy, is now falling to pieces."[1] The head of Italy's ruling Socialist Party and the justice minister had just resigned under charges of corruption. Over 150 members of Parliament were named in criminal inquiries. And 850 lesser Italian officials and businesspersons were arrested for various abuses.

Italy's unemployment rate rose from 9.9 percent in 1991 to 11 percent in 1992. The lire was devalued 7 percent by the Italian government in 1992 and further by financial markets. Exhibit 1 gives selected statistics for Italy during 1988–92. As the exhibit shows, Italy's population grew by only 600,000 during those years. More relevant to the brewing industry was the 15- to 34-year age bracket, which Italian beer industry association Assobirra called "the formative beer drinking population." This segment peaked at 18 million in 1990 and began a projected fall to 16 million in 2000 and 12 million in 2010.

The Competitors

Exhibit 2 shows all eight Italian brewers' reported production and percentage of the total in the early 1990s. Peroni and Dreher had six plants each, Moretti three, Poretti two, and the others one each. Foreign ownership of the top five in 1989 was as follows:

Dreher: Heineken, Dutch brewer (100%)

Interbrew: Stella Artois, Belgian brewer (100%)

Peroni: BSN Danone, French food group (% not known)

Moretti: John Labatt Limited, Canadian brewer (100%)

Poretti: Carlsberg, Danish brewer (50%)

Several brewers "rationalized" production in 1988–92, closing and modernizing breweries. But industry profits—and those of each major competitor—remained negative each year.

Imports and Exports of Beer

Richard Beveridge, planning and development director for Moretti, said importers were a big threat, adding, "They can sell in Italy without covering fixed costs." Exhibit 3 shows imports by country of origin for 1990–92. Imports represented 19.8 percent of consumption in 1992, up from 11.7 percent in 1981. Imports were subject to a 25 percent "value landed" tax, compared to a 19 percent tax on production costs for domestic beer. Only 2 percent of Italian beer production was exported in 1992, but this was up from 1 percent in 1981.[2]

Changing Drinking Patterns

Like other Europeans, Italians shifted to nonalcoholic beverages in the 1980s and early 1990s. From 1981–92, alcoholic drinks' "share of the throat" (percentage of total beverage consumption) in Italy fell from 39 to 25 percent, while consumption of soft drinks rose from 26 to 46 percent. Italy's per-capita beer consumption jumped 30 percent from 1980 to 1985, then flattened, easing down to 22.6 liters in 1991. Of that, 19.5 liters were "normal beer" (not less than 3 percent alcohol by volume), 2.1 liters "special beer" (not less than 3.5 percent), 0.7 liters "double malt/red beer" (not less than 4 percent), and 0.3 liters nonalcohol/low alcohol beer (less than 1 percent).[3] Beer's share of the Italian throat was 6 percent in 1992, back to its 1981 level.[4] Canadean Limited, which studied the industry, concluded:

EXHIBIT 1 *Selected Statistics for Italy*					
	1988	**1989**	**1990**	**1991**	**1992**
GDP @ mkt (L'000 bn)	1,092	1,194	1,307	1,427	1,507
Real GDP growth (%)	4.1	3.0	2.2	1.4	0.9
Consumer price inflation (%)	5.1	6.3	6.5	6.3	5.3
Population (m)	57.4	57.5	57.7	57.8	58.0
12/31 exchange rate (L/US$)	1,388	1,249	1,271	1,240	1,601
12/31 exchange rate (L/C$)	1,163	1,067	1,096	1,041	1,274

Sources of data: *The Economist* Intelligence Unit and The Royal Bank of Canada.

EXHIBIT 2 *Brewers and Reported Production in Italy for Years Ended 30 September (hl × 1,000 & % of total)*

	1990		1991		1992	
Peroni	4,117	38.3%	3,928	36.6%	3,936	36.0%
Dreher	3,243	30.2	3,040	28.3	3,266	29.8
Moretti	790	7.4	969	9.0	1,116	10.2
Poretti	983	9.2	1,081	10.1	1,095	10.0
Interbrew	749	7.0	817	7.6	736	6.7
Forst	676	6.3	695	6.5	647	5.9
Castelberg*	134	1.2	157	1.5	109	1.0
Menabrea	43	0.4	43	0.4	45	0.4
Total**	10,735	100.0%	10,733	100.0%	10,951	100.0%

Source of data: Assobirra.
*Shut down in summer 1992.
**Totals may not check, due to rounding.

The alleged replacement of wine by beer is a concept in which hardly anyone believed anymore (Italians who do not drink wine during meals have turned massively to bottled water), and beer is hardly perceived as an in-between meals and/or after dinner drink or late night drink.[5]

EXHIBIT 3 *Imports to Italy by Country of Origin for Years Ended 30 September, 1990–1992 (hl × 1,000 & % of total)*

	1990		1991		1992	
Germany	927	39.3%	969	39.8%	996	36.9%
Denmark	338	14.3	372	15.3	438	16.2
Belgium/Luxembourg	212	9.0	264	10.9	322	11.9
Holland	302	12.8	225	9.2	219	8.1
France	241	10.2	170	7.0	177	6.6
Austria	133	5.6	137	5.6	147	5.4
Great Britain	73	3.1	90	3.7	108	4.0
Mexico	6	0.3	43	1.8	100	3.7
Czechoslovakia	34	1.4	34	1.4	43	1.6
Ex-Yugoslavia	27	1.1	36	1.5	40	1.5
Switzerland	27	1.1	30	1.2	26	1.0
Ireland	16	0.7	21	0.9	26	1.0
China	9	0.4	10	0.4	16	0.6
USA	4	0.2	6	0.3	15	0.6
Spain	9	0.4	7	0.3	14	0.5
Other countries	7	0.3	22	0.9	17	0.6
Total*	2,361	100.0%	2,434	100.0%	2,703	100.0%
As percentage of consumption		18.0%		18.5%		19.8%

Source of data: Assobirra.
*Totals may not check, due to rounding.

EXHIBIT 4 *Italy's Monthly Beer Production + Imports, 1990–92 (hl × 1,000)*

	Jan.	Feb.	Mar.	Apr.	May	June	Jul.	Aug.	Sept.	Oct.	Nov.	Dec.
1990	901	976	1238	1097	1520	1521	1615	1256	1096	807	901	556
1991	1021	1058	1134	1234	1400	1337	1583	1127	1011	872	754	619
1992	889	1163	1329	1220	1404	1682	1710	987	998	n/a	n/a	n/a

Source of data: Assobirra.

Beer consumption in Italy, as elsewhere, varied through the year. Exhibit 4 shows Italy's monthly beer production plus imports for 1990–92.

Marketing Beer in Italy

Italian beer industry association Assobirra ran a "cooperative" advertising program (funded at L10 billion in 1990) for "the best category"—the ads featured multiple brands. In the 1980s, brewers began to develop their own advertising programs. In 1991, television accounted for 84 percent of Italy's media advertising expenditures for beer, and "trade press/magazines" another 8 percent. Posters and radio advertising had small, declining shares.

Retail prices for bottles, cans, and draught beer in May 1992 averaged L1,600–L2,000 per liter for "normal" beers and L2,300–L2,500 for premium ones. Each major Italian brewer produced normal and premium beers, and each had several special brands which appealed to small market segments. Exhibit 5 shows the estimated distribution of the retail price of bottled beer and the trend of each component in 1992.

Packaging of beer in Italy in the early 1990s was relatively old-fashioned by North American, or even northern European, standards. Exhibit 6 shows the types of packaging for beer sold in Italy in 1991–92. Refillable bottles were declining in use.

Of the European Community (EC) standard-size bottles (25, 50, and 75cl—cl = centliter = 0.338 fluid ounce), 25 and 50cl bottles had been introduced by Dreher and Moretti but not by other Italian brewers. Nearly all the cans were 33cl size and few kegs were sold for other than draught installations. Twist-off caps had not been introduced by domestic producers, nor had flip-in tabs for cans.[6] Glass bottles were bought from an Italian cartel, which attempted to control bottle design and supply as well as price.

Exhibit 7 illustrates the distribution channel for beer sold in Italy in 1991 and 1992. Brewers sold beer to five thousand or so "concessionaires," generally with exclusive territories. Concessionaires distributed the beer to tens of thousands of mostly small retailers. Deposits were charged on crates and returnable bottles at each level, and brewers installed and serviced draught equipment, further tying channel members together. But the relationships were not totally exclusive. Certain concessionaires also sold to other wholesalers, who delivered mixed loads of beer and other products to the tiniest outlets. Some beer was sold directly to consumers from route trucks. And an increasing percentage of beer was being purchased by *Grande Distribuzione* and *Distribuzione Organizzata* or

EXHIBIT 5 *Estimated Distribution of Retail Price of Bottled Beer, 1992*

Acquisition of prime materials and packing	7%	(stable)
Overall cost of bottles	10%	(increasing)
Production costs*	24%	(increasing)
Promotion costs	5%	(increasing)
Selling and administrative costs	7%	(stable)
Manufacturer's margin	2%	(stable)
Distributor's margins	45%	(increasing)

Source of data: Databank.
*Includes 19% value added tax (VAT), raised from 9% July 1990.

EXHIBIT 6 *Types of Packaging for Beer Sold in Italy, 1991–92*

Source: *Il Mondo Della Birra,* December 1992, p. 20.

C-73

EXHIBIT 7 *Distribution Channel for Beer Sold in Italy, 1991–92*

Source: *Il Mondo Della Birra,* December 1992, p. 30.
*Grande Distribuzione/Distribuzione Organizzata (large chains and purchasing groups)
**Sales directly to consumers from route trucks

GD/DO (centralized buying offices for chain stores and buying groups made up of large supermarkets).[7]

William Bourne, general manager of Moretti, said the concessionaire system was "consolidating" in the early 1990s—Beveridge said "disintegrating." "Now," added Beveridge, "a concessionaire may sell several competing beers, so it is less loyal than in the past. Several have merged with others or acquired them. When a concessionaire grows large enough, above 500,000 hectoliters per year, they can even import economically. Some brewers, including us, have begun to buy up concessionaires."

BIRRA MORETTI AND PRINZ IN 1989

The boxed text describes how beer is made. When acquired by Labatt, Moretti had an ancient 450,000 hl/yr brewery in Udine, in the Friuli region of extreme northeastern Italy (see Exhibit 8). Moretti's packaging plant was nine years old and was in San Giorgio, about 50 kilometers (31 miles) southwest of Udine. The company was losing money but was still owned by Luigi Moretti, a fifth-generation member of the founding family. Birra Moretti had agreed to stay out of the south for 10 years in connection with an asset sale in mid-1980. However, the company had a strong distribution system in northeastern Italy and the largest market share in that area of any brewer. The Moretti brewery was operating near capacity in 1989 and frequently dusted central Udine with a sticky, white substance which floated up from the brewing kettles. Nearby was a Moretti restaurant and bar, where a unique, nonpasteurized brew was served to the local social crowd. There was also a museum containing memorabilia from the firm's 130-year history. Labatt brewing chief Sidney Oland said Moretti's essential attraction was its "good brand" and solid distribution system constrained to a small area of Italy.

EXHIBIT 8 *Map of Italy*

How Beer Is Made

A modern brewery at first glance appears to be a simple processing plant, consisting mainly of stainless steel tanks, hoppers, dryers, filters, pumps, and so forth, connected by pipes and valves. Temperatures, pressures, and product chemistry are tightly controlled throughout, and the system is closed from the atmosphere. An on-site laboratory uses spectrographic analysis and chemical methods to test raw materials and to check the product at various points. Brewery products are also tasted regularly. Few workers are required and only an occasional technician may be observed taking a sample, recording data, or adjusting machinery.

Primary raw materials for brewing beer are water, barley malt (which provides starch for conversion to alcohol), about a fourth as much of other cereal grain (such as rice or corn), a much smaller amount of hops (which impart bitterness and aroma), and yeast (to promote fermentation). The cereals and hops are cooked in large steam-jacketed kettles to produce wort, an amber sugar solution. This takes from 2.5 to 3.5 hours, allowing seven to nine batches per day. The residue is usually sold as animal feed.

The wort is fermented in large tanks for about 4 days and the resulting beer is aged for about 16 days. Product characteristics—color, taste, alcohol content—are varied by adjusting the variety and amount of malt, grain, and hops used and by modifying the fermentation and aging regimens.

Prinz operated a modern 700,000 hl/yr brewery and packaging plant near its headquarters in Crespellano, north-central Italy, and an older 75,000 hl/yr brewery in Baragiano, far to the south. The firm was virtually bankrupt and in disarray. Both breweries were operating far below capacity in 1989, and Prinz's distribution system was collapsing. As Labatt was negotiating to buy Prinz, it discovered Prinz had been inflating sales figures by failing to account for returns, billing some product for later delivery, and even delivering presold beer to alternative customers for cash. By May 1989, prepaid customers were threatening to sue, and unpaid suppliers were refusing to ship. But Oland instructed Morgan to go ahead

with the acquisition, saying it offered "a chance to buy capacity very cheaply."

BIRRA MORETTI'S NEW CORPORATE PARENT

John Labatt Limited was Canada's leading brewer for decades before 1980. While Canada's per-capita beer consumption fell 7 percent during the 1980s, Labatt gained domestic market share, to 42.3 percent in 1989. Labatt's brewing revenues rose steadily and EBIT increased each period from FY 1985–89, both absolutely and as a percentage of sales. For FY 1989, Labatt Brewing Company reported EBIT of C$158 million on sales of C$1.8 billion.

In 1989 Labatt's arch-competitor Molson Companies Limited merged its brewing operation with Carling O'Keefe Breweries of Canada, Ltd., a unit of worldwide brewer Elders IXL Ltd. This gave Molson a 53 percent market share. Still, Oland said, "We had won the battle in Canada. We were making lots of money in brewing and had to decide what to do with it." The Molson merger? "Our weaker competitor combined with our weakest one," said Oland.

During the 1980s Labatt acquired the U.S. brewer of Rolling Rock beer and other U.S. and Canadian firms in food and nonalcoholic beverages, broadcasting, and entertainment. Labatt's total sales more than doubled in the five years before 1989. Labatt Food Company, which also included the broadcasting and entertainment activities, earned C$106 million EBIT on sales of C$3.6 billion in FY 1989 (ended March 31). About a third of Labatt's C$5.4 billion FY 1989 total revenue came from U.S. sales and about 1 percent from beer exported to Europe, nearly all to the U.K.

Labatt Breweries of Europe (LBOE) had been formed in 1987, and Oland had sent John Morgan to London to head it. Morgan chose a young Englishman, Adam Humphries, as his VP Finance and brought in a Canadian as VP Marketing. Humphries said overseas expansion was undertaken because of GATT (General Agreement on Tariffs and Trade) complaints at home and failing diversification. Indeed, the United States was preparing a charge against Canadian brewers under GATT. U.S. brewers were reportedly more efficient than the Canadians because the latter had to make beer in every province where it was sold, requiring smaller than optimal-scale plants. Further, the Food Company's

EBIT was only 5.24 percent of sales, compared to Brewing's 8.13 percent.

Whatever the reasons, Morgan and his team pressed ahead in Europe. After converting the U.K. operation to "toll brewing," hiring domestic brewers to brew beer, and joint-venture marketing, they attempted several large acquisitions, first in the U.K., then on the Continent. None worked out. One former LBOE official said "pussyfooting" by recalcitrant Labatt directors nixed the bigger deals. Humphries acknowledged, "At corporate there were those who saw European expansion as risky and who needed to be convinced." But Morgan disputed the "pussyfooting" charge, saying, "Brascan's cash needs were the reason." Brascan, part of the troubled Bronfman financial empire, owned 42.3 percent of Labatt's voting stock. In mid-1988, Morgan started the successful effort to buy Moretti and Prinz. In September that year, he hired Beveridge, then a recent graduate of the London Business School, to do financial analysis.

Before the Italian deals were closed, Labatt sold several of its businesses, ostensibly due to their lack of "strategic relevance." According to Morgan, another reason for the divestments was pressure from Brascan to "maximize cash coming up [Labatt's] corporate chain." Morgan added that Labatt was being "actively marketed" during 1988, although Oland disputed that. "Actually," Oland said, "our plan was to separate the company into brewing and entertainment divisions, both publicly traded. Labatt would own 51 percent of Brewing and 50 percent of Entertainment."

In July 1989, a month after the Moretti and Prinz acquisitions, the Labatt board gave Oland a chance to realize his vision, promoting him to president and CEO of Labatt. Oland soon announced four objectives:

1. Pursue major international growth initiatives primarily by building on the company's strength in Brewing.

2. Rationalize the Food businesses to achieve improved results in fiscal 1991 and to maximize resources for better returns longer term.

3. Divest smaller nonstrategic operations.

4. Expand the company's Broadcast and Entertainment businesses.

Before Oland's promotion, he and Taylor had "full operating responsibility" for their separate division.

But under Oland, management of the two groups was combined within the "Office of the CEO." A stated purpose of the "centralization" was to provide "strong senior management leadership in support of the company's strategic thrust toward major international expansion." Taylor was made executive vice president of Labatt.

MANAGEMENT CHANGES AT MORETTI

William Bourne, formerly Labatt's director of international development, had moved to Udine in May 1989 to become *Direttore Generale* (General Manager) of the new Birra Moretti. Although Luigi Moretti kept the title *Presidente* for a time, he took no active part in management after Bourne arrived. Morgan fired Humphries, for reasons neither chose to disclose, and himself moved back to LBOE's London headquarters. (Morgan would be promoted to president of Labatt Breweries of Canada in 1991, replaced at LBOE by Bruce E. Peer, from Canada). Beveridge stayed behind as Birra Moretti's director of planning and development, a new position. Several of the former Birra Moretti, Sp.A.'s Italian managers kept their jobs, as did most Italian supervisors and workers. In general, the Prinz management structure—to the extent it remained in existence—was dismantled, though many operating workers and salespersons were retained.

The new Birra Moretti's Commercial Department (Sales and Marketing) was placed under the direction of former Prinz commercial director Marzio Zanardi and moved to Milan in 1989. A young Italian, Michele Pecoraro, was hired as marketing director. Pecoraro's parents lived in Rome but he had attended college in Canada and worked in marketing for Procter & Gamble there.

Beveridge said, "We had a foothold on the Continent. Now, we had to make it count." Exhibit 9 outlines the ownership and organization of Labatt in July 1989.

THE NEW MORETTI'S STRATEGIC PLAN

Beveridge outlined the new Moretti's initial strategic plan as illustrated in Exhibit 10. He explained:

EXHIBIT 9 *Ownership and Organization of John Labatt Limited, July 1989*

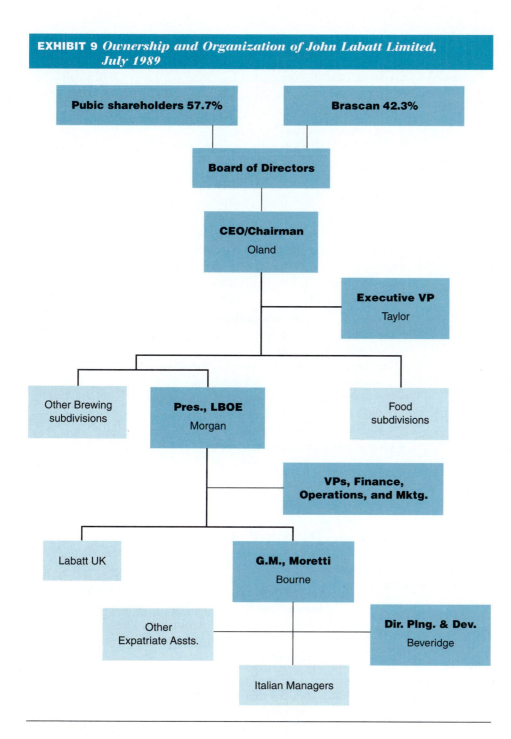

We believed that from the two organizations we could create a solid national brewer with adequate capacity to service the demand we knew Labatt marketers could generate. And there could have been a good bit of synergy with other acquisitions in Europe we expected to make.

Beveridge continued, "Prinz was the immediate concern. We had to stabilize it as we merged it into Moretti and converted it to a production operation. Prinz was a disaster." Another former member of the acquisition team added, "The integration phase was totally underestimated. Prinz was just a shell, with a

EXHIBIT 10 *Elements of Moretti's Strategic Plan, 1989*

Objectives

1. Marketing initiatives—led by marketing group in Milan.
2. Increase sales levels—"push" and "pull" strategies.
3. Increase plant utilization, mainly at Crespellano.
4. Add capacity, mainly at Crespellano.
5. Lower costs—production and distribution efficiencies.

Merger Rationale

Moretti	**Prinz**
Low-tech plants	High-tech plant
Utilized capacity	Spare capacity
Northeast plant	Central & southern plants
Strong regional distribution	Weak national distribution
Strong brand image	Weak brand image
Premium brands	Price/commodity brands
Operations-oriented	Operations-oriented

Disadvantages

1. Instability of Prinz operation
2. Lack of national credibility
3. Moretti could not sell in southern Italy before mid-1990
4. Overabundance of brands and packages
5. Communication problems (mainly language differences)
6. Lack of financial systems for combined operation
7. Lack of management information systems
8. Lack of a national sales organization

complete breakdown in management and financial systems."

Not until January 1990 did Bourne and his team focus on the operations at Udine and San Giorgio. Beveridge said:

Moretti had operated the same way for 10 years, so we thought another few months would not hurt. Actually, it did hurt. Because nothing important had changed at Udine from June through December, everyone had fallen back into the old ways.

Exhibit 11 shows the Moretti organization as it existed from 1990 to 1993. Bourne reported mainly to Peer, whose staff included directors of operations, marketing, and finance. These directors were in frequent contact with their counterparts at Moretti and at Labatt Brewing UK.

PLANT ADDITIONS AND RENOVATIONS

In 1990–91, Moretti built a new US$15 million brewery next to its packaging plant in San Giorgio. The old brewery in Udine was closed and dismantled, parts of it being used in the new facility. Beveridge said:

The movement of the brewery to San Giorgio was only a marginal capacity increase—we replaced a 450,000 hectoliter brewery with a 660,000 one. The major reason for Moretti's cash flow problems, and the reason we could buy them, was that the split site was costing them more than US$3 million per year in transport of bulk beer and overhead duplication. At present [February 1993] the overall capacity of Moretti/Prinz is only slightly more than when we started. Eventually,

EXHIBIT 11 *Birra Moretti Organization Chart, 1993*

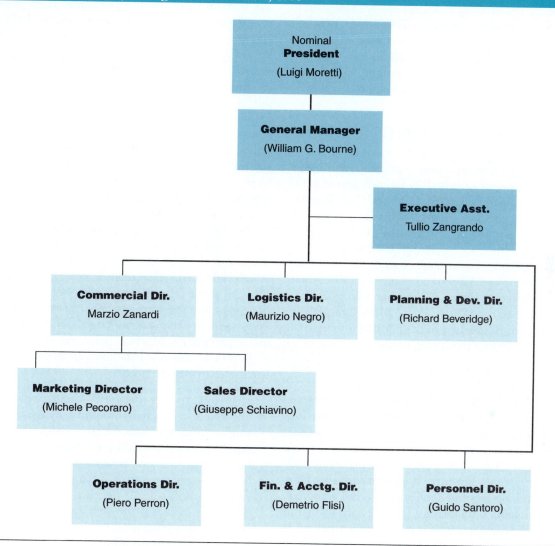

the Crespellano plant will be a minimal-mix, high productivity brewery, with fully utilized capacity, and the San Giorgio facility will be a "job shop" making shorter runs of premium products. The real benefits in capacity and costs will come as we increase the size of Crespellano.

The Crespellano brewery was renovated in 1990–91, with little change in capacity. But Beveridge said output there could be expanded by 600,000 hl/yr for about US$5 million. Starting in 1990, the brewery at Baragiano was operated only

for peak production. A Labatt official said, "We had put some value on the southern brewery but nothing there fit; in fact, in the long term we are still wondering what to do with it." Beveridge explained, "It would probably cost us more to close Baragiano than to keep it running. To replace its 70,000 hectoliters of utilized capacity and to dismiss the 30 employees there might cost US$4 million."

There were other apparent reasons the Baragiano brewery was neither closed nor expanded. It had been built partly with earthquake recovery funds, so as much as US$10 million might have to be repaid to the government if the plant were closed. Also, efforts to enlarge the brewery were reportedly suspended in 1990 after Moretti refused to hire a local official's relative in exchange for a license. Oland planned to tour the plant before the acquisition, but local officials refused to allow it. "Kidnapping," Oland said. "They were afraid I would be kidnapped."

STAFFING AT MORETTI

During the peak season, from April through August, Moretti breweries operated 24 hours a day; at other times they usually operated 16 hours. Each brewery was shut down for a month each year for maintenance, for two weeks at Christmas, and whenever necessary to limit accumulating inventories.

Moretti had 420 employees in 1993, about the same as Prinz and Moretti combined in 1989. About 50 were based in Udine, 120 in San Giorgio, 30 in Baragiano, 100 in Milan, and 120 in Crespellano. Yasmin Ferrari, assistant to the personnal director at Moretti, described the hiring process:

After a manager calls or writes us about an opening, we check the résumés on hand. If one or more of the applicants fit the job, we refer their résumés to the manager. We try to be there for the first interview, which the manager sets up. A second interview is held before hiring, usually by the manager alone. The personnel department only screens; we do not hire. If we don't find a candidate among existing applicants, we call a recruitment agency. Advertising in the paper takes too long, maybe two months by the time a person is hired. For sales jobs, the best recruiting technique is just to put the word out within the company, to take advantage of "networking." Every tenth new hire must come from the waiting list at the local labor office.

Bourne said there was no formal training program, but that there was "considerable ad hoc training, normally initiated by the function or department head."

CULTURAL CHALLENGES

Ferrari said the expatriates were bound together because "it is hard to develop relationships in the Friuli [the region surrounding Udine]. It's tough on the

non-Italians." Though of Italian parentage, Ferrari was born in Australia and lived in at least six other countries, only recently having moved to Italy. She said the expatriates were all on a first-name basis. Beveridge added, "There has, historically, been a special relationship among Bill, Michele, John Farris [financial controller, reporting to Flisi], and myself as far as dealing with the wishes of Canada, whereas Marzio [Zanardi] has been the person who really understood the dynamics of selling beer in Italy." Beveridge said, "Our goals were not only to streamline the operation and get it working, but also to go from internally oriented, production led, and top-down management to externally oriented, marketing led, and bottom-up."

Among senior managers, only Zanardi, Pecoraro, Perron, and Zangrando were bilingual, according to Beveridge, although Bourne classified Negro as "moderately bilingual." Beveridge added, "Schiavino and Flisi are about the same in English as I am in Italian, not fluent but able to get by. Bourne and Santoro are fairly weak in their second language." Most workers and supervisors at Moretti spoke only Italian.

Beveridge described the main problem he felt the expatriate managers faced:

It is this "power distance" thing, which is so imbedded in the Italian culture, as it is in all of southern Europe. Subordinates accept that bosses have power because they are bosses and not just because they are competent—although they may be. And employees do a job a particular way because the boss want it that way, not because employees believe it is the best way. Bypassing your boss is insubordination. In the traditional Italian company there is no informal "you" [*tu*] at work, only the formal you [*lei*]. Titles, status, and job descriptions become all-important.

To change that, we could change hearts, minds, or people. But in Italy you can't fire anyone except senior managers. So we have to effect massive culture change. And ultimately it has to be the Labatt culture, which involves extremely low power distance. We have to move people in and out without taking six months to learn a new way to think.

Ferrari explained the difficulty of firing anyone:

You can discharge people, but you have to pay them. For a manager above a certain level it might be a year's salary—whatever the person will accept. Workers have great protection. If you get into financial trouble you can put people on temporary layoff for up to two years, but you have to pay them almost full pay. And people don't want to "leave their chairs," as they say in Italy, even with pay.

Most employees also resisted transfer, many because their spouses worked for the government or agencies controlled by the government, such as banks, schools, and hospitals. Ferrari said:

To get one of those jobs, one must take a *concorso*, or examination. It takes perhaps a year to prepare for the *concorso*. You tend to pass if you know a member of parliament or other powerful official. Then you go on the waiting list, and may wait a year or two. Of course, all this gets circumvented for those who know the *right* officials. But when you finally get a job, it's for life, and you don't want to leave it. If you try to transfer to, say, Milan, you have to take another *concorso*. Even if you know the right people in Udine, that doesn't mean you do in Milan.

In the first half of 1990, Bourne and his team conducted meetings at each facility to explain how the new company would work. Beveridge said change came, although grudgingly, explaining:

Workers and supervisors just rolled their eyes, as if they knew nothing would really change. But things did change, and we folded Prinz into Moretti and moved toward a more externally oriented, bottom-up culture. Essentially, the marketing department in Milan is going to run this company, although it might not look like that on paper. And power distance is already [February 1993] going down. Employees of the new Moretti respect the managers, I believe, but they know competence is what counts and they are beginning to communicate up, down, and across the organization.

Beveridge felt that without continued pressure for reform, the Moretti culture would revert. He added:

I believe that's what happened at Dreher [Italian brewer which was bought by the Dutch brewer Heineken in the 1980s]. Heineken walked all over that culture and then backed off. Dreher is still aggressive, but they are having trouble respond-

ing to what we are doing, or even understanding it. If Heineken people were still running things there, it would be a different story.

Ferrari saw the change as more long lasting and attributed it mainly to replacing people and flattening the organizational structure. She explained, "The majority of the staff employees are new hires, although fewer production workers have been replaced. Only two of the senior managers are here who were here in 1989." Several of the managers had retired and others had accepted severance deals.

Ferrari also felt that employing younger people, some in newly created jobs, had made change easier to implement. She said:

Michele [Pecoraro] is 31. Only one brand manager is over 30. Most salesmen are in their twenties and most are recent hires. Even the production staff is quite young, most in their mid-thirties and younger. They know Birra Moretti aims to be a meritocracy, which means they don't get advanced based on who they know, but based on how much they contribute.

Another factor, according to Ferrari, was trying to get everyone to become part of the "family" at Moretti.

For example, the people here used to hate the annual Christmas party [for employees only]. Mr. Moretti would invite a bunch of city council members and put on a big, formal show. There would be long speeches and it would all be very boring. We had a Christmas party for everybody, spouses included, in the company in 1991—got a popular band, no city council people. The speech was limited to five minutes. Many did not come, saying it would be the same boring thing. But the ones who did come had a blast. Last Christmas, 1992, almost everybody came. One of the neat ideas was to have a singing contest between the two breweries. The San Giorgio brewery was shy and never found a contestant; so Crespellano won. San Giorgio was shamed. Next year, I hear, San Georgio is determined to win. This kind of thing has done more to change attitudes in the company than any training we could do.

But Ferrari saw less progress in her own department.

We've got a way to go on that. Santoro is from the old school, where the power distance has to be there. He speaks very little English and does not read it well. I am Santoro's assistant, but I talk with Bill Bourne often. Santoro doesn't like that, and my four Italian colleagues don't do it. They also tend to use formal titles and surnames, not first names. I am trying to introduce internal communications but finding pressure not to do it. For example, I want to post bulletin board notes when we hire a new person—giving a little personal information. Santoro keeps saying no; but he is coming toward it. I can see the fight he is going through.

MARKETING AT MORETTI

Bourne said, "Moretti has concentrated on establishing a premium position for its brands rather than competing on price simply to gain volume. . . . Aggressive marketing will remain the company's primary tool for maintaining its trend of market-share growth in the face of competitive pricing pressure." Beveridge said Moretti was also trying to reinforce the "push-type" side of its marketing program by purchasing several concessionaires.

Product Realignment

In 1990, Moretti discontinued several brands and began to focus on just three: Prinz Brau and two former Moretti brands, Birra Moretti and Sans Souci. All these were *normal* beers and all were distributed in bottles and cans. Prinz Brau and Sans Souci were also sold as draught. Moretti continued to make, but not intensely promote, a reddish "double malt" brew called La Rossa and a dark "pure malt" one, Baffo D'Oro. Baffo O'Oro was retargeted at restaurants, bars, hotels, and catering companies, mainly in southern Italy. Two of the former Prinz brands, Wolfsbrau and Castello, were made to special order only.

Prinz Brau was a "price brand" sold mainly to chain stores and buying groups. It was often marketed through "3X2" (3 for the price of 2) promotions using point-of-sale placards. Birra Moretti was a medium-light brew. Called "The Beer for Any Occasion," it was targeted at middle-aged drinkers who preferred a premium beer. Ads, as well as labels on the squat, brown Moretti bottles showed a mustachioed man in felt hat and dark suit, the "Moretti

Man," holding a mug of beer and blowing the froth aside. "*Dal 1859*" (roughly, *from 1859*) appeared on the labels along with mention of brewing by "five generations of Morettis."

Sans Souci, called Moretti's "Rock 'n Roll" beer, targeted younger drinkers. "Males 18–25 are just 7 percent of the population in the world but drink 40 percent of the beer," said Beveridge. "And males 18–35 consume 70 percent of the beer." Bottles for Sans Souci were amber medium necks. A sailing ship was shown on labels and some ads showed the face of a young woman looking out over a glass of beer. Beveridge explained:

> The positioning of Moretti and Sans Souci grew out of research into attitudes in Italy. Later, we recognized they were directly comparable to Coke's "The Real Thing" appeal for Moretti and Pepsi's "New Generation" theme for Sans Souci—and we could work by analogy to see what customers might, or might not, accept as elements of positioning. We used a sort of product story for Moretti—the man on the label and the 130-year brewing tradition—but only to emphasize the "Real Thing" idea.

By 1993, selected ads were featuring the "Moretti family" of beers, which then included Labatt Canadian Lager, imported and marketed as a "super-premium" beer. In 1992, about 20,000 hl of Moretti were exported to the United States and a little to Canada. Beveridge saw little chance of exports to the rest of Europe because, he said, "Beer flows south in Europe, not north."

Promotion

Moretti's 1991 advertising expenditures were L19 billion, most for television. Per hectoliter sold, this was more than three times Peroni's spending and over twice that of Dreher. From 1989–92, Peroni dropped 5 percent in market share and Dreher lost 2 percent, while Moretti picked up 3.2 percent.[8] Beveridge said, "Until we came, everyone was advertising the beer category, and some still are." A marketing research firm employed by Moretti said its new ads were "significantly better remembered" than those of any competitor. "It's all very encouraging," said Beveridge. In addition to its regular ad campaign for Birra Moretti, Moretti used Zucchero, Italy's leading pop singer, to promote Sans Souci, sponsor-

EXHIBIT 12 *Labatt's Estimated Investment in Moretti, March 1993*

Purchase of Prinz Brau	US$ 25 million
Purchase of Birra Moretti	75 million
Construction of San Giorgio brewery	15 million
Additional advances	35 million
Total	US$150 million

ing over 200 Zucchero concerts in FY 1993 alone. The Sans Souci brand also sponsored some concerts by lesser-known artists. Beveridge said competitors soon copied any successful strategy. He noted that Moretti intended to keep up the advertising pressure and was looking at various changes in bottle shapes and sizes, label designs, can and carton designs, and promotional appeals.

Salea and Distribution

Beginning in mid-1990, Moretti intensified its coverage of central Italy and expanded into the south. Under Giuseppe Schiavino, Moretti's national sales director, were four regional sales managers who each supervised several area managers. District sales representatives reported to the area managers. In general, sales representatives solicited orders from concessionaires, handled customer complaints, and prospected for new concessionaires. Moretti contracted with a transport company to deliver beer from its breweries to two "super depots," one outside San Giorgio and the other near Crespellano. Several regional transport companies hauled the beer to Moretti's five regional warehouses and to customer sites.

FINANCE AND MIS

By 1993, Labatt had invested an estimated US$150 million in Moretti. The estimates are broken down in Exhibit 12. Exhibit 13 presents skeleton financial data reported to the Italian government for fiscal years 1990 and 1991.[9] Beveridge said he could not confirm the data in Exhibit 13, adding:

The report to the Italian government is made according to Italian accounting principles, with Italian tax law as the prime concern. I have never wanted to see the reports after trying to disentangle them during the acquisitions—you have to make so many adjustments to get them to make sense in GAAP terms. As long as we aren't paying tax, the document has no relevance to strategic decisions. And with capital allowances, goodwill, and prior year losses it will be a long time before we are liable to tax.

For FY 1993, unit sales at Birra Moretti increased 5 percent, compared to 21 percent in FY 1992, and the company had a loss before interest and taxes of C$3 million on net sales of C$130 million.

At the time of the acquisitions, Moretti had an obsolete Texas Instruments (TI) computer and Prinz

EXHIBIT 13 *Moretti Skeleton Financial Data (billions of lire)*

	1990	1991
Net sales	40.6	68.0
Labor cost	8.5	14.5
Depreciation	4.1	6.5
Other operating costs	41.5	62.8
Operating income	−13.6	−15.8

Source of data: Databank, Milan.

had an even older IBM machine. Beveridge recruited Marcelo Cordioli as information systems manager in June 1992. They purchased a Hewlett-Packard HP9000, connecting it with PC clones through a Novell network. Beveridge said, "When this is fully working it will be a true 'distributed' computing environment—when we started from almost nothing it was as easy to go to start-of-the-art as go anywhere else."

Cordioli added, "We already [early 1993] have Crespellano, Milan, San Giorgio, and Udine on the Novell network. I hope we have all four regional offices connected by mid-year." He said he would like to see inventory computerized, "from raw materials to the super depots and the regional warehouses." Salespersons telephoned or faxed sales orders to Udine, where they were entered. "The Italian telephone system is not too good and I would not trust a remote workstation for order entry," said Cordioli. "Also, one person can enter all the orders at Udine, rather than having one at each field office."

RESTRUCTURING AT LABATT

Oland fired Morgan in July 1991. "I had good reasons," said Oland. "But you don't tell a person that if he doesn't ask. And John never asked. Anyway, it had nothing to do with Italy—he got a promotion for that." Three months later, Oland was demoted to vice chairman of Labatt and group chairman of Brewing, neither an operating position. He was replaced by George Taylor, former head of Labatt Food Company. Though no reason for Oland's demotion was made public, Oland later explained, "Brascan said I was an 'operator' and they wanted a finance person."

Labatt paid C$3 per share (C$260 million total) as a special dividend in October 1992, about C$110 million of it to Brascan. By February 1993, the remaining "nonstrategic businesses" were sold and Labatt restructured itself into Brewing and Broadcast segments. The latter included 90 percent interest in the Toronto Blue Jays. Net sales from the remaining businesses were projected to be just over C$2 billion for FY 1993, versus C$5.4 billion for all businesses in 1989. Brewing was providing about 75 percent of Labatt sales and 80 percent of earnings in FY 1993. A net loss was expected for FY 1993, ow-

ing to large losses in discontinued operations and about C$45 million in restructuring charges. The rule that Canadian brewers had to brew beer in the province where it was sold was dropped. This allowed Labatt to "rationalize" its production, an effort which had already begun, with the closing of two Canadian breweries and the announced shutdown of another.

According to Oland, the plan in 1993 was still for Labatt to be a holding company, with 51 percent of Brewing and 50 percent of Broadcast and the remainders publicly traded.

DEVELOPING AND NEGOTIATING THE FY1994 CBP

On February 4, 1993, before Labatt's FY 1993 results were known outside the company, Bourne convened a meeting of 16 key managers in Bologna to discuss Moretti's FY 1994 Comprehensive Business Plan. The CBP would include objectives by department, manpower budgets, capital expenditure plans, and market analysis as well as financial projections and brand plans. Beveridge explained the challenge he said Moretti faced:

The goal is to constantly improve. The current priority is cultural change—decentralize and reinforce the reduction of power distance, be more cost aware, and push a marketing attitude through the company. We have approached this in a stepwise way.

Initially the priority was to get basic structures in place, then to build sales: when we had spare capacity coming out of our ears there was little value in using it more efficiently. Then there was a period of radical change, particularly at San Giorgio, and it was just too difficult. Now we are basically stable but capacity is tight and it costs money to build so we have to examine the profitability of each sale more carefully—it has to cover not only the variable costs but also the capital.

The initial management group can't be everywhere at once so we have to make all the employees understand the basic tradeoffs so they can be involved. Also we want to keep momentum. Until we overtook Poretti we were pressing to be number three and had something to shoot at. It's a little harder now that we are third. Dreher is a long way away, and we need a share of about 18 percent of Italian production to get the breweries to true efficient scale. So we have to almost double sales again.

After Bourne called the meeting to order, Flisi, Zanardi, and the other directors spoke briefly. Flisi presented financial results to that time, for the company and for each department. And Zanardi discussed marketing initiatives being undertaken by Peroni and Dreher.

Bourne then handed out sheets containing the proposed departmental objectives for FY 1994. Beveridge explained:

All the individual managers had submitted their first drafts and Bill and I had rewritten them. We developed objectives, strategies, and tactics. We added objectives like "cost consciousness" to the Marketing list and "aiding Marketing in development of products" to the Purchasing list. Bill gave each manager until Monday to make further suggestions and changes.

The meeting concluded with a review of the renovation plans for the new headquarters in Milan. Beveridge said Bourne and his "direct reports" would move there in April, adding, "We think it will promote communication to have all the decision makers in the same office. Udine will become a back office. Unfortunately, Flisi, Negro, and myself will end up spending three days a week on the road visiting our departments."

Bourne and Beveridge met with Peer and his staff in London the following week. At that meeting, Bruce Peer raised the possibility of merger with Poretti, which was a subsidiary of Denmark's Carlsberg. Labatt brewed and marketed Carlsberg beer in Canada, so had good relations with that company. He said Poretti was interested, but Carlsberg would demand to control the surviving entity.

Beveridge saw little likelihood Moretti could be sold for a reasonable price, unless it was to Poretti.

Neither Peroni nor Dreher could expect to gain market share over and above the sum of the shares of the two companies by buying us. So they would have to make cost savings to generate a bid premium. And neither company has done everything they could to cut costs as they lost share in the last few years.

Beveridge suggested trying to buy Interbrew from Stella Artois. "We could add capacity and a second bottling line at Crespellano," he said. "Then, we could dispose of Interbrew's brewery and, by about 1997 or 98, the one in Baragiano."

Bourne expressed pride that Moretti "rewrote the way the beer business operated in Italy" and made the company "a strong viable entity and positioned it for future growth." He admitted Moretti would continue to lose money through FY 1994 and might need as much as US$15 million in new funding if it was to continue expanding sales. But Bourne pointed out that the rate of loss was decreasing.

The chances for continued funding seemed to improve in February 1993, when Brascan announced it had agreed to sell its Labatt stock. This eliminated the need for Labatt to throw off cash for the Bronfmans. On the other hand, Labatt was incurring huge restructuring losses as it "rationalized" production in Canada and disposed of its U.S. dairy operations. It was clear by then that Labatt would report a net loss for FY 1993, versus a C$101 million net profit the year before.

Beveridge said, "If Labatt were to refuse further funding, we'd cut marketing and capital. It's the only way to improve cash flow in the short term and would not only get us into positive cash flow but would, since sales growth would slow and maybe even stop, make rationalizing production easier. I would expect, though, that we would be losing share to some de-

---

Strategic Alternatives Discussed by Beveridge and Peer

I. Constantly improve. Place priority on cultural change, make sure sales cover both variable and capital costs, keep momentum in sales growth. *Beveridge*

II. Cut marketing and capital. Rationalize production. Close some facilities. *Beveridge*

III. Merge with Poretti. Be prepared to give up control of the surviving entity. *Peer*

IV. Attempt to buy Interbrew from Stella Artois. Add capacity and a second bottling line at Crespellano. Dispose of Interbrew's brewery and, by 1997 or 98, the one in Baragiano. *Beveridge* gree." As to closing facilities, Beveridge remarked, "The choice is, 'Horrible end or horrors without end?' I suppose in that case we would have to choose a horrible end for some facilities. Fortunately we have, until now, been able to persuade top management that we can't do the job without cash." The box summarizes the alternatives Beveridge and Peer discussed.

NOTES

1. Franco Cazzola, "Clean Hands Dip into the Tangentopoli," *The European*, 25–28 February 1993, 9.
2. Canadean Ltd., *The Beer Service Basic Report Italy* (Basingstoke, Hants, UK: Canadean Ltd., 1992), section 3.
3. Databank Sp.A., *Competitors Birra: Management Highlights* (Milan: Databank Sp.A., 1992), 7.
4. Canadean Ltd., section 1.
5. Ibid., sections 2–3.
6. Ibid., section 9, and "Dossier," *Il Mondo Della Birra*, December 1992, 30.
7. Canadean Ltd., section 8.
8. Canadean Ltd., sections 6–7.
9. Databank Sp.A., *Findas: Birra Moretti SpA* (Milan: Databank Sp.A., 1992), p. 4.

Cap Gemini Sogeti: Genesis

Marcus J. Hurt

EDHEC Graduate School of Management

THE PRAGUE RENCONTRES

It was June 26, 1992. The long-awaited "Rencontres" of the Cap Gemini Sogeti (CGS) group were finally taking place in Prague, Czechoslovakia. The European leader in information technology services had not held such a general meeting of its worldwide management since June 1990 when, at Marrakech, the group voted on major new directions. The decision had been made to aim at a global leadership position, simultaneously expanding into integrated solutions for clients and extended facilities management services as an alternative to the growing "outsourcing" being offered by major competitors such as the American firm EDS. This decision had been followed in the last two years by major acquisitions to achieve dominating positions in new services and areas of Europe. At Marrakech, it was also announced that a project to define new structures for the group would be under way, and that these new structures

Winner of the European Foundation for Management Development 1996. Case Writing Competition. Category: "European Strategy Management."

This case was written with the assistance of Gilles Serpry, of the Cap Gemini Sogeti Group. It is intended to be used as a basis for class discussion rather than to illustrate either effective or ineffective handling of an administrative situation. Copyright © EDHEC Graduate School of Management, Lille, France, March 1996.

would come into effect by January 1, 1993, with the implementation of the single European market. Thus, there was a certain tension in the audience at the opening of the Prague Recontres because the managers attending knew a major program of change for the group would be announced.

Opening Agenda

The Rencontres were the 18th meeting of the group called the Cap Gemini Sogeti. They lasted from Friday, June 26 through Sunday, June 28, 1992 and were attended by almost 700 managers of CGS companies from around the world. The number attending from each country was almost exactly equal to the percentage that each country was represented in the group's total staff of 24,500 people; 35 percent of them came from Paris and the French provinces. They were all managers of near senior status; 50 percent of those attending had between 30 and 500 people reporting to them.

The Rencontres were centered around the theme "Organize for Change." Every seat was equipped with an electronic voting box which made it possible to poll the managers for their opinions on the different decisions presented. Unlike the Marrakech Rencontres, however, no major scenarios were submitted to voting because the group's main directions had been validated at Marrakech and were not to be changed. The Prague Rencontres took place, above all, to announce and launch the series of actions that would change the group's structure and make it possible to carry through the strategic design set out two years earlier.

Over the three days of conferences and question-and-answer sessions, the changes that had taken place in the group and in the information technology service business were reviewed. Then, Serge Kampf, chairman and CEO of the group, explained the weaknesses that had become all too apparent in CGS's traditional organization and introduced the 1993 Organization for CGS as well as the program that was meant to carry through the coming organizational changes over a period of 18 months—"Genesis."

How the IT Services Profession Had Changed First, Geoff Unwin, the executive chairman of Hoskyns, reviewed the changes in the IT services profession since the Marrakech Rencontres. The industry remained complex but was no longer "foreseeable," as the managers had felt in 1990. The shift from mainframes to PCs, the commoditization of hardware, the growing literacy of IT users and the changes in their demands, the reduction in IT growth, the appearance of competition from hardware makers and accounting firms, and, above all, the globalization of the marketplace had all combined to make the environment more dynamic and less certain and to raise the stakes in the industry.

Unwin went on to point out that corporate managements now felt that information technology should be a strategic variable to be handled like any other business variable. It should lighten their corporate structures, produce savings in personnel, and improve efficiency in administration. IT vendors would have to formulate meaningful answers to customer needs by creating the right mix between technical skills and companies' processes. The general movement was toward value-added services and value chain management, where the IT manager had become architect and planner. IT vendors no longer had to provide resources, but "solutions." This meant CGS could not succeed as a series of separate branches as it had in the past.

Changes in the CGS Group Christer Ugander, chairman and CEO of Cap Gemini International Support, reviewed some of the changes that had taken place in the group since Marrakech. The group had practically doubled in size, growing from 14,000 to some 26,000 employees, including Gemini Consulting. CGS had increased its world market share from 2.5 to 3.2 percent, and its European market

share from 6.5 to 8 percent, although it had lost some market share in the United States. Yet this increase in total world market share had come mainly from acquisitions such as Hoskyns, Programator, and Volmac. Real annual growth had dropped to 9 percent in 1991, well below the optimistic 30 percent target set at Marrakech. Operating profit and net income were both down. Ugander asked if CGS had missed something in the process, or if there was something it had not had the courage to deal with. Did these changes for the worse have anything to do with bureaucracy, lack of sales aggressiveness, lack of cooperation, or attitudes and behavior?

The Traditional CGS Organization Serge Kampf was the next speaker to take the podium. He announced the changes planned in the structure of the Cap Gemini Sogeti and the new ways of working that were to be implemented. He first reviewed some of the strengths and weaknesses of the traditional CGS organization. In current structure, national operational companies, which are divided into divisions, report to operational groups, which are organized by global regions. This structure, based on a national conception of the business, was built for administrating. The branch, on which the whole structure rested, was the across-the-board responsibility of the branch manager, who was the keystone of the structure. It was designed when management of a group of DP professionals had to be efficient and when supply was short and customers plentiful. It was a management system based on annual budgets, not suited to longer-term contracts or strategies, which encouraged a competitive spirit, but not cooperation, between units. This competitive spirit had contributed to strong growth but had its downside when multidisciplinary, multinational teams needed to be created to provide services for large multinational corporations. The current structure was not suited to large projects, systems integration, or facilities management and was not conducive to a strong international image. It did, however, contribute to a growing bureaucracy.

The Agenda for Change

The New Structure for a "Transnational" CGS
The new organization, Kampf continued, should favor teamwork and manager mobility, rather than the current "fiefdoms"; abolish boundaries and territories; favor transfer of knowledge and "cross-fertilization"; mobilize resources for large projects; and build

bridges between managers. It should generally slim down the organization, reduce existing interference by intermediary staff on line managers, and permit top-level managers to devote themselves to marketing activities and interface in sales with clients at the same top level of management. It should retain a balance between excessive centralization and decentralization, but maintain the principle of "subsidiarity"; that is, decisions should be made as close as possible to the people who would implement them.

The structures that had been considered and finally rejected by the group were:

1. The geographic structure because potential clients would have been preassigned to national companies. This often was arbitrary and created a path of entry to clients through regional managers.

2. The sector structure, for four reasons: (a) There was no single European legislation for companies, which meant companies had to be established under the law of each country. (b) This kind of structure omitted the United States, and the goal was to "federate" the group. (c) Sectorization was perfectly adapted for telecoms, air traffic, and industrial chemicals, but not for other products and services. A large part of CGS's current market would have to be under "miscellaneous," which was unacceptable. (d) The sector structure represented a total turnaround of the present organization and this raised the threat of losing control of the organization.

3. The matrix structure was found to be unsuitable because, although it had the advantage of penetrating the client reservoir through two different organizations—geographic and economic sectors—it would cause a generalization of conflicts to be resolved only at the top management level.

This would create a considerable burden on the group's structures; the sector axis would need to create a technical and sales staff network to cover all CGS territory, which would duplicate the existing technical and sales staffs. Thus, it would increase the bureaucracy rather than reduce it.

The new structure that had finally been adopted was a "dual" structure with "duality of roles."

Principles. Underlying the new organization and its structure were several principles:

- There would be only two subunits at CGS: the operational divisions and the sole holding company, Cap Gemini Sogeti. All intermediary structures such as Cap Gemini Europe or Cap Sesa would eventually disappear. These operational divisions would have clients, a sales force, IT professionals to produce and deliver what was sold, a budget and income statement, and possibly—but not necessarily—the legal form of a company, with bylaws, shareholders, board, chairman, and so on. There would be at least one operational division per country, regardless of the number of employees in that division.

- The divisions would be linked directly to the CGS central core, which would be managed by a group of 25 group vice presidents who would break down the tasks of supervision, coordination, and motivation of these divisions among themselves.

- The operational divisions would make up seven strategic business areas (SBA), defined on the basis of cultural and geographical affinities.

- The seven SBAs (see Appendix F, Genesis Glossary) would be approximately numerically comparable. The seven SBAs are shown in Exhibit 1.

C-89

EXHIBIT 1 *The Seven Strategic Business Areas (SBAs)*

SBA	Location	Population
1	United States	2,600
2	United Kingdom	3,200
3	Nordic countries	3,500
4	Benelux	4,800
5	Germany	3,700
6	Ile de France (larger Paris region)	3,800
7	South (rest of France, Spain, Italy, Switzerland, and Austria)	3,400
	Approximate total CGS population	25,000

■ The SBAs would have two roles: (1) a regional role to serve clients whose decision center was located in the region covered by the territory, and (2) to develop on a transnational level—across the seven SBAs—the group's market share in the specific sector for which the SBA had responsibility because of the competencies and references it had in that sector (see Exhibits 2 and 3).

EXHIBIT 2 *Areas of Expertise of the Seven SBAs*

SBA	Location	Area of Expertise
1	United States	Oil, gas, and chemicals
2	United Kingdom	Financial services/Facilities management
3	Nordic countries	Utilities
4	Benelux	Trade, distribution, and transportation
5	Germany	Manufacturing
6	Ile de France (larger Paris region)	Telecommunications
7	South (rest of France, Spain, Italy, Switzerland, and Austria)	Aerospace

EXHIBIT 3 *The CGS Sectors*

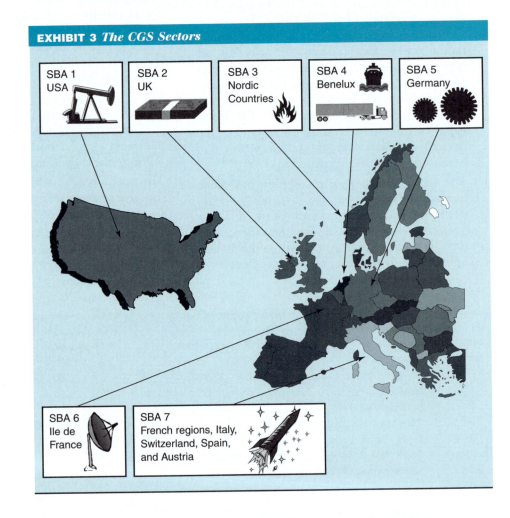

- The SBA, whenever possible, should propose and deliver to clients any and all of the services offered within the group. Because not all services could be uniformly assured by all SBAs, another SBA might be asked to assume a leadership role in providing some services—for example, the UK SBA in facilities management—and ensure their progressive dissemination and development in the group's other SBAs. Certain SBAs might also assume a leadership role in "best practices," which was defined as "best ways of doing something" in the group and which could be internally "benchmarked" (see Appendix F, the Genesis Glossary). They would have the responsibility for transferring this skill to other SBAs of the group.

- Management and the traditional reporting structure would be maintained, which would enable SBAs to measure profitability by their contribution to the group's activities as a whole.

- "Twin management" would be practiced, meaning that each SBA, except for Germany, would be headed by two managers chosen from among the 25 group vice presidents. This was based on the grouping of certain areas and divisions where two managers often had been responsible for carrying through a merger of activities. The two managers of the SBAs would imperatively avoid the splitting up of tasks, but would remain jointly responsible for both of the SBAs' dual responsibilities.

- Each SBA would be assigned a controller to assist the two VPs by ensuring follow-up on major "risks" taken by the SBA, such as large projects, joint ventures, consortiums, and so on.

- Each SBA would have an average of seven operational divisions; each division would have an average of 500 employees (see Exhibits 4 and 5).

- The traditional branch would be maintained when appropriate. However, whenever possible, Market Development Units, consisting of sales personnel only, and skill centres, consisting of all technical professionals, would be developed (see Appendix F, Genesis Glossary). These units would be devoted entirely to production and would be specialized by economic sector or technical competence. Each division could use one or the other or a mix of the three building blocks to achieve the best possible fit for the specific circumstances of its market and projects.

- The creation of additional levels of hierarchy beyond the three basic levels would be avoided.

- There would be five central functions, each headed by a group vice president: finance; group development; image and communications; manager development; and quality and innovation. There would also be a president in charge of regions, assisted by a deputy; a president in charge of sectors, assisted by a deputy; a president in charge of central function; and finally, the chairman and CEO of the group, Serge Kampf.

- A major effort would be made to fight against bureaucracy by reducing the number of meetings. Efforts would also be made to open committee meetings to new participants, to make them more like open-door forums (see Exhibit 6).

Question and Answer Session. In the hours following the announcement of the new organization, other points were raised during the question-and-answer session. Similarities between CGS's new structure and that of certain accounting and consulting firms were pointed out. Such firms often have "dual" structures, grouping their partners by two and assigning sectoral responsibility. There was some skepticism concerning the need for sectoral responsibility and the international cooperation on which the new structure was based. The great variety of regional situations within the group meant that some 40 percent of the managers were competing with smaller or medium-sized professional services groups, and not, they felt, giants such as IBM, EDS or Arthur Andersen. A minority felt that their selling performance would be helped by international cooperation or involvement of top management. Many felt that the group needed to use a single name and logo worldwide, which was currently not the case. From the standpoint of communication in the new organization, it was remarked that the group needed to change its own management information system culture. The response was that effort would be devoted to developing a comprehensive customer database and skills base on e-mail and that by January 1994 a new group MIS would be in place.

It was asked how Gemini Consulting would fit into the new organization. The consulting firm was to remain separate from CGS, but the new structure closely paralleled that of Gemini itself, which should make it easier for the two to work together. CGS and Gemini were already working together on very large accounts—*Fortune* 100 or Financial Times 100—and partnering with CGS in IT services was considered important to Gemini Consulting.

C-91

EXHIBIT 4 *The New Structure for Implementation, 1993*

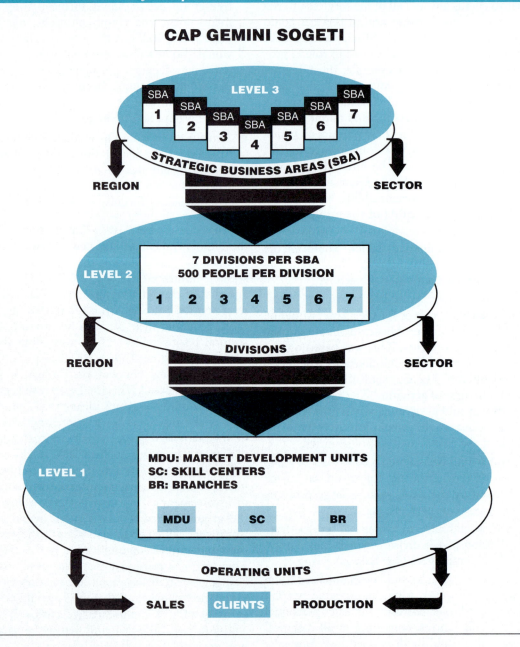

Introduction of the Genesis Project Michel Jalabert, group vice president for development and control, had been appointed Genesis project director and would be seconded by Bob Sywolski in the United States. Jalabert introduced the Genesis Project to the managers at the Prague Recontres. First, he explained that the name "Genesis" had a biological ori-gin—the gene—and demonstrated that the project literally aimed at creating a new group; it was the largest project the group had ever undertaken for it-self. It went hand in hand with the group's new de-finition, which was "helping companies be more ef-ficient in their business thanks to the use of information technology." The group's purpose was

EXHIBIT 5 *Breakdown of the Three Levels of the New Structure*

New Hierarchial Levels at CGS

no longer to master the technology per se. Jalabert continued by saying that Genesis would work on each of the three components that comprise an organization: structure, processes, and behavior.

Structure. To Serge Kampf's explanation of the new structure, Jalabert added that there were four immediate actions to be taken in building the new structure: (1) Start structuring the SBAs with the local

EXHIBIT 6 *Planning of Meetings by Level*

building blocks at a speed best suited to the local situation, shifting many forces from administration management to direct selling—one of the major purposes of the new organization. (2) Prepare to build the sectors, identifying the worldwide resources in terms of knowledge, sales delivery, and solutions. (3) Set up the new management teams with the names of the people heading the divisions (level 2) and the operating units (level 1). (4) Organize the committees and working teams by different subjects. Jalabert reminded the audience that all of this had to be done after selling hours if they did not want to lose the 1992 business year.

Processes. Jalabert explained that Gemini Consulting, which had conceived of the Genesis program, was a specialist in process redesign (see Appendix F, the Genesis Glossary). Since its creation Gemini had built a reputation in "business transformation"—leading corporate change—and reengineering. Gemini emphasized that CGS was a process-oriented company and that the group would have to have the "best practices" in all fields if it wanted to become a world leader. Excellence in all business practices everywhere would have to be built up. First, Gemini suggested setting up joint teams consisting of knowledgeable people with experience in each practice of process from each region. These joint teams, together with Gemini Consulting, would then follow a path of identifying the best internal practices. The path to building up processes would be worked out in two kinds of processes: business processes, such as sales, the CGS service offering, and delivery; and support processes, such as performance measurement and communications.

The work had already started in sales. Some 400 interviews had been conducted with people from most of the regions. They had already determined practices that provided the best chance of success in selling situations. Win–lose situations, buying networks, influences in the buy decision, and other parameters had been analyzed; with help from outside experts, a model had been designed by the joint team and submitted to the group's management for approval. The next step was to organize the pilot experiment on the basis of the selected model, analyze its results, and correct the model. It would become a model that could be "rolled out" (see Appendix F, the Genesis Glossary) and customized in all SBAs. Best practices in sales had already been identified,

but the "as-is" work had not been done in all regions. "As-is" (see Appendix F, the Genesis Glossary) was a phase in redesigning processes that analyzed how things were actually done currently and measuring the effectiveness, before setting out the "to-be" model to be piloted. What was to be delivered at the end of the process were sales manuals, sales courses, and sales management development tools to be adapted to the regions, sectors, and different service offerings.

The service offering was one of the greatest challenges. People did not use a common language or did not mean the same thing when talking to different customers and in different regions—for example, the meaning of "outsourcing." This was causing confusion and losing sales. A common language was particularly necessary as the group moved to national- and international-level contracts, where people from different regions were interfacing with the same client. The first step was to inventory the successful service offerings in each region of the group and transfer them to other parts of the group. For each individual offering, the key messages had to be defined; then sales support materials, sales management support, guidelines for marketing campaigns, and descriptions of delivery capabilities had to be built up. Two offerings had been selected for detailed analysis: applications management and technical assistance. Technical assistance, or the "renting" of skilled IT personnel to clients—called "body shopping" in industry jargon—had been the "bread and butter" of the group since its founding.

The delivery process was quite different in nature. The CGS's excellent quality system, PERFORM, which provided tools for project management, software development methods, quality control, and other areas, was not being sufficiently applied in the group. This had caused the loss of hundreds of millions of francs in previous years. The objective in working on the delivery process was to implement PERFORM. Jalabert reminded the audience that quality was not a technical concern but an overall management concern. The implementation of PERFORM did not start with the technical work, but with the very drafting of the proposal for the client.

Support processes included performance measurement and communication. Performance measurement was crucial in forecasting and tracing project benefits and as a group decision-making support process. Measuring benefits of projects and showing these benefits to the customer would allow the group to demonstrate that its prices were not high enough. Performance measurement particularly needed to take into account the specific features of Genesis, that is, the dual role of SBAs and dual reporting.

Jalabert went on to explain the need for communication in the Genesis project. Genesis was not for the 700-odd managers gathered at Prague; it was for the 25,000 employees and thousands of customers. Communicating about it was not a trivial matter. The purpose was to avoid anxiety, but also to create interest and pride. The first issue of the Genesis newspaper was already published. A road show, which would go from region to region to explain and describe Genesis, would start in the coming weeks; a hotline would be established at the Paris office to answer any questions employees had about the program; bulletin boards and press releases would be frequent.

Behavior. Jalabert stressed the need for changes in behavior—to move from selfishness and the paradigm of old ways of doing things to teamwork and openness to new ways. The new structure would help change behavior in that SBA managers would be working more with their colleagues in other countries. The new Skill Centers and Market Development Units also would require people in these two organizations to work together. Redesigning the group's processes together would also create an attitude of teamwork. Training, and more importantly, coaching would be critical to changing behavior. Rewards, performance evaluation, and problem-solving processes would all have to contribute to behavioral changes.

Conclusions Serge Kampf summarized the changes needed in the group at two levels: getting rid of ineffective habits cultivated over time and overcoming the drawbacks of cultural diversity. Poor habits had much to do with an older paradigm of business which was based on advantages that the group no longer had. Tendencies toward selfishness, narcissism, and intolerance in the traditional CGS organization had to be replaced by attitudes of greater cooperation, indulgence, and openness to the ideas of others. The marriage of a variety of activities coming from the grouping of many companies with their own cultures over the years had created a lack of understanding groupwide. Those accustomed to working on large

projects sometimes felt contemptuous of those working on time-and-material, technical assistance contracts. As a business with an engineering culture, there was often too much disparagement by technicians of salespeople, and vice versa.

Kampf described himself as "a committed European." The diversity in Europe represented a fantastic choice for the nations of Europe. It was also a great opportunity for the CGS group. He was sure this diversity would be a source for substantial enrichment and a real competitive advantage. Nevertheless, there were risks in this diversity; nationalism and prejudices—the syndrome of the systematic rejection of anything "not invented here"—had to be overcome by all companies in the group. The European companies that were set apart from their rivals by their successful handling of diversity would be those that managed common resources, clearly perceived the differences in the field, and adapted to these differences without "selling their souls." Companies had to avoid both the "imperialist temptation" of imposing a strict standard of behavior on everyone and the "Tower of Babel syndrome," where the absence of unity served as a hindrance to all action.

There were several resources for change. First, these cultural "difficulties" should be reduced by establishing a prevailing cultural norm of business behavior. Second, despite the fact that French was the mother tongue of the CGS group, Kampf stressed that the group would have an official language, which was English. Third, intercultural "internships" would have to take place to "weld" together the people taking part in them—through training at CGS University and internships outside one's home country—as well as actions involving sponsorship and "pairing" between the group's older companies and recent joiners. Fourth, manager mobility would also weld the group together; more managers should work in different parts of the world. Fifth, the internationalization of corporate headquarters was essential; already of the 25 group vice presidents, only 12 were French. Sixth, personal contacts within the group should be developed and encouraged. Finally, even if one had total antipathy to foreign languages and had no desire to establish bonds of friendship with people from other cultures, sharing the CGS "charter" of values was the foundation for overcoming diversity. (The basic values announced at Marrakech were honesty, solidarity, freedom, daring, confidence, simplicity, and fun.)

He stressed that European groups could not develop in any "monolithic" way as American and Japanese groups had, but that this impossibility constituted a real plus. He likened the future battle to a kind of crusade. It was a fight against internal enemies of bureaucracy, intolerance, selfishness, routine, and nationalism, and against external enemies such as IBM, EDS, Arthur Andersen, Computer Sciences Corporation, AT&T, and, maybe tomorrow, Hitachi or NTT.

LEADING CHANGE: IMPLEMENTATION OF GENESIS

Building a 'Transnational'

The first issue of *Genesis Today*, the group's monthly newspaper, appeared in July 1992, and announced the Genesis project to the entire world population of the CGS organization in many languages. An editorial stated that the program had two major objectives: to better serve customers and to transnationalize the company's sales and production teams. The challenges that had been becoming apparent since the Marrakech Rencontres in 1990 were now squarely addressed by the new organizational structure. First, the panoply of diverse units pieced together by a strategy of alliances and acquisitions had to be blended into a single entity; second, greater consistency in what CGS was selling and the services it provided had to be secured; third, cooperation and teamwork had to be increased by greater mobility of its managers, using the Group's references and draw-

ing on the right resources at the right time; and, finally, the organization had to be flattened by reducing layers of reporting to permit greater concentration on operations and encourage initiative. To sum up, it was no longer sufficient to be a multinational; Cap Gemini Sogeti had to become a "transnational" organization.

The seven essential activities of the Genesis project were those listed by Michel Jalabert in Prague: sales, service offerings, performance measurement, delivery, structure, sectors, and communication. The final choice of these activities was made at the end of 1992. They were the foundation for implementation of Genesis in the different SBAs.

The Phases of Genesis

Although an ambitious schedule of 18 months for total change was set, it was difficult to cascade that schedule down through the different levels of the group at the same speed in all the different business environments where CGS operated. Readjustments had to be made and differences in speed of analysis, modeling, and implementation had to be accommodated. This was accepted from the beginning; the scope of change was aimed at creating a global culture out of an acquisitions patchwork of local business methods. The varying pace of application of the process stretched on differently at divisional levels of the group because of the complexity of inventorying all the business practices in CGS worldwide. Nevertheless, the order and nature of the phases did not vary.

The five periods of Genesis's three phases were originally scheduled as shown in Exhibit 7.

EXHIBIT 7 *The Five Periods of Genesis's Three Phases*

Phases	Scheduled Periods	Tasks
Phase 1: Analysis and Design	June, July, and August 1992	Define the "as-is"
	September through October 1992	Identify best practices at the CGS group level
Phase 2: Results and Delivery	November 1992	Design the "to-be" model by workstreams
	December 1992 through part of 1993	Pilot the models
Phase 3: Implementation or "Roll-Out"	1993 to the beginning of 1994	Define the "as-is" in each operating unit
		Implement the models throughout CGS

The Genesis project followed the work process characteristic of Sogeti's Gemini Consulting subsidiary. First, the project was prepared with top management, followed by the three-phase change process of analysis and design, results and delivery, and implementation or "roll-out." Preparation activities were typically limited to a small number of people: Gemini consultants, the chairman of the client company, and a few board members or top managers. The issues typically addressed were: what problems were perceived, where the company wanted to go, what main areas of the business should be focused on in the change process, and who would be the key change actors. Then a proposal was drafted and presented to the top management. When consensus was reached with top management, analysis and design was launched. Gemini consultants acted as a driving force; it was their role to channel energies and ensure a very quick movement along two or three main tracks in the change process to prevent inertia.

Phase 1: Analysis and Design In the analysis and design phase, 10, 15, or 20 Gemini consultants would come to the client company every day for six to nine weeks. These consultants and an equal number of managers would form the "joint team." This team concentrated on looking deeply into the organization to assess the current situation—also called the "as-is"—identifying problems and opportunities for gains; understanding the market, the organizational culture, and people's feelings about changing and about the new rules that would be generated. Any proposal for change in the client company would be drafted by Gemini consultants and the joint team members.

In the Genesis project, both the preparation of the project and the beginning of the analysis and design phase had started before the Prague Recontres of June 1992. A team of 12 Gemini Consulting "investigators" had been formed to poll 110 CGS managers in eight different countries. The themes of their poll were: "What are the barriers to the group's growth? If these hurdles were raised, what growth rate could we reach?" Although the answers varied greatly, 85 of those polled requested greater cooperation between CGS units; 84 were concerned about weaknesses in marketing and the service offerings; 78 believed communication in the group was insufficiently developed; and 73 felt improvements were needed in

the management of large projects. Among the 110 managers, 87 believed an internal growth rate of 20 percent or more per year was possible if these weaknesses were corrected.

It was on the basis of this first questionnaire that the Genesis pilot team established the seven priority activities of Genesis and set up the four workstreams in sales, service offering, performance measurement and communication. A number of managers were drafted into the workstreams (see Appendix F, the Genesis Glossary), which were set up to analyze the current practices applied in all the CGS groups for the activities targeted by Genesis. Although these workstreams were formed before the announcement of Genesis in Prague, the extension of the "as-is" phase down into the divisions of the old operational groups and companies took place over a period of months; the conclusion of the "as-is" phase was not announced until October 1992 at an Open Day in Paris.

Workstreams. The workstreams were set up in the very first stages. Workstreams were international task forces that aimed to determine what practices were state of the art in the fields of sales, project management, service offering and performance measurement and to study ways of spreading the group's best competencies to all divisions. Another workstream, called the communications workstream, concentrated on sensitizing the group to the Genesis program. The workstreams were staffed internationally by people from all the divisions who had expertise in the fields under review and who could determine best practices.

■ **Sales.** The twofold objective of the sales workstream was to increase sales personnel productivity and develop existing accounts. A major concern was to determine the number of lost opportunities and reasons for them. Effective transnational teamwork was the ultimate goal. The questionnaire managers were asked to reply to during the analysis phase included questions such as: "When did we [our unit] first take control of the deal?" "Did we team up with another company?" "What do we know about the buyer's network?" "What other competitors were after the contract?" "What were the main reasons for success—or failure?" As Jalabert had said in Prague, some 400 interviews on sales had already been carried out by June 1992. Downstream results of this in-house benchmarking were to be a "Cap Gemini Sogeti business approach" based on "best practices" within the Group.

■ **Service Offering.** This workstream was to establish a Group-level definition of CGS's service offerings, develop a common structure for managing the life cycle of its products, and work out common rules for managing investment and company resources. The members interviewed managers from throughout the Group to determine if products such as facilities management were identical in France, England, and other countries served by CGS. As a senior manager of the product management group said, there was "a strong desire to create a group-level consistency of service offerings" in order to communicate with customers using the same vocabulary everywhere and increase the effectiveness of international teams.

■ **Project Management.** Planning for a groupwide implementation of the CGS quality standard PERFORM developed in 1990 by the group's international quality management committee was the project management workstream's overriding objective. The team was responsible for identifying "critical success factors" for applying PERFORM, taking into consideration cultural and linguistic barriers throughout the group and assessing the quality potential of each country where the group was present compared to PERFORM's minimum requirements.

■ **Performance Measurement.** To establish clear guidelines for measuring performance, the workstream first had to define the characteristics of the information needed for decision-making in the coming years. A common language would be needed to express key concepts. Then a suitable decision-support system could be developed, one that would fit the new CGS organization. This pm workstream was also responsible for designing measurements to follow the progress of the Genesis workstreams.

The findings of the "as-is" phase were put on display at the Open Days and presented by the workstream members. These findings pointed out weaknesses in the current practices of the target activities as well as the best practices in the group and suggested preliminary "to-be" models to be piloted in the second phase.

Phase 2: Results and Delivery "To-be" models were proposals of new ways of carrying out the group's processes. These models integrated the methods used in different parts of the group that were considered successful enough to be adopted as "best practices" by all SBAs, at least for the business offerings to which they were adapted. In the results and delivery phase, the best practices would become the final "to-be" model for everyone. At the Open Days of October 1992, which marked the end of the A & D phase, the workstreams published findings which very much confirmed the remarks made at Prague:

■ The sales workstream "found that CGS was in a strong position to meet local needs. But for large bids, there were no processes ensuring the rapid mobilization of expertise for complex, international projects." For them the "to-be" model would include being ahead of the bidding process—targeting markets and setting up selling teams to handle complex demands, rather than acting on an ad hoc basis. These selling teams would complement the clients' team-buying structure and "have the breadth and flexibility required to respond to international needs." A seven-step methodology was designed.

■ In service offering, the team identified that CGS lacked a clear overall definition of its range of business service. Applications management—which consisted of responsibility for maintaining, operating, and upgrading a client's in-house applications—existed in different forms in most newly defined SBAs. With new offers there was no coherent process to identify what service should be developed and how to bring them to market. The workstream established a new service offering management process to identify, develop, and monitor new service offerings. Applications management would be the first major transnational offer.

■ The project management workstream reported that two-thirds of interviewees believed PERFORM would improve the group's ability to deliver consistent quality, but that it was not used with the same level of understanding throughout the group and was slow to be implemented. SBA 3 and SBA 1 were targeted as pilot sites for implementation of PERFORM. After the pilot country tests, the perfected standard was to be generalized at sites all over the world.

- The performance measurement team had questioned group vice presidents and found that CGS management information systems differed all over the world and did not allow groupwide analysis. Two monitoring systems were planned to provide a "broader perspective on individual results": The "Dashboard" (see Appendix F, the Genesis Glossary), a management tool which would measure results groupwide, replacing existing methods; and a second system which would monitor the performance of Genesis itself. The latter system would provide two levels of information: an SBA level for the group vice presidents and a division-level for divisional managers.

Over the coming months, pilots were tested in different divisions of the group, and results were reported in the *Genesis Today* monthly, with feedback on progress from the different SBAs. For instance, SBA 1 in the United States reported in November 1992 that the restructuring of the eastern division had been completed; three pilot sites in New York and New Jersey had been grouped together under one division. Pilot activities had been introduced to the staff of the different subsidiaries and then transferred from headquarters to the different CGS sites. Often only parts of models were tested for "logistical reasons" at certain times of the year. This was the case with the "sales funnel" model—which was later to be adopted by CGS as the team building/team selling model for the whole group—tested by Volmac in the Benelux SBA (see Exhibit 8).

Phase 3: Implementation or "Roll-Out" The third phase was implementation or roll-out of the new models. The length of this phase varied greatly. The cascade effect down to all first-level operating units generally required a great deal of time. One hundred percent involvement of all CGS staff was not expected until 1994 (see Exhibit 9). On the other hand, some workstreams, such as the service offering and sales, had been priority areas for some years and were well under way by the Prague Rencontres. Consensus in these cases was reached early, which permitted early piloting and implementation (see Exhibit 10). Some divisions also reacted faster in the process of applying the new best practices models, since they had already been using them and may have been their originators. For instance, Hoskyns didn't need to convert from branches to skill centers and market development units since it had never used a branch structure. On the other hand, Hoskyns took a great many of the new sales approaches and much of the language coming from the sales funnel and team buying/team selling models and integrated them into its way of working.

The Actors of Change

The workstreams were chronologically the first of the major actors to play a role in the Genesis change process. The other actors to follow were to be, in order, the joint teams, the managers of change, and the trainers.

C-99

EXHIBIT 8 *The CGS Sales Funnel*

EXHIBIT 9 *Expected 100% Groupwide Application of the Genesis Project*

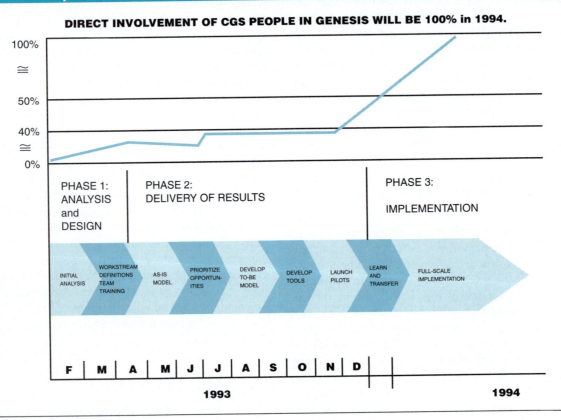

Joint Teams. The joint teams brought Gemini consultants together with CGS managers both at the level of the old operational groups—which were not dissolved until the beginning of 1993—and the divisional level. The joint teams usually had between 20 and 30 members. They would work together for six to nine weeks and draft their reports. This period was very important because the CGS team members, having drafted the change models themselves, supported the process and, indeed, carried it through their units. The joint team period also made it possible to recognize the forces in the group that would resist change.

Managers of Change (MOCs). At the CGS Kickoff Meeting, Michel Jalabert said that in the 1992 period of Genesis, Gemini consultants had acted as close partners and friends in launching the first part of the process, but that 1993 would "see CGS take the initiative in the change process" (see Exhibit 10). In early

February 1993, after short listing and interviewing, 81 MOCs—a certain number chosen from each SBA and some chosen from the central level—were sent for training at CGS University. The mission of the MOCs was to implement the new processes and communicate the change message throughout the group, so that others could carry the change further and keep the initiative for change a completely CGS-run evolution. The transferal of the change process from one group of actors to the next was compared to a motor with small gears driving ever larger gears (see Exhibit 11). The MOCs' job was to last several months and this necessitated finding replacements to handle their day-to-day work. Over a period of six weeks, from February to April 1993, all MOCs underwent two weeks of intensive training at the Cap Gemini Skill Workshop at CGS University in change management skills and new processes such as "team-buying/team-selling (TB/TS)" (see Appendix F, the Genesis Glossary). They were also given an overview of the Gen-

EXHIBIT 10 *Implementation Target for the Service Offering Model*

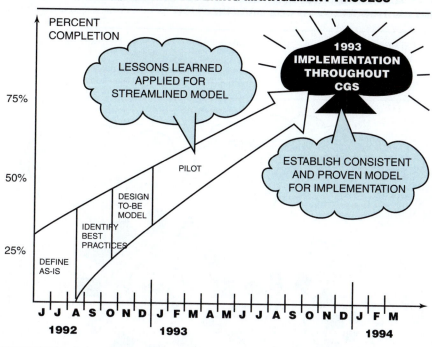

SOMP/SERVICE OFFERING MANAGEMENT PROCESS

esis program, PERFORM, the service offering portfolio, and the sales process. The first week focused on their responsibilities in the overall change process and introduced them to the new business processes. The second week concentrated on implementation in their own SBAs as well as on techniques such as guidance in conducting meetings; using tools; and developing interpersonal communications skills.

After training, the MOCs conducted intensive offsite workshops on the seven essential activities, first with division and then with unit managers. Through evening meetings, employees were given an overview of the program. During the implementation phase, the MOCs worked closely with unit management and sales professionals to make sure they assimilated the new skills. Above all they concentrated on account planning and prioritizing accounts. They were responsible for applying the TB/TS process and steering the priority accounts through the seven stages of the sales process (see Exhibit 8).

Trainers. The MOCs were responsible for coaching others who in turn would pass on the skills, the new

language, and the new models to other staff in the SBAs. In a multinational population of 25,000, the change needed more than just 81 MOCs. The latter were sent out in the field to coach division and branch managers and skill center and MDU leaders. This approach aimed to make managers in each SBA "take ownership for implementation." Group coaching took place for managers along with their own teams, and one-on-one work was assigned to some salespeople and other members of the branch team who could benefit from it.

Methods of Carrying Through Change

Above all, Genesis was based on an enormous auditing process, where hundreds of people were interviewed by the workstreams, which then reported on their findings. But information-gathering through individual interviews only set the general direction for the workstreams. A careful analysis of the "as-is" relied on the extensive use of the Gemini Consult-

EXHIBIT 11 *Perception of "Driving Change," Open Days, Paris, January 1994*

MANAGING CHANGE AT CGS
DRIVING CHANGE THROUGH CGS ORGANIZATION

REFRESHING	Containing cost
RESTRUCTURING	Clarifying roles & responsibilities
RENEWING	Regeneration of paradigms for our people
REFRAME	Reskilling and renewing our people

ing "brown paper sessions" which were later generalized throughout the CGS group to become a basic part of its problem-solving approach.

In a brown paper session a 20-foot roll of brown butcher paper was unrolled along the wall of a large room selected because it would be left accessible to all. Participants were asked to draw in detail all the steps of the business processes they were involved in. This thinking through what actually took place in the as-is situation brought to light many problem areas, which were promptly marked with post-its of various colors, depending on the nature of the comment to be made. This brown paper area was left open at any hour so people could come in and put up post-its with their comments in privacy, as their ideas came to them. Above all, this exhibition invited retracing and rethinking what people did.

PS/TB were held to get people to generate ideas.

These sessions were organized by managers of change and trainers who helped inculcate the staff with the new ways of generating ideas. Gemini consultants worked with the joint teams at every level, and weekly reviews of findings were published. There was a constant effort at synthesis and feedback, much of it through the Genesis newspaper.

Coaching was defined in Genesis as "a method of helping an individual to develop knowledge or skills. Its objective is to achieve and establish positive changes in behavior."[1] It was based on a number of principles: first, catching people winning (rather than making mistakes), then listening to them, helping them discover the problems that existed, and involving them in developing the solution. One example was given by a sales coach in *Genesis Today*: in his approach, he would first determine the behavior he wanted the trainees to pick up; then he would "warm them up" by asking them about the way they behaved and what they wanted to achieve. The move from casual conversation to coaching was made by focusing on what had been achieved so far; expectations were set for the length and the desired outcome of the session; this was followed by an exchange of feedback. The people coached were encouraged to summarize strengths and weaknesses in their skills. This coaching closely followed the transition process from an as-is analysis to a to-be model-building stage. At the end, an action plan with milestones and goals was developed and adopted as a joint commitment between the coach and trainee. Follow-up and assessment determined whether the coaching session had achieved its purposes and what follow-up coaching was needed.

The Genesis program required considerable time commitments from those most actively contributing to its implementation. Although it had been stressed that time spent on Genesis was to be after hours, obviously much time usually devoted to selling and delivery was turned to training for change. It had been decided to change the compensation policy during Genesis to prevent high-profile members of the organization who would be drafted into change manager or trainer roles from losing earning power during the project's duration. Thus the percentage of compensation paid on performance was converted from an individual basis to an operating unit basis. Although this aimed at a certain equity, some members felt that their personal earning power suffered through their efforts in assisting Genesis.

Communicating Genesis

Genesis Today. The in-house CGS newspaper created solely to communicate about the Genesis project had been conceived of by the communications workstream. The newspaper was published worldwide in all major working languages of the group. Its purpose was to act as a forum where information on the Genesis program could be relayed to the members of the CGS divisions, where the local test results of the suggestions forthcoming from the workstreams could be reported, and where "every one of the 25,000 members could enrich the project with his personal experience."

In all, 15 issues were to be published before *Genesis Today* came to an end in December 1993. Every month the newspaper ran articles on the progress of

the Genesis program, including the findings and suggestions of the workstreams, explanations on the structural changes and their applications in different areas of the world, and interviews with managers on the transition process. Emphasis was placed on communicating the new vocabulary for CGS business and service lines that was to be common worldwide. Much attention was paid to familiarizing employees with the persons involved in the process and acquainting them through articles and quiz competitions with the countries and different cultures in which CGS companies operated. Above all, the phases of change implementation were followed step by step to make the company members understand the implications of the change program.

Bulletin boards in every operating unit of the group also constantly traced developments and progress in applying new processes. Of course, brown paper operations on display at all organizational levels integrated more and more people into the reengineering effort. A hotline was set up in Paris and its number published in *Genesis Today* to encourage CGS people to call in and ask questions. The "temperature" was often taken by polls reported in the newspaper to show how CGS members felt about the change and its success.

A series of events was held in Paris and other SBA sites to mark the various phases of the Genesis program and report it to the members of the group as well as to the press. These events were called kickoff days, open days, and road shows and were characterized by "white-paper" shows—so called because the posters displayed to review progress were on white paper and not the brown paper rolls used for the auditing processes in the as-is phase.

OUTCOMES

The Beginning of a New Epoch

In 1995, three years after the launching of the Genesis project, observers would say the process was still taking place. In December 1993, *Genesis Today* was brought to an end with the announcement that "an era had ended and an epoch had begun." According to *Genesis Today's* own inventory, all 1,300 managers and salespeople had been trained in the seven-stage sales funnel process; 60 percent of the sales force had been coached on real business opportunities; 2,500 people had receiving training in PERFORM and 60 percent of project managers running responsibility projects used PERFORM as a management tool; certain new divisions had qualified for the European quality certification standard, ISO 9000; and all SBAs were working on how to offer value-added services. The cascade of change was to go on—through the new 120 MOCs, sometimes called agents of change or change drivers, who would exemplify the new types of behavior.

A plethora of concrete "tools" or approaches had been born of the Genesis project, such as team buying/team selling, the sales funnel, problem-solving/team-building, brown-paper sessions, white-paper shows, and so on. The greatest involvement by percentage of CGS population had been in the areas of sales, service offering, and PERFORM. Those polled for the last issue of *Genesis Today* said the greatest changes had been felt in the areas of corporate culture, teamwork, and communication. Pierre Hessler, who had joined the CGS group in September 1993 and was appointed Genesis project manager for 1994, said that Genesis was very ambitious and had not yet become fully synonymous with CGS. He traced Genesis's results by each of the seven essential activities:

1. In sales, the success rate for major projects had increased; there was still work to be done in cost of sales.

2. In service offering, the most significant advances were in attitude; everyone realized a well-calibrated offer was important and that speed to market was essential.

3. In delivery, PERFORM helped everyone "think quality" throughout each project phase; PERFORM still needed to be adapted to small contracts.

4. There was still a long way to go in sectors, but the approach was helping pool the group's potential.

5. In structure, it would still take time to get up to full operating speed in terms of energy and talent; the new structure was more complex than the old simple, spectacularly efficient structure.

6. In performance measurement, Genesis had proved to be very costly, but had to be maintained or the group could not reconquer its market or recover the growth figures of the past.

7. In communication, Genesis had to be integrated into everyday communication flows.

In summary, the most profound changes brought about by the group-level Genesis project may have taken place at the level of global structure itself, a concentration on transferring sectorial skills, and the creation of a veritable common identity of a global Cap Gemini Sogeti group.

Structure

The five operational groups of CGS that had been set up in 1990—Cap Gemini International Support, Cap Sesa France, Hoskyns, Cap Gemini Europe, and Cap Gemini America—continued to exist until the beginning of 1993. The half-year between the Prague Recontres and December 1992 was spent on choosing management for the new divisions and operating units created by Genesis and determining which branches would be maintained. The first wave of MOCs at the end of February 1993 really marked the beginning of full-scale implementation of the new structure as they worked with the group vice presidents to spread the change process.

The traditional branch on which CGS's growth had been based for some 25 years was a kind of small company on its own, focused on a narrow marketplace, with a branch manager, who was first and foremost a salesperson, working with a couple of other salespeople on the branch's territory. The average size of the branch ranged from 40 to 80 people, and, apart from the salespeople, was made up of technical personnel. The branch manager had always had great freedom in choosing skills he wanted for his people and had developed a name for his small company that opened doors locally. The basic business of most branches was technical assistance. This was a short-cycle business where customers needed to be called on frequently and personnel needed to be shopped for the customer's requirements. The personnel they placed with the customer were typically on contract for about 6 months, but in rare cases this might reach 10 years. Such periods were discouraged, since the personnel were losing market value, lacking exposure to enough variety of work to keep them learning.

Whereas a "do-it-yourself" approach had been suitable to the branches, Genesis was "a 180-degree turn," in the words of one top executive. "Now we say look outside to see if something has already been done by another part of the group or even outside the group. A do-it-yourself approach is going to take too long and be too costly. Now we "buy it out," preferably from within the group. CGS companies are supposed to become the architects, "buy the bricks and the cement," and put it together. This was not the branch way of operating.

In Genesis the message was clear: CGS was in a squeeze situation where the group had both small customers and large transnational companies as clients. The large transnational companies, although technical assistance customers, were tending to transform their way of using IT to a solutions approach, whereas smaller clients were less attracted by these high value-added offerings. There was no way CGS could survive trying to keep both kinds of customers; if it tried to serve both, it would lose both. The decision had been made in Marrakech to aim at world leadership and thus large accounts. The branch structure—what the press had called the "Roman Legions" at another time—was standing in the way of the group's realizing its ambition, because it only worked with medium-sized local customers and mostly in technical assistance. Nevertheless, in the reorganization, while many branches were merged into skill centers and market development units, a few were left standing because of their large customer base. They worked independently from the two new units, maintaining a kind of independent company status, and remained focused on their old core business, technical assistance. The maintenance of these branches under the new structure depended on their continued profitability.

The two new operating units were very different from the branches. Skill centers would supply services to customers as well as support on technical selling, presentations, and proposals for MDUs. Unlike the old branches, SCs were not local and needed to invest in longer cycle services by developing specific technical offers; they also needed to develop some area of excellence. SCs' offers were sometimes "vertical," that is, specific to a kind of industry—such as factory automation—or "horizontal" offers such as distributed computing systems for any industry. In the days of the branch-dominated structure, very few people had moved from one area to another for a contract. Now large numbers of people would move to design services for a customer. MDUs were not local either, and were specialized by industry, bank and insurance, public and health, and services such

as transport, defense, and telecommunications. Their responsibility was sales by sector, and they worked in constant contact with the SCs.

Sectors

The Genesis project was aimed at turning Cap Gemini Sogeti into a transnational company—a group where different competencies were best developed in different areas of the world and then transferred to other units, as opposed to a company which exported all of its competencies from its home base. This was a logical appellation for the new CGS structure, since the group had been formed by bringing together a series of companies from all over Europe and the United States with their different specializations more or less developed for market specificities. Now the globalization of needs required homogenization of the service offering of a group wishing to be a global player. The role of the sectors was indeed to gradually transfer special knowledge to all other parts of CGS's world. This was a long process and would ultimately depend on landing contracts that pulled in specialists from other countries, either physically or by Intranet—Internet adapted to in-house communications. Both the service offering and PERFORM were non-sector-specific tool sets that would make sure the group applied the same capabilities in the same language worldwide. Above all, sector idea created a kind of official support headquarters that could be called on when opportunities arose, as opposed to refusing or missing contracts when skills were lacking at the local level.

Identity

Study of the communication process of the Genesis project bears out Jalabert's statement at the Prague Rencontres that the IT would be "the largest project the group had ever undertaken for *itself*." Above all, efforts in sales methods, business lines definition, a common quality assurance method, and new methods of performance measurement were all tied together by the need to create a common identity and culture to face American monoliths such as EDS and Arthur Andersen whose growth had been far less based on acquisitions and mergers and whose cultures and languages were more homogeneous.

In retrospect, in 1995, commentators on the success of Genesis would point out that, although many people said they worked the same way as before, a common language had been instilled. Genesis had managed to make everyone in the group speak the same language to each other and to the clients. Eighteen months of constant communication and coaching and an atmosphere of change created common reference points and an awareness that the CGS group was a single entity. A kind of time-out in the long wave of acquisitions had been declared to take stock of the group and make members realize that they were part of something more than a holding company. In a sense, a group that had always grown outwardly concentrated on its internal growth for a period. One positive sign of this was the adoption of the CGS ace of spades logo by almost all the companies in the group (see Exhibit 12).

The service offering portfolio that had been launched as the "to-be" model in November 1992 and later implemented as the portfolio offered in all seven SBAs had the great advantage—like PERFORM—of consolidating the product range of all operating units in the world into one catalog on which everyone agreed (see Exhibit 13). This, along with the later coming of CGS "intra-mail," the group's worldwide internal e-mail service, facilitated cooperation on projects and finding of in-group resources for them. People were able to explain to others what their customer in another country expected

EXHIBIT 12 *Logos in Use in CGS Companies at Their National Levels, 1993*

United States

Norway

United Kingdom and Eire

Austria, Spain, Italy, Switzerland

France

Sweden, Denmark, Finland

Germany

Netherlands, Belgium, Luxembourg

EXHIBIT 13 *Redefinition of the CGS Service Offering Portfolio, Announced November 1992*

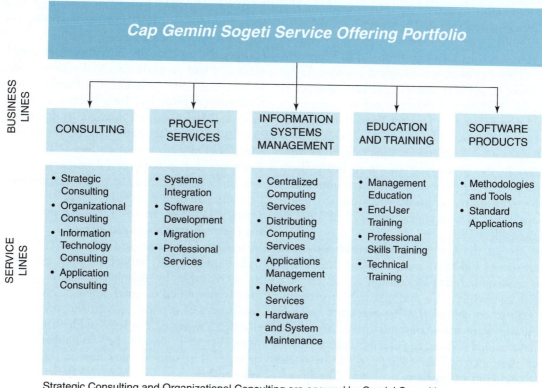

Strategic Consulting and Organizational Consulting are ensured by Gemini Consulting.

C-107

and what they had promised in terms of delivery. In the offering, strategic and organization consulting were provided by Gemini Consulting, which marked a further move toward joint efforts by the two companies. Later, the service offering portfolio was criticized for offering a tool set rather than real services, somewhat like a plumber who showed all that he had in his tool box when all the client wished was to have his leak fixed. It also offered such a panoply of services that it was not always readable by the clients; they were obliged to understand CGS's business and technology rather than be talked to in terms of their own business problems. CGS was still groping for clarity in its IT services and had not yet translated its technological skills into deliveries in the consulting business sense. Nevertheless, the tool box of 1992 had the great advantage of giving everybody in CGS the same tools and language.

CAP GEMINI SOGETI 1995

Setbacks

By the beginning of 1995, Cap Gemini Sogeti had suffered many reversals. Almost 25 years of unbroken growth and profitability had come to an end in 1992 when the group recorded FF 72 million in losses. The loss recorded that year would have been higher had the group not sold off the Sogeti Head Office building for FF 318 million. The downtrend continued in 1993 and 1994 with losses of FF 429 million and FF 94 million, respectively. This was accompanied by the selling of other nonstrategic assets that were to reach a total of FF 1 billion by the end of 1995. Throughout this period, CGS had to face a high debt burden due to its major acquisitions since 1990. Although the wave of acquisitions had stopped during Genesis, in late 1994, Geoff Unwin, chief operating officer, said the group was not ruling out smaller and highly targeted acquisitions made on the basis of CGS's new sectorial approach.

The ambitious growth rate of 30 percent per year set at Marrakech had already dropped to 9 percent in 1991. This 9 percent was mostly accounted for by acquisitions. In 1992, revenue would have dropped 4 percent in real terms if the revenues of companies acquired during the year had not been consolidated. The years 1993 and 1994 witnessed serious reductions in revenue. Administrative operating costs were too heavy in the group and efforts to bring them down did not prove to be as successful as hoped, despite the streamlining of group structures by reducing the number of companies from 270 in 1992 to 95 by the end of 1994.

The cost of the Genesis project itself was estimated at some FF 600 million, including the FF 160 million reportedly billed by Gemini Consulting for its role in the project. To the high cost of Genesis, Geoff Unwin countered that 10 percent of CGS's 1994 billings were from contracts the group would never have landed without the Genesis approach. He believed that over half the billings would be based on this new kind of business by 1996. The bread-and-butter business of technical assistance or "body shopping," which accounted for 58 percent of CGS's revenue in 1989, had slipped to 38 percent in 1993 and was expected to account for only 26 percent in 1996. Unwin said that CGS had fallen a little behind in the IT services industry due its need to acquire a strong geographical presence, rebuild its offer, and restructure by sectorial competencies. The nature of the business itself was changing very fast, which necessitated constant evolution.

A Changing Context

Obviously, other industry participants helped to bring about these changes. Major players capable of signing megacontracts such as EDS, Arthur Andersen, Computer Science Corporation, or IBM had intensified their competition at both ends of the business—the consulting end and the capital-intensive outsourcing option. EDS had made a series of acquisitions in Europe, particularly in Germany and the United Kingdom, and was moving upstream into consulting. EDS had also landed the record-breaking contract signed with the British Tax Service, whereby it would take over the running of the Tax

Service's data processing system; this outsourcing contract included putting 2,000 civil servants on the EDS payroll. IBM had taken European leadership away from CGS in 1992 and was expanding into consulting services. Sema Group, a major Anglo-French competitor, was also diversifying into consulting services and had recently acquired a strong partner in France Telecom. Although the French telecommunications operator had long been a major client of CGS and had discussed taking a sizable equity position in CGS, a deal had never been concluded and the Telecom giant turned to Sema. Thus, Daimler-Benz, which had acquired 34 percent of CGS's equity in 1991, remained the major shareholder of Sogeti, and still held an option to take full control until January 31, 1996, unless Serge Kampf bought back the German motor giant's shares.

In light of changes in the industry, CGS continued to redesign its service offering portfolio to be more readable by major clients. In 1994, it had greatly simplified its offer to be "a logical, evolving continuum of services, comprising elements chosen through a worldwide process of identifying those best practices that should be available through the group."[2] The offering was now in terms of end results rather than technological deliveries. By mid-1995, CGS was offering three major services: change management/consulting, building information systems, and managing information systems. These services provided the client company with a choice of levels of outside management of its information system—either the management of its applications or the running of its distributed information network (distributed computing services)—to free up its resources for core business activities.

In mid-1994, a joint committee was established between CGS and Gemini Consulting called the G6. The purpose of the committee was to work out a future offering common to the two companies which could be sold by both their sales forces, without necessarily obliging the client to call on both at the same time. The two were accelerating their efforts to draw on common references where both companies had provided services, such as the Spanish railways, British Telecom, or Deutsche Bundespost Telekom. In early 1995, Michel Jalabert, who now acted as executive vice president of the Sogeti holding company, stressed that between Gemini and CGS "for the time being, a merger was not in the offing," but that in the future a different business segmentation should not be ruled out. He also suggested that Sogeti itself might come to play a role beyond its current one of a simple holding company.

In assessing the success of the Genesis project, it could be said that it had brought Cap Gemini Sogeti to speak a common language and use the same selling and delivery tools worldwide. On the other hand, the sectors still had to prove that they could fulfill their mission. The service offering was still in the maturation phase. Techological changes were occurring very fast. Jean-Paul Figer, Group vice president for delivery and innovation, stated that these changes were reducing the months previously needed for development down to weeks, thus enabling new sales and delivery processes that allowed selling "benefits" to clients—and not "days of work" as technical assistance had always been billed. Speed was becoming of the essence; clients were expecting faster action and reaction from IT service providers. The CGS's new service offering was getting a lot of at-

tention from clients, but its deployment was too slow. The model for the acceleration of groupwide change was going to be the new snowball training program which very rapidly trained 10,000 CGS teachers and coaches in the group's new client/server offering between 1994 and 1995.

Yet, resistance, as well as questioning of the validity of the methods used, was still occurring. The real organization underlying the new concept of organization had not yet changed enough to permit full implementation of many Genesis principles. As discussions were taking place about launching Genesis II to speed up the process and push through implementation where it was not taking place, many were pointing out that the positive impact of Genesis on profitability had yet to be demonstrated. The group was losing money. Was it the time to attempt to accelerate the change process—or should all energies be focused on profitability?

APPENDICES

Appendix A: CGS Revenue Breakdown by Business Line for 1993

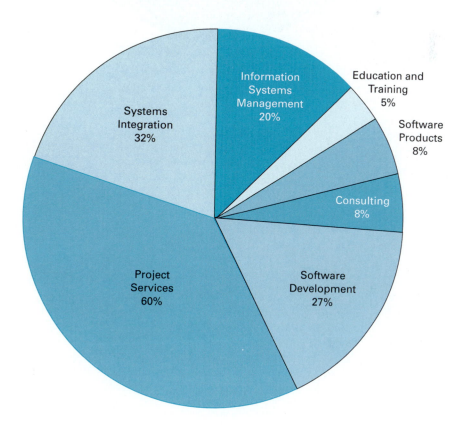

Appendix B: CGS Revenue Breakdown for 1994, Including Gemini Consulting and Debis Systemhaus (SBA 5)

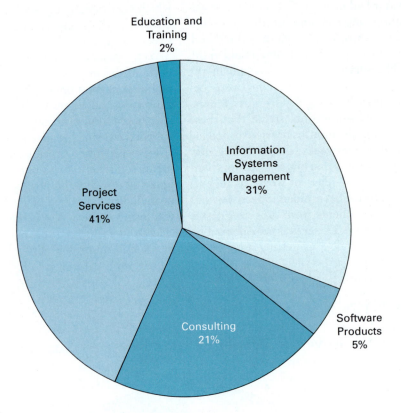

Appendix C: CGS Revenue Breakdown for 1994, Excluding Gemini Consulting and Debis Systemhaus (SBA 5)

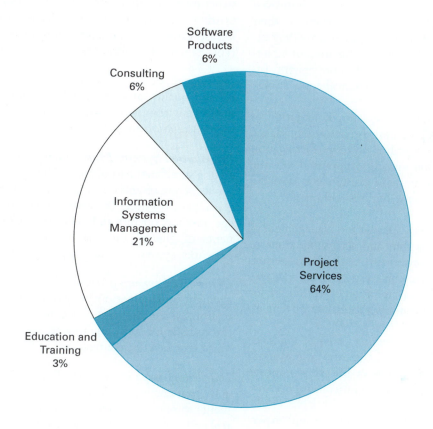

Software Products 6%

Consulting 6%

Information Systems Management 21%

Education and Training 3%

Project Services 64%

Appendix D: The CGS Service Offer Portfolio as Defined In October 1992[3]

C-112

Consulting Enable our clients to achieve improved performance through innovative solutions to their business problems and opportunities by providing expertise, knowledge and insight in the areas of strategic business planning, operational improvement, Information Technology and its practical applications.

Strategic Consulting. Design and implementation of solutions to business problems. Advice and guidance to top management regarding strategy formulation and strategic decision-making, supported by the analysis of business issues and assistance in devising corrective action, strategic options and plans.

Organizational Consulting. Design and management of change programmes within and across functions to achieve sustained improvement in business performance. Advice, guidance and expertise on management practices, people, optimisation of workflows, information management and operational improvement.

Information Technology Consulting. Advice, guidance and expertise on IT issues at the level of corporate management, IT management or IT use to improve the client's IT effectiveness and efficiency.

Application Consulting. Advice, guidance and expertise on business specifications/requirements, package selection/integration and the implementation of business applications.

Project Services A family of services designed to make a significant improvement to our clients in the execution of successful Information Systems (IS) projects.

Systems Integration. The prime contract and project management of the planning, design, and implementation of complete Information Systems solutions through the integration of multi-vendor components—hardware, software, communications, etc.

Software Development. The project management, planning, design, development and implementation for client-specific application systems on a responsibility contractual basis.

Migration. The prime contract, planning, project management and implementation of the migration of Information Systems from one technical infra-

structure to another (including the rundown of the existing environment, the establishment of the new infrastructure and the conversion, reengineering or replacement of applications).

Professional Services. The supply of pre-defined levels and quality of skills to work within the clients' project environments under controlled, flexible commercial relationships.

Information Systems Management The provision of all or a significant part of clients' Information Systems service requirements on a long-term service-level contract basis. It covers the responsibility to plan, manage, provide, operate and maintain any or all components of clients' Information Systems (equipment networks, system software, application software).

Centralized Computing Services. The continuous management and operation of data-centre-based Information System Services for clients, usually involving the transfer of staff, equipment, and assets to maximise cost savings, control, and flexibility.

Distributed Computing Services. The continuous support and maintenance of distributed computing environments to optimize clients' infrastructures and to control and maximise service, flexibility and cost savings.

Applications Management. The contracted responsibility for the management and execution of all activities related to the maintenance of applications, within well-defined service levels.

Network Services. The provision and operation of Value-Added Network (VANS) on the basis of CGS Wide Area Network (WAN) infrastructure to optimize quality, flexibility, cost effectiveness. The services include:

- Managed Data Network Services (MDNS) of complex client networks.
- Message Handling, Electronic Mail (E-Mail), Electronic Data Interchange (EDI), Image and Voice Transmission, Video Conferencing.
- Network Applications.

Hardware and System Maintenance. The contracted responsibility for continuous management and execution of overall activities related to the maintenance of hardware and system software within well-defined service levels to maximize service, flexibility and cost savings.

Education and Training A family of services designed to increase the motivation and capabilities of clients' staff in the management, use and application of Information Technology.

Management Education. The provision of education for non-IT management in order to increase the knowledge/awareness of the practical and beneficial application of IT.

End-user Training. The provision of education and training for non-IT professionals to understand and make best use of Information Technology and to become proficient in the daily usage of systems.

Professional Skills Training. The provision of training to improve the skills and capabilities of IT professionals in those aspects of their work which are independent of specific Information System environments (e.g. methods, techniques and tools).

Technical Training. The provision of training to improve the competence and performance of IT professionals to design, develop and operate systems efficiently and effectively within specific technical environments (languages, systems software, DBMS, etc.).

Software Products The provision, implementation and continuous support of ready-made, prepackaged software solutions.

Methodologies and Tools. Packaged solutions aimed at enhancing the efficiency and effectiveness of the clients' use of IT (Methodologies and Project Management, System Development, CASE and re-engineering tools).

Standard Applications. Packaged applications solutions for industry-specific and cross industry customer needs (e.g., financial control systems, personnel payroll systems, CAD systems, transport and logistics systems).

C-113

Appendix E: Importance of Common Language in Service Offerings[4]

CGS SERVICE OFFERINGS

KEY MESSAGE
"ADOPT A COMMON LANGUAGE . . . TO PRESENT OUR PRACTICES."

KEY MESSAGE
"COMBINE OUR VARIOUS KNOW-HOW . . . INTO VALUE-ADDED OFFERINGS WITH TANGIBLE BENEFITS FOR CLIENTS."

KEY MESSAGE
"SHIFT FROM SERVING CLIENT I/T TECHNICAL NEEDS . . . TO SOLVING CLIENT BUSINESS ISSUES"

Appendix F: The Genesis Glossary[5]

Account Planning. Stage 2 of the GENESIS TEAM BUYING/TEAM SELLING Sales Process: identifying the members of the clients' buying network and business opportunities.

Applications Management. A SERVICE LINE in the ISM (INFORMATION SYSTEMS MANAGEMENT) BUSINESS LINE: the contracted responsibility for managing and executing all activities related to the maintenance of applications, within well-defined service levels. To be launched in all SBAs in 1993.

As-is. A survey of current practices and their strengths and weaknesses, which can translate into opportunities for improvement.

Behaviour. One of the main aims of GENESIS is to develop new skills, and new ways of working through teamwork training, one-on-one coaching, problem solving/team building, etc. In the long term, a complete transformation of CGS culture is anticipated.

Best Practice. Identifies and documents the most effective operations in a given process, in order to provide a base for future knowledge transfer.

Blue Book. Project management tool designed to facilitate monitoring of the programme.

Branch. A type of level 1 operating unit in the CGS structure. Typically addresses a defined market (a "territory") with a range of offerings. A branch has sales and delivery responsibility.

Business Account Team. A group of people with different skills who are mobilized to sell to a given account.

Business Case. A formal document presenting the qualitative and quantitative assessment of the value-added business improvements expected from the GENESIS Programme within a given time frame.

Business Line. The highest-level definition of a generic service grouping in the CGS SERVICE OFFERING PORTFOLIO.

Change. GENESIS is a programme which aims to help restore growth and profitability by changing the structure of the CGS Group, its business management processes, and the behaviour of all its staff.

Client-Oriented. A key concept. All Group members, irrespective of their job role or hierarchical level, should ensure that customers' needs are central to everything they do.

Coaching. A mix of teaching, training and practice applied to practical business situations.

Consulting. A BUSINESS LINE which enables clients to improve performance. Innovative solutions to their business problems and opportunities are provided through expertise, knowledge and insight in the areas of strategic business planning, operational improvement, Information Technology and its practical applications.

Dashboard. A set of key performance indicators which measure improvement in a particular process.

Delivery. One of the three GENESIS business processes. The Delivery process relies on PERFORM, the unique CGS quality system guaranteeing the success of all services delivered. The ultimate goal of "excellence in delivery" is to increase client satisfaction and to build long-term relationships.

Division. Hierarchical level 2 in the CGS structure. The pivotal business unit, a division is made up of MDUs, BRANCHES and SKILLS CENTRES.

Dual. Refers to the double role of STRATEGIC BUSINESS AREAS (SBAs). Each SBA both handles the business in its regional territory and develops the market share of the whole Group in a specific economic sector.

Flight Deck. A single point for monitoring the ongoing accomplishments of the GENESIS Programme.

Genesis Project Management. The GENESIS project is complicated to manage, because of its scale—it goes right to the heart of CGS—and because of the different languages and countries it involves. The main project management body is the GENESIS Steering Committee, which meets every month for progress review and decision-making.

Hot Line. A 24-hour-a-day service for CGS staff who have questions and suggestions about the GENESIS Programme.

Implementation. The generalisation of the TO-BE process Group-wide. Also known as ROLL OUT.

Information Systems Management. One of the five BUSINESS LINES: the provision of all or a major part of clients' Information Systems service requirements on a long-term service-level contract-basis. It includes responsibility for planning, managing, providing, operating and maintaining any or all components of clients' Information Systems (equipment networks, system software, application software).

Key Account. A client identified as particularly interesting for the Group. Can be a large existing account, a high-potential account or a strategic account. It will receive special attention from a MDU.

Managers of Change (MOCs). A group of CGS managers who are trained by Gemini Consulting to become the "engine" for change within CGS.

Market Development Unit. A level 1 operating unit. Its role is to sell CGS offerings to a set of customers grouped by SECTORS. An MDU has the selling resources and capacity (sector know-how, access to skills, logistics, etc.) to generate business opportunities and follow sales leads up to contract signature. If necessary, an MDU can include IT consulting resources. Size varies from one person (i.e., a single sales person/Account Manager) to 10–15 people (with Account Managers and Consultants to support sales).

Market Planning. Stage 1 of the GENESIS TEAM BUYING/TEAM SELLING sales process. Consists of studying an operating unit's territory, assessing its existing business mix and identifying specific offerings which can help adapt the mix to market demand. Both added value and orders (hence CGS profitability) are increased.

Networking. CGS staff will establish natural connections helping them team up to respond to client needs. The networking process can exist within operational units, DIVISIONS, or SBAs and/or between two or more SBAs, in a sector.

Perform. The single comprehensive quality system used by CGS throughout all SBAs. PERFORM concentrates mainly on the DELIVERY process but can also be a very powerful selling tool. It is used in Stages 5, 6, 7 of the SALES PROCESS. PERFORMance, the PERFORM workbench, allows for easier and more complete application of the system.

Performance Measurement. Measuring performance against baselines. In 1993 CGS will be improving Group-wide measures for the six-month rolling forecast to achieve a high degree of reliability.

Pilot. A limited test of the TO-BE process in a specific area of the Group. It aims to fine-tune the TO-BE model and prepare "How To" guides for subsequent IMPLEMENTATION.

Process (Business). A process is the set of procedures and tools used to complete a task. GENESIS concentrates on three main business processes within CGS: SERVICE OFFERINGS, SALES and DELIVERY.

Project Services. One of the five BUSINESS LINES. A family of services designed to make a significant improvement to our clients in the execution of successful Information Systems (IS) projects.

Quality. The basis of PERFORM. For CGS's type of services, quality is a multi-dimensional concept: it includes complying with client needs, respecting time and money contracts, and maintaining high standards of technical achievements. All this translates into client satisfaction.

Roll-Out. See IMPLEMENTATION.

Sales Funnel. This management tool measures the progress of sales opportunities against the 7 stages of the SALES PROCESS.

Sales Process. A 7-stage sales process to increase the sales hit-rate and the overall level of orders, and potentially reduce the cost of sales through heightened team spirit, a greater level of cooperation and optimizing sales opportunities.

Sector. A Sector is a set of customers and prospects with common business requirements and (possibly) common IT needs (e.g., oil and gas, telecommunications, etc.). CGS has seven transnational sectors.

Service Lines. The main classes of offerings within each BUSINESS LINE, distinguished by function (e.g., Professional Services versus Systems Integration).

Service Offering. The specific "packaged" offers (e.g., Technical Architecture Reviews, Package Selection Studies) within each SERVICE LINE which are delivered against specific customer needs.

Service Offering Management Process (SOMP). The CGS methodology for managing the life cycle of SERVICE OFFERINGS.

Service Offering Portfolio. A description of CGS business for coherent and consistent client communication. Used internally, it forms an essential part of CGS's common language, allowing us to discuss sales opportunities, references, etc.

Skill Centre. A level 1 operating unit, primarily devoted to delivery. It can also participate in the sales process to enhance credibility and finalize solutions.

Software Products. One of the five BUSINESS LINES: the provision, implementation and continuous support of ready-made, prepackaged software solutions.

Strategic Business Area (SBA). The Level 3 operating unit. CGS has seven SBAs. Each SBA has responsibility for a Region and a SECTOR (See DUAL).

Team Buying/Team Selling (TB/TS). The matching of clients' buying networks with appropriate sales teams. This is the way in which the 7-stage SALES PROCESS is implemented.

Teamwork. One of the quintessential ingredients of the GENESIS project.

Technology Transfer. A programme within the SERVICE OFFERING process. It identifies offerings in each SBA that have high growth and profit potential transnationally.

To-Be. A model for the future of CGS based on "best practice."

Workstream. A workstream is responsible for studying a process. It consists of appropriate CGS representatives who contribute different facets of Group knowledge. A workstream is defined by its charter, objectives, deliverables and planning.

Appendix G: CGS Financial Statements, 1992–1994 (in thousands of French Francs).

Assets	1992	1993	1994
Current Assets			
Cash	550 846	364 586	516 487
Short-term investments	744 493	447 749	987 434
Accounts and notes receivables, net	3 908 399	4 082 737	3 658 963
Other receivables	369 708	337 189	288 240
Other current assets	572 877	538 064	531 821
*deferred income taxes			
*other			
Inventories and work in progress net	47 904	50 015	51 403
Total Current Assets	**6 194 227**	**5 820 340**	**6 034 348**
Noncurrent Assets			
Investments	1 762 904	1 772 863	1 701 754
*Equity investments in affiliates			
*Other investments in affiliates			
Other noncurrent assets			
Property, plant & equipment net of			
accumulated depreciation	629 212	644 551	584 740
Intangible assets	6 829 141	7 183 569	6 881 245
*Goodwill			
*Other intangible assets			
Total Noncurrent Assets	**9 221 257**	**9 600 983**	**9 167 739**
Total Assets	**15 415 484**	**15 421 323**	**15 202 087**
Guarantees given by third parties	40 693	24 802	42 084

Liabilities & Shareholders' Equity	1992	1993	1994
Current Liabilities			
Financial debt	899 231	759 266	2 122 938
Operating debt	3 396 811	3 628 185	3 076 519
Other current debt			
*deferred income taxes	23 364		
*other current liabilities	381 298	1 121 644	94 814
Total Current Liabilities	**4 700 704**	**5 509 095**	**5 294 271**
Debenture loan			995 000
Convertible bonds	1 525 548	1 525 548	41 092
Other long-term liabilities	2 481 933	2 782 597	1 961 486
Deferred income taxes			
Minority interest	1 528 473	801 701	847 027
Shareholders' equity			
*Common stock	1 678 574		
*Retained earnings	3 571 901	1 133 267	591 144
*Share capital		1 697 270	2 122 739
*Additional paid-in capital		2 401 238	3 443 608
Total shareholders' equity	5 250 475	5 231 775	6 157 491
Net income/loss for the year	(71 649)	(429 393)	(94 280)
Total Shareholders' Equity			
Before appropriation of income/loss	5 178 826	4 802 382	6 063 211
Total Liabilities and Shareholders' Equity	**15 415 484**	**15 421 323**	**15 202 087**
Commitments	3 832 541	3 889 293	2 489 331

(expressed in thousands of French francs)	1992		1993	
	Amount	%	Amount	%
TOTAL OPERATING REVENUE	**11 884 386**	**100.0**	**11 027 847**	**100.0**
Purchases	1 684 810	14.2	1 738 123	15.8
Travelling expenses	744 501	6.3	597 975	5.4
Other external charges	1 804 124	9.1	958 888	8.7
Local taxes	117 269	1.0	114 761	1.0
Salaries & social security charges	7 385 667	62.1	6 951 387	63.0
Goodwill amortization	92 084	0.8	99 170	0.9
Depreciation	299 402	2.5	302 285	2.7
Provisions	137 151	1.1	64 585	0.6
TOTAL OPERATING CHARGES	**11 545 008**	**97.1**	**10 827 174**	**98.1**
OPERATING INCOME	**339 378**	**2.9**	**200 673**	**1.9**
Financial revenue	215 935	1.8	217 807	1.9
Financial expense	(303 073)	(2.5)	(377 353)	(3.4)
NET FINANCIAL EXPENSES	**(87 138)**	**(0.7)**	**(159 546)**	**(1.5)**
NET EXCEPTIONAL ITEMS	**(148 866)**	**(1.3)**	**(373 972)**	**(3.4)**
INCOME BEFORE TAXES, EQUITY INTEREST & MINORITY INTEREST	**103 374**	**0.9**	**(332 845)**	**(3.0)**
PROVISION FOR INCOME TAXES	**(49 434)**	**(0.4)**	**(31 360)**	**0.2**
NET INCOME BEFORE EQUITY INTEREST & MINORITY INTEREST	**53 940**	**0.4**	**(364 205)**	**3.3**
Equity in undistributed earnings of affiliates	(4 602)		3 938	
Minority interest in net income	(120 987)	(1.0)	(69 126)	(0.6)
NET LOSS	**(71 649)**	**(0.6)**	**(429 393)**	**(3.9)**

C-11?

NOTES

1. *Genesis Today*, Issue 10, 24 May 1993.
2. Final Report 1994, Cap Gemini Sogeti.
3. *Genesis Today*, Issue 5, 17 November 1992.
4. *White Paper Show, Open Days*, January 1994.
5. *Genesis Today*, Issue 9, April 14, 1993.

Carnival Corporation: 1997

Michael J. Keeffe
John K. Ross III
Bill J. Middlebrook

Southwest Texas State University

Carnival Corporation is considered the leader and innovator in the cruise travel industry. From inauspicious beginnings, Carnival has grown from two converted ocean liners to an organization with two cruise divisions (and a joint venture to operate a third cruise line) and a chain of Alaskan hotels and tour coaches. Corporate revenues for fiscal 1996 (as of November 30, 1996) reached $2.2 billion; income from operations totaled $566.3 million. Carnival has several "firsts" in the cruise industry with over 1 million passengers carried in a single year and the first cruise line to carry 5 million total passengers by fiscal year 1994. Currently, its share of the cruise travel industry's market equals approximately 26 percent.

Carnival Corporation CEO and chairman Micky Arison and Carnival Cruise Lines president Bob Dickinson are prepared to maintain the company's reputation as the industry's leader and innovator. They have assembled one of the newest fleets catering to cruisers with the introduction of several "superliners" built specifically for the Caribbean and Alaskan cruise markets; four more "superliners" are to be delivered by the year 2000. Additionally, the company has expanded its Holland America Lines fleet to cater to more established cruise customers and has plans to add three more ships to its fleet in

the premium cruise segment. Strategically, Carnival Corporation seems to have made the right moves at the right time, sometimes in direct contradiction to industry analysts' expectations and cruise trends.

Cruise Lines International Association (CLIA), an industry trade group, has tracked the growth of the cruise industry for over 25 years. In 1970, approximately 500,000 passengers took cruises for three consecutive nights or more, reaching a peak of 4.6 million passengers in 1996, an average annual compound growth rate of approximately 8.9 percent. (This growth gate declined to approximately 2 percent per year over the period from 1991 to 1995.) At the end of 1996, the industry had 129 ships in service with an aggregate berth capacity of 110,000. CLIA estimates that the number of passengers carried in North America increased from 4.38 million in 1995 to 4.6 million in 1996, an approximate 5 percent increase. CLIA expects the number of cruise passengers to reach 4.9 million in 1997, and with new ships to be delivered, it will have roughly 135 vessels with an aggregate capacity of 124,000 berths in the North American market.

Carnival has exceeded the recent industry trends. For this firm, the growth rate in the number of passengers carried was 11.2 percent per year over the 1992 to 1996 period. The company's passenger capacity in 1991 was 17,973 berths and increased to 30,837 at the end of fiscal 1996. Additional capacity will be added with the delivery of several new cruise ships already on order.

Even with the growth in the cruise industry, Carnival believes that cruises represent only 2 percent of the applicable North American vacation market. This market is defined as persons who travel for leisure purposes on trips of three nights or longer involving at least one night's stay in a hotel. In a 1989 study, The Boston Consulting Group estimated that only 5 percent of persons in the North American target market have taken a cruise for leisure purposes and estimated the market potential to be in excess of $50 billion. Carnival Corporation (1996) believes that only 7 percent of the North American population has cruised. Various cruise operators, including Carnival Corporation, have based their expansion and capital spending programs on the possibility of capturing part of the 93 to 95 percent of the North American population who have yet to take a cruise vacation.

THE EVOLUTION OF CRUISING

With the replacement of ocean liners by aircraft as the primary means of transoceanic travel in the 1960s, the opportunity for developing the modern cruise industry was created. Ships no longer required to ferry passengers from destination to destination became available to investors with visions of a new vacation alternative to complement Americans' increasing affluence. Cruising, once the purview of the rich and leisure class, was targeted to the middle class, with service and amenities similar to the grand days of first-class ocean travel.

According to Robert Meyers, editor and publisher of *Cruise Travel* magazine, the increasing popularity of taking a cruise as a vacation can be traced to two serendipitously timed events. First, television's "Love Boat" series dispelled many myths associated with cruising and depicted people of all ages and backgrounds enjoying the cruise experience. It was among the top ten shows on television for many years, according to Nielsen ratings, and provided extensive publicity for cruise operators. Second, the increasing affluence of Americans and the greater participation of women in the work force gave couples and families more disposable income for discretionary purposes, especially vacations. As the myths were dispelled and disposable income grew, younger couples and families "turned on" to the benefits of

cruising as a vacation alternative, creating a large new target market for the cruise product which accelerated the growth in the number of Americans taking cruises as a vacation.

CARNIVAL HISTORY

In 1972 Ted Arison, backed by American Travel Services, Inc. (AITS), purchased an aging ocean liner from Canadian Pacific Empress Lines for $6.5 million. The new AITS subsidiary, Carnival Cruise Lines, refurbished the vessel from bow to stern and renamed it the *Mardi Gras* to capture the party spirit. (Also included in the deal was another ship later renamed the *Carnivale*.) The company's beginning was not promising, however, as on the first voyage the *Mardi Gras*, with over 300 invited travel agents aboard, ran aground in Miami Harbor. The ship was slow and guzzled expensive fuel, limiting the number of ports of call and lengthening the minimum stay of passengers on the ship required to break even. Arison then bought another old ocean vessel from Union Castle Lines to complement the *Mardi Gras* and the *Carnivale* and named it the *Festivale*. To attract customers, Arison began adding diversions on board such as planned activities, a casino, nightclubs, discos, and other forms of entertainment designed to enhance the shipboard experience.

Carnival lost money for the next three years and in late 1974 Ted Arison bought out the Carnival Cruise subsidiary of AITS, Inc., for $1 cash and the assumption of $5 million in debt. One month later, the *Mardi Gras* began showing a profit and through the remainder of 1975 operated at more than 100 percent capacity. (Normal ship capacity is determined by the number of fixed berths available. Ships, similar to hotels, can operate beyond this fixed capacity by using rollaway beds, pullmans, and upper bunks.) Ted Arison (then chairman), along with Bob Dickinson (then vice president of sales and marketing) and his son Micky Arison (then president of Carnival), began to alter the current approach to cruise vacations. Carnival sought first-time and younger cruisers with a moderately priced vacation package that included airfare to the port of embarkation and home after the cruise. Per diem rates were very competitive with other vacation packages and Carnival offered passage to multiple exotic Caribbean ports, several meals served daily with premier restaurant service, and all forms of entertainment and activities included in the base fare. The only things not included in the fare were items of a personal nature, liquor purchases, gambling and tips for the cabin steward, table waiter, and busboy. Carnival continued to add to the shipboard experience with a greater variety of activities, nightclubs, and other forms of entertainment and varied ports of call to increase its attractiveness to potential customers. The firm was the first modern cruise operator to use multimedia advertising promotions and established the theme of "Fun Ship" cruises, primarily promoting the ship as the destination and ports of call as secondary. Carnival told the public that it was throwing a shipboard party and everyone was invited. Today, the "Fun Ship" theme still permeates all Carnival Cruise ships.

Throughout the 1980s, Carnival was able to maintain a growth rate of approximately 30 percent, about three times that of the industry as a whole. Between 1982 and 1988 its ships sailed with an average of 104 percent capacity (currently the company operates at 104 to 105 percent capacity, depending on the season). Targeting younger, first-time passengers by promoting the ship as a destination proved to be extremely successful. Carnival's 1987 customer profile showed that 30 percent of the passengers were between the ages of 25 and 39 with household incomes of $25,000 to $50,000.

In 1987, Ted Arison sold 20 percent of his shares in Carnival Cruise Lines and immediately generated over $400 million for further expansion. In 1989, Carnival acquired the Holland America Line which had four cruise ships with 4,500 berths. Holland America was positioned to serve the higher-income travelers with cruise prices averaging 25 to 35 percent more than similar Carnival cruises. The acquisition also included two Holland America subsidiaries, Windstar Sail Cruises and Holland American Westours. This success, and the foresight of management, allowed Carnival to begin an aggressive "superliner" building campaign for its core subsidiary. By 1989, the cruise segments of Carnival Corporation carried over 750,000 passengers in one year, a "first" in the cruise industry.

Ted Arison relinquished the role of chairman to his son Mickey in 1990, a time when the explosive growth of the 1980s began to subside. Higher fuel prices and increased airline costs began to affect the industry as a whole. In addition, the Persian Gulf war caused many cruise operators to divert ships from

European and Indian ports to the Caribbean area of operations, increasing the number of ships competing directly with Carnival. Carnival's stock price fell from $25 in June of 1990 to $13 late in that year. The company also incurred a $25.5 million loss during fiscal 1990 for the operation of the Crystal Palace Resort and Casino. In 1991, Carnival reached a settlement with the Bahamian government (effective March 1, 1992) to surrender the 672-room Riveria Towers to the Hotel Corporation of the Bahamas in exchange for the cancellation of some debt incurred in constructing and developing the resort. The corporation took a $135 million write-off on the Crystal Palace for that year.

The early 1990s, even with industrywide demand slowing, were still a very exciting time. Carnival took delivery of its first two "superliners"—the *Fantasy* (1990) and the *Ecstasy* (1991), which were to be used to further penetrate the three- and four-day cruise market and supplement the seven-day market. In early 1991 Carnival took delivery of the third superliner, *Sensation* (inaugural sailing November 1, 1993), and later in the year contracted for the fourth superliner, *Fascination* (inaugural sailing 1994).

In 1991, Carnival attempted to acquire Premier Cruise Lines, which was then the official cruise line for Walt Disney World in Orlando, Florida, for approximately $372 million. Because the involved parties could not agree on price, the deal was never consummated. In 1992 Carnival acquired 50 percent of Seabourn, gaining the cruise operations of K/S Seabourn Cruise Lines, and formed a partnership with Atle Byrnestad. Seabourn serves the ultra-luxury market with destinations in South America, the Mediterranean, Southeast Asia, and the Baltics.

The 1993 to 1995 period saw the addition of the superliner *Imagination* for Carnival Cruise Lines and the *Ryndam* for Holland America Lines. In 1994, the company discontinued operations of Fiestamarina Lines that attempted to serve Spanish-speaking clientele. Fiestamarina was beset with marketing and operational problems and never reached continuous operations. Many industry analysts and observers were surprised at the failure of Carnival to successfully develop this market. In 1995 Carnival sold a 49 percent interest in the Epirotiki Line, a Greek cruise operator, for $25 million and purchased $101 million (face amount) of senior secured notes of Kloster Cruise Limited, the parent of competitor Norwegian Cruise Lines, for $81 million. Kloster was having financial difficulties and Carnival could not obtain common stock of the company in a negotiated agreement. If Kloster were to fail, Carnival Corporation would be in a good position to acquire some of Kloster's assets.

Carnival Corporation is expanding through internally generated growth as evidenced by the number of new ships on order (see Exhibit 1). Additionally, Carnival seems to be willing to continue with its external expansion through acquisitions if the right opportunity arises.

In June 1997, Royal Caribbean made a bid to buy Celebrity Cruise Lines for $500 million and assumption of $800 million in debt. Within a week, Carnival responded by submitting a counteroffer to Celebrity for $510 million and the assumption of debt. Two days later, the bid was raised to $525 million. However, Royal Caribbean had the inside track and announced on June 30, 1997, the final merger arrangements with Celebrity. The resulting company will have 17 ships with approximately 30,000 berths.

THE CRUISE PRODUCT

Ted and Mickey Arison envisioned a product that would offer classical cruise elegance along with modern convenience at a price comparable to land-based

vacation packages sold by travel agents. Carnival's all-inclusive package, when compared to resorts or a theme park such as Walt Disney World, often is priced below these destinations, especially when the array of activities, entertainment, and meals is considered.

A typical vacation on a Carnival cruise ship starts when the bags are tagged for the ship at the airport. Upon arriving at the port of embarkation, passengers are ferried by air-conditioned buses to the ship for boarding. Luggage is delivered by the cruise ship staff to the passenger's cabin. Waiters dot the ship offering tropical drinks to the backdrop of a Caribbean rhythm while the cruise staff orients passengers to the various decks, cabins, and public rooms. In a few hours (most ships sail in the early evening), dinner is served in the main dining rooms where wine selection rivals the finest restaurants and the variety of main dishes is designed to suit every palate. Diners can always order double portions if they decide not to save room for the variety of desserts and after-dinner specialties.

After dinner, cruisers can choose between many forms of entertainment, including live music, dancing, nightclubs, and a selection of movies; or they can sleep through the midnight buffet until breakfast. (Most ships have five or more distinct nightclubs.) During the night, a daily program of activi-

C-123

EXHIBIT 1 *Carnival and Holland America Ships Under Construction*

Vessel	Expected Delivery	Shipyard	Passenger Capacity*
Carnival Cruise Lines			
Elation	02/98	Masa-Yards	2,040
Paradise	11/98	Masa-Yards	2,040
Carnival Triumph	06/99	Fincantieri	2,640
Carnival Victory	07/00	Fincantieri	2,640
Total Carnival Cruise Lines			9,360
Holland America Line			
Rotterdam VI	09/97	Fincantieri	1,320
HAL Newbuild	02/99	Fincantieri	1,440
HAL Newbuild	09/99	Fincantieri	1,440
Total Holland America Line			4,200
Total All Vessels			13,560

*In accordance with industry practice, all capacities indicated within this document are calculated based on two passengers per cabin even though some cabins can accommodate three or four passengers.

ties arrives at the passenger's cabin. The biggest decision to be made for the duration of the vacation will be what to do (or not to do), what to eat and when (usually eight separate serving times plus 24-hour room service), and when to sleep. Service in all areas from dining to housekeeping is upscale and immediate. The service is so good that a common shipboard joke says that if you leave your bed during the night to visit the head (sea talk for bathroom), your cabin steward will have made the bed and placed chocolates on the pillow by the time you return.

After the cruise, passengers are transported back to the airport in air-conditioned buses for the flight home. Representatives of the cruise line are on hand at the airport to help cruisers meet their scheduled flights. When all amenities are considered, most vacation packages would be hard-pressed to match Carnival's prices, which range from $125 to $250 per person/per day, depending on accommodations. (Holland America and Seabourn are higher, averaging $300 per person/per day.) Occasional specials allow for even lower prices, and special suite accommodations can be had for an additional payment.

CARNIVAL OPERATIONS

Carnival Corporation, headquartered in Miami, is composed of Carnival Cruise Lines; Holland America Lines, which includes Windstar Sail Cruises as a subsidiary; Holland America Westours; Westmark Hotels; and a joint venture with Atle Byrnestad to operate Seabourn Cruise Lines. Carnival Cruise Lines, Inc., is a Panamanian corporation; its subsidiaries are incorporated in Panama, the Netherlands Antilles, the British Virgin Islands, Liberia, and the Bahamas. The ships are subject to inspection by the U.S. Coast Guard for compliance with the Convention for the Safety of Life at Sea (SOLAS), which requires specific structural requirements for safety of passengers at sea, and by the U.S. Public Health Service for sanitary standards. The company is also regulated in some aspects by the Federal Maritime Commission.

At its helm, Carnival Corporation is led by CEO and chairman Micky Arison and Carnival Cruise Lines president Bob Dickinson. A. Kirk Lanterman is the president and CEO of the Holland America cruise division, which includes Holland America Westours and Windstar Sail Cruises. (A listing of corporate officers is presented in Exhibit 2.)

The company's product positioning stems from its belief that the cruise market is actually comprised of three primary segments with different passenger demographics and characteristics and growth requirements. The three segments are called contemporary, premium, and luxury. The contemporary segment is served by Carnival ships for cruises that are seven days or shorter in length and feature a casual ambiance. The premium segment, served by Holland America, is a seven-day and longer market and appeals to more affluent consumers. The luxury segment, while considerably smaller than the other segments, caters to experienced cruise customers for seven day and longer

EXHIBIT 2 *Corporate Officers of Carnival Corporation*

Micky Arison Chairman of the Board Chief Executive Officer	Gerald R. Cahill Vice President—Finance Carnival Corporation
Robert H. Dickinson President/COO Carnival Cruise Lines	Lowell Zemnick Vice President and Treasurer Carnival Corporation
A. Kirk Lanterman President/CEO Holland America Lines	Meshulam Zonis Senior Vice President—Operations Carnival Corporation
Howard S. Frank Chief Financial Officer Vice Chairman of the Board	Pamala C. Conover Vice President—Strategic Planning Carnival Corporation

Source: Carnival Corporation, 1997.

sailings and is served by Seabourn. Specialty sailing cruises are provided by Windstar Sail Cruises, a subsidiary of Holland America.

Corporate structure is built around the "profit center" concept and is updated periodically when needed for control and coordination purposes. The cruise subsidiaries of Carnival give the corporation a presence in most of the major cruise segments and provide for worldwide operations.

Carnival has always placed a high priority on marketing in an attempt to promote cruises as an alternative to land-based vacations. It wants customers to know that the ship in itself is the destination and the ports of call are important, but secondary, to the cruise experience. Education and the creation of awareness are critical to corporate marketing efforts. Carnival was the first cruise line to break successfully from traditional print media and use television to reach a broader market. Even though other lines have followed Carnival's lead in selecting promotional media and are close in total advertising expenditures, the organization still leads all cruise competitors in advertising and marketing expenditures.

Carnival wants to remain the leader and innovator in the cruise industry and intends to do this with sophisticated promotional efforts and by gaining loyalty from former customers, refurbishing ships, varying activities and ports of call, and being innovative in all aspects of ship operations. Management intends to build on the theme of the ship as a destination given the firm's historical success with this promotional effort. The company capitalizes and amortizes direct-response advertising and expenses other advertising costs as incurred. Advertising expense totaled $109 million in 1996, $98 million in 1995, and $85 million in 1994.

FINANCIAL PERFORMANCE

Carnival retains Price Waterhouse as independent accountants. The Barnett Bank Trust Company-North America serves as the registrar and stock transfer agent. The firm's Class A Common stock trades on the New York Stock Exchange under the symbol CCL. In December 1996, Carnival amended the terms of its revolving credit facility primarily to combine two facilities into a single $1 billion unse-

cured revolving credit facility by 2001. The borrowing rate on the One Billion Dollar Revolver is a maximum of LIBOR* plus 14 basis points, and the facility fee is 6 basis points. Carnival initiated a commercial paper program in October 1996, which is supported by the One Billion Dollar Revolver. As of November 30, 1996, the Company had $307 million outstanding under its commercial paper program and $693 million available for borrowing under the One Billion Dollar Revolver.

The consolidated financial statements for Carnival Cruise Lines, Inc., are shown in Exhibits 3 and 4, and selected financial data are presented in Exhibit 5.

Customer cruise deposits, which represent unearned revenue, are included in the balance sheet when received and are recognized as cruise revenues upon completion of the voyage. Customers also are required to pay the full cruise fare (minus deposit) 60 days in advance, with the fares being recognized as cruise revenue upon completion of the voyage.

LIBOR Rate means that for an interest period for each LIBOR (London Interbank Offer Rate) rate advance comprising part of the same borrowing, the rate determined by the agent to be the rate of interest per annum rounded upward to the nearest whole multiple of 1/100 of 1 percent per annum, appearing on the Telerate screen 3750 at 11:00 A.M. (London time) two business days before the first day of such interest period for a term equal to such interest period and in an amount substantially equal to such portion of the loan, or if the agent cannot so determine the LIBOR rate by reference screen 3750, then (ii) equal to the average (rounded upward to the nearest whole multiple of 1/100 of 1% per annum, if such average is not such a multiple) of the rate per annum at which deposits in United States dollars are offered by the principal office of each of the reference lenders in London, England, to prime banks in the London Interbank market at 11:00 A.M. (London time) two business days before the first day of such interest period for a term equal to such interest period and in an amount substantially equal to such portion of the loan. In the latter case, the LIBOR rate for an interest period shall be determined by the agent on the basis of applicable rates furnished to and received by the agent from the reference lenders two business days before the first day of such interest period, subject, however, to the provisions of Section 2.05. If at any time the agent shall determine that by reason of circumstances affecting the London Interbank market (i) adequate and reasonable means do not exist for ascertaining the LIBOR rate for the succeeding interest period or (ii) the making or continuance of any loan at the LIBOR rate has become impracticable as a result of a contingency occurring after the date of this agreement which materially and adversely affects the London Interbank market, the agent shall so notify the lenders and the borrower. Failing the availability of the LIBOR rate, the LIBOR rate shall mean the base rate thereafter in effect from time to time until such time as a LIBOR rate may be determined by reference to the London Interbank market.

EXHIBIT 3 *Carnival Corporation: Consolidated Statements of Operations*

(in thousands)

Years Ended November 30,	1996	1995	1994	1993	1992	1991
Revenues	$2,212,572	$1,998,150	$1,806,016	$1,556,919	$1,473,614	$1,404,704
Costs and Expenses:						
Operating Expense	1,241,269	1,131,113	1,028,475	907,925	865,587	810,317
Selling and Administrative	274,855	248,566	223,272	207,995	194,298	193,316
Depreciation & Amortization	144,987	128,433	110,595	93,333	88,833	85,166
	1,661,111	1,508,112	1,362,342	1,209,253	1,148,718	1,088,799
Operating Income Before Affiliated	551,461					
Income from Affiliated	45,967					
Operating Income	597,428	490,038	443,674	347,666	324,896	315,905
Other Income (Expense):						
Interest Income	18,597	14,403	8,668	11,527	16,946	10,596
Interest Expense, Net of Capitalized Interest	(64,092)	(63,080)	(51,378)	(34,325)	(53,792)	(65,428)
Other Income (expense)	23,414	19,104	(9,146)	(1,201)	2,731	1,746
Income Tax Expense	(9,045)	(9,374)	(10,053)	(5,497)	(9,008)	(8,995)
	(31,126)	(38,947)	(61,909)	(29,496)	(43,123)	(62,081)
Income Before Extraordinary Item	566,302	$451,091	$381,765	$318,170	$281,773	253,824
Extraordinary Item						
Loss on early extinguishment of debt					(5,189)	
Discontinued Operations						
Hotel Casino Operating Loss						(33,173)
Loss on Disposal of Hotel Casino						(135,436)
Net Income	566,302	$451,091	$381,765	$318,170	$276,584	$84,998

Source: Carnival Corporation Annual Report, 1996, & Form 10K.

Property and equipment on the financial statements are stated at cost. Depreciation and amortization are calculated using the straight-line method over the following estimated useful lives: vessels, 25–30 years; buildings, 20–40 years; equipment, 2–20 years; and leasehold improvements at the shorter of the "term of lease" or "related asset life." Goodwill of $275 million resulting from the acquisition of HAL Antillen, N.V. (Holland America Lines) is being amortized using the straight-line method over 40 years.

During 1995, Carnival received $40 million from the settlement of litigation with Metra Oy, the former parent company of Wartsila Marine Industries, related to losses suffered in connection with the construction of three cruise ships. (Wartsila declared bankruptcy in late 1994.) Of this amount, $14.4 million was recorded as "other income" with the remainder used to pay legal fees and reduce the cost basis of the three ships.

On June 25, 1996, Carnival reached an agreement with the trustees of Wartsila and creditors for the bankruptcy which resulted in a cash payment of approximately $80 million. Of the $80 million received, $5 million was used to pay certain costs, $32 million was recorded as other income, and $43 million was used to reduce the cost basis of certain ships that had been affected by the bankruptcy.

According to the Internal Revenue Code of 1986, Carnival is considered a "controlled foreign corporation (CFC)" since 50 percent of its stock is held by individuals who are residents of foreign countries and

EXHIBIT 4 *Carnival Corporation: Consolidated Balance Sheets*

(in thousands)

Years Ended November 30,	1996	1995	1994	1993	1992
ASSETS					
Current Assets					
Cash & Cash Equivalents	111,629	$53,365	$54,105	$60,243	$115,014
Short-Term Investments	12,486	50,395	70,115	88,677	111,048
Accounts Receivable	38,109	33,080	20,789	19,310	21,624
Consumable Inventories [Average Cost]	53,281	48,820	45,122	37,245	31,618
Prepaid Expenses & Other	75,428	70,718	50,318	48,323	32,120
Total Current Assets	290,933	256,378	240,449	253,798	311,424
Property and Equipment [at cost]					
Less Accumulated Depreciation & Amortization	4,099,038	3,414,823	3,071,431	2,588,009	1,961,402
Other Assets					
Goodwill [Less Accumulated Amortization]	219,589	226,571	233,553	237,327	244,789
Long-Term Notes Receivable		78,907	76,876	29,136	
Investment in Affiliates & Other Assets	430,330	128,808	47,514	21,097	38,439
Net Assets of Discontinued Operations	61,998			89,553	89,553
	5,101,888	$4,105,487	$3,669,823	$3,218,920	$2,645,607
LIABILITIES AND SHAREHOLDERS' EQUITY					
Current Liabilities:					
Current Portion of Long-Term Debt	66,369	$72,752	$84,644	$91,621	$97,931
Accounts Payable	84,748	90,237	86,750	81,374	71,473
Accrued Liabilities	126,511	113,483	114,868	94,830	69,919
Customer Deposits	352,698	292,606	257,505	228,153	178,945
Dividends Payable	32,416	25,632	21,190	19,763	19,750
Reserve for Discontinued Operations				34,253	36,763
Total Current Liabilities	662,742	594,710	564,957	549,994	474,781
Long-Term Debt	1,277,529	1,035,031	1,046,904	916,221	776,600
Convertable Notes	39,103	115,000	115,000	115,000	
Other Long-Term Liabilities	91,630	15,873	14,028	10,499	9,381
Shareholders' Equity:					
Class A Common Stock [1 vote share]	2,397	2,298	2,276	2,274	1,136
Class B Common Stock [5 votes share]	550	550	550	550	275
Paid in Capital	819,610	594,811	544,947	541,194	539,622
Retained Earnings	2,207,781	1,752,140	1,390,589	1,089,323	850,193
Other	546	(4,926)	(9,428)	(6,135)	(6,381)
Total Shareholders' Equity	3,030,884	2,344,873	1,928,934	1,627,206	1,384,845
	5,101,888	$4,105,487	$3,669,823	$3,218,920	$2,645,607

Source: Carnival Corporation Annual Report, 1996, & Form 10K.

its countries of incorporation exempt shipping operations of U.S. persons from income tax. Because of CFC status, Carnival expects that all of its income (with the exception of U.S. source income from the transportation, hotel, and tour businesses of Holland America) will be exempt from U.S. federal income taxes at the corporate level.

The primary financial consideration of importance to Carnival management involves the control of costs, both fixed and variable, for the maintenance

EXHIBIT 5 *Carnival Corporation: Selected Financial Data by Segment*

Years Ended November 30,	(in thousands)				
	1996	1995	1994	1993	1992
Revenues					
Cruise	2,003,458	1,800,755	1,623,069	1,381,473	1,292,587
Tour	263,356	241,909	227,613	214,382	215,194
Intersegment revenues	(54,242)	(44,534)	(44,666)	(38,936)	(34,167)
	2,212,572	1,998,150	1,806,016	1,556,919	1,473,614
Gross Operating Profit					
Cruise	913,880	810,736	726,808	598,642	552,669
Tour	57,423	56,301	50,733	50,352	55,358
	971,303	867,037	777,541	648,994	608,027
Depreciation & Amortization					
Cruise	135,694	120,304	101,146	84,228	79,743
Tour	8,317	8,129	9,449	9,105	9,090
Corporate	976				
	144,987	128,433	110,595	93,333	88,833
Operating Income					
Cruise	535,814	465,870	425,590	333,392	310,845
Tour	21,252	24,168	18,084	14,274	23,051
Corporate	40,362				
	597,428	490,038	443,674	347,666	333,896
Identifiable Assets					
Cruise	4,514,675	3,967,174	3,531,727	2,995,221	2,415,547
Tour	150,851	138,313	138,096	134,146	140,507
Discontinued resort and casino				89,553	89,553
Corporate	436,362				
	5,101,888	4,105,487	3,669,823	3,218,920	2,645,607
Capital Expenditures					
Cruise	841,871	456,920	587,249	705,196	111,766
Tour	14,964	8,747	9,963	10,281	11,400
Corporate	1,810				
	858,645	465,667	597,212	715,477	123,166

Source: Carnival Corporation Annual Report, 1996, & Form 10K.

of a healthy profit margin. Carnival has the lowest break-even point of any organization in the cruise industry (ships break even at approximately 60 percent of capacity) due to operational experience and economies of scale. Unfortunately, fixed costs, including depreciation, fuel, insurance, port charges, and crew costs, which represent more than 33 percent of the company's operating expenses, cannot be reduced significantly in relation to decreases in passenger loads and aggregate passenger ticket revenue. [Major expense items are airfare (25–30 percent), travel agent fees (10 percent), and labor (13–15 per-

cent)]. Increases in these costs could negatively affect the profitability of the organization.

PRINCIPAL SUBSIDIARIES

Carnival Cruise Line

At the end of fiscal 1996, Carnival operated 11 ships with a total berth capacity of 20,332. Carnival operates principally in the Caribbean and has an assortment of ships and ports of call serving the three-, four-, and seven-day cruise markets (see Exhibit 6).

EXHIBIT 6 *The Ships of Carnival Corporation*

Name	Registry	Built	First in Company	Service Cap*	Gross Tons	Length/Width	Areas of Operation
Carnival Cruise Lines							
Carnival Destiny	Panama	1996	1997	2,642	101,000	893/116	Caribbean
Inspiration	Panama	1996	1996	2,040	70,367	855/104	Caribbean
Imagination	Panama	1995	1995	2,040	70,367	855/104	Caribbean
Fascination	Panama	1994	1994	2,040	70,367	855/104	Caribbean
Sensation	Panama	1993	1993	2,040	70,367	855/104	Caribbean
Ecstasy	Liberia	1991	1991	2,040	70,367	855/104	Caribbean
Fantasy	Liberia	1990	1990	2,044	70,367	855/104	Bahamas
Celebration	Liberia	1987	1987	1,486	47,262	738/92	Caribbean
Jubilee	Panama	1986	1986	1,486	47,262	738/92	Mexican Riviera
Holiday	Panama	1985	1985	1,452	46,052	727/92	Mexican Riviera
Tropicale**	Liberia	1982	1982	1,022	36,674	660/85	Alaska, Caribbean
Total Carnival Ships Capacity 20,332							
Holland America Line							
Veendam	Bahamas	1996	1996	1,266	55,451	720/101	Alaska, Caribbean
Ryndam	Netherlands	1994	1994	1,266	55,451	720/101	Alaska, Caribbean
Maasdam	Netherlands	1993	1993	1,266	55,451	720/101	Europe, Caribbean
Statendam	Netherlands	1993	1993	1,266	55,451	720/101	Alaska, Caribbean
Westerdam	Netherlands	1986	1988	1,494	53,872	798/95	Canada, Caribbean
Noordam	Netherlands	1984	1984	1,214	33,930	704/89	Alaska, Caribbean
Nieuw Amsterdam	Netherlands	1983	1983	1,214	33,930	704/89	Alaska, Caribbean
Rotterdam V**	Netherlands	1959	1959	1,075	37,783	749/94	Alaska, Worldwide
Total HAL Ships Capacity 10,061							
Windstar Cruises							
Wind Spirit	Bahamas	1988	1988	148	5,736	440/52	Caribbean, Mediterranean
Wind Song	Bahamas	1987	1987	148	5,703	440/52	South Pacific
Wind Star	Bahamas	1986	1986	148	5,703	440/52	Caribbean, Mediterranean
Total Windstar Ships Capacity 444							
Total Capacity 30,837							

Source: Carnival Corporation, 1997.
*In accordance with industry practice, passenger capacity is calculated based on two passengers per cabin even though some cabins can accommodate three or four passengers.
**In November 1996, Carnival Cruise Lines' cruise ship *Tropicale* was sold to the joint venture with HMM and the company chartered the vessel back until the vessel enters service with the joint venture in the spring of 1998. Holland America Line's Rotterdam V is expected to be replaced in September 1997 by the Rotterdam VI, which is currently under construction.

Each ship is a floating resort with a full maritime staff, shopkeepers and casino operators, entertainers, and complete hotel staff. Approximately 14 percent of corporate revenue is generated from shipboard activity such as casino operations, liquor sales, and sale of gift shop items. At various ports of call, passen-gers can also take advantage of tours, shore excursions, and duty-free shopping at their own expense.

Shipboard operations are designed to provide maximum entertainment, activities, and service. The size of the company and the similarity in design of the new cruise ships have allowed Carnival to achieve various economies of scale, and management is highly cost-conscious.

Although the Carnival Cruise Lines division is increasing its presence in the shorter cruise markets, the firm's general marketing strategy is to use three-, four-, or seven-day moderately priced cruises to fit the time and budget constraints of the middle class. Shorter cruises can cost less than $500 per person (depending on accommodations) up to roughly $3,000 per person in a luxury suite on a seven-day cruise, including port charges. (Per diem rates for shorter cruises are slightly higher, on average, than per diem rates for seven-day cruises.) Average rates per day are approximately $180, excluding gambling, liquor and soft drinks, and items of a personal nature. Guests are expected to tip their cabin steward and waiter at a suggested rate of $3 per person/per day, and the bus boy at $1.50 per person/per day.

Some 99 percent of all Carnival cruises are sold through travel agents who receive a standard commission of 10 percent (15 percent in Florida). Carnival works extensively with travel agents to help promote cruises as an alternative to a Disney or European vacation. In addition to training travel agents from nonaffiliated travel/vacation firms to sell cruises, a special group of employees regularly visits travel agents posing as prospective clients. If the agent recommends a cruise before another vacation option, he or she receives $100. If the travel agent specifies a Carnival cruise before other options, he or she receives $1,000 on the spot. During fiscal 1995, Carnival took reservations from about 29,000 of the approximately 45,000 travel agencies in the United States and Canada, and no one travel agency accounted for more than 2 percent of Carnival revenues.

On-board service is labor intensive, employing help from some 51 nations—mostly Third World countries—with reasonable returns to employees. For example, waiters on the *Jubilee* can earn approximately $18,000 to $27,000 per year (base salary and tips), significantly more than could be earned in their home country for similar employment. Waiters typically work 10 hours per day with approximately 1 day off per week for a specified contract period (usually 3 to 9 months). Carnival records show that employees remain with the company for approximately eight years and that applicants exceed demand for all cruise positions. Nonetheless, the American Mar-

itime Union has cited Carnival (and other cruise operators) several times for exploitation of its crew.

Holland America Lines

On January 17, 1989, Carnival acquired all the outstanding stock of HAL Antillen N.V. from Holland America Lines N.V. for $625 million in cash. Carnival financed the purchase through $250 million in retained earnings (cash account) and borrowed the other $375 million from banks at .25 percent over the prime rate. Carnival received the assets and operations of the Holland America Lines, Westours, Westmark Hotels, and Windstar Sail Cruises. Holland America currently has seven cruise ships with a capacity of 8,795 berths, with new ships to be delivered in the future.

Founded in 1873, Holland America Lines is an upscale (it charges an average of 25 percent more than similar Carnival cruises) line with principal destinations in Alaska during the summer months and the Caribbean during the fall and winter, with some worldwide cruises of up to 98 days. Holland America targets an older, more sophisticated customer with fewer youth-oriented activities. On Holland America ships, passengers can dance to the sounds of the Big Band era and avoid the discos of Carnival ships. Passengers on Holland America ships enjoy more service (a higher staff-to-passenger ratio than Carnival), have more cabin and public space per person, and have a "no tipping" shipboard policy. Holland America has not enjoyed the spectacular growth of Carnival, but has sustained constant growth through the 1980s and early 1990s with high occupancy. The operation of these ships and the structure of the crew is similar to the Carnival cruise ship model, and the acquisition of the line gave the Carnival Corporation a presence in the Alaskan market where it had none before.

Holland America Westours is the largest tour operator in Alaska and the Canadian Rockies and provides vacation synergy with Holland America cruises. The transportation division of Westours includes over 290 motor coaches comprised of the Gray Line of Alaska, the Gray Line of Seattle, Westours motorcoaches, the McKinley Explorer railroad coaches, and three-day boats for tours to glaciers and other points of interest. Carnival management believes that Alaskan cruises and tours should increase in the future due to a number of factors. These include the aging population wanting relaxing vacations with scenic beauty coupled with the fact that Alaska is a U.S. destination.

Westmark Hotels consists of 16 hotels in Alaska and the Yukon territories and also provides synergy with cruise operations and Westours. Westmark is the largest group of hotels in the region providing moderately priced rooms for the vacationer.

Windstar Sail Cruises was acquired by Holland America Lines in 1988 and consists of three computer-controlled sailing vessels with a berth capacity of 444. Windstar is very upscale and offers an alternative to traditional cruise liners with a more intimate, activity-oriented cruise. The ships operate primarily in the Mediterranean and the South Pacific, visiting ports not accessible to large cruise ships. Although catering to a small segment of the cruise vacation industry, Windstar helps with Carnival's commitment to participate in all segments of the cruise industry.

Seabourn Cruise Lines

In April 1992, the company acquired 25 percent of the capital stock of Seabourn. As part of the transaction, the company also made a subordinated secured 10-year loan of $15 million and a $10 million convertible loan to Seabourn. In December 1995, the $10 million convertible loan was converted by the company into an additional 25 percent equity interest in Seabourn.

Seabourn targets the luxury market with three vessels providing 200 passengers per ship with all-suite accommodations. Seabourn is considered the "Rolls Royce" of the cruise industry and in 1992 was named the "World's Best Cruise Line" by the prestigious Condé Nast Traveler's Fifth Annual Reader's Choice poll. Seabourn cruises the Americas, Europe, Scandinavia, the Mediterranean, and the Far East.

Airtours

In April 1996, the company acquired a 29.5 percent interest in Airtours for approximately $307 million. Airtours and its subsidiaries is the largest air-inclusive tour operator in the world and is publicly traded on the London Stock Exchange. Airtours provides air-inclusive packaged holidays to the British,

Scandinavian, and North American markets. Airtours provides holidays to approximately 5 million people per year and owns or operates 32 hotels, two cruise ships, and 31 aircraft.

Airtours operates 18 aircraft (one additional aircraft is scheduled to enter service in the spring of 1997) exclusively for its U.K. tour operators, providing a large proportion of its flying requirements. In addition, Airtours' subsidiary Premiair operates a fleet of 13 aircraft (one additional aircraft is also scheduled to enter service in the spring of 1997) that provides most of the flying requirements for Airtours' Scandinavian tour operators.

Airtours owns or operates 32 hotels (6,500 rooms) which provide rooms to Airtours' tour operators principally in the Mediterranean and the Canary Islands. In addition, Airtours has a 50 percent interest in Tenerife Sol, a joint venture with Sol Hotels Group of Spain that owns and operates three additional hotels in the Canary Islands, providing 1,300 rooms.

Through its subsidiary Sun Cruises, Airtours owns and operates two cruise ships. Both the 800-berth MS *Seawing* and the 1,062-berth MS *Carousel* commenced operations in 1995. Recently, Airtours acquired a third ship, the MS *Sundream*, the sister ship of the MS *Carousel*. The MS *Sundream* is expected to commence operations in May 1997. The ships operate in the Mediterranean, the Caribbean, and around the Canary Islands and are sold exclusively by Airtours' tour operators.

Joint Venture with Hyundai Merchant Marine Co. Ltd.

In September 1996, Carnival and Hyundai Merchant Marine Co. Ltd. signed an agreement to form a 50/50 joint venture to develop the Asian cruise vacation market. Each have contributed $4.8 million as the initial capital of the joint venture. In addition, in November 1996 Carnival sold the cruise ship *Tropicale* to the joint venture for approximately $95.5 million cash. Carnival then chartered the vessel from the joint venture until the joint venture is ready to begin cruise operations in the Asian market, targeting a start date in or around the spring of 1998. The joint venture borrowed the $95.5 million purchase price from a financial institution and Carnival and HMM each guaranteed 50 percent of the borrowed funds.

FUTURE CONSIDERATIONS

Carnival's management will have to continue to monitor several strategic factors and issues for the next few years. The industry should experience further consolidation through mergers and buyouts, and the expansion of the industry could negatively affect the profitability of various cruise operators. Another factor of concern to management is how to reach the large North American market, of which only 5 to 7 percent have taken a cruise.

With the industry maturing, cruise competitors have become more sophisticated in their marketing efforts and price competition is the norm in most cruise segments. (For a partial listing of major industry competitors, see Exhibit 7). Royal Caribbean Cruise Lines has also instituted a major shipbuilding program and is successfully challenging Carnival Cruise Lines in the contemporary segment. The announcement that the Walt Disney Company will be

EXHIBIT 7 *Major Industry Competitors*

Celebrity Cruises, 5200 Blue Lagoon Drive, Miami FL 33126

Celebrity Cruises operates four modern cruise ships on four-, seven-, and ten-day cruises to Bermuda, the Caribbean, the Panama Canal, and Alaska. Celebrity attracts first-time cruisers as well as seasoned cruisers. Purchased by Royal Caribbean on July 30, 1997.

Costa Cruise Lines, World Trade Center, 80m Southwest 8th Street, Miami FL 33131

Costa promotes itself as the Italian cruise line offering a strictly Italian experience. Costa has six refurbished ships and two modern cruise liners that offer Caribbean and Mediterranean cruises for seven days or longer. Costa's mix of ships and destinations appeal to a wide spectrum of people: first-time cruisers, young adults, and seasoned cruise passengers.

Norwegian Cruise Lines, 95 Merrick Way, Coral Gables FL 33134

Norwegian Cruise Lines (NCL), formerly Norwegian Caribbean Lines, was the first to base a modern fleet of cruise ships in the Port of Miami. It operates six modern cruise liners on three-, four-, and seven-day eastern and western Caribbean cruises and cruises to Bermuda. A wide variety of activities and entertainment attracts a diverse array of customers.

Premier Cruise Lines, P.O. Box 573, Cape Canaveral FL 32930

A former subsidiary of the Greyhound Corporation, Premier operates two refurbished cruise ships and was the official cruise line of Walt Disney World. Premier offers three- or four-day Caribbean cruises. Premier attracts families with children as well as traditional cruise passengers.

Princess Cruises, 10100 Santa Monica Boulevard, Los Angeles CA 90067

Princess Cruises, with its fleet of nine "Love Boats," offers seven-day and extended cruises to the Caribbean, Alaska, Canada, Africa, the Far East, South America, and Europe. Princess's primary market is the upscale 50-plus experienced traveler, according to Mike Hannan, senior vice president for marketing services. Princess ships have an ambiance best described as casual elegance and are famous for their Italian-style dining rooms and onboard entertainment.

Royal Caribbean Cruise Lines, 1050 Caribbean Way, Miami, FL 33132

RCCL's nine ships have consistently been given high marks by passengers and travel agents over the past 21 years. RCCL's ships are built for the contemporary market, are large and modern, and offer three-, four-, and seven-day as well as extended cruises. RCCL prides itself on service and exceptional cuisine. With the purchase of Celebrity, RCCL became the largest cruise line in the world.

Other Industry Competitors (Partial List)

American Hawaii Cruises	(2 Ships—Hawaiian Islands)
Club Med	(2 Ships—Europe, Caribbean)
Commodore Cruise Line	(1 Ship—Caribbean)
Cunard Line	(8 Ships—Caribbean, Worldwide)
Dolphin Cruise Line	(3 Ships—Caribbean, Bermuda)
Radisson Seven Seas Cruises	(3 Ships—Worldwide)
Royal Olympic Cruises	(6 Ships—Caribbean, Worldwide)
Royal Cruise Line	(4 Ships—Caribbean, Alaska, WW)

Source: Cruise Line International Association, 1996.

entering the cruise market with two 80,000-ton cruise liners by 1998 should significantly affect the "family" cruise vacation segment.

With competition intensifying, industry observers believe that the number of failures, mergers, buyouts, and strategic alliances will increase. Regency Cruises ceased operations on October 29, 1995, and filed for Chapter 11 bankruptcy. American Family Cruises, a spinoff from Costa Cruise Lines, failed to reach the family market and Carnival's Fiestamarina failed to reach the Spanish-speaking market. EffJohn International sold its Commodore Cruise subsidiary to a group of Miami-based investors that chartered one of its two ships to World Explorer Cruises/Semester At Sea. Sun Cruise Lines merged with Epirotiki Cruise Line under the name of Royal Olympic Cruises, and Cunard bought the Royal Viking Line and its name from Kloster Cruise Ltd. with one ship of its fleet being transferred to Kloster's Royal Cruise Line. All of these failures, mergers, and buyouts occurred in 1995, which was not an unusual year for changes in the cruise line industry.

The increasing industry capacity is also a source of concern to cruise operators. The slow growth in industry demand is occurring during a period when industry berth capacity continues to grow. The entry of Disney and the ships already on order by current operators will increase industry berth capacity by over 10,000 per year for the next three years, a significant increase. The danger lies in cruise operators using "price" as a weapon in their marketing campaigns to fill cabins. If cruise operators cannot make a reasonable return on investment, operating costs will have to be reduced (affecting quality of services) to remain profitable. This will increase the likelihood of further industry acquisitions, mergers, and consolidation. A worst case scenario would be the financial failure of weaker lines.

Still, Carnival's management believes that demand should increase during the remainder of the 1990s. Considering that only 5 to 7 percent of the North American market has taken a cruise vacation, reaching more of the North American target market would improve industry profitability. Industry analysts state that the problem is that an "assessment of market potential" is only an "educated guess." What if the current demand figures are reflective of the future?

China Eastern Airlines: Building an International Airline

Deborah Clyde-Smith
Peter J. Williamson

China Europe International Business School

Our objective is to make China Eastern an international airline. In six years' time, I want to see the China Eastern symbol everywhere; we must have a good global route network with more than 50% of our revenues coming from international routes.

With these words, Mr. Wang Li An, chairman of the board of China Eastern Air Group and president of China Eastern Airlines (CEA), set a challenging mission for the company. While CEA was already the 11th most profitable airline in the world, it was still relatively small compared to international giants such as American, United, British Airways, Air France, and Lufthansa. CEA's international route network was also limited. But it was already planning new routes to Vietnam, France, Germany, and Australia. Management also believed that CEA's planned flotation on the New York Stock Exchange would help increase its international visibility and stature as well as providing a new source of capital for expansion. CEA had made large strides in improving the quality of its operations and service, both on the ground and in the air, putting it in the forefront of Chinese airlines. It was planning the acquisition of new aircraft and strengthening the skills of its people through training at all levels. The question facing

management was what else would be necessary to ensure CEA could win market share in the international aviation industry—one of the most difficult businesses in the world in which to build and maintain a strong and consistently profitable position?

HISTORY OF THE INTERNATIONAL AVIATION INDUSTRY

The first flight was made by the Wright brothers in 1903; it was not until after the First World War, however, in 1919, that the first commercial airlines began to develop. These early entrepreneurs rapidly discovered that they could not survive without subsidies, mail contracts, or some kind of government support. Following the first transatlantic flight, realisation of the potential of this new form of international travel led to the Convention of Paris and later the Geneva Air Convention establishing for each state "complete and exclusive sovereignty over the airspace above its territory."

The various small airlines that developed in Europe now began to merge under their national flags. In 1933, the French government imposed the merger through which Air France was formed, and in 1938 the British government bought Imperial and British Airways and merged them to form BOAC. In Germany, several small airlines combined as Deutsche

This case was developed as the basis for class discussion rather than to illustrate either effective or ineffective handling of an administrative situation. Copyright © 1996 by China Europe International Business School.

Luft Hansa, which spearheaded the formation of the IATA, the international organisation with responsibility for coordination of schedules and the establishment of an air traffic code. In America, meanwhile, the first regular airmail service was set up by Bill Boeing, and by 1930, there were four major airlines in existence: United, American, Eastern, and TWA. During the Second World War, with Europe unable to compete, Boeing and Pan Am were able to establish a position of supremacy in the North Atlantic.

Following the war, a revived IATA became the centre of controversy regarding the new airline industry and the extent to which it should be government controlled, with each government desiring to protect its own airline in the interests of security and trade. In the 1950s, the industry boomed, but the development of efficient and inexpensive air travel in Europe was hindered by national interests and political division, while the Americans were rapidly developing new routes and advancing technology. In 1958, the Pan Am 707's inaugural flight ushered in the international jet age; in 1962, British Airways and Air France collaborated to produce the first supersonic jet, while Pan Am introduced the jumbo jet.

Between 1938 and 1978, the U.S. airline industry was controlled by a regulatory system with the chief concern of "public convenience and necessity," resulting in a system of limited competition and little incentive to improve efficiency. In 1978, the Airline Deregulation Act began the process of removing restrictions on route entry and exit; it was virtually finished by the end of 1981. By 1982, the deregulation of pricing was also complete.

With a huge increase in competition, deregulation meant, for the large carriers, an initial loss of market share, though by 1988 this trend had been reversed. In the early years, the best performers were former local service and intrastate carriers. Of the many new entrants into the market, some very aggressive, it was estimated in 1986 that two out of three had gone out of business. Some established national carriers went bankrupt; overall, the number of carriers reporting data to the U.S. Department of Transportation fell from 106 in 1985 to less than 70 by 1988. Since 1978, fares have fallen by an average of 20 percent in real terms, and up to 35 percent for long-haul routes. Industry financial results, which had reached a record $1.2 billion net income in 1978, dropped considerably following deregulation.

In Europe, from the Second World War until the 1980s, the airline industry was tightly regulated and noncompetitive. Most airlines were government owned, and governments fixed route access and fares bilaterally between themselves. In 1986, as part of the creation of the single market, the European Commission launched a three-stage liberalisation policy to open up the protected market, with consequent competition in pricing and service. Restrictive ownership rules were relaxed to allow foreign carriers to buy stakes in former national airlines, and Brussels tightened up on allowing governments to bale out their national airlines in times of trouble. Deregulation will be complete in June 1997, and by then, airlines in Europe will be allowed to fly without restriction within the single market, as well as being permitted access to all ancillary service activities. In addition, non-EU carriers and ground service providers have been able to compete in previously closed markets, a development of which North American companies in particular have taken advantage. If Europe follows the American example, deregulation will mean a proliferation of new services, with increased price and cost pressures necessitating productivity improvements. Fares are expected to fall sharply in the late 1990s; domestic German fares fell by around 20 percent in the first quarter of 1996 after price cutting by Lufthansa, which was anxious to protect its market share.

THE COMPETITIVE ENVIRONMENT IN THE 1990s

Since the 1970s, the airline industry has been subject to large swings in profitability (see Exhibit 1).

Air travel grew by 7 percent a year in the 20 years after 1970, but in 1990, the world's airlines lost a combined $2.7 billion on scheduled international services alone. In 1991, following the Gulf War, losses were close to $4 billion, and air travel worldwide declined for the first time since 1945. By 1994, following the oil embargo and the onset of a severe recession, the world's airlines had lost $15.6 billion, more than the profits earned over 75 years of international services. Problems are exacerbated by the tendency to invest heavily in aircraft during the good years, which then lie idle during hard times. In 1992,

EXHIBIT 1 *Profit Record of the International Airline Industry (IATA International Scheduled Operations)*

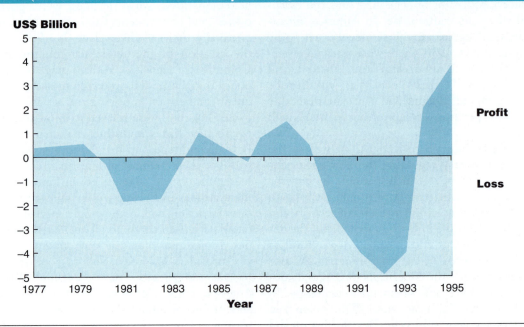

more than 1,000 aircraft, or 10 percent of the world's commercial fleet, were parked out of use. Nonetheless, forecasts continued to be bullish, with the industry anticipating a growth of 5 percent per year in air travel worldwide for the next 20 years, with new markets like Asia helping push up the overall figures.

Currently, the largest players in the world market were the American corporations, with American Airlines at the top of the list with more than $15 billion of sales, carrying over 150 million passengers a year. United and Delta were almost as large. In Europe, Lufthansa occupied the top slot, with sales of over $10 billion (global rank 4) followed by Air France, BA, and SAS, while in the Asia/Pacific region, Japan Airlines was globally ranked 7 with sales of over $8 billion, followed by All Nippon, Singapore Airlines, and Qantas.

RELATIVE SIZE OF DIFFERENT MARKETS

By 2000, the U.S. domestic market was still expected to be the largest with almost 840 billion RPKs. The market inside Asia, however, was expected to be number two in size at over 570 billion RPKs. Forecasts suggested that the Trans-Pacific market would be next largest at over 300 billion RPKs (Exhibit 2). The Trans-Pacific, Asian, and Europe-Asia markets were expected to grow the fastest (Exhibit 3).

Overall airline profit figures conceal the fact that some airlines are making healthy profits while others incur big losses. In Europe, for example, British Airways, the largest carrier of international passengers, has been successfully adapting to changes in the world market. Following privatisation, BA cut its workforce by one third between 1981 and 1984 while simultaneously adapting its management style to improve motivation, thus achieving a competitive edge over many protected and consequently less efficient European rivals. Between 1987 and 1991, BA's European turnover grew by approximately one-third, and Asian turnover by 50 percent. In contrast, Air France requested a Ffr 20 billion state aid package in 1994, prompting protests to the European commission by seven European airlines, including BA. Studies confirm that privately or partially privately owned airlines in Europe are performing best, while state-owned carriers lag behind.

EXHIBIT 2 *Major World Airline Markets (Billion RPKs)*
(McDonnell Douglas Forecasts as of 2000)

771 = Rest of the World

Laggards are therefore being forced to restructure and improve services as well as cutting costs, not only by the European Commission, but by passengers, who have less loyalty to flag carriers than governments do. Lufthansa, for example, entered on a three-year "life-saving" reorganisation plan in 1993, cutting the workforce by 17 percent and unit costs by 15 percent. Productivity rose by 31 percent in two

EXHIBIT 3 *Annual Average Passenger Growth Rate (RPKs)*
(McDonnell Douglas Forecasts to 2011)

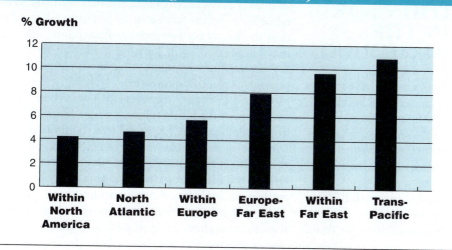

EXHIBIT 4 *Comparative Performance of Some Major Airlines*

Airline	Reporting Date	Return on Sales, %	Asset Turnover (Times p.a)	Return on Capital Employed, %*
British Airways	Mar 95	10.3	0.95	9.7
Lufthansa	Dec 94	4.4	1.59	6.9
KLM	Mar 95	11.9	0.72	8.5
Singapore Airlines	Mar 95	14.8	0.70	10.4
Cathay Pacific	Dec 94	15.5	0.73	11.3
Qantas	Jun 95	7.5	1.33	9.9
American Airlines	Dec 94	6.4	1.19	7.3
Delta Airlines	Jun 95	6.2	1.90	11.8
US Air	Dec 94	−5.9	1.94	−11.5

Source: Computed from Airlines' Annual Reports.
*Pre-tax

years, and the chairman predicted group turnover to grow by 5 percent per year until 1997, with plans to lift market share from 16.7 percent to over 20 percent. Exhibit 4 provides comparative performance statistics for some of the world's major airlines.

Slot constraints pose a further problem for airlines attempting to compete on existing routes; many of the airports in Europe, the United States, and Asia are heavily congested. This combined with overburdened air traffic control systems hinder new competitors from obtaining the take-off and landing slots needed to launch competing services. Airlines already established in a particular airport naturally fight to retain their slots, especially at peak times.

THE COMPETITION FOR PASSENGERS IN THE INTERNATIONAL MARKET

In the face of tough competition, airlines have various means at their disposal to win passengers. Service remains a key issue, despite a changing customer profile, with less business travel and more leisure passengers concerned chiefly with cheap fares. Frequent flyer programmes took off throughout the industry after American Airlines introduced its AAdvantage scheme in 1981. The computer reservations system (CRS) first developed approximately 30 years ago is now a powerful marketing tool that is indispensable to the travel

industry, while computerised structuring of fares and yield management help to maximise revenue.

Passenger mix has changed over the years in a way that adversely affects airline profits: the proportion of business travellers, who comprise the majority of those paying first- or business-class fares, fell from 52 percent in 1982 to 40 percent in 1994, and continues to decline. Exhibit 5 provides an example of the revenue contribution from different seat classes.

Customer Service

In an environment where one airline can mostly resemble all the rest, service can be crucial. Research by Singapore Airlines showed that where all other factors are equal, passengers respond most favourably to quality service. Singapore Airlines' aim was to establish this airline from a small island republic as the best in the world for service. Passengers, management impressed upon staff, were after all the reason for the airline's existence. A consequent high emphasis was placed on cabin crew training, ground services, and in-flight comforts—SIA was the first airline to provide fully reclining seats. Since SIA was not a member of IATA, it was free to ignore its rules concerning free drinks, movie headsets, and other extras. The airline has become one of the world's largest and most profitable, winning many accolades for service from travel organisations.

Service improvement has been aided by technological innovation: large-screen in-flight movies are

EXHIBIT 5 *Passenger Mix and Revenue Structure**

	British Airways		Virgin Atlantic	
Class	No. Seats	% Revenue	No. Seats	% Revenue
First	18	15%		
Upper Class			50	47%
Club Class	70	32%		
Mid-Class				
(Previously Economy)			38	14%
Economy	282	53%	271	39%

*British Airways versus Virgin Atlantic, fully loaded, London-New York flight, 1994.

C-139

being replaced by individual television screens offering a menu of different entertainment, and interactive systems are being developed to enable the traveller to communicate by telephone or fax with offices, services, and companies throughout the world. Technology has personalised service, with passengers' individual requirements being catered to using a database and information system through which they can be identified by staff. Customer loyalty is now the target, rather than simple satisfaction with service.

Computer Reservations Systems

In the United States, the longest established CRS market, an estimated 95 percent of travel agencies are linked to at least one CRS, 88 percent of all tickets are issued through a CRS, and 75 percent of tickets are bought through a travel agent. The systems are owned by airlines, and while theoretically they could give equal access to the flights of all airlines, they are in practice a sophisticated marketing tool used to promote the flights of certain carriers over those of their rivals. Some are owned by a single airline—American Airlines' Sabre, market leader in the United States with about 40 percent market share—others by a consortium of airlines, such as Galileo, owned by 11 U.S. and European airlines with a 30 percent share of the worldwide market. The big networks are becoming increasingly globally oriented: in Europe, individual countries' reservation systems are being replaced by the two rival European CRS operators (Galileo and Amadeus, operated by Lufthansa, Air France, and Iberia and linked to Worldspan, owned by Delta, Northwest, and TWA and to Abacus, run by a group of Asian carriers).

Frequent Flyer Programmes (FFPs)

First introduced by American Airlines in 1981, these incentive schemes have grown enormously popular: by 1985, FFP membership in the United States was estimated at 7.4 million, and by 1993 was around 30 million. Basically offering free flights in exchange for mileage accrual, the schemes build loyalty to a particular airline, while the database of information gathered about frequent travellers is valuable for marketing. An otherwise empty seat can be used as a marketing tool to reward customer loyalty: however, there are drawbacks, and many airlines question the effect of the schemes on revenue yields. In the United States, they push up airline costs by some $5 billion a year. There is a technical possibility of an overwhelming number of miles being claimed at once, forcing an airline into bankruptcy (which carriers strive to avoid by rules limiting when free flights can be taken). Smaller and new airlines cite problems of stifled competition and lack of market access. The newer European and Asian programmes are more cautious in approach than their American counterparts, tending to limit rewards to higher-yield first- and business-class passengers.

Fare Structure and Yield Management Systems

At a basic level, airlines attempt to fill every seat on each plane at the highest possible fare; any empty seat represents a loss. Revenue management systems are sophisticated computer programmes which can represent the difference between profit and loss for airlines operating on tight margins. Each flight has many different fares allocated to it, and these are constantly updated by the computer so that in times of peak demand fewer inexpensive seats are available, and vice versa. Major events that might increase travel demand to a particular location are taken into account, and the systems also check on rivals' fares. Various restrictions are usually applied to cheaper fares which make them less flexible and therefore less attractive to business customers.

Controlling Costs and Improving Productivity

The cost structure of a typical international airline is detailed in Exhibit 6. By comparison to the international average, China Eastern's crew (labour) costs and ground handling costs were lower (around 6 percent and 10 percent of total costs, respectively); fuel and aircraft depreciation and financing costs were significantly higher (at around 25 percent and 20 percent of total costs, respectively); while other cost components were broadly similar to the international average as a percentage of total costs. In addition to the obvious costs such as fuel, crew, and maintenance, sales costs accounted for around 20 percent of total costs.

Once an airline committed to serve a particular route and decided on flight frequency, a high percentage of the total costs were fixed. Profitability was therefore very sensitive to "load factors" (the percentage of passenger seats and cargo capacity filled). The load factor for international, scheduled flights

typically varied between an average of 60 percent up to 70 percent (see Exhibit 7).

To cut costs in a deregulated market, U.S. airlines built up large networks on a hub and spoke basis, pulling in passengers from smaller cities to larger hubs to reroute them to the more lucrative long-haul and international flights. Hubs typically generate 20 percent more revenue per plane than a comparable point-to-point flight. In Europe, smaller airlines operating out of hubs which dominate their national market but have limited international or long-haul capacity can ally with airlines with larger networks with an interest in exploiting their particular market segment.

Noncore functions such as cleaning and aircraft maintenance were increasingly being contracted out. Some major airlines now use independent caterers, which could lead to savings of up to 30 percent.

INTERNATIONAL AIRLINE ALLIANCES

In 1995, there were 401 alliances in the airline industry worldwide, twice as many as in 1991. Of these, 70 percent were national or regional arrangements, but 133 involved intercontinental links. Such links facilitate the globalisation of an industry that still is constrained by intergovernment agreements and state ownership of big carriers. These links allow airlines, by coordination with others, to offer a network of routes well beyond their own capacity, with consequent increase in revenue.

EXHIBIT 6 *Typical Airline Cost Structure*

Cost Element	% Total Cost
Crew	15
Fuel	15
Maintenance	12
Aircraft (depreciation and financing)	8
Catering	5
Ground Services—hub	10
—other end	10
Sales—own organisation	10
—commission	10
Administration	5

Source: McKinsey Quarterly 1994, no. 4.

EXHIBIT 7 *Average Load Factors for IATA Member Airlines International Scheduled Operations*

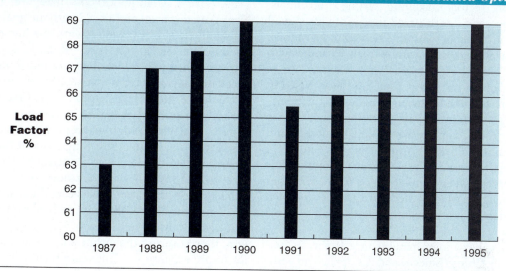

Source: IATA.

C-141

There are disadvantages, however, in terms both of passenger satisfaction with these arrangements and that of the airlines themselves: according to a study conducted by the Boston Consulting Group, less than 40 percent of regional and 30 percent of international alliances have been successful, for reasons ranging from difference in objectives to varying standards on flights.

One example of a successful partnership, initiated in 1992, is that of KLM and Northwest, in which KLM has a 25 percent stake. The developing and marketing of a joint identity and coordinating timetables increased their combined market share across the Atlantic from 7 to 11 percent, with revenue and cost saving benefits of $300 million per year, enabling Northwest to turn a $60 million loss in 1991 into a $830 million profit the following year.

The Boston Consulting Group study cites the most successful alliances as KLM/Northwest, BA/US Air/Qantas, Delta/Swissair/Singapore Airlines, and Lufthansa/United, suggesting that the more successful alliances go beyond coordination in marketing and networks to include equity stakes.

Code Sharing

The basis of most alliances is code sharing, by which airlines use the same code letters in front of flight numbers so that, for example, British Airways flights link via a hub in North America to those of US Air, in which it has a 24.6 percent stake, but the flight is listed on computer as a BA flight throughout.

For the customer, this supposedly means easier travel, with less complicated connections avoiding baggage transfer and so on, although in practice passengers are not always happy to find themselves on a different airline than they thought they had booked, especially if they consider its service to be inferior. For the airline, however, pooling traffic on less popular routes with a partner means cost reduction without loss of all the revenue, and enables it to ensnare passengers for feeder flights at both ends of long-haul routes by giving the impression of having a much larger network than is actually the case.

LINKS BETWEEN FOREIGN AIRLINES AND CHINA'S AVIATION INDUSTRY

China is the world's third largest aviation market, after the United States and Japan, with traffic growing by more than 20 percent a year, and with development and safety problems consequent upon rapid expansion of the industry. It recently announced that its aviation sector, including airlines, terminals, maintenance, and catering facilities, was to be opened to foreign investment (with a 35 percent upper limit), and several foreign airlines now plan alliances with China.

BA is cooperating with China Southern, based in Guangzhou and one of the eight largest Chinese airlines using Western aircraft. It has embarked on a joint engineering venture with China Southern and is discussing engineering, pilot training, and CRS with Shanghai-based China Eastern, hoping ultimately to forge an agreement with a Chinese carrier to coordinate services at Beijing. Qantas, in which BA has a stake, has also been targeting small regional airlines.

Lufthansa has a joint maintenance facility at Beijing with Air China (Ameco) and has opened an aeronautical training centre and shopping, office, and hotel complex in the city.

Singapore Airlines, Cathay Pacific, and Japan Airlines have invested in a maintenance facility with Xiamen Airlines south of Shanghai. SIA provides technical cooperation with regional airlines and has a stake in ground handling and catering services in Beijing.

China is seen as an area for enormous potential growth, and other links between Chinese and foreign airlines and service organisations are bound to follow.

POTENTIAL LESSONS FROM A SUCCESSFUL ENTRANT

In beginning the process of internationalising China Eastern, Mr. Wang Li An and his team examined the experience of a number of international airlines including carriers such as Singapore Airlines and JAL for whom China Eastern supplied ground handling services in Shanghai. As a new company entering the international arena, they were also interested in the lessons to be learned from the experience of other new entrants. Many newcomers to the international market, such as Braniff, People Express, and Air Europe, had rapidly run into problems, disappearing from the business altogether. One demonstrably successful entrant into the international market was Virgin Atlantic Airways.

Created by business tycoon Richard Branson in 1984, Virgin Atlantic Airways' inaugural flight to New York departed on June 22 with the goal of "providing all classes of travellers with the highest quality travel at the lowest cost." Branson knew little about the airline business, but assembled an experienced management team that he infused with his love of challenge and determination. In its first 10 years, the airline survived the worst recession in aviation history, achieving a high market profile and becoming Britain's second largest long-haul airline.

From 1986 to 1990, Virgin Atlantic expanded in a controlled fashion, with one new route of a profitable long-haul nature per year. The airline lost £14.5 million in 1992, enough to bankrupt it, but in that year Branson sold Virgin Music for £560 million, thus covering the airline's losses and providing for future expansion. (This was a relatively small loss compared with some of the major carriers; of the top six airlines, only BA was earning a profit.) In 1994, Virgin expanded its fleet with six new aircraft, commenced services to Hong Kong and San Francisco, and hired 1,000 additional employees.

The early routes were from London's Gatwick Airport to New York (Newark 1984, JFK 1988), Miami (1986), Boston (1987), and Orlando (1988). In 1989, Virgin commenced flights to Tokyo, and in 1990 to Los Angeles. In 1991, Virgin was allotted slots at London's Heathrow Airport, ending the commercial disadvantage of being confined to the smaller Gatwick. Proposed new routes include Washington, Chicago, Auckland, Singapore, Sydney, and Johannesburg.

Innovation

Branson's flamboyant style played a great part in the establishment of his airline: he used himself in various publicity stunts to promote Virgin Atlantic at every possible opportunity. The airline's image was one of informality and originality, the aim being to stand out from other services by making journeys memorable and fun. Virgin concentrated on in-flight entertainment, originally with Sony Watchmans and later by pioneering individual video screens. The services of a tailor or beauty therapist were occasionally employed, and Virgin also focused on medical requirements and on special requests—birthday cakes, champagne for newlyweds, etc. Branson introduced motorcycle rides to Heathrow for upper-class passengers—a novelty service. In 1993, the Virgin Clubhouse lounge was opened at Heathrow, providing a variety of services and comforts for passengers. It proved to be extremely popular.

Building Customer Value

In customer's minds, Virgin stands for value for their money, but according to a recent survey, is also seen as "friendly," "high quality," "fun," and "innovative." With the aim of exceeding passengers' expectations at all times, Virgin initially established itself as an economical airline appealing to the young, but since profitability depended on higher-yield business passengers, it subsequently concentrated on attracting the corporate travellers. By being able to serve both demanding executives and leisure passengers on the same flight better than its competitors, Virgin succeeded in attracting a wide range of customers, and hence attained high-yield factors relatively quickly.

Beginning with a leased second-hand Boeing 747, by Virgin's 10th anniversary, its fleet consisted of eight B747-200s, two B747-400s, and four Airbus 340s. More than half the fleet was then new. Newer planes equalled better service and image.

Service Recovery

Initially operating with a small fleet of older aircraft, Virgin was prone to delays and cancellations. To combat this customer relations disadvantage, importance was placed on prompt action: complaints from upper-class passengers were handled within 24 hours, and from economy class within a week. Dissatisfied passengers were compensated with letters or faxes of apology, free champagne, free tickets, and even occasionally a personal letter from Branson.

Cost Structure

Virgin viewed its modest size in comparison with its rivals as an advantage allowing it to react swiftly and remain innovative. A low cost structure was essential given Virgin's low fares and high level of service, and the airline is characterized by high employee productivity and high load factors in large aircraft. Management style emphasised involvement and interaction, but with strong controls, as attention had to remain on overhead and cost levels. Salaries were relatively low, but Virgin was nevertheless able to at-

tract quality staff because of its image and the importance it placed on keeping employees happy.

Staff Attitude, Productivity, and Commitment

Branson firmly believed involvement by management and staff was vital to success. The ideal employee was "informal but caring" and prepared to express constructive dissatisfaction where appropriate. The philosophy was to stimulate staff into feeling that they made a difference and into making suggestions and taking initiative as much as possible. Branson was much involved personally in discussing ideas and innovations with staff, and his presence and enthusiasm kept morale high and attitudes positive. As the airline gets older, however, it inevitably becomes vulnerable to decreasing employee motivation and enthusiasm, as it becomes more of a challenge to remain innovative, and staff may be attracted by the prestige and higher salaries of bigger airlines.

Pricing Strategy

"Offering a first class service at less than first class fares" became Virgin's slogan. The original idea was of a two-tier service, with upper-class offering many of the features of first class, but at business class prices, thus attracting both classes away from other airlines. At the same time, economy class targeted price-conscious leisure passengers. As previously discussed, a midclass was subsequently introduced when it was discovered that a high percentage of economy class passengers were in fact travelling on business.

Alliances

In 1990, Virgin launched its frequent flyer programme, Virgin Freeway, operated in partnership with SAS and other international groups. SAS also had a 35 percent stake in another Freeway partner, British Midland, into which Virgin delivered considerable traffic. These links were to enable Virgin to compete with British Airways. In April 1994, Virgin's first alliance with a major international airline, Delta, was announced. Delta bought a percentage of Virgin's seats on certain routes, which it was to price and sell independently. This alliance gave Delta Heathrow access, boosted Virgin's annual revenue by

$150 million, and greatly increased its number of U.S. destinations.

In 1994, Virgin announced a Heathrow-Sydney service in partnership with Australian-based Ansett Airlines, and in 1996 a partnership with Malaysia Airlines for a London-Kuala Lumpur route was announced.

BUILDING AN INTERNATIONAL AIRLINE

In mid-1996 it was announced that the delayed flotation of China Eastern Airlines would go forward with listings planned for the Hong Kong and New York stock exchanges. It was expected that a maximum of 35 percent of the equity would be offered for sale. China Eastern's operations continued to perform well. It would soon take delivery of three new, state-of-the-art Airbus A340 long-range aircraft. The planning for new routes to Vietnam, France, Germany, Australia, and additional cities in the United States and increased flights to Southeast Asia was underway. The company was also planning to invest around US $100 million in establishing a new base

at the new Shanghai airport being constructed in the Padong development zone. This was due for completion in 1999.

In meeting its ambitious targets for internationalisation, management was concerned about maintaining the airline's strong financial performance, with the added need to meet the stringent standards of the international financial markets following flotation. They also recognised that it was a time-consuming and challenging task to build employees' skills and adopt the advanced technology and management systems necessary to compete on the international market.

Successful international expansion involved much more than simply adding new aircraft and additional routes. How would customer service need to be further advanced? What role would innovations in computer reservations systems and yield management systems play? Should China Eastern consider entering alliances with international airlines for various aspects of its business, including possible code sharing and participation in frequent flyer schemes as well as operational areas? What would be the critical strategies and decisions to allow China Eastern to develop a large and successful international airline of which China would justly be proud?

Ciba-Geigy and Chiron: Partnerships Between Firms in the Pharmaceutical and Biotechnology Industries

Shelley Howell   Basilios A. Strmec   Jenny Wacker

In early October 1994, Chiron Corporation, a biotechnology company, came to a watershed: it must either agree to a 49 percent equity buyout alliance with Ciba-Geigy, a pharmaceutical corporation, or resist the alliance and be subject to tremendous financial pressure. Chiron had only been in existence since 1980 and had just begun to make a name for itself. Would the loss of independence from the buyout be replaced by increased operating efficiencies, or was Chiron foregoing other profitable partnerships by committing to Ciba? Soon after the initial offer on November 21, 1994, the chairmen of Chiron and Ciba announced that the two companies had signed a definitive agreement to form a strategic partnership. In the following month, Ciba purchased 11.9 million shares of Chiron stock for $2.1 billion to raise its ownership stake to 49.9 percent. Chiron issued new stock in exchange for Ciba's international Ciba Corning Diagnostics business and Ciba's 50 percent interest in the Biocine Company and Biocine SpA, which had been joint ventures in vaccines with Chiron.

Under the terms of the agreement, Ciba would guarantee up to $425 million of new debt for Chiron. Additionally, Ciba would provide between $250 and $300 million over five years for support of

research and development (R&D) at Chiron. During these five years, Ciba would not be permitted to purchase additional equity in Chiron, except to maintain its 49.9 percent ownership position. However, after five years, Ciba would have the option to increase its ownership to 55 percent. The agreement would also increase Chiron's board of directors from 8 to 11 members, with Ciba designating the additional three members.[1]

The financial structure Chiron inherited in the agreement could only increase its opportunities in R&D, and the company would benefit from Ciba's strong reputation. Chiron faced many new challenges within the new partnership with Ciba, as well as major ones in its recently expanded environment.

THE BIOTECHNOLOGY INDUSTRY

In the broadest sense, the term *biotechnology* refers to the research of organisms to obtain knowledge and develop products. More precisely, it involves the control of proteins on a molecular level within biological systems to produce specific results. The products obtained from such research range from vaccines and viruses to plasmas and other microbiological substances. Currently, the biotechnology industry can be categorized into four general segments: drugs, gene mapping, generic engineering of food, and genetic criminal identification.

This case was prepared under the direction of Professor Robert E. Hoskisson. The case is intended to be used as the basis for class discussion rather than to illustrate either effective or ineffective handling of an administrative situation.

In the 1990s, industry research concentrated on drugs and genetic mapping. Drugs developed by biotechnology companies have already helped people suffering from cystic fibrosis, heart disease, and hepatitis. Additionally, improvements have been made in efforts to cure fatal diseases such as cancer and AIDS. Achievements in gene mapping made significant contributions to the discovery and creation of these drugs. In the early 1980s, scientists had mapped only 40 genes in the human genome. However, by the early 1990s, this number increased to nearly 4,000. Mapping the entire human genome will help scientists to understand the origins of diseases and how they may be treated or even prevented.[2]

Industry Development

The concept of biotechnology originated around 7000 B.C. when people manipulated bacteria to produce food and beverages through the fermentation process. However, the biotechnology industry only recently took form and is still considered to be in its infancy. The formation of the industry followed the breakthrough discovery in 1953 of the structure of deoxyribonucleic acid (DNA) by American James Watson and Englishman Francis Crick. DNA is the genetic material controlling protein synthesis within a cell that is passed from one generation to the next. By understanding the structure of DNA, scientists were able to understand how cells produce proteins, and they then could develop theories about and methods of dealing with the manipulation of proteins. This discovery essentially created the biotechnology industry.

Another significant breakthrough occurred in 1973 when Stanley Cohen and Herbert Boyer created recombinant DNA by successfully splicing an individual piece of DNA and inserting it into a foreign piece of DNA. This genetic engineering method eventually allowed scientists to mass-produce valuable products such as hormones. The biotechnology industry experienced tremendous growth in the late 1980s largely due to the U.S. Supreme Court ruling allowing genetically engineered bacteria to be patented.[3] After this ruling, the United States emerged as the global leader in biotechnology with the United Kingdom in second position.

As U.S. biotech companies rushed to produce new products, they began to receive additional competition from other countries including France, Germany, and Japan. This surge of growth and activity in biotechnology was due largely to an increase in available capital. Investors, eagerly hoping for high returns from the next biological breakthrough, sank millions of dollars into the young industry. However, with the stock market crash of 1987 and the investing lull that followed, funding for research in the biotechnology industry declined.

Competition Among Regional Blocks

United States United States companies took an early competitive lead in the biotechnology industry and maintained their global dominance well into the mid-1900s with technological advances and strong capital funding (See Exhibit 1). Sales soared from approximately $3 billion in 1990 to $6 billion in 1992, and then to almost $8 billion in 1994. To maintain pace with this growth, R&D spending more than doubled during this period. Investors limited their capital to the 22 percent of the biotechnology-related companies in the United States that accounted for nearly 95 percent of sales in 1994.[4] However, of the 240 public biotechnology companies surveyed by Re-

EXHIBIT 1 *Leading Countries Ranked By Approximate Number of Biotech-Related Companies Active in the Early 1990s*	
1. United States	1,300 companies
2. Japan	245
3. United Kingdom	160
4. Germany	100
5. France	100

Source: *Encyclopedia of Global Industries,* 1996

combinant Capital, a San Francisco consulting firm, at least 50 percent had only enough cash to operate for 18 months.[5] This turbulent change in financing for smaller biotechnology companies opened the door for many foreign competitors.

Europe As the European leader in the biotechnology industry, the United Kingdom's success was attributed directly to financial markets as well. When the London Stock Exchange allowed biotechnology companies to trade without proving their profitability in 1993, the number of biotech companies increased dramatically. France and Germany challenged the United Kingdom's success in some areas. Large companies in these countries often had subsidiaries or smaller affiliations that benefited from foreign investments.[6]

Japan In the 1980s, Europe and the United States feared that Japan would become a dominant player in the biotechnology industry. Japan did rise to become a threatening competitor in the early 1990s, but its strength has since decreased.[7] As with some European countries, Japan entered the industry after the United States had already established its roots. In contrast to the dominance of small venture companies in the U.S. industry during the 1980s, large diversified companies helped establish the Japanese biotechnology industry. In the 1990s, many of these large companies formed alliances with U.S. companies for joint R&D. Experienced U.S. business leaders feared that these alliances would benefit only the Japanese and that the United States would give up too much of its competitive edge in technology for too little in return.[8]

Although Japan had potential for success, it made few significant contributions to biotechnology. The lack of support and cooperation between research scientists at universities and companies in the industry, as well as the lack of entrepreneurial spirit and speed, hurt the Japanese biotechnology industry. As a result, many biotech companies in Japan abandoned the industry, and the threat of Japan as a dominant competitor diminished.[9]

These three regions directly affected the evolution and development of the biotechnology industry. In aggregate, investors began to renew their interest and optimism in biotechnology in the 1990s as funding increased from $1.2 billion in 1990 to $4.4 billion in 1991.[10] Increased funds also led to increased

competition, and, by 1993, 1,500 biotechnology firms existed in the United States and Europe alone.[11]

Investors finally began to reap profitable returns in the mid-1990s as companies such as Amgen, Genentech, Biogen, and Chiron started to produce marketable products. However, these companies succeeded within a sea of unprofitable firms as industry losses swelled to $3.6 billion in 1993 from $2.2 billion in 1990.[12] Investors became frustrated and doubtful that the industry would ever provide worthwhile returns. They feared that the fragmented industry would result in inefficient duplication of research.[13] It appeared that the industry was headed toward a period of consolidation.

Investors have now shifted their attention away from risky small ventures to large, stable firms with proven experience and, thus, a greater chance of success. As a result, many of the smaller biotechnology companies are turning to larger firms for funding. The number of partnerships, joint ventures, and strategic alliances has increased dramatically in the past few years. Many even look beyond their biotechnology counterparts and seek relationships with companies in related industries, such as pharmaceuticals. According to the *Wall Street Journal*, deals between large pharmaceutical houses and biotechnology firms more than doubled in number in 1994, totaling nearly 200.[14] The 1995 transaction between Chiron and Ciba-Geigy was a typical arrangement.

THE PHARMACEUTICAL INDUSTRY

The pharmaceutical industry, in contrast to the research-centered biotechnology industry, is made up of firms engaged in the development, production, and marketing of "finished-form" drugs for human or veterinary use.[15] Since World War II, the development of life-saving medications has created a huge demand for pharmaceuticals, with high development and marketing costs being offset by patent protection and sophisticated marketing structures. By the early 1990s, the world pharmaceutical preparations market capped $250 billion in global sales, and the industry is still leading all others in the United States in terms of profit.[16] Consistent profits in the industry have been attributed to an aging population and its need for more pharmaceutical products; a growing number, innovation, and diversification of products to treat a greater number of diseases; and continued enhancement of the industry's productivity. Despite these admirable achievements, several concerns currently plague the industry, including the rising costs of R&D, the declining length of effective patent protection, and private and public pressures on profit margins.

Background

Pharmaceutical practice evolved slowly through thousands of years of practical use of herbs, minerals, and other compounds, with the major discoveries of opium and hemlock tracing back to Ancient Greece. Although progress was suppressed by the decline of the Roman Empire and the onset of the Middle Ages, the Renaissance period revived the industry in the late fifteenth century. The discovery of the "New World" introduced new plant-based medications such as belladonna, ipecacuanha, Jesuit's bark, and cocoa. Pharmaceutical practices were professionalized through the establishment of the Society of Apothecaries in London in 1617.

The modern era of the industry may be traced to the development of potent medicinal compounds that could be mass-produced in the nineteenth century. German companies dominated the industry until World War I, when other countries established their own manufacturing and research programs because of hostilities with Germany.[17] Still, Germany became the focal point of the pharmaceutical industry with the ground-breaking discoveries of products such as aspirin and Salvarsan, one of the first disease-specific medicines for treatment of syphilis.

Until World War II, most pharmaceutical companies relied on licensing and marketing agreements as well as joint ventures to access global markets. With increasingly strict import regulations, however, United States companies began to expand internationally by creating overseas affiliates. These subsidiaries imported active ingredients from the U.S. parent company and then converted them into finished products under the laws of the new country. Also out of this post-WWII era came an intense competition to develop, patent, manufacture, and market new drugs. Massive research conducted during the war spawned important pharmaceutical discoveries, including a broad-spectrum antibiotic called chloramphenicol, antidepressants, diuretics, oral contra-

ceptives, and the mass-production of penicillin. These discoveries are cited as having helped to transform the industry from a commodity chemicals business into a field relying heavily on research and marketing investments to achieve the patents and brand names that drive sales.[18]

Pharmaceutical Organization

The two categories of pharmaceutical drugs are prescription (ethical) and over-the-counter (OTC).[19] The world market in 1992 for prescription drugs was estimated at $200 billion, as compared to the $50 billion market for OTC drugs. Governments or consumers pay for prescription drugs indirectly through third parties such as health insurance companies. Prescription drugs are further broken down by their patent status into branded (patented) and generic. In-patent drugs, those with patents that have not expired, account for roughly 70 percent of the world market. These drugs command the highest profit margins but also demand high R&D and marketing expenses, amounting to anywhere from 15 to 24 percent of sales. OTC also includes branded and generic drugs. Branded drugs have the higher share of total sales, although the share for generic drugs rose 3 percent from 1992 to 1994 (see Exhibit 2).[20]

As noted in an *Organization for Economic Cooperations and Development Observer* publication, "Competitive advantage lies in innovation: high R&D costs must mostly be recovered over the short duration of the exclusive patent by means of worldwide marketing." Pharmaceutical firms use this marketing approach to maximize the profit potential of their discoveries. The firms market their drugs through distinct branding, which differentiates the products for targeted general practitioners. The marketing is then supported by a knowledgeable sales force that directs advertising efforts.

Another method of maximizing profit potential is the patent, in which all of the proceeds from the sale of a new drug are reserved for the company responsible for its development. Although the patent life of in-patent drugs often exceeds 15 years, the length of time it takes to obtain government approval often shortens the "payback" period, or effective patent protection. The government's premarket approval became more stringent, and thus lengthier, after the "Thalidomide scare" in 1962, when a drug available in Germany was found to cause severe birth defects

EXHIBIT 2 *OTC Medications Market*

This table shows the change in sales between branded and generic over-the-counter (OTC) drugs. Data are based on total sales of $55.65 billion in 1992, $58.57 billion in 1993, and $62.69 billion in 1994.

	1992	1993	1994
Branded	93%	92%	90%
Generic	7	8	10

Source: *Market Share Reported,* 1997, 664.

during its testing in the United States. Government price constraints on the sale of drugs hindered further the ability of pharmaceutical companies to maximize their profits.

Smaller manufacturers sell out-of-patent drugs under a new brand name at a lower cost after the patent for the original drug has expired. Out-of-patent drugs often face more intense price competition and lower profit margins than patented drugs. In an attempt to gain market control in this competitive environment, larger pharmaceutical companies that manufacture in-patent drugs are creating generic versions of their own patented drugs near the end of the drugs' patent lives. In doing so, these companies beat generic-drug-based competition to the market. This strategy reduces the problems of the shortened effective patent exclusivity brought on by the inefficient and time-consuming approval process.

Over-the-counter drugs include cough and cold remedies, analgesics, digestive aids, skin treatments, and nutritional supplements. The OTC segment demonstrates high advertising and low research costs since few of these are genuinely new. Generic drugs accounted for one-fifth of the total pharmaceutical sales in the early 1990s, and they were predicted to grow 6.3 percent annually from 1992 to 1997. Potential growth stems from the increase in consumer self-diagnosis and self-medication. The transfer of prescription drugs to OTC drugs by the government in an attempt to shift more cost to the patients creates additional opportunity as well.

The U.S. pharmaceutical industry emphasizes the production of biological and botanical products, medicinal chemicals, and pharmaceutical preparations. In 1991, the companies in the industry numbered 750 with a total of 60,000 employees. The industry outperforms most others in the country in terms of key performance ratios and profitability.[21] Several U.S. pharmaceutical companies have man-

aged to minimize their costs by establishing production facilities in Puerto Rico, a location with the advantages of lower taxes and lower labor costs.[22] Despite this, behind the symptom of cost pressure are major changes in the industry's environment that must be considered.

Recent Trends and Environmental Issues: The Health Care Industry

In September 1993, President Clinton introduced his detailed health care plan that would overhaul completely the entire U.S. health care system. Although his plan never passed in Congress, it triggered major changes in the health care industry. Control of the industry is moving away from traditional health care providers such as practicing doctors and hospitals to insurance companies, employers, and other third-party benefit providers. In a time of dramatically increasing health care costs (see Exhibit 3), cost minimization is of utmost importance for these groups. According to Standard and Poor's Industry Surveys, as the health care industry is becoming more and more cost-conscious, "government and third-party payers are increasingly turning to managed-care providers to control health care spending through more judicious utilization of medical products and services and increased pricing pressures."[23] Because these managed-care plans have succeeded in providing quality care at a lower cost, they will become an increasingly significant industry participant in the future. Greater pressure and competition to devise new drugs will gain the attention and support of managed-care officials.[24]

As portions of the health care industry become more selective about drug choices, pharmaceutical companies are realizing that managed-care officials don't want another "me-too" drug comparable to drugs on the market currently and are consequently

EXHIBIT 3 *Health Care Expenditures (in billions of dollars and as a percentage of GDP)*

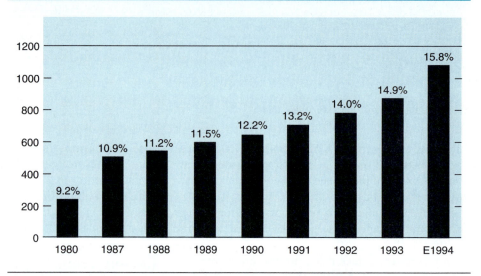

Source: Health Care Financing Administration; Department of Commerce.

spending increasing amounts each year on R&D. Health care officials cannot justify paying high premiums on similar products that are available already. As a result, companies are rushing to discover new and innovative products. R&D spending increased from $2.8 billion in 1990 to $5.7 billion in 1993, and by 1995, the biotechnology industry alone had already exhausted more than $25 billion in capital, most of which was devoted to R&D.[25]

Regulatory Environment: The Food and Drug Administration

Another source of tense, and even controversial, issues is the Food and Drug Administration (FDA). Companies in the U.S. pharmaceutical industry function within a strict regulatory environment. The industry maintains an intricate relationship with regulators that are responsible for protecting the public while simultaneously encouraging business growth. The FDA's regulation of new products demonstrates how the pharmaceutical industry and the federal government are linked at all stages of development.

The FDA is the administrative body responsible for the regulation of the pharmaceutical industry's research, production, and marketing practices. David Kessler, head of the FDA, describes the FDA as "an enforcement agency [with the goal of] keeping unsafe products away from Americans."[26] However, others believe that the FDA should focus more on making new treatments available to sick people as quickly as possible. Currently, the FDA is characterized by a slow approval process which is especially evident when compared to other countries' regulatory agencies. The slow process can threaten a company's financial stability as it waits for approval before recouping development costs in the market. One reason for the time lags lies with the limited capabilities of the 8,000-member staff which must conduct 20,000 domestic and at least 400 overseas inspections annually.

The actual process of new drug R&D is especially complex given the 1962 FDA regulatory guidelines. Company researchers must begin by screening chemicals that show potential in a certain therapeutic class, on a specific disease, or with a particular cell receptor.[27] Once the research detects a potentially beneficial chemical, the new compound is put through a series of preclinical trials using laboratory animals to determine toxicity at various doses. At this point, the company must patent the new chemical and announce to the FDA its intention to begin human trials over the course of the next several years. Upon the drug's qualification in the trials, the company submits a New Drug Application to the FDA seeking market approval for the new therapy. Even after the conditional approval, in case the drug shows adverse effects in the larger population, the result will be a total recall or new warning labels. The FDA approval process has gradually lengthened so that it now exceeds two years. Thus, most of the drug's patent years have already passed by the time the drug reaches the market. Companies then price the drug aggressively to minimize revenue lost during the approval process.

The Biotechnology Industry Organization (BIO), an organization that fights for the identity of the biotechnology industry, has called for the reform of the approval process. Included in its primary directives is a proposal requesting Congress to ease the export of unapproved U.S. drugs to countries where marketing them is legal. BIO has also proposed that the FDA be required to contract with qualified outside experts to conduct some of its own drug approval functions. BIO believes these changes would eliminate inconsistencies in how biotechnology and traditional chemical prescriptions are regulated. Finally, BIO would like to encourage the FDA to work more closely with pharmaceutical sponsors so that "one pivotal clinical trial can serve as the basis for approval of breakthrough drugs."[28]

Research and Development

Due to the pharmaceutical industry's reliance on the introduction of new products, it spends more money annually on R&D than any other industry. Additionally, pharmaceutical companies must meet the high costs of regulatory approval and of the increasing complexity of the industry's methods, including the embrace of those methods employed in the genetic engineering and biotechnology areas. In light of these efforts to move toward cutting-edge technologies, one analyst stated, "For every 5,000 substances examined, only one is likely to prove safe and effective. It takes on average $350 million to bring a new drug to market and only three out of ten prescription medicines recover that average cost."[29] Also, considering that only one in five drugs that begin clinical trials reaches the market, drug company R&D provides relatively less revenue per dollar spent than other industries.

Competing pharmaceutical manufacturers try various approaches to manage these obstacles. Some

firms focus internally to increase R&D productivity. Others employ "outcomes research" to examine the relative benefits and drawbacks of individual drug brands. One prominent firm, Eli Lilly and Company, took this concept a step further to "manage" all aspects, from drugs to hospitalization, of entire diseases for a government or health maintenance organization. The ventures of Merck and Co. demonstrate forward integration into prescription management. Still others use licensing, joint ventures, mergers, outsourcing, and other consortia to share risk and information and to maximize returns on their R&D investment.[30]

The Major Global Players

Exhibit 4 shows the largest pharmaceutical companies according to 1995 sales revenues.

Glaxo W]ellcome PLC When Glaxo PLC acquired the British drug company Wellcome for $14.8 billion in 1995, it created the largest pharmaceutical company in the world. Although the takeover was opposed by Wellcome, the merger created a firm called Glaxo Wellcome PLC. This new company had an initial 6 percent market share in the pharmaceutical industry. While pursuing the acquisition of Wellcome, Glaxo diversified into computer drug-discovery technologies by purchasing the California-based biotechnology firm Affymax NV. Arvind Desai, an analyst with Mehta & Isaly in New York, a company specializing in biotech-company research, remarked that this acquisition "will become the locomotive for [Glaxo's] future discovery effort. The whole key is to have this technology in-house so that no one else will have it."[31] However, the integration of Affymax into Glaxo has been complicated by Affymax's partnerships with competing pharmaceutical companies such as American Home Products Corporation, Marion Merrell Dow Inc., and Ciba-Geigy.

Merck & Co., Inc. As a result of the merger between Glaxo and Wellcome, U.S.-headquartered Merck fell from being the first to bring the second largest pharmaceutical company in the world. In 1993, Merck purchased Medco Containment Services for $6.6 billion. Medco is the largest pharmacy benefits management company in the United States, specializing in processing and shipping prescriptions across the nation. Unlike many of the other leading pharma-

EXHIBIT 4 *Pharmaceutical Companies Ranked by 1995 Revenue*

Company	Drug Sales* ($ billions)
Glaxo Wellcome	11.80
Merck & Co.	10.96
Novartis	10.94
Hoechst	9.42
Roche	7.82
Bristol-Myers Squibb	7.81
Pfizer	7.07
SmithKline Beecham	6.60
Johnson & Johnson	6.30
Pharmacia & Upjohn	6.26

Source: Pooling of Interests: In Big Drug Merger, Sandoz and Ciba-Geigy Plan to Join Forces, 1996, *Wall Street Journal,* March 7, A1.

*Except for Glaxo-Wellcome, figures do not represent total company revenue because they exclude sales of nondrug products.

ceutical companies, Merck believes its growth will not come from acquisitions, but instead from new drug discoveries and the expansion of Medco. In 1995 alone, Merck funneled approximately 8.2 percent of its sales into R&D. Recently, Merck expanded its international presence by creating subsidiaries in Germany, Peru, Holland, Cyprus, and South Korea. Additionally, Merck entered China through a joint venture designed to manufacture and market its products to the Chinese market.[32]

Roche In 1989, F. Hoffmann-La Roche and Sapac created Roche Holding Ltd., the fifth largest pharmaceutical company in the world and the leader in Switzerland.[33] Once dependent on its drug Valium, the company has expanded by acquiring several companies and forming biotechnology partnerships. In 1990, Roche acquired 60 percent of Genentech, a California-based genetic engineering firm, for $2.1 billion with the option to purchase the remaining shares in June 1995.[34] In 1994, Roche purchased the ailing U.S. company Syntex for $5.3 billion.[35] While laying off thousands of Syntex workers and dealing with a global restructuring in 1995, Roche was also facing the impending deadline for the Genentech option. Somewhat reluctantly, Roche decided to purchase the remaining shares at escalating prices. Some speculated that Roche hesitated due to the FDA's recent investigation into Genetech's overaggressive marketing practices. However, Genetech's CEO in-

sisted that "Roche's reluctance to exercise the option didn't signal any cold feet about the relationship between the two companies."[36]

SmithKline Beecham SmithKline Beckman and Beecham merged in 1989 to form SmithKline Beecham PLC, the world's eighth largest pharmaceutical company.[37] Unlike the other pharmaceutical giants, SmithKline Beecham committed itself publically to gene mapping and research when it decided to underwrite the gene-mapping and research project of Human Genome Sciences, Inc. (HGS) in 1993. Under the terms of the collaboration, SmithKline made an initial payment of $59 million to HGS and then would continue funding after HGS passed certain milestones. In return for financing, HGS provided SmithKline with exclusive use of its gene storehouse.[38] In July 1996, SmithKline and HGS invited three additional partners to join their effort: Schering-Plough Corp. of the U.S., Synthelabo SA of France, and Merck KGaA of Germany. William Haseltine, chairman of HGS, asserted that the additional partnerships "show that gene discoveries have created more opportunities to develop pioneer therapeutic products than either company can use on its own."[39]

International Competition

Although until recently U.S. manufacturers had a strong first position in the global pharmaceutical market, international competition has intensified. Recent evidence suggests that European and Japanese manufacturers achieve better results than those in the United States. Eight of the world's largest pharmaceutical manufacturers operate out of Europe, and nearly half of the new world-class drugs introduced between 1975 and 1989 originated there. These European firms have an advantage over their American counterparts because public ownership is held for a longer duration and is subject to less pressure of achieving high short-term earnings.

Japanese firms are now major global players seeking to expand their 3 percent of the U.S. market. They possess the capacity to innovate, develop, and market on the same level as U.S. and European firms.[40] With the world's second largest market for pharmaceuticals, the Japanese government favors new drug innovations and is implementing new patent policies and pricing structures that are conducive to the development of research-based products. Consequently, Japanese companies have changed from "imitating" to "innovating." Many Japanese firms have formed a number of joint ventures to market their discoveries in the United States and to improve their market share.

In a benchmarking study on the industry's production and manufacturing of solid-dosage forms (tablets) by the *Journal of Manufacturing Systems*, several country-specific trends emerged among the U.S., Japan, and European countries. U.S. manufacturers appeared to trail in terms of productivity per employee-hour, rating slightly lower than the European average and roughly 46 percent of the Japanese average. The European manufacturers posted the lowest average annual inventory levels in terms of dollar value while U.S. manufacturers posted the highest.[41] Research suggests that the United States maintained high inventories because prescription product manufacturers believed it was imperative to be able to satisfy demand for their product due to the life-saving and high-profit-margin considerations. U.S. manufacturers also reported the highest percentage of rejections for finished products while Japan reported the lowest rejection rate. As assumed, U.S. manufacturers produced fewer products on average than the Europeans or Japanese.

Further measures of performance included manufacturing times, in which the United States ranked the highest at an average of 15 months. This includes the time from making necessary operating arrange-

ments to the actual production of the new product. Lead times and flow times in the United States were also two to three times longer than those of Japanese and European competitors. Another significant difference among these countries was the number of years employees remain with the same company. Manufacturing workers stayed with the facility for an average of 10 years in the United States, 14 years in Europe, and 24 years in Japan.

Industry Trends

As one of the world's largest, most profitable, and fastest growing economic sectors, the pharmaceutical industry sponsors influential interest groups.[42] In the United States, the Pharmaceutical Research and Manufacturers of America (PhRMA) functions primarily as a lobbying group for government regulations and other issues, such as patent protection and capital formulation, affecting the industry. On occasion, PhRMA lobbies similar agendas to those of BIO in dealing with the media and government. However, the recent disarray in PhRMA leadership caused many of the larger pharmaceutical firms to join BIO, thereby expanding BIO's membership base at the expense of PhRMA's.[43]

The pharmaceutical industry recently experienced several constraining factors, some of which have already been mentioned. Since the early 1990s, increasingly powerful customer groups, such as pharmaceutical benefits management companies and health management organizations (HMOs), have pressed for reduced drug prices and significantly lower profit margins.[44] Simultaneously, governments around the world have added demand-side controls which further limit the firms' ability to recoup their costly operations through product pricing.

Furthermore, a lack of control in less-developed nations has discouraged investment in the pharmaceutical industry. For example, China tolerated patent pirating until 1992. To exacerbate this problem, the General Agreement on Trade and Tariffs (GATT) has proposed that developing nations wait 10 years before granting patent protection.[45] And yet, amidst increased regulation and decreased profits, the pharmaceutical industry has remained one of the world's largest and most profitable economic sectors, creating companies of international caliber such as Ciba-Geigy.

CIBA-GEIGY, LTD.

Ciba-Geigy, Ltd. (CG) of Basel, Switzerland, ranked ninth in global sales in 1993.[46] The company recorded $4.81 billion in sales during 1993 and held a 1.9 percent market share of global drug sales. Ciba-Geigy's pharmaceutical sales comprised only a fraction of its $15.31 billion total sales; most sales were generated by its interests in agrochemicals and industrial products. With its cash holdings of $5.1 billion, Ciba-Geigy was expected to acquire a generic drug company in the mid-1990s.

Early Development

The Swiss firm was established in 1758 by Johann Geigy to sell spices, natural dyes, and other products.[47] By 1859, the Geigy family entered the business of synthetic dyes, which evolved into the modern pharmaceutical industry.[48] The family was competing with Gesellschaft fur Chemische Industrie im Basel, shortened to Ciba, which was Switzerland's top-ranked chemical company by the turn of the century. Following the reestablishment of a powerful German chemical cartel, Ciba, Geigy, and Sandoz, another Basel company, formed Basel AG to share technology and markets in hopes of outperforming the German competitors. Ciba and Geigy split in 1951 only to merge again in 1970 due to increased competition within Switzerland and from other foreign competitors. In 1986, Ciba-Geigy entered into a joint venture, creating the Biocene Company with Chiron, to produce and market genetically engineered vaccines. Ciba-Geigy then acquired Maag AG, an agrochemicals company, in 1990.[49] In 1992, Ciba-Geigy and Chiron acquired the vaccine business Aclavo SpA of Siena, Italy and renamed it Biocine SpA.[50] Over the past few years, Ciba-Geigy pursued a number of research partnerships, including those with Isis Pharmaceuticals and Affymax.

At times, Ciba-Geigy's public image has suffered. In 1976, the company admitted to questionable testing practices that involved spraying six Egyptian boys in a field with the insecticide Galecron.[51] Later, in 1978, over 1,000 deaths in Japan were revealed to be linked to Ciba-Geigy's diarrhea drug. Additionally, Glaxo sued Ciba-Geigy in 1994 for alleged patent infringement of its anti-ulcer drug Zantac. Many analysts, however, saw this move as a stalling tactic to prevent Ciba from producing a generic version of Zantac.

Products

Ciba-Geigy produces health care, agricultural, and industrial products. The health care sector is composed of the ophthalmic, pharma, and self-medication divisions. Its ophthalmic interests lie with Ciba Vision, which manufactures contact lenses, lens care products, and ophthalmic medicines. Its pharma division specializes in anticancer drugs, antirheumatics, cardiovascular drugs, and neurotropics. The self-medication area of health care boasts well-known brand names such as Desenex, Doan's Pills, Efidac, and Maalox. Overall, the health care sector contributed 41 percent (9,220 SF million) of Ciba-Geigy's 1993 sales. The agricultural sector, with 21 percent of 1993 sales (8,614 SF million), develops and produces fungicides, herbicides, insecticides, parasiticides, and seeds. The third sector, industrial products, accounted for 38 percent (8,614 SF million) of Ciba-Geigy's 1993 sales. Included in this sector are products such as chemicals, composites, pigments, textile dyes, additives, polymers, and scales and balances.[52]

Ciba-Geigy excels in the research for new drug development within its industry and it has strong financial resources to support the effort. It also employs a global infrastructure in marketing, manufacturing, and regulatory registration capabilities for new health care products.[53] The infrastructure facilitates management of the international direct-selling businesses in diagnostics, vaccines, therapeutics, and ophthalmic surgical products.[54] Additionally, Ciba-Geigy has earned significant credibility with government institutions.[55]

As the fifth top pharmaceutical firm for 1995, Ciba-Geigy had established its presence in the evolving pharmaceutical industry and had made known its intention to secure more market power through its partnership with Chiron.

CHIRON

Chiron Corporation, a leading U.S. biotechnology firm headquartered in Emeryville, California, was formed in 1980 by three professors, all of whom still remain with the company. The name "Chiron" refers to the mythological Greek centaur who had great medical knowledge.[56]

Early Development

Soon after its inception, Chiron developed a network of partners. By 1986, it had collaborated with 14 other companies. One of the most significant collaborations was Chiron's joint venture with the Ortho Diagnostic Systems division of Johnson & Johnson in 1989.[57] This agreement helped expand Chiron's diagnostic line of businesses. Also of importance was Chiron's acquisition of Cetus Corporation in the summer of 1991 for $650 million in stock.[58] Cetus had developed two drugs of key interest to Chiron, Interleukin-2 and Betaseron. In another collaboration, Chiron entered into an agreement with Cephalon, Inc., in January 1994 to codevelop neurobiological drugs and technologies. The two companies formed a joint venture to produce, distribute, and market the drug Myotrophin, a genetically engineered version of an insulinlike growth factor developed by Cephalon.[59]

Chiron continued to grow significantly and to look for new partners after the collaborations. With more than 2,500 employees worldwide, in 1994 the company posted total revenues of $453 million ($18 million in net income).[60] As Chiron continued to expand, its goal was to "apply biotechnology and other techniques of modern biology to develop products

that have a goal of lowering the overall cost of health care and improving the quality of life by diagnosing, preventing, and treating disease."[61]

Products

Chiron is divided into five main lines of business: Chiron Vision, Chiron Diagnostics, Chiron Therapeutics, Chiron Biocene, and Chiron Technologies (see Exhibit 5). Two of these divisions, Therapeutics and Technologies, have recently made significant contributions to Chiron.

Chiron Therapeutics' most prominent products in the recent past originated from the acquisition of Cetus. Cetus first presented its drug to treat kidney cancer, Interleukin-2, to the FDA in 1990. In response to a confusing and unorganized presentation, the board denied approval and instead ordered further analysis. However, Chiron gained approval when it presented the drug less than two years later with more solid and organized data.[62] Chiron Therapeutics also won FDA approval in 1993 for Betaseron, another Cetus drug designed to fight multiple sclerosis.[63] Betaseron is marketed worldwide by Berlex Labs, the U.S. affiliate of Germany's Schering AG.[64] Once expected to be a blockbuster for Chiron, Betaseron has not found the intended success due to unwanted side effects.

Chiron Technologies is the company's R&D and clinical pipeline, discovering and developing new therapeutic products. Chiron Technologies devel-

EXHIBIT 5 *Chiron's Five Lines of Business*

Line	1995 Revenues ($ millions)	Products
Vision	177	Refractive and cataract surgical instruments, intraocular lenses
Diagnostics	620	Blood screening tests for hepatitis C virus, blood testing systems, immunodiagnostic systems, nucleic acid systems
Therapeutics	130	Interleukin-2, Betaseron, chemotherapies
Biocene	75	Vaccines for MMR (measles, mumps, and rubella), rabies, cholera, tuberculosis, pneumonia
Technologies	98	Hepatitis B vaccine, Myotrophin, combinatorial chemistries

Source: UBS Securities Equity Research: Chiron, August, 1996.

oped the first genetically engineered product vaccine, a hepatitis B product.[65] Active research is focused presently on new methods to quantify the amount of hepatitis virus in a diseased person using DNA probe technology. Additionally, Chiron Technologies is fine-tuning development of the drug Myotrophin with Cephalon. Not yet approved by the FDA, Myotrophin treats neurodegenerative diseases such as amyotrophic lateral sclerosis (ALS or Lou Gehrig's disease).[66] Chiron Therapeutics is also pursuing several other collaborative research efforts.

In summary, Chiron has become known as a leader in research for the biotechnology industry. Its strength lies in the discovery of new drugs, products, and technologies and their application to the prevention and treatment of various diseases.[67] It currently has more products in clinical trials than any other biotechnology company.[68] Additionally, through its use of cost-effective, quality products and technical expertise, Chiron has maintained strong relationships with customers in each of its five businesses.

Chiron's recent development within the fast-paced biotechnology industry could hardly compare to that of its new partner, Ciba-Geigy, in the established pharmaceutical industry employing a slightly altered research focus. Will the two firms be complementary in some other context?

PARTNERSHIP IN SYNTHESIS

Chiron excels in the discovery of new drugs and technology; however, as with many other biotechnology companies, its weakness is its ability to fully develop and market those ideas worldwide. Access to capital to do this almost always requires additional help in the form of financial backing and distribution expertise from another company because the cash flows of most biotech firms are allocated to R&D. Biotechnology firms often also lack the expertise required to pilot new drugs through the complex regulatory process. Compounding this problem is the recent decrease in funding by investors for the biotechnology firms. Investors seem to be shifting their money from risky, small-venture companies to large, established firms.

On the other hand, pharmaceutical companies such as Ciba-Geigy are often more skilled at developing drugs than discovering them. They have the

ability to navigate new drugs through clinical trials and the manpower to negotiate with regulatory agencies.[69] They are also adept at devising large-scale production processes and marketing products globally. However, many pharmaceutical companies are reluctant to spend the enormous amounts of risky capital needed to establish R&D structures to develop new products and technologies.

As a result of these complementary strengths of discovery and development, there has been a wave of collaborations in the form of joint ventures, strategic alliances, and partnerships between biotechnology and pharmaceutical companies. In a typical collaboration, the biotechnology partner contributes technology or a drug candidate while the pharmaceutical company contributes research funding plus compensation based on the results of the technology or drug.[70] Such collaborations allow each company to concentrate on its core competencies. The biotechnology firm can focus on drug discovery, while the pharmaceutical company can focus on manufacturing and distribution.[71]

DIVERGENCIES

Despite the 1994 alliance between Chiron and Ciba-Geigy, 1995 brought several other strategic partnerships for each firm. Chiron paid $95 million for the remaining 83 percent of Viagene Inc., a gene-therapy specialist. This deal affirmed Chiron's growing commitment to research in the gene-therapy field.[72] Also that year, Chiron acquired IOLAB from Johnson & Johnson to improve operating efficiencies and further its cataract surgery product line. A third strategic action was Chiron's license agreement for Genelab's Technology Incorporated hepatitis G virus in exchange for $24 million. These two firms agreed to develop and market diagnostic tests for the virus.[73]

Ciba had more partnerships forming on the horizon, one of which was with a direct biotechnology competitor of Chiron's. Medarex developed an innovative class of monoclonal antibodies that represents an approach to the treatment of cancer and AIDS. Ciba purchased $4 million of stock, committed up to $4 million more based on performance, and up to $31 million in R&D funding. Preceding this move, Medarex also cooperated with Merck and Co. on another cancer antibody. Ciba also joined forces with New York University, this time including

Chiron in the arrangement to conduct research in the field of genetic diseases. Both Medarex and the NYU cooperation deals were pretargeted by Ciba in a strategic plan formed two years prior to identifying potential alliance partners.[74]

One of Ciba's biggest biotech links, valued at roughly $60 million, was with Myriad Genetics Inc., a private genetic research company based in Utah. Myriad is an ideal partner in what seems to be an anticancer push from Ciba: Researchers have discovered two key genes involved in certain forms of breast cancer. The rights to develop medicines based on them were ceded to other companies and as a result limited Ciba's cooperation. Ciba created the world's third largest drug maker, Novartis, through a merger with Sandoz Ltd. Sandoz has a strong hold on the cyclosporin drug for organ transplantation, marketed under the brand name Sandimmun. Another major Sandoz drug is Clozaril for the treatment of schizophrenia, marketed as Lamisil. These drugs will soon come off patent and need Ciba's strong marketing capability to create synergies for both.

The Swiss pharmaceutical giants Roche Holding Ltd., Ciba-Geigy Ltd., and Sandoz Ltd. have expended over $7 billion in amassing biotechnology advancement, gaining a potentially decisive edge in the global race to create a new gene-based drug generation.[75] These companies have captured perhaps the biggest foreign share of the emerging U.S. biotechnology market through at least 100 companies such as Genentech and Chiron.

CONCLUSION

Which way should Chiron choose to go to become a success? A strong partnership with Ciba-Geigy would secure Chiron's presence in Europe. It would also bring the advantages of belonging to one of the three major players in the pharmaceutical industry and thus keep Chiron close to the mainstream events of the industry. Or maybe not? Might Ciba-Geigy be too large to really help Chiron develop fully?

Which other possible partners should Chiron examine? Given the rapid and abrupt changes in the industry, might smaller but more specialized partnerships be better? Is the risk of trying to stay on its own too great for Chiron? These and other questions are examples of ones that Chiron's leadership will have to face as it tries to build bridges into the next century.

C-15

NOTES

1. Chiron News Release, 1994, Chiron and Ciba-Geigy form unique global biotechnology partnership, November 21.
2. D. M. Sawinski and W. H. Mason, editors, 1996, *Encyclopedia of Global Industries*, Gale Research, 141–151.
3. Ibid.
4. Ibid.
5. R. T. King, Jr., 1995, Drug discovery: Pharmaceutical giants are eagerly shopping biotech bargain bin, *Wall Street Journal*, April 11, A1.
6. Sawinski and Mason, *Encyclopedia of Global Industries*.
7. Ibid.
8. J. Bamford, 1995, Refocus, *Financial World*, April 11, 68–69.
9. Sawinski and Mason, *Encyclopedia of Global Industries*.
10. Ibid.
11. R. Madell and C. B. Feldbaum, 1996, Bring biotech's campaign to politicians and the public, *Pharmaceutical Executive*, June, 50–60.
12. *Standard & Poor's Industry Survey*, 1995, Ciba-Geigy, 15–29.
13. Sawinski and Mason, *Encyclopedia of Global Industries*.
14. King, Drug discovery.
15. D. M. Sawinski, 1996, *U.S. Industry Profiles—The Leading 100*.
16. P. D. Sarantopoulos, T. Altiok, and E. Elsayed, 1995, Trends and perspectives: Manufacturing in the pharmaceutical industry, *Journal of Manufacturing Systems* 14: no. 6, 453.

17. Sawinski and Mason, *Encyclopedia of Global Industries*.
18. Ibid.
19. Sawinski, *U.S. Industry Profiles*.
20. *Market Share Reporter*, 1997, Gale Publishing, 664.
21. Sarantopoulos, Altiok, and Elsayed, Trends and perspectives.
22. Ibid.
23. *Standard & Poor's Industry Survey*, Ciba-Geigy.
24. King, Drug discovery.
25. Sawinski and Mason, *Encyclopedia of Global Industries*.
26. Sarantopoulos, Altiok, and Elsayed, Trends and perspectives.
27. Sawinski, *U.S. Industry Profiles*.
28. M. F. Conlan, 1995, Biotech group urges FDA to ease drug export rules, *Drug Topics*, March, 139.
29. Sawinski and Mason, *Encyclopedia of Global Industries*.
30. Ibid.
31. R. T. King, Jr., 1995, Glaxo plans to acquire Affymax for $533 million, a 67 percent premium, *Wall Street Journal*, January 27, B6.
32. P. J. Spain and J. R. Talbot, eds., 1995, *Hoover's Handbook of Emerging Companies* (Austin, TX.: The Reference Press), 143.
33. E. Tanouye, S. Lipin, and S. D. Moore, 1996, Sandoz and Ciba-Geigy plan merger of equals in $27 billion deal: Transaction is among biggest in history, and will alter the world's drug industry, *Wall Street Journal*, March 7, A1.

34. Genentech feared a stock plunge if Roche pact lapsed, 1995, *Wall Street Journal*, June 6, B6.

35. P. J. Spain and J. R. Talbot, eds., 1996, *Hoover's Handbook of American Business*, (Austin, TX.: The Reference Press).

36. Genentech feared a stock plunge, B6.

37. S. Lipin and S. D. Moore, 1996, Pooling of interests: In big drug deal merger, Sandoz and Ciba-Geigy plan to join forces, *Wall Street Journal*, March 9, A1.

38. SmithKline modifies research agreement with human genome, 1995, *Wall Street Journal*, January 9, B5.

39. Human genome sets more collaborations in gene development, 1996, *Wall Street Journal*, July 3, B6.

40. Ibid.

41. Sarantopoulos, Altiok, and Elsayed, Trends and perspectives.

42. Sawinski and Mason, *Encyclopedia of Global Industries*.

43. Madell and Feldbaum, Bring biotech's campaign, 52.

44. Sawinski and Mason, *Encyclopedia of Global Industries*.

45. Ibid.

46. Ibid.

47. Spain and Talbot, *Hoover's Handbook of American Business*.

48. Sawinski and Mason, *Encyclopedia of Global Industries*.

49. Spain and Talbot, *Hoover's Handbook of American Business*.

50. Moody's Company Data Report, 1996, Chiron Corporation.

51. Spain and Talbot, *Hoover's Handbook of World Business*.

52. Ibid.

53. Chiron news release, Chiron and Ciba-Geigy form.

54. M. Burke, 1996, Getting into bed with biotech, *Chemistry and Industry*, March 18, 200–201.

55. T. N. Cochran, 1994, A caution on Chiron, *Barron's Market Week*, December 19, MW1, 1.

56. Spain and Talbot, *Hoover's Handbook of Emerging Companies*.

57. P. E. Kelly and T. Wilson, 1996, Chiron, *UBS Securities Equity Research*, August 19, 3–50.

58. J. O. C. Hamilton, 1992, Heartbreak and triumph in biotech land, *Business Week*, February 3, 33.

59. Kelly and Wilson, Chiron.

60. Chiron Corporation, 1995, *Annual Report*.

61. Chiron Corporation Home Page, 1997, http://www.chiron.com.

62. Hamilton, Heartbreak and triumph.

63. Spain and Talbot, *Hoover's Handbook of Emerging Companies*.

64. Kelly and Wilson, Chiron.

65. Spain and Talbot, *Hoover's Handbook of Emerging Companies*.

66. Kelly and Wilson, Chiron.

67. S. D. Moore, 1995, Corporate focus: Ciba's alliance with Chiron is an open relationship, *Wall Street Journal*, June 21, B6.

68. Chiron news release, Chiron and Ciba-Geigy form.

69. Moore, Corporate focus.

70. King, Drug discovery.

71. K. Cottrill, 1996, Biotech firms aim to trigger organic growth, *Chemical Week*, September 18, S26–S27.

72. Moore, Corporate focus.

73. Health Brief—Genelabs Technologies Inc., 1995, *Wall Street Journal*, March 13, B8.

74. Moore, Corporate focus.

75. R. T. King, Jr. and S. D. Moore, 1995, Swiss stakes: Basel's drug giants are placing huge bets on breakthroughs, *Wall Street Journal*, November 29, A1.

Circus Circus Enterprises, Inc. 1997

John K. Ross III
Mike Keeffe
Bill Middlebrook

Southwest Texas State University

We possess the resources to accomplish the big projects: the know-how, the financial power and the places to invest. The renovation of our existing projects will soon be behind us, which last year represented the broadest scope of construction ever taken on by a gaming company. Now we are well-positioned to originate new projects. Getting big projects right is the route to future wealth in gaming; big successful projects tend to prove long staying power in our business. When the counting is over, we think our customers and investors will hold the winning hand.

—Annual Report, 1997

Big projects and a winning hand. Circus Circus does seem to have both. And big projects they are, with huge pink and white striped concrete circus tents, a 600-foot-long riverboat replica, a giant castle, and a great pyramid. The latest project, Project Paradise, will include a 3,800-room hotel/casino and a 10-acre aquatic environment with beaches, a snorkeling reef, and a swim-up shark exhibit.

Circus Circus Enterprises, Inc. (hereafter Circus) describes itself as in the business of entertainment, and it has been one of the innovators in the theme resort concept popular in casino gaming. The firm's areas of operation are the glitzy vacation and convention Mecca's of Las Vegas, Reno, and Laughlin,

This case was prepared for classroom purposes only, and is not designed to show effective or ineffective handling of administrative situations.

Nevada, as well as other locations in the United States and abroad. Historically, Circus's marketing of its products has been called "right out of the bargain basement" and has catered to "low rollers." Circus continues to broaden its market and now aims more at the middle-income gambler and family-oriented vacationers as well as the more upscale traveler and player.

Circus was purchased in 1974 for $50,000 as a small and unprofitable casino operation by partners William G. Bennett, an aggressive cost-cutter who ran furniture stores before entering the gaming industry in 1965, and William N. Pennington (see Exhibit 1 for the board of directors and top managers). The partners were able to rejuvenate Circus with a fresh marketing program, went public with a stock offering in October 1983, and experienced rapid growth and high profitability over time. Within the last five years (1993–1997), the average return on invested capital has been 16.5 percent and Circus had generated over $1 billion in free cash flow. Today, Circus is one of the major competitors in the Las Vegas, Laughlin, and Reno markets in terms of square footage of casino space and number of hotel rooms, despite the incredible growth in both markets. For the first time in company history, casino gaming operations (ending January 31, 1997) provided slightly less than one half of total revenues (see Exhibit 2), and Circus reported a net income of more than $100 million on revenues of $1.3 billion. During this same

EXHIBIT 1 *Circus Circus Enterprises, Inc.*

Directors

Name	Age	Title
Clyde T. Turner	59	Chairman of the Board and CEO, Circus Circus Enterprises
Michael S. Ensign	59	Vice Chairman of the Board and COO, Circus Circus Enterprises
Glenn Schaeffer	43	President, CFO, Circus Circus Enterprises
William A. Richardson	50	Executive Vice President, Circus Circus Enterprises
Richard P. Banis	52	Former President and COO, Circus Circus Enterprises
Arthur H. Bilger	44	Former President and COO, New World Communications Group International
Richard A. Etter	58	Former Chairman and CEO, Bank of America—Nevada
Michael D. McKee	51	Executive Vice President, The Irving Company

Officers

Clyde T. Turner	Chairman of the Board and Chief Executive Officer
Michael S. Ensign	Vice Chairman of the Board and Chief Operating Officer
Glenn Schaeffer	President, Chief Financial Officer and Treasurer
William A. Richardson	Executive Vice President
Tony Alamo	Senior Vice President, Operations
Steve Greathouse	Senior Vice President, Operations
Gregg Solomon	Senior Vice President, Operations
Kurt D. Sullivan	Senior Vice President, Operations
Yvett Landau	Vice President, General Counsel and Secretary
Les Martin	Vice President and Chief Accounting Officer

Source: Annual Report 1997; Proxy Statement June 24, 1997; Circus Circus News release August 13, 1997.

EXHIBIT 2 *Circus Circus Enterprises, Inc. Sources of Revenues as a Percentage of Net Revenues*

	1997	1996	1995
Casinos	49.2%	51.2%	52.3%
Food & Beverage	15.8	15.5	16.2
Hotel	22.0	21.4	19.9
Other	11.0	12.2	14.2
Unconsolidated	6.5	3.5	.5
Less: Complimentary Allowances	4.5	3.8	3.1

Source: Circus Circus 10-K, January 31, 1997.

year, Circus invested over $585.8 million in capital expenditures and anticipates another $450–550 million will be spent in fiscal year 1998.

CIRCUS CIRCUS OPERATIONS

Circus defines entertainment as pure play and fun, and works hard to ensure that customers have plenty of opportunity for both. Each Circus location has a distinctive personality. Circus Circus–Las Vegas is the world of the Big Top, where live circus acts perform free every 30 minutes. Kids may cluster around video games while the adults migrate to nickel slot machines and dollar game tables. Located at the north end of the Vegas strip, Circus Circus–Las Vegas sits on 69 acres of land with 3,744 hotel rooms, shopping areas, two specialty restaurants, a buffet with seating for 1,200, fast food shops, cocktail lounges, video arcades, and 109,000 square feet of casino space; it includes the Grand Slam Canyon, a five-acre glass-enclosed theme park including a four-loop roller coaster. Approximately 384 guests may also stay at nearby Circusland RV Park. For the year ending January 31, 1997, $126.7 million was invested in this property for new rooms and remodeling.

Luxor is another Circus project. It is an Egyptian-themed hotel and casino complex, opened on October 15, 1993, when 10,000 people entered to play the 2,245 slot and video poker games and gamble at the 110 table games in the 120,000-square-foot casino in the hotel atrium (reported to be the world's largest). By the end of the opening weekend, 40,000 people per day were visiting the 30-story bronze pyramid that encases the hotel and entertainment facilities.

Luxor features a 30-story pyramid and two new 22-story hotel towers including 492 suites and is connected to Excalibur by a climate-controlled skyway with moving walkways. Situated at the south end of the Las Vegas strip on a 64-acre site adjacent to Excalibur, Luxor features a food and entertainment area on three different levels beneath the hotel atrium. The pyramid's hotel rooms can be reached from the four corners of the building by state-of-the-art "inclinators" which travel at a 39-degree angle. Parking is available for nearly 3,200 vehicles, and includes a covered garage that contains approximately 1,800 spaces.

During 1997, the Luxor underwent major renovation costing $323.3 million. The resulting complex contains 4,425 hotel rooms, extensively renovated casino space, an additional 20,000 square feet of convention area, an 800-seat buffet, a series of IMAX attractions, five theme restaurants, seven cocktail lounges, and a variety of specialty shops. Circus expects to draw significant walk-in traffic to the newly refurbished Luxor and it is one of the principal components of the Masterplan Mile.

Located next to the Luxor, Excalibur is one of the first sights travelers see as they exit Interstate Highway 15. (Management was confident that the sight of a giant, colorful Medieval castle would make a lasting impression on mainstream tourists and vacationing families arriving in Las Vegas.) Guests cross a drawbridge, with moat, onto a cobblestone walkway where multicolored spires, turrets, and battlements loom above. The castle walls are four 28-story hotel towers containing a total of 4,008 rooms. Inside is a Medieval world complete with a Fantasy Faire inhabited by strolling jugglers, fire eaters, and acrobats, as well as a Royal Village complete with peasants, serfs, and ladies-in-waiting around Medieval theme shops. The 110,000-square-foot casino encompasses 2,442 slot machines, more than 89 game tables, a sports bar, and a poker and keno area. There are 12 restaurants capable of feeding more than 20,000 people daily and a 1,000-seat amphitheater. Excalibur, which opened in June 1990, was built for $294 million and was financed primarily with internally generated funds. In the year ending January 31, 1997, Excalibur contributed 23 percent of the organization's revenues, down from 33 percent in 1993. Yet 1997 was a record year, generating the company's highest margins and over $100 million in operating cash flow.

Situated between the two anchors on the Las Vegas strip are two smaller casinos owned and operated by Circus. The Silver City Casino and Slots-A-Fun depend primarily on the foot traffic along the strip for their gambling patrons. Combined, they offer more than 1,202 slot machines and 46 gaming tables on 34,900 square feet of casino floor.

Circus owns and operates 10 properties in Nevada and one in Mississippi and has a 50 percent ownership in three others (see Exhibit 3).

All of Circus's operations do well in Las Vegas. However, Circus Circus 1997 operational earnings

EXHIBIT 3 *Circus Circus Enterprises, Inc. Properties and Percentage of Total Revenues*

Properties	Revenues, %		
	1997	1996	1995
Las Vegas			
Circus Circus–Las Vegas	24^1	27^1	29^1
Excalibur	23	23	25
Luxor	17	20	24
Slots-A-Fun and Silver City			
Reno			
Circus Circus–Reno			
Laughlin			
Colorado Belle	12^2	13^2	16^2
Edgewater			
Jean, Nevada			
Gold Strike	6^3	4^3	NA
Nevada Landing			
Henderson, Nevada			
Railroad Pass			
Tunica, Mississippi			
Circus Circus–Tunica	4	5	3
50 Percent Ownership			
Silver Legacy, Reno, Nevada	6.5^4	3.5^4	$.5^4$
Monte Carlo, Las Vegas, Nevada			
Grand Victoria riverboat casino, Elgin, Illinois			

[1] Combined with revenues from Circus Circus–Reno.
[2] Colorado Bell and Edgewater have been combined.
[3] Gold Strike and Nevada Landing have been combined.
[4] Revenues of unconsolidated affiliates have been combined.
Revenues from Slots-A-Fun and Silver City, management fees, and other income were not reported separately.

for the Luxor and Circus Circus–Las Vegas were off 38 percent from the previous year. Management credits the disruption in services due to renovations for this decline. However, Circus's combined hotel room occupancy rates remain above 90 percent, due in part, to low room rates ($45 to $69 at Circus Circus–Las Vegas) and popular buffets. Each of the major properties contains large, inexpensive buffets that management believes make staying with Circus more attractive.

The company's other Big Top facility is Circus Circus–Reno. With the addition of Skyway Tower in 1985, this big top now offers a total of 1,605 hotel rooms, 60,600 square feet of casino space, a buffet that can seat 700 people, shops, video arcades, cocktail lounges, midway games, and circus acts. Circus Circus–Reno had several marginal years but has become one of the leaders in the Reno market. For fiscal year 1997, competition from the Silver Legacy (50 percent owned by Circus) as well as flooding, storms, and renovation reduced operating income some $13.6 million from the previous year.

The Colorado Belle and the Edgewater Hotel are located in Laughlin, Nevada, a city 90 miles south of Las Vegas on the banks of the Colorado River. The Colorado Belle, opened in 1987, features a huge paddle-wheel riverboat replica, buffet, cocktail lounges, and shops. The Edgewater, acquired in 1983, has a southwestern motif, a 57,000-square-foot casino, a bowling center, and buffet and cocktail lounges.

Combined, these two properties contain 2,700 rooms and over 120,000 square feet of casino space. These two operations contributed 12 percent of the company's revenues in the year ended January 31, 1997, down from 21 percent in 1994. Additionally, these properties saw a decrease of 17 percent in operating revenue over the previous year. The extensive proliferation of casinos throughout the region, primarily on Indian land, and the development of megaresorts in Las Vegas have seriously eroded outlying markets such as Laughlin.

Three properties purchased in 1995 and located in Jean and Henderson, Nevada, represent recent investments by Circus. The Gold Strike and Nevada Landing service the I-15 market between Las Vegas and southern California. In combination, these properties have over 73,000 square feet of casino space, 2,140 slot machines, and 42 gaming tables. Each has limited hotel space (1,116 rooms total) and depends heavily on I-15 traffic. The Railroad Pass is considered a local casino and is dependent on Henderson residents as its market. This smaller casino contains only 395 slot machines and 11 gaming tables.

Circus Circus–Tunica is a dockside casino located in Tunica, Mississippi, that opened in 1994 on 24 acres of land located along the Mississippi River approximately 20 miles south of Memphis. In 1997, operating income declined by more than 50 percent due to the increase in competition and lack of hotel rooms. Circus has decided to renovate this property and add a 1,200 room tower hotel. The casino will have a new theme to be more upscale and will be renamed the Gold Strike Casino Resort. Total cost for all remodeling is estimated at $125 million.

Joint Ventures

Circus is engaged currently in three joint ventures through the wholly owned subsidiary Circus Participant. In Las Vegas, Circus joined with Mirage Resorts to build and operate the Monte Carlo, a hotel-casino with 3,002 rooms designed along the lines of the grand casinos of the Mediterranean. It is located on 46 acres (with 600 feet on the Las Vegas strip) between the New York-New York casino and the soon to be completed Bellagio, with all three casinos to be connected by monorail. The Monte Carlo features a 90,000-square-foot casino containing 2,221 slot machines and 95 gaming tables along with a 550-seat bingo parlor, high-tech arcade rides, restaurants

and buffets, a microbrewery, approximately 15,000 square feet of meeting and convention space, and a 1,200-seat theater. Opened on June 21, 1996, the Monte Carlo generated $14.6 million as Circus's share in operating income for the first seven months of operation.

In Elgin, Illinois, Circus has a 50 percent partnership with Hyatt Development Corporation in The Grand Victoria. Styled to resemble a Victorian riverboat, this floating casino and land-based entertainment complex includes some 36,000 square feet of casino space containing 977 slot machines and 56 gaming tables. The adjacent land-based complex contains two movie theaters, a 240 seat buffet, restaurants, and parking for approximately 2,000 vehicles. Built for a total of $112 million, The Grand Victoria returned to Circus $44 million in operating income in 1996.

The third joint venture is a 50 percent partnership with Eldorado Limited in the Silver Legacy. Opened in 1995, this casino is located between Circus Circus–Reno and the Eldorado Hotel and Casino on two city blocks in downtown Reno, Nevada. The Silver Legacy has 1,711 hotel rooms, 85,000 square feet of casino space, 2,275 slot machines, and 89 gaming tables. Management seems to believe that the Silver Legacy holds promise; however, the Reno market is suffering and the opening of the Silver Legacy has cannibalized the Circus Circus–Reno market.

Circus engaged in a fourth joint venture to penetrate the Canadian market, but on January 23, 1997, the firm announced that its interests had been purchased by Hilton Hotels Corporation, one of three partners in the venture.

Circus has achieved success through an aggressive growth strategy and a corporate structure designed to enhance that growth. A strong cash position, innovative ideas, and attention to cost control have allowed Circus to operate profitably during a period when competitors were typically taking on large debt obligations to finance new projects (see Exhibits 4, 5, 6, and 7). Yet the market is changing. Gambling of all kinds has spread across the country; no longer does the average individual need to travel to Las Vegas or Atlantic City. Instead, gambling can be found as close as the local quick market (lottery), bingo hall, Indian reservation, the Mississippi River, and others. There are now almost 300 casinos in Las Vegas alone, 60 in Colorado, and 160 in California. To maintain a competitive advantage, Circus continues

EXHIBIT 4 *Selected Financial Information*

	FY 97	FY 96	FY 95	FY 94	FY 93	FY 92	FY 91
Earnings Per Share	0.99	1.33	1.59	1.34	2.05	1.84	1.39
Current Ratio	1.17	1.30	1.35	.95	.90	1.14	.88
Total Liabilities/ Total Assets	.62	.44	.54	.57	.48	.58	.77
Operating Profit Margin	17%	19%	22%	21%	24.4%	24.9%	22.9%

Source: Circus Circus Annual Reports and 10Ks, 1991–1997.

EXHIBIT 5 *Twelve-Year Summary*

Fiscal Year	Revenues (in 000)	Net Income
1997	$1,170,182	$136,286
1996	1,299,596	128,898
1995	1,334,250	100,733
1994	954,923	116,189
1993	843,025	117,322
1992	806,023	103,348
1991	692,052	76,292
1990	522,376	76,064
1989	511,960	81,714
1988	458,856	55,900
1987	373,967	28,198
1986	306,993	37,375

Source: Circus Circus Annual Reports and 10Ks, 1986–1997.

to invest heavily in renovation of existing properties (a strategy common to the entertainment/amusement industry) and continues to develop new projects.

New Ventures

Circus is involved currently with three new projects. The largest one, named Project Paradise, is scheduled for completion in late 1998 or early 1999, and is estimated to cost $800 million (excluding land). Circus owns a contiguous mile of the southern end of the Las Vegas strip which is called the "Masterplan Mile"; it currently contains the Excalibur and Luxor resorts. Located next to the Luxor, Project Paradise will aim for the upscale traveler and player and will be styled as a South Seas adventure. The resort will contain a 42-story hotel-casino with over 3,800 rooms and a 10-acre aquatic environment. The aquatic environment will contain a surfing beach, swim-up shark tank, and snorkeling reef. A stand-alone Four Seasons Resort with some 400 rooms will complement the remainder of Project Paradise. Circus anticipates that the remainder of the Masterplan Mile will be comprised eventually of at least one additional casino resort and a number of stand-alone hotels and amusement centers.

Circus also plans two other casino projects, provided all the necessary licenses and agreements can be obtained. Along the Mississippi Gulf, the firm plans to construct a casino resort containing 1,500 rooms at an estimated cost of $225 million. In Atlantic City, Circus has agreed with Mirage to develop a 150-acre site in the Marina District at an unspecified time, anticipated to cost between $600 and $800 million.

EXHIBIT 6 *Circus Circus Enterprises, Inc. Annual Income Year ended January 31 (in thousands)*

Fiscal Year Ending	1/31/97	1/31/96	1/31/95	1/31/94	1/31/93
Revenues					
Casino	$655,902	$664,772	$612,115	$538,813	$495,012
Rooms	294,241	278,807	232,346	176,001	147,115
Food and Beverage	210,384	201,385	189,664	152,469	135,786
Other	146,554	158,534	166,295	117,501	92,500
Earnings of Unconsolidated Affiliates	86,646	45,485	5,459	—	—
	1,393,727	1,348,983	1,205,879	984,784	870,413
Less Complimentary Allowances	(59,477)	(49,387)	(35,697)	(29,861)	(27,388)
Net Revenue	1,334,250	1,299,596	1,170,182	954,923	843,025
Costs and Expenses					
Casino	302,096	275,680	246,416	209,402	189,499
Rooms	116,508	110,362	94,257	78,932	68,783
Food and Beverage	200,722	188,712	177,136	149,267	128,689
Other Operating Expenses	90,601	92,631	107,297	72,802	58,917
General and Administrative	227,348	215,083	183,175	152,104	130,152
Depreciation and Amortization	95,414	93,938	81,109	58,105	46,550
Preopening Expense	—	—	3,012	16,506	—
Abandonment Loss	48,309	45,148	—	—	—
	1,080,998	1,021,554	892,402	737,118	622,590
Operating Profit before Corporate Expense	223,252	278,042	277,780	217,805	220,435
Corporate Expense	31,083	26,669	21,773	16,744	14,953
Income from Operations	222,169	251,373	256,007	201,061	205,482
Other Income (Expense)					
Interest, Dividends and Other Income (Loss)	5,077	4,022	225	(683)	820
Interest Income and Guarantee Fees from Unconsolidated Affiliate	6,865	7,517	992	—	—
Interest Expense	(54,681)	(51,537)	(42,734)	(17,770)	(22,989)
Interest Expense from Unconsolidated Affiliate	(15,567)	(5,616)	—	—	—
	(58,306)	(45,614)	(41,517)	(18,453)	(22,169)
Income Before Provision for Income Tax	163,863	205,759	214,490	182,608	183,313
Provision for Income Tax	63,130	76,861	78,204	66,419	62,330
Income Before Extraordinary Loss	—	—	—	116,189	120,983
Extraordinary Loss	—	—	—	—	(3,661)
Net Income	100,733	128,898	136,286	116,189	117,32
Earnings Per Share					
Income before Extraordinary Loss	.99	1.33	1.59	1.34	1.41
Extraordinary Loss	—	—	—	—	(0.04)
Net Income Per Share	.99	1.33	1.59	1.34	1.37

Source: Circus Circus Annual Reports and 10Ks, 1993–1997.

EXHIBIT 7 *Circus Circus Enterprises, Inc. Consolidated Balance Sheets (in thousands)*

Fiscal Year Ending	1/31/97	1/31/96	1/31/95	1/31/94	1/31/93
Assets					
Current Assets					
Cash and Cash Equivalents	$69,516	$62,704	$53,764	$39,110	$43,415
Receivables	34,434	16,527	8,931	8,673	3,977
Inventories	19,371	20,459	22,660	20,057	16,565
Prepaid Expenses	19,951	19,418	20,103	20,062	14,478
Deferred Income Tax	8,577	7,272	5,463	—	—
Total Current Assets	151,849	124,380	110,921	87,902	78,435
Property, Equipment	1,920,032	1,474,684	1,239,062	1,183,164	851,463
Other Assets					
Excess of Purchase Price over Fair Market Value	385,583	394,518	9,836	10,200	10,563
Notes Receivable	36,443	27,508	68,083	—	—
Investments in Unconsolidated Affiliates	214,123	173,270	74,840	—	—
Deferred Charges and Other Assets	21,081	17,533	9,806	16,658	9,997
Total Other	657,230	612,829	162,565	26,858	20,560
Total Assets	2,729,111	2,213,503	1,512,548	1,297,924	950,458
Liabilities and Stockholders Equity					
Current Liabilities					
Current Portion of Long-Term Debt	379	863	106	169	154
Accounts and Contracts Payable					
Trade	22,658	16,824	12,102	14,804	11,473
Construction	21,144	—	1,101	13,844	27,762
Accrued Liabilities					
Salaries, Wages, and Vacations	31,847	30,866	24,946	19,650	16,097
Progressive Jackpots	6,799	8,151	7,447	4,881	4,827
Advance Room Deposits	7,383	7,517	8,701	6,981	4,012
Interest Payable	9,004	3,169	2,331	2,278	2,098
Other	30,554	28,142	25,274	25,648	20,363
Income Tax Payable	—	—	—	3,806	708
Total Current Liabilities	129,768	95,532	82,008	92,061	87,494
Long-Term Debt	1,405,897	715,214	632,652	567,345	308,092
Other Liabilities					
Deferred Income Tax	152,635	148,096	110,776	77,153	64,123
Other Long-Term Liabilities	6,439	9,319	988	1,415	740
Total Other Liabilities	159,074	157,415	111,764	78,568	64,863
Total Liabilities	1,694,739	968,161	826,424	737,974	460,449
Redeemable Preferred Stock	17,631	18,530	—	—	—
Temporary Equity	44,950	—	—	—	—
Commitments and Contingent Liabilities					
Stockholders Equity					
Common Stock	1,880	1,880	1,607	1,603	1,599
Preferred Stock					
Additional Paid-In Capital	498,893	527,205	124,960	120,135	111,516
Retained Earnings	984,363	883,630	754,732	618,446	502,257
Treasury Stock	(513,345)	(185,903)	(195,175)	(180,234)	(125,363)
Total Stockholders Equity	971,791	1,226,812	686,124	559,950	490,009
Total Liabilities and Stockholders Equity	2,729,111	2,213,503	1,512,548	1,297,924	950,458

Source: Circus Circus Annual Reports and 10Ks, 1993–1997.

Most of Circus's projects are being tailored to attract mainstream tourists and family vacationers. However, the addition of several joint ventures and the completion of the Masterplan Mile will also attract the more upscale customer.

THE GAMING INDUSTRY

By 1997, the gaming industry had captured a large amount of the vacation/leisure time dollars spent in the United States. Gamblers lost over $44.3 billion on legal wagering in 1995 (up from $29.9 billion in 1992) at racetracks, bingo parlors, lotteries, and casinos. This figure does not include dollars spent on lodging, food, transportation, and other related expenditures that are associated with visits to gaming facilities. Casino gambling accounts for 76 percent of all legal gambling expenditures, far ahead of second-place Indian reservation gambling at 8.9 percent, and lotteries at 7.1 percent. The popularity of casino gambling may be credited to a more frequent and somewhat higher payout as compared to lotteries and racetracks; however, as winnings are recycled, the multiplier effect restores a high return to casino operators.

Geographic expansion has slowed considerably as no additional states have approved casino-type gambling since 1993. Growth has occurred in developed locations with Las Vegas, Nevada, and Atlantic City, New Jersey, leading the way.

Las Vegas remains the largest U.S. gaming market and one of the largest convention markets with more than 100,000 hotel rooms hosting more than 29.6 million visitors in 1996, up 2.2 percent from 1995. Casino operators are building to take advantage of this continued growth. Recent projects include the Monte Carlo ($350 million), New York-New York ($350 million), Bellagio ($1.4 billion), Hilton Hotels ($750 million), and Project Paradise ($800 million). Additionally, Harrah's is adding a 989-room tower and remodeling 500 current rooms, and Caesar's Palace has expansion plans to add 2,000 rooms. According to the Las Vegas Convention and Visitor Authority, Las Vegas is a destination market with most visitors planning their trip more than a week in advance (81%), arriving by car (47%) or airplane (42%), and staying in a hotel (72%). Gamblers are typically return visitors (77%), averaging 2.2 trips per year and enjoy playing the slots (65%).

For Atlantic City, besides the geographical separation, the primary differences in the two markets reflect the different types of consumers frequenting them. While Las Vegas attracts overnight resort-seeking vacationers, Atlantic City's clientele is predominantly day-trippers traveling by automobile or bus. Gaming revenues are expected to continue to grow, perhaps to $4 billion in 1997, split between 10 casino/hotels currently operating. Growth in the Atlantic City area will be concentrated on the Marina District where Mirage Resorts has entered into an agreement with the city to develop 150 acres of the Marina as a destination resort. This development will include a resort wholly owned by Mirage, a casino-hotel developed by Circus, and a complex developed by a joint venture with Mirage and Boyd Corp. Currently in Atlantic City, Donald Trump's gaming empire holds the largest market share with Trump's Castle, Trump Plaza, and the Taj Mahal (total market share is 30%). The next closest in market share is Caesar's (10.3%), Tropicana and Bally's (9.2% each), and Show Boat (9.0%).

A number of smaller markets are located around the United States, primarily in Mississippi, Louisiana, Illinois, Missouri, and Indiana. Each state has imposed various restrictions on the development of casino operations. In some cases, for example, Illinois, where there are only 10 gaming licenses available, this has restricted severely the growth opportunities and damaged revenues. In Mississippi and Louisiana, revenues are up 8 percent and 15 percent, respectively, in riverboat operations. Native American casinos continue to be developed on federally controlled Indian land. These casinos are not publicly held but do tend to be managed by publicly held corporations. Overall, these other locations present a mix of opportunities and generally constitute only a small portion of overall gaming revenues.

MAJOR INDUSTRY COMPETITORS

Over the past several years there have been numerous changes as mergers and acquisitions have reshaped the gaming industry. As of year end 1996, the industry was a combination of corporations ranging from those engaged solely in gaming to multinational conglomerates. The largest competitors, in terms of revenue, combined multiple industries to generate

C-167

EXHIBIT 8 *Major U.S. Gaming, Lottery, and Pari-Mutuel Companies 1996 Revenues and Net Income (in millions)*

	1996 Revenues	1996 Net Income
ITT	$6597.0	$249.0
Hilton Hotels	3940.0	156.0
Harrah's Entertainment	1586.0	98.9
Mirage Resorts	1358.3	206.0
Circus Circus	1247.0	100.7
Trump Hotel and Casino, Inc.	976.3	−4.9
MGM Grand	804.8	74.5
Aztar	777.5	20.6
Int. Game Technology	733.5	118.0

Source: Individual Company's Annual Reports and 10Ks, 1996.

both large revenues and substantial profits (see Exhibit 8). However, those engaged primarily in gaming could also be extremely profitable.

ITT Corporation is one of the world's largest hotel and gaming corporations, owning the Sheraton, The Luxury Collection, the Four Points Hotels, and Caesar's, as well as communications and educational services. In 1996, ITT hosted approximately 50 million customer nights in locations worldwide. Gaming operations are located in Las Vegas, Atlantic City, Halifax and Sydney (Nova Scotia), Lake Tahoe, Tunica (Mississippi), Lima (Peru), Cairo (Egypt), Canada, and Australia. In 1996, ITT had net income of $249 million on revenues of $6.579 billion. In June 1996, ITT announced plans to join with Planet Hollywood to develop casino/hotels with the Planet Hollywood theme in both Las Vegas and Atlantic City. However, these plans may be deferred as ITT fends off an acquisition bid from Hilton Hotels.

Hilton Hotels owns or leases and operates 29 hotels and manages 42 hotels partially or wholly owned by others. Twelve of the hotels are also casinos, six of which are located in Nevada, two in Atlantic City, and the other four in Australia, Turkey, and Uruguay. In 1996, Hilton had net income of $156.0 million on $3.94 billion in revenues. Although continuing with expansion at current properties, Hilton seems to want to expand through acquisition. In January 1997, Hilton commenced an offer to acquire ITT Corporation in a combination of cash and stock transactions estimated at $6.5 billion. Although ITT rejected its offer, Hilton management chose to pursue a hostile takeover. The costs of such a

takeover attempt could be extremely high for both companies.

Harrah's Entertainment, Inc., is engaged primarily in the gaming industry with casino/hotels in Reno, Lake Tahoe, Las Vegas, and Laughlin, Nevada; Atlantic City, New Jersey; riverboats in Joliet, Illinois, and Vicksburg and Tunica, Mississippi; Shreveport, Louisiana; Kansas City, Kansas; two Indian casinos and one in Auckland, New Zealand. In 1996, it operated a total of approximately 701,200 square feet of casino space with 19,011 slot machines and 941 gaming tables. With this and some 6,478 hotel rooms, Harrah's had a net income of $98.9 million on $1.586 billion in revenues.

All of Mirage Resorts, Inc., gaming operations are located currently in Nevada. It owns and operates the Golden Nugget–Downtown, Las Vegas, the Mirage on the strip in Las Vegas, Treasure Island, and the Golden Nugget–Laughlin. Additionally, it is a 50 percent owner of the Monte Carlo with Circus Circus. Net income for Mirage Resorts in 1996 was $206 million on revenues of $1.358 billion. Current expansion plans include the development of the Bellagio in Las Vegas ($1.4 billion estimated cost) and the Beau Rivage in Biloxi, Mississippi ($550 million estimated cost). These two properties would add a total of 265,900 square feet of casino space to the current Mirage inventory and an additional 252 gaming tables and 4,746 slot machines. An additional project is the development of the Marina District in Atlantic City, New Jersey, in partnership with Boyd Gaming.

MGM Grand Hotel and Casino is located on approximately 113 acres at the northeast corner of

Las Vegas Boulevard across the street from New York-New York Hotel and Casino. The casino is approximately 171,500 square feet in size and is one of the largest casinos in the world with 3,708 slot machines and 163 table games. Current plans call for extensive renovation costing $250 million. Through a wholly owned subsidiary, MGM owns and operates the MGM Grand Diamond Beach Hotel and a hotel/casino resort in Darwin, Australia. Additionally, MGM and Primadonna Resorts, Inc., each own 50 percent of New York-New York Hotel and Casino, a $460 million architecturally distinctive themed destination resort which opened on January 3, 1997.

THE LEGAL ENVIRONMENT

All current operators within the gaming industry must comply with extensive gaming regulations. Each state or country has its own specific regulations and regulatory boards requiring extensive reporting and licensing requirements. For example, in Las Vegas, Nevada, gambling operators are subject to regulatory control by the Nevada State Gaming Control Board, the Clark County Nevada Gaming and Liquor Licensing Board, and by city government regulations. The laws, regulations, and supervisory procedures of virtually all gaming authorities are based upon public policy. They are concerned primarily with the prevention of unsavory or unsuitable persons from having a direct or indirect involvement with gaming at any time or in any capacity and the establishment and maintenance of responsible accounting practices and procedures. Additional regulations typically cover the maintenance of effective controls over the financial practices of licensees, including the establishment of minimum procedures for internal fiscal affairs and the safeguarding of assets and revenues, providing reliable recordkeeping, and requiring the filing of periodic reports, preventing cheating and fraudulent practices, and providing a source of state and local revenues through taxation and licensing fees. Changes in such laws, regulations, and procedures could have an adverse effect on any gaming operation. All gaming companies are required to submit detailed operating and financial reports to authorities. Nearly all financial transactions, including loans, leases, and the sale of securities, must be reported. Some financial activities are subject to approval by regulatory agencies. As Circus moves into other locations outside of Nevada, it will need to adhere to local regulations.

FUTURE CONSIDERATIONS

Circus Circus states that it is "in the business of entertainment, with ... core strength in casino gaming," and that it intends to focus its efforts on Las Vegas, Atlantic City, and Mississippi.

Circus was one of the innovators of the gaming resort concept and continues to be a leader in that field. However, the mega-entertainment resort industry operates differently than the traditional casino gaming industry. In the past, consumers would visit a casino to experience the thrill of gambling. Now they not only gamble but expect to be dazzled by enormous entertainment complexes that are costing billions of dollars to build. The competition has continued to increase at the same time growth rates have been slowing.

For years, analysts have questioned the ability of the gaming industry to continue high growth in established markets as the industry matures. Through the 1970s and 1980s, the gaming industry experienced rapid growth. Through the 1990s, the industry began to experience a shakeout of marginal competitors and a consolidation phase. Circus Circus has been successful through this turmoil but now faces the task of maintaining high growth in a more mature industry.

BIBLIOGRAPHY

Aztar Corp. *1997 10K*, retrieved from EDGAR Data Base, http://www.sec.gov/Archives/edgar/data/

"Casinos Move into New Areas," *Standard and Poor's Industry Surveys*, March 11, 1993, pp. L35–L41.

Circus Circus Enterprises, Inc., *Annual Report to Shareholders*, January 31, 1989; January 31, 1990; January 31, 1993; January 31, 1994; January 31, 1995; January 31, 1996.

"Circus Circus Announces Promotion," *PR Newswire*, June 10, 1997.

Circus Circus Enterprises, Inc., *Annual Report to Shareholders*, January 31, 1997.

Corning, Blair, "Luxor: Egypt Opens in Vegas," *San Antonio Express News*, October 24, 1993.

"Economic Impacts of Casino Gaming in the United States," by Arthur Anderson for the American Gaming Association, May 1997.

Harrah's Entertainment, Inc. *1997 10K*, retrieved from EDGAR Data Base, http://www.sec.gov/Archives/edgar/data/

"Harrah's Survey of Casino Entertainment," Harrah's Entertainment, Inc., 1996.

Hilton Hotels Corp. *1997 10K*, retrieved from EDGAR Data Base, http://www.sec.gov/Archives/edgar/data/

Industry Surveys—Lodging and Gaming, *Standard and Poor's Industry Surveys*, June 19, 1997.

"ITT Board Rejects Hilton's Offer as Inadequate, Reaffirms Belief that ITT's Comprehensive Plan Is in the Best Interest of ITT Shareholders," Press Release, August 14, 1997.

ITT Corp. *1997 10K*, retrieved from EDGAR Data Base, http://www.sec.gov/Archives/edgar/data/

Lalli, Sergio, "Excalibur Awaiteth," *Hotel and Motel Management*, June 11, 1990.

Mirage Resorts, Inc. *1997 10K*, retrieved from EDGAR Data Base, http://www.sec.gov/Archives/edgar/data/

MGM Grand, Inc. *1997 10K*, retrieved from EDGAR Data Base, http://www.sec.gov/Archives/edgar/data/

Columbia/HCA: One-Stop Shopping in the Health Care Industry

Marc Brockhaus
Lujuanna Haynes
Jeff Ogletree
Dan Parcel

Founded in 1987, Columbia/HCA grew quickly into the largest health care provider in the United States. Seeking to provide one-stop shopping for managed care providers, Columbia's goal was to own 100 percent of any market in which it did business.[1] In 1996, Columbia/HCA managed 341 hospitals, approximately 7 percent of hospitals in the United States. The Columbia/HCA health care system recorded more than 40 million patient visits that year, more than 50 times the number logged by its nearest competitor.[2] Earnings were increasing at a rate of about 20 percent annually, and many analysts rated Columbia/HCA's stock as a top investment choice.[3]

In March 1997, allegations of misconduct within the organization diminished investor and consumer confidence. That spring, federal search warrants were served on a number of Columbia/HCA operations by authorities requesting various records and documents. The government's investigation focused on fraudulent Medicare billings in laboratory and home health care operations. On July 30, 1997, the U.S. government issued indictments against three Columbia employees for alleged false characterization of interest payments on a certain debt. These

false characterizations ostensibly resulted in overpayments to the organization by Medicare and the Department of Defense insurance program known as CHAMPUS.[4]

Richard Scott, Columbia/HCA's founder and chief executive officer, resigned in July 1997. Following Scott's resignation, more than a dozen people associated with Columbia filed separate lawsuits against the organization under federal whistleblowing laws, claiming that Columbia/HCA was engaged in a variety of schemes to defraud national health care programs. As a result of those allegations, Columbia's stock price sank to $25\frac{3}{4}$ in October 1997 from $44\frac{3}{4}$ in February 1997. During this time, patient admissions fell by an estimated 2 percent.[5]

Following Scott's resignation, Thomas Frist, M.D., was appointed chief executive officer of Columbia/HCA. Frist's immediate concerns were related to cooperating with investigating authorities while restoring investor and consumer confidence in Columbia/HCA.

To facilitate an understanding of the strategic challenges faced by Columbia/HCA, an overview of the health care industry and the political environment in which it operated follows. A discussion of Columbia's history, the organization's key players, the 1997 FBI investigation, and the ethical issues associated with physician ownership are included. In conclusion, the competitive environment facing Columbia is explored, including an overview of other medical industry suppliers.

This case was prepared under the direction of Professor Robert E. Hoskisson. The case is intended to be used as the basis for class discussion rather than to illustrate either effective or ineffective handling of an administrative situation.

OPERATING ENVIRONMENT

The predominant demographic issue affecting the health care industry in 1997 was the aging of the population. Estimates by the Bureau of the Census projected a population growth rate of more than 50 percent over the 1990 population by the year 2050, despite movement of baby boom women out of their child-bearing years. The largest age group between 1990 and 2000 is between 45 and 54 years, which is projected to increase by 44 percent. The most rapidly-growing population segment is the 85-year and older age group, which is projected to increase sixfold by the year 2050. The combined effects of increased life expectancy and increased numbers of individuals entering these age groups fuels the growth of this senior age group.[6] Culturally, increased emphasis is being placed on healthy lifestyle choices, including both healthy eating and exercising.

Politically, health care reform is an issue of growing concern. President Clinton's 1994 health care reform proposal, however, was criticized as being too sweeping and complex in nature, resulting in its failure. In 1996, Clinton scaled down the reform's initial scope, proposing a simplified version designed to provide increased health care coverage for uninsured children and workers between jobs. In August 1996, President Clinton achieved a portion of that goal when he signed into law the "insurance portability" bill. This legislation enabled workers leaving a job where they had insurance coverage to obtain coverage at their next job if their new employer offered it.[7]

Over the preceding 25 years, the health sector's share of the U.S. economy has more than doubled, reaching approximately 14 percent of the gross domestic product (GDP) in 1992. The Congressional Budget Office predicts that the health sector's share of GDP will reach 19 percent by the year 2000.[8] Annual health care costs currently approximate $2,000 per person in the United States.[9] These costs are expected to increase at twice the inflation rate.[10] An explosion in entitlement spending on Social Security and Medicare loomed on the horizon, as the baby boom generation grew closer to the age of receiving such benefits.

Economically, increasing inequality in income levels within the United States created growing concern, although the reasons for that trend were not clear.[11] As the cost of health insurance and medical care ballooned, increasing numbers of individuals were forced to forego medical care because they could not afford health insurance or the expense of uninsured medical care. In 1992, an estimated 36 million U.S. residents lacked health care insurance.[12] Increasing income inequality in the years to follow exacerbated that situation.

HEALTH CARE INDUSTRY

The health care industry consists of fragmented groups, each of which serves a different health care need. The groups are generally identified as hospitals, outpatient services, home health care services, nursing homes, and assisted living facilities.

Nonprofit hospitals are generally community owned, whereas for-profit hospitals are generally investor owned. Eighty-five percent of the hospitals in the United States are nonprofit entities; the remaining 15 percent are for-profit. Nonprofit hospitals had a 1995 median operating margin of 3.7 percent, compared to an operating margin of 9.3 percent for investor-owned hospitals.[13] That difference generally reflects the enhanced ability of investor-owned hospitals to negotiate lower prices with suppliers, attract and negotiate prices with managed care business, and generate higher volumes at a lower cost.

Home health services provide patients with routine specialized care, such as respiratory therapy and the delivery of nutrients and other drugs, in the patient's home. In response to concerns of the insurance industry over rising health care costs, the demand for home health services increased rapidly as a less expensive alternative to hospital stays. From 1994 to 1995, the number of home care agencies increased from 13,296 to 15,037.[14] The primary customer base of home health services is individuals aged 65 and older.[15]

Assisted living facilities provide long-term care for residents early in their cycle of care. Services include 24-hour assistance, emergency call systems, transportation, food preparation, and social and recreational activities. When residents require more care than that provided in assisted living facilities, they are usually moved to nursing homes. The revenues received by assisted living facilities are generally paid by private sources. Assisted living facilities are among the most rapidly growing segments of the health care industry.[16] Consumer expenditures for assisted living care were estimated at $12 billion in 1997 and are forecasted to reach $18 to $20 billion by the year 2000.[17]

Nursing homes provide resident patients with long-term specialized care including rehabilitation and social and recreational services. In 1995, 54.2 percent of people living in nursing homes were Medicaid beneficiaries and 6.4 percent were Medicare beneficiaries.[18] A growing number of nursing home patients did not require the acute care provided at full-service hospitals, but were not well enough to return home. The nursing home industry receded, however, due partially to the lower annual cost per patient of individuals residing in assisted living facilities. The annual cost per patient for those residing in assisted living facilities was $20,000 compared to $32,000 for those in nursing homes.[19]

The health care industry is regulated heavily by the states, the federal government, and municipalities. Historically, the industry consisted of doctors' individual practices and stand-alone, nonprofit hospital institutions, which were typically community owned. Government programs reimbursed health care providers for the "reasonable and necessary costs" associated with providing care for their patients.[20] Included in the reimbursed costs were amounts spent by the health care provider on training, tests, room and board, and capital costs for new facilities. Insurance companies linked the amounts they would pay for given medical services to the amounts Medicare would pay. These programs did not encourage efficiency on the part of the health care providers that were participating in the programs. Indeed, large and inefficient hospital facilities were built because significant capital expenditures increased the amount of government reimbursements. The cost of health care in the United States was spiraling upward in the early 1980s due in part to these inefficiencies.[21]

To provide incentives for health care efficiency, in 1983 Medicare switched to a "fee for service" system where each particular service provided by health care providers was reimbursed up to a predetermined maximum amount.[22] If the health care provider could not perform the particular service at a lower cost than the maximum reimbursed amount, then the health

care provider suffered a loss. In addition, managed care plans such as insurance companies, government programs, (other than Medicare), and employers purchasing health care services had begun to negotiate purchase prices with health care providers instead of "paying standard prices."[23]

The historical "reasonable cost" government payment programs resulted in approximately 40 percent overcapacity in hospital facilities in 1997.[24] The pressure from government and private programs to reduce costs in the health care industry was intense. As shown in Exhibit 1, managed care plans and governmental programs, such as insurance companies and employer plans, and Medicare and Medicaid accounted for approximately 82 percent of health care providers' total revenues. Increased cost pressures from these groups lowered the prices that health care providers could generally charge, making it more difficult for health care providers to remain profitable.

Many hospitals closed due to increased competition. To increase buying power with suppliers, increase services provided to consumers, and utilize resources more efficiently, a number of health care survivors completed mergers and acquisitions. To further reduce costs, information systems were implemented, outpatient services were expanded, and managed care products were developed. Columbia/HCA implemented a $200 million information system in 1995 for just these purposes and aggressively acquired competitors to increase the number of services provided to patients.[25] In 1995, the hospitals of such diversified health care providers boasted a 52.1 percent rate of occupancy, compared to a 49.4 percent rate of occupancy at independent hospitals.[26] Furthermore, the increased scale of the resulting hospital networks permitted those networks to negotiate discounts of approximately 5 percent with their suppliers. Columbia/HCA's cost of medical supplies was a low 14.5 percent of revenues compared to an industry average of 16 percent.[27]

Hospitals' revenues depend on inpatient occupancy levels, the extent to which ancillary services and therapy programs are provided to patients, the volume of outpatient procedures, and the charges or negotiated payment rates for such services. Charges and reimbursement rates for inpatient routine services vary significantly depending on the type of service and the geographic location of the hospital. During the preceding period, however, the industry had

EXHIBIT 1 *1995 Health Care Expenditures by Source (in billions of dollars)*

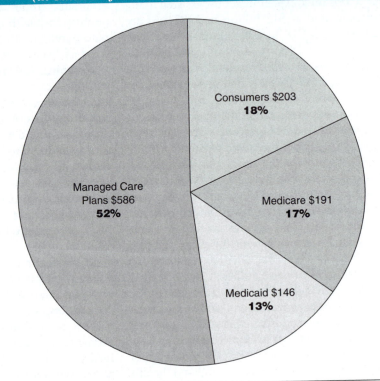

Source: 1996 Columbia Annual Report and 1995 *Journal of Health and Finance,* Summer 1997.

seen an increase in the percentage of patient revenues attributed to outpatient services. Outpatient services typically included rehabilitation, ambulatory surgery centers, physical therapy, sports medicine, and occupational health and pain management. The increase in outpatient services was primarily the result of advances in technology and acquisitions of outpatient facilities. Increased pressures from Medicare, Medicaid, health maintenance organizations (HMOs), preferred provider organizations (PPOs), and insurers to reduce hospital stays and to provide services on a less expensive outpatient basis also contributed to the increase in outpatient services.

Since 1987, Columbia/HCA has established itself as a leader in many segments of the health care industry, including home health care, hospital management, and outpatient surgery centers. The firm's expansion into the various industry segments is outlined in the following section.

COLUMBIA/HCA HISTORY

Following an unsolicited and unsuccessful $5 billion bid to assume control of Hospital Corporation of America (HCA) in 1987,[28] Richard L. Scott and Richard Rainwater joined forces to start a new hospital company from scratch. Each party invested $125,000 and Columbia Hospital Corporation was born.[29]

Beginning on September 1, 1993, Columbia initiated a series of major acquisitions with its purchase of Galen Health Care, Inc., from industry competitor Humana, Inc., at a cost of $3.2 billion (see Exhibit 2). Columbia's most significant transaction occurred on February 10, 1994, when it merged with HCA. HCA owned 97 hospitals in Florida, Texas, Tennessee, Virginia, and Georgia and generated approximately $5 billion in annual revenues. The 25-year-old HCA had long been recognized for its industry leadership,

EXHIBIT 2 *Columbia Health Care Timeline*

1968	Thomas Frist, Sr., Thomas Frist, Jr., and Jack C. Massey form Hospital Corporation of American (HCA).
1987	Scott and Rainwater make unsuccessful bid for HCA.
1987	Scott and Rainwater invest $125,000 each and form Columbia Hospital Corporation.
1993	Columbia purchases Galen Health Care, Inc., from Humana.
1994	Columbia merges with HCA.
1994	Columbia/HCA acquires Medical Care America, Inc.
1994	Columbia/HCA integrates into home health market by purchasing Keystone Home Health, Inc.
1995	Columbia/HCA acquires HealthTrust, Inc.
1997	Columbia/HCA purchases Value Health, Inc.
1997	Federal government launches investigation into Columbia/HCA.
1997	Rick Scott resigns.
1997	Thomas Frist, Jr. named new chairman of the board and CEO of Columbia/HCA.

quality hospitals, and strong physician relations.[30] The key goals of the Galen and HCA mergers were the realization of at least $160 million in annual synergies by renegotiating supply contracts, refinancing high coupon debt with investment-grade securities, and consolidating various functions.[31]

In September 1994, Columbia acquired Medical Care America, Inc., for $858 million. At the time of acquisition, Medical Care America, Inc., operated approximately 100 outpatient surgery centers. These centers were located mostly in Columbia's existing markets, such as Florida and Texas. Integrating these centers into Columbia's existing delivery network enabled Columbia to expand the scope of services available in these markets to include low-cost settings for outpatient surgical procedures. Furthermore, it served to enhance Columbia's relationship with surgeons practicing at the centers.[32]

Columbia continued its expansion into all areas of health care by purchasing Keystone Home Health, Inc., along with hundreds of independently established home care agencies. The rising popularity of home care as a hospitalization alternative fueled a proliferation of small home care providers. In response to that rapid expansion, most states enacted regulations limiting the number of home care providers. As a result, acquisition had become the only means by which Columbia could expand into new home care markets. By August 1997, approximately 6 percent of Columbia's $20 billion in annual revenues came from its home health care segment.[33]

HealthTrust, Inc., the second largest U.S. hospital chain, was acquired on April 24, 1995, for $3.6 billion in stock.[34] The addition of the HealthTrust hospitals strengthened Columbia's delivery network in several markets, including south and west Florida, New Orleans, Dallas/Fort Worth, Houston, and central Texas. This stronger market position allowed Columbia to reduce operating costs by sharing additional services and to bid aggressively for provider contracts with managed care plans and major employers. HealthTrust's suburban and sole community providers in Kentucky, Tennessee, Georgia, Alabama, and Louisiana complemented Columbia's established networks in nearby metropolitan areas. These HealthTrust facilities supported the metropolitan networks by providing a source of referrals for more sophisticated services. Furthermore, they contributed additional geographic coverage to Columbia's network, where managed care plans and major employers had coverage needs in these smaller communities.

In August of 1997, Columbia acquired Value Health in a stock deal worth $1.2 billion. Value Health is concentrated heavily in behavior health, disease management, and pharmacy benefits management.[35]

As Columbia grew, Scott invested heavily in information systems that would facilitate close monitoring of the performance of each of the company's hospitals and clinics. In September of 1997, Columbia was identified as one of the three most effective users of information technology in the United States.[36] Scott also imposed precise and highly ambitious revenue and profit goals on his nationwide team of regional and local managers, and yet allowed them considerable operating latitude.

Scott's management team openly recruited physicians to take co-ownership in its facilities. Scott believed such physician-owners would take a more active role in recruiting other physicians. He also believed they would be more motivated to improve efficiency by containing costs and evaluating capital expenditure decisions.

Columbia's decade-long strategy of aggressive acquisition was influenced strongly by the personality of its founder, Richard Scott, as well as a handful of key officers and investors. How this acquisition strategy will work relative to the strategies of competitors continues to be a long-term question. The following section describes Columbia/HCA's main competitors, including Tenet, Humana, Apria, and PacifiCare.

OVERVIEW OF THE COMPETITION

In 1997, major providers in the fragmented health care industry focused primarily on hospital management, although they continued to diversify into other medically related fields such as home care and pharmacy assistance. Smaller segment players competed within specific sectors such as home care or nursing services, rather than in all health-related fields.

Due to the size of the health care industry, Columbia had historically faced multiple competitors. As a result of numerous mergers and acquisitions, the number of competitors declined. In 1997, Columbia's major competitors included Tenet Healthcare in the hospital management segment and Humana Healthcare in the managed care segment. The third major competitor in the industry was the large number of smaller regional companies, which, although not as large, still posed a competitive threat on a regional basis.

Tenet and Humana were comparable to Columbia in several ways. Both were "national" in nature. Although not operational in each of the 50 states, they operated in several states within each geographic region of the United States. Exhibit 3 shows those states in which they competed. Furthermore, they competed head to head with Columbia in the hospital management field (until Humana sold its hospital division in 1993). Finally, they competed

with Columbia in the critical managed care area, from which 32 percent of Columbia's 1996 hospital admissions were drawn. (Comparative financial statement information is shown in Exhibit 4.)

Tenet Healthcare Systems

Tenet operated 131 health care facilities in 22 states, making it the second largest health care chain in the nation. Its primary focus was in the area of hospital management, HMOs, and home health programs. Tenet's reputation was built on the wide array of medical services it offered in the communities in which it operated. Tenet revolutionized the concept of health care systems within its operating regions, striving to make sure that the entire range of services offered was available somewhere within the members's home region network.[37]

After the start of the federal government's investigation of Columbia, Tenet considered acquiring the embattled Columbia chain. Talks were abandoned when Tenet was unable to ascertain Columbia's true value in light of potential punitive monetary damages that could be imposed by the federal government.[38] Tenet's timely membership in the AHA (American Hospital Association) gave it some political clout on the federal and state level. It also sent the message that Tenet intended to work with the not-for-profit hospitals rather than eliminate them.[39]

Tenet implemented a strategy of creating strategic alliances to serve areas it was not serving currently, as demonstrated by its alliance with Cedars-Mt. Sinai (CMS) in Los Angeles. The agreement stated that CMS would manage the facilities with Tenet's financial support, thereby leveraging CMS's familiarity with the status of medical care in that market.

Humana Healthcare

Humana was an established leader in the health care industry for many years and was known for its quality care and innovations. In 1984, public demand for higher-quality health care coupled with lower costs triggered Humana's development of a "new" concept known as the "Humana Healthcare Plan System." It consisted of a nationwide network of PPOs and HMOs. Humana continued to build its new system while managing hospitals.

By 1993, Humana had built the second largest chain of hospitals in the country (second only to

EXHIBIT 3 *Facility Locations (by competitor)*

State	Columbia	Tenet	Humana	PacifiCare	Apria
Alabama	X	X			X
Alaska	X		X		X
Arizona	X	X		X	X
Arkansas	X	X			X
California	X	X		X	X
Colorado	X			X	X
Connecticut			X		X
Delaware					X
Florida	X	X	X		X
Georgia	X	X	X		X
Hawaii					X
Idaho	X				X
Illinois	X		X	X	X
Indiana	X	X	X	X	X
Iowa	X	X			X
Kansas	X		X		X
Kentucky	X		X	X	X
Louisiana	X	X			X
Maine			X		X
Maryland					X
Massachusetts	X	X	X		X
Michigan					X
Minnesota	X		X		X
Mississippi	X	X			X
Missouri	X	X	X		X
Montana			X		X
Nebraska	X	X			X
Nevada	X	X	X	X	X
New Hampshire	X		X		X
New Jersey			X		X
New Mexico	X			X	X
New York			X		X
North Carolina	X	X			X
North Dakota					X
Ohio	X		X	X	X
Oklahoma	X			X	X
Oregon	X	X		X	X
Pennsylvania	X		X		X
Rhode Island	X		X		X
South Carolina	X	X			X
South Dakota					X
Tennessee	X	X			X
Texas	X	X	X	X	X
Utah	X			X	X
Vermont			X		X
Virginia	X				X
Washington	X	X	X	X	X
West Virginia	X	X			X
Wisconsin			X		X
Wyoming	X	X			X

EXHIBIT 4 *Comparative Financial Statements for Columbia and Competitors*

Income Statement	Columbia 1997 (First Half)	Columbia 1996	Columbia 1995	Humana 1997 (First Half)	Humana 1996	Humana 1995	PacifiCare 1997 (First Half)	PacifiCare 1996	PacifiCare 1995	Tenet 1997	Tenet 1996	Tenet 1995	Apria 1997 (First Half)	Apria 1996	Apria 1995
Sales	$10,515	$19,909	$17,695	$3,608	$6,667	$4,605	$4,225	$4,637	$3,731	$8,691	$5,559	$3,318	$587	$1,181	$1,134
Cost of Goods Sold	3,469	6,719	6,363	2,971	5,625	3,762	3,575	3,850	3,056	7,834	4,460	2,695	162	306	275
SG&A Expense	4,709	9,054	8,099	519	940	571	481	677	498	—	—	—	349	662	723
Depr/Amort.	613	1,155	981	49	98	70	55	32	29	443	321	195	67	112	103
Operating Income	1,724	2,981	2,252	69	14	202	113	79	148	414	778	428	9	101	34
Operating Margin	16.50%	15.00%	12.70%	1.90%	0.20%	4.40%	2.70%	1.70%	4.00%	4.80%	14.00%	12.90%	1.50%	8.60%	3.00%
Income	891	1,505	1,064	81	12	190	62	72	108	(207)	373	203	−10.5	33.30	−71.5
Profit Margin	8.60%	7.60%	6.00%	2.20%	0.20%	4.10%	1.60%	1.60%	2.90%	−2.38%	6.70%	6.10%	−1.70%	2.80%	
EPS Primary	0.66	2.22	1.58	0.49	0.07	1.17	0.39	2.27	3.62	(0.68)	1.78	1.04	(0.21)	0.64	(1.52)
EPS Fully Diluted	0.66	2.22	1.58	0.49	0.07	1.17	0.39	2.27	3.62	(0.68)	1.74	1.01	(0.21)	0.64	(1.52)
Assets															
Cash	$ 109	$ 113	$ 232	$ 55	$ 322	$ 182	$ 239	$ 143	$ 279	$ 35	$ 89	$ 155	$ 18	$ 27	$ 19
Receivables	3,203	3,023	2,665	256	211	131	273	170	112	1,346	838	565	367	336	258
Inventories	457	441	406	—	—	—	—	—	—	193	128	116	58	56	45
Current Assets	4,756	4,413	4,200	1,780	2,002	1,593	1,498	934	962	2,391	1,545	1,624	498	494	404
Total Assets	21,927	21,272	19,892	2,958	3,153	2,878	4,604	1,300	1,385	11,705	8,332	7,918	1,143	1,149	980
Liabilities															
Short-Term Debt	$ 267	$ 201	$ 243	—	—	—	$ 1	$ 6	$ 8	$ 28	$ 60	$ 287	$ 11	$ 12	$ 10
Long-Term Debt	7,381	6,781	7,137	3	225	399	1,091	5	12	5,022	3,191	3,273	614	623	491
Current Liabilities	2,660	2,946	2,738	1,433	1,500	1,192	1,189	471	641	1,869	1,134	1,356	162	182	205
Total Liabilities		12,663	12,763		1,861	1,591		476	653		5,696	5,932		806	696
Equity															
Common Stock	$ 8,801	$ 8,609	$ 7,129	$1,384	$1,292	$1,287	$2,135	$ 823	$ 732	$3,224	$2,636	$1,986	$364	$343	$284
Shares Outstanding	654	671	668	163.4	162.7	162.1	33.7	18.9	18.6	302.8	215.9	200	51.3	51.2	49.7

Source: Hoovers Online Annual Reports (www.hoovers.com/annuals).

Columbia), mostly through mergers and acquisitions. In a strategic move, Humana divided its hospital and health care divisions into two separate companies. Eventually, Columbia purchased the hospital division, thus removing Humana from the hospital management segment of the industry.

In July 1997, Humana had HMO/PPO core operations in 24 states (see Exhibit 3). With other operations in 14 more states, 1997 found Humana operating in a total of 38 states with a total enrollment of over 4.8 million.[40] Although it did not compete directly with Columbia in the hospital sector, Humana was large enough to pose a credible competitive threat.

Apria Healthcare

Apria is the nation's largest chain of home health care providers, operating 350 branches in all 50 states. Apria was formed as the result of a merger between the nation's number-one and number-two home health providers. It had sales of $1.1 billion in 1996; sales were projected to reach $1.3 billion in 1997. As of September 1997, Apria was available for sale. It had experienced serious financial problems as a result of an accounts receivable write-off in fiscal year 1997.[41] Following the departure of the founding CEO, Apria's president was leading the company until a buyer could be found.

PacifiCare Healthcare

PacifiCare operated the largest Medicare HMO chain in the country. By 1997, it had an enrollment of 4 million and operations in 14 states.[42] PacifiCare acquired FHP International, an HMO with branches in Illinois, Ohio, Indiana, and Kentucky, and was in the process of selling off the divisions it did not wish to incorporate into the PacifiCare network. PacifiCare was also fighting a growing class action lawsuit (started by FHP shareholders) that involved the information flow during the FHP buyout.[43]

MEDICAL INDUSTRY SUPPLIERS

The primary inputs in the health care industry consisted of labor, medical supplies/equipment, and pharmaceuticals. In 1996, labor accounted for approximately 40 percent of the industry's operating costs.[44] No labor unions dominated the industry, but the American Medical Association (AMA) exerted significant political influence within both the industry and the nation. In 1992, the AMA ranked second in size among the Federal Election Commission's top 50 political action committees.[45] In 1993, approximately 41.6 percent of the 615,000 physicians in the United States were AMA members.[46] Although AMA membership had been declining, the reduction was attributed not to the presence of fewer doctors, but to "soaring (AMA) membership fees and the proliferation of some 80 medical-specialty societies"[47] such as the American College of Physicians. The other primary source of labor was the nursing profession, with 2.1 million registered nurses in 1993.[48]

As with the industry they support, medical suppliers operate in an industry characterized by fierce competition and substantial government regulation. One supplier stands apart as an industry leader—Abbot Laboratories. Abbott is a diversified health care company operating in 130 countries, with a reputation for a lean, highly-centralized operating style and stick-to-business strategies. It developed and marketed products that are designed to improve diagnostic, therapeutic, and nutritional practices. In 1994, 25 percent of Abbott's sales were in pharmaceuticals, with the balance divided equally among hospital supplies, nutrition and diagnostics products, agricultural products, and veterinary products. In 1992, Abbott responded to the rapidly changing health care environment by creating a domestic managed care sales unit.

In the early 1980s, Baxter International, Inc. (Abbott's chief competitor) sought to increase market share by investing in increased distribution capabilities, accomplishing this with the purchase of American Hospital Supply Corp. Customers of American Hospital Supply, however, reacted negatively to having their choice of products restricted to those produced by Baxter. While Baxter was struggling to consolidate this acquisition, Abbott started a price war and gained the market leadership position. Abbott supported its market victory by standing firm in its policy of increasing its investment in research and development.[49]

Despite its market leadership position in the health care industry and the power that Columbia/HCA had attained over many industry suppliers, the summer of 1997 brought a wave of legal and political concerns to the forefront of public attention.

FBI INVESTIGATION

On March 19, 1997, Columbia's El Paso, Texas, operations were served search warrants by federal authorities requesting various records and documents.[50] This event triggered a chain of reactions that would result in Richard Scott's resignation within months.

Darla Moore, the wife of Scott's partner Richard Rainwater, claimed to have spotted trouble early on at Columbia, stating that she felt uneasy with Rick Scott's management style.[51] Late in 1996, Moore began voicing her opinions to Rainwater and Frist. Neither of them, however, was losing faith in Scott. Profits were increasing some 20 percent a year and the stock price was rising steadily; with $20 billion in revenues, Columbia was America's most admired health care company, according to *Fortune* magazine's annual survey.[52] During that time, Moore began to strengthen her alliance with Frist, who was beginning to feel shut out completely by Scott.

In June 1997, shortly after the search in El Paso, Frist gave Scott a nine-page letter outlining Columbia's problems and possible solutions. Scott never acknowledged the letter. In July 1997, Rainwater, Moore, and Frist began planning Scott's overthrow. Rainwater maintained his distance from the plan, dreading turning on his friend and partner. Moore wanted to merge Columbia with the industry's second largest company, Tenet Healthcare, and install Tenet's CEO as chief executive of the combined company. Not only did the proposal make sense financially, but it would also allow Scott to depart Columbia with relative dignity. The merger between Columbia and Tenet never occurred; the two companies could not agree on the value of Columbia's stock.[53]

On July 16, 1997, various Columbia-affiliated operations in Florida, North Carolina, Oklahoma, Tennessee, Texas, and Utah were searched pursuant to search warrants issued by the U.S. District Court in those states.[54] At that time, the investigation appeared to be focusing on laboratory billing and home health care operations. Early on the morning of July 17, 1997, Scott called Moore. During that conversation Moore told him, "It's over."[55]

At a board meeting on July 24, 1997, both Richard Scott and Columbia's chief operating officer, David Vandewater, resigned along with several other executives.[56] Thomas Frist was elected to replace Scott.

On July 30, 1997, the U.S. District Court for the Middle District of Florida, in Ft. Myers, issued an indictment against three Columbia employees.[57] The indictment related to Medicare and CHAMPUS reimbursement issues. The specific allegations related to alleged false characterization of interest payments on certain debt, resulting in overpayments to the hospitals by Medicare and CHAMPUS.

Nearly 40 percent of Columbia's patient revenues were from Medicare and Medicaid reimbursements. If found guilty, the federal government would no longer be obligated to reimburse Columbia for services rendered to Medicare recipients.

Following the issuance of the indictment, more than a dozen people associated with Columbia filed separate lawsuits against the company under federal whistle-blower laws, alleging that Columbia had engaged in a variety of schemes to defraud national health care programs. The existence of the whistle-blower suits, almost none of which were disclosed, meant that federal officials were provided with an inside look into Columbia's operations long before disclosing the existence of an inquiry.

On August 7, 1997, Frist announced several steps that would be undertaken to redefine the company's approach to its current business activities. Columbia retained the services of the law firm Latham and Watkins and the accounting firm DeLoitte & Touche and charged them with broad powers to examine the current practices of the companies, to recommend new policies and procedures, and to work with the government to resolve outstanding issues. The firm's action plan included:

- Elimination of annual cash incentive compensation for all of the company's employees.
- Sale of the home care division.
- Discontinued sale of interests in hospitals to physicians and unwinding of existing physician's interests.
- Adoption of a tough and comprehensive compliance program.
- Increased disclosures in Medicare cost reports.
- Changes in laboratory billing procedures.
- Increased reviews of Medicare coding.[58]

On August 16, 1997, Florida's State Board of Administration filed a lawsuit against Columbia, its board of directors, and key current and former executives, charging the company with mismanagement that led to stock losses for the state's public employees' pension fund. The Florida suit claimed that Columbia defrauded the government for years by intentionally inflating the cost of treating Medicare patients by "up-coding" the severity of medical procedures billed to Medicare. The suit further claimed that Columbia's hospitals showed complication rates in Medicare cases that were higher than the rates found at teaching hospitals, in some cases approaching rates of 100 percent. The suit also charged that physicians were forced by contract to meet established quotas of surgeries and office visits per month, with bonuses awarded accordingly. According to the Health Care Financing Administration, such agreements were illegal. Florida is just one of several states, including New York and Louisiana, that have filed suits on behalf of their pension funds.[59]

In September 1997, it remained too early to tell what fines Columbia might face in resolving the federal investigation. Conjecture by "those close to the investigation" estimated fines could approach $1 billion.[60] Federal officials continued to pursue a broad investigation into Columbia's billing practices, its operations, and its financial relationships with physicians.

PHYSICIAN-OWNERSHIP ISSUES

In addition to the legal allegations of fraud that Columbia faced, legal and ethical questions were also being raised in connection with the company's policy of encouraging physician ownership in the organization. Potential conflicts of interest created by physician-ownership of medical facilities such as testing labs, operating facilities, imaging centers, and home health care companies created widely divergent viewpoints regarding the medical field. Many consumers and consumer advocates questioned whether such a doctor/investor remained the patient's advocate, or whether he or she became a businessman selling his wares. Studies performed at AMA's request revealed that approximately 10 percent of physicians nationwide had ownership interests in health care entities that involved issues of self-referral.[61] Furthermore, a study by the Department of Health and Human Services found that self-

referring physicians referred patients for testing at a rate 45 percent higher than noninvesting physicians.[62]

As a proponent of physician ownership, Columbia sold physicians and hospital management up to 20 percent of the stock in its local subsidiaries, arranging low-interest loans to physicians to promote that investment.[63] Stockholders were limited to an initial investment of no more than $150,000 and were restricted to buying or selling shares directly with Columbia/HCA at a predetermined multiple of earnings.[64] Columbia argued that such ownership provided incentives for physicians to practice economical medicine.[65]

The American Medical Association viewed the problem from a similar perspective, subject to restrictions. The conflicts inherent in the practice of "self-referral" were addressed initially in 1986 and reexamined in 1989. From these examinations, the Council on Ethical and Judicial Affairs of the American Medical Association determined that the problem of self-referral was "not significantly different in principle from other conflicts presented by fee-for-service medicine" and other managed health care arrangements.[66] Despite issuing a list of safeguards designed to help ensure the protection of patients' interests, the council assumed that when a physician's financial interests conflicted with the best interests of the patient, the physician would not take advantage of the patient.[67]

Supporting the investment by physicians in health care facilities, the AMA pointed out that their special expertise gave physicians a better understanding than laypersons of the community's needs and the available technologies. It was further assumed that because they would have a better understanding of the potential returns associated with investing in health care facilities, they would also be more willing to accept the risks of such investments.[68] In 1990, the AMA did recommend, however, that physician referrals not be made to health care facilities in which that physician was an investor unless the physician was also a direct provider of services at that facility.[69] The AMA further recommended that physician investment should be made only where there was a demonstrated need in the community and alternative financing was not available.[70]

In addition to the ethical implications raised by physician-ownership of health care facilities, federal law generally prohibited health care providers from giving or receiving financial inducements for referrals of Medicare and Medicaid patients. These patients accounted for approximately 30 percent of the nation's health care expenditures in 1995 (see Exhibit 1).

KEY PLAYERS

Richard L. Scott

Co-founder and former chief executive officer of Columbia/HCA, Richard L. Scott was an intensely competitive man sometimes called a visionary in the health care field. Scott was born in 1952 and raised in a blue-collar family of five children. His stepfather was an over-the-road truck driver; his mother worked at numerous low-paying jobs to help make ends meet. Learning the value of thrift at an early age, Scott's drive was shaped by two goals: "get smart and get rich."[71] Following a brief stint in the U.S. Navy Reserves, Scott purchased his first business venture as a freshman in college. He completed his bachelor's degree in business administration in just over two years at the University of Missouri, followed by a law degree from Southern Methodist University. Upon graduating, Scott joined a large Dallas law firm where he specialized in merger-and-acquisition assignments for health care companies. He was made a partner in that firm in 1984.[72]

Scott had a vision to build a national multiservice health care chain and, in 1987, at the age of 36, he teamed with Richard Rainwater to begin executing his vision. Scott was known as a hard-working deal maker, working six-day work weeks and 12-hour days.[73] Between 1987 and 1997, Scott evolved from being a newcomer in the health care industry to becoming its voice. He developed a reputation as brazen, aggressive, thrifty, quick-minded, and sharp-tempered.[74] Peers labeled him a "cheap son-of-a-gun"[75] and a great poker player who gave nothing away.[76] In 1994, he was named Southwestern Entrepreneur of the Year by *Inc.* magazine.[77] At the time of his resignation, Scott owned 1.4 percent of Columbia's stock.[78]

During Scott's tenure at Columbia, a number of unwritten rules were imposed on those who worked for the organization. Associates understood that they were expected to dress well and work long hours. Further, Scott tolerated a negative attitude "about as long as he would suffer a fool, which is ten seconds,

tops."[79] The most important of Scott's unwritten rules, however, was the "no jerks" rule. It was the rule that must never be violated. Anyone who could not get along with people was asked to leave.[80] Despite these rules, however, employees praised his sense of fair play and his business sense, saying he was never observed to lose his composure or swear; he engendered physicians' trust by always doing what he said he would do.[81]

Thomas F. Frist, Jr., M.D.

Frist was born in Nashville, Tennessee. He received his B.A. degree from Vanderbilt University in 1961 and his M.D. degree from Washington University School of Medicine, St. Louis, in 1965. In 1968, he founded HCA along with his father, Thomas Frist, Sr., M.D., and the late Jack C. Massey. In 1977, he was named president of HCA, followed in 1987 by being named chairman, president, and chief executive officer.[82]

When Columbia and HCA merged in February 1994, Darla Moore and Richard Rainwater persuaded Frist to act as chairman of the board and allow Scott to serve as CEO. Following the resignation of Richard Scott, Frist became chairman and chief executive officer of Columbia/HCA Healthcare Corporation on July 25, 1997.[83] At the age of 59, Frist was Columbia's largest individual stockholder, with 14.6 million shares, or about 2.2 percent of Columbia stock.[84]

In the wake of Richard Scott's departure, Frist faces a plethora of challenges that must be overcome if Columbia/HCA is to remain a viable concern within the health care industry.

Darla Moore and Richard Rainwater

Richard Rainwater partnered with Richard Scott to start Columbia in 1987. At that time, Rainwater was a Fort Worth investor, having just served 16 years with Texas's Bass family. Rainwater had earned close to $100 million and was looking for new investment opportunities.

In 1993, Rainwater married banking executive Darla Moore. Soon after, she assumed control of Rainwater's investment portfolio and by 1997 had nearly tripled his net worth to $1.5 billion. Together, Rainwater and Moore owned approximately $260 million of Columbia stock,[85] or 12 million shares.

STRATEGIC CHALLENGES

A multitude of strategic challenges faced the organization in the wake of the federal government's investigation and Scott's departure. Investor confidence in the company had been shaken, despite its history of leadership in redefining the health care industry. Questions regarding the legal and ethical standards of the organization abounded, resulting in rapid erosion of its stock value. Preventing further erosion of the stock's value was crucial as Columbia faced the potential for significant financial liabilities resulting from lawsuits and the federal investigation.

In addition to the crisis in investor confidence, hospital admissions were dropping as physicians began referring patients to other hospitals. Reasons for that trend may be rooted in the legal necessity of unraveling the physician-investment relationships within the organization. As such incentives for referring patients to a Columbia facility were removed, physicians began to make greater use of facilities not owned by Columbia. Furthermore, physicians and consumers appeared to be losing faith in the organization's billing practices and ethical standards. Maintaining the organization's revenues by maintaining the level of referrals and patient admission rates was just as critical as rebuilding investor confidence.

Given the climate of general upheaval within the company, strong new leadership is vital. Scott had been a charismatic leader who offered a clear vision of the company and the industry's future. His strong personality had dominated the Columbia organization for a decade. In his absence, the organization needs an equally charismatic leader with a strong image of integrity and ethics. Frist needs to communicate a new sense of direction to network physicians, who have grown cautious of the expanding quagmire of public scorn and legal liability. He is challenged to formulate Columbia/HCA's strategic turnaround.

ENDNOTES

1. D. S. Hilzenrath, 1994, Hospital Chain Adopts a Bigger-Is-Better Strategy, *The Washington Post*, March 7, A1.
2. The King Kong of Hospital Chains Stays on Top by Gobbling Up Everything in Sight, 1997, *Money*, April 26(4), 78.
3. P. Sellers, 1997, Don't Mess with Darla, *Fortune*, September 8, 64–69.
4. K. Hundley, 1997, Three Columbia/HCA Executives Plead Not Guilty to Medicare Fraud Charges, *Knight-Ridder/Tribune Business News*, August 21, 821B1103.
5. Columbia/HCA, 1997, Form 10-Q, August 14, 3.
6. Bureau of the Census, 1993, *Population Projections of the United States by Age, Sex, Race and Hispanic Origin: 1993 to 2050*, Bureau of the Census, U.S. Department of Commerce, November, vii.
7. S. Langdon, 1996, Partisan Hurdles Lie in Wait for Expanded Coverage, *Congressional Quarterly*, November 16, 3283.
8. Congressional Budget Office, 1993, *Baby Boomers in Retirement: An Early Perspective*, Congressional Budget Office, The Congress of the United States, September, 45.
9. Physicians for a National Health Program, 1997, Newsletter Excerpts, July, *http://www.pnhp.org/news/jul97/data.html.*
10. A. Serwer, 1996, Health Care Stocks the Hidden Stars, *http://www.pathfinder.com/fortune*, October 14.
11. Bureau of the Census, 1990, *Money Income and Poverty Status in the United States*, 1989, Consumer Income Series P-60, No. 168, U.S. Department of Commerce, Bureau of the Census, 5.
12. Physicians for a National Health Program, 1997, Newsletter Excerpts, December, *http://www.pnhp.org/Data/dataD97.html.*
13. Standard & Poor's, 1997, Healthcare Facilities, *Industry Surveys*, March 27, 1–2.
14. Ibid., 5.
15. Ibid., 6.
16. Ibid., 4.
17. Ibid.
18. Ibid., 3.
19. Ibid., 5.
20. Ibid., 13.
21. Ibid., 14.
22. Ibid.
23. Columbia/HCA 1996 Annual Report, 12.
24. Standard & Poor's, *Industry Surveys*, 9.
25. Columbia/HCA 1997 Annual Report, 4.
26. Standard & Poor's, *Industry Surveys*, 13.
27. Ibid., 21.
28. Hilzenrath, *Hospital Chain*, A1.
29. A. Bianco, 1997, Is Rick Scott on the Critical List? Columbia/HCA's CEO May Have Made Too Many Enemies—Including Some of His Own Board, *Business Week*, August 4, 36.
30. Columbia/HCA 1994 Annual Report, 2.
31. Ibid., 1.
32. Ibid., 2.
33. D. Poppe, 1997, Buyers surface for Columbia's Home Health Care Unit, *Knight-Ridder/Business Tribune News*, August 21, B11.
34. K. Adams, 1994, A New Health-Care Giant, *Time*, October 17, 8.
35. Columbia/HCA 1997 Form 10-Q, filed August 14, 2.
36. Columbia/HCA Press Release, September 23, 1997.
37. Tenet Healthcare, 1997, General Facts, http://www.tenethealth.com, October 9.
38. R. Rundle, 1997, Tenet Healthcare Admits It Discussed Buying Columbia/HCA, http://www.smartmoney.com, October 1.

39. American Hospital Association, 1997, Tenet Healthcare Joins American Hospital Association, Tenet Healthcare, http://www.tenethealth.com, August 1.

40. Humana, 1997, Humana Snapshot, Humana, http://www.humana.com, August.

41. J. Greene, 1997, Apria Setting Stage for Sale: Billing Problems Lead to a Write-Off and a Search for a Buyer, *Orange County Register*, http://www.ocregister.com/news, June 27.

42. Hoover's Online, 1997, PacifiCare Health Systems, Inc., http://www.hoovers.com.

43. PacifiCare Health Systems, Inc., 1997, Class Action Suit Arising Out of Sale of FHP Int'l to PacifiCare, Talbert Medical Separation and Rights Offering and Talbert Sale to MedPartners, SmartMoney Interactive, http://www.smartmoney.com, September 26.

44. J. Fuquay, 1993, Creating the Future, *The Fort Worth Star-Telegram*, October 7, 1.

45. Physicians for a National Health Program, July.

46. M. Galen, 1993, The AMA Is Looking a Bit Anemic, *Business Week*, April 12, 70.

47. Ibid.

48. Ibid., 71.

49. M. Berss, 1994, Aloof But Not Asleep, *Forbes*, August 29, 43.

50. Columbia/HCA 1997 Form 10-Q, August.

51. Sellers, Don't mess with Darla, 65.

52. Ibid.

53. Ibid.

54. Columbia 1997 Form 10-Q, August.

55. Sellers, Don't mess with Darla, 64.

56. K. Eichenwald, 1997, Two Leaders Step Down at Health-Care Giant, *http://www.nytimes.com*, July 26.

57. Columbia 1997 Form 10-Q, August.

58. Press Release: *Columbia/HCA CEO Announces Planned Changes in Business Approach*, August 7, 1997.

59. Poppe, Buyers surface.

60. G. Jaffe and E. M. Rodriguez, 1997, In Hospital Probes, a New Focus on Bottom Line, *Wall Street Journal*, September 12, B1.

61. *Journal of the American Medical Association*, 1992, Conflicts of Interest: Physician Ownership of Medical Facilities, Council on Ethical and Judicial Affairs, Vol. 267, No. 17, May 6, 2366–2369.

62. Ibid., 2366–2369.

63. M. Walsh, 1997, Doctors with Stakes, *Forbes*, October 10, 76.

64. Ibid.

65. Ibid.

66. *Journal of the American Medical Association*, 2366.

67. Ibid.

68. Ibid., 2368.

69. Ibid.

70. Ibid.

71. B. Deener, 1993, Exec Aims High, Hits His Mark: Health Care Firm to be U.S.' Biggest, *Dallas Morning News*, October 10, A1.

72. M. Freudenheim, 1993, The Hospital World's Hard-Driving Money Man, *New York Times Biographical Service*, October, 1368–1369.

73. Ibid.

74. E. Forman, 1997, Entrepreneur Built a Giant: Columbia/HCA Founder's Firm Grew From 2 To 330 Hospitals In a Decade, *Ft. Lauderdale Sun-Sentinel*, July 26, C14.

75. P. Annin, 1993, Now, Health Care Has a Merchant King, *Newsweek*, June 28, 40.

76. Forman, Entrepreneur built a giant, C14.

77. Ibid.

78. Bianco, Is Rick Scott on the critical list?, 36.

79. Deener, 1997, U.S. Investigating Columbia Health Firm, *Dallas Morning News*, March 28, A2.

80. Ibid.

81. Ibid.

82. Columbia/HCA, 1997, Columbia Overview, Columbia/HCA, http://www.columbia.net/overview/html, September 9.

83. Ibid.

84. K. Drawbaugh, 1997, Two Top Columbia/HCA Executives Resign, *Reuters*, July 25, 1.

85. Sellers, Don't mess with Darla, 64.

Compaq: Conflicts Between Alliances

Becky Madison
Jennifer Speegle

The Compaq products exceeded our expectation [with BackOffice]. We got highly reliable systems with better performance than we ever thought possible.
—Chris Gibbons, Microsoft's CIO

Oracle InterOffice, and our alliance with Compaq, will redefine corporate computing.
—Ray Lane, President of Worldwide Operations, Oracle Corporation

As vendors of computer software and hardware recognize the need to complement each other's diverse strengths to provide better integrated solutions for customers, strategic alliances between such firms begin to form. The obvious goal of strategic partnerships is to outperform competitors, but what happens when your partners are in direct competition with each other?[1]

For the past decade, Microsoft and Compaq have worked together to form a solid alliance that has brought new and innovative products to the forefront of the computer industry. However, Compaq's alliance with Oracle is directly challenging the previously strong partnership between Microsoft and Compaq.

Compaq's dual support of Microsoft's BackOffice and Oracle's InterOffice, two competing network

This case was prepared under the direction of Professor Robert E. Hoskisson. The case is intended to be used as the basis for class discussion rather than to illustrate either effective or ineffective handling of an administrative situation.

software suites, is a source of tension for both Microsoft and Oracle. While Oracle's InterOffice appears to be the better product, Oracle fears Microsoft because it already controls the personal computer (PC) software market. Microsoft, on the other hand, is ready to abandon Compaq if it continues to support Oracle's InterOffice. Compaq has shared successes with both companies, which leaves the president and CEO of Compaq, Eckhard Pfeiffer, facing a huge dilemma.

COMPAQ'S BACKGROUND

The Compaq Computer Corporation is the fifth largest computer company in the world and the world's largest supplier of personal computers, manufacturing servers, and desktop, portable, and notebook PCs.[2] Since its founding in 1982, Compaq has boasted of many achievements; the company built the first IBM-compatible portable computer, introduced the first three-year warranty and became a *Fortune* 500 company and achieved $1 billion in sales faster than any company in U.S. history.[3]

Leading Compaq's corporate strategies and operations is president and CEO Eckhard Pfeiffer. Pfeiffer served as executive vice president, COO, and head of Compaq's international operations for eight years before becoming president and CEO in 1991.[4] Pfeiffer realizes the value of pooling resources and technology and thus has joined forces with several companies within the computer industry over the years. Compaq's most important partners include Microsoft, Oracle, SAP, Cheyenne, Novell, SCO, and Sybase.[5]

While its headquarters is located in Houston, Texas, Compaq products can be found in over 100 countries worldwide, "connecting people with people and people with information."[6] Reporting net sales of approximately $4.2 billion in 1996 (see Exhibit 1), Compaq continues to grow and plans to be among the top three computer companies in the world by 2000.[7]

To achieve such high levels of growth and success, Compaq relies on a unique organizational structure, a strong management team, and alliance partnerships. The Compaq organizational structure is divided currently into four product groups:

- PC Products—responsible for the design, manufacturing, and marketing of Compaq's desktop PC line, DeskPro.

- Consumer Products—responsible for Compaq's consumer PC family, Presario. This division focuses on the latest technology and advancements in multimedia, sound, and price performance in the growing home PC market.

- Communications Products—responsible for all of Compaq's communications businesses including the networking products businesses. This division

works to provide customers with access to people, information, and new ways to network.

- Enterprise Computing—responsible for delivering high-performance, high-availability, fault-tolerant, and tightly integrated solutions for decentralized business information systems that maintain centralized control, known as a "distributed enterprise."[8]

COMPAQ'S DISTRIBUTED ENTERPRISE ALLIANCES

In the early 1990s, the PC market was booming, but Compaq was not satisfied. It wanted to be more than a PC maker and was looking to new markets to secure future revenues. CEO Pfeiffer announced that Compaq was about to transcend its PC boundaries and move into the distributed enterprise market.[9] In this new market, Compaq is looking to achieve a complete range of high-quality products and a thorough understanding of the integration and management of business-related computer networks in order to give businesses the ability to access information across multiple platforms.[10] However, Compaq's inability to handle financing, leasing, service, and support has hindered the company from achieving a strong position in the enterprise market. There-

EXHIBIT 1 *Compaq's Income Statement*

	(in millions of dollars)	
	1996	1995
Net Revenues	$4,196	$3,388
Operating Expenses		
General and administrative	$1,912	$1,594
Research and development	$ 407	$ 207
Purchase in-process technology		$ 241
Other income and expenses, net	$ 1	$ 95
Total operating expenses	$2,320	$2,200
Income before income taxes	$1,876	$1,188
Provision for income tax	$ 563	$ 399
Net Income	$1,313	$ 789
Earnings per share (dollars)	$ 4.72	$ 2.88

Source: *Information for this exhibit found at:*
http://www.compaq.com:80/newsroom/pr/pr22019/a.html.

fore, Pfeiffer decided to build several alliances with companies that rely on industry standards to secure a strong position in the enterprise market. Compaq's strongest and most strategic partners with respect to the distributed enterprise are software vendors Microsoft and Oracle.

Microsoft's Background

From its beginning as a garage software shop in 1975, Microsoft Corporation has become the world's dominant software company.[11] Microsoft markets a broad range of products for personal computing: development tools and languages, application software, systems software, hardware peripherals, books, and multimedia applications. Microsoft's popular software products include the operating systems MS-DOS, Windows, Windows 95, and Windows NT; the programming languages Microsoft BASIC and Microsoft C++; and a variety of productivity applications for the end user, including Microsoft Word and Microsoft Excel.[12] Products such as these have helped Microsoft become the world's leading developer of personal computer software with 1996 net sales of approximately $8.7 billion (see Exhibit 2)[13]

The Alliance Between Compaq and Microsoft

Compaq and Microsoft have been informal technology partners for over a decade. For example, they worked closely together when Compaq introduced a personal computer in 1987 based on Intel's first 386-series chip, and Microsoft created its best-selling Windows software program around Compaq's specifications for the 386.[14] "Software companies get a lot out of working with very serious hardware engineers," claims Richard A. Shaffer, editor of the *Computer Letter*, a New York industry newsletter. "Microsoft has already benefited from Compaq's understanding over the years."[15]

It wasn't until April 1993 that these two powerhouse corporations extended their informal partnership into an official alliance.[16] Microsoft and Compaq's "Frontline Partnership" committed the two companies to develop products that are more advanced, yet easier to use and simpler to expand or adapt to new equipment.[17] Under the agreement, Compaq pledged to bring out a line of PCs that is optimized for the entire line of Windows products, from Windows for Workgroups to Windows NT, and Microsoft agreed to base its Windows products around Compaq's hardware specifications and stan-

C-18

EXHIBIT 2 *Microsoft's Income Statement*

	(in millions of dollars)	
	1996	**1995**
Net Revenues	$8,671	$5,937
Operating Expenses		
Cost of revenues	$1,188	$ 877
Research and development	$1,432	$ 860
Sales and marketing	$2,657	$1,895
General and administrative	$ 316	$ 267
Other income and expenses, net	$ (301)	$ (129)
Total operating expenses	$5,292	$3,770
Income before income taxes	$3,379	$2,167
Provision for income tax	$1,184	$ 714
Net Income	$2,195	$1,453
Earnings per share*	$ 1.71	$ 1.16

Source: Information for this exhibit found at:
http://www.microsoft.com/msft/annual/financials/is.html.
*Adjusted for the December 1996 two-for-one stock split. Expressed in dollars.

dards.[18] "We are removing the boundary between systems software and hardware, which is the place where a great deal of innovation is taking place, and committing the two companies to work together," said Bill Gates, chairman and CEO of Microsoft. "It's the most significant agreement we have done with a PC company in four or five years."[19] This enhanced partnership makes Compaq Microsoft's closest hardware partner. The most important part of the partnership is Compaq and Microsoft's agreement to offer joint product marketing and support, including cross-training sales personnel and sharing technical support information. As Jeff Henning, an analyst at BIS Business Strategies, stated, "This [agreement] was really an attempt to gain mind share. Compaq and Microsoft really want to show they can work together and [signal] that they're market leaders."[20]

Compaq and Microsoft were eventually able to show just how well they could work together and become market leaders. In early 1996, Compaq and Microsoft began a project with General Motors to install Compaq servers running Microsoft's Windows NT operating system at 8,400 of its dealerships to create an electronic network between these dealerships. The project, named Access Common Dealership Environment (ACDE), would supply dealers with information on one another's payroll, parts, and inventory, which would speed delivery of cars to customers.

Another alliance contract developed in late 1996. Compaq and Microsoft won a $170 million midrange distributed enterprise contract with Smith Barney Inc. and its parent company, Travelers Group.[21] This was, by far, the biggest deal to date for the "Frontline Partnership." The new contract made Compaq the primary provider of PCs and servers (20,000 Compaq DeskPro PCs and 500 Compaq ProLiant Servers) and Microsoft the primary software provider (Microsoft NT operating systems). These products will be used to create an enterprise network in order to share information among Smith Barney's 460 retail branch offices.[22]

The "Frontline Partnership" has been a very successful alliance for both Compaq and Microsoft. "Microsoft's Frontline Partnership with Compaq has delivered significant enterprise client/server [contracts] such as Smith Barney," said Jim Allchin, senior vice president of Microsoft's desktop and business systems division. "With the record-setting benchmarks announced with Microsoft's software

and Compaq's hardware, we're certain we can enhance the benefits of Compaq and Microsoft industry-standard solutions for enterprise, business-critical applications."[23] Both the General Motors and Smith Barney contracts verify the effectiveness and importance of the "Frontline Partnership" for both Compaq and Microsoft.

Oracle's Background

Oracle Corporation, the world's second largest software company, leads the world in information management software.[24] Founded in 1977, Oracle built the first commercial relational database system and sold the first products utilizing SQL (Structured Query Language), today's industry standard.[25] Today, Oracle Corp.'s Oracle 7 is the most widely used database software product in the world. Oracle's mission is to provide companies of all sizes with more productive and competitive software at a low cost.[26] In 1996, employing more than 20,000 software professionals and operating in more than 90 countries worldwide, Oracle's revenues reached over $4.2 billion (see Exhibit 3).[27]

The Alliance Between Compaq and Oracle

In July 1994, Compaq Computer Corporation and Oracle Corporation announced The Compaq/Oracle Alliance.[28] A direct result of the newly formed alliance was the establishment of the Compaq Business Unit at Oracle in Belmont, California, which aimed to provide customers with reliable, easy-to-manage, high-performance, integrated database server platforms. The unit had five key areas of focus: joint development, performance engineering, compatibility testing, customer support, and market development of Oracle software on Compaq servers.[29]

Gary Stimac, senior vice president of the Compaq Systems Division, commented on the alliance:

Oracle's Compaq Business Unit will provide our customers with proven and tested client/server solutions that are jointly engineered and supported by both companies. . . . As an outcome of the alliance, our companies are committed to delivering application and database server platforms which meet our customers' integration, performance, compatibility, and support requirements.[30]

EXHIBIT 3 *Oracle's Income Statement*

	(in millions of dollars)	
	1996	**1995**
Net Revenues	$4.223	$2.967
Operating Expenses		
Cost of revenues	$1.096	$ .779
Research and development	$ .440	$ .261
Sales and marketing	$1.549	$1.103
General and administrative	.233	.174
Other income and expenses, net	$ (.015)	$ (.009)
Total operating expenses	$3.303	$2.308
Income before income taxes	$ .920	$ .659
Provision for income tax	$ .316	$ .217
Net Income	$ .604	$ .442
Earnings per share (dollars)	$ .90	$ .60

Source: Information for this exhibit found at: http://feta.us.oracle.com:8001/corporate/annual_report/html/finstmnt.html

Oracle Corp. was excited about bringing the leading workgroup server hardware and the leading workgroup database software together. Oracle considered Compaq to be an important ally and believed that the establishment of both a dedicated business unit at Oracle and the Compaq/Oracle alliance agreement was indicative of the importance that Oracle places on its relationship with Compaq.[31]

Within a year and a half of the establishment of the Compaq Business Unit at Oracle, the two companies combined their expertise to install Oracle 7 using Compaq SmartStart (a tool used to configure, install, and optimize servers). This was the first tangible benefit to customers provided through the alliance.

In November 1995, the alliance demonstrated a first in the computer industry: the combination of an industry-standard platform and a parallel database server. The Oracle 7 Parallel Server ran on a Compaq ProLiant Server Array and provided customers with a highly scalable (meaning that it can be used in large and small computer systems) and available (easier to own) platform for running business computing systems at a price well below other available options.[32] Gene Austin, vice president of marketing at Compaq's Systems Division, enthusiastic about the parallel server technology, said that "together, Oracle and Compaq can bring highly available, reliable and resilient parallel server solutions to branch of-

fices and distributed departments at unprecedented prices. Together, we are challenging the existing notions of midrange computing solutions."[33] In December 1995, Oracle delivered the highest ever TPP-C (transaction processing performance council)[34] result on Compaq ProLiant servers and on any Intel-based configuration to date. "These record-breaking TPP-C results illustrate the power of partnership," said Stimac.[35]

As the relationship between Compaq and Oracle matured, the scope of the alliance expanded. Four key areas demanded the firms' focus with regard to product development: price/performance value, reliability and availability, scalability, and the reduced need for on-site technical support.[36] In December 1996, Compaq and Oracle signed the Global Technical Support Agreement (GTSA) to succeed in these targeted areas. The agreement resulted in mutual support between the two companies as they trained each other's support staffs to provide better service to customers, designated technical support contacts within each company to facilitate communication, and provided interchangeable problem-solving solutions through shared access to each other's support databases.[37] "The establishment of the Global Technical Support Agreement speaks directly to our mission statement, which is to ensure the business success of our customers," said Randy Baker, senior vice president of Oracle's World Wide Customer Support.[38] Addressing availability and scalability, the companies merged Oracle's FailSafe with Compaq's On-Line Recovery Server to provide a totally fail-safe system and worked together to supply Oracle Parallel Server support for Compaq Server Arrays.[39] Finally, to provide solutions requiring minimal on-site technical support, Oracle chose Compaq as the reference platform for its groupware product, the InterOffice suite.[40]

GROUPWARE

The business environment is changing at an unyielding pace, accelerating "from a gentle breeze into a hurricane,"[41] and, thus, the need to align computer infrastructures with distributed enterprise has grown. "Groupware," an application software program which enables a number of people at different computers to work together simultaneously on a common project, acts as a network information system that delivers instant access to business-critical data over a distributed enterprise.[42] It began to evolve when e-mail replaced the interoffice memo. Today, however, groupware is intended for the more serious, business-critical environment and has been described as a collaborative approach to workflow and messaging. This type of programming creates a new approach to project management while eliminating the need for constant face-to-face meetings.[43] In support of groupware software products, Dale Lowery, senior principal with Casetech, Inc., a Washington, D.C.-based VAR, stated:

> Many organizations are trying to sidestep the issue of data integration by just having departments put up Web sites and cutting and pasting information from them. That [scenario] could lead to a total mess because there is no audit trail, no attribution. I need to see the data on a database, and if you can't show me how and when you got it, I won't use it. People are being naive about the Internet. It can do a lot, but it doesn't do away with the need for enterprisewide data integration.[44]

In the beginning, Lotus dominated the groupware market with Lotus Notes. However, Novell Inc., Microsoft, and Oracle Corp. began vying for market share in the mid-1990s.[45] Novell entered the market in the spring of 1996 with its beta version of Group-Wise 5.0. This messaging system linked e-mail, calendaring, scheduling, voice mail, conferencing, shared folders, document management, and integration with the World Wide Web and runs on multiple platforms which include UNIX, Netware, Windows 3.1, Windows NT, and Macintosh.[46] As the distributed enterprise continued to grow, Lotus Notes and Novell GroupWise paved the way for new entrants into the groupware market, namely, Microsoft's BackOffice and Oracle's InterOffice.

Microsoft BackOffice

Over the years, Microsoft has come closer and closer to achieving its long-held vision of a computer on every desk and in every home.[47] But Bill Gates's vision of "windows everywhere" was one step short of being complete. For years, Microsoft played virtually no role in the development of server and workstation software (see Exhibit 4).[48] But in September 1994, Microsoft introduced BackOffice, the first suite of server applications for a distributed enterprise. BackOffice is an integrated family of server software. It is built on the Microsoft Windows NT Server operating system rather than the UNIX operating system, as Windows NT is predicted to outsell UNIX in the future (see Exhibit 5). This software package includes Windows NT Server 3.51, the network foundation for running a new generation of business applications; the SQL Server 6.0, a powerful relational database management system platform for enterprise computing; Systems Management Server (SMS) 1.1, a solution for software inventory and distribution; the Microsoft Mail Server 3.5, the messaging server; and SNA Server 2.11 for mainframe communications (see Exhibit 6).[49]

This suite of server applications is the core of an information system; it allows different offices to share information across an entire network. It provides traditional file and print services plus rich new network services on which a new generation of information applications can be built. These information applications are client/server solutions that help companies improve decision making and streamline business processes. They allow desktops to access and integrate information from a variety of sources with ease and price/performance. With Microsoft BackOffice, customers get an information system that is designed specifically to improve overall organizational productivity.

Although all of these individual applications may be effective products in their own right, they were not designed originally as an integrated package.

EXHIBIT 4 *Microsoft's Estimated Increased Sales in Server and Workstation Software*

(in billions)

Source: Information for this exhibit found at: G. Christian Hill, 1996, "Technology (A Special Report): The Battle for Control: Deja Vu? Microsoft and Intel are Trying to Do in Networks What They Did in PCs: But the War Isn't Over Yet." *Wall Street Journal,* Nov. 18, 2.

EXHIBIT 5 *The Future of Operating Systems*

Estimated Future Sales of Microsoft's NT and UNIX Servers
(in millions)

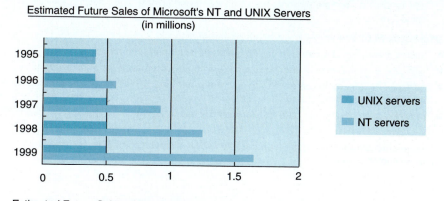

UNIX servers
NT servers

Estimated Future Sales of Microsoft's NT and UNIX Workstations
(in millions)

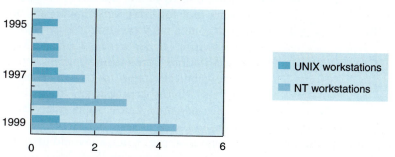

UNIX workstations
NT workstations

Source: Information for this exhibit found at: G. Christian Hill, 1996, "Technology (A Special Report): The Battle for Control: Deja Vu? Microsoft and Intel are Trying to Do in Networks What They Did in PCs: But the War Isn't Over Yet," *Wall Street Journal,* Nov. 18, 4.

EXHIBIT 6 *Microsoft BackOffice Family*

Windows NT Server 3.51—*network foundation of BackOffice*
- provides the connectivity, reliability, base services, and administrative tools necessary to deliver critical business information across a distributed network of computers
- supports nearly all desktop environments
- increased performance, improved connectivity and management tools are the highlights of the most recent release

Microsoft SQL Server 6.0—*managing and storing data*
- supports transaction processing and decision support applications when high performance, reliability, and manageability are key requirements
- increased transaction throughput
- direct support for PATHWORKS and AppleTalk networks using native protocols
- offers improved open database connectivity (ODBC) drivers as highlights of the most recent release

Microsoft SNA Server 2.12—*host connectivity*
- connects Microsoft Windows, MS-DOS Windows NT Workstations, Macintosh, and OS/2-based desktops with AS/400 and IBM mainframes
- provides flexible access to applications and data on IBM mainframe and AS/400 systems
- improved performance

Microsoft Systems Management Server 1.1—*manages PCs and servers*
- helps reduce support costs by centralizing common network administrative tasks that typically cost organizations significant amounts of time and money
- four primary functions: hardware and software inventory, automated software distribution and installation, remote systems troubleshooting and control, and network application management

Microsoft Mail Server 3.5—*distributing information*
- makes it easy for end users to create, manage, and share information
- provides a reliable messaging infrastructure with advanced tools for administrators
- easiest way to communicate with anyone, anywhere and is the foundation of a complete electronic messaging solution
- provides a direct upgrade path to Microsoft Exchange Server

Source: Information for this exhibit found at http://www.microsoft.com\:80/syspro/technet/boes/bo/bosi/technote/bf103.html

Therefore, the developers at Microsoft worked extra long hours to integrate the products that make up the BackOffice suite. The major challenge Microsoft faced was to integrate BackOffice with server hardware.

Compaq's Commitment to BackOffice

Microsoft turned to its long-standing relationship with Compaq for its integrated server hardware needs. Under this new agreement, Compaq would release new versions of its servers that would ship with the BackOffice line-up of applications for the Windows NT Server operating system.[50] The pact called for Compaq to add BackOffice support to its SmartStart tool for server installation and integration. Both companies were also to "expand joint marketing activities" under a new Compaq/Microsoft Business Solutions Partnership program and to provide joint technical support for customers using both Compaq and Microsoft products.[51] Microsoft would provide fee-based technical support to customers who licensed the Windows NT Server or BackOffice through Compaq. Compaq would provide technical support by conducting BackOffice training for over 500 of its certified systems engineers to handle customer problems and complaints.[52]

Both Microsoft and Compaq benefit from this mutual agreement. Because Compaq acts as a distribution source for Microsoft, Microsoft is able to solidify its hold on network computing by offering tightly integrated software packages that work easily on its operating systems. Compaq, on the other hand, is able to transcend its PC boundaries and enter into the distributed enterprise market by supporting the popular Microsoft Windows NT. "This [agreement] means we can put even more of our energies behind Microsoft's products," claims Mary T. McDowell, Compaq's director of systems product marketing.[53]

Oracle InterOffice

The Oracle InterOffice server software suite, formerly known as Bandwagon, represents Oracle Corp.'s stake in the "groupware" market. However, where groupware was designed strictly for PCs, InterOffice enables users to access a wide range of abilities over intranets, mobile networks, and the Internet. A tailored version of the industry-leading Oracle 7 database, the key to InterOffice's collaborative functions, includes comprehensive messaging, directory services, calendar and resource scheduling, discussion, document management, and workflow facilities (see Exhibit 7).[54] Creative Networks' Ron Rassner referred to InterOffice as "the most interesting and possibly one of the best architectures for groupware. . . . They have a single Oracle engine that can run the database, the line of business application, messaging, calendaring, and Web and intranet activities, all based on a single server platform."[55]

Oracle's InterOffice suite is targeted at *Fortune* 1000 companies, particularly those in the retail, banking, health care, finance, and insurance indus-

C-193

EXHIBIT 7 *Oracle InterOffice Family*

Messaging
- mail & directory (with synchronization)
- attachments and templates
- conferencing
- shared & public folders
- filters
- mobile support

- day & week views
- alarms
- to-do lists
- automatic meetings
- attendee freetime views
- access control
- time zones

Document Management
- any document type
- check-in & out
- version control
- full-text search
- access control
- extensible document attributes

Workflow
- graphical design
- routing
- access control
- PL/SQL engine

Scheduling

For maximum flexibility and integration with your enterprise information systems, InterOffice supports:

⇒ MAPI	⇒ OLE	⇒ XAPIA-CSA
⇒ ODMA	⇒ OCX/Active X	⇒ SPI
⇒ C/C++	⇒ CMC 1.0	⇒ other standard APIs

InterOffice supports over 25 different servers including:

⇒ NT	⇒ Sun	⇒ most RISC-based UNIX
⇒ HP-9000	⇒ IBM RS/6000	systems

Source: Information for this exhibit found at:
http://www.aberdeen.com/secure/profiles/oracle/oracle.html
http://www.interoffice.net/AboutInteroffice/index.html

tries. Because such companies usually do not have trained management information systems personnel at each office, InterOffice offers a solution for their need to organize applications across hundreds of locations.[56] InterOffice is offered in two versions: an Enterprise Edition, positioned for larger systems, and a Workgroup Edition, positioned against Microsoft's BackOffice.

The key to InterOffice is a feature which allows users to employ a single log-on and password for all applications and networks.[57] InterOffice runs on Intel-based Sun Solaris and Windows NT, and the InterOffice server supports multimedia systems and Web services, as well as LAN, WAN, and mobile computing. "Oracle has made its architecture Internet-aware," said Tim Sloane, an analyst at Aberdeen Group, Inc., in Boston. "Any desktop, any browser can have access to it. Lotus would love to say that; architecturally, they can't say that."[58] While critics contend that Oracle was late in the game since InterOffice is its third try at the market, and some feel that Oracle may be promising too much, Compaq remains faithful to Oracle and enthusiastically backs the product.[59]

Compaq's Commitment to InterOffice

Compaq supports Oracle InterOffice by optimizing the Enterprise and Workgroup InterOffice suites on Compaq server platforms. Compaq's support means that customers using InterOffice will not be faced with significant downtime or operational difficulties. With regard to Oracle InterOffice products, Pfeiffer described Compaq's commitment by saying:

A cornerstone of Compaq's [business systems] strategy is to develop strong relationships with industry market leaders to deliver integrated solutions for the distributed enterprise. . . . Using Oracle's InterOffice suite, we plan to team with Oracle to continue delivering jointly-tested, integrated and optimized networked systems. Compaq's tightly integrated solution, based on industry-standard platforms with leading price/performance, will enable branch or remote offices to further automate and increase the sophistication of their computing operation. Combine our leadership systems technology and integration expertise with Oracle's InterOffice remote management capabilities, and you have a formidable team

delivering a powerful solution for the distributed enterprise.[60]

INCREASING CONFLICTS

Microsoft BackOffice versus Oracle InterOffice

The introduction of these two network software suites has led to intense competition between Microsoft and Oracle. Oracle is particularly concerned about Microsoft, which already controls the world of PC software and is making a bid to dominate the networking business with its BackOffice software.[61] Oracle's senior vice president Jerry Baker says the introduction of InterOffice is part of "the major battle between Oracle and Microsoft." He adds that "you could definitely view [InterOffice] as a pre-emptive strike against Microsoft."[62]

As the competition between these two software corporations has increased, the InterOffice suite has slowly replaced the sales of BackOffice, which has remained only a small portion of Microsoft's overall Windows NT sales.[63] One reason for this lag in sales was poor application integration. Bundling is not as useful or cost-efficient for server software as it is for desktop applications. One example would be Microsoft's dramatically successful Office suite. In fact, a BackOffice license for all five server products cannot be divided up among several servers but must all be run on the same server.[64] "It's a concept that doesn't work well as a product, but it works well as a strategy," said Michael A. Goulde, a senior consultant at Patricia Seybold Group in Boston.[65] Many customers use one or two components and don't find it cost-effective to buy all the server software as a bundle.[66] InterOffice, however, was able to overcome this bundling problem by creating one unified software program instead of consolidating five separate packages into a server suite like BackOffice. Jerry Baker comments on the strength of InterOffice as compared to BackOffice:

Oracle InterOffice opens big doors for business computing. Small businesses and large corporations would like to capitalize on the increasing power and affordability of Intel-based hardware to integrate their entire organization, but until now, nobody has put all the right software pieces together. Microsoft tried with BackOffice, but the product is not well integrated and can't scale. Oracle InterOffice Suite brings affordable, enterprise-strength, open client/server computing to the table. It will allow a new generation of Web and multimedia-enabled applications to be mass deployed on every desktop and in every store front and branch office.[67]

The second reason that BackOffice sales have been slow is the concern with Microsoft's ability to handle and support the large-scale products on the enterprise level. "There's still a question in my mind as to Microsoft's ability to provide true enterprise support," says Allan Frank, national partner at KPMG Peat Marwick. "The only thing they [Microsoft] really have experience supporting is front-end desktop [applications]."[68] Because Oracle has had years of experience dealing with large server networking environments, it is better equipped to handle enterprise service and technical support. Lowry of Casetech, Inc., put it best when he said, "Microsoft is great on the desktop but we are not sure Microsoft 'gets it' on the enterprise level. Oracle gets it at the enterprise level."[69] These two shortcomings of Microsoft's BackOffice have left the enterprise market open for the InterOffice server software package, which can effectively integrate the entire workplace.

Compaq's Dilemma

Oracle's InterOffice Suite addresses the void in the market that is unfilled by Microsoft's BackOffice.

Sources close to Compaq say that the Oracle UNIX-based InterOffice package will fill a niche in the market and will hardly make a dent in Compaq's Windows NT business with Microsoft. But even a niche product is enough to concern Microsoft. A source close to Oracle said negotiations between Compaq and Oracle were held up because of Microsoft's opposition.[70] In fact, Bill Gates reportedly called his counterpart at Compaq, Eckhard Pfeiffer, in an attempt to stop the deal.[71] "Microsoft has had a long-term relationship with Compaq," says the source. "It doesn't look good for Microsoft's key partner to support Oracle InterOffice."[72] Microsoft has considered developing a user relationship with Dell a little closer now, possibly transferring the title of "Microsoft's closest hardware partner" from Compaq to Dell.[73]

Eckhard Pfeiffer has a difficult decision to make in regard to the conflicting Compaq alliances. It is obvious to Pfeiffer that Compaq will have to choose between these two competing alliances. He must decide whether to maintain Compaq's excellent long-term relationship with Microsoft by supporting BackOffice or continue to support Oracle's InterOffice, the promising enterprise software that challenges Microsoft's competitive position in the server software industry. If Compaq wants to maintain its strategic position in the distributed enterprise market, it must decide which alliance will best suit its future needs. An incorrect decision could jeopardize Compaq's strong position in the computer industry.

C-19!

NOTES

1. Victor Kulkosky, May 1989, "Strategic Alliances Buoy New Technology Boom," *Wall Street Computer Review*, May, no. 6(8): 18–24, 86.
2. Compaq Internet Homepage: http://www.compaq.com
3. Ibid.
4. Ibid.
5. Ibid.
6. Ibid.
7. Ibid.
8. Ibid.
9. Kelley Damore and Craig Zarley, 1996, "Compaq's New Model a Work in Progress," *Computer Reseller News*, July 15, p. 1ff.
10. Compaq Internet Homepage: http://www.compaq.com
11. Microsoft Internet Homepage: http://www.microsoft.com/jobs/guide/history.html
12. Ibid.
13. Ibid.

14. Thomas C. Hayes, 1993, "Compaq and Microsoft Plan Alliance," *New York Times*, April 13, D1.
15. Kyle Pope, 1993, "Compaq Plans to Unveil Pact with Microsoft," *Wall Street Journal*, April 9, A3.
16. Hayes, D1.
17. Steve Polilli, 1993, "Compaq-Microsoft Pact May Be All Marketing," *Infoworld*, April 19, 1.
18. Caryn Gillooly, 1993, "More Microsoft Details," *Network World*, April 19, 1.
19. Hayes, D1.
20. Polilli, 1.
21. Steve Burke, 1996, "Compaq, Microsoft win $170M Deal," *Computer Reseller News*, April 29, 26.
22. Ibid, 26.
23. Jerele Neeld, 1996, "Compaq ProLiant Server Delivers Midrange Systems Performance and Capabilities at About Half the Cost," *Business Wire*, June 3.
24. Oracle Internet Homepage: http://www.oracle.com

25. Ibid.
26. Ibid.
27. Ibid.
28. Michael Fitzgerald and Jaikumar Vijayan, 1994, "Clustering Lies at Heart of Compaq/Oracle Alliance," *Computerworld*, July 25, 28(30): 10.
29. Compaq Internet Homepage. "Compaq and Oracle Establish New Business Unit, Outline Joint Initiatives." http://www.compaq.com
30. Ibid.
31. Ibid.
32. Compaq Internet Homepage. "Oracle and Compaq Demonstrate Industry's First Parallel Database Server on Industry Standard Platforms." http://www.compaq.com
33. Ibid.
34. TPC Internet Homepage: http://www.tpc.org/csummary.html
35. Compaq Internet Homepage. "Oracle and Compaq Demonstrate Industry's First Parallel Database Server on Industry Standard Platforms." http://www.compaq.com
36. Compaq Internet Homepage. "Compaq Announces Support for Oracle 7 Release 7.3." http://www.compaq.com
37. Compaq Internet Homepage. "Compaq and Oracle Sign New Global Technical Agreement." http:/www.compaq.com
38. Ibid.
39. Oracle Internet Homepage: http://www.oracle.com
40. Ibid.
41. Ibid.
42. Isaac Peter, 1996, "Groupware Supercharges Key Word Search," *New Zealand Manufacturer*, August 12.
43. Ibid.
44. Barbara Darrow, 1996, "Oracle InterOffice Set to Ship in July," *Computer Reseller News*, June 17, no. 688: 12.
45. Anonymous, 1996, "Groupware Front-runners: Who's in Contention," *Software Magazine*, August, no. 16(8): 77.
46. Computer Time Internet Homepage. "Novell GroupWise 5-Novell Takes Microsoft and Lotus Head-on." http://www.asia1.com.sg:80/computertimes/sep96/spemo8.html
47. Ibid.
48. G. Christian Hill, 1996, "Technology (A Special Report): The Battle for Control; Deja Vu? Microsoft and Intel Are Trying to Do in Networks What They Did in PCs; But the War Isn't Over Yet," *The Wall Street Journal*, Nov. 18, 4.
49. Stuart J. Johnston, 1995, "Microsoft's BackOffice Logo Deal May Backfire," *Computerworld*, Nov. 27, 49.
50. Jacqueline Emigh, 1995, "PC Expo-Compaq to Bundle Microsoft BackOffice," *Newsbytes News Network*, June 21.
51. Ibid.
52. Kelley Damore, 1995, "Compaq Boosts Server Capabilities," *Computer Reseller News*, July 17, 135.
53. Emigh, "PC Expo-Compaq."
54. Oracle Internet Homepage: http://www.oracle.com
55. "Groupware Front-runners: Who's in contention," 77.
56. Barry D. Bowen, 1996, "Oracle Selects Solaris X86." SunWorld On-line: http://www.eu.sun.com:80/sunworldonline/swol-0101996/swol-01-oracle.html.
57. Barb Cole, 1995, "Oracle, Microsoft Shake Up Their Database Menus: InterOffice Aimed at Companies that Need to Manage Branch Office Databases," *Network World*, December 11, no. 12(50): 35–36.
58. Dan Richman and Suruchi Mohan, 1996, "Oracle Takes a Risk with Suite," *Computerworld*, January 8, no. 30(2): 43, 48.
59. Ibid.
60. Compaq Internet Homepage. "Compaq and Oracle Team to Integrate Oracle InterOffice on Compaq Servers." http://www.compaq.com
61. Neal Templin, 1995, "Oracle and Compaq Team Up on System to Boost Performance of Servers for PCs," *Wall Street Journal*, Oct. 16, 4.
62. Ibid, 4.
63. Stuart J. Johnston, 1995, "BackOffice Sales Chug Slowly," *Computerworld*, Oct. 2, 10.
64. Semich, 41.
65. Johnston, 10.
66. Ibid, 10.
67. Ibid, 10.
68. Semich, 42.
69. Barbara Darrow, 1996, "Oracle, Novell Add to Messaging," *Computer Reseller News*, Feb. 26, 71.
70. Brian Gillooly, 1995, "Compaq Serves Up UNIX," *Information Week*, Dec. 11, 22.
71. Ibid, 22.
72. Ibid, 22.
73. Ibid, 22.

Cummins Engine Company, Inc.: Relationship with KamAZ

E. Wainright Martin

Indiana University

In the early 1980s the management of Cummins Engine Company, aware that the USSR was the world's largest market for diesel engines, began exploring ways that Cummins might enter the Soviet market. In 1987, after trying unsuccessfully to develop joint ventures in Eastern Europe to gain access to this market, Cummins had its first serious contact with the KamAZ truck factory, the largest maker of heavy trucks in the world. Finding that KamAZ was one of the best-managed organizations in the USSR, Cummins began to explore possibilities for cooperation with KamAZ. In 1991, after the U.S. government loosened controls on export of technology to the Soviets, Cummins and KamAZ signed a joint venture agreement to market and manufacture Cummins-designed engines in the USSR.

There have been many difficulties implementing this agreement. Implementation problems became worse after the KamAZ engine factory burned to the ground in early 1993, destroying KamAZ's entire engine-building capacity and slowing its truck production to a trickle. As of spring 1994, KamAZ and Cummins have been unable to develop a business plan that would justify the investment required to build a factory to produce Cummins engines in Rus-

sia. Obstacles and uncertainties continue to abound, further complicating the situation.

The history of this relationship between Cummins and KamAZ, as seen from the Cummins perspective, is presented below.

THE CUMMINS ENGINE COMPANY

Cummins Engine Company, Inc., is a leading worldwide designer and manufacturer of fuel-efficient diesel engines and related products for trucks and other equipment. The company was founded in 1919 in Columbus, Indiana, where the corporate headquarters and largest engine manufacturing facility are located. Ranking 121st in sales among the Fortune 500, in 1993 Cummins reported net sales of $4.2 billion and employed approximately 23,500 persons worldwide. Henry B. Schacht is Cummins' chairman and CEO.

Since 1956 Cummins has been a multinational business, and Cummins' operations include plants, joint ventures, or license agreements in the United Kingdom, India, Mexico, Brazil, Japan, South Korea, China, Russia, Zimbabwe, Pakistan, and Turkey, as well as in the United States. During recent years Cummins' international earnings have exceeded domestic earnings. A distribution of Cummins' U.S. and international net sales over the past 13 years is depicted in Exhibit 1.

This case was written as a basis for classroom discussion. It is part of the CIBER Case Collection, sponsored by the Indiana University CIBER and distributed by the ECCH @ Babson. Copyright © 1995 by E. Wainright Martin.

EXHIBIT 1 *Net Sales*

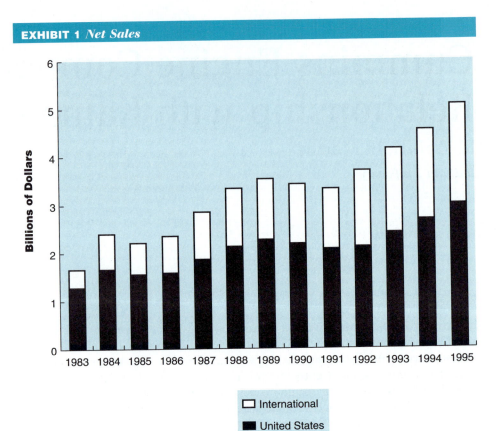

Source: Cummins 1995 Annual Report.

Cummins sells directly to original equipment manufacturers (OEMs) and to 33 distributors operating through approximately 200 locations in North America. Outside North America it sells to 110 distributors at approximately 300 locations in 130 countries. In addition, there are approximately 3,500 dealer locations in North America and a total of 5,000 worldwide at which Cummins-trained service personnel and Cummins parts are available to repair and maintain engines. Cummins has a worldwide reputation for providing outstanding service on its engines.

Products

Cummins produces large diesel engines, ranging from 76 to 2,000 horsepower. These engines power a wide variety of equipment in six key markets: heavy-duty and midrange trucks, power generation, indus-trial products, bus and light commercial vehicles, government (including military), and marine. In addition to diesel engines, Cummins' products include generator sets and alternators, electronic control systems, remanufactured engines, filters, turbochargers, and heat transfer systems.

Cummins' diesel engine product line evolved slowly over the years until 1981, when Cummins decided to design new heavy-duty truck engines that are smaller and lighter, and also to develop a new line of engines for medium and light-duty trucks. This product line overhaul required an investment of around $1 billion. The new product line has been quite successful. In 1988, Cummins introduced a line of cleaner engines, and soon thereafter added electronic fuel injection, which improved fuel efficiency and reduced truck operating costs.

With growing pressures throughout the world for reduced pollution and increased fuel efficiency, diesel engine technology is being forced to evolve rapidly. Thus, there is a growing emphasis on research and development in this industry. Because Cummins is the world's highest volume diesel engine producer, the company is well positioned to respond to these pressures. Cummins has research and development facilities in the United States, the United Kingdom, Brazil, and India. Cummins' research and engineering investments over the past 13 years are shown in Exhibit 2.

Exhibit 3 presents an overview from a sales brochure of Cummins' current line of on-highway engines. Information on the C8.3 engine from a sales brochure is shown in Exhibit 4, and the L10 engine is described in Exhibit 5.

Recent History

After World War II, the diesel engine business was a growth industry as trucking fleets converted from gasoline to diesel power. However, in the late 1970s, Cummins found itself stuck in a mature, very competitive, and highly cyclical business. In 1981, Cum-

mins' management, led by CEO Schacht, made very aggressive investments in new product development, intended to broaden its product line, so that Cummins would not be so dependent on the highly cyclical 18-wheel tractor-trailer business.

In 1985, Cummins was threatened by Japanese competitors entering the U.S. market. The Japanese had a cost structure (in dollars) that was roughly 30 percent below Cummins' cost. To meet this competition, CEO Schacht immediately reduced Cummins' prices to meet the Japanese prices and instituted a crash program to reduce Cummins' costs by 30 percent within two years. Although it took almost five years, Cummins was successful in achieving cost-reduction targets and in meeting the Japanese threat. However, this success came at the cost of substantial losses experienced during the late 1980s. Then, the early 1990's recession that struck the over-the-road truck business caused Cummins to experience continued losses.

In 1991 Cummins was faced with aggressive takeover attempts by corporate raiders. These attempts were beaten back, but CEO Schacht and the

C-199

EXHIBIT 2 *Research and Engineering Investments*

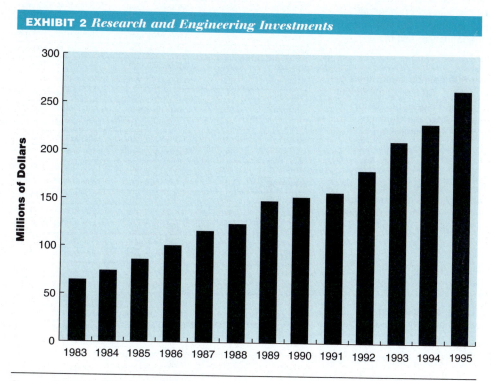

Source: Cummins 1995 Annual Report.

EXHIBIT 3

Power that's right for you.

For over-the-road power, there's a hardworking Cummins diesel that is just your style. From 105 to 460 horsepower, Cummins is the world leader in designing and manufacturing diesel engines that deliver the fuel efficiency, performance, reliability and durability you're looking for.

Because Cummins leads the way in diesel technology, you can count on your Cummins diesel to always be on the cutting edge.

N14

If you're looking for big power, the N14 has what it takes. The power to get the big loads up the big hills . . . and with Cummins C Brake™ as an option, you get strong braking power to slow you on the way down.

L10

The perfect combination of strength and fuel efficiency, the L10 has the technology to pass up every competitive diesel engine on the market today. The proven lightweight leader, the fuel-efficient L10 is one of the most popular fleet engines on the road today.

CELECT™ electronics

N14 and L10 engines are available with CELECT, Cummins totally integrated electronic control system. Through CELECT technology, you get the benefits of integrated electronic controls engineered and built to put you in total command of fuel efficiency, performance, and more.

C8.3

The C8.3 is smaller and over 600 pounds lighter than its nearest heavy-duty competitor. The C8.3's lighter weight adds up to higher payloads . . . and higher profits for you. Even though it's compact in size, the Cummins C8.3 has heavy-duty big bore design features and is built to last.

B5.9/B3.9

With over 750,000 in operation, Cummins B engines are proving they really deliver. Advanced design and modern manufacturing techniques have given Cummins B engines "big bore" engine durability in a smaller-size engine.

Power your way.

Whatever your application, there's a Cummins engine right for the job. Designed, built and backed better than any other diesels on the road today.

Choose the one that's right for you and then see your Cummins distributor or dealer, or call 1-800-DIESELS for more information.

Engine Model	Power	Torque
B3.9-105	105 hp @ 2500 rpm	265 lb-ft @ 1700 rpm
B3.9-120	120 hp @ 2500 rpm	300 lb-ft @ 1700 rpm
B5.9-160	160 hp @ 2500 rpm	400 lb-ft @ 1700 rpm
B5.9-190	190 hp @ 2500 rpm	475 lb-ft @ 1600 rpm
B5.9-210	210 hp @ 2500 rpm	520 lb-ft @ 1600 rpm
B5.9-230	230 hp @ 2500 rpm	605 lb-ft @ 1600 rpm

Engine Model	Power	Range	Torque
C8.3-210	210	1300-2400 rpm	605 lb-ft @ 1300 rpm
C8.3-250	250	1300-2400 rpm	660 lb-ft @ 1300 rpm
C8.3-250	250	1300-2200 rpm	800 lb-ft @ 1300 rpm
C8.3-275	275	1300-2200 rpm	800 lb-ft @ 1300 rpm
C8.3-275	275	1300-2000 rpm	860 lb-ft @ 1300 rpm
C8.3-300	300	1300-2400 rpm	820 lb-ft @ 1300 rpm
L10-260	260	1200-1800 rpm	975 lb-ft @ 1200 rpm
L10-260	260	1200-1950 rpm	975 lb-ft @ 1200 rpm
L10-280	280	1200-1800 rpm	1050 lb-ft @ 1200 rpm
L10-280	280	1200-1950 rpm	1050 lb-ft @ 1200 rpm
L10-280E	280	1200-1800 rpm	1050 lb-ft @ 1200 rpm
L10-300	300	1200-1950 rpm	1150 lb-ft @ 1200 rpm
L10-310	310	1200-1800 rpm	1150 lb-ft @ 1200 rpm
L10-310E	310	1200-1800 rpm	1150 lb-ft @ 1200 rpm
L10-310E	310	1200-2000 rpm	1150 lb-ft @ 1200 rpm
L10-330E	330	1200-1800 rpm	1250 lb-ft @ 1200 rpm
L10-330E	330	1200-2000 rpm	1250 lb-ft @ 1200 rpm
L10-350E	350	1200-1800 rpm	1250 lb-ft @ 1200 rpm
N14-310P	310	1100-1700 rpm	1250 lb-ft @ 1100 rpm
N14-330P	330	1100-1700 rpm	1350 lb-ft @ 1100 rpm
N14-330	330	1100-1950 rpm	1350 lb-ft @ 1100 rpm
N14-350P	350	1100-1700 rpm	1400 lb-ft @ 1100 rpm
N14-350	350	1100-1950 rpm	1350 lb-ft @ 1100 rpm
N14-370	370	1200-1800 rpm	1400 lb-ft @ 1200 rpm
N14-370	370	1200-1950 rpm	1400 lb-ft @ 1200 rpm
N14-410	410	1200-1800 rpm	1450 lb-ft @ 1200 rpm
N14-410	410	1200-1950 rpm	1450 lb-ft @ 1200 rpm
N14-430	430	1200-1800 rpm	1450 lb-ft @ 1200 rpm
N14-310E	310	1100-1800 rpm	1250 lb-ft @ 1100 rpm
N14-330E	330	1100-1800 rpm	1350 lb-ft @ 1100 rpm
N14-330E	330	1100-2100 rpm	1350 lb-ft @ 1100 rpm
N14-350E	350	1100-1800 rpm	1400 lb-ft @ 1100 rpm
N14-370E	370	1200-1800 rpm	1400 lb-ft @ 1200 rpm
N14-370E	370	1200-2100 rpm	1400 lb-ft @ 1200 rpm
N14-410E	410	1200-2100 rpm	1450 lb-ft @ 1200 rpm
N14-430E	430	1200-1800 rpm	1450 lb-ft @ 1200 rpm
N14-430E	430	1200-2100 rpm	1450 lb-ft @ 1200 rpm
N14-430E	430	1200-2100 rpm	1550 lb-ft @ 1200 rpm
N14-460E	460	1200-2100 rpm	1550 lb-ft @ 1200 rpm

EXHIBIT 4

C8.3

210-275 hp

Cummins C8.3 engines have always outclassed other engines of equal displacement. Now, with more ratings and the introduction of COMMAND technology, they give you a commanding lead over every other competitive engine in this horsepower category.

These engines offer more power, more constant torque and greater performance than ever before.

Cummins C8.3 vocational truck engine is more compact and over 600 lb lighter than the nearest heavy-duty competitor. This means more payload and bigger profits for you. And even though it's lighter in weight, this rugged COMMAND engine is built to perform . . . year . . . after year . . . after year.

Greater performance comes from design improvements in Cummins' own Holset turbocharger, which is fully integrated with the C8.3 engine. It also comes from new refinements . . . like a high-pressure, in-line fuel pump and new lift pump.

These new pumps deliver higher injection pressures through new high-strength fuel lines. Higher injection pressures help increase performance and optimize combustion.

And when it comes to durability, several technological advancements take you well into the '90s:

- Oil cooling has been improved 50% for increased life-to-overhaul.

- Lube pump has been improved to provide a 28% increase in oil flow for longer engine life.

- LF3000 combination oil filter removes contaminants more efficiently . . . for greater durability.

- Anodized crown piston helps eliminate thermal fatigue for increased durability. Dual Ni-Resist piston inserts provide better sealing and longer ring groove life than ever before.

If your operation calls for 210-275 hp, Cummins new ratings offer a powerful choice for Class 7-8 heavy-duty applications up to 80,000 lb.

Rear Engine Power Take-Off. Now available on L10 and C8.3 engines for greater productivity.

Choose Cummins' optional Rear Engine Power Take-Off (REPTO) for your L10 or C8.3 COMMAND engine, and you'll get maximum payload and continuous live power when and where it's needed . . . in mixer, refuse and other on/off highway applications.

Cummins REPTO eliminates extended frames and bumpers. This allows your wheelbase to be increased so you can handle up to 1500 lb more payload under the "Bridge Law."

Add up the advantages. You get increased productivity . . . for improved profitability . . . with Cummins REPTO.

C8.3 COMMAND Ratings for Vocational Applications

Engine Model	COMMAND Torque	COMMAND Range
C8.3-275	860 lb-ft	1300-2000 rpm
C8.3-275	800 lb-ft	1300-2200 rpm
C8.3-250	800 lb-ft	1300-2200 rpm
C8.3-250	660 lb-ft	1300-2400 rpm
C8.3-210	605 lb-ft	1300-2400 rpm

Cummins board became convinced that Cummins' long-range investment strategy was in jeopardy. Schacht decided to revise Cummins' ownership structure to place control in the hands of stable shareholders with a long-term perspective. He was successful in structuring a deal in which three important customers—Ford, Tenneco-J.I. Case, and Kubota—each paid a 25 percent premium above current stock prices to acquire a substantial stake in Cummins. Ford and Tenneco each received a seat on the Cummins board of directors. As part of the deal, Cummins' senior management agreed to work without a contract and to target a 15 percent return on equity. Together with the 10 percent stake held by company employees and a 4 percent stake by the founding Miller family, over 40 percent of Cummins' stock is in the hands of stable stockholders.

For the past decade Cummins has placed a strong emphasis on "Customer-Led Quality" which focuses on providing a comparative advantage to customers. This emphasis, supported by extensive training programs, has helped to improve product quality and significantly reduce Cummins' warranty expenses. Cummins is also experiencing better work processes emphasizing cross-functional teams and smoother product introductions. Management believes this emphasis on quality is also largely responsible for improving Cummins' financial performance. Cummins' 13-year consolidated financial summary is presented in Exhibit 6.

In early 1994 Cummins was engaged in a flurry of international activity. In addition to the relationship with KamAZ described in the next section, late 1993 brought a Cummins and Komatsu Ltd. an-

EXHIBIT 5

L10

260-330 hp

For years, you've come to recognize Cummins L10s as hardworking, long-running engines. Engines with enough power to take the steepest grades and pull you out of the toughest situations.

Now, with a much broader range of power and torque, these L10 COMMAND engines can take on more jobs . . . and tougher jobs . . . than ever before.

With Cummins' new L10 COMMAND ratings, you can choose from 260 hp and 975 lb-ft of torque all the way up to 330 hp and 1250 lb-ft of torque.

You get a greater range of power, greater torque and maximum torque that holds constant over more of the operating range. And that's only the beginning.

These engines were built to perform, with integrated design features like a Cummins Holset H2E turbocharger, perfectly matched to each and every L10 COMMAND engine. Optimum performance also comes from an overhead assembly that's been redesigned to deliver 25% higher injection pressure and improve fuel efficiency.

The L10 COMMAND engine is still one of the lightest-weight engines in its class. And the lighter the engine, the greater your payload . . . and the better your bottom line.

When it comes to durability, the new L10s are loaded with heavy-duty advancements that promote longer life-to-overhaul:

- Cylinder liner has been stiffened and press-fit reduced for better oil control.

- Cast aluminum pistons, featuring dual Ni-Resist inserts, come standard on all L10 COMMAND engines except the higher-horsepower 330Es, which have articulated pistons with forged steel crowns.

- Lube pump flow capacity has been increased by over 40% for longer engine life.

- LF3000 combination full-flow and bypass oil filter removes contaminants more efficiently for increased life-to-overhaul.

- Oil system capacity has been increased for greater protection and increased durability.

Because Cummins has led the industry with its high injection pressure fuel systems, today Cummins has the technology to offer you a choice of advanced fuel systems.

If your vocational needs are best served by a mechanical engine, Cummins offers the PT fuel system . . . the long-proven standard for mechanical fuel systems.

Cummins PT mechanical system has hydraulically controlled, mechanically activated unit injectors. It's known industry-wide for dependability and serviceability.

If electronics are right for your vocational application, Cummins gives you two choices: PT PACER and CELECT,™ integrated electronic fuel systems that will make a difference in your operation.

Consider all the choices offered by Cummins L10 COMMAND engines, including Cummins optional Rear Engine Power Take-Off (REPTO). There are five L10 vocational engines ready to put you in command.

L10 COMMAND Ratings for Vocational Applications

Engine Model	COMMAND Torque	COMMAND Range
L10-330E	1250 lb-ft	1200-2000 rpm
L10-310E	1150 lb-ft	1200-2000 rpm
L10-300	1150 lb-ft	1200-1950 rpm
L10-280	1050 lb-ft	1200-1950 rpm
L10-260	975 lb-ft	1200-1950 rpm

E designates CELECT.

---

nouncement for a joint venture to manufacture Cummins' B-series engines at a Komatsu plant in Oyama, Japan, and to manufacture Komatsu's 30-liter engines at a Cummins plant in Seymour, Indiana. Production is scheduled to begin in 1996 and is expected to produce around 40,000 engines a year by the end of the decade.

Also in 1993, Cummins and Telco, a member of the huge Tata group in India, formed a joint venture to manufacture Cummins-designed engines in India. In early 1994 they made arrangements to build a large factory in India that they expected to be one of the world's most efficient diesel engine factories.

Cummins has license agreements under which two Chinese plants produce Cummins engines. In recent years sales of those engines have doubled annually. The Chongqing Automotive Engine Plant makes heavy-duty diesel engines for work boats, electrical generator sets, and many other types of equipment. Dong Feng Motors manufactures Cummins' mid-sized truck engines. In early 1994 Cummins was negotiating with these two plants to turn the license agreements into joint ventures under which Cummins would invest additional money and technology in China. Cummins was also working on similar arrangements in Korea.

EXHIBIT 6 *Summary of Consolidated Financial Information for 13 Years*
Cummins Engine Company, Inc., and Subsidiaries

$ Millions

	1995	1994	1993	1992	1991	1990	1989	1988	1987	1986	1985	1984	1983
Results of operations:													
Net sales	5245	4737	4248	3749	3406	3462	3620	3310	2767	2304	2146	2326	1605
Cost of goods sold	3974	3551	3211	2907	2777	2857	2857	2670	2071	1758	1578	1596	1165
Gross profit	1271	1186	1037	842	629	605	663	640	698	546	568	730	440
Selling, administrative, research and engineering expenses	955	879	789	712	619	632	607	580	617	541	458	437	373
Interest expenses	13	17	36	41	43	44	52	52	52	45	28	32	34
Other expense (income), net	8	−4	7	13	13	8	−17	7	−18	−7	−18	−13	0
Restructuring and unusual charges	118	0	0	0	0	63	0	49	0	135	40	30	35
Earnings (loss) before income taxes	177	294	205	76	−46	−142	21	−48	34	−157	60	244	−2
Provision (credit) for income taxes	−47	41	22	9	17	25	22	14	16	−53	11	57	−8
Minority interest	0	0	0	0	3	−2	5	3	5	3	0	0	0
Earnings (loss) before extraordinary items and cumulative effect of accounting changes	224	253	183	67	−66	−165	−6	−63	14	−107	50	188	5
Extraordinary items	0	0	−6	−6	0	27	0	0	0	0	0	0	0
Cumulative effect of accounting changes	0	0	0	−251	52	0	0	0	0	0	0	0	0
Net earnings (loss)	224	253	177	−190	−14	−138	−6	−63	14	−107	50	188	5
Preferred and preference stock dividends	0	0	8	8	8	14	10	8	8	1	0	0	0
Earnings (loss) available for common shares	224	253	169	−198	−22	−151	−15	−72	6	−108	50	188	5
Operating percentages:													
Gross profit	24.2%	25.0%	24.4%	22.5%	18.5%	17.5%	18.8%	19.3%	25.1%	23.7%	28.5%	31.4%	27.4%
Return on net sales	4.3	5.3	4.2	−5.0	−0.4	−4.0	−0.2	−1.9	0.5	−4.7	2.3	8.1	0.3
Financial data:													
Working capital	335	458	371	271	219	263	224	306	239	285	340	371	247
Property, plant and equipment, net	1148	1090	958	929	953	921	890	911	910	841	702	567	556
Total assets	3056	2706	2390	2230	2041	2086	2031	2064	2019	1990	1705	1506	1259
Long-term debt and redeemable preferred stock	117	155	190	412	443	411	474	409	333	320	234	222	286
Shareholders' investment	1183	1072	821	501	624	669	559	702	807	770	712	648	501
Supplemental data:													
Property, plant and equipment expenditures	223	238	174	139	124	147	138	151	133	213	198	109	76
Depreciation and amortization	143	128	125	123	127	143	135	132	119	107	79	72	70
Number of common shareholders of record	5000	4800	4400	4800	5900	5900	5700	5700	5400	5500	6900	6900	6500
Number of employees	24300	25600	23600	23400	22900	24900	25100	26100	24500	23400	19600	21000	18600

Effective January 1, 1992, the company adopted changes in accounting for SFAS Nos. 108, 109 and 112. Changes in accounting in 1991 related to depreciation and inventory. The extraordinary charge in 1992 related to the early extinguishment of debt. In 1990, the purchase of a portion of the outstanding zero coupon notes resulted in the extraordinary credit.

C-203

KAMAZ

In the late 1960s the government of the USSR decided to build the world's largest truck factory on the banks of the Kama river in the small town of Naberezhnyye Chelny in the Tatarstan Autonomous Republic about 700 miles east of Moscow. (See Exhibit 7 for locations of cities in the USSR.) Ground was broken in 1969 for the Kama River Truck Factory (called KamAZ) covering about nine square miles. The target capacity of KamAZ was 150,000 trucks and an additional 100,000 replacement engines a year, which was greater than the entire capacity of North America. By 1990 Naberezhnyye Chelny had become a city with a population of about 600,000. KamAZ employed about 130,000 workers at that location and 40,000 more scattered around the former Soviet Union.

Rather than building the production equipment themselves, the Soviets decided to purchase turn-key factories and manufacturing equipment in the West. In the early 1970s, KamAZ established purchasing offices in the West, including New York, to buy technology, designs, manufacturing equipment, and plants. Many U.S. companies were eager to do business with KamAZ, but there were many restrictions imposed by the U.S. government on trade with the Soviets, which severely handicapped those efforts. For example, Mack Truck signed a protocol agreement as prime contractor for both plant and product for the first half of the planned capacity of KamAZ, which would have produced sales of around $1 billion for U.S. firms. However, Mack had to withdraw because the U.S. government did not grant permission to participate. Instead, European companies obtained lucrative contracts for machinery and equipment on the project.

Needless to say, U.S. firms that were excluded from this business were not happy, and it was readily apparent that U.S. government policy was not preventing the Soviets from building the factory. Therefore, after intense lobbying in Washington, U.S. restrictions were relaxed and over 50 U.S. firms were able to participate in the project.

The first KamAZ trucks rolled off the line in 1976. The second phase of the project began soon thereafter, and several U.S. companies won major contracts to help complete the factory. In December 1979, Soviet troops rolled into Afghanistan in KamAZ trucks. In response, in January 1980, Congress prohibited U.S. companies from doing business with KamAZ. A number of U.S. companies got badly burned. Ingersoll Rand, for example, had virtually completed the second assembly line for delivery to KamAZ, but was unable to deliver it. The Soviets went on and completed the factory by copying the first phase equipment. Although U.S. restrictions caused delays, a major impact on the Soviet Union was to enhance its local machine tool capability.

KamAZ was a huge truck *factory*, not a truck *company* in the Western sense. The trucks were designed by NAMI, the state technical institute in Moscow. The State Planning Committee told KamAZ what to produce, how much to produce, what price to charge, who its suppliers would be, and what the supplies would cost. KamAZ produced its planned quota of

EXHIBIT 7 *Map of the USSR Showing Location of Naberezhnyye Chelny*

trucks, loaded them on railroad cars, but did not know their final destination. Under the Soviet state planning system, KamAZ did no engineering, no marketing, and no servicing. It just produced growing numbers of heavy trucks and engines each year and shipped them out.

KamAZ produced a limited line of medium-heavy trucks designed for the Soviet conditions—rugged for the relatively primitive road system and capable of enduring the cold Russian winters. There were many differences in practice in operating trucks in the USSR compared to the U.S. Average speeds are lower, the roads are rougher, the temperatures are more extreme, preventative maintenance service is poor, the types of fuels and lubricating oils are different, and they do not treat their cooling water with anticorrosives.

Although KamAZ trucks were well suited to the conditions in the USSR, there was no feedback mechanism or incentive for improvement, so they were by no means world-class products. In particular, their engines were inefficient with little concern for pollution. In addition, their axles and transmissions were not up to Western standards. Because Europe was rapidly adopting U.S.-type standards for pollution control, current KamAZ engine technology would prevent the export of KamAZ trucks to most of the developed world.

KamAZ exported trucks to 30 countries around the world, most of them going to Eastern Europe, China, and Cuba. KamAZ had a foreign trade company and brochures listing places its trucks were used and showing its trucks running in different countries. But the role of the foreign trade company was largely limited to putting different shipping labels on the trucks as dictated by the bilateral trade agreements negotiated by the Soviet government. KamAZ had no direct contact with the countries before or after the trucks were shipped. However, KamAZ management did have a lot of experience in dealing with foreign companies because its people had worked with numerous companies from many nations during the construction of the KamAZ plant.

Soon after Gorbachev came to power in 1985, the path toward the disintegration of communism in the USSR began, and things began to change for huge Soviet enterprises such as KamAZ. Fortunately, KamAZ had outstanding management by Soviet standards, including Nikolai Bekh, their director general, appointed in 1986, who was exceptional.

As early as 1987, Bekh had negotiated with the central ministry in Moscow to obtain a great deal of independence for KamAZ. KamAZ was still owned by and ostensibly controlled by the central ministry, but the ministry really handed all the responsibility and authority to KamAZ management. Thus, KamAZ effectively became an independent company in 1988. In June 1990, KamAZ became the first major joint stock company in the Soviet Union (Resolution Number 616 of the Council of Ministers). This was prior to the law permitting the establishment of joint stock companies. The government created this new joint stock company as an experiment, picking KamAZ because the ministry thought KamAZ had a better chance of success than any other large enterprise in the USSR.

Bekh had the foresight to anticipate some of the upcoming challenges and to recognize strategically what he had to do to keep KamAZ functioning. He sold stock to his major suppliers, customers, and employees so that they would all have a strong interest in KamAZ's success during the radical changes that were on the horizon. Thus, KamAZ developed its own "mini-economy" linking suppliers, KamAZ, and major customers to replace the old central control network. Bekh was preparing KamAZ to operate in a market economy that began to emerge in the early 1990s.

One of Bekh's first moves after KamAZ became an independent company was to set up a wholly owned subsidiary, Avtocenter, to provide service centers for KamAZ trucks throughout the Soviet Union. Avtocenter quickly established a network of more than 200 service centers that distributed spare parts and provided service for KamAZ vehicles. KamAZ began to learn where its trucks were located, how they were used, and what their service problems were. This was a big step from the enterprise's situation under the old economic system.

Leonid Komm, the KamAZ finance director, has done an outstanding job in putting together the financial structure of KamAZ. In 1991, its first year as a joint stock company, KamAZ doubled its profits under the Soviet accounting system. KamAZ has hired DRT-Inaudit as its Western auditor and consultant to help figure out where it would stand under Western accounting systems.

As the world's largest heavy truck manufacturer, KamAZ has received attention in U.S. publications. According to a January 1994 *New York Times* article,[1]

Today KamAZ stands as a prototype for post-Soviet industry, and its experience is being studied closely in Moscow as Russia begins the process of sending its 14,000 other big state-owned enterprises—some even larger than KamAZ—into the capitalist fray.

Moreover, KamAZ has become a testing ground for a handful of pioneering companies that are gaining invaluable experience operating in Russia through joint ventures and other deals with the truck maker. Rockwell International Corporation, of Seal Beach, Calif., is negotiating to supply or coproduce a wide range of vehicle components, including axles, and is already selling factory automation equipment to KamAZ. Daimler-Benz has expressed interest in a joint venture. And KamAZ has hired American Re-insurance Company of Princeton, N.J. to develop its first property insurance program.

Domestically, KamAZ has a near-monopoly on heavy trucks and a well developed (by Soviet standards) distribution and service network that could allow a Western partner to service its products throughout the former Soviet Union. Abroad, KamAZ benefits from its currently low wage and material costs, which could allow it to price a middle-of-the-line truck for $14,000, half or less the price of similar sized Western makes.

KamAZ has come a long way toward its goal of looking and acting like a Western company. Production workers have become used to attending seminars on quality control. Engineers are preparing for a diversification into bus production. And Bekh is talking about tripling truck exports, to 40,000 a year, to compete against European and Asian rivals.

"When the Government distributes your profits and the ministry decides your future, the motivation to work is missing," Bekh said in a recent interview. "At least now, when I hold a board meeting, we're trying to focus on the right issues. All of KamAZ is now involved in adopting world standards."

But its future is by no means assured. Bekh and KamAZ employees continue to struggle not just with the nation's political spasms, but with huge business challenges. KamAZ needs hundreds of millions of dollars of outside investment to finance new products. It must begin to reduce employment to hold costs down, a politically tricky step.

It needs to shuck off responsibility to reluctant local and regional governments for financing and running schools, hospitals, mass transportation and other services that have traditionally been provided by big Russian enterprises.

It has had to build a marketing department from scratch and totally recast its financial accounting. Trade with the former Soviet republics has become more difficult, complicating relationships with key suppliers and customers. On top of everything else, a fire destroyed the company's engine factory in April 1993, crippling production for months.

HISTORY OF RELATIONSHIPS BETWEEN CUMMINS AND KAMAZ

The following history has been provided by John L. Becker, Cummins' director of international business development, who has been involved throughout Cummins' relationship with KamAZ.

As far back as the 1960s, Cummins diesel engines were being exported to the USSR through manufacturers of heavy construction and mining equipment and logging trucks. For example, Komatsu was a Cummins' licensee from 1962 to 1988, and over time around 6,500 Komatsu logging trucks and 1,000 Komatsu mining trucks with Cummins diesel engines were imported into the USSR. More than 1,000 other Cummins engines were imported into the USSR in various suppliers' mining trucks and construction equipment. Cummins had no direct involvement in the USSR at the time, but the suppliers provided sufficient maintenance and Cummins engines achieved an excellent reputation for reliability.

During the early 1970s, when the KamAZ factory was being built, Cummins was approached by the KamAZ purchasing office and encouraged to bid on providing a turn-key diesel engine factory. After careful analysis, Cummins declined to get involved. Cummins deemed this project too risky because it would have been quite large relative to Cummins' size, there were payment uncertainties, and the historical ups and down of US-USSR political relations did not bode well for the future.

Cummins' long relationship with Komatsu went through several up and down cycles over the years. In the early 1980s the U.S. government refused to allow Cummins' engines to be used in Komatsu equipment that was being exported to Russia for pipeline construction. As a result Komatsu decided to concentrate on using its own engines in its exported equipment. Soon Komatsu customers in the USSR began to complain to Cummins that they could no longer get satisfactory service on their Cummins engines through Komatsu.

Cummins' management saw the USSR as the largest diesel engine market in the world, and decided that it wanted to participate in that market in the long run. Since Cummins' reputation for reliability was being put at risk, in 1983 Cummins decided to develop its own service organization in the Soviet Union, setting up a small group in Belgium to take care of its engines in the USSR. This unit consisted of a part-time manager and three trainers who traveled around the Soviet Union teaching people how to maintain, service, and rebuild Cummins engines. This effort was very effective; before long Cummins had rebuilt and even improved its engines' excellent reputation for reliability.

In 1984 Cummins' senior management made its first contacts in the USSR while participating in a seminar sponsored by the USSR State Committee for Science and Technology. Senior-level contacts were made at foreign trade offices (FTOs), at the Ministry of Automotive Industry, and at the Ministry of Agricultural Machine Building. Also, in 1984, Chernenko took over as First Secretary of the Communist Party after the death of Andropov.

In 1985, Cummins established an unaccredited office in Moscow to coordinate service training and parts sales, sharing space with another company and staffing it on a part-time basis. The service training continued to go well as Cummins' traveling trainers established good rapport with the end users in the mining industry. The perceived reliability and durability of Cummins engines continued to exceed those of its competitors. Also in 1985, Chernenko died and Gorbachev took over the leadership of the USSR.

Since in 1985 direct investment in the USSR was not yet permitted, Cummins' management tried to penetrate the Soviet diesel market by working with equipment manufacturers in the eastern bloc that were supplying equipment to the Soviets. Cummins had serious discussions with RABA in Hungary, at-tempting to establish a joint venture to manufacture Cummins' L10 engines in Hungary for export to the USSR in Ikarus busses that were widely used in the Soviet Union. This effort failed because the partners could not work out a feasible arrangement, given the nonconvertibility of East-bloc currencies and the reluctance of the Soviets to pay for the outstanding quality of Cummins engines, since the end users had no influence on the price that the FTO was willing to pay.

In 1986, Cummins was invited by the Ministry of Agricultural Machine Building, Minsel'khozmash, to make a proposal for a turn-key factory and a license to manufacture high-horsepower diesel engines at the Cheboksary tractor factory. Cummins proposed a joint venture structure even though no law permitting foreign direct investment existed at that time. The proposal was eventually rejected, losing out to MTU from Germany that had proposed a version of the engine powering the German Leopard tank that was a mainstay of the NATO forces. According to John Becker, the Soviets offered a great deal of encouragement to Cummins when they lost this contract, saying:

> You did a great job. We are very pleased with your response, your openness, and the pricing you gave us. But nobody wins one of these things the first time around—MTU worked with us on this deal for 12 years. You will have other opportunities. Don't give up!

MTU was able to get permission from the German government and COCOM to provide the NATO tank engine to the Russians, although at that time the U.S. government was very restrictive about allowing U.S. companies to export technology to the USSR. The U.S. Commerce Department was opposed to this deal, but it was overruled by the State Department, which was typical of the disarray of U.S. foreign economic policy during this period.

In 1987 the Russian government issued its first joint-venture decree. The Soviet Ministry of Automotive Industry invited Cummins to survey Soviet diesel engine factories so that Cummins could identify potential partners for cooperation. When the Cummins team visited KamAZ, it received a very warm reception, with much interest in the Cummins engines. Although the Cummins team had expected to concentrate discussion on the 8.3 liter C engine, the Russians were especially interested in the L10.

C-207

The Cummins team was very impressed with KamAZ's facilities and with the young, competent, dynamic people operating and managing KamAZ. A second group went back to KamAZ to explore possibilities for cooperation. Things continued to progress well. In October 1987, KamAZ Chairman Nikolai Bekh and Cummins Chairman Henry Schacht met for the first time. The two chairmen immediately hit it off on a personal basis, and they agreed to try and find some way for the two companies to cooperate.

The two chairmen recognized that there were significant problems to be overcome. One set of problems was U.S. government regulations and restrictions on trade with the Soviets. There were COCOM regulations, U.S. unilateral controls such as the commodities control list, and the explicit prohibition by Congress after the Afghan invasion against U.S. companies working with KamAZ that was still in effect. The chairman agreed to begin two paths of work. First, Cummins would lobby in Washington to try modifying the U.S. government regulations. Second, the two companies would work together to try developing a viable structure for a joint venture.

Analyzing the various restrictions that might apply to cooperation with KamAZ, Cummins' people concluded that COCOM probably would not be a problem. They also knew the commodity control restrictions quite well, and they felt that they would not be a problem until they got into some sophisticated manufacturing equipment, which could be purchased from non-U.S. suppliers, if necessary. But the specific congressional restriction on dealing with KamAZ would be a major problem because it prohibited the transfer of any manufacturing technology.

Cummins mounted a lobbying effort in Washington to get the congressional restrictions on dealing with KamAZ lifted. Senior management of Cummins knew some of the top-level people in Commerce and Defense, so they were able to get good access to these organizations and had several meetings with National Security Council people. Although Commerce is responsible for administering the controls, the Defense Department recommends the controls to Congress. In the fall there was a period for public comment before the Defense Department was to recertify the need for each control, and Cummins was able to participate in those reviews. By this time the Soviets had agreed to withdraw from Afghanistan by April 1989, and Cummins was assured that Congress would lift the restrictions.

Cummins was dismayed when in January 1989, Congress voted to reimpose the controls, which meant that it would be at least another year before they could proceed with their joint venture. The year 1989 was a period of great uncertainty, not only for this reason but also because the Soviet empire was breaking up as the Warsaw Pact disintegrated and the central and eastern European countries became independent. These developments meant that the market for KamAZ trucks became more uncertain. Nevertheless, Cummins and KamAZ continued to work on defining a business relationship that made sense to both. KamAZ acquired three Cummins engines to try out in its trucks, but they were very slow in getting them installed and tested. During this period Cummins also had joint-venture discussions with other Soviet companies, which only strengthened the feeling of Cummins' management that KamAZ was the right partner.

In January 1990, Congress finally lifted the restrictions on doing business with KamAZ. In June, KamAZ became the first major joint stock company in the Soviet Union. Cummins and KamAZ began working much more energetically on defining their relationship, sharing some technical information and getting their manufacturing people involved in detailed planning.

In 1991 the U.S. government became much more favorably inclined toward cooperation with the USSR as the Russians were beginning to cooperate with the United Nations and did not oppose the Gulf War resolution. It became obvious that many Western companies would be attempting to enter the Russian market. Cummins' management decided that if it did not get something concrete done pretty soon, there would be other companies attempting to work with KamAZ and concluding an agreement might be more difficult. On the other hand, there were monumental uncertainties that made it impossible to make plausible economic projections that would justify any substantial investment at that time. Cummins did not know what the market would be, what the costs really were, what a ruble was worth, or how it could be converted to dollars. Yet Cummins' management knew that this could be a huge opportunity for the long term and felt compelled to conclude some agreement that would assure access to the largest diesel engine market in the world without making an unacceptably large investment to be at more than normal risk.

The issue of risk was a major consideration. Cummins had been going through very difficult times, with substantial losses for several years that required an extended period of aggressive cost cutting to try to become profitable. To gain approval of the Cummins board, any agreement would have to be virtually risk-free.

Cummins worked long and hard to analyze the risks and build a business case for a joint venture with KamAZ. According to Becker,

We tried and tried to do a traditional financial analysis, but we finally decided that it was meaningless because the cost and price data that we were able to use were completely unrealistic, so unrealistic that we knew it had to change in order for the economy to work.

In the end we were nonquantitative in our analysis. First, we looked at the competition in the Soviet marketplace. We concluded that in terms of weight, complexity, number of parts, power density, emissions control, fuel consumption, etc., our product was significantly better than anything that was available there.

Second, we looked at our ability to compete around the world on a manufacturing basis. We are exporting products into Japan, and we have kept the Japanese out of the U.S. We are exporting products into Germany, China, Korea—places that certainly have a reputation for efficient manufacturing and cost-effective production. We are able to compete with the best in the world anywhere. The processes for competing—the management systems, the kind of machinery, the technical processes—are things that should be implementable in the USSR. We are confident that we can compete with anyone in Russia.

Finally, we think that KamAZ is the right partner for us. They have the experience and the best management in the USSR, and their potential is enormous. The joint venture could be producing 150,000 engines in a few years if things go well. That compares to our current production of about 45,000 comparable engines in the U.S.

The key for Cummins was to structure an agreement that would limit our up-front investment and control the tremendous risk due to the monumental changes going on, and likely to continue, in Russia.

KamAZ managers had their own reasons for wanting to get something done. They knew that Cummins' technology was first rate, that Cummins had a lot of successful joint-venture experience in varied social and economic environments, and that Cummins had a presence and a good reputation for service in over 130 countries. This was important because KamAZ had no service capability outside the USSR, so Cummins' worldwide service network would be a huge start toward supporting KamAZ trucks. They also knew that, as the USSR converted to a market-based environment, Cummins' technology would provide KamAZ with a crucial competitive advantage. In fact, without better engines there was little prospect of exporting KamAZ trucks, except to the Third World.

Schacht and Bekh met in New York in May 1991 and agreed to move toward signing an agreement to establish a joint venture to manufacture Cummins engines in the USSR. Negotiations were intensified, and in October an agreement was signed by Schacht and Bekh to establish a 50-50 joint venture named KamDizel to manufacture and distribute the Cummins C-series and L-series engines in the USSR. The engines built by KamDizel were not to be exported from the USSR without permission from Cummins, but any KamAZ trucks with KamDizel engines could be exported without restriction.

The joint-venture agreement was ingeniously structured to reduce the risk associated with the many uncertainties that existed, while at the same time committing both Cummins and KamAZ to a long-term program of cooperation. The agreement defined four phases. In phase one each company invested $500,000 to establish a marketing system, a service system, and an application engineering capability in the USSR (which Cummins was already engaged in), and to import built-up engines. The second phase involved the assembly of Cummins engines by KamDizel from imported components. The third phase was to manufacture those engine components in Russia that could be produced on general-purpose manufacturing equipment. The final phase was to locally manufacture components that required dedicated equipment. At the end of the fourth phase there should be around 70 percent local content in the engines manufactured by KamDizel.

There was no specific time frame for progressing from stage to stage. Rather, the agreement established specific business targets for each phase whose attainment triggers the beginning of the next phase. These business targets involve measurable goals such as sales volume, profitability, and quality. An important characteristic of this arrangement is that it should be self-funding after the initial modest investment by each party. The second phase does not begin until the first phase has been successful in generating the necessary financing; the third phase does not begin until the second phase has been successful; and so forth. For Cummins, the payoff from this agreement was very much a long-term matter, for no tangible cash flows in either direction were contemplated until fully entering the fourth phase.

It was also clear that success in the joint venture depended on many things that were not under the control of either party. Chief among these was the assumption that the ruble would eventually become a convertible currency.

HISTORY OF KAMDIZEL

As soon as the agreement was signed, KamDizel began to get organized and staffed. Bekh assigned Ivan Kostin, director of the KamAZ engine rebuild plant, the additional title of director general of KamDizel. Cummins assigned Mike English, bus and light commercial marketing director for Europe, as the deputy general director. Kostin did not speak English, and English spoke no Russian. The KamAZ engine rebuild plant was designated as the future manufacturing site of KamDizel.

At the end of 1991 the USSR ceased to exist and was replaced by the Confederation of Independent States (CIS). This raised many questions for both KamAZ and KamDizel. What would be the future of KamAZ factories and service facilities, their suppliers, and their customer base in the other republics? These questions represented significant new uncertainties for KamDizel.

In February 1992, Yeltsin freed prices in Russia. In the first three months of 1992, prices increased three to 50-fold, depending on the product. The ruble was devalued by a factor of 70, and some of the other republics started to create their own currency to replace the ruble.

Early in 1992, Tatarstan, a region with a population of only about 3.5 million and home to KamAZ and KamDizel, voted to become "independent" from Russia. Since Tatarstan contained about one-fourth of the known oil reserves of the former Soviet Union, the decision to become independent was driven by the desire to control these valuable natural resources. At the time, no one was very specific about what "independence" would mean. But this action complicated things for KamAZ and KamDizel as some customers expressed concern about importing trucks or engines from Tatarstan. Because the local economy is so heavily dependent on the rest of the former Soviet Union, Tatarstan has continued to act as an integral part of Russia, but no one knows what the future may bring.

The old central planning relationships among suppliers, manufacturers, and customers disintegrated. But a market economy was not yet established. Consequently, much of Russia's economic activity was severely hampered. KamAZ did remarkably well under these difficult conditions, with production dropping only 12 to 20 percent, although at the end of 1992 KamAZ had substantial finished truck inventory for the first time in its history. However, in a few months KamAZ was able to work off this inventory, and by its accounting system showed a substantial profit for 1992.

Problems Perceived by Cummins

One of the first problems was establishing a satisfactory communications link between Columbus, Indiana, and Naberezhnye Chelny. The Russian telephone system was a complete disaster. Fortunately, the two companies were able to obtain permission to use the Soviet military alert communication system that was much higher quality than the civilian telephone system.

Living conditions in Naberezhyne Chelny were such that neither of the two Cummins managers at KamDizel was willing to accept a long-term assignment there; thus Cummins had a real struggle to get effective people on site. One problem was one or two American families living in isolation in a very strange and austere environment as compared to the American Midwest. Another problem was a feeling of isolation within the KamAZ culture that led to job frustration. KamAZ was a manufacturing plant, and all its values were involved with manufacturing. Because the first stage of KamDizel involved no manufacturing and had no prospect of having any manufacturing operations until the market was proved, KamAZ's operating people did not take the agreement seriously and gave it bottom priority. The Cummins people would regularly receive lectures about Cummins' go-slow step-by-step approach, how that was not the Russian way of doing things.

A major problem was that little progress was made in redesigning KamAZ trucks so that the Cummins C-series engine could be installed, which was essential to generating revenue that would allow Kam-Dizel to progress to phase two and assemble engines in Russia. Converting trucks from using the KamAZ V-8 engine to the Cummins straight six engine was by no means trivial—about 200 parts were involved for each type of truck—but it could have been done in a few months at most. But 18 months after KamDizel was established, KamAZ had not completed the modification of any of its production trucks to use Cummins engines.

Cummins' managers believed that there were a number of possible causes of this problem. First, there were the aforementioned significant cultural differences between KamAZ and Cummins. Another possible explanation for this problem was that the KamDizel board of directors was ineffective in getting things done within KamAZ. This board had several representatives from KamAZ who were in second-level positions in KamAZ. Although in a U.S. organization they would have been able to get the necessary things done, in a Soviet organization the general manager retains all authority that is not formally delegated to a subordinate. Because the problems that arose were unanticipated and could not have been delegated, the KamAZ managers on the board often did not have the authority to deal with the problems that did surface.

Perhaps the most plausible explanation of the disappointing progress was political opposition within KamAZ to the use of the Cummins engine. According to Becker,

> The major resistance was coming from the engineers. Although one of the chief engineers was on the KamDizel board of directors, we were still competing with the engines that he had devoted his life to developing. Our engines always had some difficulty or problem with installation. We couldn't solve this. We couldn't get priorities. There were just a myriad of things that we really had trouble dealing with.

For one reason or another, even though most of the KamDizel people came from KamAZ and were relatively well connected before they transferred

from KamAZ, they were treated as outsiders. It was very difficult to get the things done within KamAZ that were necessary for KamDizel to be successful.

The Engine Plant Fire

At about 7 P.M. on April 14, 1993, a fire started in the KamAZ engine and transmission plant in Naberezhnyye Chelny and burned for six days, completely destroying the plant. This was the largest engine factory in the world—approximately 700 million square feet, one kilometer long by 660 meters wide. In contrast, Cummins' largest factory is 1.2 million square feet.

This fire was a major blow to the economy of the former Soviet Union. The burned factory was the sole source of engines for KamAZ, the Fauf and Leakno bus factories, and for part of the truck production at Zil. The fire wiped out economic support for the 600,000 people in Naberezhnyye Chelny, another 400,000 people supported by KamAZ's supply base at other places, and about 500,000 people supported by the production of the smaller factories that relied on KamAZ for engines and/or transmissions. In addition, there was the effect on the Russian transportation system of losing the production of all of those vehicles that were needed by the transportation system. This fire was truly an economic disaster.

Furthermore, the factory was not insured. Under the Communist system, all production facilities were owned by the state, and the state absorbed the risk of disasters such as fires. But KamAZ had recently been privatized. Unfortunately, they had never thought about insurance.

KamAZ set up a recovery task force and announced that the factory would be back in production by the end of the year (1993). They immediately set about clearing the rubble out of the factory and locating, refurbishing, and reclaiming any of the machinery that could be salvaged. KamAZ still had a spare parts factory and Kostin's engine rebuild factory, so it still had some capacity for building parts and assembling engines. They were also able to outsource some of the components that could be produced on general-purpose equipment at other factories around the country, including military conversion factories.

The main problem was the engine cylinder block. Fortunately, the way the fire started and progressed, the block line was the least damaged area of the factory. There were two parallel cylinder block lines—

one purchased from Ingersoll Milling Machine Company of Rockford, Illinois, and the other a Russian-built copy of that line KamAZ built when the U.S. government shut off U.S. firms from participation in its Phase II expansion. By combining the salvaged machinery from the two lines and buying line components wherever they could, KamAZ managed to cobble together a block line and began to produce some engine blocks by the end of the year. This enabled KamAZ to return to limited engine production and meet its year-end target date. Everyone was amazed at the success of this truly herculean effort.

In the meantime, KamAZ did everything possible to continue to build new trucks and keep some level of operation in the factory. They recalled all of the spare parts and used engines anywhere in the KamAZ distribution network to refurbish the old engines and install them in new trucks. The Russian government, in order to help keep KamAZ afloat, gave it a purchase order for trucks without power units. Some of these trucks ended up being powered by old engines, but a lot of them sat in fields around Naberezhnyye Chelny without engines. By hook or by crook they managed to keep the KamAZ assembly line running at a reasonable pace.

The Fire's Effect on KamDizel

Immediately after the fire, Cummins offered KamAZ any kind of aid within the U.S. company's power. Cummins developed a proposal to the U.S. government and to the European Bank for Reconstruction Development (EBRD) to obtain a credit line that would finance the installation of Cummins engines in KamAZ trucks and help recover a portion of the lost production. But Cummins was turned down in both places. Despite the big splash in the Washington press about all of Clinton's aid packages to Russia, the U.S. government's Export-Import Bank said that it was up to its limit with Russian risk.

The 1991 joint-venture agreement included clauses binding Cummins to work exclusively with KamAZ in Russia and binding KamAZ to work exclusively with Cummins. Nevertheless, after the fire every engine manufacturer in the world descended on KamAZ to offer its assistance, and KamAZ undertook a fairly substantial effort to evaluate everyone's engine. KamAZ built and tested early prototype vehicles with 11 different engines in them and engaged in preliminary negotiations with some of those companies. However, in September 1993, after extensive negotiations, Kam-

AZ and Cummins concluded a new agreement under which KamDizel would build 50,000 Cummins-designed engines annually in Russia starting in 1995.

When it burned, the KamAZ engine factory had a capacity of somewhat over 200,000 engines per year. As noted previously, the KamAZ mind-set was that of a truck factory, not a profit-making truck company. Neither Cummins nor KamAZ believed that there was likely to be a market for over 200,000 engines; nevertheless the KamAZ reaction was to replace the capacity that had burned.

The KamAZ plan was to replace that capacity in three phases, called Motor 1, Motor 2, and Motor 3. The Motor 1 phase was to rebuild the firm's capacity to produce about 100,000 of the existing KamAZ engines annually. Before the fire, KamAZ engineers had designed two new engines for use in their current trucks. One was an improved version of the old V-8 engine and the other was a new in-line six engine. In the Motor 2 phase KamAZ planned to build capacity to produce 50,000 of these new engines annually. Prior to the fire, KamAZ had placed an order with East German machine tool manufacturers to produce the manufacturing line for Motor 2. However, in early 1994, the East German manufacturer had not started building that line, and no one seemed to know how it would be financed, so its status was in doubt.

The Motor 3 phase was to collaborate with a foreign partner, later determined to be Cummins, to build capacity to produce 50,000 engines annually for a new line of heavy trucks that KamAZ planned to introduce in the future. In 1993, Cummins had introduced the M11 engine, a very sophisticated upgrade of their L10 engine with fully electronic fuel injection. The M11 was the target engine for the Motor 3 phase.

The Motor 3 plan did not make business sense to Cummins, so the negotiations that led to the new agreement were intense. According to Becker,

The plans for a new heavy truck required a new engine, a new higher capacity transmission, a new higher capacity axle, a new chassis, and a new cab—a whole new vehicle. We felt that this was entirely too risky. KamAZ has not demonstrated that it is able to fund this kind of development, so we are concerned about their ability to produce a brand new truck even if the engine plant were in place. Also, KamAZ estimates that there is a market for 35 to 50 thousand heavy trucks a year in Russia, but we are not sure about that. There is some, but to utilize large numbers of heavy trucks in Russia, the heavy vehicle infrastructure would have to improve greatly. Today's KamAZ trucks are the size they are because the road infrastructure in Russia is not well developed. Furthermore, they would have to replace a lot of the loading docks and material handling systems to utilize heavy trucks.

Although there is presently no heavy truck manufacturer in Russia, Maz in Belarus and the Cremin Chug factory in Ukraine produce heavy trucks. Paccar, Caterpillar, and Zil have announced a joint venture called Nova Truck to produce a heavy duty truck in Russia, but when they might get into production is not clear. Nevertheless, KamAZ believes that it has the size, the market structure, the distribution and service system that no one else has, and that it can get virtually the entire market. This assumes that Maz doesn't sell any, Croz doesn't sell any, Roaz doesn't sell any, Nova Truck doesn't sell any, nobody imports any trucks from Western Europe, nobody imports any trucks from Hungary, Czechoslovakia, or Poland. We are highly skeptical of these assumptions.

To sum it all up, building a factory to produce the M11 engine in Russia was far too risky an investment for Cummins' taste. Our position was that KamDizel needed to manufacture the Cummins C-series engine for use in current KamAZ trucks in order for the joint venture to be profitable. We went round and round on this. KamAZ engineers did not like the C-series engine; they felt it was effectively obsolete technology and did not have a future. We believe that the C-series is very much an engine for the future that will be in our product line well into the next millennium. The debate raged on, but the KamAZ people finally understood that the only way Cummins could justify the hundreds of millions of dollars investment was to produce the C-series engine. We both agreed to compromise on a plant that would produce *both* the M11 and the C-series engine, and that was the basis for the September 1992 agreement.

The agreement took place at a policy and strategy level. Bekh and Schacht committed KamAZ and Cummins to work together to produce engines in Russia. But the agreement had to be implemented at the operational level, and there have been many difficulties in putting together a business plan that would provide a return on investment that was satisfactory to Cummins or KamAZ with an acceptable level of risk for Cummins.

Despite the difficulties, significant progress has been made. Convertibility of the ruble had been a major concern to Cummins because, based on the projected flows of engines and components and other payments, it would be necessary to get something in excess of a hundred million dollars a year of hard currency out of Russia. But, by the early part of 1994, the currency auctions seemed to be working well enough to where this problem was of less concern.

Cummins' chief financial officer, Peter Hamilton, has worked diligently with international financial institutions and with the U.S., United Kingdom, and German governments to develop financing for the project. Thanks to these efforts, the European Bank for Reconstruction Development (EBRD) and the International Finance Corporation (IFC) have each agreed to fund a major portion of the project if KamDizel can put an operating plan together that makes sense. Thus, the financing seems to be in place.

KamDizel people have also been out in the marketplace trying to determine if there is a demand for KamAZ trucks with Cummins engines. They have returned with surprisingly positive input, finding a number of people—Russians, Uzbeks, Ukrainians— who said they were willing to pay a significant premium to get a Cummins engine in a KamAZ truck, claimed they had the money to pay for them, and wanted delivery immediately. However, they did not know how much of this demand was due to trucks with KamAZ engines not being available.

Simultaneously, KamAZ finally adapted its trucks to use Cummins engines. The first 250 vehicles with Cummins engines have been produced. Moreover, KamAZ has managed to deliver hard currency to Cummins on schedule and in the amount promised to pay for these engines. So a number of very positive things have happened.

However, as of February 1994, a feasible business plan had still not been created. John Becker summarized the situation as follows:

The market is telling us that there are some number of people that are willing and able to pay a premium to buy KamAZ vehicles with Cummins engines. And KamAZ has demonstrated that it can, at least for a single payment, deliver hard currency to the West on time. But the projected financial return of the joint venture is still not acceptable either to Cummins or KamAZ, or to potential funding sources. The level of risk implicit in the current plan still exceeds Cummins'

C-213

appetite for risk and the commitment of capital is faster than we would like. So we are still working with the factors that can be manipulated to improve project return—pricing, capital investment, timing, the level of integration, etc. We are not there yet, but we are still making progress.

Additional Concerns

One of Cummins' management concerns is the politics of the situation. They have had a hard time understanding what was going on in the Russian government, with Bekh personally, between Russia and Tatarstan, and within KamAZ.

On December 12, 1993, the Confederation of Independent States (CIS) elected its first parliament, and Yeltsin's party was soundly trounced. The power of Prime Minister Viktor S. Chernomyrdin appeared to be growing, and most of the radical reformers in the cabinet have been replaced. Under the Communists, Chernomyrdin was the head of the Soviet gas industry and had an excellent reputation as a manager. He professed to be committed to continuing the market system reforms, but at a slower pace and with greater concern for the effect on the Russian people. There were many uncertainties about the future of the Russian economy, and Yeltsin's long-term role was in question.

Before the election, Bekh had spent a lot of time in Moscow and seemed to be close to Chernomyrdin. In fact, Bekh started to run for a seat in parliament as a member of Chernomyrdin's party, but withdrew just before the election. Incidentally, Bekh is Ukrainian.

As noted previously, the Tatarstan declaration of independence has been downplayed in the interest of economic realities, but Cummins' management did not understand the situation well enough to have a feel for what might happen in the future.

Cummins' management was also concerned because it did not understand the politics with KamAZ. It appeared that there had been very effective political opposition to the use of the Cummins C-series engine in KamAZ trucks, but where it came from and its future impact were unclear.

Another complication arose in late 1993. A German consortium made a proposal to the Russian government to build an engine and transmission factory to serve KamAZ and other engine and transmission

users in Russia. This consortium offered the Russian government a 1.2 billion Deutsche Mark loan to finance this proposed factory. According to Becker,

The Germans proposed that the Russian government tell Zil and KamAZ to drop their American joint venture relations and agree to use Mercedes engines and Sedif transmissions in return for German financing. Chernomyrdin summoned Bekh to Moscow and pressured him to accept that proposal. Bekh said that he would work with them on transmissions, but that he had made his engine choice. Nevertheless, with KamAZ in Tatarstan and the German consortium playing to the Russians, the politics becomes very sensitive and the Germans could wind up being powerful competitors. This has raised the question of whether the new engine plant should be located in Naberezhnyye Chelny or somewhere in Russia.

Although by 1994 Cummins' financial position had improved substantially over what it had been in 1991 when KamDizel was created, Cummins' plate was overflowing with large, important new international ventures that were competing with KamDizel for attention and resources.

Becker notes that things changed radically between 1991 and 1994:

When we signed the original joint venture agreement with KamAZ we were in a relatively stable Soviet Union with 260 million people led by Gorbachev, who had been in power for several years. Within weeks after we signed this agreement, we were in Russia with 160 million people, and within two months after that Tatarstan declared independence and we were in a country of 3.5 million people and political problems began to arise. The inflation rate went from virtually nothing to something like 25 percent a month. The currency was declared invalid a couple of times. The engine factory burned. And now the course of reform in Russia is in question. But we are still hopeful that things will work out.

NOTES

1. Excerpted with minor editing from "Russian Truck Maker Becomes a Lab for U.S. Deals," *The New York Times*, Sunday, January 16, 1994, Section F, p. 5.

Dayton Hudson Corporation

Jan Zahrly
Marshall Foote
Troy Gleason
Aaron Martin
Brent Olson
Brian Wavra

University of North Dakota

Robert J. Ulrich assumed the chairman and CEO positions of Dayton Hudson Corporation (DHC) in July of 1994 with a multitude of problems. Media coverage was negative and getting worse. Analysts' assessments were negative. Investigations by the U.S. Labor Department, earnings down seriously, key executives resigning, and merger offers from major competitors were some of the problems Ulrich faced. And each of the divisions seemed to be cannibalizing customers from the others. Ulrich joined the company in 1967 as a merchandise trainee and was one of the managers who built Target into a powerhouse but, so far, he has not been able to turn the company around.

DHC is the fourth largest discount and fashion retailer in the United States behind Wal-Mart, Sears, and Kmart. JCPenney closely trails Dayton Hudson in sales. DHC has retail operations in all segments of the discount and clothing industry. These range from a national upscale discount store chain (Target) to Mervyn's, a moderate-priced family department store chain specializing in nondurable goods. DHC also includes a Department Store Division (DSD), which is a centrally operated full-line, full-service chain of department stores emphasizing fashion leadership (under the names of Dayton, Hudson, and Marshall Fields).

This case was written solely for the purpose of stimulating student discussion. Presented at the 1995 North American Case Research Association Annual Meeting, Orlando, November 1995.

A PLETHORA OF PROBLEMS

Dayton Hudson Corporation's problems were so many that stockholders and analysts were beginning to group them into categories. First and foremost, the company could not increase profits. This was reflected in the stock price.

Second, the problems with the U.S. Labor Department were not only serious but public. Secretary of Labor Robert Reich insisted on talking about the problems on TV talk shows, and news shows covered the sweatshop raids (Chandler, 1995c).

Finally, the profit and labor problems contributed to personnel problems. Again, the problems became public knowledge when a division CEO resigned unexpectedly.

Profitability Problems

On May 16, 1995, DHC announced that first-quarter earnings fell 72 percent from the same quarter in the previous year. The company blamed weakness in its Mervyn's division and weaker than projected sales in its other department stores for the steep decline in profits.

On March 14, 1996, DHC announced that net earnings for fiscal 1995 were down 28 percent from the year before. The company cited a "tough Christmas season" and a bad year in general. Company spokesperson Jill Schmidt contended that Dayton Hudson Corporation did not plan any reorganization.

"Right now, there are no plans to sell anything. We're sticking with the plans in place," Schmidt stated (Dayton Hudson Plans No Changes, 1996).

Apparently JCPenney did not believe DHC's public statements and approached the firm about a merger in February 1996. Penney confirmed that it offered $6.8 billion for DHC, but the Dayton Hudson board promptly rejected the unsolicited offer and offered no counterproposal to discuss the possibilities of a merger. See Exhibit 1 for comparative industry data.

The Mervyn's division continued to lag the industry with 1995 profits down 51 percent from the previous year. Executives at Dayton Hudson maintained that discount and fashion retailing was in an industry slump and there was some evidence to support that argument. Apparel sales were up only 2 percent in the first half of 1995 and much of that was due to special sales (Chandler, 1995b). Analysts noted that the industry is saturated and some firms such as Target and Sears are expanding.

Legal Problems

In August of 1995, Dayton Hudson Corporation experienced trouble with the U.S. Labor Department when an El Monte, California, sweatshop was raided. Dozens of Thai nationals, who were illegal aliens, were discovered working in a shop manufacturing clothing. They were enclosed behind barbed wire and were earning less than $1 an hour. Also discovered were boxes of clothing with shipping labels for Montgomery Ward and Mervyn's stores.

"Two retail stores, from initial evidence, appear to have been dealing directly with the contractors" who managed the sweatshop, according to California Labor Commissioner Victoria Bradshaw (National Retailers Investigated, 1995).

Robert Reich, Secretary of Labor, forced a meeting in September 1995 with executives from Dayton Hudson, Sears, and Montgomery Ward to discuss ways the firms could counter the use of sweatshops (Chandler, 1995c). DHC was later excluded from a list of "Fair Labor Fashions Trendsetters" issued by the Labor Department in December 1995. The list of 31 retailers included firms that were working actively to guarantee that clothing sold by the retailers was made in shops and factories that comply with federal wage, labor, and immigration laws (Dayton Is Against Sweatshops, 1995). Secretary Reich wanted the retail industry to take an active role in enforcing fair labor and wage laws and was using public pressure to obtain retailers' compliance.

The negative publicity about Mervyn's contracting directly with sweatshops for clothing hurt DHC's image of being a socially responsible firm. *Hoover's Handbook of American Business* in 1993 listed Dayton Hudson as fifth in the nation for job creation. *Hoover's Handbook* also noted that, "Dayton Hudson has a long history as a great place to work. . . ." Because of its high-quality work atmosphere, job creation activities, and corporate charitable policies (5 percent of net income goes to local charities), Dayton Hudson was included in *The 100 Best Companies to Work For in America* in 1993.

EXHIBIT 1 *Comparative Sales and Earnings Data–1995 Discount and Fashion Retailing Industry (sales and profits in millions of $)*

	Sales	Profits	Return on Equity
Wal-Mart	$90,524	$2,827.6	20.1
Sears	$34,925	$1,025.0	25.1
Kmart	$34,572	$ 8.0	−.2
DHC	$22,564	$ 362.0	11.3
JCPenney	$22,019	$ 940.0	16.9
Industry Average			12.9

Source: *Business Week* Corporate Scoreboard, March 4, 1996.

The corporation was recognized in 1993 for its positive treatment of working parents, minorities, and those with disabilities. Dayton Hudson was listed in *The 100 Best Companies for Minorities: Employers Across America Who Recruit, Train and Promote Minorities.* Dayton Hudson was also named to "The 100 Best Companies for Working Women" by *Working Mother* magazine and "The 50 Best Companies for Hispanic Women," compiled by the Vista magazine section of *The Dallas Morning News.* Overall, Dayton Hudson, through its generous contributions and attitudes toward hiring, became one of the more identifiable good corporate citizens—until the news of the sweatshop raid became public.

Personnel Problems

In March 1996, Stephen Watson resigned abruptly as president of the Department Store Division. He had been popular with subordinates but had clashed with Chairman Ulrich (Chandler, 1996). Watson was quoted as saying he resigned because he believed the Department Store Division will soon "no longer need" a chief executive officer (Dayton Hudson Executive Resigns, 1996). He was apparently referring to the intervention of Ulrich.

At the same time Watson's resignation was announced, Linda Ahlers, one of the few women in Ulrich's inner circle, was named as the new CEO of the Department Store Division. Many outsiders and analysts believe that Ahlers "does not have much of a chance," even though she has been with Target for 19 years and has been very successful (Chandler, 1996). The department stores' profits were down by 32 percent in 1995 (compared to profits in 1994), Ahlers is under pressure to cut millions of dollars in costs, and the department stores' product line is being rejected by customers after a 1994 strategy shift to "value" products.

COMPANY HISTORY

The history of DHC dates back to the late 1800s when the J. L. Hudson Company was founded in Detroit, Michigan. The Dayton Company was founded in Minneapolis, Minnesota in 1902 and later became the Dayton Corporation. In 1956, Dayton opened the world's first fully enclosed, two-level shopping center in suburban Minneapolis, named Southdale. Meanwhile, Hudson opened the Northland Center, the world's largest shopping center at the time, in Detroit.

The shopping centers gained national attention from other retailers. Dayton and Hudson each realized they had market potential and both grew externally through acquisitions and mergers during the 1960s, 1970s, and 1980s. Dayton also developed internal growth ventures, hoping to capitalize on low-margin merchandising. The 1962 venture was the opening of three Target stores in the Minneapolis area. Dayton entered the specialty book retailing market in 1966 through the creation of the B. Dalton Bookseller stores.

In 1969, the Dayton Corporation and the J. L. Hudson Company merged to form the Dayton Hudson Corporation (DHC), making the corporation the 14th largest general merchandise retailer in the United States. DHC continued its strategy of growth. Department store expansion moved to the West through mergers and acquisitions of specialty stores and fashion retailers. In 1977, Target stores became the corporation's top revenue producer.

DHC merged with Mervyn's, a West Coast department store chain, in 1978 and became the country's 7th largest general merchandise retailer. At the same time, DHC began to shed its less profitable operations by selling regional shopping centers and entire divisions. DHC bought and sold stores in an attempt to strengthen its core business, general and fashion retailing. In 1984, Hudson and Dayton department stores combined to form the Dayton Hudson Department Store Company, the largest individual department store company in the nation. B. Dalton Bookseller was sold in the same year.

In 1990, DHC made its final major acquisition. It acquired Marshall Fields, a Midwest up-scale department store chain founded in Chicago in 1852. Mervyn's initiated a major entry into south Florida by acquiring six Jordan Marsh stores and five Lord & Taylor stores. Target expanded into key Florida markets also and opened its first of many smaller market store formats. By 1993, the Mervyn's stores were losing market share due to heavy competition.

On January 7, 1994, Retailers National Bank, a national credit card bank and a wholly owned subsidiary, was chartered. The bank acquired the outstanding accounts receivable of the Department

Store Division and Target. The bank now issues the DSD-named credit cards and a Target credit card.

INDUSTRY TRENDS

The general and fashion retailing industry is characterized by intense competition. For most of the 1970s and through the mid-1980s, retailers achieved earnings and growth by adding new units and expanding existing stores. Strong economic growth and vigorous consumer spending made this possible and feasible. With high volume, retailers were able to reduce operating costs as a percentage of sales, producing solid profits year after year.

In the wake of the recession of the early 1990s, however, the retail landscape changed. Slow economic growth, a decrease in consumer spending for nondurable goods, and an excess of retail space put American retailers to the test. Successful department stores and general merchandise chains were following corporate-level strategies of growth through acquisitions. At the same time, less successful companies were following retrenchment strategies. Successful business-level strategies were product differentiation and the two focus strategies known as focused low-cost of focused differentiation.

Retailers and customers alike grew accustomed to innovations in retailing. Upstart competitors were appearing in virtually every retailing segment. Outlet malls, for example, with their selection of brand-name apparel at value prices were luring customers away from department stores and off-price retailers. Superstores, carrying a wider variety of goods than the traditional department store, have emerged. Specialty stores evolved into "category killers" that carry a single dominant product. Examples are stores that carry many varieties of office supplies or many computer products. Specialty retail stores do not attempt to carry many different products; they want to carry all products related to a particular good or service.

Catalog retailing is expanding and at-home shopping is growing. Most of these new formats are competing on price or convenience. Different types of competition are becoming more powerful in the marketplace. Technological advances such as television, computer online services, and computer databases have opened new doors to reach consumers in their homes. Companies such as The Home Shopping

Network, America Online, and Eddie Bauer are all cashing in on this new technology.

While some consumers remain loyal to the stores they patronize, customer loyalty, in general, is eroding throughout the industry. The once powerful and extremely profitable department stores have reached a mature stage in the industry. The only segment of the retail industry that is currently in the growth stage is the discount merchandise retailer.

The retail life cycle is a natural evolutionary process and executives can do very little to counteract it. What they can do is to plan more efficiently in order to sustain profitability in the different stages. Such planning implies continuous rethinking and revision of operations. This, in turn, means that retailing will continue to be an area of turbulence and uncertainty for some time to come. (Bass, Bates, & Davidson, 1976:75)

DAYTON HUDSON CORPORATION DIVISIONS

In 1995, Dayton Hudson Corporation had three divisions, all involved in general merchandise and fashion retailing. Credit operations were consolidated in a wholly owned subsidiary, the Retailers National Bank.

Target

In 1962, the Target division was created and focused on discount prices. During the 1970s, Target expanded rapidly with internal development of stores and external acquisitions. In 1977, Target became Dayton Hudson's top revenue-producing division. One year later, Target made its first entry into a shopping mall in Grand Forks, North Dakota.

Target was the first mass merchant to use a promotional toy in 1986. More than one and one-half million Kris Kringles were sold during the 1986 holiday season. During the 1990s, Target introduced several new strategies including establishing local flexibility through micromarketing, initiating a total quality system, and focusing on efficiency through use of advanced communication technology and reduced inventory levels.

Target executives characterize the firm as an upscale discounter in the general merchandise retail

EXHIBIT 2 *Number of Stores (Year End)–Dayton Hudson Corporation*

	1995	1994	1993
Target	611	554	506
Mervyn's	286	276	265
Department Stores	63	63	63
Dayton (19)			
Hudson (21)			
Marshall Fields (23)			
Total	960	893	834

Source: *Hoover's Handbook,* 1994, 1995, 1996.

industry. The discount segment of the industry is experiencing intense growth. Target is trying to position itself by focusing on the quality of service it offers its customers. Target stores are described as having high quality at low prices, maintaining clean and attractive stores, stocking plenty of products to avoid stockouts, and offering fast, friendly, and accurate checkout procedures. Many consumers have realized that there is not much difference in the brands they can purchase at Target compared to those they might purchase at Nordstrom or Dayton.

The broad product mix is one of the reasons Target has been so successful. Target's emphasis is on basic, family-oriented merchandise. An aggressive fashion strategy enables Target to compete as a lifestyle trend merchandiser in all categories. Apparel and domestics represent approximately one-third of the product assortment. The targeted customer is 25–44 years old, typically married with children, two-wage-earner family, with income and education levels higher than the market median.

The perceived value to the consumer has been a key differentiation factor. Another less obvious differentiation factor is the millions of dollars Target and its employees donate annually to local nonprofit organizations. Through these numerous contributions, Target has established goodwill in the communities in which it operates.

At year end 1995, Target had 611 stores throughout the United States. The only region in which Target does not operate is the northeastern part of the country. Exhibit 2 lists the number of stores in each division.

Target's performance is the strength of DHC. Even though Target is a discounter and most of the products it sells make low profit margins, it is still the most profitable division of the company (see Exhibit 3).

Mervyn's

Mervyn's is a moderately priced family department store specializing in soft goods. Based in the San Francisco Bay area, Mervyn's was founded in 1949 and was purchased by Dayton Hudson Corporation in 1978. Retailer Mervyn Morris started the chain with the objective of mirroring JCPenney Co. but offering national brands and customer credit. Mervyn's still views its typical stores as smaller versions of JCPenney and Sears stores without the hardware and appliance departments.

By year end 1995, approximately 70 percent of Mervyn's senior management team was new to Mervyn's. The single purpose of the new management group was to effect a turnaround. Mervyn's profitability has been below industry averages for

EXHIBIT 3 *Target's Performance*

	1994	1993	1992
Revenues ($ in mil.)	13,600	11,743	10,393
Operating Profit ($ in mil.)	732	662	574
Net Profit Margin	5.38	5.63	5.52

Source: Dayton Hudson 1994 Annual Report.

EXHIBIT 4 *Mervyn's Performance*

	1994	1993	1992
Revenues ($ in mil.)	4,561	4,436	4,510
Operating Profit ($ in mil.)	206	179	284
Net Profit Margin	4.52	4.03	6.29

Source: Dayton Hudson 1994 Annual Report.

several years. One key addition to the management team was Paul Sauser, formerly senior vice president of merchandising at Target, now Mervyn's president and chief operating officer. Sauser, a highly regarded retail executive, was brought in to help implement Mervyn's turnaround. Mervyn's turnaround included a new pricing strategy, shrinking inventory, sprucing up stores, tailoring merchandise assortments to match the needs of the local customers, and polishing Mervyn's image among customers. The stores are being renovated with wider aisles, knowledgeable associates, less crowding, and improved store graphics.

Mervyn's recent pricing strategy is an improvement on the previous strategy which created large price differentials on many sale items. For example, a cotton blanket was regularly priced at $35.00 but carried a $17.50 sale price one week per month. Consequently, virtually all the purchases occurred when specific items were sale priced. Under the new pricing strategy, the blanket's promotional price is $17.99, with a regular price of $25.00.

Another element of the turnaround was an improvement in its image. This key element involved a return of women's career apparel and dresses, which Mervyn's dropped in 1991. Mervyn's reintroduced its female business apparel product line which sparked sales of more than $90 million in 1993. Approximately 50 percent of its merchandise is nationally known name brands. The key customer is a 25–44-year-old female, typically married with children, working outside the home. The customer tends to have a moderate household income and some college education.

Mervyn's operates in 15 states in the Northwest, West, Southwest, and Southeast. The vast majority of stores are located in California where Mervyn's derives about 50 percent of its revenues. Other major states in which Mervyn's operates are Arizona, Florida, Colorado, and Michigan. Mervyn's faces additional threats because of its strong presence in the struggling California economy. Even though Mervyn's profits and profit margin were increasing

by 1994, they continued to lag the industry and to depress company profits (see Exhibit 4).

"Mervyn's was our major disappointment" and was the fourth largest U.S. retailer, noted in its 1993 year-end earnings report. By 1995, the annual report noted that Mervyn's had made "solid improvement" because of improved markdowns, reduced initial retail prices, and improved inventory management.

Department Store Division

The Department Store Division (DSD) operates stores under the Dayton, Marshall Fields, and Hudson names. The division has goals of fashion leadership, quality merchandising, customer service, and dedication to the communities in which it operates.

The Department Store Division focuses on trends in the marketplace and new fashions and products. The emphasis placed on product mix is a strength when competing with rivals. The DSD relies on a broad assortment of trend-right, quality softlines and hardlines, national brands, and private labels to fulfill customer interest and to sustain a competitive advantage. The DSD also invests in fashion and basic merchandise in the moderate-to-better price range to renew focus on "value" offerings across the price spectrum. This broadened DSD's customer base by lowering opening price points in many departments. An example of this value-priced merchandise is the Field Gear line, introduced in 1993. While customers could still purchase higher-priced items such as Ralph Lauren and Pierre Cardin, they could also choose from the Field Gear line that prices button-down shirts at $32.

The department stores' target consumer is married, with a median age of 43, and median family income of $50,000. Approximately 40 percent have children living at home. Over half have attained at least an undergraduate degree; two-thirds hold white-collar positions.

The DSD is in the business of selling image and

maintaining a certain image. Service, human resource management, and community involvement are elements that relate to its image. DSD upholds the quality of store appearance and remodels when changes are needed or anticipated. The overall image of the DSD is that of a full-service department store, fulfilling the needs and wants of its customers.

DSD advertising places a heavy emphasis on full-color tabloids, direct mail, and occasional television and radio spots. Also, a strong special store events calendar tied to key merchandising trends and/or community events aids in specialty pricing. Finally, a strong emphasis on primary and secondary holiday advertising and promotions is utilized.

The net profit margin for the Department Store Division has improved since 1992 (see Exhibit 5). This trend is due to the increase in inventory turnover and the fact that the department stores can offer a higher price for products. Higher productivity has also resulted from the introduction of new systems that track and control the purchase and delivery of merchandise.

The Department Store Division's major markets are located in Chicago, Minneapolis/St. Paul, and Detroit. The division continues to grow. A new Dayton Store is planned for Minneapolis in 1997 as well as a new Marshall Fields unit in Columbus, Ohio. The recently resigned president of the division, Stephen Watson, said, "We wouldn't build them if we couldn't pencil in a good return" (Chandler, 1995d).

FINANCIAL POSITION

The Dayton Hudson Corporation has two main financial objectives: to produce an average 15 percent annual fully diluted earnings per share growth and to achieve an 18 percent return on equity. See Exhibits 6 and 7 for financial statements.

Dayton Hudson Corporation had average returns on equity but lower than industry returns on assets for 1994. The industry average return on equity was 17.4 percent. However, this number is inflated due to Wal-Mart's return on equity of 25.3 percent. The industry, without Wal-Mart, had a return on equity of 15.4 percent. (See Exhibit 8).

CURRENT SITUATION

Target has a strong market position in the industry. The department stores and Target carry recognizable brand-name products that give the stores credibility. Target and the department stores have a strong image in the markets in which they compete.

However, one of Dayton Hudson's main strengths could pose a problem to another aspect of its business. This is the phenomenal growth of Target. Target's growth in stores and customers may lead to cannibalization of the DSD. "After all, why should I shop in Dayton's when I can get almost the same thing for less money in Target?" said a recent Target customer who was applying for a Target credit card.

A similar problem that may arise could be the cannibalization of Target by the DSD. Since the DSD is introducing lower-priced product lines to attract a wider consumer base, it might take consumers away from Target. The department stores also use sales, with significant advertising, to attract the budget-conscious shopper.

DHC is considering the introduction of a single consolidated credit card. Currently, the corporation has three cards. The first one can be used in all of the DSD stores as well as Target. A second card is a Mervyn's card and can be used only at Mervyn's. The third card is a Target signature card which is limited to use at Target stores.

The corporation says that it is committed to the creation of value for its shareholders, despite a disappointing performance during the past 10 years. The stock price has remained flat for the last five

EXHIBIT 5 *DSD Performance*			
	1994	**1993**	**1992**
Revenues ($ in mil.)	3,150	3,054	3,024
Operating Profit ($ in mil.)	270	268	228
Net Profit Margin	8.57	8.77	7.54

Source: Dayton Hudson 1994 Annual Report.

EXHIBIT 6 *Dayton Hudson Corporation Consolidated Balance Sheets (numbers in millions)*

	1/95	1/94	1/93
Assets			
Current Assets			
Cash and cash equivalents	$ 147	$ 321	$ 117
Accounts receivable	1,810	1,536	1,514
Merchandise inventories	2,777	2,497	2,618
Other	225	157	165
Total Current Assets	4,959	4,511	4,414
Property and Equipment			
Land	1,251	1,120	998
Buildings and Improvements	5,208	4,753	4,342
Fixtures and Equipment	2,257	2,162	2,197
Construction—in Progress	293	248	223
Accumulated Depreciation	(2,624)	(2,336)	(2,197)
Net Property and Equipment	6,385	5,947	5,563
Other	353	320	360
Total Assets	$11,697	$10,778	$10,337
Liabilities and Shareholders' Investment			
Current Liabilities			
Notes payable			$ 23
Accounts payable	$ 1,961	$ 1,654	1,596
Accrued liabilities	1,045	903	849
Income tax payable	175	145	125
Current portion Long Term Debt	209	373	371
Total Current Liabilities	3,390	3,075	2,964
Long-Term Debt	4,488	4,279	4,330
Deferred Income Taxes	582	536	450
Convertible Preferred Stock	360	368	374
Loan to ESOP	(166)	(217)	(267)
Common Shareholders' Investment			
Common Stock	72	72	71
Additional paid-in capital	89	73	58
Retained Earnings	2,882	2,592	2,357
Total Common Shareholders' Investment	3,043	2,737	2,486
Total Liabilities & Common Shareholders' Investment	$11,697	$10,778	$10,337

Source: Dayton Hudson Annual Report, 1994.

years and earnings are "up just 5 percent in four years despite 45 percent growth in sales" (Chandler, 1995a). High and low stock prices for the last five years are listed in Exhibit 9.

Ulrich had his hands full. Stockholders and analysts were truly frustrated with the downward cycle of profits as well as the stock price in light of the recent bull market. The image of the firm was tarnished. Top executives were leaving suddenly. Mervyn's was a burden. Hungry competitors were circling the firm. Divisions were cannibalizing each other. Would things ever get better?

EXHIBIT 7 *Dayton Hudson Financial and Operating Data (numbers in millions except share data)*

	1/95	1/94	1/93
REVENUES	$21,311	$19,233	$17,927
Cost of sales, buying	15,636	14,164	13,129
Selling, publicity, & administrative	3,631	3,175	2,978
Depreciation	531	498	459
Interest expense, net	426	446	437
Earnings from continuing operations, net of tax	714	607	611
Income taxes	280	232	228
NET EARNINGS	434	375	383
Earnings per share	$5.52	$4.77	$4.82

Source: Dayton Hudson Annual Report, 1994.

EXHIBIT 8 *Industry Performance*

	ROE	ROA
Dayton Hudson Corp.	15.2%	3.9%
Industry Avg.	17.4%	6.6%
Industry Avg. w/o Wal-Mart	15.4%	5.1%

Source: Standard & Poor's Industry Surveys 1994.

EXHIBIT 9 *DHC Stock Prices*

	1995	1994	1993	1992	1991
Stock price high	81.00	86.88	85.00	79.25	80.25
Stock price low	63.00	64.88	62.63	58.00	53.73

Source: *Hoover's Handbook,* 1996.

BIBLIOGRAPHY

Bass, S. J., Bates, A. D. & Davidson, W. R. November-December, 1976. The retail life cycle. *Harvard Business Review:* 75.

Chandler, S. March 27, 1995a. "Speed Is Life" at Dayton Hudson. *Business Week:* 84–85.

Chandler, S. September 18, 1995b. Why Clothiers Are Feeling Pinched. *Business Week:* 47.

Chandler, S. October 16, 1995c. Look Who's Sweating Now. *Business Week:* 96–98.

Chandler, S. November 27, 1995d. An Endangered Species Makes a Comeback. *Business Week:* 96.

Chandler, S. May 20, 1996. Under the Gun at Dayton Hudson. *Business Week:* 69–70.

Corporate Scoreboard. March 4, 1996. *Business Week:* 99–122.

Dayton Hudson Corporation. 1994, 1993. *Annual Reports.* Minneapolis, MN.

Dayton Hudson Corporation. 1994. *Dayton Hudson: 1994 at a Glance.* Minneapolis, MN.

Dayton Hudson Corporation. May 1994. *History.* Minneapolis, MN.

Dayton Hudson Corporation. 1994. *Investor's Factbook.* Minneapolis, MN.

Dayton Hudson Earnings Fall. May 17, 1995. *Grand Forks Herald:* D7.

Dayton Hudson Executive Resigns. March 26, 1996. *Grand Forks Herald:* D7.

Dayton Hudson Plans No Changes Despite Profit Dip. March 15, 1996. *Grand Forks Herald:* D5.

Dayton Is Against Sweatshops. December 6, 1995. *Grand Forks Herald:* D7.

Department Store Division of Dayton Hudson Corporation. 1991. *Three Great Stores, One Great Company.* Minneapolis, MN.

Fearnley-Whittingstall, S. October 13, 1993. Outlook for Field's Northbrook opening. *WWD:* 20.

Hoover, G., Campbell, A. & Spain, P. J. 1995, 1994, 1993. Dayton Hudson Corporation. *Hoover's Handbook of American Business.* Austin, TX: Reference Press, Inc.

Keeton, L. E. & Patterson, G. A. May 17, 1995. Dayton's First-Period Profit Sank 72%: Net Fell at Penney but Rose at Wal-Mart. *The Wall Street Journal:* A8.

National Retailers Investigated in Forced Labor Case. August 10, 1995. *Grand Forks Herald:* A3.

Patterson, G. A. March 29, 1994. Mervyn's Effort to Revamp Results in Disappointment. *The Wall Street Journal:* B4.

Spain, P. J. & Talbot, J. R. 1996. Dayton Hudson Corporation. *Hoover's Handbook of American Business.* Austin, TX: Reference Press, Inc.

Standard & Poor's. 1993, 1994. *Standard & Poor's Industry Surveys:* New York.

Enron Development Corporation

Andrew Inkpen

Thunderbird, The American Graduate School of International Management

On August 3, 1995, Rebecca Mark, chairman and CEO of Enron Development Corporation (EDC), hurried to the airport to catch the first leg of a flight from Houston to Bombay. Earlier that day she had received word from India that EDC's $2.8 billion Dabhol power plant project had been canceled. Given the political situation in the state of Maharashtra, the cancellation was not completely unexpected. However, if the decision could not be reversed, EDC's potential financial losses were significant. More importantly, EDC was counting on Dabhol as a beachhead that would lead to further projects in India. India's power-generating capacity was forecast to triple in the next 15 years. The cancellation of the Dabhol project could seriously undermine EDC's participation in this massive development.

ENRON CORPORATION

Houston-based Enron Corporation (Enron), formed in 1985 in a merger between InterNorth, Inc., and Houston Natural Gas Corp., was a leading firm in the worldwide energy industries. The firm's new slo-

Copyright 1996 Thunderbird, The American Graduate School of International Management. All rights reserved. This case was prepared by Andrew Inkpen with research assistance from Katherine Johnston and assistance from Professor Arvind Phatak, Temple University, for the basis of classroom discussion only and is not intended to illustrate either effective or ineffective management.

gan was "Creating Energy Solutions Worldwide" and its stated vision was to become "The World's Leading Energy Company—creating innovative and efficient energy solutions for growing economies and a better environment worldwide."

Enron was the largest natural gas company in the United States and operated the largest gas pipeline system in the world outside of Gazprom in Russia. The firm was involved in developing more natural-gas-fired independent power plants than any other company in the world. Enron owned and operated energy facilities in 15 countries and had projects under way in 15 additional countries. In 1994, the firm had revenues of $9 billion and an operating profit of $944 million. Enron's international operations had earnings before interest and taxes of $148 million in 1994, an increase of 12 percent over the previous year. International operations represented 15 percent of the company's total sales and operating income. Exhibit 1 provides a financial summary for Enron.

Enron had five operating divisions:

- Enron Operations Corp. was responsible for U.S. interstate natural gas pipelines, operated the company's worldwide physical assets (except those owned by Enron Oil & Gas), and provided engineering, construction, and operating services expertise across all business lines.

- Enron Capital & Trade Resources Corp. conducted the majority of the firm's worldwide marketing activities for natural gas, liquids, and elec-

EXHIBIT 1 *Enron Financial Summary*

(Dollars in Millions, Except per Share Amounts)	Year Ended December 31				
	1994	1993	1992	1991	1990
Revenues	$8,894	$7,986	$6,415	$5,698	$5,460
Income Before Interest, Minority Interest and Income Taxes	944	798	767	715	662
Income Before Extraordinary Items	453	332	328	232	202
Total Assets	11,966	11,504	10,312	10,070	9,849
Long-Term Debt	2,805	2,661	2,459	3,109	2,983
Shareholders' Equity	3,257	2,837	2,518	1,929	1,856
Earnings per Common Share	1.70	1.46	1.21	0.98	0.86
NYSE Price Range					
High	$34 5/8	$37	$25	$19 1/8	$15 5/8
Low	27	22 1/8	15 1/4	12 3/8	12 1/2
Close December 31	30 1/2	29	23 3/16	17 1/2	13 5/8

Source: Enron financial statements.

tric power and was responsible for U.S. power development.

- Enron Oil & Gas was involved in exploration and production activities in natural gas and crude oil.
- Enron Global Power & Pipelines (EPP) owned and operated natural gas pipelines in emerging market countries. Enron Corporation held a 52 percent ownership interest in Enron Global Power & Pipelines.
- Enron Development Corporation (EDC) was involved in the development of international energy infrastructure projects such as power plants, pipelines, fuel transportation, and natural gas processing plants.

Enron Development Corporation EDC's focus was on natural gas projects. The firm had an international reputation as a reliable provider of turnkey natural gas projects on a timely basis. All of EDC's projects were project-financed and had long-term contracts with pricing agreements reached in advance. Revenues were tied to the U.S. dollar, and the host government or an outside agency held responsibility for currency conversions.

EDC's projects spanned the globe. On Hainan Island in China, EDC was constructing a $135 million 150-megawatt (MW) power plant. This independent power plant was the first developed by a U.S. company in China. After completion in late 1995, Enron would be the operator and fuel manager. In the Dominican Republic, EDC was completing the first phase of a 185 MW power plant. This project had a 20-year power purchase agreement with the government. In Colombia, EDC was constructing a 357-mile natural gas pipeline for the state-owned oil company. Other projects in active development included a 478 MW gas-fired power plant in Turkey; a 1,120-mile natural gas pipeline from Bolivia to São Paulo, Brazil; a 500 MW gas-fired power plant in Java, Indonesia; and a $4 billion liquefied natural gas processing plant in Qatar.

There was a close relationship between EDC and Enron Global Power & Pipelines (EPP). The parent firm had granted EPP a preferential right to acquire all of EDC's ownership interests in completed power and gas projects outside the United States. The projects under construction in which EPP had preferential rights included the firm's interest in the Dominican Republic power project, the Hainan Island power project, the Colombia pipeline, and the first and second phases of the 2,015 MW Dabhol project in India.

MARKET REFORM IN INDIA

India's population of more than 900 million inhabited the seventh largest country in the world. Issues of language and religion played a major role in Indian culture, politics, and business. Fifteen national languages were recognized by the Indian constitution and these were spoken in over 1,600 dialects. India's official language, Hindi, was spoken by about 20 percent of the population. English was the official working language and for many educated Indians, English was virtually their first language. Hinduism was the dominant religious faith, practiced by over 80 percent of the population. Besides Hindus, Muslims were the most prominent religious group, making up 11 percent of the population.

On a purchasing power parity basis, the Indian economy was the fifth largest in the world. Gross domestic product per capita was $1,300. After India gained its independence from Great Britain in 1947, and until the mid-1980s, the government pursued an economic policy of self-sufficiency. The policy was often referred to as *swadeshi*, a Hindi word meaning indigenous products or made in India. The term was first used by Mahatma Gandhi during the independence movement to encourage people to buy native goods and break the British economic stranglehold on India. To many Indians, *swadeshi* evoked images of patriotism and Indian sovereignty.

After decades of socialist-oriented/statist industrial policy focused on achieving self-sufficiency, India was financially strapped and bureaucratically bloated. High tariffs kept out imports, and official government policy discouraged foreign investment. In the 1970s, Coca-Cola and IBM were among the multinational firms that pulled out of India. During the period 1985 to 1990, foreign investment in India averaged only about $250 million annually.

Efforts to reform the Indian economy began after the 1991 federal elections. The Indian government was on the verge of bankruptcy, and foreign exchange reserves were sufficient for only three months of imports. After considerable prodding by the IMF and Finance Minister Manmohan Singh, Prime Minister Rao introduced free-market reforms in July 1991. Singh urged that India follow the free-market models of South Korea and Taiwan in achieving rapid economic development. India's economic liberalization plan moved the economy away from its traditionally protectionist policies toward actively encouraging foreign participation in the economy. As part of the plan, the prime minister's office set up a special "fast track" Foreign Investment Promotion Board to provide speedy approval for foreign investment proposals. In October 1991, the government of India opened the power industry to private-sector foreign direct investment. In February 1992, the Indian government allowed the rupee to become partially convertible. In 1994, India ratified the World Trade Organization agreement on intellectual property laws.

The economic reform program had a powerful effect. By 1995, the Indian economy was growing at an annual rate of more than 8 percent, although from 1991 to 1993 growth averaged only 3.1 percent. Exports were up by 27 percent over the previous year in the April–June quarter. The country had more than $20 billion in foreign reserves, up from $13.5 billion in 1994 and only $1 billion in 1991. Food stocks were at an all-time high and inflation was under 10 percent. Tariffs, while still high and ranging from 30–65%, were only about one-fifth what they were before liberalization. By some estimates, the government's policies had produced up to $100 billion in new entrepreneurial projects in India since 1992. In January 1995, a delegation of U.S. executives accompanied U.S. Commerce Secretary Ron Brown on a visit to India. During the trip, Brown was asked if the CEOs from the energy sector had expressed any fears about doing business in India. Brown replied, "If they had any [fears] before they came, they certainly have been dissipated by this visit."[1]

Despite these efforts to encourage market reform and economic development, many hurdles remained. In 1995, foreign direct investment in India was only $1.3 billion, as compared to $33.7 billion in China. About 40 percent of the industrial economy remained government-owned. Perhaps the greatest impediments to both rapid growth and attracting foreign investment was the lack of infrastructure that met international standards. In particular, India suffered from a substantial electricity shortage.

DEMAND FOR ELECTRICITY

The Indian population was starved for electricity. It was estimated that many of India's industries were able to operate at only half their capacity because of a lack of electric power. Frequent power outages were taken for granted. In New Delhi, the government-owned power company imposed rotating one- to two-hour blackouts periodically during the summer, when demand for electricity peaked and temperatures were often as high as 115 degrees Fahrenheit. More re-

EXHIBIT 2 *Power Demand Projections (at March 1995)*

Current capacity	78,900 MWs
Estimated growth rate of demand to 2007	approximately 9% per year
Total requirements by 2007	220,000 MWs
Likely rate of addition to 2007	3,000 MWs per year
Total capacity by 2007	115,000 MWs
Likely shortfall in 2007	107,000 MWs
Additional investment needed	Rs 5 trillion ($160 billion)

Source: The Economist Intelligence Unit, *India: 3rd Quarter Report,* EIU, 1995.

mote areas had no power at all. India's current annual electrical generating capacity was about 80,000 MWs. Demand was expected to nearly triple by 2007, as shown in Exhibit 2.

Virtually all of India's power was generated and managed by state-owned electricity boards (SEBs). It was widely acknowledged that these boards suffered from chronic managerial, financial, and operational problems.[2] As much as a quarter of the electricity generated was stolen. Government-run power plants typically operated at about 50 percent capacity. In comparison, the private power plants run by Tata Steel, an Indian company, operated at around 85 percent capacity.

Indian power rates were among the lowest in the world. Farmers paid less than 15 percent of the cost of electricity generated by new thermal power plants. In several states, small farmers paid nothing for electricity. Although the SEBs had been trying to raise rates, this had proved to be very difficult. In 1994, in the state of Gujarat, the opposition government encouraged farmers to blockade roads and burn government property after rural power rates were increased. The government was forced to back down and lower the amount of the increase.

Because of these problems and because all levels of government were so short of funds, the central government decided to turn to the private sector. The Electricity Act was amended in October 1991 to make this possible. However, the response from the private sector was poor. The act was amended again in March 1992 to provide further incentives, including a 16 percent rate of return to investors. In comparison, the Chinese government in 1994 announced a 12 percent rate of return cap on private power projects.

Still, potential investors remained skeptical of the central government's commitment to reform and were doubtful of the SEBs' ability to pay for privately generated power. The government took one more step. In May 1992, a delegation of Indian central government officials visited the United States and the United Kingdom to make a pitch for foreign investment in the power sector. The delegation included then power secretary S. Rajagopal, finance secretary K. Geethakrishan, and cabinet secretary Naresh Chandra. The visits were a major success. Many independent power producers (IPPs) immediately sent executives to India. By July 1995, more than 130 Memorandums of Understanding (MOUs) had been signed by the government of India with IPPs. Twenty-three of the 41 pending electricity projects bid on by non-Indian companies were led by American firms.

THE DABHOL PROJECT

In turning to the private sector for power plant development, the Indian government decided to give the first few private-sector projects the status of pioneer projects; later these projects became known as "fast-track" projects (of which eight such projects were eventually signed). For the fast-track projects, the central government decided not to follow the standard public tendering process. Instead, it would negotiate with IPPs for individual projects. The rationale was that the government was not in a strong negotiating position, and therefore the financial risk to the IPPs had to be reduced to entice them to invest in India. At a press conference, power secretary S. Rajagopal said the first few projects "would not be allowed to fail."

EDC's Rebecca Mark met with the Indian delegation when it visited Houston. In June 1992, Mark and several other EDC managers, at the Indian government's invitation, visited India to investigate power plant development opportunities. Within days, Enron had identified a potential site for a gas-fired power plant on the western coast of India in the port town of Dabhol, 180 miles south of Bombay in the state of Maharashtra (see map in Exhibit 3). Maharashtra was India's richest state and the center of Indian industrialization. The huge port city of Bombay was the capital and the headquarters of most of India's major companies, including Air India and

EXHIBIT 3 *Map of India*

C-22

Tata Enterprises, the largest Indian industrial conglomerate. Firms based in Bombay generated about 35 percent of India's GNP.

EDC, acting on the government's assurances that there would not be any tendering on the first few fast-track projects, submitted a proposal to build a 2,015 MW gas-fired power plant. The proposed project would be the largest plant EDC had ever built, the largest of its kind in the world, and at $2.8 billion, the largest foreign investment in India. The liquefied natural gas needed to fuel the Indian power plant would be imported from a plant EDC planned to build in Qatar. The proposal was very favorably received by both the central government and officials in the Maharashtra state government. The Maharashtra State Electricity Board (MSEB) had long wanted to build a gas-fired plant to reduce its dependence on coal and oil. Other countries with limited petroleum reserves, such as Japan and Korea, had followed a similar strategy and built coastal gas-fired power plants.

EDC was the first IPP to formally submit a proposal. Later in June 1992, EDC signed an MOU with the MSEB. A new company called Dabhol Power Company (DPC) was formed. Enron held 80 percent of the equity in Dabhol and its two partners, General Electric and International Generation Co., each held 10 percent. International Generation was a joint venture between Bechtel Enterprises Inc. (Bechtel) and San Francisco-based Pacific Gas & Electric formed in early 1995 to build and operate power plants outside the United States. General Electric was contracted to supply the gas turbines and Bechtel would be the general contractor. Exhibit 4 lists the various individuals involved with the Dabhol project, and Exhibit 5 shows the timing of the various events.

Following the signing of the MOU, EDC began a complex negotiation process for proposal approval, followed by more negotiations on the actual financial details. Officially, no power project could be developed without technical and economic clearance from the Central Electricity Authority. Typically, this process could take many months, or possibly years. The Foreign Investment Promotion Board (FIPB) was the central government's vehicle for a speedy approval process. The FIPB asked the Central Electricity Authority to give initial clearance to the Dabhol project without the detailed information normally required. However, final clearance would still be necessary at a later date.

In November 1992, EDC made a detailed presentation at a meeting chaired by the central government finance secretary and attended by various other senior government officials, including the chairman of the MSEB. (Note: The finance secre-

---

EXHIBIT 4 *Individuals Involved in the Dabhol Project*

Name	Title and/or Role
Lal Krishna Advani	President of the Federal BJP Party
Manohar Joshi	Chief Minister of Maharashtra, deputy leader of Shiv Sena
Kenneth Lay	CEO of Enron Corporation
Rebecca Mark	Chairman and CEO of EDC
Gopinath Munde	Deputy Chief Minister of Maharashtra with direct responsibility for the state energy ministry, BJP party member.
Ajit Nimbalkar	Chairman and Managing Director of Maharashtra State Electricity Board
Sharad Pawar	Former Chief Minister of Maharashtra, voted out of office March, 1995; known as the Maratha strongman
P.V. Narasimha Rao	Prime Minister of India
N.K.P. Salve	Federal Power Minister
Manmohan Singh	Federal Finance Minister, architect of free market reforms and economic advisor to PM Rao
Robert Sutton	EDC Managing Director
Balashaheb "Bal" Thackeray	Leader of Shiv Sena

EXHIBIT 5 *Timing of Events Associated with the Dabhol Project*

October 1991	Government of India invites private sector participation in the power sector
May 1992	Indian delegation visits UK and U.S.; EDC invited to India by government of India
June 1992	Maharashtra State Electricity Board signs MOU with EDC
February 1993	Foreign Investment Promotion Board (FIPB) grants approval
March 1993	Power Purchase Agreement negotiations start
November 1993	Central Electricity Authority clears Dabhol project
February 1994	Government of Maharashtra signs guarantee
September 1994	Government of India signs guarantee
March 1995	Dabhol financing completed
March 1995	Maharashtra State election results announced
April 1995	Construction begins; Government of Maharashtra orders a review; Munde Committee set up to investigate Dabhol Project
August 1995	Project canceled by Government of Maharashtra

tary was the senior civil servant in the finance department and reported directly to the finance minister.) From this meeting came a recommendation to the FIPB to approve the project. In turn, the Central Power Ministry, acting on the advice of the FIPB, asked the Central Electricity Authority to expedite the approval process. The Central Electricity Authority gave an in-principle (not final) clearance to proceed with the project since the Ministry of Finance had found the project satisfactory.

In March 1993, with the necessary government approvals largely in place, EDC was in a position to negotiate the finanical structure of the deal. The most critical element was a Power Purchasing Agreement (PPA) with the MSEB. The PPA was the contract under which EDC, as the owner of the power plant, would supply power to the MSEB electric grid. Over the next year or so, Rebecca Mark visited India 36 times. Ajit Nimbalkar, chairman and managing director of MSEB, described the negotiations:

> This is the first project of this kind that we are doing. MSEB did not have any experience in dealing with international power developers. It was a complicated exercise, for the money involved is large, and so the negotiations took a long time.[3]

MSEB turned to the World Bank for advice in the negotiations. The World Bank offered to fund a team of international consultants. The MSEB chose Freshfields, a British law firm, and the British office of the German Westdeuche Landesbank Girozentale as consultants in the PPA negotiations.

In addition to negotiating the project financial structure and gaining state and central government approvals, EDC had to obtain dozens of other government approvals, some of which were based on regulations dating back to British colonial times. For example, to get permission to use explosives on the construction site, EDC had to visit the western Indian town of Nagpur, where British Imperial forces once stored munitions.[4]

In November 1993, the Central Electricity Authority officially cleared the Dabhol project. In December 1993, the MSEB signed the Dabhol PPA. The state government of Maharashtra signed a financial guarantee in February 1994 and the central government signed a guarantee in September 1994. These guarantees provided financial protection for EDC in the event that the MSEB was unable make its payments. The central government's guarantee, which was to become very controversial, was signed with EDC before the government's guarantee policy was announced publicly.

STRUCTURE OF THE DABHOL PROJECT

Although the original plans were for a 2,015 MW project, the Maharashtra government decided to break the project into two phases. Phase I would be a 695 MW plant using distilate fuel instead of natural gas and Phase II would be a 1,320 MW gas-fired plant. The capital cost for Phase I would be $920 million, with an estimated turnkey construction cost of $527 million.[5] The second phase would cost about $1.9 billion.

Dabhol was broken into two phases because EDC had been unable to finalize its gas contracts and because the government had become concerned about the mounting criticism of the project. The shift from gas to distillate was done because distillate could be sourced from local refineries, helping deflect the criticism that gas imports would be a persistent drain on India's foreign exchange. Furthermore, using distillate instead of gas eliminated the need to build a port facility for Phase I.

The capital cost for Phase I included some costs for infrastructure items that would normally have been provided by the state, such as a pipeline. If these costs were deducted from the total capital cost, the cost per MW was comparable with the other fast-track power plant projects. However, Dabhol was the only project that had been finalized. The other projects were still going through planning and approval stages.

The Indian government generally followed what was known as a fixed rate of return model. Investors were assured a 16 percent rate of return on net worth for a plant load factor of up to 68.5 percent. Beyond 68.5 percent, the rate of return on equity would increase by a maximum of 0.70 percent for each 1 percent rise in the plant load factor. Net worth was based on the total costs of building the power plant. The main objection against this model was that it provided no incentive to minimize the capital costs of investment.

The Dabhol project used a different model. A tariff of Rs2.40 ($1 equaled about 36 rupees) per unit (kilowatt/hour) of electricity was established. The tariff, fixed in terms of U.S. dollars, consisted of a capacity charge of Rs1.20 based on the capital cost of the plant and an energy charge of Rs1.20 for the price of fuel. It was estimated that the plant would run at 80 percent capacity. By using a fixed tariff, the problems of a cost-plus system were eliminated and consumers would not be affected by increases in the capital cost of the project. For EDC and its partners, there was an incentive to become more efficient to improve shareholder returns. Based on the capital

costs per MW, Dabhol was comparable to other proposed projects in India. As to the tariff of Rs2.40, other fast-track power projects had similar tariffs, as did several recently approved public-sector projects. Several existing public-sector plants were selling power in the Rs2.15 range (although the average tariff for state electricity boards in India was Rs1.20). Enron's projected internal rate of return on the project was 26.5 percent before tax. Dabhol was granted a five-year tax holiday and the initial purchase agreement was for 20 years. Failure to achieve electricity targets would result in substantial penalty payments by the DPC to the MSEB. In the event that MSEB and DPC could not settle disagreements, international arbitration proceedings in London would be possible as specified in the PPA.

Nevertheless, because there was no competitive bidding on the Dabhol project, critics argued that the Rs2.40 per unit was too high and that the company would be making huge profits. Kirit Parekh, director of the Indira Gandhi Institute of Development and Research, was an ardent critic:

In the United States, power generated from gas-based plants is sold to utilities at 3–4 cents while Enron is charging 7 cents. It is a rip-off. The China Power Company, which is setting up a 2000 MW power plant in Hong Kong, and which will go on stream in 1996, is doing so at 15 percent less capital than Enron.[6]

Further criticism was directed at the company's lack of competitive bidding for its principal equipment supplier, General Electric, and its construction partner, Bechtel. Although General Electric and EDC had worked closely in the past, some critics suggested that foreign equipment suppliers were favored over Indian suppliers. EDC countered with the argument that it had awarded more than 60 contracts worth more than $100 million (Rs3.6 billion) to Indian companies.

EDC was also subject to criticism because of its plan to import gas for Phase II from its gas-processing plant in Qatar. When completed, this plant would be owned by a joint venture between Enron Oil & Gas and the Qatar government. Although Enron vigorously denied it, critics suggested that Enron would make excessive profits through transfer pricing and charging arbitrary prices for the fuel. From EDC's perspective, taking responsibility for fuel supply was a means of reducing its risk, since the

C-232

contract specified penalties when the plant was not able to generate electricity. Fuel supply failure would not constitute sufficient grounds for being unable to generate electricity.

The government guarantee also was criticized. A World Bank report questioned the guarantee arrangement because in its opinion, it was nothing more than a loan made by the central government on behalf of the MSEB if it could not cover its payments to Enron. EDC's Sutton countered:

> It is only after the government of India decided on a policy to give guarantees that we also decided to ask. It would have been impossible to raise money from international bankers at competitive rates without the guarantee when others are approaching the same bankers with guarantees in their pockets.[7]

THE POLITICAL SITUATION IN INDIA

India's political process was based on a parliamentary system. At the national, or central level, as it was referred to in India, the Congress (I) Party formed the current government and its leader, P. V. Narasimha Rao was prime minister. The Congress (I) Party was the descendant of the Indian National Congress, which was formed in 1855 and became the major vehicle of Indian nationalism. From 1947 to 1989, some form of the Congress Party ruled India in an unbroken string of governments. Indira Gandhi, who had been prime minister since 1964, founded the Congress (I) Party after her defeat in the 1977 election. In 1980, Indira Gandhi and the Congress (I) Party regained power. After Indira Gandhi was assassinated in 1984, her son Rajiv became prime minister. In the 1989 election, Congress (I) lost and turned power over to a minority Janata Dal government. During the 1991 election campaign, Rajiv Gandhi was assassinated and P. V. Narasimha Rao became Congress (I) Party leader. Congress (I) regained power in a minority government and although Rao was not considered to be a strong leader by opponents or supporters, he had proven to be surprisingly resilient. The next election was scheduled for May 1996. Predictions in August 1995 were that three parties—Congress (I), Left Front, and the Bharatiya Janata Party (BJP)—would each get about 150 of the 543 available seats in the Lok Sabha (House of The People).

The official opposition party was the BJP. In English, this translated to the Indian People's Party. The BJP platform emphasized support for traditional Hindu goals and values, making the party less secular than the Congress (I) Party. Many of its members belonged to the urban lower middle class and distrusted the free market reforms and modern cultural values. The BJP believed it could build support among the business community that sought decentralization and deregulation but resented intervention on the part of foreign multinationals. The BJP was considered to be the front party for a Hindu fundamentalist movement led by Rajendra Singh, known as Rashtriya Swayamsevak Sangh (RSS; translation: National Volunteers Corps). The RSS supported economic nationalism and promoted anti-Muslim, anti-feminist, and anti-English language views. In 1990, the RSS formed the Swadeshi Jagaran Manch, or National Awakening Forum, to promote economic nationalism. The forum deemed the marketing of Western consumer goods frivolous and wasteful ("India needs computer chips, not potato chips"). According to the forum's Bombay representative, "Soft drinks and instant cereals do not serve the mass of Indian people. We are not pleased with the way [Coke and Pepsi] are demolishing their rivals."[8]

The Maharashtra Election The political parties in the 25 Indian states mirrored those at the central level, although the Congress (I) was less dominant. Only five states had a majority Congress government. In two states, West Bengal and Kerala, politics had long been dominated by the Communist Party. The BJP was particularly strong in the industrial, heavily populated, and largely Hindu northern states. Decision-making was decentralized in India and many of the states had a substantial amount of power and autonomy. For example, the World Bank had secured an agreement to lend directly to individual states.

On February 12, 1995, a state election was held in Maharashtra. Results were to be announced about four weeks later because the chief election commissioner in Maharashtra had a policy of delinking voting from the counting of votes. The incumbent Congress (I) Party and an alliance between the BJP and Shiv Sena Parties were the primary contestants. State elections were normally held every five years. In the previous election in 1990, the Congress (I) Party had formed a majority government under Chief Minister Sharad Pawar. Pawar was confident of retaining power in the 1995 election.

The BJP Party was closely aligned with the national BJP Party. Shiv Sena was a Maharashtra-based party with the stated objective of protecting the economic interests and identity of Maharashtrians and safeguarding the interests of all Hindus. The official leader of Shiv Sena was Manohar Joshi, but he had limited power and openly admitted that the real authority was Bal Thackeray (sometimes referred to as Mr. Remote Control for his ability to control the party from an unofficial capacity). Thackeray was a newspaper cartoonist before he became a right-wing activist. A talented organizer and rousing orator, he set up the Shiv Sena Party in the mid-1960s to appeal to poor Hindus who resented the influence of foreigners and non-Maharashtrians, particularly those from South India. Thackeray was prone to provocative and somewhat threatening statements. He wanted to change the name of India to Hindustan and, during the Maharashtra election, talked about chasing non-Maharashtrians out of the state.

The Dabhol power project was a major campaign issue leading up to the election. Election Commission norms in India prohibited a state government from taking decisions on vital matters in the run-up to an election. However, the BJP and Shiv Sena did not make this an issue in February. Had they done so, the Election Commission might have ordered the state government to defer the decision on Dabhol.

The BJP/Shiv Sena election campaign rhetoric left little doubts as to their sentiments—one of their slogans was "Throw Enron into the Arabian Sea." The BJP platform promoted economic nationalism and sovereignty and denounced the Dabhol project. The BJP attempted to isolate Chief Minister Pawar as the only defender of Enron. The Dabhol project was described as a typical case of bad government—the failure of the ruling party to stand up to pressure from multinationals, corruption, and compromising on economic sovereignty. The BJP had always been opposed to the project for various reasons: the social and environmental aspects, alleged bribes, the project's cost, and the lack of competitive bidding. The BJP/Shiv Sena campaign strategy painted the Congress (I) Party as antipoor, corrupt, and partial to foreign firms. This platform evidently appealed to Ma-

harashtrians. On March 13 the election results were announced. The BJP/Shiv Sena coalition won 138 of 288 seats in the election and, with the help of several independent members, formed the new government. The Shiv Sena's Manohar Joshi became the new chief minister.

Not long after the election, Enron CEO Kenneth Lay noted, "If something happens now to slow down or damage our power project, it would send extremely negative signals to other foreign investors."9 Other firms with power projects under way or in planning included the Swiss firm ABB, the U.S. firms AES Corp. and CMS Energy, and Hong Kong's Consolidated Electric Power Asia.

CONSTRUCTION BEGINS

On March 2, 1995, EDC completed the financing for Phase I of the Dabhol project. Phase I financing would come from the following sources:

- A 12-bank syndication led by the Bank of America and ABN-Amro (loans of $150 million)
- U.S. Export-Import Bank ($300 million; arranged by GE and Bechtel)
- The U.S.-based Overseas Private Investment Corp. ($298 million)
- Industrial Development Bank of India ($98 million)

Construction was soon under way. But, almost simultaneously, the new state government in Maharashtra, in keeping with its campaign promises, decided to put the project under review.

THE MUNDE COMMITTEE

One week after coming to power, deputy chief minister and state BJP president Gopinath Munde ordered a review of the Dabhol project. The committee formed to carry out the review had two members from the BJP and two from the Shiv Sena. Munde, a known critic of Dabhol, was the chairman. An open invitation to individuals to appear before the committee was followed up by letters to the MSEB and Dabhol Power Company. The committee was scheduled to submit its report by July 1.

Over the next few months, the committee held more than a dozen meetings and visited the site of the power plant. The committee was assisted by five state government departments: energy, finance, industries, planning, and law. All requests for appearances before the committee were granted. Among those making depositions were environmental groups, energy economists, a former managing director of the Bombay Suburban Electric Supply Company, representatives of other IPPs, and representatives of the IPP Association. The Industrial Development Bank of India, a prime lender to the project, representatives from the former state government, and the Congress (I) Party did not appear before the committee.

During the committee hearings, the BJP continued its public opposition to Dabhol. The issue of irregularities—a euphemism for bribes—was raised. According to a senior BJP official:

Though it is impossible to ascertain if kickbacks were paid to [former Maharashtra chief minister] Pawar, even if we can obtain circumstantial evidence, it is enough. The project has been padded up and if the review committee can establish that, it is sufficient to cancel the project.[10]

Allegations of bribery were vigorously denied by EDC. Joseph Sutton, EDC's managing director in India, had told delegates at India Power '95, a conference on the power sector held in New Delhi in March, "During the three years we have been here, we have never been asked for, nor have we paid any bribes."[11]

On June 11, the RSS (the Hindu fundamentalist group) issued a directive to the BJP that it would like the party to honor its commitment to the *swadeshi* movement. The economic advisor to the Central BJP Party, Jay Dubashi said:

We think canceling this project will send the right signals. It will demonstrate that we are not chumps who can be taken for a ride. Enron probably never imagined that Sharad Pawar [former Maharashtra chief minister] would go out of power. They thought he would see the deal through.[12]

Pramod Mahajan, the BJP's All-India secretary, was also fervently against Dabhol, stating that "we will go to court if necessary and decide in the long-

term interest of the country."[13] Mahajan also ruled out paying penalities to EDC if the project were scrapped.

Meanwhile, EDC officials were shuttling back and forth between New Delhi and Bombay, trying to convince the press and the government of the viability of the Dabhol project. At one point, the U.S. ambassador to India, Frank Wisner, met with BJP President L. K. Advani. Advani refused to meet Enron officials. The issue was even discussed during U.S. Treasury Secretary Robert Rubin's visit to India in April. According to the Assistant Secretary of the Treasury, "We pushed for resolution of the issue."[14] In May 1995, the U.S. Department of Energy warned that failure to honor the contract would jeopardize most, if not all, other private projects proposed for international financing in India. Maharashtra had attracted more than $1 billion of U.S. investment, and more than half of all foreign direct investment projects in India were in this state. Furthermore, more than 25 percent of all FDI in India was from the United States.

In the meantime, Bechtel had not stopped construction. A spokesman for Bechtel said the company could not afford to have its 1,300 workers idled during a month-long review. "We have to meet a schedule; we have to provide power according to the power purchase agreement."[15]

CANCELLATION OF THE DABHOL PROJECT

The Munde Committee report was submitted to the Maharashtra government on July 15, 1995. Prior to the release of the report, N. K. P. Salve, India's power minister, stressed that the "Enron contract can be canceled only if there is a legal basis for doing so, not for any arbitrary or political reason."[16] On August 2, the Indian Supreme Court dismissed a petition by a former Maharashtra legislator challenging the Dabhol project on the grounds of secrecy.

On August 3, Chief Minister Joshi (who had visited the United States in the previous month to attract investment to India) announced to the Maharashtra legislature that the cabinet unanimously agreed to suspend Phase I of the project and scrap

Phase II. The following are excerpts from Chief Minister Joshi's lengthy statement in the Assembly:

The Enron project, in the form conceived and contracted for, is not in the best interests of the state.... Being conscious of the deception and distortion in the Enron-MSEB deal which have caused grave losses, the subcommittee is clear that the project must not be allowed to proceed. The subcommittee wholeheartedly recommends that the Enron-MSEB contract should be canceled forthwith.... Considering the grave issues involved in the matter and the disturbing facts and circumstances that have emerged pointing to extra-commerical considerations and probable corruption and illegal motives at work in the whole affair, immediate action must be initiated under the penal and anti-corruption laws by police.

The wrong choice of LNG [liquefied natural gas] as fuel and huge inflation in capital costs, along with unprecedented favours shown to Enron in different ways, including in the fuel procurement [had all resulted in an] unreasonable fuel cost to the consumers.... The documentary evidence obtained by the committee shows beyond any reasonable doubt that the capital cost of Enron Plant was inflated and jacked up by a huge margin. The committee believes that the extent of the inflation may be as high as $700 million.... Being gas-based, this project should have been cheaper than coal-based ones but in reality, it turns out to be the other way about.

I am convinced that Enron, Bechtel, and GE will sell off at least 50 percent of their equity for the recovery of their expenditures on the project plus profits and the Government would be a helpless spectator. The Government should have sought some part of this for itself.... This contract is anti-Maharashtra. It is devoid of any self-respect; it is one that mortgages the brains of the State which, if accepted, would be a betrayal of the people. This contract is no contract at all and if by repudiating it, there is some financial burden, the State will accept it to preserve the well-being of Maharashtra.[17]

Other grounds were given for cancellation: there had been no competitive bidding; EDC held secret negotiations and used unfair means to win its contract; there was potential environmental damage to a region that was relatively unpolluted; the guaranteed return was well above the norm; and there were concerns about the $20 million earmarked by EDC for education and project development. The BJP government charged that concessions granted to EDC would cause the state of Maharashtra to lose more than $3.3 billion in the future. The committee was also outraged that loose ends in the Dabhol project were being tied up by the Maharashtra government as late as February 25, almost two weeks after the state election. In effect, the contract had been made effective by an administration that had already been rejected by voters.

When the decision was announced, Prime Minister Rao was on a trade and investment promotion trip to Malaysia. He indicated that the economic liberalization policies initiated by his government would not be affected by this decision. Sharad Pawar, the chief minister of Maharashtra at the time the original agreement was signed with Enron, criticized the BJP's decision to cancel the Dabhol power project:

If the government of Maharashtra was serious about the industrialization of Maharashtra, and its power requirements for industrialization and agriculture, they definitely would have appointed an expert group who understands the requirement of power, about overall projection, about investment which is coming in the fields of industry and agriculture, legal sides, but this particular angle is totally missing here and that is why I am not so surprised for this type of decision which has been taken by the government of Maharashtra.[18]

On the day after the government's cancellation announcement, the *Saamna* newspaper, known as the voice of the nationalist Shiv Sena Party, published a headline that read, "Enron Finally Dumped into the Arabian Sea." Later that week, *The Economic Times* in Bombay reported that local villagers celebrated the fall of Enron (see Exhibit 6).

EDC'S NEXT STEPS

About 2,600 people were working on the Dabhol power project, and it was nearly one-third complete. More than $300 million had been invested in the project and estimated costs per day if the project were shut down would be $200,000 to $250,000. Cancellation of Phase II was less critical because EDC had

EXHIBIT 6 *Excerpts from* The Economic Times, *Bombay, August 7, 1995*

Villagers Celebrate 'Fall' of Enron

The "Fall" of Enron was celebrated with victory marches, much noise of slogans, firecrackers and dancing outside the gates of the Dabhol Power Project and in the neighboring villages of Guhagar, Veldur, Anjanvel and Katalwadi on Sunday.

The march was led by local BJP MLA, the boyish Mr. Vinay Natu, whose father, a former MLA, is said to have originally brought the Enron project to its present site. The younger Natu denies this and says it is Enron propaganda to defame his father.

Much action was expected at the project site by the accompanying police escort. If nothing else, the celebrators were expected to pull down the Dabhol Power Company signboards on the gates of the high fence. They had earlier trailered this in Guhagar when women pulled down a DPG signpost indicating the way to the site and trampled it with fury.

Instead, the processionists danced, threw gulai in the air, and burst long strings of firecrackers before moving on to the next gate. Behind the wire fences at the site stood the tense security staff of the project; in the distance on higher ground could be seen site engineers observing the proceedings through binoculars.

Lining the fence inside were hundreds of construction workers who came to see the show. These workers too come from the neighboring villages, including those where the celebrations were being held. And even among the processionists were many who on other days worked inside the fence area on pay much higher than anything they can get in their villages. The paradox of benefiting by the Enron project as well as protesting against it has been the most striking aspect of the controversy.

The local Congress leader, "Mama" Vaidya, was most unimpressed by the show or the opposition to the project. "This backward area needs the project," he said. As to any Congress efforts in the area to muster support for the project or economic development of the area, Mr. Vaidya said there was infighting in the party and coordinated action was not possible.

At DPC itself work goes on. There's worry on the faces of engineers, but they are determined to go on until they are told by their bosses to stop. No such order has been served yet.

C-237

not yet secured financing commitments for this portion of the project.

A few days before the Munde Committee report was made public and anticipating a cancellation recommendation, Rebecca Mark had offered publicly to renegotiate the deal. She told the media that the company would try to meet the concerns of the MSEB. On August 3, EDC announced that while it was aware of the reported announcement in the Maharashtra Assembly on the suspension of Dabhol, the company had received no official notice to that effect. The statement, issued in Houston, said:

[EDC] remains available for discussions with the government on any concerns it may have.... [EDC] has very strong legal defenses available to it under the project contracts and fully intends to pursue these if necessary. The DPC and the project sponsors would like to reiterate that they have acted in full compliance with Indian and U.S. laws.[19]

NOTES

1. N. Chandra Mohan, New Beginnings, *Business India*, January 30-February 12, 1995, p. 135.
2. Michael Schuman, India Has a Voracious Need for Electricity: U.S. Companies Have a Clear Inside Track, *Forbes*, April 24, 1995.
3. Bodhisatva Ganguli & Tushar Pania, The Anatomy of a Controversial Deal, *Business India*, April 24-May 7, 1995, p. 57.
4. Marcus W. Brauchli, A Gandhi Legacy: Clash Over Power Plant Reflects Fight in India For Its Economic Soul, *Wall Street Journal*, April 27, 1995, A6.

5. Ganguli & Pania, p. 59.
6. Ganguli & Pania, p. 58.
7. Ganguli & Pania, p. 56.
8. *AsiaWeek*, India Power Down: A Major Blow to Rao's Reform Drive, August 18, 1995.
9. Emily MacFarquhar, A Volatile Democracy, *U.S. News and World Report*, March 27, 1995, p. 37.
10. Ganguli & Pania, p. 56.
11. Ganguli & Pania, p. 55.
12. Ganguli & Pania, p. 55.
13. Ganguli & Pania, p. 55.
14. Ganguli & Pania, p. 55.
15. *San Francisco Business Times*, May 5, 1995, Sec: 1, p. 1.
16. Foreign Investment in India: The Enron Disease, *The Economist*, July 29, 1995, p. 48.
17. "Indian State Axes $2.8 BN Dabhol Power Project," in International Gas Report, *The Financial Times*, August 4; Mahesh Vijapurkar, Enron Deal Scrapped, Ongoing Work Halted, *The Hindu*, August 4, p. 1.
18. All-India Doordarshan Television, August 3, 1995.
19. Vijapurkar, p. 1.

Granada Group: A Successful Story of Mergers and Acquisitions

Jorge Costa
Gavin Eccles
Richard Teare
Tim Knowles

University of Surrey

INTRODUCTION

This case considers the hostile takeover launched by Granada Group against Forte PLC. The analysis is centred on Granada Group and covers its background and structure, recent historical development and philosophy, and the takeover bid.

COMPANY BACKGROUND

Granada is continuing to achieve good profit growth and strong cash generation throughout the group, which reflects well on a strong management team. . . . The present management has consistently pushed profits ahead, and we expect further good growth in earnings in 1995 and 1996.[1]

The history of Granada Group is one of rapid growth by means of mergers and acquisitions in recent years and the dynamism of its management team. Granada is a UK group with a diverse range of activities comprised in three business divisions: rental and computer services; television; and leisure

and services. To better understand the structure of these divisions, the activities of each division are reviewed.

Rentals and Computer Services

This division is responsible for the rent and retail of televisions, video recorders, satellite reception equipment, mobile phones, and personal computers, providing insurance and full-service backup. It also operates in the business market, supplying TV and electronic equipment services and is the largest provider of independent computer maintenance in Europe.[2] The division has 46 percent of the UK market, a figure slightly below that of its rival, owned by Thorn PLC. Computer service revenues are split into four sources: 38 percent from UK fixed-site maintenance; 12 percent from UK mobile computer services; 8 percent from various design, project management, and consultancy services in the UK; and 42 percent from similar activities to those in the UK, but based in Europe.[3] This division is responsible for 37 percent of the group's operating profits.

Television

Combined, Granada Television and London Weekend Television represent the second largest group of television franchises in the UK and together they hold the Channel 3 licenses for the North, West, and

This case is intended to be used as the basis for class discussion rather than to illustrate either effective or ineffective handling of a management situation. The case was compiled from published sources. © 1996 Jorge Costa, Gavin Eccles, Richard Teare, Tim Knowles, University of Surrey, UK.

London (weekend) regions, respectively. They are the largest supplier of programmes for the ITV network and have substantial share stakes in a number of other media companies.[2] The division makes about 66 percent of its revenue from advertising sales, 26 percent from UK programme sales, and 8 percent from other sources,[3] and is responsible for 33 percent of the group's operating profits.[2] With studios in London and Manchester, they are responsible for famous series such as "Coronation Street."

Leisure and Services

Granada Motorway Services provides a full range of services to road travellers. It is the joint largest operator of motorway service areas in the UK, with 20 motorway service areas and a market share of 35 percent. The other leisure businesses incorporate two hotels, seven nightclubs, 24 ten-pin bowling clubs, three theme parks (including Granada Studio Tours), and the Air Travel Group, a small tour operator/seat broker specialising in the Italian and Spanish tour markets. In services, Sutcliffe Catering is the third largest contract caterer in the UK, with a market share of 18 percent and around 2,400 contracts. Spring Grove is among the second tier of linen/workwear hire suppliers in the UK after BET's Initial Services. The group has contracts in the UK, Germany, and Ireland, but generates over 90 percent of its sales and profits from the UK. The division also includes Total Facilities Management (Granada) Ltd., Sterling Granada Security Services Ltd., and Granada Vending Services Ltd.[3] This division is responsible for 30 percent of the group's operating profits.[2]

CORPORATE STRUCTURE

The corporate governance of the group is carried out by the Board, the Audit Committee, the Remuneration Committee, the Nomination Committee, the Administration and Finance Committee, and the Granada Pension Scheme.[4]

The Board consists of seven executive and three nonexecutive directors and meets regularly throughout the year. A formal schedule of matters reserved

for the decision of the board covers key areas of the group's affairs, including:

- Overall group strategy
- Acquisition and divestment policy
- Approval of budgets
- Major capital expenditure projects
- General treasury
- Management policies

There are procedures to enable directors to obtain independent professional advice, and the board has delegated specific responsibilities to committees.

The Audit Committee, chaired by Michael Orr, comprised all the nonexecutive directors and meets four times a year. The committee reviews the company's interim and annual financial statements before submission to the Board for approval. The committee reviews regular reports from management and the external auditors on accounting and internal control matters. If appropriate, it also monitors the progress of action taken in relation to such matters. It also recommends the appointment and reviews the fees of external auditors.

The Remuneration Committee also comprised all the nonexecutive directors and is chaired by Ian Martin. It deals with remuneration policies including directors' remuneration packages.

The Nomination Committee is chaired by Alex Bernstein and comprised, in addition, all the nonexecutive directors and Gerry Robinson. This committee meets as required and is authorised to propose to the board new appointments of executive and nonexecutive directors.

The Administration and Finance Committee comprised the executive directors and meets as required to conduct the company's business within the clearly defined limits delegated by the Board and subject to those matters reserved for the Board.

The corporate trustee of the Granada Pension Scheme—the principal UK scheme—is Granada Trust Corporation Limited, which is chaired by Graham Parrot. Its directors include representatives nominated by the employee members of the scheme. The management of the investments of the scheme has been delegated to six independent managers, and the trustees are advised by independent actuaries and auditors. Members of the scheme receive an annual statement of their accrued benefits and a trustees' report.

HISTORICAL DEVELOPMENT

The recent historical development of Granada Group can be divided into four distinct phases.[3] The first phase is characterised by a certain financial instability; the second phase is characterised by the restructuring of the business; the third phase is characterised by a considerable profit growth; and the fourth and last phase can be characterised by the pressures of success.

The Financial Instability Phase

The first phase, from the latter part of the 1980s up to 1991, was characterised by some financial instability culminating in the collapse in profit over the 1989–1991 period. According to Winnington-Ingram and Winston,[3] the key characteristics of this period can be seen as:

■ A divisional structure that suggests at least a partial lack of central control. Beyond the core rental division there are questions as to how much control the central management team had over the actions of the divisional chairmen.

■ A rapid increase in the amount spent on investments and acquisitions, which appear to have been either poorly planned or poorly controlled. As can be seen in Exhibit 1, the rapid expansion of the group's capital expenditure over the 1987–90 period is coupled with high levels of spending on acquisitions in 1987 and 1988. The jump in Rental profit shown in 1988 suggests that the December 1987 acquisition of the Electronic Rentals Group for £245 million (completed in 1988) may not have been dilutive. However, the additions made to Granada Travel (part of the Leisure Division) in 1987, which cost £100 million, were dilutive, because Granada Travel did not produce any profits (before interest costs) until 1991. According to some financial analysts,[3] the "wisdom of acquiring" DPCE Holdings, a computer maintenance group, in 1988 for £106 million can also be questioned. In fact, initially the acquisition appears to

EXHIBIT 1 *Granada Group Performance Indicators, 1987–1991*

			(£million)		
Year to September	**1987**	**1988**	**1989**	**1990**	**1991**
Television	20.8	30.0	37.7	37.1	21.9
Rental	62.1	82.5	89.7	82.5	89.5
Computer Services	7.8	13.8	20.0	6.5	(11.8)
Leisure	25.1	30.4	38.3	39.3	23.0
Other	8.9	13.8	14.8	0.4	(2.7)
Trading Profit	124.7	170.5	200.5	165.8	125.3
Exceptionals	—	—	—	—	(15.8)
Interest Costs	(11.9)	(25.3)	(33.7)	(43.5)	(52.6)
Employee Shares	(1.7)	(2.0)	(2.7)	(1.7)	—
Pretax Profit	111.1	143.2	164.1	120.6	56.9
Fully dil. EPS (p)	24.4	27.2	29.1	21.7	11.5
Capital Expenditure	(155)	(169)	(271)	(291)	(181)
Free Cash Flow	14.3	36.8	(87.1)	(192.6)	(66.1)
Acquisitions	(141)	(545)	(44)	(8)	(40)
Cash Interest Cover	22.2	11.9	8.9	5.3	4.2
Net Debt/Equity (%)	23	63	64	97	50
ROCE (%)	22.0	22.2	22.5	16.5	15.9

Source: Winnington-Ingram and Winston, 1994.[3]

have added to profits, but the division's subsequent collapse into loss and the low levels of profit presented suggest a dilutive outcome. The dilutive effects of these acquisitions and of the poor marginal returns that the group achieved on its high levels of investment are well illustrated by the reduction in the group's return on capital employed from 22 percent to 15.9 percent over the 1987–91 period.

- High levels of cash absorbency. The high levels of spending mentioned led to increasingly high levels of free cash outflows and net debt. Gearing peaked at over 100 percent, before a 1-for-3 rights was issued in May 1991. It looks as though Granada overstretched both its finances and its management ability in the late 1980s, so that once consumer demand and asset values started to fall after 1989, Granada's future was uncertain.

The Business Restructuring Phase

By 1991 Granada's shareholders and management team realised that the situation they were facing could not go on as it was for much longer. Gearing had reached 97 percent, with cash interest cover falling to low levels. This awareness marked a turnaround in the group's strategy. The company decided to restructure the business starting with the sale of its bingo activities to Bass PLC for £147 million. The loss-making Canadian Rentals business was also sold, and the group's Computer Services division was radically restructured. A 1-for-3 rights issue also

strengthened group finances. Together with the asset sales, this issue reduced the group's year-end gearing to 50 percent.

The group's management started a period of fundamental change that cleared out the old structure, increased central control, increased cost and margin awareness, and injected much-needed strategic ability. This revolution started with the resignation of the previous group chief executive, Derek Lewis, in July 1991, and the subsequent appointment of Gerry Robinson as group managing director and chief executive in November 1991. See Exhibit 2 for more information.

The Profit Growth Phase

By this time, the new management team has been in place for long enough to make a number of demonstrable improvements to the group's strategic ability and day-to-day operating efficiencies. The measures taken by this team also had time enough to realize profit growth. Granada produced EPS growth just in excess of 100 percent in the first half of fiscal year 1993, with 56 percent growth for the full year. EPS growth was 35 percent in the first half of 1994. The group produced a free cash inflow of £127 million in 1993. As seen by Winnington-Ingram and Winston,[3] in addition to these profit and cash flow improvements, the new team has achieved:

- Improved central management control and reporting systems. The divisional fiefdom structure has been dismantled and thus the central team's

---

EXHIBIT 2 *Granada Group Management Changes, 1991–1993*

Retirees

Derek Lewis (Group Chief Executive)	Resigned 1 July 1991
William Andrews (Chairman, Leisure)	Resigned 31 Dec. 1991
David Plowright (Chairman, Television)	Resigned 29 Feb. 1992
Andrew Quinn (Managing Director, Television)	Resigned 31 Oct. 1992

Appointments

Gerry Robinson (Group MD and Chief Executive)	4 November 1991
Charles Allen (Chairman, Leisure)[1]	29 June 1992
Graham Parrot (Company Secretary)	30 November 1992
Henry Staunton (Finance Director)	1 March 1993

Source: Adapted from Winnington-Ingram and Winston, 1994.[3]
[1]Mr. Allen has subsequently become chief executive of Granada Television and chairman of the Services to Business divisions.

control of costs, capital expenditure, cash flow, and other key tools has been reestablished.

■ Greatly improved operating margins in most divisions. While sales growth remains difficult across most of Granada's activities, improved cost control has led to significantly improved margins in most parts of the group, in particular the Leisure and Television divisions.

■ Successful acquisitions and a diversification into new industries. While restructuring its existing businesses, the group acquired P&O's Business Services operations in March 1993 for £360 million and also acquired LWT Holdings in March 1994 for £811 million.

The Pressures of Success Phase

In its report from 1994, Winnington-Ingram and Winston[3] expected that by 1997 Granada would become a well-managed, cash-producing firm, still producing above-average earnings growth, but the pace of growth was continuing to slow (see Exhibit 3 for estimates). It also identified two potential questions for Granada:

■ Once it had stripped most of the excess costs out of its current activities, which parts of Granada would be the major engines of growth?

■ Based on growth and expenditure trends, Granada was expected to continue to produce escalating amounts of free cash flow from 1995 onwards. The group's balance sheet was expected to move

to a net cash position by the end of fiscal year 1997. The question then would be, What is it going to do with all this cash?

The answer to the second question, according to Winnington-Ingram and Winston, is that the group has to use its cash to make more acquisitions. In fact, it suggested that Granada needs to make regular acquisitions if it is to maintain the balance between earnings growth and cash resources. The risk is that the group might choose not to make acquisitions and instead invest ever increasing sums in its existing businesses. Overcapitalised companies that avoid making acquisitions tend to squander their resources, so that returns dip below the rate of interest that the group could get by putting this money on deposit.

BRIEF FINANCIAL REVIEW

A major achievement of Granada's new management team was the improvement in the group's free cash flow from a £188 million outflow in 1990 to a £127 million inflow by fiscal year 1993.[3] This improvement has come mostly from reduced capital expenditure. On the other hand, the very low capital requirements of most of the businesses in which the group operates mean that it works from a very low share capital base. This low capital intensity means that the group's return on capital employed is abnormally high. Rapidly accelerating levels of retained profits are in fact adding to Granada's shareholders' funds. As a consequence, it is expected that the

EXHIBIT 3 *Granada Key Performance Indicators, 1994–1998E*

Year to September	($£million$)				
	1994E[1]	1995E	1996E	1997E	1998E
Trading Profit	284.8	340.6	375.0	409.3	437.6
Interest Costs	(32.1)	(23.8)	(11.1)	5.3	23.1
Pretax Profit	252.8	316.8	363.9	414.7	460.6
Fully dil. EPS	30.5	34.9	39.9	44.6	49.0
Trading Profit Growth (%)	39.3	19.6	10.1	9.2	6.9
EPS Growth (%)	22.0	14.4	13.8	12.3	9.9
Free Cash Flow	118.9	142.6	147.7	172.3	182.8
Net Debt (Cash)/Equity (%)	58	26	5	(11)	(22)
Cash Interest Cover	12.8	19.7	45.5	N/A	N/A
ROCE (%)	31	36	38	40	40

Sources: [1]Morgan Stanley Research Estimates; Winnington-Ingram and Winston, 1994.[3]

group's capital base will achieve £1,340 million by the end of 1998.[3]

According to comments by Winnington-Ingram and Winston, made in October 1994,[3] "If Granada does not make further acquisitions, but instead just builds up a cash pile, it will be using its shareholders' funds in an increasingly inefficient manner." In March 1995, Jones et al.[1] analysed Granada's financial situation in a similar line:

> The ability of Granada management to improve returns from existing business is well proven. The uncertainty lies in how the group will deploy in the future its strong cash flow from these businesses, and from the BSkyB stake which it does not regard as a long term holding. . . . Granada has outstandingly strong cash flow, which will result in the company moving into a net cash position in mid-1997 if it does not make any acquisitions before then.

THE TAKEOVER BID

Granada's decision to launch a takeover bid over Forte PLC can be seen as a consequence of its sound financial situation as reflected in previous acquisitions. In April 1995 the group acquired Pavilion Services—a deal worth £125 million in a business comprising 27 motorway services and 9 trunk road sites.[5] Later in the year, just before launching its takeover of Forte, Granada made another acquisition in the contract catering sector with the takeover of Thames Valley-based ACMS. ACMS, a company that specialises in business and industry contracts, had 59 contracts and a turnover of £8 million a year when it was bought.[6]

In terms of Granada's offer to buy out Forte PLC, the proposed takeover worth £3.28 billion was made on November 22, 1995. The bid, which came at a time when Forte had restructured its management and was in the process of consolidating its business, was immediately rejected.[7] The reasons given by Gerry Robinson for the takeover bid were the fact that Forte was in a sector connected with his group's existing businesses, it was a worthwhile size, and it offered a significant scope for improvement. Granada also attacked Forte for the confused marketing of its hotel brands, which it described as tired.[7] The Granada attack came as it announced a 32 percent increase in pretax profits to £351 million on a 14 per-

cent rise in turnover to £2.38 billion in the year to September. Theoretically, any bid could be blocked by Forte's council, which holds Forte Trust shares and 50 percent of the voting rights, but less than 1 percent of the share capital. The council, originally created to campaign for temperance, was, however, considered unlikely to block the wishes of a clear majority of shareholders.[7]

In Granada's 1995 Annual Report and Accounts,[4] Gerry Robinson, the group chief executive, refers to the possible acquisition of Forte as an excellent addition to the group. He highlights the synergies coming from the restaurant business (predominantly roadside catering) and states the intention of focusing on two hotel brands at the budget and middle-market areas, while developing the Meridien brand and moving some of Forte's Grand hotels into that brand. Still elaborating on the hotel sector, he mentioned the Heritage and other upmarket hotels as opportunities to improve profitability by operating them as a collection, each with a separate identity but sharing a common support structure. His conclusions were based on examination of those parts of the Forte business that cannot be retained for competition reasons, such as the motorway service areas, and those from which the group does not believe satisfactory shareholder returns can be achieved (i.e., the 68 percent investment in the Savoy Group).

In a document published on December 14, 1995,[8] Granada asks Forte shareholders:

Who will create more value?

Forte, with its
- lacklustre record
- ill-conceived proposals
- lost credibility

Or

Granada, with its
- financial strength
- management skills
- proven track record

In the same document, Granada's chairman Alex Bernstein addresses Forte's shareholders and criticises Forte's arguments in the defence document. As he states:

Granada's Board believes that:

- There is little in Forte's recent record to inspire confidence in its management team.
- Forte's break-up proposals make neither commercial nor financial sense; they will not cre-

ate as much value for you as you will achieve by accepting our offer.

■ Forte lacks credibility and cannot be relied upon to deliver all that it promises.

Granada, on the other hand, has the management skills to unlock full value, the financial strength to develop the business and the track record to give it credibility.

In its increased and final offer document,[9] Granada raised its bid for Forte from £3.28 billion to £3.8 billion and announced that it had decided to sell the "more cyclical Exclusive and Meridien hotels on an orderly basis, following the completion of the acquisition." This decision represented a move from its initial intention to keep these brands. However, the emphasis on financial gains, management skills, and track record remained as can be seen by the differences between the two companies as highlighted in the document:

Value: Forte has mortgaged the future in order to create an appearance of value now and, in doing so, has materially impaired future values. Granada's Increased Offer, on the other hand, not only crystallises greater value for you now, but gives you the prospect of significant further enhancement in years to come

Strategy: Forte's management has decided to dismember the company, selling core

businesses with good prospects too cheaply and reducing Forte to just part of its hotels business. Granada would capture the benefits of owning both hotels and restaurants and release their true profit potential

Management: The track records of the two management teams differ sharply: Granada's management has provided its shareholders with significant returns; Forte's management has presided over a steady erosion of value, has failed its shareholders for too long and has lost credibility

Granada's claim is based on the certainty of the increased offer and the future promise of greater value based on its track record. It also states that its detailed plan to improve Forte's profits will result in significant earnings. Granada's analysis of its strategy shows that "Granada's strategy is firmly based on two parallel themes which are at the heart of the Group's success—*Focus* and *Breadth*. *Focus* on core businesses, to maximise growth in each of those businesses. *Breadth* across a range of related core businesses, to minimise risk to shareholders from a downturn in any core market."[9] For Granada, a successful acquisition would mean the creation of a group with four strong core activities: Leisure and Services, Television, Hotels, and Rental. The operating profits would be divided between the activities as shown in Exhibit 4.

EXHIBIT 4 *Estimated Operating Profit by Core Activity*

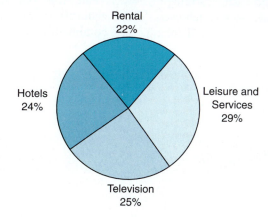

Rental 22%
Hotels 24%
Leisure and Services 29%
Television 25%

Source: Adapted from Granada Group PLC, 1996.[9]

From Granada's perspective, each of these core businesses is substantial in its own right, yet none overwhelms the others; it would have leading market positions in each sector; and the risk from economic downturn is minimised. Seeing the company as a "well-balanced group," Granada defines its current strategy as emphasising focus for growth and balance against risk.[9]

In the final document to Forte's shareholders from January 16, 1996,[10] before the deadline for acceptance (January 23, 1996), Granada once again asked Forte's shareholders: "Who can deliver greater value, both now and in the future?" To answer this question a comparison was made:

If you accept Granada's offer you get

- The best value now and in the future.
- A balanced Group with four strong businesses offering the opportunity for significant earnings enhancement.
- A management team with a track record of delivering.
- 12.5 percent Gold Card discount at Forte restaurants and hotels, including Little Chef and Travelodge.

If you reject Granada's offer you get

- A disposal of good cash generative businesses at a price that hands the upside to the buyer.
- An unbalanced company overexposed in a sector that is highly capital intensive and vulnerable to a downturn.
- Some £900 million of debt and a significant backlog of capital expenditure.
- A top management that has consistently failed to deliver adequate levels of profit and cash, even before selling cash generative businesses.
- The prospect of a falling in price.

This comparison substantiates the takeover strategy adopted by Granada which proved to be successful in previous takeovers. The two-month battle between Granada and Forte was mainly played around Granada's financial strength, management skills, and proven track record, against a company that was in the process of consolidating its business but had failed to deliver the best value for money to its shareholders.

GRANADA'S SECRET OF SUCCESS

If Granada had failed, it would have given predators much pause for thought. Its success shows the hostile bid is eminently possible—provided the bidder is prepared to pay enough and the circumstances are right: fund managers saw Forte as a company which had underperformed for many years, and its bold bid defence merely served to underline its previous inaction.[11]

A hostile bid implies that investors have to decide to back either existing management or new management. Both parties have to justify their performances, long-term strategy, and any proposed changes. The potential acquirer must also explain its strategy and how it will create long-term shareholder value.[12] From an analysis of Granada's track record in takeovers and acquisitions, it is apparent that its management team has found a success formula. In the most recent acquisitions (see Exhibit 5), the most relevant aspects have to do with the management team's strategic ability and the operating efficiencies achieved. These acquisitions were in fact earnings-enhancing.[3] The combination of strategic ability, ex-

EXHIBIT 5 *Granada's Recent Acquisitions*

Company
Forte PLC
Pavilion Services
Direct Vision Rentals
ACMS
LWT
BSkyB
Sutcliffe Group

EXHIBIT 6 *Granada's Company Directors*

Name	Position	
Alex Bernstein	Chairman	Granada Group
Gerry Robinson	Chief Executive	Granada Group
Charles Allen	Chief Operating Officer	Granada Group
Stephanie Monk	Personnel Director	Granada Group
Graham Parrot	Commercial Director	Granada Group
Henry Staunton	Finance Director	Granada Group
Graham Wallace	Chief Executive	Leisure and Services
John Ashworth	Non-Executive	
Ian Martin	Non-Executive	
Michael Orr	Non-Executive	

Source: Adapted from Granada Group PLC, 1996.[4]

cellent cash production, and the tight cost control practised by Granada are probably its major success factors.

The management team (see Exhibit 6) responsible for this confirmed success is also responsible for the internal financial control. In fact, directors have overall responsibility for the group's system of internal financial control and have established a framework designed to provide "reasonable" assurance against material misstatement or loss.[4] The main procedures supporting this framework are financial reporting, control environment, functional reporting, and investment appraisal (see Exhibit 7 for details).

EXHIBIT 7 *Granada's Internal Financial Control Procedures*

Financial reporting	A rolling three-year strategic review process which is part of a comprehensive planning system together with an annual budget approved by the board.	The results of operating units are reported monthly, compared with their individual budgets, and forecast figures are reviewed on a month by month basis.
Control environment	Financial controls and procedures, including information system controls, are detailed in policies and procedures manuals for all major subsidiaries.	As the overall quality of internal financial control across the group is directly related to the controls in individual operating units, it is a requirement for the managers of operating units and divisions to confirm each year in writing the quality of internal financial control in their area.
Functional reporting	The risks facing the business are assessed on an ongoing basis.	A number of key areas, such as treasury and corporate taxation matters, are subject to regular review by the directors. Other important areas, such as detailed insurance risk management and legal matters, come under the direct control of the executive directors and are reviewed on a continuous basis. In addition, at the end of each financial year managers of operating units and divisions are also required to provide a schedule of identified risks and action taken to minimise exposure.
Investment appraisal	The group has a clearly defined framework for controlling capital expenditure including appropriate authorisation levels beyond which such expenditure requires the approval of the board.	There is a prescribed format for capital expenditure applications which places a high emphasis on the commercial and strategic logic for the investment and due diligence requirements in the case of business acquisitions. As a matter of routine, projects are also subject to post-investment appraisal after an appropriate period.

Source: Adapted from Granada Group PLC, 1996.[4]

C-247

Granada's success can be seen as the strategy of strong leadership with clear and defined business objectives. However, the next stage will bring interesting challenges to the Granada management team, mainly the process of integrating the parts of Forte that it wants to keep. Also, the disposing of the luxury hotels in Forte's Exclusive chain and the Meridien hotels, for which there are several contenders, will be important.

NOTES

1. Jones, B., Owens, R., and Sanderson, W., *Leisure and hotel sector: Some way up already*, Smith New Court UK, London, 1995.
2. Granada Group PLC, *Annual report and accounts*, London, 1994.
3. Winnington-Ingram, R. and Winston, C., *Investment research UK and Europe: UK hotels and leisure*, Morgan Stanley & Co. International Ltd., London, 1994.
4. Granada Group PLC, *Annual report and accounts*, London, 1995.
5. Caterer and Hotelkeeper, *Granada to review its MSA business*, 20 April 1995.
6. Caterer and Hotelkeeper, *Granada group buys ACMS to work alongside Sutcliffe*, 5 October 1995.
7. Daneshkhu, S. and Snoddy, R., "Granada bids £3.3bn for Forte," *Financial Times*, Thursday, 23 November 1995.
8. Granada Group PLC, *Creating more value*, 14 December 1995.
9. Granada Group PLC, *Increased and final offer for Forte PLC*, 9 January 1996.
10. Granada Group PLC, *Delivering the promise*, 16 January 1996.
11. Dickson, M., "City plays the takeover game," *Financial Times*, Weekend, 27/28 January 1996.
12. Stevenson, H., "A question of performance," *Financial Times*, Friday, 26 January 1996.

Harold's Stores, Inc.

Craig Cockle
Jessica Winn
Neela Kulkarni
Richard Reneau

Fifty years ago, Harold's opened its first store in Norman, Oklahoma, with the goal of offering a mix of merchandise unavailable from competing stores. It has carried that strategy through to the present day with the following philosophy: "If there is a single theme to what we do at Harold's it is customer service. Our products, stores, and most of all, our people are centered around one simple goal . . . to go one step beyond what is ordinary. To treat customers as guests. To win them over and keep them for life."[1]

Since 1948, Harold's has been gradually adding new stores and increasing circulation of its direct-response catalog, nurturing a strong potential for growth and future opportunity. The company believes that its future success will be achieved by expanding the number of its women's and men's apparel stores, maintaining sales momentum at existing stores, and increasing circulation of its direct-response catalog.

To realize this potential, the company embarked recently on an aggressive expansion program, adding 11 retail stores during fiscal year 1997, thereby increasing the chain store count by approximately 44 percent.[2] The challenge of managing this expansionary phase has been placed on Rebecca Casey, chief executive officer and head buyer, and Rainey

Powell, president and chief financial officer, the daughter and son of founder Harold Powell. The company reported a second-quarter net loss of $577,000 or $.10 per share, and a cumulative net loss of $450,000 or $.08 per share for the six-month period in fiscal year 1997.[3] At the annual board of directors' meeting, Rebecca and Rainey wondered whether a publicly traded, yet family-run, business can successfully manage the increasing complexities inherent with national expansion.

HISTORY OF THE COMPANY

Harold G. Powell, founder and chairman of the board of Harold's Stores, Inc., graduated from the University of Oklahoma in 1948 and opened his first men's apparel store in Norman, Oklahoma. This first store was 1,000 square feet in a building owned by his mother.[4] For the first two years, Harold's was trying to second-guess what its customers wanted. At that time, California manufacturers influenced the predominant men's style, although when Harold's introduced Madison Avenue clothing designs, they achieved almost immediate success.

In 1958, Harold's opened a second men's clothing store in Stillwater, Oklahoma, and its first ladies' store in Norman, adjacent to the men's store. The ladies' store was a complement to the men's apparel line unit. At that time, there was an identifiable look

This case was prepared under the direction of Professor Robert E. Hoskisson. The case is intended to be used as the basis for class discussion rather than to illustrate either effective or ineffective handling of an administrative situation.

in ladies' apparel, which was primarily worn by students graduating from prominent schools in the Northeast. Going into the ladies' apparel business was an important decision, because ladies apparel today represents more than 77 percent of Harold's total volume (see Exhibit 1).[5]

Over the next several years following Harold's opening of its ladies' store, styles changed, but in an evolutionary as opposed to a revolutionary way. In 1968, Harold's opened its first store in Oklahoma City. Looking back, Powell recalls, "One store every ten years was hardly a Wall Street growth rate."[6] In 1973, the company opened its first store in Tulsa and over the next few years, stores opened in Dallas and Fort Worth, Texas; Jackson, Mississippi; and second stores in Oklahoma City and Tulsa.

In 1985, Harold's opened its first enclosed mall store in the Dallas Galleria. The Galleria was unique because it was very upscale, with stores such as Tiffany's, Ann Taylor, Laura Ashley, and Brooks Brothers. In the initial month after its opening on December 1, 1985, Harold's was first in the mall in both total sales and sales per square foot in the ladies' apparel category. It was also number one for its first year with sales over $500 per square foot in a 5,000-square-foot store.

This success made Harold's consider the possibility of expanding into similar upscale malls. Not wanting to borrow significant amounts of capital, the company contemplated an initial public offering (IPO). At that time, Harold's had nine stores with total sales of $21 million and an after-tax net profit of over $1 million. Harold's decided to pursue the IPO and became active on the exchange market on September 30, 1987. The stock opened at $8 with 833,000 shares, lost trading value over the next few days, and dropped eventually to $2.50 on "Black Monday" (October 19, 1987). The stock gradually increased to approximately $4.00 per share and remained in this range until it was decided to move from the NASDAQ to the American Stock Exchange (AMEX), where it registered as HRLD in November 1991.

Rebecca Powell Casy was chosen as president in 1987, and then served as executive vice president in merchandise and product development until her appointment as CEO in 1992. Under her leadership, as well as other top officers', Harold's has opened 27 new stores; it now has 37 stores in 17 states (see Exhibits 2 and 3). Sales were slightly above $100 million in 1997 (see Exhibit 4). Harold's is recognized in its industry for the company's product development, store design, merchandising, and personalized service.

HAROLD'S RETAILING STRATEGY AND ORGANIZATION

Harold's stores offer a wide mix of high-quality, classically inspired clothing including coordinated sportswear, dresses, coats, outerwear, shoes, and ac-

EXHIBIT 1 *Harold's Total Sales Volume*

	Fiscal 1997		Fiscal 1996		Fiscal 1995	
	(Dollar amounts in thousands)					
Women's Merchandise						
Sportswear	$ 72,808	67.3%	$65,009	69.0%	$50,464	66.6%
Shoes	5,777	5.3	5,196	5.5	3,914	5.2
Handbags, Belts and Accessories	5,422	5.0	4,962	5.3	4,438	5.9
Men's Merchandise						
Suits, Sportcoats, Slacks and Furnishings	8,815	8.1	6,493	6.9	5,338	7.0
Shoes	1,067	1.0	991	1.0	845	1.1
Sportswear and Accessories	13,547	12.5	11,256	11.9	10,337	13.6
Other	821	0.8	357	0.4	459	0.6
Total	$108,257	100.0%	$94,264	100.0%	$75,795	100.0%

EXHIBIT 2 *Harold's Individual Store Locations and Sales Revenues*

Metropolitan Area	Location	Type of Location	Product Lines	Square Footage	Sales 1995	Sales 1996	Sales 1997
Atlanta, GA	Lenox Square	Regional Shopping Center	W/M[1]	6,861	2,318,612	3,269,397	3,451,208
Atlanta, GA	Park Place	Specialty Center	W[2]	3,413	1,337,291	1,676,271	1,774,828
Austin, TX	Arboretum Market Place	Specialty Center	W	3,300	678,927	1,453,265	1,443,621
Austin, TX	8166 N. Mopac Expressway	Free Standing	W/M	13,200	4,487,151	5,255,784	4,689,014
Baton Rouge, LA	Citiplace Market Center	Specialty Center	W/M	5,200	0	774,376	3,120,185
Birmingham, AL	Riverchase Galleria	Regional Shopping Center	W/OS[3]	2,713	1,547,229	1,721,656	1,721,766
Charlotte, NC	Shops on the Park	Specialty Center	W/OS	4,000	1,340,331	2,334,944	2,164,296
Cordova, TN	Wolfchase Galleria	Regional Shopping Center	W/M	6,302	8,302	3,432,053	3,595,335
Dallas, TX	Dallas Galleria	Regional Shopping Center	W	4,974	5,009,242	5,282,102	5,527,900
Dallas, TX	Highland Park Village	Specialty Center	W/M	7,503	9,268,743	9,335,184	9,004,758
Ft. Worth, TX	University Park Village	Specialty Center	W/M	4,863	3,493,952	3,540,027	3,509,851
Germantown, TN	Saddle Creek South	Specialty Center	W/OS	3,909			
Greenville, SC	Greenville Mall	Regional Shopping Center	W/OS	5,076	0	0	1,156,068
Hillsboro, TX	Hillsboro Outlet Mall	Outlet Mall	W/M	5,160	0	571,434	3,167,769
Houston, TX	Highland Village	Specialty Center	W/M	6,189	4,423,328	5,342,348	5,451,119
Houston, TX	Town and Country Village	Specialty Center	W/M	5,883	0	0	949,545
Jackson, MS	The Rogue Compound	Free Standing	W	2,100	2,191,686	2,557,283	2,687,167
Kansas City, MO	Country Club Plaza	Regional Shopping Center	W	4,155	2,265,936	2,312,179	2,073,917
Kensington, MD	White Flint Mall	Regional Shopping Center	W/OS	4,605	917,617	1,200,105	1,167,421
Leawood, KS	Town Center Plaza	Regional Shopping Center	W/M	5,000	0	0	2,232,216
Littleton, CO	Park Meadows Mall	Regional Shopping Center	W/M	5,465	0	0	1,191,982
Louisville, KY	Mall St. Matthews	Regional Shopping Center	W/M	4,292	0	764,059	1,490,294
Lubbock, TX	8201 Quaker Avenue	Specialty Center	W/M	3,897	1,446,419	1,738,120	1,609,318
McLean, VA	Tyson's Galleria	Regional Shopping Center	W/M	5,083	0	0	1,172,994
Nashville, TN	The Mall at Greenhills	Regional Shopping Center	W/M	5,975	2,334,262	2,574,865	2,758,244
Norman, OK	Campus Corner Center	Specialty Center	W/M	9,050	2,882,896	3,061,307	3,245,619
Norman, OK	575 S. University Blvd.	Free Standing	W/M	15,421	0	0	308,889
Oklahoma City, OK	106 Park Avenue	Street Location	W/M	3,760	810,559	873,546	945,743
Oklahoma City, OK	50 Penn Place	Specialty Center	W/M	14,240	6,573,997	6,462,403	6,572,422
Omaha, NE	One Pacific Place	Specialty Center	W	3,272	9,724,459	1,246,298	1,464,548
Phoenix, AZ	Bitmore Fashion Park	Regional Shopping Center	W/M	5,033	423,541	1,939,068	1,910,473
Plano, TX (Dallas metro)	Park and Preston	Free Standing	W/M	5,525	1,283,474	3,919,319	3,742,088
Raleigh, NC	Crabtree Valley Mall	Regional Shopping Center	W/M	5,205	0	0	1,366,285
San Antonio, TX	Broadway and Austin Highway	Free Standing	W	3,312	1,861,828	2,041,001	2,196,169
St. Louis, MO	Plaza Frontenac	Regional Shopping Center	W/M	4,221	0	1,864,353	1,998,742
Tulsa, OK	Farm Shopping Center	Specialty Center	W/M	3,888	1,306,324	1,431,414	1,673,096
Tulsa, OK	Utica Square	Regional Shopping Center	W/M	4,625	2,638,285	2,747,280	2,848,805

Source: Harold's 10K Report for Fiscal Year 1997; Harold's Monthly Sales Statements.
[1]W/M Stores with the company's full-line women's and men's apparel.
[2]W Stores featuring women's apparel only.
[3]W/OS Stores with the company's full-line women's apparel and also featuring the company's "Old School Clothing Company."

EXHIBIT 3 *Harold's Store Locations*

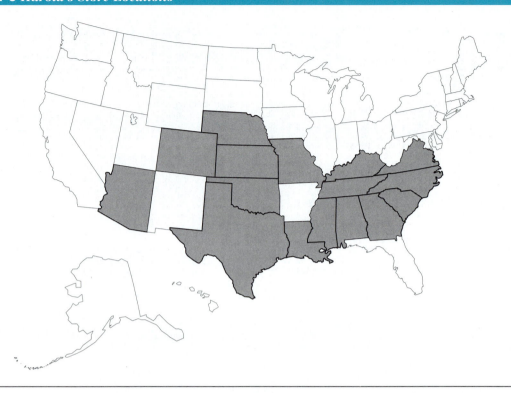

EXHIBIT 4 *Harold's Stores Inc. Detailed Annual Income Statement (in thousands of U.S. dollars)*

	52 Weeks Ending 01/29/94	52 Weeks Ending 01/28/95	53 Weeks Ending 02/03/96	52 Weeks Ending 02/01/97
Net Sales	60,940	75,795	94,264	108,257
Total Revenue	60,940	75,795	94,264	108,257
Cost of Sales	40,591	49,388	60,445	69,540
Sell./Gen./Admin.	17,449	22,594	28,722	32,519
Total Expenses	58,040	71,982	89,167	102,059
Interest Expense	−117	−274	−452	−318
Other, Net	0	0	0	0
Income Before Taxes	2,783	3,539	4,645	5,880
Income Taxes	1,171	1,451	1,858	2,352
Income After Taxes	1,612	2,088	2,787	3,528
EPS Excl. XOrd Items	0.334	0.404	0.531	0.623
Accounting Change	0	0	0	0
EPS Incl. XOrd Items	0.334	0.404	0.531	0.623
Avg Primary Shs Out.	4,826.90	5,170.15	5,250.03	5,661.57
Common Dividends/Shr	0.0000	0.0000	0.0000	0.0000
Full Dilution Adjmnt	0	0	0	0
Fully Dilutd Avg Shs	4,826.90	5,170.15	5,250.03	5,661.57
F.D. EPS Excl. Xord	0.334	0.404	0.531	0.623
F.D. EPS Incl. Xord	0.334	0.404	0.531	0.623

Source: http://www.marketguide.com.

cessories, all in updated styles. The men's product line includes tailored clothing, suits, sport coats, furnishings, sportswear, and shoes in the updated traditional fashion described as "classic styling with a contemporary influence."[7] Brand-name lines sold at Harold's include Polo, Corbin, Alden, and Kenneth Gordon. Exhibit 1 shows the percentage of sales attributable to the various merchandise categories offered. The breakdown of sales between men's and women's merchandise is approximately 22 percent and 78 percent, respectively.

Private-Label Brands

An important aspect of Harold's marketing strategy is the development of original, exclusive, and semi-exclusive apparel items. More than 90 percent of revenue can be attributed to products Harold's has created or designed. Harold's believes that this unique product mix enables it to compete with, and yet differentiate itself from, larger apparel chains by offering customers an exclusive garment at a price below that of designer and similar open-market merchandise. It is also believed that direct creation and control of merchandise enables the company to establish brand image and thus increase its initial markup. These private labels are developed and manufactured in three ways:

- By Harold's and manufactured exclusively by independent contractors.
- By Harold's and manufactured on a semi-exclusive basis.
- By vendors; Harold's private labels are affixed to nonexclusive items.

Buyers

Great emphasis is placed on researching and designing the styles and fabrics that comprise the private-label product line. Buyers travel to Europe three or four times a year to cover popular fashion markets such as Paris and Milan, searching out new styles and collecting vintage fabrics and original art for pattern development.[8] These buyers have ongoing contacts with several art studios in Europe, where artists hand paint intricate patterns and prints exclusively for Harold's. A significant portion of its merchandise also comes directly from the United Kingdom, Italy, and domestic importers from the Far East.

Product Development

A product development staff analyzes the fabric and selects the best pieces to convert into prints and patterns for each season. Once the new patterns are selected, the team develops detailed specifications of the garment's cut, fit, fabric, color, and trim. Cutting-edge, computer-aided design technology is used to create an accurate blueprint of the finalized product. This advanced computer technology enables the design team to correct inaccuracies in a design before a working sample is made. After the specifications have been finalized, material for making the product is ordered from domestic and international fabric mills. The finished fabric is shipped to manufacturers who cut, sew, and trim the completed design.

ORGANIZATIONAL STRUCTURE

Dallas

As CEO and Head Buyer for the organization, Rebecca Casey is responsible for the company's strategic direction. This includes long-term plans such as expansion and growth and short-term decisions such as which clothing styles to release next season. Her office is located in Dallas, the hub for all of the buying staff.

Corporate Offices

Harold G. Powell, chairman of the board, and his son Rainey Powell, president and chief financial officer, work in the corporate offices in Norman, Oklahoma.

Store-Level Employees

Harold's has approximately 612 full-time and 733 part-time employees, none of whom belong to labor unions. The average age of part-time employees is between 30 and 40 years old, and most are mothers who work part time. Many younger people are hired to work at the university locations, especially during holidays and summers. A typical full-line Harold's store consists of a manager, two assistant managers, one or two desk associates, and five to seven sales associates, most of whom work on a flex-time basis ranging from 20 to 25 hours per week. Sales associates are paid a commission against a draw. Commissions range from 7 to 10 percent based on the type of product sold and the associate's scale. Store managers are paid a salary plus a performance bonus based on sales-goal attainment and expense control.[9]

According to Jeff Morrell, director of human resources, the sales force, the front line to the customer, is the key component.[10] He explains, "The organization is built with a bottom-up approach . . . much like the structure that Sam Walton preached. Everyone else is there to support the efforts of the sales force." Prior to opening new stores, a trainer is sent on location to train the new sales force. The typical training program lasts three days and includes workbooks and tests. Although there is no formal evaluation system, trainers are still held somewhat accountable for the trainees' productivity.

Store managers have flexibility in setting sales goals. The first step in setting store goals is to study the previous years' sales, which are broken down by month. Store managers then approach tenured individuals (employees who have at least 18 months' experience), ask them how much they would like to earn that year, divide this amount by the commission rate, and then determine the sales that employee will have to record to achieve the goal. Jeff considers the sales associates to be much like "independent contractors; [they] don't need to be managed in this way. We want them to be recognized for what they sell. The below-optimal sellers must consider looking for a new position. Middle ones are observed most closely and given ideas for how to sell more."[11] A 3-2-9 Club sales incentive program has been set up so that employees who reach yearly sales of $329,000, $429,000, or $529,000 receive cash awards. From February to November 1997, three people reached the goal of $529,000 in sales.

INFORMATION PROCESSING

To monitor and track sales activities in the stores, an integrated point of sale (POS) inventory and management system is employed. This system automatically polls each store every 24 hours to gather pertinent data regarding the stores' merchandising activities. Information provided on a daily report includes totals of men's and women's sales and a fur-

ther breakdown of sales by category. This allows management to evaluate performance on a daily basis and implement controls and strategies as needed. This system is updated continually to add additional functionality and to aid management with store operations. For example, personnel-scheduling and time-keeping functions have been added to the system. In addition, a new customer profile function is being planned that will better identify and track consumer demographics.

Before POS machines existed, as recently as 10 years ago, sales associates had to record on a notepad the number of suits sold each day in order to track inventory. Ron Crabtree, director of MIS, describes the system as having the following advantages:

> Today, you know exactly what your points are. You can evaluate the amount of suits sold by price range; that is what the Stock Keeping Unit (SKU) is for. Management can make informed decisions with this system. Trends develop, detailing what stores want, by vendor, by station, by men's and ladies'. In our database, sales from the same day last year are automatically compared to present day sales. . . . Buyers watch purchasing trends by apparel department or classification to determine inventory stockage levels. Although the buyers are ultimately responsible for the inventory stockage levels in the stores, the store managers and buyers work together to determine sizes of clothing.[12]

STORES

Location Strategy

Harold's stores are located in either upscale, high-traffic malls, prestigious college districts, or specialty centers mainly in the southeast region (see Exhibit 2). The stores have a distinctive look, including antique fixtures, brass railings, staircases, wooden floors, and display props such as antique cars.

Harold's 37 stores range in size from 2,100 to over 15,000 square feet, with the typical store ranging from 4,000 to 6,000 square feet. Listed in Exhibit 2 are the store locations and the corresponding square footage. There are 22 full-line women's and men's apparel stores, five women's apparel stores that include a presentation of men's sportswear featuring the company's Old School Clothing brand, seven stores featuring women's apparel only, and three outlet stores to clear markdowns and slow-moving merchandise.

All of the company's stores are leased, typically for an initial 12-year term. Most include a base rent plus a contingent rent based on the store's net sales in excess of a certain threshold. Typically, this contingent rent is 4 to 5 percent of net sales in excess of the defined threshold. In fiscal 1997, 27 stores operated at sales volumes above the threshold and thus had to pay contingent rent. Exhibit 5 includes the fixed and variable components of the rent expense for the fiscal years indicated.

Existing Stores

In addition, Harold's has expanded its existing stores to provide a broader merchandise selection as well as generate the excitement of a new store opening. The Lenox (Atlanta) store has shown an increase in sales with this strategy, but the increase has not met with initial expectations. However, the Ft. Worth, Texas, store has experienced the same type of expansion and has surpassed its original expectations.

ADVERTISING

Harold's spends a considerable amount of money—approximately $8 million or 7.4 percent of sales in 1997—on advertising, primarily print advertising for daily and weekly newspapers, direct-mail pieces and other print media. This material is produced by an in-house advertising staff, that has won numerous Addie Awards at the local, district, and national level.[13]

Catalog

Harold's produces its own in-house direct-response catalog. Sales have increased from $620,000 in 1992 to almost $9 million in 1997. Management believes

that sales must reach $10 million for this operation to be profitable. The catalog has recorded a loss every year; however, it is believed to be a valuable advertising tool. It may also help in the long term because it facilitates the maintenance of an active customer list. Approximately 7.2 million copies are mailed out yearly.

INVENTORY CONTROL

According to Rebecca Casey, "A high percentage of the company's merchandise is developed internally by the company's product development team. This results in larger inventories, including work in progress, piece goods inventory and bulk purchases, than a retailer who depends primarily on branded vendor lines. Also, inventory control and planning is more complicated."[14]

Distribution Center

During an average day, approximately 25,000 boxes of merchandise are processed through one centralized distribution location. It has the current capacity to accommodate up to 120 stores, but with the future addition of a mezzanine, will be able to serve 240 stores.

Over the past three years, Harold's has made a heavy investment in this distribution center, creating a highly efficient system that uses bar coding, internal tracking, trolleys and roller systems, and individual store labeling. The error rate is quite low. UPS services 95 percent of Harold's inventory.

In November 1997, a new area opened to hold all excess clothing headed for the outlet stores. Two levels hold both the hanging and folded clothes. They are sorted by department, thus decreasing the amount of time distribution center workers spend searching among boxes sent back from the stores as excess for the outlet center and warehouse sales.

EXHIBIT 5 *Fixed and Variable Components of the Rent Expense*

	1997	1996	1995
Base Rent	$2,806,000	$2,222,000	$1,791,000
Additional Amounts Computed as a Percentage of Sales	$1,261,000	$ 112,000	$ 922,000
Total	$4,067,000	$3,334,000	$2,713,000

The distribution center has begun assisting the new store openings by price tagging, steam-cleaning, and security tagging all of the merchandise before it leaves. This helps new stores open within a three-day opening constraint.

Warehouse Sales

The Warehouse Sale, which is in its 17th year in Oklahoma City, is also held in Dallas, Tulsa, and Houston. It typically draws nearly 20,000 people at the Oklahoma State Fairgrounds Building. Catherine Cook, director of marketing, believes that "for Harold's, it's a great opportunity to expand our customer base. Our ability to offer exclusive private label merchandise at extremely competitive prices starting at $4.90, has made this sale something our customers will wait for. Conversely, it allows our company to move discontinued styles and excess merchandise."[15]

Outlet Sales

Harold's currently operates two outlet locations in Texas and recently opened a new outlet in Norman, Oklahoma. Harold G. Powell, chairman of the board, says location drives the strategy behind the company's outlet operations. These outlets offer off-price items from excess inventories, including merchandise from Harold's private-label line. By positioning outlets near major college campuses close to metropolitan areas (where regular-price Harold's stores are located), the company hopes to influence consumer buying habits early. Powell believes students appreciate the outlet's lower prices. As they graduate and move to larger cities to find work, they look to Harold's regular-price stores to update their professional wardrobe. "We want to grow up with our customers," said Mr. Powell. "We want them to rely on us for all their clothing needs, from school wardrobes to career wardrobes. It's a formula that has worked well for us in Austin, where we first began testing it in 1990."[16]

COMPETITION

Harold's believes that its major competitors fall into three categories: (1) department stores, such as Dillard's and Neiman-Marcus; (2) specialty apparel stores, such as Ann Taylor, Talbots, Today's Man, The Limited, The Gap, and Abercrombie & Fitch; and (3) catalog operations such as L.L.Bean, Land's End, and Spiegel.

General Industry Characteristics

Consumers are becoming more value-conscious. To capitalize on this trend, many of the specialty retailers, such as Ann Taylor and The Gap, have turned their strategies toward providing more moderately priced items.[17] To provide these items to consumers, many retailers have expanded their outlet businesses. The expansion has taken the form of moderate-priced stores, which serve as spin-offs of the regular retail stores. Ann Taylor is experimenting currently with its spin-off, The Ann Taylor Loft,[18] and The Gap is using the Old Navy Stores.[19]

The Gap has invested in the development of brand extensions. It now offers new product categories such as personal care in all of its divisions, linens and bed clothing for BabyGap, a home accessories line for Banana Republic, and jewelry and underwear for The Gap and Banana Republic. Talbots has also ventured into children's clothing lines. This proliferation of product categories has caused promotional activities to skyrocket, stimulating price deflation and more aggressive cross-shopping. Women's apparel prices took a record plunge in 1994, dropping 4.4 percent against 1993 prices.[20] Retailers also have been increasing inventory levels because they gear their efforts toward the same customers.

Increasingly, the fashion industry is finding that a focused merchandise mix and total wardrobe strategy—with personalized customer service, efficient store layouts, and a continual flow of new merchandise—appeals to the relatively affluent working women with limited time to shop. Customers desire consistency in their fashion, allowing them to create a wardrobe across seasons and years. Although specialty stores have been able to maintain 23 percent of the market share, the trend in shopping is toward the discounters and large department stores. Specialty stores have seen losses in 19 of 23 apparel categories since 1994. In addition, as shown in Exhibit 6, the specialty retailers only dominate in two of the five regional areas of the United States. Designer-oriented specialty stores are trying to offer merchandise in a broader array of prices.[21] Kurt Barnard, president of Bamard's Retail Report, stated, "Com-

EXHIBIT 6 *National: Specialty Stores Encounter Dog Fight, Lose Grip on West ranking by dollar market share, 1996*

Rank	National U.S.	Northeast	Southeast	Regional Midwest	Southwest	West
1	Specialty	Specialty	Discounters	Discounters	Specialty	Department
2	Discounters	Discounters	Specialty	Specialty	Discounters	Discounters
3	Department	Off-Price	Department	Department	Department	Chains
4	Chains	Department	Chains	Chains	Chains	Specialty
5	Off-Price	Chain	Off-Price	Off-Price	Off-Price	Off-Price
6	Mail Order	Mail Order	Others	Mail Order	Mail Order	Mail Order
7	Others	Others	Mail Order	Others	Others	Others

Source: http://www.sbweb2.med.iacnet.com/info

panies like Nordstrom were featuring dresses for $29 last summer."[22]

Specialty apparel stores also are attempting to gain market share through direct-order catalogs. One company that has had success with catalog operations is Talbots. In 1989, Talbots implemented a program to improve the productivity of its catalog operations by broadening its merchandise assortment and adjusting its catalog circulation to better target established and prospective buyers. This reduced catalog mailings by 36.4 percent from 1989 to 1996, increased sales per catalog by 92.6 percent during the same period, and provided savings on production and mailing costs.[23] The company utilizes computer applications, employing mathematical models to improve the efficiency of its catalog mailings. To improve customer response, Talbots has developed its own list of active customers. The company routinely updates and refines this list prior to individual catalog mailings by monitoring customer interest as reflected in criteria such as the frequency and dollar amount of purchases as well as the last date of purchase. The customer database compiled through this catalog operation provides important demographic information about potential store markets.

NATIONAL EXPANSION

Location Strategy

Harold's expansion strategy seems to contribute to the firm's success. Management tracks the orders from catalog sales of different regions to determine a potential customer region in which to expand. Then they visit that region to observe the composition of the customers in the shopping center, using criteria such as age, race, population, and income. They also look at the other stores located in the shopping center. Harold's looks for stores that have a similar customer base such as Williams-Sonoma, Pottery Barn, Ann Taylor, Talbots, and Banana Republic. In addition, they also make parking lot counts of luxury cars to determine if the selected site has the potential to provide Harold's with its targeted customers. This reduces research costs because the existing stores in the mall have already completed some activities to evaluate a location for a new store. Furthermore, the potential shopping centers often present Harold's with pertinent information, such as previous years' total sales for the mall and sales per square foot numbers of the existing stores,[24] that helps management make an informed decision about a possible store opening.

New Stores

Harold's has achieved 20 to 25 percent overall sales growth due to the continual opening of new stores. The initial plan was to open an increasing number of stores yearly to enhance overall annual sales. However, not all of the store openings have gone as planned.

Harold's earlier attempt to expand west to California proved to be an unwise decision. The expansion plan called for a move into a mall area that contained several other specialty clothing stores. The expansion turned out to be disappointing because Harold's had deviated from its traditional way of entering into new regional markets. Although it was the most expensive leasing agreement it had entered, management felt that the move would materialize into a favorable future return on investment. How-

ever, expectations for future sales proved to be optimistic. Management attributed the less than favorable sales to a competitive market in which the firm had no previous name recognition.[25]

EXHIBIT 7 *Harold's Stores Inc. Detailed Annual Balance Sheet (in thousands of U.S. dollars)*

	As of 01/29/94	As of 01/28/95	As of 02/03/96	As of 02/01/97
Assets				
Cash/Equivalents	143	109	2	433
Trade Receivables	3,580	4,238	4,687	5,476
Other Receivables	910	671	568	673
Inventory	12,647	17,847	21,647	28,544
Taxes Receivable	9	0	0	0
Prepaid Expenses	380	646	1,231	2,174
Deferred Taxes	488	622	1,010	1,615
Marketable Sec.	0	0	0	0
Total Current Assets	18,157	24,133	29,145	38,915
Land	513	590	665	665
Buildings	1,601	1,987	2,796	2,847
Leasehold Imp.	3,296	4,310	4,934	7,052
Furn./Fixtures	6,451	8,299	10,604	13,504
Constr. in Prog.	0	0	528	933
Depreciation	−3,876	−4,955	−6,097	−7,897
Other Assets	299	297	334	986
Other Receivables	0	0	0	2,603
Total Assets	26,441	34,661	42,909	59,608
Liabilities				
Notes Payable	1,475	4,902	0	0
Cur.Port.LT Debt	75	75	75	110
Accounts Payable	2,828	4,154	4,396	6,668
Redeemable Cert.	410	509	672	923
Bonus/Payroll	705	1,129	1,624	1,958
Accrued/Other	124	840	1,077	1,240
Total Current Liabilities	5,617	11,609	7,844	10,899
Long-Term Debt	669	594	9,540	12,528
Total Long-Term Debt	669	594	9,540	12,528
Deferred Tax	159	198	226	146
Total Liabilities	6,445	12,401	17,610	23,573
Shareholder Equity				
Common Stock	43	47	50	57
Paid-in Capital	13,047	17,491	20,572	31,548
Retained Erngs.	6,906	4,722	4,677	4,430
Treasury Stock	0	0	0	0
Total Equity	19,996	22,260	25,299	36,035
Shares Outstanding	5,157.65	5,179.73	5,206.09	5,713.53

Source: http://www.marketguide.com.

EXHIBIT 8 *Harold's Stores Inc. Detailed Annual Statement of Cash Flows Indirect Method (in thousands of U.S. dollars)*

	52 Weeks Ending 01/29/94	52 Weeks Ending 01/28/95	53 Weeks Ending 02/03/96	52 Weeks Ending 02/01/97
Operating Cash Flows				
Net Income	1,612	2,088	2,787	3,528
Depreciation	1,409	1,710	2,185	2,806
Accounting Change	0	0	0	0
Sale of Assets	−6	−4	1	−2
Accounts Receivable	−999	−419	−346	−798
Inventories	−1,891	−5,200	−3,800	−6,897
Taxes Receivable	37	9	0	0
Deferred Taxes	29	−95	−360	−685
Other Assets	0	2	−37	−652
Accounts Payable	−393	1,326	242	2,272
Taxes Payable	0	583	253	106
Accrued Expenses	−59	656	642	642
Prepaid Expenses	−257	−266	−585	−415
Com. Stock Bonus	9	179	254	344
Cash from Operations	−509	569	1,236	249
Investing Cash Flows				
Marketable Secs.	0	0	0	0
Investment in Secs.	0	0	0	0
Capital Expenditures	−2,909	−3,994	−5,687	−7,102
Disp. of Prop./Equip	105	42	302	96
Term Loan	0	0	0	−2,750
Payment of Term Loan	0	0	0	51
Cash from Investing	−2,804	−3,952	−5,385	−9,705
Financing Cash Flows				
Notes Payable	18,325	26,357	32,652	45,474
Pay. Notes Payable	−17,450	−22,930	−28,608	−42,451
Long-Term Debt	−615	−75	0	0
Payment Long-Term Debt	0	0	0	0
Common Stock	3,009	0	0	6,864
Fractional Shares	0	−3	−2	0
Cash from Financing	3,269	3,349	4,042	9,887
Foreign Exch. Effects	0	0	0	0
Net Change in Cash	−44	−34	−107	431
Cash Interest Paid	139	291	643	703
Cash Taxes Paid	1,025	954	1,965	2,239

Source: http://www.marketguide.com.

Harold's decided it needed to move from state to state, in small jumps, as opposed to skipping over states. The company expanded into Texas and then to the Southeast. It has even opened multiple stores in particular cities in order to utilize its name recognition.

MAJOR CHALLENGE

For Harold's to continue its aggressive expansion program, Rebecca Casey and Rainey Powell face multiple issues requiring their attention. How can this

50-year-old, family-run business survive the rising competition in the mature apparel industry market? Will the niche strategy work as Harold's expands beyond the Midwest? How can the firm expand into new areas more successfully and yet maintain its strong emphasis of private-label brands and lifelong customer relationships? Also, given its size, efficiency, and relative financial performance (see Exhibits 7 and 8), are there additional challenges requiring analysis by a firm that seeks above-average returns in a highly competitive retail environment? If so, is Harold's prepared to meet these challenges?

NOTES

1. Harold's Home Page, http://www.harolds.net.
2. Harold's Annual Report, Form 10-K, for fiscal year ended February 1, 1997.
3. Ibid.
4. Harold Powell's Speech to Oklahoma City Rotary Club, February 1997.
5. Ibid.
6. Ibid.
7. Ibid.
8. M. McMillin, 1997, Harold's Stores to open upscale apparel store in Wichita, Kansas, *Knight-Ridder/Tribune* Business News, March 19, 319.
9. Ibid.
10. Interview with Jeff Morrell, Human Resources Department, Harold's Stores, October 1997.
11. Ibid.
12. Interview with Ron Crabtree, Management Information Systems Director, Harold's Stores, October 1997.
13. Ibid.
14. Ibid.
15. Ibid.
16. Ibid.
17. S. Edelson, 1995, Move to the middle: Stores at both ends woo value shopper, *Women's World Daily*, March 2, 1.
18. Ann Taylor Annual Report, Form 10-K, for fiscal year ended February 1, 1997.
19. J. Arlen, 1996, Old Navy rocks, *Discount Store News*, September 16, 59.
20. Ibid.
21. I. Lagnado, 1995, New trends, *Women's World Daily*, May 17, 4.
22. Ibid.
23. Talbot's announces September sales; Major fall catalog sales strong while comparable store sales down 4.7%, 1997, *Business Wire*, October 9.
24. Harold's Town Meeting Questions, November 1997.
25. Interview with Bob Cole, Financial Analyst, Harold's Stores, October 1997.

Internationalization of Telefónica España, S.A.

Christian Knief
Carlos Garciá Pont
Joan E. Ricart

International Graduate School of Management

In December 1994, the Telefónica Group was a provider of telephone networking services in Spain and Latin America. Telefónica España, the Spanish parent company, was a private company traded on the Madrid, New York, London, Paris, Frankfurt, and Tokyo stock exchanges. It controlled the entire Spanish telephone services market for local, long-distance, and international calling. In 1946 the Spanish government granted Telefónica a monopoly in providing these services. At the end of 1994, Telefónica controlled US$29.5 billion in assets and was managing a network of 14,685,400 telephone lines in service, with 72,207 employees in Spain. Telefónica was the largest Spanish company in total sales, total assets, and number of employees (for financial information see Exhibit 1). Through the companies in which its subsidiary, Telefónica Internacional de España, S.A. (TI), held stakes, Telefónica managed or owned an additional 7,370,491 telephone lines and employed another 59,419 people outside of Spain, almost all of them in Latin America.

At the beginning of the 1980s the Spanish telecommunications market was national. It was characterized by a shortage of telephone lines, long waiting lists for connection to the telephone services for new customers, and a poor quality of service. During the late

1980s, under its new president Cándido Velázquez, Telefónica embarked on a major investment program to expand and improve the national telephone system. Telefónica expanded the telephone network from 10 million lines in the mid-1980s to almost 15 million lines in 1994 and eliminated the waiting list. At the same time, the company digitalized large numbers of telephone lines, decreased line failures, and improved the service quality of its operations.

The telecommunication and telephone services industry had changed during the previous 10 years (1984–1994). Industry sources expected even more change in the future. This change was driven by technological innovation and the "deregulation" of the industry at the global, European, and national levels. New technologies and competitors were already competing with Telefónica in the Spanish market. The competition was expected to increase in the long run as the Spanish market would be opened to national and international companies before the end of the century.

In response, Telefónica diversified into new businesses (mobile, multimedia, data-transmission, and information services) and international markets (the United States, Romania, Argentina, Venezuela, Peru, Columbia, Chile, Puerto Rico, and Portugal). Telefónica was active within different industries in the telecommunications sector. In addition to its national and international telephone network activities, it was a provider of data services, mobile telephone services,

Winner of the 1997 EFMD Prize as the Best Case in International Business. Case of the Research Department at IESE. Copyright © 1995, IESE.

EXHIBIT 1 *Internationalization of Telefónica España, S.A.*
Telefónica–Financial Information

		in Millions of pesetas			Avg. Growth 1993	Cum. Avg. Growth 1990–1994	in US$* 1994
	1990	1991	1992	1993	1994			
Telefónica España: Revenue								
Subscriber Charges	207,119	230,885	253,751	276,280	287,373	4.00%	8.50%	2,181
Data and Image Transmission	87,628	103,852	115,669	112,433	103,213	−8.20	4.20	783
Domestic Automatic Services	374,472	465,584	539,564	579,671	616,461	6.30	13.30	4,679
Trunk Calls Through Operators	1,642	2,266	2,861	3,271	4,018	22.80	25.10	30
International Service	113,857	124,492	135,005	132,672	140,162	5.60	5.30	1,064
Mobile and Maritime Services	8,696	14,255	25,989	32,754	44,518	35.90	50.40	338
Advertising	8,506	10,017	12,806	15,007	15,519	3.40	16.20	118
REVENUE FROM SERVICES	801,920	951,351	1,085,645	1,152,088	1,211,264	5.10	10.90	9,194
Connection Fees and Other Items	50,622	56,680	69,051	67,998	72,272	6.30	9.30	549
REVENUE FROM OPERATIONS	852,542	1,008,031	1,154,696	1,220,086	1,283,536	5.20	10.80	9,743
Telefónica Internacional	n.a.	333	1,767	18,338	221,451	n.a.	n.a.	1,681
Remaining Subsidiaries	n.a.	134,488	156,395	161,106	179,080	11.20	10.00	1,359
Sales Among Group	n.a.	−93,854	−103,920	−102,091	−105,217	3.10	3.90	−799
CONSOLIDATED REVENUE	n.a.	1,048,998	1,208,938	1,297,439	1,578,850	21.70	14.60	11,985

Source: Telefónica España Annual Report.
*Figures in US$ million; at the Exchange Rate of Dec. 30, 1994: $1.00 = Ptas. 131,739.

satellite communications, and value-added services. At the same time, Telefónica was divesting its holdings in several Spanish telecommunications equipment producers.

Since the late 1980s, Telefónica had expanded into new geographic markets and diversified into new products. By 1994, with its subsidiary TI, the company controlled operations in Chile, Argentina, Peru, Venezuela, Puerto Rico, the United States, Portugal, Colombia, and Romania. One of the critical issues facing Telefónica España in the context of internationalization was the emergence of strategic alliances. Just recently, Telefónica España formed a strategic alliance at the European level with Unisource. At the same time, Telefónica Internacional was negotiating a strategic alliance for its Latin American operations.

The Spanish government had been thinking about selling its 23.8 percent stake in TI. If this were to happen, it would allow the entry of an ally into the company. The main concern of Telefónica's management was the compatibility of the future partner. They were looking for a company with similar strategic goals to become a major player in Latin America. Also, they were interested in gaining access to new technologies, especially in the multimedia and cellular telephone businesses. Finally, it was important for Telefónica to play an active role in the alliance.

THE CHANGING TELECOMMUNICATION SERVICES INDUSTRY

The telecommunications industry had been relatively stable before 1984, when the American market was deregulated. Initially, telecommunication services had to rely on a wire-based infrastructure. This required significant investments in infrastructure to guarantee universal service within the different national markets. Because governments saw this as an important issue, these services were initially provided by public utilities or companies that held government-granted monopolies. Internationally, this led to an industry characterized by domestic monopolies with little competition across borders. However, with the onset of deregulation, the industry became very dynamic.

In the 1990s, telecommunication service compa-

nies basically provided telephone connections. Owing to the technological structure of the telephone system, three different services could be distinguished: local telephone services, long-distance telephone services, and international telephone services. In most countries, these services were provided by one company; however, in other countries, long-distance and international calling was open to competition. In the United States, for example, AT&T, Sprint, and MCI competed in the provision of long-distance and international telephone services, while regional companies had monopolies for their local telephone networks.

The local operator basically provided two types of service. The first, the local telephone service, consisted of telephone connections between customers within their cities and regions. These were local or regional telephone calls. The second service was the exchange access service, which provided access to other networks such as the long-distance and international telephone networks. This service included all calls in or out of the local telephone exchange. The providers of local telephone services had to undertake large infrastructure investments because they needed to install a telephone connection to each individual customer.

The long-distance service was quite different from the local telephone service in terms of infrastructure requirements. The reason was that long-distance installations accounted for a small part of the mileage in a country's phone system, while the wire network for local calling represented the greater part of the telephone infrastructure. It was not economically feasible for long-distance service operators to wire directly to their customers' homes and businesses. Telephone customers accessed long-distance services through their local service. When local and long-distance services were controlled by different companies, as was the case in the United States, the long-distance carrier paid the local telephone companies an exchange access fee.

International calling was again different from local and long-distance calling. Technically, international calling was similar to long-distance calling. The important difference between long-distance and international services arose from bilateral agreements that had to be signed between one operator in the country of origin and another operator in the country of destination. Once the connection between two countries was established, calls accessed the international services from the national long-distance, local or mobile services. The international operator then provided an exchange access service to long-distance, local, or mobile services in the country of destination.

Technological Changes

Since the mid-1980s, the industry had experienced dynamic change along the technical and regulatory dimensions. The first important aspect was the application of new transmission technologies. Cellular radio transmission technology was introduced and opened up new possibilities to access customers. Further, the interaction between computer technology and telecommunications allowed the incorporation of more complex telecommunication services. Finally, fibre-optics-based networks were installed, allowing the transfer of large amounts of data and thereby providing data-intensive services for final customers.

Mobile telephone systems were not very different, from an operations perspective, from the local telephone system. Like the local telephone system, they were organized into geographic regions called cells. However, customers moved around in these cells, or "roamed," in the industry jargon. Important activities included the planning of network structure, the installation and maintenance of transmission systems, and the assignment of user numbers. The main difference in the operation of these systems was that the technology was more sophisticated, incorporating a greater number of more highly complicated functions (such as caller location and roaming) into the system.

When a call originated in one cell and was destined in the same cell, the operator of the cell provided a kind of a local calling service. Also, if the call was between two cells operated by the same company, one operator completed the communication. However, when the customer used long-distance or international calling services, the standard telephone, or another cellular telephone system, the call went outside of the mobile telephone network and the cellular telephone operator provided an exchange access service to the other operator.

The local telephone network and the mobile telephone system were the backbones of the overall telecommunication system as all calls originated or terminated in one of the two systems. Because of the lower penetration of cellular systems, the main function was still carried out through the conventional wired telephone system. However, as the use of mobile personal communications grew rapidly all over the world, mobile telephony was becoming more important. In countries with little fixed line infrastructure in place, mobile networks would play a much bigger role in building the basic telecommunications infrastructure. In the long run, analysts expected that mobile services would be preferred over fixed network services.

The merging of telecommunication and computer technology not only allowed the incorporation into telephone services of new features such as detailed customer billing or call waiting, but also led to the creation of new services. An important new service was national and international voice and data transmission for multinational enterprises. This service addressed the needs of large national and multinational companies. It included the planning and operation of national and international communication networks. In this market, the customer would outsource all its data and communication networks to a single service provider. This service provider then guaranteed the functioning of the corporate network.

Furthermore, international telephone services and corporate networks might share the same infrastructure, as both voice and data could be transferred digitally. There would be no further need for separate infrastructures. However, whether both services would be provided using the same infrastructure would depend on regulators' decisions.

In the near future, the installation of fibre optics networks would create another means to access customers. As optical cables allowed the transmission of large amounts of digital information, the fibre optics network would allow companies to provide multimedia products to the final customers. In the long run, the application of this technology would lead to the creation of a multimedia industry. This also would allow the cable television companies to offer telephone services. Telephone service providers in the future would be only one of several information distributors.

Regulatory Changes

The second dimension along which the industry had changed was regulation. Telecommunication had traditionally been viewed as critical infrastructure for a nation. In the past, most nations had wanted to guarantee a universal telecommunication service in their national markets. Also, many governments had promoted the cross-subsidization of local calls through long-distance and international calls for political reasons. For these reasons and because of the large investments in fixed infrastructure, governments had granted monopolies in order to attract investments. During the 1980s, many countries began to recognize that the quality of telecommunications infrastructure could benefit countries economically as it played an important role in the economic development of a nation.

A well-developed telecommunications system stimulated economic activity as it facilitated economic transactions. Also, it gave a country a comparative advantage as a location for companies. This had led nations to reconsider the regulation of their telecommunication sectors. Among them were the United States, Great Britain, Japan, and some developing nations.

Most of the industrialized nations were deregulating their industries, trying to increase the level of competition to improve service quality. Many developing countries were opening (or would open in the near future) their borders to direct foreign investments in order to attract capital to build the basic telecommunications infrastructure.

Internationalization

These technological and regulatory changes were opening international opportunities for established players. These companies were opening international routes as well as entering those local market segments that did not need large infrastructure investments.

At the same time, telecommunications companies were forming a large number of strategic alliances. Local telephone service providers teamed up with cable television companies to access fibre optics technology. Companies with experience in the provision of cellular telephone services entered into strategic alliances to introduce cellular telephone systems in newly opened markets. International consortia, including financial institutions and telecommunications companies, entered the markets of developing countries to revamp their underdeveloped telecommunications infrastructure. Last, but not least, utilities and companies with countrywide networks at-

tempted to enter the long-distance and data-transmission business.

TELEFÓNICA ESPAÑA, S.A. (TELEFÓNICA)

In December 1994, Telefónica was the provider of telephone networking services in Spain. Its sales totalled 6.5 billion pesetas in 1994. The company controlled the complete Spanish telephone market for local, long-distance, and international calls. In comparison with other telephone operators, Telefónica was a medium-sized company. In Europe it was neither small nor large. The three big telecoms operators, BT, Deutsche Bundespost Telekom (DBT), and France Télécom, were much larger than Telefónica, while the telecommunications operators in the smaller countries such as The Netherlands, Belgium, or Denmark were much smaller (Exhibit 2). The Spanish market had been one of the fastest growing in recent years, as the penetration of telephone services had only recently reached the levels achieved in the northern European nations. In particular, the Spanish markets for mobile calling and networking services offered opportunities.

Since the beginning of the 1990s, regulations in Spain had changed significantly, opening more markets to competition (Exhibit 3). In addition, new product markets such as cellular telephone services and data-transmission services had grown rapidly (Exhibit 4). Due to the changes expected in the regulatory environment in the near future, new competition was expected to emerge.

Through the increase of the installed base during the late 1980s, Telefónica had improved its competitive position in its domestic markets. At the same time, with the emergence of new technologies, the company had started to actively pursue research and development for new services. In addition, it had expanded internationally through investments in Latin America and the participation in a strategic alliance.

In 1994, Telefónica began to reorganize. The company created nine units: eight businesses and a corporate center. The logic of this reorganization was to decentralize the company so that the managers responsible for the business units assumed more initiative. Top management hoped that this would also improve efficiency.

EXHIBIT 2 *Internationalization of Telefónica España, S.A.*
International Telecommunications Companies

Ranking		Company (Country)	Revenues Total in million US$		Changes		Telephone Lines Total in 1000s		Changes	
1993	1994		1993	1994	(92–93)	(93–94)	1993	1994	(92–93)	(93–94)
1	1	NTT (Japan)	60,100	68,900	2.80%	14.64%	58,500	59,800	2.00%	2.22%
2	2	AT&T (USA)	39,900	43,400	0.70	8.77				
3	3	DBT Telekom (Germany)	35,700	37,700	9.30	5.60	36,900	39,200	4.20	6.23
4	4	France Télécom (France)	22,400	23,300	3.60	4.02	30,800	31,600	3.00	2.60
5	5	British Telecom (UK)	20,500	21,300	3.30	3.90	26,200	27,100	2.10	3.44
8	6	SIP (Italy)	14,900	18,000	8.60	20.81	24,200	24,500	1.90	1.24
6	7	GTE (USA)	17,200	17,400	–2.00	1.16	17,700	17,400	1.50	–1.69
7	8	BellSouth (USA)	15,900	16,800	4.50	5.66	19,300	20,200	3.70	4.66
9	9	Bell Atlantic (USA)	12,500	13,800	3.70	10.40	18,600	19,200	2.60	3.23
10	10	MCI (USA)	11,900	13,300	12.90	11.76				
9	11	Nynex (USA)	13,400	13,300	1.70	–0.75	16,100	16,600	2.70	3.11
13	12	Sprint (USA)	11,400	12,700	23.20	11.40	6,100	6,400	4.80	4.92
12	13	Ameritech (USA)	11,700	12,600	5.00	7.69	17,600	18,200	3.30	3.41
14	14	SW Bell (USA)	10,600	11,600	6.70	9.43	13,200	13,600	3.40	3.03
15	15	US West (USA)	10,000	11,000	4.80	10.00	13,800	14,300	3.70	3.62
18	16	Telstra (Australia)	8,600	9,800	3.50	13.95	8,500	8,900	3.40	4.71
16	17	Telefónica (Spain)	9,500	9,600	5.70	1.05	14,200	14,700	3.30	3.52
17	18	Pacific Telesis (USA)	9,200	9,200	–7.00	0.00	14,900	15,300	2.20	2.68
19	19	Telmex (Mexico)	7,200	8,700	17.60	20.83	7,400	8,500	12.70	14.86
20	20	Telbras (Brasil)	6,900	7,800	n.a.	13.04	10,500	11,800	8.6	12.38
TOTAL		The 20 largest operators	349,500	380,200	2.90%	8.78%	354,500	367,300	3.20%	3.61%

Ranking 1992	Company (Country)	Revenues Total million ECU	Telephone Lines Total in 1000s	Personnel Total
1	DBT Telekom (Germany)	26,616	33,600	231,000
2	France Télécom (France)	18,010		170,000
3	British Telecom (UK)	17,845	29,100	155,300
4	SIP (Italy)	13,475	23,100	87,475
5	Telefónica (Spain)	8,689	13,300	74,437
6	PTT Telecom (Netherlands)	4,000	7,200	
7	Belgacom (Belgium)	2,172	4,100	27,700
8	Teledanmark (Denmark)	1,996	3,000	17,829
9	Mercury (UK)	1,248		
TOTAL	The nine largest operators	94,051		

EXHIBIT 3 *Internationalization of Telefónica España, S.A.*
Changes in the Legal Framework

European Directives

Spanish Legislation

	European Directives	Spanish Legislation
1987	■ Green Paper on Telecommunications Act	■ Telecommunications Act (LOT)
1988	■ Liberalization of terminals	
1990	■ Liberalization of services and ONP	
	■ Liberalization of voice telephony for Groups Closed User and Business Networks	
1991		■ Liberalization of terminals
1992	■ ONP leased circuits Directive	■ Modification of LOT
		■ Radiopaging service open to competition
1993	■ Agreement for liberalization of voice services by January 1, 1998	■ Data transmission, Closed Group radio telephony and local radiopaging services open to competition
		■ Correos and Retevisión awarded support service for VSAT
1994	■ Agreement on liberalization of infrastructure by January 1, 1998	■ Automatic Mobile Telephony open to competition
	■ Resolution on Universal Service	■ Trunking licenses granted
	■ Infrastructure Green Paper (part I)	■ Second GSM license granted
		■ Correos and Retevisión granted circuit leasing for TMA (GSM)
		■ Public Telephony open to competition (except public booths)
1995	■ Satellite communications open to competition	■ Resale of leased circuit capacity authorized
	■ Infrastructure Green Paper (part 2)	■ Liberalization of VSAT services
		■ Cable Telecommunications Bill (1995)
1996	■ Automatic Mobile Telephony open to competition	
1998		■ Basic Telephony and Infrastructure open to competition

C-26

EXHIBIT 4 *Internationalization of Telefónica España, S.A.*
Forecast: Evolution of the Spanish Telecommunications Market by Main Sub-Sectors 1991–2000
(in billions of ptas.)

	1991	1992	1993	1994	1995	1996	1997	1998	1999	2000
Basic Telephone		939	1,040	1,124	1,277	1,419	1,685	1,935	2,128	2,416
Data Transmission		116	129	149	169	212	251	322	355	446
Value Added Services		15	17	18	21	25	30	44	48	59
Mobile Telephone		31	37	41	51	64	75	88	129	223
Other Services		30	34	36	41	47	55	64	71	82
Services Subtotal	1,049	1,131	1,256	1,369	1,559	1,776	2,097	2,454	2,731	3,227
Equipment	341	240	266	284	319	351	417	478	493	491
TOTAL Market	1,390	1,371	1,523	1,653	1,879	2,117	2,097	2,932	3,225	3,717

Source: *Business Spain,* May 1994, No. 72.

The parent company, Telefónica, would contain three of the nine units: corporate center, basic telephone services, and international telephone traffic. The corporate center had the task of defining the strategy of the group as a whole and coordinating and controlling the different businesses to take advantage of the synergies available and avoid squandering resources. The Basic Telephone Services unit would incorporate local and long-distance calling in the Spanish market, which were Telefónica's core activities. At the end of 1994, the International Telephone Traffic unit was still part of Telefónica, though it was expected that the unit would soon be transferred to an independent company.

The other businesses would be organized in existing or newly incorporated companies. The remaining six units included the international division

TI, Mobile-Telephone Services, Data-Transmission, Multimedia, Public Telephones, and the Information and Advertising Division (Exhibit 5).

Basic telephone services and international telephone traffic were the most important of Telefónica's businesses because the company generated around 85 percent of its revenues from these markets. Under European Community conditions, Telefónica could retain its monopoly in basic phone services until 1998. At the same time, some of the services that were traditionally incorporated within basic telephone services, such as data and voice transmission in corporate networks, would be opened to competition earlier.

Telefónica Internacional de España (TI) was Telefónica's largest subsidiary and coordinated all international expansion activities (see section on TI on page C-270).

EXHIBIT 5 *Internationalization of Telefónica España, S.A. Organizational Structure*

Cellular Telephony was among the businesses grouped outside Telefónica. This business was growing at a very high rate. Also, it was expected that the cellular telephone system would be the main competitor to Telefónica's wire-based telephone network in the coming decades. Since 1988, the number of subscribers had increased rapidly, from 13,000 in 1988 to almost 411,930 customers, with an increase of 154,669 customers in 1994 alone. This was roughly equivalent to a penetration rate of about 1 percent of the Spanish population, and was low compared with the European average.

In addition, Telefónica's monopoly of cellular telephone services expired at the end of 1994. In 1994, several companies and alliances lined up to bid for the second license to be granted by the Spanish government. They included several international telecommunications companies: Ameritech and Pacific Telesis International (two Regional Bell Operating Companies, RBOCs, from the United States), Mercury Communications (competitor of BT in the United Kingdom) and GTE (the largest U.S. local telephone company). Airtel, a consortium of Spanish companies, won the bidding. It planned to start offering its services by October 1995. The technology was supplied by Airtouch, a North American cellular telephone company.

The second unit grouped outside of Telefónica was the Data-Transmission business. The unit was operating in an attractive market with growth potential. The Spanish market for data-transmission services had been deregulated in 1993. However, Telefónica still had a de facto monopoly because competition had not materialized as of the end of 1994. A consortium with the partners BT and Banco Santander planned to enter the market and invest about 80.2 billion pesetas over the next 10 years, capturing a market share of about 20 percent in the same time frame. At the same time, Telefónica was negotiating a possible transfer of its assets in this business into Unisource, a strategic alliance with three European PTTs (post, telegraph, and telephone companies).

Another important area in which Telefónica planned to expand was the Multimedia business. This business included the installation and operation of fiber optics cables that made it possible to transmit large amounts of data to the end customer. This would provide the infrastructure for services such as home shopping and video on demand. In 1994, Tele-

fónica Multimedia S.A. had been formed with the aim of offering marketing and leisure services. Initially, this division would offer cable TV services, but would later move into interactive multimedia services. All of these services would use Telefónica networks.

Telefónica had already invested in a fiber optics network, which at the end of 1995 reached 7.3 million households. The company planned to invest between 350 billion and 700,000 billion pesetas within the next 15 years in cable TV and Multimedia services, depending on how the market developed. Three major issues remained to be resolved. First, Telefónica needed to find out whether there was any demand among Spanish customers for services such as video on demand, video games, home shopping, educational programs, etc. Second, Telefónica needed software to integrate the different services provided over the cable TV system. Third, regulatory issues were still unresolved because the law for cable TV was under discussion.

To address the first issue, Telefónica planned to undertake a pilot test of services through cable TV. This was scheduled for spring 1995 and included 100 households in the north of Madrid. Regarding the second issue, Telefónica was in contact with several companies as potential allies. Finally—and most importantly—cable TV laws were under revision. Telefónica might have the opportunity to cover the whole of the Spanish market. The Spanish government planned to allow two operators into the cable market. It was possible that Telefónica would receive a national license while regional operators would be allowed to compete with Telefónica in locally defined markets. The regional operators would acquire their license through a public bidding contest, and six months after the license was allocated, Telefónica would be allowed to offer services by cable. The competitors saw this as an unfair advantage for Telefónica, as they could not possibly install a cable system in 6 months and also they were not allowed to offer telephone services over TV cable until 1998.

Public Telephony included all those activities related to the installation and operation of public telephone booths, pay phones, and telephone centers. By the end of 1994, 53,147 telephones and 1,315 telephone centers were available.

The Information and Advertising division published telephone directories and supplied information and advertising services. In 1994, 19 phone di-

C-269

rectories were published, representing an edition of more than nine million volumes.

Besides preparing the group by expanding into new businesses, Telefónica also expanded by investing heavily in Latin America and forming a strategic alliance with Unisource.

TELEFÓNICA INTERNACIONAL DE ESPAÑA, S.A. (TI)

As of December 1994, TI was the largest subsidiary of Telefónica. It generated profits of US$192 million and had assets of US$7.63 billion. Seventy-six percent of TI's capital was held by Telefónica and the remaining 24 percent was owned by the Spanish government. The division incorporated all of Tele-

fónica's international investments. At the end of 1994 these were predominantly equity positions in Latin American telephone companies (Peru, Chile, Colombia, Argentina, Venezuela, and Puerto Rico). Furthermore, TI had small investments in Romania, Portugal, and the United States (Exhibit 6).

TI was the division in charge of the internationalization of Telefónica. The primary tasks of TI were analysing new markets, bidding on new contracts, financing, and managing the different international investments. In addition, TI attempted to take advantage of the synergies between the different investments.

TI's corporate strategy focused on the provision of telecommunication services outside of the Spanish market. The unit competed in four businesses: the privatization of basic telecommunication services, mobile telephones, international data and voice networks, and multimedia services. The operating

EXHIBIT 6 *Internationalization of Telefónica España, S.A.*
Telefónica Internacional—International Activities

Company, Dec. 94	Number of Lines in Service (000)	Number of Subscribers to Cellular Service	Number of Subscribers to Cable TV Service	Revenues '000 US$	Net Income '000 US$
TASA	2,719	92,151		2,099	392
CTC	1,545	43,350	49,407	869	249
Telefónica Peru	772	26,532	4,598	689	29
CANTV	2,334	130,651		1,164	−44
TLD				63	−1
COCELCO		18,860		18	−7
Telefónica Romania		2,768		4	1
Publiguías				65	9
Contactel		18,954		5	−3
TOTAL	7,370	333,266	54,005	4,976	625

priorities were, first, to concentrate on the business in Latin America; second, to consolidate the position in the European market; and third, to open new opportunities in the United States.

TI was a corporate center for its operating companies. It provided management systems for its companies. TI also supported the operating companies in the commercialization of new services and managed their relationships with international organizations and other operators. It administered the purchasing of supplies.

TI operated as a holding company. It had 254 employees; 71 in Spain, mainly in administrative, technical, and managerial positions, and 183 outside of Spain. Of these, 91 were active in Argentina. Of the remainder, 60 worked in Peru, 18 in Venezuela, 4 in Chile, 2 in Romania, and the rest in other countries. In total, the operating companies had about 60,000 employees, controlled more than 7 million telephone lines, and had 50,000 cellular telephone customers in rapidly growing markets.

The privatization of the basic telecommunication service, TI's most important activity, included the upgrading of existing telephone networks and the installation of new networks in developing countries. This business ranged from planning of telephone networks, laying telephone lines, and installing switching equipment, to connecting the equipment on the customer's premises. Once the technical systems were in place, the operating company ran and serviced the network. The basic service involved local, long-distance, and international calling.

Having started the 1980s with high levels of debt and stagnant economies, many of the developing nations seized on privatization as a step toward debt relief, economic reform policy, and infrastructure investments. Latin American telephone companies, which had been trapped in cycles of underinvestment and poor earnings, quickly became the first target of the region's economic revolution. However, markets in eastern Europe and Asia opened slowly as well. This allowed foreign competitors the opportunity to enter new markets.

TI held equity in several local service providers in Latin America. In Chile, it controlled CTC, which provided 90 percent of local calls in its domestic market. In Argentina, TI controlled TASA, which operated the local telephone service in Buenos Aires and the southern part of the country. In Peru, TI controlled 100 percent of local calling. Finally, in

Venezuela it participated in the Venworld consortium, led by GTE with AT&T. In these markets, TI faced no direct competition, as it either had a monopoly granted by the government or dominated the market.

In most Latin American countries, long-distance services were provided by the same companies that provided local calling services. TI was active in the long-distance markets of Argentina, Venezuela, Peru, and Chile. In addition, TI owned TLD in Puerto Rico, which provided long-distance calls between the island and the continental United States, and international connections with the rest of the world, without operating a local network. In Chile and Puerto Rico, TI's operation faced competition. Its subsidiary CTC competed with Entel-Chile, Chilesat, and VTR, among others. In Chile, Entel dominated the market for long-distance calls. Initially, the company belonged to TI, but TI had to sell the operation in response to the demands of the national government. CTC was investing to build and expand its position in this market.

TI operated cellular networks in Chile, Argentina, Colombia, Peru, and Venezuela. In several of these markets the operating companies were in direct competition with national consortia and subsidiaries of North American telephone companies. Bell South operated cellular telephone networks in Argentina, Chile, and Venezuela. GTE operated a cellular telephone network in Argentina. Other American companies also participated in cellular networks in Latin America.

International voice and data transmission included the planning and operation of international communication networks. TI was active in this market in Argentina, Chile, Peru, and Puerto Rico.

The multimedia business included operations that were related to telecommunications, such as the publishing of yellow pages or the provision of cable TV. TI controlled yellow pages companies in Chile, Venezuela, and Argentina. In addition, it held stakes in a Chilean and a Peruvian cable TV company.

Furthermore, the company had a stake in a Portuguese paging operation and a cellular telephone service in Romania and controlled a small equity position in a data-services provider in the United States.

These foreign investments changed the structure of the telephone industry in Latin America. Several competitors were active across different geographic markets and businesses. Besides the two European competitors, TI and France Télécom, six large North American telephone companies had invested in Latin America. Among them were AT&T; the three RBOCs, Southwestern Bell, Bell South, and Bell Atlantic; and GTE (Exhibit 7).

EMERGING INTERNATIONAL COMPETITION IN TELECOMMUNICATIONS

The telecommunications industry was internationalizing through the development of data-transmission services for multinational customers. Mobile telephone services would be provided across borders, thus increasing foreign direct investment. The Telefónica group was one of several operators that were competing in different national markets.

In the future, Telefónica planned to compete on the European level, and with TI in Latin America. At the same time, it would seek cooperation with other companies to access new technology and enter new markets.

Telefónica's management expected that future competitors would have different characteristics. Local competitors would limit their operations exclusively to their home markets. They would lose customers in their home markets to outside competitors and lose importance from a global perspective. The global operators would internationalize and try to enter new geographic markets and offer new international services. They would seek advantages from coordination across national markets. However, only the largest telephone companies had the potential to become international players. Only they had the resources to expand and compete in a large number of geographic product markets.

Nippon Telegraph and Telephone Corporation (NTT)

NTT was the largest telephone company in the world. In 1994, it generated sales of approximately US$69 billion and profits of US$500 million, with US$122 billion in assets. NTT had 215,629 employees at that time. The Ministry of Finance held more than 65 percent of the company's shares.

NTT was established in 1952 as a state-owned public telecommunications corporation in Japan. In 1986 it was privatized as the largest telecommunications company in the world in terms of revenues and local customers. NTT and its subsidiaries provided a wide range of telecommunications services. Telephone services accounted for 73 percent of 1994 revenues. The company also leased circuit services, telegraph and telex services, and paging services. The company had eight subsidiaries in Japan and 136 subsidiaries overseas, which focused mainly on international calling services.

NTT operated in a competitive home market. By mid-1991, 67 new entrants were providing long-distance, rural, mobile, and international telecommunications services. To respond to these competitive pressures, NTT decided to reformulate its strategy as an international company. It subsequently invested US$2 billion in Thailand and negotiated its entry into the Worldpartners alliance with AT&T.

AT&T

With US$79 billion in assets, US$75 billion in sales, US$4.7 billion in profits, and about 305,000 employees, AT&T was the largest telephone company in the United States. It provided telecommunication services and products as well as network equipment and computer systems. Its customers were businesses, consumers, other telecommunication service providers, and government agencies. AT&T had joint ventures and alliances with prominent telecom companies in most major foreign markets. Telecom services generated more than 58 percent of the company's revenues. About 10 percent of its revenues were generated outside of the United States. It had subsidiaries in more than 50 countries, most of them active in the international voice-transmission business.

AT&T had a long tradition as an operator of telephone systems. It had operated in the industry since its incorporation in 1885. In its first 50 years, in addition to making telephone services available to virtually every American, AT&T had established its first subsidiaries and alliances with companies in more than a dozen countries. Before its divestiture of the Regional Bell Operating Companies (RBOCs) at the end of 1983, AT&T had grown to more than one million employees and its stock had been by far the most widely held in the United States. In 1984, af-

EXHIBIT 7 *Internationalization of Telefónica España, S.A. Competition in Latin America*

	Local Telephone Services	Long-Distance Telephone Services	International Telephone Services	Mobile Telephone Services	Data Transmission Services	Multimedia Services
Telefónica Internacional	South-Argentina Chile Peru Venezuela	Argentina Chile Peru Puerto Rico Venezuela	Argentina Chile Peru Puerto Rico Venezuela	Argentina Chile Colombia Peru Venezuela	Argentina Chile Colombia Peru Venezuela	Argentina Chile Peru soon Argentina
Head-to-Head Competition		Chile Entel, and others Puerto Rico AT&T, MCI, Sprint	Chile Entel, and others all AT&T, MCI, Sprint	Argentina AT&T, Bell-South, GTE Chile BellSouth Venezuela BellSouth	Argentina IMPSAT & others Colombia IMPSAT & others Venezuela IMPSAT & others	Argentina TCI & others Chile TCI & others
Presence In Latin America	North-Argentina France Télécom & Stet Mexico France Télécom & Southwestern Bell	North-Argentina France Télécom & Stet Mexico France Télécom & Southwestern Bell	North-Argentina France Télécom & Stet Mexico France Télécom & Southwestern Bell	Dominican Republic GTE Mexico Bell Atlantic, Bell-South, Iusacell, Motorola Uruguay BellSouth Colombia McCaw & AT&T		

C-273

ter separation from the Baby Bells, AT&T concentrated on long-distance and international calling.

By 1994, AT&T's home market was highly competitive. Two companies, MCI and Sprint, competed for market share in long-distance and international calling. Recently, AT&T had acquired McCaw, the largest cellular telephone services provider in the United States. From this acquisition, it had gained access to three million cellular telephone service subscribers in 12 states. The company was also exploring opportunities in multimedia and cable TV services. In Latin America, AT&T competed in three counties. In Argentina, it owned 10 percent of CTI, a provider of cellular telephone services. CTI held a license for all of Argentina, except the Buenos Aires area. In Brazil, AT&T held 47 percent of AT&T network systems. In Venezuela, it had three investments: it held a 5 percent stake in the Venworld consortium, of which GTE and TI were also partners, and operated two subsidiaries, AT&T-Erlom and AT&T Telesis. AT&T also participated in several consortia investing in submarine fiber optic cables. However, the company did not have a very strong position in Latin America, as none of the companies played a decisive role in its market, nor did AT&T have a stake large enough to exercise control.

Deutsche Bundespost Telekom (DBT)

DBT provided telephone services in Germany. In 1994 it reorganized its mobile telephone services and separated them into an independent company, DT Mobil. Voice telephony generated about 80 percent of DBT's US$39.5 billion in revenues in 1994. The company had 225,000 employees who operated about 39.2 million access lines and assets valued at US$107 billion. Profits of US$0.8 billion made DBT the best-performing government-controlled enterprise. DBT also offered a variety of value-added services such as video text, electronic mail, and telemetry. None of these services had achieved their market penetration goals.

Internationally, DBT was expanding into western and eastern Europe through alliances. As a result of its control over the former East German telephone authority, DBT was a member of both major satellite organizations, Intelsat in the west and Interspudnik in the east. It had agreements with the national carriers of Poland, the Czech Republic, and

Hungary for building an eastern European fiber optic cable. It was bidding against BT and France Télécom for a digital cellular license in Hungary. DBT was the most important link to the telecommunications market in eastern Europe. Through its strategic alliances with France Télécom, DBT was also a key player in western Europe.

France Télécom

In 1994, France Télécom was the second largest telecommunications company in Europe, with US$51 billion in assets, sales of US$23.8 billion and profits of 4,804 million francs. The company's 154,548 employees managed 30.8 million telephone lines. The company operated a cellular network with 430,000 subscribers. It provided basic telephone services, cellular telephone services, data-transmission services, and cable TV. In addition, it operated a large video text network which provided value-added services to households (Multitel). Telephone services and related activities accounted for about 84 percent of 1994 revenues; dedicated lines and networks, 7 percent; mobile services, 2 percent; and information services, another 2 percent. Over 95 percent of the company's revenues was generated in France, with the majority coming from the provision of basic telephone services.

Since the beginning of 1991, France Télécom had evolved from a publicly administered government apparatus, DGT (Direction Générale des Telecommunications), into a state-owned company. The Ministry of Finance had given it control over budgets and employee compensation. In addition, it was allowed to develop its corporate strategy independently of the Ministry.

Since its incorporation, the company had made several international investments in eastern Europe, Asia, and Latin America and had negotiated a strategic alliance with DBT.

Its Latin American investments included partial ownership of two companies. In Mexico, it owned part of Telmex, the operator of basic telephone services in Mexico. Telmex itself was one of the 20 largest telephone operators in the world and was expected to grow rapidly with the development of Mexico. In Argentina, France Télécom owned part of Telecom Argentina, which operated the basic telephone services in the northern half of the country.

British Telecom (BT)

BT provided domestic and international telephone services in the United Kingdom. The company generated a net income of US$2.8 billion with sales of about US$22 billion. Besides basic telecommunication services, BT provided global communication-related services. Of its 156,000 employees, 2,100 were employed outside the United Kingdom. In 1994, domestic telephone calls accounted for 38 percent of revenues, telephone line leasing generated 18 percent, international calling generated 14 percent, and supplying equipment for customers' premises provided 7 percent. The remaining 35 percent was generated by other activities.

At the domestic level, BT was becoming more market-driven and efficient. It had a large advantage over other European companies because of the early liberalization of the British market.

BT's effort at developing customer-oriented services was reflected in an attempt to build its international business. For example, in November 1990 it launched an international virtual private network service that linked North America and Europe. In order to coordinate its U.S. activities, BT had merged all U.S. subsidiaries into a single unit called BT North America. In addition, the company acquired a large stake in McCaw, the leading cellular telephone services provider in the United States.

In 1992, BT changed its international strategy dramatically. First it sold its stake in McCaw Cellular to AT&T for US$1.8 billion, and then it announced a US$4.3 billion strategic alliance with MCI, buying 20 percent of the company. BT's strategy was to become one of the two or three global carriers by the end of the decade.

GTE

GTE corporation was not one of the RBOCs, but had always been an independent telecommunication company. It had more than 111,000 employees. With assets of more than US$42 billion, it generated sales of US$20 billion and profits of US$2.4 billion. GTE's telephone operations served approximately 17.4 million access lines in 28 states throughout the United States.

Its telephone activities generated about 80 percent of revenues in 1994. Telecommunication products

and services provided the bulk of the remaining 20 percent. Within the American market for cellular telephone services, the company held second place in terms of market share. Its U.S. telephone operations were undergoing restructuring. For example, in 1993 GTE cut 26,000 salaried employees from its payroll. Also, it consolidated its local networks, selling US$1.1 billion worth of local exchange properties, which included about 500,000 customer access lines in nine states. GTE tried to "cluster" its operations and focus on regions where it possessed a larger market share. The proceeds from these sales were used to reduce the company's debt.

In addition to its national operations, GTE invested internationally. It operated several cellular systems, competed in the publishing of directories, and provided related marketing and consulting services. According to a GTE top manager, the company had always been operationally decentralized, so its various units had each pursued international investment opportunities individually. The company aimed to coordinate these international investments.

GTE operated several telecommunications subsidiaries outside of its home market. In Latin America it operated in three countries. In Venezuela it led the consortium Venworld, with a 51 percent stake, and operated a cellular system. In Argentina it held 23 percent of a cellular telephone services consortium. Finally, in the Dominican Republic, GTE owned 100 percent of Codetel, also a provider of mobile cellular services.

BellSouth

BellSouth was one of the RBOCs that had been separated from AT&T at the end of 1983 in the deregulation of the U.S. telecommunications industry. It had more than 92,121 employees. With sales of US$16.8 billion and profits of US$2.1 billion, it was the largest of the seven Bell operating companies.

BellSouth competed in telecommunication services and telecommunication system products. Telecommunication network services and related activities accounted for 72 percent of its revenues. In addition, it operated directory advertising and publishing services, which generated 9 percent of its total sales. Wireless communication services accounted for another 12 percent of the company's revenues.

BellSouth's territory of nine southeastern states had outperformed the rest of the United States economically since the break-up of AT&T in 1984. As a result, there had been a strong demand for its telecommunication services throughout the 1980s. Like most of the other RBOCs, BellSouth had cut costs and had reduced the number of employees to increase efficiency and respond to increased competition in its regional market.

The company's goal was to become a leading international provider of wireless services. It invested in Europe, Asia, and Latin America. In Latin America, BellSouth provided cellular telephone services in Argentina, Chile, Mexico, Uruguay, and Venezuela.

Bell Atlantic

Bell Atlantic employed about 72,300 people in its operations. In 1994, the company generated US$13.7 billion of revenues and earned net income of almost US$1.4 billion, with US$24.3 billion in assets.

The company's main business was telecommunication services, including network and related services. A subsidiary provided wireless communication services and products. Over 90 percent of Bell Atlantic's sales and more than 95 percent of its profits were generated in the area of communications and related services.

Bell Atlantic's goal was to become a leading communications and information company. It was diversifying from its core business into wireless services, multimedia, and new geographic markets.

In Latin America, Bell Atlantic bought a 23 percent stake in Iasucell,the leading provider of cellular systems in Mexico. Due to established facilities and the cash infusion from Bell Atlantic, industry sources expected Iasucell to win Mexico's second long-distance license, to be granted in 1996.

MCI

MCI operated the second largest long-distance telephone system in the United States. The company had about 40,000 employees and assets valued at US$16 billion; it generated sales of about US$13 billion and had profits of US$582 million. The United States was its main market.

MCI provided domestic and international telecommunications services, primarily through its own microwave and fiber optics networks. The company accessed most of its customers through local interconnection facilities. These facilities were managed by local exchange telephone companies and competitive access providers, which connected the transmissions between MCI and its customers.

In 1993, MCI decided to enter the local telephone market. It planned to spend US$2 billion on the installation of local phone networks in 20 cities, including the competitive regional markets of New York, Atlanta, and Los Angeles. It had the rights for another 200 cities in the United States.

Internationally, MCI had an alliance with BT. In 1992, BT had acquired a 20 percent stake in MCI for US$4.3 billion. The two partners invested US$1 billion in a joint venture to offer worldwide network services to international corporations. In addition, MCI undertook several other direct foreign investments. In Mexico, it negotiated a US$450 million partnership with the Mexican bank Banacci to compete with Telmex. Furthermore, MCI provided digital private network services in Argentina, Brazil, Chile, Colombia, Costa Rica, Ecuador, Mexico, and Peru. In the future this could become a basis to offer international networks and to handle business customers' data and voice traffic.

Southwestern Bell

Southwestern Bell was the third RBOC active in Latin America. The company had 58,750 employees and assets worth US$24 billion. It generated a profit of $1.4 billion from US$10.7 billion in revenues. It controlled 9 million residential and 4 million business access lines in five states.

As a communications holding company, Southwestern Bell had business activities including basic telephone services, yellow pages and directory services, cellular and cable TV services, and telecommunications equipment. In 1993 the company generated more than half of its total sales in local telephone services, 25 percent in network access for other services, 10 percent in long-distance services, and 10 percent in directory advertising.

Internationally, Southwestern Bell had two investments. In Mexico, it participated with France Télécom in the privatization of Telmex, which provided local and cellular telephone services. It also operated several cable TV franchises in the United Kingdom and directory publishing in Australia and Israel.

US West

US West was a diversified global communications company engaged in telecommunications, directory publishing, marketing, and most recently, entertainment services. The company generated sales of US$11 billion and a net income of US$1.426 billion, with assets of about US$23.2 billion. The company's 61,505 employees were able to provide telecommunication services to more than 25 million residential and business customers in the 14 midwestern and western states. Directory publishing, marketing, and entertainment services were provided by other US West subsidiaries to customers both inside and outside the US West region.

The strength of US West was in the multimedia business. In 1994, the company acquired a cable TV company. It also had a joint venture with Telewest International and an alliance with TeleCommunications Inc., which is the largest U.S. cable TV company. It reached 58 million households in the United States. Furthermore, US West had a 25 percent stake in Time Warner Entertainment, a large media conglomerate.

Internationally, US West was focusing on building wireless networks, personal communication networks, and broad-band networks to deliver multimedia services. Besides operations in the United Kingdom and Japan, it had several operations in Eastern Europe. In the Czech Republic, Hungary, Russia, Slovakia, Japan, and the United Kingdom it was offering cellular services. In the United Kingdom, the company operated 23 cable TV franchises. US West also participated in data transmission services in the Czech Republic and Slovakia and provided international gateway services in Lithuania and Russia.

Pacific Telesis

Pacific Telesis was one of the seven RBOCs formed after AT&T's divestiture. It served over 22 million customers in the southwest area of the United States. With assets of US$23 billion, the company generated sales of approximately US$9 billion and a net income of US$20 million, after more than US$1 billion per year at the beginning of the 1990s. The company employed around 60,000 people.

Its other subsidiaries provided paging, cellular, and directory printing services. The company also planned to enter video and multimedia services and lobbied for a liberalization of the cable TV and telecommunications industries in its home market.

Internationally, the goal of Pacific Telesis was to be a premier provider of wireless telecommunications services in the world's most attractive markets. The company had participated in cellular and digital cellular services in Belgium, France, Germany, Portugal, Spain, Sweden, and Japan.

STRATEGIC ALLIANCES IN THE TELECOMMUNICATIONS INDUSTRY

At the end of 1994, the international telecommunication industry was characterized by the formation of strategic alliances. Many competitors were scrambling to establish cooperative agreements in the industry. More than 100 alliances were in the formation process. These alliances took different forms, from simple cooperative agreements to outright 100 percent takeovers. They involved partners from different industries: telecommunications companies, utilities, banks, and publishing houses. The partners often included domestic and international companies.

Telefónica negotiated several alliances. At the European level the company was finalizing an agreement with Unisource regarding the provision of services in the European market. Its subsidiary TI was negotiating an agreement for its operations in Latin America. Also, several of the subsidiaries were involved in negotiations. The Spanish cable TV division was dealing with several U.S. companies regarding the provision of technology.

Unisource

Telefónica was a partner in one cross-border strategic alliance. In November 1993 management had signed a letter of intent to become a partner of Unisource. Telefónica joined the alliance in July 1994, acquiring a 25 percent ownership stake. However, as of December 1994 many contractual issues still needed to be resolved.

Unisource was founded in 1992 by the PTTs from The Netherlands, Sweden, and Switzerland. The initial partners were three comparatively small telecommunications companies. Unisource was formed to compete with the large European competitors in the provision of cross-border services. It concentrated on four businesses: data transmission and the provision of services for large corporate networks, satellite services, mobile telephone services, and payment transfer services.

Unisource's most important business was the provision of border-spanning backbone networks that aimed at delivering services to corporate customers. This market was growing because deregulation of telecommunication monopolies around the world permitted international network management. In the past, services of this kind were too expensive. After years of poor service and excessive prices, potential customers were now looking forward to improved conditions.

These services responded to the needs of the multinationals and addressed the issue of seamless global communication and information technology infrastructure. The competitors were offering managed global network services that would come under the umbrella of outsourcing and facilities management. This included global coverage, one-stop shopping, and billing in the currency, language, and country of the customer's choice. It relieved the customers from having to manage their networks. These services were only now being made available, with mergers and acquisitions taking place on a global scale. There were only a few groups that would be capable of providing these services on an international scale.

The four partners envisaged transferring infrastructures to the alliance when regulation allowed them to do so. The entry of Telefónica allowed Unisource to offer its clients the best pan-European solutions available in the market. In the future, an extension of this alliance to other businesses such as international calling depended on the progress the alliance made and the development of regulation in Europe. At the same time, Unisource was negotiating an alliance with Worldpartners to provide data-transmission services globally.

The international data-transmission and global networking services industry was just taking shape. Most of the alliances were in the process of being formed, and the market for the outsourcing of corporate networks was relatively new. Most of the services were still undefined. A further liberalization and realignment could be expected. As a consequence,

new companies were expected to enter the competition. Others would be taken over or pushed out.

Alliances Competing with Unisource

Several companies were particularly aggressive in preparing to provide European and global carrier services. Among the most aggressive were AT&T, BT, MCI, Sprint, Deutsche Telekom, and France Télécom (see Exhibit 8).

At the European level, DBT and France Télécom formed the joint venture Eunetcom in 1992. Although strong, Eunetcom was regarded as a more regionally focused, newly emerging provider of global network services. Both companies were still in the process of privatization. While DBT was to be sold in 1998, there was no indication that the French government would sell its holding in France Télécom to private investors.

At the global level, three alliances were competing in this business: Worldpartners, Concert, and Atlas/Sprint. The desire to increase geographic coverage was the overriding reason for the alliance activity in this market segment. A global operator had to have a presence in most, if not all, of the major centers of industry and commerce. The formation of alliances promised dense network coverage and potentially good local support in many countries—something that national operators failed to deliver before. The success of the alliances depended on how effectively they provided a solution to the problems of corporate network managers in implementing a global data networking and telecommunication strategy.

AT&T formed the Worldpartners alliance in 1993 with KDD of Japan and Singapore Telecom. Since then, Telecom New Zealand International, Telstra of Australia, and Hong-Kong Telecom had become members of the association. In order to extend its range of services to Europe, Worldpartners negotiated an alliance with Unisource (at that time still excluding Telefónica).

Worldpartners made use of the member carriers' transmission lines and switching equipment. AT&T's investments in the alliance were estimated to be worth US$450 million, US$350 million of which were channeled into Europe and US$100 million to the Pacific Rim. The investments were going into technological changes that ensured a seamless network infrastructure. For example, if Unisource joined Worldpartners, the software for the switches

EXHIBIT 8 *Internationalization of Telefónica Espanña, S.A. International Telecommunications Alliances in Corporate Communication Services*

	Worldpartners	Concert	Atlas/Sprint
AT&T	●		
British Telecom		●	
Deutsche Bundespost Telekom			●
France Télécom			●
Hong Kong Telecom	●		
KDD (Japan)	●		
MCI		●	
Nippon Information and Communication		●	
Norwegian Telecom		●	
Singapore Telecom	●		
Sprint			●
Stentor (Canada)		●	
Telecom New Zealand	●		
Telstra (Australia)	●		
UNISOURCE*	●		
Unitel (Canada)	●		

Source: *Data Communications,* November 21, 1994.
*UNISOURCE plans on taking an equity stake in AT&T Worldpartners.

connecting the transmission lines needed to be upgraded to ensure compatibility.

Concert was the main competitor of AT&T's Worldpartners. It had been formed in June 1993 by BT and MCI as an independent joint venture. BT invested US$4.3 billion in acquiring 20 percent of MCI. MCI, on the other hand, bought the majority of the assets of BT North America for US$125 million. The terms of the joint venture gave BT and MCI 75 percent and 25 percent, respectively, of Concert. The companies expected to invest US$1 billion in Concert until June 1997. These investments were to be channeled into the business and would upgrade the existing BT networks

Founded in 1994, Atlas/Sprint was a partnership among Sprint, the third largest U.S. long-distance carrier, France Télécom, and DBT. In this joint venture, each partner was to be responsible for its own region, with two other joint ventures covering the rest of Europe and the rest of the world. Like the alliance between Worldpartners and Unisource, this alliance still needed the permission of regulators in the United States and Europe.

In December 1994, none of the alliances offered global services. With the addition of Unisource as a European partner, the AT&T Worldpartners association would have the largest geographic reach—good U.S. coverage, adequate European coverage, and strong coverage in the Pacific Rim. Both Concert and Atlas/Sprint had a drawback in that they had no partner in the Pacific Rim. However, regulatory issues still needed to be resolved.

Strategic Alliance for TI

At the same time, TI was negotiating a strategic alliance for its operations in Latin America. As the Spanish government was thinking about selling its 23.8 percent stake in TI, this would allow the entry of an ally into the subsidiary of Telefónica. The alliance between Telefónica and Unisource did not include TI, so the unit was free to choose any partner.

Management's main concern was the compatibility of the future partner. It was looking for a company with similar strategic goals to become a major player in Latin America. At the same time, it was interested in gaining access to new technologies, especially in the multimedia and cellular telephone businesses. Finally, it was important for TI to play an active role in the alliance.

TI was mainly looking for a North American partner, as the United States was the market with the most highly developed multimedia services and the most competitive cellular telephone operators. Companies that seemed interested in an alliance with TI included AT&T, GTE, and the RBOCs.

Management was wondering whether TI should actually enter into a strategic alliance and with whom, what advantages this offered the company, and what the company would bring to the negotiating table. Also, it was considering whether and how this alliance could contribute to operations in Spain and Europe. Finally, it did not know what the impact of such a strategic alliance might be on the global telecommunications industry.

Jefferson-Pilot Corporation

Lew G. Brown
Michael J. Cook

University of North Carolina at Greensboro

A STRATEGIC REVIEW

David Stonecipher, president and CEO of Jefferson-Pilot Corporation (J-P), took his seat at the large conference table in the firm's corporate offices in downtown Greensboro, North Carolina. Joining him were Ken Mlekush, executive vice president for individual life insurance; Ron Ridlehuber, senior vice president for independent marketing, and Bill Seawell, senior vice president for ordinary marketing.

Stonecipher had joined J-P in late 1992, taking over as president and CEO in early 1993. He knew that J-P's board expected him to reinvigorate the financially strong company that had experienced several years of relatively lackluster sales performance. Stonecipher recruited Mlekush and Ridlehuber to join him on the management team and promoted Seawell from his position as an agency manager in J-P's career insurance sales force. He also asked a major consulting firm that specialized in working with life insurance companies to conduct a strategic marketing review of the firm.

Now, in early 1993, he had assembled his new management team to hear the consulting firm's report. He knew this report would provide a basis for the strategic decisions the group would have to make if the company were going to meet the board's and the shareholders' expectations. The managers knew that a key focus of the report and of the decisions facing them would be how J-P should structure and manage its sales force because life and annuity sales would need to grow dramatically to increase revenues significantly.

J-P distributed its individual insurance products through three separate systems: career agents, independent producing general agents, and financial institutions. J-P hired career agents and provided them with extensive training, an office, and full staff support. The company paid the agents a salary subsidy during their training year and then changed them to a commission-only basis. The agents earned a commission on the premiums each policy generated. The commission rate was higher on the first-year premium, then was reduced on renewal premiums thereafter as the policyholder renewed the policy year after year. The career agents were very loyal. In fact, the company was very selective in choosing career agents. Becoming one was difficult, and those who were successful were very proud of their position. But growth based on a career system was slow, and the costs of maintaining the sales force were high.

In early 1993, J-P had approximately 800 career agents. They sold about 90 percent of the firm's life insurance policies. On average during 1992 agents wrote about 30 policies and earned approximately $26,000 in first-year commissions (the commissions paid on the policy's first-year premium). The first-year commission rate averaged 50 percent of the first-year's premium. The average career agent earned total income, including commissions on renewal policies, in the high $40,000 range. Bill Seawell was responsible for managing the career sales force.

At the beginning of 1993, there were approximately 1,400 independent producing general agents (PGAs) distributing J-P's life and annuity products. Twelve salaried regional directors recruited about 15 to 20 PGAs each year, seeking agents who were already established in the insurance business. Although the independent agents did not work directly for J-P, the company provided extensive training and support. The PGAs allowed J-P to extend its marketing operations (in a limited way) beyond its core geographic distribution areas. Although there were more PGAs than career agents, many of them sold few J-P policies each year. They had contracts with J-P as well as with other insurance companies and could sell policies offered by any company they represented. First-year commission rates on policies PGAs sold were in the 80 to 85 percent range. These rates were higher than those for career agents because J-P did not pay any of the PGAs' expenses, as it did for career agents. Ron Ridlehuber was responsible for managing the independent sales force.

J-P also used an additional distribution channel consisting of 19 relatively small community banks and savings institutions that contracted to distribute life and annuity products. J-P designed the annuity products for these institutions and controlled pricing.

Exhibits 1 and 2 present financial data on Jefferson-Pilot. Appendices I and II present background information on the life insurance industry and Jefferson-Pilot.

David Stonecipher glanced around the conference room to make sure everyone was ready. "Well, gentlemen, let's begin."

THE CONSULTANTS' PRESENTATION

Aaron Sherman and Larry Richardson, who directed the project for the consulting firm, began the presentation.

"Gentlemen, I have given each of you a detailed report summarizing our findings. We wanted to meet with you today to present an overview of the key points and to answer any questions you have," Sherman began. "As you are aware, we began this process by holding a workshop with J-P's executives at which we asked them to rate issues the company faces. The number-one issue they identified was the fact that your annualized premiums have declined during the

past five years while most of your major competitors' revenues have grown. Although J-P has an excellent core of field and home-office people and is in excellent financial condition, our analysis highlights areas where you need to take action."

"In conducting our analysis, we looked at a group of 13 companies, 7 of which we call 'managerial peers' and 6 of which we call 'target companies.' The target companies are those you face on a day-to-day basis in competing for policyholders and new agents. Some of these operate using a 'general agent,' that is, an independent agent who is not a company employee. The managerial peer companies are those you compete with when you sell policies or recruit agents, but all of them use a career system like J-P, with agency managers who are responsible for the agents who work out of their offices. J-P has the highest rating in terms of claims-paying ability from both A. M. Best and Standard and Poor's rating services. Only 5 of the 13 peer companies have similar ratings. Some of your agents see the company's financial strength as a competitive weapon, while some others question whether the company has been too conservative. This overhead [Exhibit 3] presents a summary of your operating performance over the 1987–91 period as compared with the 13 companies. As you can see, premium income and net gain before dividends have grown more slowly than the target group's average but faster than the managerial peers' average. Over this same period, the number of J-P's career-ordinary life agents has shrunk from 1,186 to 546. As a result, you have seen a decline in the percentage of your total premium income coming from life insurance. This results also from a decline in the number of policies written and in the face amount per policy. It also appears that the productivity of your agents has lagged behind competitors. Additionally, you rely heavily on the business you develop in North and South Carolina and Virginia, as this overhead indicates" [Exhibit 4].

"Next, we looked at your customers. This overhead [Exhibit 5] first compares J-P and the peer groups on the basis of premium per policy and average size per policy. Then, we break down your customers into male, female, and juvenile groups. As you can see, J-P has a lower premium per policy, average size policy, and premium per $1,000 coverage than do the peer companies. As with the peers, however, your typical customer is a male, under 35 years old, who is employed in a professional or executive

EXHIBIT 1 *Consolidated Statements of Income*
Jefferson-Pilot Corporation and Subsidiaries

(Dollar Amounts In Thousands Except Per Share Information)	Year Ended December 31		
	1990	1991	1992
Revenue			
Life premiums and other considerations	$238,326	$230,369	$230,034
Accident and health premiums	375,872	382,624	383,552
Casualty and title premiums earned	$47,078	45,270	44,815
Total premiums and other considerations	661,276	658,263	$658,401
Net Investment income	342,053	352,772	360,882
Realized investment gains	28,201	33,963	48,170
Communications operations	127,330	125,045	129,734
Other	3,753	3,433	5,142
Total Revenue	1,162,613	1,173,476	1,202,329
Benefits and Expenses			
Death benefits	111,444	104,131	105,013
Matured endowments	5,223	4,455	4,576
Annuity benefits	13,903	14,912	15,054
Disability benefits	1,224	1,151	1,185
Surrender benefits	59,297	47,174	38,485
Accident and health benefits	322,922	318,876	317,350
Casualty benefits	34,605	36,657	30,025
Interest on policy or contract funds	89,651	93,995	94,106
Supplementary contracts with life contingencies	4,997	5,346	5,637
(Decrease) in benefit liabilities	(10,050)	(764)	(1,292)
Total benefits	633,216	625,933	610,139
Dividends to policyholders	16,950	16,598	16,997
Insurance commissions	63,396	57,237	54,382
General and administrative	125,101	124,470	128,501
Net (deferral) of policy acquisition costs	(15,745)	(12,214)	(11,536)
Insurance taxes, licenses and fees	22,750	24,351	24,660
Communications operations	95,356	92,334	93,560
Total Benefits and Expenses	941,024	928,709	916,703
Income before income taxes	221,589	244,767	285,626
Income taxes (benefits)			
Current	68,031	77,839	88,889
Deferred	(4,079)	(8,759)	(6,501)
Total Taxes	63,952	69,080	83,388
Net Income	$157,637	$175,687	$203,238
Net Income Per Share of Common Stock	$2.94	$3.42	$3.99

Source: Jefferson-Pilot Annual Report, 1992.

C-28

position. Your career agents sell 91 percent of your policies, but the policies they sell are smaller in terms of size and premium than those sold by your PGAs."

"Because adult males account for a little over half of your policies and 70 percent of your premiums, we wanted to look more closely at this group. This overhead [Exhibit 6] shows the occupation, age, and income distribution for your male customers and those of the peer companies. Although we saw earlier that your typical customer is under 35 years old,

EXHIBIT 2 *Jefferson-Pilot Segment Information*

(Dollars in Thousands)	1990	1991	1992
Revenue			
Life insurance	$946,262	$956,426	$965,862
Other insurance	55,164	53,472	53,907
Communications	127,330	125,045	129,734
Other, net	33,857	38,533	52,826
Consolidated	$1,162,613	$1,173,476	$1,202,329
Income before income taxes			
Life insurance	$179,725	$202,349	$217,635
Other insurance	6,576	919	7,820
Communications	16,902	18,023	24,262
Other, net	18,387	23,476	35,909
Consolidated	$221,589	$244,767	$285,626
Identifiable assets at December 31			
Life insurance	$4,132,811	$4,535,398	$4,817,482
Other insurance	136,449	147,309	158,741
Communications	111,130	102,836	99,938
Other, net	74,518	139,677	159,676
Consolidated	$4,454,908	$4,925,220	$5,235,837
Depreciation and amortization			
Life insurance	$ 5,031	$ 5,741	$ 6,055
Other insurance	155	209	194
Communications	9,980	10,013	8,425
Other, net	324	327	172
Consolidated	$15,490	$16,290	$14,846

Source: Jefferson-Pilot Annual Report, 1992.

you will note that the peer companies have larger percentages of their customers in this group and that you have a higher percentage of your customers over 45 years old. This would suggest that you should have higher premiums per policy, yet your premiums per policy are lower in both the younger and older groups and overall. Our analysis indicates that your typical male customer has a median income of $37,500."

"Why do you think our premiums are typically lower than those of the peer companies?" Ken Mlekush asked.

"That's a good question, Ken," Richardson responded. "Our feeling is that the lower premiums are the result of your company's concentration in the Southeast, where incomes are generally lower than in the Northeast. A number of the peer companies have a major presence in the Northeast. Also, some of your agents may not be capitalizing on the op-

portunities in their markets, but we believe the regional difference is the key factor."

"If that answers your question, Ken, we'll move on to our discussion of your products," Sherman resumed. "Our next overhead [Exhibit 7] presents an analysis of J-P's product mix, based on first-year commissions, as compared with the peer companies. As the exhibit shows, J-P has been steadily selling less life insurance, down from 76 percent of first-year commissions to 63 percent, just since 1989. The other companies' life insurance shares have held relatively constant over this time. Your salespeople are selling considerably more disability income and health insurance and annuities than are the other companies."

"Why do you think our agents are selling more annuities and disability income policies?" David Stonecipher asked.

"Our experience indicates that agents find it easier to sell disability income and annuities as com-

EXHIBIT 3 *Jefferson-Pilot's Summary of Operations 1987–1991*

(Dollar Amounts in Millions)	1987	1988	1989	1990	1991
Premiums and annuity considerations	$648.1	$718.0	$716.3	$727.2	$768.9
Net investment income	250.1	295.3	313.0	326.6	338.7
Other income	32.0	25.8	24.1	28.0	26.8
Total income	930.2	1,039.1	1,053.4	1,081.8	1,134.4
Total expenses	802.3	916.8	890.0	896.9	930.6
Net gain before dividends	127.9	122.3	163.4	184.9	203.8
Dividends to policyholders	18.8	25.3	24.7	23.8	22.5
Net gain after dividends	109.1	96.9	138.7	161.1	181.3

(Dollar Amounts (in Millions)	Change from 1987–1991			Average Annual Percent Change		
	J-P	Target Group Average	Managerial Peers Average	J-P	Target Group Average	Managerial Peers Average
Premiums and annuity considerations	$120.8	$850.9	$3,182.0	4.4%	7.5%	11.7%
Net investment income	88.6	371.7	723.4	7.9%	9.1%	6.2%
Total income	204.2	796.5	3,590.1	5.1%	4.7%	8.6%
Deductions	(128.3)	(528.9)	(3,337.8)	(3.8)%	(3.5)%	(8.8)%
Net gain before dividends	75.9	267.6	252.3	12.4%	14.4%	6.3%

Source: Jefferson-Pilot.

pared to life insurance," Sherman answered. "Consumers can understand these policies better and salespeople find them easier to explain. Thus, the salespeople go for the easy sale. What is more important to understand, however, is that it is unusual for a company with a large career sales force to stress universal life. Whole-life policies provide more support for the field sales force because consumers tend to keep the policies in force longer and the renewal premiums are higher."

"How do our salespeople feel about the products we give them to sell?" Bill Seawell asked.

Larry Richardson responded by presenting an overhead (Exhibit 8). "This overhead summarizes our findings on that question. As you can see, relative to the norm for other companies we have surveyed, your agents were less pleased with the variety of products and were significantly less pleased with new product development. They also seemed to feel that the company is not as market driven as it should be."

"Larry, while we are on the subject of how the salespeople feel, how did we stack up relative to recruitment and retention of the sales force?" Ron Ridlehuber wondered.

"That's an important question, Ron. Our study shows that only 35 percent of J-P's new agents made it through the first year, 15 percentage points below the industry average, and only 24 percent made it through the first two years. Moreover, only 7 percent stay more than four years."

"This overhead [Exhibit 9] summarizes your situation pretty well. The first part of the overhead shows that in 1991, recruits represented 48 percent of your base sales force, as compared with 29 percent and 38 percent for the two peer groups. Further, as we've noted, your base sales force has been declining while your peers' sales groups have been stable or increasing. Likewise, your turnover rates have been consistently higher than your peers'. Finally, the overhead shows that only 35 percent of your sales force has been with you more than five years as compared with

EXHIBIT 4 *Jefferson-Pilot 1991 Market Share for Selected States*

	J-P Share of Ordinary Life Insurance			J-P's Ordinary Life Premiums (000)
	% Premium	% Issues	% In-Force	
Core Southeastern states:				
North Carolina	3.97%	2.86%	3.57%	$ 63,794
South Carolina	2.08	1.62	1.86	15,884
Virginia	0.94	0.54	0.88	13,017
Other major Southern states:				
Texas	0.58	0.36	0.50	19,368
Florida	0.37	0.19	0.35	10,268
Georgia	0.59	0.39	0.55	8,785
Tennessee	0.57	0.30	0.52	5,865
Louisiana	0.51	0.52	0.55	4,352
Alabama	0.36	0.07	0.28	3,108
Mississippi	0.63	0.29	0.68	2,794
Kentucky	0.33	0.35	0.31	2,181
Outside the South:				
Virgin Islands	3.73	0.60	3.28	433
Puerto Rico	2.58	1.15	1.89	3,853
California	0.07	0.03	0.05	3,738
U.S. Total	**0.32%**	**0.20%**	**0.29%**	**$175,446**

Source: Jefferson-Pilot.

46 percent and 40 percent for the two comparison groups. And after five years, we expect agents to be in their most productive period."

"Larry, what did you determine about our agents' productivity versus the peer groups'?" David Stonecipher asked.

"We looked closely at the issue of productivity. We found that J-P agents earned on average lower first-year commissions (not including renewal commissions) in each year as compared with the peers. Your base sales force had average first-year commissions of about $22,000 versus $31,000 for the target group and almost $25,000 for the managerial peer group. When we looked at number of policies sold, we also found that your agents sold fewer individual life policies."

"Do you have any ideas as to why our productivity is lower, Larry?"

"Yes, David. Although there are many factors that affect productivity, it seems to the project team that J-P's production standards are low compared to the peers' standards. This may cause more experienced

agents to place less business with J-P. They may meet their performance goals with you and then place other business with other firms in order to meet goals there."

"There is also evidence that the agents feel that the production levels are too low. As this overhead [Exhibit 10] shows, your managers believe that they help agents set high but attainable goals, yet slightly less than half of the agents feel that way. In looking at the validation requirements, the performance standards that first-year agents must meet, 69 percent of the agents believed they were modest or too low. Finally, your agents had considerably less activities in direct mail, telephone prospecting, etc., than did agents from the peer companies. Many salespeople don't like to perform these activities, but experience shows that the activities are a key part of building a clientele."

"Your managers and agents also seem to have different perspectives on what is required of new agents. This overhead [Exhibit 11] indicates that over 90 percent of your managers felt they give a realistic pic-

EXHIBIT 5 *Comparison of Premiums and Average Size Per Policy*

PREMIUM/POLICY SIZE

	Jefferson-Pilot	Target Group	Managerial Peers
Premium per policy	$889	$1,211	$966
Average size policy	$101,470	$126,940	$91,580
Premium per $1,000	$8.76	$9.54	$10.55

Percent of Policies (Premium Per Policy)

CUSTOMER DEMOGRAPHICS

	Jefferson-Pilot	Target Group	Managerial Peers
Male	51%	57%	53%
	($1,213)	($1,567)	($1,257)
Female	38	33	36
	($639)	($879)	($744)
Juvenile	11	10	11
	($233)	($255)	($303)

BY WHOM SOLD

	Full-Time Agents	PGAs
Percent of policies	91%	9%
Premium of policy	$837	$1,439
Average size policy	$100,920	$127,580
Premium per $1,000	$8.29	$11.28

Source: Jefferson-Pilot.

C-287

ture of an agent's career to an agent they are recruiting, yet only 32 percent of the agents felt that way. Moreover, when we asked the managers which activities they required of a new agent prior to signing a contract with them, we got a very different set of responses than we got when we asked the new agents the same question. Seventy-three percent of your new hires have not been full-time life agents previously, so it is not hard to understand that they might not fully understand what being a career agent requires."

"How did we compare as far as marketing costs, Aaron?"

"Ken, our analysis indicates that your marketing costs are generally in line with the managerial peer group. As you know, because of the one-time cost of issuing a policy and the high first-year sales commission, it costs J-P about $1.65 for each $1.00 of premium income in the first year. In other words, you lose $.65 for every dollar of premium income in the

first year. That's why it is so important to keep policies on the books. The second and third years are required for the company to earn money on the policy."

"Your $1.65 figure compares with $1.66 for the managerial group, but it is higher than the target group's average of $1.45. We think that comes from your having more smaller offices. When we controlled for office size, your costs seemed to be in line. This overhead [Exhibit 12] shows the elements of your costs as compared with the peer companies. Your costs are higher for both producer (agent) compensation and management compensation due to your competitive bonus structure and your agent financing plan. Your home office expenses are probably higher simply because you are a smaller company than some of the peers, and there are certain fixed costs you have to bear. You should be able to grow and spread those fixed costs. To help you compare your agencies' costs with the peer group's, I prepared this overhead [Exhibit 13]. It shows that your agen-

EXHIBIT 6 *Analysis of Adult Male Consumer by Occupation, Income, and Age*

Adult Males
Percent of Policies
(Premium Per Policy)

OCCUPATION	Jefferson-Pilot	Target Group	Managerial Peers
Executive	37%	36%	28%
	($1,756)	($2,003)	($1,728)
Professional	33	41	28
	($1,234)	($1,651)	($1,492)
Blue Collar	21	18	38
	($710)	($884)	($772)
Clerical	9	5	6
	($866)	($1,664)	($734)
INCOME			
Under $25K	26%	14%	24%
	($625)	($582)	($603)
$25K–49.9K	45	41	51
	($841)	($811)	($956)
$50K or over	29	45	25
	($2,421)	($2,400)	($2,541)
AGE			
Under 35	39%	47%	47%
	($561)	($671)	($688)
35–44	31	32	27
	($1,169)	($1,647)	($1,034)
45 or over	30	21	26
	($2,056)	($3,536)	($2,494)

Source: Jefferson-Pilot.

cies are on average about one-third the size of the average peer agency."

"How do our agents feel about their compensation, Larry?"

"Bill, I prepared this overhead to summarize our findings on that point [Exhibit 14]. As you can see, your full-time agents are below the norm in every category for all agents in our survey. On the other hand, your managers are above the norm in each category except for how secure they feel about their income."

"David, I think that about covers the points we wanted to present at this time. We will, of course, be available to answer additional questions you have as you proceed with your planning," Larry concluded.

"Thank you, Larry and Aaron. Your work will be very helpful. We'll let you go now while we continue our discussion."

OPTIONS

"Well, I don't know that any of the consultants' findings surprised us, but hearing them all together is certainly sobering," David began. "We've got our work cut out for us if we are going to achieve the growth and profitability goals the board has set. It wants us to grow earnings per share by 10 percent per year and achieve above average returns on capital. Ken, what do you think our options are?"

"David, even if we choose the option of continuing to have the same kind of company we've had—that is, one focused primarily on using the career agent to sell our products—we've got to make a number of changes to address the issues in the report. We seem to be in a cycle of declining performance. Fewer agents lead to less new business. This causes an expense problem. Due to that problem, we don't

EXHIBIT 7 *Product Mix Trends*
(Percent of First-Year Commission)

	1989	1990	1991
Jefferson-Pilot			
Life	76%	70%	63%
DI/health	9	12	12
Annuities	11	13	17
Investment products	4	5	7
Group	0	0	0
Total	100%	100%	100%
Target Group			
Life	78%	75%	75%
DI/health	7	6	6
Annuities	4	6	7
Investment products	5	6	8
Group	7	7	5
Total	100%	100%	100%
Managerial Agency Peers			
Life	76%	78%	77%
DI/health	5	5	5
Annuities	8	9	9
Investment products	3	3	4
Group	7	6	4
Total	100%	100%	100%

Source: Jefferson-Pilot.

do the things we need to do to develop competitive products. It's a vicious cycle. Don't you agree, Bill?"

"Yes, Ken. But I think it is important for us to remember that our career-agent system is our key strength. We are known as a company because of that system. We have many long-term, loyal agents. As you know, my father worked here and was in charge of our career agents. We need to improve the quality of our recruits, train them better, and keep them with us. If we can do those things, we will grow faster and be more profitable."

"That's true, Bill," Ron joined in, "but it seems to me that we need to look more closely at complementing the career system by increasing our empha-

EXHIBIT 8 *Sales Force's Ratings of J-P's Products*
(Percent of Agents Agreeing)

Agents' Overall Assessment of Companies' Products	Jefferson-Pilot	Norm
I am pleased with the variety of products our company offers.	66%	78%
I am satisfied with our company's development of new products.	33	65
Our company is market driven, responding to the needs of its target market with appropriate products and services.	25	66

Source: Jefferson-Pilot.

EXHIBIT 9 *Sales Force Recruitment and Retention*

RECRUITS AS A PERCENT OF BASE FORCE

	Rate	No. of Recruits	Target Group	Managerial Peers
		Jefferson-Pilot		
1991	48%	280	29%	38%
1990	58	378	31	41
1989	34	316	30	40
1988	40	459	30	45
1987	42	501	33	41

PERCENT CHANGE IN BASE FORCE

	Jefferson-Pilot*	Target Group	Managerial Peers
1991	−6%	−1%	−1%
1990	−11	+	2
1989	−31	+	1
1988	−2	+	9
1987	−2	1	6

TURNOVER RATE

1991	36%	24%	28%
1990	44	24	28
1989	48	23	28
1988	30	23	25
1987	31	24	25

DISTRIBUTION OF SALES AGENTS BY YEARS OF SERVICE

Years of Service

1	35%	24%	29%
2	15	14	15
3	10	9	9
4	5	7	7
5+	35	46	40

Source: Jefferson-Pilot.

*The field force has declined from 1,161 to 546 full-time agents.

$^+$Less than $\frac{1}{2}$ of −1 percent

sis on the independent agent. We have many independent agents now, and the report shows that they are very productive. But they have never been the focus of our system. Under a new system we would contract with existing insurance agents, allowing them to offer our products. This avoids the problem of having to hire and train new recruits, and it would allow us to expand our geographic coverage more quickly. Further, we would not have to pay the office costs and associated salaries. We could pay these independent agents on a commission-only basis. Instead of using our 12 regional directors to recruit, we could license independent marketing organizations to recruit for us, with them earning an override commission on sales their agents made."

"Ron, I know you used this kind of system at Southland, but it would be such a radical change for J-P," Bill responded. "If you increased the size of our sales force substantially by using independent agents, I'm not sure how our career force would react. I'm afraid they'd be terribly threatened. And the folks in the home office are used to working with career agents.

EXHIBIT 10 *Results of Agent Survey–Production Goals*

**In Our Agency, a Good Job Is Done of Helping Agents
Set Challenging but Attainable Production Objectives**

	Percent Agreement
Agency manager	88%
Sales manager	73
Agent	49
Norm for FT agent	52%

**If Validation Requirements Were a Production Level
Goal Toward Which I Was Working, I Would See It As:**

	Jefferson-Pilot	Target Group	Managerial Peers
Challenging	30%	40%	48%
Modest	51	35	33
Too low	18	23	14
Too high	1	2	5

In The Past Month, How Many:

	Jefferson-Pilot	Target Group	Managerial Peers
Prospects have you mailed to	99	231	278
Prospects have you phoned	113	211	147
Cold calls have you made	41	74	63
Appointments have you had	29	49	41
Fact-finders have you completed	22	17	17
Closing interviews have you done	17	18	18

Source: Jefferson-Pilot.

C-29

The independents would not be loyal to the company. We would have less control over what they sell and over the quality of their work with policyholders. And can you imagine what will happen the first time one of our career agents runs into an independent agent trying to sell the same product to the same customer!"

"David, you asked about options," Ken continued. "I guess this exchange points out that we could continue with a predominantly career-based system, move to a predominantly independent system, or have a combination of the two approaches. We're going to have to make significant changes under any of the options, and I'm sure there will be problems we'll have to address. A final growth option, of course, is to acquire other insurance companies. We certainly have the financial strength to do that, but even then we are going to have to address the issue of how we distribute and how we sell our products to our policyholders."

"Yes, Ken, distribution is a key issue. I can see that there are many issues we need to think carefully about before we make a decision. Here's what I'd like for you to do. I'd like for each of you independently to consider our situation and develop recommendations as to how we should proceed. I'd like to meet again in two weeks to hear your presentations. I'll call you to set up a specific time once I check my calendar."

APPENDIX I–THE LIFE INSURANCE INDUSTRY

Life Insurance

People buy life insurance for many reasons, but mainly to provide financial protection for their families if the policyholder should die prematurely. Life insurance provides support for the insured's survivors

EXHIBIT 11 *Results of Agent Survey—Precontract*

In Our Agency, New Agents Are Given a Realistic Picture of the Agent's Career

	Percent Agreement
Agency Manager	100%
Sales Manager	93
Agent	32
Norm for FT agent	39%

Managers: Which Activities Do You Typically Require of Producers Prior to Contract?

	Jefferson-Pilot	Target Group	Managerial Peers
Learn a sales talk	100%	63%	83%
Make joint calls	93	57	60
Market opinion surveys	93	74	78
Complete sales	81	57	53
Basic insurance knowledge	70	79	77
Become licensed	59	82	93

Agents: Which of the Following Activities Were You Required to Complete Prior to Being Contracted?

	Jefferson-Pilot	Target Group	Managerial Peers
Market opinion surveys	64%	24%	39%
Basic insurance knowledge	51	54	51
Become licensed	49	62	66
Complete sales	47	28	27
Learn a sales talk	39	36	40
Make joint calls	30	19	18
None	8	17	12

Source: Jefferson-Pilot.

EXHIBIT 12 *Components of Marketing Costs: 1991 (Per $100 of Weighted New Premiums)*

	Jefferson-Pilot	Target Group	Peer Group
Producer compensation[1]	$61	$55	$62
Management compensation[2]	26	23	19
Field expenses paid by company[3]	37	36	43
Field benefits	17	17	24
Subtotal	**141**	**131**	**148**
Home office marketing expenses	24	14	18
Total	**$165**	**$145**	**$166**

Source: Jefferson-Pilot.

[1]Includes all compensation *other than* renewal commissions; includes first-year commissions on management personal production.

[2]Includes compensation paid to agency managers and second-line supervisors.

[3]Includes all operating expenses paid by company (e.g., clerical salary, rent, postage, telephone, etc.).

EXHIBIT 13 *1991 Average Agency Characteristics*

	Jefferson-Pilot	Peers
Manager income*	$100,913	$150,145
Agency first-year commission revenue	$247,941	$778,431
Managers' years of service	9.9	6.1
Number of agents	11.1	32.9
Number of recruits	5.7	11.2
Number of 2nd-line managers	1.5	2.2
2nd-line manager income*	$23,489	$52,075
Number of agencies	35	473

Source: Jefferson-Pilot.

*Excludes personal production.

and pays any estate obligations at the time of death; accumulates funds for retirement, emergencies, and business use; and defers or avoids income taxes. A person can use life insurance to create or add to an estate and then can protect that estate by maintaining the policy.

Historical Background Ancient Babylonians and the early Greeks developed the concept of insurance. Under Babylonian law, a person could adopt a son, raise him, and then depend on him for support in later years, thereby providing a type of retirement insurance. The Greeks belonged to various religious sects to which they paid monthly dues. As a benefit, the sect promised a decent burial according its rites, as well as money to pay the deceased's obligations. If members fell behind in their monthly premiums, they had to pay fines.

The Romans furthered the concepts of burial insurance and settlement of obligations. They began

EXHIBIT 14 *Attitudes Toward Compensation*

Full-Time Agent Responses
(Percent Agreement)

	Jefferson-Pilot	Norm
I have a secure income.	39%	46%
I have a good compensation plan.	46	58
My compensation plan is competitive.	38	49
My compensation plan is clear and understandable.	51	53
I have good fringe benefits.	51	64

Managers' Responses
(Percent Agreement)

	Jefferson-Pilot	Norm
I have a secure income.	33%	58%
I have a good compensation plan.	67	65
My compensation plan is competitive.	56	55
My compensation plan is clear and understandable.	66	57
I have good fringe benefits.	44	73

Source: Jefferson-Pilot.

C-293

to place less emphasis on the religious aspects and opened membership to the general public. They created a special society for soldiers that provided death benefits and pensions for disability or old age.

However, the development of modern insurance did not begin until the early 14th century. In 1310, the first insurance company was chartered in Flanders. Life insurance first appeared in the United States in 1759, with the formation of "The Corporation for Relief of Poor and Distressed Widows and Children of Presbyterian Ministers." This company, now Covenant Life Insurance Company, is the oldest life insurance company in continued existence in the world. In 1794, the Insurance Company of North America became the first chartered general life insurance company in the United States. In 1840, the New York State Legislature enacted a law that protected a widow's life insurance proceeds from creditors' claims, strengthening a life insurance policy's protective power. In 1859, New York State established the first state government insurance department; and, in 1869, the U.S. Supreme Court upheld states' rights to regulate insurance companies. In 1911, companies introduced the first group life insurance policies for purchase by companies for their employees. In 1944, the U.S. Supreme court held that life insurance companies were subject to federal laws because they were engaged in interstate commerce.

Classes of Life Insurance Companies offer several classes of life insurance. The classes differ in type of customers, policy amounts, cash values, methods of computing and collecting premiums, underwriting standards, and marketing methods.

Ordinary Life Insurance. Companies usually issue life insurance in amounts of $1,000 or more with premiums payable annually, semiannually, quarterly, or monthly. The ordinary department of most life insurers is their largest department, and many insurers write only ordinary life insurance. Ordinary insurance accounts for 51 percent of life insurance in force in the United States and about 76 percent of the insurance purchased annually. Term, whole life, and universal life are all types of ordinary life insurance.

Term Insurance. Term insurance is the most basic type of life insurance. Term insurance provides only temporary protection, for a specified time period, such as 1, 5, or 10 years, or until the insured reaches a specified age, such as 65. Term insurance policies provide pure protection and do not accumulate cash values or offer any savings element. Most term insurance is both renewable and convertible. "Renewable" means that the policyholder can renew the policy for additional periods without evidence of insurability. "Convertible" means that the policyholder can exchange the policy for some type of cash value life insurance with no evidence of insurability. Term life insurance premiums increase as the policyholder ages. Purchasers use term insurance for three general situations: if their income is limited, if they have temporary needs, or if they want to guarantee future insurance availability.

Term insurance has two major limitations. First, because term insurance premiums increase with age, premiums often became unaffordable at older ages. Second, because term insurance has no cash value or savings element, they do not help the insured save money for certain purposes, such as for retirement or for their children's education.

Whole Life Insurance. Whole life insurance has fixed premiums and provides lifetime protection. The most common types of whole life insurance are called ordinary life and universal life.

Ordinary life insurance has level premiums and lifetime protection to age 100. If the insured is still alive at age 100, the insurance company pays the policyowner the policy's face amount. Under an ordinary life policy, the premiums paid during the early years of the policy are higher than necessary to pay death claims, while the premiums paid during the later years are lower than necessary for paying death claims. Because of the higher-than-necessary early premiums, an ordinary life policy develops a legal reserve. The legal reserve becomes a liability item on the insurance company's balance sheet that formally recognizes the overpayment of premiums. The life insurer then has to accumulate assets to offset the legal reserve's liability.

Because the policyholder pays premiums that are larger than necessary, his or her policy develops a "cash value." Insurance companies use the cash value from their polices to make investments so they will be able to pay policy claims and also pay interest on the policyowners' savings. If the policyowner no longer wants the insurance, the policyowner can surrender the policy for its cash value. Although the cash surrender values are relatively low during the early years, they can accumulate to sizable amounts over time.

Thus, an ordinary life policy allows the insured to provide for insurance and saving needs all in one policy.

Ordinary life policies also have disadvantages. Because ordinary life insurance is relatively expensive in the early years, some policyowners can still be underinsured. Additionally, ordinary life policies have some disadvantages as savings vehicles. Insurance companies do not have to state the rate of return on the cash value specifically when they issue the policy. Rates of return are relatively low on some policies. Finally, cash values are not legally required until the end of the third year. Thus, the amount of saving during the early years is relatively small, and the policyholder can incur a substantial loss if he or she allows the policy to lapse or if he or she surrenders the policy during the early years.

Universal Life Insurance. Universal life insurance is a relatively new, rapidly growing form of whole-life insurance. Companies often sell universal life policies as investments that combine insurance protection with savings. Universal life insurance is a flexible premium deposit fund combined with monthly renewable term insurance. The policyowner pays a specified initial premium. The company credits the gross premium less expenses to the policy's initial cash value and deducts a monthly mortality charge for the pure insurance protection. The company then pays interest at a specified rate on the remaining cash value. Fundamentally, universal life insurance serves as a combination of a savings account and monthly renewable term insurance.

Universal life policies are very flexible. Policyholders can increase or decrease the premiums, skip premium payments as long as the cash value is sufficient to cover mortality costs and expenses, increase or decrease death benefits, add to the cash value at any time, and borrow money based on the cash value.

Special Purpose Policies and Riders In addition to the basic policy types, life insurance companies offer several special policies. These policies are usually combinations of policies designed to meet specific life insurance needs. Many policies are designed as inflation-era products to help policyowners cope with the need for increasing death protection and savings as the value of the dollar declines. Many of these special policies provide coverage for more than one person, usually entire families. Others provide for payment of mortgages and so forth.

Insurance companies often add supplemental agreements, called riders, to life insurance policies. Some riders add more life insurance, such as level, increasing, or decreasing term, to a basic whole-life policy. Others deal with the waiver of premium payments in the event of disability, accidental death and dismemberment benefits, and the guaranteed right to purchase additional insurance. Some riders even increase or decrease the amount of insurance to reflect cost-of-living changes measured by the consumer price index.

Annuities Annuities are another form of insurance that consumers can use to provide income. An annuity represents an investment that provides regular periodic payments for the owner's life or for a specific period. An annuity providing lifetime income is called a life annuity. A life annuity is true life insurance because it insures against outliving financial resources. Life annuities are important instruments in planning for financial security during retirement.

A consumer purchasing an annuity commits to make a specified payment each month for a specified period. Each payment adds to the annuity's cash value, and the account earns interest on that value. The owner can structure an annuity so that, at retirement, the annuity will be sufficient to make a certain monthly payment to the owner for the remainder of his or her life. Each payment has three components: interest, principal, and an insurance benefit. The interest earned declines each year as the principal is gradually liquidated through payments. Therefore, as years go by, more of the payment comes from principal and less from interest. If the owner's principal runs out before he or she dies, the payments then consist of an insurance benefit. When the owner dies, the remaining principal and accrued interest become part of his or her estate.

Life Insurance in the 1990s

Consumers purchased $1.6 trillion in life insurance in 1991, up 5.7 percent from 1990. Sales of ordinary life insurance accounted for nearly two-thirds of that amount. Purchases of whole life were 56 percent, down from 61 percent three years earlier. Universal and variable life insurance accounted for 21 percent of ordinary sales, down from a high of 40 percent in 1985.

In 1991, life insurance in force reached an all-time high, $9.98 trillion, up 6.3 percent from 1990. The average amount of life insurance per U.S. household was $102,700, some $4,300 more than in 1990. Eighty-one percent of American households owned life insurance. Approximately 70 percent of adult Americans owned some form of life insurance.

In 1991, benefit payments, excluding health insurance, reached a record $91.6 billion, up 3.6 percent. Payments to beneficiaries in 1991 totaled $25.4 billion. Companies paid about $29.6 billion to life insurance policyholders and $36.6 billion to annuity owners.

U.S. life insurance companies' assets were $1.6 trillion at year-end 1991. This was an increase of $143 billion, or 10.2 percent, from year-end 1990. Policy loans outstanding rose slightly in 1991, and totaled $66.4 billion. They accounted for 4.3 percent of assets—the lowest proportion since 1965. Life insurance companies' largest percentage increase in investments was in stocks, up 28.0 percent over year-end 1990. The net rate of investment earnings before federal taxes (excluding separate accounts) continued to decline, to 9.09 percent, the lowest since 1983.

Life Insurance Purchases in 1991

Of the nearly 30 million new life insurance policies and certificates issued during 1991, 13.5 million were ordinary policies, 112,000 were industrial policies, and 16.2 million were group certificates. The average size of the ordinary policies continued to increase. In 1981, for example, the average new ordinary policy was $30,430; by 1986, the amount had increased to $55,540; in 1990, to $76,050; and in 1991, to $77,320. A sample survey of ordinary life insurance purchased by Americans in 1991 showed that 50 percent of all new policies sold were for people between the ages of 25 and 44.

In terms of the number of policies sold, term insurance accounted for 20 percent in 1991, down from 25 percent in 1987. Variable and universal policies dropped from 26 percent of sales in 1987 to 16 percent in 1991. Traditional whole life and combination sales continued to increase, to 64 percent of policies in 1991, but were still below the 69 percent share of 1982.

Life Insurance Companies' Earnings

Life insurance companies produce revenue from two main sources: premiums paid by policyholders and earnings on investments. There is a close relationship between these income elements. Part of each

premium payment becomes available for investment. In calculating premiums, companies take into account the anticipated investment earnings, thereby reducing the price of life insurance.

In 1991, total income of all U.S. life insurance companies was $411 billion, with 64.2 percent from premium receipts and 28.9 percent from investment earnings. The remaining 6.9 percent came from other sources, including payments for supplementary contracts.

Premium receipts and annuity considerations totaled $263.8 billion. Americans spent the equivalent of 4.81 percent of total disposable income in 1991 for life insurance and annuities, compared with 5.07 percent during 1990.

Life insurance accounted for about 30 percent of all premium receipts in 1991. This proportion had declined in relation to the income received from annuities. In 1971, the proportion was 56.3 percent; by 1981 the proportion had dropped to 43.8 percent.

Ordinary policy premiums accounted for $62.8 billion, or 79.2 percent of the life insurance premiums in 1991. Most ordinary premiums were renewals. Group insurance premiums amounted to $14.3 billion, or 18 percent of all life insurance premiums, while industrial premiums accounted for $527 million, or 0.7 percent. Annuity considerations totaled $123.6 billion in 1991, down from $129.1 billion in 1990.

U.S. life insurance companies' policy reserves totaled $1.3 trillion at the end of 1991. These reserves represented the funds set aside to meet the companies' future obligations to policyholders and their beneficiaries. State laws required each company to maintain its policy reserves at a level that would assure payment of all policy obligations. Regulators calculated the reserve amount based on actuarial tables that took into account the funds from future premium payments, interest earnings, and expected mortality experience.

Life insurance companies' total reserves at the end of 1991 included $372.1 billion for life insurance policies, $38.3 billion for health insurance policies, and $894.5 billion for annuities and supplementary contracts.

Life Insurance Company Assets

In 1991, U.S. life insurance companies' assets, including those held in separate accounts, totaled

$1.55 trillion, an increase of 10.2 percent during the year, compared to an increase of 8.3 percent in the previous year. Net investments in U.S. capital markets by life insurance companies totaled $90.2 billion in 1991. Life insurance ranked second among private domestic institutional sources of funds, supplying 18.1 percent of the total funds flowing into financial markets. Companies' investments were primarily in corporate debt issues, government securities, mortgages, and preferred and common stocks.

Life Insurance Companies

In 1991, there were 2,105 U.S. life insurance companies and approximately 50,000 life insurance agents. The number of companies reached an all-time high in 1988 but had been declining steadily. Most companies that discontinued operations did so by merging with other insurers or had all their outstanding business reinsured in other life insurance companies. The remaining companies terminated for various reasons, including conversion to nonlife company status.

The majority of new companies formed in recent years remained in business. By specializing in meeting the needs of families in specific regions, many had been able to compete successfully with older and larger companies whose operations encompassed larger areas.

Trends

In the late 1970s and early 1980s, the industry had to contend with high inflation and increasing interest rates. New money market funds were paying 17 percent interest compared to only 5 percent for conventional whole life policies. Consumers shifted their insurance purchases to less expensive term insurance and invested the premiums they saved at higher rates elsewhere. Policyholders terminated their policies and took out low-rate policy loans. This aggravated insurers' liquidity problems and undermined profitability.

On the other hand, the high interest rates allowed the industry to realize higher returns on investments. As interest rates began to drop in the late 1980s, the industry once again faced financial difficulties. These problems were magnified by the real estate market's decline in the early 1990s. Many life insurance com-

panies began increasing their real estate holdings in the early 1980s in order to improve investment returns. Unfortunately, the market slowed considerably, and commercial vacancy rates rose to the 20 percent level. Many companies were stuck holding nonperforming assets.

Analysts expected competition in the life insurance segment to increase. Aging "baby boomers" would increase the demand for products that provided retirement income and health care financing. Additionally, life insurance companies would have to face competition from banks, mutual funds, and other financial institutions that were able to offer products that competed with life insurance products.

APPENDIX II–JEFFERSON-PILOT CORPORATION

History

J-P had its origins in the Worth-Wharton Real Estate & Investment Company, which was incorporated in Greensboro in 1890. In 1905, the owners changed the name to Southern Life and Trust Company; and in 1924, the company reorganized as Pilot Life Insurance Company. A separate company, The Jefferson Standard Life Insurance Company, began operations in Greensboro in 1907. The North Carolina business and civic leaders who founded these companies believed they could meet the needs of the region better than existing competitors. They wished to keep capital in the area to support economic development.

Both companies succeeded and rapidly extended their initial reach, eventually achieving national significance. Jefferson Standard's equity interest in Pilot dated to 1931, and, in 1945, Jefferson Standard acquired all of Pilot's stock. Both companies accelerated their expansion after World War II.

The two companies were complementary. Jefferson Standard focused on a single product line, individual ordinary life insurance, while Pilot, which began as an ordinary life company, entered the home service business in 1945, thus becoming a multiple-line company. The companies' distinctiveness lay in marketing. Jefferson Standard sold through company-owned regional agencies staffed with career agents, while Pilot's primary marketing channel was through independent general agencies.

With the formation in 1968 of J-P Corporation, both Jefferson Standard and Pilot became wholly-owned subsidiaries of that company. Following that, the two companies drew closer together, and, through a joint planning process, coordinated their business strategies closely. The companies jointly developed products, and each company's agents began selling the other's products. Their common interests led to the formation of subsidiaries providing services to both in investment management, data processing, pension plan sales and administration, and investor services.

As the positive aspects of the dual marketing system became evident, the owners decided to merge the two companies. On January 1, 1987, Jefferson Standard Life Insurance Company and Pilot Life Insurance Company combined to form the Jefferson-Pilot Life Insurance Corporation.

The J-P Corporation had five major business segments at year-end 1992:

- **Individual Insurance.** This segment offered life insurance, annuities, disability income, mutual funds, and 401-Ks. The primary markets were estate planning, income protection, retirement planning, and investment. Individual insurance accounted for 68.1 percent of J-P's operating profits in 1992. Over 2,200 career agents, personal producing agents, independent brokers, and managers, along with 470 home service agents and managers, 12 individual health regional sales and service offices, and 19 financial institutions distributed J-P's individual insurance products.

- **Group Insurance.** This segment offered many products and services, including employee and dependent term life, mass-marketed payroll deduction universal life, short-term and long-term disability income, dental benefits, vision benefits, accidental death and dismemberment, prescription drug benefits, and managed care. Group insurance has its primary markets in employee groups with more than 10 people, with the greatest concentration on companies with 25 to 1,000 employees. Group insurance products and services were distributed by 85 sales and service representatives, 22 regional sales and service offices, and the company's agents and independent brokers. The group insurance segment accounted for 23.3 percent of J-P's 1992 total operating profits.

- **Casualty and Title Insurance.** This segment offered commercial insurance lines such as worker's compensation, commercial property, commercial auto, and general liability. This segment also marketed personal insurance lines such as automobile, homeowner's insurance, and title insurance. Six regional sales offices and 303 professional independent agents distributed the products. This segment contributed 4.1 percent of J-P's total operating profits in 1992.

- **Communications.** This segment contained three elements: broadcasting properties, Jefferson-Pilot Sports, and J-P Data Services. J-P owned two television stations and six radio stations. Jefferson-Pilot Sports produced broadcasts of Atlantic Coast Conference and Southeastern Conference football and basketball games. J-P Data Services provided information to television and radio broadcasters, cable networks, and advertising agencies and representatives. The communications segment provided 8.3 percent of J-P's operating profits in 1992.

- **Investments.** Although this segment did not directly produce or deliver a product or service, its objective was to invest premium income. The net investment income was $361 million in 1992, despite a low interest rate.

As of December 31, 1992, J-P had approximately 3,900 employees with revenues of $1.2 billion. The average number of outstanding shares in 1992 was 51 million and these shares were held by 9,881 stockholders. Besides its executive offices in Greensboro, it also owned facilities in Colorado, Florida, Georgia, California, and Virginia. J-P held licenses to operate in 39 states, the District of Columbia, Puerto Rico, and the Virgin Islands.

(Exhibits 1 and 2 present J-P's summary financials.)

Jefferson-Pilot: 1993

On February 28, 1993, Roger Soles, J-P's president, chairman of the board, and chief executive officer for the last 25 years, retired. Soles had used a strong leadership style to guide J-P during his tenure. Decision making and management had a top-down focus, and Soles exercised a high level of control. However, revenues had been basically flat for the last five years (1988–92). Low interest rates, which affected investment earnings, and declining life insurance sales contributed to the sluggish revenues and earnings. The corporate culture also seemed resistant to change and fixed on retaining the status quo—the traditional way of doing things.

J-P's board of directors felt the company needed aggressive new leadership if the company were to be a market leader. The board selected David A. Stonecipher, previous president and CEO of Life of Georgia, to replace Soles. Stonecipher had a reputation as an aggressive, outgoing leader who was will-

ing to change and try new things. He realized that increased sales would be the key to J-P's revenue growth. With that in mind, one of his first acts was to appoint Kenneth Mlekush as executive vice president for individual insurance. Mlekush, who had previously served as president of Southland Life, brought extensive experience to the position and specialized in marketing individual life and annuity products. Ken later asked Ron Ridlehuber, who worked with him at Southland, to join J-P.

Královopolská: The Search for Strategy

Karen L. Newman
Stanley D. Nollen

Georgetown University

In early 1996, Zdeněk Pánek, the general director of Královopolská, reviewed his predecessor's words in the company's 1992 annual report.

> Management intends to concentrate its efforts on the long-term development of the company, to increase productivity to a level that is five times its current status by 1997, to increase the value of the company by 30 percent every year, and to pay dividends to its shareholders starting in 1994.

Pánek smiled. So much had changed since these words were written, just three years ago. Goals to become more productive and pay dividends were typical for many Czech companies immediately following the "Velvet Revolution" of 1989.[1] Královopolská was making the transition from central planning to market economy fairly successfully; it was among the top third of large Czech companies in business performance, Pánek thought. But after declining profits in 1992, the company reported losses in 1993 and 1994. Profits returned in 1995 but they were small (3 percent of assets) and the company's gross margin from production was negative. Pánek knew that Královopolská had to focus its business strategy, but

he was not sure how. It was critical to answer this question now because the management team he headed had just purchased 51 percent of Královopolská via a leveraged buyout. Pánek was not only the president, but now also an owner.

THE COMPANY AND ITS BUSINESS

Královopolská was a medium-sized producer of industrial equipment for a diverse range of end users. The company was located in Brno, the second largest city in the Czech Republic (population 400,000 in 1990), about 200 kilometers (120 miles) southeast of Prague. Sales revenue in 1994 was Kč 3.5 billion (about US$122 million), and employment was 3250.

Královopolská was established in 1889 at Královo Pole (King's Field) on a greenfield site as a machinery works, first making railway carriages and storage tanks, and soon adding steam boilers, woodworking machinery, and cranes. Employment was 300 to 400 people in the nineteenth century. The company's production program did not change throughout the World War I and II periods. Czechoslovakia's post-World War II government nationalized Královopolská in 1945 and enlarged it by combining six facilities in addition to the original plant in 1948. The company stopped producing railway carriages but added chemical plant equipment during the first 5-year plan imposed by the Communist government

By Karen L. Newman and Stanley D. Nollen, Georgetown University. Research for this case was supported by the Pew Foundation and Georgetown University's Center for International Business Education and Research, School of Business, and Graduate School. We are indebted to Vladimír Relich and the managers of Královopolská for their informative cooperation.

beginning in 1949. The company's product lines were expanded in 1958 with the addition of steel structures and in 1961 with water treatment plant equipment.

In 1958, the Czechoslovak government consolidated the country's chemical and food processing industries. Královopolská manufactured equipment for the industries, and in addition was given responsibility for directing and controlling the activities of other enterprises in the industries, including two research and development institutes, a design engineering firm, and a construction firm. Seven years later, in 1965, Královopolská lost its central role and its independent status when the government reorganized the chemical and food equipment industries and placed the enterprises under the control of CHEPOS [a type of holding company with an acronym from the Czech words for chemical (chemick´), food (potrava), and machinery (strojirna)]. Královopolská regained its independence from CHEPOS in 1988 but remained primarily an equipment manufacturer.

From 1958 to 1965, as the head of the Czechoslovak chemical and food equipment industries, Královopolská developed the capability to manage turnkey projects—to design, engineer, manufacture, deliver, install, and service entire water treatment and chemical manufacturing facilities in cooperation with other enterprises. The turnkey business diminished substantially in 1965. A small turnkey operation, later known as the RIA Division, survived. (RIA stands for Realizace Investičních Akcí, translated literally as "realization of investment activities," but more meaningfully rendered in the company's reports as comprehensive plant equipment delivery.)

At the time of the Velvet Revolution, Královopolská primarily manufactured equipment for the chemical industry, which accounted for half its production volume. Nuclear power stations purchased about another quarter of its output, and water treatment plant equipment and cranes and steel structures each accounted for less than 10 percent of Královopolská's production.

PRIVATIZATION

Centrally planned economies in eastern and central Europe with communist governments functioned very differently from market economies. Central planning business methods may have been well-adapted to that system, but they were not suitable for firms in market economies. Companies in eastern and central Europe had to adjust when central planning ended, and Královopolská was no exception. (Features of business under central planning are detailed in Exhibit 1). The first order of business after the Velvet Revolution was to privatize the economy.[2]

Královopolská's management urged the Ministry of Privatization to support early privatization of the company. In the words of one manager, "We wanted to be free of the state method of management as soon as possible." Initial privatization for Královopolská occurred in May 1992 during the first wave of voucher privatization. About 30 percent of the company's 1,004,000 shares were sold to individuals and investment funds (the shares began trading one year later). The National Property Fund (NPF), the state agency that held shares pending the completion of privatization, retained 66 percent of the shares. The legal status of the company changed from that of state plant (s.p.) to joint stock company (a.s.).

In March 1995 a partnership called KENOP, created by Pánek and six other managers from Královopolská, bought shares from the NPF to create a 51 percent stake to complete privatization. (Individuals held 22 percent and investment funds held the remaining 27 percent of the company's shares.)

BUSINESS CONDITIONS DURING THE TRANSITION

The transition from central planning to a market economy caused many hardships and brought severe challenges to all Czech companies. Macroeconomic conditions made business difficult. Real gross domestic product in Czechoslovakia dropped by 26 percent between the Velvet Revolution and 1993, and industrial production fell by 44 percent, thus reducing demand for the company's products from the domestic market. In 1991, the government allowed the market to set prices, and inflation soared to 58 percent. Between 1991 and 1993 short-term financing was scarce and nominal interest rates were around 14 to 15 percent. The government devalued the currency from Kč 15 per US$1 to about Kč 29 per US$1 in 1991 and pegged the exchange rate to the German mark and U.S. dollar with 60 to 40 weights. (Exhibit 2 shows the change in the Kč/US$ ratio during the years 1989 to 1995.)

EXHIBIT 1 *Business under Central Planning*

From 1946 to the end of 1989, the Czechoslovak economy was nearly totally state-owned, and mostly closed to trade and investment with the West. Most industries had only a few large enterprises, and in many instances they were monopoly producers of individual products. This meant that enterprises were typically very big (relative to the size of the market) and specialized in the production of just one product or a narrow product line. Enterprises in an industry were typically combined under a single *konzern* such as CHEPOS. The needs of the Soviet Union shaped the production program of many enterprises.

Producers in centrally planned economies typically were only manufacturing plants (an enterprise was termed a *statni podnik,* or state plant). They were producers, but they did not do other business functions such as marketing and finance. Distribution and sales were handled by separate state-owned trading companies, research and development was either centralized or assigned to a separate enterprise, and capital investment decisions were made by the state. Banks disbursed funds and collected "profits" but did not make lending decisions. There were no capital markets.

The goal of any firm, one that all managers understood, was to meet the production plan set by the central ministry. Successful managers were those who could skillfully negotiate a favorable plan and who knew how to produce the required quantity. Another goal imposed on firms by the state was to provide employment for everyone. There was little concern about costs, prices, money, or profits.

Most managers were technically trained, and all top managers were necessarily members of the Communist Party; selection depended on political as well as business considerations.

Enterprises were centralized and hierarchical, and typically had a functional organizational structure in which the production function was the biggest and most important. Other functions usually included a technical function, a commercial function (this was mainly order filling and shipping), an economy function (mainly financial record keeping), a personnel function, and others depending on the company's type of business.

Large enterprises during the socialist era typically provided a wide range of housing, recreation, education, and medical services to their employees. For example, Královopolská had 579 flats (apartments) for workers and a "staff quarters building" with 478 beds (later to become the company hotel); four recreation centers, a youth pioneer camp, and a heated swimming pool near the factory (open to townspeople as well); three kindergartens and one nursery that could accommodate all employees' children; a clinic located within the plant area staffed by 13 full-time and 5 part-time medical doctors; and two kitchens that prepared hot meals for all three shifts, served in 10 dining rooms on the grounds.

Export Markets

Královopolská was a relatively low-cost producer. Low labor wages outweighed low labor productivity. At the same time, Královopolská had a reputation as a manufacturer of good, serviceable products. The company won medals at industry fairs in Brno despite the fact that the central planners had authorized no significant investment in technology or equipment during the 20 years prior to the Velvet Revolution. Královopolská produced equipment that met the prevailing specifications in the East. Nevertheless, the combination of price and quality gave Královopolská a potential advantage in international markets because it could underprice Western producers (by about 10 to 15 percent, some managers estimated), and make affordable products for developing countries.

In 1989, Královopolská earned three-quarters of its revenue from exports, and of that total, about 70 percent came from business with the Soviet Union and Iraq. In August 1990, the United Nations embargo against Iraq stopped those exports; and, in August 1991, the Soviet Union collapsed and went into a steep economic decline. Královopolská's exports dropped sharply to 9 percent of sales in 1991 and 16 percent in 1992. A recovery to 48 percent of sales in 1993 was partly illusory because Slovakia became a separate country in January 1993 so that formerly domestic sales became export sales.

EXHIBIT 2 *Economic Conditions in Czechoslovakia, 1989–1995*

Variable	1989	1990	1991	1992	1993*	1994*	1995*
Gross domestic product, real %	0.7†	−3.5	−15.0	−7.1	−0.9	2.6	4.6
Industrial production, real %	0.9	−3.7	−23.1	−12.4	−5.3	2.3	9.0
Consumer price inflation, %	1.4	10.0	57.8	11.5	20.8	10.0	8.9
Interest rate, %‡	5.5	6.2	15.4	13.9	14.1	13.1	12.8
Exchange rate, Kč/US$, annual average	15.1	18.0	29.5	28.3	29.3	28.8	26.3
Unemployment rate, %	na	0.3	6.8	7.7	3.5	3.2	3.0

Sources: Economist Intelligence Unit, *Country Report: Czech Republic and Slovakia,* 1st Quarter 1996; 2nd Quarter 1994; 2nd quarter 1993, 2nd Quarter 1990. London, 1996, 1994, 1993, 1990; International Monetary Fund, *International Financial Statistics,* March 1996, January 1994, March 1994. Washington D.C., 1996, 1994.

*Czech Republic only.

†Net material product.

‡Lending rate to state enterprises.

Through this period, some of Královopolská's exports to Russia continued, despite that country's economic hardship, because the products were furnaces and replacement parts for oil refineries, which Russia needed to generate its own hard currency exports. Russia continued to buy these products from Královopolská and paid for them in U.S. dollars. Exports to Russia accounted for about 10 percent of Královopolská's production volume in 1993.

The company found it difficult to develop new export business. As with many large Czech firms, Královopolská did not own or control its distribution channels so it had few direct relationships with customers. Fifty percent of its exports were handled through one state trading company, Technoexport, before the Revolution. The other half was exported indirectly via the engineering firms that actually constructed power plants, chemical plants, and water treatment facilities.

Other factors made export development difficult as well. Much of western Europe was in the midst of recession in the early 1990s and west European technical standards were different from those that Královopolská followed. In some cases, price was less important than established relationships with customers. Here, Královopolská was at a disadvantage because it had very little Western business experience. In some developing countries, on the other hand, the problem was national, political and economic instability. Královopolská developed new export business in Iran, accounting for about a quarter

of all exports in 1993, but this business encountered its own problems—the Iranian government defaulted on payments in 1994. Other business was developed in Syria, Egypt, and Iraq.

The Domestic Market

Like other Czech firms, Královopolská had been a monopoly producer in most of its domestic businesses, including chemical equipment, industrial cranes, and water treatment plant equipment. However, its domestic monopoly in water treatment facilities eroded after the Revolution as new privatized firms entered the business. In addition, water treatment equipment was readily available outside the Czech Republic and could be imported after the Revolution.

Nevertheless, the water treatment plant business was of special interest to Královopolská. Over the last 40 years, there had been little improvement in municipal and industrial water treatment systems. According to a government study, roughly half of all city water supplies were below standard in water quality. A new effort to reduce environmental pollution and improve water quality led to government regulations and investments in water purification and sewage treatment facilities, effectively expanding one of Královopolská's markets. Growth in this business helped to counter declines from the depressed chemical and nuclear power industries and contributed to increased revenues for the RIA Division in particular.

Financial Results

Královopolská posted better financial results than many other companies in the 1991–1993 transition years, though the firm was not without its troubles. (Exhibits 3 and 4 provide selected financial data for the years 1989–1995.) Revenue decreased in 1990 and 1991, and the high rate of price inflation in 1991 meant that revenue in real terms declined about 40 percent in that year. However, revenue went up both in nominal and real terms in 1992 and 1993, counter to the trend in the economy as a whole. Královopolská was profitable throughout the transition period until 1993, when it incurred a loss of Kč 103 million (about US$3.5 million). This loss was largely a result of a first-time charge for reserves of Kč 180 million. Its loss of Kč 54 million in 1994 was partly due to the fact that little new business had been booked in 1992 and 1993 and partly the result of changes in financial reporting made to bring ac-

counting standards in line with Western financial reporting methods. Sales were up substantially in 1995, with a small profit of Kč 162 million (US$6 million).

Czech companies faced a serious financial threat during the transition because of the lack of trade credit. The Czech government followed a conservative fiscal and monetary policy from 1991 onward, resulting in tight credit and high nominal interest rates. In the absence of a functioning banking system, and lacking trade credit from banks, firms financed sales to customers by simply not paying their bills from suppliers, creating huge balances of both accounts payable and receivable. In 1993 the sum of all receivables in the Czech Republic was Kč 200 billion (US$7 billion).

Královopolská was in relatively good shape during this period because it managed to keep its receivables under control (which also helped its posi-

EXHIBIT 3 *Královopolská's Selected Income Statement Data for 1989 to 1995 (Kč Million Current)*

	1989	1990	1991	1992	1993	1994	1995
Revenue							
Sales of products and services to external customers	1826	1737	1560	1915	2430	2304*	3143
Other revenue	1	8	82	114	155	1204	1041
Total revenue	1827	1745	1642	2029	2585	3508*	4184
Costs							
Cost of purchased inputs and services	na	na	1145	1360	994	1987*	2105
Labor, depreciation, reserves	448	—	459	461	731	1018	1072
Wages	—	244	263	261	322	327	311
Change in inventory and work in process	−132	153	−438	−97	710	−169	617
Total costs of production	na	na	1166	1724	2435	2836*	3794
Other costs	na	na	270	104	253	723	226
Total costs	1788	1625	1436	1828	2688	3559*	4020
Profits							
Gross margin from production (sales of products less costs of production)	na	na	394	191	−5	−532	−651
Profits before taxes (total revenue less total costs)	39	120	204	201	−103	−51	162

Source: Královopolská *Annual Reports* 1992, 1993, 1994, 1995.

*Data for 1994 include internal sales of one division to another, and costs of purchased inputs by one division from another; therefore, these figures cannot be compared to 1993 or earlier data. However, profit figures are comparable.

Other revenue includes sale of fixed assets, penalties received, and interest from financial investments. Reserves were first set aside in 1993 for plant and equipment repair and upgrades in the amount of Kč 180 million. Change in inventory and work-in-process appears in the revenue section of the income statement in the company's annual reports as is the German custom; we have moved it to the costs section. Other costs include costs of selling fixed assets, penalties paid, gifts, write-off of accounts receivable, interest paid on loans, and exchange rate losses.

EXHIBIT 4 *Královopolská's Selected Balance Sheet Data for 1989 to 1995 (Amounts in Kč Million Current)*

	1989	1990	1991	1992	1993	1994	1995
				Assets			
Accounts receivable	485	781	717	1008	796	697	779
Inventories	2698	2942	1471	832	1567	1515	1747
Total current assets	3287	3741	4797	5244	4323	4336	3914
Total fixed assets	640	654	1114	1105	1130	1098	1116
Total assets	3927	4394	5910	6349	5453	5435	5030
				Liabilities			
Accounts payable	133	456	941	1050	1041	1223	1424
Bank loans	1065	1284	1016	972	1167	371	224
Total liabilities	—	3689	4409	5185	4180	4202	3672
Equity capital	—	705	1501	1164	1273	1232	1378
Total liabilities and equity	—	4394	5910	6349	5453	5435	5050

Sources: Královopolská *Annual Reports* 1991, 1992, 1993, 1994, 1995.

Note: Changes in accounting systems from the central planning era to western standards require some balance sheet data to be interpreted with care.

tion with banks). Receivables exceeded payables in 1989 and 1990, but not after that. Královopolská managers attacked the receivables problem vigorously, sending its sales force to customers to work out swaps of receivables, sometimes in three-way trades facilitated by the Ministry of Finance or assisted by consultants from Brno Technical University, who provided computer tracking. As a result, Královopolská's receivables were less than payables in the critical years 1991–1993, thus easing its cash flow problem and reducing its need for bank credit to cover receivables.

It was almost impossible for firms to obtain long-term loans. Komerčni Banka (Commerical Bank), Královopolská's bank, "is very good if we don't ask for anything," said finance director, Jiří Cupák, in 1993. "Getting credit is very difficult. We need 100 percent collateral for loans. This is new for us. It is uncomfortable. Before the Revolution it was no problem to pay off loans. Now we have trouble. Sometimes we are late. We only get one-year loans now."

However, Královopolská was more fortunate than other companies. It was able to obtain short-term credit because, according to one manager, "We pay our interest." The Czech government was cooperating with Královopolská in long-term financing and trade credit for major export business, notably equipment for the aluminum refinery on which Iran later defaulted.

When asked about the effect of his country's economic condition on Královopolská in 1993, Zdenčk Pánek said, "I cannot change the economic conditions. If I want to cross a dirty river I either have to build a bridge or jump in and swim." He knew he could not "clean the river" himself, so he had to find another way to the other side and was likely to get a bit muddied in the process.

MANAGEMENT'S ACTIONS DURING THE TRANSITION

After initial privatization in 1992, Královopolská changed its top management, which acted quickly to reorganize the company, to try to instill a new corporate culture, to improve technology and quality, and to develop new markets.

The Managers

Královopolská managers reported that even before the Velvet Revolution, people were promoted more on the basis of merit than on Party membership.

Technical qualifications were always more important than political favor. In this way Královopolská was different from the central planning norm. After the Revolution, political history was not a major factor in top management succession. Former Communist Party officials left the company, but technically qualified rank-and-file Party members stayed. None of the new top managers was old enough to have been deeply involved in the failed Prague Spring of 1968 or the reprisals that followed it. The average age of the 11 top managers in 1992 was only 43.

Karel Jelínek was Chairman of the Board, a position the company established in 1992. He simultaneously served as the company's strategy director. Jelínek was the only top manager after privatization who was also a top manager in 1989, when he was production director (before that he was the company's technical director). He was also unusual by being just over 50 years old in 1993. Together, Pánek and Jelínek, who was technically educated, ran Královopolská.

The board appointed Zdenčk Pánek to be the new general manager in July 1992 after initial privatization (his predecessor had served just 1½ years and then left the company). Pánek, 37, was the director of the RIA Division at the time, but was not in top management of the company when the Velvet Revolution occurred. Pánek was unusual because he was trained in economics rather than engineering. Before becoming head of the RIA Division, he had been a field sales engineer. Pánek had no Western-style management training, and spoke neither German nor English. However, he mandated that all top managers learn English in company-provided classes (although he himself did not do so). Pánek had a keen sense of the importance of customers' needs and of the necessity to change the corporate culture to one that rewarded quality, customer orientation, financial performance, and initiative rather than longevity or Party membership.

The rest of the management team was composed of engineers who had devoted their entire working life to Královopolská. Vladimír Relich was typical. He was educated at Brno Technical University in engineering. He started at Královopolská as a designer, then became head of a department (chemical equipment), then head of all design, then head of central product development, and finally technical director and a member of top management in 1992.

Organizational Structure

Until 1991, Královopolská was organized by function, as was the case with most Czech firms. The functional departments were production, technical, economy, commercial, personnel, and training. The economy function under central planning involved record keeping for cash, production, and wages. Královopolská eliminated this function in 1991 and created instead a finance function. The former commercial function was remade and renamed as the strategy function (headed by Jelínek); a marketing function, for which there was no need before, was added.

The company reorganized in 1991 into six product divisions: (1) Water, Wood, and Light Chemical Equipment, (2) Heavy Chemical Equipment, (3) Specialty (Nuclear) Chemical Equipment, (4) Cranes and Steel Structures, (5) Metallurgy, and (6) RIA. (Exhibit 5 shows company organization after initial privatization in 1992.) The first three of these divisions manufactured tanks and pipes for sale to engineering and construction firms. RIA was a small engineering and construction firm for water treatment plants, purchasing some of its product from the Water, Wood, and Light Chemical Equipment Division.

In 1992, three more functions were added to the organization: quality assurance, information systems, and legal. After initial privatization, Královopolská created an inside board of directors to whom the general manager was responsible, and an outside advisory board, consistent with Czech law.

By 1993, the RIA division had become the largest division in terms of revenue generated from external customers. However, other divisions sold some of their output to RIA, so that the reckoning of division size in terms of revenue understates the size of the other divisions in terms of volume. (See Exhibit 6.)

In 1994, the first three product divisions, distinguished primarily by the technical aspects of their products (e.g., size and specifications) and their end use (e.g., petrochemical plants, water treatment plants, or nuclear power stations) were combined into one division. The intent was to eliminate unproductive interdivisional competition, combine similar technologies and production processes, make all divisions into strategic business units with decentralized profit responsibility, and move further away from technologically determined collections of products to a customer focus. (Exhibit 7 shows the company's organizational chart in 1995.)

EXHIBIT 5 *Organization Chart for 1992 after Initial Privatization*

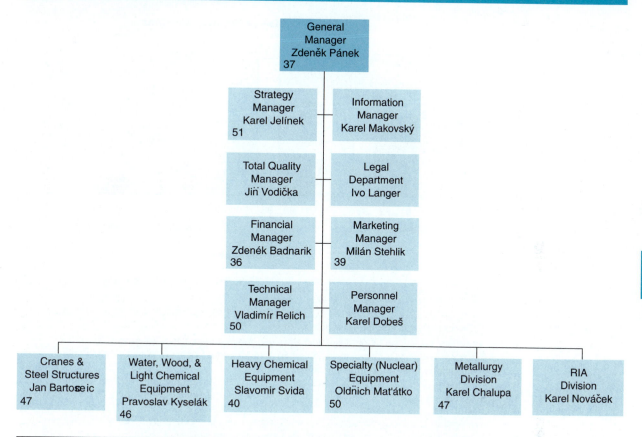

Incumbents' ages shown in bottom left area of box, when known.

New Market Development

Královopolská made progress in new market development and marketing after 1991. The company's objectives were to build business relationships with large Czech chemical and construction companies, to create new distribution channels for export business independent of its former export trading company, and to focus on west European markets for both export and joint venture opportunities while also maintaining its trade links with Russia.

The company succeeded in setting up a joint venture with seven other Czech companies for trading with Russia, and it established country-level trading entities in Slovakia, Poland, and Italy. However, gaining new customers, especially in new markets, was difficult in this industry because most relationships between equipment makers and customers were long-standing. Attractive brochures and new, modern logos for each division made a good impression, nevertheless.

Quality Initiatives and Competitiveness

Quality, customer-orientation, and competitiveness became the mantra of top management. Královopolská started a companywide quality assurance program in 1992, and obtained ISO 9000 and other relevant certifications by the end of 1994. The technical director, Vladimir Relich, said, "Our products were always high quality; but they did not meet west European standards. Now we have certificates of quality according to west European standards. Our products are higher in quality than Italian products." The

EXHIBIT 6 *Královopolská Divisions*

Relative Size of Product Divisions

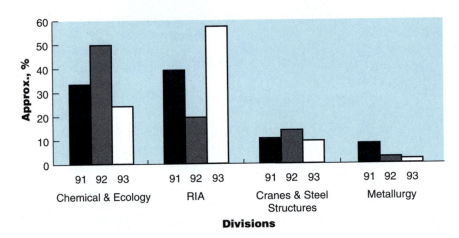

Chemical and Ecology Division

The Chemical and Ecology Division was formed in 1994 by consolidation of three former divisions. It consisted of three subdivisions:

Water, Wood, and Light Chemical Division: Tanks, tubes, filters, pumps, evaporators, agitators, furnaces, and other small equipment for water treatment plants, wood-working machinery, and light chemical industries

Heavy Chemical Division: Tanks, towers, reactors, heat exchangers, hydrogenerators, extractors, autoclaves, steam reformers, and other large-scale equipment for the chemical and petrochemical industries

Special Chemical (Nuclear) Division: Special-purpose, highly engineered steel, alloy, and plastic equipment for nuclear power stations and water treatment plants.

Cranes and Steel Structures Division

Bridge cranes, gantry cranes, special cranes, steel buildings, and road and railway bridges for industrial and commercial applications designed in accordance with customers' requirements and erected on-site.

Metallurgy Division

Production of tubes, elbows, castings, forgings, steel and alloy ingots, and annealing, tempering, and surface treatment of metallurgic products for the chemical and other industries.

RIA Division

Design, engineering, production, delivery, installation, commissioning, and maintenance of complete water treatment, chemical, and nuclear plants as turnkey jobs.

Source: Královopolská *Annual Reports*. Division-level data not available after 1993.

company produced glossy brochures with eye-catching graphics and text that illustrated Královopolská's commitment to quality in every interaction with customers. The brochures included language about the firm's trust in its employees.

Relich conducted an international competitive analysis of every Královopolská product in 1993 and 1994, including the products' technical specifications, quality, price, and perceptions of customer service. Competitors included companies from France, Italy, and Germany. The competitive analysis yielded six categories of products: those that were excellent (7 percent), competitive (44 percent), needed innovation (11 percent), needed a price reduction (21 per-

EXHIBIT 7 *Organization Chart for 1995 after Final Privatization*

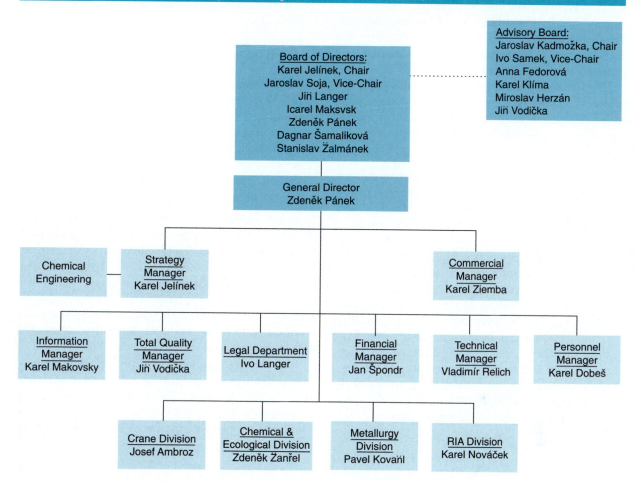

C-309

cent), needed marketing support (7 percent), and those that were not competitive (11 percent). The competitive analysis served as an important guide for investment and divestment decisions during 1994 and 1995.

Research and Technology

Before the change in governments, Královopolská obtained research and development services centrally from the CHEPOS organization, as was usual in centrally planned economies. However, the breakup of CHEPOS during privatization meant that its R&D unit began competing with Královopolská. Královopolská began to build its own R&D capability through alliances with universities and technical colleges and through a newly created internal R&D

group. This would, inevitably, be a slow process, according to Relich.

"We need to buy or license technology," said Relich. "It is an acute problem. We need a partner who does not need a return right away." While no such licensing deal occurred immediately, Královopolská did in fact make commercial agreements with firms in Austria and Finland for long-term purchases of high-technology components by Královopolská that would enable it to make, sell, and deliver new products.

Corporate Culture

Královopolská's managers identified the company's culture as a persistent challenge. The history of the firm favored manufacturing. "Production was king," said one manager. "Management tries now to put sales on top and production next. We are still learning to make what the customer wants." He went on to say, "Our main problem is not on-time delivery. The problems are inside the company—deciding that one contract is more important than another and writing a contract that we can fulfill."

Karel Jelínek, speaking in 1994, discussed the difficulty Královopolská was having in changing the corporate culture from one that focused on following orders to one that focused on customers, quality, and initiative.

We are trying to change the corporate culture, and have been trying hard for three years. The easy thing is to write it down. The hard thing is to persuade the people so that they are convinced about the company. We want our customers to feel the corporate culture from every employee. This is the basis of a market-based approach. . . . We introduced a motivation system. It is too early to show results. People don't like to take responsibility for their own decisions. They expect other signatures on decisions [an attitude left over from the Communist era]. We are trying to find people who are not afraid of big decisions. I like people who make me lose sleep because of the possible bad results of their decisions. I prefer these people to those who wait for my approval.

Královopolská was attempting to create a new corporate culture in several ways. In addition to public statements by the general manager and the chairman of the board, Královopolská used management training, competitive analyses, merit-based performance appraisal, and incentive pay (with "disappointing results so far," said one manager in 1994) to create a more customer-, quality-, and performance-oriented climate. Pánek's observations in 1993 illustrate the challenge.

All of top management went through training to use human and democratic elements of management. But these management techniques can't be applied completely. We need order. To make order we use a direct system which is supported by control. The old system was disorder.

We want a new organizational culture in our new company. The new culture is presented on video. Each meeting of managers begins with the video. They see the video until order is there. In the worst cases they work on Saturdays seeing the

video. After three Saturdays it is okay because even the worst cases don't want to come in for a fourth Saturday.

Pánek's frustration with the pace of change echoed Jelínek's:

The hardest problem is changing the people. In one year we worked out all of our quality control manuals with detailed descriptions about quality and activities. Now we fight the human factor. Even though we describe the changes in detail, people don't behave that way. They go back to the old system in which they were raised. We change people with pressure.

Královopolská also needed to create an awareness of costs, prices, profits, and financial discipline. Cupák noted, "We have a problem with management internally—with financial controls. They [financial controls] are good discipline but managers don't like them." Královopolská created a company bank to stimulate accountability and competition among divisions for corporate resources. Each division was required to show a profit or risk being sold.

Královopolská steadily reduced its employment during the 5 years after the Velvet Revolution, from 5,469 in 1989 to about 3,250 at the end of 1994. Top management planned to reduce employment by about 400 people per year for at least 2 more years.

Strategic Options

One of the Královopolská top management goals, according to a company document produced during the transition, was to determine "a clear strategy of development for the company with the objective of creating an added value very close to the value usual in the prosperous companies in the developed European countries." When Pánek became general manager in 1992, his first effort was to create a genuine business plan. Working with people from the Consulting Institute of the Prague School of Economics, top managers addressed a number of key issues, among them the objectives of the company, its strategy, and its structure. At this early stage, top management agreed to focus on quality, customer orientation, and improved discipline and motivation among employees. "We will increase productivity by 15 percent, decrease costs by 10 percent, increase efficiency by 10 percent, and extend our business into new markets," said Pánek.

In another company document, *Královopolská Strojáirna Brno 1992*, Královopolská managers repeated a gem of Czech management wisdom from the 1930s, a period that predated the central planning era, attributed to the famous Czech industrialist, Thomas Bat'a:

> We follow the well-known—and nearly forgotten but today often repeated Czech saying: "Our customer, our master.

Pánek's emphasis on "order" and incentive pay was also part of the Bat'a philosophy.

Královopolská undertook business transformation largely without the help of Western consultants. Pánek believed that Western consultants were too interested in the consultant's way of doing things and not familiar enough with Czech business practices, circumstances, and culture to be of much use. One negative early experience with a German consulting firm that delivered a product (for DM 38,000) that was little more than copies of publicly available documents supported his point of view. "Consultants," he said, "don't respect Czech management. They forget that we did not just jump down from the trees." He added, "We think, therefore we are." His allusion to philosophy in this statement was his way of emphasizing the cultural sophistication and intellect of Czech managers.

Pánek elaborated his view of consultants. While admitting that Královopolská needed help with financial management and business strategy, he did not want to hire consultants. "I would prefer that no one give us company-to-company advice. If someone wants to share the risk with us they should become our employee and solve problems together."

He also was determined not to use foreign trade companies, as had been the practice prior to the Revolution. Instead, he wanted his own sales people.

> The goal of the new business policy is to build up a high-quality sales network of our own people in the Czech Republic. Also outside the Czech Republic. In this region [western Europe] we don't know the markets and don't have enough qualified people. Our philosophy is our employees will become qualified. We will hire people from abroad rather than consultants. We will pay them in their currency.

Exactly how Královopolská could best achieve its business objectives was yet to be determined in 1995. Two questions needed to be resolved: What should the company's main business be? On what basis could the company best compete?

The company's long history, pride in Czech management, and skepticism of Western advice indicated that it should try to remain independent and evolve its current lines of business. Exports to Russia could be expected to continue, although they were not very large.

Progress was being made in developing new business in the Middle East, a natural market for Královopolská's products and prices, and one in which it had some experience from central planning times. However, this market was unstable.

Domestically, Královopolská was fortunate that one of its businesses, water treatment plant equipment, was in a growth industry. The Czech government adopted a policy of extending long-term, low-interest loans to municipalities to help them finance improved water treatment facilities. Laws passed in 1992 mandated ecologically sound water systems which adhered to environmental regulations and which required Czech company participation. Company managers projected an expenditure of Kč 16 billion (about US$575 million) on municipal water treatment projects in the Czech and Slovak Republics over the 5-year period 1993–1998.

One of the options that especially interested Pánek and Jelínek was to develop vigorously the RIA Division and become a full-service engineering company that would design, engineer, manufacture, and build complete projects, especially water treatment projects with which RIA already had some experience. Both industrial waste water treatment and purification of drinking water would be included. The RIA Division was small (only 280 employees in mid-1993), marginally profitable (Kč 16 million in 1992, amounting to about 3 percent of its sales), but already it was growing rapidly. Pánek thought a reasonable goal for the RIA Division was that it should account for 70 percent of total company revenue by 1997; in 1995, it reached two-thirds.

However, Pánek believed that Czech investment in water treatment facilities would begin to decrease in the next few years, and he recognized the value in turnkey capability for chemical plants and steel construction. To this end, Královopolská established a small chemical engineering group reporting directly to Jelínek in 1994 and a small engineering capability in the cranes division at the same time. Relich, when asked about the company of the future, said,

We will be in all our businesses [in the next five years] but we must change the base of our divisions. I hope the new chemical engineering department will be a separate division and will support production in the shops by getting orders and work in the field [within five years]. We will operate as an engineering company with a majority of the company moving toward turnkey projects in cranes, water, and chemical plants. We will start with small projects and learn for bigger projects, step by step. Technology knowhow has to be purchased because it is owned by big American and German companies.

The RIA Division purchased many of its components from the other divisions. About 30 percent of the Chemical and Ecological Division's output went to RIA. In early 1995 the RIA Division opened every job to outside suppliers for bids. "Suppliers must compete for every RIA job. When the internal price is competitive, our division will get the job. Now RIA buys more products from other companies than from our division," said one manager.

However, the RIA Division faced growing competition for the water treatment business from former state-owned enterprises that now also were privatized and restructured. One of the competitors was Sigma Engineering in Olomouc (a large town near Brno), which was strong in industrial waste water treatment, the forecasted fastest-growing market segment. Sigma also posed a threat to RIA internationally because it had a good foreign sales unit and an international network left over from its role as a hard currency earner before 1989. Another competitor was Vitkovice in Ostrava (a steel town near Poland), which was expert in small water treatment plant projects for villages of 1200 or fewer inhabitants, a segment in which Královopolská acknowledged it was less efficient and less experienced. However, Vitkovice relied on outside installers and thus did not do complete turnkey projects. Three other potential competitors—Kunst, Eko, and Fontana—were created in 1992 out of a larger former state plant, but they were hampered by quality problems with their biological water treatment products. Because they were new, they did not have the name recognition and reputation that Královopolská had.

Numerous engineering and manufacturing firms were potential competitors in western Europe. For example, Královopolská benchmarked itself against 40 firms that manufactured equipment for water treatment plants, among them English firms (A. G. Tapsell, Ltd., Contra-Shear Development, Ltd., Jones Attwood Ltd., Kee Services Ltd., and Three Star Environmental Engineering Ltd.), German firms (Durr GmbH, Eisenbau Heilbronn GmbH, Fischtechnik GmbH, Handke Stengelin GmbH, Kary GmbH, Preussag Hoell GmbH, and Windolf AG, among others), and Dutch firms (Hubert Stavoren BV, Kopcke Industrie BV, and Landustrie Maschinenfabrik BV).

For Královopolská to maintain world standards, it needed newer technology, and, like all Czech companies, it needed capital for plant modernization. For these reasons Královopolská explored the possibilities of a foreign partnership. A joint venture between the RIA Division and a west European partner was sought, as this would improve access to west European markets that were proving difficult to enter.

Discussions took place in 1993 with a French firm in which the RIA Division was especially interested. The business of the proposed joint venture would be to build water treatment facilities in the Czech Republic. The French company was interested in the venture because it needed a Czech partner to satisfy government requirements for domestic participation. Královopolská saw the joint venture as a means of obtaining technology—the French firm would license its technology to the joint venture—and capital. Technology included not only physical processes and hardware, but also management techniques such as cost accounting. Capital was needed for investment in new plant and equipment. In addition, Královopolská's Chemical and Ecological division might be able to sell its products to the French parent. The risk of doing business with the French firm was that it allowed easy access to the potentially large Czech and Slovak markets—possibly trading away future business for current business. In the end, the two firms failed to reach an agreement. Though revenue for the joint venture was projected to grow rapidly, profits were expected to be too small and too far in the future for the French firm.

When the management buyout occurred in January 1995, the company's financial situation captured more of Pánek's attention than ever before. Cash flow and debt repayment had to become priorities.

The company was the collateral for the bank loan used for the purchase. More profitable business was needed soon. When asked about the future, one top manager said:

> Královopolská is among the top third of all Czech companies. Our products are competitive. We have good equipment and well-trained people. . . . The future is relatively good for us, but the next two years are important for us. It is necessary to change people's minds. The highest level people have changed but it is necessary to go to the lowest level. . . . We will change the base of our business. We want to become an engineering company. Results from turnkey projects will be two times higher in five years. We will buy parts from outside Královopolská. The result will be a more competitive environment within our own divisions.

Pánek reviewed Královopolská's position in mid-1995. He knew he would have to harness Královopolská's resources quickly to return to profitability, but he was not sure what his priorities should be. How would the domestic and international environments change in the near future? What opportunities and threats would those changes present to the firm? What resources and capabilities did Královopolská possess now or need to develop for the future? What were the firm's strengths and weaknesses? Should the firm emphasize a particular product line? Should business development efforts focus on the domestic Czech market, on Western Europe, on Eastern Europe, or on the developing countries? What additional internal organizational and cultural changes would be needed? Pánek was sure of only one thing: a specific business plan mapping out the next steps was vital to Královopolská's future success.

REFERENCES

The readings given below are not required to analyze the case. They provide a useful context for discussion.

Fogel, D. S. (ed.) *Managing in Emerging Market Economies: Cases from the Czech and Slovak Republics.* Boulder, CO: Westview Press, 1994. See especially Chapters 1 and 2.

Fogel, D. S. (ed.) *Firm Behavior in Emerging Market Economies: Cases from the Private and Public Sectors in Central and Eastern Europe.* Aldershot, UK: Avebury, 1995.

Journal of Economic Perspectives, vol. 5, no. 4, 1991. Special issue on privatization in eastern Europe.

Mann, C. L. "Industry Restructuring in East-Central Europe: The Challenge and the Role for Foreign Investment." *American Economic Review*, vol. 81, no. 2, 1991, pp. 181–184.

Maruyama, M. "Some Management Considerations in the Economic Reorganization of Eastern Europe." *Academy of Management Executive*, vol. 4, no. 2, 1990, pp. 90–91.

Matesová, J. "Country Overview Study: Czech and Slovak Republics. Will the Manufacturing Heart Beat Again?" *Eastern Europe Economics*, vol. 31, no. 6, 1993, pp. 3–35.

Newman, Karen L., and Stanley D. Nollen, "Managerial Challenges During Organizational Re-Creation: Industrial Companies in the Czech Republic." In A. A. Ullmann and A. Lewis (eds.) *Privatization and Entrepreneurship: The Managerial Challenge in Central and Eastern Europe.* Binghampton, NY: Haworth Press, 1997, pp. 115–140. This chapter contains a brief analysis of Královopolská as a case in discontinuous change.

Newman, Karen L., and Stanley D. Nollen. "Zetor Tractors (A) and (B)." *Case Research Journal*, vol. 15, no. 1, 1995, pp. 10–33.

Sacks, P. M. "Privatization in the Czech Republic." *Columbia Journal of World Business*, vol. 28, no. 1, 1993, pp. 189–194.

Shama, A. "Management under Fire: The Transformation of Managers in the Soviet Union and Eastern Europe." *Academy of Management Executive*, vol. 7, no. 1, 1993, pp. 22–35.

Svejnar, J. (ed.) *The Czech Republic and Economic Transition in Eastern Europe.* San Diego: Academic Press, 1995.

Williams, C. 1993. "New Rules for a New World: Privatization of the Czech Cement Industry. *Columbia Journal of World Business*, vol. 28, no. 1, 1993, pp. 62–68.

World Bank 1993. *Enterprise Behavior and Economic Reforms: A Comparative Study in Central and Eastern Europe.* Washington, D.C.: World Bank, 1993.

NOTES

1. The Velvet Revolution occurred in late November and early December of 1989, a few months after the fall of the Berlin wall. The name "Velvet Revolution" comes from the fact that the existing Communist government resigned without bloodshed, after massive peaceful demonstrations in Prague, giving way to a democracy almost overnight. The first post-Communist government was led by Václav Havel, a playwright who had been imprisoned under the former regime for his political views. Havel, though inexperienced in government, was a strong symbol of the moral underpinnings of the Velvet Revolution and the future for Czechoslovakia.

2. The Czech economy was the most state-controlled of all Soviet bloc countries (97 percent of industry was state-owned). However, the Czech Republic had a history of capitalism. Between World Wars I and II, it was among the ten largest economies in the world. Privatization of large state-owned enterprises began in 1992. In some cases, foreign companies bought Czech firms in deals brokered by the government (e.g.,

Volkswagen bought Skoda), or foreign companies established joint ventures with Czech companies [e.g., ABB, the Swiss-Swedish multinational, and První Brněnska Strojírna (PBS) created a new 67 percent–33 percent joint venture company from part of the formerly state-owned PBS]. However, the largest share of Czech industry was privatized by vouchers. Because the government wanted to privatize industry quickly but Czech citizens had insufficient funds to buy companies, enterprises were practically given away. Each citizen could buy a voucher book for Kč 1000, which was about one week's pay for the average industrial worker at that time. Vouchers could be spent on shares of stock in companies or sold to investment funds that purchased shares. The vast majority of large firms were privatized via this voucher method between 1992 and 1995.

The Lincoln Electric Company, 1996

Arthur Sharplin

Waltham Associates, Austin, Texas

John A. Seeger

Bentley College

It was February 29, 1996. The Lincoln Electric Company, a leading producer of arc welding products, had just celebrated its centennial year by reporting record 1995 sales of over $1 billion, record profits of $61.5 million, and record employee bonuses of $66 million. This performance followed two years of losses—the only losses in the company's long history—stemming from a seemingly disastrous foray into Europe, Asia, and Latin America. (Exhibits 1 and 2 tabulate operating results and ratios for recent years.)

Headquartered in the Cleveland suburb of Euclid, Ohio, Lincoln Electric was widely known for its Incentive Management System. According to the *New York Times*, thousands of managers visited Lincoln's headquarters each year for free seminars on the system, which guaranteed lifetime employment, paid its production people only for each piece produced, and paid profit-sharing bonuses which had averaged 90 percent of annual wages or salary for the sixty years from 1934 to 1994.[1] James Lincoln, the main archi-

By Arthur Sharplin, of Waltham Associates, Austin, Texas, and John A. Seeger, of Bentley College. The authors thank Richard S. Sabo of Lincoln Electric for help in the field research for this case, which is written solely for the purpose of stimulating student discussion. Management exerted no editorial control over content or presentation of the case. All events and individuals are real. All rights are reserved to the North American Case Research Association (NACRA) or jointly to the author and NACRA. Copyright © 1997 by the *Case Research Journal* and Arthur Sharplin and John A. Seeger.

tect of the Incentive Management System, had been dead 30 years by 1995, but he remained a dominant influence on the company's policies and culture.

Record sales and profits, however, were not a cause for complacence. Lincoln Electric had gone public during 1995 to reduce the substantial debts it incurred during its two losing years; now the company was subject to public scrutiny and such publications as the *New York Times* and *Business Week* questioned whether the famous Incentive Management System was consistent with the firm's obligations to its public stockholders. Dividends for 1995 amounted to $9.1 million, while bonuses had totalled $66 million. Even at $66 million, however, bonuses equalled only 56 percent of employees' annual pay. Some workers complained loudly that the average $21,000 payment in December was far short of what it should have been.

Lincoln's hometown newspaper, the Cleveland *Plain Dealer*, saw the worker complaints as a sign of increasing strain between management and workers. Characterizing Lincoln's work pace as ". . . brutal, a pressure cooker in which employees are constantly graded and peer pressure borders on the fanatical," reporter Thomas Gerdel said Lincoln "faces growing discontent in its workforce."[2] *Business Week* said, ". . . Lincoln increasingly resembles a typical public company. With institutional shareholders and new, independent board members in place, worker bonuses are getting more of a gimlet eye." Chairman and CEO Donald F. Hastings had set up a commit-

EXHIBIT 1 *Five-Year Operating Results*

	1995	1994	1993	1992	1991
			Year Ended December 31		
			(in thousands of dollars, except per share data)		
Net sales	$1,032,398	$906,604	$845,999	$853,007	$833,892
Income (loss) before cumulative effect of accounting change	61,475	48,008	(40,536)	(45,800)	14,365
Cumulative effect of accounting change			2,468		
Net income (loss)	$ 61,475	$ 48,008	$ (38,068)	$ (45,800)	$ 14,365
Per share:					
Income (loss) before cumulative effect of accounting change	$ 2.63	$ 2.19	$ (1.87)	$ (2.12)	$ .67
Cumulative effect of accounting change			.12		
Net Income (loss)	$ 2.63	$ 2.19	$ (1.75)	$ (2.12)	$ .67
Cash dividends declared	$ .42	$ .38	$ .36	$ .36	$ .30
Total assets	$ 617,760	$556,857	$559,543	$603,347	$640,261
Long-term debt	$ 93,582	$194,831	$216,915	$221,470	$155,547

tee and hired Price Waterhouse to study the bonus program and the company's productivity.

"If Lincoln can adapt to new times without sacrificing employee good will," said *Business Week*, "another model pay plan may yet emerge."[3]

A HISTORICAL SKETCH

In 1895, having lost control of his first company, John C. Lincoln took out his second patent and began to manufacture an improved electric motor. He opened his new business with $200 he had earned redesigning a motor for young Herbert Henry Dow (who later founded the Dow Chemical Company). In 1909, John Lincoln made his first welding machine (Exhibit 3 describes the welding process). That year, he also brought in James, his younger brother, as a salesman. John preferred engineering and inventing to being a manager, and in 1914 he appointed James vice president and general manager. (Exhibit 4 shows a condensed history of the firm.)

James Lincoln soon asked the employees to form an "Advisory Board." At one of its first meetings, the Advisory Board recommended reducing working hours from 55 per week, then standard, to 50. This was done. In 1934, the famous Lincoln bonus plan

was implemented. The first bonus averaged 25 percent of base wages. By 1940, Lincoln employees had twice the average pay and twice the productivity of other Cleveland workers in similar jobs. They also enjoyed the following benefits:

- An employee stock purchase plan providing stock at book value,
- Company-paid life insurance,
- An employees' association for athletic and social programs and sick benefits,
- Piece rates adjusted for inflation,
- A suggestion system with cash awards,
- A pension plan,
- A policy of promotion from within,
- A practice, though not in 1940 a guarantee, of lifetime employment,
- Base pay rates determined by formal job evaluation,
- A merit rating system which affected pay, and
- Paid vacations.

During World War II, the company suspended production of electric motors as demand for welding products escalated. Employee bonuses averaged $2,250 in 1942 (about $20,000 in 1995 dollars). Lincoln's original bonus plan was not universally ac-

EXHIBIT 2 *Financial Ratios, 1992–1995*

Fiscal Year Ending December 31:	1995	1994	1993	1992
Quick Ratio	0.89	0.95	0.74	0.89
Current Ratio	2.12	2.17	1.85	2.16
Sales/Cash	102.35	86.97	41.51	41.35
SG&A/Sales	0.28	0.29	0.33	0.35
Receivables: Turnover	7.33	7.19	7.66	7.66
Receivables: Day's Sales	49.11	50.04	47.02	46.98
Inventories: Turnover	5.65	5.84	5.89	4.98
Inventories: Day's Sales	63.77	61.66	61.14	72.27
Net Sales/Working Capital	5.48	5.35	5.65	4.94
Net Sales/Net Plant & Equipment	5.02	4.92	4.99	4.09
Net Sales/Current Assets	2.89	2.89	2.60	2.66
Net Sales/Total Assets	1.67	1.63	1.51	1.41
Net Sales/Employees	172,066	159,249	140,159	134,714
Total Liability/Total Assets	0.46	0.64	0.73	0.64
Total Liability/Invested Capital	0.67	0.92	1.13	0.92
Total Liability/Common Equity	0.87	1.90	3.01	2.13
Times Interest Earned	9.07	6.09	−1.66	−0.84
Long-Term Debt/Equity	0.28	1.00	1.51	1.11
Total Debt/Equity	0.29	1.02	1.58	1.19
Total Assets/Equity	1.87	2.87	3.90	3.04
Pre-Tax Income/Net Sales	0.10	0.09	−0.06	−0.04
Pre-Tax Income/Total Assets	0.16	0.14	−0.08	−0.06
Pre-Tax Income/Invested Capital	0.24	0.21	−0.13	−0.08
Pre-Tax Income/Common Equity	0.31	0.43	−0.35	−0.19
Net Income/Net Sales	0.06	0.05	−0.04	−0.05
Net Income/Total Assets	0.10	0.09	−0.07	−0.08
Net Income/Invested Capital	0.15	0.12	−0.11	−0.11
Net Income/Common Equity	0.19	0.26	−0.28	−0.25
R & D/Net Sales	NA	NA	NA	NA
R & D/Net Income	NA	NA	NA	NA
R & D/Employees	NA	NA	NA	NA

Source: Disclosure, Inc., Dow-Jones On-Line News Service.

cepted: the Internal Revenue Service questioned the tax deductibility of employee bonuses, arguing they were not "ordinary and necessary" costs of doing business, and the Navy's Price Review Board challenged Lincoln's high profits. But James Lincoln overcame the objections, loudly refusing to retract the firm's obligations to its workers. Also during World War II, Lincoln built factories in Australia, South Africa, and England.

In 1951, Lincoln completed a new main plant in Euclid, Ohio; the factory remained essentially unchanged in 1995. In 1995, Lincoln again began making electric motors, but they represented only a small percentage of the company's revenue through 1995.

Executive Succession

William Irrgang, an engineer and longtime Lincoln protégé, was president when James Lincoln died in 1965. By 1970, Lincoln's annual revenues had grown to $100 million, and bonuses were averaging about

EXHIBIT 3 *What Is Arc-Welding?*

Arc-welding was the standard joining method in shipbuilding for decades and remained so in 1995. It was the predominant way of connecting steel in the construction industry. Most industrial plants had their own welding shops for maintenance and construction. Makers of automobiles, tractors, and other items employed arc-welding. Welding hobbyists made metal items such as patio furniture and barbecue pits. The popularity of welded sculpture was growing.

Arc-welding employs electrical power, typically provided by a "welding machine" composed of a transformer or solid-state inverter connected to a building's electrical system or to an engine-driven generator. The electrical output may vary from 50 to 1,000 amps at 36–60 volts (for comparison, a hair dryer may use 10 amps at 120 volts) and may be alternating or direct current (AC or DC) of varying wave patterns and frequencies. The electrical current travels through a welding electrode and creates an arc to the item being welded. This melts the actual surface of the material being welded, as well as the tip of the electrode, resulting in deposit of the molten metal from the electrode onto the surface. When the molten metal re-freezes, the pieces being joined are fused into one continuous piece of steel.

Welding electrodes—called "consumables" because they are used up in the welding process—are of two main types: short pieces of coated wire (called "stick" electrodes or "welding rods") for manual welding and coils of solid or tubular wire for automatic and semiautomatic processes. The area of the arc must be shielded from the atmosphere to prevent oxidation of the hot metal. This shielding is provided by a stream of inert gas which surrounds the arc (in "MIG," or metallic-inert gas welding) or by solid material called "flux" which melts and covers the liquefied metal surface. Flux often contains substances which combine with the molten metal or catalyze chemical reactions. The flux may be affixed as a coating on welding rods, enclosed inside tubular welding wire, or funneled onto the weld area from a bin (in "submerged-arc" welding). Arc-welding produces sparks, heat, intense light, and noxious fumes, so operators usually wear face, body, and eye protection and, if ventilation is inadequate, breathing devices.

Other types of welding include oxy-fuel welding, which uses a flame to melt metals together; tungsten-inert gas (TIG) welding, which employs a tungsten electrode to create an arc to melt a welding rod; induction welding, which uses electrical coils to induce currents in the metal being welded, thereby heating it; resistance welding, which heats the weld joint by passing current directly through it; and plasma-arc welding, which is similar to arc-welding but involves higher temperatures and a more tightly constrained arc. Related processes include cutting metals with oxy-fuel torches, laser beams, and plasma-arc systems.

$8,000 per employee each year (about $30,000 in 1995 dollars). Irrgang was elevated to chairman in 1972 and Ted Willis, also an engineer and protégé of James Lincoln, became president. In 1977, Lincoln completed a new electrode plant a few miles from Euclid, in Mentor, Ohio; this doubled the capacity for making welding wire and rods.

Lincoln's net sales were $450 million in 1981, and employee bonuses averaged $20,760 (about $34,000 in 1995 dollars) that year. But sales fell by 40 percent in the next two years owing, Lincoln management said, to "the combined effects of inflation, sharply higher energy costs, and a national recession." By 1983, the firm's net income and

bonuses had collapsed to less than half their 1981 levels. (Exhibit 5 lists bonus amounts from 1981 to 1995.)

But there was no layoff. Many factory workers volunteered to do field sales work and customer assistance. Others were reassigned within the plants, some repairing the roof of the Euclid factory, painting, and cleaning up. The work week, previously averaging about 45 hours, was shortened to 30 hours for most nonsalaried workers. Several new products, that had been kept in reserve for just this kind of eventuality, were brought to market. Sales, profits, and bonuses began a slow recovery.

Bill Irrgang died in 1986. Ted Willis took over as

EXHIBIT 4 *Condensed History of Lincoln Electric Company*

1895	Company founded by John C. Lincoln.
1909	James Lincoln joins as salesman. (General Manager, 1914)
1934	Bonus plan implemented, at 25 percent of base earnings.
1940	Employees earning double the area's average wage.
1942–1945	Factories built in South Africa (later closed), England (later sold to employees), and Australia. Motor production discontinued.
1951	Main factory built in Euclid, Ohio.
1955	Motor production resumed.
1958	Historic guaranteed employment policy formalized.
1965	James Lincoln's death. William Irrgang named president.
1970	Annual revenues reach $100 million for the first time.
1972	Irrgang named chairman/CEO. Ted Willis becomes president.
1977	New electrode factory built in Mentor, Ohio.
1982–1983	Recession slashes revenues. Employees on 30-hour weeks. ESAB begins global expansion.
1986	Willis named chairman/CEO. Don Hastings becomes president. International operations include five plants in four countries.
1992	Foreign operations include 21 plants in 15 countries. Long-term debt at $220 million. Hastings named chairman/CEO. Fred Mackenbach named president.
1992–1993	Global recession. First losses in Lincoln's history. International retrenchment begins.
1995	International operations include 16 plants in 11 countries. Public stock issue provides funds for debt reduction. New motor factory built.

chairman and Don Hastings became president, taking primary responsibility for domestic operations.

THE LINCOLN PHILOSOPHY

Throughout the tenures of these CEOs, the business philosophies first articulated by James Lincoln remained in effect, forming the foundation of the company's culture and providing the context within which the Incentive Management System worked. Lincoln's own father had been a Congregationalist minister, and the biblical Sermon on the Mount, with Jesus' praise of meekness, mercifulness, purity of heart, and peacemaking, governed his attitudes toward business. James never evangelized his employees, but he counseled truthfulness in speech, returning evil with good, love of enemies, secret almsgiving, and quiet trust and confidence.[4]

Relationships with Customers

In a 1947 speech, James Lincoln said, "Care should be taken . . . not to rivet attention on profit. Between 'How much do I get?' and 'How do I make this better, cheaper, more useful?' the difference is fundamental and decisive." He later wrote, "When any company has achieved success so that it is attractive as an investment, all money usually needed for expansion is supplied by the customer in retained earnings. It is obvious that the customer's interests, not the stockholder's, should come first." He added,

EXHIBIT 5 *The Lincoln Electric Company Bonus History*

Year	Total $ Millions	Number Employees	% of Wages	Average Gross Bonus	W-2 Average Earnings Factory Worker
1981	59.0	2684	99.0	22,009	
1982	41.0	2634	80.1	15,643	
1983	26.6	2561	55.4	10,380	
1984	37.0	2469	68.0	15,044	
1985	41.8	2405	73.2	17,391	
1986	37.7	2349	64.8	16,056	
1987	44.0	2349	70.5	18,791	
1988	54.3	2554	77.6	21,264	
1989	54.5	2633	72.0	20,735	47,371
1990	56.2	2701	71.2	20,821	47,809
1991	48.3	2694	65.0	17,935	39,651
1992	48.0	2688	61.9	17,898	40,867
1993	55.0	2676	63.9	20,585	48,738
1994	59.0	2995	60.2	19,659	55,757
1995	64.4	3396	55.9	*21,168	57,758

Source: Lincoln Electric Company document.
*Employees with more than 1 year of service.

The Christian ethic should control our acts. If it did control our acts, the savings in cost of distribution would be tremendous. Advertising would be a contact of the expert consultant with the customer, in order to give the customer the best product available when all of the customer's needs are considered. Competition then would be improving the quality of products and increasing efficiency in producing and distributing them; not in deception, as is now too customary. Pricing would reflect efficiency of production; it would not be a selling dodge that the customer may well be sorry he accepted. It would be proper for all concerned and rewarding for the ability used in producing the product.

Lincoln's pricing policy, often stated, was "Price on the basis of cost and keep downward pressure on cost." C. Jackson Graham, founder of The American Productivity Institute, said prices of Lincoln products, on average, grew at only one-fifth the rate of inflation in the decades after 1930. Some prices actually went down. For example, Lincoln welding electrodes which sold for $0.16 per pound in 1929 were $0.05 in 1942. And Lincoln's popular SA-200 welder decreased in price from 1958–1965.

Until the 1990s, Lincoln was the dominant U.S. producer of arc-welding products and was able to keep market prices low, especially for consumables. That changed after Miller Welding Co. grew to match Lincoln in U.S. sales of machines, and ESAB became the world's largest supplier of consumables and materials. In 1984, Don Hastings said,

Right now we are paying the price of not having enough capacity in Mentor [Ohio] to supply our customer demand. We are spending money now. But if we had spent it last year, we would not be having the shortages that we're having right now. We're also allowing our competition to raise prices because there's nothing we can do about it without more capacity.

Lincoln quality was legendary. In the refinery and pipeline industries, where price was seldom the main consideration in purchasing, Lincoln welders and electrodes were almost universally specified for decades. Warranty costs at Lincoln typically averaged under one-fourth of one percent of sales. A Lincoln distributor in Monroe, Louisiana, said he had sold hundreds of Lincoln welders and had never had a warranty claim.

Lincoln sold its products directly to major customers and indirectly through distributors, most of which were welding supply stores. Lincoln also licensed hundreds of service centers and trained their personnel to do maintenance and warranty work on Lincoln machines. The company maintained a system of regional sales offices, which serviced both direct customers and distributors. In keeping with James Lincoln's principle that salespersons should be "expert consultants," sales jobs at Lincoln were open only to graduate engineers until about 1992, when Hastings changed the policy; he began to recruit majors in liberal arts, business, and other disciplines into the sales force.

Hastings instituted Lincoln's Guaranteed Cost Reduction (GCR) program in 1993. Under GCR, Lincoln sent teams of engineers, technical representatives, and distributors to customer facilities with a goal to "find ways to improve the customer's fabrication procedures and product quality as well as methods to increase its productivity." Hastings promised, "The Lincoln Electric Company will guarantee in writing that your company's annual arc welding fabrication costs will be reduced by a specified amount when you use Lincoln products and methods. If you don't save that amount, a check will be written for the difference." Lincoln cited these "successes" in its literature promoting GCR:

A fabricator of steel buildings found GCR savings of $25,000/year and, as a result of the program, developed an improved welding cost analysis system. A manufacturer of heavy grading equipment verified savings in excess of $50,000/year and productivity gains from 50 to 90 percent. An automotive manufacturer produced productivity increases, in specific welding operations, exceeding 20 percent. Resultant savings totaled over $1,000,000 a year.

Relationships with Employees

The company professed to still adhere to the basic precepts James Lincoln set down early in his development of the incentive system:

The greatest fear of the worker, which is the same as the greatest fear of the industrialist in operating a company, is the lack of income ... The industrial manager is very conscious of his company's need of uninterrupted income. He is completely oblivious, evidently, of the fact that the worker has the same need.

He is just as eager as any manager is to be part of a team that is properly organized and working for the advancement of our economy ... He has no desire to make profits for those who do not hold up their end in production, as is true of absentee stockholders and inactive people in the company.

If money is to be used as an incentive, the program must provide that what is paid to the worker is what he has earned. The earnings of each must be in accordance with accomplishment.

Status is of great importance in all human relationships. The greatest incentive that money has, usually, is that it is a symbol of success ... The resulting status is the real incentive ... Money alone can be an incentive to the miser only.

There must be complete honesty and understanding between the hourly worker and management if high efficiency is to be obtained.

"I don't work for Lincoln Electric; I work for myself," said Lester Hillier in the 1994 *New York Times* article. "I'm an entrepreneur," added Hillier, a welder at Lincoln for 17 years. Other workers, asked in April of 1995 about why people worked so hard and what motivated them, responded:

Joe Sirko, machine operator since 1941:

People want their bonus. And a decent job. No layoffs. I wanted a job where I could spend all the money I make all year and then I get the bonus. I still do that. I go out and live it up. I go to the races. I go everywhere.

When I came here—under James Lincoln—the jobs were given to family. Almost everybody in here was family. My brother got me in. Somebody else's brother got them in or their dad got them in. It was all family. And J.F. backed that a hundred percent. Family, right on down. If you had someone in your family, they were in. Now, they have three different interviewers down there. They all interview.

They hired a lot of people once, to reduce the overtime, remember, and they had all them people when it slowed down. They were sweeping and cleaning—and they didn't know what to do with them. When James Lincoln was alive, he always got up when he gave the bonus and told them— they would be complaining about overtime—he told them that they would either work, because he didn't want to over hire all them extra people. He believed in all the overtime.

Kathleen Hoenigman, wiring harness assembler hired in 1977:

I worked in factories before and the factories I worked at either went out of business or moved to another state. I will have to say that my money is more here, but I did always make good money. This is much more, because of the bonus. I invest. I also bought a house. Right now, I give my mother money.

I feel that people here that are making all this money, they work so hard for it that they don't want to spend it stupidly and what they do is invest, for the future. And they also, you know, take care of their family.

I like the challenge. I also like the money and the fact that the money is tied to my own output. You have to be motivated yourself. You want the company to succeed, so you want to do better. By having guaranteed employment, the company has to be strong. To me, guaranteed employment means if there's a slowdown you always have a job. Like they'll always take care of you. Back in 1982, when sales slumped, they put me on the roof carrying buckets of tar.

Scott Skrjanc, welder hired in 1978:

Guaranteed employment is in the back of my mind. I know I'm guaranteed a job. But I also know I have to work to get paid. We don't come in and punch a card and sit down and do nothing.

Linda Clemente, customer service representative hired in 1986:

Well, I guess the biggest thing is guaranteed employment. And I think most people want to be the best that they can be. For other people, maybe the motivation is the money, because they are putting kids through college and things like that. I mean, it's definitely a benefit and something everybody works for.

Relationships with Unions

There had never been a serious effort to organize Lincoln employees. While James Lincoln criticized the labor movement for "selfishly attempting to better its position at the expense of the people it must serve," he still had kind words for union members. He excused union excesses as "the natural reactions of human beings to the abuses to which management has subjected them." He added, "Labor and management are properly not warring camps; they are parts of one organization in which they must and should cooperate fully and happily."

Several of the plants Lincoln acquired during 1986–1992 had unions, and the company stated its intention to cooperate with them. No major Lincoln operation had a union in 1995, although 25 of the Ohio employees did attend a union presentation by the United Auto Workers in December, after the announcement of the 1995 bonus rate. "The attendance, out of a total of 3,400 workers, was disappointing even to organizers," said the Cleveland *Plain Dealer*. Lincoln spokesman Bud Fletcher said, "The secret to avoiding those types of situations is that management has to work twice as hard to provide all the elements that membership in an organization like a union would have. We've got to listen, we've got to sit down, we've got to take our time."

Relationships with Stockholders

Through 1992, Lincoln shareholders received dividends averaging less than 5 percent of share price per year, and total annual returns averaged under 10 percent. The few public trades of Lincoln shares before 1995 were at only a small premium over book value, which was the official redemption price for employee-owned stock.

"The last group to be considered is the stockholders who own stock because they think it will be more profitable than investing money in any other way," said James Lincoln. Concerning division of the largess produced by Incentive Management, he wrote, "The absentee stockholder also will get his share, even if undeserved, out of the greatly increased profit that the efficiency produces."

Under Hastings, Lincoln Electric gave public shareholders more respect. Dividends, while limited under certain credit agreements, were increased in 1994 in preparation for the public issue, and again in 1995. And the presence of new outside directors on the Lincoln board (see Exhibit 6) seemed to protect public shareholder interests.

EXHIBIT 6 *Officers and Directors of Lincoln Electric Company*

DIRECTORS

Donald F. Hastings, 67, *1980
Chairman of the Board and
Chief Executive Officer

Frederick W. Mackenbach, 65, *1992
Retired President and Chief Operating
Officer

Harry Carlson, 61, *1973
Retired Vice Chairman

David H. Gunning, 53, *1987
Chairman, President and Chief
Executive Officer of Capitol American
Financial Corp.

Edward E. Hood, Jr., 65, *1993
Former Vice Chairman of the Board
and Executive Officer of The General
Electric Co.

Paul E. Lego, 65, *1993
President of Intelligent Enterprises

Hugh L. Libby, 70, *1985
Retired Chairman of the Board and
Chief Executive Officer of Libby Corp.

David C. Lincoln, 70, *1958
Retired Chairman of the Board and
Chief Executive Officer of Lincoln Laser
Co. and President of Arizona Oxides LLC

Emma S. Lincoln, 73, *1989
Retired Attorney in private practice

G. Russell Lincoln, 49, *1989
Chairman of the Board and Chief
Executive Officer of Algan, Inc.

Kathryn Jo Lincoln, 41, *1995
Vice President of The Lincoln
Foundation, Inc. and Vice
Chair/Secretary of The Lincoln
Institution of Land Policy

Anthony A. Messaro, 52, *1996
President and Chief Operating Officer

Henry L. Meyer III, 46, *1994
Chairman of the Board of Society
National Bank and Senior Executive
Vice President and Chief Operating
Officer of KeyCorp

Lawrence O. Selhorst, 63, *1992
Chairman of the Board and
Chief Executive Officer of American
Spring Wire Corporation

Craig R. Smith, 70, *1992
Former Chairman and
Chief Executive Officer of Ameritrust
Corporation

Frank L. Steingass, 56, *1971
Chairman of the Board and
President of Buehler/Steingass, Inc.

*Date elected as a director.

OFFICERS

Donald F. Hastings, 67, *1953
Chairman and Chief Executive Officer

Anthony A. Massaro, 52, *1993
President and Chief Executive Officer

David J. Fullen, 64, *1955
Executive Vice President,
Engineering and Marketing

John M. Stropki, 45, *1972
Executive Vice President
President, North America

Richard C. Ulstad, 56, *1970
Senior Vice President,
Manufacturing

H. Jay Elliott, 54, *1993
Senior Vice President,
Chief Financial Officer and Treasurer

Frederick G. Stueber, 42, *1995
Senior Vice President,
General Counsel and Secretary

Frederick W. Anderson, 43, *1978
Vice President,
Systems Engineering

Paul J. Beddia, 62, *1956
Vice President,
Government and Community Affairs

Dennis D. Crockett, 53, *1965
Vice President,
Consumable Research and
Development

James R. Delaney, 47, *1987
Vice President
President, Lincoln Electric Latin
America

Joseph G. Doria, 46, *1972
Vice President
President and Chief Executive Officer,
Lincoln Electric Company of Canada

Paul Fantelli, 51, *1970
Vice President,
Business Development

Ronald A. Nelson, 46, *1972
Vice President,
Machine Research and Development

Gary M. Schuster, 41, *1978
Vice President,
Motor Division

Richard J. Seif, 48, *1971
Vice President,
Marketing

S. Peter Ullman, 46, *1971
Vice President
President and Chief Executive Officer,
Harris Calorific Division of Lincoln
Electric

Raymond S. Vogt, 54, *1996
Vice President,
Human Resources

John H. Weaver, 57, *1961
Vice President
President, Lincoln Africa, Middle East
and Russia

*Year joined the Company.

C-32

THE LINCOLN INCENTIVE MANAGEMENT SYSTEM

Lincoln's Incentive Management System was defined by the firm's philosophy and by the rules, regulations, practices, and programs that had evolved over the 60 years since its origination.

Recruitment. Every job opening at Lincoln was advertised internally on company bulletin boards and any employee could apply. In general, external hiring was permitted only for entry-level positions. Often, applicants were relatives or friends of current employees. Selection for these jobs was based on personal interviews—there was no aptitude nor psychological testing and no educational requirement—except for engineering and sales positions, which required a college degree. A committee consisting of vice presidents and supervisors interviewed candidates initially cleared by the Personnel Department. Final selection was made by the supervisor who had a job opening. From over 3,500 applicants interviewed by the Personnel Department in 1988, fewer than 300 were hired. The odds were somewhat better in 1995, as Lincoln scrambled to staff its new electric motor factory and to meet escalating demand for its welding products.

Training and Education. New production workers were given a short period of on-the-job training and then placed on a piecework pay system. Lincoln did not pay for off-site education unless specific company needs were identified. The idea behind this policy was that not everyone could take advantage of such a program, and it was unfair to spend company funds for a benefit to which there was unequal access. Recruits for sales jobs, already college graduates, were given an average of six months on-the-job training in a plant, followed by a period of work and training at a regional sales office.

Sam Evans, regional manager for international, described the training program when he joined Lincoln in 1953 as an electrical engineering graduate:

> A few months into the training, I decided to move to sales. During those days, the training program was about a year—several months learning to weld, several months on the factory floor, and in other departments. I got the MBA while I was working in Buffalo as a Sales Engineer.

Merit Rating. Each manager formally evaluated subordinates twice a year using the cards shown in Exhibit 7. The employee performance criteria—"quality," "dependability," "ideas and cooperation," and "output"—were considered independently of each other. Marks on the cards were converted to numerical scores, which were forced to average 100 for each specified group, usually all the subordinates of one supervisor or other manager. Thus, any employee rated above 100 would have to be balanced by another rated below 100. Individual merit rating scores normally ranged from 80 to 110. Any score over 110 required a special letter to top management. These scores (over 110) were not considered in computing the required 100 point average for each evaluator. Point scores were directly proportional to the individual's year-end bonus.

Welder Scott Skrjanc seemed typical in his view of the system. "You know, everybody perceives they should get more. That's natural. But I think it's done fairly."

Under Lincoln's early suggestion program, employees were given monetary awards of one-half of the first year's savings attributable to their suggestions. Later, however, the value of suggestions was reflected in merit rating scores. Supervisors were required to discuss performance marks with the employees concerned. Each warranty claim was traced to the individual employee whose work caused the defect, if possible. The employee's performance score was reduced, or the worker could repay the cost of servicing the warranty claim by working without pay.

Compensation. Basic wage levels for jobs at Lincoln were determined by a wage survey of similar jobs in the Cleveland area. These rates were adjusted quarterly in response to changes in the Cleveland Area Wage Index, compiled by the U.S. Department of Labor. Wherever possible, base wage rates were translated into piece rates. Practically all production workers—even some fork truck operators—were paid by the piece. Once established, piece rates were changed only if there was a change in the methods, materials, or machinery used in the job. Each individual's pay was calculated from a daily Piecework Report, filled out by the employee. The payroll department, responsible for paying 3,000 employees, consisted of four people; there was no formal control system for checking employees' reports of work done.

EXHIBIT 7 *Lincoln's Merit Rating Cards*

————— Increasing Output —————▶

OUTPUT

This card rates HOW MUCH PRODUCTIVE WORK you actually turn out.

Days Absence ◯

It also reflects your willingness not to hold back and recognizes your attendence record.

This rating has been done jointly by your department head and the Production Control Department in the shop and with other department heads in the office and engineering.

EM-629A REV. 1988

————— Increasing Ideas & Cooperation —————▶

IDEAS & COOPERATION

This card rates Cooperation, Ideas and Initiative

New ideas and new methods are important to your company in our continuing effort to reduce costs, increase output, improve quality, work safely and improve our relationship with our customers. This card credits you for your ideas and initiative used to help in this direction.

It also rates your cooperation — how you work with others as a team. Such factors as your attitude towards supervision, co-workers, and the company, your efforts to share your expert knowledge with others; and your cooperation in installing new methods smoothly, are considered here.

This rating has been done jointly by your department head and the Time Study Department in the shop and with other department heads in the office and engineering.

EM-629A REV. 1988

————— Increasing Dependability —————▶

DEPENDABILITY

This card rates how well your supervisors have been able to depend upon you to do those things that have been expected of you without supervision.

It also rates your ability to supervise yourself including your work safety performance, your orderliness, care of equipment, and effective use you make of your skills.

This rating has been done by your deparment head.

EM-629A REV. 1988

————— Increasing Quality —————▶

QUALITY

This card rates the QUALITY of the work you do.

It also reflects your success in eliminating errors and in reducing scrap and waste.

This rating has been done jointly by your department head and the Quality Assurance Department in the shop and with other department heads in the office and engineering.

E17-629A REV. 1988

In December of each year, bonuses were distributed to employees. Lincoln reported that incentive bonuses from 1934 to 1994 averaged about ninety percent of annual wages; the total bonus pool typically exceeded after-tax (and after-bonus) profits. Individual bonuses were determined by merit rating scores. For example, if the Board of Directors authorized a bonus equal to 80 percent of total base wages paid, a person whose performance score averaged 95 in the two previous evaluation periods received a bonus of 76 percent (0.80×0.95) of base wages.

Because of company losses in 1992 and 1993, the bonus was about 60 percent of base wages, and management was forced to borrow $100 million to pay it. After Lincoln's turnaround in 1994, the 60-percent bonus rate was continued as $63 million was used to repay principal and interest on the borrowed money. Average compensation of Lincoln's Cleveland employees in 1994 was about $35,000 before bonuses, and the average bonus was $20,000—$12,000 less than if the 90 percent average had applied. Some felt that employees were paying for management's mistakes.

Continuous Employment. In 1958 Lincoln formalized its guaranteed continuous employment policy, which had already been in effect for many years. Starting in 1958, every worker with over two years' longevity was guaranteed at least 30 hours per week, 49 weeks per year. The requirement was changed to three years' longevity in the recession year of 1982, when the policy was severely tested. In previous recessions the company had been able to avoid major sales declines. However, sales plummeted 32 percent in 1982 and another 16 percent the next year. Management cut most of the nonsalaried workers back to 30 hours a week for varying periods of time. Many employees were reassigned, and the total workforce was slightly reduced through normal attrition and restricted hiring. The previous year had set records, and some employees grumbled at their unexpected misfortune, to the surprise and dismay of some Lincoln managers.

Among employees with a year or more of service, employee turnover ran only four percent at Lincoln Electric. Absenteeism, too, was extremely low; critics in the press noted this was understandable, since workers were not paid for sick days. They noted, too, that 25 to 30 percent of new hires quit in their first six months of work, in spite of Lincoln's intensive

interview process. In 1995, Lincoln's Cleveland workers were averaging over 45 hours a week on the job. Employee turnover after the first year was under 1 percent per year, excluding retirements. "The vast majority that quit do so before their first bonus," said Dick Sabo, director of corporate communications. "Once they see the dollars, they realize they are extremely well paid for their efforts." The average length of service of Lincoln's Cleveland workers in 1995 was approximately 14 years.

Stock Ownership by Employees. James Lincoln said that financing for company growth should come from within the company—through initial cash investment by the founders, through reinvestment of earnings, and through stock purchases by those who work in the business. He claimed this approach gave the following advantages:

1. Ownership of stock by employees strengthens team spirit. "If they are mutually anxious to make it succeed, the future of the company is bright."

2. Ownership of stock provides individual incentive because employees feel they will benefit from company profitability.

3. "Ownership is educational." Owner-employees "will know how profits are made and lost; how success is won and lost."

4. "Capital available from within controls expansion." Unwarranted expansion would not occur, Lincoln believed, under his financing plan (which did not allow for borrowing capital for growth).

5. "The greatest advantage would be the development of the individual worker. Under the incentive of ownership, he would become a greater man."

6. "Stock ownership is one of the steps that can be taken that will make the worker feel that there is less of a gulf between him and the boss."

Under Lincoln's Employees' Stock Purchase Plan, each employee could buy a specified number of shares of restricted common stock from the company each year, with company financing. The stock was priced at "estimated fair value" (taken to be book value), and the company had an option to repurchase it. Lincoln had always exercised its option to repurchase shares tendered by employees, and many employees felt it was obligated to do so. In 1992, approximately 75 percent of the employees owned over 40 percent of the total stock of the company. Lincoln family members and former Lincoln executives owned about half the remainder.

As Lincoln was preparing to report its first quarterly loss in August 1992, the directors voted to suspend repurchases under the Stock Purchase Plan in order to prevent wholesale tendering of shares by employees at a time when Lincoln was short of cash. The change in policy meant that employees could sell their stock in the open market as unrestricted stock if they wished to convert it to cash. At that time, book value (and therefore market value) was about $19 per share. As it turned out, only 11 percent of the restricted shares were converted.

In preparation for the public issue of stock in 1995, the Employees' Stock Purchase Plan was terminated on March 30, automatically converting all shares issued under it to unrestricted stock. Market value of the shares at that time was about $40. After the public issue, shareholders approved a new stock purchase plan permitting employees to purchase up to $10,000 per year in open-market shares without brokers' commissions.

Vacations. Lincoln's plants were closed for two weeks in August and two weeks during the Christmas season for vacations, which were unpaid. Employees with over 25 years of service got a fifth week of vacation at a time acceptable to superiors. When Lincoln was unable to meet its customers' orders in 1994, most employees agreed to work overtime through the August vacation period. Some of the employees were given vacations at alternate times.

Fringe Benefits. Lincoln sponsored a medical plan (with the cost deducted from the annual bonus pool) and a company-paid retirement program. At the main plant, a cafeteria operated on a break-even basis, serving meals at about sixty percent of outside prices. The Employee Association, to which the company did not contribute, provided disability insurance and social and athletic activities. Dick Sabo commented.

The company maintains traditional fringe benefits which include life insurance, health care, paid vacations, an annuity program (401K), and a variety of employee participation activities. All of these programs, of course, reduce the amount of

money which otherwise could be received by the employees as bonus. Each employee is, therefore, acutely aware of the impact of such benefit items on their overall earnings in each year.

He also cautioned,

When you use "participation," put quotes around it. Because we believe that each person should participate only in those decisions he is most knowledgeable about. I don't think production employees should control the decisions of the chairman. They don't know as much as he does about the decisions he is involved in.

The primary means of employee participation beyond an employee's immediate work environment were the suggestion program and the Advisory Board. Members of the Advisory Board were elected by employees and met with President Fred Mackenbach every two weeks. Unlike James Lincoln and Bill Irrgang, CEOs Willis and Hastings did not regularly attend these meetings. Responses to all Advisory Board items were promised by the following meeting. Exhibit 8 provides excerpts from minutes of the Advisory Board meeting of March 14, 1995 (generally typical of the group's deliberations).

The Advisory Board could only advise, not direct, although its recommendations were taken seriously. Its influence was shown on December 1, 1995, when Lincoln reversed a two-year-old policy of paying lower wages to new hires. Veteran workers had complained loudly. *Business Week* quoted Joseph Tuck, an inspector with 18 years' service: "If an individual shows he can handle the workload, he should be rewarded" with full pay.[5]

INTERNATIONAL EXPANSION

Internationally, the welding equipment industry was highly fragmented but consolidating. No global statistics reported total economic activity or companies' market shares in various countries, but many developed economies had local suppliers. Two U.S. producers—Lincoln and Miller Electric—and one European firm, ESAB (the largest welding firm in the world by 1996), were present in most markets. (Exhibit 9, adapted from the 1995 annual report, shows Lincoln's recent sales by region.)

EXHIBIT 8 *Excerpts From Advisory Board Minutes, March 14, 1995*

Mr. Mackenbach opened the meeting by welcoming three new members to the Board. He called on Mr. Beddia to inform the Board about the Harvest for Hunger food drive.

Prior Items

1. Could all air-cooled engines be covered when we receive them? Answer: The Material Handling Department will cover the top pallet of each stack when the engines are unloaded.

2. Could the 401K contributions from bonus be included in the year-to-date totals on the remaining regular December pay stubs? Answer: Yes, it will be.

3. An employee was almost hit by a speeding electric cart in Bay 16. Could a slow speed sign be posted? Answer: Signs cautioning pedestrians regarding Towmotor traffic have been installed. Additional changes are being reviewed.

New Business

1. Why was an employee of the Motor Division penalized for a safety issue when he performed his job as instructed? Answer: Referred to Mr. Beddia.

2. Has our total percent of market share increased? Answer: In the past, we could provide a precise answer. Some of our competitors no longer provide the required information to NEMA. However, in our judgment, we are increasing our percent of market share in both consumables and equipment.

3. Could an additional microwave unit be installed in the Bay 24 vending area? Answer: Referred to Mr. Crissey.

4. Could we consider buying an emergency vehicle instead of paying between $300 and $500 per ambulance run to the hospital? Answer: When we use the services of the Euclid Fire and Rescue Squad, there is a charge of approximately $350. While in general this charge is covered by hospitalization insurance, we will ask Mr. Trivisonno to review this with city officials.

5. When will the softball field be completed? Answer: A recreational area on the EP-3 site will become a reality, although certain issues with the city must be resolved first. We will show the preliminary layout at the next meeting.

6. Is a member of the Board of Directors being investigated for fraud? Answer: We are not aware of any investigation of this type.

7. Is our investment in Mexico losing value? Could we have an update as to how our Mexican operation is doing? Answer: Yes. An update will be provided at the next meeting.

8. Could something be done to eliminate the odor created when the septic tank is cleaned? Answer: Referred to Mr. Hellings.

Until 1986, Lincoln Electric held to James Lincoln's original policy toward international ventures, according to Sam Evans, regional manager of international and a 40-year Lincoln veteran. James Lincoln had felt his company could manufacture in any English-speaking country. Otherwise, he let others promote Lincoln products internationally. Evans described the approach:

We dealt with Armco International, which was a division of Armco Steel. Lincoln licensed Armco to manufacture and market our products in Mexico, Uruguay, Brazil, Argentina, and in France. It was electrodes, but included assembly of machines in Mexico. Armco also marketed Lincoln products along the Pacific Rim and in a few other areas of the world. At one point, we also had a joint venture with Big Three Corporation in Scotland.

In 1986, Lincoln Electric faced a newly aggressive Scandinavian competitor, ESAB Corporation, part of the Swiss-Swedish engineering/energy group Asea Brown Boveri. ESAB had bought up welding products manufacturers throughout the world during the industry downturn of 1982–1985. Starting in 1986, ESAB began to penetrate the U.S. market, buying several U.S. welding products companies (trade names acquired by ESAB included Oxweld, Genuine

EXHIBIT 9 *Financial Results by Geographic Sector, 1993–1995 (in thousands of dollars)*

	United States	Europe	Other Countries	Total*
1995				
Net Sales to Unaffiliated Customers**	$711,940	$201,672	$118,786	$1,032,398
Pre-Tax Profit (Loss)	79,737	10,171	10,956	99,584
Identifiable Assets	404,972	194,319	80,921	617,760
1994				
Net Sales to Unaffiliated Customers	$641,607	$156,803	$108,194	$906,604
Pre-Tax Profit (Loss)	68,316	7,891	4,062	80,168
Identifiable Assets	350,012	165,722	76,129	556,857
1993				
Net Sales to Unaffiliated Customers	$543,458	$211,268	$91,273	$845,999
Pre-Tax Profit (Loss)	42,570	(68,865)	(22,903)	(46,950)
Identifiable Assets	389,247	172,136	69,871	559,543

*Totals for Profit/Loss and Identifiable Assets will not cross-add due to elimination of intercompany transactions.

**Net Sales reported for the United States include materials exported to unaffiliated customers, amounting to $81,770 in 1995; $64,400 in 1994; and $58,100 in 1993. Net Sales excludes intracompany sales to Lincoln's overseas branches.

Heliarc, Plasmarc, Allstate Welding Products, Alloy Rods, and the former Lindy Division of Union Carbide). ESAB opened an electrode plant less than a mile from Lincoln's Cleveland headquarters.

In the global recession of the early 1980s, ESAB's movement toward consolidation threatened to give the firm a volume base large enough to provide economies of scale for research and development programs. Dick Sabo said Lincoln's CEO, Ted Willis, was concerned and met with the chairman of ESAB in 1986, hoping "that we could work together." The relationship soon soured, however, and Willis decided to challenge ESAB internationally.

From 1986–1992, Lincoln purchased controlling interests in manufacturing and marketing operations in 16 countries. It took over most of the operations previously licensed to Armco and Big Three. It put a factory in Brazil, where ESAB had an estimated 70-percent market share. Lincoln expanded into gas welding and cutting by buying Harris Calorific Corporation, which made oxyacetylene cutting and welding equipment in the U.S., Italy, and Ireland. Lincoln's largest new investment was the purchase of Messer Griesheim's welding products business in Germany, considered ESAB's most profitable terri-

tory. Altogether, Lincoln opened or expanded plants in England, France, the Netherlands, Spain, Norway, Mexico, Venezuela, and Japan. The expansion required heavy borrowing; for the first time, James Lincoln's conservative financial policies were discarded. Long-term debt rose from zero in 1986 to over $220 million in 1992. (Exhibit 10 summarizes Lincoln financial statements for 1986–1995.)

Separate Lincoln-type incentive management plans remained in place at the company's factories in Australia, Mexico, and the U.S., but attempts to implement such plans in other countries were largely unsuccessful. Sabo said the main problem was that Europe lapsed into recession. He added, "Germany started to fail within two months after we purchased Griesheim. The country had 27-percent unemployment. So we didn't implement the system at all. We didn't get a chance to." In Brazil, Willis learned that regulations defined incentive bonuses to be part of base salaries, which could not be reduced during downturns, so the Lincoln system was not installed there.

Welder Scott Skrjanc, a 17-year veteran of the production force, had another idea about why the system did not work out overseas:

EXHIBIT 10 *Summaries of Lincoln Financial Statements, 1986–1995**

BALANCE SHEETS	12/86	12/87	12/88	12/89	12/90	12/91	12/92	12/93	12/94	12/95
Assets										
Cash and Equivalents	47.0	61.0	23.9	19.5	15.5	20.3	20.6	20.4	10.4	10.1
Receivables	46.0	61.7	90.9	100.8	127.3	118.0	111.3	110.5	126.0	140.8
Inventories	52.3	74.7	116.3	120.5	164.4	206.3	171.3	143.7	155.3	182.9
Other Current Assets	9.4	9.1	12.0	14.4	14.5	17.5	18.0	51.1	21.7	23.3
Total Current Assets	154.8	206.4	243.1	255.1	321.7	362.1	321.2	325.7	313.4	357.1
Gross Plant	153.2	195.7	274.8	328.2	387.7	422.9	435.2	406.7	444.5	490.6
Accumulated Depreciation	93.4	121.2	148.6	170.2	193.1	213.3	226.8	237.0	260.3	285.0
Net Plant	59.8	74.5	126.3	158.0	194.7	209.6	208.4	169.7	184.2	205.6
Long-Term Investments	11.5	0.3	0.0	0.0	0.0	0.0	0.0	0.0	0.0	0.0
Intangible and Other Assets	13.1	13.4	33.8	42.6	55.9	68.6	73.7	64.1	59.2	55.1
Total Assets	239.2	294.7	403.2	455.8	572.2	640.3	603.3	559.5	556.9	617.8
Liabilities & Equity										
Short-Term Debt	4.6	6.6	39.2	41.6	40.6	50.7	27.1	33.4	18.1	29.8
Accounts Payable	11.2	23.4	36.8	40.0	44.3	46.6	44.2	43.5	54.8	53.9
Other Current Liabilities	25.1	32.7	38.1	41.0	52.4	61.3	77.2	99.0	71.2	85.0
Total Current Liabilities	41.0	62.7	114.2	122.6	137.3	158.6	148.5	175.9	144.1	168.7
Long-Term Debt	0.0	5.7	17.5	30.2	109.2	155.5	221.5	216.9	194.8	93.6
Other Long-Term Liabilities	11.7	9.7	15.3	16.6	24.0	20.3	17.8	15.3	17.0	20.1
Minority Interests	4.0	11.9	31.4	42.6	47.4	41.7	16.8	7.9	6.8	5.5
Total Liabilities	56.7	90.0	178.4	211.9	317.9	376.1	404.6	416.0	218.6	287.9
Common Equity	182.6	204.7	224.8	243.8	254.3	264.1	198.7	143.5	194.1	329.9
Total Equity Capital	182.6	204.7	224.8	243.8	254.3	264.1	198.7	143.5	194.1	329.9
Total Liabilities & Capital	239.2	294.7	403.2	455.8	572.2	640.3	603.3	559.5	556.9	617.8
INCOME STATEMENTS										
Net Sales	370.2	443.2	570.2	692.8	796.7	833.9	853.0	846.0	906.6	1,032.4
Cost of Goods Sold	245.4	279.4	361.0	441.3	510.5	521.8	553.1	532.8	556.3	634.6
Gross Profit	124.8	163.8	209.2	251.5	286.2	312.1	299.9	313.2	350.3	397.8
SG&A Expense	100.3	119.7	165.2	211.1	259.2	270.5	280.3	273.3	261.7	289.8
Operating Profit	24.5	44.1	44.0	40.4	27.0	41.6	19.6	39.9	88.6	108.0
Restructuring Charge	0	0	0	0	0	0	−23.9	−70.1	2.7	0
Non-Recurring Oper. Exp.	0	0	0	0	0	0	−18.9	−3.7	0	0
Other Income	6.1	7.1	14.4	15.7	14.4	8.5	7.5	4.5	4.5	3.9
EBIT	30.6	51.2	58.4	56.1	41.4	50.1	−15.7	−29.4	95.9	111.9
Interest Expense	1.0	1.3	2.6	7.6	11.1	15.7	18.7	17.6	15.7	12.3
Pre-tax Earnings	29.6	49.9	55.9	48.5	30.4	34.4	−34.4	−47.0	80.2	99.6
Income Taxes	13.7	22.3	21.5	21.0	19.3	20.0	11.4	−6.4	32.2	38.1
Accounting Change	0	0	0	0	0	0	0	2.5	0	0
Net Income	15.8	27.6	34.4	27.6	11.1	14.4	−45.8	−38.1	48.0	61.5

*Source of Data, McDonald and Company and SEC reports.

Their culture, as I understand it, was so much different from ours. Their work ethic and work habits, I guess, aren't like the United States. They have a saying in German that means, "slowly, slowly, but good." And I guess that's how they perceive it. Here, we do high-quality work, but we work fast—and smart. As you get older, you get wiser and work smarter.

Sam Evans, who managed Lincoln's operations in Eastern Europe until cancer forced his return to Cleveland for successful treatment, gave his view of CEO Willis' performance in the international expansion:

Ted Willis' belief—and I think it was a very good belief, although he is often criticized by Lincoln people—was that we needed a stronger world organization. The welding industry was consolidating in the world market, much like the steel industry did in the 1930s. He felt we needed this larger sales base so that we could invest in the research and development to maintain our position in the industry. I think that has succeeded. Even though we have had failures internationally, we have grown with our base.

We are coming out with a lot of new items—the new square-wave machines, which control the actual wave form, the new stainless products, the inverter technology in motors and machines. We are moving rapidly ahead of the industry. That was Mr. Willis' vision, and it was a good one. His financial vision wasn't so good—perhaps.

Retrenchment and Turnaround under Hastings

Willis retired in 1992 and Don Hastings became chief executive officer. Hastings set about "consolidating and reorganizing" the foreign operations. He agreed with ESAB to close the Lincoln factory in Brazil and to license ESAB to make Lincoln products there. Similarly, ESAB closed its Spanish electrode plant, and Lincoln used its excess capacity in that country to supply ESAB's needs. Lincoln mothballed its German plant, losing an estimated $100 million there. It also shut down factories in Venezuela and Japan. Practically all of Lincoln's international operations that were not closed were scaled back. By 1996 ESAB, now owned by Britain's Charter Group, was recognized as the largest welding vendor in the world, with key markets in East and Western Europe, South America, and the Far East; it had the "leading position in stick electrodes (a declining market) and an even bigger position in fluxed core wires (a rapidly growing market)."[6]

In 1992 and 1993, Lincoln wrote off approximately $130 million of its foreign assets and reported its first-ever net losses—$46 million and $38 million respectively. Citing the profitable performance of the firm's U.S. workers, Hastings convinced the Board of Directors to give them incentive bonuses averaging $19,000 each year in spite of the overall losses. Dividends were cut by nearly 40 percent from the 1991 level. In 1994, Hastings told the U.S. employees, "We went from five plants in four countries in 1986 to 21 plants in 15 countries in 1992. We did it too fast, we paid too much, we didn't understand the international markets or cultures, and then we got hit by a tremendous global recession." By mid 1995, Lincoln was down to 16 plants in 11 countries. Dick Sabo described the company's new relationship with ESAB:

So the animosity has ended. We're still competitors, but we are more like the U.S. competitors. In the US, we've always had a competitive situation, but we're friendly competitors. So, overall, the strategy that Ted Willis originated was good. The implementation was poor. That's where the problem was.

Rank and file employees commented on the results of the attempt at international expansion. Stenographer Dee Chesko, a 27-year employee, said she had heard no bitterness voiced about the losses:

What I was hearing was people were disappointed—that they felt upper management should know, per se, what they're doing. You know, how could this happen? Not bitterness . . . a little frustration. But, if companies are to expand and be global, this has to be expected.

Assembler Kathleen Hoenigman, hired in 1997, added:

They say, "We want to be number one. We want to be number one." So we are going to keep buying and buying and buying. I think we will be investing more overseas. And I think we are going to be number one internationally, not just in the U.S., but the manufacturing will be done here. The expansion helped. We lost money, but I think it

C-331

helped. You know what, if we didn't do as we did, we wouldn't be known as well as we are right now. Because we were staying just like a little . . . a little pea, while everybody was building up around us.

Sabo said Lincoln expected to continue expanding internationally, "But we're going at it a little differently." He explained,

Under Willis, we bought a manufacturing site with the intent of creating the marketing demand. Under Hastings, we're developing the marketing demand with the anticipation that we'll build the manufacturing site to meet the demand. So what we're trying to do is take the existing facilities that we have and sell a lot of product and create enough demand so that we have to buy—or build—more facilities to service that demand.

We're just getting there in terms of being global. We're global to the extent that we market in 123 countries. We're global to the extent that we have distributors in 86 different countries. We're global because we have manufacturing sites in ten countries. Are we global in our management style? No. We're just starting to develop that.

THE U.S. WELDING PRODUCTS INDUSTRY IN 1995

The welding products market of the mid 1990s was classified as "mature and cyclical." In the United States, annual sales volume had ranged between $2.5 and $2.7 billion since 1988 (see Exhibit 11). The main arc-welding products were power sources and welding machines; consumable items such as welding electrodes; accessories such as protective clothing; automated wire feeding systems; and devices to manipulate or position the electrodes, such as robots.

After the downturn in 1982–1983, when industry sales fell 30–40 percent, the U.S. welding products industry consolidated. By 1995, at least 75 percent of machine and consumables sales could be attributed to just four companies: Lincoln, Miller Electric Company (which did not sell consumables), ESAB Corporation, and Hobart Brothers, Inc. ESAB was now owned by Britain's Charter Group; both Miller and Hobart had recently been acquired by Illinois Tool Works, Inc. Lincoln and Miller were thought to have about equal unit sales of machines and power

supplies, about double Hobart's volume. Hundreds of smaller companies marketed various niche products, and several international firms sold limited lines of transformer- and inverter-based machines in the U.S. and elsewhere. Over 600 exhibitors were registered to show their wares at the 1996 annual Welding Show in Chicago, where 25,000 potential customers would attend.

Starting in the early 90s, Lincoln, Miller, and Hobart each began buying similar articulated-arm robots and adapting them to welding applications. The size of the robotics segment of the welding products market was unclear in 1995, but Chet Woodman, head of Lincoln Automation, said his unit had robotics sales of about $7 million in 1994 and predicted $50 million annual revenue by the year 2000.

ESAB, Lincoln, and Hobart each marketed a wide range of continuous-wire and stick electrodes for welding mild steel, aluminum, cast iron, and stainless and special steels. Most electrodes were designed to meet the standards of the American Welding Society (AWS) and were thus essentially the same as to size and composition from one manufacturer to another. Price differences for similar products among the three companies amounted to only a percent or two. Low-price competitors were well represented in the market, however, as imported consumables that purported to meet AWS standards were commonly available. There was no testing system to confirm a product's conformance to the standards.

Every electrode manufacturer had a limited number of unique products, which typically constituted only a small percentage of its total sales. There were also many producers of specialized electrodes for limited applications, such as welding under water and welding space-age alloys, and several international companies marketed general-purpose electrodes. Wire for gas-shielded (MIG) welding was thought to be the biggest-selling welding consumable. ESAB claimed to have the largest share of the global welding consumables and materials market.

LINCOLN'S MANUFACTURING PROCESSES

Lincoln made about twice as many different products in 1995 as it had ten years earlier. Its net sales per employee in 1994 were $159,248. For U.S. em-

EXHIBIT 11 *Trends and Forecasts: Welding Apparatus (SIC 3548) (in millions of dollars except as noted)*

	1987	1988	1989	1990	1991	1992[1]	1993[2]	1994[3]
Industry Data								
Value of shipments[4]	2,105	2,498	2,521	2,684	2,651	2,604	2,576	—
Total employment (000)	18.7	19.7	19.0	19.2	19.5	19.4	19.5	—
Production workers (000)	11.5	12.3	11.6	12.0	11.8	11.7	11.7	—
Average hourly earnings ($)	12.10	12.45	12.67	13.15	13.07	—	—	—
Capital expenditures	45.4	49.3	59.1	67.7	50.5	—	—	—
Product Data								
Value of shipments[5]	1,918	2,263	2,298	2,475	2,434	2,374	2,340	—
Value of shipments (1987 $)	1,918	2,135	2,077	2,154	2,034	1,935	1,874	1,954
Trade Data								
Value of imports	—	—	480	365	478	381	458	458
Value of exports	—	—	491	566	597	621	661	671

			Percent Change (1989–1994)			
	88–89	89–90	90–91	91–92	92–93	93–94
Industry Data						
Value of shipments[4]	0.9	6.5	−1.2	−1.8	−1.1	—
Value of shipments (1987 $)	−3.3	2.5	−5.2	−4.1	−3.0	3.9
Total employment (000)	−3.6	1.1	1.6	−0.5	0.5	—
Production workers (000)	−5.7	3.4	−1.7	−0.8	0.0	—
Average hourly earnings ($)	1.8	3.8	−0.6	—	—	—
Capital expenditures	19.9	14.6	−25.4	—	—	—
Product Data						
Value of shipments[5]	1.5	7.7	−1.7	−2.5	−1.4	—
Value of shipments (1987 $)	−2.7	3.7	−5.6	−4.9	−3.2	4.3
Value of exports	747	15.3	5.5	4.0	8.1	11.3

C-333

Source: U.S. Department of Commerce: Bureau of the Census; International U.S. Industrial Outlook January, 1994.
[1]Estimate, except exports and imports.
[2]Estimate.
[3]Forecast.
[4]Value of all products and services sold by establishments in the welding apparatus industry.
[5]Value of products classified in the welding apparatus industry produced b.

ployees only, the number was approximately $225,000. About two-thirds of net sales was represented by products made in the Cleveland area.

Fortune magazine declared Lincoln's Euclid operation one of America's ten best-managed factories, and compared it to a General Electric plant also on the list:

Stepping into GE's spanking new dishwasher plant, an awed supplier said, is like stepping "into the Hyatt Regency." By comparison, stepping into

Lincoln Electric's 33-year-old, cavernous, dimly lit factory is like stumbling into a dingy big-city YMCA. It's only when one starts looking at how these factories do things that similarities become apparent. They have found ways to merge design with manufacturing, build in quality, make wise choices about automation, get close to customers, and handle their work forces.[7]

As it had for decades, Lincoln required most suppliers to deliver raw materials just as needed in production. James Lincoln had counseled producing for stock when necessary to maintain employment. For many years after his death, however, the firm manufactured only to customer order. In the late 1980s, Hastings decided to resume maintaining substantial finished goods inventories. Lincoln then purchased its finished goods warehouse.

Outsourcing

It was James Lincoln's policy to keep Lincoln as insulated as possible from work stoppages in supplier plants, especially unionized ones. He also felt Lincoln quality was higher than that most suppliers could provide. So instead of purchasing most components from outsiders, Lincoln made them from basic industrial raw materials such as coils of steel sheet and bar, pieces of metal plate, spools of copper and aluminum wire, and pallets of paints and varnishes. Lincoln even made its own electronic circuit boards, to assure their performance in outdoor, cold, dirty conditions; commercial suppliers were accustomed to making circuit boards for warm, clean computers. At one point the firm had contemplated buying its own steel rolling mill. President Ted Willis, however, was concerned over the mill's union affiliation, and the purchase was not completed.

As an exception to on-site manufacture of components, gasoline and diesel engines for the engine-driven machines were purchased. Like its main competitors, Lincoln used Wisconsin-Continental, Perkins, and Deutz engines in 1995.

Welding Machine Manufacture

In the machines area, most engine-driven welders, power supplies, wire feeders, and so forth, were assembled, tested, and packaged on conveyor lines. Almost all components were made by numerous small "factories within a factory." Various of these small factories—mostly open work areas—made gasoline tanks, steel shafts, wiring harnesses, and even switches, rheostats, and transformers. The shaft for a certain generator, for example, was made from round steel bar by two men who used five machines. A saw cut the bar to length, a digital lathe machined different sections to varying diameters, a special milling machine cut a slot for the keyway, and so

forth, until a finished shaft was produced. The operators moved the shafts from machine to machine and made necessary adjustments and tool changes. Nearby, a man punched, shaped and painted sheet metal cowling parts. In another area, a woman and a man put steel laminations onto rotor shafts, then wound, insulated, and tested the rotors. Many machines in the factory appeared old, even obsolete; James Lincoln had always insisted on a one-year payback period for new investments, and it appeared the policy was still in effect.

Consumables Manufacture

The company was secretive about its consumables production, and outsiders were barred from the Mentor, Ohio plant (which made only electrodes) and from the electrode area of the main plant. Electrode manufacture was highly capital intensive, and teams of Lincoln workers who made electrodes shared group piece rates. To make electrodes, rod purchased from metals producers, usually in coils, was drawn down to make wire of various diameters. For stick electrodes, the wire was cut into pieces, most commonly 14″ long, and coated with pressed-powder "flux." Dick Sabo commented,

> The actual production of a stick electrode has not changed for at least forty years. Bill Irrgang designed that equipment. As to the constituents which make up the electrodes, that may change almost daily. There are changes in design from time to time. And every new batch of raw material has a little different consistency, and we have to adjust for that. We make our own iron oxide [a main ingredient of many fluxes]. We have had that powder kiln in operation since about the 1930s. We may have the largest production facility for iron oxide pellets in the world. At first, we contemplated selling the pellets. But we decided not to give our competition an edge.

Stick electrodes were packaged in boxes weighing two to 50 pounds. Continuous-wire electrode, generally smaller in diameter, was packaged in coils and spools, also two to 50 pounds each, and in drums weighing up to half a ton. Some wire electrode was coated with copper to improve conductivity. Lincoln's Innershield wire, like the "cored" wire of other manufacturers, was hollow and filled with a material similar to that used to coat stick electrodes.

The New Electric Motor Factory

In 1992, Lincoln saw an opportunity to become a major factor in the electric motor business by purchasing the assets of General Motors' AC-Delco plant in Dayton, Ohio. New government regulations on motors' energy efficiency made it necessary to redesign whole product lines; GM decided instead to exit the industry. Lincoln's intent was to combine AC-Delco's technology and product line with Lincoln's manufacturing expertise and cost structure in the Dayton plant. Don Hastings offered to involve the existing union in its operation of the plant if it were retained. Dick Sabo described the implementation efforts:

> We asked the AC-Delco employees if they wanted to adopt the Lincoln Incentive System and keep their plant open—and their jobs. They voted overwhelmingly not to adopt the system. And they knew all about us. We put a lot of effort into telling them about Lincoln, even brought some employees up here to tour our plant and talk to Lincoln people. What struck Mr. Hastings as odd was that people would vote themselves out of work rather than knuckle down and put in the effort that it takes to be in the motor business. That was sort of an eye opener for Lincoln Electric.

In mid-1995, Lincoln's new electric motor factory, close to the main plant, was near completion and in partial operation. The plant was designed to make motors from one-third to 1,250 horsepower, in custom configurations as well as standard specifications, with shipment six days after customer orders. Lincoln's net sales of electric motors in 1994 totaled about $50 million, and the goal was $100 million in sales by the year 2000.

Robotics

Adjacent to the electric motor factory was a smaller building housing Lincoln's Automation unit. There, work teams of two or three put together robotic welding units that combined Fanuc (Japanese) articulated arms with Lincoln automatic welders. In operation, the robot arm manipulated the wire electrode much as a human operator would, but faster and more accurately. The system priced at about $100,000, could be purchased with a laser "eye" to track irregular seams and could be programmed to follow any three dimensional path within the arm's reach. Chet Woodman, head of Lincoln Automation, was a former Hobart executive with over a decade of experience in robotics manufacturing and marketing.

MANAGEMENT ORGANIZATION

James Lincoln stressed the need to protect management's authority. "Management in all successful departments of industry must have complete power," he said, "Management is the coach who must be obeyed. The men, however, are the players who alone can win the game." Examples of management's authority were the right to transfer workers among jobs, to switch between overtime and short time as required, and to assign specific parts to individual workers. As to executive perquisites, there were few—crowded, austere offices, no executive washrooms or lunchrooms or automobiles, and no reserved parking spaces, except for visitors. Even CEO Hastings and President Mackenbach paid for their own meals, normally in the employee cafeteria.

James Lincoln never allowed preparation of a formal organization chart, saying this might limit flexibility. Irrgang and Willis continued that policy. During the 1970s, Harvard Business School researchers prepared a chart reflecting the implied management relationships at Lincoln. It became available within the company, and Irrgang felt this had a disruptive effect. Only after Hastings became CEO was a formal chart prepared. (Exhibit 12 shows the official chart in 1995 and Exhibit 6 lists officers and directors.) Two levels of management, at most, existed between supervisors and Mackenbach. Production supervisors at Lincoln typically were responsible for 60 to over 100 workers. Hastings, who was 67, had recruited experienced managers from outside the company and appointed a number of new, young vice presidents, mainly from the field, so they could compete for the top jobs.

Promotion from Within

Until the 1990s, Lincoln had a firm policy of promotion from within and claimed to hire above the entry level "only when there are no suitable internal applicants." In 1990, all senior managers at Lincoln

EXHIBIT 12 *Lincoln Organization Chart, 1995*

were career Lincoln employees—and all directors were present or former employees or Lincoln family members. However, when Lincoln purchased Harris Calorific in 1992, its CEO, Paul F. Fantelli, was retained and later became vice president, business development of Lincoln. A number of other acquired company officials were integrated into Lincoln's management structure.

Lincoln's CFO in 1996, H. Jay Elliott, came from Goodyear in 1993; General Counsel Frederick Stueber came from a private law firm in 1995; and Anthony Massaro, the nominated successor to Fred Mackenbach as president, joined Lincoln from his position as group president of Westinghouse Electric Co. in 1993. Several outside directors were also

elected, including the CEO of Capitol American Financial Corporation, a former vice chairman of General Electric, a former CEO of Westinghouse, and the CEO of Libby Corporation. Still, there were no announced plans to hire more managers from outside. And insiders and Lincoln family members retained a clear majority on the board.

Lincoln managers received a base salary plus an incentive bonus. The bonus was calculated in the same way as for workers. The only exceptions were the three outsiders Hastings hired as managers in 1993–1995 and the chairman and chief executive officer. The former outsiders had special employment contracts. Sabo explained how the CEO was compensated:

James Lincoln set the chairman's salary at $50,000 plus 0.1 percent of sales. After Willis became chairman, it was based on a percentage of sales plus a percentage of profit. It became apparent that when the company started losing money it was difficult to pay someone based on losses. So they changed the approach for Don Hastings. [Through the lean years] Don has somewhere around $600 thousand base salary plus incentives.

For 1995, Hastings was paid $1,003,901.[8]

LOOKING TO THE FUTURE

When Lincoln in the spring of 1995 announced plans to raise capital with a public issue of stock, Dick Sabo said that certain Lincoln family members were afraid the family would lose control of the company. "Paranoid, I guess, is the proper term," he remarked. Sam Evans added,

I hope the public issue is handled in such a manner that those public owners understand that the success of this company is based on the incentive system. For sixty or seventy years, that has been our success—through the contribution of the employees. We have succeeded because we had a good product, good R&D, and excellent management for most of that period. But we've also had great contribution from the employees.

With the public issue accomplished and a record year in the books, noted *Business Week*,

. . . executives are now considering ways to move toward a more traditional pay scheme and away from the flat percentage-bonus formula. "The bonus is a good program, and it has worked well, but it's got to be modified some," says Director David C. Lincoln, whose father John C. Lincoln founded the company in 1895. Adds Edward E. Lawler, who heads the University of Southern California's Center for Effective Organizations: "One of the issues with Lincoln is how [its pay plan] can survive rapid growth and globalization."

C-337

NOTES

1. Feder, Barnaby J. "Rethinking a Model Incentive Plan," *The New York Times*, September 5, 1994, Section I, p. 33.
2. Gerdel, Thomas W. "Lincoln Electric Experiences Season of Worker Discontent," *Plain Dealer*, December 10, 1995.
3. Schiller, Zachary, "A Model Incentive Plan Gets Caught in a Vise," *Business Week*, January 22, 1996, p. 89.
4. Eiselen, F.C., E. Lewis, and D.G. Downey, eds. *The Abingdon Bible Commentary*, Nashville, TN: The Abingdon Press, Inc., 1929, pp. 960–969.
5. Schiller, *op. cit.*
6. Utley, N., *et al.*, Greig Middleton & Co., Ltd. Company report number 1674211, *Charter 12/12/95*. Investext 02/23.
7. Bylinsky, Gene. "America's Best-Managed Factories," *Fortune*, May 28, 1984, p. 16.
8. Baltimore, MD, Disclosures, Inc. (Via Dow Jones News Service).

Lockheed and Martin Marietta: The Defense Megamerger

Jeremy Wait
Chintan Gohil
Allison Daniel
Sayed Mahmood Ahmed

These are Darwinian times in our industry, failure to change is failure to survive.
—Chairman Norman R. Augustine, Martin Marietta Corporation.

OVERVIEW

On March 15, 1995, two of the giants of the aerospace defense industry, Lockheed and Martin Marietta, merged formally into a single company, Lockheed Martin. In June 1995, Lockheed Martin announced that the new company would lay off 15,000 employees and close a dozen manufacturing and research facilities nationwide. Yet even as the company painfully streamlined, the leadership insisted that this was part of a long-term strategy to redefine the company to ensure its continued survival and long-term positioning.

[Chairman and chief executive officer Daniel] Tellep insists on looking at the benefits of the merger in the advantages offered in the long term. The company's "vision statement" defines what they see as their critical success factors in the industry [see Exhibit 1]. He says, "Anybody who looks at us and says what does it mean during the next two years is really missing the broader point of the merger, which is all about positioning ourselves for the long haul."[1]

Tellep made it clear that the merger was only part of the firm's continuing evolution to meet the

challenges of a hostile environment. He voiced Lockheed Martin's commitment to continue looking for opportunities when he said, "We are conducting a thorough review of our business portfolio to determine appropriate investment and divestiture strategies."[2]

However, the future was full of potential hazards. The defense contracts on which both Lockheed and Martin Marietta had depended traditionally for a majority of revenue were drying up. Defense companies were consolidating rapidly to achieve larger shares of the smaller pie. Lockheed and Martin Marietta had previously moved away from the commercial aircraft market. Lockheed Martin would have to stake out aggressively its position in the rapidly changing world. How should the company position itself for long-term growth and profitability? Will the merger help Lockheed Martin achieve a stronger competitive position or did the two companies overdiversify by merging?

LOCKHEED MARTIN

Lockheed Martin is a diversified corporation now organized into five sectors: aeronautics; electronics; environmental systems and technology; information and technology services; and space and strategic missiles. (See Exhibit 2 for a more complete company structure.) When the corporations merged, they reorganized to take advantage of potential synergies

This case was prepared under the direction of Professor Robert E. Hoskisson. The case is intended to be used as the basis for class discussion rather than to illustrate either effective or ineffective handling of an administrative situation.

EXHIBIT 1 *Lockheed Martin Vision Statement*

Our vision is for Lockheed Martin to be recognized as the world's premier systems engineering and technology enterprise. Our mission is to build on our aerospace heritage to meet the needs of our customers with high-quality products and services. And, in so doing, produce superior returns for our stockholders and foster growth and achievement for our employees.

Overarching Principles

In realizing our vision, we will adhere to the highest standards of ethical conduct in everything we do. We will achieve mission success for our customers, create opportunity for our employees, provide strong returns for our stockholders, and serve the communities where we live and work. Our actions are guided by certain unifying principles:

- Ethical conduct in dealing with our colleagues, customers, stockholders, suppliers, and the public, providing the basis for earned trust.
- Mission success as we carry out our responsibility to achieve superior performance and to provide our customers the quality products and services they have a right to expect.
- Technological leadership in all disciplines that contribute to fulfilling our vision.
- Financial strength and profitability to meet the expectations of our stockholders and enable us to aggressively pursue new business opportunities.
- Competitiveness through attention to cost, efficiency and continuous improvement.
- Fair treatment and candid communication with the diverse workforce from whom our enterprise derives its strength.
- Decisiveness and responsiveness in addressing our internal and external challenges.
- Active, responsible citizenship to the nation and the communities in which we live and work.

and to group the businesses into more manageable and related sectors.

In its aeronautics division, for example, Lockheed Martin provides several advanced aircraft for specialty purposes. Its P-3 is used by many countries for maritime patrols, and its versatile C-130 Hercules is a large rugged transport plane used for both hunting hurricanes and icebergs and transporting relief supplies (21 tons in one flight). Lockheed Martin's F-16s, the world's lowest-cost, high-capability, multi-role fighter is used by the air forces of five countries. The company also has experience with stealth technology and is involved with several projects seeking to improve or modify aircraft with this capability.[3]

Lockheed Martin's space and strategic missiles sector has a worldwide presence with commercial satellites and launch vehicle operations, as well as TIROS weather satellites, which provide data to 140 nations. Additionally, its satellite system, INTELSAT VIII, will serve the communications needs of more than 125 national customers worldwide. In a strategic partnership with France's Matra Marconi Space and Korea's Goldstar and Korean Air,

Lockheed Martin is designing, producing, and delivering a two-satellite system for broadcasting and telecommunications services for South Korea. With Russia's Khrunichev Enterprise and NPO Energia, Lockheed Martin is jointly marketing the services of the Atlas and Proton rockets to give commercial customers reliable systems and greater schedule flexibility in launching spacebound payloads. Most recently, Lockheed Martin was chosen to provide a satellite-based mobile telephone system for Southeast Asia known as ACES.

Lockheed Martin's electronics sector produces the L-Band, solid-state FPS-117 radar, a worldwide standard for long-range aerial surveillance. The information and technology services sector produces aircraft simulators for air force customers in Europe, Asia, and the Middle East. The energy and environment sector is involved in new methods of hazardous waste cleanup and the development of new materials such as advanced ceramics for use in automobile engines. These are just a few examples among many (see Exhibit 3 for more products and services the firm offers and Exhibit 4 for a list of Lockheed Martin compa-

EXHIBIT 2 *Lockheed Martin Organization Chart*

nies). Lockheed Martin has created a global presence and has a presence in most significant markets.

HISTORICAL BACKGROUND OF LOCKHEED AND MARTIN MARIETTA

Lockheed History

After two failed ventures, Allen Lockheed formed a successful aircraft company in 1927. Although the company faced lean times during the Depression,

during World War II it found a niche as a military contractor. By May 1943, Lockheed had built a total of 19,297 aircraft for the Allied war effort, 9 percent of the United States' total production.

After World War II, Lockheed moved smoothly back into commercial production. It resumed manufacturing some of its civilian aircraft designs that had been suspended during the war and redesigned some of its military aircraft for civilian use. It also retained various military contracts.

The company expanded during the 1950s, built new plants, improved and expanded old ones, and continued to innovate. Lockheed projects were used extensively in the Korean conflict, and the Cold War proved to be a boon for the company.

EXHIBIT 3 *Lockheed Martin Corporation*

Sector	Products/Services	Description
Aeronautics Sector	<ul><li>F-16 fighter aircraft</li><li>F-22 tactical fighter</li><li>X-33 reusable launch vehicle (under development)</li></ul>	<ul><li>Technologically advanced fighter cargo and transport planes</li></ul>
Electronics Sector	<ul><li>AEGIS combat systems (phased array radar)</li><li>BSY-2 submarine combat system</li><li>APG-67 airborne radar</li><li>LANTRIN low-altitude navigation and targeting system</li></ul>	<ul><li>Military radar</li><li>Automated air traffic control</li><li>Flight and engine control</li><li>Mission planning</li><li>Fire control combat systems</li><li>Electronic warfare</li><li>Radar and sensor systems</li></ul>
Environmental Systems and Technology Sector	<ul><li>Emerging technologies: microengines</li><li>Computer security (for Information Superhighway)</li><li>Developing nickel and iron aluminides</li><li>Leader in supercomputing simulations (example: simulations of car crashes to check safety and efficiency)</li></ul>	<ul><li>Systems integrator for nation's nuclear weapon stockpile management program</li><li>National engineering and testing research center</li><li>Produces prototype of new products for commercialization</li></ul>
Information and Technology Services Sector	<ul><li>Host hardware platform for Sega</li><li>CASS (U.S. Navy standardized test equipment)</li><li>Supports government agencies<ul><li>Social Security Administration network</li><li>EPA network</li><li>Defense Department network</li><li>Knolls Atomic Power Laboratory</li></ul></li></ul>	<ul><li>Supports the other sectors with IT</li><li>Develops large complex information systems such as distributed client/server systems</li><li>Designs, manufactures, and markets computer graphic products</li><li>High-capacity data storage products</li><li>Integrated modular software and turnkey operations</li><li>Leading parking and traffic ticket company</li><li>Electronic toll collection and automated weigh station provider</li><li>Manages collection services for child support debt</li></ul>
Space and Strategic Missiles Sector	<ul><li>Launch services</li><li>Space launch vehicle manufacturing</li><li>Satellite manufacturing</li><li>Supporting ground services for all of the above</li><li>Hubble space telescope</li><li>Ballistic missiles</li><li>Titan and Atlas payload deployment rockets</li></ul>	<ul><li>Provides a full range of systems and services for access to space</li><li>Builds satellites for International Telecommunications Satellite Organization (INTELSAT)</li><li>Environment monitoring satellites</li></ul>

In 1953, the company formed Lockheed Missiles & Space Company. Because some U.S. administrations felt that nuclear weapons provided "more bang for the buck," missiles quickly became as important to Lockheed as aircraft. Lockheed was primarily responsible for several generations of submarine-launched nuclear missiles such as the Polaris and the Poseidon, as well as many other projects deemed vital to national security. By 1968, this division was active in such diverse areas as space exploration, oceanographic vessels, and tactical missiles.[4]

EXHIBIT 4 *Lockheed Martin Operating Units*

Subsidiaries and Other Investments	Martin Marietta Materials, Inc.
	Airport Group International, Inc.
	Space Imaging, Inc.
	Lockheed Martin Finance, Inc.
Aeronautics	Lockheed Martin Skunk Works, Palmdale, California
	Lockheed Martin Aircraft Services, Ontario, California
	Lockheed Martin Logistics Management, Arlington, Texas
	Lockheed Martin Aeronautical Systems, Marietta, Georgia
	Lockheed Martin Tactical Aircraft Systems, Fort Worth, Texas
	Lockheed Martin Aero & Naval Systems, Baltimore, Maryland
Electronics	Lockheed Martin Armament Systems, Burlington, Vermont; Milan, Tennessee
	Lockheed Martin Communications Systems, Camden, New Jersey
	Lockheed Martin Control Systems, Binghamton, New York
	Lockheed Martin Defense Systems, Pittsfield, Massachusetts
	Lockheed Martin Communications Systems, Camden, New Jersey
	Lockheed Martin Electronics & Missiles, Orlando and Ocala, Florida; Troy, Alabama
	Lockheed Martin Government Electronic Systems, Moorestown, New Jersey
	Lockheed Martin Ocean, Radar & Sensor Systems, Syracuse and Utica, New York
	Sanders, A Lockheed Martin Company, Nashua, New Hampshire
	Lockheed Martin Advanced Technology Laboratories, Camden, New Jersey
	Lockheed Martin Canada, Kanata, Ontario
	Lockheed Martin Electronics Laboratory, Syracuse, New York
	AV Technology, LLC, Chesterfield, Michigan
Energy and Environment	Lockheed Martin Energy Systems, Oak Ridge, Tennessee
	Lockheed Martin Idaho Technologies, Idaho Falls, Idaho
	Sandia Corporation, A Lockheed Martin Company, Albuquerque, New Mexico
	Lockheed Martin Environmental Systems and Technologies, Houston, Texas
	Lockheed Martin Utility Services, Bethesda, Maryland
Information and Technology Services	Lockheed Martin Specialty Components, Largo, Florida
	Lockheed Martin IMS, Teaneck, New Jersey
	Lockheed Martin Management and Data Systems, Valley Forge, Pennsylvania; Reston, Virginia
	Lockheed Martin Manned Space Systems, Michoud, Louisiana
	Lockheed Martin Space Operations, Titusville, Florida
Information Services Group	Formtek, A Lockheed Martin Company, Pittsburgh, Pennsylvania; Palo Alto, California
	Lockheed Martin Enterprise Information Systems, Orlando, Florida
	Lockheed Martin Information Systems, Orlando, Florida
Lockheed Martin Services Group	KAPL, A Lockheed Martin Company, Nisakayuna and West Milton, New York; Windsor, Connecticut
	Lockheed Martin Services Company, Cherry Hill, New Jersey; Houston, Texas
Lockheed Martin Commercial Products Group	Access Graphics, A Lockheed Martin Company, Boulder, Colorado
	CalComp, A Lockheed Martin Company, Anaheim, California
	Lockheed Martin Commercial Electronics, Hudson, New Hampshire
	MountainGate, A Lockheed Martin Company, Reno, Nevada
Space and Strategic Missiles	Lockheed Martin Missiles and Space, Sunnyvale, California
	Lockheed Martin Astronautics, Denver, Colorado
	Lockheed Martin Astro Space, East Windsor, New Jersey; Valley Forge, Pennsylvania
	Lockheed Martin Technical Operations, Sunnyvale, California

Lockheed also recognized that electronics were critical to keeping its products on the technological frontier. Although it had been developing broad, companywide competence in the area, Lockheed acquired Stavid Engineering in 1959 to fortify its electronics capability. It immediately merged much of its own electronics activities with those of Stavid to form Lockheed Electronics.[5] Lockheed immediately began leveraging the increased knowledge into its defense and commercial products. By 1969, Lockheed Electronics' volume was nine times that of the independent company before the acquisition.

With its wealth of military contracts, Lockheed dropped out of the commercial aircraft market in 1957. In 1967, Lockheed reentered this market with the introduction of a widebody jetliner, the L-1011 Tristar. The initial design was problematic; several airline companies complained of design flaws and equipment failures. By 1971 the firm was facing a liquidity crisis so severe that the federal government extended a loan guarantee to Lockheed. (The firm was considered critical to national security and could not be allowed to go bankrupt.) The company tenaciously upgraded the design; in 1980, the Federation Aeronautique Internationale, a worldwide aviation organization, praised Lockheed "for the highly scientific design concept of the L-1011 Tristar family of transport aircraft, which successfully introduced advanced technologies for significant fuel savings and operational efficiencies into commercial airline service."[6] A protracted downturn in commercial aircraft demand in 1981 crushed all hope of recovering the investment. When this became clear, Lockheed withdrew from the commercial aircraft market in December of that year.

In the 1980s, Lockheed continued to work with the U.S. government; it won a contract to integrate the systems of the Hubble telescope as well as work on some of its subsystems. (It was not responsible for the embarrassing mirror flaw.)[7] Lockheed was also the single largest recipient of grants relating to the Strategic Defense Initiative (SDI) in its first five years.[8]

During this decade, Lockheed also ventured into another industry: information systems. In the early 1980s, Lockheed made a string of acquisitions in software, information services, and graphics systems, culminating in its 1986 acquisition of Sanders Associates, Inc., for $1.17 billion.[9] Although it subsequently sold off many of the individual business units in this industry during its restructuring in 1989–1990, information technology remains a large and important part of Lockheed Martin's sales.

In the late 1980s, the government came under extreme pressure to control cost overruns in defense contracts. As a result, the government began to award "fixed-price contracts," which forced defense contractors to absorb any expenditures over budget.

Although fixed-price contracts were discontinued after intense lobbying by the defense industry, backlogs of these contracts ensured that Lockheed had a profit of only $2 million on sales of almost $10 billion in 1989.[10]

Because of the low profits, Harold Simmons, a corporate raider, organized dissatisfied investors and fought a proxy battle. In early 1990, he forced CEO Daniel Tellep to give institutional investors more influence in selecting board members. To fend off more aggressive moves, Tellep cut 9,500 employees and instituted other cost-saving measures. As a result, the 1990 profits jumped to $335 million, a display that impressed and satisfied the agitated investors and ensured Tellep's continued leadership. The measures also ensured that Lockheed entered the new decade leaner and fitter than it had been in years.[11]

Martin Marietta History

Early in the century, Glenn Martin started a small airplane factory. After missing opportunities during World War I, Martin invested heavily in selling bombers to the military. Support from the government allowed Martin to develop the B-10 bomber.

The Martin Company was prepared for World War II and produced thousands of aircraft. After World War II ended, Martin continued to manufacture aircraft for the military. It produced the B-57 bomber and a number of scout and patrol planes, all while expanding its interest in rockets and missiles. By the 1960s the company was a leader in the manufacture of second-generation rockets.

Because it was smaller than many of its competitors, Martin decided to specialize in developing unique aeronautic equipment and weapons. Eventually, it decided to concentrate on missiles, including the Bullpup, Matador, Titan, and Pershing. Its last airplane rolled off the production line in December 1960.

To get away from selling one product to one customer, the company merged with American-

Marietta Corporation in 1961. Marietta was a manufacturer of chemical products, such as paints, inks, household chemicals, and construction materials. The company again expanded its base in 1968 with the purchase of Harvey Aluminum.

During the 1970s the company won many NASA contracts and became known for its space projects. In spite of its focus on expanding this business, it remained a leader in construction materials and aluminum.

In an attempt to tighten its controls, in 1982 Martin Marietta decided to restructure the company. During this reconstruction, Bendix Corporation launched a hostile takeover bid but was unsuccessful. Martin Marietta emerged intact, independent, and, because the takeover aided its restructuring efforts, more tightly managed and efficient. However, Martin Marietta also accumulated a $1.34 billion debt defending itself from the takeover attempt.

In 1982, Martin Marietta was a diversified set of businesses. One-third of its revenue came from aerospace, and two-thirds were generated by construction materials, aluminum, and chemicals. To deal with the debt, the company sold off some of the specialty chemical operations and the company's cement holdings, reducing its debt in 1983 to $613 million. In 1986 the company sold its aluminum subsidiary. This further reduced the debt to a manageable $220 million.

Again expanding its horizons, Martin Marietta became active in the design, manufacture, and management of energy, electronics, communication, and information systems, including artificial intelligence. In spite of these attempts to diversify, in 1992 the company still made 69 percent of its sales to the Department of Defense and another 17 percent of its sales to NASA and civilian government agencies.[12]

Recent Activity of Lockheed and Martin Marietta

In the early 1990s, with the scalebacks in military spending and less public demand to conquer space, the aerospace industry feared a shakeout would occur. Both Lockheed and Martin Marietta sought to ensure their survival by a series of acquisitions that gave them greater size and leverage for the lean years ahead.

Lockheed's most important acquisition during this period was its December 1992 purchase of General Dynamics' Tactical Military Aircraft business for more than $1.5 billion. This unit included the F-16 Falcon fighter, a favorite combat jet of the U.S. Air Force and foreign buyers.[13]

Martin Marietta was even more aggressive. The company acquired materials companies, broadening its commercial base. In April 1993 it acquired the aerospace division of General Electric in a $3.05 billion deal,[14] and in December of the same year, the Space Systems Division of General Dynamics Corporation for $208.5 million.[15] The merger of Lockheed and Martin Marietta will make the firm the second largest aerospace firm in the world and the largest defense contractor.

EXTERNAL ENVIRONMENT

Government and Defense Spending

Lockheed Martin's single largest customer is the Department of Defense. Because of this, the company is subject to cyclical booms and busts depending on the state of the world, the priorities of the party with power in Congress, and the agenda of the President of the United States. As a result of these factors, government expenditures on defense vary from one congressional session to next.

After World War II, the state of the former Soviet Union and the world in general was volatile enough to justify huge levels of military spending by the United States and other NATO countries. Even up until the 1970s the percentage of the federal budget spent on defense was as high as 43 percent of the government's total outlays (see Exhibit 5). After the Vietnam War ended, the defense sector saw a major decline in spending throughout the 1970s. In 1978 defense spending was at a low point, constituting only 24 percent of the overall U.S. budget. As international tensions increased in 1979, starting with the Suez Canal crisis, spending again began to increase.

In 1981 President Ronald Reagan entered the Oval Office and made military superiority his number-one foreign policy objective in part to contain the spread of communism. The defense industry experienced the largest buildup since World War II. As programs such as the Strategic Defense Initiative, commonly referred to as "Star Wars," were initiated, defense spending increased significantly. From the

EXHIBIT 5 *Defense Spending as Percentage of Total U.S. Federal Government Budget*

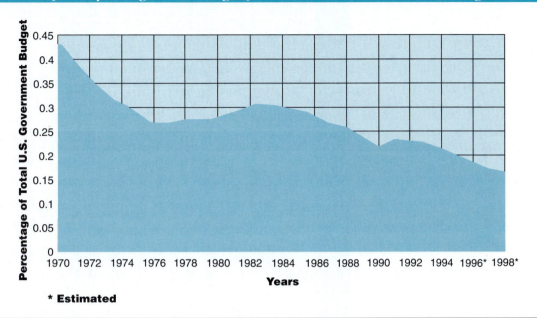

* Estimated

time Reagan took office to the time he left, military spending increased as a percentage of government spending from 24 percent to its high of 29.3 percent in 1987 (see Exhibit 5). That year the United States spent almost $300 billion on national defense (see Exhibit 6). Even today Lockheed continues to draw revenue for 10- to 15-year contracts made during the mid-to-late 1980s.

The effects of these changes on the defense industry were evident. Companies such as McDonnell Douglas and Lockheed earned record profits during the 1980s and expanded heavily into high-technology frontiers with little regard for possible commercial applications of their research and development. They did not have a strategic plan for what to do when and if demand decreased.

In 1989, after Reagan left office, defense contractors saw indications of trouble ahead. The main reason for defense buildup, the Cold War, seemed to be coming to an end. The former Soviet Union was in economic ruin and had become a second-rate power. The "Iron Curtain" fell and with it the great enemy of the United States. Companies came to a staggering realization that they could no longer depend on the U.S. military for contracts.

In 1990 the "peace dividend" was cut out of the defense spending budget and aggregate spending ac-

tually took a downturn from $318 billion to $314 billion in fiscal year 1990 (see Exhibit 7). This was the first time since 1970 that aggregate spending had decreased. However, when the Gulf War erupted in 1991, defense spending increased back up to 1989 levels.

Since 1993, defense spending has declined steadily as a percentage of total government spending. In fiscal year 1994, the total spending was at its lowest since 1970, representing only 20 percent of the overall outlay by the government. Forecasted figures for 1995 through the year 2000 project spending on defense to be reduced to around 15 percent of the total budget.

These cuts come during times when the government is being scrutinized. Government has come under increasing pressure to spend its money efficiently. This comes amidst a ballooning revolution within government—"the reinvention of government."

Future Direction of Defense Market

As projected by the Defense Department, the spending on defense as a percentage of government outlay will decline further by the year 2000. However, this does not mean that defense technology has no future. Although the revenues may shrink, it is the

C-346

EXHIBIT 6 *U.S. Defense Expenditures*
(all figures, other than percentages, in millions $)

	1970	1971	1972	1973	1974	1975	1976	1977	1978	1979
Defense-military	80,123	77,497	77,645	75,033	77,864	84,852	87,917	95,147	102,259	113,605
Defense-civil	4,064	4,763	5,415	6,099	6,816	8,296	9,427	10,506	11,754	13,198
Total defense spending	84,187	82,260	83,060	81,132	84,680	93,148	97,344	105,653	114,013	126,803
Total government spending	195,649	210,172	230,681	245,707	269,359	332,332	371,792	409,218	458,746	504,032
Military spending as % of total government spending	0.430296	0.391393	0.360064	0.330198	0.314375	0.280285	0.261823	0.258182	0.248531	0.251577

	1980	1981	1982	1983	1984	1985	1986	1987	1988	1989
Defense-military	130,912	153,868	180,714	204,410	220,928	245,154	265,480	273,966	281,935	294,880
Defense-civil	15,161	16,892	17,927	18,891	19,540	18,770	20,254	20,684	22,029	23,450
Total defense spending	146,073	170,760	198,641	223,301	240,468	263,924	285,734	294,650	303,964	318,330
Military spending as % of total government spending	0.247184	0.251765	0.266362	0.276232	0.282290	0.278874	0.288522	0.293502	0.285642	0.278462

	1990	1991	1992	1993	1994	1995*	1996*	1997*	1998*	1999*
Defense-military	289,755	261,925	286,632	278,574	268,635	260,269	250,045	246,070	244,178	249,639
Defense-civil	24,975	26,543	28,270	29,266	30,407	31,207	31,934	32,642	33,607	35,364
Total defense spending	314,730	288,468	314,902	307,840	299,042	291,476	281,979	278,712	277,785	285,003
Total government spending	1,252,705	1,323,441	1,380,856	1,408,675	1,460,914	1,538,920	1,612,128	1,684,709	1,745,185	1,822,180
Military spending as % of total government spending	0.251240	0.217968	0.228048	0.218531	0.204695	0.189402	0.174911	0.165436	0.159172	0.156407

*Estimated

EXHIBIT 7 *Total U.S. Defense Spending*

* Estimated

government's responsibility to protect its population in an increasingly factionalized and unpredictable world. Furthermore, new technologies threaten to change radically the military capabilities critical to winning an armed conflict. Long-held strategies must soon be reworked or scrapped.

Military strategy experts believe that war as it is fought today will soon change completely. In a Pentagon simulation war between China and the United States in 2020, the United States was badly bloodied. China had a twenty-first century military bought off the shelf, whereas the United States had an updated version of its Gulf War force. Satellite-guided antiship missiles hit the U.S. fleet, which was exposed to Chinese surveillance sensors in space. As fast as the United States could destroy these inexpensive satellites, the Chinese would launch more. The aircraft and aircraft carriers on which much of today's defense strategy is based were forced to stay too far off the battlefield area and thus were rendered ineffective.[16]

Andrew Marshall, a Pentagon strategist since 1949, warns that the United States needs "to avoid the fate of other nations whose overconfident militaries slid from triumph to obsolescence."[17] His thinking is commanding top-level attention in Washington as the end of the Cold War and mind-boggling technological leaps have spurred a willingness to reexamine long-held military assumptions.

Military strategists envision a smaller, more professional force packing more firepower. Airplanes will be drones and targeting information will be communicated directly to a computer on board or straight into a pilot's helmet. For example, Marshall and many other strategists believe that current strategic mainstays such as aircraft carriers, fighters, bombers, and tanks are all "sunset systems." Warfare has not changed much since World War II; even Desert Storm was a late industrial age conflict with only hints of a high-tech future. It was an example of using new equipment in old ways, says Marshall. The new arena of warfare is going to be in information technology and how it can facilitate accurate and deep strikes on key enemy strongholds. Ironically, these strongholds will be information and communication centers as well.

POTENTIAL NEW MARKETS

Although the defense industry will always exist in some form and has potential in the near future as the United States and its allies modernize, it will probably never reach the levels of the past. To continue to grow, Lockheed Martin must look to other markets.

Lockheed's chief, Daniel Tellep, intends to pursue potential new markets aggressively. He sees the company, which is currently 50/50 in terms of defense and nondefense, headed to a 40/60 split in five years because of the uncertainty of the defense budgets and the host of emerging opportunities in the nondefense sectors. He believes the merger between the defense giants increases Lockheed Martin's ability to pursue these new opportunities by increasing the competitiveness of its complementary businesses such as electronics, information services, missiles, and space technologies.[18]

High Technology

One of the major thrusts the new firm envisions is technology transfer into new markets. In an interview, Tellep alluded to new commercial technology that Lockheed Martin is developing based on digital wideband electronic warfare work. "I won't be more specific than that, but it's really exciting. The point is, what slowly is coming into focus is how to apply some of our defense-derived technologies into markets that you never would have imagined two or three years ago"[19] (see Exhibit 8). However, he points out specifically that the new opportunities that will be explored and undertaken will be defined by the sector presidents.

Communications

One of the areas in which Lockheed Martin has been less secretive is communications. In 1993, the firm undertook an ambitious project in which it plans to launch satellites into higher orbits in order to provide high-speed communication capabilities to anyone in any place.[20] The projections of cash flows from the operation are high but so are the risks. The estimates range from $6 to $10 billion during the next five years.

The system has many proponents as well as opponents. Some opponents of the system do not think such a network has much chance of success. They conclude that given the current cellular networks that span the country, subscribers would not pay the steep prices that these satellite services would demand. The process for satellite communications is in the range of $2,000 to $3,000 for a hand-held unit and upwards of $3 a minute for calls.[21] Compared to current cellular rates of 25 to 95 cents per minute and hand-held units given away free with a service signup, the success of such a high-stakes gamble seems unlikely. However, the proponents of the system claim that the increasing use of computer communications would make the satellite system a better choice due

---

EXHIBIT 8 *Lockheed Martin S2 Strategy: Strength with Speed*

Leverage technology breadth, employee talent, corporate scale, global market access, and financial strength.
- Realize corporate-wide synergies: invest in our people.
- Focus technology and investments on true market differentiators.
- Capitalize on corporate resources as targeted competitive advantage.

Improve competitiveness, profitability and agility.
- Drive costs down at all levels—reduce cycle times.
- Embrace commercial practices wherever beneficial.
- Foster a change-oriented, high-performance environment.

Grow leadership positions in core businesses.
- Focus on superior people, technology, performance, and affordability.
- Continuously improve mission success and customer satisfaction.
- Benefit from industry consolidation opportunities.

Expand into related domestic and international growth markets.
- Apply premier technology base to meet emerging market needs.
- Capitalize on international presence with broader products and services.
- Adopt innovative approaches for profitable market penetration.

Consistently deliver superior stockholder value growth.

to the higher quality and faster transfer of data, lowering the overall costs. Cellular networks can transmit 100 million bytes of data per second; the satellite networks could transfer more than one billion bytes per second.[22] The companies that are involved in this satellite network project are scrambling to have their networks available first, because they know that not everyone who enters this market will survive. With potential losses for failure reaching into the billions of dollars, companies are pursuing cautious strategies.[23]

In April 1991, LMSC (Lockheed Martin Satellite Communication) and Motorola announced that they are teaming up on a 77-satellite iridium system to bring personal communication services to virtually any spot in the world, which is especially important in remote regions that now lack telephone services.[24] Martin Space Development announced in May 1993 that it will begin development of a new family of three launch vehicles designed to accommodate payloads from 2,300 to 8,000 pounds. In August 1993, LMSC signed a contract with Motorola Satellite Communications Division (SATCOM). The contract is for the development of key elements of a constellation of 66 spacecraft, which will form the basis of a revolutionary global telecommunications system named Iridium TM/SM.[25]

NASA

Lockheed Martin has announced an agreement to form a joint venture with Rockwell International Corporation to serve NASA. NASA has stated that it would like to restructure the U.S. space shuttle program and deal with only one prime contractor, and the Lockheed Martin Rockwell joint venture believes that it has a strong chance of winning this distinction.

U.S. Aircraft Manufacturing Industry

U.S. industry is the world's leading supplier of aircraft with two American suppliers, McDonnell Douglas and Boeing, supplying 71 percent of the market and the European Airbus Industries supplying the remainder. U.S. jet engines led the world in production with annual sales of $34 billion per year.

Faced with sluggish passenger growth, lower profits, and tighter credit conditions, the number of planes ordered between 1991 and 1992 declined and

those on order were renegotiated. Sales on parts and spares have also declined, especially for engine manufacturers. The decline in aircraft manufacturing has a historical background. The market is known to be cyclical. A similar downturn occurred during the 1980s but was masked by increasing military orders. Due to new political pressures and world markets, military orders did not make up the difference during the 1991–1992 downturn. The orders placed in 1992 did not produce significant cash flows until 1995 due to the long lead times in the industry; thus, an upturn in the industry seems unlikely before 1998. The near future requires tight control and tough choices by aircraft manufacturers. If they cut back too little at this time, they face serious losses now; if they cut back too much, they face higher future costs of rebuilding the workforce and supply lines when orders improve, in addition to missing the opportunity of future sales.

The decline in aircraft orders further intensifies competitive pressures. The new markets are not only emphasizing lower prices and good financial terms, they also want technological and design enhancements that help increase the operating efficiency and productivity of the airlines that buy them. The three main manufacturers of passenger planes are continually seeking to strengthen their individual competitive positions.

COMPETITION

Given the dynamic environment of the newly evolved defense industry, many participants were left scrambling for market positioning as defense budgets declined and the industry became laden with overcapacity. The reactions of Lockheed Martin's competitors have repercussions not only on the overall shape of the defense sector but also on Lockheed Martin itself. As the defense industry changed, so did the major firms in the market, and an inability to adapt meant certain doom. To survive and be successful in this new market, Lockheed and Martin Marietta merged to create the largest defense company in the world. The array of decision criteria regarding where to go in the future is affected largely by the external environment in which competitors operate and how they leverage their resources to maneuver effectively around possible setbacks to make gains from the opportunities created. In addition to the many market challenges and opportunities that face Lockheed Martin, competition from other aerospace and defense companies necessitates constant repositioning and rethinking of strategic direction.[26]

Northrop

In March 1994, Northrop made a cash counteroffer for Grumman Corporation's outstanding shares valued at $2.04 billion. This bettered Martin Marietta's offer of $55 per share, totaling $1.9 billion. Consequently, the offer was accepted, which created Northrop Grumman Corporation. Northrop officials said that the decision to acquire Grumman was based on industry trends and the advantage of being the first to move.

Northrop believed that it needed to achieve "critical mass" to succeed in this new competitive defense environment. Kent Kresa, CEO of Northrop Corporation, said that the move to consolidate Grumman and Northrop will give the new firm the "staying power necessary to compete in this new defense environment, enabling the firm to retain critical defense industry skills and jobs." According to Grumman's CEO Caporali, the firm would not have survived without making a substantial strategic move.[27]

The acquisition catapulted Northrop into the top six aerospace defense contractors with approximately $8 billion in sales. Because both Northrop and Grumman were both unusually dependent on the U.S. government for sales, however, the resulting corporation will make almost 90 percent of its sales to one customer. It currently operates in four major businesses: military aircraft, aerostructures, systems integrations, and electronics and data systems.

McDonnell Douglas

In recent years, McDonnell Douglas has been beleaguered on many sides. In late 1990 and early 1991, it incurred a liquidity crisis that severely threatened the company. The crisis forced the company to embark on significant cost reductions. It also sold off many of its noncore businesses, including some of its financial services and all of its information services. Although the company has recently posted healthier results, it appears to use an accounting system that allows it to defer expenses indefinitely. This makes

it difficult to accurately assess the firm's true financial condition, although it is less sound than its balance sheet would suggest.[29]

Even before the Lockheed Martin merger in 1993, Lockheed's aggressive acquisition strategy pushed McDonnell Douglas out of its position as the largest military contractor in the world.[30] Although it now appears that the company has its debt under control, McDonnell Douglas received a great deal of criticism because its financial position prevented it from participating in the first round of acquisitions and mergers in the defense industry. The overall company strategy garnered mixed reviews; some industry analysts asserted that the company was not proactive enough to remain competitive in the long run,[31] while others cite Douglas as one of the firms that will probably survive the industry changes due to its sheer size.[32]

Hughes

Hughes is a subsidiary of General Motors and has played an aggressive role in the industry consolidation. It acquired the tactical missile business of General Dynamics and, by consolidating and downsizing, it recouped its investment in just 18 months.[33] Many analysts expect the company to be extremely competitive in avionics, missiles, and space technology when the industry takes its final form.

Boeing

Boeing is the largest aerospace company in the world, with sales of more than $21 billion in 1994 (down from more than $30 billion in 1992). It has consistently ranked as one of the nation's top three exporters and is one of the most financially sound companies in the industry with a debt-to-capital ratio of only 18 percent. The company has chosen to concentrate on the highly cyclical commercial aircraft market; it receives about 80 percent of its revenue from commercial transport sales. However, it also is a substantial competitor in the military arena. Although the combined defense and space divisions were only profitable once over the four years from 1989 to 1992, the technology spillovers alone are valuable enough for Boeing to continue pursuing military contracts.[34] Boeing's government contracts include space systems, helicopters, military airplanes, missile systems, electronic systems, and information systems management.[35]

European Competitors

The reduced demand for defense technology is not strictly an American phenomenon. From the mid-1980s to 1994, France's budget for conventional land-based munitions fell from about $550 million to $180 million. During the same period, comparable German spending also decreased approximately two-thirds to about the same level.[36] As American firms consolidate to survive, European firms are faced with the same environment but without the same opportunities. Most of the aerospace and defense companies are national concerns and many are state owned, which means that future consolidations will have to overcome political obstacles to merge across national borders.[37] However, most of Europe's leaders are not willing to trust their nation's defenses to a multinational corporation and are, therefore, understandably reluctant to allow consolidation that most have admitted must occur.

As an alternative, many European manufacturers have turned to cooperative ventures to pool their resources without sacrificing their sovereignty. The most successful result of international aerospace cooperation is the four-nation consortium of aircraft manufacturers comprising Airbus. Airbus is one of the three major manufacturers of civil aircraft along with Boeing and McDonnell Douglas and, as such, is not a direct competitor with Lockheed Martin. However, the members of the Airbus consortium are also armaments suppliers, and various cooperative ventures are beginning to crystallize among the members and among other firms in these areas as well. Daimler-Benz Aerospace, a German firm, and Aerospatiale, a French corporation, have recently agreed to merge their missile and satellite divisions under a new, jointly owned organization. British Aerospace and Matra Defense, British and French firms, respectively, have also agreed to merge their tactical missile subunits.[38] Although these deals only reflect industry imperatives, it is still possible for political concerns to block the initiatives. However, eventually economic forces will probably compel a consolidation or cooperation in European defense and aerospace. When this occurs, the new players are likely to be substantial competitors.

THE CHALLENGES PRESENTED TO LOCKHEED MARTIN BY THE MERGER

Given the ever-changing global environment in this industry and the moves undertaken by its main competitors, Lockheed and Martin Marietta joined forces to cope with the declining defense market demand and industry overcapacity. The two companies also saw opportunities for future expansion through synergies created by their union.

The proposed merger between Lockheed and Martin Marietta, after receiving government and shareholder approval, became official on March 15, 1995. However, those two hurdles were only the first of many challenges faced by the company.

The benefit most often cited by both Lockheed and Martin Marietta for the consolidation move is the cost savings realized by reducing duplication. The combined corporation expects to be able to reduce staff on the payroll and sell a number of plants. The new chief of information systems believes the company can save $700 million in internal information systems costs alone over the next five years.[39] Overall, Lockheed Martin estimates that the consolidation effort will cost $1.7 billion by the middle of 1997, but, when complete, will yield annual savings of $1.8 billion.[40]

The proponents of the merger also believe that Lockheed and Martin Marietta had offsetting strengths and weaknesses that will result in a much stronger competitive position with the combined line of products and services. For example, Martin Marietta had emerged as the leader in the space-launch industry by dominating U.S. heavy- and medium-lift launch programs. However, that position will be strengthened by Lockheed's alliance with Russian producers and the addition of its line of light-launch vehicles.[41]

In other businesses, the consolidation will give the corporation new economies of scale by combining the smaller shares built by the separate companies. For example, Lockheed and Martin Marietta had been trying to grow their segments in environmental remediation and information services. The leadership hopes that the resulting consolidated business units will achieve the critical mass needed for continued viability and increased competitiveness.[42]

In spite of the optimistic view taken by the company, not all observers agree. Harry C. Stonecipher, president and chief executive of McDonnell Douglas, says that the merger is, in most ways, an expansion into totally new markets for both of the companies and adds, "I don't know where the synergy is."[43]

Another challenge to the united leadership of the company is improving the low employee morale. Although layoffs would have been inevitable even without the merger, they are expected to be deeper and more far reaching now that duplication needs to be eliminated. In June 1995, Lockheed Martin an-

C-352

EXHIBIT 9 *Lockheed Martin Corporation Consolidated Financial Data (in millions, except per share)*

	1994	1993	1992	1991	1990
Income Statement					
Sales	22,906	22,397	16,030	15,871	16,089
Costs and expenses	21,127	20,857	14,891	14,767	15,178
Earnings from operations	1,779	1,540	1,139	1,104	911
Other income and expenses	200	44	42	−49	34
EBIT	**1,979**	**1,584**	**1,181**	**1,055**	**945**
Interest expense	−304	−278	−177	−176	−180
Income before taxes	1,675	1,306	1,004	879	765
Income tax expense	620	477	355	261	161
Earnings before acct. changes	1,055	829	649	618	604
Cum. effect on acct. changes	−37		−1,010		
Net Earnings (Loss)	**1,018**	**829**	**− 361**	**618**	**604**
Dividend per common share					
Assuming no dilution	5.12	3.99	−1.84	3.05	2.97
Assuming full dilution	4.66	3.75	−1.84	3.05	2.97
Cash dividends	1.14	1.09	1.04	0.98	0.90
Common shares outstanding	199.1	197.9	194.1	201.4	200.7
Consolidated Balance Sheet					
Current assets	8,143	6,961	5,157	5,553	5,442
Property, plant & equipment	3,455	3,643	3,139	3,155	3,200
Intangible assets related to contract and programs acquired	1,971	2,127	42	52	59
Costs in excess of net assets acquired	2,831	2,697	841	864	882
Deferred income taxes		283	392		49
Other assets	1,649	1,397	1,256	895	834
Total Assets	**18,049**	**17,108**	**10,827**	**10,519**	**10,466**
Current liabilities—others	5,350	4,845	3,176	3,833	4,235
Current maturities of long-term debt	285	346	327	298	30
Long-term debt	3,594	4,026	1,803	1,997	2,392
Post-retirement benefit liabilities	1,756	1,719	1,579	54	
Other liabilities	978	971	460	112	38
Stockholders equity	6,086	5,201	3,482	4,225	3,771
Total Stockholders Equity & Liabilities	**18,049**	**17,108**	**10,827**	**10,519**	**10,466**

nounced that it would eliminate 15,000 of its 170,000 workers over two years. This is less than the 25,000 many outsiders had predicted,[44] but still a dismaying number to those threatened.[45]

Perceived inequities are also hard to avoid. The employees of the former Lockheed are grumbling especially loudly because in this "merger of equals," Martin employees seem to have an advantage. For example, the former Lockheed had satellite manufacturing facilities at Sunnyvale, California, while Martin maintained installations in Denver, Colorado; Valley Forge, Pennsylvania; and East Windsor, New Jersey.[46] Up to two of these may be closed; and, according to industry observers, the high-cost, highly regulated Sunnyvale plant is a logical candidate.[47] And, although Martin employees are not immune to layoffs, the executives of the former Martin Marietta are dividing up an $82.4 million windfall payment triggered by the "change in control of the corporation."[48]

The merger of Lockheed and Martin Marietta created the largest defense contractor in the world with sales of approximately $23 billion (see Exhibit 9). Their combined assets totaled $18 billion. This consolidation of capital and assets may enable Lockheed Martin to take advantage of economies of scale in an industry that is riddled with overcapacity. But was it wise to merge with another company also heavily involved in the same declining industry? Where should the company be heading for the long term? Should it continue to invest its resources in defense, or should it place more emphasis on commercial applications? Will Lockheed Martin be able to take advantage of the opportunities presented by the merger without falling victim to the pitfalls? The leadership will continue to struggle with these and other questions during the next few years.

C-35?

NOTES

1. A. L. Velocci, 1994, Merger partners poised to fulfill strategic plan, *Aviation Week & Space Technology*, November 14, 40.
2. A. Pasztor, 1995, Lockheed Martin to cut 15,000 jobs, fewer than expected, over 2 years, *Wall Street Journal*, June 27, A2.
3. Lockheed Corporation, 1993, *Annual Report*, 8–12.
4. Lockheed Corporation, 1968, *Annual Report*.
5. *Moody's Industrial Manual*, 1974, 2752.
6. Lockheed Corporation, 1980, *Annual Report*, 10.
7. Lockheed Corporation, 1978, *Annual Report*, 21.
8. Anonymous, 1988, Lockheed cited as top contractor in first five years of SDI program, *Aviation Week & Space Technology*, March 21, 17.
9. Anonymous, 1986, Sanders accepts Lockheed bid . . . , *Electronic News*, July 14, 1.
10. M. Tharp, 1991, The education of Daniel Tellep, *U.S. News & World Report*, May 25, 55.
11. E. Schine, 1991, Lockheed: Oh, what a difference a year makes, *Business Week*, February 25, 37.
12. Martin Marietta, 1993, *Annual Report*, 59.
13. M. duBois, 1994, Defense mergers in U.S. raise issue in Europe; fractured industry abroad to face stiffer rivalry; speculation lifts stocks, *Wall Street Journal*, September 1, B6.
14. Anonymous, 1992, GE deal stresses defense turmoil, *Flight International*, December 8, 6.
15. A. L. Velocci, 1994, Northrop, Martin battle for Grumman, *Aviation Week & Space Technology*, March 14, 26.
16. T. E. Ricks, 1994, Warning shot . . . , *Wall Street Journal*, July 15, A1.
17. Ibid.
18. Velocci, Merger partners poised to fulfill strategic plan.
19. Ibid.
20. J. J. Keller, 1993, Phone space race has fortune at stake, *Wall Street Journal*, January 18, B1.
21. Ibid.
22. Ibid.
23. R. L. Hudson, 1993, Technology: Finding and feeding . . . , *Wall Street Journal*, May 24, R11.
24. Lockheed Martin home page.
25. Ibid.
26. Ibid.
27. Velocci, Northrop, Martin battle for Grumman.
28. E. M. Print and Rachel Schmidt, 1994, *Financial Condition of U.S. Military Aircraft Prime Contractor*, RAND Corporation, 55–70.
29. Ibid.
30. Anonymous, 1994, Lockheed leapfrogs McDonnell, *Defense News*, July 18, 8.
31. Anthony L. Velocci, Jr., 1994, Proactive strategy, *Aviation Week & Space Technology*, March 14, 44.
32. J. Cole, 1994, Taking aim . . . , *Wall Street Journal*, March 14, A1.
33. A. L. Velocci, Jr., 1994, Consolidation outlook stormy, *Aviation Week & Space Technology*, March 14, 43.
34. Print and Schmidt. Financial Condition.
35. The Boeing Company home page.
36. C. Covault, 1995, German, French firms merge armament units, *Aviation Week & Space Technology*, January 30, 25.
37. M. J. Bollinger, 1994, What Lockheed Martin means to Europe, *Interavia*, October, 10.
38. P. Sparaco, 1995, European companies to strengthen ties, *Aviation Week & Space Technology*, June 5, 28.
39. J. King, 1995, Lockheed Martin plans to slash IS budget by $700 M, *ComputerWorld*, March 27, 4.
40. Pasztor, Lockheed Martin to cut 15,000 jobs.

41. J. Cole, 1994, Joining forces: Merger of Lockheed Martin and Martin Marietta pushes industry trend, *Wall Street Journal*, August 30, A1.

42. Velocci, Merger partners poised to fulfill strategic plan.

43. J. Cole, 1995, Corporate focus: Lockheed Martin totes heavy baggage on honeymoon . . . , *Wall Street Journal*, March 16, B4.

44. Ibid.

45. King, Lockheed Martin plans to slash IS budget by $700 M.

46. Anonymous, 1995, Lockheed Martin Corp. official ready to ax, *Space News*, March 20, 6.

47. Anonymous, 1995, Taking a painful plunge: Lockheed Martin prepares to let people and plants go, *Washington Post*, April 16, H1.

48. A. L. Velocci, Jr., 1995, New merger looks certain, *Aviation Week & Space Technology*, March 13, 31.

Motorola in China

Christine C. Mayo
Gregory L. Richards
Kate Sumpter
Basilios A. Strmec

"China basically looked to us as a friend, and the time you need a friend most is when you're in hot water." These sentiments surrounded Motorola's 1989 operating expansion into China at the same time that a peaceful demonstration turned into a bloody massacre in Beijing's Tiananmen Square.[1]

Robert W. Galvin, Motorola's former CEO, began negotiations with the Chinese government to enter into the Chinese electronics industry. However, Galvin did not want to pursue the traditional joint-venture method of entry into China, which Chinese officials had proposed. Instead, he wanted to establish a wholly owned subsidiary in Beijing.

The Tiananmen Square incident turned out to be the saving grace Motorola needed to win in the negotiations for its wholly owned subsidiary. While other foreign companies were pulling out of deals and breaking contracts because of the student demonstration, Motorola decided to remain in China. Once the smoke cleared, negotiations reconvened and Chinese officials stood ready to offer almost anything to Motorola, including the wholly owned subsidiary it desired.

Motorola has since expanded even more broadly in the Chinese market through joint ventures and other alliances. As a result of the company's support

for China during the Tiananmen incident, Motorola has enjoyed increased concessions for its operations from the Chinese government. In almost every one of its new ventures, Chinese officials have been there to help ease the way for Motorola. Current projects in the country include construction of a Greater China Headquarters facility in Beijing, a wafer fabrication plant in Tianjin, and a research and design center in Hong Kong. With each new facility, Motorola strengthens its claim that it is in for the long haul with the Chinese people.[2]

Despite Motorola's successes in China since the Tiananmen incident, certain issues are causing concern for the firm's managers. Historically, Motorola's core competencies in the wireless communications and semiconductor sectors have provided much profit for the growing company. Now the firm is producing and selling personal computers through licensing and sublicensing agreements as well as through joint ventures. In addition to this technological expansion, Motorola wants to expand even further into China through direct foreign investment.

Motorola's increased expansion has raised three concerns. First, should Motorola move away from its core businesses of wireless communications and semiconductors toward its new ventures in computers? A second concern, relating to the diversification issue, involves Motorola's decision to align with Apple to create Mac-compatible systems. The final issue facing Motorola concerns its investment of $1.2 billion in China, which seems to increase every year.

This case was prepared under the direction of Professor Robert E. Hoskisson. The case is intended to be used as the basis for class discussion rather than to illustrate either effective or ineffective handling of an administrative situation.

BACKGROUND ON MOTOROLA

Motorola leads the world in manufacturing advanced electronic systems, communication components, and semiconductors. Its major businesses include cellular telephones, paging and data communications, two-way radios, automotive electronics, personal communications, defense and space electronics, and computers. Motorola semiconductors are used in communication devices, computers, and millions of other electronic products. Conducting business on six continents, Motorola employs more than 142,000 people and maintains manufacturing facilities throughout the world.[3]

Motorola's fundamental objective is total customer satisfaction through quality, speed, technology, and teamwork.[4] In meeting this objective, Motorola concentrates on "respecting the individual, maintaining uncompromising integrity, and focusing on a vision of a world in which everyone can reach their full potential."[5] With these basic goals and principles, Motorola seeks to achieve "what you never thought possible."[6]

History

Paul V. Galvin founded Motorola in 1928 as the Galvin Manufacturing Corporation. The company's first product was a "battery eliminator" that enabled customers to operate their radios with home electricity instead of batteries. The Galvin Manufacturing Corporation commercialized car radios in the 1930s under a new brand name, Motorola. The company also began to advertise nationally to strengthen its success in the home radio market. In 1947, Galvin Manufacturing Corporation officially changed its name to Motorola, Inc. Motorola's management decided to study solid-state electronics and enter into government work. By 1959, Motorola had developed a strong presence in consumer electronics and had built its first semiconductor facility. At the same time, it was a leader in military, space, and commercial communications equipment. While Motorola was expanding rapidly in the domestic market, it was also positioning itself to expand internationally and was determined to become and then remain the global industry leader.[7]

In 1959, Paul Galvin passed away and his son Robert W. Galvin assumed control of the company. Under Robert's leadership, Motorola began a new era, shifting its focus away from domestic consumer electronics toward new international markets. The company sold its color television receiver business in order to concentrate its energies on high-technology markets spanning government, commercial, and industrial fields. In the following decades, Motorola quickly developed into the leading worldwide supplier of cellular telephones. This electronic evolution continued into the 1990s with marketing contracts for a satellite-based global personal communication system.[8]

Structure

Motorola's high degree of decentralization enabled it to expand rapidly. Its business operations are divided into four sectors and two groups to provide flexibility and utilize expertise. The four sectors include General Systems; Semiconductor Products; Messaging, Information, and Media; and Land Mobile Products. The two main groups are the Automotive, Energy, and Controls Group and the Government and Space Technology Group. Another component of Motorola's organizational structure is the New Enterprises organization, which guides the company into new strategic alliances to capitalize on emerging high-technology and high-growth opportunities.[9]

Strategy

Two key beliefs underlie Motorola's fundamental strategy for total customer satisfaction: respect for the dignity of the individual and uncompromising integrity.[10] These beliefs provide stability and strength, creating an environment of empowerment. To remain competitive, Motorola's management encourages long-term investment in technology. Consequently, the company has increased sales per employee by 3.2 percent per year and has reduced in-process defect levels 250 times. Investments of over $4 billion in research and development have resulted in over 400 new patents since 1991. In 1995, sales increased 22 percent to $27 billion. Additionally, earnings jumped from $1.56 billion to $1.78 billion with 63 percent of sales being generated in markets outside the United States (see Exhibit 1).[11]

EXHIBIT 1 *Motorola Financial Information*

Income Statement

	1995	1994
Net sales	$27,037,000	$22,245,000
COGS	17,545,000	13,760,000
Gross profit	9,492,000	8,485,000
Selling, general, and administrative expenses	4,642,000	4,381,000
Depreciation and amortization	1,919,000	1,525,000
Interest expense	149,000	142,000
Income before taxes	2,782,000	2,437,000
Provision for income taxes	1,001,000	877,000
Net income	$ 1,781,000	$ 1,560,000

Statement of Cash Flows

	1995	1994
Operating activity	$ 3,287,000	$ 2,552,000
Investing activity	(4,579,000)	(3,968,000)
Financing activity	1,276,000	1,271,000
Net cash flow	$ (16,000)	$ (145,000)

Balance Sheet

	1995	1994
Assets		
Cash	$ 725,000	$ 741,000
Marketable securities	350,000	318,000
Receivables	4,081,000	3,421,000
Inventories	3,528,000	2,670,000
Other current assets	1,826,000	1,775,000
Total current assets	10,510,000	8,925,000
Net property, plant, and equipment	9,356,000	7,073,000
Deposits and other assets	2,935,000	1,538,000
Total assets	$22,801,000	$17,536,000
Liabilities & Stockholders' Equity		
Notes payable	$ 1,605,000	$ 916,000
Accounts payable	2,018,000	1,678,000
Accrued expenses	4,170,000	3,323,000
Total current liabilities	7,793,000	5,917,000
Deferred charges/income	968,000	509,000
Long-term debt	1,949,000	1,127,000
Other long-term liabilities	1,043,000	887,000
Total liabilities	11,753,000	8,440,000
Net common stock	1,774,000	1,764,000
Capital surplus	1,813,000	1,415,000
Retained earnings	7,461,000	5,917,000
Shareholder equity	11,048,000	9,096,000
Total liabilities and shareholders' equity	$22,801,000	$17,536,000

Source: Motorola Financial Statements, 10K, SEC Disclosure, 1995.

Communications and Semiconductor Industries

Motorola, which is the market leader in cellular telephones, pagers, and two-way radios, commands the largest share of wireless communications equipment sales in the world.[12] Motorola also has dominant positions in the semiconductor market in many of the areas it serves. The cellular telephone market has grown to 85 million subscribers, and Motorola's sales in this industry account for about 29 percent of its total revenue. Additionally, with almost half of the world's population aware of its paging services, Motorola has captured a large portion of the paging market's 95 million users.[13] Pagers, cellular telephones, and personal communication equipment are being used throughout the world and are driving Motorola's expansion. The semiconductor business is now developing the technologies that will reshape the electronics industries. These new technologies are faster, stronger, cheaper, and more reliable. Motorola also leads the world in several of the fastest-growing semiconductor segments. It is flourishing in the energy and industrial sectors, the automotive sector, multimedia set-top boxes, personal computer printers, and interactive, microcontroller-based smartcards.

In addition to the growth in its semiconductor segment, Motorola has made advances in satellite communications. The firm created the Iridium global wireless communications network to serve hand-held telephones and permit voice, data, fax, or paging messages to reach their destinations almost anywhere on the earth's surface.[14] Other recent technological innovations include "streaming video," which makes movies accessible on a PC, and the software program VocalTech, which allows phone calls over the Internet.[15]

Motorola Computer Group

The Motorola Computer Group (MCG) continues to find new and inventive ways to add value to the company. MCG is composed of three areas of focus: embedded technologies, technical OEM systems, and commercial systems. Its strategy is to deliver high-performance PowerPC platforms and solutions in graphics-intensive applications for Macintosh, Windows NT, and AIX operating systems.[16] MCG is now venturing internationally, specifically into

China, to expand its operations, cultivate a broader knowledge and research base, and gain access to a potentially colossal market. Motorola hopes its investment in China can help launch its computer sales and technology into the 21st century.

CHINA

The high-tech electronic industry is witnessing the birth of a new player. As China draws the world's attention, many corporations are investing billions of dollars in the Chinese market. China is expected to emerge as the world's largest consumer of electronic products, buying everything from computers and radios to telephones and televisions. Because of its market potential, growing labor force, and expanding economy, China is expected to emerge as a major competitor in the micro-electronics industry for the production of semiconductors, two-way radios, and computers.[17]

Economic Conditions in China

One must understand the evolution of the Chinese economic system to comprehend the nature of business in China and how Motorola operates in this volatile nation. Prior to market reforms, the government State Planning Commission developed and implemented policies that outlined the short- and long-term objectives of the national program. To allocate the economic resources to various units and regions, the commission created ministries organized by economic units and provinces organized by geographic regions.

The horizontally connected ministries often overlapped resources and pursued redundant measures. However, the reforms of 1978 changed the way the ministries, the provinces, and the commission interacted and dealt with each other. More reforms are in progress, encompassing both the bureaucratic and the individual worker as entities of the economic system. As a result of these reforms, employees now receive promotions and compensation increases based more on performance levels than on political issues and seniority. These increased incentives encourage employees at all levels to work harder and to improve work quality, thus improving product quality.

A major aspect of the Chinese reforms concerns the establishment of Special Economic Zones (SEZs), which encourage increased foreign investment, especially from firms involved in light manufacturing industries. Foreign firms choosing to locate in a SEZ receive special tax treatment and special facilities in terms of infrastructure and government services. Business dealings within a SEZ are decentralized so that the province has direct control over the transactions in its respective zone. This reduces the levels of bureaucracy a firm must go through to perform its operations. Special benefits provided by locating within an SEZ include allowances in corporate income taxation, factory site choices, and import duty waivers. Many expatriates living within a zone may receive special personal benefits as well, such as special housing, better living conditions, and preferential tax treatment.[18]

Electronic Future

The expected emergence of China as a leader in the high-tech field of electronics stems from the ongoing changes the Chinese government has been pursuing since the 1978 reforms. The political framework created by the changes will allow China to participate in a dynamic global economy as both a consumer and a producer. As the number of graduating scholars from China's universities increases, so does the rate at which the Chinese people demand more high-tech products. Thus, Chinese industries

are scrambling to produce consumer electronic products to meet the rising demand. The universities in China are encouraging increased enrollment in hopes of securing the nation's future by cultivating the knowledge and skills needed to progress in the volatile electronics industry.

Supporting China's move into electronics is increasing foreign investment by companies such as Northern Telecom, Philips, and Intel in Shanghai; Ericsson in Nanjing; IBM in Shenzen; and Motorola in Beijing, Tianjin, Hong Kong, and Nanjing.[19]

MOTOROLA IN CHINA

Motorola is taking giant strides to ensure its presence in the Chinese market. By encouraging the Chinese economy through direct foreign investment and by supporting the Chinese people through education programs and community projects, Motorola is staking a claim in China's future. Therefore, as China grows, Motorola will grow too, especially in the areas of research, design, manufacturing, and sales. China and Hong Kong already comprise 12 percent of the firm's total sales, and Motorola's managers expect this figure to increase (see Exhibit 2).[20]

Thus, Motorola brings new technologies into a culture that has not caught up completely with the rest of the world. The firm encourages its Chinese

EXHIBIT 2 *Market Sales, 1995*

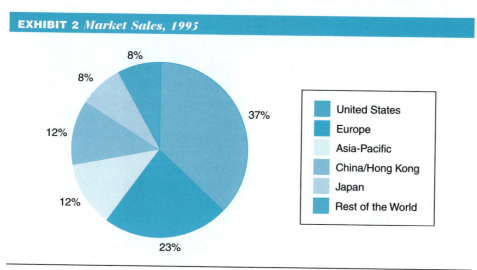

Legend: United States, Europe, Asia-Pacific, China/Hong Kong, Japan, Rest of the World

37%, 23%, 12%, 12%, 8%, 8%

Source: http://www.mot.com/General/China/facts96.html

employees to take an active role in their work. This practice gives Motorola a better image in the eyes of the Chinese. In fact, Gary Tooker, a high-ranking Motorola official, is considered a head of state when he visits China.[21] This honor is rarely given to foreigners, especially in business.

Motorola contributes to its standing in the Chinese electronics industry by indicating that it will remain in China for the long term. Currently, about 6,000 locals are employed in the various manufacturing and research facilities throughout the nation,[22] and its investment in China surpassed $1.2 billion in 1995 (see Exhibit 3).[23] These additional investments place Motorola as the number-one foreign investor in the growing Chinese electronics market. Nevertheless, there are still tremendous risks involved in dealing with the Chinese political system, which is relatively unstable and plagued by corruption. Although the Chinese reforms improved the political situation, government officials pay little respect to copyrights and many basic human rights. In addition, sociopolitical instability, labor unrest, inadequate energy supply, underdeveloped infrastructure, limited local financing, and low labor productivity intimidate many foreign investors. However, Motorola continues to invest significantly in the Chinese economy. This concerns many investors because Motorola would lose most of its Chinese investment if China's economy fails.[24]

Locations

Strategically planned sites for the Motorola facilities in China underscore the firm's operations in this nation. The main focus of Motorola's operations include Beijing City and Tianjin, as well as Hong Kong, which rejoined China in 1997 (see Exhibit 4).

Beijing Beijing serves as the headquarters for all ongoing operations in China. In 1986, Motorola opened its first facility there as a representative office to test the Chinese market.[25] In 1995, Motorola (China) Electronics Ltd. (MCEL)[26] purchased a high-tech modern office building to house the future Greater China headquarters, furthering Motorola's long-term commitment to China. Rick Younts, the executive vice president of MCEL, states:

> The purchase of this building and the locating of Motorola's future Greater China headquarters in Beijing is a vote of confidence by Motorola in the future of China and indeed the future of Greater China. Long-term success requires long-term commitment. Motorola's vision is of a vigorous and mutually beneficial partnership with all of

EXHIBIT 3 *Investment Growth in China*

Source: http://www.mot.com/General/China/test1/eng/invest.html

EXHIBIT 4 *Motorola Plant Locations*

Source: http://www.mot.com

China. Beijing—a city of tremendous history, culture, and resources—will be the base from which we build that future and a more prosperous tomorrow.[27]

Tianjin Since the initial entry into China through Beijing, Tianjin has evolved into the manufacturing center of Motorola's operations in China (see Exhibit 4). Motorola broke ground for the first manufacturing plant in Tianjin in June 1992 in the Tianjin Economic Development Area (TEDA).[28] Operations began there in March 1993 and expanded in 1995 with construction of an advanced submicron wafer fabrication facility in the XiQing Economic Development Zone (XEDZ). Rick Younts believes this investment supports the Beijing actions:

The establishment of this wafer fabrication plant is important because it signifies our long-term commitment to China. This indicates that Motorola is full of confidence in the modernization of China and also indicates our sincerity in the active assistance and involvement in establishing China's micro-electronics industry at world-class level.[29]

Motorola authorities chose a prime site for this plant. The XEDZ lies along the outskirts of Tianjin City, close to major roads and highways. Downtown is

only 10 km away, the airport is approximately 15 km away, and the original Motorola plant in TEDA is about 45 km away from the fabrication plant. Scheduled to open in late 1997 or early 1998, 400 to 500 people were to be employed in the initial stages of operations at this facility.[30]

"We are focusing on high growth areas, and we are adding capacity to capitalize on opportunities across our major product lines,"[31] says C. D. Tam, the Motorola Asia Pacific Semiconductor Group senior vice president and general manager. He feels that this new facility supports Motorola's objective of creating total customer satisfaction by increasing its operating advantages.

Quality Standards and Education

Motorola executives know that they need to invest heavily in education to succeed in the global market. In the 1980s, they realized that unless they improved production quality they would lose market share. A higher-quality standard demanded a better educated work force. A training program was started to improve their employees' performance. In their Illinois production facilities, company leaders were stunned to find that 60 percent of their manufacturing employees had trouble with simple arithmetic. Understanding the language was another challenge at many sites. When a plant in Florida offered English as second language designed for 60 people, about 500 registered for the program.[32] Consequently, Motorola learned how to communicate with and train people who are overcoming language barriers. Investments in the training amounted to $60 million a year in the early 1990s.[33]

Better education of the work force helps Motorola achieve the ambitious quality goals of Six Sigma. In its efforts to achieve total customer satisfaction, Motorola (China) Electronics Ltd. (MCEL) has adopted Six Sigma and is performing well. This quality standard calls for every process to produce no more than 3.4 defects for every one million parts manufactured.[34] Six Sigma has been incorporated into every aspect of Motorola's operations. The current achievement rate of 99.9996% accuracy owes some of its success to the Quality and Speed Policy to which the employees adhere (see Exhibit 5).[35]

The achievement of global leadership in quality is based on the continual training of the work force in new technologies.[36] In the words of a Motorola executive, "Whenever we reach a certain level of expertise or performance, there's always another one to go for." Even though challenges exist, Motorola has been able to bring its culture of continuous education and high-quality results to China. It spends about $4.5 million annually in training courses for its staff at Beijing and Tianjin.[37] In addition to internal training, the company has encouraged higher education by sponsoring 2,000 scholarships in the last four years at top Chinese technical universities, including Beijing University, Tianjin University, and Fudan University.[38]

Community

Motorola views its operations in China not only as a business opportunity, but also as a chance to assume an active role in the local community and environment. In addition to the 6,000 jobs it provides for the Chinese people, Motorola has organized Project Hope[39] in an effort to increase the standard of living for the local people (contributions amounted to $820,000 in 1996).[40] Currently, this project is building schools in 16 rural villages while continually looking for new ways to expand its reach.[41]

STRATEGIC ALLIANCES

Although historically Motorola has relied on strategic alliances and joint ventures to pursue direct foreign investment, it entered different markets in China through wholly owned subsidiaries, alliances, and partnerships. To coordinate its investment projects in China, the firm established Motorola (China) Investment Ltd. as a holding company. For specific examples of Motorola's alliances in China, see Exhibit 6.

Motorola and Apple

Apple Computer, Inc., the company that produces the Macintosh operating system, has had limited suc-

---

EXHIBIT 5 *Motorola Asia Pacific Semiconductor Products Group Quality and Speed Policy*

- Every employee strives for continuous improvement in Quality and Speed of products and services that we provide our customers.
- We recognize that we all serve a Customer, whether internal or external to Motorola.
- Our goal is to surpass our Customers' expectations and be Best-in-Class. To this end we continuously monitor their Key Indices of Performance as well as our own.
- We continuously strive to Streamline our operations and eliminate Non-Value-Added Processes.
- Every employee is aware that only through Empowered, Cross-Functional Teamwork can we achieve continuous success.
- We are committed to Do-It-Right-the-First-Time and to use all appropriate tools and methods to help us exceed Beyond Six Sigma Performance in everything we do.

Source: http://www.apspg.com/quality.html

EXHIBIT 6 *Motorola's Alliances in China*

Chinese Company	Sector
Joint Ventures:	
Leshan Radio Factory	Semiconductors
Panda Electronics Group	PowerPC computers
Shanghai Radio Communications Equipment Manufacturing Ltd.	Pagers
Shanghai Instrumentation Group	Automotive components
Hangzhou Communications Equipment Factory	Cellular telephones
Learning Alliances:	
Legend Group	Software development
Computer Integrated Manufacturing System-Engineering Center at Qinghua University (Beijing)	Manufacturing research
MPT Datang Telecommunications	Cellular telephone equipment
China PowerPC Consortium	Chinese language operating system development

Source: http://www.mot.com/General/China/facts96.html, March 6, 1997.

cess in the past few years. In hopes of regaining the market share it lost to Microsoft's Windows, Apple entered into alliances and licensing agreements. For example, Apple entered into an alliance with IBM and Motorola (the AIM Alliance) to develop the PowerPC platform, also known as the Common Hardware Reference Platform (CHRP). The CHRP will run multiple operating systems including AIX, Mac OS, and Windows NT.[42]

Licensing Agreement Motorola signed a licensing agreement with Apple in February 1996 which allows Motorola to sell computers that bear its own brand name and rely on the Macintosh operating system (Mac OS). The licensing agreement also allows Motorola to sublicense, which empowers it to grant other hardware manufacturers the right to use the Mac OS without permission from Apple. Ron Rogers, director of Motorola Computer Group, commented: "Basically, the sublicensing agreement allows [MCG] to sell systems in a multitiered distribution environment. In effect, we have open licensing of the Mac OS."[43]

As a result of its ability to develop and sell PowerPCs based on the Mac OS, Motorola developed a new line of Macintosh clones. This line, known as the StarMax family, utilizes high-performance Pow-

erPC microprocessors and features a multimedia-rich feature set and a five-year warranty. Motorola Computer Group's corporate vice president and general manager Joe Gugliemi stated: "We know there is a demand for high-performance, quality systems; customers can feel confident that the StarMax systems they purchase meet the impeccable Motorola standards of quality."[44]

Motorola's decision to enter the PC market via the licensing agreement with Apple has been questioned since the firm's core competencies have traditionally focused on the communications and semiconductor markets. Skeptics suggest that Motorola may be straying from its "bread and butter" industries by building entire computer systems. Gugliemi expressed his endorsement when he stated, "We believe the Mac-compatible market is an important opportunity for us, and also for Apple. This will make customers more at ease in buying Mac platform products."[45]

Motorola also feels that it can utilize its manufacturing, engineering, and marketing expertise to spark demand for the waning Mac systems. Although the Mac system is already considered the most user friendly operating system and maintains a certain portion of the computer industry market share, Motorola believes it can add value to the system by offering stronger products, more choices, and competitive prices. Motorola plans to offer desktop systems with the Mac OS in China through its alliance with Panda Electronics Group. Gilbert Amelio, Apple's chairman in 1996, indicated that he hopes Apple can build a big following in China. "We live in a world where only about half the people alive have used a telephone, much less a computer. The fact that a small segment of users uses another platform . . . hardly matters," Amelio said. "Our intention is to get as many people excited and using the Macintosh operation around the world as we can."[46]

The licensing agreement with Motorola will certainly promote excitement. The question still remains, however, whether manufacturing Mac-based systems is the best way for Motorola to enter the computer market. Can Motorola help the Mac system break IBM and Intel's stronghold in China, or will Motorola simply be wasting millions of dollars on an unmarketable computer system of the past?

Motorola and Panda

Panda Electronics Group is one of the largest electronics enterprises in China. It was founded in 1936 and produces shortwave communication systems, satellite communications systems, mobile communications systems, video cassette recorders, radio/audio tape recorders, and component audio products. In 1994, Panda's revenues amounted to US $540 million.[47]

Nanjing Power Computing Ltd. Motorola announced its major joint venture with Panda Electronics Group on October 31, 1995. Panda Electronics Group is one of China's leading electronics companies, and Motorola International Development Corporation (MIDC) is Motorola's wholly owned subsidiary in Schaumburg, Illinois. The two companies formed Nanjing Power Computing Ltd. The overall purpose of the joint venture is to develop, produce, and sell computer systems based on PowerPC microprocessors with Motorola investing 60 percent and Panda Electronics Group investing 40 percent.[48] Motorola's part in the alliance involves shipping electronic circuit boards to Nanjing Power Computing where the boards will be packaged into final computers and sold in Chinese markets. Through this alliance, Motorola will gain access to Panda's extensive distribution network and be able to market its StarMax line to consumer and educa-

tion markets. Achieving the overall goal will help to empower Nanjing Power Computing to develop new RISC PCs for China and other markets in Asia.

China's Marketing Division of the Electronic Computer Micro-electronic Research (CCID) of the Ministry of Electronics Industry reported that the PC computer market in China was entering a rapid growth stage. In 1995, the division expected computer sales to increase by 50.4 percent with a 25 percent average increase over the next five years.[49] Therefore, with Panda serving as Nanjing's distribution arm throughout China, Nanjing Power Computing will be able to capitalize on this growth because of its superior computing technology, manufacturing expertise, and distribution channels.

Edward Staiano, executive vice president of Motorola, Inc., and president and general manager of Motorola's General Systems Sector, commented:

> We are extremely excited with the development of this joint venture as it brings for the first time the strength of the PowerPC architecture to a market with vast opportunity. The computer market in China is clearly moving toward an integrated multi-media environment that combines graphics, audio and telecommunications functionality which is fully supported by our PowerPC microprocessor-based platforms. We believe that PowerPC will dramatically change the face of desktop computing in China.[50]

Chen Xiang Xing, chairman of the board of Panda Electronics Group, also expressed his support and enthusiasm.

> This cooperation between two powerful giants will be a major force in contributing to, and participating in, China's national development policy for the country's computer industry. Motorola, as one of the leading global corporations in the electronics industry, and Panda, one of China's largest and most comprehensive electronics enterprises, form a powerful union which will introduce state-of-the-art and technologically advanced PC computers to the Chinese marketplace.[51]

Motorola and Panda decided to base the management, engineering, and manufacturing organizations of Nanjing Power Computing Ltd. in the Jianging Economic and Technology Development Zone. The first products manufactured at this site were scheduled to reach the Chinese market in 1996. Nanjing

Power Computing will be capable of producing in excess of 100,000 multimedia PC systems annually.[52]

In addition to establishing production schedules, Nanjing needed an organizational structure designed to meet both Motorola and Panda's expectations. Nanjing Power Computing installed a management structure with a general manager reporting to a board of directors that consists of seven members, four appointed by Motorola and three by Panda.[53] Nanjing Power Computing then established its own marketing department to provide support to the existing sales channels of Panda Electronics Group in China.

Production in China protected Motorola from the 1997 Asian financial crash and kept profit margins somewhat higher than analysts had predicted.[54] More importantly, however, the Chinese market continues to evolve, and the world watches with great anticipation. Two billion people comprise a relatively untapped, seemingly infinite market.

STRATEGIC CHALLENGES AND QUESTIONS

From two-way radios to wireless communications and from television receivers to semiconductors, every new business opportunity Motorola, Inc., embarks upon seems to succeed. Most recently, Motorola has entered the computer market through the AIM Alliance and the Apple licensing agreement. Today, Motorola Computer Group is expanding its computer operations into China through its partnership with Panda Electronics.

However, a question arises as to whether Motorola should move away from its core businesses of wireless communications and semiconductors to its new ventures in computers. Overdiversification could pose potential organizational problems for the firm; however, the computer industry could provide Motorola with significant new opportunities, particularly in Asian countries.

A second concern relating to the diversification issue involves Motorola's decision to align with Apple and create Mac-compatible systems. Apple's difficulty in competing with IBM and IBM-compatible systems might be a problem that transfers to Motorola's computer business. Thus, the question exists as to whether Motorola can successfully create new demand for the Mac OS.

A final issue facing Motorola concerns its investments in China. The company has not only invested in manufacturing operations; it also has invested in the well-being of the Chinese people through supporting higher education and other community programs. The concern surrounding this issue deals with the lack of infrastructure in China as well as the low income of its citizens. Sociopolitical instability, labor unrest, inadequate energy supply, underdeveloped infrastructure, limited local financing, and low labor productivity still intimidate foreign investors.[55] Is China the rising star of tomorrow? Is the Nanjing joint venture with Motorola the right approach in China? Should Motorola invest so heavily in China when there is at least doubt about the potential of the Chinese market?

Motorola has been successful in its past ventures into new arenas. Will it be successful in the computer market? More specifically, will it be successful competing with IBM-compatible computers by producing Mac-compatible computers? Finally, should Motorola invest so heavily in China when there is doubt about the potential of the Chinese market?

C-365

NOTES

1. Karl Schoenberger, 1996, Motorola bets big on China, *Fortune*, May 27: 119.
2. Ibid.
3. http://www.mot.com/General/facts96.html, March 7, 1997.
4. Leigh Ann Klaus, 1997, Motorola brings fairy tales to life, *Quality Progress*, June, vol. 30, no. 6: 24–25.
5. http://www.apspg.com/about.html, March 7, 1997.
6. http://www.mot.com, March 6, 1997.
7. J. Morone, 1997, *Winning in High Tech Markets: The Role of General Management*, Harvard Business School Press, Cambridge, Mass.
8. http://www.mot.com/General/facts96.html, March 7, 1997.
9. http://www.mot.com/GSS/MCG/products/systems/ds/starmax/smaxqas.html, March 6, 1997.
10. http://www.apspg.com/about.html, March 7, 1997.
11. http://www.mot.com/General/facts96.html, March 7, 1997.
12. Ibid.
13. Ibid.
14. Ibid.
15. Jan Ozer, 1997, Streaming video: A welcome reception, *PC Magazine*, October 7, vol. 16, no. 17.
16. Ken Presti, 1996, "Motorola unveils Macintosh clones," *Computer Reseller News*, September 23, 16.
17. Schoenberger, Motorola bets big on China.

18. James E. Austin, Francis Aguilar, and Jian-sheng Jin, *Nike in China* (Abridged), Harvard Business School (9-390-092), August 12, 1993.

19. Schoenberger, Motorola bets big on China.

20. http://www.mot.com/General/China/facts96.html, March 6, 1997.

21. http://www.mot.com/MU/Opportunities/Q396Perspective. html, March 6, 1997.

22. http://www.mot.com/General/China/speech.html, March 6, 1997.

23. http://www.mot.com/MU/Opportunities/Q396Perspective. html, March 6, 1997.

24. Schoenberger, Motorola bets big on China.

25. http://www.mot.com/General/China/facts96.html, March 6, 1997.

26. http://www.mot.com/General/China/eng/hopemain.html, February 13, 1998.

27. http://www.design-net.com/press/html/PR951116A.html, March 6, 1997.

28. http://www.mot.com/General/China/facts96.html, March 6, 1997.

29. http://www.design-net.com/press/html/PR951114C.html, March 6, 1997.

30. Ibid.

31. Ibid.

32. William Wiggenhorn, Motorola U: When training becomes an education, in Robert Howard, 1997, *The Learning Imperative*, Harvard Business School Press, Cambridge, Mass.

33. Ibid.

34. http://www.apspg.com/tianjin/quality.html, March 7, 1997.

35. http://www.apspg.com/quality.html, March 7, 1997.

36. Robert J. Browman, 1997, The joy of six sigma, *Distribution*, vol. 96, no. 9: 62–64.

37. Peter Wonacott, 1997, Foreign firms spend heavily in race to train staff in China, *The Asian Wall Street Journal Weekly*, October 13: 21.

38. http://www.mot.com/General/China/facts96.html, March 6, 1997.

39. http://www.mot.com/General/China/eng/facts96.htm, February 13, 1998.

40. http://www.apspg.com/quality.html, March 7, 1997.

41. http://www.mot.com/MU/Opportunities/Q396Perspective. html, March 6, 1997.

42. Bob Francis and Lisa Picarille, 1996, PowerPC trio aims for 600-Mhz chips, *Computer World*, August 5: 14.

43. Joshua Piven, 1996, Motorola first to sublease Mac OS, motherboards, private label systems to manufacturers, *Computer Technology Review*, April: 1, 16.

44. Terri Thorson, 1996, Motorola Computer Group introduces new PowerPC-based Mac OS-compatible systems, *Business Wire*, September 17.

45. Presti, Motorola unveils Macintosh clones.

46. Elizabeth Corcoran, 1996, Apple gives Mac license to Motorola, *Washington Post*, February 20.

47. Ibid.

48. http://www.mot.com/GSS/MCG/new/press_rel/panda.html, March 6, 1997.

49. Ibid.

50. Ibid.

51. Ibid.

52. Ibid.

53. Ibid.

54. Carol Huber, 1998, Motorola sees shift in Japan, China, *Electronic News*, January 19.

55. Jacob Chacko and Piotr Chelminski, 1996, An investigation of the business environment of China: Recommendations for foreign investors, *American Business Review*, June.

Pasta Perfect, Inc.

Joan Winn
John W. Mullins

University of Denver

"This is a tough call," said Jim Leonard, director of Pasta Perfect, Inc., to Tom Walker, president of Pasta Perfect. "Clearly, our results in the retail stores are not what we'd like them to be, and that concerns me a great deal. On the other hand, I'm not sure we have what it takes to succeed in supermarkets, and to put our funds there is not what we told the shareholders we would do with their money when we raised the last round of capital."

It was October 1988, and the Pasta Perfect board was discussing a change in strategy, from development of a chain of specialty retail shops to selling fresh pasta and sauces through supermarkets. Pasta Perfect, headquartered in St. Louis, Missouri, operated 14 fresh pasta shops in the St. Louis and Chicago metropolitan areas. In spite of its rapid growth, the company had not reached profitability. While everyone in the small company was frustrated about the firm's poor performance, no one felt the frustration more acutely than did Tom Walker. He conceived the idea of a chain of fresh pasta stores; he put to-

gether a management team and he recruited a board of directors, including Jim Leonard, a venture capitalist. Tom Walker also had convinced investors to provide several rounds of capital to build the business. Now it appeared that these investors, who included friends and family as well as almost 7,000 shareholders in the now publicly held firm, were at risk of losing their entire investment in Pasta Perfect. To Tom, it was clear that something had to change. "I've tried everything that my 15 years in retailing have taught me, and except for store #102, we just can't seem to turn the corner to positive contribution from the stores. I don't like to admit it, but I'm afraid we need to find another path."

THE CHANGING PASTA MARKET

The first American pasta factory had opened in 1848 in Brooklyn, New York. By 1981, the average American was consuming about 12 pounds of pasta per year, or about one serving a week. For years, pasta had been considered a starchy, inexpensive belly stuffer.[1] Spaghetti or macaroni and cheese made an economical dinner at the end of the week; canned ravioli was a quick, hot lunch.[2] But as people started paying closer attention to health, exercise, and nutrition in the early 1980s, pasta's image began to change to one of a healthy gourmet food.

This case was originally presented at the North American Case Research Association Annual Conference in New Orleans, November 1994. This case is intended for use as the basis for class discussion rather than to illustrate the effective or ineffective handling of a managerial situation. All events and individuals in this case are real, but names and locations have been disguised. All rights reserved jointly to the authors and the North American Case Research Association (NACRA). Copyright © 1994 by Joan Winn and John W. Mullins.

Throughout the 1980s, pasta sales enjoyed a steady five percent per year growth as pasta became a featured item in gourmet restaurants and cookbooks. In 1982, Morisi & Sons in Brooklyn, New York, began manufacturing flavored dried pasta. That same year, fresh pasta appeared in supermarkets in New York City and Los Angeles. As the pasta market grew in sales and in its upscale appeal, these developments created new market niches. The dried pasta category remained a hotly competitive one, with consumers shopping largely based on price and retailers demanding price promotions from manufacturers. The new specialty pastas, including flavored dried pastas and an expanding variety of fresh pastas, were viewed differently, however, by both consumers and retailers. These specialty products catered to upscale urban and suburban adults who sought convenient, yet nutritious and tasty meals. These products were generally marketed in the higher-margin deli sections of supermarkets, instead of in the grocery aisle, to avoid competition with lower-cost dried pasta.[3] Such products were also found in small Italian food shops in urban neighborhoods with large Italian populations.

THE PASTA INDUSTRY IN THE LATE 1980s

By 1987, American pasta factories were producing nearly 3 billion pounds of pasta—$1.6 billion at wholesale prices—per year. Average per capita consumption had grown to more than 16 pounds annually. This was an increase of 6 percent from 1986, and an average increase of 4 to 5 percent per year since 1980. The National Pasta Association predicted consumption of 24 pounds per person or 192 servings annually by 1995. In 1988, more than 40 percent of sales came from the retail dry packaged pastas; 60 percent came from the prepared pasta market, which included frozen, canned, and jarred pasta products.[4]

In spite of this growth pattern, dried pasta was viewed as a commodity business, with retail prices averaging less than $1 per pound. No brand had achieved national distribution, and even the companies with big market savvy had been unable to successfully establish strong brand identities. "The game of price is really the game of pasta," observed Hugh Peters, senior product manager for Mueller's Pasta

Products. Timothy Dunn, senior investment officer with PNC Financial, saw pasta as "a volume business. Name recognition is important, but I don't think people really see much difference between [brands]. . . . They'll buy whatever they can get a deal on."[5]

In 1987, the top five leading brands were Mueller's with sales of $154 million, Creamette with sales of $125 million, General Foods' Ronzoni with $92 million in sales, San Giorgio with $67 million in sales, and Prince with sales of $59 million. Together, however, these five brands accounted for only about one-third of the pasta sold nationally, with the remaining share of the market spread across a variety of regional brands.

Although the growth of the dry pasta market had been steady but unspectacular, the growth of refrigerated fresh pasta had been tremendous. Sales of refrigerated fresh pasta, which was soft and flexible, rather than dried into rigid sticks, had risen 30 percent per year since 1985 and was approaching $100 million in 1988. Sales were predicted to top $150 million by 1990 and $250 million by 1995. This rapid growth occurred in spite of retail prices averaging over $3 per pound, more than three times the price of dried pasta.

In early 1987, the American Italian Pasta Company (AIPC) in Excelsior Springs, Missouri, began supplying Kroger supermarkets, a large midwestern chain, with private-label packages of refrigerated fresh pasta. AIPC provided merchandising support, including in-store product demonstrations and mobile pasta cart display units. AIPC founder Richard Thompson planned to launch is own brand, Pasta LaBella, by 1989. Also in 1987, Vivace, another small manufacturing newcomer, started marketing fresh pasta to Houston area supermarkets.[6]

By late 1987, there were over 50 manufacturers of refrigerated pasta that marketed their products outside of their immediate neighborhood. Because fresh pasta was relatively new, these regional brands were not well entrenched. Carnation's Contadina Fresh, which went national after Nestlé acquired a small New York-based fresh pasta producer in 1986 for $56 million, was the only brand that enjoyed more than a local following. Carnation's plans were for Contadina's pasta sales to exceed $60 million in 1988, serving 37 metropolitan markets nationally.

This rapid growth of refrigerated fresh pasta had been made possible by the recent development of gas-flushed packaging technology that extended the product's shelf life. The soft fresh pasta was manufactured using new, high-tech equipment, that gently folded the pasta and placed it in an attractively labeled clear plastic container, which was then filled with a mixture of nitrogen and other gases. This packaging prevented the growth of mold and kept the pasta fresh and appealing for 90 days.

MARKETING OF PASTA PRODUCTS

Pasta was advertised mainly through radio and newspaper ads, coupons and reduced prices, and in-store demonstrations and sampling. Most of the advertising dollars were spent on sauce, rather than pasta. National advertising for pastas was rare, because there were distinct regional differences in customer preferences. Most dry pasta brands did not advertise, because profit margins were thin and purchasing tended to be dictated by price. Creamette was projected to spend about $7 million in advertising in 1988, more than $5 million more than anticipated by second-place spender Prince.

Most media advertising was directed toward sauces, partly because sauces commanded a higher profit margin, but also because they could be differentiated from each other. Ragu, founded in 1937 in Rochester, New York, had gone national in 1969 when it was acquired by Chesebrough-Ponds. In 1982, Campbell's introduced Prego, and the sauce wars intensified. Unilever acquired Chesebrough-Ponds in 1987, spending more than $20 million in advertising, $15 million of that on network TV. Ragu was the industry leader, having successfully captured more than half of the sauce market, with over $400 million in sales in 1987. Hunt's had introduced Prima Salsa in the mid-1970s, but pulled it off the shelves in the early 1980s due to stiff competition from Ragu. Other sauce competitors included various regional brands such as Progresso, sold mostly in the Northeast, and Contadina, which was sold in the refrigerated section of the store next to its pastas.

THE ORIGINS OF PASTA PERFECT

In 1983, Tom Walker saw the potential for growth and profitability in the fresh pasta market. Walker, who had recently left his vice president's position with a major specialty apparel retailer and moved to St. Louis, had been looking for a niche in which to build a specialty retail business of his own. "When we lived on the East Coast, there was a fresh pasta store that Jan and I frequented at least once a week. The pasta and sauces were wonderful. And because fresh pasta cooks in just two minutes, we could have a gourmet meal on the table in 10 minutes when we got home from work." With the growth he saw in the pasta market, combined with the burgeoning trends toward fitness and nutrition and his retailing background, Walker decided he had found his niche. "I knew that consumers were increasingly interested in freshness, whether in fresh-baked chocolate chip cookies in the shopping mall, freshly ground coffee from the grocery store, or other food products. I also saw that fresh products could command a price premium over conventional packaged products. And I knew from that little store back east just how good fresh pasta really is." Tom could barely contain his enthusiasm and excitement as he began to work on planning a chain of retail stores that would sell fresh pasta and sauces to take home. He envisioned small, attractive shops in high-traffic areas, targeted at upscale consumers who wanted a convenient meal that they could quickly purchase and prepare at home. Italian cuisine was popular in St. Louis, so Tom was convinced that there was ample demand for his product. And, because pasta was made largely from inexpensive ingredients—semolina flour, eggs, and water—Tom felt that gross margins were likely to be attractive enough to cover the costs of operating small stores.

Confident in the future of fresh pasta, Tom decided to devote his full-time attention to his new venture. He wrote a business plan, found partners with time and money to invest (one of whom came from an Italian family), and set out to raise the additional money needed to start his business. He talked to family and friends and quickly sold several of them on his idea. With $35,000 raised and his partner's family sauce receipes adapted to large quantity production, he was ready to launch Pasta Perfect.

The first store opened in May 1984 in St. Louis, Missiouri. By September 1985, there were five Pasta Perfect stores in the St. Louis area. By October 1988, there were ten stores in St. Louis and four in Chicago, with the newest Chicago store having opened in June.

The company's plan was to cluster groups of stores in large metropolitan areas. This would provide economies of scale in preparation and delivery, as well as in advertising and store supervision, and allow the company to maintain the high standards for product quality, freshness, and customer service for which it was becoming increasingly well known. The young company's growth was helped along by favorable articles in the St. Louis newspapers, with the food writers praising Pasta Perfect's products.

As of late 1988, Pasta Perfect encountered little direct competition in its offerings of fresh pasta products. Several stores specializing in fresh pasta products emerged in New York and California, but Pasta Perfect was the only specialty retail chain in Missouri and Illinois. Packaged, refrigerated fresh pasta was just starting to appear in St. Louis and Chicago supermarkets.

THE PASTA PERFECT STORE CONCEPT

Pasta Perfect stores were designed with two-income families in mind, where time savings and quality were more important than price in home-food purchasing decisions. Pasta Perfect stores were located in high-traffic urban locations or in strip shopping centers anchored by major supermarket chains for easy access. Because fresh pasta sold at a premium price over the conventional dried pasta products found on supermarket shelves, it was important for Pasta Perfect stores to look attractive and inviting, with an atmosphere that conveyed quality, freshness, and convenience.

Each Pasta Perfect store was decorated in green and white with natural wood furnishings and a prominently displayed Pasta Perfect logo. Displays of the products offered for sale were planned with eye appeal in mind. Seven of the stores featured limited seating for 8 to 15 people, and offered, in addition to Pasta Perfect's assortment of take-home products, a light lunch menu consisting of cold sandwiches, soups, pasta salads, desserts, and beverages. Seating had been planned for these stores because Pasta Perfect had found it difficult to lease locations as small as the 400 to 500 square feet needed. Thus, some stores were as large as 2,000 square feet.

The stores' furniture and equipment consisted principally of a pasta-cutting machine, refrigerators, display and storage cases, counters, display and storage shelving, and various types of smaller equipment such as a cash register, scale, bowls and jars for product display, and utensils. Stores that served prepared items also contained tables and chairs.

Pasta Perfect offered fresh pasta in five regular flavors—egg, herb, spinach, black pepper, egg-free—plus weekly specials such as lemon and tomato basil. Pasta was delivered to each store in whole sheets and then cut to order for each customer, wrapped in butcher paper, and sealed with a bright red and green label that gave cooking instructions. Pasta Perfect's best-selling pastas were fettucini (wide), linguine (narrow), tagliarini (thin), and angel hair (fine). Pasta Perfect also sold its own sauces for pasta, plus various fresh and frozen specialty products including salads and other Italian specialties such as ravioli, manicotti, and lasagna. The assortment of sauces for its fresh pasta included tomato, meat, white clam, alfredo (heavy cream with freshly grated cheeses), and bolognese (tomatoes with Italian sausage, wine, and fresh vegetables). Pasta Perfect also offered other food and nonfood products, including fresh bread, various imported and domestic food products, Italian cookbooks, and utensils.

Operations

Stores were open from 11:00 A.M. to 7:00 P.M. six days a week; most of them were open from 11:00 to 5:00 on Sundays as well. For each store, the company employed a full-time manager who was responsible for two to four part-time employees. To assure that individual stores were operated at a high level of quality, Pasta Perfect took great care in its selection and training of managers and provided a detailed training and operations manual to each manager.

Most of the products sold in Pasta Perfect stores were prepared at Pasta Perfect's commissary, located in a St. Louis suburb. This central preparation center served all of the stores in the metropolitan area in an effort to reduce the investment and space needed for each store and to increase control over product quality, freshness, and costs.

Pasta was prepared daily and delivered to the St. Louis area stores in a refrigerated truck designed to hold the products at desired temperatures. Sauces were packaged in microwave-safe and freezer-safe containers. Fresh pasta for the Chicago stores was produced in a back kitchen area in one of those stores. Sauces and other refrigerated and frozen products were prepared in St. Louis and shipped to the Chicago stores via refrigerated common carrier. Because fresh pasta has a shorter shelf life than dried pasta, careful rotation of stock and effective management of inventory levels were necessary to maintain product freshness and control waste.

PASTA PERFECT FINANCIAL PERFORMANCE

Pasta Perfect financed its operations and growth by raising several rounds of capital. Its first five stores were funded by private investors, whom Tom Walker was able to interest in purchasing equity or providing convertible debt to his young company. In December 1985, Pasta Perfect raised $1.5 million in an initial public offering. In April 1988, another $800,000 was raised in a second public offering in which all shareholders were offered "rights" to purchase additional shares. This offering had been made possible by the relatively strong sales of the new Chicago stores, compared to the St. Louis stores, in spite of the fact that the company had yet to earn a profit. Exhibit 1 shows balance sheet information as of April 1988 (adjusted to include the capital raised in April 1988). Exhibit 2 shows the company's profit and loss history. Individual store performance data is shown in Exhibit 3, and the planned operating performance of Pasta Perfect stores is shown in Exhibit 4.

In the fiscal year ended April 1, 1988, only two of the St. Louis stores and one Chicago store were contributing positively to overhead and profit; but, two of these three were barely profitable (see Exhibit 4). Results for the current fiscal year to date were similar to those in FY 1988. Over the four years of the company's existence, a series of steps had been taken to address Pasta Perfect's poor operating performance.

In late 1986 and early 1987, a series of productivity enhancements and personnel changes at Pasta Perfect's St. Louis commissary led to significant reductions in the labor portion of product costs as well as improved quality and consistency of the company's pasta and sauce products. These enhancements and changes resulted in a reported commissary contribu-

tion of $43,000 in FY 1987 (see Exhibit 3), compared to an expected break-even performance. Because products were passed from the commissary to the stores at transfer prices intended to recover the full variable and fixed costs to make them, these transfer prices were reduced at the beginning of FY 1988 so that the margin improvements (about 4 percent of retail sales) would be reflected in store operating performance figures.

More generally, new flavors of pasta and sauces were developed and offered on a rotating basis, in order to encourage more frequent customer visits to the stores. Lunch menus and espresso were added in the larger stores, and delivery and some catering were tested. Radio advertising and newspaper coupons were developed to expand consumer awareness and bring new customers into the stores, and sales contests and other employee incentives were established.

In 1987 and early 1988, approximately $200,000 was spent on a radio advertising campaign designed to stimulate lagging sales in the St. Louis stores. (Advertising expenses are included in the regional overhead figures reported in Exhibit 3.) While the campaign did increase awareness of Pasta Perfect in St. Louis and had a modestly positive impact on sales, the overall result was a significant increase in the size of St. Louis operating losses in the year ended April 1988 compared to the year ended April 1987 (see Exhibit 3). The lack of success of this effort coupled with steadily worsening economic conditions in St. Louis led Walker to conclude that significant improvement in operating performance in St. Louis was extremely unlikely in the short run. While some St. Louis stores could be closed to mitigate these losses, rent would still be due unless landlords could find new tenants for the spaces, something Walker deemed unlikely in the deteriorating economic environment in St. Louis.

In Chicago, the picture was somewhat brighter, at least in terms of revenue. Given its sales problems in St. Louis (see Exhibit 3), Pasta Perfect had decided to secure the best possible locations for its stores in Chicago. All three Chicago stores were opened in upscale neighborhoods with busy foot traffic passing the store, in contrast to the strip shopping center approach that had been used in St. Louis. This decision paid off in sales, as average per-store sales in Chicago were 75 percent higher than in St. Louis. "Such locations do not come cheap, however," said Walker. In fact, store rent averaged $35,000 per year

EXHIBIT 1 *Pasta Perfect, Inc. Balance Sheet*

For the 52-Week Year Ending:	March 29, 1985	March 28, 1986	April 3, 1987	April 1, 1988
Assets				
Current assets				
Cash and temporary cash investments	$ 1,673	$1,115,647	$ 301,158	$ 701,185
Notes receivable	800			
Accounts receivable	516	1,936	14,461	2,758
Inventories	9,372	19,351	45,644	41,418
Prepaid expenses	706	7,411	1,056	2,838
Receivable on exercise of common stock purchase warrants			150,000	
Total current assets	$ 13,067	$1,144,345	$ 512,319	$ 748,199
Property and equipment				
Furniture and equipment, at cost	$ 47,195	$ 194,543	$ 389,780	$ 399,529
Leasehold improvements	17,978	106,571	291,586	261,769
Less accumulated depreciation	(6,079)	(24,417)	(81,419)	(155,362)
Net property and equipment	$ 59,094	$ 276,697	$ 599,947	$ 505,936
Other assets:				
Organizational expense	$ 2,643	$ 1,906	$ 1,168	—
Deposits	1,945	7,792	16,414	18,340
Total other assets	4,588	9,698	17,582	18,340
Total assets	$ 76,749	$1,430,740	$1,129,848	$1,272,475
Liabilities and Stockholders' Equity				
Current liabilities				
Notes payable	$ 25,672	$ 4,602	—	—
Accounts payable	10,257	37,624	130,856	66,459
Accrued liabilities	27,684	14,922	61,879	137,199
Long-term debt due within one year	2,470	8,963	32,370	47,352
Total current liabilities	$ 66,083	$ 66,111	$ 225,105	$ 251,010
Long-term debt due after one year	$ 4,269	$ 49,963	$ 151,260	$ 173,960
Subordinated debentures	60,000	—	—	—
Total liabilities	$130,352	$ 116,074	$ 376,365	$ 424,970
Stockholders' equity				
Common stock	$ 6,286	$ 42,249	$ 43,788	$ 51,507
Capital in excess of par value	56,264	1,648,827	1,781,095	2,467,283
Accumulated deficit	(116,153)	(376,410)	(1,071,400)	(1,671,285)
Total equity (deficit)	(53,603)	1,314,666	753,483	847,505
Total liabilities & equity	$ 76,749	$1,430,740	$1,129,848	$1,272,475

in Chicago, compared to $13,000 in St. Louis. In addition, Walker had to pay $5,000 more in salary in Chicago to attract competent store managers. The additional rent and payroll costs, together with somewhat lower gross margins due to lower levels of production in Chicago and freight costs on goods shipped from St. Louis, consumed the majority of the extra revenues. Thus, the Chicago region was not profitable either.

While Walker hoped that the Chicago market could be profitable for Pasta Perfect, his hopes were contingent on getting a few more stores opened to expand Pasta Perfect's market presence and permit economies of scale in pasta production and store su-

EXHIBIT 2 *Pasta Perfect, Inc. Statement of Profit and Loss*

For the 52-Week Year Ending:	March 29, 1985	March 28, 1986	April 3, 1987	April 1, 1988
Gross sales	$130,180	$303,458	$1,009,723	$1,289,037
Promotional discounts	(10,156)	(23,034)	(111,521)	(136,344)
Net sales	$120,024	$280,424	$ 898,202	$1,152,693
Operating costs and expenses:				
Cost of sales*	$ 86,938	$194,753	$ 440,195	$ 525,369
Selling, general, admin**	132,522	362,894	1,164,653	1,204,373
	219,460	557,647	1,604,848	1,729,742
Operating loss	($99,436)	($277,223)	($706,646)	($577,049)
Other income (expense):				
Interest income	$ 447	$ 22,173	$ 39,266	$ 8,547
Interest expense	(6,967)	(8,543)	(29,440)	(33,250)
Miscellaneous income	7,270	3,336	1,830	1,867
	750	16,966	11,656	(22,836)
Net loss	($98,686)	($260,257)	($694,990)	($599,885)

*Full cost of products sold in Pasta Perfect stores, including both fixed and variable commissary costs associated with the manufacture of Pasta Perfect's pasta and sauce products.

**Includes all store-level expenses other than cost of sales and all regional and headquarters expenses.

pervision. He and his leasing agent had identified two promising locations. Neither was vacant currently, but the current tenants' leases were expiring within 90 to 120 days and would not be renewed. More importantly, however, his company was running out of time. "To open, say, three new stores will consume about $120,000 of our remaining capital, assuming equipment from underperforming stores in St. Louis is moved to Chicago. And, by the time we get the new stores built out and open—six months or so from now—our current burn rate will leave us perilously low on cash."

In October 1988, Pasta Perfect's cash reserves stood at $450,000, and the company was losing $45,000 per month in cash, or $540,000 per year. Tom Walker had prepared a summary (see Exhibit 5) of the company's current cash flow performance, and he realized that the company's cash would not last long if things continued as they were.

At this point, it does not seem realistic to think we can turn around our store operations fast enough. Though our Chicago store sales are much better than our sales in St. Louis, our higher rent, payroll, and supervision costs eat up all the extra revenues. We can't seem to make money in our stores, even in Chicago. And, while we sure wouldn't have come this far without the public offerings, it costs a lot of money to be publicly held (see Exhibit 5). I believe we have no choice but to consider alternatives to our present strategy. I'm really frustrated at our inability to make our stores economically viable!

PASTA PERFECT'S FUTURE

Tom Walker proposed two options for the board to consider. First, Pasta Perfect could continue to open additional stores in Chicago. Opening more stores in St. Louis was out of the question, because the St. Louis economy had continued to sour in the last year. Many shopping centers in metropolitan St. Louis, including some where Pasta Perfect stores were located, were losing tenants; unemployment was rising, and other economic indicators pointed to a prolonged economic slump in the area. All of the St. Louis stores but two were losing money. Prospects in Chicago seemed brighter, because sales volumes in the new Chicago stores were so much higher than in the St. Louis stores. On the other hand, the higher

EXHIBIT 3 *Pasta Perfect, Inc. Comparative Store Data*

	52-Week Year Ending April 1, 1988		52-Week Year Ending April 3, 1987		Increase	
	Net Sales	**Contribution**	**Net Sales**	**Contribution**	**Net Sales**	**Contribution**
St. Louis Stores						
#101	$55,881	($9,751)	$77,335	($6,636)	($21,454)	($3,116)
#102	$158,655	$33,611	$165,597	$21,451	($6,943)	$12,160
#103	$139,082	($11,074)	$119,077	($22,518)	$20,005	$11,444
#104	closed	closed	$27,725	($20,386)	$27,725	($20,386)
#106	$107,956	$1,614	$117,154	($2,890)	($9,199)	$4,505
#107	$59,345	($21,809)	$56,703	($19,639)	$2,643	($2,169)
#108	$40,066	($10,965)	$77,618	($12,420)	($37,551)	$1,455
#109	$105,825	($8,861)	$91,748	($5,433)	$14,077	($3,428)
#110	$60,125	($19,478)	$64,129	($6,385)	($4,004)	($13,092)
#111	$64,546	($8,181)	$24,232	$43	$40,315	($8,223)
	$791,481	($54,894)	$821,317	($74,815)	($29,837)	$19,921
Wholesale	$13,336	$4,059	$12,387	$3,237	$2,649	$821
SL commissary*	-0-	$11,475	-0-	$43,227		($31,752)
SL region overhead**		($95,901)		($209,322)		$113,421
St. Louis totals	$804,817	($135,261)	$833,704	($237,673)	($28,887)	$102,411
Chicago Stores						
#201†	$122,692	($14,276)	$30,989	($5,204)	$91,703	($9,072)
#202†	$162,705	$525	$33,509	$723	$129,195	($198)
#203††	$62,480	($2,728)	-0-	-0-	$62,480	($2,728)
	$347,876	($16,480)	$64,498	($4,481)	$283,378	($11,998)
Chgo commissary*	-0-	($6,325)	-0-	$242		($6,567)
Chgo region overhead**		($50,749)		($29,122)		($21,627)
Chicago totals	$347,876	($73,554)	$64,498	($33,361)	$283,378	($40,193)
Administration†††		($245,237)		($395,523)		$150,286
Store Closing Cost		($122,997)		($35,466)		($87,531)
Other		($22,837)		$7,032		($29,869)
Total Company	$1,152,693	($599,885)	$898,202	($694,990)	$254,491	$95,105

*No sales are shown for the commissaries, since all their products are shipped to the stores and booked as intracompany transfers.

**Region overhead consists of advertising and the salary and expenses of a regional manager.

†Stores #201 and #202 opened in February 1987.

††Store #203 opened in October 1987.

†††The decline of administrative expense from FY 1987 to FY 1988 is due largely to the elimination of a former vice president of marketing position and a store procedures and training position at headquarters, and a reduction in expense associated with new store openings, together with other administrative efficiencies. See Exhibit 5 for detail of administration expense.

operating costs in Chicago were troublesome and seemingly largely out of Tom's control, given the high levels of rent and manager salaries that prevailed in Chicago. "I must admit," said Walker, "that I am not at all confident that the Chicago stores as a group, much less the company as a whole, can be made profitable before we run out of cash."

Walker's second option was to change the direction of the company, shifting from a specialty store retailing strategy to one of selling pasta and sauces in supermarkets. Contadina refrigerated fresh pasta had recently appeared in St. Louis supermarkets, but there were no well-established competitors. Individual supermarkets in Chicago had just begun experi-

EXHIBIT 4 *Pasta Perfect, Inc. Business Model Per Store*

Sales		$150,000
Cost of goods sold		60,000
Gross margin		90,000
Store operating expenses		
Payroll and benefits	33,000	
Store rent	12,000	
Equipment lease expense	7,000	
Occupancy costs*	3,000	
Other store operating	3,000	
Total store operating expenses		58,000
Store contribution to overhead and profit		32,000
Regional overhead per store**		10,000
Contribution to overhead and profit		$ 22,000

*Utilities and real estate taxes.
**Advertising and regional manager salary and expense.

menting with local pasta brands. Tom had read in a trade magazine that the national fresh pasta market was projected to reach something like $125 million in 1991. He figured that he could estimate the market potential in Pasta Perfect's markets by comparing their population to that of the United States in total (see Exhibit 6). It seemed likely that Contadina would secure the leading market share, given its head start, but Tom thought a 20 percent share for Pasta Perfect might be within reach by the end of calendar year 1989.

To enter the supermarket distribution channel would require that Pasta Perfect's products be packaged using the same gas-flushed technology em-

ployed by Contadina. The manufacturing and packaging line necessary would cost about $250,000 to install, and a small facility would have to be leased to accommodate it. No one in Pasta Perfect understood this technology, and the company lacked sophisticated food manufacturing expertise. Alternatively, Walker could contract, at least at the outset, with either of two firms located in Alabama and Iowa which were already in gas-flushed pasta manufacturing and packaging. Doing so would save cash and perhaps partially mitigate the risks.

Walker reasoned that there would be room for the Pasta Perfect brand on the supermarket shelves, and that Pasta Perfect's good reputation might make it

EXHIBIT 5 *Pasta Perfect, Inc. Sources of Annual Negative Cash Flow as of October 1988*

St. Louis Region Operations	$135,000
Chicago Region Operations	80,000
Costs of Being Public Company[1]	80,000
Store Equipment Lease Payments	120,000
Other General and Administrative[2]	175,000
Total	$590,000

Note: Store rent expenses, which are included in the operations figures above, totaled $130,000 per year for the St. Louis region (10 stores) and $140,000 per year for the Chicago region (4 stores). The leases were due to expire at various dates from 1989 through 1993.
[1]Includes cost of audited financial statements, legal fees, and expenses associated with reporting to Pasta Perfect's 7,000 public shareholders.
[2]Includes salaries of president, controller, two accounting clerks, secretary, and office expenses.

EXHIBIT 6 *Pasta Perfect, Inc. Demographic Data–Pasta Perfect Markets*

Geographic Area	Population
Metropolitan St. Louis	2,493,000
Metropolitan Chicago	8,240,000
Missouri	5,117,000
Illinois	11,431,000
United States	248,710,000

Source: *Statistical Abstract of the United States,* U.S. Department of Commerce, 1994.

possible to secure shelf space. He had spoken to a merchandise manager at the leading supermarket chain in St. Louis, and she seemed open to the idea of carrying Pasta Perfect products in her chain's 60 stores. However, the potential margins were less certain. Heavy promotional costs and probable inefficiencies while Pasta Perfect installed and attempted to master the new technology (or lower margins if production were outsourced) could easily reduce margins (net of these costs) to as little as 20 percent of sales until all the problems were solved.

There were several additional risks and barriers to adopting the supermarket strategy. The first was that Tom's skills and past experience were in retailing. He and others on the management team knew relatively little about selling *to* supermarket retailers. (Exhibit 7 shows profiles of the company's officers and directors.) Walker had managed groups of stores for a large apparel chain, so he knew how to set up store systems and attract and motivate store employees, skills which had enabled Pasta Perfect to grow quickly. But, he had little experience on the buying side of the business, and his direct selling experience was limited to selling barbecue accessories to chain retailers in a previous entrepreneurial venture. No one on the board or the management team had any previous manufacturing experience, and manufacturing expertise was certain to be among the critical success factors for a supermarket-driven strategy. Tom wondered whether he could attract a strong manufacturing person given the company's financial condition.

Additionally, many supermarket chains required substantial promotional allowances, including slotting allowances (fees paid to gain shelf space for new products, sometimes as high as $300 per item per store to introduce new items) and introductory deals, before they would place new products on their shelves. While Walker had heard that slotting allowances were sometimes waived for small local suppliers, the totality of these marketing costs was likely to make it very expensive to change to a supermarket strategy. And even if the company were to close its retail stores to focus on supermarkets, the company remained liable for store rents and payments on equipment leases (see Exhibit 5). Walker did not know how quickly his company could reduce these obligations.

A final concern was that, in the prospectus for the recent rights offering, the company had indicated that it would use the proceeds of the offering to expand its retail chain. Using the proceeds in another manner could lead shareholders to believe that the company had misled them in the rights offering prospectus, and thereby lead to the possibility of shareholder lawsuits against the company and/or its officers and directors personally. Tom knew his intentions were honorable in proposing the supermarket strategy, but he also knew that two of his directors served on the boards of other small firms, and they could not afford even the appearance of impropriety.

The board faced a difficult choice. The specialty stores were losing money. Unless these stores became profitable, the company's 7,000 shareholders would probably lose their entire investments. On the other hand, the supermarket channel, while potentially more attractive, carried substantial risks as well, and exposed the directors to possible personal liabilities if the new strategy failed, and shareholders sued them based on the company's failure to disclose its planned use of funds from the rights offering.

Time was of the essence, because the company's cash reserves were dwindling. "I'm really troubled by our choices," said Jim Leonard. "I've lost some confidence in our retailing strategy, in spite of the fact

EXHIBIT 7 *Pasta Perfect, Inc. Officers and Board of Directors*

Thomas L. Walker, president and director, age 42, founded the company in 1983. Mr. Walker has approximately 15 years' experience in the retailing industry. From 1980–1983 Mr. Walker managed . . . a marketer of barbecue products, and Walker Associates, a retail management consulting firm. From 1977–1980 he was employed by [a large apparel retailer] where he was responsible initially for implementing store systems, procedures, and training programs for new stores organized by that corporation, and later for the general management of one division of stores. Mr. Walker received an MBA degree from the Stanford University Graduate School of Business.

Lloyd W. Anderson, age 39, has served as controller of the company since January 1986, and was elected secretary and treasurer in January 1988. Mr. Anderson has over 13 years of accounting and finance experience. From 1983–1985 he was a consultant for . . . a large residential land developer. From 1978–1983 he worked for . . . , last serving as vice president of finance. Mr. Anderson is a certified public accountant and member of the American Institute of Certified Public Accountants.

James P. Leonard, director, age 35, has been a principal or general partner of . . . a venture capital firm since 1983. From 1979 to 1983 he was president of [a medical equipment company]. Mr. Leonard is also secretary, treasurer, and a director of [several companies]. Mr. Leonard is a graduate of Boston College.

William R. Patrick, director, age 45, is a private investor and is president of . . . a consulting firm. Mr. Patrick was a founder, chief executive officer, and chairman of the board of directors of . . . a publicly held company. Mr. Patrick received an MBA degree from the Harvard Business School.

Principal Shareholders

Name	Number of Shares
Thomas L. Walker	66,030,556[1]
James P. Leonard	33,159,518[2]
William R. Patrick	2,333,723
Venture Capital Company 1	36,459,794
Venture Capital Company 2	33,159,518
Total Shares Outstanding	525,456,630

[1]Does not include options to purchase up to an additional 22,500,000 shares contingent upon profits being achieved by the company. Mr. Walker's shares are held jointly with his wife, Jan H. Walker.

[2]Mr. Leonard owns no shares of record personally, but may be considered the beneficial owner of the 33,159,505 shares owned by Venture Capital Company 2.

that our products are head-and-shoulders above anybody else's. I think supermarkets could sell our stuff, but I don't know that we can get it on the shelf, I don't know how long our learning curve might be with the new technology, and I'm concerned about doing something different with our shareholders' money than we said we would do. We're between a rock and a hard place, I'm afraid."

NOTES

1. Bagot, Brian. (June 1989). Mangia! Mangia! *Marketing & Media Decisions*, 83–93.
2. Huffman, Frances. (June 1990). The Pasta Payoff, *Entrepreneur*, 72–78.
3. Eppinger, Josh. (February 5, 1990). Pasta LaBella's Fight to Become a Major National Brand, *Adweek's Marketing Week*, 28.
4. Myers, Marilyn. (October 1991). America's pasta passion, *Food Arts*, 70.
5. Bagot, Mangia! Mangia!, 83.
6. Huffman, The Pasta Payoff, 72–78.

Prvni Brněnská Strojirna (PBS): The Joint Venture Decision

Stanley D. Nollen
Karen L. Newman
Jacqueline M. Abbey

Georgetown University

Richard Kuba had led his company to a decision. A joint venture proposal between Prvni Brněnská Strojirna (PBS), of which he was the general manager, and Asea Brown Boveri (ABB), the Swiss-Swedish engineering company, was on the table. Kuba had worked more than a year on these negotiations. A majority of his board members had been opposed to a joint venture with ABB and initially rejected it. Now ABB had a new proposal to offer. Kuba and his board would reconsider the joint venture decision in a new board meeting. The decision would not be easy.

As the general director (chief executive officer) of a sizeable Czech company struggling to make the transition from central planning to market economy, Kuba was in uncharted managerial waters. He believed that PBS had to take a decisive step to adapt to the challenge of international competition in the post-Soviet era. He felt responsible for the welfare of his employees and fellow managers and a sense of national duty. PBS, a power plant equipment engineering and manufacturing company, had a continuous history from its founding in 1814 (the company name means "First Brno Machinery") through two world wars and the recently ended Communist period. Now PBS once again had to adapt in order to survive.

We acknowledge with thanks the assistance of managers of ABB PBS, advisors of IFC, Dagmar Petrová, and Theodore Moran. Case preparation was supported in part by the Pew Economic Freedom Fellows Program, Georgetown University. The authors are responsible for errors of fact or interpretation.

PBS—ITS BUSINESS AND ITS PROBLEMS

The Company's Business

At the time of the Velvet Revolution,[1] PBS's principle business was the manufacture of turbines and boilers, which accounted for a large majority of its revenue. The company also built complete power and heating plants, serviced and reconstructed old plants, and manufactured miscellaneous industrial parts. The company listed its product lines as follows:

Turbines: Steam turbines for industrial heating and power plants, small to mid-size gas turbines, turbochargers, and accessories.

---

[1]The Velvet Revolution occurred in late November 1989 in Czechoslovakia, a few months after the fall of the Berlin Wall. The name, Velvet Revolution, comes from the fact that the existing Communist government resigned without bloodshed, after massive peaceful demonstrations in Prague, giving way to a democracy almost overnight. The first post-Communist government was led by Václav Havel, a playwright who had been imprisoned under the former regime for his political views. Havel, though inexperienced in government, was a strong symbol of the moral underpinnings of the Velvet Revolution and the future for Czechoslovakia. One of the first orders of business was rapid transformation of the economy (one of the 10 largest in the world between World Wars I and II) from the most thoroughly state-owned of all Soviet bloc economies to a market economy based on private ownership of property.

Boilers: Oil-fired, gas-fired, and coal-burning industrial boilers and accessories.

Power plants: Complete power and heating plants made on a turn-key basis; service and reconstruction of existing plants.

Other products: Burners, heaters, railcar shock absorbers, power plant measurement and regulation instruments, gas meters, castings, and forgings.

In 1992, the year of Kuba's decision, PBS booked orders worth Kčs 4,857 million (about $175 million) (Exhibit 1) and earned revenue of Kčs 3,472 million (about $125 million). Profit was Kčs 365 million ($13 million). The level of employment was just under 8,000 and falling steadily (Exhibit 2).

The company's headquarters and most of its manufacturing facilities were in Brno, where it had manufactured steam turbines for 90 years and gas turbines for 35 years. Four plants were located in smaller towns in Moravia, dating from post-World War II years. The plant in Trebič made boilers and accessories (burners, heaters), and the plant in Mikulov made blades for turbines. The plant in Velká Bíteš made turbochargers and had received most of the new capital investment that came to PBS from the central planning authorities during the 1980s. This plant's output was exported mostly to the Soviet

Union until its breakup in 1991; its business then fell by 80 percent. The plant in Oslavany made a variety of products and parts, such as railcar shock absorbers, nuts, bolts, and screws that were not central to PBS's main turbine and boiler businesses.

By 1992, PBS had begun to concentrate on environmentally friendly power plant and heating plant systems. Much of its recent boiler business involved overhauling and reconstructing existing boilers to meet higher regulatory standards.

In pre-Communist Czechoslovakia, PBS was a leader in the power generation equipment industry and had a reputation for quality products and service. The early years of central planning were economically satisfactory as well. However, relative competitive decline set in at PBS after the "normalization" that followed Prague Spring in 1968.[2] Investment in plant and equipment and new technology was insufficient for over 20 years. By 1992, PBS product quality was below Western standards, concern for the customer was low, and employee willingness to take initiative was lagging.

[2]Prague Spring refers to the liberalization efforts of Alexander Dubček in the spring of 1968. The reforms were put down by an invasion of troops and tanks from Russia and other Soviet client states in August 1968. Many business leaders who sympathized with Prague Spring reforms were punished.

EXHIBIT 1 *PBS Sales Booked by Product Line, 1990–1992 (Kčs million current)*

Product	1990	1991	1992
Total sales	1484	3307	4857
Turbines	527	1080	783
Steam turbines	234	270	557
Gas turbines	63	54	27
Turbochargers	230	756	198
Boilers	549	724	1823
Industrial boilers	415	563	1099
Piping	134	161	724
Assemblies	85	288	299
Repairs	171	191	162
Central heating equipment	68	111	119
Aircraft equipment	101	14	18
Other (see text)	282	898	1653

Source: Prvni Brněnská Strojirna (PBS), Annual Report, 1992.
Notes: Freeing of prices in 1991 resulted in 58 percent price inflation in Czechoslovakia in that year. Gas turbines includes expansion turbines.

EXHIBIT 2 *Selected Financial and Operating Data for PBS, 1990–1992 (Kčs million current except where indicated otherwise)*

Variable	1990	1991	1992
Total revenue	2052	3412	3472
Production revenue	1842	3207	3255
Profit	224	369	365
Total assets	3338	5399	6187
Fixed assets	2246	2688	2972
Trade receivables	377	1411	1635
Trade payables	322	814	857
Bank loans	752	1107	931
Exports as percentage of booked sales—to COMECON	20	19	10
Exports as percentage of booked sales—worldwide	24	28	53
Employees (number)	9564	8857	7946
Labor productivity (Kčs 000 revenue per employee)	215	385	437
Average monthly wages (Kčs)	3629	4410	5299

Source: Prvni Brněnská Strojirna (PBS), Annual Report, 1992, and communication with PBS managers.

Notes: Data include the Velká Bíteš plant. Figures for revenue in this table do not match sales figures in Exhibit 1 because the figures in Exhibit 1 represent sales orders booked, not revenue received.

Yet PBS was better off than many other Czech companies that also suffered from little investment, aging capital equipment, and outdated products. Unlike most companies during central planning, PBS had its own engineering capabilities in-house and, as a result, had developed its own coal-fired boiler and steam turbine technology. In addition, PBS had a long-standing but small turn-key business. It not only made boilers and turbines, but also did all the work necessary to construct or reconstruct complete electric power generation plants and steam heating plants. PBS was not just a manufacturing plant.[3]

Distribution

Before 1989, PBS used two state trading companies for export sales, Škodaexport and Technoexport. Exports accounted for about one-quarter of PBS's business, about three-quarters of which went to Soviet Bloc countries. Domestic sales of turbines and boilers were uncomplicated, partly because the product was tailor-made; also, there were few potential customers, orders were big, and there were no direct domestic competitors. PBS's customers were the contractors that built the power plants or end users (usually companies or city governments) if PBS did the project on a turn-key basis.

Employee Wages and Production Costs

Wage rates at PBS, as in all Czech companies, were quite low—an average of Kčs 5,400 per month in 1992 (about $190). The skill level of the work force was very good. However, productivity was also quite low PBS managers asserted, because of the lack of investment in recent years. However, PBS did not have a production cost advantage compared to German companies. As one manager said:

We figured the German company's hourly rate for value added to engineer and produce turbine blades. We added up their wage rates and rental rates and depreciation rates, but we excluded the price of raw materials and parts they purchased

[3]Prior to the Velvet Revolution, PBS was part of the Škoda Koncern group of companies, which consisted of Škoda Pizen (a heavy machinery maker with 30,000 employees), PBS (10,000 employees), CKD (a maker of railroad cars with 4,000 employees), SES (a Slovak company with 8,000 employees), and several smaller companies. Škoda Koncern was organized differently from most other Czech industrial groups insofar as it did not separate research and engineering from manufacturing units. Each company was a stand-alone enterprise.

from outside suppliers. Then we did the same calculation for ourselves. We found that our hourly rate was one-third of theirs. But then we looked at how long it took the Germans to make the turbine blades compared to how long it took us. It turned out that the German company used one-third the time that our company used. So our production costs were about the same as theirs.

Managers

The top managers at PBS were mostly technically educated (as expected in Czech industrial companies), and most had been employed at PBS for their entire careers. Richard Kuba, the first postrevolution general manager, fit this pattern.

Richard Kuba joined PBS in 1965 after graduating from Brno Technical University, where he studied power generation and turbine design. Early in his career he spent some time in PBS's turn-key business. In 1968, Kuba began to attend economics courses at the Prague School of Economics, but when Prague Spring was crushed and tighter government control was reasserted, he dropped his studies.

Kuba's ascent to the upper levels of PBS management was slow because he chose not to join the Communist Party. Despite his refusal to join the party, he was given the opportunity to travel abroad and work with foreign customers in Bulgaria, Romania, Sweden, and Syria. After completing graduate studies in power grid management in 1989, he was promoted to director of the engineering department in the power plant division. His promotion to general manager in 1990 at the age of 47 (he was selected by the head of Škoda Konzern) came as a surprise, even to Kuba himself.

The Investment and Finance Problem

During the years of central planning, investment decisions from the Czechoslovak government were heavily influenced by the needs of major national or Soviet projects (e.g., the development of nuclear energy or the construction of a natural gas pipeline). Profits earned by enterprises were remitted to the State and new investment capital came from the State, but with no linkage between the two. In the case of PBS, most of the investment that came to it went into the outlying plants, especially the plant at Velká Bíteš which made turbochargers, mainly for

the Soviet Union. However, these investments were of little value in 1992 because they were designed for the Soviet market that diminished so rapidly and dramatically. Conversion of these plants to meet Western needs was difficult and costly because of differences in product specifications.

Interest rates were quite high in Czechoslovakia during this time, even in real terms, and loanable funds were very scarce. Short-term financing was also difficult to obtain, and a liquidity crisis ensued during 1992 and 1993. Since trade credit was scarcely available, many companies responded by simply not paying their bills. In PBS's case, trade receivables at their worst exceeded payables by a factor of two, and were Kčs 1,635 million ($57 million) at the end of 1992, just below half of that year's sales revenue (Exhibit 2).

Privatization

PBS was converted to a joint stock company to become PBS a.s. in 1991. All of the shares in the company were owned by the National Property Fund (NPF) which was the Czech government agency established to hold shares of enterprises until they could be sold to private buyers. The company, which had the usual functional structure of large enterprises in centrally planned economies (Exhibit 3), reorganized into a divisional structure of product-centered businesses (Exhibit 4). The Ministry of Industry put PBS a.s. into the first wave of voucher privatization in 1992. Thirty-six percent of PBS a.s. shares were purchased by individuals and investment funds, 60 percent remained with the NPF, and 4 percent were set aside for restitution, which was the standard practice.[4] The fact that the NPF held the majority of PBS shares meant that privatization was not complete and that further ownership changes would occur.

---

[4]The Czechoslovak government's objective was to transfer most of the country's large enterprises to widespread private ownership quickly. Because local citizens did not have the financial resources to "buy the economy" overnight, much of it was "given away." Under voucher privatization, each adult citizen was entitled to buy a book of vouchers containing 1,000 points for Kčs 1,000 (which in early 1992 was an average week's wages). The voucher holder could bid for shares of individual companies or spend voucher points on mutual funds that in turn bought shares of companies. Other methods of privatization included auction (for small companies), tender offers (usually with conditions attached about future employment levels), management buyouts, direct sale to a predetermined buyer, transfer at no cost to a municipality, and restitution to the family from which property had been confiscated by the State.

EXHIBIT 3 *PBS Organization Chart (Partial) in 1989*

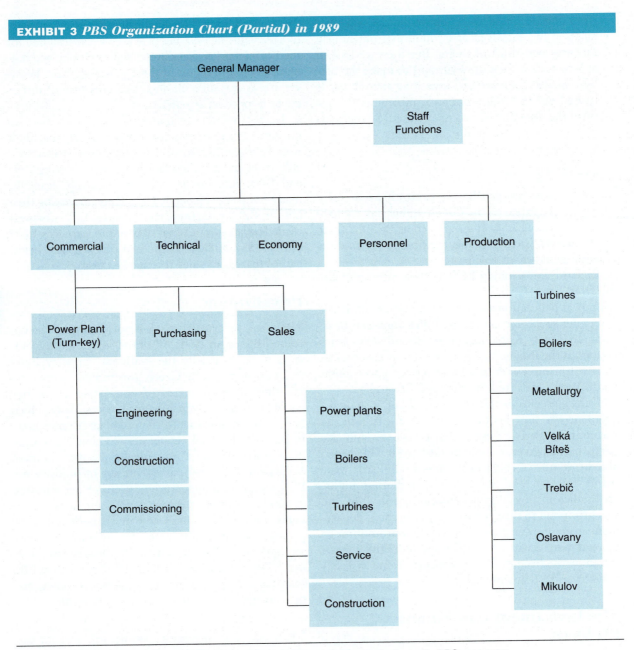

Source: Prvni Brněnská Strojirna (PBS), Annual Report, 1991, and communication with PBS managers.

The Search for a New Business Strategy

To successfully make the transition from central planning and become competitive in world markets, PBS managers proposed two different types of strategies. PBS had been an industry leader before the central planning era. Some managers believed it could regain this position through increased efficiency and product innovation. These people, who included most of the deputy general directors and department heads, placed their hopes for PBS in an ambitious new business strategy that called for maintaining independence and becoming more competitive by increasing quality

EXHIBIT 4 *PBS Organization Chart in 1992*

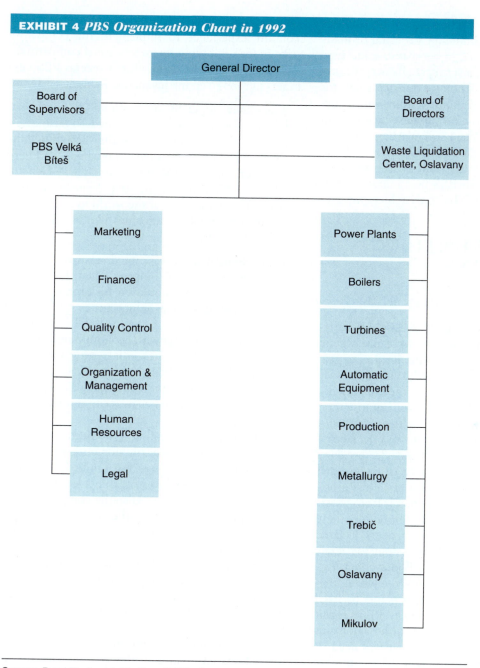

C-38

Source: Prvni Brněnská Strojirna (PBS), Annual Report, 1992.

standards, cutting production costs, manufacturing products to meet international environmental standards, improving the fuel efficiency of products, and creating a climate for change within the company.

Financing this strategy, however, was a problem. There was very little capital available from Czech banks in the form of multiyear loans at reasonable interest rates, and PBS had not met with success in finding affordable financing from Western banks.

Other managers believed that the best strategy was to choose from several alternative relationships with other companies. They thought a go-it-alone approach could not succeed. The range of possibilities included some type of technology licensing or manufacturing link with a foreign company, some type of marketing agreement, a strategic alliance of some sort that would have technology transfer gains for PBS, the establishment of a joint venture with a foreign or domestic company, or purchase by a foreign or domestic company. When several Western companies—including General Electric, GEC-Alsthom, Deutsche Babcock, Siemens, and ABB—discussed business relationships with PBS beginning in 1991, PBS management listened, but only reluctantly.

THE JOINT VENTURE NEGOTIATIONS

Points of View and Kuba's Role

When foreign companies initially discussed partnership proposals with PBS, managers were ambivalent. They knew they needed capital to modernize, to gain access to Western technology, and to get assistance in developing export markets. But they also had a strong wish to remain independent and not lose their brand name. PBS was, according to the Czechoslovak Ministry of Privatization, the "family silver." Most managers were unwilling to consider breaking up the company or entering into a relationship that rendered PBS "just an equipment manufacturer." Many of the initial partnership proposals from Western companies would have led to one or both of these unattractive outcomes. Some PBS managers declared that the company had operated successfully for nearly two centuries and could survive without any Western equity partners. The trend toward environmentally clean power plants and heating plants by itself would bring substantial new business to PBS's repair and reconstruction unit. The PBS order book was full in 1991. Maybe no foreign partner was needed.

Richard Kuba, however, thought differently. He knew that PBS did not have the latest technology. He discovered that Western companies could deliver a product in 25 percent less time than PBS could. While Kuba thought that PBS could upgrade its technology by itself, it would take more than five years because the investment capital was not available. With a foreign partner, it would go faster. In addition, turnover among young engineers at PBS was making internal technology development harder.

Kuba also believed PBS did not have the market economy experience to implement the company's strategy for improving its international competitiveness. In 1991 and 1992, he visited several PBS customers in foreign countries such as Pakistan and Iran.

They knew about Škoda Pizen and Škodaexport, but not about us. Škoda Pizen had 10 businesses. If one of their businesses fails, they have nine others. We had one, and we had no name. . . . There are four big international companies—General Electric, Siemens, ABB, and Mitsubishi—that control a big majority of the world market. There are tens of smaller companies like us, and some will not survive.

Kuba thought PBS was not diversified, so if its one business failed, the company failed. He learned that world markets did not know his product. These facts, he believed, were as important as the need for technology updates.

The Czech economy, with economic reforms initiated in January 1990, was still getting worse. Industrial production had fallen about 40 percent since the Velvet Revolution, and GDP was off 26 percent (Exhibit 5). An upturn in business conditions was not predicted until 1994.

Kuba came to believe that it would be necessary to bring in a foreign investor, for both technology and market reasons. "I was not enthusiastic about bringing in a foreign investor, but I knew that we had to do it if we wanted to keep the company whole and not split it up. To keep the company together was more important than keeping it independent." Although the company could survive for several more years on the strength of its existing assets, order book, work force, and customer base, he thought that only a strong Western partner could ensure that PBS would flourish and remain the pride of the Czech Republic.

As was common practice in the centrally planned Czechoslovakian economy, the general director of PBS decided most issues of company policy himself within the framework of the five-year plan. In 1992, Kuba was, in theory, accountable to a board of directors elected by the shareholders of PBS and the State. In practice, however, these bodies had little experience with corporate governance. Committing the assets of PBS to a venture with a Western company that meant a foreign ownership stake was a controversial decision with major ramifications. Kuba

EXHIBIT 5 *Economic Conditions in Czechoslovakia, 1989–92*

Variable	1989	1990	1991	1992
Gross domestic product, real %[a]	0.7	−3.5	−15.0	−7.1
Industrial production, real %	0.9	−3.7	−23.1	−12.4
Consumer price inflation, %	1.4	10.0	57.8	11.5
Interest rate, %[b]	5.5	6.2	15.4	13.9
Exchange rate, Kč/$, annual average	15.1	18.0	29.5	28.3
Unemployment rate, %	na	0.3	6.8	7.7

Sources: Economist Intelligence Unit, *Country Report: Czech Republic and Slovakia,* 2nd quarter 1993, 2nd quarter 1990. London, 1993, 1990; International Monetary Fund, *International Financial Statistics,* March 1994. Washington DC, 1996, 1994.
[a]Net material product.
[b]Lending rate to state enterprises.

expected to be criticized no matter which course the company chose. Therefore, he would not make this decision alone.

The International Finance Corporation

At the recommendation of the Czech Ministry of Industry, which was keenly interested in the fate of PBS, Kuba met with advisors from the International Finance Corporation (IFC), the consulting arm of the World Bank. The first meeting occurred in March 1992. Kuba was impressed with the work the IFC advisors had done earlier in the Czech Republic, particularly in facilitating the conclusion of Škoda Pizen's joint-venture negotiations. Kuba hired the IFC to structure a tender process and oversee negotiations for a joint venture.

The IFC advisors made two important recommendations to Kuba. First, PBS should secure government approval to enter into a joint venture with a Western partner in advance of negotiations. This would ensure that PBS, not the State, would be the ultimate decision maker. PBS acted on this recommendation immediately.

Second, the IFC advised PBS to separate its turbine, boiler, and turn-key businesses from its other activities. Only by packaging the core businesses together, without adding in peripheral businesses and unrelated assets of dubious value, would PBS attract a Western partner. The advisors explained that they were trying create an auction-like situation, and in order to do that they had to package the most valuable parts of the company separate from the rest. Though most managers and board members were very skeptical, Kuba convinced them to allow the IFC advisors to restructure the company on paper in order to find the best potential partners.

Kuba remained noncommittal throughout the discussions, supporting the IFC advisors and facilitating negotiations, but always in the name of "exploring options." He communicated that he was willing to take a risk to improve the company's prospects, but did not challenge the sometimes passionate objections of his fellow managers to the need for a foreign investor in the company.

As the discussions continued, General Electric proposed to license technology to PBS, but would have imposed conditions that were unattractive and would not have invested any equity. The other potential partners fell into secondary positions. Siemens, GEC-Alsthom, and Deutsche Babcock did not put forward sufficiently comprehensive proposals, or they did not offer enough technology transfer. The remaining contender was ABB.

ABB

ABB, formed by the 1988 merger of Asea of Sweden and Brown Boveri of Switzerland, was one of the world's major engineering and industrial equipment companies. It had revenue of $29.6 billion in 1992 and net income of $505 million, which gave it a return on equity of 11.8 percent (from ABB Web site, http://www.abb.ch/abbgroup/investor). The company, with 213,000 employees, came out on top of

C-385

both the 1994 and 1995 Financial Times-Price Waterhouse polls of European executives as the most respected company in the world (*Financial Times*, September 19, 1995).

ABB had five main businesses: industrial and building systems, power generation, power transmission and distribution, transportation, and financial services. The power generation business, into which PBS's business would fall, was the second largest of ABB's businesses, accounting for one-quarter of all ABB revenue. This business had experienced rapid growth; it had nearly tripled its revenue since 1988, despite declining prices. ABB's main competitors in its main businesses were Siemens of Germany, GEC-Alsthom of Britain and France, Mitsubishi of Japan, and General Electric of the United States.

ABB was a truly global corporation. The company had product-oriented business units with worldwide responsibilities ranging from design through manufacturing to marketing and customer service. ABB had a very small headquarters group in Zurich, and dozens of wholly owned or majority-owned companies on six continents.

ABB was no stranger to negotiating foreign joint ventures. Its approach to negotiations—which emphasized relationship building, patient persistence, and resolving issues one at a time—had been honed through experience. In the power generation business, its corporate strategy was to locate the complete range of boiler production, turbine production, and power plant design activities into each of several ABB companies around the world rather than to separate boilers from turbines and put them in different companies. This approach allowed ABB to reduce the high costs of engineering labor and to compete in the high value-added turn-key plant market.

The company began investing in the Czech Republic in 1991, drawn by the country's skilled work force, low relative labor costs, proximity to Western Europe, and successful conservative government. PBS would be the fourth and largest of seven Czech companies in the ABB network; other acquisitions had already been made in Poland, Hungary, and Romania.

In particular, ABB identified four main attractions of a joint venture with PBS:

1. ABB expected the market for power plants in the Czech Republic and in other central and east European countries to develop over time and be-

come large, stimulated by the effort to clean up old plants; ABB wanted to be a "local" company inside this market.

2. ABB needed to develop a low-cost export platform to export components to other ABB companies and to export complete products to other countries. Low-cost east European components could be combined with high-cost German or Swedish components to make an attractive total product package.

3. PBS had boilers and turbines in one company (one location), while ABB did not have boiler capacity in Europe. (It is easier to build a power plant if boiler and turbine production are located together because they frequently communicate with each other.)

4. PBS had considerable installed capacity to service; this would provide good short-run business even though the Czech Republic was not a major growth market in the power plant business at present.

ABB gave no thought to a licensing arrangement. According to an ABB negotiator:

It is not the ABB way. We wanted equity. Anyway, in this case, we wanted just about the whole company, and that is not as easy to license as, say, the production of gas turbines like General Electric does.... We wanted to develop the power generation business in east and central Europe, and that required the hands-on management that only a controlling interest in a joint venture allowed.

The ABB team made it clear that they sought to buy into both the turbine and boiler businesses and to expand the turn-key operations. The other bidders were interested in smaller segments of the business. The ABB team's desire to incorporate both the turbine and boiler business made it more attractive to PBS management. ABB presented opportunities for technology transfers, training, market access, and investment capital that could build up PBS instead of simply absorbing it.

ABB sent representatives from its Power Ventures unit to negotiate the deal. Their task was to establish the joint venture and to manage its start-up. The representatives had contact with PBS management and employees at different levels. Meetings with

ABB's top corporate executives, including a lunch in Zurich with Percy Barnevik, the chief executive officer, were arranged for Kuba. ABB also engaged the head of its Prague office to emphasize to PBS management the advantages that ABB offered as a joint venture partner, and ABB's vision for creating with PBS an efficient engineering firm capable of serving the turbine, boiler, and turn-key markets using advanced technologies and creative engineering solutions. ABB recognized PBS's capabilities in coal-fired power plants and intended to keep the joint venture a full-fledged company, not just a manufacturing plant. ABB also included environmental indemnifications in its offer. Substantial sums were invested in developing and presenting the pitch.

Among all potential Western partners, only ABB was seemingly unfazed by PBS's lack of unified commitment to the concept of a joint venture. ABB sought to identify specific concerns of PBS management and responded with detailed presentations.

THE DECISION

After several months of negotiations, PBS managers had all the information needed to make a decision and several proposals before them to consider, the most attractive of which was from ABB. The meeting of the PBS board to decide on the proposals was held in late December 1992; it lasted 12 hours and became contentious. Everyone realized the gravity of the situation.

The board members returned to the issue of whether or not PBS should enter into a joint venture with a large Western partner. Strong concerns were voiced; many of the managers had worked for PBS for decades and feared that by surrendering its independence PBS was inviting ruin. They feared the intrusion of Western management. They saw the joint venture proposals as giving up, and they weren't ready to do that. Finally, after several hours, one member stood

up and said, "I'm going to say what I think everyone else is afraid to say—we don't like it. We don't want a deal." The board took a poll, and decided that PBS should reject all joint venture proposals.

After the poll, the IFC advisors addressed the board for a further six hours, emphasizing that PBS's negotiating position was not likely to improve with time. Its market position would decline in the absence of needed investment and technology improvement. Further, if they simply broke off negotiations with the companies that were courting them now, they should expect that any future discussions on cooperation would meet with a much less favorable response. In short, PBS's negotiating leverage would steadily decrease over time and eventually, given its economic prospects, the company would be forced to accept a much less desirable arrangement than was currently available. The time to form a joint venture was now; the company needed to decide whether it would pursue its business objectives without a foreign partner or communicate to the existing bidders why their proposals were not satisfactory and invite revised bids. After further deliberation, the board resolved to solicit improved bids.

ABB responded quickly with a multifaceted approach, directing its attention not only to the board members but also to managers at lower levels and employees whose voices they knew could flow upward to persuade board members to change their minds in favor of a deal. Several ABB executives and engineers arrived in Brno the weekend following the marathon board meeting to address the issues that PBS had identified as most troublesome. They arranged to meet with employees at several different levels in order to hear and address the most common concerns. They believed it was important to provide a formal avenue for the these employees to express their fears and reservations.

The ABB team presented a new proposal within a few days. A new board meeting was scheduled in which a decision would be made.

Rover Group–The Indonesian National Car Programme

Keith J. Perks

University of Brighton

Garry Smith

Rover Group Ltd.

THE SITUATION IN OCTOBER 1995

In October 1995, the executives of the business development function of the Rover Group were considering their next move after the Indonesian government had cancelled the Memorandum of Understanding signed in 1993. The Indonesians had decided to develop the Indonesian National Car with new partners, the Australian government and a consortium of Australian automotive companies. As they reflected on the situation, the members of the Rover team all had their own views as to why the joint venture had collapsed. In general, they agreed that some lessons had to be learned for the future.

In particular, the business development team wanted to know how much of this situation was outside of their control. Could they have anticipated the cessation of the agreement? Had they been ill prepared for the cultural aspects of the negotiations? Was the relationship poorly managed? How big a role did political influence play in determining the Indonesian decision? It was clear now to the business development function that for Rover Group to salvage a position in the Indonesian market, something had to be done. But what?

This case is intended to be used as the basis for class discussion rather than to illustrate either effective or ineffective handling of a management situation.

ROVER GROUP'S RECENT HISTORY AND TURNAROUND IN THE UK MARKET

The Rover Group's business development team was about to embark on a new chapter in the restructuring and turnaround of the UK-based Rover car and Land Rover producer. The company had recovered its position in the home market based on a strategy that was driven by what top management called "Extraordinary Customer Satisfaction," through the use of Total Quality Management and, more importantly, a radical change in company culture. It shifted from a confrontational management style to the adoption of the consensus model, which brought with it employee participation and involvement in the survival, then growth of the company.

The company's top management had put its faith in its employees to deliver the quality product required to underpin its niche marketing strategy. Focusing on the Rover brands, the company targeted the premium end of each car segment in which it operated. The company was able to offer this quality through a major programme of investment in manufacturing technology, learning from its cross-share holding joint venture with Honda, employee involvement, the recruitment of the best young graduates, and a supplier and dealer development programme to improve the quality and cost of components and customer service. The capability to deliver a high-quality car was further supported by an advertising and promotion strategy that increased the pull demand for the Rover brands. The Rover dealer network and sales force were motivated to sell this new breed of car that gradually improved its image among the British buying public who, a few years before, had lost faith in the car maker because of poor design and manufacturing quality.

Exhibit 1 gives the BL/Rover Group sales turnover and profit figures between 1988 and 1993. Exhibit 2 outlines the BL/Rover Group production volumes and number of models between 1970 and 1994, with the reduction in volumes and number of models reflecting the shift in their strategy toward focus on the Rover name and selling fewer cars at the premium end of each car and vehicle segment.

THE CONSOLIDATION PERIOD AND EXPANSION INTO EUROPEAN MARKETS

From 1986 to 1993, the Rover Group, under the initial leadership of Sir Graham Day and the subsequent ownership of British Aerospace, concentrated on delivering its quality cars and embarked on a new product development programme in which time to market was reduced drastically by the use of special multifunctional project teams and early supplier involvement. In addition to the new product programme, Rover started to develop a European and international business strategy and in 1992 created

three new divisions—Rover Europe, Rover Marketing, and Rover International—as part of the implementation process. Exhibit 3 gives details of the responsibilities of each division.

THE CONTRIBUTION OF INTERNATIONAL SALES TO THE ROVER GROUP

In 1995, Rover's total world sales were up 2 percent to 483,000 vehicles, reflecting the lack of growth in some key continental European markets. Total exports outside Europe were 38 percent higher at 93,000 vehicles (*Financial Times*, January 26, 1996). This was a result of an export drive in the Asia-Pacific region (excluding Japan), which saw sales leap to 40,000 vehicles, four times the level of 1993. Mr. B. Pischetsrieder, BMW's chairman, is focusing on Rover vehicles to develop sales in emerging markets. As such, any future growth is highly dependent on Rover's success in achieving sales growth internationally, outside of the UK and other European markets.

THE ROVER GROUP'S INTERNATIONAL BUSINESS STRATEGY

The establishment of a Rover international business development function for the international markets signalled the Rover Group's commitment to internationalising its business in an attempt to shift the

C-389

EXHIBIT 1 *BL/Rover Turnover and Profits, 1981–1993*		
Year	Turnover (£m)	Profit (Loss) (£m)
1988	1,179*	35.0
1989	3,430	64.0
1990	3,785	55.0
1991	3,744	(52.0)
1992	3,684	(49.0)
1993	4,301	56.0

Source: Company Report and Accounts.
*Part year from BAe Report.

C-390

EXHIBIT 2 *BL/Rover Production Volumes and Number of Models, 1970–1994*

Year	Production Volume	Number of Models Made
1970	788,700	20
1971	886,721	22
1972	916,218	21
1973	873,839	22
1974	738,503	22
1975	605,141	22
1976	687,875	18
1977	651,069	17
1978	611,625	17
1979	503,767	15
1980	395,820	10
1981	398,763	11
1982	383,074	10
1983	445,364	8
1984	383,324	7
1985	465,104	7
1986	404,454	8
1987	471,504	7
1988	474,687	7
1989	466,619	8
1990	464,612	9
1991	395,624	9
1992	378,797	9
1993	406,804	11
1994	452,500	10

Source: Various SMMT (Society of Motor Manufacturers and Traders) Year Books. 1994 figure from BL/Rover Group Annual Report and Accounts (1994).

EXHIBIT 3 *Rover's Divisions*

Rover Europe	Headquarters Rover Bickenhill
	National sales companies in France, Germany, Holland, Italy, Spain, Belgium, Portugal, and Luxembourg
Rover International	Headquarters Rover Bickenhill
	National sales companies in Japan, North America, and Australia
	Business and market development outside of Europe
Rover Marketing	Coordination of marketing and product management UK, Europe, and International

Source: Rover Group Internal Document.

company away from export orientation to establishing an operating presence in non-European markets. The company had already established national sales companies in Japan, North America, and Australia and had plans to establish subsidiaries in South Africa, Korea, and Mexico in the future.

The company had a long tradition of exporting cars; in the 1950s, the Morris Minor car was the largest single product export from the UK. However this export business fluctuated and the company was unable to sustain positions in foreign markets throughout the next four decades. For the company to develop sustainable international sales, one of the key issues was how to reenter and penetrate foreign markets. Having established a strong home base, the Rover Group needed to expand in international markets to reduce the dependence on British and other European markets, which were saturated and subjected to intense rivalry from U.S., other European, and Asian producers. Additionally, the costs of new designs and improved quality of its products required heavy commitment of financial and human resources, and the Rover Group needed additional sales volume and profits to recover these investments.

THE SITUATION IN 1992

The prospects of developing international business for Rover was a challenge for the Rover international business development team, who saw the turnaround and evolution of the Group as a milestone. The Rover Group had set a sales target of 100,000 units per year within three years for Rover International, which was a substantial increase on the actual 1992 sales of 24,000. In taking on this challenge, there were many options for the team. It had to consider the resource implications for any chosen strategy. This growth aspiration required a radical change from the pure export mode of international marketing, and other means of growing the business had to be developed. Furthermore, decisions had to be made about which regions and markets in the world on which the company should focus. In conducting research, the team had examined the international environment, collecting and analysing the regional and country macroeconomic and political data, before considering the market specific data such as market size, growth, and competition. In considering the Rover international business strategy, the team was

aware that in some markets the company had already established business links and previous sales. The initial strategy was to build on these positions before choosing new markets, with one key market being Indonesia. The country also fell within the Southeast Asian region that was attractive because of the rapid growth in member country economies of ASEAN (Association of South East Asian Nations).

BACKGROUND TO ROVER GROUP'S INVOLVEMENT IN THE INDONESIAN MARKET

The Land Rover company had been present in the Indonesian market since the mid-1950s, selling its products through an Indonesian distributor. Vehicles were assembled in the UK and exported to Indonesia to meet the demand for retail and government orders.

In 1976 the Indonesian government banned imports of completely built vehicles and imposed heavy duties on imported components for knock-down vehicles (CKD, i.e., vehicles supplied in kit form requiring local assembly). Land Rover did not have a local assembly partner and as a consequence saw its position in the market erode. Since 1976 the business has been limited to occasional orders for military vehicles or wholesaling as many vehicles as possible in years when import barriers were lifted to meet the demand for particular categories of vehicles. In 1981 a number of Land Rovers were supplied in CKD form with final assembly being carried out by the distributor.

Over the intervening 20 years, competitive products, particularly Japanese, were gaining market dominance by setting up assembly plants and producing vehicles from CKD kits. By establishing local assembly plants, the Japanese were able to keep the key technologies for their vehicles within their Japanese operations. The Indonesian government saw no long-term sustainable benefit from local assembly, as all engineering and development was undertaken in Japan and the local assembly plants were managed by Japanese personnel. From the Japanese manufacturers' point of view, there were the benefits of a low-cost labour force and the Indonesian government benefited from the revenue received from import duties and corporate taxes. This did not

C-391

resolve the Indonesian government's long-term fear that the Japanese would move their assembly operations to another low-wage economy if Indonesian labour rates increased.

THE INDONESIAN VEHICLE-CAR MARKET

The Indonesian car-vehicle market has the potential to be one of the fastest growing in Southeast Asia. With over 190 million people, Indonesia ranks fourth largest in population after China, India, and the United States. GDP growth is currently 7 percent

per annum with inflation under 10 percent. In 1994 the vehicle market grew by over 50 percent from 210,000 units to 320,000 units. By 2000 it is projected to double to 600,000 units and to expand to 800,000 by 2003. The vehicle market structure is unusual because of the small proportion of cars and the preference for light commercial vehicles (LCVs), instead of passenger cars due to the more favourable tax levels on LCVs. The structure is expected to change in the next decade as Indonesia attempts to develop its own car industry. The car market (sedans in local terms), totalled 40,000 units in 1994, or less than 15 percent of vehicle sales, but this is projected to rise to 40 percent (250,000 units) in 2000 and 50 percent (400,000 units) in 2003 (see Exhibit 4).

EXHIBIT 4 *Indonesia Car Market–TIV Forecasts to 2003*

Volumes	1990	1991	1992	1993	1994	1995	1996	1997	1998	1999	2000	2001	2002	2003
Cars	56.4	45.8	30.6	32.2	40.2	50	65	100	150	200	250	300	350	400
Off Road			18.5	26.9	47	55	60	64	68	72	76	80	84	88
CVs			122.8	151.6	234.6	245	255	266	272	268	274	285	296	312
Vehicles	275.4	267.1	171.9	210.7	321.8	350	380	430	490	540	600	665	730	800

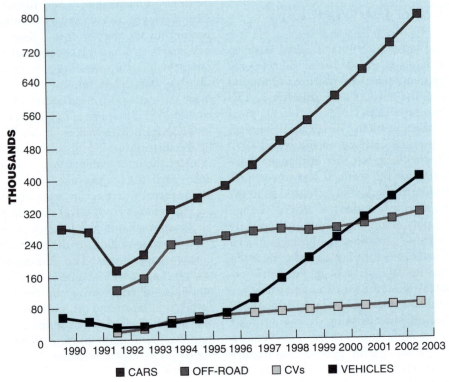

Source: Rover Group Market Research.

There was a significant market for off-road vehicles totalling 47,000 units in 1994, which was expected to grow to 76,000 units per annum by 2000. However, the true 4 by 4 market (General Purpose Vehicles, GPVs in local terms) is currently a small proportion of this, less than 6,000 units or 12.5 percent in 1994, having fallen from over 10,000 units and 50 percent of the segment in two years. There has been a shift to 2WD vehicles, which are classed as commercial and therefore are subject to less tax.

Imports of built-up vehicles are only allowed in exceptional circumstances at present, for example, by diplomats or VIPs, and virtually all of the vehicles sold in Indonesia are locally assembled. There are currently 27 vehicle assemblers in Indonesia, with 20 of them producing cars and 8 producing off-road vehicles. Most of the competitors have been established in the market for some years, but there have been some recent new entrants, notably the Korean producers Hyundai and Daewoo, which have been joined by Kia after the announcement of a planned U.S. $400 million investment in a new plant to produce 50,000 Sephia cars and sports models per year. Another recent addition is Jeep now that it is capable of building a right-hand-drive version of the Cherokee. The Land Rover Defender is positioned well above the closest local competition in the market, the Daihatsu Rocky-based Taft and Hi-Line models. The relative pricing of 4WD models is shown in Exhibit 5.

ROVER'S OPPORTUNITY TO DEVELOP A JOINT COOPERATIVE VENTURE WITH THE INDONESIAN GOVERNMENT

Identifying the Indonesian government's apprehension about dependence on the Japanese manufacturers for the supply of cars and that little or no Indonesian capability or expertise was being developed in the manufacture of components, Rover's overseas business strategy department entered into discussions with the Ministry of Research and Technology.

The Indonesian government, headed by president Suharto, had a vision for the country based on the

EXHIBIT 5 *Pricing of 4WD Vehicles in the Indonesian Market*

Model	Price (Rupiah millions)	1994 Volume
Daihatsu Taft 2.8D	52.0	3,552
Daihatsu Rocky 2.8D	54.3	—
Suzuki Vitara 1.6	66.3	190
Land Rover Defender 90 PUP	78.1	83
Nissan Pathfinder 2.4	86.2	62
Land Rover Defender 90 PUD	86.3	—
Chevrolet Trooper 2.3	86.5	652
Land Rover Defender 90 HTP	88.0	—
Jeep Wrangler 4.0	91.0	—
Land Rover Defender 110 PUD	93.3	—
Land Rover Defender 90 HTD	95.8	—
Land Rover Defender 110 HTD	109.2	—
Jeep Cherokee 4.0 Sport	112.0	936
Land Rover Defender 110 HTP V8	119.3	—
Jeep Cherokee 4.0 Limited	125.0	—
Toyota Land Cruiser 4.2 STD	130.0	2
Toyota Land Cruiser 4.2 Turbo	174.9	—
Mercedes Benz 300GE	248.3	104

Source: Internal Rover Document, 1995.

development of high-technology industries utilising high-technology processes in design and manufacture. The Rover Group, however, wanted to use the relationship to develop a local manufacturing programme for the Land Rover Defender, which while a capable off-road vehicle, is not a high-technology product and can be assembled in very basic manufacturing facilities. This was a potential area of mismatch between the objectives of the two partners.

Another important consideration from Rover's point of view was who should undertake the assembly of the vehicle and where? Clearly, an existing local assembler could produce the Land Rover vehicles, but who would market the product and would it create a position of preference among Indonesian consumers and the Indonesian authorities? Would this be a platform for developing sales volumes for the Rover product range as a whole?

While discussions regarding the Defender were going on, the Indonesian government revealed that it wanted to develop its own automobile. This was of interest to Rover and discussions started. The intention was for Rover to become the consultant in the development of an Indonesian national car. The Indonesian government stipulated that it required a high-technology, low retail price, small passenger car that would have its own unique identity and would be manufactured in Indonesia using locally made components.

THE LAND ROVER DEFENDER LOCAL ASSEMBLY PROJECT

The Defender Knock-Down (KD) project was aimed at the civilian market, where a need was identified for the rugged qualities and ultimate off-road ability of the vehicle in such industries as forestry, agriculture, mining, and construction. Land Rover Defender sales averaged 80 units per annum in the three years preceding 1994.

The discussions on the Land Rover Defender presented an ideological problem for the Indonesians. Early conversations, from the Rover point of view, were aimed at understanding the objectives of the Indonesians in the longer term. Clearly the Defender did not meet the aspirations for a high-tech product produced in high volume in high-tech manufacturing facilities. However, the vehicle more than matched

the driving conditions to be encountered in normal operating environments throughout the country, and would provide an automotive workhorse in support of the massive infrastructure projects on which Indonesia was about to embark.

The outcome of these early discussions was an understanding that the longer-term ambition was for Indonesia to have an indigenous, independent automotive capability, but in the short term it needed a vehicle that would create a pull demand on component suppliers.

The agreement that followed this understanding was for Rover to provide the technology transfer necessary for Indonesia to gain manufacturing process/vehicle design experience (by working on product development programmes) and to experience and develop supply chain logistics in support of automotive projects. In the longer term, an Indonesian specification for the product, managed and implemented by Indonesians, was discussed as a possibility. Given the Indonesian government's high foreign debt, the Defender was appealing as a low-capital-cost project. From Rover's point of view, a low-cost minimal risk project was also appealing.

To implement the project, Rover agreed to work with one of the 10 BPIS companies. By working with a government department, Rover also believed that it would gain credibility and confidence in the private sector, which would act as the component manufacturing base. In addition, as a partner the Indonesian government would be able to amend existing regulations or pass new ones to ensure the viability of the programme. Furthermore, given the relatively small capital requirement it would be easier for the government to fund the project, and if not, commercial funding would be readily available with the state as a borrower. The advantages of the project in terms of sales would be a government and semistate preference for purchasing the Defender.

Throughout 1993 and 1994, the Rover and BPIS teams worked together to develop vehicle specifications and production facility plans that would be capable of delivering an initial 1,500 vehicles per year, with production commencing six months after the contract signing. However, the project encountered one delay after another, and by the end of 1994 the Indonesians were unable to move into the implementation phase. In a final effort to implement the project with BPIS, two specialist Rover engineers went to the proposed assembly site in early 1995, and with the Indonesians prepared a report on the new capital requirements (five figures US$) to establish the assembly facility. Despite this low investment, the Indonesians did not move into the implementation phase, and as a result Rover cancelled its agreement with BPIS and sought a partner in the private sector. The companies were selected for discussions on the basis of their available cash, government contacts and influence, and their nonassociation with established automotive producers in Indonesia. After the partner selection was made, the project work moved quickly, and the new manufacturing facility became operational in mid-1996, with a total capacity of 70,000 units per year.

POSSIBLE REASONS FOR THE BREAKDOWN IN THE AGREEMENT BETWEEN ROVER AND THE INDONESIAN GOVERNMENT

It remains unclear as to why the arrangement with BPIS failed to materialise. Discussions were cordial, with problems and disagreements always being resolved.

However, it was suspected but never confirmed, that there was disagreement and rivalry within BPIS that prevented a consensus and commitment to the Land Rover Defender plan. Given the national trait of not saying no and having to save face, it would have been an anathema for the Indonesians to admit to the disagreements. As a consequence, they were relieved when the agreement was cancelled. Some time later, a senior member of the Indonesian team confided that the project would never have succeeded because of BPIS's inability to achieve open consensus on the objectives and the details of pursuing them.

THE INDONESIAN NATIONAL CAR PROGRAMME: THE MALEO PROJECT

The Maleo Project was created to develop a small car for Indonesia based on the Rover 100 and its con-

stituent components such as the K-series engine. The car would be built and sold as an Indonesian product, without the Rover identity, and as such the joint venture was considered a stand-alone exercise that was not part of Rover's overall corporate and long-term product and marketing strategy. However, the project would build a positive and unique relationship with the Indonesian government, which could prove beneficial for Rover Group-branded products in Indonesia.

The National Car Programme, if it was to be successful, needed to address a broad range of issues, and the disparate organisations involved had to be committed and fully engaged in the process. The Indonesian objectives for the programme can be summarised as follows:

- An Indonesian car.
- A self-sufficient indigenous automotive design capability.
- An efficient and competitive automotive component supplier base in Indonesia.
- Development of exports of vehicles and components around the world.

In meeting these objectives, the Indonesian government accepted that certain compromises would have to be made, particularly if it wanted to finish the programme in the desired time frame. The advantages of basing the national car on the Rover Metro were understood by the initial Indonesian team:

1. It would produce a rapid vehicle introduction because the major systems in the vehicle were already available; additional design and engineering work would be confined to the car's visual appearance.

2. Eighty percent of the components would be identical to those of the Metro; therefore, supplier development could be undertaken by partnering the current Rover supplier base with future Indonesian suppliers. The technology transfer could then happen at a controlled pace dictated by Indonesian capability and product complexity. The disadvantages were that the Indonesians would not be involved in a completely new design and consequently would miss the opportunity to develop their own vehicle structure.

In addition to the design and engineering of the car, a number of other supporting specialties had to be marshalled. For example, in order for the Indonesians' automotive capability to be sustainable, the programme had to include a training and development dimension. To support this activity, colleges and universities in the UK had to be brought into the programme to ensure that by the launch date there was a sound automotive base not only in the assembly plant, but also in the local dealer service operations to provide the all important after-sales backup to the product.

The Early Phase of the National Car Programme

The discussions on the National Car Programme were held with representatives from the Ministry of Research and Technology headed by Minister B. J. Habibie. Habibie remains the longest serving minister in the same post having been recalled to Indonesia by President Suharto in 1974 to lead Indonesia out of an agrarian economy into an industrial economy. Habibie's strategy was to focus on high-technology industries, concentrating on aerospace and ships. The Ministry of Research and Technology has two main divisions: the Agency for the Assessment and Application of Technology (BPPT) and the Agency for Strategic Industries (BPIS). BPIS has 10 member companies, the most prominent being IPTN. In the 18 years since its formation, in addition to assembling aircraft under licence, it has undertaken a joint aircraft programme with CASA of Spain and achieved the maiden flight of its own designed, engineered, and built turbo prop fly-by-wire passenger aircraft. During the same period, PT PAL, the shipbuilding company, launched a passenger liner.

BPIS was chosen by the Indonesian government to deliver the National Car Programme and Minister Habibie visited the Rover Longbridge factory in June 1993. During that visit, he was shown the Rover Low Pressure Sandcasting system and the "K" series engine plant, which represent the latest level of technology in both design and manufacturing. The opportunity was also taken to put the Minister into every one of the Rover Group products. At the end of the visit, Habibie proclaimed that he wanted Rover to work with BPIS in jointly developing the Indonesian car, which should be based on the Rover Metro. The car should be available for sale in Indonesia by August 1995 to coincide with the 50th anniversary of the Indonesian declaration of independence.

Following this statement, Rover worked with BPIS to establish a team composed of personnel from the various strategic industries that would develop the car programme. In September 1993, the Indonesian team arrived in the UK for a two-week working session during which they were shown the manufacturing processes, design issues, and constraints for the existing Rover Metro.

The joint Rover-BPIS team developed three design themes for the Indonesian national car, which everybody believed could be delivered in under two years. A single design theme was selected for presentation to Minister Habibie.

In November 1993, Minister Habibie returned to the UK and declared at a meeting that the design theme submitted still looked too much like a Rover Metro, and he wanted a unique identity for the car. The Rover negotiation team explained the development process for a car and why a radical design change could not be achieved in the two years left before August 1995. Having discussed the issues in detail, Habibie accepted the conflict between his aims for the product and the desired time scale, and the meeting concluded with a Memorandum of Understanding being signed, which appointed Rover as the technology partner to jointly develop the car for sales launch in September 1997.

Competitor Positioning and the National Car Programme

The prospect of an Indonesian national car stimulated a great deal of interest in the automotive world. In general, the companies interested in these programmes fell into two categories:

1. Companies that offered to establish a manufacturing facility in Indonesia and "donate" one of their second-generation models to be badged (branded) as the Indonesian car.

2. Companies that wanted the programme to fail and/or believed that it would not succeed given the Indonesians' record of slow progress and difficulty in completing previous engineering projects.

The competitors in the first category included Mazda that, in 1990, launched the MR90, an abbreviation for Mobile Raykat (People's Car). The vehicle was the old rear-wheel-drive Mazda 323 that had been toned down in specification to be marketed at the low selling price in Indonesia of 16 million rupiah (US$8,000). The vehicle was marketed by Mazda as the Indonesian People's Car, but without the support of the Indonesian government.

The vehicle never reached substantial sales volumes and was quickly upgraded to a fully specified vehicle, rebadged as "Baby-Boomer" and sold at 27 million rupiah. In this form, the vehicle sold in small volumes until it was replaced by a new model. Companies in the first category were primarily European manufacturers or Japanese companies that were struggling to increase their volumes through sales of their own branded products (see Exhibit 6).

In contrast, the competitors in the second category were already well established in Indonesia and could lose sales volume in competition with a national car.

BMW AND THE INDONESIAN MARKET

BMW's entry into the Indonesian market was through a partnership with PT Gaya Motors, a part of the Astra Group, the largest vehicle assembler in Indonesia. PT Gaya assembles the BMW 3 and 5 series, which doubled in sales in the upper medium and executive sectors between 1992 and 1994, when BMW volumes reached nearly 3,000 cars (2,200 3-series and 700 5-series). However, BMW was outperformed by Mercedes Benz, that sold over 3,300 cars (up from 1,000 in 1993) following the introduction of the C-class in 1994.

Competitive pressures from both of these groups was evident from the beginning of the Rover discussions. The competition from the first group was intense through the initial stages, until the signing of the Memorandum of Understanding. In the aftermath of the agreement, competitive actions were strongest from the category two players, which were using their capacity and capabilities to argue that Indonesia could not afford and did not need a national car. These companies also attempted to find out as much about the programme as they could to plan their own product strategy.

Implementation and the Development of the Car Design

The next stage of the process was to develop the style for the car, but clearly within the parameters set by the original Metro design. Between January and October 1994, the joint team worked in Indonesia on developing the design of the car.

The major difficulty in working together was to achieve the compromise between what the Indonesian stylist wanted for aesthetic reasons with what was feasible within the time scale, budget restrictions, manufacturing feasibility, and compatibility with the carry over design from the "parent" car. The UK members of the team adopted a patient approach and engaged in discussions with their Indonesian colleagues to explain the practicality of ideas and courses of action, and then allowed the Indonesians to make the decision. By October 1994, a full-size model of the proposed car was ready to present to Minister Habibie.

The car was presented to the minister and senior officials from Indonesia by the joint team, but led by the Indonesian members. They explained how they had arrived at the design, why certain features could not be changed, and the proposed model line up for introduction, including trim options and engine variants to be available. On the basis of the model and the presentation, Minister Habibie agreed that the programme should continue, but that the relationship between BPIS and Rover should be made more formal. The Indonesian government and Rover agreed that when Minister Habibie visited the UK at the end of the year, the two organisations would sign a contract detailing their relationship and obligations throughout the remainder of the programme. Senior officials from BPIS and Rover discussed and drafted a framework agreement, completed a few days before a signing ceremony on December 22, 1994, which was presided over by the British Minister for Trade and Industry in London. The agreement provided both sides with the confidence to commit fully to the programme in terms of both resources and relationship development.

The Car Clinic: Indonesian Consumers' Reaction to the New Car

The next stage was to test potential customer reaction to the car. To do this, the full-size model was taken to Indonesia and subjected to scrutiny and comparison with two competitor vehicles by an invited audience of target customers. This exercise, the first car clinic to be conducted in Indonesia, generated a great deal of constructive comments about the car against which the design could be reappraised to

EXHIBIT 6 Indonesian Car and Commercial Prices, September 1995

PRICES Rupiah (mills)	1994 Volume			
Van/Bus				
SUZUKI CARRY	36649	1.0	1.3	Van
DAIHATSU ZEBRA	26457	PU		Espass
MITSUBISHI COLT T120	15085		Std	Baby Boomers
MAZDA VANTREND	2988		SX SSX	LGX
TOYOTA KIJANG	62420		PU SS	HGL
ISUZU PANTHER	26827			
Commercial List		1.3		
SUZUKI KATANA/JIMNY	17303	)		1.6
SUZUKI ESCUDO			2.0	
KIA SPORTAGE		)	Std SE Semi Long	
DAIHATSU FEROZA	23779	)	PU	GTL 4x4
DAIHATSU HI-LINE		)		
Small Car				
MAZDA MR90	499	1.4	1.4	
FIAT UNO	246		1.3 Winne	Classy
DAIHATSU CHARADE	1904		1.3	1.6
SUZUKI SWIFT/ESTEEM	1918		1.0 1.3	Ltd
TOYOTA STARLET	3163			1.6
Lower Medium Car				
HYUNDAI ELANTRA	0		1.6 Auto	
OPEL ASTRA/OPTIMA	264		Optima	
FORD LASER/M323	3378		1.6 1.8 Ghis	Supreme Genesis
NISSAN SENTRA	1144		1.6 SE	1.6 Auto
TOYOTA COROLLA	7022		1.6 1.8	GTi Auto
MITSUBISHI LANCER	2036		3 dr 4 dr	1.6 4dr Auto
HONDA CIVIC/GENIO	3137			
Upper Medium Car			STi Auto LeMars	
PEUGEOT 405	589		2.0 STi	
OPEL VECTRA	480		Brilliant Challenge	
FORD TELSTAR	105		2.0 2.5	
MAZDA 626/CRONOS	273		1.6 2.0 2.0 Auto	
TOYOTA CORONA	1209		V6 V6 Auto	
MITSUBISHI GALANT	1524		VR4	Auto
HONDA ACCORD/CIELO	5189		22 Ciel	320A 3201 Ltd 3201 Ltd Auto
BMW 3-SERIES	2757		3201	
MERCEDES C-CLASS	2463		C180 Classic	C180 Esprit
Executive Car				
VOLVO 850/960	572		960 GL	960 Royal
TOYOTA CROWN	298		850 GLT Man Auto	5201 Auto 4
BMW 5-SERIES	924		520 A 530 A	A
MERCEDES E-CLASS	1629		E220	E120
Leisure 4x4				
DAIHATSU TAFT	3552	2.8GT Rocky	1.6	
SUZUKI VITARA	190		90PUP 90PUD 90HTD	
L-R DEFENDER	83		110HTD 1.0 HTP V8	
CHEVROLET TROOPER	652		UBS 16	
NISSAN TERRANO	936		Limited Sport 4.0 Ltd	
JEEP CHEROKEE			Wrangler STD	Turbo
TOYOTA LANDCRUISER				300 GB
MERCEDES G-WAGON	104			
PRICES Rupiah (mills)	Volume			

Source: Rover Group Market Research.

match customer requirements and preferences as closely as possible.

It was also recognised that the car programme needed comprehensive political support from the Indonesian government if the car was to be launched. Therefore, while the model was in Indonesia, it was shown to the cabinet ministers and their reactions to the design were discussed. The most important objective was to show the model to President Suharto and gain his support for the car design programme; this was achieved in mid-February 1995. The car model was then returned to the UK for design revision and to ensure that the programme was completed for the launch date of September 1997.

In April 1995, the Indonesians appointed a full-time project director for their team, replacing the previous leader who was the head of the Agency for Strategic Industries, and with whom a strong relationship had been formed over the previous two years. Until this point, the daily operational activities had been led by the Rover project team, demonstrating the trust that existed at that time.

At the same time, Rover also appointed a project director from the vehicle engineering function, to replace the Rover International commercial organisation that had originally established the relationship. The next major milestone in the programme was the completion of the fully engineered and styled model for the car, scheduled for September 1995. Work on the project accelerated from April onwards with the joint team growing to nearly 100 engineers based in Indonesia and the UK. The level of demand for change to the features of the vehicles grew dramatically over this period, and eventually the two sides became increasingly polarised. The two new project directors were no longer focused on a common objective. One was devoted to producing a low-risk but credible quality product, while the other was deter-

mined that a new vehicle be made in totally new facilities in Indonesia. Between them, they were unable to resolve the disparity.

In September 1995, the engineered model design milestone was achieved, but the Indonesian team insisted that the programme be halted while Minister Habibie was consulted. In October of 1995, the agreement signed the previous December was cancelled by the Indonesian government.

The Award of the National Car Programme to the Australian Automotive Industry

A third group of competitors emerged after the signing of the Memorandum of Understanding. This group consisted of parties who either did not know about the National Car Programme earlier or did not believe the Indonesians were seriously committed to the programme.

Once the agreement between Rover and BPIS was public knowledge, this group became active and joined the competitive arena, with the benefit of being able to appraise the various approaches and the proposal that finally won. The main competitor in this group turned out to be the Australian government, in the form of the Department of Industry, Science and Technology, which formally invited Mr. Habibie to Australia. In May 1995 he was taken on a tour of the Australian automotive facilities and capabilities. In June 1995, Senator Cook, the Australian Minister for Industry, led a delegation of managing directors of automotive companies to Jakarta. The Australians continued their lobbying through 1995 at the national car project director level, and in October 1995 Rover was informed that the Australians were the new partners on the Indonesian programme.

Sanyo Manufacturing Corporation: 1977–1990

Suresh Kotha
Roger Dunbar

New York University

Tanemichi Sohma was the vice president for administration and personnel at Sanyo Manufacturing Company's (SMC) facility in Forrest City, Arkansas. In 1988, after a decade in this position, he could look back on many press reports that documented how he had done everything in his power to make the work environment at SMC attractive and supportive for its American workers. In addition, he had attempted to build good relations with the broader community. As a result, he had expected that the American work force would show loyalty to their employer at its time of need.

Instead, when SMC needed support, the employees had gone on strike. They had gone even further and carried placards with racist, anti-Japanese slogans. Instead of helping SMC as it faced brutal competition from Korean and Taiwanese firms, the American employees demanded more financial incentives and were unwilling to consider management's proposals for wage concessions. In fact, from SMC's standpoint, the employees had always seemed to demand more and, in return, gave little back to benefit.

COMPANY BACKGROUND

Sanyo Electric is a large Japanese consumer electronics firm headquartered in Osaka, Japan. In the late 1960s and early 1970s, the firm had no manufacturing facilities in the United States but was exporting increasingly large numbers of TVs to Sears, Roebuck & Co (Sears). At the time, however, Sears had a joint venture with Warwick Electronics, a subsidiary of the Whirlpool Corporation, to produce TVs. This venture's main production facility, 25 percent owned by Sears, was located in Forrest City, Arkansas, where it had served as a captive Sears supplier of color TVs.[1] During the 1960s, output at the Forrest City plant had grown, and at one point over 2,500 employees were employed by Warwick.

However, the Warwick plant was unable to meet the new quality and technology standards and the much more competitive prices that heralded the arrival of Japanese competition in the mid-1960s. Because of customer returns and complaints about quality, Sears soon became dissatisfied with the TVs produced by Warwick. It preferred to buy its TVs from Japan rather than from its U.S. joint venture partner. As a result, output at the Warwick plant started to decline and over time, four of the five assembly lines were closed, equipment was allowed to run down, and employment was cut to less than 400. Losses mounted (over $9 million in 1975 on sales of $71 million) as demand for TVs ebbed. Morale fell to an all-time low. An employee described the situation at Warwick as follows:

> This was really a desolate place then. . . . People were continually being laid off, and the handwriting was on the wall for everyone to see. There

This was was prepared as the basis for class discussion rather than to illustrate either effective or ineffective handling of an administrative situation.

was no money, so we were letting equipment run down. We were having terrible quality problems and spending nights and weekends reworking sets so that we could keep up with our delivery schedules. The management group was working as hard as it could, and yet things kept getting worse. It was really demoralizing.[2]

Many of Sears's imported TVs were manufactured by Sanyo Electric. Sears approached Sanyo with a request that it give Warwick some technical help. Sanyo countered, instead, with an offer to buy out Whirlpool's share of the joint venture for $10.3 million. With Sears's agreement and support, therefore, the Forrest City plant was taken over by Sanyo on January 1, 1977. Sears agreed to loan Sanyo $9 million at 6 percent. The loan was due in four annual installments of half-a-million dollars each beginning December 31, 1978, with the balance due at the end of 1982.[3] The new subsidiary and the Warwick facility were renamed the Sanyo Manufacturing Company (SMC).

According to a senior executive, Sanyo Electric's move to the United States was spurred on by the restrictions on color television imports that were about to be imposed and which were, at the time, in the process of being worked out by U.S. and Japanese negotiators.[4] To better appreciate the conditions that faced Sanyo Electric when it entered the United States, it is important to describe how the U.S.-television industry had evolved from the 1960s through the 1970s into the early 1980s.

THE U.S. TV INDUSTRY

In the 1950s, U.S. television technology was state of the art and U.S. manufacturers dominated world TV output. This U.S. leadership was the result of a sequence of technological developments that dated back to 1879 and Edison's invention of the phonograph. In addition to their dominance in the U.S. market, many U.S. manufacturers invested heavily in European production facilities in order to supply the growing European demand for TVs. They were unable to build facilities in Japan, however, because of prohibitions imposed by the Japanese government. These were put in place by the government to protect the fledgling domestic TV industry as the country attempted to rebuild its industrial base after World War II.

In response to this situation, many U.S. firms decided to license their technology to the Japanese and, in this way, generate additional revenues. In the 1950s, firms such as RCA, GE, and Westinghouse transferred their monochrome technology to Japan. RCA licensed its color technology to Japanese firms in 1962. This technology transfer steadily accelerated as the American firms, in an attempt to reduce their costs even further, encouraged the Japanese and other manufacturers to develop their capacity to manufacture TV parts and components.[5]

In 1956, the fledgling Japanese television manufacturers came together to form the Home Electronic Appliance Market Stabilization Council. This council was an effort to coordinate Japanese sales of televisions, radios, and other electronic products in the Japanese domestic market and, also, to exclude foreign imports from Japan.[6] To promote the growth of Japanese TV producers, the council set minimum price levels for products designated for domestic sale, and in the process established industry levels for profit margins. They also acted to boycott nonmembers who tried to venture in by working with the government to raise tariff and nontariff barriers designed to deny foreign firms (mostly American) access to Japanese distribution channels. Recently, some authors have noted:

> In the late 1960s Japanese television sets cost about twice as much in Japan as they did in the United States. Higher prices at home helped the Japanese manufacturers generate the capital they needed to maintain a healthy growth rate in spite of the low prices they were charging to gain market share in the United States. At that time, American television makers were prevented from selling their products in the protected Japanese market.[7]

Although the council was theoretically subject to legal challenge by the Japanese Fair Trade Commission established during the U.S. occupation, the Japanese government agreed with the council's approach and disagreed with the mandate established for the Trade Commission. As a result, the Japanese government instituted a policy of benign neglect in so far as the antitrust statutes were concerned. Instead, they encouraged the colluding behavior of the domestic producers. According to published reports:

> In Japan's home market the Japanese Federal Trade Commission conducted a number of in-

vestigations. One of these looked into the activities of three secret consumer-electronics groups that each met monthly for many years. The groups included representatives from Matsushita (Panasonic), Hitachi, Mitsubishi, Sanyo, Sharp, and Toshiba—most of the major television manufacturers. . . . This major Japanese price-fixing investigation ended in the 1970s, owing in part to "the passage of time," according to the Trade Commission. American firms alleged that the collusion had produced enormous profits that were used to subsidize dumping in the United States.[8]

In the early 1960s, MITI went further and targeted the consumer electronics industry for government support and development to help its efforts to sell overseas. To coordinate these export efforts, the Japanese TV manufacturers organized the Television Export Council in 1963.

Exports to the US Markets

Through improved transistor technology, the Japanese manufacturers had been able to simplify the manufacturing of TVs and improve their performance (see Exhibit 1). In fact, their technological success and progress in production techniques far exceeded what had been achieved by their former teachers, their U.S. manufacturing competitors.[9] Supported by MITI, therefore, the Japanese were keen to enter and establish a strong presence in the large U.S. TV mar-

ket. Their competitive advantages included superior technology, better manufacturing process, lower price, and a generally higher-quality product. They offered these superior TVs to importers such as Sears and other large retailers at prices that were well below those of U.S. producers. They not only offered TVs to importers at prices which U.S. manufacturers believed were below cost but, in addition and as a further enticement, they offered rebates of up to $40 per set and additional payments for "market research." Although the U.S. manufacturers were appalled at Japanese tactics, many U.S. importers liked the arrangements. They willingly agreed to import Japanese TVs and, by the late 1960s, Japanese TVs were flooding into the United States in large volumes (see Exhibit 2).

Some U.S. manufacturers protested the Japanese tactics to the U.S. federal government, but it was slow to respond. As a result, U.S. employment in television production fell quickly, dropping 50 percent between 1966 and 1970, another 30 percent between 1971 and 1975, and a further 25 percent between 1977 and 1981.[10] The U.S. manufacturers realized the Japanese television sets were not just technically better, but the additional financial incentives that the Japanese manufacturers were offering importers were considered illegal in the United States. In the process, however, and with the collusion of U.S. importers such as Sears, the Japanese firms were effectively gaining a dominant market share of the U.S. market (see Exhibit 3).

EXHIBIT 1 *TV Production Cost Structure and Reliability Estimates*

	Japan	U.S.	South Korea	West Germany	U.K.
Average man-hours	1.9	3.6	5	3.9	6.1
Employment costs (£/hour)	3.0	2.45	0.3	3.85	1.74
Direct labor costs (£)	5.7	8.8	1.5	15.1	10.6
Material costs (£)	100.0	NA	113	119	126
Plant overheads (£)	11.0	NA	2.0	17.0	20.0
Total Production Costs (£)	116.7	NA	116.5	151	156.5

Comparative Color TV Reliability Measures

	Japan	U.S.	U.K.
Field call rate (calls per set)	.09–.26	1.0–2	1.2–3.0
Production fall-off rate (faults per set on the assembly line)	.01–.03	1.4–2	1.8–2.9

Source: M. E. Porter, 1983. The U.S. Television Set Market, 1970–1979.

EXHIBIT 2 *U.S. TV Production and Imports*

	1973	1974	1975	1976
Black and white (Units M)	7.3	6.87	4.42	5.94
Color (Units M)	10.07	8.41	6.22	8.19
Black and white ($ M)	560	543	371	528
Color ($ M)	3097	2658	2121	3269
Imports				
Black and white (Units M)	4.99	4.66	2.97	4.33
From Japan	0.877	0.775	0.647	1.385
Color (Units M)	1.4	1.28	1.21	2.83
From Japan	1.06	0.917	1.04	2.53
Saturation (% Households owning)				
Black and White				
Total	99.9	99.9	99.9	99.9
1st Set	38.3	31.4	28.3	NA
2nd Set	52.7	58.3	NA	NA
Color				
Total	67.1	71.5	74.4	77.7
1st Set	57.7	64.7	68.8	NA
2nd Set	5.1	6.8	NA	NA

Source: Porter, 1983.

EXHIBIT 3 *U.S. Market Shares of Major TV Manufacturers*

	Black and White TVs		Color TVs	
Manufacturer	1973	1977	1973	1977
Zenith	17.00	17.00	22.50	22.0
RCA	12.00	14.00	20.30	20.0
Matsushita	8.00	15.00	2.10	8.00
Motorola	6.00	10.00	8.00	6.00
GE	11.00	10.00	6.00	7.50
Sears	9.00	9.80	7.80	9.00
GTE	2.50	5.30	5.00	5.50
Philco-Ford	4.80	—	2.90	2.50
Sony	4.00	4.00	4.00	7.50
Admiral	5.60	4.30	3.50	2.50
Sanyo	1.50	1.90	0.50	1.80
Wards	1.70	3.00	1.30	2.50
Sharp	2.20	2.50	0.90	2.00
Hitachi	1.50	2.20	0.80	1.60
Penncrest (JCP)	1.45	1.70	0.90	2.00
Magnavox	4.00	2.00	8.00	7.00
Packard-Bell	0.70	—	0.70	—

Source: M. E. Porter, 1983.

U.S. manufacturers requested protection from the government. In 1968, for example, the Import Committee of the U.S. Electronics Industries Association filed a petition with the U.S. Treasury Department alleging Japanese TV sets were being dumped on the U.S. market. The U.S. Treasury Department launched an investigation of Japanese manufacturers such as Sony, Sharp, Matsushita, Toshiba and Hitachi. These firms responded by stonewalling requests for information. In 1970, the National Union Electric (NUE) Corporation (with brand names such as Emerson and Dumont) filed another antitrust suit charging the Japanese companies with conspiracy to restrain competition and to drive firms like NUE out of business. Finally, in 1971, the Treasury Department responded to the complaints and officially charged the Japanese firms with dumping TVs. This finding meant that antidumping levies could be collected from the firms to offset the advantage they gained. But, again, the calculation of such levies required accurate information from the Japanese firms and this was something they were not prepared to provide. Although it was possible to theoretically calculate such figures, doing so created a dilemma for U.S. trade officials. Specifically, such levies invited retaliation and a trade war. Therefore, the U.S. Treasury did nothing. It was speculated therefore that "both the Democratic and Republican administrations concluded that it was better to settle trade disputes between governments rather than through litigation."[11]

By 1975–76, there was a veritable minefield of proceedings and investigations facing the Japanese firms (e.g., Hitachi, Mitsubishi, Sanyo, Sharp, and Toshiba). To resolve these legal challenges, the Japanese hired Mr. Malmgren who had been the deputy special trade representative for the Nixon and Ford administrations. Within three months, he worked out a compromise known as the Orderly Marketing Agreement (OMA). In the agreement, the Japanese agreed to limit their exports from Japan to the United States to 1.5 million units a year for three years. It also permitted the Japanese firms to use manufacturing facilities they owned in the United States to fill any demand they had that exceeded this quota. Many Japanese manufacturers also hired additional consultants and advisors from among ex-U.S. government officials who had worked on television issues. Their objective was to have immediate access to experts who could protect them from such legal concerns in the future.[12]

The Japanese response to the OMA was to quickly establish manufacturing facilities in the United States. Sanyo's acquisition of Warwick in 1977 with Sears's support is an example. Earlier in 1974, Matsushita had bought out Motorola's production facility and renamed its brand Quasar. In addition, Mitsubishi opened a plant in California, Toshiba built a $6 million color TV plant in Lebanon, Tennessee, and Hitachi and GE announced a TV production joint venture. In fact, all of the major Japanese TV manufacturers began producing color TVs in the United States around this time (see Exhibit 4). With the exception of Sony, which owned its own proprietary tube, these firms also decided to use U.S. firms as the source of their color tubes. According to published reports:

The Japanese had not restricted themselves to producing color TVs, and many had begun or were about to begin making a number of products in the United States, including microwave ovens,

EXHIBIT 4 *U.S. Color TV Production by Japanese Firms*

	1973	1974	1975	1976	1977	1978	1979
Sony	130	250	275	370	400	450	475
Matsushita	—	—	300	400	460	600	700
Sanyo	—	—	—	—	300	600	680
Toshiba	—	—	—	—	—	60	175
Mitsubishi	—	—	—	—	—	60	120
Hitachi	—	—	—	—	—	—	20
Sharp	—	—	—	—	—	—	100
	130	250	575	770	1160	1770	2270

Source: M. E. Porter, 1983.

stereos, and some appliances, such as vacuum cleaners and small refrigerators.[13]

In 1951, at the start of the television era, there were over 90 U.S.-owned firms that manufactured TVs. By 1968, this number had been reduced to 28 firms and, by 1976, only six U.S.-owned firms remained. Faced with severe Japanese competition in

the early 1970s, U.S. firms such as Admiral and Westinghouse were sold or closed, while others, such as Magnavox, were sold to Phillips NV of the Netherlands. Other U.S.-owned TV manufacturing businesses that had been household names, such as Philco, Sylvania, RCA, and GE, were either sold or closed down during the 1980s (see Exhibit 5). By the late 1980s, Zenith remained as the lone U.S.-owned

EXHIBIT 5 *What Ever Happened to the Brands of TV's Golden Age?*

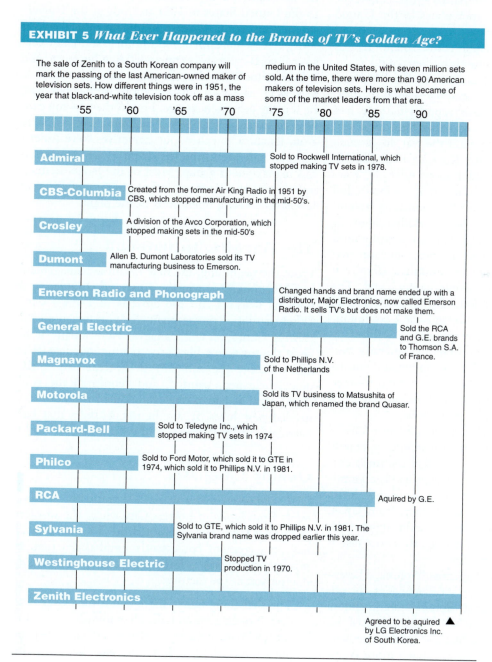

Source: David Lachenbruch, *Television Digest.*

TV manufacturer. In July 1995, a majority stake in Zenith was sold to Korean interests (LG Electronics) so that now there is no U.S. manufacturer of TVs.[14]

SANYO AT FORREST CITY

Forrest City, the location of Sanyo's first experience with manufacturing and labor issues in the United States, is located in northeast Arkansas, just west of Memphis in the Mississippi cotton delta. It was founded in 1866 by the flamboyant hero of the Confederate cavalry, General Nathan Bedford Forrest. General Forrest is remembered for several reasons. During the Civil War, he is reputed to have had about 20 horses shot out from under him. After settling down in Forrest City after the war, he became the first grand wizard of the Ku Klux Klan (KKK). He resigned this position after about a decade, however, when he became concerned that the intent and the direction of the KKK was becoming too violent.

With cotton prices high and unskilled labor always needed, the region was relatively wealthy until the 1950s. With the advent of cotton-picking machines, however, the need for unskilled labor was eliminated, leaving many people unemployed. The city had a stable population of just under 15,000 equally divided between white and black communities. About a third of the city population is illiterate, and about 30 percent are on welfare. Generally, residents' incomes are low, with unemployment consistently hovering around 20 percent.[15] Due to such conditions, the city welcomed the establishment of the Warwick facility in the early 1960s.

Similarly, SMC was welcomed to Forrest City in the 1970s. People realized that the town desperately needed jobs and they were afraid that the main employer, Warwick, would disappear, as had been gradually occurring. To run its Forrest City facility, SMC sent over 26 managers and technicians from Japan. They were given instructions to live throughout the city and to behave, eat, play, and go to school just as they found the Americans did.

During SMC's entry, Tanemichi Sohma, a Japanese national, was appointed vice president for administration and personnel. Sohma's command of the English language was better than that of his Japanese colleagues. As he had also gone to university in the United States, he was much more familiar with how things generally worked. He warned the Japanese technicians who worked with the plant employees, for example, that they must be patient with the workers and not be too bossy.

Although Satoshi Iue was SMC's president, it was Sohma who was in charge of day-to-day operations and, in particular, managed the relations between the Japanese managers and local employees, and between the plant and the local community. Sohma had come to the United States in 1951 to study at the University of Southern California. While his official title at SMC was vice president for administration and personnel, SMC observers concluded that his power and influence locally within the plant belied his title. At least as far as day-to-day operations were concerned, he was the person in charge. Five of the new top echelon of executives at SMC, including Sohma, were from Japan. The other four executives were American and had been inherited from Warwick's previous management group. Most of the Japanese managers and technicians worked at a variety of different levels supervising operations in the plant.

The Warwick Turnaround

From the beginning, the new Japanese management of SMC sought to win the trust and confidence of both its workers and the citizens of Forrest City. When it took over the plant, SMC retained all the existing employees and managers. Additionally, it invited the town to a big party to announce its arrival and welcome the company to Forrest City. SMC quickly cleaned, painted, and renovated the rundown plant it had taken over. When the company needed new hires, it sought out workers that had been laid off by Warwick and rehired them.

Quality Emphasis

SMC imported many of its TV transistor components from Japan to Forrest City where the workers in Forrest City then assembled the TV sets. SMC's new management consistently emphasized that its prime concern was to improve quality. According to one person at the factory:

The first thing Sanyo did when it took over [was that] it retained essentially all employees and managers who were there. . . . Sanyo moved some people around, though. For example, they took the former manager of Quality Control—who really had been taking a lot of heat from everybody during the previous two years, because of quality problems—and made him the plant manager. That, by the way, was just one of the signals the company gave that the number-one priority for the plant was improving quality. All the managers talked about was quality.[16]

In pursuing SMC's approach to quality, many of the Japanese managers and technicians spent a lot of their time simply standing very close to the employees, watching what they did, and correcting and training them as SMC thought necessary. The employees reported that they found this behavior somewhat amusing at times, but that the Japanese were very fussy and always wanted everything to be done exactly their way. They noted that they had installed quality checks everywhere. In addition to the regular checks on the assembly line, they installed "tumblers" (devices that threw the sets into the air) to see if any screws came loose. If a screw came loose, the failure was traced back to the particular worker who assembled the set. The error was then pointed out and the way to avoid such errors in the future was patiently reexplained.

Sanyo not only guided the workers inside the plant in order to improve quality but also the vendors outside to ensure that the quality of its supplies also improved. Again, a meticulous, time-consuming, and detailed approach was consistently in evidence. Like the plant employees, some of the suppliers found this approach annoying and several questioned why it was necessary. But in time all had to acknowledge that, uniformly, the quality of the plant's production had significantly improved. Pride in the quality of work they were doing began to characterize workers' attitudes.

Building a Happy Family

More than 60 percent of the workers at the plant were black. Those among them who were hourly workers were organized by the International Union of Electrical Workers (IUE). Sohma met with the union and explained that the company sought a partnership with it. He requested that the union talk with management about its production policies, methods, and goals and to join with management in implementing a start-to-finish quality program that guar-

anteed that no defective TV ever left the plant. Every time Sohma talked, he mentioned that it was his and his firm's intent to promote quality. Initially, the union was pleasantly shocked but a little at a loss as to how to respond. The Warwick management had always said production policies were management's prerogative, and they had always closed their eyes to the many defective TVs that everyone could see were leaving the plant.

The work style that developed at SMC was noisy, busy, and casual. Believing little things counted, Sohma and his managers noticed anything that caused employees discomfort. Whenever they could, they remedied the matter immediately. In turn, the workers were likewise expected to immediately correct anything they noticed wrong on the assembly line. Similarly, managers tried to be consistently sensitive to workers' feelings and needs as well as to manufacturing requirements. As equipment was found to be lacking, it was purchased. As workers made mistakes, they were counseled rather than discharged. According to reports published at that time, "Sanyo set out to create a 'big happy family' atmosphere to enhance morale at the plant."[17]

Sohma recognized, too, that the Warwick custom of firing people after the Christmas season had been very disturbing to workers, destroying whatever loyalty they might have developed toward the firm. He pledged to the labor union that Sanyo would seek to smooth out production so that over time it would eventually be possible to phase out the need for the repeated layoffs and recalls that had plagued plant relations in the past. Several people were impressed by this commitment and the combination of cooperation, on the one hand, and authority on the other, that seemed to be demonstrated. They observed that although Sohma always sought mutuality, he did not eliminate hierarchy.

Additionally, Sohma also sought out the labor union's help to solve certain issues. For example, Sohma explained to the union that Japanese managers were repelled by workers who smoked while working on the line. He then worked out a plan with the union to successfully phase out smoking among those working on the line.[18]

Operating Management

In keeping with Sanyo's desire to share the management process, a management committee was chosen to supervise operations. This committee consisted of three U.S. and three Japanese managers. Decision making in this committee turned out to be very slow and difficult, however. The Japanese would allude to or imply things rather than specifically say what they wanted. The Americans would not recognize the cues. They would continue to wait for instructions, not knowing that they had already been given. Unable to solve these communication difficulties, the committee eventually had to be abandoned.

THE 1979 STRIKE AND AFTERMATH

Although to local people Sohma seemed to be the person in charge in Forrest City, in fact, many decisions at SMC had to be referred back to headquarters in Japan for confirmation and approval. This sometimes created problems because of unanticipated delays. Another problem was the lack of familiarity on the part of top executives at Sanyo Electric headquarters concerning some of the assumptions that were taken for granted about business life and how things are done in the United States. This became an issue in 1979 when there was an eight-week union strike over cost-of-living increases, an unresolved problem that Sanyo management had inherited from the Warwick administration.

Sohma explained what the strike was about to his bosses back in Japan. This was difficult to do as, first, his superiors in Japan could not understand what the issues were and, second, Japanese firms have very few strikes and they last but a day or two.[19] When the strike in Forrest City entered its third week, management in Osaka felt something was terribly wrong. Reasoning that Sohma must surely have gravely offended the workers, they advised him to call his work force together immediately, to humble himself before them, and to apologize for whatever terrible things he had done. Sohma refused. He was rebuked by his Japanese bosses, who informed him he had become too Americanized.

The 1979 strike was soon resolved. But cultural differences between the Americans and the Japanese were starting to emerge as SMC management found it could not completely keep commitments it had made. According to Nakai, SMC's managing director in 1981:

Given different American conditions, we haven't been totally able to transplant the Japanese way to America. There are good periods and also slow periods, with heavy sales focused on November and December for the Christmas season. We've naturally had to adjust our production schedule and lay off some workers, as do other American manufacturers.[20]

In discussing the 1979 strike and emerging cultural differences between the Japanese managers and U.S. workers, Nakai said:

American workers maintain a much looser relationship toward their company compared with the Japanese. . . . However, we learned some lessons from that [1979 strike] and are now trying to improve the situation. In Japan, the union lives with the company and never pulls the trigger unless it finds itself in an extremely serious situation. It tries as much as possible to work with us on the same ground, because its members' future and prosperity are directly linked to ours. The important question for us right now is how to instill this concept in our American workers.[21]

The Japanese managers were also aware that despite their successful efforts to improve quality at the Forrest City plant and the local admiration these efforts had earned, Sanyo's plants back in Osaka achieved similar quality, but were also 25 percent more efficient than the Forrest City plant. Hence, they demanded that workers do better at Forrest City. However, the U.S. employees had seen the vast improvements in quality, efficiency, and volume that the Japanese had brought about relative to the Warwick period, and they wondered why the Japanese managers were still concerned. Reflecting on the situation, Nakai noted:

On the subject of productivity, the key element is teamwork, with the responsibility resting squarely on management to motivate its workers. The reason there are workmanship problems in the US, I believe, is the different concept of teamwork. In a Japanese plant there is much more dialogue between blue-collar and white-collar workers; in fact the rapport is so natural, we take it for granted. Such however, is not the case in the US.

Soon, along with the production of TVs, microwave ovens were added to the product line. Production levels actually increased tenfold while the numbers of workers increased only threefold. By 1981, the plant employed 1,750 workers making televisions, 350 in the plant furniture shop, and 250 making microwave ovens. Defects caught during final inspection had dropped by 75 percent. Highly satisfied, Sears provided Sanyo with a new five-year contract and agreed to purchase at least 70 percent of its annual requirements of color TVs for sale in the United States.[22]

In 1982, Forrest City was declared a foreign trade subzone to facilitate further expansion of the plant. The designation meant that Sanyo did not have to pay duty on imported parts, just on the foreign content of the sets later shipped. In total, Sanyo seems to have invested around $60 million in the Forrest City plant. In 1982, the union contract was renegotiated without further incident.

In addition to working with U.S. suppliers, Sanyo allied itself with political leaders of the surrounding community to attract more Japanese investment to the area. In 1981, for example, Sanyo helped orchestrate a tour by Arkansas Governor White intended to attract firms from the Far East to establish plants in Arkansas. In response to Sanyo's recommendation, a number of additional Japanese and Far Eastern firms decided to locate their manufacturing and servicing facilities around Memphis and in the surrounding area of northeast Arkansas.

THE 1985 STRIKE AND AFTERMATH

In 1984 U.S. production capacity was 13.1 million TV sets while actual production had been 11.5 million sets, around 89 percent of capacity. By 1987, however, production capacity had grown by almost 50 percent to more than 17 million TV sets. This resulted from large capacity expansion efforts undertaken by most of the Japanese firms as well as some new entrants from Korea and Taiwan (see Exhibit 6 for dropping TV prices in the United States and Exhibit 7 for increasing penetration of Korean and Taiwanese firms in the United States). In contrast, actual production dropped in 1987 to 11.2 million sets, or only 66 percent of the expanded capacity.

It was clear that a shake out in the industry was about to occur. At the time, there were around 20

firms producing televisions in the United States. Most were foreign owned; many were Japanese subsidiaries, but several were recently established subsidiaries of Korean and Taiwanese multinationals who were prepared to compete fiercely on quality and price criteria, just as the Japanese had done 15 to 20 years earlier.[23] As a result, this rapidly established overcapacity ensured higher costs and lower prices as fierce competition came to dominate the attention of industry managers. From 1985 to 1987, firms moved from making good profits to having to sustain some substantial losses.

It was under these approaching competitive conditions that SMC negotiated with its labor union in 1985. SMC, still feeling the need to increase efficiency to match the performance of its Japanese plants, sought changes that would organize the plant more like a Japanese facility. SMC pressed for relaxing the union rules on seniority rights and for greater worker flexibility as well as reduced medical benefits and insurance costs. But SMC was unable to convince the union leaders that such concessions were necessary. Increasingly, the union was convinced that the company only wanted to squeeze more production out of its workers. The atmosphere became bitter and poisoned. According to published reports:

> The demands [of the Japanese management] sparked a 21-day strike. Pickets carried signs that read: "Japs go home" and "Remember Pearl Harbor." Windows were broken, guns were fired, a car was overturned, and at one point the plant was nearly overrun by strikers.[24]

Wilford W. Banks, Jr., was president of Local 1106 of the IUE. He had watched employment increase at the Arkansas plant from 300 to 1,500 but he was not pleased. He felt the company had made the workers work too hard. He felt the "happy family" theme was just a way to extract more work and more employee ideas out of his members without providing them with additional compensation. The union, while pleased to cooperate on the operating side with Sanyo, felt it still had to be militant and launch a strike in order to protect its members' contract rights.

Further, the racism implicit in Forrest City's history also came to the fore. Police arrested the people picketing and the truckers delivering supplies that hit the strikers with their trucks as they entered the plant. Eventually, the strike was ended by a new

C-40

EXHIBIT 6 *Television Set Prices vs. Total Sales of All Goods & Services 1974–1978*

Annual Consumer Price Index U.S. 1974–1992

Television Sets ------ Total U.S. (G & S)

Source: Based on figures provided in *The U.S. Consumer Electronics Industry in Review*, 1993 Edition.

42-month contract. But, many acknowledge that there is a legacy of bitterness from this strike.

A year after the strike, SMC had grown to be the largest Japanese TV producer in the United States. It employed 1,700 people and was producing 1.2 million TV sets and 500,000 microwave ovens. Its annual sales amounted to $40 million. However, due to the increased competition resulting from industry overcapacity and the fierce price competition, the firm had no profits, but instead posted a loss of $14 million.

These losses prompted SMC to ask its employees to accept a 20 percent wage cut as a sign of solidarity and loyalty to the firm. The union responded by

EXHIBIT 7 *Imported Television Sets: Japan vs. Korea and Taiwan 1980–1987*

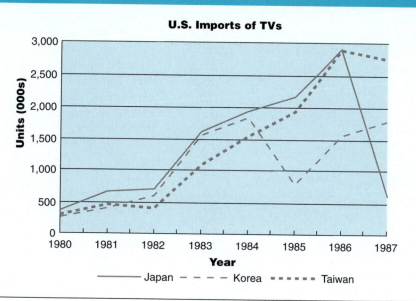

Source: Based on figures provided in Collis (1988).

asking its auditor to examine the firm's books and to assess SMC's justification and need for the wage cut. He reported that the company's problems had, in fact, little to do with its labor costs. As a result, the union rejected the firm's request for a wage cut although it did agree to forego a 3 percent wage increase along with cost-of-living increases. It also agreed to allow SMC some freedom to assign employees to tasks that were not included in their job descriptions.

There was growing frustration among Sanyo management with American workers' "way of thinking." Faced with fierce competition, externally, and after years of attempting to work with the union to improve quality and build loyalty and commitment in its work force, the managers were highly frustrated by the fact that in this time of obvious firm need there was no corresponding readiness to sacrifice on the part of the workers. As Sohma said, summarizing management's sentiments:

They come here for eight hours' work and to get eight hours' pay. . . . As long as they get that, they don't care what happens to our production. Here, there's no sacrifice. . . . Union leaders are destructive. I want the union to be strong, but I want

it to be intelligently strong to help instead of stirring up things.

Moving Production Abroad

In 1988, with high labor costs, continuing industry overcapacity, intense competition, and rapidly sinking prices for TV products, questions arose at Sanyo headquarters in Osaka as to whether it was desirable to maintain the Forrest City facility. Given the pressures, it seemed imperative to relocate the production facilities to a place where it would be possible to reduce costs so Sanyo could compete successfully in the U.S. market. Sanyo decided to drastically scale back the size of its operations in Forrest City to the point of closing it down.

Employment dropped from 1,200 in 1986 to 650 in 1988, including just 190 hourly workers. Sanyo decided to shift some labor-intensive production to a maquiladora in Tijuana, Mexico, where labor costs were about an eighth of those in Arkansas (see Exhibit 8 for a list of other Japanese firms operating out of Mexico and Exhibit 9 for top TV and microwave makers in 1993).

According to Annette Bradley, a worker at SMC during the time:

EXHIBIT 8 *Plants Located on the Mexican Side of the Border Zone in 1990*

Company	Location	Employees	Products
Goldstar	Mexicali	1,000	13″ and 19″ TVs
Hitachi	Tijuana	1,000	TV and audio
Matsushita	Tijuana	2,000	TVs, tuners, chassis
Murata Erie.	Juarez	150	yokes, transformers
Philips	Juarez	3,000	9–20″ TVs, CD players
Sanyo	Tijuana	530	small-screen TVs, chassis
Sony	Tijuana	1,500	13–27″ TVs, projection TVs, chassis
Thomson	Juarez	3,500	chassis and kits
	Torreon	2,000	yokes, transformers
Tocabi	Tijuana	1,000	cabinets
Toshiba	Juarez	800	chassis
Zenith	Juarez	3,200	furniture, wood cabinets*
	Reynosa	6,000	components, 9–20″ TVs
	Matamoros	3,700	TV components
	Agua Prieta	900	parts and service

Source: *Television Digest,* July 23, 1990.
*Some TVs are also reportedly made here.

"I don't know if it was bad management, or bad parts, but I know one thing was they could get cheaper labor in Mexico.... I feel bad. They're taking jobs from the U.S. to Mexico because of cheaper labor, and it hurts the States and it hurts the people. I know they're human, they're out to make a dollar just like the rest of us are, but it's just that it would have been better if they would have just tried to work a little bit more with us, instead of just ship everything out."[25]

EXHIBIT 9 *Top Television Makers in 1993*
(Shares are shown based on total sales of 21 million units for 1993.)

Company	Share, %
Thomson (GE/RCA)	22.0
NAP (Magnavox, Sylvania)	13.0
Zenith	13.0
Matsushita (Panasonic, Quasar)	7.0
Sony	7.0
Sharp	6.0
Emerson	5.0
Sanyo	5.0
Toshiba	5.0
Mitsubishi	4.0
JVC	2.0
Samsung	2.0
Curtis Mathes	1.0
Goldstar	1.0
Hitachi	1.0
Others	6.0

Source: *Appliance Manufacturer,* February 1994, p. 38.

EXHIBIT 9 *Microwave Oven Manufacturers*
(cont.) *(Manufacturer shares are shown in percent based on the 7,967,000 unit market in 1992.)*

Company	Share, %
Sharp	20
Samsung	18
Matsushita (Panasonic, Quasar)	17
Electrolux (Frigidaire)	10
Goldstar	10
Sanyo Fisher	7
Maytag (Magic Chef)	6
Raytheon (Amana)	4
Whirlpool	3
Toshiba	1
Others	4

Source: *Appliance Manufacturer,* February 1993, p. 18.

C-41

Responding to this move by SMC, Bill Clinton, governor of Arkansas at the time, made a personal appeal to Sanyo Electric's chairman in Osaka to keep the Forrest City facility open for the benefit of the local community. According to *The Economist* magazine:

> Indeed, some say that Sanyo did not pull out altogether only because Mr. Clinton, on a trip to Japan, appealed to Sanyo's chairman in person to save the plant. He intervened again when Sears cut back on its Sanyo orders, arranging a new retailing deal with the Wal-Mart chain (which is based in Arkansas).[26]

The Situation in 1988

The decision of headquarters back in Japan was to pack up and leave the United States. Reports of the ungrateful and disloyal U.S. work force had not helped. As the Arkansas governor could be a very persuasive man, his appeal to SMC's president would be given appropriate consideration. But an appeal to save jobs was unlikely to bring about much change in the ongoing thrust to move SMC's manufacturing outside the United States.

At best a symbolic presence would be maintained in Arkansas. Most of SMC's operations in Forrest City were sure to be shut down.[27] Facing current competition, SMC needed a work force it could rely on. And despite Sohma's Herculean efforts, such loyalty had not been forthcoming at Forrest City.

It is not clear that this had to be the outcome. Demonstrated loyalty had been a critical requirement from SMC's standpoint. Had such a demonstration been forthcoming, workers at Forrest City might have had both their jobs and money. Because of the impression they made of being disloyal to SMC and calculative about their own immediate rewards, workers lost both.

NOTES

1. R. Hayes, and K. Clark, Sanyo Manufacturing Corporation—Forrest City, Arkansas. *Harvard Business School Case #9-682-045,* 1981.
2. Ibid, p. 2.
3. Ibid, p. 3.
4. B. Krisher, *Fortune,* June 15, 1981, pp. 97–99.
5. M. L. Dertouzos (1989), *Made in America: Regaining the Productive Edge,* Cambridge, MA: MIT Press, p. 223.
6. P. Choate, *The Washington Post,* September 30, 1991.
7. Dertouzos (1989), p. 224.
8. Ibid, p. 224.
9. M. Porter, The US Television Market, in *Cases in Competitive Strategy,* Free Press, New York, 1983.
10. This decline in U.S. manufacturing employment is sometimes attributed primarily to higher wage rates in the United States. However, "in the late 1960s, when domestic television man-

ufacturers were being underpriced in the marketplace by the Japanese, assembly labor was less than 15 percent of the direct costs in the United States. During this period U.S. import duties were 8 percent, and the costs of transportation and insurance added about 10 percent more to imported goods, for a total cost differential of 18 percent. Thus, the lower prices could not be attributed solely to lower labor costs" (Dertouzos et al., 1989, p. 223).

11. Dertouzos et al., p. 225.
12. P. Choate.
13. M. Porter, pp. 502–3.
14. B. J. Fedder, *The New York Times*, July 18, 1995.
15. The news and television media have often highlighted the racial tensions that have pervaded Forrest City and the surrounding county. Court-ordered integration, that occurred in Arkansas schools in 1965, had a direct impact on the area. In 1969, students at the local black high school rioted when a favorite teacher was fired for "insubordination." A curfew was imposed. Blacks began picketing white businesses; four black men were charged with raping a teenager. Another infamous story tells of how another alleged rapist was castrated by vigilantes and his testicles then turned up in a jar which was kept on the local sheriff's desk. A private school called Forrest City Academy was founded in the 1970s for whites only, but proved to be a temporary phenomenon and soon closed its doors in the 1980s. In 1988, the Forrest City High School held its first integrated prom. There were no incidents and the news media, which were watching the event closely, pronounced it an outstanding success.

16. Quoted in Hayes and Clark, p. 3.
17. T. R. Reid, *The Washington Post*, September 2, 1977.
18. While he gained an agreement whereby workers were not allowed to smoke in the plant, some Japanese executives still did so. The executives also had exclusive and personal reserved parking spots for themselves. Workers were also forbidden to play radios and tape decks in the plant.
19. Strikes in Japan are usually symbolic expressions of a breakdown in relations between management and workers. Having effectively signaled such a concern by wearing armbands on the job and working even harder than usual, for example, workers then call off their strike.
20. B. Krisher.
21. Ibid.
22. Hayes and Clark, p. 3.
23. In Japan, the necessary industry retrenchment would have been managed through discussions with MITI. But in the United States, there is no equivalent organization and, anyway, not all the producers were Japanese.
24. J. A. Byrne, *Business Week*, July 14, 1988.
25. J. Risen, *The Los Angeles Times*, August 16, 1988.
26. *The Economist*, March 6, 1993.
27. Although much of SMC's production was moved to Mexico, the Forrest City plant continued to make large TVs. For the first time since it was established, it began shipping these sets to Japan.

Sonic: A Success Story

Sarah Gordon
Clayton Newman
Yuling Qian
Loren Schrader

J. Clifford Hudson is the president and chief executive officer of Sonic Drive-In, a popular drive-in restaurant chain. Now headquartered in Oklahoma City, Sonic was founded in Shawnee, Oklahoma, in 1953. Hudson and his predecessor, C. Stephen Lynn, presided over the resurrection of Sonic after its struggles in the early 1980s. Today, both Wall Street and Main Street value the firm's current performance and future potential.

At Sonic, customers order from and dine in their cars. A roller-skating carhop brings customers' orders to them. Sonic defies those who dismiss drive-ins as a concept so rooted in America's past that they have no future role. Far from fading away, Sonic has experienced exponential growth and tremendous customer loyalty. The company has matured such that its marketing campaign is no longer based solely on nostalgic appeals to the 1950s. Sonic continues to sell hamburgers and hotdogs to American families as drive-ins did in the days of Eisenhower and the "Ed Sullivan Show."

With success comes the challenge of continuing growth. Hudson and his management team are preparing their plan for "Sonic 2000," a series of bold initiatives that builds on the historic reasons for Sonic's past success and links it to the future. Hudson enjoys a unique perspective from his Oklahoma City office, a place where he once had to battle high

inflation and apathetic franchisees to keep Sonic financially viable. Now he must convince members of the successful chain that to continue their success they must be willing to take risks.

THE FAST FOOD RESTAURANT INDUSTRY

Fast food is convenient, predictable, and quick. As a result, it has become a part of the busy American lifestyle. More than 300,000 fast food restaurants in the United States[1] serve menu items ranging from sandwiches, chicken, pizza, seafood, and Mexican food to baked goods and various specialty coffees. The largest segment of the fast food restaurant industry is the hamburger segment, with annual sales of $40 billion.[2] Not only is it the largest, but its revenues are also growing faster than those of any other segment.

Cost Structures

Pricing in the fast food industry is extremely competitive. The most successful fast food restaurants in the hamburger segment all operate at high volumes of sales with low mark-up. The trend within this industry is vertical integration of the supply function to control costs. The market leaders own a combination of large numbers of company-owned restaurants and franchise restaurants. The fast food indus-

Prepared for discussion purposes only under the direction of Dr. Robert E. Hoskisson.

EXHIBIT 1 *Composite Stock Price Movements*

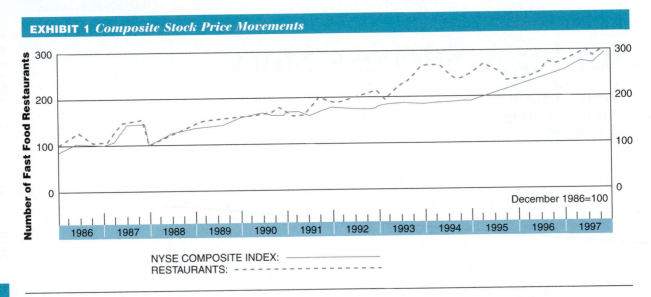

NYSE COMPOSITE INDEX: ———————
RESTAURANTS: - - - - - - - - - - - - -

Source: *Moody's Industry Review*, September 19, 1997.

try is mature and strives to maintain economies of scale for operating efficiency. The market leader, McDonald's, defines and sets the prices that the remainder of the industry follows.[3]

Product Markets

Competitors seek to differentiate themselves with unique menu offerings, as well as emphasizing quality and customer service. As a result, advertising and marketing are extremely important to remaining competitive.

However, it would be difficult for any new fast food restaurant to effectively compete with the industry market leaders, which are established and already have defined territories. Market leaders have established brand name loyalty, maximized demographically based locations, vertically integrated their supply functions, learned how to engage in competitive pricing, and learned how to gain efficiencies and economies of scale due to volume of business and number of operating units.

As the population grows, the potential for additional growth within this industry increases as well. The target consumers within the hamburger segment of the fast food restaurant industry are males aged 18 to 40 and families with young children. According to the 1990 U.S. Census, the number of families in the United States has doubled since 1960. The predic-

tions for 1996 to 2050 are that over 50 percent of the population will be less than 44 years of age.[4]

COMPANY HISTORY

The Beginning

Troy Smith, an entrepreneur from Shawnee, Oklahoma, had two unsuccessful restaurants before owning his first drive-in restaurant in 1953. Smith acquired property in Shawnee that included a steak house and a root beer stand. His plans were to operate the small drive-in root beer stand until he was ready to tear it down and replace it with a parking lot for the steak house. Oddly enough, the root beer stand, the Top Hat Drive-In, was more profitable than the attractive steak house.

While traveling in Louisiana, Smith spotted a hamburger stand with homemade speakers that allowed customers to order through an intercom system without leaving their cars. Smith hired the creator of these speakers to make a set for his Top Hat Drive-in and hired stereo technicians to install them. Smith also installed a parking canopy and introduced the concept of carhop service in 1953. The changes to the restaurant made it much more convenient for customers and created the concept that eventually led to Sonic Drive-Ins.

Charles Pappe, manager of the Shawnee, Oklahoma, Safeway supermarket, approached Smith about opening his own Top Hat Drive-In. Together, the two businessmen opened three more Top Hat Drive-Ins. Other individuals began approaching the two men about opening an outlet, but the name "Top Hat" was copyrighted. So the two selected the name "Sonic," which embodied the meaning of their slogan "Service with the Speed of Sound." Smith and Pappe helped the new franchisees, who signed a short, one-and-a-half page doubled-spaced agreement, with site selection, store layout, and operations. They charged royalty fees of one penny per sandwich bag used by the franchisee. The terms negotiated in the franchise agreements were limited, with no mention of territorial rights or contribution to marketing. Pappe died in 1967, and Smith carried on the responsibilities of running the company along with two franchisees that joined his team to take charge of Sonic's centralized supply and distribution system.

In 1973, Sonic, which now had 165 stores systemwide, was restructured by a group of 10 franchisees who were selected to serve as the company's officers and board of directors. These directors bought the rights to the company, which included intangibles such as names and symbols and the centralized supply and distribution division. Shares of stock were offered to each drive-in operator; thus, the company was owned by its franchisees and became a publicly traded company. Sonic experienced significant growth in the 1970s, opening more than 800 outlets between 1973 and 1978. During this high-growth period, the company introduced the Sonic Advertising Trust and formalized training for drive-in management.[5]

The Downturn

High inflation characterized the United States economy in 1979 and contributed to Sonic's 21 percent drop in net profit by the end of the fiscal year. In 1980, the company struggled with a net operating loss of approximately $300,000 and, as a result, closed 28 company-owned stores. Sonic management attempted to brace itself to combat the inflation problems and introduced a $5 million advertising campaign while holding its first national convention in 1980. In 1984, there were only 968 Sonic Drive-Ins located in 19 states and systemwide sales were about

$300 million. Although Sonic had begun a national advertising campaign, there was no systematic cooperative advertising program. In addition, the company did not have a national purchasing program. Management was able to get 200 company-owned and franchised stores to agree to spend about 1 percent of sales on advertising and join in a national purchasing program for a year. In return, Sonic management made a strong commitment to these operators to attempt to increase sales by 15 percent and cut food costs by 3 percent.[6]

Leveraged Buyout: The Beginning of the Turnaround

Prior to 1986, the company had been owned by its franchisees. A leveraged buyout in 1986 marked the beginning of a major turnaround for the company. A management team took out loans and bought the company for $10 million.[7] This buyout enabled managers to make more focused strategic decisions because it gave them greater control and removed them from the direct scrutiny of franchisees. Corporate management and store operators were also beginning to form a cooperative partnership, evidenced by 36 percent of the entire chain contributing $300,000 to cover advertising costs.[8] Management focused its efforts on making changes at the corporate level that could have positive effects throughout the restaurant chain.

Executives with significant national fast-food chain experience were recruited and brought Sonic to the "cutting edge" in marketing, purchasing, technology, and finance. For example, Dennis H. Clark, who was vice president of operations in the late 1980s, currently serves on Sonic's board of directors. Clark instituted the concept of giving minority partnership interests in company-owned restaurants to outlet managers and supervisors.[9] This gave employees in leadership positions incentive to succeed in restaurant management by making them partial owners: not in the whole firm, but in the specific store in which they worked.

An initial public offering in 1991 raised $52 million, which added to Sonic's working capital, paid off debt, and bought out venture capital investors. A secondary public offering in 1995 (fiscal year ending August 31, 1996) raised an additional $28.2 million, which was used to pay off long-term debt.[10] In the late 1990s, the company pursued an aggressive expansion strategy; the dollars spent for investment in property and equipment almost doubled over each two-year period, generated by the addition of new company-owned units to the system.[11]

C. Steven Lynn, chief executive officer for the 10 years following the buyout, and J. Clifford Hudson, chief operating officer during the latter years of Lynn's tenure as CEO and Lynn's successor since fiscal year 1995, have contributed significantly to Sonic's successful turnaround. The two executives understood what needed to be done to benefit the company on both the corporate and individual store level. The changes they made included increased communication with drive-in management and emphasizing teamwork, which helped develop the relationships with store management that were required for improved decision-making systemwide.

Corporate employees, including executives, were sent, as part of their training, to one of the restaurants to work for up to a week performing duties such as grilling hamburgers, making shakes, or mopping floors. Said CFO Scott McLain of his "on-the-job" experience, "I was assigned to operating the fountain, which included making milkshakes. Apparently, I wasn't very good at making chocolate shakes, because customers kept sending them back. I was putting in the set amount of chocolate syrup as dictated by corporate management and that just wasn't enough chocolate."[12] Keeping in touch with restaurant operations helped make a difference in setting operational policies and making strategic decisions by bringing needs, such as centralized marketing and brand development efforts, to upper-level managers' attention.

Brand Development and Marketing

In the late 1980s, the company began to focus on coordinated nationalized advertising and promotional campaigns, bringing in Frankie Avalon as a spokesperson. Television commercials, such as those featuring Avalon in a yellow-feathered chicken suit, gave the chain a national brand identity, as opposed to the image of a local, small-town hangout for teenagers and a highlight of the "drag" route. The company also used nostalgia to establish its identity, which targeted the baby-boom generation.

The company later dropped Avalon as its spokesperson and moved toward a "Beach Boys" theme for commercials and brand development. Many of the drive-in restaurants had stereo systems that played the same Beach Boys-style music featured on television and radio commercials. However, in keeping with the times, television commercials for Sonic now feature more modern music and customers in modern-day convertibles. (See Exhibit 2 for a history of marketing expenditures from 1992 to 1996.) The stereos at the restaurants now play more contemporary music. The company's target consumer has shifted from members of the baby-boom generation to young adult males.[13] In effect, the company has had to redefine its identity to appeal not only to baby boomers, but also to generation X.

An important part of establishing a strong brand identity for Sonic was the transition to menu consistency in the mid-1990s. All Sonic Drive-Ins began offering the same basic products, with deviations appearing under a special menu heading entitled "Local Favorites." This consistency gave consumers the

EXHIBIT 2 *Financial Highlights*

	1996	1995	1994	1993	1992
Company revenues	$151,130,000	$123,760,000	$ 99,704,000	$ 83,790,000	$ 66,676,000
Net income	$ 16,560,000	$ 12,484,000	$ 10,058,000	$ 8,644,000	$ 6,814,000
Earnings per share	$ 1.23	$ 1.05	$ 0.84	$ 0.72	$ 0.58
Stockholders' equity	$109,700,000	$ 63,400,000	$ 54,400,000	$ 46,800,000	$ 36,000,000
Marketing expenditures	$ 28,000,000	$ 24,000,000	$ 20,000,000	$ 15,000,000	$ 12,000,000
Systemwide sales	$984,784,000	$880,521,000	$776,347,000	$691,490,000	$600,044,000
Systemwide average sales per restaurant	$ 648,000	$ 615,000	$ 585,000	$ 562,000	$ 523,000
Stores in operation	1,567	1,464	1,369	1,274	1,191

Source: Sonic Annual Reports, 1994, 1995, and 1996.

benefit of knowing that the Sonic in a rural Oklahoma town has the same menu items as a Sonic in a large city in Florida. When Sonic standardized its menu, it also unveiled a new product line, "Frozen Favorites," which has experienced overwhelming success, dominating even Dairy Queen, fast-food's reigning ice cream favorite.[14]

Sonic is also moving toward a more futuristic style—called "Sonic 2000"—for its stores. The new drive-in style is a retrofitted design with larger menu housings and a large drive-through ordering board and lane. These drive-ins also provide the additional benefit of reducing capital outlay and operating costs by fitting the same equipment used in a traditionally designed Sonic Drive-In onto one-half the amount of floor space.[15]

Consolidated Purchasing

Another significant factor in Sonic's turnaround was the development of an effective centralized purchasing division. Through centralized purchasing, Sonic has solidified stronger relationships with its suppliers. These new relationships provide better bulk-rate prices and economized or custom packaging and produce more consistent product quality. For example, Sonic recently began purchasing hamburger patties in 25-pound boxes instead of 10-pound boxes, with a savings of $.50 per box.[16] Also, through the centralized purchasing program, Sonic has implemented a policy of consistent packaging. The new packaging spreads the same logo throughout the chain and provides higher-quality food benefits, such as better heat retention for hot food items.

Employee Issues–Training and Motivation

While the fast food industry as a whole has tremendous difficulty with employee turnover, Sonic has enjoyed relative success in retaining drive-in employees. The introduction of the annual Sonic Games, recently sponsored by soft drink supplier Dr. Pepper, has been credited with much of this success. The Sonic Games, which challenge drive-in employees in areas such as operation of the grill and soda fountain and carhop service, serve as a year-round motivation for the participating employees. The events score employees both on speed and quality of service. Drive-ins whose employees participate in these

games not only experience less employee turnover within their restaurants, but also typically achieve better sales results than nonparticipating drive-ins.[17] In addition to the Sonic Games, the company provides formalized training for drive-in management that teaches not only operational skills, but focuses heavily on leadership and team-building skills.

Information Technology

Enhanced information technology also played a role Sonic's success. Sonic's corporate management has successfully developed its own point-of-sale (POS) system, which takes advantage of information that is generated from the moment a customer pushes the button on a "squawk box" and places his or her food order. The POS system tracks operational and financial information that is provided to store-level and corporate management. The information, which gives details about matters such as sales revenue by item and specific food and paper costs, provides management with the information needed to make strategic decisions in areas such as marketing and purchasing. For example, inventory information is processed through the system and is used to make better purchasing decisions. In the past, this information would have been gathered by hand or not at all.[18]

THE COMPETITION

Although Sonic has made a successful turnaround, it is important to understand its competitive environment. The restaurant industry in general and the fast food segment in particular are highly fragmented. The 10 largest fast food chains account for only about 15 percent of all units and 23 percent of sales. McDonald's remains the industry sales leader by a wide margin, with its U.S. systemwide sales of $15.9 billion in 1995 representing about 7 percent of total U.S. restaurant sales. In comparison, runner-up Burger King had U.S. systemwide sales of $7.8 billion. According to estimates by *Nation's Restaurant News*, there are about 20 restaurant chains with annual U.S. sales of at least $1 billion.[19] The fast food restaurants compete on the basis of price and service and by offering quality food products. Management at Sonic views the following four restaurants as their primary competition: McDonald's, Burger King, Wendy's, and Hardee's (see Exhibit 7).[20]

McDonald's

McDonald's was founded in San Bernardino, California, by two brothers, Maurice and Richard McDonald, in 1937. Today, McDonald's is the largest and best-known global food-service retailer with more than 21,000 restaurants in 104 countries. In the United States, about 424,000 restaurants generate nearly $238 billion in annual sales. McDonald's accounts for about 2.7 percent of those restaurants and approximately 6.9 percent of those sales. At the end of 1996, there were 12,094 McDonald's restaurants in operation in the United States and 8,928 in other countries and territories. Of these restaurants, 13,428 were operated by company franchisees, 4,357 by the company, and 3,237 by affiliates (operating under joint-venture agreements).[21]

McDonald's restaurants offer a standardized menu consisting of hamburgers and cheeseburgers, including the Big Mac, Quarter Pounder with Cheese, and Arch Deluxe; the Fish Filet Deluxe, Grilled Chicken Deluxe, and Crispy Chicken Deluxe; french fries; and soft drinks and other beverages. The key factors contributing to McDonald's leading position are its large number of outlets and convenient locations. Other factors include its intensive advertising programs and its low price strategy. McDonald's vision is to dominate the global food-service industry. To achieve this goal, McDonald's is expanding rapidly both domestically and internationally. In 1996, 2,642 restaurants were added systemwide. Over the past five years, McDonald's has added 5,800 foreign restaurants. These foreign operations continue to contribute an increasing percentage to financial results. International sales rose 10 percent in 1996 and 27 percent in 1995. For the first six months of 1997, McDonald's net income grew 8 percent, net income per common share grew 10 percent, and one new restaurant opened every six hours around the world. For fiscal year 1996, total systemwide sales within the United States were $16,370,000,000, while total systemwide sales outside the United States were $6,096,000,000. McDonald's is trying to expand its leadership position through convenience, superior value, and excellent operations.

Burger King

Burger King Corporation was founded in 1954 in Miami, Florida. In 1967, Pillsbury Company acquired Burger King Corporation as a subsidiary for $18 million. In 1988, Grand Metropolitan PLC acquired Pillsbury Company and its subsidiaries, including Burger King Corporation, for $5.79 billion.[22]

Since its Florida beginning more than 42 years ago, when a Burger King hamburger cost $.18 and a WHOPPER® sandwich cost $.37, Burger King Corporation has established restaurants around the world—from Australia to the Bahamas and from Venezuela to Seoul. As of March 31, 1997, there were 7,166 Burger King restaurants in operation in the United States and 1,863 internationally.

Just as the WHOPPER® sandwich was an immediate hit when introduced in 1975, each of the company's products provide the quality and convenience sought by today's consumers. The BK BROILER®, a grilled chicken sandwich introduced in 1990, already has captured a following of its own, selling up to a million daily immediately following its launch. Still, the WHOPPER® sandwich, one of the best-known hamburger sandwiches in the world, remains a perennial favorite. More than 1.5 billion WHOPPER® sandwiches are sold annually.

Burger King was the first fast food chain to introduce a dining room, allowing customers a chance to eat inside. Drive-through service was introduced in 1975 and now accounts for 60 percent of Burger King's business. "Take-out" represents another 15 percent of off-premises dining. Burger King has always taken great care in the design and construction of its restaurants so they will add to the attractiveness of communities in which they are located.

One of the factors that has helped to increase the company's expansion and growth has been the sale of restaurant franchises. Burger King's advertising campaigns have also contributed to its success. For fiscal year 1995 and 1996, Burger King's systemwide sales were $9.0 billion and $8.4 billion, respectively.[23]

Wendy's

Wendy's International is one of the industry's biggest comeback stories. After slumping in the mid-1980s, Wendy's saw its net income climb from less than $4 million in 1987 to more than $100 million in 1995. The ingredients of Wendy's success include a series of popular advertisements featuring founder Dave Thomas. Also important is its diverse menu that includes $.99 "value" items and limited time offers of specialty sandwiches.

Wendy's is accelerating its development of new units. At year-end 1995, Wendy's acquired the breakfast-oriented Tim Hortons chain, which has more than 1,100 outlets. At the end of 1996, there were 4,993 Wendy's restaurants in operation in the United States and in 33 other countries and territories. Of these restaurants, 1,315 were company owned and 3,618 were franchised. In addition, its franchisees operated 1,384 Tim Hortons restaurants in Canada and the United States. The total revenue for 1996 was almost $1.9 billion, with a net income of $156 million.[24]

Each Wendy's restaurant offers a relatively standard menu featuring hamburgers and filet of chicken sandwiches, which are prepared to order with the customer's choice of condiments. Wendy's menu also includes a salad bar, chili, baked potatoes, french fries, prepared salads, desserts, soft drinks, and a child's meal. Wendy's advertises on television and radio, and in newspapers with a variety of promotional campaigns. The company strives to maintain quality and uniformity throughout all of its restaurants. Wendy's does this by publishing detailed specifications for food products, preparation, and service. The company also continually conducts in-service training of employees and sponsors field visits from company supervisors. The company has registered certain trademarks and service marks in the United States Patent and Trademark Office and in similar offices in international jurisdictions.

Hardee's

Hardee's Food Systems is based in Rocky Mount, North Carolina, and currently operates a system of 3,080 quick-service restaurants in 39 states and 11 foreign countries, of which 790 are company owned and 2,290 are Hardee's franchisees. Hardee's became the indirect wholly owned subsidiary of Imasco Limited in 1981. In 1997, CKE Restaurants, Inc., acquired Hardee's Food Systems, Inc. as its wholly owned subsidiary.[25]

Hardee's menu consists of hamburgers, french fries, and soft drinks. In 1988, Hardee's became the first major fast food chain to completely switch to cholesterol-free vegetable oil for all fried products. Based on customers' desires for big burgers, Hardee's introduced the Monster Burger, which has two quarter-pound meat patties, three slices of American cheese, and eight strips of bacon, served on a seeded bun with mayonnaise. For the hungry breakfast customer, Hardee's offers the Breakfast Hoagie, which features bacon, eggs, and cheese on a toasted hoagie roll.

Hardee's results have been disappointing in recent years. Its systemwide sales in 1995 exceeded $4.5 billion, while in 1996 it only had $4 billion in sales.[26] However, putting Hardee's together with a strong and growing restaurant company such as CKE represents a unique opportunity to accelerate the recovery process and enhance growth prospects in what will become a nationwide restaurant operation.

Hardee's international development efforts are in the very early stages. It has restaurants in Hong Kong, Korea, the Middle East, and Latin America. International operations may provide an opportunity for franchising operations on a global basis.

SONIC'S STRATEGY

Sonic has established a dominant position in the drive-in hamburger business. It has a unique service delivery system that is fast and convenient, with personalized carhop service. This, together with its unique menu, offering high-quality, made-to-order food and specialty items, has enabled the company to post the leading average-unit sales growth for the industry.

Sonic has many unique products and services that differentiate it from its competition. The firm's drive-in concept eliminates waiting in lines at a drive-through window. In addition, there is no getting in and out of the car for on- or off-premises dining. Sonic's food is made to order upon arrival, unlike many of its competitors which "pre-cook" and place food under heating lamps. Sonic employs carhops who deliver the food directly to the customers' cars, emphasizing customer service; and, the company carries many unique menu items such as Extra Long Cheese Coney, Steak Sandwich, Tater Tots, Onion Rings, Cherry Limeades, Ocean Water, Slushes, Banana Splits, Hot Fudge Sundaes, Floats, and Flurrys.

Customers

According to industry surveys, Sonic has had the highest customer frequency rate for several consecutive years. Sonic customers are also extremely loyal and readily identify with the Sonic brand. In a recent poll of 4,000 consumers conducted by *Restaurants & Institutions* magazine, Sonic maintained its leadership in the hamburger segment of the fast food industry.[27]

Locations

In January 1997, the 1,600th Sonic Drive-In opened. With stores in 27 states, Sonic ranks as the nation's largest drive-in restaurant chain, and is the second largest hamburger chain in the Southwest. Exhibit 8 shows the number of Sonic restaurants in each state. As of August 31, 1997, the number of Sonic Drive-ins was 1,680. Of those, 256 were company owned and 1,424 were franchised. Sonic has greatly accelerated its program of opening company-owned restaurants. Over the last four fiscal years, the company has more than doubled the number of company-owned restaurants it operates.[28]

Franchises

In November 1996, *Forbes* named Sonic to the "200 Best Small Companies in America" for the third consecutive year.[29] Sonic is the fifth largest hamburger chain in the United States. It currently has franchising opportunities available for markets in

California, Colorado, Florida, Georgia, Illinois, Indiana, Nevada, North Carolina, South Carolina, and Virginia. The current franchise fee is $30,000, with an initial investment ranging from $245,000 to $325,000. This excludes land, site work, and building costs. The minimum financial requirements are $1,000,000 net worth and $300,000 in liquid assets. The royalty and advertising fees are 1.5% and 4 percent of restaurant sales, respectively. Experience with prior or current successful multiunit operations is required. The Sonic franchise term is 20 years.[30]

CURRENT FINANCIAL POSITION AND OPERATING RESULTS

The financial results of the turnaround changes can be explored in Exhibits 2 through 6. The current market value of Sonic is estimated at more than $260 million. From 1995 to 1996, revenues increased 22 percent, sales by company-owned restaurants increased 32 percent, net income increased 33 percent, earnings per share increased 17 percent, and working capital decreased 18 percent. During the same

EXHIBIT 3 *(dollars in thousands, except per share amounts and number of restaurants)*

	1996	1995	Percent change
Operations, for the Year			
Company revenues	$151,130	$123,760	22%
Income from operations	$ 27,080	$ 21,631	25
Net income	$ 16,560	$ 12,484	33
Net income per share	$ 1	$ 1	17
Return on average stockholders' equity	18.6%	21.2%	
Financial Position, at Year's End			
Total assets	$147,444	$105,331	40
Stockholders' equity	$109,683	$ 63,357	73
Systemwide Information			
Total sales	$984,784	$880,521	12
Average unit sales	$ 648	$ 615	5
Company-owned restaurants (year's end)	231	178	30
Franchised restaurants (year's end)	1,336	1,286	4
Total restaurants (year's end)	1,567	1,464	7

Source: Sonic Annual Report, 1996.

EXHIBIT 4 *Income Statement Data [n](in thousands, except per share amounts)*

	Year ended August 31,						
	1996	**1995**	**1994**	**1993**	**1992**	**1991**	**1990**
Sales by company-owned restaurants	$120,700	$91,438	$72,629	$58,228	$44,335	$36,370	$30,574
Franchised restaurants							
Franchise fees	1,453	1,409	1,144	1,513	1,251	819	627
Franchise royalties	23,315	20,392	14,703	12,872	10,580	8,644	7,138
Equipment sales	3,743	9,076	9,602	9,797	8,975	6,833	6,419
Other	1,919	1,445	1,626	1,380	1,535	1,214	1,102
Total revenues	151,130	123,760	99,704	83,790	66,676	53,880	45,860
Costs and expenses:							
Cost of restaurant sales	92,663	72,275	56,967	45,961	34,301	28,436	23,726
Cost of equipment sales	3,101	7,354	7,775	8,082	7,304	5,751	5,398
Selling, general and administrative	14,498	13,260	10,918	9,572	8,625	7,529	7,540
Depreciation and amortization	8,896	5,910	4,165	2,918	2,130	1,802	1,793
Provision for litigation costs	—	—	—	300	—	—	—
Minority interest in earnings of restaurant partnerships	4,806	3,259	2,723	2,640	2,678	2,169	1,888
Provision for impairment of long-lived assets	8,627	71	4,153	246	271	176	333
Income from operations	18,539	21,631	13,003	14,071	11,367	8,017	5,182
Interest expense	1,184	1,823	1,084	799	666	2,115	3,684
Interest income	(708)	(409)	(309)	(383)	(549)	(387)	(178)
Income before income taxes and extraordinary expense	18,063	20,217	12,228	13,655	11,250	6,289	1,676
Provision for income taxes	6,819	7,733	4,585	5,011	4,436	2,568	735
Income before extraordinary expense	$ 11,244	$12,484	$ 7,643	$ 8,644	$ 6,814	$ 3,721	$ 941
Extraordinary expense, net	—	—	—	—	—	594	—
Net income	$ 11,244	$12,484	$ 7,643	$ 8,644	$ 6,814	$ 3,127	$ 941
Earnings per share:							
Income before extraordinary expense	$ 0.84	$ 1.05	$ 0.64	$ 0.72	$ 0.58	$ 0.39	$ 0.13
Extraordinary expense, net	—	—	—	—	—	(0.06)	—
Net income	$ 0.84	$ 1.05	$ 0.64	$ 0.72	$ 0.58	$ 0.33	$ 0.13
Weighted average shares outstanding	13,449	11,842	11,954	11,970	11,803	9,662	7,527

Source: Sonic Annual Reports, 1994, 1995, and 1996.

EXHIBIT 5 *Balance Sheet Data (in thousands)*

	Year ended August 31,				
	1996	**1995**	**1994**	**1993**	**1992**
Working capital	$ 3,491	$ 4,249	$ 7,314	$ 7,383	$ 9,486
Property, equipment and capital leases, net	100,505	70,171	40,979	31,695	20,050
Total assets	147,444	105,331	76,982	63,517	50,303
Obligations under capital leases, net of current portion	8,985	5,793	6,351	5,400	4,866
Long-term debt, net of current portion	11,884	24,795	6,334	1,182	1,099
Stockholders' equity	109,683	63,357	54,377	46,750	35,964

Source: Sonic Annual Reports, 1994, 1995, and 1996.

EXHIBIT 6 *Restaurant Operating Data (dollars in thousands)*

	1996	1995	1994	1993	1992
Company-owned restaurants[1]	231	178	142	120	91
Franchised restaurants[1]	1,336	1,286	1,227	1,154	1,100
Total	1,567	1,464	1,369	1,274	1,191
Systemwide sales	$984,784	$880,521	$776,347	$691,490	$600,044
Percentage increase[2]	11.8%	13.4%	12.3%	15.2%	15.7%
Average sales per restaurant:					
Company-owned	601	577	558	547	526
Franchise	657	620	592	n/a	n/a
Systemwide	648	615	585	562	523
Change in comparable restaurant sales:[3]					
Company-owned	4.9%	1.9%	2.5%	5.3%	8.9%
Franchise	5.1%	3.9%	2.9%	n/a	n/a
Systemwide	5.0%	3.6%	2.8%	6.2%	8.0%

[1]Number of restaurants open at end of period.
[2]Represents percentage increase from the comparable period in the prior year.
[3]Represents percentage increase for restaurants open in both the reported and prior years.
Source: Sonic Annual Reports, 1994, 1995, and 1996.

EXHIBIT 7 *Largest U.S. Hamburger Chains*

Chain	Parent company	Fiscal year ending	Systemwide U.S. sales (mill. $)	Total Units at fiscal year end
McDonald's	McDonald's Corporation	12/96	16,370	21,022
Burger King	Grand Metro. Plc	9/96	8,400	9,029
Wendy's	Wendy's Int'l	12/96	5,389	4,993
Hardee's	Imasco Ltd.	12/96	4,000	3,083
Sonic Drive-In	Sonic Corp.	8/96	985	1,567

Sources: McDonald's Annual Report, 1996, p. 18; http://www.burgerking.com/company/facts.htm; Wendy's Annual Report, 1996, http://www.wendys.com/annual.htm; http://www.hardeesrestaurants.com/hardees/history/timeline/data.html; Sonic Annual Report, 1996. Http://www.sonicdriven.com/s13.htm.

time period, systemwide sales increased 11.8 percent, and same-store sales increased 4.9 percent for company-owned stores and 5.1 percent for franchise stores.[31]

In addition, Sonic's cost of operations declined from 79.0 percent of sales in 1995 to 76.8 percent of sales in 1996. This change was attributable to a combination of a 2.5 percent average price increase, a 10% reduction in promotional menu price discounting, reduction in food and packaging costs because

of market changes, purchasing consolidation and stronger purchasing negotiations, and improved cost controls on an operational level.

STRATEGIC CHALLENGES

J. Clifford Hudson, president and chief executive officer of Sonic Corp. & Subsidiaries, and his management team are confronted with an enormous

EXHIBIT 8 *Sonic Drive-In Locations as of August 31, 1997*

State	Franchise Drive-Ins[a]	Company-Owned Drive-Ins[b]
Alabama	20	35
Arkansas	103	15
Arizona	33	0
California	4	0
Colorado	21	0
Florida	2	11
Georgia	23	2
Iowa	1	0
Illinois	5	0
Indiana	3	0
Kansas	88	7
Kentucky	23	9
Louisiana	80	15
Missouri	99	28
Mississippi	88	0
North Carolina	14	16
Nebraska	2	0
New Mexico	56	0
Nevada	7	0
Ohio	3	0
Oklahoma	168	22
South Carolina	31	0
Tennessee	113	26
Texas	433	63
Utah	1	0
Virginia	2	7
West Virginia	1	0

Source: Sonic Corporation.
[a]1,424 franchise drive-ins
[b]256 company-owned drive-ins

challenge. They must decide how to make a successful company remain successful.

Sonic has begun to develop a strong brand name. In the 16th annual "Choice of Chains," a survey of fast food consumers conducted by *Restaurant & Institutions*, it trailed only Wendy's.[32] Sonic is now considering selling clothing with its brand name to exploit this new-found loyalty.[33] The question for Hudson and his management team is how they can strengthen this brand image and increase sales.

Another positive trend for Sonic is its success in repeat customer business. CREST (Consumer Reports on Eating Share Trends) surveys indicate that Sonic has the highest ratio of customer frequency in

the industry. But, can Sonic continue to compete against the increasingly sophisticated menu offerings of industry leaders? Sonic's relatively narrow focus in the hamburger segment has been successful so far. The question is whether Hudson's management team will be creative and innovative enough with menu offerings in this increasingly competitive industry.

Hudson's management team must also determine appropriate growth pace and locations. As Sonic continues to build 12 company-owned units per quarter, the organizational skills to manage these large numbers must grow as well.[34] Hudson has so far successfully "stolen" talent from other fast food chains and developed it internally as well. In addition to number of units, location is a pressing issue. Sonic has acquired a significant presence in the Sunbelt but has not yet penetrated the northern United States (see Exhibit 8). A northward expansion will include special challenges to a drive-in chain because of the significantly different climate. If Sonic chooses to go northward, should it build "dine-ins"? If it does build "dine-in" seating space, will Sonic be abandoning its competitive focus?

Finally, Hudson and his team need to address whether or not to continue the Sonic philosophy of building a "partnering relationship." This special relationship is unique to Sonic; other market leaders keep a tighter grip on franchisee management. This relationship undoubtedly benefited the company in its turnaround effort in the late 1980s and in its exponential growth in the 1990s. But is this the kind of relationship that will work in the hyper-competitive fast food industry in the future? What makes Sonic successful in the future may be different from what made it successful in the past.

NOTES

1. Lisa Litzenberger, 1997, *Fast Food Facts*, Office of the Minnesota Attorney General, October, p. 1(4).
2. *Moody's Industry Review*, Restaurants, September 19, 1997 v. 16, no. 12: 5.
3. Ibid.
4. *1996 Technomic Top 100: Update & Analysis of the 100 Largest U.S. Chain Restaurant Companies*, Technomic Information Services, Appendix D-1.
5. http://www.govcensus.com. (Resident Population Projection by Age and Sex: 1996–2050; Households, Families, Subfamilies, Married Couples, and Unrelated Individuals.)
6. http://www.sonicdrivein.com/s07.htm#Long. *The Long and Winding Road—Sonic Turns 40.*
7. Ibid.
8. Interview with Steve Vaughan, Sonic Controller, November 13, 1997.
9. http://www.sonicdrivein.com/s07.htm#Long. *The Long and Winding Road.—Sonic Turns 40.*
10. Interview with Steve Vaughan, Sonic Controller, November 13, 1997.
11. *Sonic 1994 Annual Report*, p. 18 and *Sonic 1996 Annual Report*, p. 19.
12. Interview with Scott McLain, Sonic Chief Financial Officer, August 10, 1996.
13. Interview with Luwanna Haynes, Sonic Administrative Assistant, October 14, 1997.
14. Ibid.
15. Interview with Mark Inman, Sonic Internal Auditor, July 15, 1996.
16. Anita Lienert, 1996, Setting off a Sonic boom, *Management Review*, December, v. 85, no. 12: 3.
17. Ibid.
18. *Sonic 1994 Annual Report*, p. 10.
19. Challenges and Opportunities in the Graying '90s, *Standard & Poor Industry Surveys*, April 18, 1996, p. 53.
20. Interview with Luwanna Haynes, Sonic Administrative Assistant, October 14, 1997.
21. *McDonald's 1996 Annual Report*, p. 18.
22. http://www.burgerking.com/company/history.htm.
23. http://www.burgerking.com/company/facts.htm.
24. http//www.wendys.com/annual.htm. *1996AnnualReport.*
25. http://www.hardeesrestaurants.com/hardees/history/timeline/data.html.
26. http://www.hardeesrestaurants.com/hardees/news/releases/data9.html.
27. http://www.sonicdrivein.com/s0l.htm. *Investing in America's Drive-In*, p. 2.
28. http://www.sonicdrivein.com/s13.htm. *Where's Sonic* (as of August 31, 1997), p. 1.
29. http://www.sonicdrivein.com/s10.htm. *A Franchise Success Story*, p. 1.
30. Ibid.
31. *Sonic 1996 Annual Report*, p. 12.
32. Anita Lienert, 1996, Setting off a Sonic boom, *Management Review*, December, v. 85, no. 12, p. 2.
33. Interview with Luwanna Haynes, Sonic Administrative Assistant, October 14, 1997.
34. http://www.sonicdrivein.com/s01.htm.

Southwest Airlines, 1996

Andrew Inkpen
Valerie DeGroot

Thunderbird, The American Graduate School of International Management

In January 1996, Southwest Airlines (Southwest) entered the Florida and southeastern U.S. markets. The company planned to operate 78 daily flights to Tampa, Fort Lauderdale, and Orlando by August of the following year. With the expansion into Florida, the northeast remained the only major U.S. air traffic region where Southwest did not compete. The northeast U.S. market had generally been avoided by low-fare airlines such as Southwest because of airport congestion, air traffic control delays, frequent inclement weather, and dominance by a few major airlines. Airports such Logan International in Boston, J. F. Kennedy International in New York, and Newark International were among the busiest and most congested airports in the country. Continental Airline's attempt to introduce widespread, low-fare operations in the East during 1994–1995 was a financial disaster.

With the move into Florida and the potential challenges associated with the northeastern market, questions were being raised about Southwest's ability to maintain its position as America's most consistently profitable airline. In particular, there were concerns whether Southwest was growing too fast and deviating from its proven strategy. Would entry into the Florida market and possibly the northeastern market

jeopardize 25 years of success? Success resulted in a focused strategy based on frequent flights, rapid turnarounds at airport gates, and a careful selection of markets and airports that avoided ground and air traffic control delays. Herb Kelleher, the charismatic president, co-founder, and chief executive officer of the airline, wrote to his employees in 1993: "Southwest has had more opportunities for growth than it has airplanes. Yet, unlike other airlines, it has avoided the trap of growing beyond its means. Whether you are talking with an officer or a ramp agent, employees just don't seem to be enamored of the idea that bigger is better."[1]

THE U.S. AIRLINE INDUSTRY

The nature of the U.S. commercial airline industry was permanently altered in October 1978 when President Jimmy Carter signed the Airline Deregulation Act. Before deregulation, the Civil Aeronautics Board regulated airline route entry and exit, passenger fares, mergers and acquisitions, and airline rates of return. Typically, two or three carriers provided service in a given market, although there were routes covered by only one carrier. Cost increases were passed along to customers, and price competition was almost nonexistent. The airlines operated as if there were only two market segments: those who could afford to fly and those who couldn't.[2]

Copyright 1997 Thunderbird, The American Graduate School of International Management. All rights reserved. This case was prepared for the basis of classroom discussion only and is not intended to illustrate either effective or ineffective management.

Deregulation sent airline fares tumbling and allowed many new firms to enter the market. The financial impact on both established and new airlines was enormous. The fuel crisis of 1979 and the air traffic controllers' strike in 1981 contributed to the industry's difficulties, as did the severe recession that hit the United States during the early 1980s. During the first decade of deregulation, more than 150 carriers, many of them new start-up airlines, collapsed into bankruptcy. Eight of the major 11 airlines dominating the industry in 1978 ended up filing for bankruptcy, merging with other carriers, or simply disappearing from the radar screen. Collectively, the industry made enough money during this period to buy two Boeing 747s (Exhibit 1).[3] The three major carriers that survived intact—Delta, United, and American—ended up with 80 percent of all domestic U.S. air traffic and 67 percent of trans-Atlantic business.[4]

Competition and lower fares led to greatly expanded demand for airline travel. By the mid-1990s, the airlines were having trouble meeting this demand. Travel increased from 200 million travelers in 1974 to 500 million in 1995, yet only five new runways were built during this time period. During the 1980s, many airlines acquired significant levels of new debt in efforts to service the increased travel demand. Long-term debt-to-capitalization ratios increased dramatically: Eastern's went from 62 to 473 percent, TWA's went from 62 to 115 percent, and Continental's went from 62 to 96 percent. In contrast, United and Delta maintained their debt ratios at less than 60 percent, and American Airline's ratio dropped to 34 percent.

Despite the financial problems experienced by many fledgling airlines started after deregulation, new firms continued to enter the market. Between 1992 and 1995, 69 new airlines were certified by the FAA. Most of these airlines competed with limited route structures and lower fares than the major airlines. The new low-fare airlines created a second tier of service providers that save consumers billions of dollars annually and provided service in markets abandoned or ignored by major carriers. One such start-up was Kiwi Airlines, founded by former employees of the defunct Eastern and Pan Am airlines. Kiwi was funded largely by employees: pilots paid $50,000 each to get jobs and other employees paid $5,000.

Despite fostering competition and the growth of new airlines, deregulation created a significant regional disparity in ticket prices and adversely affected service to small and remote communities. Airline workers generally suffered, with inflation-adjusted average employee wages falling from $42,928 in 1978 to $37,985 in 1988. About 20,000 airline industry employees were laid off in the early 1980s, while productivity of the remaining employees rose 43 percent during the same period. In a variety of cases, bankruptcy filings were used to diminish the role of unions and reduce unionized wages.

Industry Economics

About 80 percent of airline operating costs were fixed or semivariable. The only true variable costs were travel agency commissions, food costs, and ticketing fees. The operating costs of an airline flight depended primarily on the distance traveled, not the number of passengers on board. For example, the crew and ground staff sizes were determined by the type of aircraft, not the passenger load. Therefore, once an airline established its route structure, most of its operating costs were fixed.

Because of this high fixed-cost structure, the airlines developed sophisticated software tools to maximize capacity utilization, known as *load factor*. Load factor was calculated by dividing RPM (revenue passenger miles—the number of passengers carried multiplied by the distance flown) by ASM (available seat miles—the number of seats available for sale multiplied by the distance flown).

On each flight by one of the major airlines (excluding Southwest and the low-fare carriers), there were typically a dozen categories of fares. The airlines analyzed historical travel patterns on individual routes to determine how many seats to sell at each fare level. All of the major airlines used this type of analysis and flexible pricing practice, known as a *yield management system*. These systems enabled the airlines to manage their seat inventories and the prices paid for those seats. The objective was to sell more seats on each flight at higher yields (total passenger yield was passenger revenue from scheduled operations divided by scheduled RPMs). The higher the ticket price, the better the yield.

Although reducing operating costs was a high priority for the airlines, the nature of the cost structure limited cost-reduction opportunities. Fuel costs (about 13 percent of total costs) were largely beyond the control of the airlines, and many of the larger

C-428

EXHIBIT 1 *Airline Operating Data, 1986–1994*

Seat-Miles Flown

	American	America-West	Continental	Delta	Eastern	Northwest	Pan-American	SouthWest	TransWorld	United	USAir	Total All Majors
1994	110,658	17,852	49,762	98,104		52,110	0	29,624	27,938	95,965	58,311	540,324
1993	117,719	16,980	49,690	99,852		52,623	0	34,759	25,044	98,652	55,918	551,237
1992	114,418	18,603	49,143	100,904		52,430	0	21,371	30,483	89,605	56,027	532,984
1991	104,616	19,460	48,742	94,350		48,847	9,042	18,440	29,684	88,092	56,470	517,743
1990	102,864	18,139	48,385	87,748	25,299	47,210	12,157	16,456	33,942	86,085	58,014	536,299
1989	98,638	13,523	47,107	82,440	15,489	44,372	11,670	14,788	35,246	82,758	40,652	486,683
1988	88,620	11,994	53,343	79,719	41,126	39,349	10,331	13,370	35,024	84,240	28,234	485,350
1987	77,724	10,318	54,626	71,504	50,156	41,499	8,217	11,457	33,566	86,246	20,014	465,327
1986	66,901	4,296	27,778	50,448	52,556	27,561	8,901	9,712	29,534	78,568	18,254	374,509
Total	**882,158**	**131,165**	**428,576**	**765,069**	**184,626**	**406,001**	**60,318**	**169,977**	**280,461**	**790,211**	**391,894**	**4,490,456**

Revenue per Passenger-Miles (RPMs) (in cents)

	American	America-West	Continental	Delta	Eastern	Northwest	Pan-American	SouthWest	TransWorld	United	USAir
1994	13.11	10.81	11.50	13.93		13.93	0	11.65	12.67	11.81	15.92
1993	13.65	11.13	11.97	14.66		13.06	0	11.92	12.78	12.49	17.94
1992	12.03	10.36	11.01	14.02		12.21	0	11.78	11.13	11.88	16.97
1991	13.11	10.00	11.79	14.30		12.79	10.02	11.25	11.31	12.21	16.93
1990	12.86	11.14	12.48	14.21		13.24	11.65	11.48	12.34	12.71	16.37
1989	12.27	11.84	12.04	13.91	11.71	13.02	11.98	10.49	12.10	12.18	15.83
1988	11.92	10.52	10.61	13.52	12.00	12.54	10.94	10.74	11.47	10.86	15.33
1987	11.06	9.66	9.34	131.10	11.02	11.73	9.97	10.02	11.02	10.10	14.91
1986	10.23	9.90	8.56	13.54	11.26	10.48	10.12	10.59	10.07	9.87	14.93

Passenger Load Factor (percent)

	American	America-West	Continental	Delta	Eastern	Northwest	Pan-American	SouthWest	TransWorld	United	USAir
1994	63.25	67.99	62.48	64.68		64.88	0.00	66.80	62.73	69.80	62.02
1993	59.21	65.56	62.20	61.52		63.51	0.00	68.09	62.38	63.80	58.59
1992	63.12	61.62	63.14	60.59		62.24	0.00	64.52	62.94	66.15	58.60
1991	60.86	64.94	61.80	59.95		62.90	60.53	61.14	60.94	64.23	58.22
1990	61.48	60.99	58.42	57.98	60.80	62.53	60.00	60.60	58.90	63.85	59.54
1989	63.6	57.7	60.3	63.6	61.9	60.9	61.2	62.7	59.4	65.4	61.2
1988	63.1	57.9	58.8	57.6	61.8	61.8	63.4	57.7	59.9	67.4	61.3
1987	63.7	56.1	60.7	55.5	65.3	61.8	64.1	58.9	62.0	65.0	65.3
1986	65.6	61.0	62.7	57.4	60.6	54.9	51.4	58.3	59.5	65.6	61.1

Source: Department of Transportation.

C-429

EXHIBIT 1 *Airline Operating Data, 1986–1994 (cont.)*

Operating Revenues, in millions of dollars

	American	America-West	Continental	Delta	Eastern	Northwest	Pan-American	SouthWest	TransWorld	United	USAir	Total All Majors
1994	10,631	1,414	4,091	9,514		5,325		2,417	2,555	8,966	6,394	51,307
1993	10,828	1,332	4,128	9,653		4,928		2,067	2,325	8,794	6,364	50,419
1992	9,902	1,281	3,840	9,164		4,464		1,685	2,510	7,861	5,974	46,681
1991	9,429	1,359	4,014	8,593		4,356	596	1,314	2,464	7,790	5,895	45,810
1990	9,203	1,322	4,036	7,697		4,298	946	1,187	2,878	7,946	6,085	45,598
1989	8,670	998	3,896	7,780	1,295	3,944	957	1,015	2,918	7,463	4,160	43,096
1988	7,548	781	3,682	6,684	3,423	3,395	804	860	2,777	7,006	2,803	39,763
1987	6,369	577	3,404	5,638	4,054	3,328	625	699	2,668	6,500	2,070	35,932
1986	5,321	330	1,676	4,245	4,093	1,815	553	620	2,064	5,727	1,787	28,231
Total	**77,901**	**9,394**	**32,767**	**68,968**	**12,865**	**35,853**	**4,481**	**11,864**	**23,159**	**68,053**	**41,532**	

Net Operating Income (Loss), in millions of dollars

	American	America-West	Continental	Delta	Eastern	Northwest	Pan-American	SouthWest	TransWorld	United	USAir	Total All Majors
1994	432	146	(145)	123		725		290	(81)	262	(466)	1,286
1993	357	121	56	335		268		281	(63)	184	(143)	1,396
1992	(251)	(64)	(183)	(225)		(203)	(186)	182	(191)	(354)	(397)	(1,686)
1991	40	(79)	(218)	(115)		17	(280)	62	(233)	(412)	(233)	(1,357)
1990	103	(32)	(191)	(176)		(132)	(118)	82	(134)	(34)	(437)	(1,231)
1989	709	48	124	677	(666)	57	(181)	98	10	302	(239)	1,002
1988	794	18	(87)	441	(187)	19	(260)	86	113	461	144	1,621
1987	483	(35)	(56)	383	66	72	(283)	41	79	97	263	1,133
1986	378	4	91	212	61	(25)		81	(77)	51	164	657
Total	**3,045**	**127**	**(609)**	**1,655**	**(726)**	**798**	**1,308**	**1,203**	**(577)**	**557**	**(1,344)**	

Source: Department of Transportation.

airlines' restrictive union agreements limited labor flexibility. Although newer aircraft were much more fuel efficient than older models, most airlines had sharply lowered their new aircraft orders to avoid taking on more debt. At the end of June 1990, U.S. airlines had outstanding orders to buy 2,748 aircraft. At the end of June 1996, orders had fallen to 1,111.[5] (A new Boeing 737 cost about $28 million in 1995.)

To manage their route structures, all of the major airlines (except Southwest) maintained their operations around a "hub-and-spoke" network. The spokes fed passengers from outlying points into a central airport—the hub—where passengers could travel to additional hubs or their final destination. For example, to fly from Phoenix to Boston on Northwest Airlines, a typical route would involve a flight from Phoenix to Northwest's Detroit hub. The passenger would then take a second flight from Detroit to Boston.

Establishing a major hub in a city like Chicago or Atlanta required an investment of as much as $150 million for gate acquisition and terminal construction. Although hubs created inconveniences for travelers, hub systems were an efficient means of dis-

tributing services across a wide network. The major airlines were very protective of their so-called "fortress" hubs and used the hubs to control various local markets. For example, Northwest controlled more than 78 percent of the local traffic in Detroit and 84 percent in Minneapolis. When Southwest entered the Detroit market, the only available gates were already leased by Northwest. Northwest subleased gates to Southwest at rates 18 times higher than Northwest's costs. Southwest eventually withdrew from Detroit, one of only three markets the company had abandoned in its history. (Denver and Beaumont, Texas, were the other two.)

Recent Airline Industry Performance

U.S. airlines suffered a combined loss of $13 billion from 1990 to 1994 (Exhibit 1).[6] High debt levels plagued the industry. In 1994, the earnings picture began to change with the industry as a whole reducing its losses to $278 million.[7] Overall expansion and health returned to the industry in 1995 and 1996. In 1996, net earnings were a record $2.4 billion (see Exhibit 2 for 1995 airline performance and Exhibit 3 for

C-431

EXHIBIT 2 *Airline Performance*

	Revenue (in $000s)	Net Profit (in $000s)	RPM (in 000s)	ASM (in 000s)
American	15,501,000	167,000	102,900,000	155,300,000
United	14,943,000	349,000	111,811,000	158,569,000
Delta	12,194,000	510,000	86,400,000	130,500,000
Northwest	9,080,000	392,000	62,500,000	87,500,000
USAir	7,474,000	119,000	37,618,000	58,163,000
Continental	5,825,000	224,000	40,023,000	61,006,000
TWA	3,320,000	(227,400)	25,068,683	38,186,111
Southwest	2,872,751	182,626	23,327,804	36,180,001
America West	1,600,000	53,800	13,300,000	19,400,000
Alaska	1,417,500	17,300	9,335,000	15,299,000
American Trans Air	715,009	8,524	4,183,692	5,951,162
Tower Air	490,472	10,689	1,208,001	1,455,996
Mesa	454,538	14,012	1,179,397	2,310,895
Conair	418,466	N/A	1,187,706	2,274,695
ValuJet	367,800	67,800	2,600,000	3,800,000
Hawaiian	346,904	(5,506)	3,171,365	4,238,320
Atlantic Southeast	328,725	51,137	763,000	1,700,000
Midwest Express	259,155	19,129	1,150,338	1,794,924
Reno Air	256,508	1,951	2,090,017	3,322,475

Source: *Business Travel News,* May 27, 1996, and *Air Transport World,* March 1996.

EXHIBIT 3 *Airline Market Shares*

1995 Company Rankings	% Market Share	1985 Company Rankings	% Market Share
United	21.0	American	13.3
American	19.3	United	12.5
Delta	16.0	Eastern	10.0
Northwest	11.7	TWA	9.6
Continental	7.5	Delta	9.0
USAir	7.2	Pan Am	8.1
TWA	4.7	NWA	6.7
Southwest	4.4	Continental	4.9
America West	2.5	People Express	3.3
American Trans Air	1.2	Republic	3.2
Others	4.5	Others	19.4
Total	100.0	Total	100.0

Sources: Department of Transportation and Standard & Poor's, cited by *Industry Surveys*, February 1, 1996.

1995 market share ratings). For 1996, revenue forecasts were $7.2 billion with a net profit of $3 billion.

In 1996, for the first time in 10 years, the industry had a profitable first quarter ($110 million). Numerous statistics indicated that the industry was in good shape: load factors were up to 68–69 percent in 1996; fares were up 5 percent; and yields were up to 13.52 cents per passenger mile. The break-even load factor fell 2.5 points to about 65 percent and unit costs dropped by 0.4 percent in 1995.[8] The expiration of a 10 percent domestic ticket tax resulted in net lower-priced tickets to customers despite increased fares. Traffic growth outpaced the 1.7 percent industry rise in capacity.

Future Pressures on the Industry

Despite the recent positive financial performance, concerns over fare wars, overcapacity in some markets, increased fuel prices, and the possibility of economic recession created significant uncertainty about the future. In particular, cost pressures were expected from several factors:

1. *Labor costs.* The average salary per airline employee from 1987 to 1996 rose at a rate faster than the increase in the CPI index (4.4 percent increase in labor costs compared with a 3.7 per-

cent CPI increase over the same period).[9] Pressure from labor was expected to increase as employees sought a share of the airlines' recent record profits. The possibility of new federal regulations concerning aircrew flight and duty time requirements were also an issue. It was estimated that the potential costs from regulation changes could be as high as $1.2 billion in the first year and $800 million in each subsequent year.

2. *Aircraft maintenance.* The aging of the general aircraft population meant higher maintenance costs and eventual aircraft replacement. The introduction of stricter government regulations for older planes placed new burdens on those operating them.

3. *Debt servicing.* The airline industry's debt load of approximately 65 percent greatly exceeded U.S. industry averages of about 40 percent.

4. *Fuel costs.* Long-term jet fuel cost was uncertain. Prices had risen 11 cents per gallon from July 1995 to May 1996. Proposed fuel taxes could cost the industry as much as $500 million a year.

5. *Air traffic delays.* Increased air traffic control delays caused by higher travel demand and related airport congestion were expected to negatively influence airlines' profitability.

SOUTHWEST AIRLINES BACKGROUND

In 1966, Herb Kelleher was practicing law in San Antonio when a client named Rollin King proposed starting a short-haul airline similar to California-based Pacific Southwest Airlines. The airline would fly the "Golden Triangle" of Houston, Dallas, and San Antonio and by staying within Texas, avoid federal regulations. Kelleher and King incorporated a company, raised initial capital, and filed for regulatory approval from the Texas Aeronautics Commission. Unfortunately, the other Texas-based airlines, namely Braniff, Continental, and Trans Texas (later called Texas International) opposed the idea and waged a battle to prohibit Southwest from flying. Kelleher argued the company's case before the Texas Supreme Court, which ruled in Southwest's favor. The U.S. Supreme Court refused to hear an appeal filed by the other airlines. In late 1970, it looked as if the company could begin flying.

Southwest began building a management team and purchased three surplus Boeing 737s. Meanwhile, Braniff and Texas International continued their efforts to prevent Southwest from flying. The underwriters of Southwest's initial public stock offering withdrew and a restraining order against the company was obtained two days before its scheduled inaugural flight. Kelleher again argued his company's case before the Texas Supreme Court, which ruled in Southwest's favor a second time, lifting the restraining order. Southwest Airlines began flying the next day, June 18, 1971.[10]

When Southwest began flying to three Texas cities, the firm had three aircraft and 25 employees. Initial flights were out of Dallas' older Love Field airport and Houston's Hobby Airport, both of which were closer to downtown than the major international airports. Flamboyant from the beginning, original flights were staffed by flight attendants in hot pants. By 1996, the flight attendant uniform had evolved into khakis and polo shirts. The "Luv" theme was a staple of the airline from the outset and became the company's ticker symbol on Wall Street.

Southwest management quickly discovered that there were two types of travelers: convenience, time-oriented business travelers and price-sensitive leisure travelers. To cater to both groups, Southwest developed a two-tiered pricing structure. In 1972, Southwest was charging $20 to fly between Houston, Dallas, and San Antonio, undercutting the $28 fares of the other carriers. After an experiment with $10 fares, Southwest decided to sell seats on weekdays until 7:00 P.M. for $26 and after 7:00 P.M. and on weekends for $13.[11] In response, in January 1973, Braniff Airlines began charging $13 for its Dallas-Houston Hobby flights. This resulted in one of Southwest's most famous ads, which had the caption "Nobody's going to shoot Southwest out of the sky for a lousy $13." Southwest offered travelers the opportunity to pay $13 or $26 and receive a free bottle of liquor. More than 75 percent of the passengers chose the $26 fare and Southwest became the largest distributor of Chivas Regal scotch whiskey in Texas. In 1975, Braniff abandoned the Dallas-Houston Hobby route. When Southwest entered the Cleveland market, the unrestricted one-way fare between Cleveland and Chicago was $310 on other carriers; Southwest's fare was $59.[12] One of Southwest's problems was convincing passengers that its low fares were not just introductory promotions but regular fares.

SOUTHWEST OPERATIONS

Although Southwest grew to be one of the largest airlines in the United States, the firm did not deviate from its initial focus: short-haul (less than 500 miles), point-to-point flights; a fleet consisting only of Boeing 737s; high-frequency flights; low fares; and no international flights. In 1995, the average Southwest one-way fare was $69. The average stage length of Southwest flights was 394 miles, with flights of 600 miles making up less than 2.5 percent of the airline's capacity. Kelleher indicated in an interview that it would be unlikely that the company's longer flights (those more than 600 miles) would ever exceed 10 percent of its business.[13] On average, Southwest had more than 40 departures per day per city, and each plane flew about 10 flights daily, almost twice the industry average.[14] Planes were used an average of 11.5 hours a day, compared with the industry's 8.6 hours per day average.[15] Southwest's cost per available seat mile was the lowest in the industry (Exhibit 4) and the average age of its fleet in 1995 was 7.9 years, the lowest for the major carriers. Southwest also had the best safety record in the airline business.

EXHIBIT 4 *Cost Per Available Seat Mile Data*

Short-Haul Costs*
(Based on standardized seating, 500-mile hop)

Company	Plane	Cost (in cents)	Percent
American	F-100	12.95	202
USAir	F-100	12.05	187
USAir	737-300	11.49	179
United	737-300	11.17	174
American	MD-80	11.02	171
Continental	737-300	10.18	158
Northwest	DC-9-30	10.18	158
TWA	DC-9-30	9.67	150
Continental	MD-80	9.58	149
Delta	MD-80	8.77	136
Northwest	MD-80	8.76	136
TWA	MD-80	8.29	129
America West	737-300	7.96	124
Alaska	MD-80	7.59	118
ValuJet	DC-9-30	6.58	102
Reno Air	MD-80	6.53	102
Southwest	737-300	6.43	100

Long-Haul Costs
(Based on standardized seating, 1,400-mile hop)

Company	Plane	Cost (in cents)	Percent
USAir	757	6.72	134
American	757	6.70	134
United	757	6.51	130
Northwest	757	5.83	116
Continental	757	5.70	114
Delta	757	5.61	112
American Trans Air	757	5.40	108
America West	757	5.02	100

Source: Roberts Roach & Associates, cited in *Air Transport World,* June 1996, p. 1.
*Second Quarter 1995 data.

Southwest was the only major airline to operate without hubs. Point-to-point service provided maximum convenience for passengers who wanted to fly between two cities, but insufficient demand could make such nonstop flights economically unfeasible. For that reason, the hub-and-spoke approach was generally assumed to generate cost savings for airlines through operational efficiencies. However, Southwest saw it another way: hub-and-spoke arrangements resulted in planes spending more time on the ground waiting for customers to arrive from connecting points.

Turnaround time—the time it takes to unload a waiting plane and load it for the next flight—was 15 minutes for Southwest, compared with the industry average of 45 minutes. This time savings was accomplished with a gate crew 50 percent smaller than that of other airlines. Pilots sometimes helped unload bags when schedules were tight. Flight attendants regularly assisted in the cleanup of airplanes between flights.

Relative to the other major airlines, Southwest had a "no frills" approach to services: reserved seating was not offered and meals were not served. Customers were handed numbered or color-coded boarding passes based on their check-in order. Seating was first come, first served. As a cost-saving measure, the color-coded passes were reusable. As to why the airline did not have assigned seating, Kelleher explained: "It used to be we only had about four people on the whole plane, so the idea of assigned seats just made people laugh. Now the reason is you can turn the airplanes quicker at the gate. And if you can turn an airplane quicker, you can have it fly more routes each day. That generates more revenue, so you can offer lower fares."[16]

Unlike some of the major carriers, Southwest rarely offered delayed customers a hotel room or long-distance telephone calls. Southwest did not use a computerized reservation system, preferring to have travel agents and customers book flights through its reservation center or vending machines in airports. Southwest was the first national carrier to sell seats from an Internet site. Southwest was also one of the first airlines to use ticketless travel, first offering the service on January 31, 1995. By June 1996, 35 percent of the airline's passengers were flying ticketless, at a cost savings of $25 million per year.[17] The company was a 1996 Computerworld Smithsonian Awards Finalist for the rapid development and installation of its ticketless system within a four-month time frame.

Over the years, Southwest's choice of markets resulted in significant growth in air travel at those locations. In Texas, traffic between the Rio Grande Valley (Harlingen) and the "Golden Triangle" grew from 123,000 to 325,000 within 11 months of South-

west's entering the market.[18] Within a year of Southwest's arrival, the Oakland-Burbank route became the 25th largest passenger market, up from 179th. The Chicago-Louisville market tripled in size 30 days after Southwest began flying that route. Southwest was the dominant carrier in a number of cities, ranking first in market share in more than 50 percent of the largest U.S. city-pair markets. Exhibit 5 shows a comparison of Southwest in 1971 and 1995.

Southwest's Performance

Southwest bucked the airline industry trend by earning a profit in 23 consecutive years (see Exhibit 6 for Southwest's financial performance). Southwest was the only major U.S. airline to make a profit in 1992. Even taking into account the losses in its first two years of operation, the company averaged an annual 12.07 percent return on investment. In 1995, for the fourth year in a row, Southwest received the coveted Triple Crown award given by the U.S. Department of Transportation for having the best on-time performance, best luggage handling record, and fewest customer complaints. No other airline achieved that record for even one month.

Southwest accomplished its enviable record by challenging accepted norms and setting competitive thresholds for the other airlines to emulate. The company had established numerous new industry standards. In 1991, Southwest flew more passengers per employee (2,318 versus the industry average of 848) than any other airline, while at the same time having the fewest number of employees per aircraft

C-435

EXHIBIT 5 *Southwest 25-Year Comparison*

	1971	1995
Size of fleet	4	224
Number of employees at year-end	195	19,933
Number of passengers carried	108,554	44,785,573
Number of cites served	3	45
Number of trips flown	6,051	685,524
Total operating revenues	2,133,000	2,872,751,000
Net income (losses)	(3,753,000)	182,626,000
Stockholders' equity	3,318,000	1,427,318,000
Total assets	**22,083,000**	**3,256,122,000**

Source: K. Freiberg and J. Freiberg, 1996, *Nuts: Southwest Airlines Crazy Recipe for Business and Personal Success,* Austin, TX, Band Press, p. 326.

EXHIBIT 6 *Southwest Airlines 10-Year Financial Summary*

Selected Consolidated Financial Data[1]
(in thousands except per share amounts)

	1995	1994	1993	1992	1991	1990	1989	1988	1987	1986
Operating revenues:										
Passenger	$2,760,756	$2,497,765	$1,144,421	$973,568	$1,267,897	$1,144,421	$973,568	$828,343	$751,649	$742,287
Freight	65,825	54,419	42,897	33,088	26,428	22,196	18,771	14,433	13,428	13,621
Charter and other	46,170	39,749	37,434	146,063	84,961	70,659	65,390	17,658	13,251	12,882
Total operating revenues	2,872,751	2,591,933	2,296,673	1,802,979	1,379,286	1,237,276	1,057,729	860,434	778,328	768,790
Operating expenses	2,559,220	2,275,224	2,004,700	1,609,175	1,306,675	1,150,015	955,689	774,454	747,881	679,827
Operating income	313,531	316,709	291,973	193,804	72,611	87,261	102,040	85,980	30,447[9]	88,963
Other expenses (income), net	8,391	17,186	32,335	36,361	18,725	(6,827)[6]	(13,696)[7]	620[8]	1,374[10]	23,517
Income before income taxes	305,140	299,523	259,637	157,443	53,886	80,434	115,736	85,360	29,073	65,446
Provision for income taxes[3]	122,514	120,192	105,353	60,058	20,738	29,829	41,231	27,408	8,918	15,411
Net income[3]	$182,626	$179,331	$154,284[4]	$97,385[5]	$33,148	$50,605	$74,505	$57,952	$20,155	$50,035
Income per common and common equivalent share[3]	$1.23	$1.22	$1.05[4]	$.68[5]	$.25	$.39	$.54	$.41	$.14	$.34
Cash dividends per common share	$.04000	$.04000	$.03867	$.03533	$.03333	$.03223	$.03110	$.02943	$.02890	$.02890
Total assets	$3,256,122	$2,823,071	$2,576,037	$2,368,856	$1,854,331	$1,480,813	$1,423,298	$1,308,389	$1,042,640	$1,061,419
Long-term debt	$661,010	$583,071	$639,136	$735,754	$617,434	$327,553	$354,150	$369,541	$251,130	$339,069
Stockholders' equity	$1,427,318	$1,238,706	$1,054,019	$879,536	$635,793	$607,294	$591,794	$567,375	$514,278	$511,850
Consolidated financial ratios[1]										
Return on average total assets	6.0%	6.6%	6.2%[4]	4.6%[5]	2.0%	3.5%	5.5%	5.1%	1.9%	4.8%
Return on average stockholder's equity	13.7%	15.6%	16.0%[4]	12.9%[5]	5.3%	5.4%	12.9%	10.3%	4.0%	10.3%
Debt as a percentage of invested capital	31.7%	32.0%	37.7%	45.5%	49.3%	35.0%	37.4%	39.4%	32.8%	39.8%

Consolidated Operating Statistics[2]

Revenue passengers carried	44,785,573	42,742,602[12]	36,955,221[12]	27,839,284	22,669,942	19,830,941	17,958,263	14,876,582	13,503,242	13,637,515
RPMs (000s)	23,327,804	21,611,266	18,827,288	13,787,005	11,296,183	9,958,940	9,281,992	7,676,257	7,789,376	7,388,401
ASMs (000s)	36,180,001	32,123,974	27,511,000	21,366,642	18,491,003	16,411,115	14,796,732	13,309,044	13,331,055	12,574,484
Load factor	64.5%	67.3%	68.4%	64.5%	61.1%	60.7%	62.7%	57.7%	58.4%	58.8%
Average length of passenger haul	521	506	509	495	498	502	517	516	577	542
Trips flown	685,524	624,476	546,297	438,184	382,752	338,108	304,673	274,859	270,559	262,082
Average passenger fare	$61.64	$58.44	$59.97	$58.33	$55.93	$57.71	$54.21	$55.68	$55.66	$54.43
Passenger revenue yield per RPM	11.83¢	11.56¢	11.77¢	11.78¢	11.22¢	11.49¢	10.49¢	10.79¢	9.65¢	10.05¢
Operating revenue yield per ASM	7.94¢	8.07¢	8.35¢	7.89¢	7.10¢	7.23¢	6.86¢	6.47¢	5.84¢	6.11¢
Operating expenses per ASM	7.07¢	7.08¢	7.25¢[13]	7.03¢	6.76¢	6.73¢	6.20¢	5.82¢	5.61¢	5.41¢
Fuel cost per gallon (average)	55.22¢	53.92¢	59.15¢	60.82¢	65.69¢	77.89¢	59.46¢	51.37¢	54.31¢	51.42¢
Number of employees at year end[14]	19,933	16,818	15,175	11,397	9,778	8,620	7,760	6,467	5,765	5,819
Size of fleet at year end[14]	224	199	178	141	124	106	94	85	75	79

[1]The Selected Consolidated Financial Data and Consolidated Financial Ratios for 1992 through 1989 have been restated to include the financial results of Morris. Years prior to 1989 were immaterial for restatement purposes.

[2]Prior to 1993, Morris operated as a charter carrier; therefore, no Morris statistics are included for these years.

[3]Pro forma for 1992 through 1989 assuming Morris, an S-Corporation prior to 1993, was taxed at statutory rates.

[4]Excludes cumulative effect of accounting changes of $15.3 million ($.10 per share).

[5]Excludes cumulative effect of accounting changes of $12.5 million ($.09 per share).

[6]Includes $2.6 million gains on sales of aircraft and $3.1 million from the sale of certain financial assets.

[7]Includes $10.8 million gains on sales of aircraft, $5.9 million from the sale of certain financial assets, and $2.3 million from the settlement of a contingency.

[8]Includes $5.6 million gains on sales of aircraft and $3.6 million from the sale of certain financial assets.

[9]Includes TranStar's results through June 30, 1987.

[10]Includes $10.1 million net gains from the discontinuance of TranStar's operations and $4.3 million from the sale of certain financial assets.

[11]Includes a gain of $4 million from the sale of aircraft delivery positions.

[12]Includes certain estimates for Morris.

[13]Excludes merger expenses of $10.8 million.

[14]Includes leased aircraft.

(79 at Southwest compared with the industry average of 131).[19] Southwest maintained a debt-to-equity ratio much lower than the industry average. The ratio was 50 percent in 1995, with cash holdings of $400 million. In addition, Southwest had a credit rating of "A," with a $460 million line of credit in 1995. Southwest was the only airline with an investment-grade credit rating.

Southwest's fleet of 737s had grown to 224 by 1995, up from 106 in 1990 and 75 in 1987. New aircraft deliveries were expected to average 22 per year until 2000, split equally between purchases and leases.[20] Revenues more than doubled between 1987 and 1995. Profits grew even faster during the same period. In 1994, Southwest tripled annual capacity growth, measured by available seat miles, to 30 percent and flew to 46 cities in 22 states. The number of flights per day in 1995 was 2,065 serving 46 cities, up from 1,883 flights in 1994.

HERB KELLEHER

Southwest's CEO, Herb Kelleher, managed the airline with a leadership style of flamboyance and fun and a fresh, unique perspective. Kelleher played Big Daddy-O in one of the company videos, appeared as the King of Rock (Elvis Presley) in in-flight magazine advertisements, and earned the nickname "High Priest of Ha-Ha" from *Fortune* magazine.[21] Although Kelleher was unconventional and a maverick in his field, he led his company to consistently new standards for itself and for the industry. Sincerely committed to his employees, Kelleher generated intense loyalty to himself and the company. His ability to remember employees' names and to ask after their families was just one way he earned respect and trust. At one point, Kelleher froze his salary for five years in response to the pilots agreeing to do the same. Often when he flew, Kelleher would help the ground crew unload bags or help the flight crew serve drinks. His humor was legendary and served as an example for his employees to join in the fun of working for Southwest. He was called "a visionary who leads by example—you have to work harder than anybody else to show them you are devoted to the business."[22]

Although Kelleher tried to downplay his personal significance to the company when questions were raised about succession, many analysts following Southwest credited the airline's success to Kelleher's unorthodox personality and engaging management style. As one analyst wrote, "the old-fashioned bond of loyalty between employees and company may have vanished elsewhere in corporate America, but it is stronger than ever at Southwest."[23]

THE SOUTHWEST SPIRIT

Customer service far beyond the norm in the airline industry was not unexpected at Southwest and had its own name—Positively Outrageous Service. Some examples of this service included: a gate agent volunteering to watch a dog (a Chihuahua) for two weeks when an Acapulco-bound passenger showed up at the last minute without the required dog crate; an Austin passenger who missed a connection to Houston, where he was to have a kidney transplant operation, was flown there by a Southwest pilot in his private plane. Another passenger, an elderly woman flying to Phoenix for cancer treatment, began crying because she had no family or friends at her destination. The ticket agent invited her into her home and escorted her around Phoenix for two weeks.[24]

Southwest Airlines customers were often surprised by "Southwest Spirit." On some flights, magazine pictures of gourmet meals were offered for dinner on an evening flight. Flight attendants were encouraged to have fun: songs, jokes, and humorous flight announcements were common. One flight attendant had a habit of popping out of overhead luggage compartments as passengers attempted to stow their belongings, until the day she frightened an elderly passenger who called for oxygen.[25] Herb Kelleher once served in-flight snacks dressed as the Easter Bunny.

Intense company communication and camaraderie were highly valued and essential to maintaining the *esprit de corps* found throughout the firm. The Southwest Spirit, as exhibited by enthusiasm and extroverted personalities, was an important element in employee screening conducted by Southwest's People Department. Employment at Southwest was highly desired. When the company held a job fair in Oklahoma City, more than 9,000 people attended in four days.[26] In 1995, 5,444 employees were hired from the 124,000 applications received and 38,000 interviews held.[27] Once landed, a job was fairly secure. The airline had not laid off an employee since 1971. Employee turnover hovered around 7 percent, the lowest rate in the industry.[28] More than half of Southwest's 22,000 employees had been hired after 1990. In 1990, Southwest had only 8,600 employees and less than 6,000 in 1987.

During initial training periods, efforts were made to share and instill Southwest's unique culture. New employee orientation, known as the new-hire celebration, included Southwest's version of the Wheel of Fortune, scavenger hunts, and company videos including the "Southwest Airlines Shuffle" in which each department introduced itself, rap style, and in which Kelleher appeared as Big Daddy-O.

Advanced employee training regularly occurred at the University of People at Love Field in Dallas. Various classes were offered, including team building, leadership, and cultural diversity. Newly promoted supervisors and managers attended a three-day class called "Leading with Integrity." Each department also had its own training department focusing on technical aspects of the work. "Walk-a-Mile Day" encouraged employees from different departments to experience first hand the day-to-day activities of their co-workers. The goal of this program was to promote respect for fellow workers while increasing awareness of the company.[29]

Employee initiative was supported by management and encouraged at all levels. For example, pilots looked for ways to conserve fuel during flights, employees proposed designs for ice storage equipment that reduced time and costs, and baggage handlers learned to place luggage with the handles facing outward to reduce unloading time.

Red hearts and "Luv" were central parts of the internal corporate culture, appearing throughout company literature. A mentoring program for new hires was called CoHearts. "Heroes of the Heart Awards" were given annually to one behind-the-scenes group of workers, whose department name was painted on a specially designed plane for a year. Other awards honored an employee's big mistake through the "Boner of the Year Award." When employees had a story about exceptional service to share, they were encouraged to fill out a "LUV Report."

Southwest placed great emphasis on maintaining cooperative labor relations. Within the firm, almost 90 percent of all employees were unionized. The company encouraged the unions and their negotiators to conduct employee surveys and to research their most important issues prior to each contract negotiation. Southwest had never had a serious labor dispute. The airlines' pilot union, SWAPA, represented 2,000 pilots. At its 1994 contract discussion, the pilots proposed a 10-year contract with stock options in lieu of guaranteed pay increases over the first five years of the contract. In 1973, Southwest was the first airline to introduce employee profit sharing.

SOUTHWEST IMITATORS

Southwest's low-fare, short-haul strategy spawned numerous imitators. By the second half of 1994, low fares were available on more than one-third of the industry's total capacity.[30] Many of the imitators were new start-up airlines. The Allied Pilots Association (APA) claimed that approximately 97 percent of start-ups resulted in failures. According to the APA, only 2 of 34 start-up airlines formed between 1978 and 1992 were successful, with success defined as surviving 10 years or longer without bankruptcy. The two successful firms, Midwest Express and America West, had both been through Chapter 11 bankruptcy proceedings. APA's prognosis for newer airlines was equally pessimistic, with only Frontier and Western Pacific of the 19 start-ups formed since 1992 perceived as having good prospects for long-term survival.[31] Three of the 19 had already folded by 1996, and ValuJet was grounded after its May 1996 crash in the Florida Everglades.

The major airlines had also taken steps to compete directly with Southwest. The Shuttle by United, a so-called "airline within an airline," was started in October 1994. United's objective was to create a new airline owned by United with many of the same operational elements as Southwest: a fleet of 737s, low fares, short-haul flights, and less restrictive union rules. Although offering basically a no-frills service, the Shuttle provided assigned seating and offered access to airline computer reservation systems. United predicted that the Shuttle could eventually account for as much as 20 percent of total United U.S. operations.

United saturated the West Coast corridor with short-haul flights on routes such as Oakland-Seattle, San Francisco-San Diego, and Sacramento-San Diego. Almost immediately, Southwest lost 10 percent of its California traffic. Southwest responded by adding six aircraft and 62 daily flights in California.

In April 1995, United eliminated its Oakland-Ontario route and proposed a $10 fare increase on other flights. By January 1996, United had pulled the Shuttle off routes that did not feed passengers to its San Francisco and Los Angeles hubs. In early 1995, United and Southwest competed directly on 13 percent of Southwest's routes. By 1996, that number was down to 7 percent.[32]

Cost was the major problem for United in competing with Southwest. The Shuttle's cost per seat mile remained at about 8 cents, whereas Southwest's cost was close to 7 cents. Two factors were largely responsible for the Shuttle's higher costs. First, many passengers booked their tickets through travel agents, which resulted in commission fees. Second, many of the Shuttle's flights were in the San Francisco and Los Angeles markets, both of which were heavily congested and subject to costly delays. In addition, the Shuttle was unable to achieve the same level of productivity as Southwest. Nevertheless, by launching the Shuttle, United was able to gain market share in the San Francisco and Los Angeles markets, largely at the expense of American, USAir, and Delta.

Continental Lite (CALite) was an effort by Continental Airlines to develop a low-cost service and revive the company's fortunes after coming out of bankruptcy in April 1993. CALite began service in October 1993 on 50 routes, primarily in the Southeast. Frequency of flights was a key part of the new strategy. Greenville-Spartanburg got 17 flights a day and in Orlando, daily departures more than doubled. CALite fares were modeled after those of Southwest and meals were eliminated on flights less than 2.5 hours.

In March 1994, Continental increased CALite service to 875 daily flights. Continental soon encountered major operational problems with its new strategy.[33] With its fleet of 16 different planes, mechanical delays disrupted turnaround times. Various pricing strategies were unsuccessful. The company was ranked last among the major carriers for on-time service and complaints soared by 40 percent. In January 1995, Continental announced that it would reduce its capacity by 10 percent and eliminate 4,000 jobs. By mid-1995, Continental's CALite service had been largely discontinued. In October 1995, Continental's CEO was ousted.

Delta was developing its "Leadership 7.5" campaign, intended to cut costs by $2 billion by mid-1997 and lower its ASM costs to 7.5 cents. Western Pacific (WestPac) was one of the newest domestic start-up airlines building on Southwest's formula, while adding its own twists. WestPac began flying out of a new airport in Colorado Springs in April 1995. WestPac's fleet consisted of 12 leased Boeing 737s. The airline started with 15 domestic destinations on the West Coast, East Coast, Southwest and Midwest, and all medium-length routes. Offering an alternative to the expensive Denver International Airport, business grew quickly. The company made a profit in two of its first four months of operation. Load factors averaged more than 60 percent in the first five months of operation, and were 75.9 percent in August. Operating cost per available seat mile averaged 7.37 cents during the early months and dropped to 6.46 cents within five months. The Colorado Springs airport became one of the country's fastest growing as a result of WestPac's market entry. WestPac had one-third of the market share and had flown almost 600,000 passengers during its first seven months.

One of WestPac's most successful marketing efforts was the "Mystery Fare" program. As a way to fill empty seats, $59 round-trip tickets were sold to one of the airline's destinations, but which one remained a mystery. Response greatly exceeded the airline's expectations; thousands of the mystery seats were sold. "Logo jets," also known as flying billboards, were another inventive approach by the start-up company. Jets painted on the outside with client advertising raised more than $1 million in fees over a one-year period. The airline also benefited from recent advances in ticketless operations. A healthy commission program to travel agents and a diverse, nonunion work force were other features of WestPac operations.[34]

Morris Air, patterned after Southwest, was the only airline Southwest had acquired. Prior to the acquisition, Morris Air flew Boeing 737s on point-to-point routes, operated in a different part of the United States than Southwest, and was profitable. When Morris Air was acquired by Southwest in December 1993, seven new markets were added to Southwest's system.

SOUTHWEST'S MOVE INTO FLORIDA

In January 1996, Southwest began new flights from Tampa International to Fort Lauderdale, Nashville,

New Orleans, St. Louis/Lambert International Airport, Birmingham, Houston/Hobby Airport, and Baltimore/Washington International Airport. Saturation and low initial fares were part of Southwest's expansion strategy. Some of the routes would have as many as six daily flights. In April, service began from Orlando International airport, with 10 flights headed to five different airports. Southwest's goal was to operate 78 daily flights to Tampa, Ft. Lauderdale, and Orlando.

Availability of assets and staff was a potential restriction on the airline's expansion possibilities. Ground crews were being transferred from other Southwest locations, with pilot and flight attendants coming from Chicago and Houston bases to cover the Florida expansion. Ten new Boeing jets were on order for the Florida routes.

EXPANSION INTO THE NORTHEAST

With Southwest established as a leader in many aspects of the industry, continued success was hard to doubt. Yet, Southwest had shown itself to be vulnerable, at least for a short time, to the well-planned competition from Shuttle by United on the West Coast. New airlines, such as WestPac, had also proved capable of innovating and quickly becoming profitable.

The proposed entry into the northeastern region of the United States was, in many respects, the next logical move for Southwest. The Northeast was the most densely populated area of the country and the only major region where Southwest did not compete. New England could provide a valuable source of passengers to Florida's warmer winter climates. Southwest's entry into Florida was exceeding initial estimates. Using a low-fare strategy, ValuJet had, until its crash, built a strong competitive base in important northeastern markets.

Despite the large potential market, the Northeast offered a new set of challenges for Southwest. Airport congestion and air traffic control delays could prevent efficient operations, lengthening turnaround time at airport gates and wreaking havoc on frequent flight scheduling. Inclement weather posed additional challenges for both air service and car travel to airports. Southwest had already rejected some of the larger airports as too crowded, including LaGuardia, JFK International, and Newark International airports. Some regional airports lacked facilities required by a high-volume airline. For example, Stewart International Airport, near Newburgh, New York, and north of New York City lacked basic facilities such as gates and ticket counters.

The critical question for Southwest management was whether expansion to the Northeast, and particularly New England, was premature. Or, would the challenge bring out the best in a firm with a history of defying conventional wisdom and doing things its own way?

NOTES

1. K. Freiberg and J. Freiberg, 1996, *Nuts: Southwest Airlines' Crazy Recipe for Business and Personal Success*, Austin: TX: Bard Press, p. 61.
2. Ibid., p. 28.
3. P. S. Dempsey, 1984, Transportation Deregulation: On a Collision Course, *Transportation Law Journal* 13: 329.
4. W. Goralski, 1996, Deregulation Deja Vu, *Telephony*, June 17: 32–36.
5. A. Bryant, 1996, U.S. Airlines Finally Reach Cruising Speed, *New York Times*, October 20, Section 3: 1.
6. *Business Week*, August 7, 1995, p. 25.
7. C. A. Shifrin, 1996, Record U.S. Airline Earnings Top $2 Billion, *Aviation Week & Space Technology*, January 29: 46.
8. P. Proctor, 1996, ATA Predicts Record Year for U.S. Airline Profits, *Aviation Week & Space Technology*, May 13: 33.
9. Ibid., p. 33.
10. Freiberg and Freiberg, pp. 14–21.
11. Ibid., p. 31.
12. Ibid., p. 55.
13. More City Pairs Await Southwest, 1995, *Aviation Week & Space Technology*, August 7: 41.
14. K. Labich, 1994, Is Herb Kelleher America's Best CEO?, *Fortune*, May 2: 47.
15. Freiberg and Freiberg, p. 51.
16. Herb Kelleher, http://www.iflyswa.com/cgi-bin/imagemap/swagate 530.85.
17. *Computerworld*, June 23, 1996, p. 98.
18. Freiberg and Freiberg, p. 29.
19. Southwest Airlines Charts a High-Performance Flight, 1995, *Training & Development*, June: 39.
20. A. L. Velocci, 1995, Southwest Adding Depth to Short-Haul Structure, *Air Transport*, August 7: 39.

21. Labich, p. 45.
22. 24th Annual CEO Survey: Herb Kelleher, Flying His Own Course, 1995, *IW*, November 20: 23.
23. Labich, p. 46.
24. *IW*, p. 23.
25. B. O'Brian, 1992, Flying on the Cheap, *Wall Street Journal*, October 26: A1.
26. B. P. Sunoo, 1995, How Fun Flies At Southwest Airlines, *Personnel Journal*, June: 66.
27. Freiberg and Freiberg, p. 72.
28. *Training & Development*, June p. 39.
29. A. Malloy, 1996, Counting the Intangibles, *Computerworld*, June: 32–33.

30. Industry Surveys, 1996, *Aerospace & Air Transport*, February 1: A36.
31. E. H. Phillips, 1996, GAO Study: Demographics Drive Airline Service, *Aviation Week & Space Technology*, May 13: 37.
32. S. McCartney and M. J. McCarthy, 1996, Southwest Flies Circles Around United's Shuttle, *Wall Street Journal*, February 20: B1.
33. B. O'Brian, 1995, Heavy Going: Continental's CALite Hits Some Turbulence in Battling Southwest, *Wall Street Journal*, January 10: A1, A16.
34. Rapid Route Growth Tests WestPac's Low-Fare Formula, 1995, *Aviation Week & Space Technology*, December 4: 37–38.

Starbucks Corporation

Melissa Schilling
Suresh Kotha

University of Washington

Starbucks Corporation is a Seattle, Washington-based coffee company. It roasts and sells whole-bean coffees and coffee drinks through a national chain of retail outlets/restaurants. Originally only a seller of packaged, premium, roasted coffees, the bulk of the company's revenue now comes from its coffee bars where people can purchase beverages and pastries in addition to coffee by the pound. Starbucks is credited with changing the way Americans view coffee, and its success has attracted the attention of investors nationwide.

Starbucks has consistently been one of the fastest growing companies in the United States with over 1,006 retail outlets in 1996. Over a five-year period starting in 1991, net revenues increased at a compounded annual growth rate of 61 percent. In fiscal 1996, net revenues increased 50 percent to $696 million from $465 million for the same period the previous year (see Exhibit 1). Net earnings rose 61 percent to $42 million from the previous year's $26 million. Sales for Starbucks have been continuing to grow steadily, and the company is still a darling of investors with a PE ratio of 58.

To continue to grow at a rapid pace, the firm's senior executives have been considering international expansion. Specifically, they are interested in Japan and other Asian countries, where Starbucks has lit-

tle or no presence. Japan, the world's third largest coffee consumer after the United States and Germany, represented both a challenge and a huge opportunity to the firm. To explore what changes in Starbucks' strategy were required, and the questions that might arise during expansion, this case looks at the firm's entry strategy into Japan and the nature of issues facing the firm during early 1997.

COMPANY BACKGROUND

In 1971, three Seattle entrepreneurs—Jerry Baldwin, Zev Siegl, and Gordon Bowker—started selling whole-bean coffee in Seattle's Pike Place Market. They named their store Starbucks, after the first mate in *Moby Dick*. By 1982, the business had grown to five stores, a small roasting facility, and a wholesale business selling coffee to local restaurants. At the same time, Howard Schultz had been working as vice president of U.S. operations for Hammarplast, a Swedish housewares company in New York, marketing coffee makers to a number of retailers, including Starbucks. Through selling to Starbucks, Schultz was introduced to the three founders, who then recruited him to bring marketing savvy to the company. Schultz, 29 and recently married, was eager to leave New York. He joined Starbucks as manager of retail sales and marketing.

A year later, Schultz visited Italy for the first time on a buying trip. As he strolled through the piazzas

This case was prepared as the basis for class discussion rather than to illustrate either effective or ineffective handling of an administrative situation.

EXHIBIT 1 *Selected Financial Data (in thousands, except earnings per share)*

As of and For the Fiscal Year Ended:	Sept 29, 1996 (52 Wks)	Oct 1, 1995 (52 Wks)	Oct 2, 1994 (52 Wks)	Oct 3, 1993 (52 Wks)	Sept 27, 1992 (52 Wks)
Results of Operations Data:					
Net revenues					
Retail	$600,067	$402,655	$248,495	$153,610	$ 89,669
Specialty Sales (Institutional Customers)	78,655	48,143	26,543	15,952	10,143
Direct Response (Mail Order)	17,759	14,415	9,885	6,979	3,385
Total Net Revenues	696,481	465,213	284,923	176,541	103,197
Operating Income	56,993	40,116	23,298	12,618	7,113
Provision for Merger Costs[1]	—	—	3,867	—	—
Gain on Sale of Investment in Noah's[2]	9,218	—	—	—	—
Net Earnings	$ 42,128	$ 26,102	$ 10,206	$ 8,282	$ 4,454
Net Earnings per Common and Common Equivalent Share—Fully Diluted[3]	$ 0.54	$ 0.36	$ 0.17	$ 0.14	$ 0.09
Balance Sheet Data:					
Working Capital	$238,450	$134,304	$ 44,162	$ 42,092	$ 40,142
Total Assets	726,613	468,178	231,421	201,712	91,547
Long-Term Debt (Including Current Portion)	167,980	81,773	80,500	82,100	1,359
Redeemable Preferred Stock	—	—	—	4,944	—
Shareholders' Equity	451,660	312,231	109,898	88,686	76,923

Source: From the consolidated financial statements of the company.

[1]Provision for merger costs reflects expenses related to the merger with The Coffee Connection, Inc., in fiscal 1994.

[2]Gain on sale of investment in Noah's of $9,218 ($5,669 after tax) results from the sale of Noah's New York Bagel, Inc., stock in fiscal 1996.

[3]Earnings per share is based on the weighted average shares outstanding during the period plus, when their effect is dilutive, common stock equivalents consisting of certain shares subject to stock options. Fully-diluted earnings per share assumes conversion of the Company's convertible subordinated debentures using the "if converted" method, when such securities are dilutive, with net income adjusted for the after-tax interest expense and amortization applicable to these debentures.

of Milan one evening, he was inspired by a vision. He noticed that coffee was an integral part of the romantic culture in Italy; Italians start their day at an espresso bar, and later in the day return with their friends. (For a history of the coffeehouse, see Exhibit 2.) There are 200,000 coffee bars in Italy, and about 1,500 in Milan alone. Schultz believed that given the chance, Americans would pay good money for a premium cup of coffee and a stylish, romantic place to enjoy it. Enthusiastic about his idea, Schultz returned to tell Starbucks' owners of his plan for a national chain of cafés stylized on the Italian coffee bar. The owners, however, were less enthusiastic and did not want to be in the restaurant business. Undaunted, Schultz wrote a business plan, videotaped dozens of Italian coffee bars, and began looking for investors.

By April 1985, he had opened his first coffee bar, Il Giornale (named after the Italian newspaper), where he served Starbucks coffee. Following Il Giornale's immediate success, Schultz opened a second coffee bar in Seattle and then a third in Vancouver. In 1987, the owners of Starbucks agreed to sell to Schultz for $4 million. The Il Giornale coffee bars took on the name of Starbucks.

Convinced that Starbucks would one day be in every neighborhood in America, Schultz focused on expansion. In 1987 he entered Chicago, four years later he opened in Los Angeles, and in 1993 he entered the District of Columbia. Additionally, he hired executives away from corporations such as PepsiCo. At first, the company's losses almost doubled, to $1.2 million from fiscal 1989 to 1990 as overhead and op-

EXHIBIT 2 *The History of the Coffee House*

Coffee made its way up the Arabian peninsula from Yemen 500 years ago. At that time, coffee houses were regularly denounced as "gathering places for men, women and boys of questionable morals, hubs of secular thought, centers of sedition and focal points for such dubious activities as the reading aloud of one's own poetry."

In Turkey and Egypt, coffee houses were meeting places for "plotters and other fomenters of insurrection." In Arabian countries, it was considered improper for a Muslim gentleman to sit at a coffee house—it was deemed a waste of time and somewhat indecent to gather and discuss secular literature, though these activities later became the rage in European coffee houses.

In 17th-century London, coffee houses were suggested as an alternative to the growing use of alcohol. Coffee houses were a very popular place for the masses to gather since in a coffee house, a poor person could keep his seat and not be "bumped" if a wealthier person entered. Coffee houses became known as "penny institutions" where novel ideas were circulated.

Around the turn of the century, espresso was invented in Italy. The name refers to the method of forcing high-pressure water through the coffee grounds, rather than the standard percolation techniques. Espresso and cappuccino rapidly became the preferred beverage of the coffee house; today most Italians and many other Europeans spurn the canned coffee that has been so popular in America.

Sources: *Chicago Tribune,* February 28, 1993; *Los Angeles Times,* December 6, 1992.

C-445

erating expenses ballooned with the expansion. Starbucks lost money for three years running, and the stress was hard on Schultz, but he stuck to his conviction not to "sacrifice long-term integrity and values for short-term profit."[1] In 1991, sales shot up 84 percent, and the company turned profitable. In 1992 Schultz took the firm public at $17 a share.

Always believing that market share and name recognition are critical to the company's success, Schultz continued to expand the business rather aggressively. Notes Schultz: "There is no secret sauce here. Anyone can do it." To stop potential copycats, he opened 100 new stores in 1993 and another 145 in 1994. Additionally, he acquired the Coffee Connection, a 25-store Boston chain, in 1994.

Everywhere Starbucks has opened, customers have flocked to pay upwards of $1.85 for a cup of coffee (latte). Currently, the firm operates stores in most of the major metropolitan areas in the United States and Canada, including Seattle, New York, Chicago, Boston, Los Angeles, San Francisco, San Diego, Austin, Dallas, Houston, San Antonio, Las Vegas, Philadelphia, Pittsburgh, Cincinnati, Minneapolis, Portland, Atlanta, Baltimore, Washington, D.C., Denver, Toronto, and Vancouver, B.C. Its mail-order business serves customers throughout the United States. Enthusiastic financial analysts predict

that Starbucks could top $1 billion by the end of the decade (see Appendix A).

In 1996, Starbucks employed approximately 16,600 individuals, including roughly 15,000 in retail stores and regional offices, and the remainder in the firm's administrative, sales, real estate, direct-response, roasting, and warehousing operations. Only five of the firm's stores (located in Vancouver, British Columbia) out of a total of 929 company-operated stores in North America were unionized. Starbucks has never experienced a strike or work stoppage. Management was confident that its relationship with its employees was excellent.

Currently the firm is organized as a matrix between functional and product divisions. The firm's functional divisions include Marketing; Supply Chain Operations (manufacturing, distribution, purchasing); Human Resources; Accounting; International; Planning and Finance; Administration (facilities, mail); Communications and Public Affairs; and Merchandising (the group that focuses on product extensions for food and beverages). The firm's product-based divisions include Retail North America (this division accounts for the bulk of the company's business and is split into regional offices spread throughout the United States); Specialty Sales and Wholesale Group (handles large accounts such as restaurants); Direct Response (a division that focuses on mail-order/Internet-related orders); International; and Licensed Concepts Unit. Because of the overlap in these divisions (e.g., Marketing and Retail North America), many employees report to two division heads. Notes Troy Alstead, the company's director of international planning and finance, "We have avoided a hierarchical organization structure, and therefore we have no formal organization chart." Exhibit 3 provides a partial list of Starbucks' top management.

MARKET AND COMPETITION

Americans have a reputation for buying the cheapest coffee beans available. Most American coffee buy-

---

EXHIBIT 3 *Top Management at Starbucks*

Howard Schultz is the founder of the company and has been chairman of the board and chief executive officer since its inception in 1985. From 1985 to June 1994, Mr. Schultz was also the company's president. From September 1982 to December 1985, Mr. Schultz was the director of retail operations and marketing for Starbucks Coffee Company, a predecessor to the Company; and from January 1986 to July 1987, he was the chairman of the board, chief executive officer, and president of Il Giornale Coffee Company, a predecessor to the Company.

Orin Smith joined the company in 1990 and has served as president and chief operating officer since June 1994. Prior to June 1994, Mr. Smith served as the company's vice president and chief financial officer and later, as its executive vice president and chief financial officer.

Howard Behar joined the company in 1989 and has served as president of Starbucks International since June 1994. From February 1993 to June 1994, Mr. Behar served as the company's executive vice president, sales and operations. From February 1991 to February 1993, Mr. Behar served as senior vice president, retail operations, and from August 1989 to January 1991, he served as the company's vice president, retail stores.

Scott Bedbury joined Starbucks in June 1995 as senior vice president, marketing. From November 1987 to October 1994, Mr. Bedbury held the position of worldwide director of advertising for Nike, Inc. Prior to joining Nike, Inc., Mr. Bedbury was vice president for Cole and Weber Advertising in Seattle, Washington, which is an affiliate of Ogilvy and Mather.

Michael Casey joined Starbucks in 1995 as senior vice president and chief financial officer. Prior to joining Starbucks, Mr. Casey served as executive vice president and chief financial officer of Family Restaurants, Inc., from its inception in 1986. During his tenure there, he also served as a director from 1986 to 1993, and as president of its El Torito Restaurants, Inc., division from 1988 to 1993.

Vincent Eades joined Starbucks in April 1995 as senior vice president, specialty sales and marketing. From February 1993 to April 1995, Mr. Eades served as a regional sales manager for Hallmark Cards, Inc. From August 1989 to February 1993, Mr. Eades was general manager of the Christmas Celebrations business unit at Hallmark Cards, Inc.

Sharon E. Elliott joined Starbucks in 1994 as senior vice president, human resources. From September 1993 to June 1994, Ms. Elliott served as the corporate director, staffing and development, of Allied Signal Corporation. From July 1987 to August 1993, she held several human resources management positions with Bristol-Myers Squibb, including serving as the director of human resources—corporate staff.

E. R. (Ted) Garcia joined Starbucks in April 1995 as senior vice president, supply chain operations. From May 1993 to April 1995, Mr. Garcia was an executive for Gemini Consulting. From January 1990 until May 1993, he was the vice president of operations strategy for Grand Metropolitan PLC, Food Sector.

Wanda J. Herndon joined Starbucks in July 1995 as vice president, communications and public affairs, and was promoted to senior vice president, communications and public affairs, in November 1996. From February 1990 to June 1995, Ms. Herndon held several communications management positions at DuPont. Prior to that time, Ms. Herndon held several public affairs and marketing communications positions for Dow Chemical Company.

David M. Olsen joined Starbucks in 1986 and has served as the company's senior vice president, coffee, since September 1991. From November 1987 to September 1991, Mr. Olsen served as its vice president, coffee, and from February 1986 to November 1987, he served as the company's director of training.

Deidra Wager joined Starbucks in 1992 and has served as the company's senior vice president, retail operations, since August 1993. From September 1992 to August 1993, Ms. Wager served as the company's vice president, operation services. From March 1992 to September 1992, she was the company's California regional manager. From September 1988 to March 1992, Ms. Wager held several operations positions with Taco Bell, Inc., including having served as its director of operations systems development.

Source: Starbucks Corporation, 1997.

ers have to fight growers to keep them from just showing them the culls. Much of the canned coffee on American supermarket shelves is made from the robusta bean—considered to be the lowest quality coffee bean with the highest in caffeine content. Japanese, German, and Italian buyers, in contrast, are known for buying the best beans, primarily Arabica. There are many different types and grades of Arabica and robusta beans, though for years Americans have treated them as a generic commodity.[2]

The U.S. Coffee Industry

U.S. coffee consumption peaked in 1962. At that time Americans were drinking an average of 3.1 cups per day. However, from the 1960s to the 1980s coffee consumption declined, bottoming out at an average consumption of 1.8 cups per day, or $6.5 billion annually. Over the past decade, coffee demand has been stagnant, with growth only occurring in some of the specialty coffees (see Exhibit 4). Whereas three-fourths of all Americans were regular coffee drinkers in the 1960s, today only half of the U.S. population consumes coffee.[3]

There has been a marked consumer trend toward more healthful fare, causing overall coffee consumption to decline. Although the coffee industry had expected decaffeinated coffee brands to increase, decaffeinated sales in the grocery stores have been steadily dropping, making decaffeinated coffee one of the fastest-declining categories in the supermarket.[4] Industry observers note that many consumers are disappointed with the flavor of decaffeinated coffees and have opted to give up coffee entirely. Demand for better-tasting coffees has also hurt the instant coffee market, with sales of instant coffee declining as well. While the instant coffee technology impressed consumers following its introduction in 1939, younger coffee consumers appear to be spurning instants.

Growth of the Gourmet Segment

The more faithful coffee drinkers have turned to the gourmet decaffeinated coffees, specialty flavors, and whole-bean coffees. According to the Specialty Coffee Association of America (SCAA), the gourmet coffee segment grew by more than 30 percent each year for the past three years. The SCCA predicts that by

1999 specialty coffee will capture about 30 percent of the market (up from 17 percent in 1988) for combined retail sales of $5 billion. Also by 1999, the number of espresso bars and cafés is expected to grow to more than 10,000, up from 4,500 in 1994 and 1,000 in 1989.

Sales of specialty coffee have climbed steadily. For instance, in 1969 the retail sales volume of specialty coffee totaled just under $45 million. However, sales grew to more than $2.0 billion in 1994. During 1994, the specialty coffee segment represented about 19 percent of all coffee sold. This figure was up from 10 percent in 1983. However, by 1996 about 30 percent of all coffee drinkers consumed specialty coffees. This amounted to a customer base of approximately 35 million people in the United States. Today, specialty coffees such as espressos and lattes have become so popular that they are being offered in drive-through cafés and coffee stands throughout many parts of the United States.[5]

Some analysts attribute the explosive growth in specialty coffees to the poor economy. They note that as people scale back in other areas, they still need their "minor" indulgences. Although many people cannot afford a luxury car, they can still afford a luxury coffee.[6] Despite this growth, some analysts anticipate trouble on the horizon for the specialty coffee business. As evidence, they cite several indicators. For instance:

■ In many markets some of the smaller coffee houses have closed due to excessive competition.

■ In Los Angeles, the city council (in response to complaints about rowdy late-night patrons) was considering an ordinance that would require coffee houses open past midnight to obtain a license. This move, suggest analysts, is a sign that the coffee business is maturing.

■ The cost of coffee beans is expected to rise in the near future, tightening margins for coffee merchants. Coffee farmers are switching to more profitable fruit and vegetable crops, reducing the world's supply of coffee beans.

Competition for the Gourmet Segment

Starbucks faces two main competitive arenas: retail beverages and coffee beans. Starbucks whole-bean

EXHIBIT 4a *U.S. Consumption of Coffee and Other Beverages*

	1985	1986	1987	1988	1989	1990	1991	1992	1993	1994	1995
Total Coffee	1.83	1.74	1.76	1.67	1.75	1.73	1.75	na	1.87	na	1.67
By Sex:											
Male	1.91	1.80	1.89	1.86	1.85	1.86	1.92	na	2.11	na	1.81
Female	1.76	1.68	1.64	1.50	1.66	1.60	1.59	na	1.64	na	1.54
By Age:											
10–19 years	0.12	0.09	0.11	0.14	0.11	0.16	0.12	na	0.15	na	0.16
20–29 years	1.24	1.06	0.99	0.94	0.99	0.96	0.83	na	0.89	na	0.69
30–59 years	2.65	2.43	2.56	2.35	2.46	2.34	2.40	na	2.62	na	2.35
60 plus	2.20	2.40	2.18	2.17	2.30	2.32	2.44	na	2.38	na	2.11

Source: *National Coffee Association of U.S.A.,* 1995 Report.
na = not available.

EXHIBIT 4b *U.S. Specialty Coffee Consumption*

% of the Population Drinking:	1993	1995	Male*	Female*
Espresso	0.6%	0.9%	0.9%	0.9%
Cappuccino	1.1	1.2	0.7	1.6
Latte	0.5	0.4	0.3	0.5

Source: *National Coffee Association of U.S.A.,* 1995 Report.
*Based on 1995 figures.

EXHIBIT 4c *U.S. Consumption in Gallons*

	1990	1991	1992	1993	1994E	1995P
Soft Drinks	47.6	47.8	48	49	50.6	51
Coffee*	26.2	26.6	26.5	25.4	23.4	21.2
Beer	24	23.3	23	22.9	22.6	22.5
Milk	19.4	19.4	19.1	18.9	18.9	18.8
Tea*	7	6.7	6.8	6.9	7.1	7.4
Bottled Water	8	8	8.2	8.8	9.2	9.6
Juices	7.1	7.6	7.1	7	7	7
Powdered Drinks	5.7	5.9	5.8	5.5	5.4	5.3
Wine**	2	1.9	2	1.7	1.7	1.6
Distilled Spirits	1.5	1.4	1.3	1.3	1.3	1.3
Total	148.5	148.6	147.8	147.4	147.2	145.7

Source: John C. Maxwell Jr., *Beverage Industry, Annual Manual* 1995/1997.
*Coffee and tea data are based on a three-year moving average to counterbalance inventory swings, thereby portraying consumption more realistically.
P = Projected, E = Estimates.

coffees compete directly against specialty coffees sold at retail through supermarkets, specialty retailers, and a growing number of specialty coffee stores. According to senior executives at Starbucks, supermarkets pose the greatest competitive challenge in the whole-bean coffee market, in part because supermarkets offer customers the convenience of not having to make a separate trip to "a Starbucks' store." A number of nationwide coffee manufacturers, such as Kraft General Foods, Procter & Gamble, and Nestlé, are distributing premium coffee products in supermarkets, and these products serve as substitutes for Starbucks' coffees. Additionally, regional specialty coffee companies also sell whole-bean coffees in supermarkets.

Starbucks' coffee beverages compete directly against all restaurant and beverage outlets that serve coffee and a growing number of espresso stands, carts, and stores. Both the company's whole-bean coffees and its coffee beverages compete indirectly against all other coffees on the market. Starbucks' management believes that its customers choose among retailers primarily on the basis of quality and convenience and, to a lesser extent, on price.

Starbucks competes for whole-bean coffee sales with franchise operators and independent specialty coffee stores in both the United States and Canada. There are a number of competing specialty coffee retailers. One specialty coffee retailer that has grown to considerable size is Second Cup, a Canadian franchiser with stores primarily in Canada. In 1996 there were 235 Second Cup stores in Canada. Second Cup also owns Gloria Jean's Coffee Bean and Brother's Gourmet, both franchisers of specialty coffee stores that are primarily located in malls in the United States. Gloria Jean's, founded in 1979, operated 249 retail stores with about $125 million in annual sales in 1996. Brother's Gourmet is a Florida-based coffee chain with almost 250 franchisee-owned locations in the Chicago area.

Seattle's Best Coffee (SBC) competes fiercely with Starbucks on Starbucks' own turf, Seattle. This firm is following Starbucks' lead in national expansion. However, unlike Starbucks, SBC sells franchise rights to its stores in order to expand rapidly with limited capital. SBC takes advantage of Starbucks' market presence by waiting for Starbucks to invest in consumer education. Then, once customers are familiar with the concept of gourmet coffees, SBC en-

ters that market. In following this approach, the firm has had an easier time finding franchisees. SBC intends to operate 500 stores by 1999.

Starbucks also competes with established suppliers in its specialty sales and direct-response (mail-order) businesses, many of which have greater financial and marketing resources than Starbucks. Lately, competition for suitable sites to locate stores has also become intense. Starbucks competes against restaurants, specialty coffee stores, other stores offering coffee stands within them (e.g., bookstores, clothing retailers, kitchenware retailers) and even espresso carts for attractive locations. In many metropolitan areas, a single square block may have four or five different coffee beverage stores. This level of competition prompted Brother's Gourmet Coffee to abandon its 1995 expansion plans after it determined that the market was almost saturated and that Starbucks was already in all of their markets. Finally, the firm also competes for qualified personnel to operate its retail stores.

THE STARBUCKS LEGACY

In establishing Starbucks' unique approach to competition, Schultz had four companies in mind as role models: Nordstrom, Home Depot, Microsoft, and Ben & Jerry's. Nordstrom, a national chain of upscale department stores based in Seattle, provided a role model for service and is part of the reason that each employee must receive at least 24 hours of training. Home Depot, the home improvement chain, was Schultz's guideline for managing high growth. Microsoft gave Schultz the inspiration for employee ownership, resulting in Starbucks' innovative Bean Stock Plan. And Ben & Jerry's was his role model for philanthropy; Starbucks sponsors community festivals, donates money to CARE for health and literacy programs in coffee-growing countries, and donates to charity any packages of coffee beans that have been open a week.

Schultz's goal is to "Establish Starbucks as the premier purveyor of the finest coffee in the world while maintaining uncompromising principles as we grow." He has since articulated six guiding principles to measure the appropriateness of the firm's decisions (see Exhibit 5).

EXHIBIT 5 *Starbucks' Mission Statement and Guiding Principles*

Mission Statement:

Establish Starbucks as the premier purveyor of the finest coffee in the world while maintaining our uncompromising principles as we grow.

Guiding Principles:

- Provide a great work environment and treat each other with respect and dignity.
- Embrace diversity as an essential component in the way we do business.
- Apply the highest standards of excellence to the purchasing, roasting and fresh delivery of our coffee.
- Develop enthusiastically satisfied customers all of the time.
- Contribute positively to our communities and our environment.
- Recognize that profitability is essential to our future success.

Securing the Finest Raw Materials

Starbucks' coffee quality begins with bean procurement. Although many Americans were raised on a commodity-like coffee composed of Arabica beans mixed with less-expensive filler beans, Starbucks coffee is strictly Arabica, and the company ensures that only the highest-quality beans are used. Dave Olsen, the company's senior vice president and chief coffee procurer, scours mountain trails in Indonesia, Kenya, Guatemala, and elsewhere in search of Starbucks' premium bean. His standards are demanding and he conducts exacting experiments in order to get the proper balance of flavor, body, and acidity. He tests the coffees by "cupping" them—a process similar to wine tasting that involves inhaling the steam ("the strike" and "breaking the crust"), tasting the coffee, and spitting it out ("aspirating" and "expectorating").[7]

From the company's inception, it has worked on developing relationships with the countries from which it buys coffee beans. Traditionally, most of the premium coffee beans were bought by Europeans and Japanese. Olsen has sometimes had to convince coffee growers that it is worth growing premium coffees—especially since American coffee buyers are notorious purchasers of the "dregs" of the coffee beans. In 1992 Starbucks set a new precedent by outbidding European buyers for the exclusive Narino Supremo bean crop.[8] Starbucks collaborated with a mill in the tiny town of Pasto, located on the side of the Volcano Galero. There they set up a special operation to single out the particular Narino Supremo bean, and Starbucks guaranteed to purchase the entire yield. This enabled Starbucks to be the exclusive purveyor of Narino Supremo, purportedly one of the best coffees in the world.[9]

Vertical Integration

Roasting of the coffee bean is close to an art form at Starbucks. The company currently operates three roasting and distribution facilities: two in the Seattle area, and one in East Manchester Township, York County, Pennsylvania. In the Seattle area, the company leases approximately 92,000 square feet in one building located in Seattle, Washington, and owns an additional roasting plant and distribution facility of approximately 305,000 square feet in Kent, Washington.

Roasters are promoted from within the company and trained for over a year, and it is considered quite an honor to be chosen. The coffee is roasted in a powerful gas-fired drum roaster for 12 to 15 minutes while roasters use their sight, smell, hearing, and computers to judge when beans are perfectly done. The color of the beans is even tested in an Agtron blood-cell analyzer, with the whole batch being discarded if the sample is not deemed perfect.

The Starbucks Experience

According to Schultz, "We're not just selling a cup of coffee, we are providing an experience." As Americans reduce their alcohol consumption, Schultz hopes to make coffee bars their new destination. In order to create American coffee enthusiasts with the dedication of their Italian counterparts, Starbucks provides a seductive atmosphere in which to imbibe.

Its stores are distinctive and sleek, yet comfortable. Though the sizes of the stores and their formats vary from small to full-size restaurants, most are modeled after the Italian coffee bars where regulars sit and drink espresso with their friends.

Starbucks' stores tend to be located in high-traffic locations such as malls, busy street corners, and even grocery stores. They are well lighted and feature plenty of light cherry wood. Further, sophisticated artwork hangs on the walls. The people who prepare the coffee are referred to as *baristas*, Italian for bartender. And jazz or opera music plays softly in the background. The stores range from 200 to 4,000 square feet, with new units tending to range from 1,500 to 1,700 square feet. In 1995, the average cost of opening a new unit (including equipment, inventory, and leasehold improvements) was about $377,000. The firm employs a staff of over 100 people whose job is to plan, design, and build the unique interiors and displays. The Starbucks' interiors have inspired a slew of imitators.

Location choices so far have been easy; Starbucks opens its cafés in those cities where their direct-mail business is strong. By tracking addresses of mail-order customers to find the highest concentration in a city, Starbucks can ensure that its new stores have a ready audience. Although this would normally imply cannibalizing their mail-order sales, mail-order revenues have continued to increase.

The packaging of the firm's products is also distinctive. In addition to prepared Italian beverages such as lattes, mochas, and cappuccinos, the retail outlets/restaurants offer coffee by the pound, specialty mugs, and home espresso-making machines. *Biscotti* are available in glass jars on the counter. Many of the firm's stores offer light lunch fare including sandwiches and salads, and an assortment of pastries, bottled waters, and juices. Notes George Reynolds, a former senior vice president for marketing, Starbucks' "goal is to make a powerful aesthetic statement about the quality and integrity of their products, reaffirming through their visual identity the commitment they feel to providing the very best product and service for customers."

The company has also developed unique strategies for its products in new markets; for instance, for its passport promotion, customers receive a frequent buyer bonus stamp in their "passport" every time they purchase a half-pound of coffee. Each time a customer buys a different coffee, Starbucks also validates their "World Coffee Tour." Once a customer has collected 10 stamps, he or she receives a free half-pound of coffee. The passport also contains explanations of each type of coffee bean and its country of origin.

Despite the attention to store environment and coffee quality, Starbucks' effort at bringing a premium coffee and Italian-style beverage experience to the American market could have been lost on consumers had the company not invested in consumer education. Starbucks' employees spend a good portion of their time instructing customers on Starbucks' global selection of coffee and the different processes by which the beverages are produced. Employees are also encouraged to help customers make decisions about beans, grind, and coffee/espresso machines and to instruct customers on home brewing. Starbucks' consumer education is credited with defining the American espresso market, paving the way for other coffee competitors.[10]

Building a Unique Culture

While Starbucks enforces almost fanatical standards about coffee quality and service, the policy at Starbucks toward employees is laid back and supportive. They are encouraged to think of themselves as partners in the business. Schultz believes that happy employees are the key to competitiveness and growth:

> We can't achieve our strategic objectives without a work force of people who are immersed in the same commitment as management. Our only sustainable advantage is the quality of our work force. We're building a national retail company by creating pride in—and a stake in—the outcome of our labor.[11]

Schultz is also known for his sensitivity to the well-being of employees. Recently when an employee told Schultz that he had AIDS, Schultz reassured him that he could work as long as he wanted, and when he left, the firm would continue his health insurance. After the employee left the room, Schultz reportedly sat down and wept. He attributes such concern for employees to memories of his father:

> My father struggled a great deal and never made more than $20,000 a year, and his work was never valued, emotionally or physically, by his employer. . . . This was an injustice. . . . I want our employees to know we value them.

A recent article on the firm in *Fortune* points out:

Starbucks has instituted all sorts of mechanisms for its Gen X-ers to communicate with headquarters: E-mail, suggestion cards, regular forums. And it acts quickly on issues that are supposedly important to young kids today, like using recycling bins and improving living conditions in coffee-growing countries. To determine the extent to which Starbucks has truly identified and addressed the inner needs of twentysomethings would require several years and a doctorate. But anecdotally, the company appears to be right on the money.[12]

On a practical level, Starbucks promotes an empowered employee culture through employee training, employee benefits programs, and an employee stock ownership plan.

Employee Training Each employee must have at least 24 hours of training. Notes *Fortune*:

Not unlike the cultural blitz of personal computing, Starbucks has created one of the great marketing stories of recent history, and it's just getting started. The company manages to imprint its obsession with customer service on 20,000 milk-steaming, shot-pulling employees. It turns tattooed kids into managers of $800,000-a-year cafés. It successfully replicates a perfectly creamy caffee latte in stores from Seattle to St. Paul. There is some science involved, and one of its primary labs happens to be Starbucks' employee training program.[13]

Classes cover everything from coffee history to a seven-hour workshop called "Brewing the Perfect Cup at Home." This workshop is one of five classes that all employees (called partners) must complete during their first six weeks with the company. This workshop focuses on the need to educate the customer in proper coffeemaking techniques.

Store managers (who have gone through facilitation workshops and are certified by the company as trainers) teach the classes. The classes teach the employees to make decisions that will enhance customer satisfaction without requiring manager authorization. For example, if a customer comes into the store complaining about how the beans were ground, the employee is authorized to replace them on the spot. While most restaurants use on-the-job training,

Starbucks holds bar classes where employees practice taking orders and preparing beverages in a company training room. This allows employees to hone their skills in a low-stress environment, and also protects Starbucks' quality image by allowing only experienced baristas to serve customers.[14] Reports *Fortune*:

It's silly, soft-headed stuff, though basically, of course, it's true. Maybe some of it sinks in. Starbucks is a smashing success, thanks in large part to the people who come out of these therapy-like training programs. Annual barista turnover at the company is 60% compared with 140% for hourly workers in the fast-food business. "I don't have a negative thing to say," says Kim Sigelman, who manages the store in Emeryville, California, of her four years with the company. She seems to mean it.[15]

Employee Benefits Starbucks offers its benefits package to both part-time and full-time employees with dependent coverage available. Dependent coverage is also extended to same-sex partners. The package includes medical, dental, vision, and short-term disability insurance, as well as paid vacation, paid holidays, mental health/chemical dependency benefits, an employee assistance program, a 401k savings plan, and a stock option plan. The firm also offers career counseling and product discounts.[16]

Schultz believes that without these benefits, people do not feel financially or spiritually tied to their jobs. He argues that stock options and the complete benefits package increase employee loyalty and encourage attentive service to the customer.[17] Notes Bradley Honeycutt, the company's vice president, human resources services and international: "[Our] part-timers are on the front line with our customers. If we treat them right, we feel they will treat (the customers) well."[18] Sharon Elliot, human resources senior vice president, offers another explanation, "Most importantly, this is the right thing to do. It's a basic operating philosophy of our organization."

Despite the increased coverage, Starbucks' health care costs are well within the national average, running around $150 per employee per month. This may be due, in part, to the fact that its employees are relatively young, resulting in lower claims. Half of the management at Starbucks is under 50, and retail employees tend to be much younger. Starbucks is betting on the increases in premiums being largely offset by lower training costs due to the lower attrition rate. Comments *Fortune:*

> It has become boilerplate public relations for corporations to boast about how much they value their people. But Starbucks really does treat its partners astonishingly well. The pay—between $6 and $8 an hour—is better than that of most entry-level food service jobs. The company offers health insurance to all employees, even part-timers. . . . Walk into just about any Starbucks, and you'll see that these are fairly soft hands: Some 80% of the partners are white, 85% have some college education beyond high school, and the average age is 26.

The Bean Stock Plan Employee turnover is also discouraged by Starbucks' stock option plan, known as the Bean Stock Plan. Implemented in August of 1991, the plan made Starbucks the only private company to offer stock options unilaterally to all employees. After one year, employees may join a 401k plan. There is a vesting period of five years; it starts one year after the option is granted, then vests the employee at 20 percent every year. In addition, every employee receives a new stock-option award each year and a new vesting period begins. This plan required getting an exemption from the Security Exchange Commission, since any company with more than 500 shareholders has to report its financial performance publicly—a costly process that reveals valuable information to competitors.

The option plan did not go uncontested by the venture capitalists and shareholders on the board. Craig Foley, a director and managing partner of Chancellor Capital Management Inc. (the largest shareholder before the public offering), noted that, "Increasing the shareholders substantially dilutes our interest. We take that very seriously." In the end he and others were won over by a study conducted by the company that revealed the positive relationship between employee ownership and productivity rates, and a scenario analysis of how many employees would be vested. Foley conceded: "The grants are tied to overachieving. If you just come to work and do your job, that isn't as attractive as if you beat the numbers."[19]

Since the Bean Stock Plan was put into place, enthusiastic employees have been suggesting ways to save money and increase productivity. The strong company culture has also served as a levy against pilferage; Starbucks' inventory shrinkage is less than half of 1 percent.

In 1995, Starbucks demonstrated that its concern for employee welfare extended beyond U.S. borders. After a human rights group leafleted the stores complaining that Guatemalan coffee pickers received less than $3 a day, Starbucks became the first agricultural commodity importer to implement a code for minimal working conditions and pay for foreign subcontractors.[20] The company's guidelines call for overseas suppliers to pay wages and benefits that "address the basic needs of workers and their families" and to only allow child labor when it does not interrupt required education.[21] This move has set a precedent for other importers of agricultural commodities.

Leveraging the Brand

Multiple Channels of Distribution While Starbucks has resisted offering its coffee in grocery stores, it has found a variety of other distribution channels for its products. Besides its stand-alone stores, Starbucks has set up cafés and carts in hospitals, banks, office buildings, supermarkets, and shopping centers. In 1992, Starbucks signed a deal with Nordstrom to serve Starbucks coffee exclusively in all of its stores. Nordstrom also named Starbucks as the exclusive coffee supplier for its restaurants, employee lunchrooms, and catering operations. As of 1992, Nordstrom was operating 62 restaurants and 48 espresso bars. A year later, Barnes & Noble initiated an agreement with Starbucks to implement a "café-in-a-bookshop" plan.

Other distribution agreements have included office coffee suppliers, hotels, and airlines. Office coffee is a large segment of the coffee market. Associated Services (an office coffee supplier) provides Starbucks coffee exclusively to the 5,000 northern California businesses it services. Sheraton Hotel has also signed an agreement to serve Starbucks coffee. In 1995, Starbucks signed a deal with United Airlines to provide Starbucks coffee to United's nearly 75 million passengers a year.[22]

While Starbucks is the largest and best-known of the coffee-house chains and its presence is very apparent in metropolitan areas, the firm's estimates indicate that only 1 percent of the U.S. population has tried its products. Through these distribution agreements and the new product partnerships it is establishing, Starbucks hopes to capture more of the U.S. market.

Brand Extensions In 1995, Starbucks launched a line of packaged and prepared teas in response to growing demand for tea houses and packaged tea. Tea is a highly profitable beverage for restaurants to sell, costing only 2 to 4 cents a cup to produce.[23]

Starbucks coffee is not sold in grocery stores, but its name is making its way onto grocery shelves via a carefully planned series of joint ventures.[24] An agreement with PepsiCo brought a bottled version of Starbucks' Frappuccino (a cold, sweetened coffee drink) to store shelves in August 1996. A similar product released a year before, called Mazagran, was a failure and was pulled from the shelves; however, both Starbucks and PepsiCo had higher hopes for Frappuccino.[25] Starbucks also has an agreement with Washington-based Redhook Ale Brewery to make a product called Double Black Stout, a coffee-flavored stout. In another 50–50 partnership, Dreyers Grand Ice Cream Inc. distributes seven quart-products and two bar-products of Starbucks coffee ice cream.

Other company partnerships are designed to form new product associations with coffee. For instance, Starbucks has collaborated with Capitol Records, Inc., to produce two Starbucks jazz CDs, available only in Starbucks stores. Starbucks is also opening tandem units with Bruegger's Bagel Bakeries and bought a minority stake in Noah's New York Bagels in 1995. This minority stake has since been sold.

INTERNATIONAL EXPANSION

From the beginning, Schultz has professed a strict growth policy. Although many other coffee houses or espresso bars are franchised, Starbucks owns all of its stores outright with the exception of license agreements in airports.[26] Despite over 300 calls a day from willing investors, Schultz feels it is important to the company's integrity to own its stores. Further, rather than trying to capture all the potential markets as soon as possible, Starbucks goes into a market and tries to completely dominate it before setting its sights on further expansion. As Alstead points out, "Starbucks hopes to achieve the same density in all of its markets that they have achieved in Seattle, Vancouver and Chicago."

In 1996, the firm opened 307 stores (including four replacement stores), converted 19 Coffee Connection stores to Starbucks, and closed one store. In 1997, Starbucks intends to open at least 325 new stores and enter at least three major new markets in North America including Phoenix, Arizona, and Miami, Florida. Moreover, Schultz plans to have 2,000 stores by the year 2000.

Some analysts believe that the U.S. coffee bar market may be reaching saturation. They point to the fact that there have been some consolidations as bigger players snap up some of the smaller coffee bar competitors.[27] Further, they note that Starbucks' store base is also maturing, leading to a slowdown in the growth of unit volume and firm profitability. Higher coffee costs have also cut into margins, intensifying the competition in what has now become a crowded market. Recognizing this, Starbucks has turned its attention to foreign markets for continued growth. Notes Schultz, "We are looking at the Asia-Pacific region as the focus of our international business."

Expansion into Asian Markets

In 1996, Starbucks invested $1.5 million and established a subsidiary called Starbucks Coffee International, Inc. The focus of this subsidiary will be on penetrating the Asia-Pacific region. According to Kathie Lindemann, the director of international operations at Starbucks:

> We are not overlooking Europe and South America as areas for future expansion. But, we feel that expanding into these regions is more risky than Asia. The Asia-Pacific region we feel has much more potential for us. It is full of emerging markets. Also consumers' disposable income is increasing as their countries' economies grow. Most important of all, people in these countries are open to Western lifestyles.

This international subsidiary consists of 12 managers located primarily in Seattle, Washington. Together these managers are responsible for developing new businesses internationally, financing and planning of international stores, managing international operations and logistics, merchandising in international markets and, finally, training and developing of Starbucks' international managers. Since its establishment, this subsidiary has been responsible for opening Starbucks' coffee houses in Hawaii, Japan, and Singapore.[28]

Lindemann, commenting on Starbucks' approach to Asian markets, notes:

At Starbucks we don't like the concept of franchising. Therefore, we decided to work with partners in Japan and other Asian countries. Our approach to international expansion is to focus on the *partnership first, country second.* Partnership is everything in Asia. We rely on the local connection to get everything up and working. The key is finding the right local partners to negotiate local regulations and other issues.

When asked to list the criteria by which Starbucks chose partners in Asia, Lindemann highlighted six points:

We look for partners who share our values, culture, and goals about community development. We are trying to align ourselves with people, or companies, with plenty of experience. We are primarily interested in partners who can guide us through the process of starting up in a foreign location. We look for firms with: (1) similar philosophy to ours in terms of shared values, corporate citizenship, and commitment to be in the business for the long haul, (2) multi-unit restaurant experience, (3) financial resources to expand the Starbucks' concept rapidly to prevent imitators, (4) strong real-estate experience with knowledge about how to pick prime real estate locations, (5) knowledge of the retail market, and (6) the availability of the people to commit to our project.

Entry into Japan In October 1995, Starbucks entered into a joint venture with Tokyo-based Sazaby, Inc. This firm was expected to help Starbucks open 12 new stores in Japan by the end of 1997. This joint venture, amounting to 250 million yen ($2.33 million) in capitalization, is equally owned by Starbucks Coffee International and Sazaby. Sazaby, often recognized as a leader in bringing unique goods to the Japanese, operates upscale retail and restaurant chains throughout Japan. Commenting on this joint venture, the president of Starbucks International, Howard Behar, noted:

This powerful strategic alliance, which combines two major lifestyle companies, will provide the Japanese consumer a new and unique specialty

coffee experience. . . . We look at this venture as though we're starting all over again, and in many ways, we are.

With Sazaby's assistance, the firm opened two stores in Tokyo in September 1996. The first outlet was in Tokyo's posh Ginza shopping district. The Ginza store was planned so that Japanese customers could have the same "Starbucks experience" offered in U.S. stores. The firm's second store was located in Ochanomizu, a student area cluttered with colleges, bookstores, and fast-food restaurants. Starbucks hopes that students and office workers in the neighborhood will come in for a cup of coffee and a light snack. At both stores, customers can eat in the store or take out their purchases.

The food-and-drink menus in the firm's Japanese coffee houses are similar to those in the United States. The firm offers 15 types of beverages, snacks such as cookies and sandwiches, coffee beans, and novelty goods such as coffee mugs and T-shirts. The firm's single-shot-short latte costs 280 yen in Tokyo (about $2.50, a price that is roughly 50 cents more than in the United States). According to an August 1996 industry report, a cup of coffee in Tokyo costs about 399 yen, on average, in August 1996.

Although the Japanese are not used to Italian-style coffee beverages, Starbucks' executives believe that Japanese consumers are ready to embrace the Starbucks concept.[29] A report in the *Wall Street Journal* suggests that breaking into the Japanese market may not be easy (see Exhibit 6 and Exhibit 7):

The Japanese haven't developed a taste for espresso drinks like caffe latte and caffe mocha; they drink a lot of instant coffee or ready-to-drink coffee in cans, as well as American-style hot coffee. Moreover, the Japanese coffee market may be saturated with many coffee shops and vending machines serving hot coffees. Coca-Cola alone has more than 800,000 vending machines that sell canned coffee.[30]

Similarly, a report in the *Nikkei Weekly* points out:

Though Japan is the world's third largest coffee consumer, its coffee shops constitute a declining industry, with high operating costs knocking many small operators out of business. In 1992, there were 115,143 coffee shops in Japan, according to the latest government survey available. That figure is nearly 30% less than the peak in 1982.[31]

C-455

EXHIBIT 6 *Japan Consumer Preferences**

	1980	1985	1990	1994
Instant Coffee	57.6%	59.2%	50.6%	45.4%
Regular Coffee	33.3%	29.4%	33.1%	37.4%
Canned Coffee	9.1%	11.4%	13.1%	17.3%
Total (Cups per Week)	7.4	9.02	9.52	10.36
Place of Consumption				
Home	55.8%	58.3%	56.6%	54.7%
Coffee Shop	24.6%	11.6%	8.9%	8.0%
Work/School	15.4%	21.8%	23.9%	26.4%
Other	4.2%	8.3%	10.6%	10.9%

Source: *Tea & Coffee Trade Journal,* August 1995.
*Based on a survey from October 20 through November 7, 1994, by the All Japan Coffee Association. The survey reported that men aged between 25–39 years consumed the most coffee at 16 cups per week and girls between 12–17 years consumed the least at 3 cups.

EXHIBIT 7 *Canned Coffee Sales in Japan (US $ Millions)*

	Market Share	1991	1992	1993	1994	1995
Coca Cola	40%	2,718	2,396	2,635	2,899	3,189
UCC	12	653	718	790	869	965
Pokka	11	599	658	724	797	877
Daido	10	544	599	658	724	797
Nestlé	7	381	419	461	507	558
Others	20	1,089	1,198	1,317	1,449	1,594
Total	100	5,445	6,990	6,589	7,248	7,972

Source: *Advertising Age,* 1996.
Notes: Canned coffee accounts for approximately 40% of total beverage sales in Japan, including soft drinks.

Japan's coffee culture revolves around the *kissaten,* a relatively formal sit-down coffee house. According to the *All Japan Coffee Association,* while U.S. and German consumers consumed 18.1 and 10 million bags, respectively, of coffee in 1994, the Japanese consumed 6.1 million coffee bags (one bag of coffee contains 60 kilograms of coffee beans).

Despite the absolute size of the Japanese coffee market, knowledgeable analysts note that Starbucks is likely to face stiff competition and retaliation from well-established players in Japan. Two of Japan's well-established coffee chains are the Doutor Coffee Company and the Pronto Corp.

Started in 1980, Doutor Coffee Company is Japan's leading coffee bar chain. In 1996, it had over 466 shops in and around Tokyo. At times, consumers refer to this firm as the McDonald's of coffee houses since it provides a limited menu and emphasizes self-service. In Doutor's shops, seating is limited and counters are provided where customers can stand while they consume their beverages. The focus is on speed of service and quick turnover of customers. The average customer stay in a Doutor Coffee Shop is about 10 minutes, about one-third the stay in a typical *kissaten.* Close to 90 percent of the Doutor's coffee houses are operated by franchisees, while the remaining 10 percent of the shops are operated directly by Doutor. A standard cup of coffee at Doutor costs 180 yen. The firm serves other refreshments, such as juice, sandwiches, and pastries. It is reported that nearly 10 million customers per month visit Doutor coffee houses. The firm has five shops in Ginza, where Starbucks opened its first store.[32]

Pronto Corp. is Japan's second largest coffee bar chain. The firm opened its first shop in Tokyo in 1987. In 1996, it operated over 95 outlets, most of them in Tokyo. The firm's coffee houses serve coffee and light snacks during the day, and at night they switch to neighborhood bar-type operations, serving alcoholic drinks and light meals. At Pronto, a standard cup of coffee costs 160 yen. Reacting to Starbucks' entry into Japan, Seiji Honna, president of Pronto Corp., notes: For the past few years, we've had this nightmare scenario that espresso drinks are going to swallow up Japan's coffee market. . . . And we won't know how to make a good cup of espresso. . . . [And now Starbucks' entry], if they really mean business, I think they'll probably put some of us out of business.[33]

But he goes on to comment:

I don't think that the opening of the first Starbucks store in Japan would immediately be a threat to our business. . . . But Starbucks could become a strong competitor if it is able to gain consumer recognition in the next three years or so. In order to do so, Starbucks will need to have about 30 to 50 stores in the Tokyo area.[34]

Yuji Tsunoda, president of Starbucks Coffee Japan Ltd., indicates that the company intends to have 100 directly owned coffee bars in major Japanese cities in the next five years.

According to Kazuo Sunago, an analyst from Japan's leading advertising firm Dentsu Inc., Japanese coffee bars lack the creativity to stop a firm like Starbucks from making inroads in the Japanese coffee market.

As traditional mom-and-pop coffee shops die off, big chains are looking for more attractive formats. . . . But they are like a dry lake bed—void of new ideas. That's why the whole industry is stirred up about Starbucks.[35]

Comments Alstead: "The issue facing Starbucks is how, as we expand geographically and through expanding channels, will we be able maintain the Starbucks' culture."

NOTES

1. *Success*, April 1993.
2. *Chicago Tribune*, July 1, 1993.
3. According to the *Berkeley Wellness Letter*, a newsletter from the University of California, 53 percent of all coffee in the United States is consumed at breakfast. Further, 11 percent of the U.S. population drink decaf coffee, and 10 percent drink instant coffee. Of the people who drink instant coffee, most are over the age of 55.
4. *Wall Strret Journal*, February 25, 1993. According to the National Coffee Association, brewed coffee accounted for 85 percent of all coffee consumed in the United States during 1995. This was followed by espresso-based drinks (14 percent) and express coffee (1 percent).
5. Espresso, despite its potent flavor, is lower in caffeine than the canned coffees offered in supermarkets. It is made with Arabica beans that are lower in caffeine content, and the brewing method yields less caffeine per cup.
6. *Wall Street Journal*, February 25, 1993.
7. *Sacramento Bee*, April 28, 1993.
8. This Columbian coffee bean crop is very small and grows only in the high regions of the Cordillera mountain range. For years, the Narino beans were guarded zealously by Western Europeans who prized their colorful and complex flavor. It was usually used for upgrading blends. Starbucks was determined to make them available for the first time as a pure varietal. This required breaking Western Europe's monopoly over the beans by convincing the Columbian growers that it intended to use "the best beans for a higher purpose."
9. *Canada Newswire*, March 1, 1993.
10. Though *Consumer Reports* rated Starbucks coffee as burnt and bitter, Starbucks customers felt otherwise, and most of Starbucks' early growth can be attributed to enthusiastic word-of-mouth advertising. The typical Starbucks customer is highly proficient in the science of coffee beans and brewing techniques. The coffee bars even have their own dialect; executives from downtown Seattle businesses line up in force to order "tall-skinny-double mochas" and "2% short no-foam lattes."
11. *Inc.*, January 1993.
12. *Fortune*, December 9, 1996.
13. *Fortune*, December 9, 1996.
14. *Training*, June 1995.
15. *Fortune*, December 9, 1996.
16. The decision to offer benefits even to part-time employees (who represent roughly two-thirds of Starbucks' 10,000 employees) has gained a great deal of attention in the press. According to a Hewitt Associates L.L.C. survey of more than 500 employers, only 25 percent of employers offer medical coverage to employees working less than 20 hours a week. It was difficult to get insurers to sign Starbucks up since they did not understand why Starbucks would want to cover part-timers.

17. *Inc.*, January 1993.
18. *Business Insurance*, March 27, 1995, p. 6.
19. *Inc.*, January 1993.
20. *Wall Street Journal*, April 4, 1995.
21. *Wall Street Journal*, October 23, 1995.
22. In the past, one interesting outlet for Starbucks coffee was Starbucks' deal with Smith Brothers, one of the Northwest's oldest dairies. Smith Brothers used to sell Starbucks coffee on its home delivery routes. The idea for the alliance actually came from the dairy, a supplier for Starbucks. Management at Smith Brothers began to wonder if Starbucks' rapid growth might prompt the company to look for other dairies to supply its milk. A report in the *Seattle Times* (November 6, 1992) noted that Earl Keller, sales manager for Smith Brothers, got the idea that "Maybe if we were a good customer of theirs, it would be more difficult for them to leave us." In 1992, Smith delivered 1,000 pounds of coffee beans a week. The coffee was sold at the same price as in Starbucks' retail stores, and the only complaint has been that Smith does not carry all 30 varieties. The company no longer sells coffee through Smith Brothers.
23. *Nations Restaurant News*, July 10, 1995.
24. According to Troy Alstead, "We are evaluating whether to offer our coffee in grocery stores, and we have done some private labeling of Starbucks coffee for Costco." The Specialty Coffee Association of America predicts that by 1999 supermarkets will account for 63 percent of all coffee sold in America. This will be followed by gourmet stores (14%), mass market (11%), mail order (8.0%) and other (8%).
25. Coke and Nestlé have signed a similar agreement to produce single-serving cold coffee drinks in specialty flavors such as french vanilla, mocha, and café au lait to compete with the Starbucks product.
26. Airports often grant exclusive concessions contracts to a single provider, such as Host Marriott. Because Starbucks wanted to tap these markets, it negotiated licensing arrangements with Marriott to run Starbucks stands in the airports that Marriott has under contract.
27. *Washington Post*, August 1, 1995.
28. The Hawaii entry is based on a joint venture with The Mac-Naugton Group, a real estate development firm that has been responsible for the successful introduction of several well-known mainland firms such as Sports Authority, Office Max and Eagle Hardware stores into the Hawaiian Islands. Using this joint venture, the firm plans to develop approximately 30 stores throughout the Hawaiian Islands over the next three to four years. Starbucks' entry into Singapore is based on a licensing agreement with Bonvests Holdings Limited, a firm involved in property and hotel development, investment, related management services, waste management and building maintenance services, food and beverage retailing and marketing of branded luxury products in Singapore. Under this agreement (completed in December 1996), ten Starbucks coffee stores are expected to open within the first 12 to 15 months.
29. *Puget Sound Business Journal*, June 21–27, 1996.
30. *Wall Street Journal*, September 4, 1996.
31. *Nikkei Weekly*, September 23, 1996.
32. According to a report in the *Nihon Keizai Shimbum* (June 18, 1988), Doutor is good at segmenting the coffee market. For instance, the firm has a coffee shop for just about every taste and service level. The low-end shops are located near train stations and busy areas where people are in a hurry. In residential locations, the firm operates Cafe Colorado where people can sit and chat for a while. The price of coffee in Cafe Colorado is double that of the firm's inexpensive coffee houses. The firm also caters to more upscale customers via Cafe Doutor, where the ambiance is more elegant and the coffee price is much higher.
33. According to a report in the *Wall Street Journal*, Honna spent time last year gathering intelligence on Starbucks' method in the United States. He reportedly visited, incognito, more than 20 Starbucks coffee shops along the West Coast.
34. Reuters World Service, August 1, 1996.
35. *Wall Street Journal*, September 4, 1996.

APPENDIX A *Starbucks Corporation—A Brief History*

1971 Starbucks Coffee opens its first store in the Pike Place Market—Seattle, Washington's, legendary, open-air farmer's market.

1982 Howard Schultz joins Starbucks as director of retail operations and marketing. Starbucks begins providing coffee to fine restaurants and espresso bars in Seattle.

1983 Schultz travels to Italy, where he's impressed with the popularity of espresso bars. Milan, a city the size of Philadelphia, hosts 1,500 of these bars.

1984 Schultz convinces the original founders of Starbucks to test the coffee bar concept in a new Starbucks store on the corner of 4th and Spring in downtown Seattle. Overwhelmingly successful, this experiment is the genesis for a company that Schultz will found in 1985.

1985 Schultz founds Il Giornale, offering brewed coffee and espresso beverages made from Starbucks coffee beans.

1987 In August, with the backing of local investors, Il Giornale acquires the Seattle assets of Starbucks and changes its name to Starbucks Corporation. The company has fewer than 100 employees and opens its first stores in Chicago and Vancouver, B.C. **Starbucks store total = 17**

1988 Starbucks introduces mail-order catalog, offering mail-order service in all 50 states. **Starbucks store total = 33**

1989 Opens first Portland, Oregon, store in Pioneer Courthouse Square. **Starbucks store total = 55**

1990 Starbucks expands corporate headquarters in Seattle and builds a new roasting plant. **Starbucks store total = 84**

1991 Starbucks opens first stores in Los Angeles, California. Announces Starbucks' commitment to establish a long-term relationship with CARE, the international relief and development organization, and introduces CARE coffee sampler.

Becomes the first U.S. privately owned company in history to offer a stock option program, Bean Stock, that includes part-time employees. **Starbucks store total = 116**

1992 Starbucks opens first stores in San Francisco, San Diego, Orange County, and Denver. Specialty Sales and Marketing Division awarded Nordstrom's national coffee account. Completes initial public offering, with common stock being traded on the NASDAQ National Market System. **Starbucks store total = 165**

1993 Opens premier East Coast market: Washington, D.C., Specialty Sales and Marketing Division begins relationship with Barnes & Noble, Inc., as national account. Opens second roasting plant located in Kent, Washington. **Starbucks store total = 275**

1994 Opens first stores in Minneapolis, Boston, New York, Atlanta, Dallas, and Houston. Specialty Sales and Marketing Division awarded ITT/Sheraton Hotel's national coffee account.

The Coffee Connection, Inc., becomes wholly owned subsidiary of Starbucks Corporation in June.

Starbucks announces partnership with Pepsi-Cola to develop ready-to-drink coffee-based beverages.

Completes offering of additional 6,025,000 shares of common stock at $28.50 per share.

Schultz receives Business Enterprise Trust Award recognizing the company's innovative benefits plan. **Starbucks store total = 425**

1995 Starbucks opens first stores in Pittsburgh, Las Vegas, San Antonio, Philadelphia, Cincinnati, Baltimore, and Austin. Specialty Sales and Marketing Division begins relationship with United Airlines.

Starbucks and Redhook Ale Brewery introduced Double BLACK™ STOUT, a new dark roasted malt beer with the aromatic and flavorful addition of coffee.

Acquires minority interest in Noah's New York Bagels, Inc.

Starbucks stores begin serving Frappuccino® blended beverages, a line of low-fat, creamy, iced coffee beverages.

Starbucks opens state-of-the-art roasting facility in York, Pennsylvania, serving East Coast markets.

Announces alliance with Chapters Inc. to operate coffee bars inside Chapters' superstores in Canada.

Announces partnership with Star Markets to open Starbucks retail locations within Star Market stores.

Develops framework for a code of conduct as part of a long-term strategy to improve conditions in coffee origin countries.

Starbucks Coffee international signs agreement with Sazaby, Inc., a Japanese retailer and restaurateur, to form a joint venture partnership that will develop Starbucks retail stores in Japan. The joint venture is called Starbucks Coffee Japan, Ltd.

Forms long-term joint venture with Dreyer's Grand Ice Cream, Inc., to develop revolutionary line of coffee ice creams. **Starbucks store total = 676**

C-460

APPENDIX A *Starbucks Corporation—A Brief History (cont.)*

1996 Opens first stores in Rhode Island, Idaho, North Carolina, Arizona, Utah, and Toronto, Ontario. Specialty Sales and Marketing Division awarded Westin Hotel's national coffee account.

Starbucks Coffee Japan, Ltd. opens first location outside North America in the Ginza District, Tokyo, Japan. Announces plans to develop 10 to 12 additional stores in the Tokyo metropolitan area over the next 18 months.

Starbucks Coffee International signs agreement forming Coffee Partners Hawaii, which will develop Starbucks retail locations in Hawaii.

First Starbucks store in Honolulu opens at Kalala Mall.

Starbucks Coffee International signs licensing agreement with Bonstar Ptc. Ltd. to open stores in Singapore.

First Licensed Singapore location opens at Liat Towers.

Direct Response Division reaches over seven million America Online (AOL) customers through Caffé Starbucks, a marketplace channel store that offers select Starbucks catalog products.

Announces that all Coffee Connection locations in the Boston area will become Starbucks stores during fiscal 1996.

Announces development agreement with three leading digital media companies—Digital Brands, Inc., Watts-Silverstein & Associates and Cyberstruction, Inc.—to develop a wide-ranging online strategy.

Unveils prototype store at Comdex Convention and Trade Show, Las Vegas, with Intel Corp., showcasing some of the technologies Starbucks will be testing in several stores over the next year.

Forms licensing arrangement with ARAMARK Corp. to put licensed Starbucks operations at various locations operated by ARAMARK.

Starbucks and Dreyer's Grand Ice Cream, Inc., introduce six flavors of Starbucks™ ice cream and Starbucks ice cream bars, available in grocery stores across the United States. Starbucks ice cream quickly becomes the number-one brand of coffee ice cream in the United States.

North American Coffee Partnership (between Starbucks and Pepsi-Cola Company) announces a bottled version of Starbucks popular Frappuccino™ blended beverage will be sold in supermarkets, convenience stores, and other retail points of distribution on the West Coast.

Starbucks commemorates the first anniversary of the Blue Note Blend coffee and CD with Blue Note 2, an encore collection of jazz from the Blue Note® Records label. The Blue Note Blend coffee also returns for a limited engagement in the company's coffee lineup.

Celebrates the company's 25th Anniversary with marketing program featuring the art, music, and culture of 1971, the year Starbucks was born. **Current Starbucks store total = 1,100**

Steinway & Sons

Suresh Kotha

University of Washington

Roger Dunbar

New York University

A Steinway is a Steinway.... There is no such thing as a "better" Steinway. Each and every Steinway is *the best Steinway.*

—Theodore Steinway

The 1990s were a period of change for the music industry. Foreign competition in the mid-price upright piano market was intense. In addition to well-entrenched players from Japan (Yamaha and Kawai), two South Korean firms (Young Chang and Samick) were emerging as strong competitors. Moreover, Yamaha and Young Chang had already established a presence in China. Forecasts indicated that the future market for pianos will be concentrated in Asia.

This case discusses Steinway & Sons' history, the evolution of its value system, and the current market conditions facing the firm. It highlights the issues faced by Steinway & Sons as its top management formulates its strategy toward the growing Chinese piano market.

This case was prepared with assistance from Joseph H. Alhadeff (Stern MBA, 1995), Gerald Tennenbaum (Stern MBA, 1995), and Professor Xavier Martin (Stern) as the basis for class discussion rather than to illustrate either effective or ineffective handling of an administrative situation. Copyright © 1996 Kotha and Dunbar. All rights reserved.

COMPANY BACKGROUND

The Steinway Family Years—1853 to 1971

Steinway & Sons was founded in 1853 by Henry E. Steinway, Sr., and his sons, Henry Jr., Charles, and William. In 1854, the firm entered and won its first competition. A year later it won first prize at the American Institute Fair in New York. By 1860, Steinway & Sons built a manufacturing facility at 52nd Street and Fourth (now Park) Avenue, on the site now occupied by the Waldorf Astoria Hotel. Here 350 men produced 30 square pianos and 5 grands per week. In 1864, the firm opened a showroom on 14th Street, and in 1865, sales topped $1,000,000.

From the beginning, piano building at Steinway & Sons was a family affair. Each Steinway son concentrated on gaining expertise in a different aspect of piano manufacturing: William was a "bellyman" who installed the piano soundboards, Henry Jr. focused on piano "finishing," and Charles concentrated on "voicing" the piano. By 1854, the Steinways were employers, and the family members had become managers. Henry Sr. was in charge overall, while Henry Jr. focused on research and development, Charles managed the plant, and William concentrated on marketing.

Music historians consider the competition at the 1867 Paris Exhibition as the turning point in the piano industry because it was there that the "American" system of cast-iron frames, heavier strings, solid construction, and more powerful tone took the competitive honors from European pianos. The jury report gave the Steinway piano a slight edge over that of the other major U.S. manufacturer, Chickering & Sons, due to its expression, delicate shading, and a variety of accentuations.

With this recognition, Steinway's domestic piano sales and exports grew rapidly, requiring greater production capacity. In 1870, under William's leadership, the firm purchased 400 acres of remote farmland in Astoria, Queens, with the idea of moving the factory from Manhattan. By 1873, the new factory was operating, and Steinway-sponsored employee housing, transport, and other facilities were built. Two years later, the firm opened a showroom in London. Ten years later, to avoid U.S. labor issues and build a global presence, the firm built a factory in Hamburg, Germany. Pianos manufactured there were marketed in Europe and exported to the rest of the world. Today, these two factories remain the firm's only manufacturing centers.

In the 1870s, low-cost piano producers were a significant competitive threat. Conflict emerged between William and Theodore concerning the best way to respond. (C. F. Theodore was the founder's fourth son and had joined the firm in 1865 following his brothers' deaths.) The choice was to continue to emphasize class and high quality, as William favored, or to make inexpensive models, as advocated by Theodore. William's view won out. Ever since, the firm has remained steadfast in its focus on the high-end segment of the market.

At the turn of the century, the public developed an interest in player pianos. Steinway & Sons, however, showed no interest in these add-on technologies. Sales of player pianos plummeted after radio broadcasting began in 1920. In contrast, Steinway's sales continued to climb. They were supported by extensive advertising and a generous sponsorship program that deployed 600 Steinways to support concert artists.

Successive generations of Steinways sought to follow the founder's advice: "We provide customers with the highest quality instrument and services, consistent with Steinway's reputation for excellence, by building the finest piano in the world and selling it at a reasonable profit." This approach was threatened when the U.S. economy entered a depression in the

1930s, and the firm's survival was at stake. To market pianos to people of more modest means with smaller homes, Steinway developed and introduced two new models, a five foot, one inch "baby grand" and a 40-inch upright piano. At the outbreak of World War II, production was stopped.

When piano making resumed in 1946, the television set was at the center of the American home. The task of rebuilding Steinway & Sons fell to Henry Z. Steinway, a fourth-generation family member, who assumed responsibility for manufacturing. His brother John took over promotions and marketing. To help consolidate the firm financially, Henry Z. sold Steinway Hall on 57th Street in Manhattan (the company's showroom) and leased back the lower two floors.

In the 1960s, new competition emerged from Asia. Yamaha and Kawai began exporting thousands of pianos to the United States. A Yamaha piano sold for about one-half the price of the equivalent Steinway model. By the early 1970s, the Japanese threat raised doubts about the future of Steinway & Sons and the entire U.S. piano industry. Henry Z. decided to sell:

Among the active family members, none were getting younger. And no young Steinways were interested in the firm. In the mid-twenties, two stockholder managers could get in a room and do anything they wanted. With the depression, shares were diluted bringing many new owners. The New York factory was located in an area hostile to manufacturing. Other piano makers had moved South to where they appreciated manufacturers. If we chose to move, we needed lots of capital.

In 1972, the firm was sold and merged into the CBS Musical Instruments Division. Henry Z. observed:

Japan represents both an opportunity and a menace. As the largest market in the world for new pianos, having surpassed the U.S., possibly Steinway could enter that market effectively with the aid of CBS. Conversely, free from restraints imposed by antitrust legislation in the U.S., one huge company [Yamaha] has the avowed purpose of overcoming Steinway. Why CBS and not General Motors or U.S. Steel? CBS wanted us at a price we thought right. More importantly, we thought CBS could and would handle our product in the right way.

The CBS Years—1972 to 1985

CBS increased capital spending from $100,000 annually to between $1 and 2 million. Workers received the same medical and retirement benefits as other CBS employees. These were a big improvement over what had been provided previously. To facilitate continuity, Henry Z. remained as president. Nevertheless, concerns soon arose. According to industry reports:

Once CBS entered upon its own period of decline, Steinway was plagued by bureaucratic confusion, changing strategies and parades of efficiency experts. There were four Steinway presidents in [16 years]. "Quality control" slipped. . . . There were pianists who began to say that the Steinway was no longer a great instrument; the market for half-century old rebuilt Steinways boomed.[1]

Recalling top management changes under CBS, Henry Z. Steinway observed:

Each new [division] president wanted to do something different. It was like riding a different horse every six months—first it was quality, then it was volume, then it was automation. The firm was drifting from one program to another. Also, I got so many memos from the parent corporation [CBS Musical Instruments Division] that after a while, I simply ignored them. I also thought it was rather amusing that I reported to the head of the division in California who, in turn, reported to a guy at the [CBS] headquarters just a few blocks from our offices in Manhattan.

Further, CBS often showed little regard or understanding for Steinway's established traditions. Steinway tradition, for example, encouraged workers to bring their relatives to work for the firm. Steinway believed this was a good way of preserving established skills and also encouraged loyalty and a reliable, motivated work force. Under CBS, however, such nepotism was strictly forbidden. Annoyed, Henry Z. retired from the firm in 1980.

During the early 1980s, under the fourth CBS president, quality was revived and the firm introduced a new upright. This new 52-inch piano was targeted to institutions and music schools. Then CBS decided to divest all of its music businesses. *Smithsonian* magazine reported:

That announcement alone nearly completed what earlier sloppiness and mismanagement could not. . . . In 1985, the year of the sale, Steinway was earning $8 million on $60 million in revenues. The sale, involving at least 18 interested parties, dragged out over a period of ten months. There were rumors that the factory would be sold for its real estate value. CBS claimed to be concerned over the future of the company, but finally it needed cash to fend off attempts to take it over. And so CBS sold Steinway & Sons in haste, along with three other musical instrument companies, for less than $50 million—a much smaller sum than was offered earlier by serious devotees of the instrument.[2]

This brought morale among Steinway workers to an all-time low.

The Birmingham Years—1985 to 1995

CBS sold Steinway & Sons and the rest of its Musical Instruments Division in December 1985 to John and Robert Birmingham, two brothers from Boston who had made their fortune through a family-owned heating-oil business. The Steinway work force, which had just survived the uncertainty and confusion of the CBS years, was not predisposed to trust strangers.

Lloyd Meyers, the last CBS president, had tried to organize a leveraged buyout. Following the firm's acquisition, he left, as did the chief financial officer. Bruce Stevens became president. The sales force, which had been managed by a two-day-a-week manager, was placed under Frank Mazurco, a long-time Steinway district sales manager. The number of U.S. dealers was reduced from 152 to 92. Stevens established a program to strengthen the ties between Steinway & Sons and its dealers. A formal five-day program for technicians was established to provide hands-on training at the New York and Germany plants. Additionally, the firm instituted a three-year strategic planning process. To instill more "discipline" into manufacturing, top management replaced the factory manager with Daniel Koenig, a manufacturing engineer who had spent 21 years at GE.

Under Koenig, the firm introduced state-of-the-art machines for manufacturing such components as hammers so that tolerances could be brought within carefully established limits. The whole "action-mechanism" department was reorganized and moved to a single location. New programs, such as statistical process control, were introduced. Engineers were hired and provided with state-of-the-art computer-aided design technology. The goal was to document the design and manufacturing process using old Steinway drawings, many of which dated back to the turn of the century.

These changes were viewed as controversial by some employees, music critics, and other followers of the firm. They observed that the changes top management introduced to increase efficiency were working to the detriment of Steinway's historical tradition of craftsmanship and quality. Steinway management countered by arguing that employing a modern, scientific approach to manufacturing was not a break with, but a continuation of, Steinway traditions.

In 1991, Steinway & Sons introduced a new line— the Boston Pianos—designed to compete in the mid-range $10,000 piano market. This line was designed by Steinway & Sons and manufactured at Kawai's factory in Japan. According to Bruce Stevens:

> Steinway dealers had suggested that a logical step-up strategy to a Steinway piano was needed. The availability of many competent lower-priced pianos made making a Steinway sale to a novice pianist harder to justify. We decided that a new line of mid-priced pianos was necessary.

Steinway dealers now had a piano they could offer to compete against similarly priced pianos made by Yamaha, Young Chang, Kawai, and Samick. Currently, the Boston line includes four grand piano models ranging in length from 5 feet, 4 inches to 7 feet, 2 inches, as well as four upright models ranging in height from 44 to 52 inches. The line does not include a full-size concert grand. As they were originally intended strictly as an export from Japan, Boston pianos sell for 25 percent more than Japanese domestic pianos.

According to John Birmingham, perhaps the most important ingredient that the new owners brought to Steinway was their attitude. Noted John:

> We did not purchase the company to move it and make a fortune in real estate, or to silk-screen Steinway t-shirts, or to go public and make a killing on the stock offering. It was our intention

to operate the Steinway piano business in a vigorous and creative way. Our guiding principle has been to guard and nurture the quality and integrity of the Steinway piano.

During the Birminghams' tenure, worker morale was gradually reestablished. Discussions between management and workers evolved so appropriate modernization of technical equipment occurred while respect for the unique aspects of the craft mode of production associated with a Steinway piano was maintained. In 1995, one of the firm's harshest critics from *The New York Times* acknowledged the following:

> A recent tour of the Steinway's factory in Queens showed an apparently serious effort to improve the instrument. The final stages of manufacture receive more attention than they did a few years ago. Outside technicians have also reported improvements in Steinways, a heartening sign.[3]

Enter Selmer Company, 1995

In 1995, Steinway & Sons was purchased by the Selmer Company for nearly $100 million. This Elkhart, Indiana, firm had manufacturing facilities in La Grange, Illinois; Cleveland, Ohio; and Monroe, North Carolina. The Steinway & Sons management team installed by the Birminghams remained intact and in charge.

Commenting on the merger, Dana Messina, an investment banker and a controlling shareholder of Selmer's parent corporation, noted:

> The combination of Steinway and Selmer is an exciting opportunity for both of the companies and their employees. Our extensive investigation has made it clear that Steinway's New York factory today produces excellent instruments of a quality unequaled in many years, and the Steinways made in the company's Hamburg factory continue to dominate the European and Asian concert scene. . . . We intend to continue the mission of producing great instruments that has been pursued by Steinway.

The new owners made an IPO stock offering to raise $60 million in August 1996.

THE STEINWAY LEGACY

There are two fundamentals in understanding the origins of the Steinway legacy: technical innovation and marketing. Around 1800, the piano's identity was still in a formative stage, but by the 1850s, the instrument's basic structure had been defined. Taking the basic structure as a given, the Steinways improved the piano and, ultimately, the entire industry.

Building Technical Capabilities

In 1850, producers were working to make piano performance more reliable and louder. New piano works were developed by romantic composers and they demanded a broader range of tones. In addition, larger concert halls were being built. These developments served to establish a need for pianos with a louder tone. The general objective of Steinway & Sons' efforts was to develop reliable pianos that offered a more powerful tone.

Experimentation at Steinway & Sons was done primarily by two of the founder's sons, Henry Jr. and Theodore. These Steinway brothers experimented and developed theories about improvements to both the design and the manufacture of pianos. In 1911, Alfred Dolge described Theodore's approach as follows:

> Step by step he invaded the fields of modern science, investigating and testing different kinds of wood in order to ascertain why one kind or another was best adapted for piano construction, then taking up the study of metallurgy, to find a proper alloy for casting iron plates which would stand the tremendous strain of 75,000 pounds of the new concert grand piano that was already born in his mind, calling chemistry to his aid to establish the scientific basis for felts, glue, varnish oils—in short, nothing in the realm of science having any bearing on piano construction was overlooked.[4]

Over a 50-year period starting in 1857, the firm obtained 58 patents for various innovations to piano design. At international exhibitions in Europe, the Steinways proudly showed off their new methods and basked in the resulting acclaim. One consequence was that their methods were copied widely, especially in Europe. By the 1870s, the "Steinway system" was well recognized, and by the end of the century it became the *de facto* industry standard.

During the mid-19th century, new industrial technologies emerged to cause a revolution in piano manufacturing. Steinway & Sons was at the forefront of these developments, implementing innovative and unique approaches to piano manufacturing. At their large facility, opened in 1860, they standardized various parts of the piano to facilitate volume manufacturing, refitting, and servicing. Though the firm used increased mechanization to produce standardized components, it retained a "craft" approach for other components and for assembling pianos. The combination of the mechanized technologies and individual craft skills quickly became a hallmark of the Steinway approach to piano manufacture.

Building Reputation

From the beginning, Steinway & Sons faced intense competition from rivals such as Chickering & Sons and Mason & Hamlin in the United States and Erard and Broadwood in Europe. Facing this competition, the firm sought to highlight not only the unique construction of the Steinway piano but its "superior" sound.

To do this, the firm entered its pianos in contests that compared manufacturers' products. In 1854, for example, the firm exhibited a square piano at the Metropolitan Fair held in Washington, D.C., and received a prize medal. A year later Steinway & Sons entered the American Institute Fair at the Crystal Palace in New York and the judges awarded it first prize from among 19 competitors.

> [Steinway & Sons'] great triumph came at the great fair of the American Institute in New York in 1855, where their overstrung square piano with full iron frame created a sensation in the piano world. As a result their business expanded so rapidly that in 1859 the erection of that mammoth factory on Fifty-Third Street and Fourth Avenue, New York, became a necessity.[5]

To gain international recognition, Steinway & Sons, along with 130 other manufacturers, entered the International Exhibition held at the Crystal Palace in London in 1862. Steinway & Sons was recognized as the best American manufacturer and was awarded a major prize. The main prize went to

C-465

Broadwood. In 1867, the firm entered the Paris Exposition, along with 178 other firms. Both Steinway and Chickering were awarded gold medals at this exposition.

Winning by Not Competing At the major manufacturers' competition held in Vienna in 1873, around two-thirds of the pianos exhibited were built according to the Steinway system. Steinway & Sons did not compete, however, having reached an agreement with Chickering in order to avoid continuation of the shrill accusations that had arisen between the two rivals after the Paris Exposition.[6] With the competition over, however, the judges issued a statement regretting that "Steinway & Sons, the celebrated inaugurators of the new piano-making system, had chosen not to exhibit." From the standpoint of enhancing its reputation for making a superior piano, Steinway & Sons "won" in Vienna by not competing.

Industry rivalries also persuaded Steinway & Sons and 15 other piano-making firms from the eastern United States to boycott the 1893 World's Fair in Chicago. As expected, W. W. Kimball, a Chicago piano manufacturer, won the highest award. At the time, however, Steinway & Sons was promoting a U.S. tour of the Polish virtuoso, Ignance Jan Paderewsky. Paderewsky was invited to play at the exhibition's inauguration, but only if he would play on a piano entered in the competition. Paderewsky countered that he could only play on a piano he was used to playing. The organizers relented and Paderewsky played his Steinway. Again, unfolding events enabled Steinway & Sons to enhance its reputation by not competing.

A Steinway Is a Steinway Steinway & Sons always sought to establish a reputation for itself as the firm that built the best piano for musicians, especially concert artists. It also sought to establish itself as being a contributor, supporter, and leader in the cultural arts. As Dolge noted:

> They never relaxed in letting the public know that they manufactured a fine piano. William Steinway, with farseeing judgment, was not satisfied only to use printer's ink with telling effect, but he also began to educate the public to appreciate good music. Steinway Hall was erected, the Theodore Thomas orchestra generously supported and the greatest piano virtuosos from Rubinstein to Joseffy engaged for concerts, not only in New York but in all large cities of the United States and Canada.[7]

Steinway Hall, designed and built by William Steinway in 1866, was the largest concert hall in New York City. Notes Dolge:

> The opening of this hall was the inauguration of a new era in the musical life of America. Anton Rubinstein, Annette Essipoff, Teresa Carreno, Fannie Bloomfield-Zeisler, Rafael Joseffy, Eugene D'Albert, Leopold Damrosch and Anto Seidl made their bows to select audiences from the platform of Steinway Hall. William Steinway knew that the American people needed musical education. He provided it.[8]

Steinway & Sons used concert artist endorsements to convince the public that its pianos were superior. Initially, the effort at Steinway & Sons was largely opportunistic and informal. But the benefits of more large-scale efforts were recognized as a result of the 215-concert U.S. tour in 1872 by virtuoso Anton Rubinstein, who was sponsored by Steinway & Sons. Rubinstein and his Steinway dazzled audiences. In 1891, the Steinway-sponsored concert tour of Ignace Jan Paderewsky was also a great success. Paderewsky cleared an unprecedented $200,000 from his tour, and the promotional value to Steinway & Sons was immeasurable.

These concerts, the artists involved, and the sponsor all received extensive press coverage and acclaim. In 1912 Charles Steinway, the president of Steinway & Sons, observed: "It was without doubt the most effective of all advertising methods we employed, since it not only made the piano and its maker widely known, but assisted in laying the foundation for a broad national culture."

Although Steinway & Sons never offered to reduce the price of its pianos, it sought endorsements from New York's social elite.[9] To this and other groups, the firm presented itself as offering a high-quality product worthy of a high price. Today, Steinway pianos are priced the highest in the industry. Often this price is nearly double that of an equivalent Yamaha, the firm's most competitive rival in the United States.

Steinway & Sons has consistently emphasized its commitment to the cultural enrichment of the nation and the world. The firm's promotions argue, for example, that the act of buying a piano is not the same as the act of buying a Steinway. Buying a Steinway is depicted as an indication of appreciation for high cultural taste and, hence, was a sign of high achievement. The firm also built upon its international presence. Dolge noted:

> Having established the fame of his piano in America beyond dispute, William [Steinway] looked for other worlds to conquer, and opened a branch house in the city of London about the year 1875. Steinway Hall in London was formally opened in 1876. In 1880 Hamburg factories were started, to supply the ever-growing European trade.[10]

The Hamburg facility was established primarily to challenge the domination of European piano markets by companies such as Bechstein, Bluthner, and Ibach. At the time, the firm was the only piano maker that served all well-known concert artists in every major city in America and in Europe. According to D. W. Fostle, an author and keyboard expert, "A Steinway piano soon became recognized as an admired cultural icon in any refined home, a necessary element on any prominent concert stage, and part of the necessary baggage of any prominent pianist."[11]

Building a Marketing Approach

As with its competitors, Steinway & Sons originally sought out and paid for endorsements from prominent concert artists. Over time, Steinway and other firms ceased this practice. Concert artists, however, still chose to endorse the Steinway piano. Today, more than 90 percent of all classical music concerts featuring a piano soloist are performed on a Steinway concert grand piano.[12] This endorsement has remained stable for many decades. Music schools and conservatories such as Juilliard, Oberlin, and Indiana University have always showed a great fondness for Steinways.

Steinway & Sons sought to be associated with high culture, style, status, and class. In 1855 the firm started advertising daily in *The New York Times*. Gradually, Steinway & Sons moved to much more extensive advertising campaigns.

> To the astonishment and chagrin of the older and more conservative houses in the piano trade, William [Steinway] started an aggressive and heretofore unheard-of advertising campaign. As a

competent judge he knew that his factories turned out the best pianos that could possibly be made, and he was bent not only on letting the world know it, but on making the world believe it, as he did. This was revolutionary, even shocking, but William persisted until he carried his point.[13]

Steinway as an Investment In 1900, Steinway & Sons hired N. W. Ayer & Son, the oldest full-service advertising agency in the country, to promote Steinway pianos. Ayer & Son emphasized that many potential Steinway buyers were not only interested in music but were greatly interested in class and status. Their interest in owning a Steinway would increase if the class and status associated with the Steinway name was emphasized.

Systematically, Steinway broadened the message in its promotions. The firm's advertising emphasized, for example, that one did not "buy" but "invested" in a Steinway, that there was no such thing as a better Steinway for a Steinway was the best, that owning a Steinway was more important than being able to play it, and that a Steinway piano was always made just a little bit better than was necessary. Steinway advertising was targeted to emphasize family values, the firm's contributions to art and music, its technical excellence, or some combination of these. Forging a link with the art community, the firm commissioned paintings showing famous artists and composers, past and present, linked to the Steinway piano. The "timeless" excellence of a Steinway was emphasized.

> The commission and use of modern art in Steinway ads of the 1920s was an extension of the advertising style that the New York firm had employed for decades. . . . With Steinway the association was natural. However much another product's image was improved by its proximity to art, it remained a mere product. The Steinway itself became art.[14]

In the 1920s, the program to make sure that all outstanding concert artists used a Steinway grew to include more than 600 supported artists. With a consistent and overwhelming advertising message and its U.S. competition in retreat, the firm convinced the public that a Steinway was the only "artistic" piano.[15]

According to *Forbes*, a Steinway piano outperforms Mercedes-Benz automobiles, power boats, wine, and gold as luxury items for investment. A Steinway created between 1929 and 1958 is now worth nearly six times its original cost; for those dating from 1959 to 1978, the factor of appreciation currently stands at nearly three times. Piano rebuilders are known to scour the world in search of old Steinways because, regardless of its age or neglect, a Steinway grand can often be restored to its original magnificence.

The 1970s and 1980s saw new competition emerge from Asian competitors. Of particular interest was Yamaha's announced intention to overtake the status associated with a Steinway. Yamaha's president claimed this would be done by promoting Yamaha's sound quality and tone along with the status and class associated with the Yamaha name. Despite Yamaha's avowed threat to overtake the status of Steinway & Sons, the firm's reputation as producer of the best-sounding piano has remained intact. In 1991, Dolge noted:

> Just as a most masterful copy of a Raphael or Correggio will ever be only a copy and far from the original, so it has proved impossible to produce a piano equal to the Steinway piano, even though the Steinways were copied to the minutest detail. No art product can be duplicated by copying.

MANUFACTURING STEINWAYS

Manufacturing a Steinway piano is a labor-intensive and time-consuming process. A Steinway concert grand piano is one of the world's most complex pieces of hand-built machinery. It consists of over 12,000 parts and requires about a year to complete. Approximately 300 craftspeople have a hand in its development.

The 44,000-square-foot manufacturing facility manufactured about 67 percent of Steinway pianos sold in 1995. This facility consists of many linked buildings that house the factory and Steinway's offices. In 1985, 260 direct workers and 61 nondirect workers were involved in manufacturing pianos. The production workers are represented by Local 102 of the United Furniture Workers, a small two-company local that has bargained with Steinway management for decades. In 1986, wages averaged approximately $9 per hour ($12 including fringe benefits). About 25 percent of the skilled artisans are paid via piece

rates, while other workers are paid on a straight-time basis. Throughout the factory there are workers who represent families that have been with the firm for generations. Currently, the work force has a multinational cast of first-generation immigrants. Over 17 languages are spoken in the factory.

The factory is part lumber mill, part fine-cabinet works, part manual-crafts assembly line, and part studio for industrial craftspeople working on art acquired through many years of apprenticeship. Although the buildings have undergone significant changes over the years, the piano-making operations have hardly changed in the last century.

The Lumber Mill The mill, the factory's lumber yard, carries approximately 1.5 million board-feet of select woods (costing approximately $2 million) such as hard rock maple and sitka spruce. Twice a year, the firm's wood technologist, Warren Albrecht, goes to Canada and the American Northwest to identify wood of sufficient quality and grain to be used by Steinway. These woods are air-dried in the open for about 18 months, and then kiln-dried using recently installed computer-controlled equipment. Reduction of the wood's moisture content through drying is essential for the instrument's acoustics. Through years of trial and error, the firm has managed to establish ideal moisture content and drying times for each of the instrument's various wooden components. It is here, via the world's finest woods, that the foundation of what eventually becomes a Steinway piano begins.

Rim-Bending Operations This operation focuses on the piano's rim (the curved sideboard giving grand pianos their shape and support). A concert grand's rim requires a 22-foot-long, three-and-one-half-inch-wide board of hard rock maple. Because boards of this length rarely occur in nature, thin slats of maple laminates (18 layers thick) are glued together to form the piece. When bent, this wooden piece forms the piano's familiar outer and hidden inner rims that extend below the sound board and frame. Steinway's processes for bending the inner and outer board remain unique in the industry. According to Henry Z. Steinway, it is this process that provides the instrument with greater strength and durability.

The rim-bending room consists of eight piano-shaped forms of steel whose perimeters are fitted with screws and clamps. With the glue holding the 18 layers of laminates still wet, the piece is manually pressed against the form and secured by iron pinions.[16] The bent rim is then heated by high-frequency radio waves. Although the rim is technically ready for the next process in minutes, it remains in the iron form for 24 hours. Once removed, the piece is stacked in a humidity-controlled environment for 10 weeks. This curing period ensures that the rim retains its bent form. Following the waiting period, the rim is planed, sanded, and cross-braced and then the key-bed and pin-block are inserted. Slowly the rim is transformed into a unitary piano case.

The Sound Board Assembly In another part of the factory, highly skilled woodworkers create the piano's sound board. The sound board consists of 20 spruce boards, selected from the same lot of wood, meticulously cleared of any imperfections. These boards are matched for grain and color and glued along their lengths. Once glued, the board is thinned in certain places and tapered toward the ends. By the application of support ribs to its underside, the board is also slightly crowned. Then a bridge, the clef-shaped support for the strings, is affixed.

The Action Mechanism The "guts" of the piano consist of the keys and the action. Together, they constitute the mechanism by which the act of depressing the key causes the corresponding hammer to strike the string and return to its original resting place.[17] Once assembled, the actions are mated with the piano's keys and the entire "key-action assembly" mechanism is regulated to ensure proper movement. After being regulated, the key-action assembly is moved to another part of the factory where the keys are weighted to ensure they provide the appropriate touch and recoil. Proper touch and recoil result in the piano's "even feel," an important trait of the legendary Steinway experience. The mechanism is then fitted into a piano case. The foundation that supports the key-action assembly is the spruce key bed.

The Final Assembly The joining of the piano case and an iron plate to support the strings is carried out in the factory's "belly" room. The bellying process involves attaching the iron plate and the sound board to the inner rim of the piano case. This process takes up to eight hours over the course of two days. During this process, the sound board is affixed securely to the piano case using a special hot glue that ensures a good seal between the board and the piano case. The board installation process is critical for the proper resonance of the strings, and multiple measurements are taken to ensure a proper fit.

Once the hot glue sets and the clamps holding the board in place are removed, the cast iron plate is lowered into the case. Accurate installation of the plate ensures the proper bearing of the bridge, which then helps maintain the right pressure on the piano's strings. Too little or too much pressure results in an instrument that sounds weak or muffled. With the sound board and iron plate installation complete, the piano is ready for stringing.

The stringing process involves hammering pins into a pin-block underneath the iron plate and inserting about 243 strings. After the instrument is strung, it passes through a "banger" which mechanically pounds every key about 8,000 times within a 45-minute period. This "aging" process ensures that the sound notes emanating from the instrument are stable. The instrument is then regulated to ensure its moving parts (the key-action mechanism) interact properly.

The Steinway piano comes in flat and glossy finishes. The flat finish is the trademark of the Queens factory, and the glossy finish is typical of the Hamburg factory. Each piano receives five coats of lacquer prior to the insertion of the sound board and iron plate, but is not truly finished until it is shipped. Once assembled, pianos are polished and rubbed in a manually intensive process.

The Tone Regulating Department Many of the sound-related operations are carried out in the tone regulation department by a group of Steinway's most skilled technicians. Highly skilled artisans (as the firm prefers to call them) optimize the final tone of the piano and do all the fine-tuning. For the concert grands, this process can take as long as a week per piano.

Tuning involves adjusting the piano strings to get the proper tonal quality, and "voicing" entails final adjustments to the shape of the hammer, the feel of the felt, and the movement and position of the actions. With the personality or voice of the piano exposed, final adjustments are completed to optimize the instrument's sound qualities. The time taken to complete this process varies from 8 to 24 hours. Variations in the production process are accommodated during the tuning and voicing processes and contribute to the distinctive sound of each Steinway piano. Given the nature of the craft production process, each step is contingent upon the success of the previous steps and there is little room for error. Each piano sounds and feels different. The firm encourages prospective buyers to play several pianos and then to pick the one they think sounds best.

By the time a piano is assembled, strung, tuned, and voiced, it has gone through 25 to 30 quality checkpoints. The workers responsible for sound board placement, stringing, tone adjustment, and other big jobs often signed their work. According to one Steinway tuner, "It's an aspiration of everybody to be immortal, and so, like an artist who signs his painting, I sign the piano. I put into the piano the best of myself."[18] In the 1980s, John Steinway observed:

> A Steinway is a Steinway only because we don't cut any corners. My great-grandfather started that 135 years ago. I often say we're probably thick-headed and stubborn; we stick to our principles. But it works.[19]

Arthur Loesser has chronicled the history of the piano and describes the sound of the Steinway concert grand piano most eloquently:

> The end result of the Steinway effort was a tone-producing tool of matchless strength and sensitiveness. . . . It was a marvelous kind of sound for the music that people loved then: thick, thundering piles of chord, booming batteries of octaves, and sizzling double jets of arpeggios. But the single Steinway tone, struck gently and held, also worked its ineffable spell, taking an endless, yearning time to die.[20]

In 1986, the total direct-labor costs for a grand piano averaged between $1,350 and $2,050, and for vertical pianos, between $600 and $800. The material costs for a grand piano averaged between $1,900 and $3,600, and for upright pianos, between $1,200 and $2,200. The firm produced 2,698 pianos in 1994.

Historically, grand pianos have accounted for the bulk of Steinway's production. Steinway offers eight models of grand pianos that range in length from 5 feet, 1 inch for a baby grand to 9 feet for the largest concert-style piano. Grand pianos are at the pre-mium end of the piano market in terms of quality and price, with the Steinway grands dominating the high end of the market. Retail prices range from $27,600 to $101,200 in the United States.

THE MARKET AND COMPETITION

According to a 1990 survey conducted by the Gallup Organization for the American Music Conference, slightly more than 4 in 10 (43 percent) U.S. households contained at least one amateur instrumental musician. The survey reported that about 42 million music-making households exist in the United States. However, the proportion of households with one or more amateur musicians dropped from 46 percent in 1985 to 43 percent in 1990. About 44 percent of piano players were male and 56 percent were female.

Generally, players were under the age of 35 (the median age was 28). Among musical instruments, piano and the guitar topped the survey's list with about 40 percent of players choosing the piano and 17 percent the guitar. Amateur musicians came from households that had a higher median income level ($45,860) than the total population ($37,640) and were headed by an adult with more than a high school education.[21]

Domestic Competition

In the 1960s, U.S. piano manufacturers were confronted with Japanese piano imports for the first time. The Japanese firms offered high-quality pianos at a much lower price than U.S. manufacturers. By 1968, two Japanese firms, Yamaha and Kawai, were selling 10,000 units annually. Together they captured 5 percent of U.S. upright piano sales and 28 percent of U.S. grand piano sales.

The 1980s saw further significant change in the U.S. piano market. Yamaha introduced the first all-digital synthesizer, which could effectively produce a range of high-quality sounds. Yamaha's introduction of the synthesizer effectively undercut the low-end acoustic piano market. In fact, sales of acoustic pianos declined from a high of 233,000 units per year at the beginning of the 1980s to 50,000 units annually in 1994. As sales of upright pianos decline, the number of grand pianos sold has increased (see Exhibits 1 and 2).

EXHIBIT 1 *Annual Sales of Steinway & Sons Pianos (1946–1994)*

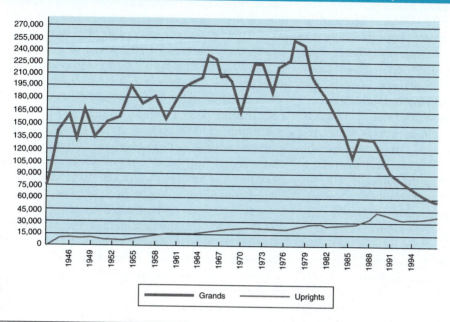

Legend: Grands, Uprights

Although Japan and Korea held 11 percent of the U.S. market in 1980, they held 38 percent of it by 1985. Several U.S. firms have closed, and, currently, only two U.S. firms, Steinway & Sons and Baldwin, continue to make pianos. Several foreign firms now have U.S. manufacturing facilities: Kawai operates a plant in North Carolina and Samick has a manufacturing facility in California. Currently, the high-volume producers are located in Japan, Korea, China, and the former Soviet Union. Total U.S. production is in third place—at about the same level as that of South Korea.

EXHIBIT 2 *Sales of U.S. Pianos by Product Type—1992 and 1987*

Product Type	1992			1987		
	Firms with Shipments of $100,000 or More	Units*	Value* (mil.)	Firms with Shipments of $100,000 or More	Units*	Value* (mil.)
Verticals, uprights, consoles, 37″ or less in height	1	—	—	3	40,900	$38.5
Verticals, uprights, consoles, more than 37″ in height	7	53,700**	$84.1**	5	52,100	$75.1
Grand pianos	3	5,500	$53.5	3	7,700	$58.2

SOURCE: U.S. Bureau of Census, 1992.
*No. of units shipped and value of shipments reported are for all producers in the industry, not just for those with shipments valued at greater than $100,000.
**Represents combined figures for all verticals and uprights. Figures for pianos 37″ or less are not available separately.

U.S. Piano Market in 1995 In 1995, the musical instrument industry in the United States generated retail sales of approximately $5.5 billion. The acoustic piano segment, which represents approximately 11 percent of the total musical instrument industry, had retail sales of $598 million in 1995, up 7 percent from 1994.[22] This included an 11 percent increase for grand pianos over five feet in length. During the period from 1991 to 1995, total dollar sales of grand pianos increased at an average annual rate of over 7 percent from $288 million to $372 million. Upright piano dollar sales, in contrast, increased at an average rate of only 1.5 percent during the same period.

Steinway's domestic market share of the grand piano market was approximately 7 percent in 1995. Approximately 90 percent of Steinway unit sales were made on a wholesale basis, with the remaining 10 percent sold directly by Steinway at one of its five company-owned retail locations. Steinway & Sons operates five retail stores in New York, New Jersey, London, Hamburg, and Berlin. The West 57th Street store in New York City, known as Steinway Hall, is one of the largest and most famous piano stores in the world. Steinway pianos are sold by dealers in 45 states across the country. The firm's leading markets are in and around major metropolitan areas. The two largest regions in terms of sales are California and New York, which together accounted for approximately 20 percent of domestic wholesale revenues in 1995 (see Exhibit 3). The institutional segment of the U.S. piano market, which includes music schools, conservatories, and universities, represented less than 10 percent of Steinway's domestic sales.[23] Steinway's largest dealer accounted for approximately 8 percent of sales in 1995, while the top 15 accounts represented 28 percent of sales.

In 1994, the firm sold 2,698 grand pianos worldwide (see Exhibit 4 for a history of Steinway grand piano sales). During the same year, the firm reported a net income of $3.1 million on sales of $101 million (see Exhibit 5). Approximately 50 percent of Steinway's total sales were in the United States, 37 percent were in Europe, and the remaining 13 percent were in Asia. Steinway's market share in Japan and Korea combined is less than 1 percent. Germany, Switzerland, France, the United Kingdom, and Italy accounted for the greatest percentage of sales outside the Americas. Steinway's largest European markets were Germany and Switzerland.

Steinway pianos are primarily purchased by affluent individuals with annual incomes over $100,000. The typical customer is over 45 years old and has a serious interest in music. Steinway's core customer base consists of professional artists and amateur pianists, as well as institutions such as concert halls, conservatories, colleges, universities, and music schools. Customers purchase Steinway pianos either through one of the firm's five retail stores or through independently owned dealerships. Over 90 percent of the firm's piano sales in the United States are to individuals. In other countries, sales to individuals are a smaller percentage of the total sales.

EXHIBIT 3 *Steinway's Top Ten U.S. Markets (1994, 000s)*

City	Sales
New York City	$6,007
Los Angeles	2,643
Baltimore/Washington D.C./Virginia	2,250
Dallas	1,642
Phoenix	1,438
Boston	1,144
San Francisco	1,078
Salt Lake City	848
Minneapolis/St. Paul	793
Detroit	605

Source: Steinway & Sons.

EXHIBIT 4 *Historical Steinway Unit Sales (1965–1994)*

Year	U.S. Grands	Foreign Grands	Total Grands	Year	U.S. Grands	Foreign Grands	Total Grands
1994	1,720	978	2,698	1979	1,815	1,357	3,172
1993	1,631	887	2,518	1978	1,819	1,334	3,153
1992	1,344	917	2,261	1977	1,590	1,372	2,962
1991	1,550	1,438	2,988	1976	1,908	1,241	3,149
1990	2,117	1,459	3,576	1975	1,875	1,160	3,035
1989	2,096	1,385	3,481	1974	2,001	937	2,938
1988	2,144	1,283	3,427	1973	1,919	1,131	3,050
1987	2,144	1,237	3,381	1972	1,809	1,212	3,021
1986	1,763	1,369	3,132	1971	1,540	1,173	2,713
1985	1,337	1,291	2,628	1970	1,470	1,142	2,612
1984	1,876	1,340	3,216	1969	1,806	1,163	2,969
1983	2,036	1,263	3,299	1968	1,932	1,250	3,182
1982	1,677	1,141	2,818	1967	1,603	1,043	2,646
1981	2,041	1,394	3,435	1966	1,770	1,056	2,826
1980	1,897	1,349	3,246	1965	1,659	1,259	2,918

Source: Steinway & Sons.

C-473

Baldwin In 1862, Dwight H. Baldwin, a music teacher, founded this firm as a retail piano business in Cincinnati, Ohio. In 1865, Baldwin hired Lucien Wulsin as a bookkeeper and made him a partner in 1870. Until his death in 1912, Wulsin shaped the firm's development.

Branch stores were opened in Indianapolis, Indiana, Louisville, Kentucky, and other towns in Ohio. In 1887, when M. Steinert & Company, a Steinway franchisee, opened a retail store in Cincinnati, the Steinways canceled Baldwin's Steinway franchise. Wulsin responded by planning Baldwin's first manufacturing facilities, and production started in Chicago in 1889. To sell Baldwin pianos, Wulsin introduced a dealer consignment program whereby the dealer only paid for the piano after it sold. The company also experimented with installment sales contracts. This combination of consignment selling and installment contracts led to the firm's rapid growth at the turn of the century. Baldwin's successful approach was copied by most other piano manufacturers.

The firm's rapid growth in the 1950s and the inadequacies of the company's manufacturing facilities in Cincinnati convinced the owners to move south. Eventually, five plants were opened—three in Arkansas and one each in Mississippi and Juarez, Mexico. Baldwin's offering included a line of high-quality grand pianos and a line of relatively inexpensive uprights assembled in the firm's highly automated Arkansas plants.

During the 1970s, the firm transformed itself into a conglomerate—Baldwin-United Corp.—and acquired banks, savings and loans, and insurance companies. But the acquisitions also ran up a sizeable debt. Unable to repay the debt, the firm filed for bankruptcy protection in 1983. A year later, R. S. Harrison and Harold Smith led a $55 million leveraged buyout of the company's piano and organ operations and reestablished the firm as a dedicated keyboard manufacturer.

Baldwin has over 800 dealers in the United States. Its dealership base and broad product line help attract students and other low-end users who generally stay with a Baldwin piano as they upgrade. In 1987, the firm sold 175,000 pianos, a figure well below the 282,000 units it sold a decade ago. With excess capacity in its Arkansas facility, Baldwin obtained a contract from Yamaha to manufacture the Everett piano line. Actions for Baldwin pianos are assembled at the Juarez plant. In 1995, the firm reported a net income of $3.9 million on sales of $122 million (see Exhibit 6).

EXHIBIT 5 *Steinway & Sons–Income Statement and Balance Sheet (000s)*

	1990	1991	1992	1993	1994
Income Statement Data					
Net Sales	$92,037	$98,816	$89,240	$89,714	$101,896
Gross Profit	33,673	35,586	30,759	26,139	31,636
Operating Income	10,096	9,124	4,556	1,919	8,795
Income (Loss) from Continuing Operations	3,077	2,753	(2,930)	(3,009)	2,847
Net Income (Loss)[1]	3,618	2,825	(10,335)	(3,009)	3,115
Ratio of Earnings to Fixed Charges[6]	2	2	1	[7]	2
Other Data					
EBITDA[2]	$13,500	$13,535	$9,591	$6,067	$13,068
Nonrecurring Charges[3]	1,861	2,319	2,532	2,047	1,658
Interest Expenses, Net	3,448	3,186	3,307	4,390	3,842
Depreciation and Amortization[4]	1,669	2,099	2,675	2,695	2,664
Capital Expenditures[5]	2,451	1,889	1,936	1,237	1,145
Steinway Grand Pianos Sold (in units)	3,558	3,282	2,648	2,245	2,569
Margins					
Gross Profit, %	37	36	44	29	31
EBITDA, %	15	14	11	7	13
Balance Sheet Data					
Current Assets	$68,306	$70,120	$73,300	$56,259	$58,760
Total Assets	85,701	87,832	91,784	72,677	76,019
Current Liabilities	30,327	32,078	45,602	31,896	32,969
Long-Term Debt	31,921	29,395	28,715	26,394	25,379
Redeemable Equity	3,614	4,227	1,471	1,000	270
Stockholders' Equity	9,066	10,606	3,690	767	4,935

[1]Net loss for the fiscal year ended June 30, 1992 includes loss from discontinued operations of $7,405 as a result of Steinway's September 14, 1992 disposition of its Gemeinhardt Company, Inc. Subsidiary

[2]EBITDA represents earnings before tax expense (benefit), adjusted to exclude certain non-recurring charges and charges related to previous ownership, which are not expected to recur. While EBITDA should not be construed as a substitute for operating income or a better indicator of liquidity than cash flow from operating activities, which are determined in accordance with generally accepted accounting principles, it is included herein to provide additional information with respect to the ability of the Company to meet its future debt service, capital expenditure and working capital requirements. EBITDA is not necessarily a measure of the Company's ability to fund its cash needs. See the Consolidated Statement of Cash Flows of Selmer and Steinway and the related notes thereto included in this Prospectus. EBITDA is included herein because management believes that certain investors find it to be a useful tool for measuring the ability to service debt.

[3]Nonrecurring charges represent certain costs and expenses primarily consisting of certain executive compensation and benefits and office related expenses of Steinway which, as a result of the merger, are not expected to recur.

[4]Depreciation and amortization for the fiscal year ended June 30, 1994 excludes approximately $563 of amortization of deferred financing costs written off pursuant to a debt refinancing effected in April 1994 (see note 6 to Steinway's financial statements).

[5]Capital expenditures of Steinway exclude expenditures for additions to the Concert and Artist Piano Bank.

[6]For purposes of this computation, fixed charges consist of interest expense and amortization of deferred financing costs and the estimated portion of rental expense attributable to interest. Earnings consist of income (loss) before taxes plus fixed charges.

[7]Earnings were inadequate to cover fixed charges by $3,065 for the year ended June 30, 1993.

EXHIBIT 6 *Baldwin Piano & Organ Company (Figures in US$, 000s)*

This firm is the largest domestic manufacturer of keyboard musical instruments that manufactures or distributes all major product classes of pianos and electronic organs.

	1995	1994	1993
Sales	$122,634	$122,347	$120,658
Net Income	3,960	345	4,561
Total Assets	101,429	97,460	89,928
Stockholders' Equity	54,114	50,154	49,892

Source: Compact Disclosure Database, 1996.
Note: The company also manufactures grandfather clocks, wooden cabinets and printed circuit boards utilized in a wide variety of products outside of the music industry. Musical products and other accounted for 72% of 1995 revenues; electronic contracting, 23.2% and financing services, 4.7%.

Japanese Competitors

In the early part of the century, there was little piano manufacturing in Japan due to a lack of quality components, impoverished circumstances, and a work force that was uninformed about the subtleties of instrument design and construction. After World War II, however, two Japanese companies, Yamaha and Kawai, quickly became important piano manufacturers. Figures for the 1980s indicate that together these two firms made more pianos than manufacturers in any other nation. In 1954, only 1 percent of Japanese homes owned a piano; currently, more than 20 percent do. In contrast to Steinway & Sons, the Japanese approach to piano manufacturing emphasizes automation and assembly-line operations.

Yamaha Corporation Founded in 1887 as Nippon Gakki, Yamaha's main plants are near Hamamatsu. From the time of its founding, the firm has built pianos.[24] It first exported pianos to the United States in 1960. By the 1970s, Yamaha had developed a strong reputation for making high-quality pianos. In the United States, it took significant market share away from U.S. producers. The company uses innovative engineering and automated manufacturing to produce its pianos. The firm markets its pianos worldwide.

In 1987, its centenary year, Yamaha was the world's leading musical instrument maker. It commanded 30 percent of the world piano market, 40 percent of the organ market, and 30 percent of the wind instrument market. Currently, the firm markets a line of grands, uprights, consoles, and studio pianos manufactured

in either Georgia in the United States, or Hamamatsu in Japan. These pianos are the company's pride. Concert grands represent the measure of its aspirations. Yamaha currently commands around 55 percent of the Japanese piano market.

In 1983, Genichi's son, Hiroshi Kawakami, took over the leadership of Yamaha. Under his direction, Yamaha established several close working relationships with other firms in the late 1980s and 1990s. In 1984, Yamaha subcontracted Kemble & Co. of England to make pianos. In 1986, the firm subcontracted Baldwin to make the Everett piano line. In 1988, Yamaha established Tienjin Yamaha Electronic Musical Instruments for production in China. Further, it obtained an option to buy 25 percent of Schimmel Pianofortefabrik in Germany. More recently, Yamaha held a 60 percent ownership of a $10 million joint venture with Jiangzhu Piano, China's largest piano manufacturer, located in Guangzhou. In 1996, the joint venture started producing pianos at a monthly rate of 1,300 units. In 1995, the firm reported a net income of $61.6 million on sales of over $5.5 billion (see Exhibit 7).

Kawai Musical Instruments In 1889, while he was an employee of Yamaha, Koichi Kawai, the founder of Kawai Musical Instruments, began his piano research. He developed the first rudimentary assembly line to make pianos. He was the first in Japan to design and build a piano action. Prior to his effort, all Japanese manufacturers had imported their actions from the United States or Germany. Kawai began production of upright pianos a year after building his first piano action. It was the cost advantage of his do-

EXHIBIT 7 *Yamaha Corporation (Figures in US$, 000s)*

The firm products include pianos, electronic organs, digital musical instruments, wind instruments and percussion instruments, and audio equipment.

	1995	1994	1993
Sales	$5,576,860	$4,348,744	$4,210,910
Net Income	61,665	−38,854	15,913
Total Assets	5,327,507	4,518,696	4,151,752
Stockholders' Equity	1,702,343	1,424,758	1,353,630

Source: World Scope Database, 1996.
Note: Audio and musical instruments accounted for 61% of fiscal 1995 revenues; electronic equipment and metal products, 18%; household utensils, 12%; and other, including sports goods and housing equipment, 9%. The company has 58 consolidated subsidiaries, 26 in Japan and 32 overseas. Overseas sales accounted for 30.5% of fiscal 1995 revenues.

mestically produced action that gave him a foothold in the fledgling Japanese market. Soon he began building grand pianos.

In 1955, Koichi's son, Shigeru Kawai, took over as president and has since overseen the firm's growth and the introduction of modern technology. In 1956, the firm had one plant with 546 employees and production capacity was 1,776 units. By 1996, Kawai had nine factories and employed over 7,000 people who produced about 100,000 pianos. The firm's main manufacturing center, Ryuyo Grand Piano Facility, opened in 1980, and is known for the efficient methods its has developed to build grand pianos. Kawai emphasizes the engineering, research, and development; quality control; technological innovation; and skill that goes into its pianos. Koichi's son, Hirotaki Kawai, is expected to take over leadership of the firm.

In its advertising, Kawai emphasizes the number of institutions and music venues (prominent universities, symphony orchestras, opera companies, music centers, theater companies, churches, music studios, and hotels) around the world that have purchased the Kawai piano. In 1995, however, the firm reported a loss of $2 million on sales of $877 million. This loss was attributed to the lingering economic recession facing Japanese firms (see Exhibit 8).

Korean Competitors

In 1964, the Korean government decided to promote musical instrument manufacture. To support this effort, it passed a prohibitive tariff on imported luxury goods such as pianos. Three firms immediately benefited from this protection. They included Samick,

EXHIBIT 8 *Kawai Musical Instruments (Figures in US$, 000s)*

This second largest musical instruments firm in Japan is also an OEM supplier of pianos to the Boston Piano Co., wholly-owned subsidiary of Steinway Musical Properties.

	1995	1994	1993
Sales	$877,742	$881,114	$899,657
Net Income	(2,733)	(2,200)	1,180
Total Assets	—	—	530,666
Stockholders' Equity	—	—	235,114

Source: Japan Company Handbook.
Note: Pianos accounted for 25% of fiscal 1995 revenues; electronic equipment and metal products, 8%; other including musical instruments, 9%; metallic parts for electronic instruments, 13%; other products, 10%; and music schools, 35%. Overseas sales accounted for 11% of fiscal 1995 revenues.

which had already established its piano manufacturing facility; Young Chang, which formed a joint venture with Yamaha; and Sojin, a division of Daewoo. Industry assessments state that "despite a harsh environment and a lack of Western musical tradition, Young Chang and Samick made the transformation from primitive manufacturers to global powerhouses in record time. Over the past century, no other manufacturers have come so far so fast."[25] Recently, Hyundai also became a Korean piano manufacturer. In the 1990s, with growing labor and raw material shortages, Samick and Young Chang have shifted their production to locations with either lower costs or better access to raw materials or markets.

Samick Established in 1958 by Hyo Ick Lee, Samick has grown into the world's largest producer of pianos, with its main plant in Inchon. The firm produced 18,000 grand pianos in 1995. Samick pianos feature cabinets designed by Kenneth Benson and incorporate a high-tension imperial-German scale. In making its pianos, Samick makes extensive use of computer-controlled equipment to shape parts and perform finishing operations.

In 1989, Samick Music Corporation, a wholly owned subsidiary of Samick, opened a 85,000-square-foot facility in California to assemble upright pianos. In 1991, monthly production at the facility had reached 325 units. While case parts were American, all actions, backs, and hardware were imported by Samick.

Recently, Samick opened parts-producing facilities in Indonesia and China. Components and subassemblies from these plants are then shipped to the firm's main plant at Inchon for assembly. These new facilities have allowed Samick to hold costs down and minimize price increases. Samick offers the best warranty in the industry—10 years on the piano, plus a

lifetime warranty on the iron plate, the sound board, and the pin block. In 1995, the firm reported a net income of $13 million on sales of $291 million (see Exhibit 9). At the end of 1996, Samick filed for bankruptcy protection due to financial difficulties.

Young Chang Young Chang was founded by three brothers. Jai-Sup Kim had studied engineering, Jai-Young Kim had studied finance at New York University, and Jai-Chang Kim had studied music. In 1956, they began to produce pianos in a small storefront in Seoul, South Korea. They also secured distribution rights to Yamaha pianos in South Korea. In 1962, they became the first musical instrument manufacturer in South Korea and built their first assembly plant in Seoul in 1964.

In 1967, they entered into a partnership with Yamaha Corporation, receiving technical assistance to acquire the production skills necessary to create instruments capable of competing with those made in Japan, the United States, and Europe. In 1971, they began exporting. In 1975 Yamaha and Young Chang parted ways, and in the next year Young Chang opened its second factory in Inchon, which was expanded in the late 1980s. In 1979, Young Chang America was established.

Young Chang's economies of scale, in combination with its advanced manufacturing processes, have resulted in one of the best price/value offerings in the market today. With an annual production capacity of 200,000 pianos, Young Chang is also the largest piano manufacturer in the world. The firm produces around 110,000 units annually, including 13,000 grand pianos. It holds over 50 percent of the expanding Korean market (around 150,000 units per year) and currently has over 4,000 employees. It offers a complete line of upright and grand pianos, as well as guitars. The firm sees piano manufacturing

EXHIBIT 9 *Samick Corporation (Figures in US$, 000s)*			
	1995	**1994**	**1993**
Sales	$291,512	$243,287	$254,125
Net Income	13,350	225	14,062
Total Assets	477,887	474,387	414,575
Stockholders' Equity	31,037	26,737	25,000

Note: Pianos accounted for 54.5% of fiscal 1995 revenues; guitars, 28.5%; amplifiers, 16.8%; and other, 0.2%.

as a totally integrated activity and has facilities for making all the significant parts of a piano.

In 1990, Young Chang acquired Kurzweil, a music keyboard manufacturer, for $20 million. In 1993, Young Chang acquired its own timber mill in Tacoma, Washington, for $32 million. In 1995, it opened a $40 million production facility in Tienjin, China, with an annual production capacity of 60,000 units. As J. S. Kim observed:

In the short term, our balance sheet would look stronger if we were to stay out of China. But it is obvious that the future for the piano industry is in China and companies not willing to make the investment are in great jeopardy.

The firm anticipates that the Chinese market will eventually be the world's largest. In 1995, the firm reported a net income of $9.6 million on sales of $262 million (see Exhibit 10).

European Competitors

Although German piano manufacturers make high-quality, high-priced pianos, they have been severely tested by their low-priced Asian competitors. As a consequence of this competition, the number of piano makers has fallen from several hundred to around 10. All surviving firms faced financial difficulties in the 1990s. In 1995, total annual production in Germany was over 20,000 units, with 20 percent being grand pianos. Bechstein Gruppe, the manufac-

turer of Bechstein and Zimmerman pianos, had annual sales of around DM30 million. Recently, the group has been working its way out of bankruptcy protection.

Other firms included Blüthner of Leipzig, which produced about 400 pianos annually with 50 percent marked for export, and Schimmel in Braunschweig, which has held around 11 percent of the German market. Schimmel has a close relationship with Yamaha, which has marketed Schimmel pianos in Japan. Steinway & Sons of Hamburg produces approximately 1,000 grands and 200 uprights annually and exports around 300 grand pianos to Japan.

While English firms were world-renowned piano manufacturers during Steinway's formative years, today there is little piano making in England. The manufacturing that does occur involves subcontracting from non-British makers. The most prominent is Kemble & Co., a firm that employs 100 people and makes pianos for Yamaha (Japan) and Schiedmeyer (Germany).

In Austria, Bösendorfer continues to make a limited number of high-end concert grands and upright pianos for its parent, Kimball International. Until recently, Kimball was a U.S. domestic piano maker with a single plant in Indiana. This facility, however, closed in 1995.

Significant numbers of pianos are made in the former Soviet Union. Until recently, few of these pianos have appeared in the United States; however, some imports have started to appear. Perhaps the best known brand is the Belarus piano from Borisov.

EXHIBIT 10 *Young Chang (Figures in US$, 000s)*

This firm produces pianos, guitars, electronic organs and other musical instruments. The company has six subsidiaries, two each in the United States and China, and one each in Canada and Germany.

	1995	1994*	1993
Sales	$262,158	$258,489	$225,716
Net Income	965	8,209	3,368
Stockholders' Equity	131,818	135,698	126,536
Total Assets	302,437	292,172	233,889

Source: World Scope Database, 1996.
*In 1994, export sales accounted for 37% of total revenues. Acoustic and digital pianos for 80% of fiscal 1995 revenues: synthesizers, 5.5%; guitars, 2%; and other, 12.5%.

ISSUES FACING STEINWAY'S MANAGEMENT

Domestic grand piano sales increased 42 percent from 1992 to 1995. This increased growth was largely attributable to economic recovery in the United States as well as increased marketing efforts by the major piano producers.

Growing Importance of China

Industry forecasts indicate that the future market for pianos will be concentrated in Japan, Korea, and China. Bruce Stevens acknowledged:

> Although the Steinway Piano has an excellent reputation in Asia and is the piano of choice in virtually every Japanese concert venue, Steinway has not historically focused significant selling or marketing efforts in these markets.

According to Bob Dove, however, the situation was changing:

> The Boston Piano currently has around 5 percent of the Japanese market in terms of units, and a higher percentage, about 8 percent, in terms of value (since the Boston line is more expensive than your average piano). We are optimistic about future sales of both Boston and Steinway pianos in Japan. We believe the Boston piano is significantly better than that offered by competitors at similar prices.

The recent ownership changes and the growth of Asian markets had increased Steinway's interest in finding ways to achieve an advantage in these developing situations. Bob Dove said:

> The merger of Steinway & Sons with the Selmer Company and its woodwind and band instruments has introduced a number of new strategic possibilities. The future demand for the band instruments made by Selmer is predictable from demographic data, peaking as larger cohorts of children enter high school. So this gives the new company a predictable source of demand for its products. So far as growth is concerned, pianos are important and there is no doubt that growth in demand for pianos will occur mainly in Asia and so this is the current focus of company attention. . . . There are also other instruments that have high quality standards and which have high sales and growth rates, e.g. guitars. These may be areas which offer new opportunities for the enlarged firm. Finally, the Steinway brand name, itself, is unsurpassed in terms of its positive reputation. In the future, this too could be used in a number of different ways.

Additionally, the developing situation in China was intriguing. Estimates indicated that the Chinese domestic production of pianos had risen from 43,000 units in 1987 to more than 100,000 units in 1994. The Chinese government's policy of one child per family has encouraged parents to spend more money on their children. This, many observers believe, may keep unsatisfied demand for pianos relatively high. Moreover, school children are being taught to appreciate music and this will have a positive impact on demand.

In 1994, there were four main piano-producing centers in China, including Beijing (30,000 units), Shanghai, Guangzhou (50,000 units), and Yingkuo in Liaoning Province. In 1996, Tienjin in North China also became a center of acoustic piano production when Young Chang established a plant there. Dove, however, was skeptical:

> All expect that China will be the world's largest market for pianos. However, since the price of pianos is currently set very low [the average price of a piano in China was around $1,100] the reported levels of untapped demand there are probably a bit illusory. Further, there are already large piano-making facilities in China such as Young Chang's and Yamaha's factories. It is not clear there is a need for additional production capacity.

Although the demand at current prices far outstrips supply, it is uncertain how an increase in prices might affect demand. Bob Dove believes that Steinway's current approach is appropriate:

> Given the emphasis on culture in China, the country's rapidly growing income levels, the small families and the interest parents have in their children, one can expect the usual developments to occur so far as piano penetration is concerned. But this takes time and people don't start off their interest in music by buying a Steinway. Rather, they work up to a Steinway. We already have an active

Steinway dealership in Hong Kong and this firm has opened a branch in Shanghai. Currently, [therefore], we should be just watching to see how things develop.

Moreover, he is optimistic about other Asian markets:

Other Southeast Asian countries like Japan, South Korea, Hong Kong, Taiwan and Singapore have already achieved higher general wealth levels and have meaningful piano penetration into homes. These countries, therefore, should be more immediate targets for both the Steinway and Boston line of pianos.

Among the many proposals Steinway & Sons is considering is the possibility of building a plant in Asia, perhaps in China. This new facility could help service the demand for pianos in Asian markets. Dove commented:

Ideally, because quality is such an important issue and the desire to "do the job right" is so strong,

it would be better for all Steinways to be built in one place. Perhaps standardized and mass-produced components could be supplied from different sources and could reduce costs, but for assembly and to do the other processes involving specialist skills, it would be better to have the Steinway piano built in a single place.

Irrespective of the approach the firm decides to pursue with respect to China and other Asian markets, Dove commented that:

In considering what to do, Steinway & Sons has to remember two things. First, the company has built up a tremendous brand name and enjoys an unsurpassed reputation for quality. So first, anything we do must be consistent with the idea that we are the "keepers of the flame." Second, as Henry Z. Steinway said, "Capital loves growth." To generate growth, we also have to know where we are adding value.

NOTES

1. E. Rothstein. "To Make a Piano It Takes More Than Tools," *Smithsonian*, November 1988.
2. Ibid.
3. E. Rothstein. "Made in the USA, Once Gloriously, Now Precariously," *The New York Times*, May 28, 1995.
4. A. Dolge, *Pianos and Their Makers* (Covina, CA: Covina Publishing Company, 1911), p. 303.
5. Ibid., p. 302.
6. Both Chickering and Steinway attempted to depict the results of the Paris Exposition as confirming that it (not its rival) was the leading U.S. piano manufacturer. This competition escalated into a notorious series of claims and counterclaims as each firm claimed additional endorsements and awards in their efforts to convince the public that it was they who had "really won" in Paris.
7. Dolge, p. 174.
8. Dolge, p. 309.
9. As judges, newspaper proprietors, music publishers, teachers, clergy, music critics, or others prominent in New York social or cultural circles indicated they would like to buy a Steinway, the firm offered them generous credit terms to encourage the purchase. By having a Steinway in influential New York homes, Steinway & Sons calculated that its status by association tended to grow.
10. Dolge, p. 309.
11. D. W. Fostle, *The Steinway Saga* (New York: Scribners, 1995).
12. Currently, the Concert Artists' Department maintains a bank of 330 Steinway concert-grand pianos spread around in 160 cities. Once an artist achieves sufficient stature to be considered eligible by Steinway & Sons to receive concert service,

he or she is offered the opportunity to use Steinway pianos for all performances. The only expense to the artist is the cost of hauling the piano to the recital hall.
13. Dolge, p. 309.
14. C. H. Roell, *The Piano in America, 1890–1940* (Chapel Hill: The University of North Carolina Press, 1989), p. 180.
15. The firm's ads necessarily were—and are—devoted to maintaining an appeal to a minority audience of high culture that has not been swept into mass society. Hence the promotion of Steinway as art. According to the classical pianist Jose Feghali: "Steinways are a work of art; if they weren't, we wouldn't be playing them. . . . You can walk into a room with 10 pianos and it's like playing 10 different instruments."
16. To prevent damage and facilitate conductivity, a brass strap equal to the length of the piece is placed on the exterior side. The wet glue, along with the wood's slightly elevated moisture content, permits the laminates that formed the wooden piece to slide against each other just enough to permit bending.
17. The piano key covers are made from a mock ivory polymer in deference to the ban on ivory imports. The action consists of 17 different wooden parts including machined wooden parts, Brazilian deer hide, felt-covered maple hammers, metal pins, and Teflon impregnated wool bushings. The components of the action are milled on the third floor and then assembled on the second floor. The design of the actions, much like the rest of the piano, only works if all of the milled parts fit together perfectly. Employees are trained in determining the exact fit and, also, to spot problems through visual and physical inspection of the action components.

18. "Steinway's Key . . . One at a time," *Associated Press International*, 1985.

19. Ibid.

20. Quoted in R. V. Ratcliffe, *Steinway & Sons* (San Francisco: Chronicle Books, 1985), p. 102.

21. American Music Conference, *Music USA, 1991*, pp. 21–23.

22. The U.S. acoustic piano market consisted of two important segments—grands and uprights. Grand pianos are larger and give a louder, more resonant sound. The grands were more expensive and the market for such pianos was generally smaller than that for uprights, and fewer firms were involved in their manufacture.

23. Steinway provides restoration services and sells piano parts from its New York, London, Berlin, and Hamburg locations. It also provides tuning and regulating services. Restoration, repair, tuning, and regulating services are important because they lead to potential new customers. In 1995, restoration services and piano parts accounted for approximately 7 percent of revenue, with gross margins of approximately 29 percent.

24. In 1950, Genichi Kawakami took over the leadership of the firm from his father. In 1953 Genichi toured the United States and Western Europe and was struck by the emphasis being placed on recreational products and the waning interest in musical instruments. He returned home determined to stimulate an interest in musical instruments in Japan and opened a chain of franchised music schools that have since graduated 4 million students. There are currently 10,000 franchised schools, and many have a showroom for Yamaha instruments on the ground floor.

25. *The Music Trades*, January 1991.

Textron Inc. and The Cessna 172

Robert N. McGrath
Blaise P. Waguespack, Jr.
George A. Wrigley

Embry-Riddle Aeronautical University

The situation did not promise inevitable success. The corporation had a reputation for state-of-the-art aerospace technologies, yet it was rejuvenating a vintage 1950s product design. The product had become a venerable cash cow in the past, but its rejuvenation was to cost at least $75 million. Its target market had collapsed by over 95 percent since its peak in the 1970s, a demise that was accompanied by a serious deterioration in the relevant consumer infrastructure. The product always had, and again was planned to have, some of the dullest performance features in its class. In recent years, many more economical variants had appeared at the low end of its market, and the high end was dominated by far newer technologies. Head-to-head competition would likely be dominated by—of all things—its own established base. A rapidly globalizing economy had changed the nature of the competition from an oligopolistic triad of U.S. firms to the inclusion of strong international players, some of which were spilling over from other industries and was certain to change the nature of competition. Consumers would surely see the product as, by and large, the same old thing, yet its production would be in a brand new facility, restarted after a 10-year production moratorium, guided by a management philosophy that was wholly new to the division, and would incorporate a solid handful of small but important technological improvements related to the safe operation of the product. Any quality imperfections at all were almost certain to become the subject of catastrophically expensive lawsuits.

History showed that just the cost of protecting the firm from product liability claims, when distributed across total production, was a per-unit figure that could easily exceed any competitive selling price.

Yet announcement of the product was highly praised by internal corporate management, consumers of the product type, Wall Street, and just about every other interested observer except, of course, its probable competition. Not only was market success predicted as certain, but so was market leadership. Could one change in product liability statutes, which supplied immunity only to products at least 18 years old, possibly have such an effect and the other dismal signs could largely be ignored?

PRODUCT LIABILITY IN GENERAL AVIATION

The term *product liability* addresses the issue of who bears risks associated with accidents (Huber & Litan, 1991; Eichenberger, 1994; Stern, 1994; Barnard, 1985; Harrison, 1995; Truitt & Tarry, 1995). In effect, this amounts to determining which party is at fault (and the extent of that responsibility) when a product fails to perform to a required standard or reasonable expectation. In principle, the objectives of liability statutes include the compensation of victims, the deterrence of injuries, the equitable spreading of risks, and the stimulation of safety-related innovation. In an important 1963 case, the U.S. Supreme

Court ruled that even if a manufacturer took reasonable care in the production of its goods and had no prior knowledge that a product was defective in its manufacture or design, the manufacturer was nevertheless responsible and wholly liable for associated damages. This "strict" interpretation of liability inaugurated a decades-long precedent where an increasing number of liability burdens were shifted consistently from consumers to producers.

Because of the technological complexity of aircraft, their operating environments, and the egregious injuries that resulted from accidents, product liability expenses became enormous in the general aviation industry after the 1963 decision. Legal defenses became not only difficult but easy to distort. For example, full compliance with Federal Aviation Administration (FAA) standards became understood by precedent to be merely the accomplishment of design and manufacture minimums; that is, plaintiffs successfully argued that manufacturers producing to FAA standards were trying to do as *little* as possible. The best efforts of the manufacturers' scientists and engineers, so difficult for lawyers and judges to understand, not to mention juries, were easily assailed.

It was sometimes argued that in this environment, innovation was stymied rather than stimulated, because the risks of newness became so much greater than the risks of holding on to the status quo. It was entirely possible, though difficult to show conclusively, that flight safety in general aviation was retarded, not improved, because of the "strict" liability standard. Nevertheless, immediate consumer sovereignty reigned supreme.

By the late 1980s, the average amount per claimant per occurrence was approximately $10 million; the total cost (losses plus defense expenses) averaged about $530,000. Even though manufacturers won over 80 percent of the cases that went to trial, general aviation's Big Three asserted that the annual cost incurred from all product liability expenditures was from $70,000 to $100,000 *per aircraft delivered*. Consequently, liability insurance expenses skyrocketed, from an industrywide $24 million in 1978 to $210 million in 1985. The problem became so acute that insurers became reticent to accept this business at all. Quipped one official of Lloyd's of London, "We are quite prepared to insure the risks of aviation, but not the risks of the American legal system" (Truitt & Tarry, 1995: 56). In this environment, Cessna withdrew from the single-engine aircraft market alto-

gether, Beech substantially reduced levels of production, and Piper was forced to file for Chapter 11 status.

Many industry participants and followers felt that the demise of general aviation manufacturing was principally the result of legal conditions and responded eventually with successful attempts to rectify the situation. Lobbyists [e.g., General Aviation Manufacturers Association (GAMA) and the Aircraft Owners and Pilots Association (AOPA)] convinced legislators such as Representatives Dan Glickman and Nancy Kassebaum (both Republicans from Kansas) to introduce product liability reform bills. Consumer groups, organized labor, and the Association of Trial Lawyers of America (ATLA) successfully battled these movements for several years, but eventually the General Aviation Revitalization Act of 1994 was signed into law by President Bill Clinton on August 17 of that year (Banks, 1994; *Business Week*, 1995; *Design News*, 1995).

The most significant effect of this bill was to relinquish manufacturers from the liability for products more than 18 years old. This relief may seem benign, but it was viewed as a significant breakthrough for several reasons. First, since the average age of a general aviation aircraft was more than 28 years, a very substantial window of litigation opportunity was erased. Second, because the most recent surge in production occurred in the late 1970s, a larger number of general aviation aircraft necessarily would become immune from liability in the near future. Therefore, advocates hailed this legislation as the beginning of a renaissance for general aviation aircraft development and manufacturing and predicted the creation of as many as 25,000 new jobs. Detractors, of course, decried the deterioration of consumer sovereignty and, from one side of legal theory, innovation incentive.

THE GENERAL AVIATION INDUSTRY: BACKGROUND

The term *general aviation* was not entirely definitive, but had become understood by what it generally included and excluded (Truitt & Tarry, 1995; *FAA Aviation Forecasts*, 1996; *GAMA Report*, 1996). The general aviation industry included a light aircraft segment, a business aviation segment, and a regional/charter aircraft segment; it excluded the commercial

C-48

airlines (with some ambiguities regarding regional/local carriers) and the military. In effect, this primarily differentiated private from commercial aviation. On the production side, it clearly distinguished firms such as Boeing, Lockheed-Martin, and McDonnell-Douglas from the "Big Three" of general aviation: Beech, Cessna, and Piper. During the 1980s, Cessna manufactured about 100,000 general aviation aircraft; Piper manufactured about 50,000, and Beech manufactured about 24,000.

More specifically, general aviation aircraft were considered to be single- and multipiston-engine-powered fixed-wing airplanes weighing less than 12,500 pounds (i.e., "light" aircraft) and some turboprop and jet-powered aircraft (i.e., business or executive aircraft). U.S. airframe manufacturers traditionally dominated this industry.

By the mid-1990s, the industry was a more important component of the American economy than many people appreciated. In a clear economic sense, the production and sale of general aviation aircraft, avionics, and many other types of equipment, as well as associated services including finance, insurance, flight instruction, maintenance, airport services, and so forth, accounted for $40 billion annually and employed 540,000 people with approximately a $10 billion aggregate payroll. In less quantifiable terms, the industry also served to accommodate various social needs of its 120 million annual consumers that the "market imperfections" of other aviation sectors might otherwise have been economically pressured to leave unresolved, such as the costly transportation of live human organs that were needed urgently for surgical transplants.

Historically, the industry was earmarked by cyclical patterns, tied to the larger national economic picture. For example, aircraft sales plummeted after the economic recessions of 1960, 1970, and 1975, followed by industry recoveries that paralleled recoveries of the national economy.

There have been two major slumps in production. Immediately following the at-large overexpansion of the 1960s (aircraft sales peaked at 15,768 in 1966), only 7,242 aircraft were sold in 1970. More recent developments were even more dramatic. After a recovery of 125 percent in a six-year period (1977 sales totaled 17,000) and an industry peak of 17,811 aircraft sold in 1979, production then crashed by 95.5 percent, to a point where only 811 aircraft were sold in 1993, and 444 in 1994. During the same period,

the number of U.S. manufacturers fell from 29 to 16; meanwhile, elsewhere in the world, the number of manufacturers rose from 15 to 29. In 1980, U.S. manufacturers employed 40,000 people; in 1991, the figure was 21,580. Whereas, U.S. firms traditionally captured 20 to 30 percent of the world market in addition to their dominance at home, in 1981 the United States became a net importer of general aviation aircraft, and by 1988 net importation of foreign aircraft accounted for $700 million of the national trade imbalance. Whereas 3,395 aircraft were exported in 1979, 440 were exported in 1986. U.S. manufacturers held 100 percent of home market share in 1980; by the mid-1990s this figure was less than 70 percent.

INTERPRETATIONS: "WHERE YOU STAND DEPENDS ON WHERE YOU SIT"

In 1989, Russell Meyer, president of Cessna, noted that Cessna suspended production of piston aircraft because of the cost of product liability. Moreover, Meyer indicated that Cessna would not build another piston aircraft unless a way could be found to reduce the ongoing cost of product liability.

There was no question that the demise of the general aviation industry in the United States was coincident with the dynamics associated with the prosecution of product liability claims, within the larger legal framework of extant laws. What was more arguable was the extent to which the coincidences contained a causal element. That is, while some stakeholders viewed product liability dynamics as the smoking gun in the industry's demise, others saw the product liability issue as only one explanatory factor among many others.

As described earlier, the industry was cyclical, and its fortunes were strongly tied to the national economy. Here, some observers noted that various oil embargoes and crises, the relatively high inflation rates experienced during the 1970s, and the prolonged recessionary periods that occurred during the 1980s all had negative effects on the industry. Moreover, in recent decades, disposable incomes generally fell, hurting all industries that depended on these dollars.

A growing general skepticism about economic futures had a related effect on the demand for luxuries.

Some factors were extended effects of more basic explanations. In addition to the crippling effect of record-high oil prices, costs of maintenance and flight instruction also continued to rise substantially. Elimination of the investment tax credit, in essence, increased the absolute cost of purchasing an airplane. The heyday of production during the boom periods caused a glut during the slow years, creating an aftermarket that competed directly with new aircraft sales. Manufacturers were pressured economically to offer financial arrangements not only to their customers (dealers), but directly to consumers as well, exacerbating their cost problems.

Some parts of the overall explanation were truly idiosyncratic to the industry. For example, American citizens who served in the armed forces during World War II and the Korean conflict were subsidized under the version of the GI Bill to pursue flight training. A substantial portion of these many thousands of veterans took advantage of this benefit, transforming fundamental skills learned during military service into civilian occupations and hobbies. As time progressed, however, this population aged and fewer and fewer eligible veterans took advantage of the benefit. Meanwhile, changes to the GI Bill eliminated the benefit for younger veterans. The net result was far fewer general aviation pilots of both the small-business and recreational variety. And pilots, after all, were obviously the nexus of demand for general aviation airplanes.

Technologically, the advent of reliable "kit" airplanes helped largely eliminate the low end segment of general aviation aircraft manufacturing. What was once viewed as the purview of backyard eccentrics became legitimized by actions such as the FAA's ever-expanding certification of worthwhile kit models and by the advocacy of organizations such as the Experimental Aircraft Association and the Small Aircraft Manufacturers Association—all of which helped change the public's perception of flying as a luxurious hobby (typical kit planes could be purchased for $45,000 to $80,000). Exhibit 1 shows the primary use of aircraft and the average hours used for each purpose.

Profit margins on kit planes were low, however, so the understandable reaction of industry incumbents to these relatively unproven technologies was abandonment of the market they served in favor of the high-profit, technologically safer, high-end (upscale business) segment. Overall, manufacturers netted over $2 billion in sales in 1990 on sales of 1,144 aircraft; in 1993, sales rose by about $140 million, but it was on sales of only 964 aircraft. Here, only about 5 percent of sales was accounted for by piston-powered aircraft; turboprop and jet aircraft dominated.

Cessna and Beech in particular profited from this shift in emphasis. Not coincidentally, Beech had become a subsidiary of Raytheon and Cessna had been acquired by Textron (both technological conglomerates tuned to corporate and military markets). Thus, decisions to abandon high-risk, low-return segments of the general aviation industry seemed consistent only with "bigger pictures" and overall corporate strategies.

Some industry observers viewed these events as being the natural symptoms of an industry that had transitioned from a general period of growth to a period of maturity. The "demise" might have been nothing more than an ordinary shakeout, the kind that economists and market analysts often predict. Even if this was true, however, industry incumbents and other stakeholders were apparently determined to not let the industry slip into decline without a fight.

INDUSTRY FUTURE

As of 1995, the outlook for the general aviation industry was mixed (*U.S. News & World Report*, 1995; *FAA Aviation Forecasts*, 1996; *GAMA Report*, 1996). One of the more important factors was the trend regarding the size and nature of the pilot population. As of January 1, 1995, the total number of private pilots was 284,236, a modest increase of 0.2 percent from the year before, but a reversal of a steady decline in the previous five years. The number of student pilots (96,254) fell by a disturbing 7.1 percent, however, a figure which was below 100,000 for the first time since 1962.

In terms of manufacturing, there were signs that the production of general aviation aircraft had bottomed out in 1994. New aircraft shipments totaled 980 in 1995, with billings of $3 billion—30.5 percent higher in one year, attributable to the rising unit value of aircraft. More specifically, 234 turboprop aircraft were shipped (up 15.3 percent from the year before),

EXHIBIT 1 *General Aviation Active Aircraft by Primary Use (top) and Hours Flown (bottom) (Both figures in thousands)*

Use Category	1994	1993	1992	1991	1990
Corporate	9.7	9.9	9.4	10.0	10.1
	2,548	2,659	2,262	2,617	2,913
Business	25.6	27.8	28.9	31.6	33.1
	3,005	3,345	3,537	4,154	4,417
Personal	100.8	102.1	108.7	115.1	112.6
	8,116	7,938	8,592	9,685	9,276
Instructional	14.6	15.6	16.0	17.9	18.6
	4,156	4,680	5,340	6,141	7,244
Aerial application	4.2	5.0	5.1	7.0	6.2
	1,210	1,167	1,296	1,911	1,872
Aerial observation	4.9	4.8	5.6	5.1	4.9
	1,750	1,750	1,730	1,797	1,745
Sightseeing	1.3	1.6	n/a	n/a	n/a
	323	412	n/a	n/a	n/a
External load	0.1	0.1	n/a	n/a	n/a
	172	105	n/a	n/a	n/a
Other work	1.2	1.0	1.7	1.7	1.4
	226	175	343	471	572
Air taxi	3.9	3.8	4.6	5.5	5.8
	1,670	1,452	2,009	2,241	2,249
Other	4.2	4.2	3.5	3.9	4.1
	640	656	358	473	475
Total	170.6	175.9	183.6	198.5	198.0
	23,866	24,340	25,800	29,497	30,763

Source: *FAA Aviation Forecasts.*

241 jet aircraft were shipped (up 8.1 percent), and 505 piston aircraft were shipped (up 4.3 percent). Exports, however, still showed signs of industry deterioration. Only 286 general aviation aircraft were exported in 1995, a one-year decline of 2.4 percent; billings declined 23.2 percent to $637.3 million. Exports represented 29.2 percent of total aircraft shipped and 21.4 percent of billings, figures that fell 33.8 percent and 36.4 percent in one year, respectively.

In a larger sense, the total number of "active" aircraft (i.e., the number of aircraft flown at least once during the previous year) indicated continuing decline. The number of active single-engine piston aircraft declined in one year (1993 to 1994) from 130,687 to 123,332 (down 5.6 percent), the number of multiengine piston aircraft fell from 16,406 to 15,577 (down 5.1 percent), and the number of turboprop aircraft fell from 4,359 to 4,207 (down 3.5

percent). However, numbers regarding turbojet, experimental, and "other" categories showed significant improvement. The number of active turbojets increased from 3,859 to 4,073 (up 5.6 percent), the number of experimental aircraft increased from 10,938 to 12,852 (up 17.5 percent), and the number of "other" aircraft increased from 5,247 to 6,169 (up 17.6 percent). Exhibits 2 and 3 depict the current and projected use of different types of aircraft.

The number of hours flown showed a somewhat different pattern than the number of active aircraft. From 1993 to 1994, the number of hours flown in multipiston aircraft (2.6 million hours) rose 3.6 percent; the number in turbojet aircraft (1.2 million) rose 6.5 percent; the number in experimental aircraft (0.7 million) rose 1 percent; and the number in "other" aircraft (0.4 million) rose 12.8 percent. Meanwhile, the number of hours flown in single-

EXHIBIT 2 *General Aviation Active Aircraft (top) and Hours Flown (bottom) (Both figures in thousands)*

Aircraft Type	1994	1993	1992	1991	1990
Piston	138.9	147.1	162.1	175.3	175.2
	18,370	19,029	21,251	24,102	25,832
Turboprop	4.2	4.4	4.7	4.9	5.3
	1,106	1,227	1,478	1,513	2,319
Turbojet	4.1	3.9	4.0	4.4	4.1
	1,241	1,165	1,072	1,236	1,396
Fixed Wing—Total	147.2	155.3	170.8	184.6	184.5
	20,717	21,421	23,801	26,851	29,546
Rotorcraft	4.4	4.5	5.8	6.3	6.9
	2,006	1,832	2,283	2,757	2,209
Other	6.2	5.2	7.8	7.6	6.6
	424	376	410	459	341
Experimental	12.9	10.9	n/a	n/a	n/a
	718	711	n/a	n/a	n/a
Total	170.6	175.9	183.6	197.8	196.9
	23,866	24,340	25,800	29,497	30,763

Source: *FAA Aviation Forecasts.*

engine piston aircraft (15.8 million) fell by 4.5 percent, and the number flown in turboprop aircraft (1.1 million) fell 9.9 percent. Since most hours were accounted for by flying in single-engine piston aircraft (66.1 percent), total hours flown in general aviation aircraft fell from 24.3 million to 23.9 million hours (down 2 percent overall).

General aviation aircraft were most often flown for personal use. In 1994, personal flying accounted for 34 percent of total general aviation flying, up an impressive 32.6 percent from the previous year. The second most popular use was in instructional flying, which in 1994 accounted for 17.4 percent of the total, a decline of 11.2 percent from the previous year. Business and corporate flying (as a combined category, 23.3 percent) also fell by 7.5 percent.

EXHIBIT 3 *Active General Aviation and Air Taxi Hours Flown Forecast (millions)*

Aircraft Type	1996	1997	1998	1999	2000	2001	2002	2003	2004	2005	2006
Piston											
Single Engine	15.3	15.2	15.3	15.5	15.7	15.8	15.9	16.0	16.0	16.1	16.2
Multiengine	2.5	2.5	2.6	2.6	2.6	2.6	2.7	2.7	2.7	2.7	2.7
Turboprop	1.1	1.2	1.2	1.2	1.2	1.3	1.3	1.3	1.3	1.4	1.4
Turbojet	1.3	1.3	1.4	1.4	1.4	1.5	1.5	1.5	1.6	1.6	1.6
Rotorcraft											
Piston	0.3	0.3	0.3	0.3	0.3	0.3	0.3	0.3	0.3	0.3	0.3
Turbine	1.6	1.7	1.7	1.7	1.7	1.7	1.8	1.8	1.8	1.8	1.8
Experimental	0.7	0.8	0.8	0.8	0.8	0.8	0.8	0.8	0.8	0.8	0.9
Other	0.4	0.4	0.4	0.4	0.4	0.5	0.5	0.5	0.5	0.5	0.5
Total	23.2	23.4	23.7	23.9	24.1	24.5	24.8	24.9	25.0	25.2	25.4

The mid-1990s also were a period of general decline in the general aviation industry infrastructure. A subtle but important point was the interaction between the decline in single-engine piston aircraft activity and overall industry health. Historically, pilots found their way into the industry through single-engine piston aircraft and then progressed to more sophisticated technologies. Statistics regarding single-engine piston aircraft, therefore, served as a bellwether for long-term industry health. For example, it was probably no coincidence that the flight training and flight instructor infrastructure was also in decline, and many of the physical facilities devoted to training showed obvious signs of encroaching dilapidation.

By the mid-1990s, the industry and many of its stakeholders had acted to improve overall industry strength. The federal government restored some of the subsidization of veterans' flight training programs. Congress restored the investment tax credit, giving incentives for the purchase of general aviation aircraft as well as many other durable goods. The FAA developed a comprehensive plan for industry improvement, consistent with its overall mission of advocating all aviation interests. The plan aimed at improving general aviation's image while reducing some of the regulatory burden that the agency itself imposed. The AOPA launched a project designed to attract 10,000 new student pilots and achieved this goal. The National Business Aircraft Association (NBAA) actively promoted the added value that business flying had the potential to bring to individual firms, under the catchy slogan, "No plane, No gain." Expansion of university programs in aviation-related degrees and actual flight training programs expanded

significantly. Exhibits 4 and 5 depict the number of active pilots by type of certificate and factors affecting people's interest in learning to fly.

TEXTRON AND CESSNA

Dozens of acquisitions, divestitures, reorganizations, and other moves peppered Textron's history. Its origins could be traced to the establishment of the Franklin Rayon Corporation in 1928, which became known as Textron American, Inc., in 1955, after a merger with the American Woolen Company and Robbins Mills, Inc. (*Moody's Industrial Manual, 1995*). In subsequent decades, the corporate profile changed greatly and purposively. By the mid-1990s, Textron was known as a high-tech conglomerate, employing about 53,000 people in almost 60 subsidiaries operating in two major business sectors: manufacturing (in 1994, 70 percent of total revenues and 53 percent of total profits) and financial services (30 percent of total revenues and 47 percent of total profits).

Textron was renowned as one of the nation's largest defense contractors (sales to the U.S. government represented 18 percent of the total revenues) and was also a significant exporter (18 percent of revenues). Generally, management's aim was to (1) achieve balanced diversification so that the corporation would not be vulnerable to economic cycles, and (2) to establish a dependable bedrock that would allow the firm to pursue growth opportunities and advanced technologies.

The manufacturing segments concentrated on the following product types: aircraft, automotive, industrial, and systems and components. The aircraft seg-

EXHIBIT 4 *Active Pilots by Type of Certificate (thousands)*

Type	1996	1997	1998	1999	2000	2001	2002	2003	2004	2005	2006
Students	95.0	94.6	96.4	98.2	100.1	101.9	103.2	104.7	105.8	106.6	107.4
Balloon	0.2	0.3	0.3	0.3	0.3	0.4	0.4	0.4	0.4	0.5	0.5
Private	280.5	278.4	281.4	284.5	287.6	290.5	292.7	294.8	297.1	299.0	300.5
Commercial	137.3	135.9	137.2	138.6	140.0	140.7	141.4	142.1	142.8	143.6	144.3
Airline	118.6	120.4	122.2	124.3	126.8	129.3	131.3	13.2	134.9	136.6	138.3
Helicopter	8.5	8.5	8.6	8.7	8.8	8.8	8.9	9.0	9.1	9.1	9.2
Glider	8.6	8.7	8.8	8.8	8.9	8.9	9.0	9.0	9.1	9.1	9.2
Total	648.7	646.8	654.9	663.4	672.5	680.5	686.9	693.2	699.2	704.5	709.4

Source: *FAA Aviation Forecasts.*

EXHIBIT 5 *Market Survey Results*

Category	Total	Male	Female	Likely Student
Factors That Would Make Survey Targets Much More Interested in Learning to Fly				
Fly at twice speed of driving	44	43	45	48
Weekend adventure	43	41	50	46
Get license in 6 months	42	41	44	46
Available mentors	42	41	44	47
Entertain family/friends	42	41	45	47
Rent for $50/hour	41	37	52	39
Recreational license	34	34	34	37
Make friends	32	30	36	37
Safer than biking	32	31	35	34
Airplane clubs	32	33	31	36
High self-esteem	29	28	32	30
Career	23	24	21	24
Learning cost $3,500	21	20	26	26
Used planes for $30,000	18	18	16	21
Survey Target's Participation in Other Activities				
Bicycling	64	62	70	68
Fishing	59	64	46	61
Boating	55	56	51	64
Golf	40	45	26	44
Backpacking	39	39	37	46
Water skiing	35	38	27	41
Tennis	31	31	32	32
Motorcycling	29	32	19	32
Scuba diving	29	23	18	29
Mountain climbing	21	21	20	24
RV touring	19	18	19	22
Auto racing	18	19	14	17
Skydiving	9	8	9	12
Ballooning	5	4	8	7
Hang gliding	4	4	4	5

Source: *GAMA Final Report.*

C-489

ment consisted of Bell Helicopter and Cessna. The most exciting program in Bell Helicopter was the continuing development of the V-22 tilt rotor aircraft. It had been in development for many years and always seemed to be on the verge of landing huge contracts with the U.S. Department of Defense. Such contracts, if landed, would probably help launch much more business on an international scale. Overall, this business segment performed well in both civilian and military markets. It was adept at marketing its products through its own worldwide sales force as well as through a network of independent representatives. Key success factors were price, financing terms, product performance, reliability, and long-term product support. Bell Helicopter typically accounted for 11 to 14 percent of total corporate revenues.

Cessna was well known as the world's largest designer and manufacturer of general aviation aircraft; in particular, Cessna designed and manufactured light and mid-sized business jets and single-engine utility turboprop aircraft. Cessna was a fairly recent acquisition, having been purchased on February 28, 1992, from the General Dynamics Corporation for $605 million in cash. Two efforts were particularly exciting: the development of the Citation X, a large business jet scheduled for delivery in 1996; and the decision to restart production of Cessna models 172, 182, and 206 piston-engine aircraft in new manufacturing facilities located in Kansas. In 1994, Cessna delivered about 115 Citation business jets, for sales of approximately $850 million; sales were projected to top $1 billion by 1996. As with Bell Helicopter, Cessna marketed its products through both its own worldwide sales force and independent representatives, principally relying on product reliability, product support, and superb brand name recognition. Additionally, both Bell and Cessna were making positive contributions to the corporation as a whole; in the most recent years, this was attributable to improved margins, lowered product development expenses, lowered administrative expenses in the establishment of new business, and higher sales.

The automotive sector supplied components to automotive original equipment manufacturers (OEMs) and competed on the basis of price, product quality, and delivery. Several divisions of the industrial segment competed similarly in industries less oligopolistic than the automotive sector on the basis of price, product quality, product performance, brand name recognition, and delivery. The systems and components segment supplied the civilian aerospace and military industries, operating its own sales force and competing on price, reliability, product performance, and product support.

Textron's situation and overall philosophy were well summarized in CEO James F. Hardyman's letter to shareholders published in the 1994 annual report:

Textron's record of consistent growth continued in 1994, as earnings per share increased 14 percent over 1993 and the fourth quarter was our 21st consecutive quarter of year-to-year income improvement . . .

Significantly, we achieved consistent improvement in results over the last five years despite an array of challenges, including cutbacks in defense spending, a slump in the commercial aviation industry and disappointments in the disability insurance business. . . .

Our ability to deliver consistent growth stems from Textron's two defining characteristics:

- We are a multiindustry company focused on maximizing the benefits of diversification.
- We are committed to disciplined and aggressive management of our businesses and our business mix. . . .

Diversification is a source of strength, providing a foundation that supports growth and enables us to manage risk. . . .

Textron's presence in diverse industries helps achieve balance and stability in a variety of economic environments by providing insulation from business and industry cycles. More specifically, we were able to maintain consistent growth in 1994 in part because the growth of our Aircraft, Automotive, Industrial and Finance businesses more than offset the downturns in the Systems and Components segment and Paul Revere's disability insurance business. . . .

Finally, Textron's mix of businesses is a unique management resource, providing a depth and breadth of management expertise that is shared throughout our operating units, strengthening the corporation overall. For example, in the JPATS competition to build the new training aircraft for the Air Force and Navy, three of our key Textron divisions shared their significant experience in government contracts with Cessna. This, combined with Cessna's technical expertise, led to a comprehensive proposal. Our constant search for "best practices" applies our most successful methods for operation to all our businesses. . . .

Textron is focused on operations. We believe that long-term objectives are attained by coupling strategically driven planning with an intense concentration on day-to-day execution. Throughout the organization, the management philosophy instills a clear focus on the ultimate goal—building value for shareholders—with execution tailored to the unique characteristics of each of our businesses.

We translate this philosophy into action by relying on four basic principles:

- **Short- and Long-Term Planning.** We conduct a continuous, corporatewide strategic planning process centered on setting clear, challenging financial and operating objectives.
- **Continuous Improvement.** We are making major improvements in operations, but we will never be satisfied. . . .

- **Consistent Management.** We measure our commitment to building value on a monthly basis. All of our divisions use the measurement of return on invested capital relative to the cost of capital as their standard.

- **Accountability of Performance.** We relentlessly follow up to ensure that goals are achieved. . . .

Five key strategies . . . guide our commitment to building value:

- **Internal Growth.** Textron's market-driven businesses create products that meet customer needs for quality, reliability and value. . . .

- **Acquisitions.** Our acquisitions strategy targets growth and an increased presence in industrial components manufacturing. . . . [W]e are capitalizing on the strengths of our core markets: market leadership, competitive advantage and the ability to generate sustained economic value for our shareholders. . . .

- **Increased International Presence.** Geographic diversification is a key element in achieving our growth objectives. Our goal is to increase international sales from about one-fourth of our business to more than one-third by the end of this decade. . . .

- **Restructuring/Redeploying.** We are making the tough decisions to bring underperforming businesses up to standard—improving the businesses that can meet our requirements, selling those that do not and managing businesses for cash when divestiture is not appropriate. Over the last five years, we have restructured 11 commercial aerospace and defense businesses—closing or selling 254 plants—to meet profitability goals in the face of continued weakness in the defense and commercial aviation markets. . . . We take these steps only when global pressures make them necessary. . . .

- **People/Culture.** We are also changing our culture to ensure that it supports our shared values of respect, trust, integrity and the pursuit of excellence. . . . [W]e are developing a corporate culture in which every member of the Textron team is constantly finding ways to make us better and faster. . . . [W]e are creating a Textron that is recognized for its multi-

industry strength, market leadership and consistent growth.

Textron's financial performance is depicted in Exhibits 6 and 7.

THE CESSNA 172

The Cessna 172 was introduced to the general aviation market in 1955; even then, it was not entirely original, because it shared many engineering features and components with other Cessna models (Charles, 1986; *Aviation Week*, June 5, 1995; Stewart, June 1995; Stewart, October 1995). Key to its success in the early years was aggressive advertising that presented the plane as being comparable, in ease of operation, to the automobile. It had doors on both sides and a steering wheel-like pilot control yoke, rather than the control sticks that were still ubiquitous at the time. More superficially, interior furnishings and exterior paint jobs emulated the automotive fashions of the day.

The first year the Cessna 172 was on the market, it outsold its cash-cow predecessor Cessna 170 by a margin of ten to one, prompting management to discontinue the old model in favor of the new, recognizing it as the company's future in general aviation. (Most significantly, the Cessna 170 was a "taildragger," while the Cessna 172 featured a "tricycle" landing gear configuration.) Virtually no design changes were deemed necessary until 1960, when the tail design was changed to a more swept-back look—a feature incorporated for aerodynamic reasons, but one which was immediately popular for its look as well. Minor changes occurred roughly each year thereafter, such as better streamlining (the distinguishing characteristic of the 172B Skyhawk, perhaps the version that most clearly embedded itself in general aviation history), shorter landing gear struts, a wrap-around rear window, electric flaps, a baggage door, a larger fuel tank, and new contours that improved its range.

The airplane's original engine was the Continental O-300; it was very expensive to repair and overhaul and troublesome because of its tendency for valve failures and carburetor icing. This engine was replaced in 1968 by the Lycoming O-320-E2D, a proven design that was instantly popular when installed in the 172. In 1977, another engine change was made, but this time for the worse; the Lycoming O-320-H2AD caused camshaft and valve damage and

EXHIBIT 6 *Textron's Consolidated Statement of Cash Flows ($000)*

	1994	1993
Net income	379,000	(355,000)
Effect of changes in accounting principles	—	679,000
Depreciation and amortization	424,000	397,000
Provision for losses on receivables	195,000	196,000
Insurance policy liabilities	342,000	309,000
Deferred income taxes	28,000	37,000
Commercial and U.S. government receivables	(27,000)	(2,000)
Changes in inventories	176,000	55,000
Additions to insurance policy acquisition costs	(235,000)	(205,000)
Increase in other assets	(80,000)	(22,000)
Accounts payable	108,000	(50,000)
Accrued liabilities	(11,000)	20,000
Other	1,000	(17,000)
Net cash provided by operating activities	1,300,000	1,042,000
Securities to be available for sale	(220,000)	—
Securities to be held to maturity	(1,497,000)	(1,846,000)
Other purchases	(27,000)	(17,000)
Sales of securities available for sale	205,000	—
Sales of securities held to maturity	173,000	737,000
Mature and calls	768,000	743,000
Proceeds from other investments	42,000	27,000
Finance receivables originated or purchased	(5,011,000)	(4,853,000)
Finance receivables repaid or sold	4,253,000	4,212,000
Cash used in acquisition of business	(139,000)	(905,000)
Proceeds from sale of minor interests	175,000	—
Capital expenditures	(252,000)	(217,000)
Other investing activities	27,000	(15,000)
Net cash used by investing activities	(1,503,000)	(2,134,000)
Short-term debt	485,000	(50,000)
Proceeds from issuance of long-term debt	1,669,000	2,913,000
Principal paid on long-term debt	(1,954,000)	(1,780,000)
Receipts—interest sens insured products	193,000	142,000
Return of balance—interest sens product	(105,000)	(88,000)
Stock options	19,000	34,000
Dividends paid	(110,000)	(98,000)
Net cash provided by financing activities	197,000	1,073,000
Effect of foreign exchange rate change on cash	1,000	—
Net change in cash	(5,000)	(19,000)
Cash at beginning of year	31,000	50,000
Cash at end of year	26,000	31,000

Source: *Moody's, 1995.*

EXHIBIT 7 *Textron's Consolidated Balance Sheet ($000)*

	0/01/94	1/02/93
Assets		
Cash	26,000	31,000
Investments	4,764,000	4,152,000
Receivables, net	8,240,000	7,731,000
Inventories	1,488,000	1,648,000
Property, plant, & equipment	1,269,000	1,183,000
Unamortized insurance policy acquisition costs	784,000	696,000
Goodwill, net	1,437,000	1,366,000
Other assets	1,650,000	1,559,000
Total assets	19,658,000	18,367,000
Liabilities		
Accounts payable	614,000	489,000
Accrued postretirement benefits	1,033,000	981,000
Other accrued liabilities	2,268,000	2,072,000
Insurance reserves and claims	4,091,000	3,615,000
Textron parent company borrowing group	2,025,000	2,283,000
Finance and insurance subsidiaries	6,847,000	6,440,000
Total debt	8,872,000	8,723,000
Total liabilities	16,878,000	15,879,000
Pfd stk $2.08 cum conv, ser A	9,000	11,000
Pfd stk $1.40 cum conv, ser B	7,000	8,000
Common stock	12,000	11,000
Capital surplus	687,000	661,000
Retained earnings	2,209,000	1,940,000
Other	52,000	52,000
Total	2,872,000	2,579,000
Less cost of treasury shares	92,000	91,000
Total shares equity	2,780,000	2,488,000
Total liabilities and stock equivalents	19,658,000	18,367,000
Book value	$15.08	$12.53

Source: *Moody's, 1995.*

was plagued by abrupt engine failures related to the design and operation of oil pumps and accessory drive gears. A product recall in 1977–78 corrected some of these problems; a complete resolution was accomplished in 1981 with the installation of the Lycoming O-320-D2J engine.

Cessna's management did not foresee in 1955 that the 172 would become the world's most popular airplane. In the ensuing 31 years, some 36,010 individual aircraft would be sold, the largest number of aircraft of any single type of aircraft sold in aviation

history. From its introduction to the mid-1980s, models A through P were introduced. By the mid-1980s, however, prospects in the general aviation industry were so dire that Cessna pulled out of the single-engine piston product line altogether.

As soon as production ceased, the marketplace missed the Cessna 172. Consumers loved this airplane so much that numerous hobbyists emerged, focused on keeping the 172 alive. The 172 had become something of a legend. Owners of the 172 discovered that as long as their airplanes were maintained well, they actually appreciated in value. Simple supply and demand evidenced itself in a very strong "used" market for 172s. Most editions of *Trade-A-Plane*, for example, featured one or two pages of advertisements for the Cessna 172; asking prices were consistently at bluebook value. Strangely, value was not directly related to age, but was more a function of specific model type. Models sold from 1968 to 1976 were considered outstanding; models from the 1956 to 1967 era were considered to be fair, and models from the 1977 to 1980 era were considered to be terrible, relative to other models of the 172. The airplane's continuing popularity stemmed from its excellent safety record, operating economy, and low maintenance costs. Of course, in terms of performance it was always somewhat ho-hum, being the "family car" of general aviation.

Inspired by the 1994 tort reform, Cessna Aircraft Company CEO Russell Meyer (not coincidentally, a key lobbyist in the movement to reform aviation liability statutes) announced in 1994 that Cessna would introduce a new version of the venerable 172. Start-up costs would be approximately $75 million. The new 172s would be produced by the company's Pawnee division and manufactured in new facilities located in Independence, Kansas. The first deliveries were planned for the summer of 1996 (in 1997, larger single-engined Cessna models 182, 206, and Turbo 206 were also to be introduced). The new facility would be about 480,000 square feet, with room for final assembly, painting, flight test, delivery, and market functions. Though this new facility meant an important shift from Cessna's traditional Wichita production site, it also meant lower overhead costs (first, the Wichita facility produced Cessna's jet aircraft; second, the Independence site would be new both physically and philosophically, being benchmarked against GM's Saturn methods of production) and better local flight testing conditions.

Plans called for the eventual manufacture of about 2,000 planes per year. The 600 planes produced in the first year would earn approximately $300 million. (This forecast also assumed the simultaneous sale of 400 Cessna 182s and 250 Cessna 206s per year; international sales were forecast at about 300 Cessna 172s, 200 Cessna 182s, and 250 Cessna 206s per year. College, government, military, and civil patrol orders were expected to account for another 300 Cessna 172s.) The new business was expected to increase Cessna's work force from 6,000 to over 7,500

employees. Instant market leadership was expected, and full-scale production margins were expected to be double-digit.

The "new" 172 would have a similar appearance to the 172 legend, with only a few aerodynamic improvements to reduce drag. The most significant improvements would be a quieter engine; an electronic ignition with back-up magneto; an all-metal fluorescent-lit instrument panel; a standard backup instrument vacuum system; a gravity-feed, 50-gallon wet wing; improved interior crashworthiness (improved seat tracking and seat adjustment system); standard step-ladders, handles, toe-steps, and hand-grips; redesigned cowling fasteners; corrosion-proofing; more modern avionics (the electronic components in airplanes); an improved autopilot; and a "derated" (200 hp to 160 hp) fuel-injected, four cylinder, Lycoming IO-360 engine; the derating would be accomplished by installing low-compression pistons and by limiting takeoff power to 2,500 rpm.

Decisions regarding these changes were based on the thousands of hours of operating experience accumulated on previous models and, of course, cost considerations. Meyer estimated that the nonrecurring costs of developing an airplane of this type "from scratch" through to FAA certification, would have been close to $25 million, and would optimistically have taken about three and a half years. Even these assumptions were based on traditional aluminum construction; state-of-the-art airframes partially fabricated of space-age composite materials were much more costly, difficult, and time-consuming to produce and certify.

Well into 1995, decisions regarding the total configuration of the aircraft and its selling price were still at hand. The effects of a renewed regulatory environment were not entirely foreseeable; a backlog of hundreds of liability cases that needed clarification and resolution remained. Even Edward W. Stimpson, president of the General Aviation Manufacturer's Association, admitted "the market's very confused right now."

Other than the continuing evolution of safety/liability issues, it was also not certain that the industry would return to its relatively stable condition of a Big Three oligopoly, especially with Piper just emerging from Chapter 11 status. The world had changed a great deal since 1986. Firms such as the Commander Aircraft Co. (Bethany, Oklahoma), the French Aerospatiale group, and even Toyota had "invaded," or were poised to invade, what was once fairly secure Big Three territory.

Ironically, some of the strongest competition was certain to come from the used market. A Cessna 172 purchased new in the 1970s for $50,000 could typically garner a $75,000 resale price in the 1990s, if its condition was good. Taking inflation into account, and the added value of improved avionics and other "new" features, it seemed that Cessna's management would need to think in terms of a $100,000 price tag if the new 172 was to compete favorably with its own past success.

REFERENCES

Banks, H. 1994. "Cleared for Takeoff," *Forbes*, September 12: 116–122.

Barnard, T. 1985. "Courts and Crashes: Why $70,000 of an Aircraft's Cost Is for Product Liability Insurance," *Canadian Aviation*, July: 33–35.

Charles, B. 1996. "Something's Coming," *Air Progress*, January: 14–15.

"Clearing a Runway for Planemakers," *Business Week*, March 20, 1995: 94–95.

Eichenberger, J. 1994. "The Day After," *The Aviation Consumer*, October 1: 16–17.

FAA Aviation Forecasts: Fiscal Years 1996–2007. 1996. Washington, D.C.: United States Department of Transportation.

"First 'New' C-172s to Fly in Late 1996," *Aviation Week & Space Technology*, June 5, 1995: 64–65.

"General Aviation Experiences a Rebirth," *Design News*, September 11, 1995: 27–28.

Harrison, K. H. 1995. "Drastic Insurance Rate Hikes Sock It to General Aviation," *Aviation International News*, May 1: 25–28.

Huber, P. W. & R. E. Litan (eds.). 1991. *The Liability Maze*. Washington, D.C.: The Brookings Institute.

Moody's Industrial Manual, 1995. New York: Moody's Investor's Services, Inc.

Revitalizing the Piston-Powered Aircraft Industry: Final Report of the General Aviation Manufacturers Association, March 26, 1996. 1996. Washington, D.C.: General Aviation Manufacturers Association.

Stern, W. M. 1994. "A Wing and a Prayer," *Forbes*, April 25: 42–43.

Stewart, C. 1995. "Affordable Classic," *Air Progress*, October: 30–43.

Stewart, C. 1995. "Restart 172," *Air Progress*, June: 12–13.

"The Takeoff in the Small-Plane Market," *U.S. News and World Report*, August 21, 1995: 50.

Truitt, L. J., & S. E. Tarry. 1995. "The Rise and Fall of General Aviation: Product Liability, Market Structure, and Technological Innovation," *Transportation Journal*, Summer: 52–70.

Tootsie Roll, Inc.

Sharon Ungar Lane
Alan N. Hoffman

Bentley College

Tootsie Roll's good fortunes are an accumulation of many small decisions that were probably made right plus bigger key decisions, such as acquisitions, that have been made right, and a lot of luck.

—Mel Gordon
CEO, Tootsie Roll, 1993

INTRODUCTION

Tootsie Roll Industries, Inc., a niche candy maker, has often been voted one of *Forbes* magazine's "200 Best Small Companies of America." A top-quality producer and distributor of Tootsie Rolls and other candy, Tootsie Roll Industries maintains a 50 percent market share of the taffy and lollipop segment of the candy industry, and sales have increased each year for the past 19 years. The world's largest lollipop supplier, the company produces approximately 16 million lollipops and 37 million individual Tootsie Rolls per day.

EARLY HISTORY

In 1896, Leo Hirschfield, a young immigrant from Austria, set up a small shop in Brooklyn, New York, to make candy from a recipe he brought from Europe. As he rolled the sweet, chewy chocolate candies, his thoughts wandered to his young daughter, Clara "Tootsie" Hirschfield, and he named his new confection the "Tootsie Roll." He wrapped the Tootsie Rolls individually in paper to keep them clean and sanitary and priced them at a penny each.

Hirschfield's Tootsie Rolls were an immediate success, and demand quickly outpaced supply. Hirschfield realized he would need additional capital to promote and expand his business. After just one year, he merged his operation with a local candy manufacturer, Stern & Saalberg, which incorporated eight years later and officially changed its name to the Sweets Company of America in 1917.

From 1922 to 1966, the Sweets Company of America established manufacturing facilities around the United States to meet growing demand for Tootsie Roll products. Having captured America's sweet tooth with the Tootsie Roll, the company expanded its product line in the 1930s, developing a series of companion products such as the first soft-centered lollipop, the Tootsie Pop, which had a Tootsie Roll center and a hard candy outside.

In 1962, Ellen and Melvin Gordon took over as president/chief operating officer and chief executive officer/chairman of the board, respectively. In 1966, the Gordons changed the company name to Tootsie Roll Industries, Inc., and opened a large manufacturing facility in Chicago (which subsequently became the company's world headquarters). In the late 1960s, Tootsie Roll began exploring foreign markets, establishing a subsidiary in Mexico and licensing a firm in the Philippines to produce and distribute Tootsie Rolls. After a positive response in both of these countries, the company expanded to Canada in 1971.

Amazingly, as the Tootsie Roll celebrates its 100th birthday in 1996, the candy still tastes exactly as it did when it was first hand-rolled by Leo Hirschfield. The company's success, as 19 consecutive years of record sales and 14 consecutive years of record earnings confirm, is based on strong consumer awareness of the Tootsie Roll brand name and strategic acquisition of other well-positioned and highly recognized brand names to leverage its existing operations. The Gordons own 66 percent of the voting rights and 47 percent of the company's stock and continue to control the firm, which remains exclusively a candy company making the very best quality candy for the market it knows best.

THE CANDY INDUSTRY

The United States' largest manufacturing sector, the processed food and beverage industry, is composed of two primary segments: lower value-added and higher value-added food processors. Higher value-added processors, such as candy manufacturers, make retail-ready, packaged, consumer brand name products that have a minimum of 40 percent of the industry shipment value added through sophisticated manufacturing. Candy is a $20 billion retail industry worldwide and accounts for about one-third of the dollar value of the snack-food market (the largest market niche in the higher value-added segment). Tootsie Roll Industries occupies a niche market within the Standard Industrial Classification (SIC) code 2064 (candy and other confectionery products), which includes taffies, lollipops, and chewing gum. The U.S. confectionery market generates approximately $9.7 billion in annual sales.

Candy is not yet a "mature" industry in the United States. The compound annual growth rate for candy in the past 10 years has been close to 6 percent a year, a very solid gain in an industry that is supposedly mature. In fact, within the chocolate confectionery subcategory, the United States ranks 11th in the world in per capita consumption and fifth in the world in growth since 1980. Based on current demographics, many analysts believe that there will be further growth for confectioneries. A "baby boomlet" is on the way, significantly increasing the teenage population. By the time the population bulge peaks

in 2010, it will top the baby boom of the 1960s in both size and duration. According to government statistics, the percentage of children between the ages of 5 and 14 will rise during the 1990s, increasing from 14.2 percent of the population in 1990 to 14.5 percent in 2000. This trend will serve as a strong foundation for increasing consumption of confectionery products through the end of the century. Nevertheless, spending for food and drink as a percentage of all personal consumption is declining in the United States, and most manufacturers recognize that future opportunities will be derived from using domestic profits to penetrate foreign markets.

Many U.S. producers now use complex processing methods and efficient, automated manufacturing operations that yield comparable quality at lower cost. Also, there is a growing international market for candy products. Despite recessionary economic conditions and reduced discretionary income, foreign consumers purchase U.S. higher value-added foods and beverages because U.S. products compare favorably with similar products made elsewhere, offering equal or better quality at a lower price. Today, the top five importers of U.S. products are Japan, Canada, Mexico, South Korea, and the Netherlands. Foreign demand for U.S.-produced higher value-added products (including candy) has increased since 1993, thanks primarily to the rapid growth of the middle class in developing and emerging nations and growth in the new markets of the former Soviet bloc nations.

However, the candy industry has recently faced several industry curbs. Nutritional labeling requirements were imposed by the Food and Drug Administration in 1990 to regulate serving size, health messages, and the use of descriptive terms such as "light" and "low fat." The Federal Trade Commission also developed stringent sale-date requirements and strict guidelines for documenting environmental claims on packaging. These new regulations were imposed under costly, disruptive, difficult to meet deadlines, and posed a particular threat to many foreign food and beverage processors, that are not accustomed to such extensive product analysis and disclosure. For Tootsie Roll, this major packaging revision was costly and involved detailed laboratory analysis and package modification of every item the company produces.

Candy is still a treat for all ages. People that loved Tootsie Rolls when they were children often buy them for their children; thus, the Tootsie Roll perpetuates itself. The baby boom generation grew up with Tootsie Roll products, therefore name recognition is very high among this group. While parental purchases may increase because of brand recognition, the baby boomers are becoming increasingly more concerned with their health and their children's diet. As a result, baby boomers are purchasing less candy for themselves and their children. Thus, as people become more health and weight conscious, their demand for sugar-based products decreases. Additionally, as this consumer group ages, its concern for dental health grows. Candy has been identified as a major cause of dental decay, and hard, sticky, or chewy snacks, such as Tootsie Rolls, cannot be eaten by people who have had various kinds of dental work. Also, some parents do not buy candy because they are concerned that sugar causes hyperactivity in some children.

Children are Tootsie Roll's primary target market. Children aged 6 to 17 create the greatest demand for confectionery products. Candy is the second most requested snack food among 6- to 12-year-olds; only ice cream is higher in demand according to a study by the Good Housekeeping Institute. This group (ages 6 to 17) spends $60 billion of its own money annually with two-thirds of this spending on candy, snacks, and beverages.

TOOTSIE ROLL–1996

Tootsie Rolls are unique and occupy a niche of the candy market that includes taffies, lollipops, and chewing gum. Tootsie Roll Industries' competition is other candy and ready-to-eat snack food manufacturers. Tootsie Roll Industries commands 2 to 3 percent of the overall market as the eighth largest candy manufacturer following Hershey (27 percent), M&M Mars (25 percent), Nestlé (10 percent), Brach (6 percent), Huhtamaki (4 percent), Storck (3 percent), and RJR Nabisco (3 percent) (see Exhibit 1). Although Tootsie Roll has captured only 2 to 3 percent of the total candy market, it continues to be the leader in its own segment where it maintains a 50 percent market share. Tootsie Roll's strengths are brand loyalty, established shelf space, state-of-the-art manufacturing facilities, and the fact that there are fixed price ceilings for candy products. Also, as the United States becomes a more nutrition-oriented society, Tootsie Rolls have another advantage because they contain no cholesterol and have less saturated fat than other leading candy bars.

Tootsie Roll uses many suppliers for sugar, corn syrup, cocoa, and milk, and adapts to fluctuations in commodity prices by changing the formula and size of its products to keep total costs relatively constant.

EXHIBIT 1 *Top Ten Candy Brands, Five-Year Average Market Share*

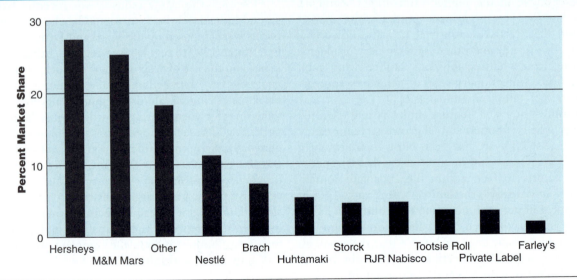

For example, Tootsie Roll can substitute corn syrup for some of the necessary sugar, thereby reducing its dependency on a given commodity or supplier. Tootsie Roll also controls costs through ownership of its own refinery. The company can thus buy raw sugar and make, rather than buy, processed sugar, decreasing its dependence on processed sugar suppliers. When natural disasters affect the availability or price of one of its ingredients, for instance, sugar or cocoa, as did floods along the Mississippi River in 1993, the company usually reduces the size of its product to keep the selling price constant.

Tootsie Roll Industries' vertically integrated structure supports its drive for competitiveness, keeping total costs down and maintaining its leading edge in technology. In addition to the sugar refinery, Tootsie Roll owns its own advertising agency so that commissions flow back to it. The company also makes the sticks for its lollipops, has a print shop for color printing, and owns a machine shop where new machinery is manufactured and existing machinery is rebuilt. Tootsie Roll Industries also constantly upgrades its manufacturing equipment to maintain the utmost efficiency.

Tootsie Roll's objectives, which have made it one of America's strongest companies, are and have always been:

1. Run a trim operation.
2. Eliminate waste.
3. Minimize cost.
4. Improve performance.

To be competitive in the world candy market, where margins are limited, one must produce top-quality candy highly efficiently. Tootsie Roll has spent millions of dollars on state-of-the-art expansion and automation of its five production facilities (Chicago, Massachusetts, New York, Tennessee, and Mexico). Much of its equipment is designed specifically for Tootsie Roll. As Mel Gordon, CEO and chairman of the board of Tootsie Roll Industries explains,

> Anybody can buy machinery and in that way become state-of-the-art, but if you develop your own adaptations to the machinery so that it runs faster and runs better for your products, or you develop in-house machinery that does what nobody else in the market can do, then you're ahead of state-of-the-art. We've strived in the last 15 years to be ahead of state-of-the-art.

However, the company has not been able to control the power of its packaging material suppliers. Increased demand has led to dramatic price increases in paper, board, plastics, and foil. To insulate itself from price fluctuations, Tootsie Roll has, whenever possible, negotiated fixed-price contracts with its packaging suppliers.

ACQUISITIONS

Tootsie Roll Industries often generates more cash than it requires for internal growth and can therefore consider complementary acquisitions. Following strict criteria, such as a strong brand name, and a preference for nonchocolate (such as hard candies and chewy candies) over chocolate so as not to compete in its own niche, Tootsie Roll has made several key acquisitions of proven brands to expand its product line, increase its shelf space, and spur growth. As President Ellen Gordon explains, "We add new lines only when it benefits our product in quality and efficiency."

Two of Tootsie Roll's earliest acquisitions (1972) were the Mason Division of Candy Corporation of America, with such well-known products as Mason Mints, Mason Dots, Mason Licorice Crows, and Mason Spice Berries; and the Bonamo Turkish Taffy Company. In 1985, Tootsie Roll acquired Cella's Confections which makes chocolate covered cherries; and, in 1988, it acquired the Charms Company, thereby becoming the world's largest manufacturer of lollipops. Charms' principal product, the Blow Pop, a lollipop with a bubble gum center, complements nicely the highly successful Tootsie Pop. Shortly after the acquisition of the Charms Company, Mel Gordon observed,

> We specialize in hard candies such as Tootsie Pops and Blow Pops and all the flat pops that Charms makes. That's a big niche for us, to be the world's largest manufacturer of pops. Also, we're in chewy candy with the Tootsie Roll and the growing Frooties and Flavor Roll lines. We feel that in those two areas we have a certain dominance and we'd like to keep our expertise focused in those areas.

C-499

In November 1993, Tootsie Roll purchased the chocolate and caramel division of the Warner-Lambert Company, which makes the popular brands Junior Mints, Charleston Chew, Sugar Daddy, Sugar Babies, and Pom Poms. The acquisition of these new lines places Tootsie Roll Industries in more direct competition with other major chocolate manufacturers such as Hershey and M&M Mars and provides it with a number of new products that clearly complement its "chewy" candy product lines. Over the years, Tootsie Roll has carefully and selectively acquired 17 popular candy brands, enlarging its niche in the candy and other confectionery segment of the higher value-added products market.

DISTRIBUTION/ ADVERTISING

Tootsie Roll Industries uses over 100 public and contract brokers to distribute its products to nearly 15,000 customers. To market the newly acquired Warner-Lambert brands more effectively, Tootsie Roll created new packaging for them which resembled the packaging of its more established Tootsie Roll products and capitalized on the synergies of Warner-Lambert products with its existing lines.

In addition to using its distribution network to increase sales of Warner-Lambert products, Tootsie Roll is pushing those products generally associated with movie theatres, such as Junior Mints, into mainstream retail outlets: convenience stores, grocery stores, drug chains, and warehouse club stores. Convenience stores and supermarkets have traditionally been the dominant candy retailers, but recently have been losing sales to discount stores and drug store chains. Currently, all four venues share equally in confectionery sales. However, most candy purchases are impulse buys made while waiting in line at a store; many supermarkets have switched to candy-free aisles, thus reducing these impulse sales. As impulse sales opportunities diminish, the customer must search for the product. A consumer is unlikely to undertake a search unless desire is heightened through advertising. Parents are the target market that advertisements must reach. However, marketing efforts often focus on children, who are not the primary purchasers. Children normally purchase candy through and with the acceptance of their parents.

Recently, Tootsie Roll has focused its sales efforts on the more rapidly growing classes of trade such as warehouse clubs. In the candy industry, it is difficult to gain shelf space particularly when competing with large companies such as Hershey and M&M Mars. Tootsie Roll has begun to make progress toward this objective. Tootsie Rolls are beginning to appear in warehouse stores, such as Sam's, BJ's Warehouse, and COSTCO, with large packages of traditional Tootsie Rolls and bags of multicolored Tootsie Roll pops.

Candy regularly shows the strongest gains from promotion and merchandising, clearly evident by the significant increases in candy sales during major holiday periods—Valentine's Day, Easter, Halloween and Christmas. In fact, candy has shown a stronger response to promotions than any other snack category.

The third quarter has always been the strongest for Tootsie Rolls due to increased Halloween sales. However, Halloween is changing. Grocery retailers report that there is a noticeable shift in consumer behavior because of concern for child safety. In the last several years, Halloween celebrations have moved from the streets, "trick or treating" door to door, to indoor parties sponsored by schools, churches, and more recently enclosed shopping malls, thereby reducing purchases of candy that is to be given to trick or treaters. Also, parents have been reluctant to purchase products that can be tampered with easily, particularly at Halloween. The way Tootsie Roll products are packaged creates a potential concern. Individually wrapped and unsealed products can be tampered with and are thus negatively affected by events such as the 1982 Tylenol poisoning. In fact, Tootsie Roll sales suffered in the wake of that national scare.

While Tootsie Roll's 100-year history has contributed to its wide product recognition, a tradition of national advertising begun in the early 1950s on television programs such as "The Mickey Mouse Club" and "Buffalo Bob" has successfully made "Tootsie Roll" a household word, establishing its domestic market; schedules continue to be regularly placed in both electronic and print media. Although the Tootsie Roll and Charms brands are well known, as Ellen Gordon puts it, "it's important to keep them in front of the public." In Tootsie Roll's memorable 1970s advertising campaign, "How Many Licks?", a little boy asks a wise owl, "How many licks does it take to get to the Tootsie Roll center of a Tootsie Pop?" Although the company has had several successful advertising campaigns since then, it currently spends very little on advertising (approximately 2 percent of sales, concentrated on television), relying instead on nostalgia and its 100-year-old brand. Internationally, however, aggressive advertising programs support the brands in Mexico as well as in the Pacific Rim markets and certain Eastern European countries.

THE GORDONS

Since 1962, Tootsie Roll Industries, Inc., has been run by the husband and wife team of Ellen Gordon, president and chief operating officer, and Melvin Gordon, chairman of the board and chief executive officer. The couple own 47 percent of the company stock, most of which was inherited by Ellen Gordon, whose family has been Tootsie Roll's largest shareholder since the early 1930s.

Ellen and Melvin Gordon have been working together since the 1960s. They are quick to state that they have an open-door policy, but often do not attend annual meetings, saying that they already know what has happened. Together with five other executives, they plan all of the company's marketing, manufacturing, and distribution strategies, but the Gordons alone determine Tootsie Roll's corporate vision by controlling strategic planning, decision making, and the setting of corporate goals. Ellen, 64, and Melvin, 75, have no immediate plans to retire and insist they want to continue working, though on a number of occasions, they have expressed the desire to have one of their four daughters (none of whom currently works for Tootsie Roll) take over the management of the company. "We hope that our children or the management that we are building up in the company will be able to run the company someday," the Gordons claim, but they have no definite strategic plan for passing on the succession.

Tootsie Roll's strong performance and superior balance sheet should make it a prime target for a takeover, but the Gordons' determination to maintain control over Tootsie Roll Industries may be one reason why Wall Street has shown little interest in the company. (See Exhibits 2 and 3 for more detailed reports on the firm's financial status.) The majority of Tootsie Roll's voting stock, 66 percent, is con-

trolled by the Gordons, and the couple says they have no intention of selling the company. Ellen Gordon explains, "We're busy making Tootsie Roll products and selling them. We're kind of conservative and we don't make projections."

Tootsie Roll does not intend to sacrifice long-term growth for short-term gains. Its strategy has been to focus on making Tootsie Rolls, rather than on preparing forecasts or strategic planning. Over the years, several key acquisitions have enhanced Tootsie Roll's product line. But, these acquisitions have generally been based on opportunities that have surfaced within the firm's market niche, and not necessarily as part of a well-thought-out strategic plan. The Gordons remain arrogant in their view of the market; Ellen Gordon repeatedly states, "No one else can make a Tootsie Roll."

Recently, Tootsie Roll Industries took advantage of an opportunity related to the location of its headquarters in Chicago. The lease on its 2.2 million-square-foot facility was due to expire, and the landlord was not willing to renew it. Tootsie Roll faced the possibility of relocating to a less expensive territory because with a low ticket item such as candy, every penny counts; but the company did not wish to relocate. At the same time, the city did not want Tootsie Roll Industries to leave because it feared the resulting increase in unemployment. Thus, Ellen Gordon was able to leverage the firm's 850 jobs into a lucrative package of incentives to remain headquartered in Chicago. The deal signaled a national trend: small companies are more likely to receive major tax concessions and other perks as city economies increasingly depend on them. The Gordon's negotiations garnered $1.4 million in state and local tax exemptions over the next 15 years, a $20 million low-interest loan to purchase the Tootsie Roll plant, $200,000 in job training funds, and the creation of a state enterprise zone located in the plant for tax breaks on machinery and utilities. In turn, the Gordons agreed to add 200 workers over five years and start a loan program for employees to purchase homes in Chicago.

Tootsie Roll has remained an independent company for its 100-year history, and Ellen Gordon feels that its independence has been a great strength: "As we have grown beyond a small entrepreneurial company we have been able to retain some of our entrepreneurial philosophy and way of doing business." The Gordons are determined to continue as an in-

EXHIBIT 2 *Consolidated Statement of Earnings and Retained Earnings, Tootsie Roll Industries, Inc. and Subsidiaries (in thousands except per share data)*

	For the Year Ended December 31,		
	1994	**1993**	**1992**
Net sales	$296,932	$259,593	$245,424
Cost of goods sold	155,565	133,978	127,123
Gross margin	141,367	125,615	118,301
Operating expenses			
Marketing, selling, and advertising	44,974	40,096	38,958
Distribution and warehousing	20,682	17,655	16,959
General and administrative	13,017	12,837	13,186
Amortization of the excess of cost over acquired net tangible			
assets	2,706	1,510	1,265
	81,379	72,098	70,368
Earnings from operations	59,988	53,517	47,933
Other income, net	1,179	4,193	3,989
Earnings before income taxes	61,167	57,710	51,922
Provision for income taxes	23,236	22,268	19,890
Net earnings	37,931	35,442	32,032
Retained earnings at beginning of year	96,647	90,285	83,507
	134,578	125,727	115,539
Deduct:			
Cash dividends ($.42, $.35 and $.27 per share)	4,580	3,769	2,947
Stock dividends	22,235	25,311	22,307
	26,815	29,080	25,254
Retained earnings at end of year	$107,763	$ 96,647	$ 90,285
Earnings per common share	$3.50	$3.27	$2.95
Average common and class B common shares outstanding	10,848	10,848	10,848

dependent company "for generations to come," but Ellen claims, finally, that the key to their success is "fun. Whenever I tell people I work in a confectionery company there's always a smile. That's very important—the magic of candy." Five-year histories of sales and net income are presented in Exhibits 4 and 5, respectively.

GLOBAL OPPORTUNITIES

The United States accounts for 90 percent of Tootsie Roll's sales; the remaining 10 percent of Tootsie Roll products are sold in foreign markets. Mexico is Tootsie Roll's second largest market; Canada is third. However, because U.S. consumer spending for food and drink as a percentage of all personal consumption is declining, Tootsie Roll and other candy man-

ufacturers have begun to recognize that future growth opportunities exist in penetrating foreign markets. Thus, Tootsie Roll needs to increase its sales and distribution internationally to continue to grow as the U.S. market moves toward maturity. As trade barriers are reduced or eliminated, Tootsie Roll's opportunities to expand internationally are increasing, especially because foreign demand for U.S.-produced higher value-added products, including candy, has increased significantly since 1993. The predicted reduction or elimination of the European Community confection tariffs and variable levies on ingredient composition may also facilitate export growth into Eastern Europe.

Tootsie Roll Industries has begun slowly and cautiously working toward worldwide market penetration, targeting export growth to the Far East and Europe, where per capita confectionery consumption is

EXHIBIT 3 Consolidated Statement of Financial Position, Tootsie Roll Industries, Inc. and Subsidiaries (in thousands)

	December 31,	
	1994	1993
Assets		
Current Assets		
Cash and cash equivalents	$ 16,509	$ 1,986
Investments held to maturity	45,861	54,217
Accounts receivable, less allowances of $1,466 and $2,075	22,087	20,656
Inventories:		
Finished goods and work-in-process	16,704	17,186
Raw materials and supplies	12,464	12,108
Prepaid expenses	3,094	3,667
Deferred income taxes	2,168	2,094
Total current assets	118,887	111,914
Property, Plant, and Equipment, at cost		
Land	6,672	4,231
Buildings	26,982	25,347
Machinery and equipment	109,438	107,685
Leasehold improvements	6	10
	143,098	137,273
Less accumulated depreciation and amortization	57,450	50,574
	85,648	86,699
Other Assets:		
Excess of cost over acquired net tangible assets, net of accumulated amortization of $9,966 and $7,260	98,668	101,375
Other assets	6,880	3,952
	105,548	105,327
Total Assets	$310,083	$303,940
Liabilities and Shareholders' Equity (in thousands except per share data)		
Current Liabilities		
Notes payable to banks	$ —	$ 22,601
Accounts payable	6,124	6,259
Dividends payable	1,219	1,026
Accrued liabilities	17,046	17,919
Income taxes payable	1,872	3,057
Total current liabilities	26,261	50,862
Noncurrent Liabilities:		
Deferred income taxes	7,716	6,364
Postretirement health care and life insurance benefits	4,993	4,498
Industrial Development Bonds	7,500	7,500
Term notes payable	20,000	20,000
Other long-term liabilities	3,152	2,373
Total noncurrent liabilities	43,361	40,735
Shareholders' Equity:		
Common stock, $.69-4/9 par value—		
25,000 shares authorized		
7,306 and 7,069, respectively, issued	5,074	4,909
Class B common stock, $.69-4/9 par value		
10,000 shares authorized		
3,542 and 3,465, respectively, issued	2,459	2,406
Capital in excess of par value	132,997	111,108
Retained earnings, per accompanying statement	107,763	96,647
Foreign currency translation adjustment account	(7,832)	(2,727)
	240,461	212,343
Commitments	—	—
Total Liabilities and Shareholders' Equity	$310,083	$303,940

EXHIBIT 4 *Tootsie Roll Industries, Five-Year Sales History*

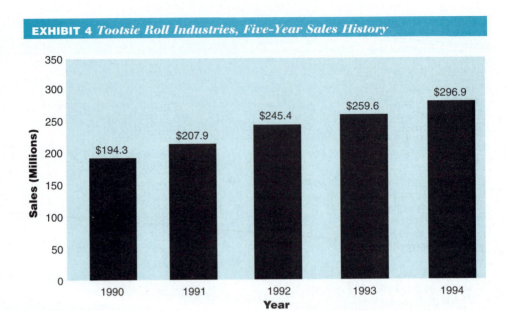

EXHIBIT 5 *Tootsie Roll Industries, Five-Year Net Income History*

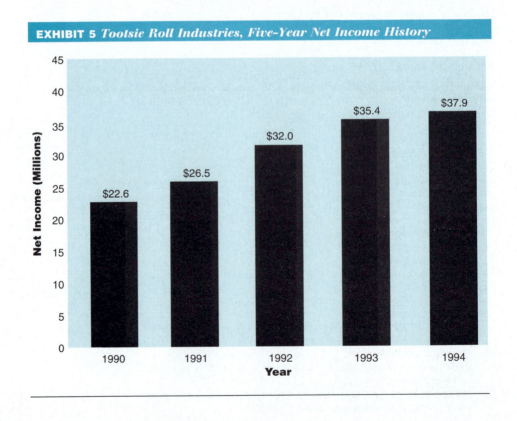

EXHIBIT 6 *Tootsie Roll Industries, Percent of Foreign Sales*

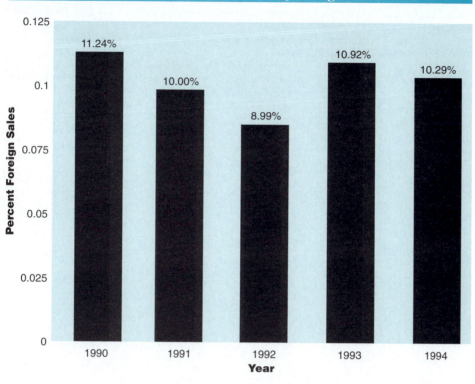

40 percent higher than in the United States. Tootsie Roll currently holds licenses in several countries and regions including the Philippines, Colombia, Europe, the Far East, and Latin America. In addition, the company opened a sales office in Hong Kong in 1992 for sales to China, Korea, and Taiwan and exports products to the Middle East, Eastern Europe, and Central and South America. However, this international activity remains a very small percentage of Tootsie Roll's total sales. (See Exhibit 6.)

Because the Gordons are not becoming younger, the future of Tootsie Roll will depend on several key decisions they will make over the next few years. Perhaps the time has come for Mel and Ellen to think ahead while their company is achieving marketplace success.

REFERENCES

Bloomberg, New York, March 1995.

Brown, R. H., & Garten, J. E., *Forecasts for Selected Manufacturing and Service Industries: U.S. Industrial Outlook 1994*, U.S. Department of Commerce, January 1994.

Dow Jones Stock Quote Reporter Service.

Hershey Foods, Inc. Annual Report, 1994.

Industry Norms and Key Business Ratios—One Year, Dun & Bradstreet Information Services, 1993–1994.

Jorgensen, J., *Encyclopedia of Consumer Brands.* Detroit: St. James Press, 1994.

Keith, H., "Green" Package Blues, *Snack Food*, February 1995: 58–61.

Keith, H., Packaging 2000: Virtually Real, *Snack Food*, January 1995: 52–53.

Kimbrell, W., Way to Grow, *Snack Food*, May 1994: 22–25.

Labate, J. Tootsie Roll Industries. *Fortune*, January 10, 1994: 109.

Littman, M., & Rogers, P., Snack Food Salutes the Top 100 Manufacturers in the Industry, *Snack Food*, December 1994: 32–37.

Market Share Reporter—1995, New York: Gale Research, 1991.

Marketing, *Wall Street Journal*, August 26, 1992: B-1.

Moody's Industrial Manual. New York: Moody's Investors Services, 1994.

Moskowitz, M., Levering, R., & Katz, M., *Guide to Company Profiles.* New York: Bantam Doubleday Dell Publishing Group, Inc., 1990.

Sparks, D., Tootsie Roll: Don't Bite Yet, *Financial World*, April 26, 1994: 16.

Springen, K., Bigger Breaks for Small Business. *Working Woman*, November 1993: 17–18.

Standard NYSE Stock Reports, Vol. 61, No. 241, Sec. 50, New York: McGraw-Hill, Inc.

Stauffer, C., Formulating the Fat Out, *Snack Food*, January 1995: 46–48.

Tootsie Roll Industries, Inc., Annual Report, 1994.

Value Line

Warner-Lambert Co., *Snack Food*, December 1994: 40.

When Employees Own Big Stake, It's a Buy Signal for Investors, *Wall Street Journal*, February 13, 1992: C-1.

Tyson Foods, Inc.

Loretta Ferguson Cochran

Clemson University

Tyson's Real Asset: The people of Tyson are the people who work in the plants, in the feed mills and in the offices. We live in the deep South, on the East Coast and overseas—everywhere we have operations. We are as diverse as our work.

We work in live swine production. We catch fish in the Bering Sea. We load pallets of product to be shipped to customers in places such as Hong Kong and Russia, as well as 41 other countries.

Every day, all 55,800 of us work not only to keep the company number one in the poultry category, but to expand other growing areas such as our beef, pork, fish, corn and flour operations.

We take responsibility for our work. Together we manage both people and capital. But most important is how we build our company by taking chances, doing new things, working as a team, sharing credit and keeping an eye on the bottom line.

We are always challenging ourselves. Our philosophy is that if we're doing things the same way we did yesterday, chances are there's room for improvement.

We continue to believe that our people are our number one asset. We believe that if we take care of our people, they will take care of our customers, which ultimately takes care of our shareholders. It's simple, but it works.

—Don Tyson (1994 Annual Report)

Tyson Foods, Inc., is the world's largest fully integrated producer, processor, and marketer of poultry-based food products. In addition, it is a significant producer and marketer of other "center-of-the-plate" (entrée) and convenience food items.[1] Tyson's stated strategy is to "Segment, Concentrate, and Dominate." According to Don Tyson, CEO, "We (Tyson Foods, Inc.) find something we can do, focus on it, and aim to be #1."[2]

POULTRY PROCESSING INDUSTRY

Poultry production is a major component of agricultural production throughout the world, with poultry serving as a source of high-quality protein for the world's population.[3] The poultry industry, unlike most agricultural production, is highly vertically integrated. Beginning in the 1950s, poultry farmers combined feed mills and processing plants to create efficient operation complexes.[4]

The industry produces three distinct processed poultry meat products. First, fresh carcass products are packaged as the whole bird and as parts (i.e., a package of chicken legs). Second, formed products, both whole and chopped, consist of deboned meat shaped into a specific form and held in place while being cooked into that shape. In whole products, the whole muscle is left intact or in large pieces to retain the intact muscle tissue texture; in chopped products, the meat is finely chopped to the point where it loses the characteristics of muscle tissue. Third, in emulsified products, the meat has been pureed into a batter and forced into a product casing to form items such as frankfurters and bologna. These items are typically cooked, smoked, or cured.[5]

Poultry producers sell directly to large grocery and restaurant chains such as Winn Dixie and McDonald's, but use food wholesalers to reach smaller chains and sole proprietorships.

Processed poultry meats have emerged as a low-fat alternative (substitute) to red meats. Prior to the 1970s, consumer demand was for commodity chicken, marketed and distributed through grocery store outlets. In the mid- to late 1970s, demand began to shift to convenience-type products, such as formed patties. Presently, the slow growth in whole fryers and parts has continued, and the demand is continuing to strengthen for processed parts and formed products which are available as prepared food in restaurants and as ready-to-eat products in grocery stores.

try consumption per person is listed in Exhibits 4 and 5.

Feed prices have a significant effect on the cost of raising poultry and, therefore, on the profitability of poultry farmers and processors. Given the latest bumper (feed) crops, feed prices have declined recently, which should widen profit margins on poultry even if selling price per pound falls slightly.[6] Seventy percent of the industry cost of producing a ready-to-cook chicken is from the feed ingredients. It is the single most influential factor on poultry industry cycles.[7] To some extent, vertically integrated firms are able to control the influence of feed suppliers by producing their own feed. However, floods and droughts, which also increase feed costs, are beyond their control. Exhibits 6 and 7 show the fluctuation in price of mill feed and of poultry from September 1993 to September 1994.

INDUSTRY SALES AND PROFITS

The industry shipments for poultry processing (SIC 2015) are listed in Exhibits 1 through 3. Annual poul-

COMPETITORS

Exhibit 8 includes 1993 market share, revenues, and net income (in millions of dollars) for the top 10 companies in poultry processing.[8] The revenue and net

EXHIBIT 1 *Poultry Processing Shipments (in millions of dollars)*

1987	1988	1989	1990	1991
14,912	16,598	20,283	20,928	21,703

Source: *U.S. Industrial Outlook 1994.*

EXHIBIT 2 *Poultry Processing Shipments (percent change)*

1987–88	1988–89	1989–90	1990–91
11.3	22.2	3.2	3.7

Source: *U.S. Industrial Outlook 1994.*

EXHIBIT 3 *Product Shipments, Exports, and Imports (millions of dollars)*

Product Shipments		Value of Exports		Value of Imports	
1990	1991	1990	1991	1990	1991
20,353	21,246	717	879	32	37
% Change	4.4%		22.6%		15.6%

Source: *U.S. Industrial Outlook 1994.*

EXHIBIT 4 *Per Capita Consumption of Chicken and Turkey (in pounds)*

	1983	1984	1985	1986	1987	1988	1989	1990	1991	1992
Chicken	50.7	52.4	54.1	55.4	58.5	58.7	60.6	63.0	65.6	68.4
Turkey	11.8	11.8	11.6	12.9	14.7	15.7	16.6	17.6	18.0	18.0

Source: *Dairy and Poultry Statistics,* Washington, D.C.: U.S. Government Printing Office, 1993.

EXHIBIT 5 *Per Capita Consumption (percent change)*

	1983–84	1984–85	1985–86	1986–87	1987–88	1988–89	1989–90	1990–91	1991–92
Chicken	3.35	3.24	2.4	5.6	0.34	3.24	4.0	4.13	4.27
Turkey	0	−.02	11.2	14.0	6.8	5.7	6.02	2.3	0

Source: *Dairy and Poultry Statistics,* Washington, D.C.: U.S. Government Printing Office, 1993.

income figures are for the entire corporation, which often includes more than poultry processing. Market share is based on 289.5 million pounds of ready-to-cook poultry product produced each week in 1993.

The top four producers capture less than 40 percent of the market, which indicates a moderate level of fragmentation in the industry. In addition, half of the firms listed in Exhibit 8 are privately held. Poultry processing is fragmented in part due to the way

vertical integration of the industry developed. When firms began integration, there were significantly fewer barriers to entry. As the product experienced moderate growth, firms became more automated and efficient. Smaller firms tend to have less extensive vertical integration, while the larger firms maintain a high degree of vertical integration.

Competition tends to focus on price and quality, with brand name recognition being an avenue for

EXHIBIT 6 *Mill Feed Prices, 1993–94*

EXHIBIT 7 *Commodity Poultry Prices, 1993–94*

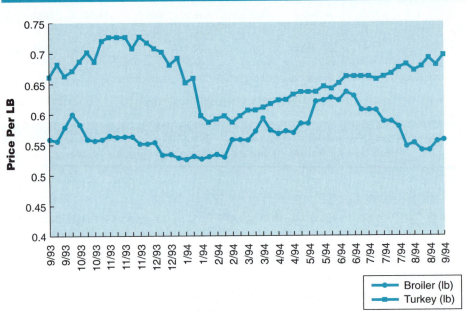

capturing market share. The significance of brand name recognition was evidenced when Tyson acquired Holly Farms in 1988. This acquisition was important because Holly Farms held 19 percent of the brand-name chicken sold in grocery markets. Name recognition is vital in obtaining shelf space and subsequent market share for branded products. The Holly Farms acquisition also increased Tyson's supply of chickens and processing capacity, which were needed because of Tyson's rapid growth in supplying the fast-food industry.

Geographical competition is also present for the best contract growers.[9] Contracts growers are individuals with broiler houses that raise company-

EXHIBIT 8 *Competitor Information*

Company	Market Share (percent)	Revenue ($ million)	Net Income ($ million)	Operating Margin (percent)
Tyson Foods	15.4%	4,707.40	180.33	11.7%
ConAgra	9.4	21,519	399.5	5.6
Gold Kist	6.7	1,561	*	*
Perdue Farms	5.6	1,020	*	*
Pilgrim's Pride	4.2	887.87	22.3	6.32
Hudson Foods	3.5	920.50	15.9	6.2
WLR Foods	3.0	617	14.6	9.0
Foster Farms	2.9	1,160	*	*
Wayne Poultry	2.9	11	*	*
Townsends	2.1	270	*	*
Others	44.3			

*Data unavailable for private firms; their sales figures are estimates.

provided chicks to market-size broilers. These growers are served by a company representative that checks on chick development. The growers own the houses and pay utilities, but the company supplies the feed and supplements for the birds. The growers are paid for the broilers by a formula that includes weight, feed conversion, mortality rate, and other factors. Within a geographic region, there can be several broiler complexes from various companies.

These complexes include a hatchery, a feed mill, and a processing plant. Each complex is affiliated with egg and broiler producers. There is competition among complexes for the best contract producers.

This sort of geographical association supports poultry as a regional industry in terms of ownership, with broiler production predominantly in the southern region. Exhibit 9 outlines the top five states in 1992 in terms of production.[10] Exhibit 10 provides a

EXHIBIT 9 *Geographical Regions of Production*

State	Percentage
Arkansas	15.3%
Alabama	13.5
Georgia	13.2
North Carolina	9.9
Mississippi	7.5
Total % of Market Accounted for	88.2

EXHIBIT 10 *Location of Publicly Held Firms' Processing Facilities*

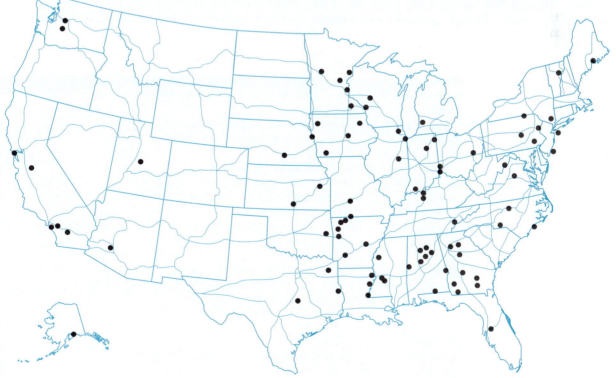

geographical layout of the locations of processing facilities for publicly held firms.

Historically, each division of the poultry industry (broilers, layers, turkeys) functioned as a sector industry with independent hatcheries, feed suppliers, and processors.[11] For example, broiler growers purchased chicks and feed from different suppliers than do layer and turkey growers. Individual farmers negotiated price with processors who then handled the sale of their products to retailers. Eventually, the poultry industry developed binding contracts between producers, feed suppliers, and processors—particularly in the broiler segment—along with more reliable scheduling and product commitments. In the broiler segment, individual producers own the birds but agree to do business with a specific feed supplier and processor. Over the past 40 years, these relationships among hatcheries, feed suppliers, and processors have developed into vertical integration, as strategic alliances have emerged between companies and contract growers (Exhibits 11 and 12).[12] The company owns a hatchery, a feed mill, and a processing plant. Vertical integration dominates the industry; over 95 percent of commercial broilers are produced by vertically integrated firms.[13]

Strategic alliances have developed between the contract growers and the affiliated company. The broilers from the hatchery are grown by independent "contract farms" or company-owned farms. Company-owned farms account for a very small percentage of chickens grown. The company is not the grower; it just facilitates broiler production.

Vertical integration has consolidated the marketing, sales, quality standards, and administrative functions that were present in each sector before integration. This has had a positive effect on demand and profitability by maintaining efficient processes and reducing costs. Establishing quality standards between a company and a supplier in today's market is important for those companies that adhere to universal product standards such as ISO 9000, since the quality standards extend to suppliers. These types of supplier-customer relationships existed years ago in the poultry industry and have improved the process of growing a uniform bird.

Economies of scale have also been created in scheduling, distribution, coordinating facilities, and controlling production. Many of the costs of vertical integration have been avoided so far, partially because past integration developed through acquisitions that were perceived as beneficial to both companies, and were, therefore, not opposed by stakeholders. The level of vertical integration is different from economies of scale. Feeds, chicks, and other necessary materials for production enjoy a reduction in per unit cost when purchased in larger

EXHIBIT 11 *An Example of Vertical Integration: Tyson Foods*

Step	Description	
Foundation Breeder Flock	Pedigree flocks that yield the highly productive line of breeder hens and roosters.	
Hatchery Supply Flock	Breeder houses where roosters and hens produce broiler eggs.	
Commercial Hatchery	Environmentally controlled nurseries where eggs hatch.	
Feed Mill	Hammer and grinding mills where train loads of grain are mixed and trucked to nearby farms	Independently owned farms operate as strategic alliances, not part of the company's vertical integration.
Broiler Growout Farms	Long, narrow houses (company owned) where flocks of chickens are raised.	
Processing Plant	Automated factories where birds are processed into poultry staples and byproducts.	
Distribution Channels	Massive freezer warehouses and trucking fleets deliver products.	

EXHIBIT 12 *Vertical Integration of the Poultry Processing Industry*

amounts. Vertical integration allows firms to own everything from the feed mill and processing plant to the distribution process and facilities.[14] The costs are lower than if the units were operating separately, with each demanding a markup in price.

GLOBAL ISSUES

Three countries accounted for over 55 percent of worldwide broiler exports in 1992:[15] United States (26 percent), France (16 percent), and Brazil (15 percent). In 1992, the largest importers of U.S. poultry were Japan ($130 million), Hong Kong ($127 million), Canada ($90 million), and Mexico ($71 million). Larger processors are penetrating foreign markets by buying into foreign poultry processing concerns.

Tyson holds a majority interest in Trasgo, S.A. de C.V., Mexico's third largest poultry processor.[16] Cargill has moved into European markets with Cargill France, which has opened a processing plant in France to supply McDonald's with chicken products.

The effect of the North American Free Trade Agreement (NAFTA) and General Agreement on Tariffs and Trade (GATT) on expanding markets may be twofold. First, these agreements may open up international markets and relieve some international subsidies on poultry products. Second, both agreements include new labeling regulations that contain extensive disclosure requirements. These agreements, along with the enforcement of the Nutrition Labeling and Education Act by the Food and Drug Administration, may benefit the poultry processing industry by highlighting the "healthier" nature of poultry over other meat products, and possibly by giving U.S. firms an advantage because of previous experience with this type of regulation.[17]

SAFETY ISSUES

New regulations on handling, cooking, and inspecting poultry have been created in response to recent attention by the media to the poor standards of inspection and unsafe working conditions in the poultry processing industry. The enforcement of laws regulating labor conditions has included the imposition of fines and jail sentences on those responsible for labor law violations.

Performance of firms with respect to these safety and health standards varies considerably across the industry. For example, a Reidsville, N.C., Equity Meats facility has above-standard programs for safety and health, while the Imperial Foods Hamlet operation had no safety program. The Hamlet facility burned in 1991 with locked exit doors and no sprinkler system, killing 25 workers and injuring 55 others.[18] Members of the management team were held responsible for the incident with fines and jail terms.

TECHNOLOGICAL TRENDS

Today, the poultry processing industry is much more capital intensive. With broilers now grown to a uniform size and shape, highly automated processing facilities have emerged to set new industry production and quality standards. Line speeds of 140 chickens per minute are normal for plants that are automated and efficient.[19] Other processing developments include feather plucking technology and improved disinfectant bird-bathing processes.

Technological advances are used in product development as well. A technological development being tested currently is a meat analog product that is made from washed poultry meat. This is finely ground meat that is mixed with buffers that remove soluble protein fraction from the muscle tissue. The insoluble protein fraction that remains is formed and cooked into the designed shape. The resulting product is high in protein and low in fat and can be flavored in such a way as to serve as a substitute product for other meats such as lobster and crab.[20]

LABOR UNIONS

Labor unions such as Laborers' International Union of North America (LIUNA) and United Food and Commercial Workers International Union (UFCW) are organizing poultry facilities all across the South, and membership is growing at a rapid rate. Only 7 of the 63 Tyson plants are unionized. In contrast, 7 of 14 Hudson Foods plants are unionized. Unionized labor could have a significant effect on the availability and cost of labor which will drive up prices.

OTHER PRODUCTS

An emerging substitute for chicken appears to be ostrich.[21] If chicken is viewed as the healthy alternative to red meat, then ostrich surpasses it. Exhibit 13 outlines the nutritional information on various types of meat for a 3-ounce serving. As ostrich has become more available, prices have fallen. If this trend continues, ostrich could compete directly with poultry.

EXHIBIT 13 *Comparison of Various Meat Products*			
Meat	**Calories**	**Cholesterol**	**Fat**
Ostrich	82.5	50.7g	0.5g
Chicken	140	73g	3g
Beef	240	77g	15g
Pork	275	84g	19g

Consumer reaction to ostrich has been less than favorable, but growers remain optimistic. According to growers, the most significant challenge is finding a way to convince consumers to taste ostrich meat.

TYSON FOODS, INC.

Tyson Foods and its subsidiaries produce, market, and distribute various food products. These products serve the function of providing nourishment. The firm's product mix consists of value-enhanced poultry; fresh and frozen poultry; value-enhanced beef and pork products; fresh and frozen pork products; value-enhanced seafood products; fresh and frozen seafood products; and flour and corn tortillas, chips, and other Mexican food-based products. Other products and processes include live swine, animal feed, and pet food. Value-enhanced products have added value in some fashion (deboned, seasoned, cooked, etc.) for a food service firm or have been processed (patties, frankfurters, etc.) and packed for the retail shelf.

The vertically integrated operations consist of breeding and rearing chickens and hogs and harvesting seafood, followed by processing, further processing, and marketing these food and beef products.[22] Poultry production and subsequent processing, marketing, and distribution capture the greatest percentage of Tyson Foods' revenue. The breakdown of Tyson's business units in terms of sales mix for 1994 is shown in Exhibit 14.

Markets served by Tyson products, as outlined in Exhibit 15, include food service, retail, wholesale club, international, and other. Food service customers include hotels, cafeterias, fast-food chains, and food service distributors. Retail products on supermarket shelves include Tyson Holly Farms Fresh Chicken, a variety of Weaver brand products, Louis Kemp Crab and Lobster, and several ready-to-eat Roasted Chicken and "Complete" meal kits. Annual sales are highlighted with gross margin in Exhibit 16.

COMPANY CHARACTERISTICS

Following is a brief overview of Tyson Foods, Inc. The data is taken from the 1994 Annual Report, year ending October 31, 1994, and from Moody's Company Data Report on Tyson Foods from October 1994.[23]

Tyson Foods was incorporated in Delaware in 1986 to distinguish it from the company originally incorporated in Arkansas on October 7, 1947. The company is headquartered in Springdale, Arkansas, with production and distribution operations as shown in Exhibit 17.

C-515

EXHIBIT 14 *1994 Sales (by percentage)*

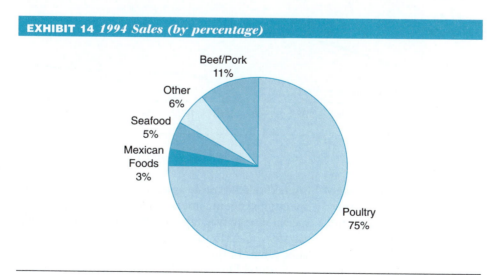

EXHIBIT 15 *1994 Sales (by percentage)*

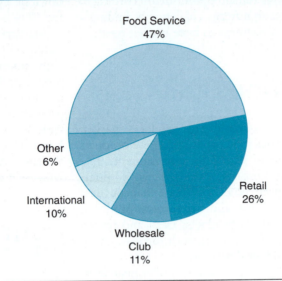

EXHIBIT 16 *Tyson Foods Inc. (in thousands)*

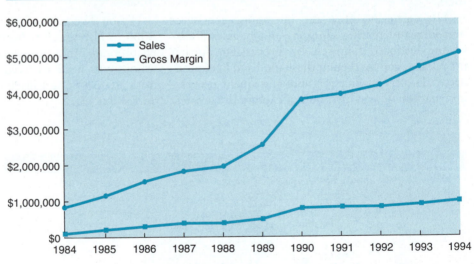

In addition, international facilities or joint ventures are shown in Exhibit 18. The diverse international locations are due principally to Trasgo and Cobb-Vantress. Exhibits 19 and 20 outline Tyson's acquisition history and current subsidiaries.[24]

Sales for 1994 peaked at a historic $5,110,270,000. Due to a one-time special charge of $214 million (pretax) related to the assets of Arctic Alaska seafood operations, net income was a loss of $2,128,000. The special charge was taken in the third quarter of fiscal 1994 to write-down the goodwill and impaired asset values of the Arctic Alaska Fisheries portion of the Seafood Division. The write-down was necessary because of unanticipated production overcapacity,

EXHIBIT 17 *Location of U.S. Operations*

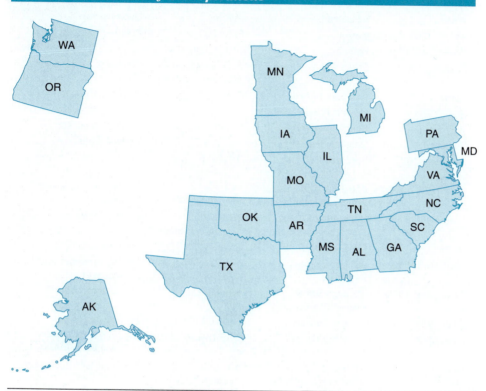

C-517

EXHIBIT 18 *International Locations*

China
Hong Kong
India
Indonesia
Japan
Philippines
South Africa

Argentina
Brazil
Denmark
Mexico
Spain
Venezuela
United Kingdom

EXHIBIT 19 *Tyson's Acquisition History*

Date	Acquired	Price	Description
March 1963	Garrett Poultry Co.	$300,000	Poultry producer
September 1966	Washington Creamery	$1,500,000	Poultry distributor
November 1967	Franz Foods Producers	53,196 shares common stock	Poultry producer and processor
1969	Prospect Farms	*	Poultry producer
April 1972	Ocoma Foods	*	Poultry processor
July 1972	Krispy Kitchens	*	Poultry processor
August 1973	Cassady Broiler Co.	*	Poultry processor
February 1974	Vantress Pedigree	*	Genetic research and breeding farm
July 1978	Wilson Foods Poultry Division	*	Poultry producer and processor
January 1981	Honeybear Foods	$3,100,000 cash and stock	Poultry producer
1983	Mexican Original	*	Flour/corn tortillas
October 1984	90% of Valmac Industries	$70,723,815	Poultry producer and processor
December 1985	Heritage Valley Processing Division	$9,400,000	Poultry processor
May 1986	Lane Processing	$107,000,000	Poultry processor
July 1989	Holly Farms	$1.5 billion	Integrated poultry producer and processor
June 1991	Arkansas-California Livestock Company	100,000 shares Class A stock	Beef and swine producer
October 1992	Arctic Alaska Fisheries	242,700,000 cash and stock	Seafood producer and processor
October 1992	Louis Kemp Seafood	$19,300,000	Seafood processor
November 1992	Swine plants	*	Swine processor
December 1992	Brandywine Foods	*	Swine processor
January 1994	George's Food Service	*	Beef processor for food service
April 1994	Majority ownership of Trasgo, S.A. de C.V.	*	Poultry producer and processor
July 1994	Culinary Foods	*	Processor of value-added specialty frozen foods
August 1994	Increased to 100% ownership of Cobb-Vantress	*	Supplier of breeding stock for broilers

*Some information was unavailable. Acquisitions were made in cash unless otherwise noted.

intense competition for a decreasing number of fish, shorter fishing seasons, and less production per vessel. Total assets are at $3,668,000,000 and long-term debt is $1,381,481,000.

Tyson, along with the rest of the poultry processing industry, is heavily automated, especially in value-added further processing facilities. Value-added products, such as chicken nuggets sold to fast-food chains, require processing beyond whole fryer, commodity chickens. Additional processing is necessary to add ingredients and shape the products. Value-added further processed products are packed

EXHIBIT 20 *Subsidiaries*

Subsidiary	Description
AAFC Holdings, Ltd. (Canada)	Poultry processing
AAFC Intl., Inc. (Virgin Islands)	Poultry processing
Arctic Alaska Fisheries Corp.	Seafood division
Global Employment Services	Internal employment services
Southeast Health Plan of AR	Internal self-insured employee health plan
Trasgo, S.A. de C.V. (Mexico)	Poultry processor
Tyson Breeders, Inc.	Breeder flock
Tyson Export Sales	Export sales division
Tyson Farms, Inc.	Complex division
Tyson Foods, Inc.	Processing division
Tyson Holding Company	Acquisition division
Tyson Marketing	U.S. marketing division
Tyson Marketing, Ltd. (Canada)	Canadian marketing division
We Care Workers Compensation	Internal workers' compensation
WLR Acquisition Corp. (failed)	Failed takeover division

products ready for the retail consumer; Tyson frozen and children's meals are examples.

Tyson Foods is committed to making the customer aware of each product's advantages. From the beginning, Tyson's intention has been to convince customers that precooked food is more practical than home-prepared dishes. In this way, Tyson has been instrumental in facilitating market acceptance of the value-added products that provide today's growth.

Tyson serves as the industry leader in technology and processing innovation and change. Tyson is protective of its processes and discourages all facility tours. Automated hatcheries and capital-intensive processing facilities highlight Tyson's commitment to technology. The company's shift from internal combustion to electric forklifts is eliminating emissions problems. These forklifts operate in their processing plants and distribution facilities, saving Tyson a significant amount in maintenance costs.[25]

Tyson's corporate philosophy is one of growing shareholder value. The return on a $100 investment in Tyson Foods (including dividend reinvestment) for a 10-year period ending October 1, 1994, yielded 34.2 percent annually. The 10-year compounded annual growth rates for the period ending October 1, 1994, for three indices pale in comparison: 16.9 percent for the Dow Jones Industrial Average, 16.4 percent for the Wilshire 5000, and 14.6 for the Standard & Poor's 500. In addition, Tyson closed 1994 with record sales of approximately $5.1 billion.

Tyson has chosen to focus on the needs of its customers with the largest segment being the food service industry. Tyson has responded positively with product and service improvements to meet customer concerns over labor shortages, food costs, and food safety. For example, food service customers, such as institutions, needed products that require the least amount of labor and time to prepare. Further processed products have allowed Tyson to reduce these customers' preparation time and manpower needs.

Recent Tyson acquisitions include Culinary Foods and George's Food Service, Inc., both of which are important to expanding sales and service in the growth market of the food service industry. Tyson also purchased Upjohn's interest in Cobb-Vantress, becoming the sole owner. It is a world leader in supplying broiler breeding stock, with 90 percent of its sales outside the United States.

Tyson claims to be an industry leader in employment practices and work-force policies. Management displays a commitment to training and other benefits that are unmet in the industry. This commitment enables Tyson to maintain a work force of the best and brightest in the business, from field representatives to vice presidents. In general, Tyson salaries are not the highest in the industry, but the benefits package of insurance and bonuses is unequaled. The attractiveness of the total package is a unique advantage due to the growing importance of these "additional" compensation packages that complement salary. Tyson is committed to career path development for each employee, and cross-training serves as the vehicle for developing new leaders. Tyson places high expectations on employees and has been able to hire individuals willing to meet and exceed those expectations.

Employee skills are at various levels. First, the line workers, who handle the broilers, are relatively unskilled or low-skilled labor. Maintenance and technical employees have a high degree of industrial/mechanical skill that is necessary to maintain the highly automated systems. Management has a training center located in Russellville, Arkansas, that provides a basic introduction to company culture and practices for each member of management (regardless of level).

Tyson employees work in the safest facilities in the poultry industry. Tyson has the best safety record in the industry, which is five times safer than the industry average. In 1994, one plant logged 3 million man-hours without a lost-time accident, and six other plants logged 1 million man-hours without a lost-time accident. A lost-time accident is a category of OSHA recordable accidents.[26]

Union activity at the Tyson facilities has been minimal. Less than 1 percent of Tyson employees nationwide are unionized. This small percentage is in sharp contrast to Hudson Foods which has 7 of its 14 plants unionized.

Another stakeholder is the University of Arkansas, Fayetteville, where the multimillion-dollar expansion of the poultry science program is a direct result of Tyson Food's investment. Tyson considers this an investment in research and development that will result in a competitive advantage in product quality.

Tyson's philosophy is simple: to increase shareholder value. The strategy is to "Segment, Concentrate, and Dominate." Through acquisition and internal expansion, Tyson first segments the particular product market then concentrates on technological innovation and vertical integration to dominate that market segment. This vision of domination in the primary food markets should make Tyson the industry leader.

Examples of achieving this strategy though acquisition are easy to find in Tyson's history. Holly Farms

was a competitor until Tyson won a bidding war with ConAgra over its acquisition. Tyson failed in its recent bid for WLR, a competitor, but it continues to search for other acquisitions.

Tyson's mission has evolved with the company. Prior to the 1970s, most of the company's sales were from commodity chicken, marketed and distributed through grocery store outlets. John Tyson maintained a production-oriented strategy during the early days. During the 1950s and 1960s, the company focused on expanding production facilities and competitive technological innovation and completed vertical integration in the broiler industry. In 1964, Don Tyson offered a signal to the company's changing focus. He concluded that the optimal way for the company to grow was to buy assets with profit-making potential at values under its own earnings per share. At first, these acquisitions were within the poultry industry; however, by the late 1980s and early 1990s, Tyson had expanded into related fields of swine and beef. By doing so, Tyson established a product diversification plan centered around new product introduction.[27] The 1970s were a time of growth and poultry product diversification. During this time, Tyson emerged as an industry leader in new product introduction. By 1979, it had 24 specialty poultry products. In addition, the processing plants were industry leaders in technological improvements.

All along, Tyson has achieved the majority of its vertical integration through successful acquisitions. The company has been successful in gaining the cost and productivity savings and efficiencies from these acquired concerns. According to Don Tyson, efficiency and improved product quality in processing is a direct result of putting killing facilities and processing plants together.[28] Through successful vertical integration including feed producers, feed costs at Tyson account for only 40 percent of production costs. Tyson maintains freezer/warehouse facilities that use an inventory system tied into the Springdale mainframe and subsequently linked to processing levels and activities. The status and location of any product are always available. This information integration is a skill Tyson continues to improve. In 1980, the firm consolidated its further processing efforts into a product line that consisted of chicken that was quick and easy to prepare. Currently, Tyson holds the philosophy that change is necessary for improvement and dominance in the marketplace.

VALUE-ADDED CHAIN

Tyson has achieved success through vertical integration with timely acquisitions and synergistic results from the acquired businesses. Tyson has a level of vertical integration unmatched by other poultry companies. As previously noted, seven levels are incorporated into the poultry processing business. First, Tyson has the foundation breeder flocks from which the breeder hens and roosters are obtained. Next, the hatchery supply flock is responsible for the broiler eggs. Then, in the controlled hatchery environment, the eggs hatch. The feed mills supply both the hatcheries and the grower farms. Next, the automated plants process the broilers. The warehouse and truck fleet system delivers the product either to the customer or to a further processing facility. One exception to this model is the broiler growout farm. Broilers are typically grown by contract farmers that are in a strategic alliance with Tyson and are not part of the company's vertical integration. An additional level is the recently completed purchase of Upjohn's 50 percent stake in Cobb-Vantress, Inc. Cobb-Vantress is a genetic engineering farm where varieties of broilers are developed that will grow uniformly and quickly, which produces a bird that is genetically efficient.

An example of how Tyson has made these acquisitions work is present in Cobb-Vantress. Tyson is able to take the birds that are developed but not qualified for breeding stock and absorb them into Tyson's processing volume. Tyson is the primary but not sole customer of Cobb-Vantress at the present time. Tyson has been able to capitalize on the benefits of vertical integration and has negated many of the costs by creating a highly efficient operation along with greatly improving the quality of the product. Tyson facilities are top of the line and pristine compared to the industry average and the firm's closest competitors.

The complete vertical integration has developed an unparalleled advantage for Tyson in that it has controlled the majority of the factors that affect poultry prices and, at the same time, made them efficient and productive through automation. Complexes have a feed mill and processing facility, typically with a warehouse and freezer unit connected. Normally, growers are within a 60-mile radius of the facility.[29]

STAKEHOLDERS

Principal internal stakeholders are long-time senior managers that have been with Tyson since the early days in the 1960s. The members of general management are identified in Exhibit 21.

Tyson, Tollett, and Wray are the key players within the company and have been together for over 30 years. Tollett and Wray are the balancing forces that complement Tyson's aggressive ideas for future

C-521

EXHIBIT 21 *Tyson Management*

Individual	Company History
Don Tyson	1952 to present. Was president and CEO, then chairman of the board and CEO; is currently chairman of the board; will step down in April 1995, to become senior chairman.
Leland Tollett	1961 to present. Was vice president, then COO, then president and COO; is currently vice chairman, president, and CEO. In April 1995 will become chairman.
Donald Wray	1959 to present. Was vice president of marketing, then executive VP sales and marketing, then senior VP processing sales and marketing, then senior VP sales and marketing; is currently COO.
Gerald Johnston	1970 to present. Was vice president, and currently is executive VP finance.
David Purtle	1971 to present. Was group vice president operations, and is currently senior VP operations.
Wayne Britt	1973 to present. Was secretary/treasurer vice president, then treasurer VP; is currently senior VP of international sales and marketing.

growth. Tyson sets the corporate direction and long-term goals. These men are committed to Don Tyson's vision of "Segment, Concentrate, and Dominate" as the way to increase shareholder wealth though acquisition.

There are 900,000,000 shares of Class A common stock authorized outstanding. These shares have one vote per share. Don Tyson, founder John Tyson's son, controls 99.9 percent of the 900,000,000 shares of Class B stock. These shares have 10 votes per share and can be converted to Class A stock.

GROWTH

Growth at Tyson is a result of the desire to evolve into a company that produces chicken-based foods that are free from market fluctuations. Regardless of the acquisition source, as long as it is within a select field of expertise, the company will try it if Tyson can grow it.

Recent success for Tyson has been based on a decreasing focus on commodity products and movement into further processed and value-added poultry. Tyson desires to meet customer wants with top-quality products. To be the preferred producer, future growth plans must remain flexible and subject to change. The company's success is indicated by its need to match production to sales activity.

Tyson's new product development is not subject to the same strict budgetary controls as the rest of the corporation. Due to management's style of risk taking and financial support, the company has been able to introduce products with development times well below the industry average. Tyson has used marketing strategies described as defensive, offensive, niche, and guerrilla in its operation. The goal is to make Tyson a recognized household name with brand loyalty second to none.

New products have a relatively short and fairly predictable product life cycle. Tyson is aware of these factors, and therefore has a range of products in development at different stages of the process. Tyson is committed to remaining with what it does best. For example, it sold off its fast-food venture because a fast-food market emerged for its other products, and it has avoided the seasonal turkey market because it did not fit into the overall corporate strategy.

The purchase of Prospect Farms in 1969 was Tyson's first attempt at growth into value-added

products on a large scale. Tyson was able to enter into food service products where sales were relatively unaffected by fluctuations in the chicken market. Consumer demand for value-added food service products began to include the retail markets. Not all market development efforts have succeeded. The Looney Tunes line of children's meals was pulled in 1994, in part because the customers the product targeted were too young to operate the microwave. However, top management accepts that when seeking first mover advantages, there will be some missteps.

Tyson had a vertically integrated system in the late 1960s, when firms were failing during extreme market swings. Major acquisitions were made when firms were financially depressed or overextended. Companies are purchased when it is easier and cheaper to buy than to build.

Not all acquisition targets are success stories. The 1994 attempt to acquire WLR failed because of WLR's purchase of Cuddy (turkey) Farms, which pushed WLR above the limit in terms of cost for Tyson. In addition, not all purchases have led to increased profits. The Arctic Alaska Fisheries acquisition resulted in a $191 million special charge for excess of investment over net assets acquired in addition to the $23 million for impaired long-lived assets. This resulted in a special charge, after tax, of $205 million or $1.38 per share in 1994. In addition, government restrictions and legal troubles are on the horizon for Arctic. Seafood is a related product to Tyson's core business of poultry; therefore, this business unit, as problematic as it seems, is a part of the company's growth strategy. The only positive result is that management has taken an early and preemptive financial charge in hopes of initializing a recovery.

In concert with the corporate strategy of "Segment, Concentrate, Dominate," marketing has specific sales approaches for a wide range of products and customers. In food service, for example, there are 23 purchase points that have been identified—separate markets being served that each require a different marketing effort.

As a function of operations, Tyson has a staff of employees that works closely with independent food service distributors and brokers. The company helps train these individuals to sell Tyson products and to have command of every detail about each product, at no charge to the distributor. In addition, Tyson is one of only a few companies that offers food service customers such as restaurants three-year contracts with price protection.

Tyson will not introduce a product or enter a market if a company using Tyson products is already established there. Tyson is not in the food service industry, as the largest portion of its sales go to that industry. The only rule is to respect the customer. This noncompete attitude has been a key to the success of the company's growth through acquisition. However, Tyson will not necessarily leave its established niche when a current competitor becomes a customer. For example, the chicken-based frozen entrée market is not a policy conflict. Tyson marketed its own brand of frozen entrées before it began providing chicken ingredients to other companies for their frozen dinners.

Tyson Foods has made related diversification moves into the swine and beef businesses. The swine operation is the largest hog farming operation in the country. Tyson enjoys increased efficiencies by utilizing the poultry freezer and distribution system in swine production.

INTEGRATED STRATEGY

Tyson's competitive strategy has shifted over the years from low cost to integrated differentiation and low cost. This strategy has been consistent with the market and demand shifts and supports the company's segment, concentrate, dominate theme. Tyson competed on price in the 1950s when the main

products were commodity chicken. Now, Tyson's products are increasingly further processed and value added (items that are higher priced with larger margins). However, Tyson's vertical integration has afforded it the advantage of also being the lowest-cost producer of value-added products. Product quality is the primary dimension on which these products are differentiated. In addition to Tyson's channel dominance and low-cost advantage, this differentiation into convenience chicken products has introduced another barrier to entry for competitors. The initial investment for a new competitor would be enormous. Potential problems arise when competitors such as ConAgra have the resources to compete and imitate Tyson's products. ConAgra and Tyson have a long-standing rivalry that discourages other companies from entering the poultry market.

FINANCIAL INFORMATION

With the exception of the special charge this year, Tyson's financial data indicate that not only is it a leading producer, it is a leading firm in terms of financial strength. Tyson's profitability ratios, shown in Exhibits 22–26, are compared to those of two competitors: ConAgra and Hudson Foods. It appears that the competitive advantage Tyson has over ConAgra is a result of the improved efficiency that may not be noticed if only sales are considered, as ConAgra is a larger company. As a performance measure of profitability, operating margin attempts to

C-523

EXHIBIT 22 *Operating Margin*

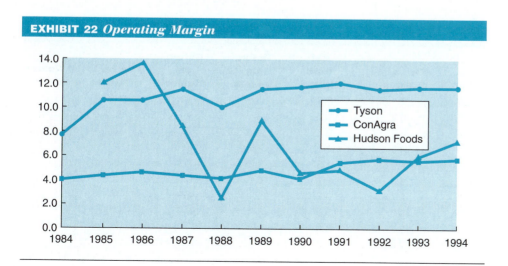

EXHIBIT 23 *Net Profit Margin*

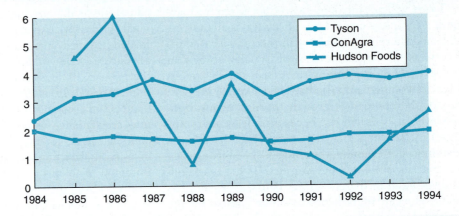

EXHIBIT 24 *ConAgra*

Year	Operating Margin	Net Profit Margin	Return on Assets	Return on Equity	Current Ratio	Quick Ratio
1994	5.7%	1.9%			1.06	0.48
1993	5.6	1.8	2.21%	17.2%	1.08	0.48
1992	5.7	1.8	2.15	16.7	1.05	0.48
1991	5.3	1.6	4.06	20.1	1.1	
1990	4.1	1.5	5.36	22.4	1.1	
1989	4.8	1.7	5.27	22.5	1.1	
1988	4.1	1.6	6.22	20.1		
1987	4.4	1.7				
1986	4.6	1.8				
1985	4.4	1.7				
1984	4.1	2.0				

EXHIBIT 25 *Hudson Foods*

Year	Operating Margin	Net Profit Margin	Return on Assets	Return on Equity	Current Ratio	Quick Ratio
1994	7.1%	2.6%			1.87	0.69
1993	6.2	1.7			2.22	0.82
1992	3.2	0.3			1.61	0.66
1991	4.9	1.1	2.6%	6.5%		
1990	4.7	1.3	3.0	7.3		
1989	9.0	3.7	8.1	23.6		
1988	2.7	0.7	1.4	4.9		
1987	8.6	3.0	5.7	20.8		
1986	13.7	6.0				
1985	12.0	4.6				

EXHIBIT 26 *Tyson*

Year	Operating Margin	Net Profit Margin	Return on Assets	Return on Equity	Current Ratio	Quick Ratio	Debt Ratio	Asset Turnover
1994	11.7%	4.0%	−58%	NEG	2.34	0.94	0.40	1.39
1993	11.7	3.8%	5.5%	13.3%	1.54	0.26		1.45
1992	11.5	3.9	6.1	16.4	1.46	0.33		1.59
1991	12.0	3.7	5.8	17.7	1.20			1.48
1990	11.8	3.1	4.6	18.1	1.21			1.53
1989	11.6	4.0	11.3	22.5	1.60			0.98
1988	10.0	3.4	10.1	23.9	2.40			2.18
1987	11.5	3.8	8.9	25.1	1.23			2.21
1986	10.5	3.3	6.6	24.7	1.20			1.98
1985	10.5	3.1	7.4	22.5	1.23			2.41
1984	7.7	2.4	6.1	21.5	1.34			2.52

EXHIBIT 27 *Industry Ratios*

Industry (SIC 2015), 1993	Upper Quartile	Median	Lower Quartile
Quick Ratio	1.1	0.8	.05
Current Ratio	2.2	1.4	1.1
ROA	10.2	5.6	1.4
ROE	24.6	10.9	3.4

standardize sales. Net profit margin also indicates the advantage of integration for Tyson, and highlights the weight of ConAgra's other businesses.

Compared to the industry (Exhibit 27), Tyson's net profit margins are on target, as the industry net profit is 2.6 percent (1993).[30] Return on equity is in the median range for the industry, which is not surprising given the nature of acquisitions. Return on assets and return on equity support earlier conclusions.

NOTES

1. Tyson Foods, (1995, January 30). "Tyson Foods Reports Record First Quarter Sales and Earnings: First Quarter 1995 Operating Results." Springdale, AR: Tyson Foods.
2. Schwartz, M. (1991). *Tyson, From Farm to Market.* Fayetteville, AR: University of Arkansas Press.
3. Scanes, C. G., & Lilburn, M. (1994). *Poultry Production,* In *Encyclopedia of Agricultural Science, Vol. 3,* pp. 441–450, New York: Academic Press.
4. Kemp, G. (1994). "International Poultry Show: Poultry Marketing and Packaging Trends." *Quick Frozen Foods International,* 35(4): 95.
5. Scanes & Lilburn, 1994.
6. Tyson Foods (1994, November 18). *ValueLine Investment Survey.* Volume I, Number 10, Part 3, Page 1489. New York: Value Line Publishing.
7. Schwartz, 1991.
8. Poultry & Egg Marketing from National Broiler Council as cited in Gale Research, Inc., *Market Share Reporter,* 1995.
9. Scanes & Lilburn, 1994.
10. Ibid, 1994.
11. Ibid, 1994.
12. Ibid, 1994.
13. Ibid, 1994.
14. Ibid, 1994.
15. Ibid, 1994.
16. Tyson Foods Company Report (1994, August). Source: Stephen's, Inc.
17. U.S. Industrial Outlook, 1994.

18. PRNewswire (1994, October 18). Laborers' Union Hams It Up in North Carolina. P. 1018DC019.
19. Ibid, 1994.
20. Sams, A. R. (1994). *Poultry Processing and Products*, In *Encyclopedia of Agricultural Science, Vol. 3*, pp. 433–440, New York: Academic Press.
21. McCarrell, P. (1994, August 26). Ostrich breeders confront chicken-and-egg situation. *Puget Sound Business Journal.*
22. Moody's (1995, February). Moody's Company Data Report on Tyson Foods, Inc.
23. Tyson's 1994 Annual Report; Moody's, 1995.
24. Porter, M. E. (1985). *Competitive Advantage.* New York: Free Press.
25. Rice, J. (1993, June). "Electric forklifts slash maintenance costs at Tyson; Handle 3,000-lb. loads over extended lift cycles." *Food Processing*, Vol. 54, No. 6, pp. 123–125.
26. Schwartz, 1991.
27. Ibid, 1991.
28. Moody's, 1995.
29. Schwartz, 1991.
30. S & P Industry Surveys, 1994.

United Colors of Benetton

Christian Pinson
Vikas Tibrewala

INSEAD

It was October 1995. Luciano Benetton, chairman of Benetton Group SpA, prepared to address yet another audience of business leaders. This tall, smiling yet reserved man with very blue eyes and longish hair was the guest speaker at a dinner held by the Italian Chamber of Commerce for France in Paris. Over the past 40 years, Benetton had become famous for its technological advances and novel approach to retailing. By 1995, it had become one of the world's best-known brands, with 8,000 shops worldwide, and a successful winning Formula One racing team. (Key financial data can be found in Exhibit 1.) For most people, however, Benetton was synonymous with its communication strategy—one of the world's most visible and controversial, almost always provoking reactions of outrage or praise and, quite often, both.

Rather than advertising its products, Benetton used its communications budget to provoke debate on broad social issues such as racism, AIDS, war and poverty. A number of observers had criticised its "use of social problems to sell knitwear." Luciano knew that he would have to explain one more time why he spent Benetton's L115 billion[1] communication budget on "penetrating the barriers of apathy," and

This case was prepared by Professor Christian Pinson and by Professor Vikas Tibrewala as a basis for class discussion rather than to illustrate either effective or ineffective handling of an administrative situation. Reprinted with the permission of INSEAD-CEDEP. Copyright © 1996 INSEAD-CEDEP, Fontainebleau, France.

that, inevitably, some of his audience would remain unconvinced.

THE FORMATIVE YEARS

Luciano Benetton was born in 1935 in Ponzano, a village in a depressed rural area near the northern Italian cities of Treviso and Venice. Like millions of Italians of his class and generation, his father, Leone, left Italy. In 1937 he emigrated to Ethiopia, then an Italian colony, leaving behind his wife Rosa, Luciano, and three smaller children: Giuliana, Gilberto and Carlo. In Ethiopia, Leone was robbed of the small business he had managed to build and returned home poorer than when he had left. After his death in 1945, from malaria contracted in Ethiopia, the family eked out a living by doing odd jobs and selling, one by one, the small plots of land they owned.

Luciano's sister, Giuliana, joined a knitwear workshop when she was 11 years old. Luciano worked before and after school, selling soap door-to-door and carrying 30 kilos of newspapers to sell at Treviso train station before dawn. At 14, Luciano left school to work in a clothing store in Treviso, where he learned the rudiments of retailing:

The Dellasiega shop was typical of Italy in those times. A long counter separated the sales assistant from the client and the goods were usually hidden away except for a few models in the shop window or on a hanger. The customer needed to have

EXHIBIT 1 *Benetton Group SpA: Financial Highlights 1986–1995 (millions of lire)[1]*

	Italy	Other Europe	The Americas	Other Countries	Consolidated
1986 Revenues	388,872	470,530	173,322	19,558	1,089,983
Operating profits	99,680	86,160	16,180	4,030	206,050
Net Income					113,029
Share price/MIB[2]					15,900/104.8
1987 Revenues	437,101	609,973	222,780	12,050	1,261,077
Operating profits	108,426	117,071	8,928	(2,526)	249,839
Net Income					130,291
Share price/MIB					10,460/99.6
1988 Revenues	641,633	702,462	236,372	35,266	1,475,282
Operating profits	111,937	115,196	16,134	(2,361)	239,673
Net Income					130,171
Share price/MIB					10,560/80.3
1989 Revenues	665,530	672,635	222,874	96,460	1,657,519
Operating profits	120,986	99,462	(637)	5,560	225,307
Net Income					115,412
Share price/MIB					8,720/99.3
1990 Revenues	749,930	819,825	220,463	268,830	2,059,048
Operating profits	147,477	142,820	(8,265)	9,952	266,180
Net Income					133,271
Share price/MIB					8,580/100.0
1991 Revenues	790,339	933,751	215,409	364,265	2,303,764
Operating profits	150,374	151,368	(12,255)	35,123	311,757
Net Income					164,783
Share price/MIB					10,320/84.7
1992 Revenues	862,495	987,603	237,798	424,745	2,512,641
Operating profits	170,770	172,533	(12,029)	43,106	356,639
Net Income					184,709
Share price/MIB					13,870/70.5
1993 Revenues	850,609	1,062,823	270,021	568,005	2,751,458
Operating profits	165,003	204,150	(22,418)	74,490	407,926
Net Income					208,038
Share price/MIB					26,730/83.5
1994 Revenues[3]	882,744	1,019,478	227,302	658,148	2,787,672
Operating profits	151,153	175,040	(19,318)	93,841	388,740
Net Income					210,200
Share price/MIB					12,038/104.1

Note: Results for 1995: revenues of L2,940 billion with net income of L220 billion. Share price on 31.12.95: 18,890 lire.

[1]Exchange rate Lire/US$: 1986 = 1358; 1987 = 1169; 1988 = 1306; 1989 = 1271; 1990 = 1130; 1991 = 1151; 1992 = 1471; 1993 = 1704; 1994 = 1626.

[2]MIB = MIB Index, calculated by the Milan Stock Exchange and based on the average of all stocks traded on that exchange, 1900 = 100.

[3]On 1 February 1994, Benetton had a capital issue of 10 million shares at L 26,500/share.

at least a vague idea of what she was looking for, and describe it to the sales assistant . . . Clothes were sold like medicine—by prescription only.[2]

In provincial postwar Italy, clothes were still very much dictated by a person's occupation and social class. Traditional social structures were, however, beginning to break down, following the end of the war and the downfall of Mussolini. But despite a growing interest in leisure and sports, casual clothes were not available nor were there specific clothes for young people, who often wore hand-me-downs from their parents. During his long days at Dellasiega's shop, Luciano became convinced that there was a market for a youthful, casual range of clothing. In 1955 he and Giuliana set up their own workshop. He was 20 years old, she was 18. To buy a knitting machine, Luciano sold his concertina, while his brother Gilberto sacrificed his bicycle. Working in the evenings, Giuliana produced a collection of 20 knitted sweaters, helped by Gilberto, aged 14, and Carlo, aged 12. Rosa assembled and ironed the jumpers, and Luciano spent his evenings cycling from door-to-door to sell them under the trademark *Très Jolie*. Luciano recalled:

> Our first collection featured very simple designs: high-neck, turtle-neck, V-neck, all in combed wool, English-style . . . but . . . we used pale blue, green or yellow wool, colours that nobody wore. We were the first to use them, and we realised that people were starved of colour, as if it had been rationed during the war.

Six months later, Giuliana left her daytime job to concentrate on their family business. The following year she bought a second knitting machine and hired two girls aged 11 and 12. In 1957 Luciano left Dellasiega's to devote himself full time to *Très Jolie*. Gilberto joined in 1963 to look after the firm's finances. Luciano, aware that Italy lagged behind its competitors in terms of quality, visited knitwear plants in England and Scotland, and adapted some of their processes to improve his own products. The real breakthrough came when Luciano and Ado Montana, an impoverished dye specialist from Trieste, discovered a way to dye fully assembled sweaters.

Hitherto, knitwear had been produced using predyed yarn as it was generally believed that the high temperatures necessary to dye wool would cause holes or severe shrinkage in the assembled garment.

The new process enabled the Benettons to respond quickly to changes in fashion and customer demand.

THE YEARS OF GROWTH

Throughout the 1960s, Italy experienced an unprecedented economic boom, and the Benettons found themselves unable to keep up with demand. They obtained a bank loan to build a factory in Ponzano Veneto. The avant-garde plant, with luxuries such as landscaped grounds and air conditioning, resembled a spaceship set down in the fields near Ponzano, and was designed by Tobia and Afra Scarpa, a husband-and-wife team of inexperienced architecture students. As the firm continued to grow, the plant soon proved to be too small, even before it was finished.

In 1964, Luciano was approached by Piero Marchiorello, a penniless but enthusiastic 25-year-old from the small town of Belluno. Marchiorello wanted to open a shop that would sell only *Très Jolie* jumpers. At the time, the concept of a one-brand, one-product shop was unheard of in Italy. The small shop, called *My Market*, was inauspiciously located in a cul-de-sac in Belluno, which Luciano described as "the worst site I had ever seen." Marchiorello was more upbeat: "Look on the bright side—if it works here, it can work anywhere!" The name *My Market* was chosen to evoke the swinging English fashion scene of the time, with open-air "Carnaby Street"-type associations. The shop was an immediate success. As Marchiorello explained to Luciano: "When clients enter, they stand frozen, as if they were drinking in the colours."

The second *My Market* store opened in 1965 in Cortina d'Ampezzo, a trendy skiing resort and had no counter—a decision seen by Afra Searpa as symbolising the removal of social barriers. "Instead, there was a small table for the cash register, . . . all the [decorative] colour came from the clothes." Realising that the name *Benetton* sounded "English to the English, French to the French, and so on for Italians, Germans, Americans," and was easy to pronounce in all languages, it was decided to label the knitwear with a logo featuring *Benetton* in white characters on a dark green background, and a stylised knot of yarn. As sales continued to grow, Luciano decided to expand into each new city by opening two or three shops rather than just one:

It made more sense to compete with ourselves than with others. So we asked Scarpa to design several store interiors to appeal to different clients and varying local tastes. The *Merceria* design was classic in feel, oriented to the mothers of our *My Market* customers. *Tomato* was all glossy, chrome and ultra-modern. *Fantomax* had the feel of Art Nouveau and Swinging London.[3]

Within four years, Benetton had 500 stores across Italy. In 1969, Benetton opened its first store abroad, in Paris's Latin Quarter. Profits grew from L800m in 1970 to L8 billion in 1979. But in Italy the *anni di piombo*, "the lead years" of the 1970s, were marked by the onset of terrorism and frayed relations with trade unions. Luciano was himself the target of a kidnapping attempt, the violence of which haunted him for years. The Benettons decided to keep a low profile, as explained by Luciano:

> In Italy, even if in 1975 a thousand retailers sold our product exclusively, they did not know much about us. We remained invisible, refused to grant interviews, kept financial information strictly to ourselves and never published an annual report. Because of our use of sub-contractors and the fact that many stores were called *Sisley*, *Tomato* or *Merceria* rather than Benetton, our real scale and scope remained unknown to the public.

The 1980s saw a dramatic improvement in Italy's economic and political situation. In 1983, Benetton recruited Aldo Palmeri, a 36-year-old banker with a master's degree from the London School of Economics, to introduce modern management structures and methods to the family firm. Before this, Luciano had considered management education to be "a luxury reserved for bureaucrats with nothing better to do." Palmeri put in place a Board of Directors, an Executive Committee, and a supporting management structure. He implemented a worldwide state-of-the-art information technology system. Senior managers with international experience were recruited and external consultants were brought in as needed. Benetton entered new markets such as the Soviet Union and Eastern Europe, and acquired holdings in various other businesses. The creation of In Holding SpA marked Benetton's foray into the financial services sector, enabling them to offer a comprehensive service to their partners.[4] In 1986 Benetton, which had recently published its first annual report, secured a listing on the Milan stock exchange. The stock was later listed on five exchanges worldwide: London, Frankfurt, New York, Toronto and Tokyo. *The New Yorker* remarked: "It is worth remembering that Benetton, all but unknown in most places less than a decade ago, now owns one of the world's most recognised brand names, as familiar as Coca-Cola and Reebok."[5]

THE BENETTON GROUP

In 1994, the textiles and clothing industry turned over US$250 billion in the European Union; it employed over 2.5 million people, produced a trading surplus of over US$2 billion, and was second only to the automotive sector in terms of value added in manufacturing.[6] Germany, France and Italy were the leading producers. Despite a recent surge in mergers and acquisitions, the industry remained fragmented with over 100,000 producers—the top 20 percent of whom accounted for about 80 percent of industry sales. Most clothes were bought in boutiques or department stores, although some variations existed across countries (see Exhibit 2).

Benetton Group SpA was the world's biggest consumer of wool and Europe's largest clothing concern, with 1994 sales of L2,788 billion and net income of L210 billion. Its largest markets were Italy (34% of sales), Germany (12%), Japan (11%) and France (9%). Sixty-four million items were sold worldwide in 1994, up 12.7 percent from 1993. Outside the EU, the increase was 36 percent. Aided by several devaluations of the Lira, Benetton had cut prices by up to 40 percent over the previous two years. Luciano was now the Group's chairman and main spokesman, Giuliana was in charge of design, and Gilberto and Carlo looked after finance and production, respectively.[7]

In 1995, the newspaper *Milano Finanza* listed the Benettons as the richest family in Italy. While clothes manufacturing remained the core of the family activities, they also, in 1989, began to acquire controlling stakes in a number of other companies. These businesses were regrouped as the family-owned Edizione Holding, chaired by Gilberto and with an aggregate turnover of nearly L10,000 billion in 1994 (see Exhibit 3).[8] In addition to its range of clothing and accessories, Benetton licensed the manufacture of products such as sunglasses and spectacle frames, stationery, cosmetics, household linens, lingerie,

EXHIBIT 2 *Clothes Buying Behavior in Europe, 1994 (A Time Magazine Study)*
Methodology: questionnaire sent on 8 March 1994 to a panel of 5,500 Time magazine subscribers in 11 countries (500 per country).

"Where do you usually buy your clothes?"

N = 2,151 respondents	Country												Sex		Age				
	B	CH	D	DK	E	F	I	NL	P	S	UK	EUR	M	F	<25	25-34	35-44	45-54	55+
Boutiques	46	34	40	50	46	60	55	37	60	37	10	43	40	52	51	51	46	43	35
Department stores	34	52	56	50	57	43	38	40	36	46	68	47	48	46	44	43	52	46	47
Designer retail outlets	18	20	14	11	14	14	15	24	12	15	20	16	17	13	15	10	16	19	18
Catalogues/Direct mail	5	17	15	4	6	16	3	7	5	7	25	10	8	18	11	9	13	9	10
Tailor	2	3	4	2	2	1	2	1	4	1	3	2	3	—	2	—	—	2	5
All other	2	1	3	2	2	1	3	3	2	1	4	2	2	4	2	1	1	2	3
Can't say/it varies	17	16	15	13	12	12	9	20	17	19	10	15	14	17	14	19	14	12	15

"How important are each of the following factors and features when buying clothes?"

N = 2,151 respondents	Country												Sex		Age				
	B	CH	D	DK	E	F	I	NL	P	S	UK	EUR	M	F	<25	25-34	35-44	45-54	55+
Quality of material	8.34	8.47	8.29	8.13	8.31	8.11	8.70	8.36	8.60	8.30	8.17	8.34	8.29	8.51	8.21	8.23	8.23	8.36	8.52
Style	8.03	7.81	7.78	7.18	8.02	7.97	8.48	7.74	8.10	7.57	7.71	7.85	7.60	8.70	8.29	8.17	7.99	7.74	7.53
Cut	7.78	7.90	7.67	7.22	7.70	7.93	8.16	7.50	8.25	7.72	7.80	7.79	7.58	8.46	7.59	7.75	7.76	7.88	7.80
Colour	7.52	7.98	7.59	7.58	7.28	7.59	8.01	7.68	7.84	7.69	7.66	7.68	7.54	8.14	7.81	7.76	7.65	7.64	7.63
Price	7.11	6.87	6.97	6.73	7.30	7.20	7.35	7.05	7.38	6.28	7.36	7.06	6.94	7.47	7.02	7.34	7.18	6.87	6.97
Season	5.40	5.37	4.77	4.54	5.45	5.30	6.07	5.18	6.45	5.00	4.06	5.23	5.17	5.45	5.59	5.46	5.42	5.23	4.89
Partner's influence	5.43	4.33	5.10	4.78	4.47	5.04	4.88	5.98	4.43	4.90	4.84	4.93	5.25	3.83	4.63	4.96	4.97	4.95	4.92
Country of origin	2.85	3.13	2.99	2.99	3.23	3.73	3.68	3.17	3.63	3.47	3.09	3.27	3.38	2.92	3.41	3.05	3.23	3.33	3.34
Prestigious name	2.70	2.47	2.44	2.43	3.43	2.81	3.17	2.76	3.87	2.44	2.65	2.84	2.94	2.52	3.80	2.84	2.80	2.93	2.53
Loyalty to designer	2.57	2.37	2.09	1.94	3.23	2.63	2.98	2.64	3.33	2.24	2.00	2.55	2.65	2.20	3.14	2.63	2.33	2.58	2.49
Advertising	2.34	2.27	2.33	2.47	2.66	2.15	2.38	2.58	3.13	2.28	2.20	2.44	2.52	2.17	2.85	2.62	2.42	2.47	2.20

Source: Images of Fashion and Fragrance 1994, *Time* Magazine Opinion Poll.
Average scores based on a scale of 1–10, where 1 = not at all important and 10 = extremely important.
Code: Europe (EUR), Belgium (B), Switzerland (CH), Germany (D), Denmark (DK), Spain (E), France (F), Italy (I), Netherlands (NL), Portugal (P), Sweden (S), United Kingdom (UK).

C-531

EXHIBIT 3 *Major Investments and Controlling Interests Held by Edizione Holding*

Benetton Group SpA	Clothing, 71% owned, turnover L2788bn, net profit L210bn
Benetton Sportsystem	Sporting equipment, 100% owned, turnover L1150bn, operating profit L31bn:
■ Nordica	Ski boots, 33% of total turnover
■ Rollerblade	Roller skates, 30%
■ Prince	Tennis rackets, 20%
■ Kästle	Skis, 9%
■ Asolo	Mountain boots, 4%
■ Killer Loop	Glasses and snow boards, 4%
GS-Euromercato	Supermarkets, 60% owned,[1] L4350bn turnover
Autogrill	Highway restaurants, 60% owned,[2] L1400bn turnover
21 Investimenti	Partnership or minority interests in diversified sectors, 75% owned
United Optical	Spectacle frames, 100% owned
Divarese	Shoes, 85% owned, turnover L60bn, profit L230m
Verdesport	Sporting activities, 100% owned
Edizione Property	Commercial and nonindustrial properties, including ranches in Patagonia and Texas, 100% owned
Minority Investments	1% of Banca Commerciale Italiana and others

Note: Data reflect the situation in March 1996. Edizione was itself 100% owned by the Benetton family.
[1]Partnership with Del Vecchio Group.
[2]Partnership with Mövenpick Group.

watches, toys, steering wheels or knobs for gearshifts, golf equipment and luggage. These products provided net income of L9 billion in 1993. In 1995, Benetton was asked by Motorola to design and market a range of pagers. These colourful units, first launched in the UK, were intended to develop the youth market for pagers and were priced at £99, in competition with the Swatch pager, priced at £119. A joint-venture in Japan for the sale of designer condoms ("Benetton's smallest item of clothing") was expected to contribute $40m to turnover.

In 1995, Benetton had three main brands:

- United Colors of Benetton (clothing for men and women) which also included Blue Family (with an emphasis on denim) and Benetton Undercolors (underwear and beachwear): 60.8% of sales

- 012 United Colors of Benetton (clothing for children under 12) including Zerotondo (clothing and accessories for babies): 18.5% of sales

- Sisley (higher-fashion clothing): 11.8% of sales

Over two-thirds of the firm's clothing was for women, who represented 80 percent of Benetton's shoppers. Fabrizio Servente, head of product development, commented:

The "objective" target for the adult Benetton stores is the 18–24-year-old, but of course there is no age ceiling. Our product takes into account quality and price. Its clean, international, with a lot of attention to design. It can be worn just as easily by Princess Diana and by her maid, or her maid's daughter. The way young people dress is becoming more and more "uniform," but there are differences from one region to another. Benetton must still be Italian in Italy, Brazilian in Brazil, Indian in India.

Industry observers felt that Benetton had no clearly identifiable worldwide competitor. While Esprit, The Gap, Next, Stefanel, or Zara were often cited, it was generally agreed that they did not have the same geographical spread as Benetton. Servente's view was that Benetton had many competitors, and none:

> *The* Benetton competitor doesn't exist. On the other hand, we have plenty of local competitors. In Italy, it might be Stefanel. In France, Kookaï—although they target a different age group. In Britain, Next. In the U.S., Esprit. No [global] competitor can offer the same quality and cost as we can. A shop owner in Treviso may order jumpers in Hong Kong, and clearly he will be cheaper than us since he has lower fixed costs. If that is a competitor, then we have 10,000 of them. There are many that we keep an eye on, but not any one in particular.

THE BENETTON SYSTEM

Benetton today operates through a complex system of over 500 sub-contractors and several joint ventures specialising in design, cutting, assembling, ironing or packaging, plus thousands of independent retail outlets. Benetton's success has been largely attributed to this ability to combine fashion with industry.

Production

While the pressure to reduce costs had led a number of clothing firms to move their production to the developing world, Benetton, which operates factories worldwide, has kept over 80 percent of its production in Italy, a strategy made possible by its emphasis on automation and continuous modernisation.

The Castrette (Treviso) production centre currently covers an area of 190,000 square metres, including new twin facilities which are among the most advanced in the world, producing cotton outerwear: shirts, jackets, shirts, and jeans. They are Benetton's latest technological accomplishment. Afra and Tobia Scarpa employed a suspension technique hitherto used in naval architecture to reduce the number of supporting pillars, allowing space to be organised according to production needs. A computerised system regulates humidity and lighting to limit energy waste and minimise colour distortions. The plants can produce 80 million items per year, with 800 staff. A fibre-optic communications network links the plants to Benetton's automated distribution centre nearby.

A computerised network provides the Group's central system in Ponzano with real-time data from retail points all over the world and interlinked retailing, production units, and warehousing. The L42 billion distribution centre in Castrette is the length of a football pitch, with robots handling up to 30,000 boxes a day. On each box, a bar-coded label specifies the particular shop to which it is to be sent. The robots read the bar codes, sort the boxes, and store them while a staff of five specialists monitor their movements on a computer. Benetton can produce and deliver garments anywhere in the world within 10 days of orders being taken.

All purchasing activities are centralised, since this is the main source of economies of scale in the clothing industry. From the beginning Benetton has used natural fibres—virgin wool and cotton. "The Group can contemplate its own production of cotton and wool, with a complete cycle from sheep to sweater," said Carlo Benetton, the Group's production chief. Benetton owns a 3,600-hectare (8,900 acres) cotton farm in Texas and is the largest producer of wool in Patagonia, with ranches spread over 700,000 hectares. Although Benetton uses only 10 percent of the wool it produces, running these ranches enables it to understand and improve the technology of wool production, and to strengthen its negotiating power with suppliers.

Hundreds of subcontractors perform knitting, assembly and most of the finishing (about 70 percent of the production process). They account for close to 30 percent of total manufacturing and distribution costs and often have less than 15 employees in order to save on Social Security costs. Most of them work exclusively for Benetton, which provides technical know-how, financial consulting and other services and exerts strict quality control throughout production. A senior executive commented:

> [They] provide our much-vaunted flexibility. With minimum investment, we can double production one season, then halve it the next season with no personnel or machinery costs to us.

Strategic, capital-intensive, and complex operations such as design, cutting, and dyeing are performed internally. Every year, an international team of 200 stylists and designers prepares two worldwide collections and two reassortment collections under Giuliana's supervision—a total of 4,000 models. The designers are given contracts for a maximum of six

C-533

seasons (three years) in order to encourage a constant flow of new ideas. Most of the production is assembled undyed, and colour decisions can then be made late in the production cycle. This process is slightly more expensive but it allows the company to produce 30 percent of its output at almost the last moment. Benetton uses the latest CAD-CAM (computer-aided design and manufacturing) systems, allowing a new design to be created and moved into production in a matter of hours. A new software programme, developed by Benetton in collaboration with Japanese specialists, makes it possible to produce a seamless knitted sweater ("a concept which could revolutionise the industry") in half an hour.

Retailing

Benetton's unique distribution philosophy was another important reason for its success. "We didn't want to become directly involved in the selling side," Luciano Benetton has said,[9] "so in the beginning it was friends with financial resources who moved into this part of the business." By 1995, from over 8,000 retail outlets (see Exhibit 4), Benetton owned and operated fewer than 50 "flagship stores" in cities such as Milan, New York, Paris, and Düsseldorf. The rest were owned by independent retailers who typically ran five or six outlets.

The company deals with these retailers through a network of 83 agents, controlled by seven area managers reporting to Benetton's commercial director. The agents, who are independent entrepreneurs, have exclusive rights over a territory; they select store owners and receive a 4 percent commission on orders placed with them. They supervise operations in their territory, keep an eye on the market and offer guidance to store owners on product selection, mer-

chandising and the location of new stores, making sure that Benetton's policies are respected. Another important responsibility of the agents is to find new retailers who "fit" the Benetton culture. They are themselves encouraged to reinvest their earnings in new stores of their own.

Upon entering a new market, the site for a "lead" store is selected, after which the agent tries to blanket the area with several other shops offering Benetton products. (Milan alone has over 45 stores.) Luciano Benetton commented:

> I discovered that, even if the brand was unknown, seeing three or four of our shops in one town would give a feeling of security equivalent to a good advertising campaign. . . . We prefer small spaces . . . a very limited selection, in a store that's always crowded, if possible. We want a lot of people looking at the same thing, watching others buying clothes.[10]

Some retailers have complained that Benetton was "sticking too many stores together" or that "the Benetton agent put us in the wrong location." Shop owners have to sell Benetton products exclusively but they do not sign franchise agreements; neither do they have to pay Benetton a fee for use of its name or a royalty based on a percentage of sales or profits. Luciano Benetton explained:

> We selected them on the basis of personal knowledge and individual capability, rather than commercial experience. . . . [Their] prior career was of no importance, but [they] had to have the right spirit. . . . Many of them were friends, or friends of friends, we didn't ask them to give us a percentage of profits. . . . Frankly, I was uncomfortable with the idea of American-style contracts.[11]

EXHIBIT 4 *Number of Benetton Points-of-Sale, 1982–1994[1]*													
Region	**1982**	**1983**	**1984**	**1985**	**1986**	**1987**	**1988**	**1989**	**1990**	**1991**	**1992**	**1993**	**1994**
Europe	1,823	2,180	2,388	2,708	3,103	3,646	3,846	4,007	4,846	5,378	5,949	5,881	5,651
(Italy)	(1,165)	(1,227)	(1,253)	(1,279)	(1,390)	(1,470)	(1,505)	(1,601)	(1,806)	(1,969)	(2,089)	(2,044)	(2,031)
The Americas	41	71	207	432	708	903	1,225	1,214	1,187	1,306	1,075	1,175	1,144
(USA)	(32)	(66)	(190)	(400)	(640)	(n.a.)	(700)	(630)	(650)	(480)	(294)	(429)	(421)
Far East and others	53	45	49	62	85	99	412	651	1,299	1,204	1,109	1,458	1,443
Total	1,917	2,296	2,644	3,202	4,102	4,995	5,483	5,872	7,332	7,888	8,133	8,514	8,238

[1]As of 1990, the figures include "shops-in-shop," corners, and concessions.

In 1995, the retailers could choose from several store layouts designed by Scarpa, some of which are shown in Exhibit 5.[12] Benetton supplied point-of-sale advertising material; shops could advertise in the local press once the company had checked the advertisement. Prices were suggested by Benetton, markdowns outside the sales periods had to be agreed with the agent. Stock control and cash flow management were major concerns for the retailers since Benetton produced to order six months ahead, did not take back unsold merchandise and required direct payment within 90 to 120 days of delivery. The importance of the end-of-season "sales" periods, which accounted for up to 40 percent of total revenue, was growing.

During these periods, the usual 120 percent markup could fall to zero, or even to a 10 percent loss.

Senior executives travelled constantly, visiting shops, talking to consumers, and observing competitors. Luciano Benetton himself spent two weeks every month flying around the world in his private jet. An executive explained how new products and store concepts were tested:

We don't do a lot of market studies. We find an entrepreneur who believes in the product and the brand, and who invests his own money. We give him all the support we can, and he opens a shop. If it works, we go for it.

EXHIBIT 5 *Major Benetton Store Layouts, 1995*

Mega Benetton	Area	>400 square metres
	Location	Main business and residential areas with good purchasing power
	Target	Young and very young, but not only
	Assortment	Most clothing lines and licensed products
Blue Family/Fil di Ferro	Area	>100 square metres
	Location	Main business zones and areas frequented by students with average purchasing power
	Target	Very young clientele
	Assortment	Blue Family line of clothing, accessories, and licensed products
Benetton Uomo **(Benetton for Men)**	Area	>70 square metres
	Location	Main business zones and residential areas with good purchasing power
	Target	Youthful informal, classic informal
	Assortment	Benetton's men's line of clothing, accessories, and licensed products
Benetton Donna **(Benetton for Women)**	Area	>150 square metres
	Location	Main business zones and residential areas with good purchasing power
	Target	Youthful informal, classic informal
	Assortment	Benetton's women's line of clothing, accessories, and licensed products
012	Area	>100 square metres
	Location	Main business zones and residential areas with good purchasing power
	Target	0 to 12 years of age
	Assortment	Newborn and children's clothing, accessories, and licensed products
Sisley	Area	>100 square metres
	Location	Main business zones and residential areas with average and above-average purchasing power
	Target	Sporty, outdoor, and fashion-conscious lifestyles
	Assortment	Sisley line of clothing, accessories, and licenses products

In recent years, Benetton had encouraged retailers to either upgrade existing stores to larger "megastores" where the whole range was displayed, or start selling smaller, specialised collections.[13] Palmeri felt that this change posed a new challenge:

> Most people running today's stores are not ready to face a new strategy.... They became very rich with the Benetton system. Others don't have the money to invest.... Anybody can run a store of 50 square metres. It's a completely different thing to run a system of 10 superstores each with 1,000 square metres.[14]

While international expansion had generally been successful, the United States proved to be a difficult market. Benetton opened its first store in New York in 1979 but had to wait till 1983 to see sales take off. Growth peaked in 1988 with a total of 700 stores, but by 1995 Benetton had only 150 stores[15] in the U.S.[16] However, the selling square footage had doubled over the preceding five years, due to the opening of megastores. Two strong markets were California and the Northeast where, according to Luciano Benetton, "consumers were more European."

Industry observers attributed Benetton's U.S. difficulties to a number of factors including high prices; increased competition from firms such as The Gap, The Limited, and Lands' End; and a weak understanding of American customer service norms. For example, American consumers were frustrated that they could not return a Benetton product bought at one store to another, even in the same city. Further, Benetton's unique "no written contract/no franchise" culture proved difficult to import and had led to several legal disputes. Other critics cited Benetton's policy of two collections a year versus that of The Gap which changed styles every four to six weeks. This was seen as hurting Benetton, especially among teenagers. An industry analyst commented, "The trend is clearly going towards a much more continuous change of product and Benetton just has to learn that." However, Luciano dismissed these concerns, insisting "two collections a year is perfect."[17]

Benetton's approach to international expansion is twofold: through its own independent agents or through local partners with whom it sets up a licence agreement and develops a joint venture for the local market. The Group hoped to be present in "as many countries as competed in the Olympics." In 1995, it had stores in unusual outposts such as Albania, Cuba and Libya, where it was "the only store of its kind," according to Luciano. The Group was also targeting several other promising markets: China, where it planned to open 300 outlets by 1997 and where it saw a potential market of 120 million customers; India, with 80 million potential consumers; Latin America, with 70 million; Turkey with 60 million; and Southeast Asia with 50 million. On 12 September 1995, a Benetton store was opened in Sarajevo, the besieged capital of war-torn Bosnia. Its manager, Vesna Kapidzic, commented, "Anyone can open a store after the war. We think it is nice to open this store during the war."[18]

Benetton's Communication

Benetton's early advertisements were rather conventional, focusing on the product and stressing the quality of wool.

The logo, a stylised knot of yarn, and the word "Benetton" were later united within a green rectangle with rounded corners. During the 1970s, the company reduced its advertising consistent with its decision to adopt a low profile in Italy. The first U.S. advertising campaigns, handled by a small agency (Kathy Travis), stressed the European origins and international success of Benetton. "Last year we made 8,041,753 sweaters ... sold through 1573 Benetton stores internationally." These campaigns contributed less to Benetton's breakthrough in the U.S. than the runaway success among students of a simple model (the rugby polo) and the awakening of Americans to fashion "Made in Italy."[19]

In 1982, Luciano Benetton met Oliviero Toscani, a well-known fashion and advertising photographer who lived in Tuscany and had studios in Paris and New York. His clients included, among others, Jesus Jeans, Valentino, Esprit, Club Med and Bata. Toscani convinced Luciano that Benetton ought to promote itself as a lifestyle, not a clothing business. At Toscani's suggestion, Benetton retained Eldorado, a small Paris agency with which Toscani had often worked as a photographer.

All the Colours in the World The first campaigns were conventional in style, stressing social status and conformism and featuring groups of young people wearing Benetton clothing. The real departure came in 1984 with a new concept, "All the Colours in the

World." This campaign showed groups of teenagers from different countries and ethnic groups dressed in colourful knitwear. The print and billboard campaign was distributed by J. Walter Thompson (JWT) in 14 countries.

The campaign was greeted with enthusiasm and Benetton received hundreds of letters of praise. But it prompted shocked reactions in South Africa, where the ads were carried only by magazines catering to the black community. A few letters from England and the U.S. reflected hysterical racism. "Shame on you!" wrote one correspondent from Manchester in the north of England, "You have mixed races that God wants to keep apart!"

United Colors of Benetton In 1985, a UNESCO official visited the studio where Toscani was photographing a multiracial group of children and exclaimed: "This is fantastic, it's the United Colors here!" This became the new slogan: "United Colors of Benetton." The posters reconciled instantly recognisable "enemies": a German and an Israeli, a Greek and a Turk, and an Argentinean and a Briton. Another poster showed two small black children bearing the U.S. and Soviet flags.

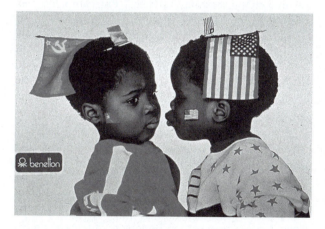

The multiracial message was made clearer still with the theme chosen for the 1986 and 1987 campaigns: "the globe." One ad showed a white adolescent dressed as an Hassidic Jew holding a money box full of dollar bills, next to a black teenager dressed as an American Indian. "In the eyes of Eldorado's directors, all of them Jewish, the picture was humorous enough to make it clear that we were taking aim at the stereotype [of the money-grabbing Jew]," wrote Luciano Benetton.[20] Benetton was flooded

with protests, mostly from France and Italy. In New York, Jewish groups threatened to boycott Benetton shops. Benetton replaced the ad with a picture of a Palestinian and a Jew, which was also criticised.

Luciano commented:

I was a bit discouraged, but I had learned a fundamental lesson. We had chosen to promote an image that touched very deep feelings, identities for which millions of people had fought and died. We had reached the limits and felt the responsibilities of commercial art. Everybody was now watching us, and even a small dose of ingenuity could hurt us and irritate others. I promised myself I would control our image even more rigorously.[21]

The 1987 autumn/winter campaign, "United Fashions of Benetton," showed models wearing Benetton clothes with accessories that evoked the great names in fashion. "United Superstars of Benetton" was the slogan for the 1988 campaign, featuring pairs dressed up as Joan of Arc and Marilyn Monroe, Leonardo da Vinci and Julius Caesar, or Adam and Eve—two long-haired teenagers dressed in denim.

A Message of Racial Equality

Nineteen eighty-nine marked a turning point in Benetton's communication activities. The company terminated its relationship with Eldorado.[22] "From the beginning, Luciano Benetton wanted image to be an in-house product, so that it would reflect the company's soul," Toscani explained later. United Colors Communication would soon handle all aspects of Benetton's communication including production and media buying. The entire process was managed by less than ten people; Toscani's visuals would be discussed by the advertising team, then shown to Luciano for final approval. This allowed Benetton to produce advertisements which cost about one-third of those of its competitors.[23] Benetton did not usually advertise on television because of the high costs but used print and outdoor media extensively. It limited itself to two series of campaigns (Spring and Fall). Each campaign would typically last a couple of weeks and consist of a small number of visuals shown in an increasing number of countries. By 1995, Benetton spent about 4 percent of turnover on communication, which included campaigns for United Colors of Benetton and Sisley; sports sponsorship; a quarterly magazine, *Colors;* and funding for its communications school, *Fabrica.*

This shift to in-house communications was accompanied by a radical change in approach. The 1989 ads no longer showed the product, didn't use a slogan, and replaced the knot logo with a small green rectangle that was to become the company's trademark. Hard-hitting images began to deliver an unambiguously political message championing racial equality. One ad showing a black woman nursing a white baby generated controversy in South Africa and in the U.S., where it was seen as a throwback to the era of slavery. Benetton withdrew the ad in the U.S., explaining that "the campaign is intended to promote equality, not friction."

This became Benetton's most praised visual ever, winning awards in five European countries. Another ad, showing a black man and a white man handcuffed together, offended British blacks, who thought it showed a white policeman arresting a black. London Transport refused to show the poster in its network.

The 1990 campaign continued the theme, with softer images: the hand of a black child resting in a white man's hand; a white wolf and a black lamb; a small black child asleep amid white stuffed bears; the hand of a white relay runner passing a baton to a black teammate.

Benetton's attempt to show two babies on their potties on a 770-square-meter billboard opposite Milan's cathedral was banned by the city authorities and the Roman Catholic cardinal. That year, Benetton won its first advertising award in the United States.

Social Issues

By 1991 Benetton's campaigns, which now tackled issues beyond racism, were reaching audiences in more than 100 countries. A picture showing a military cemetery, released at the start of the Gulf war, was turned down by all but one newspaper, *Il Sole 24 Ore* in Italy.

An ad displaying brightly coloured condoms ("a call for social responsibility in the face of overpopulation and sexually transmitted disease") was intended to "demystify condoms by displaying them in a playful and colourful way, like fashion items."

Simultaneously, condoms were distributed in Benetton's shops worldwide. Benetton also distributed HIV guides in the shanty towns of Rio "because it was important that even people who could

never buy a Benetton sweater should get the basic communication."

Other ads included a white boy kissing a black girl, a group of Pinocchio puppets in different hues of wood, and a multiethnic trio of children playfully sticking out their tongues. While this last ad won awards in Britain and Germany, it was withdrawn from display in Arabic countries, where it was considered offensive.

Later that year, Toscani chose to focus on: "love, the underlying reason for all life." The campaign featured, among others, a priest and a nun kissing; and Giusy, a screaming new-born baby, with her umbilical cord still attached.

In the U.S., the Anti-Defamation League condemned the priest-and-nun ad for "trivialising, mocking, profaning and offending religious values," and several magazines rejected it.

In France, the Bureau de Vérification de la Publicité (BVP), a self-regulating advertising body, recommended the removal of the priest-and-nun ad in the name of "decency and self-discipline," whilst in England, it won the Eurobest Award. Others were also positive: Sister Barbara Becker Schroeder from Alzey, Germany, wrote to Benetton: "I feel the photo expresses great tenderness, security and peace. . . . I would be grateful if you would let me have one or more posters, preferably in different sizes."[25] In November 1991, Benetton won a court case initiated by AGRIF (L'Alliance générale contre le racisme et pour le respect de la famille française) where it was accepted that the nun and priest poster was not racist or anti-Christian.

In Britain, Benetton ignored a warning issued by the Advertising Standards Authority (ASA) concerning the Guisy ad and within days, the authority received some 800 complaints. The offending posters were withdrawn—and replaced with an ad showing an angelic blond-haired child next to a black child whose hair was styled to evoke horns, which the ASA also criticised.

In the United States, Giusy elicited some negative reactions but was accepted by *Parenting, Self,* and *Vogue*. It was rejected by *Child, Cosmopolitan,* and *Elle*. The posters were not displayed in Milan where the city officials complained of "the excessive impact and vulgarity of the subject." The local High Court ruled that "the picture offended public order and general morality." Giusy was also banned in France, Germany, and Ireland, where the advertising space was donated to the Association for the Fight Against Cancer. These reactions surprised Benetton, as well as a number of others:

> We should ask ourselves the question of why such a natural, vital and basic image as that of a baby being born, offends the public. Every day we are confronted with pictures of death, often meaningless, and we put up with them in silence, or very nearly. Yet we are afraid to see an image of life. (*L'Unita*, 10/9/91)
>
> Why must beer be drunk topless on the deck of a sailing boat and the smiling, happy mum always be half-naked as she swaddles the baby in a nappy like a scented pastry? Isn't all this rather ridiculous? (*Il Giornale Nuovo*, 26/10/91)

According to Benetton, "Once the period of rejection was over, the picture began to be understood and appreciated." Giusy won an award from the Société Générale d'Affichage in Switzerland and Bologna's General Clinic asked for a copy to decorate its labour room.

The "Reality" Campaigns In 1992, Benetton broke new ground with two series of news photographs on issues such as AIDS, immigration, terrorism, violence, and political refugees. The use of real-life pictures showing, for example, a bombed car, Albanian refugees, a Mafia-style killing, and a soldier holding a human bone provoked controversy around the world, despite Benetton's repeated claim that it was trying to prompt debate of serious social issues.

This claim was supported by Patrick Robert, a photographer with the Sygma agency, some of whose pictures had been used in the campaigns: "the ab-

sence of an explanatory caption on my photographs [soldier with human bone, truck bulging with refugees] does not bother me. . . . For me the objective of the campaign is reached . . . to draw the public's attention to these victims.[26]

A picture showing David Kirby,[27] an AIDS patient, surrounded by his family on his deathbed, stirred particularly strong emotions.

In Britain, the ASA described the ad as "obscene" and "a despicable exploitation of a tragic situation" and asked magazines to reject it. Benetton donated the use of 500 paid UK poster sites to the charity *Trading*. Maggie Alderson, the editor of the UK edition of *Elle*, which ran a statement on two blank pages instead of the ad, commented:

> It is an incredibly moving image in the right context, but to use it as an advertisement for a fashion store selling jumpers is incredibly insulting. They have stepped out of the bounds of what is acceptable and what makes this so sickening is that they have touched up the photograph to make it look biblical because the AIDS victim resembles Jesus Christ. (*The Guardian*, 24/1/92).

In France, the BVP took an unprecedented step: without even waiting for the ad to be printed, it threatened to exclude any publication that dared carry it. One publication ignored the ban: *Max*, a magazine for young people. Its editor, Nicolas Finet, commented, "Our readers, those between 15 and 30 years old, are directly affected by this topic. This campaign is one way of approaching the AIDS problem whilst avoiding the socio-medical aspect. Our readers' letters have shown that we were not wrong" (quoted in the French advertising weekly *Stratégies*, 18/2/92). In Switzerland, *Schweizer Illustrierte* decided to accept the ad saying that it did not hurt mass sensitivity but "wounded only one thing: the rules of the games according to which the message must be dull, stale even."

Many organisations and advocacy groups for homosexuals charged Benetton with callous exploitation, saying it offered no information about prevention. However, some AIDS activists felt it gave the issue a higher public profile, an opinion which others shared:

> For the large majority of the population which thinks that AIDS is not their business, Benetton's ads will be a slap in their face . . . and I am sure it will be more effective than every campaign to

date by any public or private body. (*L'Unita*, 25/1/92)

The company estimates that between 500 million and one billion people have seen the AIDS image, far more than ever saw it when it came out in *Life*. A public that is reading fewer newspapers and believing fewer broadcasts might begin to swallow tiny doses of information between the ads for liqueur and lingerie. (Vicky Goldbert *in The New York Times*, 3/5/92)

The picture . . . has done more to soften people's heart on the AIDS issue than any other I have ever seen. You can't look at that picture and hate a person with AIDS. . . . As far as the comment that it was "touched up to look like Jesus Christ" . . . I know that at Pater Noster [hospital], several times, with several patients through the years, nurses have made the same comment, "he looks like Jesus." (Barb Cordle, David Kirby's nurse in *Interview*, 4/92)

The Economist (1/2/92) felt that the ads targeted the young and,

what better means to appeal to them than by offending their elders . . . expect no repentance, or tamer ads, from Benetton unless its sales start to drop.

Asked about the campaign's impact on sales, Peter Fressola, Director of Communications, Benetton Services, New York, emphasised that individual ads were not geared to boost sales and that Benetton was aware that

people are not going to look at an image of a burning car, and then make a best-seller out of our fuschia sweater. (*The Wall Street Journal*, 28/5/92)

Reacting to the charges of exploitation, Benetton argued that the David Kirby visual increased awareness of the need for collective and personal solidarity with AIDS patients, created a media tribune for HIV organisations and others involved in the issue, and encouraged a debate on how best to communicate on AIDS.[28] They also stressed that David's family was in favor of the photo being used. In support of the ad, the Kirby family went on the record:

It is what he would have wanted. . . . We don't feel used. Rather it is we who are using Benetton. David is speaking louder now that he is dead than when he was alive. (*Il Mattino*, 22/3/92)

The second 1992 campaign once more used hard-hitting news pictures: an oil-covered bird from the Gulf; an albino Zulu woman ostracised by other Zulus; a grime-smeared Salvadoran child carrying a white doll; pigs in a trash heap in Peru; children building a brick wall; KGB agents arresting a suspect; an empty electric chair in a U.S. jail.

The *Financial Times* commented:

Like its previous campaign, Benetton has again focused on the downbeat and the unhappy, this time selecting a set of apparent outcasts to sell its colourful jumpers. (17/9/92)

The Clothing Redistribution Project The spring 1993 campaign showed Luciano Benetton, newly elected to the Italian Senate and named as Italy's leading entrepreneur, stark naked, modestly screened by a caption reading "I want my clothes back." A second ad followed: "Empty your closets."

People were invited to donate clothes of any brand at Benetton stores. The campaign, which ran in about 1,000 magazines and 150 dailies, was widely welcomed: "It is a clear break from Benetton's self-serious attitude of the past. It also marks the first time the company has engaged in direct action to support a cause (*The Wall Street Journal*, 27/1/93).[29]

Some 460 tons of clothes were collected in 83 countries and redistributed worldwide with the help of charities such as Caritas, the International Red Cross, and the Red Crescent.

The Venice Triptych In June 1993, Toscani exhibited a 400-square-meter triptych at the Venice Biennial art show. A specially restored chapel housed the work, which showed 56 close-up photos of male and female genitals—blacks and whites, adults and children. Benetton added its logo and published the picture as an ad in *Libération*.

That day the newspapers sold an extra 40,000 copies. The BVP threatened to sue. Two days later, French men's underwear-maker Eminence published a double page in *Libération* showing as many (male) crotches with the same layout and the slogan: "We like dressing them."

The HIV-Positive Campaign A near-unanimous outcry greeted the fall 1993 campaign, which consisted of three stark photographs showing an arm, buttock and crotch, each branded with the words "HIV Positive."

Benetton explained that the pictures referred to the three main avenues for infection, as well as to the ostracism of AIDS victims. In Singapore, Danny Chow (President, ASA) dismissed the ads as "easily another ploy to get free publicity" (*Straits Times*, 27/9/93). The Italian advertising watchdog, the Giuri della Pubblicità, condemned the campaign for "not respecting the dignity of human beings."

The AIDS association LILA (*Lega Italiana per la Lotta contro l'AIDS*) didn't approve of it but took a pragmatic approach and decided to use it in its fight against AIDS. In the United States, reactions were mostly negative. David Eng (Gay Men's Health Crisis, New York) felt that "the ad can fuel hatred and disempowerment. . . . People can get the message that this [i.e. branding] is what we should be doing to people who are HIV positive" (*The New York Times*, 19/9/93). The *National Review* refused the ad without seeing it. The British ACET (AIDS Care Education and Training) demanded the ad's withdrawal.

The *Association Française de la Lutte contre le Sida* (AFLS), a French government-sponsored AIDS group, sued Benetton, for "hijacking a humanitarian cause for commercial ends." Four HIV sufferers joined in the lawsuit, with charges of "humiliation" and "debasement." According to their lawyers, the brandings were an implicit call to discriminate against patients, and evoked the Nazi death camps.[30] A representative of AIDES, another French association, felt the ad could be misinterpreted: "It is clearly stated that sodomy or intravenous drug abuse are the [major] causes of AIDS. . . . Such short cuts are misleading and stupid" (*CB News*, 20/9/93).

The brother of one sufferer bought a full-page ad in *Libération* and published a picture of his brother's emaciated face with the caption: "During the agony, the selling continues. For the attention of Luciano Benetton, from Olivier Besnard-Rousseau, AIDS sufferer, terminal phase." There were increasingly strident calls to boycott the firm, including one from a former cabinet minister. Arcat Sida, a French AIDS support group headed by Pierre Bergé, CEO of Yves Saint Laurent, sponsored a poster showing a condom stuffed with bank notes next to a "United Boycott" logo in Benetton's signature typeface and green colour. Stores were vandalised and sprayed with graffiti leading some store owners to complain that "Mr. Benetton listens to nobody" (*Le Nouvel Observateur*, 20/12/93).

Luciano Benetton was himself surprised and hurt by the violence of these reactions. In the Group's defence, its long-standing commitment to the fight against AIDS and the extent of its actions were cited. On December 1, 1993 (World AIDS Day), Benetton, in cooperation with the association Actup had a 22 metre pink condom placed over the obelisk in the Place de la Concorde in Paris. Other Benetton actions against AIDS are presented in Exhibit 6. In early 1994, Luciano received an award given by the President of South Korea in recognition of the consciousness-raising role played by the company.

The Known Soldier In February 1994, a Benetton ad showing bloodied battle fatigues appeared on billboards and in newspapers across 110 countries. The clothes had belonged to a Croatian soldier killed in Bosnia, as a caption in Serbo-Croat indicated:

> I, Gojko Gagro, father of the deceased Marinko Gagro, born in 1963 in the province of Citluk, would like that my son's name and all that remains of him be used in the name of peace against war.

The advertisement was greeted by an immediate uproar. While it became an instant success in Sarajevo, where the *Oslobodenje* newspaper printed it, leading dailies such as the *Los Angeles Times*, *Le Monde*, and the *Frankfurter Allgemeine Zeitung* refused to carry it, and the Vatican denounced Benetton for "image terrorism." Reactions among the combatants and people in the war zones depended on whether Gagro was seen as a victim or an aggressor and whose cause the ad was perceived as helping. Indignation reached a climax in France, where the minister for human rights and humanitarian action urged consumers to stop buying Benetton clothes and to "rip them off the backs of those who wear them." Once again, several Benetton stores were vandalised, causing a growing sense of unease among some retailers.

The French advertising weekly *Stratégies* announced it would not write about Benetton's advertising as long as it remained in the same vein: "Besides the disgust it causes, this [latest] ad raises the issue of the responsibility of advertisers. Can one do anything, use anything, to attract attention?" (25/2/94). Marina Galanti, Benetton's spokeswoman reacted to the outcry: "If we were trying to sell T-shirts, there probably would not be a worse way of doing it. We are not that naïve. It's meant to question the notion of institutionalised violence and the

EXHIBIT 6 *Some of Benetton's Actions Against AIDS (1991–1995)*

1991	In parallel with Coloured Condoms ad, free condoms distributed in Benetton stores in Europe and USA. $50,000 donation to HIV/AIDS Education Fund, a high school educational programme in New York City.
1992	Gigantic painted version of Coloured Condoms (26m × 26m) displayed in a Milan square. Donation made to the hospital to which David Kirby was admitted. Coloured Condoms posters displayed in Amsterdam during an international conference on AIDS. In South Africa, gigantic Coloured Condom posters hung outside five hospitals in Cape Town, Durban and Pretoria (at the Medical Research Council's request). Coloured Condoms used as part of national prevention campaign sponsored by AIDES organisation in France. Helped raise $600,000 for AIDS charities in USA.
1992–1993	Produced and distributed guides to safe sex in collaboration with a number of associations: Gay Men's Health Crisis (USA); Lega Italiana per la Lotta Contro l'AIDS (Italy); Japanese Foundation for AIDS Prevention; Fundai (Argentina); Gapa (Brazil); Shine and The Guardian (Caribbean); Proyecto Alerta (Chile); Fundacion Amor (Columbia); Conasida (Mexico); Fundacion Marco Aguayo (Paraguay); FranSida and National AIDS Programme (Uruguay). In Germany, sponsored the first major AIDS fund-raising project in 100 nightclubs (in collaboration with Deutsche AIDS Stiftungen); was one of two founding partners of the Deutsche AIDS Hilfe Communications Fund, created during an international AIDS conference in Berlin.
1993	200 HIV organisations worldwide were contacted to explore possible joint communication projects. In Brazil, organised a concert for the benefit of a hospital for children with AIDS in Latin America, special projects (fashion shows, musical and cultural events) were dedicated to AIDS. Sponsored the Films on Drugs Festival in Vienna, Austria. Sponsored the Gay Film Festival in Turin, Italy. In Portugal, donated outdoor advertising space to the HIV organisation Abraço. In France, supported survey on the sexual behaviour of young men with *20 Ans* magazine. On Dec 1 (World AIDS day), a 22-metre pink condom was placed over the Obelisk on Place de la Concorde in Paris (in cooperation with the group Act Up). Also participated in a major national campaign to promote the use of condoms, in collaboration with AIDES, the national nongovernmental organization. Was the first company to sign the UK Declaration of Rights for People with HIV and AIDS. Sponsored "Stopping AIDS Together," a fashion show to help raise funds for AIDS research and care in USA and Canada.
1994	An entire issue of *Colors* (No. 7) was dedicated to AIDS (over 500,000 copies distributed worldwide). Sponsored "10th World Aids Conference" in Yokohama, Japan and organised fund-raising operations. Sponsored Gay Film Festival in Turin and the Ripensare l'AIDS Convention in Bologna, Italy. Also donated T-shirts to the organisation SAMAN. In the UK, participated in the "Quilts of Love" demonstration and developed a pamphlet on AIDS prevention with various organisations (125,000 copies distributed). Co-produced one of ten award-winning films for the SIDATHON day in France. Organised distribution of free condoms during the Rio carnival in Brazil.
1995	In India, produced and distributed posters and leaflets on AIDS prevention.

role of advertising" (*The Guardian*, 16/2/94). The autumn 1994 worldwide campaign featured in print media and billboards showed a mosaic of 1000 faces arranged to softly highlight the word AIDS at its centre. This campaign attracted little attention.

The Alienation Campaign The spring 1995 campaign featured two visuals based on the theme of "alienation." One showed lines of barbed wire, coming from a variety of troubled countries such as Bosnia, Lebanon, and Israel as well as from private gardens. The other showed a jungle of TV antennae symbolising the "invisible barriers erected by the overcrowding of video images, which not only affect interpersonal relationships, but also people's perception of reality." Billed as "an invitation to an open discussion on real and virtual prisons, on the mental and televisual dictatorships which restrict freedom," the campaign did not elicit strong reactions. Benetton denied that the ads reflected a softer, toned-down communications strategy.

Around the same time, Benetton's U.S. retailers launched a campaign developed by Chiat/Day of New York, designed to appeal to more conservative audiences. The new U.S. campaign focused on clothing and included TV spots as well as eight-page magazine inserts. Luciano explained that this initiative was not an alternative to their international campaign, but an additional support to its U.S. store owners.

The German Lawsuits The furor over the recent Benetton campaigns reached a peak in Germany. Here 12 retailers being sued by Benetton for non-payment[31] defended their case by accusing Benetton of provoking adverse reaction in consumers through their ads, with a consequent drop in sales. Benetton stated that "total sales in Germany have remained stable in 1994 . . . 1992 was a record year . . . 8 million items were sold in 1993 and 1994 versus 4 million in 1985." While the group of retailers claimed that the number of Benetton stores had dropped from 650 to 500, with 100 more dropouts expected, Benetton maintained that it had 613 stores in Germany in 1994 as opposed to 650 in 1993. Marina Galanti explained that, "What we are talking about is a lawyer's trick to use a *cause célèbre* as a peg on which to hang every kind of grievance . . . these store owners may not like the ads, but the Frankfurt Museum of Modern Art has them on permanent exhibition" (*The Independent*, 6/2/95).

Threats of legal action in France and other European countries had also been made. A body called The Benetton Retailers Interest Group had been formed to coordinate the various actions against Benetton. However, other retailers formed the "Pro-Benetton" group in Germany to "fight the discredit done to Benetton by the disgruntled retailers."

In October 1995, Luciano indicated that all 12 cases had been won by Benetton and that "the affair was now over."[32] Financial analysts were generally optimistic about Benetton's prospects as they felt the markets had already discounted any possible negative impact due to the controversies. Salomon Brothers issued a "Buy" recommendation on Benetton stock on 17 October 1995.

Benetton's Communication Philosophy

Benetton argued that its communication philosophy was born out of a need to develop a distinctive image targeted at a global customer base and to make the most of its limited resources. The company claimed that "various studies have shown . . . that consumers are as concerned by what a company stands for as they are about the price-value relationship of that company's products" (*Financial Times*, 20/4/92). Further, the general feeling within Benetton was that the 8,000 Benetton outlets in 120 countries constituted the best advertising for its products in the streets of the world's main cities. "This is where we promote the products and the prices. Not in the ads" (Luciano Benetton, *CB News*, 28/6/93). Benetton also explained that the sheer diversity of their product range made it impossible to design individual product campaigns for each market.

Benetton had received several major awards for its advertising campaigns (Exhibit 7) and some of its ads were displayed in museums worldwide. Even its critics acknowledged that "it had achieved probably more visibility than any print campaign in world advertising history," to quote Robin Wright, chairman of the advertising agency WCRS (*Campaign* 25/3/94). Nonetheless, its communication approach had created a raging debate among advertisers:

Advertising should sell happiness. . . . This pair [Toscani and Benetton] have understood that society is adrift, and they have chosen the easy path: instead of extending a lifebuoy, they are pushing society's head down further under water, rubbing its nose in sex, in AIDS. . . . (Jacques Séguéla, Euro-RSCG, interviewed on *Antenne 2*, 16/9/93)

Benetton's banal expressions of moral outrage were not bold, but transparent. Not courageous, but cowardly. Not socially responsible, but socially irresponsible—a cynical publicity gimmick contrived to horrify the many in order to sell pricey T-shirts to the few. (Bob Garfield, *Advertising Age*, 27/3/95)

EXHIBIT 7 *Some Major National Awards Received by Benetton*

Year	Country/Award
1984	**Netherlands**—Avenue Award
1985	**France**—Banque de l'Union Publicitaire
	France—Stratégies Grand Prix (Best Campaigns) and Awards in the Magazine, Outdoor and Textiles/Clothing categories
	Netherlands—Avenue Award
1986	**Netherlands**—Avenue Award
1988	**Austria**—Kulturamt der Stadt Wien Award
	Italy—Confindustria Print Italia and Pubblicità Successo Awards
	Netherlands—Avenue Award
	UK—Eurobest Awards
1989	**Austria**—Kulturamt der Stadt Wien Award
	Denmark—Årets Guldkrone Award
	France—Stratégies Grand Prix (Outdoor category)
	Italy—Finedit, IGP, Confindustria Print Italia Grand Prix Awards
	Netherlands—Avenue Award
1990	**Austria**—Kulturamt der Stadt Wien Award
	France—Art Directors' Club of Europe Grand Prix
	Italy—Art Directors' Club Award (outdoor category) and Confindustria Print Italia Award
	Netherlands—Avenue Award
	UK—Media and Marketing Europe Award
	USA—International Andy Award of Excellence
1991	**Austria**—Kulturamt der Stadt Wien Award
	Finland—Maximedia Special Award (outdoor category)
	France—Cannes International Golden Lion Award
	Germany—Art Directors' Club of Europe Award
	Italy—Art Directors' Club Award
	Netherlands—Avenue Award
	Spain—AEPE Award (out-door category)
	Switzerland—Société Générale d'Affichage Grand Prix
	UK—Epica and Eurobest Award
	USA—International Andy Award of Excellence (magazine and international retail category), Institute of Outdoor Advertising OBIE Award International Center for Photography (ICP) Jury Award
1992	**Europe**—FEPE (European Federation of Outdoor Advertising) Award (Best Poster for Italy)
	France—Cannes International Golden Lion (outdoor category)
	Ireland—Best Out-door Campaign Award
	USA—ICP Infinity Award, Institute of Outdoor Advertising's Fiftieth OBIE Award
1993	**Austria**—Kulturamt der Stadt Wien Award
1994	**Austria**—Kulturamt der Stadt Wien Award
	France—French Retailers Association's "Enseigne d'Or" Award
	Japan—Art Directors' Club of Japan Award
	Turkey—Kuzguncuk Lions Club Award
	USA—Art Directors' Club of New York Medal
1995	**Switzerland**—Swiss Federal Department of the Interior Award

[Toscani's] "advertising" is totally irrelevant to the products he is meant to be selling. . . . You can put a four-letter word in a headline and it will certainly be noticed, but it doesn't mean I like you for it. (Ced Vidler, Lintas Worldwide)[33]

Benetton has restated a truth about successful advertising . . . that to create a distinctive "culture" around a brand is . . . often more important than a practical selling benefit. (James Lowther, Saatchi & Saatchi)

This is obviously a company with profound understanding of how advertising really works. . . . Cynics say Benetton is using shock value to sell sweaters. Benetton counters they are doing important consciousness-raising. I would say both are right. . . . They sell a little product. They do a little good. Most advertising does neither. (Marty Cooke, Chiat/Day)

Toscani was extremely critical of traditional advertising and was seen as a maverick:[34]

Advertisers have done a lot of social damage . . . using fake images and fake dreams to sell us their products, so that today if you are a girl you really are a nobody if you don't look like Isabella Rossellini. . . . With the amount large multinationals spend on advertising they could make the best campaign in the world against drug abuse, for example. (*Financial Times*, 28/1/93)

Advertising is the richest and most powerful form of communication in the world. . . . Ad agencies are obsolete. . . . They create a false reality and want people to believe in it. We show reality and we're criticised for it. Our advertising is a Rorschach test of what you bring to the image. . . . Shocking violence in the news is normal. But when you take the same photo out of the news and put a Benetton logo on it, people pause and reflect. . . . When they can't come to terms with it, they get mad at us. . . . The more real a thing is, the less people want to see it.[35]

The advertising industry has corrupted society. . . . One day there will be a Nuremberg trial of advertisers. . . . I will sit on it, I will be the prosecution and the public. (*The Independent*, 16/12/92)

Today, kids get killed on the road because they have been convinced by the promise of happiness suggested by some car makers in their ads. But that doesn't stop them "selling whilst they're dying." Right now, I am exhibiting my posters on a 6,000 square metre surface in Brussels. . . . 48,000 visitors have been to see these posters, already seen in the street. Next door, there is an exhibition of Flemish painters . . . they have had 3,200 visitors. (*Jeunes à Paris*, January 1995)

Toscani saw himself not as an advertiser, but as a reporter-photographer.

Benetton gives me the world's largest museum— the street, tens of thousands of posters in a hundred countries—every artist's dream. . . . An artist must help change things. . . . I want to show what people do not want to see. . . . I am a modern illiterate. I don't read any books, almost never watch television, but I devour dozens of newspapers every day, dailies only, from all countries. . . . Luciano is my patron, my Lorenzo de Medici. (*Le Monde*, 17/2/95)

The company believed that its most controversial ads were considered scandalous not because of what they showed, but because of the Benetton signature. Claude Torracinta, a Swiss TV journalist commented: "twenty years ago, the picture of a child dying of hunger provoked a strong reaction. . . . What Toscani is telling me . . . is that it has become banal to talk of the world's suffering [on TV news] . . . this does not affect people anymore. If you want to touch them, you need a *mise en scéne*, an escalation in the presentation.[36]

In Benetton's mind, the images they used therefore had more impact than if they were featured by public or state organisations. Laura Pollini, Benetton's Image and Communications Director, stressed that their advertisements were intended to remain "open" to all interpretations—including negative ones—another reason for not subjecting them to traditional advertising tests.[37] Pascal Sommariba explained: "Ads are usually a totally closed text. What we thought was interesting was to have the text disappear totally . . . so that people had to write their own text. . . . The pictures became rich through the interface with the public."

Benetton itself never performed prelaunch tests nor analysed a campaign's impact. Toscani explained:

Research? We try to do the very opposite. . . . If you do research, you get yesterday's results. If they had done research 500 years ago, they would never have discovered America. They would have found out that the world is flat. You have to have the courage to make mistakes. . . . Luciano didn't test the market for a taste in coloured sweaters.

The instructions I received didn't indicate selling as a target. Therefore I am free to create as I see fit. (*Mainichi Shimbun*, 11/9/91)

You see, Luciano owns the company. No company run by a manager would accept what I ask, they would say, . . . "We must know before if it will work." That way they get something mediocre. (*The Times*, 26/1/93)

The visibility and uniqueness of Benetton's communications had prompted a number of advertising agencies and publishing and market research companies to conduct independent studies of their effectiveness, very often without Benetton's knowledge. These studies evaluated specific Benetton campaigns (Exhibits 8 and 9) together with the image of Benetton and other leading brands across a variety of countries (Exhibits 10 to 13).

Other Communication Activities

The Benettons have long been involved in sponsoring sports and the Benetton Treviso basketball and rugby teams and Sisley Volley are among Italy's top players in their respective national championships. In 1983, the company inaugurated the Palaverde complex, a venue for concerts, shows, cultural displays, and sporting events. The 18-hectare Ghirada Sports Centre, built on the outskirts of Treviso in 1985, welcomes thousands of children every year to its gyms, basketball and volleyball courts, and rugby fields. The centre also includes a golf course and physical rehabilitation unit.

Luciano realised that Formula One Grand Prix racing attracted a worldwide audience and decided, in 1983, to sponsor the Tyrrell team at a cost of $6 million. In 1984, Benetton sponsored Alfa Romeo Euroracing, with mixed results. Benetton bought the Toleman team for L4 billion in 1985 and decided to compete directly under the *Benetton Formula* colours.

All the characteristics of Grand Prix racing— speed, colour, internationality, excitement, plus

the irresistible combination of high technology and the human factor—are a perfect expression of our corporate philosophy. This affiliation has been effective in creating an image for us in some countries before we had established a commercial presence.[38]

Benetton Formula, with the German driver Michael Schumacher, won the Formula One World Championship in 1994 and 1995.

In 1992, Benetton launched *Colors*, a large-format magazine sold in five bilingual editions in over 100 countries and dedicated to racial integration. Its editor-in-chief is Toscani and the artistic editor is Tibor Kalman, an influential New York graphic designer. It rarely shies away from controversy, using, for example, computer imagery to show Queen Elizabeth II of the UK and Arnold Schwarzenegger with black skin, Pope John Paul II as an Asian or Ronald Reagan as an AIDS victim. *Colors*, which was initially distributed free in Benetton stores, has a print run of 400,000 and includes paid advertising for brands such as Kenwood, Philips, and Alfa Romeo. MTV Europe is responsible for the sale of advertising space in *Colors*.

In 1993 Toscani set up *Inedito*, which he described as a "fashion pictures production pool," in Paris. *Inedito* produced quality ready-made fashion magazine articles featuring 30 percent Benetton clothes and accessories and made them available to magazines worldwide. Each feature, complete with headlines, captions and full credits, is available in three languages.

In July 1995, 21 Investimenti, the investment arm of Edizione Holding, bought a local Milan TV station and renamed it *Sei Milano* (Milan 6).

And so, where next? *Fabrica*, another brainchild of Toscani, opened near Treviso in the autumn of 1995. This communications research centre can host up to 50 promising young designers and artists from around the world. The institution is housed in a Palladian villa restructured by the Japanese architect Tadao Ando, the 1995 Pritzker prize winner. Luciano has said that "It [*Fabrica*][39] will be a school without professors and textbooks. We want to see what creativity produces. Benetton's future communication will be *Fabrica*."

EXHIBIT 8 *Ipsos Tests of Benetton Campaigns in France (billboards, Paris and suburbs), 1985–1995*

Date of Campaign: 1–20/3/85
Date of Test: 20/9/85
Cost[1]: 2,000,000 FF and 4,000,000 FF ($223,000 and $446,000)

	Recognition[2]	Attribution[3]	Confusion[4]	Liked	Disliked
Overall sample					
(N = 300)	57	29	3	73	23
18–34 year olds					
(N = 150)	63	36	3	73	21

Date of Campaign: 1989
Date of Test: 28/9 to 3/10/89
Cost: 2,396,000 FF ($375,543)

N = 301	Recognition	Attribution	Confusion	Liked	Disliked	Indifferent
Overall sample	75	64	2	79	20	1
Gender						
Men	75	60	3	77	23	1
Women	75	68	1	81	17	2
Age group						
18–24	81	77	1	83	16	1
25–34	81	76	1	83	15	3
35–55	69	53	3	75	25	—
Income group						
Higher	83	72	3	81	18	1
Medium	72	60	2	77	22	1
Lower	65	58	2	77	20	3
Ipsos standards[5]	43	18	—	60	35	5

Ad depicting a black woman nursing a white baby

Source: Ipsos Publicité, Paris, France.
[1]Estimated cost of the campaign in French Francs (US$). This refers only to billboards and does not include print.
[2]Respondents were shown a folder containing several ads with the brand name blocked out. As they leafed through, they were asked which ads they remembered seeing. The recognition score is the % of respondents remembering having seen (at least one of) the ads listed.
[3]For each ad recognised, respondents were asked whether they remembered the name of the brand blocked out.
[4]Percentage of respondents who incorrectly identified the brand.
[5]Average score of all other billboard campaigns tested by Ipsos within the same industry and with similar budgets.

EXHIBIT 8 (continued) *Tests of Benetton Campaigns in France (billboards, Paris and suburbs)*

Date of Campaign: 12/3–20/3/90
Date of Test: 22/3/90
Cost: 2,319,000 FF ($425,872)

$N = 301$	Recognition	Attribution	Confusion	Liked	Disliked	Indifferent
Overall sample	88	75	2	90	8	2
Gender						
Men	85	69	2	89	9	3
Women	91	81	1	91	8	1
Age group						
18–24	90	82	—	94	6	—
25–34	92	83	—	91	9	—
35–55	85	68	3	89	7	3
Income group						
Higher	91	81	2	92	6	2
Medium	89	74	2	90	9	1
Lower	81	67	—	86	11	3
Ipsos standards	43	18	—	59	35	6

Date of Campaign: 3/9–16/9/90
Date of Test: 20–24/9/90
Cost: 2,001,000 FF ($367,473)

$N = 305$	Recognition	Attribution	Confusion	Liked	Disliked	Indifferent
Overall sample	83	72	2	88	10	2
Gender						
Men	81	68	3	88	9	3
Women	84	76	1	88	11	1
Age group						
18–24	94	90	1	95	5	—
25–34	91	85	2	90	9	1
35–55	75	58	2	94	6	—
Income group						
Higher	82	75	2	89	11	1
Medium	84	72	2	85	10	4
Lower	82	64	2	94	6	—
Ipsos standards	43	18	—	59	35	6

EXHIBIT 8 (continued) *Tests of Benetton Campaigns in France (billboards, Paris and suburbs)*

Date of Campaign: 11/3–20/3/90
Date of Test: 21/3/91
Cost: 2,176,000 FF ($385,672)

$N = 301$	Recognition	Attribution	Confusion	Liked	Disliked	Indifferent
Overall sample	83	69	4	70	28	2
Gender						
Men	79	62	5	74	26	1
Women	87	77	2	67	30	3
Age group						
18–24	93	90	1	82	17	1
25–34	91	80	5	79	20	1
35–55	75	58	3	61	36	3
Income group						
Higher	87	75	5	74	25	1
Medium	78	67	1	66	31	3
Lower	84	63	6	69	27	3
Ipsos standards	43	18	—	59	35	6

Date of Campaign: 2/9–11/9/91
Date of Test: 19/9/91
Cost: 2,440,000 FF ($432,463)

$N = 302$	Recognition	Attribution	Confusion	Liked	Disliked	Indifferent
Overall sample	79	72	1	32	66	2
Gender						
Men	76	67	1	34	64	2
Women	83	77	—	30	69	1
Age group						
18–24	84	75	1	34	64	2
25–34	80	77	1	38	62	—
35–55	79	67	1	26	70	3
Income group						
Higher	80	71	—	44	56	1
Medium	82	78	1	23	75	3
Lower	75	63	2	27	71	2
Ipsos standards	43	18	—	59	35	6

C-550

EXHIBIT 8 (continued) *Tests of Benetton Campaigns in France (billboards, Paris and suburbs)*

Date of Campaign: 2/9–11/9/91 and 14/10–21/10/91

Date of Test: 24/10/91

Cost: 2,440,000 ($432,463) and 1,097,000 FF ($194,431)

Ad featuring a priest and a nun kissing.

$N = 193$	Recognition	Attribution	Confusion	Liked	Disliked	Indifferent	Incites to Buy[6]	Does not incite to Buy
Overall sample	64	59	1	59	38	3	36	61
Gender								
Men	67	60	1	60	38	2	35	61
Women	60	58	—	58	39	3	38	60
Age group								
18–24	65	63	—	65	29	6	41	59
25–34	67	65	—	60	36	4	38	60
35–55	60	53	1	58	41	1	35	61
Income group								
Higher	67	63	1	56	43	1	41	55
Medium	60	53	—	66	30	4	36	60
Lower	66	62	—	48	48	3	21	79
Ipsos standards	43	18	—	59	35	6	—	—

[6]The percentage of respondents who said that the campaign has created in them a positive or negative desire to buy the product. Ipsos reports the following standards for incitation to buy: 27% positive "desire to buy" when ad liking is below 45%; 49% positive when liking is between 45% and 60%; 52% positive when liking is above 60%.

Date of Campaign: 2/9–11/9/91 and 14/10–21/10/91

Date of Test: 24/10/91

Cost: 2,440,000 ($432,463) and 1,097,000 FF ($194,431)

$N = 193$	Recognition	Attribution	Confusion	Liked	Disliked	Indifferent	Incites to Buy	Does not incite to Buy
Overall sample	72	67	1	70	28	2	40	56
Gender								
Men	64	57	1	69	29	2	33	61
Women	80	78	—	71	28	1	48	51
Age group								
18–24	86	82	—	76	24	—	43	55
25–34	77	73	—	72	26	2	42	55
35–55	69	62	1	68	31	1	39	57
Income group								
Higher	67	66	1	64	34	1	38	56
Medium	73	69	—	74	25	1	47	52
Lower	79	69	—	76	21	3	31	66
Ipsos standards	43	18	—	59	35	6	—	—

EXHIBIT 8 (continued) *Tests of Benetton Campaigns in France (billboards, Paris and suburbs)*

Date of Campaign: 18/3–29/3/92
Date of Test: 2/4/92
Cost: 2,125,000 ($401,413)

$N = 301$	Recognition	Attribution	Confusion	Liked	Disliked	Indifferent	Incites to Buy	Does not incite to Buy
Overall sample	79	72	—	39	58	3	19	78
Gender								
Men	81	70	1	42	54	4	19	79
Women	78	74	—	36	61	3	18	76
Age group								
18–24	83	81	—	44	51	5	26	73
25–34	85	81	—	42	54	4	23	75
35–55	74	63	1	36	61	3	14	81
Income group								
Higher	76	71	1	37	61	2	16	79
Medium	82	74	—	37	59	4	19	78
Lower	80	71	—	45	50	5	23	76
Ipsos standards	43	18	—	59	35	6	—	—

Date of Campaign: 22/9–29/9/92 and 19/10–26/10/92
Date of Test: 5/11/92
Cost: 2,000,000 and 2,527,000 FF ($377,800 and $477,350)

$N = 301$	Recognition	Attribution	Confusion	Liked	Disliked	Indifferent
Overall sample	77	73	1	42	54	4
Gender						
Men	77	73	1	52	42	6
Women	76	74	—	33	65	2
Age group						
18–24	84	83	—	44	55	1
25–34	84	82	—	42	56	2
35–55	70	65	1	42	52	6
Income group						
Higher	80	78	1	40	57	3
Medium	76	71	—	39	55	6
Lower	75	69	1	49	48	3
Ipsos standards	43	18	—	65	30	5

Ad showing an albino Zulu woman ostracized by other Zulus.

EXHIBIT 8 (continued) *Tests of Benetton Campaigns in France (billboards, Paris and suburbs)*

Date of Campaign: 14/9 to 21/9/93

Date of Test: 23/9/93

Cost: 2,200,000 FF ($388,473)

$N = 301$	Recognition	Attribution	Confusion	Liked	Disliked	Indifferent
Overall sample	81	77	2	23	70	7
Gender						
Men	78	72	3	22	70	8
Women	85	81	1	24	70	6
Age group						
18–24	86	84	—	21	69	10
25–34	82	79	1	22	71	7
35–55	81	75	3	24	68	7
Income group						
Higher	86	85	1	20	75	6
Medium	82	75	4	25	68	7
Lower	69	60	—	28	62	10
Ipsos standards	44	21	—	61	31	8

Ad consisting of two stark photographs showing an arm and a buttock, each branded with the words "HIV Positive."

Date of Campaign: 22/2–28/2/94

Date of Test: 3/3/94

Cost: 1,754,000 FF ($315,900)

Ad showing bloodied battle fatigues.

$N = 302$	Recognition	Attribution	Confusion	Liked	Disliked	Indifferent	Incites to Buy	Does not incite to Buy
Overall sample	60	55	1	27	71	2	14	86
Gender								
Men	63	56	1	28	71	1	14	86
Women	56	54	—	27	70	3	15	85
Age group								
18–34	66	64	—	28	72	1	14	86
35–55	54	46	1	27	70	3	15	85
Income group								
Higher	65	64	1	25	75	1	9	91
Medium	53	50	—	31	67	2	17	83
Lower	63	52	1	25	72	3	16	84
Ipsos standards	44	20	—	61	31	8	—	—

EXHIBIT 8 (continued) *Tests of Benetton Campaigns in France (billboards, Paris and suburbs)*

Date of Campaign: 18/10–31/10/94
Date of Test: 3/11/94
Cost: 3,400,000 FF ($612,400)

$N = 300$	Recognition	Attribution	Confusion	Liked	Disliked	Indifferent
Overall sample	86	80	1	59	32	9
Gender						
Men	86	80	1	58	28	13
Women	86	81	2	60	35	5
Age group						
18–34	93	90	1	66	26	7
35–55	79	70	2	52	37	11
Income group						
Higher	87	81	1	61	29	10
Medium	86	80	2	58	35	6
Lower	84	79	—	57	29	14
Ipsos standards	44	20	—	61	31	8

Date of Campaign: 21/2–6/3/95
Date of Test: 9/3/95
Cost: 3,600,000 FF ($720,000)

$N = 301$	Recognition	Attribution	Confusion	Liked	Disliked	Indifferent
Overall sample	82	78	1	37	60	4
Gender						
Men	83	77	1	37	58	5
Women	81	79	—	36	62	2
Age group						
18–34	86	85	—	42	55	3
35–55	79	72	1	31	65	4
Income group						
Higher	80	75	2	35	62	3
Medium	84	83	—	38	59	3
Lower	82	74	—	35	58	7
Ipsos standards	47	23	—	63	30	7

EXHIBIT 9 *Test of Benetton Billboard Campaign in Switzerland, 1991 (a Société Générale d'Affichage study)*

Campaign tested: "Giusy, the new-born baby"—Date of test: 9–12 August, 1991

Methodology: This SGA study tested the impact of 10 new outdoor advertising campaigns prior to their national launch in Switzerland. These campaigns were displayed in two metropolitan areas in greater Lausanne and Bern during a two-week period (29 July–11 August, 1991) on 30 and 38 "B12" billboards respectively. The test campaigns included Benetton's "new-born baby" campaign as well as nine other campaigns. The test occured seven weeks prior to the national launch in Switzerland of the "new-born baby" campaign. The 10 test campaigns (a) had not appeared anywhere previously; (b) were only displayed on "B12" billboards, and (c) were the only campaigns run by these brands for two weeks prior to and after the test display period. The sample was representative of all persons aged 15 to 74 living in the greater Lausanne and Bern areas.

A. Unaided Recall[1]

Lausanne sample (N = 401)		Bern sample (N = 402)	
Brands	**Recall, %**	**Brands**	**Recall, %**
1 Benetton[2]	18.0	1 Benetton[1]	33.8
2 Marlboro	7.5	2 Stop AIDS	8.0
3 Stop AIDS	5.7	3 SBB	3.5
4 Camel	4.7	4 Stimorol[2]	2.5
5 SBB	3.7	5 Migros	2.5
6 McDonald's	3.0	6 Der Bund[2]	2.2
7 Clin d'oeil[2]	2.7	7 700th Anniversary	2.2
8 700th Anniversary	2.7	8 Circus Knie	2.0
9 AMAG/VW	2.7	9 Levi Jeans	1.7
10 Comptoir Suisse[2]	2.5	10 Marlboro	1.7

B. Recognition[3] and Company/Product Familiarity[4] for All 10 Test Campaigns

	Lausanne Sample			Bern Sample		
	Recognition			**Recognition**		
Brands	**Seen for sure, %**	**Perhaps, %**	**Familiarity, %**	**Seen for sure, %**	**Perhaps, %**	**Familiarity, %**
Benetton	55.1	12.2	90.3	60.4	4.7	87.8
Heine	28.2	14.5	38.7	39.8	11.7	51.2
Providentia	20.7	18.0	70.1	27.1	9.7	57.2
Stimorol	34.9	23.4	91.8	45.3	10.4	92.0
SGA	25.9	15.2	46.4	25.9	10.0	40.5
Clin d'Oeil[5]	40.1	17.0	75.1			
Comptoir Suisse[5]	26.2	15.5	92.8			
L'Hebdo[5]	51.1	20.2	90.3			
Der Bund[5]				68.9	9.7	95.3
Wartman[5]				39.1	11.2	85.8

Source: "Billboards B12," Société Générale d'Affichage (SGA), Switzerland, 1992, and Martial Pasquier "Conscience et Comportement," Arbeitspapier Nr 21, Institut für Marketing and Unternehmungsführung, Universität Bern, 1994.

[1]Respondents were asked: "Can you spontaneously give examples of posters or billboards which you have seen during the last 2 weeks?"
[2]One of the 10 test campaigns.
[3]Respondents were asked: "Here are photos of billboards. Are there any among them which you remember having seen during the past two weeks? Please tell us which ones you have seen 'for sure,' 'perhaps' or 'not at all.'"
[4]Respondents were asked: "For each billboard, please say if the product or the company is familiar to you."
[5]Ad displayed only in French-speaking Lausanne or German-speaking Bern.

EXHIBIT 9 (continued) *Test of Benetton Billboard Campaign in Switzerland, 1991*

C. Variation of Benetton Total Recognition[1] by Sex and Age

	Lausanne Sample, %	Bern Sample, %
Men	65.0	60.1
Women	69.5	69.9
15–29	78.9	68.2
30–49	67.2	67.4
50–74	54.8	58.2

D. Liking/Disliking[2] of Benetton Campaign

	Lausanne Sample		Bern Sample		Lausanne Sample			Bern Sample		
					Reasons for Disliking[3] (%)					
	Dislike, %	Like, %	Dislike, %	Like, %	A	B	C	A	B	C
Overall	58	15	62	12	23	39	54	32	44	38
Men	58	17	63	11	23	34	51	25	45	40
Women	59	15	64	12	23	43	57	37	42	35
15–29	52	24	55	14	19	33	51	32	44	39
30–44	59	15	68	12	26	37	56	37	49	32
45–74	65	9	68	10	18	44	56	27	39	41

[1]Total recognition: "seen for sure" + "seen perhaps."

[2]Respondents were asked to indicate whether they liked or disliked the ad using a 6-point scale (1 = does not like at all; 6 = likes a lot). Here, dislike scores correspond to 1–2 answers and like scores correspond to 4–6 answers.

[3]People with a negative reaction were asked one or more of the following reasons for their dislike. A: use of the subject for commercial purposes; B: the image is shocking; C: the relationship between the subject and the brand.

EXHIBIT 10 *Awareness, Liking, and Usage of Some Fashion Brands in Five European Countries, 1990 (A Euroka Project–Brigitte Magazine Germany)*

Methodology: "Omnibus" surveys in West Germany, France, Great Britain, Italy, and Spain involving a random sample of 2,000 women, 14–64 years old, April–May 1990.

Clothing Brands	Germany			France			Great Britain			Italy			Spain		
	Aware-ness, %	Liking, %	Usage, %	Aware-ness, %	Liking, %	Usage, %	Aware-ness, %	Liking, %	Usage, %	Aware-ness, %	Liking, %	Usage, %	Aware-ness, %	Liking, %	Usage, %
Benetton	68	42	28	73	30	26	61	26	14	92	65	57	53	21	17
Armani	28	11	4	6	1	0	18	6	2	81	41	28	9	2	1
Esprit	73	46	33	3	1	1	20	4	1	8	2	1	6	0	0
Jil Sander	68	37	14	5	1	0	2	0	0	12	3	1	2	0	0
Triumph	91	60	53	49	6	8	43	10	6	31	10	10	30	7	12
Schiesser	93	64	56	2	0	0	2	0	0	3	1	1	2	0	0

Benetton Awareness (Aided), Liking, and Usage by Age Group

Awareness

Liking

Usage

EXHIBIT 11 *Image of Benetton and Some Other Clothing Brands in France, 1994 (A Sofres Survey)*

Brands	Population	Aided Awareness[1]	Evocation[2]	Perceived Quality[3]	Conviction[4]	Refusal[5]	Influence[6]	Influence Ratio[7]	Usage[8]
Chanel	1,000	969	782	863	250	226	476	1.11	130
Lacoste	1,000	961	798	865	249	148	397	1.68	255
Benetton	1,000	871	661	574	122	247	369	0.49	106
Chevignon	1,000	814	607	582	106	252	358	0.42	80
Armani	1,000	298	167	157	24	102	126	0.24	17
Boss	1,000	263	145	148	24	95	119	0.25	16
Average 300 Brands	1,000	825	591	539	168	223	391	0.75	254

Basis: Total population rescaled to 1,000.

Source: SOFRES, France. Data extracted from "SOFRES Megabrand System 1994" database. The Megabrand system covers 300 international brands across a variety of goods and services with a representative national sample of 3,000 French respondents.

[1]Aided awareness: number of individuals who indicate that they "know the brand from amongst those presented, if only by name."

[2]Number of individuals for whom this brand evokes "many things," "some things," or "a few things" (as opposed to "nothing").

[3]Number of individuals for whom the brand is the "best available quality" or "better than others" as opposed to "inferior to others" or "worst quality available."

[4]Number of individuals who state they "would definitely choose" this brand (as opposed to "probably," "probably not," "certainly not").

[5]Number of individuals who state they "would *definitely not* choose this brand."

[6]Number of individuals who are not indifferent to this brand (influence = conviction + refusal).

[7]Influence ratio = conviction/refusal.

[8]Number of individuals who use "almost only" this brand, or "more than any other," as opposed to "less than others" or "almost never."

EXHIBIT 12 *Images of Some Leading Fashion Companies in Europe, 1994 (A* Time *Magazine Study)*

Methodology: questionnaire sent on 18 March 1994 to a panel of 5,500 *Time* magazine subscribers in 11 countries (500 per country). Respondents were presented with a list of 40 fashion and/or fragrance houses and asked their perceptions of these companies. Only the top 10 fashion companies are shown in this exhibit.

"Overall familiarity with the company"

	N = 2151 respondents	Country	EUR %	B %	CH %	D %	DK %	E %	F %	I %	NL %	P %	S %	UK %
1	Benetton	I	80	84	83	87	64	87	87	89	69	90	67	69
2	Christian Dior	F	74	78	80	73	64	81	89	77	64	83	67	58
3	Lacoste	F	72	73	75	80	67	76	88	86	55	81	71	44
4	Burberrys	UK	72	70	73	61	79	85	74	73	62	76	72	65
5	Yves Saint Laurent	F	70	76	70	68	59	78	86	79	59	76	63	58
6	Chanel	F	68	65	71	61	59	66	88	80	63	82	55	63
7	Giorgio Armani	I	56	53	50	62	35	73	40	93	32	67	58	49
8	Hugo Boss	D	49	40	59	76	57	35	39	38	43	73	49	32
9	Karl Lagerfeld	F	47	46	48	67	46	39	60	33	43	47	55	36
10	Hermès	F	47	51	61	37	21	55	85	61	31	40	33	39

"Prestigious image"

	N = 2151 respondents	Country	EUR %	B %	CH %	D %	DK %	E %	F %	I %	NL %	P %	S %	UK %
1	Christian Dior	F	62	73	69	61	55	58	79	63	47	66	56	60
2	Yves Saint Laurent	F	56	66	64	49	43	61	75	59	38	63	55	50
3	Chanel	F	49	55	51	39	32	54	79	52	35	66	35	41
4	Giorgio Armani	I	46	50	36	53	26	63	28	73	24	56	42	52
5	Burberrys	UK	41	39	41	30	33	58	39	46	29	49	36	54
6	Karl Lagerfeld	F	38	49	40	57	29	30	48	17	31	40	39	36
7	Hermès	F	35	41	46	31	14	47	62	37	24	30	20	32
8	Lacoste	F	31	30	30	36	29	40	30	31	29	47	25	18
9	Calvin Klein	US	26	26	24	30	26	21	14	10	26	32	31	49
10	Nina Ricci	F	24	26	31	12	9	32	45	26	21	35	18	12
...														
15	Benetton	I	20	15	11	16	18	33	10	16	18	40	18	22

"Reputation for quality"

	N = 2151 respondents	Country	EUR %	B %	CH %	D %	DK %	E %	F %	I %	NL %	P %	S %	UK %
1	Burberrys	UK	54	47	58	54	64	60	60	46	43	50	53	63
2	Lacoste	F	34	26	30	33	25	47	50	38	28	45	33	15
3	Hugo Boss	D	26	24	28	48	32	19	24	15	16	43	23	15
4	Aquascutum	UK	25	16	44	13	26	18	18	38	12	26	11	56
5	Chanel	F	24	23	28	17	17	29	37	23	24	30	16	20
6	Yves Saint Laurent	F	24	22	17	22	17	26	42	26	15	35	17	28
7	Giorgio Armani	I	23	16	17	23	13	29	21	44	13	31	23	25
8	Benetton	I	23	22	18	16	26	24	24	36	14	26	17	29
9	Christian Dior	F	23	18	21	17	17	33	34	27	16	27	13	26
10	Hermès	F	22	20	24	17	5	29	45	24	15	23	15	19

EXHIBIT 12 (continued) *Images of Some Leading Fashion Companies in Europe, 1994*

"Is more high fashion"

	N = 2151 respondents	Country	EUR %	B %	CH %	D %	DK %	E %	F %	I %	NL %	P %	S %	UK %
1	Christian Dior	F	42	41	46	38	34	42	61	38	41	40	32	48
2	Karl Lagerfeld	F	30	38	33	37	22	29	41	24	23	26	20	33
3	Giorgio Armani	I	30	36	30	36	18	42	21	42	14	28	28	30
4	Yves Saint Laurent	F	30	30	27	33	29	31	45	28	32	25	16	35
5	Calvin Klein	US	25	19	31	28	20	20	20	24	23	27	16	44
6	Chanel	F	21	25	22	16	16	25	37	30	22	22	9	22
7	Jean-Paul Gaultier	F	19	25	23	16	9	18	32	19	14	24	13	20
8	Kenzo	F	15	17	24	21	11	9	25	16	12	12	13	2
9	Benetton	I	15	11	16	25	16	13	9	12	11	11	15	27
10	Nina Ricci	F	11	10	9	7	3	17	23	14	3	15	9	6

"Caters for my style"

	N = 2151 respondents	Country	EUR %	B %	CH %	D %	DK %	E %	F %	I %	NL %	P %	S %	UK %
1	Burberrys	UK	17	9	19	17	15	22	16	15	18	20	11	25
2	Giorgio Armani	I	12	8	6	14	8	18	7	21	5	10	14	16
3	Lacoste	F	12	15	10	10	9	20	16	17	9	14	7	4
4	Hugo Boss	D	10	11	6	20	12	8	9	3	6	20	9	4
5	Ralph Lauren	US	9	7	11	9	9	10	5	10	8	11	8	12
6	Benetton	I	9	11	5	9	9	12	13	15	6	10	1	7
7	Yves Saint Laurent	F	8	5	5	6	4	11	14	7	5	9	8	10
8	Calvin Klein	US	6	3	4	5	8	9	4	4	8	9	3	12
9	Aquascutum	UK	6	3	11	5	4	2	3	7	4	9	1	15
10	Chanel	F	6	3	9	6	3	7	8	10	9	4	5	4

"Would buy for day/work wear"

	N = 2151 respondents	Country	EUR %	B %	CH %	D %	DK %	E %	F %	I %	NL %	P %	S %	UK %
1	Benetton	I	38	35	40	45	30	37	44	58	33	44	24	24
2	Lacoste	F	27	31	37	28	23	37	40	29	11	34	18	13
3	Burberrys	UK	26	24	26	25	23	39	30	21	17	28	24	27
4	Hugo Boss	D	18	22	23	37	15	15	20	17	6	22	13	10
5	Ralph Lauren	US	16	11	16	15	12	22	15	17	13	22	11	16
6	Giorgio Armani	I	14	11	7	16	8	20	13	30	3	16	15	19
7	Daniel Hechter	F	13	17	15	29	8	10	37	9	2	7	9	3
8	Aquascutum	UK	12	7	21	9	10	8	9	18	5	13	2	27
9	Calvin Klein	US	12	11	11	15	10	11	7	8	15	14	6	19
10	Yves Saint Laurent	F	11	8	8	11	6	18	23	14	4	13	9	9

Source: Images of Fashion and Fragrance 1994, *Time* Magazine Opinion Poll.
Code: Europe (EUR), Belgium (B), Switzerland (CH), Germany (D), Denmark (DK), Spain (E), France (F), Italy (I), Netherlands (NL), Portugal (P), Sweden (S), United Kingdom (UK).

EXHIBIT 13A *Overall Awareness and Use of Some Clothing Brands in 21 Countries, 1994 (A Young & Rubicam Brand Asset™ Valuator Study)*

	Benetton		Chanel		Dior		Esprit		Gap		Armani		Lacoste		YSL	
	Aware[1]	Use[2]	Aware	Use	Aware	Use	Aware	Use	Aware	Use	Aware	Use	Aware	Use	Aware	Use
Australia	59	2/81	93	4/84	94	11/73	87	7/63	12	1/93	43	2/95	74	4/65	82	16/76
Brazil	54	3/81	51	1/93	42	4/86	30	0/98	9	0/98	20	1/97	29	6/85	34	5/88
Canada	61	2/78	97	11/69	89	2/89	83	22/58	57	5/79	60	2/92	41	2/78	84	15/64
Czech Rep.	69	1/77	92	3/38	91	6/36	32	1/45	23	1/70	22	0/47	51	1/57	37	2/44
France	91	8/53	98	16/64	98	14/65	21	1/96	25	2/91	37	3/91	97	24/30	99	19/58
Germany	71	8/51	80	5/66	83	3/70	68	8/54	19	1/79	44	4/72	66	4/54	63	2/71
Hungary	73	3/87	78	3/90	75	7/87	31	2/95	13	1/95	35	2/93	60	4/67	45	4/91
Italy	94	21/35	85	15/67	83	13/68	25	1/97	16	1/96	93	25/49	86	19/37	73	14/70
Japan	75	3/64	98	21/63	93	27/50	47	3/93	28	1/90	75	6/85	88	6/36	93	29/49
Mexico	66	8/74	90	13/63	79	17/59	73	5/86	22	4/86	33	7/82	60	7/57	47	14/69
Netherlands	74	1/53	93	10/70	86	5/73	66	3/41	11	0/10	36	3/31	78	2/54	78	6/64
P.R.China	19	2/95	15	1/97	23	1/98	6	0/99	12	0/99	7	0/100	9	0/99	13	1/98
Poland	40	0/81	69	2/50	58	4/52	13	0/59	9	0/76	31	2/57	27	1/70	32	2/55
Russia	17	0/99	53	4/91	67	4/91	5	1/99	11	1/98	22	1/98	22	0/93	12	1/98
S.Africa	25	3/88	29	3/91	49	13/72	56	3/89	25	1/89	12	1/97	29	2/86	22	5/88
Spain	73	9/48	85	6/69	86	7/65	28	1/79	12	2/77	55	5/72	87	18/36	59	7/66
Sweden	74	0/62	93	1/65	92	1/61	54	1/74	14	1/91	58	1/74	89	18/42	83	2/63
Switzerland	89	11/50	91	14/56	93	14/63	69	11/55	19	2/92	65	12/68	89	10/50	87	14/61
Thailand	55	3/18	51	3/25	64	5/37	14	1/6	37	2/12	23	0/12	49	6/20	39	2/17
UK	88	2/65	96	7/78	94	7/77	35	1/93	27	1/87	70	5/85	55	2/78	87	8/77
US	53	1/30	90	11/51	86	15/51	76	16/58	77	12/24	61	5/51	51	2/23	70	12/51

Source: A Young & Rubicam Europe, Brand Asset™ Valuator Study, 1994.

Note: The database consists of a survey of 30,000 consumers in 21 countries across 6,000 global and local brands and 120 product categories.
[1] Awareness: respondents were asked to rate on a 7-point scale (1 = never heard of, 7 = extremely familiar) their "overall awareness of the brand as well as their understanding of what kind of product or service the brand represents." The figures correspond to the % of respondents answering 2 or above.
[2] First figure: % of respondents indicating that they "use or buy regularly/often"; 2nd figure: % of respondents indicating that they have "never used or bought."

Methodology: Correspondence analysis of respondents' ratings of the brand on 24 image attributes.

How to read the map: The further away a country is plotted from an attribute, the less the people in this country associate that attribute with the brand. Countries that are close to each other tend to have a similar perception of the brand. Two dimensional maps are presented. The percentage of variance explained by the third dimension is 13.1% for Benetton, 14.6% for Esprit, 12.9% for The Gap, 11.2% for Lacoste.

Benetton
% of variance explained: horizonal axis (factor 1): 39%, vertical axis (factor 2): 15.4%

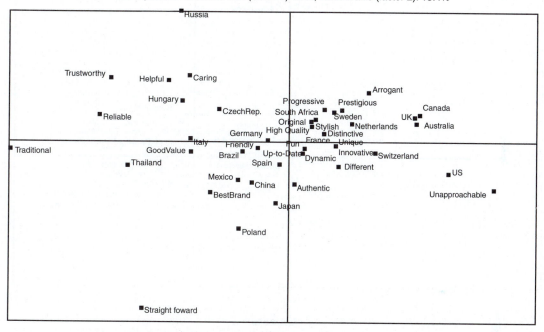

Esprit
% of variance explained: horizontal axis (factor 1): 20%, vertical axis (factor 2): 18%

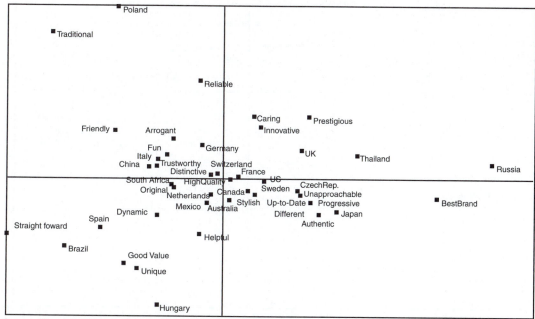

Source: Young & Rubicam Europe, Brand Asset™ Valuator, 1994

C-561

EXHIBIT 13B (continued) *A Perceptual Map of Benetton, Esprit, The Gap and Lacoste in 21 Countries (A Young & Rubicam Europe, Brand Asset™ Valuator Survey)*

The Gap
% of variance explained: horizontal axis (factor 1): 22%, vertical axis (factor 2): 15.4%

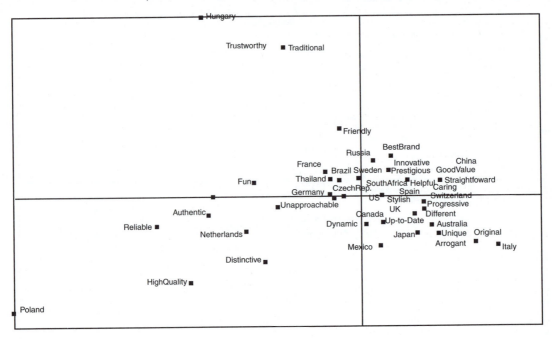

Lacoste
% of variance explained: horizontal axis (factor 1): 31.7%, vertical axis (factor 2): 17.9%

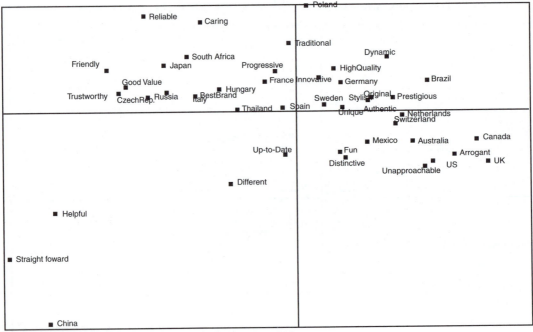

Source: Young & Rubicam Europe, Brand Asset™ Valuator, 1994

EXHIBIT 13C *The Benetton Brand Power Grid Across 21 Countries*

Methodology: The Power Grid plots respondents' perceptions of a brand on two dimensions: Brand Vitality and Brand Stature. Brand Vitality is a combination of Differentiation and Relevance while Brand Stature combines Esteem and Familiarity. *Differentiation:* The extent to which the brand is perceived to be "Distinctive," "Unique," and "Different"; *Relevance:* The extent to which respondents perceive the brand to be "appropriate [for them] personally"; *Esteem:* The extent to which respondents "think or feel highly about the brand" or consider it to be "best brand in its category"; *Familiarity:* Overall awareness of the brand as well as understanding what kind of product or service the brand represents.

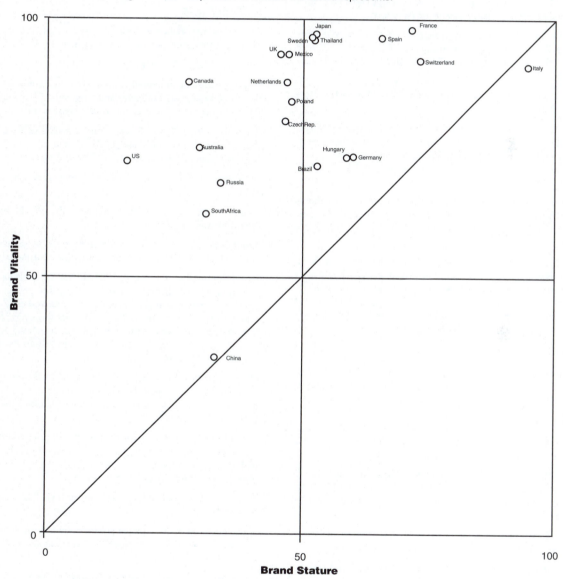

Source: Young & Rubicam Europe, Brand Asset™ Valuator, 1994

C-563

NOTES

1. On 16 October 1995, US$ 1 = L1602.10

2. Quotes not otherwise attributed in this section and the next are from: Luciano Benetton and Andrea Lee, *Io e i miei fratelli*, Sperling e Kupfer Editori, 1990 (translated by the authors).

3. In 1996, there were still a few *Merceria* shops and a very small number of shops called *Tomato* or *Fantomax*.

4. "We quickly realised that finance was not for us. We came out of it in 1987, just before the crash, having made a few tens of billions of lire," Gilberto Benetton in *Les Echos*, 20–21 January 1994.

5. A. Lee, "Profiles: Being Everywhere," *The New Yorker*, Nov. 10, 1986.

6. In 1994, European Union member countries were as follows: Belgium, Denmark, France, Germany, Ireland, Italy, Greece, Luxembourg, Netherlands, Portugal, Spain, United Kingdom. Austria, Finland, and Sweden joined the EU on 1 January 1995.

7. Disagreements over the globalisation strategy led to Palmeri's amicable departure in 1990. He returned in 1992 to leave again in February 1995. He was replaced by Carlo Gilardi, a career banker.

8. Asked by the *Daily Telegraph* (27/2/95) about the link between clothing and these activities, Gilberto answered, "There is no synergy with textiles but this group must grow and be developed." He also told *Libération* (9/3/95), "Growth in our traditional areas had limits. . . . We need to develop our heritage. . . . we have many [14] children."

9. *Io e i mei fratelli.*

10. Luciano Benetton, "Franchising: How Brand Power Works," in P. Stobart, ed., *Brand Power*, New York University Press, 1994.

11. *Io e i mei fratelli.*

12. Full-scale models of these layouts can be seen on a mock "Benetton Street" at Benetton's headquarters.

13. In March 1995, London-based Nota Bene, in collaboration with the UK's largest mail-order company, Grand Universal Stores, secured exclusive rights to sell Benetton products through mail order in the UK.

14. W. Ketelhohn, "An Interview with Aldo Palmeri of Benetton," *European Management Journal*, September 1993.

15. In addition, Benetton had 271 "shops in stores" and concessions in the U.S.

16. In the same period, The Gap grew from 900 to 1,400 stores.

17. "The Faded Colors of Benetton," *Business Week*, International Edition, 10 April 1995.

18. "Bosnia: Store Opening Symbolises Sarajevo's Reawakening," *Los Angeles Times*, 13 September 1995.

19. Benetton's sales have always relied upon a few highly successful models. For example, in 1994, the crew-neck navy blue pullover accounted for 40 percent of the winter sales in France.

20. *Io e i mei Fratelli.*

21. *Io e i mei Fratelli.*

22. Two years later, Benetton fired JWT and set up United Colors Communication as a full-service agency.

23. *Financial World*, 17 September 1991, p. 41.

24. In 1993, spending amounted to 5.7 percent to finance the TV launch of Tribù, a line of scents and cosmetics. The complete Benetton fragrance business was restructured in 1995.

25. This is one of 100 letters (positive and negative) published at Benetton's initiative in P. Landi and L. Pollini, eds. *Cosa C'entra L'Aids Con i Maglioni?*, A. Mondadori Editore, 1993.

26. In *Benetton par Toscani*, Musée d'Art Contemporain, Lausanne, 1995.

27. The photographer, Therese Frare, won the World Photo Award for this picture.

28. Around this time, Benetton started advertising in gay magazines, which were generally ignored by major corporations.

29. Pascal Sommariba, Benetton's International Advertising Director, countered charges of a lack of charitable giving, saying: "If a company makes 10 percent profits and takes 20 percent of it for charity, this is 2 percent of its turnover. If you take just one-third of a communication budget of, say 5 percent of turnover, you are already there and it does not look like a charitable company, it is fairer."

30. On 1 February 1995, a Paris court ruled against Benetton and awarded damages of about US$32,000. On 6 July 1995, a German court ruled that these pictures offended the dignity of HIV-infected people.

31. Ulfert Engels, the lawyer co-ordinating the 12 cases said: "Our tactic was to get Benetton to sue, otherwise we would have had to fight in an Italian court and we prefer to fight in Germany." *Marketing Week*, 3 February 1995.

32. "Germany: Benetton ends dispute with retailers." *Handelsblat*, 12 October 1995.

33. This and the next two quotes are from the article "For and Against the Benetton Approach," *Media International*, September 1993.

34. Nonetheless, he was considered "a pillar of Benetton's success" by Ciro Tomagnini, analyst with Merill Lynch in London. Rumors of Toscani's resignation on 18 April 1994 caused a drop of almost 8 percent in Benetton's share price (*The Wall Street Journal Europe*, 20 April 1994).

35. In Tamotsu Yagi, "*United Colors of Benetton: A Global Vision*," Robundo, 1993.

36. Benetton par Toscani.

37. I. G. Evans and S. Riyait, "Is the Message Being Received? Benetton Analysed," *International Journal of Advertising*, 1993, 12, 291–301 recommended adding a text to aid the interpretation as some Benetton ads could yield different interpretations by different national or cultural groups.

38. Luciano Benetton, "Franchising: How Brand Power Works."

39. In summer 1995, Benetton extended its use of Toscani's controversial images to its first global campaign for Benetton SportsSystem, the sports equipment subsidiary of Edizione.

VOS Industries: Entrepreneurship in the New Russia

J. G. Gallagher
R. S. Scott

Napier University

INTRODUCTION

For hundreds of years the Russians lived under centralising, autocratic regimes. In April 1985, Gorbachev's Perestroika was to change this. Perestroika introduced the seeds of a democratic political system and the beginnings of a market economy that was to supplant the failing Marxist model. Inevitably, the outcome was a situation of unparalleled complexity.

The All Russia Association of the Blind (VOS) had been established in 1925. The creation of such an organisation reflected the view commonly held in the developed world that disabled members of society should be given employment opportunities, whether in open industry or under specialised supervision. The aim was to ensure their full participation in life.

VOS was structured around "enterprises" that were training and manufacturing centres employing visually impaired workers. These enterprises also acted as the focus for the delivery of the organisation's welfare services. The level of provision varied from enterprise to enterprise and included health services, schools, recreation and leisure facilities, housing, holidays, and free or subsidised food.

As expected of an organisation founded during the old regime, it had a bureaucratic structure. There were, in 1995, 189 specialised enterprises spread throughout Russia supported by a central board and a training centre, both in Moscow (see Exhibit 1).

The Central Board, in the centre of Moscow directly opposite the old KGB Headquarters, has an elected president who wields absolute power. Since 1986 this position has been held by Alexander Neumavakin, a former tank commander who was blinded in a military accident.

Soon after his appointment, Neumavakin restructured the Central Board and in the process cut staff levels from 210 to 100. A former employee suggested that the motive was not increased efficiency but rather the creation of circumstances under which the president's own salary could be increased. It was certainly true that the trappings of power and wealth were still important: in 1994 Neumavakin ordered a top-of-the-line Saab as his official car.

The enterprises were engaged in production and teaching. They had both an employment and a social welfare role. The welfare activities were financed jointly by the government, VOS, and the employees' pension fund. The enterprises employed over 200,000 people, 50 percent of whom were visually handicapped.

The problems facing VOS were:

- **Legislation:** The flow of new legislation and accompanying regulations created many problems as directors struggled to understand the system within which they worked.

This case is intended to be used as the basis for class discussion rather than to illustrate either effective or ineffective handling of a management situation. The case was made possible by the co-operation of VOS. © 1996 J.G. Gallagher and R.S. Scott, Napier University, Edinburgh, UK.

EXHIBIT 1 *Structure of VOS*

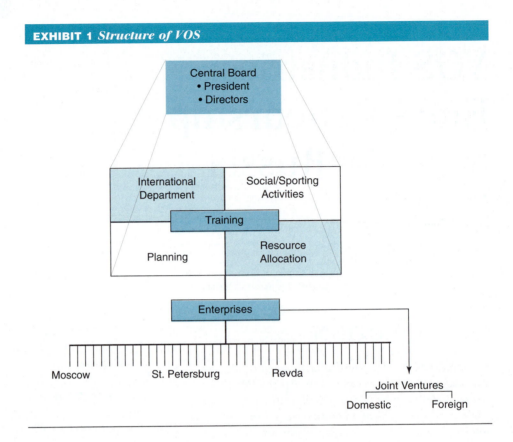

- **Economic issues:** Management and control of the economy; monetary financial systems; banking; integration into a hard currency system; customs regulations; attempts to stimulate foreign trade—all these changes added individual and collective pressures.

- **Psychological problems:** There had been generations of managers and workers that were not familiar with competitive market conditions; socialism had masked inefficiencies and ignored problems; the leadership in VOS was unprepared for the new environment.

The organisation was pulled in new directions. This created tensions and led some of those involved to question the reason for the existence of VOS. The changing circumstances required that VOS enterprises produce competitive products and, to achieve this, introduce new technologies. However, these new technologies were not seen to co-exist readily with the technologies appropriate to workshops for the blind.

In the 1980s, it had been "business as usual." This meant that the enterprise operated in a stable and predictable environment. The VOS enterprises were supported within the government's overall plan and thus were guaranteed raw material supplies and market outlets. By 1989, that environment was changing. By 1993, it had changed to such an extent that approximately 80 percent of the VOS enterprises were insolvent. The winds of free enterprise and the competitive market had blown away the security that monopoly and privilege had bestowed on the enterprises. From that time on, these enterprises had to operate competitively with all the implied opportunities and threats. The cosy, comfortable Say's Law, which says that supply creates its own demand, no longer operated.

State subsidy still existed. For example, no taxes were paid on profits, soil (rates), or social and medical insurance. VOS enterprises did pay the full charge for energy—heat, light, and power. In 1990, one kilowatt of energy cost 40 kopecks. In 1995, the cost was 180 roubles. General inflation in February 1995 was running at between 15 and 30 percent per month.

The central organisation continued to control aspects of the enterprises' activities and continued to benefit from their profits. The profits of the individual enterprises were distributed as follows:

	100 Units of Profit, %
Social programmes	5
VOS Centralised Fund	30
Taxes	10–15 (roads, etc.)

The percentage of profit going to the central organisation was reduced for enterprises experiencing difficulties, and loans were made available from the Centralised Fund. When the reduction in profits was widespread, the VOS structure was affected.

Exhibit 2 shows the tripartite relationship within VOS. The enterprise in Box A generates its profit. From this profit, 30 percent is paid to the VOS Centralised Fund—Box B. The Central Board then redistributes this flow of income to cover its central services, for example, to the Training Centre—Box C.

A direct outcome of the changed conditions was the emerging commercialisation of the training arm of VOS. Here the shortfall in revenue forced a reorientation toward commercially viable activities such as providing hotel services and rented accommodations. Of more significance to the enterprises was that they now had to pay full market rate for any training they commissioned.

ENTERPRISE 13

One of the most successful of the VOS enterprises was Enterprise 13 based in South Eastern Moscow and run by Alexander Ovtin. It was established in 1948, shortly after the end of the Second World War, and by 1995 had some 400 employees.

Ovtin, who is blind, joined the enterprise as deputy director in 1973 and became director in 1980. When he became director, there was some restructuring in the enterprise resulting in job changes and dismissals. These changes were designed to improve the enterprise's operation.

The staff, from shop floor to deputy director, held Ovtin in high regard. He was seen as someone who truly appreciates the difficulties faced by the employees and he sought to do everything in his power to look after them. He was supported by a close team that had a genuine regard for the social and welfare needs of the employees and not only an interest in the "bottom line."

1995: Meeting the Challenge

For Ovtin, the chief concern was finding a way of meeting fluctuating demand with products priced competitively enough to bring an acceptable profit to the enterprise. In this sense, his dilemma was that of any business leader operating in a free market economy.

Alexander Ovtin's Attempt to Cut the Gordian Knot
In 1993, the enterprise had many debtors and few creditors. Ovtin closed the enterprise for one month

EXHIBIT 2 *Tripartite Relationship Within VOS*

to reevaluate the strategic position and direction. After the withdrawal of guarantees of raw materials and markets, the new order was fluctuating demand and competitive pricing. Rationalisation—not of employees but of equipment—was needed for the organisation to cope with these changes. An attempt was made to attract private sector investment. At the same time, the Department of Labour and Employment was approached for investment capital. No funds were raised from the private sector, but by arguing that 50 percent of the work force would otherwise be laid off, Ovtin obtained a loan of 102 million roubles at 30 percent interest from the Department of Labour and Employment. This was provided to reequip the enterprise and to create new workstations. (In the early months of 1994, the interbank rate was 200 percent.)

The steps Ovtin took to address the problems he faced were subject to and conditional upon the following:

1. **The ethos of the enterprise would not allow wholesale staff reduction. Full employment was an unbreachable parameter.**

Incentive systems were acceptable. Pay was comprised of a basic wage plus a piece rate on work completed. In 1995, the enterprise was operating at full capacity on a single seven-hour-per-day shift system. The basic rate of pay was 281 roubles per hour, or 41,400 roubles per month.

The minimum wage set by the government at that time was six times a minimum wage figure based on the price of bread: this was 20,000 roubles per annum. The actual minimum wage was therefore 120,000 roubles per annum. However, achieving basic living standards required 180,000 roubles per annum. If an enterprise paid its workers above this minimum rate, say at the cost of living level of 180,000, then a tax was levied on the difference between the minimum rate and the actual rate paid. In such a case 60,000 roubles would be taxed—at 40 percent.

The general inflation rate during the week of January 31 to February 7, 1995, was 103.8 percent, and 122.2 percent from the beginning of the year. The average cost of a basket of essential food supplies was 142,000 roubles per month. This represented an increase of 5.1 percent during the week, or 32 percent from the beginning of the year. The Ural districts experienced the lowest rise in food prices—2.2 percent. In Moscow, the cost of a basket rose by 6.7 percent during that week and cost 173,000 roubles.

Early in February, the prices of nonfood items were increasing more slowly than those on food and services. The rise was 2.8 percent in the first week in February, a slight increase over the 2.6 percent rise in January.

Late in 1994 a proposal was put before the Duma (Parliament) to increase the minimum wage to 154,000 roubles per annum. At the time it was feared that this would not be promulgated as it would cost the government too much in lost revenue.

In the period from December 1994 to February 1995, Enterprise 13 suffered losses. It was trying to maintain competitive, stable prices by not passing on the inflationary increases in its own costs. It had been able to do this because of the advance orders it had received. In February 1995, it was working on orders for August. It had no other orders on its books beyond that time.

Despite this lack of orders, Ovtin decided that wages rates, which inevitably lagged behind inflation, should be doubled from February 1995. On Thursday, February 9, 1995, the Federation Council (Duma's upper chamber) rejected the proposal to raise the national minimum wage. The decision was reversed the following day and the new minimum was 51,000 roubles per month.

2. **Improving the efficiency of the three main workshops.**

The activities undertaken in the workshops are procurement, assembly (manufacture), packing, auxiliary services (repairs), appliance manufacture for the disabled, and outwork.

The product range had been reduced significantly. Only those products that were seen to satisfy market demand were retained. New products or services, such as galvanic plating, were pursued actively on the evidence of an emerging market. The product range at that time covered furniture accessories (door hinges), low-voltage micro-circuit switches, fishing lines and weights, and circular knitting needles.

In the previous five years roughly 45 percent of output had consisted of products developed within that five-year period. Until 1993, the primary product was a micro-switch. The annual plan called for output of 3.5 million units. As government orders, particularly the special orders of the military, dried up, new customers were sought. This proved difficult to achieve and stocks began to rise. By 1994 stocks were between 700,000 and 800,000 switches. Ovtin continued to seek new outlets and to explore other applications. Some success was achieved by developing a new elevator switch to be used on old elevators still in service. New outlets were found for furniture accessories, such as door hinges. This latter item became the dominant product for the enterprise in 1993, and resources were moved from micro-switch production to door-hinge production.

In 1994, the output was approximately 6,000 hinges per day with a maximum possible output of 9,000 per day. The total 1994 output was 2 million hinges. In the first half of 1995 the output was 3 million hinges.

3. **Recognizing that the human resource is the critical element in the life of an enterprise and one that influences every operational and strategic decision.**

The average age of employees in the enterprise was 52 years. Labour turnover rates were very low. In the immediate past, no new visually disabled employees were taken on. This was mostly because the cessation of the Afghan War meant that there were fewer instances of visual impairment. The actual number of visually disabled people is determined by the Employment and Medical Commission. After 1994, a number of physically disabled workers were employed.

For VOS as a whole, this change in the composition of the work force—in particular the reduction in the provision of the number of jobs for the partially sighted—led to a regrouping of resources. Prior to 1993, a reduction in jobs would have meant that those over 70, and possibly those over 60, would have been retired. After 1993, the aim was to encourage the young visually disabled to go into business for themselves. Of a loss of 16,000 jobs, 8,000 of those concerned started their own businesses. Despite this, VOS still hoped the government would restore the lost jobs.

The ability of the enterprise to change product design was limited by the availability of technology and by the adaptability of the work force. When a new product or process was introduced, visually disabled employees were allowed one month to master it. No output norms were applied during this month. If the employee was sighted, the period was reduced to two weeks.

Ovtin recognised that such changes affected employees directly and showed his concern by ensuring that he saw some of his workers every day and by touring the factory at least once a week. He held reg-

ular meetings with the workers to inform them of plans and developments. He regularly met the trade union representative who kept him informed of workers' views. Despite the limited power of the trade union and its mainly social role, Ovtin continued to use it as a channel of communication to and from the work force.

4. **Bringing the financial affairs of the business under control.**

Between 1989 and 1995 the customer base fell by 25 percent. The level of customer default increased markedly. The government solution was a decree, in 1993/94, requiring enterprises (industrial customers) to pay in advance for finished products. Unfortunately, few enterprises were in a position to do this. For Enterprise 13 this meant that it had to extend credit to good customers and establish account chasing as a vital operating function.

Bad debts became a major feature of business life. In 1994, a further government decree allowed debts outstanding for more than three months to be written off against profits. The debt was effectively transferred to the government.

In 1994, turnover was 912 million roubles. The profit on individual products varied, but overall was approximately 42 percent. Losses on stockpiling of products amounted to over 450 million roubles.

	Stock Turnover, Days
1993	47
1994	86

In 1994, for the whole of the VOS enterprises, approximately 43 billion roubles were tied up in stock of unsold goods. In this same year, some 500 new products were introduced in an attempt to create business to replace the previously guaranteed state enterprise orders. Prior to 1993 Enterprise 13 could have expected between 74 and 76 percent of its output to go to guaranteed state enterprise orders. At the end of 1994, this figure had fallen to 25 percent.

5. **Clearly identifying the market location.**

Enterprise 13's customers were chiefly in the Moscow area, although some were in other conurbations such as St. Petersburg.

There were about 10 competitors in the main product area of furniture accessories (hinges). These firms had furniture factories employing able-bodied workers. The Enterprise 13 management believed that its own products were of better quality than those of the competition. In 1992, management held a similar view about the competitor's quality of output in the production of micro-switches.

Conclusion Ovtin's solution to the enterprise's problems was to seek new markets and introduce new products. He established a marketing department. A computer system was introduced to monitor and control distribution and to record and classify customers. A definite move was made to identify and approach furniture makers with a view to supplying them with hinges. Advertisements were placed in newspapers and on television and radio and leaflets were published.

Ovtin's efforts were boosted by further legislation passed on February 10, 1995, in which government support was pledged for the disabled of all categories. Of particular benefit was the guarantee of favourable tax rates, including some exemptions.

REVDAN ENTERPRISE

Ivan Boormatov was born in 1944, the year the first workshops at Revda were built. He was the second of five children of an ordinary peasant family. After service in the army, Ivan graduated from the Urals Polytechnic Institute. From there he went to work at a copper smelting plant. After 15 years, in 1979, he joined the Revdan enterprise as chief engineer. In 1990, he became the director.

The Revdan enterprise, located in the Central Urals, was established in 1948. The area is rich in natural resources and has a history of industrial activity stretching back to the late 18th century. In 1995, the enterprise employed some 1,250 workers of whom 430 were visually disabled. Its location was such that it served an immediate regional market of 4.5 million people; 1.5 million of these lived in Ekaterinburg, some 30 kilometres to the east.

Prior to 1990, as with all other enterprises in the VOS system, the Revdan enterprise operated in a stable and predictable environment: all VOS enterprises were accommodated within an overall government plan and were guaranteed raw materials supplies and market outlets.

The VOS enterprises suffered from the collapse of the industrial base of the Commonwealth of Independent States (CIS). The Revdan enterprise suffered an 80 percent reduction in demand for its prod-

ucts. Boormatov's approach to this problem was to introduce new products based on new technologies. His objective was to employ 50 percent visually disabled and 50 percent able-bodied people. Some of the new technologies could not be staffed by the visually disabled. This led him to make another decision: he created new enterprises that were legal entities and that, mostly, employed only the able-bodied.

These enterprises were set up to produce plastic moulds, painting, galvanic coatings, arts paintings, and stone processing.

The new enterprises would be taxed under the general taxation rules. It was therefore Boormatov's policy that the enterprises should not record a profit but should show only sufficient revenue to cover their wages and other costs. Any profits would be attributed to the Revdan enterprise.

In periods of difficulty for an enterprise, the percentage of profit going to VOS may be reduced progressively. For Revda this meant a reduction from 30 percent to 10 percent in the percentage of profit paid. However, no loans were obtained from the VOS Central Board to aid the development and introduction of new technologies.

1995: Meeting the Challenge; Ivan Boormatov's Cutting of the Gordian Knot

In 1990, the Revdan enterprise had two products. Boormatov decided that Perestroika would lead to a reduction in demand for these products:

> Perestroika was a decay process, many enterprises had large stock piles which allowed them to survive for some time. However, without new approaches our enterprise would not have survived. This process of change was inevitable if we were to survive.

During 1991/92 Boormatov held meetings to try to generate ideas for the new era. As a result, four areas were identified as being crucial and needing immediate attention:

- Development of new technologies
- Development of new products
- Computerisation, particularly in-house software
- Introduction of automation and automatic-control equipment in factories

EXHIBIT 3 *Steps Taken to Revitalize the Revdan Enterprise*

C-573

The steps Boormatov took to support his survival plan are discussed below and illustrated in Exhibit 3.

New technologies were developed and introduced. From these new technologies new products and product ranges were cultivated. A promotional effort was initiated to ensure that acceptable sales levels were achieved.

In February 1995, there were 160 items in the product range. Perhaps more importantly, lessons had been learned in the process of development. One such lesson was becoming aware of the dangers of technological failure; another was the realisation that sales and production had to be coordinated. This latter problem was tackled by dedicating 1995 as the year of marketing.

In addition to accepting the importance of the consumer, Boormatov also was aware that further work had to be done. A new orientation for management was required. He had to build a management team that could adjust to the new environment and adapt to the new philosophies that were part of the new market conditions. For a time the team constantly changed as he tried to achieve the right blend of what was a very scarce commodity: flexible and qualified personnel.

Boormatov saw the lack of good staff at the management level as a major constraint on the enterprise.

My life is not long enough for me to teach them the skills they need. They are the future, therefore, we need to train, develop, and allow them to maximise their opportunities. We communicate with educational institutions which allows me to gain knowledge of potential graduate employees. However, psychologically, my staff fears responsibility. We establish enterprises but I can't find the leaders for them.

Boormatov had a personal assistant named Vasilli. He joined the enterprise in 1982 as civil defence supervisor. He had worked in the Middle Urals Copper Smelting Factory where Boormatov was his brigade leader. He was also a product of the Urals Polytechnic Institute, graduating the same year as his director. Boormatov's comments about Vasilli were:

Vasilli feared promotion to director. Two years ago he turned it down, even though I showed him the future, mapping out the enterprise's growth— 10 people now, 30 in two years and hopefully then 100. Lack of good staff is a drawback.

Vasilli's views on the changes that had taken place and on Boormatov were revealing:

It is almost impossible to compare the enterprise with 1982. When Ivan became director, things changed drastically. He reads a lot, he always studies and organises and teaches the staff. Before Perestroika, Boormatov predicted what would happen. He sees over the mountain.

Boormatov saw communication and learning as vital aspects of the director's job. Every Monday he made sure he had no appointments that would take him away from the enterprise. This left him free to talk to the staff and production managers and to walk around the enterprise, observe, and learn. His learning took place on a broader front. He traveled to Germany, China, and the United Kingdom. From each he borrowed ideas. He read widely, particularly business periodicals but, as he said, "not textbooks."

Each Tuesday he met with his deputy directors and workshop supervisors and engineers. At these meetings strategies were discussed. He also had further private meetings, conversations, and brainstorming sessions, especially on weekends. When combined with an openness and honesty in communication, these actions made all levels of the enterprise feel well informed.

Boormatov quoted Napoleon to illustrate the cultural change he was trying to achieve.

> Every person should be a leader. Each employee should be able to achieve more for themselves than they do at present.

1993: "Everything Is in a State of Flux." (Heraclitus, 513 B.C.)

As the market for industrial lighting dried up, Boormatov decided to produce domestic lighting and to widen the product range as rapidly as possible. In the enterprise there was no experience in the production of domestic lighting. His aim was to develop a niche in the market that could be exploited. He observed:

> I had seen other plants lose their market outlets and fail. Ours was an intuitive decision to choose this product. Perhaps it was an amaetur approach but it allowed us the time to develop the courage to tackle the problem.

Boormatov and the management team became aware that growth brings its own problems. There was difficulty in increasing production in a period of inflation. Weak spots appeared regularly in both finance and production. The enterprise outgrew its structure. Originally it had only two workshops and centralised control. In 1995, it had seven workshops, five sections, and five independent enterprises and the prospect of a further five.

A clear manifestation of the turmoil created by the events of 1993 was the financial bottleneck that developed. Revda's sources of finance were as follows:

1. Investment in equipment was absorbed into costs.
2. Profit was ploughed back into the business.
3. Credit from VOS or banks was received.

Virtually all the profits made had been directed toward development and the purchase of raw materials. Wages were suppressed.

In 1994, the financial group within the enterprise was given the status of a department. Its basic functions were credit control, interpayments (barter or countertrade), and analysis of future plans and activities.

The department used manual methods to process data and, with a large information flow, found it difficult to analyse the data coming to it. This was particularly serious when the rules on taxation were changing daily and there were 1,500 suppliers and 2,000 customers.

Seventy percent of transactions were conducted on a countertrade basis. These included payments for raw materials, electricity, transport, and containers for transport. Transport costs alone accounted for 10 percent of total cost.

The enterprise obtains its energy requirements from the neighbouring copper smelting factory in exchange for which it barters or pays the factory's debt to others by barter with whatever goods it has acquired. A consequence of this system was that the enterprise opened seven retail shops in urban areas to sell the goods it had bartered as well as those it manufactured.

The enterprise started to acquire its own raw materials. With no restrictions on its choice it found its own suppliers. The major problem was that every supplier wanted payment in advance. In 1994, the enterprise met all its needs for raw materials and created a reserve for 1995. This allowed it to plan for normal working in the first quarter of 1995.

Seventy to eighty percent of the payment for its raw materials was made by countertrade. This trade was negotiated by value. Agreement on prices and on specific products was fixed and a contract was developed. For example, the Natalinsk Glass Factory (NGF) that supplies the Revda enterprise had spare capacity. Its market was all of the Russian federation where it had 30 large and 50 small customers. This had shrunk to 5 large and 40 small customers. Lack of demand for its output meant a shortage of money for NGF. Revda took over 50 percent of NGF's output. In turn, NGF took fuel, raw materials, and stock for its shop from Revda. NGF itself gave products in place of 40 percent of wages due. If such countertrade had stopped, both parties would have suffered. The flexibility of the system allowed the parties to benefit.

The countertrade chain was often very long, with five or six parties involved. Under these circumstances, calculating profit was extremely difficult. It required the determination of initial manufacturing costs, estimation of expected profit, and calculation of the changes in the rate of exchange of the rouble. As a consequence of this process, the profit levels fluctuated, and the real profit was always less than the calculated profit on which tax was paid. This was a consequence of the accounting system's inability to cope with the quantity and complexity of information.

	Profit (Roubles)
1990	650,000
1995	7 billion, 770 million

On average, business to a value of three billion roubles was carried out by countertrade. In 1994, this represented 68 percent of profit.

Products

Boormatov had a simple strategy: "Quantity then Quality." Supporting this strategy was a strong emphasis on cost control and efficiency. When the market for industrial lighting collapsed, the enterprise was saved by converting to the production of domestic lighting. The new product—hand-decorated lamps—did not have a rival in the market when it was introduced. By 1995, 60 people were producing these items. They were engaged on a competitive basis—their artistic skill. They were not employed directly by the enterprise; rather they constituted a separate enterprise.

The production norm for the shade decoration section was 100 pictures per day. A smaller experimental unit, employing two art school graduates, tried to produce higher quality artwork. Here there were no norms. Lamp shades in total account for 30 percent of the volume of the enterprise's output. An increased volume of output was made possible by the

purchase of an adjoining gym from a failed enterprise. Space had been at a premium in the enterprise.

Operational and functional skills were developed in the process of developing lamp shade production. These skills could then be transferred to other areas. The production philosophy that underpinned this development and that was applied progressively to other areas was to create the products in micro-sections of workers. It was an idea that originated in a stone-cutting shop set up in 1992 under the guidance of a graduate of the art school. The system of organising the work was transferred to the lamp-painting section and it worked. Boormatov believed that the system created a culture and a team spirit that led the micro groups to fight to keep their identities. It also made it easier for the enterprise to retain its skilled workers.

Markets

The markets for Revdan products extend throughout Russia and into Belorussia, the Ukraine, Kazakstan, and the Far East. In these markets, too, financial restrictions constrained market development and so a wide range of Revdan goods and spare parts were exchanged for raw materials. The VOS network helped to establish contacts so that a total of six regions and two republics were served.

The range of products was split into domestic and industrial. Domestic items, such as leather goods, stoneware, wooden products, and domestic lamp shades, were sold directly to the retail trade and made a higher profit than industrial products such as street lamps. The enterprise retained street lamps as a product because it expected its fortunes to revive in the future.

Despite the uncertainties of the market, product branding became an issue. All products received a certificate for sale if they met a minimum quality standard. Without the certificate, they could not be sold. By 1995, the enterprise had obtained 36 certificates and was expecting to be awarded a further 10 in the next year.

Physical distribution had been a problem. Boormatov's solution was for Revda to have its own fleet of vehicles. It had 65 lorries and control of transport costs—approximately 100,000 roubles per month. As part of the marketing effort, representatives of the enterprise attended trade fairs and exhibitions in every region. Advertising was done through newspapers, radio, and television and by using the Register on Enterprise. All the VOS enterprises made 1995 the Year of Marketing. Boormatov said, "We introduce new items but without an effective marketing programme we will fail."

The process of computerisation, which could help marketing, was slow. There was computer equipment but it was underused. In marketing it was mainly used for processing low-grade work such as advertising support or producing leaflets or labels and packaging artwork.

Technology

The low level of technology used within the enterprise was a major weakness. Boormatov's solution was to buy better technology. Manufacturers in the West either refused to build the needed equipment or priced it out of reach of Revda. Boormatov decided that the equipment needed could be built in-house.

Equipment that was built in-house included an electrostatic plating system, a vacuum extrusion system, and elevators. The West would have taken a year to build and install an electrostatic plating system. By creating his own experimental brigade to design and build the system, the cost was held to 50 million roubles and the time was cut by three-quarters.

In January 1995, new, fully automatic, thermoplastic machines were introduced (made internally) to produce car mirrors, etc. The machines which they replaced had been purchased second hand from the Ukraine in 1991. Initially, lack of experience of their use resulted in a number of explosions.

The enterprise manufactured about 50 percent of its requirement of nonstandard machinery using its own designs. The next project the experimental brigade will tackle will be the production of glass-making equipment.

Boormatov's next project is uncertain but could be revolutionary, in a free market sense.

Walt Disney Co.

Anthony Claro
Michelle Hill
Eric Maxwell
Russell Porter
Angela West

INTRODUCTION

At the March 3, 1997, stockholders' meeting, Michael Eisner, CEO of Walt Disney Co., made a startling acknowledgment. "People are assuming that Walt Disney Co. is going to keep growing at the same rate as it has in the past. We're having some problems with ABC, and I just wouldn't assume that."[1] This acknowledgement indicates that Disney may have reached a crossroads and that its growth may be leveling off. In 1996, the company's earnings were lower than they were the previous year, a first in the Eisner era. Some analysts say that Disney's $19 billion acquisition of Cap Cities/ABC has placed a strain on its growth potential.[2]

Even more startling than Eisner's comment was the stockholders' dissatisfaction, given that Disney's stock price had risen $19 in the six months prior to the meeting. The stockholders' dissatisfaction stemmed from several sources. First, the stockholders expressed dismay at the $100 million payout to former Disney president Michael Ovitz. They also expressed concern over Eisner's new contract, which ties his compensation to earnings per share over a target growth rate of 7.5 percent. Eisner's previous contract had tied his earnings to return on equity.

This case was prepared under the direction of Robert E. Hoskisson. The case is intended to be used as the basis for class discussion rather than to illustrate either effective or ineffective handling of an administrative situation.

Furthermore, the stockholders were unhappy with the results of the Cap Cities/ABC merger. ABC's ratings continued to lag behind other networks, and its ad revenues were falling. As a result of ABC's poor performance, Disney's net income decreased from approximately $1.4 billion in 1995 to $1.2 billion in 1996 (see Exhibits 1, 2, and 3).[3]

Eisner faces three major challenges to satisfy stockholders. First, he must formulate a growth strategy. Second, he must continue to create synergies between each of the divisions and find ways to integrate ABC. Third, Eisner must develop successors that can continue Disney traditions and growth in his absence.

MEDIA AND ENTERTAINMENT INDUSTRY: DEREGULATION, TECHNOLOGY, AND DEMAND

The large-scale consolidation of the media and entertainment industry largely has been attributable to the anticipation of regulatory changes. The recent broad changes in broadcasting regulations have caused many networks and other media organizations to position themselves for major strategic realignments. This regulatory environment influences the

EXHIBIT 1 *Consolidated Statement of Income (in millions, except per share data)*

Year ended September 30,	1996	1995	1994
Revenues	$18,739	$12,151	$10,090
Cost and expenses	−15,406	−9,685	−8,118
Accounting changes	−300		
Operating income	$3,033	$2,466	$1,972
Corporate activities and other	−309	−239	−279
Interest expense	−479	−178	−120
Investment and interest income	41	68	130
Acquisition-related costs	−225		
Income before income taxes	$2,061	$2,117	$1,703
Income taxes	−847	−737	−593
Net income	$1,214	$1,380	$1,110
Earnings per share	$2	$3	$2

Source: Walt Disney Co. Annual Report, 1996.

size of networks, which may cause media companies and others seeking to diversify to reevaluate future options. Certain regulations are now being considered that undoubtedly will change the strategic focus of firms competing in the entertainment industry.

In October 1995, the cable industry changed when Congress repealed the 1984 Communications Act. The Communications Act of 1984 was outdated and no longer addressed the realities and capabilities of current and projected communications technologies.[4] Now known as the Communications Act of 1995, the bill permits companies to own more than one station in a marketplace and increases the allowed viewership of a station group to 35 percent of the national audience.[5] In addition, the act opened phone service to competition, freed cable rates, allowed phone companies to carry video, and approved the use of V-chips to block out programs not suitable for children.[6] This congressional act and its implementation by the Federal Communications Commission (FCC) was intended to increase cable television competition, thus decreasing the rates for cable TV. As an industry deregulation, the bill will spur new investments in cable-TV systems and TV stations. This is critical to cable providers because they are now able to expand cable lineups and move into the telephone business, thus increasing competition.[7] At this time, many large media companies were positioning themselves for this radical change. Many "megamergers," such as the Disney/Cap Cities/ABC merger and Westinghouse's acquisition of CBS, took place at this time.

The Telecommunications Act of 1995 has also played a role in the redefinition of the communications industry. With the merger of Walt Disney and Cap Cities/ABC, the FCC had to review the applicability of the Telecommunications Act. Under the act, the current policy states that any newspaper-broadcast cross-ownership is prohibited. The FCC stated that it would make a ruling about ownership rules within the next 12 months. At present, the FCC has given Disney a temporary waiver until the matter can be reviewed further.

The four major networks, including ABC, have been experiencing competition from new sources. The recent advancement in satellite technology will increase the possible number of channel outlets to 500 in the near future. Furthermore, cable networks continue to gain market share from the four major network television stations, FOX, ABC, CBS, and NBC. In the 1970s, the big three (excluding FOX) held 91 percent of the market. That share dwindled from 61 percent in 1994 to 57 percent in 1995.[8] However, brand image is needed to compete effectively in such a diverse environment, and the networks still reach 98 percent of U.S. households.[9] Thus, the networks remain an instantaneous way to achieve a distribution channel for the mega-media players such as Disney, Time Warner, and News Corp.

EXHIBIT 2 *Consolidated Balance Sheets (in millions)*

September 30,	1996	1995
Assets		
Cash and cash equivalents	$ 278	$ 1,077
Investments	454	866
Receivables	3,343	1,793
Inventories	951	824
Film and television costs	3,912	2,099
Theme parks, resorts and other property, at cost		
Attractions, buildings and equipment	11,019	8,340
Accumulated depreciation	−4,448	−3,039
	6,571	5,301
Projects in process	1,342	778
Land	118	111
	8,031	6,190
Intangible assets, net	17,978	
Other assets	2,359	1,757
	37,306	14,606
Liabilities and Stockholders' Equity		
Accounts payable and other accrued liabilities	6,374	2,843
Income taxes payable	582	200
Borrowing	12,342	2,984
Unearned royalty and other advances	1,179	861
Deferred income taxes	743	1,067
Stockholders' equity		
Preferred stock, $.01 par value; $.025 at September 30, 1995		
Common stock, $.01 par value; $.025 at September 30, 1995	8,576	1,226
Retained Earnings	7,933	6,990
Cumulative transaction and other adjustments	39	38
	16,548	8,254
Less Treasury Stock, at cost 8 mill. shares and 51 mill. shares	462	1,603
	16,088	6,651
	37,306	14,606

Source: Walt Disney Co. Annual Report, 1996.

The growing U.S. economy has had a profound effect on the revenue streams of the entertainment industry in general and the four major networks in particular. Optimism by analysts for the demand of major consumer products such as cars, movies, retail, and fast-food categories has led to a greater desire to advertise these products.[10] According to Larry Hoffner, head of network sales for NBC, "Network television is the single most valuable marketing tool."[11] "Upfront" sales, which are advertising time slots sold before the television season begins, reached $6 billion for the first time.[12] NBC, with the popular Thursday Night "Must See TV" lineup, had the most upfront sales for 1997 with $2.1 billion, and ABC was second with $1.6 billion.[13]

While upfront sales account for 80 percent of a network's revenues, other factors determine broadcaster competitiveness. Broadcasters compete for subscribers, viewers, and listeners. Affiliates, the local stations that networks supply with creative content, and independent stations, those that lack an affiliation with the major networks, comprise the

EXHIBIT 3 *Consolidated Statement of Cash Flows (in millions)*

Year ended September 30,	1996	1995	1994
Net Income	$ 1,214	$1,380	$1,110
Change to Income Requiring Cash Outlay			
Amortization of film and television cost	2,966	1,383	1,199
Depreciation	677	470	410
Amortization of intangible assets	301		
Accounting changes	300		
Other	22	133	231
Changes In (Including the impact of ABC acquisition)			
Investments in trading securities	85	1	
Receivables	−426	−122	−280
Inventories	−95	−156	−59
Other assets	−160	−288	−81
Accounts and taxes payable and accrued liabilities	−455	415	136
Unearned royalty and other advances	274	161	−141
Deferred income taxes	−78	133	283
	3,411	2,130	1,698
Cash Provided by Operations	4,625	3,510	2,808
Investing Activities			
Acquisition of ABC, net of cash acquired	−8,432		
Film and television cost	−3,678	−1,886	−1,434
Investments in theme parks, resorts, and other property	−1,745	−896	−1,026
Purchases of marketable securities	−18	−1,033	−953
Proceeds from sales of marketable securities	409	1,460	1,494
Other		67	−968
	−13,464	−2,288	−2,887
Financing Activities			
Borrowings	13,560	786	1,866
Reduction of borrowings	−4,872	−772	−1,315
Repurchases of common stock	−462	−349	−571
Dividends	−271	−180	−153
Exercise of stock options and other	85	183	76
	8,040	−332	−97
Increase (Decrease) in cash and cash equivalents	−799	890	−176
Cash and cash equivalents, beginning of period	1,077	187	363
Cash and cash equivalents, end of period	278	1,077	187
Supplement disclosure of cash flow information			
Interest paid	379	123	99
Income taxes paid	689	557	320

Source: Walt Disney Co. Annual Report, 1996.

television market. Affiliates and independent stations have different cost structures. Affiliates receive payment for broadcasting network shows. The prime-time slots during the evening hours are the peak hours for showcasing network television. Because affiliates receive payment for broadcasting and the prime-time hours are filled with network television, their operating costs are low as compared to those of independents. Independents must fill prime-time slots with syndicated television because network television such as United Paramount Network (UPN) or Warner Brothers (WB) is limited. Independents must pay for syndicated shows, which increases their operating costs. Despite the higher costs, independents have more local advertising time to allot since national advertising occurs primarily on the network affiliates. A Standard & Poor's industry survey projects a 5.3 percent growth in television advertisement revenue compounded annually over the next five years. Radio advertising revenue is expected to increase 7.9 percent over the same time period.[14]

Both cable and direct satellite broadcasters (DSBs) receive the bulk of their revenues from subscriber fees.[15] The cable industry has a long history of providing inferior service to customers. However, despite quality issues and the maturity of the industry, the number of subscribers is expected to increase 3 percent annually over the next four years.[16] The cable industry also expects a 13.4 percent increase in advertisement in 1997 to $6.85 billion.[17] DSB subscribers mushroomed 152 percent from 1995 to 1996.[18] Standard and Poor's expects revenues to grow at an annual rate of 46.7 percent from 1996 to 2000.

COMPETITIVE ENVIRONMENT

The major shift toward consolidation of media enterprises involves the integration of content-driven companies such as Disney with distribution-driven companies such as ABC. These realignments have created powerful media conglomerates including Disney, News Corp., and Time Warner (see Exhibit 4). Media include outlets other than the four major networks, such as publishing, movies, cable, music, and retail products. Other considerations, such as diversification at Westinghouse, have driven this merger frenzy.

Disney is a primary example of a media company leveraging its core competencies from movie production to the retail outlet. Disney distributes a movie such as *Hercules* and uses its animation property rights to market toys, clothes, and other items related to the movie. Although not considered media, theme parks complement large media conglom-

erates by increasing brand recognition. Disney has a unique advantage in this area.

Unlike a media outlet, physical travel is required to experience a theme park. Furthermore, theme parks cater to different market segments. Parks such as Six Flags, Sea World, and Busch Gardens are more regional and can be experienced in one day. Disney World and Universal Studios are national, if not global, attractions. Visitors expect to spend up to a week at these theme parks/resorts. Theme parks allow media companies an opportunity to promote their brand image through life experiences, such as meeting Mickey Mouse at Disney World. This is becoming a more popular method of attaining brand recognition. For instance, Six Flags has an alliance with Warner Bros. to provide Looney Tunes characters to enhance the park's atmosphere.

Disney is the dominant competitor in the theme park industry. The Disneyland development gave Disney a first-mover advantage it has yet to relinquish. Its progress into other park creations keeps it ahead of its primary competitors: Universal Studios, Six Flags, and Busch Gardens. Although important, the trend toward theme parks is a less significant issue for Disney than the broader industry dynamics of creative content and finding appropriate channels of distribution, that is, broadcasting.

Time Warner

Turner Broadcasting merged with Time Warner (TW) in 1995. Ted Turner became the vice chairman of Time Warner, Inc., and Gerald Levin remained chairman and CEO. According to the Time Warner Home Page, "Time Warner journalists and artists create one new product for every half-hour of the day." Time Warner believes it creates value through "three interlocking fundamentals: creativity, libraries, and branded content combined with branded distribution."[19] Time Warner was able to increase the size of its animated library with the addition of Hanna-Barbara to its Warner Bros. line. With the acquisition of Turner Broadcasting, quality news channels such as CNN and award-winning journalists became a part of the Time Warner family. CNN complements the large publishing arm of TW, including *Time* and *Sports Illustrated* magazines. Furthermore, TW gains access to many more cable channels through brand name recognition provided

EXHIBIT 4 *Holdings of Disney and Competitors*

Company/ Holding	Time Warner Inc.	The Walt Disney Co.
Television	WB television network; Warner Bros. Television; international Warner Bros. Programming	Walt Disney Television (International); Touchstone Television; Walt Disney Television Animation; Buena Vista Television; ABC Inc.: ABC Television Network (ABC News and ABC Sports); 10 TV Stations; Disney/ABC International Television
Cable	CNN: Headline News, CNN/SI (sports net), CNN Airport, CNNfn (The Financial Network); HBO: HBO Family Channel, HBO Animation; Cinemax; TNT; TBS Superstation; Cartoon Network; Turner Classic Movies (TCM)	ESPN; The Disney Channel; A&E Networks: A&E, The History Channel; Lifetime Television
Radio		ABC Radio Network (ABC News and ABC Sports); 26 Radio Stations: 11 AM, 15 FM; working to start Radio Disney (24-hour children's radio)
Feature Films	Warner Bros. Studios; Warner Home Video; Warner Bros. International Theaters	Walt Disney Motion Picture Groups: Walt Disney Pictures, Touchstone Pictures, Hollywood Pictures, Caravan Pictures, Miramax Films; Buena Vista Pictures Distribution: Buena Vista International, Buena Vista Home Video, Buena Vista Home Entertainment
Publications	Time Inc.: *People, Sports Illustrated, Time, Entertainment Weekly, Fortune,* specialized magazines; Time Warner Trade Publishing; Time Life Books; Warner Books; Little Brown Publishing; books; international magazines	Daily newspapers; 50 trade publications; W. magazine; Discover magazine; family magazines; books; comics
Music	Warner Music Group: Atlantic, Elektra, Warner Bros., Warner Music International, Warner/Chappell Publishing Co., 50% of Columbia House	Walt Disney Records; Hollywood Records
Retail	Warner Bros. Consumer Products; 161 Warner Bros. Studio Stores Worldwide	101 Disney Stores worldwide; clothing; toys; licensing ventures
Misc.	Book-of-the-Month Club Inc.; Warner Bros. theme parks; CNN Interactive	Disney theme parks: Walt Disney World, Disneyland, Epcot Center, building Disney's Animal Kingdom and Disney's Calfornia Adventure, parks in Europe and Asia; Walt Disney Imagineering; Anaheim Sports: Anaheim Mighty Ducks NHL team; Walt Disney Theatrical Productions; Disney Online; ABC Online; Disney Interactive (CD-ROMs and online products); Disney Cruise Line
Investments/ joint ventures		25% of Anaheim Angels baseball team; interests in international broadcasting companies; partnership with Ameritech to develop new cable TV networks

Source: The Top 25 Media Groups, *Broadcasting and Cable,* July 7, 1997, 22–28.

EXHIBIT 4 *continued*

News Corp. Ltd. (FOX)	Viacom (Paramount)	General Electric (NBC)	Westinghouse Electric Corp. (CBS)
Fox Broadcasting Co.: 23 U.S. TV stations; Fox broadcast network; Fox News Productions Inc.; 20th Century Fox Television; Twentieth Century Fox/Astral Television Distribution Ltd.; Evergreen Television Productions Inc.; Fox Children's Network Inc.	Television Signal Corp.; Riverside Broadcasting Co.; 13 TV stations; Paramount Communications Inc.; 75% of Spelling Entertainment Group, Inc.	NBC; 11 TV stations	CBS TV Network; CBS Entertainment; 14 TV Stations; CBS News/Sports
Fox Pay-Per-View services; fX Networks	MTV; Showtime; Nickelodeon/Nick at Nite; VH1; USA Networks; Comedy Central; All News Channel 12 radio stations	Seven cable/satellite networks including CNBC and Court TV	77 radio stations
Fox Motion Pictures; 20th Century Fox Film; Columbia TriStar Films; 21st Century Fox Film; Cinemascope Products; Fox Animation Studios; Mirror Pictures; Van Ness Films; Fieldmouse Production; Fox West Pictures; San Antonio Film Features; Fox Home Video; 20th Century Fox Home Entertainment	Paramount Pictures; Viacom Productions		
HarperCollins US Inc.; Murdoch Publications; News T Magazines; News America Publications Inc.	Simon & Schuster; Macmillan Publishing USA; technical and professional books		
Fox Music; Fox Records; Fox Children's Music Inc.; Fox Film Music; Fox On Air Music; Fox Broadcast Music	Music By Video Inc.		
	Blockbuster Entertainment Corp.: home video, music		
Fox Movietone News; Fox Net; Fox Sports Productions	Discovery Zone; Paramount Parks (5 theme parks); audio/visual software; Games Productions Inc.		
			MSNBC

by TNT, Cartoon Network, TBS, and HBO. Time Warner officials point out that "in the 1995/96 season, cable networks grew to 30% share of the total primetime viewing audience."[20]

News Corp. (FOX)

Rupert Murdoch has established a worldwide media conglomerate. In 1985, News Corp. chairman and CEO Murdoch acquired FOX. Historically a movie producer, Murdoch set out to utilize FOX as a television distribution outlet as well. FOX network was initially a lowly regarded fourth player in the network television market. Since its advent, FOX has produced such popular shows as "The Simpsons," "Married with Children," and "COPS." A high degree of "titillation television" led to ratings growth at the expense of the other three networks. By the mid 1990s, the FOX network enhanced its legitimacy with the procurement of National Football League and Major League Baseball television rights. Murdoch continued to increase the visibility of FOX and News Corp. with the acquisition of the Los Angeles Dodgers, a national cable sports network, and Pat Robertson's Family Channel. Furthermore, News Corp. is actively fostering the worldwide Direct Satellite Broadcasting (DSB) market.

Viacom (Paramount Pictures)

Viacom's largest holding is Paramount Pictures, a major motion picture studio that has existed since 1912.[21] A major portion of Viacom's assets is the Paramount movie library, which includes hits such as *The Ten Commandments*, *The Godfather* series, and *Forrest Gump*. But, movies are not Paramount's only business. The Paramount television studio is responsible for the "Star Trek" series. "Cheers," "I Love Lucy," and "The Honeymooners" are also a part of the Paramount TV library. Other Viacom franchises include MTV, Nickelodeon, and VH1. As a consequence, Viacom is a major participant in the music and children's television industries. Furthermore, Viacom has a large publishing arm; Simon & Schuster "is the world's largest English-language, educational, and computer book publisher."[22] In 1994, Viacom acquired Blockbuster Entertainment, a large retail outlet for movie videocassettes and music prod-

ucts. Thus, Viacom is a vertically integrated producer, distributor, and multimedia operator.

Westinghouse (CBS)

Westinghouse diversified its holdings with the purchase of CBS. Unlike the integration of content and distribution with the competitors described above, Westinghouse's purchase of CBS integrated two distribution companies. This purchase included local CBS television and radio stations. Industry insiders view the merger negatively. Former CBS executive Laurence Tisch was notoriously conservative. The CBS vision was considered reactive as the firm was selling its major assets, which resulted in considerable immediate earnings for CBS. Shareholders and Tisch benefited from management's actions in the short term. Westinghouse will have to revive the CBS network with an infusion of investment capital. This will be more difficult than liquidating parts of the firm to increase earnings. Despite CBS's internal problems, sporting events such as the NCAA Basketball Tournament, Master's golf tournament, and NCAA football are popular programs. In addition, television shows such as "The Price Is Right" and "The Late Show with David Letterman" are mainstays.

General Electric (NBC)

NBC is the top-rated network in the television marketplace. Its ability to continually market new situation comedies around the success of a few mainstays is one example of its competitiveness. For instance, the slogan "Must See TV" started with the network's Thursday night lineup of "Seinfeld" and "Frasier." NBC's weekend programming is filled with sports shows, such as the NFL, Major League Baseball, and the increasingly popular National Basketball Association, which have loyal viewers. General Electric, much like Westinghouse, holds NBC as a part of its diversification strategy. The financial strength of General Electric (unlike Westinghouse) increases NBC's competitiveness. NBC executives have created cable channels such as CNBC and MSNBC, which compete for the CNN-type viewer. MSNBC is unique in that it is a joint venture with software power Microsoft. This strategic alliance is designed to integrate the television medium with the information superhighway, the Internet.

HISTORY AND CURRENT BUSINESS

Walt Disney

Walter Elias Disney was born in Chicago on December 5, 1901. Walt was one of five children and came from a family that encouraged hard work and tight purse strings. As he was growing up, Walt amused himself by drawing. At the age of 14, he enrolled in the Kansas City Art Institute and began making small animated films. However, Walt never made any profits from the films because he lacked financial knowledge and business acumen.[23]

In 1923, Walt moved to California to join his brother, Roy Disney. Together they began producing animated films. Their first major hit was *Oswald the Lucky Rabbit*. However, to continue to produce these films, they had to borrow money from a New York distributor. As the character became increasingly popular, the costs to produce the films increased. Therefore, Walt asked the distributor for a raise. Instead of receiving a raise, Walt was told that he did not own the rights to Oswald, the New York distributor did. So, Walt and Roy developed the now-famous Mickey Mouse character.

To develop Mickey Mouse, Walt and Roy formed a partnership in which their mission was to provide the public with a quality product. However, their plans were often bigger than their resources and they had to take Walt Disney Productions public in 1940. Walt Disney Productions was known for taking risks and striving continuously to venture into innovative forms of entertainment. With the support of the growing Walt Disney Productions company, Walt and Roy decided to open a theme park in 1955 called Disneyland Park. This park introduced a whole new form of entertainment, the outdoor theme park. As a result, the company began to be perceived as being on the leading edge of the entertainment industry.[24]

After Walt

At the time of Walt's death in 1966, the plans for Walt Disney World in Orlando had just begun. At first, Walt's death did not affect the company; he still had a strong presence in the company and had shared his vision so well that the corporate officers were able to carry on, as Walt had once said, "after Disney."

However, this growth eventually began to slow and changes could be seen within the corporation. The company was no longer taking risks on new ventures and projects and was gradually losing touch with what the public perceived as quality and innovative entertainment. The synergy between the different divisions of the Walt Disney Company had once been considered a key strength, but now it was weakening. At this time, Saul Steinberg initiated a takeover bid for the company. However, Disney's officers were able to maintain control of the company with the help of many loyal stockholders.[25]

Michael Eisner

In 1984, Michael Eisner left Paramount to become the CEO of the Walt Disney Company.[26] Eisner's original strategy was to change the company, venture into new businesses, and make acquisitions. His goal was to "continue to nurture and protect the Disney brand and to reaffirm core values such as our commitment to quality and service."[27] Eisner's first priority was to revamp Disney's film and production division and develop original and creative full-length animated films.[28] Not only did Eisner reinvent the film and production division, he also turned Disney into a premier entertainment giant with enough revenue and power to acquire Capital Cities/ABC, Inc. The majority of growth Eisner achieved came from businesses (see Exhibit 5) that did not exist prior to his tenure as the firm's CEO.[29] These businesses stemmed from acquisitions and internal ventures.

Theme Parks and Resorts

Disney's theme parks and resorts include the Walt Disney World Resort in Florida and Disneyland Park in California. The company also owns a National Hockey League team called the Mighty Ducks of Anaheim and has part ownership of and general management responsibility for the Anaheim Angels baseball team. Disney also receives royalties from its partially owned theme parks in Tokyo and Paris (Tokyo Disneyland and Disneyland Paris). The theme parks and resort division grew 13 percent in 1996, which brought revenues to $4.5 billion. This growth is expected to increase with the 1998 addition of another theme park at the Walt Disney World Resort in Florida, Disney's Animal Kingdom. Eisner also expects Disney to profit from the company's addition

EXHIBIT 5 *Disney's Expansions Since Eisner Became CEO in 1984*

- International film distribution
- Television broadcasting
- Television station ownership
- Expanded ownership of cable systems
- Radio and radio network broadcasting
- Ownership of radio stations
- Newspaper, magazine, and book publishing
- The Disney Stores
- The convention business
- Live theatrical entertainment
- Home video production
- Interactive computer programs and games
- Online computer programs
- Sites on the World Wide Web
- Ownership of professional sports teams
- Telephone company partnership
- Disney Regional Entertainment
- Disney Cruise Line

Source: Walt Disney Co. Annual Report, 1996.

of a Wide World of Sports Complex in Orlando. This complex will be the home of the Amateur Athletes Union and the Harlem Globetrotters. It will also serve as the spring training site for the Atlanta Braves. With the help of Disney's new regional entertainment division, Disney Regional Entertainment, the company will continue to offer a diverse range of entertainment and educational experiences to children and families around the world. Disney Regional Entertainment will be in charge of operating a variety of entertainment experiences across the United States using sports concepts, interactive entertainment centers, and children's play centers. The division will run these businesses with the help of Disney's creative entertainment talents and the popularity of the Disney brand.[30]

Film

Disney's film and television division had numerous successes in 1996. It released several hit films such as *Toy Story* (Disney), *Con Air* (Touchstone Pictures), and *G.I. Jane* (Hollywood Pictures). Almost one out of four movie tickets sold each day in North America is for a Disney movie. This is not hard to believe because Disney has several different film and televi-

sion companies within this division. When Eisner became CEO in 1984, his goal was to reinvent this division. In 1984 Disney released only two live-action motion pictures. However, under Eisner's leadership, in 1996 Disney increased this number to 29, which does not include the 36 films released by the Disney-owned Miramax. However, because the film market is saturated, Disney plans to reduce the number films it releases annually. This strategy will allow Disney to focus on releasing more "high-impact, star-driven films with greater potential."[31]

Broadcasting

Disney's broadcasting division has grown significantly over the last two years. February of 1996 brought about the completion of the Disney and Capital Cities/ABC merger. Upon this merger, Disney transferred three of its units to this division: The Disney Channel, Buena Vista Television, and Disney Television International. With the Capital Cities/ABC merger, Disney gained control of several distribution channels, including ESPN, A&E Networks, and Lifetime Television. Combined, these three channels have over 90 million subscribers. ESPN is the most widely distributed cable programming network in the country. Combining Disney Television International and ABC allows Disney to form a powerful distribution operation.[32]

Consumer Products

Disney's consumer products division continues to be fueled by the popularity of the company's main characters such as Mickey Mouse, Donald Duck, Goofy, and Minnie Mouse. It also has experienced sales gains from its new animation characters such as the Little Mermaid, 101 Dalmatians, Hercules, and the Lion King. The consumer products division includes The Disney Stores, Disney Interactive, and Disney Online. Under Eisner's leadership, The Disney Stores, which promote all of the Disney characters, now have 550 units in 11 countries. Disney is also taking advantage of its merger with Capital Cities/ABC by opening an ESPN store in Southern California and a Club Disney in Thousand Oaks, California. The ESPN store will be a theme retail store offering sports merchandise with logos of various professional and college teams, sports memorabilia, and a large number of items with the ESPN logo.[33] Club Disney will offer children a virtual-reality-type play site to enjoy with their families.

Disney Interactive has increased its market share to 15 percent in the education category with its Animated Story Books. It has already released five of the best-selling children's software titles in history, such as the "Toy Story Animated Storybook" and the "Lion King Activity Center." Disney Online's goal is to increase the firm's presence on the World Wide Web via its two Web sites, Disney.com and Family.com. Disney.com acts as Disney's primary marketing and promotional Web site, while Family.com is considered a site for parents and children to visit and enjoy together.[34]

Walt Disney Imagineering

The Walt Disney Imagineering division is responsible for planning, creating, and developing all Disney resorts, theme parks, communities, and regional entertainment sites. It uses its cutting-edge creative, technical, and development abilities to update the appearance and design of all the theme parks and to create cutting-edge and creative themes for the new resorts. As a new project, the division has aided in the creation of the community outside of Walt Dis-

ney World in Florida called Celebration. This community will combine the latest telecommunication and personal computer technology with the essence of a comfortable community atmosphere. Also, this division is currently working on Disney's restoration of the New Amsterdam Theater in New York City.[35] Through the restoration of the New Amsterdam Theater, Disney hopes to lead others in an effort to recreate 42nd Street as the Main Street USA of show business.[36]

LEADERSHIP AND GOVERNANCE

In 1994, two major events occurred that changed Eisner's outlook. First, there was the accidental death of Eisner's good friend and number two man, Frank Wells. Several months later, Eisner himself had a brush with death when he suffered a heart attack and required bypass surgery. These events were complicated by shakeups at Disney. Jeffrey Katzenberg, then head of Walt Disney Studios, left Disney after Eisner refused to give him Wells's job. (Wells was president of Disney.) In addition, Katzenberg took several key executives with him. However, Eisner came back from these events with a renewed focus and a new plan.[37]

Eisner appointed Richard Nanula, then CFO, as president of Walt Disney Stores and then made an unusual move by bringing in someone from outside of the entertainment industry. He recruited Steve Bollenbach from Marriott to fill the position of CFO. Bollenbach was known for his ability to finance deals, and it was Bollenbach who convinced Eisner to go ahead with the ABC acquisition.

The building block of Eisner's diversification strategy was the acquisition of Capital Cities/ABC, Inc. The Disney-ABC merger combined a content company with a distribution company. Through ABC, Disney acquired distribution capabilities in radio, television, and print. ABC owned 20 radio stations as well as network and cable television distribution channels. ABC's network television capability included eight television stations and foreign stations. ABC's cable television holdings included ESPN, A&E, and Lifetime. Finally, ABC's print distribution operations included a wide variety of magazines.

To implement Disney's diversification strategy,

Eisner recruited long-time friend Michael Ovitz to serve as president of Walt Disney, Inc. Ovitz came from Creative Artists Agency, the talent agency he founded and led. Ovitz was known for his ability to recruit talent and complete business transactions. For example, Ovitz was instrumental in the Sony/MCA merger and the MCA/Seagrams merger.[38]

Eisner also appointed Bob Iger president of ABC, Inc. At the time of the merger, Iger was six months from succeeding Tom Murphy as CEO of ABC, Inc. Iger had spent his entire career at ABC.[39]

Amid controversy, Ovitz left Disney with a $100 million settlement just over a year after he signed with Eisner. Reasons cited for Ovitz's departure included Eisner's hands-on approach to management.

In addition, Bollenbach and Iger reported to Eisner rather than to Ovitz, which Ovitz claimed made it difficult to run things. Therefore, this new top-management team quickly broke apart.

Eisner has not replaced Ovitz. Instead, he has focused on building a team of number-twos (see Exhibit 6). Rather than having just one number-two person, Eisner decided to have several number-two persons for each segment of the business: Joe Roth, Walt Disney Motion Pictures; Bob Iger, ABC; Gerry Laybourne, Disney/ABC cable; Steve Bornstein, ESPN/ABC Sports; Judson Green, Walt Disney attractions; and Richard Nanula, president and CFO.[40] (Nanula was moved back to the position of CFO when Bollenbach left Disney for other opportunities.)

EXHIBIT 6 *Disney Management and Board of Directors*

Corporate Officer:
- Michael D. Eisner, Chairman and Chief Executive Officer
- Richard D. Nanula, President and Chief Financial Officer
- Sanford M. Litvack, Senior Executive Vice President and Chief of Corporate Operations

Major Subsidiaries, Divisions and Affiliates
- Robert A. Iger, President, ABC, Inc.
- Steven M. Bornstein, President and Chief Executive Officer, ESPN, Inc./President, ABC Sports
- Geraldine Laybourne, Executive Vice President, Disney/ABC Cable
- Judson C. Green, President, Walt Disney Attractions
- Joe Roth, Chairman, Walt Disney Motion Pictures

Board of Directors
- Reveta F. Bowers, Headmistress, Center for Early Education
- Roy E. Disney, Vice Chairman of the Company
- Michael D. Eisner, Chairman and CEO of the Company
- Stanley P. Gold, President and CEO, Shamrock Holdings, Inc.
- Sanford M. Litvack, Senior Executive Vice President and Chief of Corporate Operations of the Company
- Ignacio E. Lozano, Jr., Chairman, La Opinion
- George J. Mitchell, Attorney, Former U.S. Senator
- Thomas S. Murphy, Former Chairman and CEO, Capital Cities/ABC, Inc.
- Richard A. Nunis, Chairman, Walt Disney Attractions
- Leo J. Donovan, President, Georgetown University
- Sidney Poitier, Actor, Director, and Writer
- Irwin E. Russell, Attorney
- Robert A. Stern, Senior Partner, Robert A. M. Stern Architects
- E. Cardon Walker, Former Chairman and CEO of the Company
- Raymond L. Watson, Vice Chairman, The Irvine Co.
- Gary L. Wilson, Chairman, Northwest Airlines Inc. and Northwest Airlines Corp.

Source: Corporate Yellow Book, 1997.

The lack of a successor at Disney is a major concern of shareholders and analysts. Eisner is noted for his ability to manage every aspect of the entertainment business. His previous experience at Paramount and ABC trained him in everything from movie production to television programming. Eisner is credited with being "one of those rare executives who is a shrewd businessman with keen creative skills."[41] Many wonder if anyone can fill his shoes. Still, Eisner refuses to appoint a successor and Disney's board of directors has been criticized for seemingly sitting idle. Some believe that Disney would benefit from having a board of directors that will stand up to Eisner's forceful dual CEO/chairman role and demand that he create a successor plan.

There are other areas of Disney's corporate governance that concern shareholders and analysts. Under Eisner's 1989 contract, his bonus was tied to the company's return on equity. Since Eisner took over, Disney has achieved average return on equity of about 20 percent a year, bringing Eisner a bonus of $9.9 million in 1994 and $14 million in 1995. Eisner's new contract abandons the return-on-equity formula. Instead, the bonus is now tied to his ability to increase earnings per share over a target growth rate of 7.5 percent. Also included in Eisner's contract is the option for 8 million Disney shares (3 million premium options and 5 million regular options) with an estimated value of anywhere from $195 to $400 million.[42] The premium options have an exercise price higher than the fair market value at the time of the grant, meaning that they become valuable only if the company's stock price rises substantially.[43]

During the annual meeting in 1997, shareholders sent a strong message about executive pay, independence of the board of directors, and the multimillion-dollar payout to former president Michael Ovitz. About 8 percent of the shareholders voted against Eisner's new contract, which will keep him at the company until 2006.[44] Approximately 12.7 percent of the company's institutional and individual investors voted to withhold their support to reelect five members of the company's board.[45] This withholding for reelection of incumbent directors represents the largest "no" vote against a major U.S. corporation since Archer-Daniels-Midland Co.'s annual meeting in October 1995.[46] When expressing disappointment about the company's payout to Ovitz, one investor suggested that Eisner personally pay for the loss.

In response to shareholders' discontent, Eisner acknowledged that Ovitz's tenure at Disney was "a mistake." Eisner said that "because he did not make it in our company, we had to give Mr. Ovitz his stock options". At another point in the meeting, Eisner brought investor Warren Buffett, who has a large stake in Disney, onstage to deliver a short speech about how happy he is with the company. "I advise you to keep your stock," Mr. Buffet said.[47]

H. Carl McCall, who controls 3.4 million Disney shares as sole trustee of New York's public pension fund, said he was voting the fund's shares against the two proposals, in part, because of the $100 million plus severance package paid to Ovitz. In addition, 24 of the 103 pension funds belonging to the Council of Institutional Investors are voting against the board reelections, the Eisner pay package, or both. The pension funds, including the California Public Employees' Retirement System and New York's Common Retirement Fund, hold at least 22 million of Disney's more than 680 million outstanding shares.[48]

McCall argues that the board has not demonstrated sufficient independence, which corresponds with criticism that is heard frequently about Disney. Twelve of the sixteen members of the Disney board have personal or professional ties to Eisner or the company. These ties include Eisner's personal lawyer, the principal of an elementary school Eisner's children attended, a Disney-commissioned architect, and three former Disney executives.[49] John Dreyer, a Disney spokesman, responds to McCall by indicating that Disney's stock performance has appreciated 2,000 percent during Eisner's $12\frac{1}{2}$ years, and that the market cap has risen to $53 billion from $2 billion. Dreyer maintains that the board should be measured ultimately by the performance of the company, not by some other, arbitrary standards. He argues: "I'm sure (the pensions) have what they would consider more independent boards in their holdings that are not performing well. If they really don't think the company is a good investment, they really should sell their stock."[50]

COMPETITIVE CHALLENGES

Television Disney's television holdings (ABC, ESPN, Disney Channel, Lifetime, A&E, and E!) have varied success rates. ABC currently is experiencing record low ratings and profits. However, the other channels are thriving. The critical issue is whether ABC can revive its prime-time schedule to compete against NBC and CBS. ABC's programming problems are compounded by unclear leadership. Insiders say that "Jamie's [Jamie Tarses, president, ABC Programming] the figurehead. If you've got a big piece of business, you call Iger. Eisner's going to set the tone and the strategy—and he'll set the schedule."[51] The big question is who will lead ABC in its effort to regain market share.

Movie Studios Can Disney achieve its goal of producing fewer but better films than the competition? Disney must continue to compete in all markets: adults (Miramax, Hollywood Pictures, Caravan, and Touchstone), adolescents (Touchstone and Hollywood Pictures), and children (Disney and Touchstone). In addition, Disney must deal with increas-

ing competition in animation pictures from Fox and Dreamworks SKG.

Consumer Products Consumer product success is tied to Disney's animated film success. Because of Disney's lack of hit animation films in the last year, retailers no longer see Disney products as guaranteed hits.

Theme Parks Disney faces increasing competition in the theme park segment. The challenge for Disney is to sustain the first-mover advantage by expanding the Disney experience more quickly and efficiently than competitors.

Will Michael Eisner be able to satisfy stockholders? What should his growth strategy be? Will he be able to manage the complexity that is associated with the size and maturity of Disney as a result of the ABC acquisition? Should he continue his current expansion strategy? What implications do the firm's corporate governance practices have for top management's strategy?

NOTES

1. D. Turner, 1997, Disney's go-go growth days may be going, going, gone, *Los Angeles Business Journal*, March 3, 1.
2. Ibid.
3. Ibid.
4. N. M. Minow, The Communications Act, *Vital Speeches of the Day*, April 15, 1995, 389–392.
5. W. Cohen and K. Hetter, 1995, Tomorrow's media today, *U.S. News & World Report*, August 14, 47–49.
6. M. Levinson, 1995, Mickey's wake-up call, *Newsweek*, August 14, 27.
7. M. Burgi, 1995, Still bound by big brother, *Mediaweek*, May 15, 25–27.
8. Ibid.
9. Ibid.
10. E. Rathbun and D. Petrozzello, 1996, Infinity: Only the beginning?, *Broadcasting and Cable*, July 1, 7.
11. Ibid.
12. Ibid.
13. Ibid.
14. Standard & Poor's Industry Survey, "Broadcasting & Cable," June 26, 1997, 1.
15. Ibid, p. 2.
16. Ibid.
17. Ibid, p. 3.
18. Ibid, p. 7.
19. http://www.pathfinder.com
20. Ibid.
21. http://www.viacom.com
22. Ibid.
23. L. Maltin, 1995, *The Disney Films*, 3rd Edition (New York: Jessie Film Ltd.), 1–2.
24. L. Marabele (ed.), 1990, *The Walt Disney Company, International Directory of Company Histories* (Chicago: St. James Press), 2:172–174.
25. Ibid.
26. "Eisner, Michael" Microsoft® Encarta® 1996 Encyclopedia © 1993–95 Microsoft Corporation.
27. Walt Disney Co. Annual Report, 1997.
28. "Eisner, Michael" Microsoft® Encarta® 1996 Encyclopedia © 1993–95 Microsoft Corporation.
29. Walt Disney Co. Annual Report, 1997.
30. Ibid.
31. Ibid.
32. Ibid.
33. Turner, Disney's go-go growth days may be going, going, gone, 1.
34. Walt Disney Co. Annual Report, 1997.
35. Ibid.
36. F. Rose, 1996, "Can Disney tame 42nd Street?", *Fortune*, June 24, 94–98.
37. M. Meyer, 1995, How Eisner saved Disney and himself, *Newsweek*, August 14, 28.
38. E. S. Reckard, 1996, Ovitz out as Disney president, *Associated Press Online*, December 12.

39. M. Gunther and J. McGowan, 1997, Can he save ABC? Robert Iger faces the toughest challenge of a charmed career, *Fortune*, June 23, 90.

40. R. Grover, 1997, Michael Eisner defends the kingdom, *Business Week*, August 4, 73.

41. S. Coe, 1995, Disney's Michael Eisner: No Mickey Mouse CEO, *Broadcasting & Cable*, August 7, 16.

42. Turner, Disney's go-go growth days may be going, going, gone, 1.

43. B. Orwall, 1997, Disney chief's stock options exercise irks some, but street remains calm, *Wall Street Journal Interactive Edition*, http://www.wsj.com December 5.

44. B. Orwall, 1997, Shareholders express anger over pay to Ovitz and Eisner, *Wall Street Journal Interactive Edition*, http://www.wsj.com February 25.

45. Holders of 12.7% of Disney shares oppose 5 directors, *Dow Jones Newswires*, February 25, 1997.

46. B. Orwall, 1997, Shareholders express anger over pay to Ovitz and Eisner.

47. Ibid.

48. McCall to vote NY Pension Fund 3.4M shares against Disney board, *Dow Jones Newswires*, February 24, 1997.

49. New York State—2-: Disney says criticisms are misguided, *Dow Jones Newswires*, February 24, 1997.

50. Ibid.

51. Gunther and McGowan, 1997, Can he save ABC? Robert Iger faces the toughest challenge of a charmed career, *Fortune*, June 23, 90.

C-591

Warner-Lambert Company

Andrew Inkpen

Thunderbird, The American Graduate School of International Management

On August 1, 1991, Melvin Goodes became chairman and chief executive officer of Warner-Lambert Company (WL). In 1990, WL enjoyed the most successful year in its history. Worldwide sales rose 12 percent to $4.7 billion, earnings per share increased 18 percent, and shares in WL stock appreciated by 17 percent. Each of WL's three core businesses—ethical pharmaceuticals, nonprescription health care products, and confectionery products—generated increased sales. In international markets, WL continued to make new inroads.

Despite the success of recent years, Goodes was convinced that trouble was looming at WL. In March, the U.S. Food and Drug Administration (FDA) turned down the company's approval application for the Alzheimer's drug Cognex. WL had hoped that Cognex would be its next blockbuster drug. With the patent expiring on Lopid, WL's best-selling drug, in early 1993, the Cognex decision was a major blow. At the same time, the growth of private-label health care products in the United States was slowing the expansion of powerful brands such as Listerine mouthwash and Schick razors. Without a major new drug and with domestic sales slowing, restructuring at WL looked unavoidable. Of in-

creasing priority was the need to restructure WL's international operations. Although a proposal to globalize the company had been shelved by the board in 1989, Goodes knew that he could no longer afford to wait. Given the changing configuration of global markets and pressures for increased operating efficiencies, globalization appeared to be a necessity for WL.

WARNER-LAMBERT BACKGROUND

WL's origins can be traced to 1856 when William Warner opened a drugstore in Philadelphia. After 30 years of experimenting with the formulation of pharmaceutical products, Warner closed his retail store and started a drug-manufacturing business.

William Warner & Co. was acquired in 1908 by Henry and Gustavus Pfeiffer. Gustavus later wrote, "We changed thinking locally to thinking nationally." For the next 30 years the company made many acquisitions and, by 1939, had 21 marketing affiliates outside the United States and several international manufacturing plants. The largest acquisition was Richard Hudnut Company, a cosmetics business, which was sold in 1979.

During the 1950s and 1960s, the company continued to make acquisitions, both in the United States and overseas. In 1952, the company, now known as Warner-Hudnut, acquired Chilcott Labo-

Copyright 1996 Thunderbird, The American Graduate School of International Management. All rights reserved. This case was prepared with research assistance from Chris Hormann and with assistance from Professor John Zerio for the basis of classroom discussion only and is not intended to illustrate either effective or ineffective management.

ratories, a pharmaceutical company founded in 1874. In 1955, with sales at $100 million, Warner-Hudnut merged with the Lambert Company to form the Warner-Lambert Pharmaceutical Company. The Lambert Company's best-selling product was *Listerine* mouthwash, a product developed in 1879.

In 1962, WL acquired American Chicle. American Chicle was formed in 1899 with the consolidation of three major chewing gum producers. The Halls cough tablets brand was acquired in 1964. In 1970, Schick wet-shave products were acquired. Also in 1970, WL merged with the pharmaceutical firm Parke, Davis, & Company (Parke-Davis). Parke-Davis was founded in 1866 in Detroit. In the 1870s, Parke-Davis collaborated with the inventor of a machine to make empty capsules for medications. This established the forerunner of WL's Capsugel division, the world's largest producer of gelatin capsules. In 1901, Parke-Davis introduced the first systematic method of clinical testing for new drugs. In 1938, Parke-Davis introduced the drug Dilantin for the treatment of epilepsy and 1946, began marketing Benadryl, the first antihistamine, in the United States. In 1949, Chloromycetin, the first broad-spectrum antibiotic, was introduced.

The 1980s was a period of restructuring for WL. The company divested more than 40 businesses, including medical instruments, eyeglasses, sunglasses, bakery products, specialty hospital products, and medical diagnostics. The divested businesses accounted for $1.5 billion in annual sales but almost no profit. In 1991, WL had operations in 130 countries and, of its 34,000 employees (down from 45,000 in 1981), nearly 70 percent worked outside the United States. WL had 10 manufacturing plants in the United States and Puerto Rico and 70 international plants in 43 countries. Over the previous five years, WL's earnings grew 15 to 20 percent annually. In 1990, sales growth occurred in both the U.S. and international markets and in all worldwide business segments. About 52 percent of company sales were in the United States. Exhibits 1 and 2 provide a summary of financial information.

WARNER-LAMBERT BUSINESS SEGMENTS

In 1990, WL had three core business segments: ethical pharmaceuticals; nonprescription health care products, commonly referred to as over-the-counter (OTC); and confectionery products. Beyond these segments, WL had several other product sectors: empty gelatin capsules for the pharmaceutical and vitamin industries, wet-shave products, and home aquarium products. Exhibit 3 shows sales by region and business segment. Exhibit 4 describes the segments and the leading brands in each.

The Ethical Pharmaceutical Industry

The ethical pharmaceutical industry involved the production and marketing of medicines that could be obtained only by prescription from a medical practitioner. Seven markets (United States, Japan, Canada, Germany, United Kingdom, France, and Italy) accounted for about 75 percent of the world market, with the largest single market, the United States, accounting for approximately 30 percent of the total. The pharmaceutical industry was very fragmented, with no single firm holding more than a 4 percent share of the market. The five largest firms—Merck (U.S.), Bristol-Myers Squibb (U.S.), Glaxo (U.K.), SmithKline Beecham (U.K.) and Hoechst (Germany)—accounted for less than 15 percent of world market share.

The pharmaceutical industry was also highly profitable. Between 1986 and 1989, the industry ranked first in the United States on both ROS and ROI. With new medical advances on the horizon and an aging population in the developed countries, the industry was expected to continue growing steadily. However, significant challenges were facing the drug companies. The cost and time to develop new drugs had increased substantially. The drug development cycle from synthesis to regulatory approval in the United States was 10 to 12 years. The average development cost per drug was $230 million (up from $125 million in 1987), with various phases of testing and clinical trials accounting for roughly 75 percent of the cost.

There was significant risk associated with pharmaceutical R&D. It was estimated that for every 10,000 compounds discovered, 10 entered clinical trials and only one was developed into a marketable product. Of those brought to market, only about 20 percent generated the necessary sales to earn a positive return on R&D expenditures. In 1990, the FDA approved just 23 new drugs, 15 of which were

EXHIBIT 1 *Warner-Lambert Financial Information*

	1990	1989	1988	1987	1986
	(Dollars in millions, except per share amounts)				
Results for Year					
Net Sales	$4,687	$4,196	$3,908	$3,441	$3,064
Cost of Goods Sold	1,515	1,383	1,352	1,170	1,053
Research and Development Expense	379	309	259	232	202
Interest Expense	69	56	68	61	67
Income Before Income Taxes	681	592	538	493	446**
Net Income	485	413	340	296	309**
Net Income per Common Share	$ 3.61	$ 3.05	$ 2.50	$ 2.08	$ 2.09**
Year-End Financial Position					
Current Assets	$1,559	$1,366	$1,265	$1,253	$1,510
Working Capital	458	335	240	279	540
Property, Plant, and Equipment	1,301	1,13	1,053	960	819
Total Assets	3,261	2,860	2,703	2,476	2,516
Long-Term Debt	307	303	318	294	342
Total Debt	537	506	512	444	585
Stockholders' Equity	$1,402	$1,130	$ 999	$ 874	$ 907
Common Stock Information					
Average Number of Common Shares					
Outstanding (in millions)*	134.3	135.3	136.1	142.5	148.0
Common Stock Price per Share:*					
High	$70 3/8	$59 3/8	$39 3/4	$43 3/4	$31 9/16
Low	49 5/8	37 1/4	29 15/16	24 1/8	22 1/2
Book Value per Common Share*	10.44	8.38	7.36	6.37	6.32
Cash Dividends Paid	204	173	147	127	118
Cash Dividends per Common Share*	$ 1.52	$ 1.28	$ 1.08	$ .89	$ .80
Other Data					
Capital Expenditures	$ 240	$ 218	$ 190	$ 174	$ 138
Depreciation and Amortization	$ 120	$ 105	96	$ 79	$ 68
Number of Employees (in thousands)	34	33	33	34	31

Source: Warner-Lambert Annual Report, 1990.
*Amounts prior to 1990 were restated to reflect a two-for-one stock split effected in May 1990.
**Includes a net nonrecurring credit of $8 million pretax (after-tax $48 million, or $0.32 per share) in 1986.

approved already in Europe. Nevertheless, R&D was the lifeblood of the industry, as explained by a senior WL manager:

Product renewal is critical. Firms must continue to generate a stream of new products. These need not be blockbusters. The key is new products. Eventually, each of these products will become a generic [unbranded] product so in any given year, there must be a certain percentage of new products.

If a firm did develop a blockbuster drug, the rewards were enormous. New drugs sold at wholesale prices for three to six times their cost. Zantac™, an ulcer drug sold by Glaxo, had worldwide sales of $2.4 billion in 1990. This was Glaxo's only product in the top 200 best-selling prescription drugs. Tagament™, a competing ulcer drug produced by SmithKline Beecham, had 1990 sales of $1.2 billion.

Two other challenges faced pharmaceutical companies. Spiraling health care costs in the major markets brought increased pressure on the companies to

EXHIBIT 2 *Warner-Lambert Financial Information by Business Segment*

(Millions of Dollars)

Segment	Net Sales			Operating Profit			Research and Development Expenses		
	1990	1989	1988	1990	1989	1988	1990	1989	1988
Health Care									
Ethical Products	$1,555	$1,324	$1,213	$560	$465	$420	$(299)	$(240)	$(204)
Nonprescription									
Products (OTC)	1,526	1,370	1,296	367	311	305	(38)	(35)	(27)
Total Health Care	3,081	2,694	2,509	927	776	725	(337)	(275)	(231)
Confectionery	1,054	1,003	918	208	195	187	(17)	(15)	(13)
Other Products	552	499	481	119	101	92	(25)	(19)	(15)
Research and Development Expenses				(379)	(309)	(259)	$(379)	$(309)	$(259)
Net Sales and Operating Profit	$4,687	$4,196	$3,908	875	763	745			
Interest Expenses				(69)	(56)	(68)			
Corporate Expenses				(125)	(115)	(139)			
Income Before Income Taxes				$681	$592	$538			

(Millions of Dollars)

Segment	Identifiable Assets			Depreciation and Amortization			Capital Expenditures		
	1990	1989	1988	1990	1989	1988	1990	1989	1988
Health Care									
Ethical Products	$1,063	$ 892	$ 916	$ 43	$ 39	$ 36	$ 88	$ 71	$ 72
Nonprescription									
Products (OTC)	619	513	489	20	16	15	49	37	37
Total Health Care	1,682	1,405	1,405	63	55	51	137	108	109
Confectionery	564	490	459	23	21	20	44	33	33
Other Products	442	406	387	24	20	19	41	42	40
Subtotal	2,688	2,301	2,251	110	96	90	222	183	182
Corporate	573	559	452	10	9	6	18	35	8
Total	$3,261	$2,860	$2,703	$120	$105	$96	$240	$218	$190

Source: Warner-Lambert Annual Report, 1990.

hold down their prices. The growing use of price controls and restricted reimbursement schemes in international markets were reducing the drug companies' flexibility to recoup R&D investments. Finally, there was competition from generic drugs once a patent expired. Legislation passed in the United States in 1984 made it very easy for generic drugs to enter the market after the patent on the original drug expired. In the United States, 50 percent decreases in sales were not uncommon in the first year after a patent expired. In Europe, the degree of generic erosion was not as dramatic because once a branded drug was on a list of officially sanctioned drugs eligible for state reimbursement, a long lifespan for the drug was reasonably certain.

Although the chemical compounds of the major drugs were identical around the world, the pharmaceutical industry structure varied tremendously from country to country. In Europe, each of the 12 EC member states had different regulations for

EXHIBIT 3 *Warner–Lambert Financial Information by Geographic Segment ($000,000)*

	Ethical Pharmaceuticals	Nonprescription Health Care	Confectionery Products
United States	$ 871	$1066	$ 507
Canada	60	95	107
Mexico	11	49	88
Latin America (excluding Mexico)	47	100	127
Japan	80	122	80
Asia/Australia (excluding Japan)	66	115	16
Europe/Middle East/Africa	582	369	129
Total	$1717	$1916	$1054

Note: The figures in Exhibits 2 and 3 show different totals for the Ethical Pharmaceutical and Nonprescription Health Care segments. In 1991, WL redefined its business segments. The Capsugel business ($162 million in sales) was reclassified to the Pharmaceutical segment. The wet-shave and *Tetra* businesses ($390 million in sales) were reclassified to the Nonprescription Health Care segment.

EXHIBIT 4 *Warner-Lambert Care Businesses and Primary Products*

Business Segment

1. Ethical Pharmaceutical Products (Parke-Davis)
   - Brand-name pharmaceuticals and biologicals, including analgesics, anesthetics, anti-inflammatory agents, antihistamines, anticonvulsants, influenza vaccines, cardiovascular products, lipid regulators, oral contraceptives, psychotherapeutic products
   - Generic pharmaceuticals (Warner Chilcott), manufacturer and marketer of generic pharmaceutical products

2. Nonprescription Health Care (OTC)
   - Over-the-counter pharmaceuticals marketed under the Parke-Davis name

   - Other consumer health care products

3. Confectionery (Gums and Mints)
   - Chewing gum, breath mints, sugarless gum, bubble gum, chocolate candy

4. Other Products
   - Empty hard-gelatin capsules for use in pharmaceutical manufacturing (used by Warner-Lambert and other companies)
   - Wet-shave products
   - Home aquarium products

Leading Brands

Dilantin (epilepsy), *Dilzem* (angina and hypertension), *Lopid* (lipid regulating), *Accupril* (hypertension), *Loestrin* (contraceptive), *Ponstan* (analgesic)

Benadryl (antihistamine), *Benylin* (cough syrup), *Sinutab* (sinus medication), *Anusol* (hemorrhoid treatment)
Listerine (mouthwash), *Efferdent* (denture cleanser), *Lubriderm* (skin lotion), *Rolaids* (antacid), *Halls* (cough drop)

Chiclets, Dentyne (chewing gum), *Certs, Clorets* (breath mints and chewing gum), *Trident* (sugarless gum), *Bubblicious* (bubble gum), *Junior Mints* (chocolate candy)

Capsugel

Schick

Tetra

registering, pricing, and marketing drugs. Government health care systems paid for a majority of the consumer's cost of drugs, and the prices of drugs were fixed in negotiations between the drug companies and the government. The result was different prices in different countries and a growing problem with parallel imports. Consumers in France and Spain paid about 72 percent of the EC average, and in Ireland and the Netherlands, prices were about 130 percent of the average. Most European governments had the legal authority to force the transfer of a drug patent from one firm to another in the event that the firm with the patent was unwilling to manufacture the drug.

There was also national differences in the type and amount of drugs consumed. In France, the consumption of drugs was the highest per capita in the world. In Japan, physicians made most of their income by dispensing drugs. Moreover, the Japanese government allowed high prices for breakthrough drugs to stimulate medical innovation. As well, many of the drugs used in Japan were unique to that market. For example, several best-selling Japanese drugs dilated blood vessels in the brain on the unproven theory that this reversed senility. In other parts of the world, the lack of controls over intellectual property made it very difficult for drug companies to operate.

WL's Pharmaceutical Business WL's ethical pharmaceutical line was marketed primarily under the Parke-Davis name. Included in the pharmaceutical sector was Warner-Chilcott, a manufacturer of generic prescription drugs primarily for the United States. Sales of WL ethical products were $1.6 billion in 1990, a 17 percent increase over the previous year. WL ranked 17th among the world's leading drug firms by turnover.

WL's best-selling drug was Lopid, which reduces cholesterol. In 1991, projected sales for Lopid exceeded $480 million. Dilantin, an antiepileptic drug, had sales of $145 million and was a worldwide leader in its category. Other leading drugs were Loestrin, a contraceptive, and Accupril, a cardiovascular drug. Although the FDA postponed approval of Cognex by asking for additional data, WL continued to have high expectations for the product and clinical testing continued.

The firm's drug discovery program was focused on two areas: cardiovascular diseases, such as hyper-

tension and congestive heart failure, and disorders of the central nervous system. In recent years, WL had made a major effort to strengthen its pharmaceutical R&D. Over the past five years, the number of scientists had increased 60 percent to 2,600, and 1991 R&D spending for pharmaceuticals was expected to be close to $350 million, an increase of 12 percent over 1990. These efforts were beginning to pay off: WL had several new pharmaceutical products awaiting FDA approval.

OTC Industry

The OTC health care industry was structured very differently from the ethical drugs industry. With ethical drugs, there was a unique relationship between consumer and decision maker: consumers paid for the drugs but physicians made the buying decisions. As a result, the marketing of ethical pharmaceuticals was directed at prescribing physicians, who were not particularly concerned about prices. With OTC products, the consumer made the buying decision, although often based on advice from a physician or pharmacist. To compete successfully with OTC products, significant investments in consumer marketing and distribution were required. Some of the largest drug companies, such as Glaxo, had a corporate policy of avoiding the OTC market on the grounds that selling directly to consumers was different from the medically oriented marketing of ethical drugs.

There were two broad classes of OTC health care products: (1) drugs that were formerly prescription drugs and (2) health care products developed for the nonprescription market, such as toothpaste, mouthwash, and skin care products. Moving a prescription drug to the OTC market required regulatory approval in most countries. The shift also required marketing expenditures of as much as $30 million a year and extensive consultation with physicians and pharmacists. Even though a prescription was not required, many OTC drugs would not succeed without continued physician recommendations, particularly in highly controlled retail environments such as Germany and Japan. Pharmacists' recommendations were also important. When WL switched the antihistamine, *Benadryl*, to the OTC market in 1985 after 40 years as a prescription drug, the company devised an extensive program for pharmacists based on product samples and promotional literature.

Between 1982 and 1990, global demand for OTC drugs grew at about 7 percent annually and was expected to remain strong, particularly with increased pressure to reduce health care costs. In the developing nations, shortages of more expensive prescription products made OTC drugs very popular. Among the major types of OTC products were analgesics; antacids; cough, cold, and sinus medicines; skin preparations; and vitamins.

The OTC drug industry was even more fragmented than the ethical pharmaceutical industry, particularly in Europe. According to one report, there were 15,000 registered brands in the European OTC market but only 10 could be purchased in seven or more countries.[1] For example, the Vicks-Sinex™ cold remedy could be purchased in British supermarkets; in Germany, it was available OTC but only in pharmacies; and in France, it was available only by prescription. In Latin American countries where the state paid for drugs, there was little distinction between ethical pharmaceuticals and OTC drugs. In the United States, nonprescription products could be sold in any retail channel. In Canada, the United Kingdom, and Germany, some nonprescription drugs could be sold only in pharmacies.

WL's OTC Business Reflecting the increasing global acceptance of nonprescription health care products, WL's OTC sales increased 11 percent in 1990 to $1.5 billion. The largest product lines were Halls cough tablets with sales of $320 million and Listerine mouthwash with sales of $280 million. Other leading brands included Rolaids antacid (the number-one brand in the United States), Benadryl antihistamine (the number-one OTC allergy product in the United States), Lubriderm skin lotion (the number-three brand in the United States), and Efferdent dental products.

During 1991, WL planned more than 20 new OTC product introductions in non-U.S. markets. It was often necessary to adapt products to local markets to account for differences in product usage and government regulations. For example, there were more than 50 different formulations of Halls around the world. Halls was considered a cough tablet in temperate climate areas and a confection in tropical areas. In Thailand, Halls had a much greater amount of menthol than in most countries because Halls was

sold as a cooling sweet. In some of the Asian and Latin American countries, a large volume of Halls was sold by the individual tablet, as opposed to by the package. Benylin cough medicine also had more than 50 different formulations, leading to the question raised by a WL manager: "There are not 50 different kinds of coughs, why do we need 50 different formulations?"

The Confectionery Industry

The confectionery industry consisted of four main segments: chocolate products (approximately 53 percent of the industry), nonchocolate products such as chewing gum (23 percent), hard candy (18 percent), and breath mints (6 percent). WL competed primarily in the chewing gum and breath mint segments.

The confectionery industry was highly concentrated on a global basis with the chewing gum segment the most concentrated. Although WL's American Chicle Group had once been the leading firm, the largest chewing gum company in 1991 was William Wrigley Jr. Co. (Wrigley) with $1.1 billion in annual sales in more than 100 countries. Wrigley's strategy had been focused and consistent for many years—sticks of gum sold at low prices. Wrigley's three main brands, Spearmint™, Doublemint™, and Juiceyfruit™, were ubiquitous around the world. In the United States, Wrigley had the largest market share (48 percent), followed by WL (25 percent) and RJR/Nabisco's Beechnut™ brands. Canada was the only English-speaking country in the world where Wrigley products did not have a leading market share. WL had about 55 percent of the Canadian gum market, compared with Wrigley's 38 percent. A major trend in the food market in recent years had been toward healthy eating. This trend was reflected in the shift toward sugarless gum. In the United States, sugarless gum accounted for 35 percent of the chewing gum market, and in Canada, it was 55 percent, the highest percentage in the world.

Although most breath mints were sugared confections, the breath mint category was referred to as candy plus because the mints contained additional breath-freshening ingredients. In this segment, RJR/Nabisco was the largest firm, with brands sold by the Lifesavers™ division holding about 40 percent of U.S. market share. WL brands held about 36 percent of the market. Tic Tac™, a brand produced by the Italian company Ferrero, had a 12 percent share of the U.S. market. Several other brands with minimal U.S. sales were strong in international markets, such as Fisherman's Friend™, a U.K. product. In other countries such as Germany, Argentina, and Colombia, there were strong local competitors.

Confectionery companies operated on the premise that the majority of sales were by impulse. There were several factors critical to success in this type of market: display and distribution, superb value, and excellent advertising. The most important factor, according to WL confectionery managers, was display and distribution. Thus, there was a strong emphasis on packaging, on developing a wide distribution base, and on in-store display. In the United States, Germany, and France, confectionery distribution to the consumer was dominated by large, efficient retailers (such as Wal-Mart in the United States). In contrast, in Italy, Spain, Greece, South and Southeast Asia, and Latin America, the retail environment was very fragmented with many kiosks and mom-and-pop stores. A strong retail sales force was essential in these areas.

The major challenge faced by firms producing gums and mints was the threat of new market entrants. Traditionally, gums and mints generated higher profit margins than other confectionery segments. As a result, other firms in the candy industry, as well as snack food companies such as PepsiCo, were making an effort to penetrate the gum and mint markets. In many of the developing countries and in particular Latin America, the imitation of best-selling brands by local firms was a regular occurrence.

WL's Confectionery Business Although historically focused on chewing gum and breath mints, WL had started to seek niche opportunities in other confectionery segments. Sales of WL confectionery products increased 5 percent to $1.1 billion in 1990. The leading brands were Trident (sales of $225 million and the world's leading brand of sugarless gum) and Clorets gums and breath mints ($130 million). Other major brands were Adams brand Chiclets (candy-coated chewing gum), Certs (breath mints), and Bubblicious (chewing gum). Trident was the product WL would likely lead with as a new market entry. Other brands had regional strengths; Chiclets was a major brand in Latin America and French Canada but a minor U.S. brand. The strongest market for Clorets was Southeast Asia.

Overall, WL's confectionery business had its largest market shares in the United States, Canada, Mexico, and other countries of Latin America. In Europe, the confectionery business was strongest in Greece, Portugal, Spain, and Italy. The company also had a strong presence in Japan and Southeast Asia. WL's customer mix varied from region to region. In the United States and Canada, customers tended to be adults using products with functional purposes, such as breath mints and sugarless gum. In Latin America, where the emphasis was on fun products marketed mainly to young people, Chiclets, Bubblicious, and Bubbaloo were leading brands.

Global product expansion had been a key objective in recent years. Outside the United States, the Clorets brand had become the largest selling confection product. Clorets was introduced in the United Kingdom and Portugal in 1990 and in France in 1991. The company had high expectations that Trident sugarless gum could be built into a major global brand by capitalizing on concerns for health and fitness. In China, where WL introduced its first three confectionery products in 1991, a new confectionery plant was under construction. Over the previous several years, an aggressive marketing effort in Japan had established a solid market position in chewing gum. To increase penetration into the Italian market, a joint venture was formed in 1990. Alivar, the new company, became Italy's second largest nonchocolate confectionery company.

Organizational Structure

WL was organized into four major divisions reporting to the president and COO, Lodewijk de Vink: Parke-Davis Group, American Chicle Group, Consumer Health Products Group, and International Operations. All four groups had their headquarters in Morris Plains, New Jersey. See Exhibit 5 for an organization chart and Exhibit 6 for short biographies of the five members of WL's office of the chairman.

The Parke-Davis Group included the U.S. pharmaceuticals operations, the Warner-Chilcott generics business, and the Pharmaceutical Research Division. The Research Division, based in Ann Arbor, Michigan, operated facilities in Michigan, Canada, the United Kingdom, and Germany. Parke-Davis manufactured in three plants in the United States, one in Canada, and two in Puerto Rico.

EXHIBIT 5 *Warner-Lambert Organization*

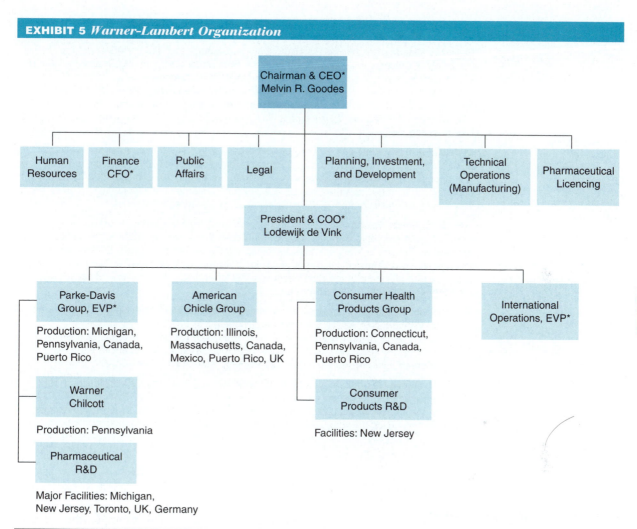

*Member, Office of the Chairman.

Warner-Chilcott production came from a plant in the United States. Parke-Davis was responsible for U.S. pharmaceutical regulatory affairs.

The American Chicle Group was responsible for the U.S. confectionery business. American Chicle manufactured in two U.S. plants and outsourced to plants in Canada, Mexico, Puerto Rico, and the United Kingdom.

The Consumer Health Products Group was responsible for U.S. consumer health care and shaving products. Consumer health care included the OTC pharmaceuticals marketed under the Parke-Davis name plus other OTC products such as Listerine and Lubriderm. Products were manufactured in two U.S. locations, Canada, and Puerto Rico. This group managed a R&D division that performed research for both the Consumer Health Products and American Chicle Groups. The division also performed a significant amount of research for WL's international affiliates.

The International Operations Group was responsible for the manufacture and marketing of WL's pharmaceutical and consumer products outside the United States. Capsugel and Tetra, WL's two businesses that were operated on a global basis, reported to the International Operations Group.

EXHIBIT 6 *Members of the Warner-Lambert Office of the Chairman*

Melvin R. Goodes was born in Hamilton, Ontario, Canada, and had an MBA from the University of Chicago. After several years at the Ford Motor Company of Canada, he joined WL in 1964 as a new product development manager in confectionery. After various senior international positions, including regional director of European confectionery operations and president of WL Mexico, he was appointed president of the Consumer Product Division in 1979. In 1985, he became WL president, COO, and a director of the company and, in 1991, chairman and CEO.

Lodewijk J. R. de Vink was a native of Amsterdam, The Netherlands. After completing an MBA at American University, he joined Schering-Plough Corporation in 1969. In 1981, he was appointed vice president of Schering Laboratories and, in 1986, president of Schering International. In 1988, he joined WL as vice president, International Operations. In 1991, he was appointed president and COO and elected to the board of directors.

Joseph E. Smith was born in Buffalo and had an MBA from the Wharton School. He worked for several years with International Multifoods and Ross Laboratories before joining Johnson & Johnson in 1965. In 1986, he joined the Rorer Group and held several senior management positions, including executive vice president. He joined WL in 1989 as a vice president and president of the Pharmaceutical Sector and, in 1991, became executive vice president and president, Parke-Davis Group.

John Walsh, a native of Worcester, Massachusetts, had an MBA from Seton Hall University. He joined WL as a cost analyst in corporate accounting in 1967. In 1978, he became controller of the American Chicle Group and, in 1980, vice president, finance, Consumer Products Group. In 1989, he became president of the Canada/Latin American Group and, in 1991, executive vice president of WL and president, International Operations.

Robert J. Dircks was born in New York and held an MBA from the City University of New York. He joined WL in 1951 as an accountant in the Nepera Chemical Company. In 1962, he joined the Consumer Products Group as an accounting supervisor. In 1974, he became vice president, finance, Parke-Davis Group. In 1986, he was appointed executive vice president and CFO.

International Operations

International Operations was divided into three operating groups responsible for 45 operating affiliates: Asia/Australia/Capsugel Group, Canada/Latin America Group, and Europe/Middle East/Africa Group. Exhibit 7 shows the countries in which each of the groups had affiliates and the number of employees in each affiliate. The general manager, or country manager, for each affiliate reported directly to one of the geographic group presidents, who in turn reported to the head of International Operations. Below the geographic group presidents were staff managers responsible for the lines of business, such as the Europe/Middle East/Africa head of pharmaceuticals. Geographic group presidents also had staff functions, such as sales and human resources, reporting to them.

In some regions, multiple affiliates were grouped together for management and reporting purposes under one general manager. For example, the German general manager was responsible for the German, Austrian, and Swiss affiliates. Other grouped affiliates included the United Kingdom and Ireland; France, Belgium, and Netherlands; Spain and Portugal; and Italy and Greece.

Across all three of WL's main business segments, acquisitions of confectionery or pharmaceutical firms had accounted for much of WL's international growth. As a result, most of the international affiliates were dominated by either a pharmaceutical or confectionery business. The result was an inconsistent mix of market penetration around the world. For example, the German affiliate had 95 percent of its sales in ethical pharmaceuticals, 5 percent in OTC products, and no confectionery business. In Switzerland, WL was a market leader in several confectionery lines. In the affiliates in France, Italy, and the United Kingdom, pharmaceuticals were dominant

EXHIBIT 7 *Warner-Lambert International Operations'*

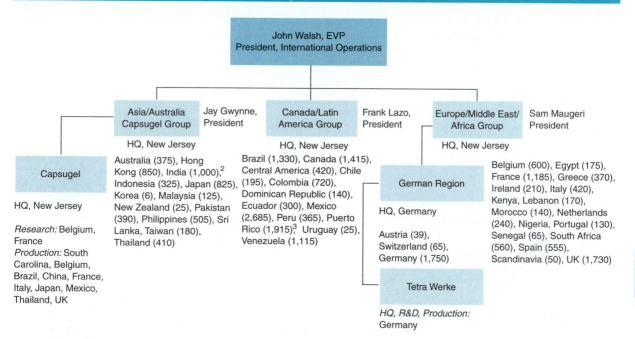

[1]The numbers after each affiliate show the number of employees in the affiliate.
[2]The affiliate in India was a joint venture in which WL had a 40 percent interest.
[3]The Puerto Rico operation was primarily a manufacturing center. The actual affiliate had about 50 employees.

but there was also a reasonably strong confectionery presence. In Spain, Portugal and Greece, confectionery was the primary sector. In Japan, the largest business was Schick, with about 65 percent of the wet-shave market, by far the highest share in the various countries where Schick was marketed. The affiliate in Canada was unique in that the pharmaceutical, confectionery, and consumer health care businesses were all mature, viable businesses with strong managers in each sector. In that sense, the Canadian unit was very similar to WL's operations in the United States.

The country managers managed a full functional organization (marketing, finance, human resources, etc.) and were responsible for all WL products marketed in their country. In most of the affiliates, the country manager's background corresponded with the affiliate's dominant business sector. According to a senior WL manager:

In our affiliates we have only a handful of country managers capable of managing a diverse busi-

ness. Very few managers can move from pharmceuticals to consumer products or vice versa. In one Latin American affiliate, we had a business dominated by confection products. We put in a manager with a pharmaceutical background and the business failed. In Germany, we have tried several times to expand the consumer business and failed each time. In Australia, we have problems with confectionery. Japan is one of the few exceptions. We had a country manager with a pharmaceutical background who successfully grew a confectionery business.

Because the affiliates tended to be dominated by managers from either the confectionery or pharmaceutical side of the business, managers involved in the nondominant businesses struggled to obtain resources. As a WL manager commented:

If, for example, you are a confectionery manager in a country with a small confectionery business, you're treated like the poor stepchild. Because these managers are not given the resources to grow their businesses, there is a tremendous amount of frustration. It is very hard to retain good managers because they are not given the opportunity or the resources to do the things you have to do to be successful.

To illustrate international operations, brief descriptions of the German and Brazilian affiliates are provided.

Germany

WL's operations in Germany, Austria, and Switzerland were managed from Gödecke, A.G., WL's German affiliate. Gödecke, a pharmaceutical firm founded in 1866, was acquired by WL in 1928. In 1997, Parke-Davis's German affiliate was merged with Gödecke. Prior to this, Parke-Davis and Gödecke were operated as separate organizations.

Within Germany, the Gödecke name was far more well known than WL. Employees considered themselves Gödecke employees and the Gödecke name, along with Parke-Davis, was prominent in promotional literature and corporate communications. In 1991, Gödecke had approximately 1,400 employees, with 230 working in pharmaceutical R&D. Gödecke's business was primarily in ethical pharmaceuticals. There was one sales force for OTC and ethical products because in Germany, the OTC market was very small. Because prescription drugs were reimbursable, Germans tended to use drugs that were prescribed by their doctors, even if the drug was available as an OTC product.

Gödecke had no confection business. According to a senior manager in the German affiliate, "WL has never been willing to spend significant long-term money to develop the confection market, which is puzzling since Germany has one of the largest confection markets in the world." Gödecke also had a very limited business in consumer health care products. With respect to the potential of Listerine in Germany, the manager commented:

If you bring a product like that into the market it is not enough to just advertise the product, you have to change people's minds. To do that we would need to spend a lot of money, maybe as much as DM130-140 million. . . . People always see Germany as a market with huge potential but what they don't see is that you need to invest in this market first. Another mistake people keep making is that U.S. tastes will work in Germany. Germans are not mouthwash users.

Brazil

American Chicle entered the Brazilian market in the 1940s. When WL acquired American Chicle in 1962, the confectionery business in Brazil was well established under the Adams brand. A strong pharmaceutical business based on Parke-Davis products was also established in Brazil. However, the hyperinflation in the 1970s and the government's attempts to control inflation through price controls resulted in significant losses in the pharmaceutical business. WL decided to discontinue manufacturing and marketing pharmaceutical products in Brazil and licensed the Parke-Davis line of drugs to another Brazilian company. Since the products were marketed under the Parke-Davis name, WL maintained a close relationship with the licensing company for quality assurance purposes. The licensee, however, had complete control over which products to produce and how to manage production, marketing, and distribution.

The Brazil affiliate had about 1,300 employees and virtually all were involved in the confectionery business. The largest brand in Brazil was Halls, which was marketed as a confectionery product (a "refreshing experience") rather than a cough tablet. The affiliate had a small consumer health care business; Listerine was one of the products sold.

The relationship between headquarters and the affiliate was described by a senior Brazilian manager:

They are in charge of the strategy and we are in charge of the operations. We have a strategic plan in place, we discuss it with headquarters, they give us direction on which areas to engage in and which areas not to do anything, and the implementation is left to us.

Aside from product line extensions, such as changes in flavor or packaging, very little new product development was done in Brazil. One exception was the development of a liquid-center chewing gum called Bubbaloo. A leading brand in Brazil and several other Latin American countries, Bubbaloo was developed by the Brazilian affiliate for the Brazilian market.

THE MANAGEMENT OF INTERNATIONAL OPERATIONS

The Country Managers

Within WL, the country managers were akin to "kings" because, as one manager explained:

> These people are rulers. They control every asset and every decision that is made. The mindset is "I am managing France or Spain or wherever and I will manage it any way I like."

In the larger affiliates, country managers were usually nationals of that country. In Western Europe, most of the country managers had backgrounds in pharmaceuticals. In other regions, many of the country managers had confectionery backgrounds. In the smaller European countries and in the developing countries, country managers were often expatriates using the country manager position as a training ground for higher-level appointments within WL.

Comments from a former country manager illustrate life at the top of an affiliate:

> It was a wonderful life. I was left alone because I was growing the business by 15 percent a year. I learned to run a business from the ground up and I could experiment with ideas very easily. I turned down two promotions because I was having such a great time being king. . . . I had a great deal of autonomy and could ride over most of the staff people. I remember one time when we were planning a new product introduction in an area outside our traditional product lines. Someone from the international division told me "you can't do that." I did it anyway. Before we launched the product, I was told that international would send someone down to help us launch the product. I said fine but I won't be here if you do. So they left me alone. The new product outsold the dominant product in the market and was a huge success.

New Product Development

New product development is critical in the pharmaceutical business. Some new product initiatives in the affiliates were the result of coordinated efforts with headquarters. Others occurred independently in the affiliates. Drugs that were successful in the United States did not always achieve success in the affiliates. For example, Lopid was a huge success in the United States but only moderately successful internationally, despite a significantly increased international marketing effort in recent years. Nevertheless, Lopid represented WL's first truly international pharmaceutical product. Some drugs were introduced outside the United States because of less time-consuming regulatory processes. For example, Accupril was available in 23 countries outside the United States; WL anticipated FDA approval for the U.S. market by the end of 1991.

Because WL had a relatively small number of proprietary ethical pharmaceutical products, licensing was an important developmental activity in the United States and in the affiliates. The major affiliates had their own approaches to licensing strategy. According to one manager:

> Licensing is an ad hoc process—it is done one way in the United States and one way in each of the affiliates. The affiliates try to find products that work in their region. Germany licenses a drug from Italy, Italy from France, and so on. We've ended up with a hodgepodge of drugs in the different regions.

As an example, WL's best-selling drug in Germany and seventh largest among all drugs was Valoron *N*, a painkiller for chronic and acute pain. This drug was licensed by the German affiliate and was not marketed by WL outside the German region.

Both the background of the country manager and the dominant business segment within the affiliate influenced new product development at the affiliate level. In particular, WL had experienced considerable difficulty in convincing the affiliates with dominant pharmaceutical businesses to adopt new consumer health care or confection products. Germany, for example, with its strong pharmaceutical business, had a series of country managers with pharmaceutical backgrounds. For some time, WL had been interested in introducing Listerine in Germany, even though mouthwash was not a recognized product category. The German affiliate leadership believed that the market was too small to justify the $15 million it would take to launch the product, even though Listerine was WL's second leading brand worldwide.

Global Integration

There was very little interaction among the senior U.S. pharmaceutical, OTC, and confectionery managers and their international counterparts. For instance, the U.S. head of pharmaceuticals would meet with the European head of pharmaceuticals once a month. There was virtually no other contact between these senior managers. The affiliate managers also rarely interacted. The affiliates reported to one of the three international groups, and there were no reporting relationships between the units. Once a year, general managers from the affiliates and the United States hold an annual meeting attended by about 250 people, characterized by one manager as follows:

> Some silly situations happen at the meetings. For example, Uruguay, an affiliate doing a few million dollars worth of business, might have a new strategic plan. The Uruguay general manager might get the same amount of air time as the head of Consumer Health Care Products in the United States.

The primary objective for country managers was maximizing the performance of their affiliates. A senior WL manager explained:

> Each affiliate is making decisions on a country basis. For example, say there is a strong shaving business in a country where the country manager is focused on building the local pharmaceutical business. If shaving exceeds its profit targets, the country manager could be tempted to shift cash from shaving to pharmaceutical. The global shaving industry is not his concern. In another country the opposite situation may be happening. The local shaving business is not doing well this year so the country manager borrows money from pharmaceuticals to do some advertising in shaving. This cross borrowing across business lines is sub-optimizing our business lines.... Country managers are not concerned with company growth; they are concerned with affiliate growth. Strategic decisions are not made about products and brands; the whole thinking process is strictly local—how do I maximize my bonus and my performance?

Manufacturing and raw materials sourcing were largely done locally by the affiliate, particularly in those affiliates that were acquired, such as Germany, Spain, Italy, and the United Kingdom. Advertising was also done primarily at the affiliate level. Because the affiliates varied so much in size, the quality of the advertising was often less than satisfactory. Although there was an effort to standardize packaging and graphics, particularly with confectionery products, it was not always successful. For example, when Halls was introduced in Brazil, a third-party manufacturer was used. Because the firm did not have the proper equipment to manufacture square mints, a rectangular shape was used. As the Halls brand grew, the rectangular shape became the standard for mints in Brazil. In the rest of the world, the Halls mint was square.

Two lines of business were exceptions to the lack of global integration—the Capsugel and Tetra divisions. In the early 1980s, the Capsugel business was organized on a geographic basis with the various international units reporting through the country managers. However, because the gelatin capsule market was essentially a commodity business and extremely competitive on a global scale, the geographic structure was considered ineffective and inconsistent with a fast-moving global business. In the mid-1980s, a global structure was created for Capsugel. A similar structure was already in place for Tetra.

International Operations Staff

To coordinate WL's far-flung international businesses, there were approximately 250 International Operations staff members working in the New Jersey headquarters. Included in this number was a small headquarters staff for Capsugel and staff for Tetra's U.S. operations.

Officially, the role of the International Operations staff was to assist the country managers in implementing strategy by communicating information between HQ and affiliates and consolidating the huge amounts of data that were generated. As one manager commented:

> The staff function is "to make order out of chaos." In New Jersey, the international staff coordinates the three large geographic reporting organizations. Each geographic area has its own hierarchical structure of staff managers marketing, finance, and so on working out of New Jersey.

Although the international staff was expected to act in an advisory role to the affiliates, their advice was not always taken, or even wanted. A manager explained:

If a marketing manager in International Operations wants to launch a new product in a particular country, he or she must convince the country manager to make the investment. The country manager may say "I don't want it." The international manager might be three levels below the country manager in the organizational hierarchy. What can the staff person do?

The country managers run their affiliates like hardware stores. They can have 10 different people telling them we would like you to sell this particular drug or this new confectionery product. The guy leaves and the country manager goes back to doing what he wants to do. Their attitude toward the staff marketing people is "I don't need them, what value are they bringing? Get them out of the mix."

It has always been a blurred vision as to the responsibility of some of the international staff functions. At the international operations level it is supposed to be strategic and visionary; leave the day-to-day running of the business to the line managers in Europe, Asia, etc. The staff people would be responsible for oversight, monitoring, cross fertilization and linking Germany with what is going on in France, with what is going on in the UK and hopefully, bringing that knowledge to other geographic areas by feeding that knowledge up to International Operations. The International Operations Group is also supposed to be coordinating with R&D, which is primarily based in the United States.

EARLIER REVIEWS OF THE INTERNATIONAL STRUCTURE

Concerns that there were problems with the structure of WL's international operations first surfaced in the early 1980s. At that time, a consulting report recommended that the company disband its geographic structure and move to a line-of-business organization. Although senior management agreed in principle with a global line-of-business structure, there were concerns that a full-scale reorganization of international operations was too drastic. WL tried a different approach to internationalization several years later. The objective was to put a global strategic planning process in place and merge this with lo-

cal operating plans. In other words, the strategy would be global and tactics would be local. This approach was largely unsuccessful. Despite the attempt to put global plans into action, the realities were that a global vision had not been established and local objectives took precedence.

In 1989, a task force headed by Melvin Goodes was established to develop a globalization plan. The task force was made up of senior managers from the pharmaceutical, confectionery, and consumer segments. A plan based on global lines of business was developed, but for several reasons the plan was not implemented. At some levels in the organization, there was the belief that WL was still not ready for major international restructuring. In addition, WL was enjoying record profits with sales growth of 15 to 20 percent per year. Change was viewed as disruptive and unnecessary. There was a sense that "if it is not broken, why fix it?" Given WL's performance, it was not clear that the competitive marketplace had created a strategic imperative for reorganization.

THE NEXT STEPS

As the new CEO of WL, Melvin Goodes was quite prepared to act and now had the authority. From his perspective, the existing organization was inconsistent with an increasingly competitive global environment. As he explained:

> Our decision making is too slow. For example, we had the opportunity to make an acquisition in Germany. The process started when the German country manager identified the investing opportunity. After he reviewed it, it went to the European Group. It then went to the International Group. Finally, it made its way to corporate in New Jersey. By this time a year had passed and the opportunity was gone.

The next step was to identify priorities and establish an implementation plan. There were many issues to be resolved. Should changes in structure and reporting relationships involve the entire organization? How quickly should change proceed? What would happen to the kings and the international operations staff in a new structure? Should the same international structure be established for each business segment? Should New Jersey remain the headquarters for each business segment?

NOTES

1. *The Financial Times*, July 23, 1991, Survey, p. 1.

EXTERNAL INFORMATION SOURCES

Archer, Alan, "Alliances Offer a Model: Restructuring the Industry," *Financial Times*, July 23, 1991, Survey, p. 2.

Cookson, Clive, "Pharmaceuticals: Successful but Cautious," *Financial Times*, July 23, 1991, Survey, p. 1.

Esposito, Michael A., Gunnar F. Hesse, and Nicholas E. Mellor, "Survival of the Fittest in the EC Pharmaceuticals Market," *The Journal of European Business*, 1991, May/June, pp. 31–38.

Lynn, Matthew, "Drug Companies in a Fix," *International Management*, 1991, October, pp. 62–65.

Malnight, Thomas A., "Globalization of an Ethnocentric Firm: An Evolutionary Perspective," *Strategic Management Journal*, 1995, 16, pp. 119–141.

O'Reilly, Brian, "Drugmakers Under Attack," *Fortune*, July 29, 1991, pp. 48–63.

Shon, Melissa, "Pharmaceuticals 94: Industry, Heal Thyself," *Chemical Marketing Reporter*, March 7, 1994, Special Report.

Teitelmann, Robert, "Pharmaceuticals," *Financial World*, May 30, 1989, pp. 54–80.

Whirlpool's Quest for Global Leadership

Arieh A. Ullmann

State University of New York at Binghamton

In the Chairman's Letter of Whirlpool Corporation's 1995 Annual Report, David R. Whitwam, chairman of the board and chief executive officer, stated his disappointment with the company's recent performance:

> On a relative basis, 1995 was a good year for Whirlpool Corporation and we continued to strengthen our position as the global leader in the major home appliance industry. That said, we should have done better. On an operating basis, and compared to our own very high performance expectations, the year was disappointing—for me, our global team and you, our shareholders.[1]

Whitwam attributed this disappointing performance partly to manufacturing inefficiencies and start-up costs of a new refrigerator in the United States, and partly to restructuring difficulties in Europe, along with raw material cost increases and minimal growth or even declining demand in North America and Europe. This statement was quite a change in tone compared to his pronouncement a year earlier, when at the same place he had boldly stated that the company had achieved both primary objectives—to produce "strong, short-term results" and to build "competitive advantage by continuing our expanding

worldwide enterprise at all levels, and to leverage its best practices and Whirlpool's cumulative size."[2] (For key performance data, see Exhibit 1.)

THE U.S. APPLIANCE INDUSTRY

Home appliances were generally classified as laundry (washers and dryers), refrigeration (refrigerators and freezers), cooking (ranges and ovens), and other appliances (dishwashers, disposals, and trash compactors). Many appliance manufacturers also made floor-care goods such as floor polishers and vacuum cleaners.

Manufacturing operations consisted mainly of preparation of a metal frame to which the appropriate components were attached in automated assembly lines and by manual assembly. Manufacturing costs comprised approximately 65 to 75 percent of total operating cost, with labor representing less than 10 percent of total cost. Optimal-sized assembly plants had an annual capacity of about 500,000 units for most appliances except microwave ovens. Unlike other industries such as textiles, variable costs played an important role in the cost structure; changes in raw material and component costs were also significant. Component production was fairly scale sensitive. Doubling compressor output for refrigerators, for instance, reduced unit costs by 10 to 15 percent. There were also some economies of scale in assem-

Copyright © 1995 by Arieh A. Ullmann, Associate Professor, Binghamton University. Prepared as the basis for class discussion rather than to illustrate either effective or ineffective handling of an administrative situation.

EXHIBIT 1 *Whirlpool Corporation: Key Performance Measures*

Year	Earnings per Share[1]	Return on Equity[2]	Total Return to Shareholders[3]	P/E Ratio
1990	$1.04	5.1%	2.8%	22.6
1991	$2.45	11.6	6.7	15.9
1992	$2.90	13.1	17.0	15.4
1993	$3.19	14.2	25.8	20.8
1994	$2.10	9.4	12.0	23.9
1995	$2.80	11.6	20.8	19.0

[1]Earnings from continuing operations before accounting change.
[2]Earnings from continuing operations before accounting change divided by average stockholders' equity.
[3]Five-year annualized.

bly, but the introduction of robotics tended to reduce those while improving quality and performance consistency and enhancing flexibility.

Distribution of major appliances occurred either through contract sales to home builders and to other appliance manufacturers directly or indirectly through local builder suppliers. Traditionally, these customers were very cost conscious and thus preferred less expensive appliance brands. Retail sales represented the second distribution channel, with national chain stores and mass merchandisers, such as Sears, department, furniture, discount, and appliance stores acting as intermediaries. The consolidation of the appliance distributors during the past 10 years led to the current situation where about 45 percent of the total appliance volume was being sold through 10 powerful mega-retailers, with Sears leading with a market share at approximately 29 percent. A third, less visible channel was the commercial market (laundromats, hospitals, hotels, and other institutions).

Industry Structure

Since World War II, when over 250 firms manufactured appliances, several merger waves consolidated the industry while sales grew and prices held. The most recent consolidation occurred in 1986 when within less than one year Electrolux purchased White Consolidated, Whirlpool acquired KitchenAid, and Magic Chef was purchased by Maytag. Maytag's acquisition of Jenn-Air and Magic Chef increased its overall revenues by giving it brand-name appliances at various price points. Likewise, Whirlpool's acqui-

sition of KitchenAid and Roper broadened its presence at the high end and low end of the market. By the end of 1995, the number of domestic manufacturers varied by type of product between 4 for dishwashers and 15 for home refrigeration and room air-conditioning equipment.

In the 1980s, the market continued to grow primarily due to booming sales of microwave ovens that tripled from 1980 to 1989, while washer and dryer sales increased 34 and 52 percent, respectively. Appliance manufacturers realized that they must offer a complete line of appliances even if they did not manufacture all of them, which was one reason for the merger activity and practice of interfirm sourcing. For example, Whirlpool made trash compactors for Frigidaire (Electrolux/White Consolidated); General Electric manufactured microwave ovens for Caloric (Raytheon), Jenn-Air, and Magic Chef (Maytag).

By 1992, five major competitors, each of which offered a broad range of product categories and brands targeted to different customer segments, controlled 98 percent of the core appliance market. With 33.8 percent domestic market share, Whirlpool was ahead of GE (28.2 percent), a reversal of the leadership position two years earlier. Whirlpool was especially strong in washing machines (1995, 53% share), whereas GE led in refrigerators, dishwashers, and electric ranges. In terms of overall market share, Electrolux followed (16 percent), then Maytag (14 percent) and Raytheon (6 percent).

Throughout the 1980s and into the 1990s, competition in the United States was fierce. Industry demand depended on the state of the economy, disposable income levels, interest rates, housing starts, and the consumers' ability to defer purchases. Saturation levels remained high and steady; over 70 percent of households had washers and over 65 percent had dryers (Exhibit 2). Refrigerator demand stagnated while sales of electric ranges slowed as the microwave oven bloomed. Microwave sales, which had jumped from 3.5 million units in 1980 to over 10 million by 1989, began to level out, while sales of ranges dropped off drastically due to market maturity.

Factors of Competition

In this environment, all companies worked hard to restrain costs. Investments in efficient manufacturing facilities were one method used to control costs. Over four years, for example, Electrolux spent over $500 million to upgrade old plants and build new ones for its acquisition, White Consolidated Industries. General Electric automated its Louisville, Kentucky, plant which, over 10 years, halved the work force and raised output by 30 percent.

Toward the end of the 1980s, it became even more important to lower costs, monitor margins, and achieve economies of scale. The Big Four were ren-

ovating and enlarging existing facilities. Maytag built new facilities in the South to take advantage of lower-cost, nonunion labor. Others built twin-plants on the Mexican border to profit from cheap labor. A third trend was toward the use of focus factories where each plant produced one product category in all price ranges.

Also, all competitors started to move into the upper-end segment of the market which was more stable and profitable. Once the domain of Maytag, it became increasingly crowded with the appearance of GE's Monogram line, Whirlpool's acquisition of KitchenAid, and White's Euroflair models. Quality became an important competitive feature. Maytag used quality effectively in its famous ad featuring the lonely repairman. Defects rates dropped from 20 per 100 appliances made in 1980 to 10 per 100 12 years later. Relationships with suppliers changed as companies used fewer of them than in years past. Contracts were established over longer terms to improve quality and restrain costs through just-in-time deliveries.

Recently powerful distributors demanded faster delivery. Distributors sought to curtail inventory costs, their largest expense. As a consequence, manufacturers began to improve delivery systems. For instance, General Electric created its Premier Plus Program that guaranteed three-day delivery. Sales departments

EXHIBIT 2 *Global Home Appliance Industry: Saturation Levels by Region, Demand, and Market Growth, 1994–2004*

	North America	Europe[1]	Latin America	Asia
Home Appliances				
Refrigerators	100	100	70	30
Cooking Equipment	100	96	90	—
Clothes Washers	74	82	40	20
Clothes Dryers	70	18	—	—
Dishwashers	51	30	—	—
Microwave Ovens	80	40	5	8
Room Air Conditioners	41	—	10	8
Compactors	5	—	—	—
Freezers	40	40	—	—
Population (million)	380	1,100	380	2,900
Annual Demand (million units)	46	75	17	56
Est. Annual Growth Rate	3%	3%	6–8%	8–9%

Source: Whirlpool Corporation. 1994 Annual Report.
[1]Includes Eastern Europe, Africa, and the Middle East.

were reorganized so that one sales representative could cover all of a manufacturer's brands in a given product category. Customer information services via 800-telephone lines were also strengthened.

Innovation

Two developments, government regulation and advances in computer software, combined with intense competition, accelerated product innovation. New energy standards stipulated by the 1987 National Appliance Energy Conservation Act limited energy consumption of new appliances with the objective of reducing energy usage in appliances by 25 percent every five years. At the same time, the possible ban on ozone-depleting chlorofluorocarbons (CFCs) in refrigerators by 1995 was forcing the industry to redesign its refrigerators. Pressure was also exerted to change washer and dishwasher designs to reduce water consumption and noise levels. In 1989, the Super Efficient Refrigerator Program Inc. (SERP) offered a $30 million award for a refrigerator prototype free of CFCs that was at least 25 percent more energy-efficient than the 1993 federal standards required. The winner had to manufacture and sell over 250,000 refrigerators between January 1994, and July 1997.

As the industry globalized, more stringent government regulations outside of the United States became an issue. For example, there was a concern that the more stringent environmental standards prevailing in the European Community would become law in the United States as well. While Whirlpool supported the more stringent standards, the other competitors, notably GE, opposed them.

Regarding advances in computer technology, new programs using fuzzy logic or neural networks that mimicked the human brain's ability to detect patterns were being introduced in many industries including white goods. In Asia, elevators, washers, and refrigerators using fuzzy logic to recognize usage patterns were already widespread. In late 1992, AEG Hausgeräte AG, then a subsidiary of Daimler Benz's AEG unit, introduced a washer using fuzzy logic to automatically control water consumption based on load size and to sense how much dirt remained in clothes.

There were also other innovations. In the late 1980s, new technologies in cooking surfaces were introduced, including ceramic-glass units, solid elements, and modular grill configurations. Other new customer-oriented features were the self-cleaning oven, automatic ice cube makers, self-defrosting refrigerators, pilotless gas ranges and appliances that could be preset. Also, manufacturers worked hard to reduce the noise level of dishwashers and washing machines. Consumers became more concerned with the appearance of appliances. Sleek European styling became fashionable with smooth lines, rounded corners and electronic controls. Another trend was the white-on-white appearance, suggesting superior cleanability.

Outlook

Future demand conditions in the United States continued to be unattractive with growth rates estimated around 3 percent based on a 1994 demand of 46 million units (Exhibit 2). At the prevailing saturation levels demand was primarily replacement purchases (79 percent) with the remainder based on new housing and new household formation. The industry was so competitive that no individual manufacturer could keep an innovation from being imitated within a year without a patent. One of the competitors summarized the situation in the North American appliance industry as follows:

> In the 1980s, four manufacturers accounted for almost all major home appliance sales in the United States, a market where approximately 40 million appliances are sold annually. Each was a tough, seasoned competitor fighting for greater sales in a market predicted to grow little in the decade ahead.[3]

THE GLOBALIZATION OF THE APPLIANCE INDUSTRY

Foreign Competition

The white goods industry was as American as baseball and apple pie. In 1992, 98 percent of the dishwashers, washing machines, dryers, refrigerators, freezers and ranges sold in America were made in America. Exports represented around five percent of shipments. The manufacturing plants of the industry leaders were located in such places as Newton, Iowa (Maytag), Benton Harbor, Michigan

(Whirlpool), and Columbus, Ohio (White Consolidated Industries). Combined, these companies virtually dominated the market for each major appliance with one exception—microwave ovens. These represented the major share of imports that were approximately 17 percent of total appliance sales.

The acquisition of White Consolidated Industries by AB Electrolux of Sweden in 1986 marked a major change in the industry. Until then, foreign competition in the United States was restricted largely to imports of microwave ovens, a segment that was controlled by Far Eastern competitors from Korea (Goldstar, Samsung) and Japan (Sharp, Matsushita). Aware of other industries' fate, many expected that it was only a matter of time before these companies would expand from microwave ovens and compact appliances into other segments.

Europe

U.S. manufacturers were particularly attracted to the European market. Since 1985, Western Europe was moving rapidly toward a unified market of some 320 million consumers and was not nearly as saturated as the markets in Canada and the United States. Appliance demand was expected to grow at 5 percent annually. Political changes in Eastern Europe integrated these countries into the world trade system and thus added to Europe's long-term attractiveness.

During the 1970s and 1980s, the European white goods industry had experienced a consolidation similar to that in the United States. According to Whirlpool, in 1995 the number of manufacturers in Western Europe was 35, most of whom produced a limited range of products for a specific geographic region.[4] However, since the late 1980s, six companies—Electrolux Zanussi, Philips Bauknecht, Bosch-Siemens, Merloni-Indesit, Thompson, and AEG—controlled 70 percent of the market (excluding microwave ovens and room air conditioners). Until the mid-1980s, most companies were either producing and selling in only one national market or exporting to a limited extent from one country to many European markets. Observed Whirlpool's CEO Whitwam: "What strikes me most is how similar the U.S. and European industries are."[5] Research by Whirlpool also indicated that washers were basically the same in terms of working components around the globe.[6]

The European market was very segmented and consumer preferences differed greatly from country to country with regard to almost every type of appliance. For example, the French preferred to cook foods at high temperatures, splattering grease on oven walls. Thus, oven ranges manufactured for France should feature a self-cleaning ability. However, this feature was not a requirement in Germany where lower cooking temperatures were the norm. Unlike Americans, who preferred to stuff as many clothes into the washer as possible, Europeans overwhelmingly preferred smaller built-in models. Northern Europeans liked large refrigerators because they preferred to shop only once a week; consumers in the south of Europe preferred small ones, because they visited the open-air markets daily. Northerners liked their freezers at the bottom of the refrigerators, southerners on top. In France, 80 percent of washing machines were top-loaders, while elsewhere in Western Europe, 90 percent were front-loaders. Also, European washers frequently contained heating elements and the typical European homemaker preferred to wash towels at 95 degrees Celsius. Gas ranges were common throughout Europe, except for Germany where 90 percent of all ranges sold were electric.

Given these differences in terms of consumers' preferences, some observers were skeptical about the possibility of establishing pan-European models that would yield a sustainable competitive advantage through manufacturing, procurement, and marketing efficiencies. They claimed that the European market was actually made up of many smaller individual markets corresponding to the respective countries. Furthermore, they reasoned, many of these national markets featured strong competitors.

Distribution of white goods in Europe was different than that in North America. The larger channel, known as the retail trade, comprised independent retailers many of which were organized through buying groups or as multiple-store chains. The second channel, the kitchen trade, was primarily comprised of kitchen specialists that sold consumers entire kitchen packages. The kitchen trade was focused mainly on built-in units and was not involved in laundry appliances.

AB Electrolux had 25 percent market share in all of Europe. Over 20 years, the $14 billion multinational from Sweden completed more than 200 acquisitions in 40 countries which spanned five businesses: household appliances, forestry and garden products, industrial products, metal and mining, and commercial services. Its expertise in managing acquisitions and integrating the newly acquired units into the organization was unequaled. For example, in 1983, Electrolux assumed control of a money-losing Italian white goods manufacturer with 30,000 employees, 50 factories, and a dozen foreign sales companies. Within four years, the Swedes turned this company that in 1983 lost Lit. 120 billion into an efficient organization netting Lit. 60 billion. The acquisitions of Zanussi of Italy, Tricity in Britain, and three Spanish companies in anticipation of the changes in Western Europe marked the beginning of a new era in this mature industry as Electrolux sought to establish a pan-European approach to the appliance market. However, in 1993, Electrolux's pan-European strategy experienced trouble. The recession combined with Europe's market fragmentation reduced profits far below the targeted 5 percent margin.

In Germany, Bauknecht (Philips), Bosch-Siemens, and AEG-Telefunken were dominant; Britain's GEC Hotpoint and France's Thompson-Brandt also were credible competitors. Merloni from Italy pursued a different approach by flooding Europe with machines produced in Italy with lower-cost labor. In 1987, Merloni acquired Indesit, an Italian producer in financial trouble, to enlarge its manufacturing base and exploit Indesit's marketing position in many European countries. In the late 1980s, no brand had more than 5 percent of the overall market, even though the top 10 producers generated 80 percent of the volume.

In 1989, the Americans landed in Europe. General Electric formed an appliance joint venture with Britain's General Electric Corporation (GEC), which had a strong presence in the low-price segment of the European market, especially in the United Kingdom, and thus complemented GE's high-end European products. In the same year, Maytag acquired the Hoover Division through the purchase of Chicago Pacific. Hoover, best known for its vacuum cleaners, also produced washers, dryers, and dishwashers in the United Kingdom. However, these products were not readily accepted in other European markets. Hoover was also present in Australia and, through a trading company, serviced other parts of the world. In 1989, Whirlpool and N.V. Philips of the Netherlands formed a joint venture that included all of Philips' European appliance division. Thus, within a short time the Americans closed the gap relative to Electrolux's geographical scope. In spite of concerns regarding differing consumer preferences in Europe, the largest U.S. appliance manufacturers established themselves before the 1992 EU Program became a reality. European Community rules required 60 percent local content to avoid tariffs which, combined with the fear of a "Fortress Europe" protected by communitywide tariffs after 1992, excluded exports as a viable strategy.

Within a short time, further agreements greatly reduced the number of independent competitors in Europe. AEG started cooperating with Electrolux in washer and dishwasher production and development and, in 1994, became part of Electrolux; Bosch-Siemens formed an alliance with Maytag; the European Economic Interest Group combined several manufacturers with France's Thompson-Brandt as the leader. In spite of this trend toward consolidation in the early 1990s, Whirlpool estimated the number of European manufacturers of home appliances to be around 100.[7]

Asia

Asia, the world's second largest home appliance market, was likely to experience rapid economic growth in the near future primarily because of the booming economies of the Pacific Rim countries. Home appliance shipments were expected to increase at least 6 percent per annum through the 1990s (Exhibit 2). The biggest promise, of course, was the huge markets of the world's most populous nations—China and India. However, incomes in these two markets were only approaching levels at which people could afford appliances. The Asian market was dominated by 50 widely diversified Asian manufacturers, primarily from Japan, Korea, and Taiwan, with no clear leader. Matsushita, the market leader, held less than 10 percent outside Japan.

Consumer preferences in Asia were quite different from those in North America and Europe and varied widely from country to country. For example, typical Asian refrigerators ranged from 6 to 10 cubic feet due to the lack of space. Because owning a refrigerator was a status symbol, refrigerators were often placed in the living room. Such a prominent display created a demand for stylish colors and finishes. In India, for example, refrigerators in bright red or blue were popular. Both direct-cool and forced-air models were common in Asia, whereas direct-cool prevailed in Europe and the forced-air version was preferred in North America. Clothes washers had to be portable because living quarters tended to be small and had no basement. Washers could not be hooked up permanently to a water supply and drain. Often, they were stored in an outside hallway and moved into the bathroom and kitchen for use. Also, they had to be delivered to large apartment blocks with no elevators and thus had to be carried up many flights of stairs. Therefore, washers tended to be designed as lightweight products on wheels equipped with handles for easy relocation. Technological designs varied, even though vertical axis machines dominated. The clothes also represented a challenge because they ranged from the yards of fabric used in Indian saris to simple cotton dress and Western-style clothing. Clothes dryers were virtually unknown. Washing habits were different, too. For instance, Japanese usually washed with cold water. To get their clothes clean, Japanese machines have soak cycles that can range from 30 minutes to several hours. Two-burner, tabletop cooking units replaced the ranges used in North America and Europe, reflecting the differences in cooking styles. In addition, kitchens were much smaller and baking was virtually unknown. Dishwashers were also unheard of. In air conditioning, split-system units were the dominant version in Asia. In regions where air conditioners were used during most of the year, consumers didn't want to block out limited window space. Split-system units were installed high on the wall, often out of reach, making remote controls an important feature.

Latin America

Another market promising attractive growth in appliances was Latin America, once these countries emerged from decades of political instability, economic mismanagement, and hyperinflation. Indeed, much of this was happening in the 1990s accompanied by efforts to lower tariffs, which would stimulate trade. In 1994, the white goods industry in Latin America comprised about 65 competitors. Whirlpool expected appliance shipments to expand at a faster pace than in North America and Europe.[8]

WHIRLPOOL CORPORATION

Company Background

In early 1996, Whirlpool Corporation, headquartered in Benton Harbor, Michigan, was one of the world's leading manufacturers and marketers of major home appliances. The company's plants were located in 12 countries and it distributed its products in over 140 countries under 28 brand names (Exhibits 3 through 7). Fifteen years earlier, Whirlpool executives had perceived the world primarily as consisting of the U.S. and Canadian markets, with some marginal sales in Latin America and limited export opportunities. Today, Whirlpool's world encompasses four major regions: North America with 46 million units sold annually (1994), consisting of Canada, Mexico, and the United States; Europe with 50 million units (Western, Central, and Eastern Europe, Africa, and the Middle East); Asia, representing a total demand of 56 million units; and Latin America comprised of the Caribbean and Central and South America with 17 million units.

Whirlpool was founded in St. Joseph, Michigan, in 1911. At the time, it was producing motor-driven wringer washers under the name Upton Machine, with the hopes of selling them in quantities to large distributors. In 1916, the first order from Sears, Roebuck and Co. marked the beginning of an enduring relationship with Sears as the oldest and largest customer representing 20 percent of Whirlpool's 1995 sales. In 1948, the Whirlpool-brand automatic washer was introduced. This established the dual distribution system—one product line for Sears, the other for Nineteen Hundred. The Nineteen Hundred Corporation was renamed Whirlpool in 1950 with the addition of automatic dryers to the product line. In 1955, Whirlpool merged with Seeger Refrigerator Co. of St. Paul, Minnesota, and the Estate range and air-conditioning divisions of RCA. In 1957, Whirlpool entered the foreign market through the purchase of equity interest in Multibras S.A. of São Paulo, Brazil, later renamed Brastemp S.A. In 1967, Whirlpool was the first competitor in the industry to take advantage of AT&T's new 800-line service and created the Cool-Line Telephone Service that provided customers a toll-free number to call for answers to questions and to receive help with service.

EXHIBIT 3 *North American Appliance Group in Early 1996*

Principal Products	Major Brand Names	Principal Locations	
Automatic dryers	Acros[1]	**Corporate, Regional:**	**Sales Offices:**
Automatic washers	Admiral (Canada)	**Research, and Engineering Center:**	**U.S.A.**
Built-in ovens	Chambers	Benton Harbor, Michigan	Atlanta
Dehumidifiers	Crolls[1]	**Subsidiaries:**	Boston
Dishwashers	Coolerator	Inglis Ltd.	Charlotte
Freezers	Estate	Mississauga, Ontario	Chicago
Ice makers	Inglis	Whirlpool Financial Corp.	Dallas
Microwave ovens	KitchenAid	Benton Harbor, Michigan	Dayton
Ranges	Roper	**Affiliates:**	Denver
Refrigerators	Speed Queen (Canada)	Vitromatic S.A. de C.V.	Kansas City
Room air conditioners	Supermatic[1]	Monterrey, Mexico	Knoxville
Trash compactors	Whirlpool	**Manufacturing Facilities:**	Little Rock
		Benton Harbor, Michigan	Los Angeles
		Celaya, Mexico	Miami
		Clyde, Ohio	Minneapolis
		Evansville, Indiana	New York City
		Findlay, Ohio	Orlando
		Forth Smith, Arkansas	Philadelphia
		Greenville, Ohio	Pittsburgh
		Lavergne, Tennessee	Santurce (Puerto Rico)
		Marion, Ohio	San Francisco
		Mexico City, Mexico	Seattle
		Montmagny, Quebec	**Canada**
		Monterrey, Mexico	Laval, Quebec
		Oxford, Mississippi	Missisauga, Ontario
		Puebla, Mexico	Vancouver, British Columbia
		Reynosa, Mexico	**Mexico**
		Tulsa, Oklahoma	Guadalajara, Jalisco
			Mexico City, Distrito Federal
			Monterrey, Nuevo León

[1] Affiliate owned.

In the mid-1980s, the limited growth potential of its established markets motivated Whirlpool to undertake a major examination of the industry. Top management decided "to remain focused on major home appliances but to expand into markets not already served by Whirlpool."[9] In 1986, the KitchenAid division of Hobart Corporation was purchased from Dart & Kraft marking Whirlpool's entry into the upper-end segment of the appliance market as well as into small appliances. In the same year, Whirlpool sold its central heating and cooling business to Inter-City Gas Corp. of Canada. In 1985, Whirlpool purchased the assets of Mastercraft Industries Corp., a Denver-based manufacturer of kitchen cabinets. A year later a second cabinet maker, St. Charles Manufacturing Co., was acquired through the newly formed Whirlpool Kitchens, Inc. However, in March 1989, Whirlpool Kitchens was sold due to lack of fit.

North American Appliance Group

The North American Appliance Group (NAAG) was formed in 1989 out of Whirlpool's operations in the United States, Canada, and Mexico (Exhibit 3).

EXHIBIT 4 *Whirlpool Europe B.V. in 1996*

Principal Products	Major Brand Names	Principal Locations	
Automatic dryers	Bauknecht	**European Operations Center:**	**Sales Offices:**
Automatic washers	Ignis	Comerio, Italy	Athens, Greece
Dishwashers	Laden		Barcelona, Spain
Freezers	Whirlpool	**Subsidiaries:**	Brussels, Belgium
Microwave ovens		Whirlpool Europe B.V.	Budapest, Hungary
Ranges		Eindhoven, Netherlands	Comerio, Italy
Refrigerators		Whirlpool Tatramat a.s.	Dublin, Ireland
		Poprad, Slovakia	Eindhoven, Netherlands
		Manufacturing Facilities:	Espoo, Finland
		Amiens, France	Herlev, Denmark
		Calw, Germany	Lenzburg, Switzerland
		Cassinetta, Italy	Lisbon, Portugal
		Naples, Italy	London, UK
		Neunkirchen, Germany	Moscow, Russia
		Norrköping, Sweden	Oslo, Norway
		Poprad, Slovakia	Paris, France
		Schorndorf, Germany	Poprad, Slovakia
		Siena, Italy	Prague, Czech Republic
		Trento, Italy	Stockholm, Sweden
			Stuttgart, Germany
			Vienna, Austria
			Warsaw, Poland

C-617

EXHIBIT 5 *Latin American Appliance Group in 1996*

Principal Products	Major Brand Names	Principal Locations
Automatic washers	Brastemp[1]	
Dishwashers	Consul[1]	**Regional Headquarters:**
Dryers	Eslabon de Lujo	São Paulo, Brazil
Freezers	Semer[1]	**Subsidiaries:**
Microwave ovens	Whirlpool	Latin American Sales and
Ranges		Service Company, Miami
Refrigerators		South American Sales Company,
Room air conditioners		Grand Cayman
		Whirlpool Argentina S.A.,
		Buenos Aires, Argentina

[1]Affiliate owned

After several plant closings and a reshuffling of product lines between plants, a streamlined organization with a unified strategy was formed, originally around four brands. In 1992, Whirlpool reorganized its North American operations behind a strategy to create a "dominant consumer franchise" (DCF). For Whirlpool, a DCF existed "when consumers insist on our brands for reasons other than price, when they view our products as clearly superior to other appliances, [and] when they demonstrate strong loyalty in

EXHIBIT 6 *Asian Appliance Group in 1996*

Principal Products	Major Brand Names	Principal Locations	
Automatic washers	Bauknecht	**Regional Headquarters and Technology Center:**	**Manufacturing Facilities:**
Microwave ovens	Ignis	Singapore	Beijing, China
Refrigerators	KitchenAid		Faridabad, India
Room air conditioners	Raybo	**Regional Offices:**	Pondicherry, India
	Roper	Hong Kong	Shanghai, China
	Whirlpool	New Delhi, India	Shenzhen, China
		Singapore	Shunde, China
	Under license:		
	Kelvinator (India)	**Subsidiaries:**	**Sales Offices:**
	Narcissus	Beijing Whirlpool Snowflake	Auckland, New Zealand
	SMC	Electric Appliance Co.,	Bangkok, Thailand
	Snowflake	Ltd., Beijing	Guanzhow, China
	TVS	Kelvinator of India	Ho Chi Minh City, Vietnam
		New Delhi, India	Hong Kong
		Whirlpool Narcissus	New Delhi, India
		(Shanghai) Co. Ltd.,	Noble Park, Australia
		Shanghai, China	Petaling Jaya, Malaysia
		Whirlpool Washing Machines,	Shanghai, China
		Ltd., Madras, India	Seoul, South Korea
			Singapore
		Affiliates:	Tokyo, Japan
		Great Teco Whirlpool Ltd.,	
		Taipei, Taiwan	
		Beijing Embraco Snowflake	
		Compressor Co. Ltd.,	
		Beijing, China	

their future purchase decisions."[10] Such a strategy required, above all, a better understanding of consumer needs; merely improving product quality and keeping costs low was deemed necessary but not sufficient. The objective was to become more customer focused, entailing a functional organization that deals with four core processes: product management, brand management, trade partner management, and logistics. Unlike the traditional functional organization, the new approach employed cross-functional teams within each function with product business teams at the center.

To support its DCF strategy, Whirlpool announced a multitude of new products aimed at six discrete appliance consumer segments labeled: (1) the Traditionalist; (2) the Housework Rebel, (3) the Achiever, (4) the Self-Assured, (5) the Proven Conservative, (6) the Homebound Survivor.[11] KitchenAid-brand appliances were marketed to upscale consumers who look for style and substance, typically found among Achievers; Whirlpool was positioned as the brand that helps consumers to manage their homes better, for instance Housework Rebels. Roper-brand appliances were value-priced and offered basic styling and features and were a match for the Self-Assured. The Estate brand line was limited to a few high-volume models and distributed through warehouse club outlets. The Kenmore Appliance Group was dedicated to serve Whirlpool's single largest customer—Sears, Roebuck and Co.

In June 1993, Whirlpool was selected as the winner in the $30 million Super Efficient Refrigerator Program, a success CEO Whitwam attributed to the multidisciplinary team that had been assembled from all over the world. The SERP models eliminated CFCs completely by using a different refrigerant. Also, an environmentally safe blowing agent was used to expand foam insulation between the walls of the refrigerator liner and cabinet. Energy efficient gains were achieved through better insulation, a

EXHIBIT 7 *Changes in Whirlpool's Global Presence, 1988–1995*

	1988	1995
Revenues	$4.41 billion	$8.35 billion
Market position	Leader in North America	#1 in North America
	Affiliates in Brazil, Canada, India, and Mexico	#1 in Latin America
		#3 in Europe
		Largest Western appliance company in Asia
Manufacturing locations (incl. affiliates)	4	12
Brands (incl. affiliates)	14	28
Market presence (number of countries)		>140
Employees	29,110	45,435

high-efficiency compressor, and an improved condenser fan motor in conjunction with a microchip-controlled adaptive defrost control that incorporated fuzzy logic. Whirlpool had entered the SERP contest because it was consistent with the company's strategy to exceed customer expectations. Jeff Fettig, vice president, group marketing and sales, for NAAG commented:

> The SERP program allowed us to accelerate the development process and bring these products to the market sooner. Future products will be designed with these consumer expectations [regarding environmental friendliness] in mind, giving people even more reason to ask for a Whirlpool-built product next time they are in the market for a major home appliance.[12]

After an energy-efficient refrigerator with a CFC-free sealed system was launched in March 1994, the company announced that it would introduce a new clothes washer in 1996 that would use a third of the water and energy of a conventional washer. The company hoped that consumers would be willing "to pay a premium price for the new washer."[13] In its 1993 Annual Report, Whirlpool announced that since 1988 NAAG had increased its regional market share by nearly a third also thanks to Inglis, Ltd., the Canadian subsidiary, and Vitromatic S.A., the Mexican affiliate.

In late 1994, Whirlpool initiated a major restructuring, closing plants and reducing the workforce in an effort to reduce costs. In 1995, Montgomery Ward, the second largest home appliance retailer in the United States, became a Whirlpool customer.

Whirlpool's Globalization

In 1995, Whirlpool's efforts to establish a global presence were more than 10 years old. In its 1984 Annual Report, Whirlpool announced that it had concluded a two-year study and adopted a plan for the next five years. Among the steps mentioned were developing new international strategies and adding new businesses that would complement existing strengths. The strategy was based on the assumption that in spite of the differences in consumer habits and preferences, it was possible to gain competitive advantage by leveraging a global presence in the various regional markets. In the 1987 Annual Report, CEO Whitwam elaborated on the company's rationale for globalization:

> The U.S. appliance market has limited growth opportunities, a high concentration of domestic competitors and increasing foreign competition. Further, the U.S. represents only about 25% of the worldwide potential for major appliance sales.
>
> Most importantly, our vision can no longer be limited to our domestic borders because national borders no longer define market boundaries. The marketplace for products and services is more global than ever before and growing more so every day.

Consumers in major industrialized countries are living increasingly similar lifestyles and have increasingly similar expectations of what consumer products must do for them. As purchasing patterns become more alike, we think that companies that operate on a broad global scale can leverage their strengths better than those which only serve an individual national market. Very likely, appliance manufacturing will always have to be done regionally. Yet the ability to leverage many of the strengths of a company on an international basis is possible only if that company operates globally.[14]

Whirlpool Trading Corporation was formed to consolidate existing international activities and explore new ventures. In January 1985, the company increased its equity interest in Inglis, which dated back to 1969, from 48 to more than 50 percent. In the following year, Aspera S.r.l. in Torino, Italy, a large compressor maker, was purchased from Fiat.

In the late 1950s, Whirlpool had undertaken the first expansion beyond U.S. borders when it entered Brazil; its next expansion was into Canada in 1969 (Exhibit 8). In 1976, Whirlpool strengthened its position in Brazil. However, Whirlpool became a global organization in the 1980s when it decided to compete in Mexico, India, and Europe through formation of a series of joint ventures. The moves into South America and Asia were motivated by the expectation that climbing disposable incomes in these regions would result in a growing demand for appliances that would "at least partially mirror the American consumer boom of the 1950s and 1960s."[15]

Among Whirlpool's top-level managers, David R. Whitwam was known as a champion of Whirlpool's globalization. Whitwam had succeeded Jack Sparks, who had retired in 1987 after 47 years of service, including five as CEO. Sparks had given Whirlpool the focus it lacked. It was not an easy task to follow in the footsteps of such a distinguished leader.

Born in Madison, Wisconsin, Whitwam graduated with honors from the University of Wisconsin with a B.S. in economics. After eight years in the U.S. Army and the Wisconsin National Guard, he joined Whirlpool as a marketing management trainee in July 1968. One year later, he was named territory sales manager of the South California sales division, and from there the job descriptions did not

change, only the locations. Whitwam spent time in New York and in Southern California.

Whitwam moved to corporate headquarters in 1977 when he was named merchandising manager for range products. From that post came a promotion to director of builder marketing, and then vice president, Whirlpool sales, in 1983. In 1985, he was elected to the company's board of directors. On December 1, 1987, he assumed his current position as president, CEO, and chairman of the board of Whirlpool Corporation. Thereafter, he transformed a domestically oriented $4 billion company into a $8 billion global force. Whirlpool's corporate vision, which was displayed in many of its publications and throughout its facilities, clearly communicated this orientation:

Whirlpool, in its chosen lines of business, will grow with new opportunities and be the leader in an ever-changing global market. We will be driven by our commitment to continuous quality improvement and to exceeding all of our customers' expectations. We will gain competitive advantage through this, and by building on our existing strengths and developing new competencies. We will be market driven, efficient and profitable. Our success will make Whirlpool a company that worldwide customers, employees and other stakeholders can depend on.

Whirlpool Europe B.V.

David Whitwam was strongly convinced of the promise of the European market: "The only people who say you can't have a pan-European brand are the people who don't have one themselves."[16] On August 18, 1989, Whirlpool announced a joint venture with N.V. Philips, the second largest appliance manufacturer in Europe behind Electrolux, with a broad presence in many markets throughout Europe and Latin America. The deal was for a 53 percent interest in Philips' worldwide Major Domestic Appliance Division for $361 million in cash; the new company was called Whirlpool International B.V. In July 1991, Whirlpool exercised its option to purchase from Philips the remaining interest in WIBV and changed the name to Whirlpool Europe B.V. (WEBV) (Exhibit 4). By 1994, with 13 percent market share, WEBV occupied the third position in

EXHIBIT 8 *Milestones of Whirlpool's Globalization*

1957 Whirlpool invests in Brazilian appliance market through purchase of equity interest in Multibras S.A., renamed Brastemp S.A. in 1972.

1969 Entry into the Canadian appliance market through a 52% equity interest in Inglis, Limited. Sole ownership established in 1990.

1976 Increased investment in Brazil through purchase of equity interests in Consul S.A., an appliance manufacturer, and Embraco S.A., a maker of compressors.

1986 Purchase of majority interest in Aspera S.r.l. of Fiat S.p.A., a manufacturer of compressors, located in Turin and Riva, Italy.

1987 Entry into the Indian appliance market through TVS Whirlpool Limited, a 33% each joint venture company formed with Sundaram-Clayton Limited of Madras.

Ownership in Inglis, Limited, increased to 72%.

1988 Vitromatic, S.A. de C.V. is formed with Vitro, S.A., of Monterrey, Nuevo León, to manufacture and market major home appliances for Mexican and export markets. Whirlpool has a 49% interest.

Whirlpool operates a maquiladora, Componentes de Reynosa, in Reynosa, Tamaulipas, to manufacture components for final assembly in the United States.

1989 Whirlpool and N.V. Philips of the Netherlands consummate an agreement under which Whirlpool acquires a 53% interest in a joint-venture company made up of Philips' former major domestic appliance division. The new company, Whirlpool International B.V. (WIBV), will manufacture and market appliances in Western Europe. The joint-venture brand names are Bauknecht, Philips, Ignis, and Laden.

North American Appliance Group formed from streamlined U.S., Canadian, and Mexican operations.

Affiliates in Brazil, India, and Mexico complete construction of facilities and start producing the "World Washer."

1990 A program is launched to market appliances in Europe under the dual brands Philips and Whirlpool. Formation of a joint-venture company with Matsushita Electric Industrial Co. of Japan to produce vacuum cleaners for the North American market.

Creation of Whirlpool Overseas Corporation as a wholly owned subsidiary to conduct industrial and marketing activities outside North America and Western Europe.

Inglis Limited becomes a wholly owned subsidiary.

1991 Whirlpool acquires remaining interest in WIBV from Philips Electronics N.V.

Creation of two global business units: Whirlpool Compressor Operations and Whirlpool Microwave Cooking Business.

1992 Creation of Whirlpool Tatramat in the Slovak Republic. Whirlpool Tatramat a.s. will manufacture clothes washers for Slovakia and neighboring countries and import other WIBV major appliances for sale.

Begins gradual phase-out of dual-branded advertising to sole Whirlpool brand by removing the Philips name in Europe.

Whirlpool assumes control of SAGAD S.A. of Argentina from Philips.

Reorganization of Whirlpool Europe. The name is changed from WIBV to WEBV.

Creation of a global small appliance business unit.

1993 Reorganization of NAAG.

WOC is replaced by two separate regional organizations in Latin America and Asia.

Start of the implementation of a new Asian strategy with Tokyo as headquarters and regional offices in Singapore, Hong Kong, and Tokyo.

Sales subsidiaries are opened in Greece, Poland, and the Czeck Republic.

Inglis Ltd. becomes Canada's leading home appliance manufacturer.

To streamline European operations, WEBV sells its Spanish refrigerator plant to IAR/Sital of Italy.

1994 In May, Whirlpool announces a joint venture with Teco Electric & Machinery Co., Ltd., of Taiwan to market and distribute home appliances in Taiwan.

Whirlpool becomes a stand-alone brand in Europe.

Brazilian affiliates Consul and Brastemp merge to form Multibras.

Acquires controlling interest in Kelvinator of India, Ltd., and assumes controlling interest in TVS Whirlpool Ltd.

Whirlpool's Asian headquarters moved to Singapore; number of regions increased from three to four.

Whirlpool exits vacuum cleaner business by selling its minority interest in the joint venture with Matsushita.

Acquires majority ownership in SMC Microwave Products Co., Ltd., and Beijing Whirlpool Snowflake Electric Appliance Company, Ltd.

Creation of the Microwave Oven Business Unit as a global business unit.

1995 Formation of South American sales company.

New joint venture formed to produce washers called The Whirlpool Narcissus (Shanghai) Co., Ltd.

Acquired majority interest in Raybo Air Conditioner Manufacturing Company.

Approval obtained for a joint venture with Sehnzhen Petrochemical Holdings Co. to produce air conditioners.

Creation of the Global Air treatment unit as a global business unit.

Europe behind Electrolux (25%) and Bosch-Siemens (15%).

Soon after the formation of WIBV, Philips' decentralized organization was phased out and WIBV was split into customer-focused business units. Brands were positioned to fit the niches and conditions in Europe, an approach employed earlier in the United States. Bauknecht—Philips' most profitable brand—was aimed at the high end of the market, the dual-branded Philips/Whirlpool at the middle, and Ignis was designed for the lower end. Later, in 1995, Whirlpool terminated its successful $110 million brand-transfer effort and dropped the Philips brand name. The Bauknecht and Philips/Whirlpool Appliance Groups received centralized sales and marketing functions that supported all of Whirlpool's European brands. National sales subsidiaries were consolidated into three sales regions to take account of the growing European cross-border trade. The marketing function included separate, brand-oriented components to strengthen brand identity while at the same time ensuring internal coordination. Manufacturing and technology activities were reorganized around product groups and development centers with Germany focusing on laundry and dishwashing products and Italy on refrigeration and cooking. Key support functions (Consumer Services, Information Technology, Logistics, Planning) were maintained as separate, centrally managed entities. Distribution was reconfigured toward a pan-European approach and 10 out of 28 finished goods warehouses were closed. Explained WEBV president Hank Bowman: "The idea is to put systems support in place so we can deliver products more accurately and in a more timely manner."[17] WEBV also assumed responsibility for the Middle East and Africa, which accounted for $100 million in sales mainly in the form of kits, in an attempt to boost local content and thus preempt the emergence of domestic-content rules. In late 1994, yet another reorganization was started to streamline operations on a pan-European basis in conjunction with similar efforts in North America in the hope of achieving annual cost savings of approximately $150 million per year starting in 1997.

In 1992, WIBV started a four-year effort to redesign its products in order to increase manufacturing efficiency, and improve product quality and customer satisfaction. The goal was to renew the entire product line by 1996. Whirlpool had identified what it called a "value gap" in Europe. When benchmarking the European industry's performance against best-in-class North American and Asian companies, managers found that European producers experienced significantly lower levels of customer satisfaction. Also, Europeans paid more for their appliances than did their U.S. counterparts. Explained Ivan Menezes, vice president, group marketing, WEBV:

> When Whirlpool first came to Europe, the typical appliance cost 50 percent to 100 percent more in terms of daily income. In the U.S., for example, a typical consumer could, in 1991, earn the necessary dollars for a dishwasher in 3.8 days, whereas in Europe, it would have taken 7.5 days. Today that gap has closed by 15 percent to 20 percent for all appliances.[18]

A global outlook was forged in the management team. Managers were rotated between Europe and the United States to foster global thinking. The first time this move paid off was in 1991 when the VIP Crisp microwave oven, developed by a new "advanced global technology unit" in Norrköping, Sweden, was introduced and quickly became Europe's best-selling model. The VIP Crisp had a heated base plate which allowed Italians to bake crisp pizza crusts and the British to fry eggs. Subsequently, the company started to import the VIP Crisp to the United States.

WEBV also made a series of moves to establish itself in the emerging markets of Central and Eastern Europe, which in 1991 represented about 11 percent of the world appliance market and promised attractive growth opportunities over the long term. Bauknecht was first in setting up a distribution system in East Germany after the opening of the border. In early 1992, WEBV developed distribution networks in the entire region and established a wholly owned sales subsidiary in Hungary. In May 1992, Whirlpool took a 43.8 percent minority investment in Whirlpool/Tatramat a.s., a joint venture in the Slovak Republic, which manufactured and sold automatic washers and marketed products assembled at other WEBV locations. In 1994, WEBV took a controlling interest in this joint venture. A year earlier, sales subsidiaries were opened in Poland and the

Czech Republic, adding to WEBV's position in Eastern Europe, and Greece in Southeastern Europe, followed by Russia in 1995. Expansions into Romania and Bulgaria were planned for 1996.

Latin American Appliance Group

Whirlpool's overseas foray began in Latin America in 1957 when it purchased an equity interest in Multibras S.A. of Brazil, a manufacturer of major appliances. Whirlpool's strategy in Latin America called for taking full advantage of this large emerging market by optimally positioning its brands across the entire spectrum based on in-depth consumer research in an attempt to cultivate "Customers for Life."

In the crucial Brazilian market, accounting for about half of all appliances sold in Latin America in 1994, Whirlpool held equity positions in three Brazilian companies: (1) Multibras, which in 1994 merged three sister appliance makers into one organization; with annual sales of $800 million, this firm held the market leader position in Brazil; (2) Embraco was one of the world's largest manufacturers of compressors that exported to 50 countries on four continents; (3) Brasmotor S.A., was a holding company with a majority interest in Multibras and a minority interest in Embraco. Whirlpool claimed that, based on its own research, it has the second highest brand recognition after Coca-Cola.

In January 1992, Whirlpool strengthened its position in South America by taking over SAGAD, Philip's white goods operation in Argentina. Outside of Brazil and Argentina, the South American Sales Company, a subsidiary of LAAG, was responsible for sales throughout the region.

Originally, Whirlpool's Latin American operations were part of the Whirlpool Overseas Corporation (WOC) which was formed in Spring 1990 as a wholly owned subsidiary to conduct marketing and industrial activities outside North America and Europe. It included U.S. Export Sales, the Overseas Business Group acquired from Philips in the WIBV transaction, and three wholly owned sales companies in Hong Kong, Thailand, and Australia. Industrial activities encompassed technology sale and transfer, kit and component sales, joint venture manufacturing, and project management for affiliates.

Key responsibilities of WOC also included feeding new technologies from Whirlpool's bases in North America and Europe to its other units; ensuring optimal brand positioning in each country; and analyzing specific appliance designs for their suitability to various markets. Conditions could vary greatly from country to country. For instance, the company sold so-called giant ovens in Africa and the Middle East. These ovens were 39 and 42 inches wide compared to the standard 30 inches in the United States and were large enough to roast a sheep or goat.

In 1993, after exhaustive and detailed analysis of world markets, the company decided that its global business interests would be better served by establishing two stand-alone business units, one for Latin America called LAAG, the other, the Whirlpool Asian Appliance Group for Whirlpool's Asian operations (Exhibits 5 and 6).

Whirlpool Asian Appliance Group

When Whirlpool began to pursue perceived business opportunities in Asia, it was not new to the market. It had exported home appliances to the region for over 30 years from the U.S. With the acquisition of Philips' appliance business, it gained broadened access to Asian markets. However, Whirlpool realized that a viable position in Asia implied more than selling imports from NAAG and WEBV, having kits assembled by licensees, or having appliances built to specification by local manufacturers.

Whirlpool's Asian strategy rested on the "Five Ps"—partnerships, products, processes, people, and a pan-Asian approach. The strategy was batched into three phases: start-up, building, and market leadership. Based on extensive market research, Whirlpool decided to base its foray into Asia on four specific appliance products, the so-called "T-4": refrigerators, clothes washers, microwave ovens, and air conditioners. For a household with no appliances, a refrigerator was usually the first purchase when income increased. A clothes washer came next. Air conditioners were important because of the heat and humidity in much of the region. Microwave ovens had become a truly global appliance with essentially standardized features and design. Whirlpool focused its efforts on China and India, the most populous countries. Market entry was supposed to occur through joint ventures, to be followed later by "greenfield" plants. Based on commonalties identified in the region, Whirlpool planned to use a pan-Asian platform, with modifications made for specific areas given regional preferences. In contrast to other regions, only one brand name—Whirlpool—would be used because the market was not considered mature enough to allow for a multibrand approach.

In 1987, Whirlpool created a joint venture in India with Sundaram-Clayton, Ltd., called TVS Whirlpool, Ltd., which began to operate a plant producing semiautomatic clothes washers, the so-called "World Washer," and twin-tub washers for the Indian market.

Whirlpool's Asian expansion gained momentum in 1993 with the creation of the Whirlpool Asian Appliance Group (WAAG) (Exhibit 6) supported by a $10 million investment. A regional headquarters was established in Tokyo and later moved to Singapore, which also became the home of a pan-Asian marketing, product development, and technology center. The Asian market was further subdivided first into three, then four operating regions: Greater China, based in Hong Kong (Peoples Republic, Hong Kong); South Asia, based in Delhi (India, Pakistan, and surrounding markets); North Asia, based in Tokyo (Japan, Korea, Philippines, Taiwan), and Southeast Asia, based in Singapore (Australia, New Zealand).

In 1994, Whirlpool's investment in Asia increased to over $200 million. Whirlpool announced a joint venture with Teco Electric & Machinery Co., Ltd., to market and distribute home appliances in Taiwan as an insider. In February 1994, Whirlpool acquired a controlling interest in Kelvinator of India, Ltd., one of the largest manufacturers and marketers of refrigerators in that country. Also, Whirlpool obtained a controlling interest and day-to-day management of its existing Indian-based venture, TVS Whirlpool, Ltd. In its 1995 Annual Report, the company announced that in the forthcoming year it would create an efficient, customer-responsive "Whirlpool of India" organization.

Also, China became the center of a series of joint ventures combined with plant expansions and upgrades which marked an important milestone by completing Whirlpool's T-4 strategy in China (for details see Exhibit 8.)

The creation of a technology center in Singapore was essential for the long-term strategy. A new generation of products would be designed for the Asian market and could tap into Whirlpool's expertise gained around the globe. As was the case in Latin America, the Worldwide Excellence System was adapted to the regional circumstances and provided a strong integrating mechanism.

To accelerate the process, Whirlpool assembled global product teams, offered foreign assignments for key personnel within the global organization, and began to hire aggressively within the region.

ORCHESTRATING THE STRATEGY GLOBALLY

Although Whirlpool was a global force by the end of 1995, its U.S. exports were less than 10 percent of gross revenues. As Whirlpool expanded its geographic reach, it became more and more critical to lay the groundwork so that the company could utilize effectively its experience worldwide in product technology and manufacturing processes and transfer it quickly to wherever it was needed. Thus, it could leverage its global presence to gain sustainable competitive advantage. For this purpose, a number of projects and organizational functions and arrangements were put in place.

Global Business Units

Two product groups were managed and organized on a global platform. The Microwave Oven Business Unit managed microwave oven production and development activities on a global basis with manufacturing and product development facilities in Norrköping, Sweden, and a second, low-cost source in development in China. Whirlpool claimed that once the Shunde facility started operating, it would be one of the world's top five microwave oven manufacturing sites.

In late 1995, Whirlpool created the Global Air Treatment Unit which relied on the LaVergne Division in Tennessee and Shenzhen Whirlpool Raybo Air-Conditioner Industrial Co. Ltd., which had become part of the company a few months before. With an aggressive growth strategy, the company anticipated quadrupling the increase in sales in the first half of 1996 relative to the same period a year earlier.

In addition, Whirlpool Financial Corporation, established in 1957, served manufacturers, retailers, and consumers in the United States, Canada, and

Europe. With assets exceeding $1.9 billion in 1995, it provided inventory and consumer financing to support product sales from the point of manufacture through the market channel to the consumer.

The World Washer

The World Washer was an effort to create a lightweight compact washer with few parts that could be produced in developing countries where manufacturing technology was not as advanced. The washer could be sold at a price that put it within reach of many more households than the designs marketed in the industrialized world. The goal of the World Washer effort was to develop a complete product, process, and facility design package versatile enough to satisfy conditions and market requirements in various countries but with low initial investment requirements. At the same time, the World Washer became a major competitor, especially against the Far Eastern rivals. Some did not share Whirlpool's vision of global products. Commented Lawrence A. Johnson, a corporate officer of General Electric's Appliance Division: "We're not in an industry where global products work well. . . . There is also no such thing as a global brand, and it's unlikely that there will be. It's hard to change decades of brand commitment."[19]

As the name indicated, a common design was envisaged for India, Brazil, and Mexico where the washer was to be produced and marketed. Originally, Whirlpool planned to replicate the project design in each of the three countries; however, it eventually proved necessary to develop three slightly different variations. Costs also varied widely, further affecting both product and process decisions. "In India, for example, material costs may run as much as 200 to 800 percent higher than elsewhere, while labor and overhead costs are comparatively minimal," added Lawrence J. Kremer, senior vice president, global technology and operations.[20]

The plants also varied subtly from each other, although the goals were identical, minimizing facility investment and avoiding big finish systems and welding stations requiring extensive machinery for material cleanup and environmental safety. In Brazil, the plant was constructed of precast concrete. It was designed with a creative convection cooling system to address the high humidity. In India, the new facility was built in Pondicherry, just 12 degrees north of the equator. Although the plant looked similar to that in Brazil—except for the overhead fans—the method of construction was different. Concrete was hand mixed on location then carried in wicker baskets to forms constructed next to the building site. The Indian construction crew cast the concrete, allowed it to cure and then, using five or six men, raised each three-ton slab into place using chain, block, and tackle.

Worldwide Excellence System

Established in 1991, the Worldwide Excellence System (WES) was the company's blueprint for how it approached quality, customers, and continuous improvement worldwide. WES combined elements of other well-known quality systems: ISO 9000, the Deming approach used in Asia, and the Baldridge system used in the United States. As with the Baldridge system, WES used a point system to measure success of implementing the program. WES had seven categories (Exhibit 9). The Leadership and Whirlpool People categories described the involvement of people at all levels in moving the corporation to excellence. Fact-Based Management, Strategic Planning, and Quality of Process & Products outlined the major internal processes for achieving excellence. Measurement and Results explained the methods used to determine what customers expected and to assess how well they were being satisfied. The continuous monitoring of Customer Satisfaction was used to improve activities and processes.

Technology Organization

Several of Whirlpool's functions were organized to take advantage of the company's technical know-how which was scattered around the globe. The goal was to develop advanced, innovative products and move them to market quickly. As mentioned previously, an early success in this area occurred in late 1991 when the VIP Crisp microwave oven, developed in Norrköping, Sweden, was introduced and quickly became Europe's best-selling model.

A Global Procurement organization bought all material and components to support the company's appliance production facilities. From procurement centers in the United States, Italy, and Singapore, it purchased finished products, commodities sourced

EXHIBIT 9 *Worldwide Excellence System*

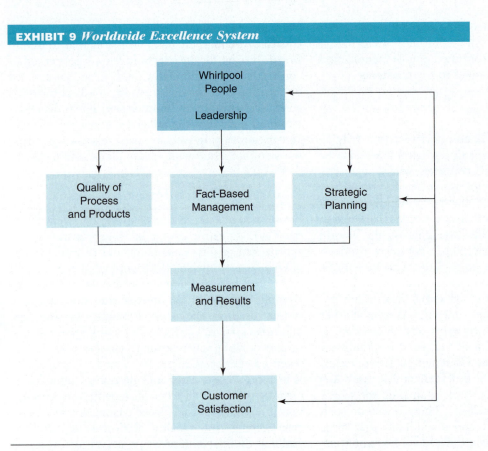

on a regional or global basis, and standardized parts and components. Most other parts and material were outsourced to suppliers located near the production facilities where they were used. In developing countries, this often implied educating and assisting local suppliers so they could satisfy Whirlpool's standards.

Corporate Technology Development developed product and process technology capabilities and provided technical services to Whirlpool businesses. While centrally managed from the corporation's technology center in Benton Harbor, technology development activities were geographically dispersed in Europe, Asia, and North America.

Advanced Product Concepts looked beyond current product needs for appliances Whirlpool was making. It was responsible for developing new product concepts that were identified through market research.

Advanced Manufacturing Concepts was responsible for bringing new manufacturing processes into the corporation and identifying and developing simulation tools and best practices to be used on a global basis.

Strategic Assessment and Support identified and evaluated nontraditional new product opportunities in cooperation with other Whirlpool units. Also, it established corporate policy regarding product safety, computer-aided design, and manufacturing and addressed environmental and regulatory issues and intellectual property rights.

THE RACE FOR GLOBAL DOMINANCE

Whirlpool was not alone in its effort to establish a strong global position. In fact, competitors throughout the industry were pursuing similar strategies.

Electrolux, the leader in Europe, continued to expand aggressively using its strong pan-European as well as local brands. Plans included establishing market share leadership in Central and Eastern Europe by 2000. A $100 million investment in China included joint ventures to manufacture water purifiers, compressors, and a vacuum cleaner plant. Vacuum cleaner manufacturing capacity was also increased in South Africa. In India, Electrolux established itself through acquisitions of majority holdings in production facilities for refrigerators and washing machines. In Thailand, Indonesia, Malaysia, and Singapore, the Swedish giant rapidly developed a strong position through a network of retailers. In Latin America, the company recently acquired a minority interest in Brazil's second largest white goods manufacturer, Refripar.

Besides trying to strengthen its position in North America through its alliance with Maytag, Bosch-Siemens Hausgeräte GmbH (BSHG) also vied for a larger share in other regions. In China, BSHG had acquired a majority in Wuxi Little Swan Co., a leading manufacturer of laundry appliances. In Brazil, BSHG purchased Continental 2001, a large appliance producer with sales of $294 million. In Eastern Europe, it recently completed the construction of a washing machine factory in Lodz, Poland.

General Electric Appliances, a $6 billion giant in 1994, was also working diligently to become a global player: "We're focusing our efforts on the world's fastest growing markets, including India, China, Southeast Asia and South America. . . . We're also strengthening our alliances in Mexico and India, and we developed a number of new products specifically for global markets," explained J. Richard Stonesifer, GEA's president and CEO.[21]

EPILOGUE

For fiscal year 1995, Whirlpool reported per share earnings of $2.80, up from the previous year but still below the 1993 high. (For a summary of financial results, see Exhibits 1 and 10–12.) A combination of events and trends contributed to these results. First, in North America, product shipments had declined by 1.4 percent while operating profits dropped by 16 percent. In Europe, rising raw material costs, fierce competition, and a shift by consumers to cheaper brands and models reduced Whirlpool's shipments by 2 percent while the industry grew by 1 percent. Volume in Latin America was up because of robust growth in Brazil; in contrast, in Argentina industry shipments plummeted by as much as 50 percent fueled by the Mexican economic collapse. Whirlpool Asia reported an operating loss due to the continuing expansion, while shipments increased by 193 percent and revenues by 83 percent. David Whitwam said that the company was ahead of schedule in its restructuring effort in Europe and North America and that he anticipated significant improvements in operating efficiency for next year. Evidently, Whirlpool was confident about its position in the industry, as indicated by the quote in Whitwam's 1995 Letter to Shareholders, in spite of the lackluster short-term results.

EXHIBIT 10 *Twelve-Year Consolidated Financial Review (Year Ended December 31, Millions of Dollars Except per Share Data)*

	1995	1994	1993	1992	1991	1990	1989	1988	1987	1986	1985	1984
Consolidated Operations												
Net sales	$8,163	$7,949	$7,368	$7,097	$6,550	$6,424	$6,138	$4,306	$4,104	$3,928	$3,465	$3,128
Financial services	$ 184	$ 155	$ 165	$ 204	$ 207	$ 181	$ 136	$ 107	$ 94	$ 76	$ 67	$ 63
Total revenues	$8,347	$8,104	$7,533	$7,301	$6,757	$6,605	$6,274	$4,413	$4,198	$4,004	$3,532	$3,191
Operating profit	$ 396	$ 397	$ 482	$ 479	$ 393	$ 349	$ 411	$ 261	$ 296	$ 326	$ 295	$ 288
Earnings from continuing operations												
before income taxes												
and other items	$ 242	$ 292	$ 375	$ 372	$ 304	$ 220	$ 308	$ 233	$ 280	$ 329	$ 321	$ 326
Earnings from continuing operations	$ 209	$ 158	$ 231	$ 205	$ 170	$ 72	$ 187	$ 161	$ 187	$ 202	$ 182	$ 190
before accounting change	$ 209	$ 158	$ 51	$ 205	$ 170	$ 72	$ 187	$ 94	$ 192	$ 200	$ 182	$ 190
Net earnings	$ 480	$ 418	$ 309	$ 288	$ 287	$ 265	$ 208	$ 166	$ 223	$ 217	$ 178	$ 135
Net capital expenditures	$ 282	$ 246	$ 241	$ 275	$ 233	$ 247	$ 222	$ 143	$ 133	$ 120	$ 89	$ 72
Depreciation	$ 100	$ 90	$ 85	$ 77	$ 76	$ 76	$ 76	$ 76	$ 79	$ 76	$ 73	$ 73
Consolidated Financial Position												
Current assets	$3,541	$3,078	$2,708	$2,740	$2,920	$2,900	$2,889	$1,827	$1,690	$1,654	$1,410	$1,302
Current liabilities	$3,829	$2,988	$2,763	$2,887	$2,931	$2,651	$2,251	$1,374	$1,246	$1,006	$ 781	$ 671
Working capital	$ (288)	$ 90	$ (55)	$ (147)	$ (11)	$ 249	$ 638	$ 453	$ 444	$ 648	$ 629	$ 632
Property, plant, and equipment-net	$1,779	$1,440	$1,319	$1,325	$1,400	$1,349	$1,288	$ 820	$ 779	$ 677	$ 514	$ 398
Total assets	$7,800	$6,655	$6,047	$6,118	$6,445	$5,614	$5,354	$3,410	$3,137	$2,856	$2,207	$1,901
Long-term debt	$ 983	$ 885	$ 840	$1,215	$1,528	$ 874	$ 982	$ 474	$ 367	$ 298	$ 125	$ 91
Total debt—appliance business	$1,635	$ 965	$ 850	$1,198	$1,330	$1,026	$1,125	$ 441	$ 383	$ 194	$ 64	$ 53
Stockholders' equity	$1,877	$1,723	$1,648	$1,600	$1,515	$1,424	$1,421	$1,321	$1,304	$1,350	$1,207	$1,096
Per Share Data												
Earnings from continuing operations												
before accounting change	$ 2.80	$ 2.10	$ 3.19	$ 2.90	$ 2.45	$ 1.04	$ 2.70	$ 2.33	$ 2.61	$ 2.72	$ 2.49	$ 2.59
Net earnings	$ 2.80	$ 2.10	$ 0.67	$ 2.90	$ 2.45	$ 1.04	$ 2.70	$ 1.36	$ 2.68	$ 2.70	$ 2.49	$ 2.59
Dividends	$ 1.36	$ 1.22	$ 1.19	$ 1.10	$ 1.10	$ 1.10	$ 1.10	$ 1.10	$ 1.10	$ 1.03	$ 1.00	$ 1.00
Book value	$25.08	$22.83	$22.80	$22.67	$21.78	$20.51	$20.49	$19.06	$18.83	$18.21	$16.46	$14.97
Closing stock price, NYSE	$53 1/4	$50 1/4	$66 1/2	$44 5/8	$38 7/8	$23 1/2	$ 33	$24 3/4	$24 3/8	$33 7/8	$24 11/16	$23 1/4

EXHIBIT 11 *Business Unit Revenues and Operating Profit (millions of dollars)*

	1995	1994	1993
Revenues			
North America	5,093	5,048	4,559
Europe	2,502	2,373	2,225
Latin America	271	329	303
Asia	376	205	151
Other	(5)	(6)	130
Total Appliance Business	8,163	7,949	7,368
Operating Profit			
North America	445	522	474
Europe	92	163	139
Latin America	26	49	43
Asia	(50)	(22)	(5)
Restructuring[1]	—	(248)	(23)
Business Dispositions[2]	—	60	(8)
Other	(147)	(154)	(116)
Total Appliance Business	366	370	504

[1]Consolidation and reorganization of European and North American operations in 1993 and 1994 and closure of two North American manufacturing facilities in 1994.

[2]In 1994, the minority interest in Matsushita Floor Care Company was sold, as were the European compressor operations to its Brazilian affiliate Embraco and its refrigerator plant in Barcelona.

C-630

EXHIBIT 12 *Business Segment Information (millions of dollars)*

	North America	Europe	Other and (Eliminations)
Net Sales			
1995	$5,093	$2,502	$ 586
1994	5,048	2,451	450
1993	4,547	2,410	411
1992	4,471	2,645	185
1991	4,224	2,479	54
1990	4,157	2,405	43
Operating Profit			
1995	$ 314	$ 90	$ (38)
1994	311	43	16
1993	341	129	34
1992	359	101	19
1991	314	82	(3)
1990	269	86	(6)
Identifiable Assets			
1995	$2,031	$2,104	$2,033
1994	2,046	1,824	1,410
1993	1,742	1,758	1,154
1992	3,511	1,917	690
1991	3,672	2,284	489
1990	3,216	1,905	493
Depreciation Expense			
1995	$ 140	$ 105	$ 8
1994	141	98	4
1993	137	101	1
1992	142	132	1
1991	129	104	—
1990	140	107	—
Net Capital Expenditures			
1995	$ 262	$ 186	$ 29
1994	269	135	12
1993	188	116	3
1992	174	111	3
1991	183	104	—
1990	158	106	1

BIBLIOGRAPHY

"A Portrait of the U.S. Appliance Industry 1992," *Appliance* (September 1992).

Appliance Manufacturer (February 1990), pp. 36–37.

Babyak, R. J., "Strategic Imperative," *Appliance Manufacturer*, Vol. 47, No. 2 (Special Section) (February 1995), pp. 19–24.

Botskor, I., M. Chaouli, and B. Müller, "Boom mit Grauwerten," *Wirtschaftswoche*, No. 22 (May 28, 1993), pp. 64–75.

Bower, J. L., and N. Dossabhoy, "Note on the Major Home Appliance Industry in 1984 (Condensed), Case #385-211, Harvard Business School, mimeo.

Bray, H., "Plugging into the World," *Detroit Free Press* (May 17, 1993), pp. 10–11F.

Bylinsky, G., "Computers That Learn by Doing," *Fortune* (September 6, 1993), pp. 96–102.

DuPont, T., "The Appliance Giant Has a New President and a Global Vision," *The Weekly Home Furnishings Newspaper* (July 2, 1987), p. 1.

DuPont, T., "Whirlpool's New Brand Name," *The Weekly Home Furnishings Newspaper* (April 11, 1988).

Echikson, W., "The Trick to Selling in Europe," *Fortune* (September 20, 1993), p. 82.

Fisher, J. D., "Home Appliance Industry," *Value Line* (December 22, 1989), p. 132.

"Fleet of Foot," *Appliance Manufacturer*, Vol. 46, No. 5 (May 1994), pp. 35–38.

Ghoshal, S. and P. Haspeslagh, "The Acquisition and Integration of Zanussi by Electrolux: A Case Study," *European Management Journal*, Vol. 8, No. 4 (December 1990), pp. 414–433.

Hunger, J. D., "The Major Home Appliance Industry in 1990: From U.S. to Global," mimeo, 1990.

Jackson, T., "European Competition Hurts Whirlpool," *Financial Times* (October 14/15), p. 6.

Jancsurak, J., "Holistic Strategy Pays Off," *Appliance Manufacturer*, Vol. 47, No. 2 (Special Section) (February 1995), pp. 3–6.

Jancsurak, J., "Marketing: Phase 2," *Appliance Manufacturer*, Vol. 47, No. 2 (Special Section) (February 1995), pp. 8–10.

Jancsurak, J., "Big Plans for Europe's Big Three," *Appliance Manufacturer*, Vol. 47, No. 4 (April 1995), pp. 26–30.

Jancsurak, J., "Wanted: Customers for Life," *Appliance Manufacturer*, Vol. 47, No. 2 (Special Section) (February 1995), pp. 36–37.

Kindel, S., "World Washer: Why Whirlpool Leads in Appliance: Not Some Japanese Outfit," *Financial World*, Vol. 159, No. 6 (March 20, 1990), pp. 42–46.

Maruca, R. F., "The Right Way to Go Global," An Interview with Whirlpool CEO David Whitwam, *Harvard Business Review* (March-April 1994), pp. 135–145.

Naj, A. K., "Air Conditioners Learn To Sense If You're Cool," *Wall Street Journal* (August 31, 1993), p. B1.

R. J. B., "Demystifying the Asian Consumer," *Appliance Manufacturer*, Vol. 47, No. 2 (Special Section) (February 1995), pp. 25–27.

R. J. B., "Multifaceted Strategy," *Appliance Manufacturer*, Vol. 47, No. 2 (Special Section) (February 1995), pp. 28–29.

Remich, N. C. Jr., "A Kentucky Thoroughbred That Is Running Strong," *Appliance Manufacturer*, Vol. 47, No. 7 (Special Section) (July 1995), pp. 3–6.

Remich, N. C. Jr., "Speed Saves the Day," *Appliance Manufacturer*, Vol. 47, No. 7 (Special Section) (July 1995), pp. 25–29.

Schiller, Z, "The Great Refrigerator Race," *Business Week* (July 5, 1993), pp. 78–81.

Schiller, Z, "GE Has a Lean, Mean Washing Machine," *Business Week* (November 20, 1995), pp. 97–98.

Standard & Poor's Corp., "Waiting for the Next Replacement Cycle," *Industry Surveys*, Vol. 2 (November 1991), pp. T102–105.

Standard & Poor's Corp. "Poised for a Moderate Recovery," *Industry Surveys*, Vol. 2 (November 1992), pp. T96–101.

Stewart, T. A., "A Heartland Industry Takes on the World," *Fortune* (March 2, 1990), pp. 110–112.

Tierney, R., "Whirlpool Magic," *World Trade* (May 1993).

Treece, J. B., "The Great Refrigerator Race," *Business Week* (July 15, 1993), pp. 78–81.

Weiner, S., "Growing Pains," *Forbes* (October 29, 1990), pp. 40–41.

Whirlpool Corporation, Annual Reports 1987–1995.

Whirlpool Corporation, Form 10-K, 1992, 1994, 1995.

Whirlpool Corporation, 1992, Proxy Statement.

Whirlpool Corporation, Profile, 1994, 1995.

Whirlpool Corporation, "Whirlpool 'World Washer' Being Marketed in Three Emerging Countries," News Release, Updated.

Whirlpool Corporation, "Whirlpool Corporation Named Winner in $30 Million Super-Efficient Refrigerator Competition," undated.

Zeller, W., "A Tough Market Has Whirlpool in a Spin," *Business Week* (May 2, 1988), pp. 121–122.

NOTES

1. Whirlpool Corporation, 1995, Annual Report, p. 4.
2. Whirlpool Corporation, 1994, Annual Report, p. 2.
3. Whirlpool Corporation, 1995, Profile.
4. Whirlpool Corporation, 1995, Form 10-K.
5. Stewart, "A Heartland Industry . . ."
6. Kindel, "World Washer . . ."
7. Whirlpool Corporation, 1994, Form 10-K.
8. Whirlpool Corporation, 1992, Annual Report.
9. Whirlpool Corporation, 1994, Profile.
10. Whirlpool Corporation, 1994, Annual Report, p. 9.
11. "Fleet of Foot."
12. Whirlpool Corporation, World Washer News Release.
13. Whirlpool Corporation, 1994, Annual Report, p. 10.
14. Whirlpool Corporation, 1987, Annual Report, p. 5.
15. Whirlpool Corporation, 1989, Annual Report, p. 9.
16. Stewart, "A Heartland Industry . . ."
17. Tierney, "World Washer . . ."
18. Jancsurak "Marketing: Phase 2."
19. Remich, "Speed Saves the Day," p. 129.
20. Whirlpool Corporation, World Washer News Release.
21. Remich, "A Kentucky Thoroughbred. . . ," p. 4.

Name Index

Nussbaum, B., 469
Nystrom, P. C., 79

O'Reilly, Anthony, 449
O'Reilly, B., 40, 80, 501–502
O'Bannon, D, P., 468
Oberton, Will, 457
Ocasio, W., 198
O'Donnell, S., 388
Ogletree, J., 41
Ohmae, K., 38, 199
Okuda, Hiroshi, 103, 483
O'Leary, Michael, 283
Olian, J. D., 468
Oliver, C., 39, 119, 157
Olk, P., 347
O'Neal, D., 501
O'Neill, H. M, 430
O'Neill, R. M., 470
Ono, Y., 258
O'Reilly, Anthony J. F., 362–363, 420–421, 449
O'Reilly, B., 501–502
Ortega, B., 80, 269
Orton, J. D., 501
Orwell, B., 120
Osnos, E., 158
Oster, S. M., 80
Osterland, A., 382, 389
Ouchi, W. S., 345
Oughton, C., 234
Oum, T. H., 346
Overholt, M. H., 430
Oviatt, B. M., 306, 501
Ovitz, Michael, 365–366
Owen, D., 431
Oxley, J. E., 345
Ozanne, M. R., 121

Paez, B. L., 235
Paine, L. S., 81
Palepu, K., 234, 464
Palia, K. A., 120
Palmer, A. T., 158
Pan, Y., 307, 345
Pandit, B. L., 502
Pantzalis, C., 307
Pappas, B., 457
Parcel, D., 41
Park, D., 40, 80, 201, 306, 308, 347, 42, 502
Park, Seung-Ho., 80, 307, 344–346
Parke, A., 348
Parsons, C. K., 470
Patel, P., 501
Pavitt, K., 502
Pearce, J. A., II, 469
Pearson, A. E., 41
Pearson, Andrall, 215, 258
Peffers, K., 80
Pereira, I., 199
Perry, N. J., 159
Perser, J. H., 200
Person, J., 307
Peteraf, M. A., 81, 119, 199, 233
Petzinger, T., Jr., 40, 502

Pfeffer, J., 119, 266, 469
Pfeifer, Eckhard, 179–180, 439
Phan, P. H., 268
Pieke, F. N., 501
Piercy, N. F., 345
Pinches, G. E., 266, 500
Pine, B. J., II, 80
Pinsker, B., 199
Pisano, G., 40, 79, 119–120, 234, 268, 306, 430
Planck, Max, 284
Platt, Louis E., 368, 370
Poitier, Sidney, 352
Pollack, A., 104
Polonsky, M. J., 4
Pope, K., 327
Porac, J. F., 199
Porras, J. I., 469
Porter, James, 110
Porter, M. E., 38–39, 61, 81, 87, 106, 119–121, 136, 139, 145, 157–159, 198, 233–234, 267, 280, 298, 306–308, 319, 380, 389, 431
Pouder, R., 336, 347, 430
Prahalad, C. K., 38, 40–41, 119, 121, 198, 233, 468, 502
Prasad, S. B., 235, 389
Prasad, V. K, 307
Prasso, S., 234
Preble, J. F., 79
Premeaux, S. R., 470
Prescott, J. E., 347
Pressley, J., 345
Preston, L. F., 40
Price, Michael, 389, 376
Price, R., 500
Price, Sol, 109
Priem, R. L., 79, 119, 468
Provan, K. G., 313, 344, 430
Prudom, J. J., 198
Puffer, S. M., 347
Pulliam, S., 238
Punnett, B. J., 305–307
Puri, S., 388

Quelch, J. A., 307
Quick, R., 238
Quinlan, J. P., 306
Quinn, J. B., 120, 468
Quint, M., 235
Quintanilla, C., 189, 266

Raghavan, A., 266
Rahweddeer, C., 432
Rajagopalan, N., 39–40, 157, 46"69
Rajan, M. V., 306, 431
Ramaswamy, K., 233, 2 66
Ramo, J, C., 39
Ramstad, E., 199, 327, 347, 389, 468
Rangan, U. S., 307, 346
Rasheed, A. M. A., 79, 468
Ravenscraft, D. J., 235, 267, 269
Rawsthorn, A., 231, 235
Rayport, J. F., 157
Reddy, S., 267, 307, 346
Redenbacher, Orville, 158

Rediker, K. J., 387–388
Reed, R., 120
Reger R. K., 81, 159
Rehbeing, K. A., 81
Rehfeld, B., 388
Reibstein, D. J., 157–158, 198, 200
Reichheld, F. F., 120
Reichhng, Gary, 492
Reilly, P. M., 2 34
Reimann, B. C., 500
Reingold, J., 388–389, 468
Reinhardt, A., 38, 119
Reitman, V., 306, 431, 484
Render, B., 200
Reuer, J. J., 347
Reuter, Edzard, 223
Rheem, H., 119
Ricart, J., 346
Rice, F., 158
Richman, L. S., 79
Ricks, D. A., 305–307
Riley, B., 389
Robbie, K., 502
Roberts, H. V., 183, 200
Robey, D., 121
Robins, J., 431
Robinson, G., 79
Roche, Gerard, 436
Rock, L., 268
Rock, R. H., 268
Rodriguez, E. M., 470
Roe, M. J., 388
Roesner, J. B., 80
Rogers, D. M. A., 501
Rohwedder, C., 432
Roll, R., 267
Romer, Paul M., 200
Roos, D., 500
Rose, F., 158
Rose-Ackerman, S., 235
Rosen, B., 200, 388
Roseno, A., 231, 233, 235
Rosenstein, S., 388
Ross, D., 234
Ross, Steven J., 33, 41
Rossan, J. , 4, 234, 242
Roth, K., 388
Rothwell, R., 502
Routamo, R., 503
Rowe, W. G., 233, 430–431
Rowley, T. J., 347
Rudnitsky, H., 470
Rugman, A., 306–307, 313, 344, 347
Rumelt, R. P., 38–41, 157–158, 205, 233–235, 389, 430–431
Rusakova, Ludmila, 495
Russell, R. S., 159, 200
Russo, M., 345

Sager, I., 113, 119, 158, 468–469, 501
Sakakibara, M., 198, 347
Sakano, T., 347
Salk, J. E., 307
Saloner, G., 347
Salter, M. S., 502
Sanchez, C., M., 268

I-7

I-8

Company Index

Subject Index

Photo Credits